September 19–21, 2011
Tokyo, Japan

Association for
Computing Machinery

Advancing Computing as a Science & Profession

ICFP'11

Proceedings of the 2011 ACM SIGPLAN International Conference on Functional Programming

Sponsored by:

ACM SIGPLAN

Supported by:

CiTRiX, Credit Suisse, Erlang Solutions, Galois, IIJ, Jane Street, Microsoft Research, NII, Univ Paris Diderot - Sorbonne Paris Cité, Standard Chartered, Tsuru Capital, and Twitter

Association for
Computing Machinery

Advancing Computing as a Science & Profession

The Association for Computing Machinery
2 Penn Plaza, Suite 701
New York, New York 10121-0701

ISBN: 978-1-4503-0865-6

Additional copies may be ordered prepaid from:

ACM Order Department
PO Box 11405
New York, NY 10286-1405

Phone: 1-800-342-6626 (USA and Canada)
+1-212-626-0500 (all other countries)
Fax: +1-212-944-1318
E-mail: acmhelp@acm.org

ACM Order Number: 565110

Printed in the USA

Foreword

Welcome to the 16th ACM SIGPLAN International Conference on Functional Programming – ICFP'11.

The picture, on the front cover, is of Mount Fuji, seen from the 20th floor of the National Institute of Informatics (NII). It was taken by Sebastian Fischer in January 2011. In Japanese, the characters "human" and "lambda" have a similar shape, and the text is a combination of famous Japanese proverbs where all occurrences of "human" have been replaced by "lambda". It translates as follows:

> Lambda has a history
> Lambda exists in the place where virtue is
> Respect heaven and love lambda
> One lambda is worth a thousand (things)

This bouquet of proverbs was composed by Zhenjiang Hu and the local organizers at NII, and has benefited from the kind assistance of Kenichi Asai and Jacques Garrigue. It was written by Isao Sasano's calligraphy teacher, Keigai Nukata.

There were 112 submissions this year: 92 research papers, 8 functional pearls, and 12 experience reports. The Program Committee selected 33 research papers (1/3), 2 functional pearls (1/4), and 3 experience reports (1/4). Out of the 112 submissions, 8 were "forces majeures" (acts of God) related to the earthquake in Japan. Among those, 4 were selected. In addition to this selection, the PC also chose to invite Andrzej Filinski and Makoto Takeyama. For simplicity, there were no submissions by PC members.

Each submission was reviewed by at least 3 PC members. In addition, we consulted 113 external reviewers. All PC members attended the PC meeting, which took place on May 26–27, Avenue d'Italie, in Paris, courtesy of the PPS Laboratory (Preuves, Programmes et Systèmes) at the University of Paris 7. Notifications were sent within hours of the completion of the PC meeting, and updated reviews in the course of the following week.

It has been a pleasure to team up with General Chairs Manuel Chakravarty and Zhenjiang Hu, and to interact with Zhenjiang Hu's team at NII and with Soichiro Hidaka (local arrangements) and Wouter Swierstra (publicity). Also, throughout, Ian Zerny has been a selfless and first-rate help with the submission web site (HotCRP). Our PC meeting has received the support of PPS Director Thomas Ehrhard and of Microsoft Research, and its local organization has rested on Alexis Saurin and Marine Meyer's resourceful shoulders. The ICFP steering committee was its usual helpful, friendly, and level-headed self. I have also benefited from the wisdom of previous program chairs: Stephanie Weirich, Andrew Tolmach, Peter Thiemann, Norman Ramsey, Julia Lawall, Benjamin C. Pierce, Kathleen Fisher, and Philip Wadler as well as Greg Morrisett. Overall, running ICFP'11 was thrilling: an intense feeling of service and scientific contribution, and a continued amazement at the diversity and health of the functional-programming community, from authors to external reviewers to PC members. My heartfelt thanks to all.

Olivier Danvy
ICFP'11 Program Chair

On Submissions and Resubmissions

At ICFP 2011, and with the approval of the ICFP steering committee, I ran the following experiment about resubmissions:

> Authors of re-submissions can attach a confidential *revision history*, i.e., an annotated copy of the reviews of the previous submission(s) specifying how each point in each review was addressed. If one of the reviewers of a previous submission is asked to review the re-submission (and assuming that he has kept a copy of his review even if he has discarded the corresponding submission), this re-reviewer sends his original review to the program chair, who sends back the annotated copy. This way, the re-reviewer directly sees how the previous review was addressed, and can start reviewing the re-submission on an informed footing. Nobody else knows that a submission is a re-submission or is brand new before completing his own review. No new reviewer of a re-submission sees the annotated reviews of the initial submission.

The declaration that [the submission was brand new, or was the revision of a previous submission] was optional. There were 12 such declared resubmissions. One submission presented itself as brand new, but was subsequently identified as a resubmission (which was not counted against it). So among 112 submissions, at least 13 were resubmissions, i.e., 11%.

Enclosing the revision history was also optional. Among the 12 declared resubmissions, 5 had annotated copies of previous reviews, and 7 did not:

- among the 7 that did not, at least 3 were reviewed by a reviewer of the previous submission;

  all 7 were accepted;

- among the 5 that did,
  - 3 reviewers identified themselves as a previous reviewer, and asked me for a copy of the previous review;
  - 1 (sub-)reviewer suggested the resubmission be rejected on the ground that it still had problems, which I spotted while going through this review; I then asked the reviewer for a copy of his previous review, and I sent him the corresponding annotated reviews; this sub-reviewer then realized that his main issue had actually been addressed. This made him change his mind and suggest the submission be accepted – which it was.

  Among these 5, 4 were accepted.

At the PC meeting, the reviewers appeared to be neutral about whether a submission was brand new or was a resubmission. All re-reviewers, however, were interested about how their initial review had been addressed.

Conclusion: This experiment suggests that attaching a revision history to a resubmission has a positive effect:

- It forces the authors to spell out how they have addressed (or not) the previous reviews.
- It makes it possible for the re-reviewer to read – or not – the annotated copy of the previous review, so that (s)he has the choice of starting either on a fresh footing, or on an informed footing. And if the reviewer chooses not to read the annotated copy of his/her previous review, it is with the knowledge that the points of this previous review *were* considered (though of course not necessarily addressed) by the authors.
- The time invested in writing a review is better spent, particularly if there is a concrete prospect of seeing the points of the review being addressed in the future.

The experiment also illustrates the value of reading through reviews and responses to the reviewers.

Olivier Danvy
ICFP'11 Program Chair

Table of Contents

Keynote Address 2

Session 6: Proof Assistance

Session 7: Implementation

Session 8: Derivation and Synthesis

Session 9: Types

Session 10: Distributed Programming

Session 11: Applications

Session 12: Naming

Session 13: Semantics

Session 14: Program Transformation

Session 15: Imperative Programming

Session 16: Correctness

ICFP 2011 Conference Organization

General Chairs: Manuel Chakravarty *(University of New South Wales, Australia)*
Zhenjiang Hu *(National Institute of Informatics, Japan)*

Program Chair: Olivier Danvy *(Aarhus University, Denmark)*

Local Arrangements Chair: Soichiro Hidaka *(National Institute of Informatics, Japan)*

Workshop Chairs: Gabriele Keller *(University of New South Wales, Australia)*
Derek Dreyer *(MPI-SWS, Germany)*

Programming Contest Chair: Eijiro Sumii *(Tohoku University, Japan)*

Publicity Chair: Wouter Swierstra *(Radboud University Nijmegen, The Netherlands)*

Steering Committee: Amal Ahmed *(Indiana University, USA)*
Manuel Chakravarty *(University of New South Wales, Australia)*
Olivier Danvy *(Aarhus University, Denmark)*
Robby Findler *(Northwestern University, USA)*
Fritz Henglein *(University of Copenhagen, Denmark)*
James Hook *(Portland State University, USA)*
Zhenjiang Hu *(National Institute of Informatics, Japan)*
Paul Hudak *(Yale University, USA)*
Graham Hutton *(University of Nottingham, UK)*
John Launchbury *(Galois, USA)*
Greg Morrisett *(Harvard University, USA)*
Wouter Swierstra *(Radboud University Nijmegen, The Netherlands)*
Peter Thiemann *(Universitat Freiburg, Germany)*
Andrew Tolmach *(Portland State University, USA)*
Philip Wadler *(University of Edinburgh, UK)*
Stephanie Weirich *(University of Pennsylvania, USA)*

ICFP 2011 External Reviewers

Michael D. Adams
Thorsten Altenkirch
Sandra Alves
Torben Amtoft
Thomas Arts
Robert Atkey
Patrick Baillot
Thibaut Balabonski
Vincent Balat
Edoardo S. Biagioni
Mathieu Boespflug
Carl Friedrich Bolz
Antonio Bucciarelli
Swarat Chaudhuri
James Cheney
Olaf Chitil
Aske Simon Christensen
William D. Clinger
Ezra Cooper
Ben Delaware
Christopher Dutchyn
Manuel Fahndrich
Jean-Christophe Filliâtre
Andrzej Filinski
Matthew Flatt
Nate Foster
Alain Frisch
Marco Gaboardi
Jeremy Gibbons
Michael Greenberg
Jim Grundy
René Rydhof Hansen
Michael Hanus
Stephan Herhut
Stefan Holdermans
Cătălin Hriţcu
Frank Huch
Liyang Hu
Graham Hutton
Keigo Imai
Jun Inoue
Mauro Jaskelioff
Jean-Baptiste Jeannin
Pierre Jouvelot
Koji Kagawa
Ohad Kammar
Jerzy Karczmarczuk
Andrew Kennedy
Oleg Kiselyov
Sunil Kothari
Robbert Krebbers
Jim Laird
Julia L. Lawall
Hai Liu
Florian Loitsch
Pedro Lopez-Garcia
Victor Luchangco
Ian Mackie
José Pedro Magalhães
Geoffrey Mainland
Gregory Malecha
Moe Masuko
Damiano Mazza
Conor McBride
Lambert Meertens
Arie Middelkoop
Akimasa Morihata
Guillaume Munch
Shin-Cheng Mu
Madan Musuvathi
Anders Møller
Aleksandar Nanevski
Henrik Nilsson
Michael Norrish
John O'Donnell
John O'Leary
Bruno C. d. S. Oliveira
Dominic Orchard
Nicolas Oury
Scott Owens
Leaf Petersen
Emmanuel Polonowski
Yann Régis-Giannas
Tillmann Rendel
Morten Rhiger
Kristoffer Rose
Claudio Russo
Mathias Schwarz
Manuel Serrano
Peter Sestoft
Robert J. Simmons
Matthieu Sozeau
Vincent St-Amour
Alley Stoughton
T. Stephen Strickland
Kohei Suenaga
Wouter Swierstra
Jaroslav Ševčík
Keishi Tajima
Hayo Thielecke
Peter Thiemann
Jakob G. Thomsen
Sam Tobin-Hochstadt
Laurence Tratt
Aaron Turon
Daniele Varacca
Jeff Vaughan
Jérôme Vouillon
Dimitrios Vytiniotis
Philip Wadler
Ryan Wisnesky
Jeremy Yallop
Tetsuo Yokoyama
Noam Zeilberger
Ian Zerny

ICFP 2011 Sponsor & Supporters

Sponsor: acm SIGPLAN

Supporters:

CITRIX®

CREDIT SUISSE
Quantitative Strategies

Erlang SOLUTIONS

galois

IIJ
Internet Initiative Japan

JANE STREET

Microsoft Research

NII
National Institute of Informatics

université PARIS DIDEROT PARIS 7

Standard Chartered

TSURU CAPITAL

twitter

Towards a Comprehensive Theory of Monadic Effects

Andrzej Filinski
DIKU, University of Copenhagen
andrzej@diku.dk

Abstract

It has been more than 20 years since monads were proposed as a unifying concept for computational effects, in both formal semantics and functional programs. Over that period, there has been substantial incremental progress on several fronts within the ensuing research area, including denotational, operational, and axiomatic characterizations of effects; principles and frameworks for combining effects; prescriptive vs. descriptive effect-type systems; specification vs. implementation of effects; and realizations of effect-related theoretical constructions in practical functional languages, both eager and lazy. Yet few would confidently claim that programs with computational effects are by now as well understood, and as thoroughly supported by formal reasoning techniques, as types and terms in purely functional settings.

This talk outlines (one view of) the landscape of effectful functional programming, and attempts to assess our collective progress towards the goal of a broad yet coherent theory of monadic effects. We are not quite there yet, but intriguingly, many potential ingredients of such a theory have been repeatedly discovered and developed, with only minor variations, in seemingly unrelated contexts. Some stronger-than-expected ties between the research topics mentioned above also instill hope that there is indeed a natural, comprehensive theory of monadic effects, waiting to be fully explicated.

Categories and Subject Descriptors F.3.2 [*Logics and Meanings of Programs*]: Semantics of Programming Languages—Denotational semantics, Operational Semantics, Program Analysis

General Terms Languages, Theory

Keywords Monads, Computational Effects

ICFP'11, September 19–21, 2011, Tokyo, Japan.
ACM 978-1-4503-0865-6/11/09.

Just do It:
Simple Monadic Equational Reasoning

Jeremy Gibbons and Ralf Hinze

Department of Computer Science, University of Oxford
Wolfson Building, Parks Road
Oxford, OX1 3QD, England
http://www.cs.ox.ac.uk/{jeremy.gibbons,ralf.hinze}/

Abstract

One of the appeals of pure functional programming is that it is so amenable to equational reasoning. One of the problems of pure functional programming is that it rules out computational effects. Moggi and Wadler showed how to get round this problem by using monads to encapsulate the effects, leading in essence to a phase distinction—a pure functional evaluation yielding an impure imperative computation. Still, it has not been clear how to reconcile that phase distinction with the continuing appeal of functional programming; does the impure imperative part become inaccessible to equational reasoning? We think not; and to back that up, we present a simple axiomatic approach to reasoning about programs with computational effects.

Categories and Subject Descriptors D.2.4 [*Software/Program Verification*]: Correctness proofs, Programming by contract; F.3.1 [*Specifying and Verifying and Reasoning about Programs*]: Assertions, Logics of programs, Pre- and post-conditions, Specification techniques; F.3.3 [*Studies of Program Constructs*]: Functional constructs.

General Terms Languages, Theory, Verification.

Keywords Monads, equational reasoning, Lawvere theories, algebraic specification.

1. Introduction

Pure functional programming languages are good for equational reasoning [36]: non-strict semantics supports algebraic manipulation through the principle of 'substitution of equals for equals'. But on the face of it, purity is very limiting: many programs of interest involve impure computational effects, such as mutable state and nondeterminism. Famously, Moggi [16] and Wadler [38] showed how *monads* can be used to neatly encapsulate these effects. A pure program can assemble a representation of an effectful computation as a plain value, which can then be executed at the top level instead of being printed out—'Haskell is the world's finest imperative programming language' [21].

ICFP'11, September 19–21, 2011, Tokyo, Japan.

Nevertheless, little work has been done on the combination of equational reasoning and programs exhibiting computational effects. Current practice involves simulating an effectful computation as a pure function, and conducting the reasoning on this pure value; for example, a recent paper by Hutton and Fulger [9] presents a proof of correctness of a stateful computation using equational reasoning in terms of pure state-transforming functions. This works, but it is unsatisfactory in a number of ways: for one thing, it breaches the abstraction boundary provided by the monadic interface, inhibiting any reuse of proof efforts across programs using different classes of effect; and for another, not all computational effects can be adequately simulated in this way.

In this paper, we present a simple axiomatic approach to equational reasoning with monadic programs, preserving the monadic abstraction. The key idea is to exploit the algebraic properties of both the generic monad interface (the 'return' and 'bind' operators, and their associativity and unit laws) and the specific operations used to support a particular class of effects (for example, the 'put' and 'get' operations of mutable state, or the 'choice' points in nondeterministic computations). In essence, this is an approach based more on the 'algebraic theory' interpretation of universal algebra within category theory [13] than on the later 'monad' interpretation [14] more familiar to functional programmers. Either can be used to model computational effects in a pure setting [10], with nearly equivalent expressiveness, but the 'algebraic theory' interpretation emphasizes the specifics of a particular class of effects, whereas the 'monad' interpretation focusses on the general notion of effectful computations and says little about specific effects.

In passing, we present (what we believe to be) a novel approach to reasoning about programs that exploit both nondeterministic and probabilistic choice. The monad of nondeterminism (that is, the list functor, or more accurately the finite powerset functor) is very familiar to functional programmers [38, 20]. Less well known in functional programming circles, but nevertheless well established in programming language semantics, is the monad of probability distributions [5, 11, 27, 3]. We show that these two monads combine neatly, providing a simple unified model of nondeterminism and probability, supporting the same simple equational reasoning as any other monad. Models for this combination of effects have been given before (see for example [15]), but we believe that none are as straightforward as ours.

The remainder of the paper is structured as follows. We warm up in Section 3 with a discussion of a simple problem involving effectful computation—counting the disc moves in the Towers of Hanoi puzzle. In Sections 4, 5, and 6 we consider some more interesting effects: nondeterminism, exceptions, and mutable state, respectively. In Section 7 we look at programs that combine two classes of effect, nondeterminism and state; and in Section 8 we look at probabilistic computations, and their combination with nondeterminism. Finally, we return to Hutton and Fulger's tree relabelling problem in Section 9, and Section 10 concludes. But we start in Section 2 with some background on monads.

2. Background

As is well known [16, 38], the categorical notion of a *monad* precisely expresses an abstraction of sequential computations, which is necessary for controlling the consequences of computational effects in a lazy functional programming language. The 'return' and 'bind' methods model the identity and sequential composition of computations, respectively. They are captured in the following type class:

$$\begin{array}{l}\textbf{class}\ \mathit{Monad}\ m\ \textbf{where}\\ \quad \mathit{return} :: a \to m\ a\\ \quad (\gg\!=) :: m\ a \to (a \to m\ b) \to m\ b\end{array}$$

The two operations are required to satisfy three laws, corresponding to the monoidal properties of sequential composition:

$$\begin{array}{ll}\mathit{return}\ x \gg\!= k & = k\ x\\ \mathit{mx} \gg\!= \mathit{return} & = \mathit{mx}\\ (\mathit{mx} \gg\!= k) \gg\!= k' & = \mathit{mx} \gg\!= (\lambda x \to k\ x \gg\!= k')\end{array}$$

We will make use of two important specializations of the operations associated with a monad, which more precisely match the idea of the identity computation and sequential composition:

$$\begin{array}{ll}\mathit{skip} & :: \mathit{Monad}\ m \Rightarrow m\ ()\\ \mathit{skip} & = \mathit{return}\ ()\\ (\gg) & :: \mathit{Monad}\ m \Rightarrow m\ a \to m\ b \to m\ b\\ \mathit{mx} \gg \mathit{my} & = \mathit{mx} \gg\!= \mathit{const}\ \mathit{my}\end{array}$$

We will also make significant use of the derived operator

$$\begin{array}{l}\mathit{liftM} :: \mathit{Monad}\ m \Rightarrow (a \to b) \to m\ a \to m\ b\\ \mathit{liftM}\ f\ \mathit{mx} = \mathit{mx} \gg\!= \mathit{return} \circ f\end{array}$$

The reader may enjoy checking that the unit and associativity properties imply that *liftM* satisfies the map laws of a functor:

$$\begin{array}{ll}\mathit{liftM}\ \mathit{id} & = \mathit{id}\\ \mathit{liftM}\ (f \circ g) & = \mathit{liftM}\ f \circ \mathit{liftM}\ g\end{array}$$

An uncurried version of Haskell's *liftM2* can be defined as $\mathit{liftM}\ f \circ \mathit{pair}$, where *pair* sequences a pair of monadic computations:

$$\begin{array}{l}\mathit{pair} :: \mathit{Monad}\ m \Rightarrow (m\ a, m\ a) \to m\ (a,a)\\ \mathit{pair}\ (\mathit{mx},\mathit{my}) = \mathit{mx} \gg\!= \lambda x \to \mathit{my} \gg\!= \lambda y \to \mathit{return}\ (x,y)\end{array}$$

2.1 Imperative functional programming

The return and bind operations of the *Monad* class are sufficient to support a very convenient monad comprehension or '**do**' notation for computations, offering an elegant imperative programming style [37, 23]. The body of a **do** expression consists of a non-empty sequence of *qualifiers*, which may be *expressions*, *generators*, or *local definitions*—except for the last qualifier, which must be an expression. In this paper, we restrict attention to patterns consisting of simple variables or tuples of such; then the **do** notation can be defined in terms of just $\gg\!=$ and ordinary **let** (and *return*, which is usually needed for the final expression):

$$\begin{array}{ll}\textbf{do}\ \{e\} & = e\\ \textbf{do}\ \{e; es\} & = e \gg \textbf{do}\ \{es\}\\ \textbf{do}\ \{x \leftarrow e; es\} & = e \gg\!= \lambda x \to \textbf{do}\ \{es\}\\ \textbf{do}\ \{\textbf{let}\ \mathit{decls}; es\} & = \textbf{let}\ \mathit{decls}\ \textbf{in}\ \textbf{do}\ \{es\}\end{array}$$

For example, an alternative definition of *pair* is

$$\mathit{pair}\ (\mathit{mx},\mathit{my}) = \textbf{do}\ \{x \leftarrow \mathit{mx}; y \leftarrow \mathit{my}; \mathit{return}\ (x,y)\}$$

(More generally, the pattern match against a generated value might be refutable; then some mechanism for handling failed matches is necessary. In Haskell, the *Monad* class has an additional operation *fail* for this purpose; we will do without.)

The **do** notation makes it clearer that the monad laws are not awkward impositions, but properties essential for manipulating sequential compositions and blocks:

$$\begin{array}{ll}\textbf{do}\ \{y \leftarrow \mathit{return}\ x; k\ y\} & = \textbf{do}\ \{k\ x\}\\ \textbf{do}\ \{x \leftarrow \mathit{mx}; \mathit{return}\ x\} & = \textbf{do}\ \{\mathit{mx}\}\\ \textbf{do}\ \{x \leftarrow \mathit{mx}; y \leftarrow k\ x; k'\ y\} & = \textbf{do}\ \{y \leftarrow \textbf{do}\ \{x \leftarrow \mathit{mx}; k\ x\}; k'\ y\}\end{array}$$

where, in the third law, x is not free in k'. The first two laws state that *return* is a unit of sequential composition, and the third that nested blocks can be flattened, given appropriate care over bound variables.

3. A counter example: Towers of Hanoi

The *Monad* class specifies only the very basic general-purpose plumbing of sequential composition. To obtain any interesting computational effects, one must augment the interface with additional methods. In this paper, we will consistently do this by defining subclasses of *Monad*, rather than by declaring instances of *Monad* with additional operations; and we will studiously program and reason according to the interface, not to a particular implementation.

For example, here is a class of monads supporting a simple effect of counting:

$$\begin{array}{l}\textbf{class}\ \mathit{Monad}\ m \Rightarrow \mathit{MonadCount}\ m\ \textbf{where}\\ \quad \mathit{tick} :: m\ ()\end{array}$$

And here is a program for solving the Towers of Hanoi problem—it ticks the counter once for each move of a disc.

$$\begin{array}{ll}\mathit{hanoi} :: \mathit{MonadCount}\ m \Rightarrow \mathit{Int} \to m\ () & \\ \mathit{hanoi}\ 0 & = \mathit{skip}\\ \mathit{hanoi}\ (n+1) & = \mathit{hanoi}\ n \gg \mathit{tick} \gg \mathit{hanoi}\ n\end{array}$$

We claim that

$$\mathit{hanoi}\ n = \mathit{rep}\ (2^n - 1)\ \mathit{tick}$$

where *rep* repeats a unit computation a fixed number of times:

$$\begin{array}{ll}\mathit{rep} :: \mathit{Monad}\ m \Rightarrow \mathit{Int} \to m\ () \to m\ () & \\ \mathit{rep}\ 0 \qquad \mathit{mx} & = \mathit{skip}\\ \mathit{rep}\ (n+1)\ \mathit{mx} & = \mathit{mx} \gg \mathit{rep}\ n\ \mathit{mx}\end{array}$$

(This is a type specialization of the function *replicateM_* in the Haskell standard library.) Note that

$$\begin{array}{ll}\mathit{rep}\ 1 \qquad \mathit{mx} & = \mathit{mx}\\ \mathit{rep}\ (m+n)\ \mathit{mx} & = \mathit{rep}\ m\ \mathit{mx} \gg \mathit{rep}\ n\ \mathit{mx}\end{array}$$

The verification of *hanoi* is by induction on n. The base case is trivial; for the inductive step, we assume the result for n, and calculate:

$$\begin{array}{ll} & \mathit{hanoi}\ (n+1)\\ = & \quad [\![\ \text{definition of } \mathit{hanoi}\ ]\!]\\ & \mathit{hanoi}\ n \gg \mathit{tick} \gg \mathit{hanoi}\ n\\ = & \quad [\![\ \text{inductive hypothesis}\ ]\!]\\ & \mathit{rep}\ (2^n - 1)\ \mathit{tick} \gg \mathit{tick} \gg \mathit{rep}\ (2^n - 1)\ \mathit{tick}\\ = & \quad [\![\ \text{property of } \mathit{rep}\ ]\!]\\ & \mathit{rep}\ ((2^n - 1) + 1 + (2^n - 1))\ \mathit{tick}\\ = & \quad [\![\ \text{arithmetic}\ ]\!]\\ & \mathit{rep}\ (2^{n+1} - 1)\ \mathit{tick}\end{array}$$

This is a very simple example, because the additional algebraic structure in *MonadCount* is free—no laws were imposed on *tick*, and the only equivalences between counting programs are those induced by the monoidal structure of sequential composition. In the rest of the paper, we will look at more interesting classes of effect.

4. Nondeterministic computations

Nondeterministic programs are characterized by the ability to choose between multiple results, and (sometimes) by the possibility of returning no result at all. We express these as two separate subclasses of *Monad*.

4.1 Failure

We consider failure first, because it is the simpler feature:

$$\textbf{class}\ Monad\ m \Rightarrow MonadFail\ m\ \textbf{where} \\ \quad fail :: m\ a$$

The *fail* operation is a left zero of sequential composition:

$$fail \gg m = fail$$

but not a right zero—a computation of the form $mx \gg fail$ might yield some effects from mx before failing, and so be different from *fail* alone.

Note that this is a different design from that in Haskell standard [22], which provides a *fail* method in the *Monad* class itself (as discussed in Section 2.1), as well as an *mzero* method as part of a more extensive *MonadPlus* class (which we will discuss below)—but which is silent on the properties expected of *fail*. There is a proposal dating from 2006 on the Haskell Wiki [39] to reform the standard along the lines we have chosen, but the situation is still open.

We will make significant use of the function *guard*, which checks that a boolean condition holds, and fails if it does not:

$$guard :: MonadFail\ m \Rightarrow Bool \to m\ () \\ guard\ b = \textbf{if}\ b\ \textbf{then}\ skip\ \textbf{else}\ fail$$

and, later on, a related function that takes a predicate:

$$assert :: MonadFail\ m \Rightarrow (a \to Bool) \to m\ a \to m\ a \\ assert\ p\ mx = \textbf{do}\ \{x \leftarrow mx; guard\ (p\ x); return\ x\}$$

4.2 Choice

Choice is modelled by the class *MonadAlt*:

$$\textbf{class}\ MonadAlt\ m\ \textbf{where} \\ \quad (\Box) :: m\ a \to m\ a \to m\ a$$

subject to the axiom that $\Box$ is associative, and composition distributes leftwards over it:

$$(m \Box n) \Box p \quad = m \Box (n \Box p) \\ (m \Box n) \gg\!= k = (m \gg\!= k) \Box (n \gg\!= k)$$

Following [7], and in contrast to the 'additive monads' of Goncharov *et al.* [6], we do not always require composition to distribute *rightwards* over choice: in general,

$$m \gg\!= \lambda x \to k_1\ x \Box k_2\ x \neq (m \gg\!= k_1) \Box (m \gg\!= k_2)$$

As was the case above with *fail* on the right of a composition, this is a dubious proposition when m has non-idempotent effects, such as writing output: on the left-hand side above, the effects happen once, and on the right, twice. Sometimes, though, we do want this distributivity property; Section 7 is a case in point.

4.3 Nondeterminism

We model nondeterministic programs as those using the combination of failure and choice features:

$$\textbf{class}\ (MonadFail\ m, MonadAlt\ m) \Rightarrow MonadNondet\ m\ \textbf{where}$$

There are no additional operations; the body of this class definition is empty, and the operations of *MonadNondet* are just those of *MonadFail* (namely *fail*) together with those of *MonadAlt* (namely $\Box$). However, there are additional laws, beyond those of *MonadFail* and *MonadAlt* considered in isolation: *fail* should be a unit of $\Box$, giving a monoidal structure altogether.

The obvious model of the specification (indeed, the initial one) is given by lists:

$$\textbf{instance}\ Monad\ [\,]\ \textbf{where} \\ \quad return\ a \;\; = [a] \\ \quad mx \gg\!= k = concat\ (map\ k\ mx)$$

$$\textbf{instance}\ MonadFail\ [\,]\ \textbf{where} \\ \quad fail = [\,]$$

$$\textbf{instance}\ MonadAlt\ [\,]\ \textbf{where} \\ \quad (\Box) = (+\!\!+)$$

However, sometimes we do not want to treat the ordering of elements as significant, so we might sometimes impose an additional axiom that $\Box$ is commutative, in which case finite bags form the initial model. And sometimes we do not want to treat multiplicity of results as significant either, so we add the axiom that $\Box$ is idempotent; then finite sets form the initial model.

Note that *MonadNondet* is rather like the Haskell standard's *MonadPlus* class [22]. However, as we shall see in Section 5, there is an alternative interpretation of the same monoidal structure—intuitively, as exceptions rather than nondeterminism. The signatures of the operations are the same, but the laws are different, so the two interpretations should most definitely not be confused with each other. (In particular, it makes no sense at all to suppose that the *catch* operator in exception handling is commutative!)

4.4 Permutations

Here is a simple example of a nondeterministic program. The function *select* takes a non-empty list and nondeterministically chooses an element, returning that element and the remaining list; it fails on the empty list.

$$select :: MonadNondet\ m \Rightarrow [a] \to m\ (a,[a]) \\ select\ [\,] \qquad = fail \\ select\ (x:xs) = return\ (x,xs)\ \Box \\ \qquad\qquad\qquad \textbf{do}\ \{(y,ys) \leftarrow select\ xs; return\ (y,x:ys)\}$$

Using *select*, the function *perms* nondeterministically generates a permutation of a (finite) list.

$$perms :: MonadNondet\ m \Rightarrow [a] \to m\ [a] \\ perms\ [\,] = return\ [\,] \\ perms\ xs = \textbf{do}\ \{(y,ys) \leftarrow select\ xs; zs \leftarrow perms\ ys; return\ (y:zs)\}$$

We will exploit the laws of nondeterminism in Section 7 and 8.

5. Exceptional computations

Before we explore the ramifications of reasoning about nondeterminism monadically, it is worth pausing to consider again the importance of the laws associated with a class. There is another interpretation of the signature of the class *MonadNondet*, namely a monad with an imposed monoidal structure; but the additional laws are quite different, and hence so of course is the computational behaviour.

We have in mind the class of effect called *exceptions*. As with nondeterminism, there is a special constant *fail*, which is a left zero of composition. There is also a binary operator, which we will call *catch*, which forms a monoid in conjunction with *fail*. We capture the latter by means of a distinct subclass *MonadExcept* of *MonadFail*:

$$\textbf{class}\ \mathit{MonadFail}\ m \Rightarrow \mathit{MonadExcept}\ m\ \textbf{where}$$
$$\quad \mathit{catch} :: m\ a \rightarrow m\ a \rightarrow m\ a$$

The idea is that *fail* raises an exception, and that *catch m h* executes body *m*, but passes control to the handler *h* if an exception is raised during the execution of *m*. This operational intuition is expressed axiomatically by the laws—that *catch* and *fail* form a monoid:

$$\begin{aligned} &\mathit{catch}\ \mathit{fail}\ h &&= h \\ &\mathit{catch}\ m\ \mathit{fail} &&= m \\ &\mathit{catch}\ m\ (\mathit{catch}\ h\ h') &&= \mathit{catch}\ (\mathit{catch}\ m\ h)\ h' \end{aligned}$$

that unexceptional bodies need no handler:

$$\mathit{catch}\ (\mathit{return}\ x)\ h = \mathit{return}\ x$$

and that exceptions are left-zeros of sequential composition:

$$\mathit{fail} \gg \mathit{mx} = \mathit{fail}$$

No other properties are expected; in particular, we expect that in general distributivity of composition over exception handlers will fail:

$$(\mathit{catch}\ m\ h) \gg\!= k \neq \mathit{catch}\ (m \gg\!= k)\ (h \gg\!= k)$$

—exceptions raised by *k* on the left-hand side may be erroneously handled on the right-hand side. Conversely, with nondeterminism there is no requirement that pure computations are left zeros of $\square$.

5.1 Fast product

We can illustrate reasoning with exceptions via the 'fast product' algorithm, which multiplies the elements of a list of integers, but raises an exception if it finds a zero, subsequently catching the exception and returning zero for the overall product. We define

$$\mathit{fastprod} :: \mathit{MonadExcept}\ m \Rightarrow [\mathit{Int}] \rightarrow m\ \mathit{Int}$$
$$\mathit{fastprod}\ \mathit{xs} = \mathit{catch}\ (\mathit{work}\ \mathit{xs})\ (\mathit{return}\ 0)$$

where *work* is specified by

$$\mathit{work} :: \mathit{MonadFail}\ m \Rightarrow [\mathit{Int}] \rightarrow m\ \mathit{Int}$$
$$\mathit{work}\ \mathit{xs} = \textbf{if}\ 0 \in \mathit{xs}\ \textbf{then}\ \mathit{fail}\ \textbf{else}\ \mathit{return}\ (\mathit{product}\ \mathit{xs})$$

And we calculate:

$$\begin{aligned} &\mathit{fastprod}\ \mathit{xs} \\ =\ &\quad [\![\ \text{definition of } \mathit{fastprod}\ ]\!] \\ &\mathit{catch}\ (\mathit{work}\ \mathit{xs})\ (\mathit{return}\ 0) \\ =\ &\quad [\![\ \text{specification of } \mathit{work}\ ]\!] \\ &\mathit{catch}\ (\textbf{if}\ 0 \in \mathit{xs}\ \textbf{then}\ \mathit{fail}\ \textbf{else}\ \mathit{return}\ (\mathit{product}\ \mathit{xs}))\ (\mathit{return}\ 0) \\ =\ &\quad [\![\ \text{lift out the conditional}\ ]\!] \\ &\textbf{if}\ 0 \in \mathit{xs}\ \textbf{then}\ \mathit{catch}\ \mathit{fail}\ (\mathit{return}\ 0) \\ &\qquad\qquad \textbf{else}\ \ \mathit{catch}\ (\mathit{return}\ (\mathit{product}\ \mathit{xs}))\ (\mathit{return}\ 0) \\ =\ &\quad [\![\ \text{laws of } \mathit{catch}, \mathit{fail}, \text{and } \mathit{return}\ ]\!] \\ &\textbf{if}\ 0 \in \mathit{xs}\ \textbf{then}\ \mathit{return}\ 0\ \textbf{else}\ \mathit{return}\ (\mathit{product}\ \mathit{xs}) \\ =\ &\quad [\![\ \text{arithmetic: } 0 \in \mathit{xs} \Longrightarrow \mathit{product}\ \mathit{xs} = 0\ ]\!] \\ &\textbf{if}\ 0 \in \mathit{xs}\ \textbf{then}\ \mathit{return}\ (\mathit{product}\ \mathit{xs})\ \textbf{else}\ \mathit{return}\ (\mathit{product}\ \mathit{xs}) \\ =\ &\quad [\![\ \text{redundant conditional}\ ]\!] \\ &\mathit{return}\ (\mathit{product}\ \mathit{xs}) \end{aligned}$$

Thus, *fastprod* is pure, never throwing an unhandled exception. Moreover, *work* may be refined separately, to eliminate the multiple traversals; one can use the universal property of *foldr* to derive

$$\mathit{work} = \mathit{foldr}\ \mathit{next}\ (\mathit{return}\ 1)\ \textbf{where}$$
$$\quad \mathit{next}\ n\ \mathit{mx} = \textbf{if}\ n == 0\ \textbf{then}\ \mathit{fail}\ \textbf{else}\ \mathit{liftM}\ (n\times)\ \mathit{mx}$$

The two steps of the calculation concerning conditionals depend only on pure reasoning: for non-bottom boolean *b*, we have:

$$\begin{aligned} &\textbf{if}\ b\ \textbf{then}\ f\ x\ \textbf{else}\ f\ y = f\ (\textbf{if}\ b\ \textbf{then}\ x\ \textbf{else}\ y) \\ &\textbf{if}\ b\ \textbf{then}\ x\quad \textbf{else}\ x\quad = x \end{aligned}$$

6. Stateful computations

Perhaps the foremost class of effect that springs to mind is that of stateful computations. These are captured by the interface

$$\textbf{class}\ \mathit{Monad}\ m \Rightarrow \mathit{MonadState}\ s\ m \mid m \rightarrow s\ \textbf{where}$$
$$\quad \mathit{get} :: m\ s$$
$$\quad \mathit{put} :: s \rightarrow m\ ()$$

Here, the class *MonadState s m* denotes monads *m* involving functions that transform a state of type *s*; the declaration includes a functional dependency, declaring that *m* determines *s*. The operation *get* yields a copy of the current state, and *put* overwrites the state with a new value (returning unit); they are related by four axioms:

$$\begin{aligned} &\mathit{put}\ s \gg \mathit{put}\ s' &&= \mathit{put}\ s' \\ &\mathit{put}\ s \gg \mathit{get} &&= \mathit{put}\ s \gg \mathit{return}\ s \\ &\mathit{get} \gg\!= \mathit{put} &&= \mathit{skip} \\ &\mathit{get} \gg\!= \lambda s \rightarrow \mathit{get} \gg\!= k\ s &&= \mathit{get} \gg\!= \lambda s \rightarrow k\ s\ s \end{aligned}$$

6.1 Eight queens

As an example of a stateful computation, we consider a few programs for the '*n* queens' problem. First, we start with a purely functional implementation, implicitly placing one queen in each column of the board, and explicitly assigning the rows of the queens from the permutation of the column numbers, so that by construction it is only the diagonals that are potential threats. The main data structure we manipulate is a pair of lists recording the up-diagonals and down-diagonals threatened by the queens to the right of a given column, where a queen in position (c,r) threatens up-diagonal $r-c$ and down-diagonal $r+c$.

For notational brevity, we define

$$\textbf{type}\ \mathit{Square}\ a = (a,a)$$

$$\mathit{square} :: (a \rightarrow b) \rightarrow (\mathit{Square}\ a \rightarrow \mathit{Square}\ b)$$
$$\mathit{square}\ f\ (a,b) = (f\ a, f\ b)$$

and write 'a^2' and 'f^2' for '*Square a*' and '*square f*', respectively.

The essence of the program is the following function *test*, which takes a (column, row) position for a queen, and lists of already threatened up- and down-diagonals, and returns a pair consisting of a boolean for whether this queen position is safe, and updated lists of threatened up- and down-diagonals.

$$\mathit{test} :: \mathit{Int}^2 \rightarrow [\mathit{Int}]^2 \rightarrow (\mathit{Bool}, [\mathit{Int}]^2)$$
$$\mathit{test}\ (c,r)\ (\mathit{ups},\mathit{downs}) =$$
$$\quad (u \notin \mathit{ups} \wedge d \notin \mathit{downs}, (u : \mathit{ups}, d : \mathit{downs}))$$
$$\qquad \textbf{where}\ (u,d) = (r-c, r+c)$$

Predicate safe_1 checks a putative placement of queens for safety, using a fold from right to left over the list of column-row pairs. The carrier $(\mathit{Bool}, [\mathit{Int}]^2)$ of the fold consists of a boolean indicating whether the queens to the right, which have already been checked, are safe, and the up- and down-diagonals under threat from the queens considered so far.

$$\mathit{safe}_1 :: [\mathit{Int}]^2 \rightarrow [\mathit{Int}^2] \rightarrow (\mathit{Bool}, [\mathit{Int}]^2)$$
$$\mathit{safe}_1 = \mathit{foldr}\ \mathit{step}_1 \circ \mathit{start}_1$$

$$start_1 :: [Int]^2 \to (Bool, [Int]^2)$$
$$start_1\ updowns = (True, updowns)$$

$$step_1 :: Int^2 \to (Bool, [Int]^2) \to (Bool, [Int]^2)$$
$$step_1\ cr\ (restOK, updowns) = (thisOK \wedge restOK, updowns')$$
$$\quad \textbf{where}\ (thisOK, updowns') = test\ cr\ updowns$$

To allow convenient expression below of the relationship between $safe_1$ and some later variants, we have factored out the initial value $([\,],[\,])$ for the threatened diagonals, and have not projected away the final diagonals; so the actual test for whether a list *crs* of column-row pairs is safe is $fst\ (safe_1\ ([\,],[\,])\ crs)$. In particular, the safe arrangements of n queens can be computed in a generate-and-test fashion, nondeterministically choosing row lists as permutations and discarding the unsafe ones:

$$queens :: MonadNondet\ m \Rightarrow Int \to m\ [Int]$$
$$queens\ n$$
$$\quad = \textbf{do}\ \{ rs \leftarrow perms\ [1\,..\,n];$$
$$\qquad guard\ (fst\ (safe_1\ empty\ (place\ n\ rs)));return\ rs \}$$

$$place\ n\ rs = zip\ [1\,..\,n]\ rs$$
$$empty \quad = ([\,],[\,])$$

6.2 Queens, statefully

Rather than do the whole safety computation as a pure function, we now consider a version that uses a stateful computation to build up the sets of up- and down-diagonals threatened by the queens considered so far. The function returns a boolean, while statefully constructing the lists of threatened diagonals.

$$safe_2 :: MonadState\ [Int]^2\ m \Rightarrow [Int^2] \to m\ Bool$$
$$safe_2 = foldr\ step_2\ start_2$$

$$start_2 :: MonadState\ [Int]^2\ m \Rightarrow m\ Bool$$
$$start_2 = return\ True$$

$$step_2 :: MonadState\ [Int]^2\ m \Rightarrow Int^2 \to m\ Bool \to m\ Bool$$
$$step_2\ cr\ k$$
$$\quad = \textbf{do}\ \{ b' \leftarrow k; uds \leftarrow get; \textbf{let}\ (b, uds') = test\ cr\ uds;$$
$$\qquad put\ uds'; return\ (b \wedge b') \}$$

In Figure 1, we prove using the axioms of *get* and *put* that

$$safe_2\ crs$$
$$\quad = \textbf{do}\ \{ uds \leftarrow get; \textbf{let}\ (ok, uds') = safe_1\ uds\ crs;$$
$$\qquad put\ uds'; return\ ok \}$$

by showing that this **do** expression satisfies the universal property of the fold in $safe_2$. This explains how the stateful computation $safe_2$ relates to the pure function $safe_1$. However, in order to revise the definition of *queens* to use $safe_2$ instead of $safe_1$, we need to reconcile the different computational settings: *perms* is nondeterministic, and $safe_2$ is stateful. We could flatten the stateful computation to a pure function: if we assume also the existence of a reification function

$$run :: MonadState\ s\ m \Rightarrow m\ a \to (s \to (a, s))$$

then we have

$$run\ (safe_2\ crs)\ updowns = safe_1\ updowns\ crs$$

and obtain a plug-in replacement for the use of $safe_1$ in *queens*. We will not do that; instead, we will lift the two components *perms* and $safe_2$ into one unified setting, providing both nondeterministic and stateful effects.

7. Combining effects

One distinct advantage of the axiomatic approach to reasoning with effects is that it is straightforward to take reasoning conducted in one setting and reuse it in another—that is, indeed, the general benefit of 'programming to an interface'.

In the case of the n-queens problem, we have a nondeterministic program generating candidate solutions (namely, permutations of the rows of the chessboard), and a stateful program testing those candidates (namely, the safety check acting on a pair of lists of diagonals). To that end, we name the combination of effects:

$$\textbf{class}\ (MonadState\ s\ m, MonadNondet\ m) \Rightarrow$$
$$\quad MonadStateNondet\ s\ m \mid m \to s$$

There are no additional operations; *MonadStateNondet*'s operations are just those of *MonadState* (namely, *get* and *put*) together with those of *MonadNondet* (namely, *fail* and $\square$). But, as with *MonadNondet* itself earlier, we need to specify how the two classes of effect interact. In this case, we want *backtrackable state*, with nondeterministic behaviour taking priority over stateful behaviour—a failing computation should discard any accumulated stateful effects, and choice points should be explored from a common starting state. This is captured equationally by stipulating that failure is a right zero of sequential composition:

$$m \gg fail = fail$$

and that composition distributes rightwards over choice:

$$m \gg\!= \lambda x \to k_1\ x \,\square\, k_2\ x = (m \gg\!= k_1) \,\square\, (m \gg\!= k_2)$$

Recall that the *MonadNondet* class already requires *fail* to be a left zero of composition, and composition to distribute leftwards over choice. It would be unreasonable to require the additional two laws in general, because not all effects are backtrackable; but this is not an issue for state transformations. The alternative is to 'keep calm and carry on'—state persists over failure, and is threaded linearly through choice points—but this is not what we want for the n-queens problem. (Failure happens in selecting from the empty list when generating a permutation, and when discovering that a putative queen position is already threatened, and in both cases we should abandon that alternative and try an alternative. Choices take place between permutations, and each permutation should be checked starting from a clean slate.) The types $s \to [(a, s)]$ and $s \to ([a], s)$ are both models of stateful and nondeterministic computations, but only the first is a model of backtrackable state.

A crucial consequence of failure being a left and right zero of composition (and *skip* being a left and right unit) is that guards commute with anything:

$$guard\ b \gg m = m \gg\!= \lambda x \to guard\ b \gg return\ x$$

Indeed, the same applies for any expression involving only the effects of *MonadFail*: if *mx* has type $MonadFail\ m \Rightarrow m\ a$ and *my* has type $MonadStateNondet\ m \Rightarrow m\ b$, then

$$\textbf{do}\ \{ x \leftarrow mx; y \leftarrow my; return\ (x, y) \}$$
$$= \textbf{do}\ \{ y \leftarrow my; x \leftarrow mx; return\ (x, y) \}$$

7.1 Queens, statefully and nondeterministically

Now, from the axiom of state that $get \gg\!= put = skip$, we have

$$queens\ n = \textbf{do}\ \{ s \leftarrow get; put\ s; queens\ n \}$$

and from that we can calculate using basic properties of monads, together with the fact that *perms* is independent of the state and so commutes with *put*, that

$$queens\ n$$
$$\quad = \textbf{do}\ \{ s \leftarrow get; rs \leftarrow perms\ [1\,..\,n]; put\ empty;$$
$$\qquad ok \leftarrow safe_2\ (place\ n\ rs); put\ s; guard\ ok; return\ rs \}$$

This program is a little clumsy, but it does accurately capture the relationship with the non-stateful version of *queens*: when interpreted

For the empty list, we have:

$$
\begin{array}{l}
\quad \mathbf{do}\ \{ uds \leftarrow get ; \mathbf{let}\ (ok, uds') = safe_1\ uds\ [\,] ; put\ uds' ; return\ ok \} \\
= \quad [\![\text{ definition of } safe_1 \ ]\!] \\
\quad \mathbf{do}\ \{ uds \leftarrow get ; \mathbf{let}\ (ok, uds') = start_1\ uds ; put\ uds' ; return\ ok \} \\
= \quad [\![\text{ definition of } start_1 \ ]\!] \\
\quad \mathbf{do}\ \{ uds \leftarrow get ; \mathbf{let}\ (ok, uds') = (True, uds) ; put\ uds' ; return\ ok \} \\
= \quad [\![\text{ lifting the } \mathbf{let}\text{; } get \gg\!= put = return\ () \ ]\!] \\
\quad return\ True \\
= \quad [\![\text{ definition of } safe_2 \ ]\!] \\
\quad safe_2\ [\,]
\end{array}
$$

while for non-empty lists, we have:

$$
\begin{array}{l}
\quad \mathbf{do}\ \{ uds \leftarrow get ; \mathbf{let}\ (ok, uds') = safe_1\ uds\ (cr : crs) ; put\ uds' ; return\ ok \} \\
= \quad [\![\text{ definition of } safe_1 \text{ as a } foldr \ ]\!] \\
\quad \mathbf{do}\ \{ uds \leftarrow get ; \mathbf{let}\ (ok, uds') = step_1\ cr\ (safe_1\ uds\ crs) ; put\ uds' ; return\ ok \} \\
= \quad [\![\text{ introduce a } \mathbf{let} \ ]\!] \\
\quad \mathbf{do}\ \{ uds \leftarrow get ; \mathbf{let}\ (b', uds'') = safe_1\ uds\ crs ; \mathbf{let}\ (ok, uds') = step_1\ cr\ (b', uds'') ; put\ uds' ; return\ ok \} \\
= \quad [\![\text{ definition of } step_1 \ ]\!] \\
\quad \mathbf{do}\ \{ uds \leftarrow get ; \mathbf{let}\ (b', uds'') = safe_1\ uds\ crs ; \mathbf{let}\ (b, uds''') = test\ cr\ uds'' ; \mathbf{let}\ (ok, uds') = (b \wedge b', uds''') ; put\ uds' ; return\ ok \} \\
= \quad [\![\ put\ s \gg put\ s' = put\ s' \ ]\!] \\
\quad \mathbf{do}\ \{ uds \leftarrow get ; \mathbf{let}\ (b', uds'') = safe_1\ uds\ crs ; \mathbf{let}\ (b, uds''') = test\ cr\ uds'' ; \mathbf{let}\ (ok, uds') = (b \wedge b', uds''') ; put\ uds'' ; put\ uds' ; return\ ok \} \\
= \quad [\![\text{ move two of the } \mathbf{let}\text{s} \ ]\!] \\
\quad \mathbf{do}\ \{ uds \leftarrow get ; \mathbf{let}\ (b', uds'') = safe_1\ uds\ crs ; put\ uds'' ; \mathbf{let}\ (b, uds''') = test\ cr\ uds'' ; \mathbf{let}\ (ok, uds') = (b \wedge b', uds''') ; put\ uds' ; return\ ok \} \\
= \quad [\![\ put\ s \gg get \gg\!= k = put\ s \gg k\ s \ ]\!] \\
\quad \mathbf{do}\ \{ uds \leftarrow get ; \mathbf{let}\ (b', uds'') = safe_1\ uds\ crs ; put\ uds'' ; \\
\qquad uds'''' \leftarrow get ; \mathbf{let}\ (b, uds''') = test\ cr\ uds'''' ; \mathbf{let}\ (ok, uds') = (b \wedge b', uds''') ; put\ uds' ; return\ ok \} \\
= \quad [\![\text{ associativity of } \gg\!= \ ]\!] \\
\quad \mathbf{do}\ \{ b' \leftarrow \mathbf{do}\ \{ uds \leftarrow get ; \mathbf{let}\ (ok, uds'') = safe_1\ uds\ crs ; put\ uds'' ; return\ ok \} ; \\
\qquad uds'''' \leftarrow get ; \mathbf{let}\ (b, uds''') = test\ cr\ uds'''' ; \mathbf{let}\ (ok, uds') = (b \wedge b', uds''') ; put\ uds' ; return\ ok \} \\
= \quad [\![\text{ definition of } step_2 \ ]\!] \\
\quad step_2\ cr\ (\mathbf{do}\ \{ uds \leftarrow get ; \mathbf{let}\ (ok, uds'') = safe_1\ uds\ crs ; put\ uds'' ; return\ ok \})
\end{array}
$$

Figure 1. Proving the relationship between $safe_2$ and $safe_1$

in a stateful setting, it amounts to remembering the current state s, executing a stateful version of *queens*, and restoring the original state s again.

7.2 Queens, exploratively

There is a more natural generate-and-test algorithm for the n-queens problem: rather than computing a boolean *ok* for whether an arrangement of queens is safe, and then asserting *ok*, we explore the possible threats to each queen in turn, and immediately abandon this arrangement if ever two queens conflict. How does this algorithm relate to the previous one? Very straightforwardly, as it turns out.

Since guards commute with anything, in the version of the *queens* program from Section 7.1, the *put s* and *guard ok* in particular commute, and we have:

$$
\begin{array}{l}
queens\ n \\
\quad = \mathbf{do}\ \{ s \leftarrow get ; rs \leftarrow perms\ [1\,..\,n] ; put\ empty ; \\
\qquad\quad ok \leftarrow safe_2\ (place\ n\ rs) ; guard\ ok ; put\ s ; return\ rs \}
\end{array}
$$

Let us therefore define

$$safe_3\ crs = safe_2\ crs \gg\!= guard$$

so that

$$
\begin{array}{l}
queens\ n \\
\quad = \mathbf{do}\ \{ s \leftarrow get ; rs \leftarrow perms\ [1\,..\,n] ; put\ empty ; \\
\qquad\quad safe_3\ (place\ n\ rs) ; put\ s ; return\ rs \}
\end{array}
$$

Now, let us investigate $safe_3$. Recall that $safe_2$ is a fold. Moreover, $(\gg\!= guard)$ combines with that fold using the fusion property, as we now show. The initial value is simple:

$$start_2 \gg\!= guard = guard\ True = skip$$

For the inductive step, we have:

$$
\begin{array}{l}
\quad step_2\ cr\ k \gg\!= guard \\
= \quad [\![\text{ definition of } step_2 \ ]\!] \\
\quad \mathbf{do}\ \{ b' \leftarrow k ; uds \leftarrow get ; \mathbf{let}\ (b, uds') = test\ cr\ uds ; \\
\qquad put\ uds' ; return\ (b \wedge b') \} \gg\!= guard \\
= \quad [\![\ \mathbf{do}\text{-notation} \ ]\!] \\
\quad \mathbf{do}\ \{ b' \leftarrow k ; uds \leftarrow get ; \mathbf{let}\ (b, uds') = test\ cr\ uds ; \\
\qquad put\ uds' ; guard\ (b \wedge b') \} \\
= \quad [\![\ guard \text{ distributes over conjunction }]\!] \\
\quad \mathbf{do}\ \{ b' \leftarrow k ; uds \leftarrow get ; \mathbf{let}\ (b, uds') = test\ cr\ uds ; \\
\qquad put\ uds' ; guard\ b ; guard\ b' \} \\
= \quad [\![\ guard\text{s commute with anything }]\!] \\
\quad \mathbf{do}\ \{ b' \leftarrow k ; guard\ b' ; uds \leftarrow get ; \mathbf{let}\ (b, uds') = test\ cr\ uds ; \\
\qquad put\ uds' ; guard\ b \} \\
= \quad [\![\text{ associativity of } \gg\!= \ ]\!] \\
\quad \mathbf{do}\ \{ (k \gg\!= guard) ; uds \leftarrow get ; \mathbf{let}\ (b, uds') = test\ cr\ uds ; \\
\qquad put\ uds' ; guard\ b \} \\
= \quad [\![\text{ definition of } step_3 \text{ (see below) }]\!] \\
\quad step_3\ cr\ (k \gg\!= guard)
\end{array}
$$

where we define

$step_3\ cr\ m = m \gg$
$\quad \mathbf{do}\ \{uds \leftarrow get\,;\mathbf{let}\ (b,uds') = test\ cr\ uds\,;put\ uds'\,;guard\ b\}$

Therefore, by fold fusion, we have

$safe_3\ crs = foldr\ step_3\ skip$

We have derived this 'exploratory' version of the n-queens algorithm from the merely 'stateful and nondeterministic' one using plain old-fashioned equational reasoning. Of course, it is still a rather inefficient algorithm; we have simply used the problem as a vehicle for demonstrating the modularity achievable using the axiomatic approach to specifying effects.

8. Probabilistic computations

The observation that probability distributions form a monad is fairly well known; the first published description appears to date from 1981 [5], but (as with so many things) the credit seems to go back to an observation by Lawvere twenty years earlier [12]. Jones and Plotkin [11] use this theory to construct a powerdomain of probability distributions, allowing them to give a semantics to recursive programs with probabilistic features; Ramsey and Pfeffer [27] use it to define a probabilistic lambda calculus for finitely supported distributions; Erwig and Kollmansberger [3] describe a little monadic Haskell library for programming with finitely supported distributions.

We suppose a type *Prob* of probabilities (say, the rationals in the closed unit interval), and define a type class of finitely supported probability distributions by:

$\mathbf{class}\ Monad\ m \Rightarrow MonadProb\ m\ \mathbf{where}$
$\quad choice :: Prob \rightarrow m\ a \rightarrow m\ a \rightarrow m\ a$

The idea is that *choice p mx my* behaves as *mx* with probability p and as *my* with probability $1-p$. From now on, we will write '$\bar{p}$' for $1-p$, and following Hoare [8], write choice in infix notation, '$mx \lhd p \rhd my$', because this makes the laws more transparent. We have two identity laws:

$mx \lhd 0 \rhd my = my$
$mx \lhd 1 \rhd my = mx$

a skewed commutativity law:

$mx \lhd p \rhd my = my \lhd \bar{p} \rhd mx$

idempotence:

$mx \lhd p \rhd mx = mx$

and quasi-associativity:

$mx \lhd p \rhd (my \lhd q \rhd mz) = (mx \lhd r \rhd my) \lhd s \rhd mz$
$\quad \Longleftarrow p = r\,s \wedge \bar{s} = \bar{p}\,\bar{q}$

(As informal justification for the associativity law, observe that the likelihoods of mx, my, mz on the left are $p, \bar{p}q, \bar{p}\,\bar{q}$, and on the right are $rs, \bar{r}s, \bar{s}$, and a little algebra shows that these are pairwise equal, given the premise.) Moreover, bind distributes leftwards and rightwards over choice:

$(mx \lhd p \rhd my) \gg\!= k \qquad = (mx \gg\!= k) \lhd p \rhd (my \gg\!= k)$
$mx \gg\!= \lambda x \rightarrow k_1\ x \lhd p \rhd k_2\ x = (mx \gg\!= k_1) \lhd p \rhd (mx \gg\!= k_2)$

where, in the second law, x is assumed not to occur free in p.

For example, here is a function to generate a uniform distribution from a finite list of outcomes:

$uniform :: MonadProb\ m \Rightarrow [a] \rightarrow m\ a$
$uniform\ [x] \qquad = return\ x$
$uniform\ (x:xs) = return\ x \lhd {}^{1}/_{length\ (x:xs)} \rhd uniform\ xs$

Note that *uniform xs* is side-effect-free ($uniform\ xs \gg m = m$), because bind distributes leftwards over choice.

8.1 The Monty Hall Problem

As an example, consider the so-called Monty Hall Problem [28], which famously caused a controversy following its discussion in Marilyn vos Savant's column in *Parade* magazine in 1990 [35]. Vos Savant described the problem as follows (quoting a letter from a reader, Craig F. Whitaker):

> *Suppose you're on a game show, and you're given the choice of three doors: Behind one door is a car; behind the others, goats. You pick a door, say No. 1, and the host, who knows what's behind the doors, opens another door, say No. 3, which has a goat. He then says to you, "Do you want to pick door No. 2?" Is it to your advantage to switch your choice?*

Implicitly, the car is equally likely to be behind each of the three doors, the car is the prize and the goats are booby prizes, the host always opens a door, and it always differs from the one you pick and always reveals a goat, and you always get the option to switch.

We might model this as follows. There are three doors:

$\mathbf{data}\ Door = A \mid B \mid C\ \mathbf{deriving}\ (Eq, Show)$

$doors :: [Door]$
$doors = [A,B,C]$

First, the host hides the car behind one of the doors, chosen uniformly at random:

$hide :: MonadProb\ m \Rightarrow m\ Door$
$hide = uniform\ doors$

Second, you pick one of the doors, also randomly:

$pick :: MonadProb\ m \Rightarrow m\ Door$
$pick = uniform\ doors$

Third, the host teases you by opening one of the doors—not the one that hides the car, nor the one you picked—to reveal a goat, choosing randomly among the one or two remaining doors:

$tease :: MonadProb\ m \Rightarrow Door \rightarrow Door \rightarrow m\ Door$
$tease\ h\ p = uniform\ (doors \setminus\!\setminus [h,p])$

(Here, the expression $xs \setminus\!\setminus ys$ denotes the list of those elements of xs absent from ys.) Fourth, the host offers you the choice between two strategies—either to switch to the door that is neither your original choice nor the opened one:

$switch :: MonadProb\ m \Rightarrow Door \rightarrow Door \rightarrow m\ Door$
$switch\ p\ t = return\ (head\ (doors \setminus\!\setminus [p,t]))$

or to stick with your original choice:

$stick :: MonadProb\ m \Rightarrow Door \rightarrow Door \rightarrow m\ Door$
$stick\ p\ t = return\ p$

(In either case, you know p and t but not h.) Here's the whole game, parametrized by your strategy, returning whether you win the car:

```
play :: MonadProb m ⇒ (Door → Door → m Door) → m Bool
play strategy =
  do
    h ← hide              -- host hides the car behind door h
    p ← pick              -- you pick door p
    t ← tease h p         -- host teases you with door t (≠ h,p)
    s ← strategy p t      -- you choose, based on p and t
    return (s == h)       -- you win iff your choice s equals h
```

We will show below that the switching strategy is twice as good as the sticking strategy:

$$\begin{aligned}
&\mathit{play\ switch} = \mathit{uniform}\ [\mathit{True},\mathit{True},\mathit{False}]\\
&\mathit{play\ stick}\ \ = \mathit{uniform}\ [\mathit{False},\mathit{False},\mathit{True}]
\end{aligned}$$

The key is the fact that uniform choices are independent, in the sense that choosing consecutively from two uniform distributions is equivalent to choosing simultaneously from their cartesian product:

$$\mathit{pair}\ (\mathit{uniform}\ x, \mathit{uniform}\ y) = \mathit{uniform}\ (\mathit{cp}\ x\ y)$$

where

$$\begin{aligned}
&\mathit{cp} :: [a] \to [b] \to [(a,b)]\\
&\mathit{cp}\ x\ y = [(a,b) \mid a \leftarrow x, b \leftarrow y]
\end{aligned}$$

We omit the straightforward proof by induction.

Expanding definitions and exploiting independence of uniform choices, we have

$$\begin{aligned}
&\mathit{play\ strategy}\\
&\quad = \mathbf{do}\ \{(h,p) \leftarrow \mathit{uniform}\ (\mathit{cp\ doors\ doors}); t \leftarrow \mathit{tease}\ h\ p;\\
&\qquad\quad s \leftarrow \mathit{strategy}\ p\ t; \mathit{return}\ (s == h)\}
\end{aligned}$$

So we calculate:

$$\begin{aligned}
&\mathit{play\ stick}\\
=\ &\quad [\![\ \text{definition of } \mathit{play}\ ]\!]\\
&\mathbf{do}\ \{(h,p) \leftarrow \mathit{uniform}\ (\mathit{cp\ doors\ doors});\\
&\qquad t \leftarrow \mathit{tease}\ h\ p; s \leftarrow \mathit{stick}\ p\ t; \mathit{return}\ (s == h)\}\\
=\ &\quad [\![\ \mathit{stick}\ p\ t = \mathit{return}\ p\ ]\!]\\
&\mathbf{do}\ \{(h,p) \leftarrow \mathit{uniform}\ (\mathit{cp\ doors\ doors});\\
&\qquad t \leftarrow \mathit{tease}\ h\ p; \mathit{return}\ (p == h)\}\\
=\ &\quad [\![\ t \text{ unused, and } \mathit{uniform} \text{ side-effect-free; } \mathit{liftM}\ ]\!]\\
&\mathit{liftM}\ (\mathit{uncurry}\ (==))\ (\mathit{uniform}\ (\mathit{cp\ doors\ doors}))\\
=\ &\quad [\![\ \text{naturality of } \mathit{uniform}; \text{ definition of } \mathit{cp}, ==\ ]\!]\\
&\mathit{uniform}\ [\mathit{True},\mathit{False},\mathit{False},\mathit{False},\mathit{True},\mathit{False},\mathit{False},\mathit{False},\mathit{True}]\\
=\ &\quad [\![\ \text{simplifying: three } \mathit{True}\text{s, six } \mathit{False}\text{s}\ ]\!]\\
&\mathit{uniform}\ [\mathit{True},\mathit{False},\mathit{False}]
\end{aligned}$$

and

$$\begin{aligned}
&\mathit{play\ switch}\\
=\ &\quad [\![\ \text{definition of } \mathit{play}\ ]\!]\\
&\mathbf{do}\ \{(h,p) \leftarrow \mathit{uniform}\ (\mathit{cp\ doors\ doors}); t \leftarrow \mathit{tease}\ h\ p;\\
&\qquad s \leftarrow \mathit{switch}\ p\ t; \mathit{return}\ (s == h)\}\\
=\ &\quad [\![\ \mathit{switch}\ p\ t = \mathit{return}\ (\mathit{the}\ (\mathit{doors} \setminus\!\setminus [p,t]))\text{—see below}\ ]\!]\\
&\mathbf{do}\ \{(h,p) \leftarrow \mathit{uniform}\ (\mathit{cp\ doors\ doors}); t \leftarrow \mathit{tease}\ h\ p;\\
&\qquad s \leftarrow \mathit{return}\ (\mathit{the}\ (\mathit{doors} \setminus\!\setminus [p,t])); \mathit{return}\ (s == h)\}\\
=\ &\quad [\![\ \mathit{return} \text{ is left unit}\ ]\!]\\
&\mathbf{do}\ \{(h,p) \leftarrow \mathit{uniform}\ (\mathit{cp\ doors\ doors});\\
&\qquad t \leftarrow \mathit{tease}\ h\ p; \mathit{return}\ (h == \mathit{the}\ (\mathit{doors} \setminus\!\setminus [p,t]))\}\\
=\ &\quad [\![\ \text{case analysis on } h == p\text{—see below}\ ]\!]\\
&\mathbf{do}\ \{(h,p) \leftarrow \mathit{uniform}\ (\mathit{cp\ doors\ doors});\\
&\qquad \mathbf{if}\ (h == p)\ \mathbf{then}\ \mathit{return\ False}\ \mathbf{else}\ \mathit{return\ True}\}\\
=\ &\quad [\![\ \text{lift out conditional; booleans}\ ]\!]\\
&\mathbf{do}\ \{(h,p) \leftarrow \mathit{uniform}\ (\mathit{cp\ doors\ doors}); \mathit{return}\ (h \not= p)\}\\
=\ &\quad [\![\ \text{definition of } \mathit{liftM}\ ]\!]\\
&\mathit{liftM}\ (\mathit{uncurry}\ (\not=))\ (\mathit{uniform}\ (\mathit{cp\ doors\ doors}))\\
=\ &\quad [\![\ \text{naturality of } \mathit{uniform}; \text{ definition of } \mathit{cp}, ==\ ]\!]\\
&\mathit{uniform}\ [\mathit{False},\mathit{True},\mathit{True},\mathit{True},\mathit{False},\mathit{True},\mathit{True},\mathit{True},\mathit{False}]\\
=\ &\quad [\![\ \text{simplifying: three } \mathit{False}\text{s, six } \mathit{True}\text{s}\ ]\!]\\
&\mathit{uniform}\ [\mathit{False},\mathit{True},\mathit{True}]
\end{aligned}$$

For the second step above, note that t is by construction distinct from p, and so $\mathit{doors} \setminus\!\setminus [p,t]$ is a singleton; we therefore introduce the function *the* such that $\mathit{the}\ [a] = a$.

Now for the case analysis. For the case $h = p$, we have:

$$\begin{aligned}
&\mathbf{do}\ \{t \leftarrow \mathit{tease}\ h\ p; \mathit{return}\ (h == \mathit{the}\ (\mathit{doors} \setminus\!\setminus [p,t]))\}\\
=\ &\quad [\![\ \text{using } h = p\ ]\!]\\
&\mathbf{do}\ \{t \leftarrow \mathit{tease}\ h\ p; \mathit{return}\ (h == \mathit{the}\ (\mathit{doors} \setminus\!\setminus [h,t]))\}\\
=\ &\quad [\![\ h \text{ is not in } \mathit{doors} \setminus\!\setminus [h,t]\ ]\!]\\
&\mathbf{do}\ \{t \leftarrow \mathit{tease}\ h\ p; \mathit{return\ False}\}\\
=\ &\quad [\![\ t \text{ unused, and } \mathit{uniform}\ x \text{ side-effect-free}\ ]\!]\\
&\mathbf{do}\ \{\mathit{return\ False}\}
\end{aligned}$$

And for the case $h \neq p$, we have:

$$\begin{aligned}
&\mathbf{do}\ \{t \leftarrow \mathit{tease}\ h\ p; \mathit{return}\ (h == \mathit{the}\ (\mathit{doors} \setminus\!\setminus [p,t]))\}\\
=\ &\quad [\![\ \text{definition of } \mathit{tease}\ ]\!]\\
&\mathbf{do}\ \{t \leftarrow \mathit{uniform}\ (\mathit{doors} \setminus\!\setminus [h,p]);\\
&\qquad \mathit{return}\ (h == \mathit{the}\ (\mathit{doors} \setminus\!\setminus [p,t]))\}\\
=\ &\quad [\![\ h \neq p, \text{ so } \mathit{doors} \setminus\!\setminus [h,p] \text{ is a singleton}\ ]\!]\\
&\mathbf{do}\ \{\mathbf{let}\ t = \mathit{the}\ (\mathit{doors} \setminus\!\setminus [h,p]);\\
&\qquad \mathit{return}\ (h == \mathit{the}\ (\mathit{doors} \setminus\!\setminus [p,t]))\}\\
=\ &\quad [\![\ h \neq p, \text{ and } t \neq h,p; \text{ so } t,h,p \text{ distinct}\ ]\!]\\
&\mathbf{do}\ \{\mathbf{let}\ t = \mathit{the}\ (\mathit{doors} \setminus\!\setminus [h,p]); \mathit{return}\ (h == h)\}\\
=\ &\quad [\![\ t \text{ unused}\ ]\!]\\
&\mathbf{do}\ \{\mathit{return\ True}\}
\end{aligned}$$

This concludes our proof that vos Savant was right, and that the many mathematics PhDs who wrote in to *Parade* magazine chastizing her were—at best—thinking about a different problem.

8.2 Probability and nondeterminism

One might argue that a more accurate representation of the Monty Hall scenario allows the host a *nondeterministic* rather than probabilistic choice in hiding and teasing: Monty is in charge, and nobody says that he has to play fair.

The interaction of nondeterministic and probabilistic choice is notoriously tricky [40, 15], but it turns out to be mostly straightforward to give a model in terms of monads. We combine the two classes *MonadAlt* (interpreted commutatively and idempotently) and *MonadProb* of effects:

$$\mathbf{class}\ (\mathit{MonadAlt}\ m, \mathit{MonadProb}\ m) \Rightarrow \mathit{MonadAltProb}\ m\ \mathbf{where}$$

As before, there are no new operations. But there is an additional law, relating the two kinds of choice—probabilistic choice should distribute over nondeterministic:

$$m \triangleleft p \triangleright (n_1 \,\square\, n_2) = (m \triangleleft p \triangleright n_1) \,\square\, (m \triangleleft p \triangleright n_2)$$

Intuitively, no freedom is lost from the program on the left by making the nondeterministic choice before the probabilistic one rather than afterwards.

As a consequence of this distribution property, the semantic model is roughly as sets of distributions, as for example with the probabilistic predicate transformer work of McIver and Morgan [15]. But not quite sets; in order to retain the idempotence of probabilistic choice

$$mx \triangleleft p \triangleright mx = mx$$

we have to live with equivalence up to *convex closure* [33]—that is, if a computation may yield any two distributions d, d', then it may also yield their convex combination $r \times d + \bar{r} \times d'$ for any r with $0 \leqslant r \leqslant 1$. This is intuitively reasonable; if d, d' are possible outcomes of an experiment, then a sequence of experiments may yield any combination of ds and d's. The alternative solution, promoted by Varacca [34], is to abandon idempotence; this is unappealing to us, because it means that unused choices, such as Monty's *tease* in the face of the *stick* strategy, cannot be discarded.

As a simple example of a computation that mixes nondeterministic and probabilistic features, consider the basic operations of a fair coin toss [15]:

$$\begin{aligned}
&\mathit{coin} :: \mathit{MonadProb}\ m \Rightarrow m\ \mathit{Bool}\\
&\mathit{coin} = \mathit{return\ True} \triangleleft {}^1\!/_2 \triangleright \mathit{return\ False}
\end{aligned}$$

and an arbitrary boolean choice:

$$\begin{array}{l} \mathit{arb} :: \mathit{MonadAlt}\ m \Rightarrow m\ \mathit{Bool} \\ \mathit{arb} = \mathit{return}\ \mathit{True} \,\square\, \mathit{return}\ \mathit{False} \end{array}$$

sequentially combined in either order:

$$\begin{array}{l} \mathit{arbcoin}, \mathit{coinarb} :: \mathit{MonadAltProb}\ m \Rightarrow m\ \mathit{Bool} \\ \mathit{arbcoin} = \mathbf{do}\ \{ a \leftarrow \mathit{arb}; c \leftarrow \mathit{coin}; \mathit{return}\ (a == c) \} \\ \mathit{coinarb} = \mathbf{do}\ \{ c \leftarrow \mathit{coin}; a \leftarrow \mathit{arb}; \mathit{return}\ (a == c) \} \end{array}$$

These two differ; informally, in *coinarb* the nondeterministic choice can depend on the result of the coin toss, whereas in *arbcoin* it cannot—and of course, the fair probabilistic choice does not depend on the arbitrary nondeterministic choice either—otherwise it wouldn't be fair. As sets of distributions (here represented as weighted lists), *arbcoin* has two possible outcomes, both being a 50–50 distribution, so really only a single possible outcome:

$$\mathit{arbcoin} = \{ [(\mathit{True}, {}^1\!/_2), (\mathit{False}, {}^1\!/_2)], [(\mathit{False}, {}^1\!/_2), (\mathit{True}, {}^1\!/_2)] \}$$

whereas *coinarb* offers four possible outcomes—a 50–50 distribution, in two different ways, or always *False* or always *True*:

$$\begin{array}{l} \mathit{coinarb} = \{ [(\mathit{True}, {}^1\!/_2), (\mathit{False}, {}^1\!/_2)], [(\mathit{False}, {}^1\!/_2), (\mathit{True}, {}^1\!/_2)], \\ \qquad [(\mathit{False}, {}^1\!/_2), (\mathit{False}, {}^1\!/_2)], [(\mathit{True}, {}^1\!/_2), (\mathit{True}, {}^1\!/_2)] \} \end{array}$$

whose convex closure is in fact the set of all boolean distributions; that is, the nondeterministic choice in *arbcoin* provides no flexibility, but the one in *coinarb* can engineer any distribution whatsoever.

Returning to the Monty Hall problem, we could allow the host to make nondeterministic rather than probabilistic choices:

$$\begin{array}{l} \mathit{hide} :: \mathit{MonadAlt}\ m \Rightarrow m\ \mathit{Door} \\ \mathit{hide} = \mathit{arbitrary}\ \mathit{doors} \\[1ex] \mathit{tease} :: \mathit{MonadAlt}\ m \Rightarrow \mathit{Door} \rightarrow \mathit{Door} \rightarrow m\ \mathit{Door} \\ \mathit{tease}\ h\ p = \mathit{arbitrary}\ (\mathit{doors} \setminus\!\setminus [h, p]) \end{array}$$

where

$$\begin{array}{l} \mathit{arbitrary} :: \mathit{MonadAlt}\ m \Rightarrow [a] \rightarrow m\ a \\ \mathit{arbitrary} = \mathit{foldr}_1\ (\square) \circ \mathit{map}\ \mathit{return} \end{array}$$

As it happens, making this change has no effect on the game. The first two choices—the host's choice of where to hide the car, and your initial choice of door—can still be combined, because bind distributes leftwards over nondeterministic choice:

$$\begin{array}{ll} & \mathit{pair}\ (\mathit{hide}, \mathit{pick}) \\ = & [\![\text{ let } k = \lambda h \rightarrow \mathit{liftM}\ (h,)\ \mathit{pick}\ ]\!] \\ & \mathit{hide} \gg\!= k \\ = & [\![\text{ definition of } \mathit{hide}\ ]\!] \\ & (\mathit{return}\ A \,\square\, \mathit{return}\ B \,\square\, \mathit{return}\ C) \gg\!= k \\ = & [\![\text{ distributivity }]\!] \\ & (\mathit{return}\ A \gg\!= k) \,\square\, (\mathit{return}\ B \gg\!= k) \,\square\, (\mathit{return}\ C \gg\!= k) \\ = & [\![\ \mathit{return} \text{ is left unit }]\!] \\ & k\ A \,\square\, k\ B \,\square\, k\ C \\ = & [\![\text{ definition of } k\ ]\!] \\ & \mathit{liftM}\ (A,)\ \mathit{pick} \,\square\, \mathit{liftM}\ (B,)\ \mathit{pick} \,\square\, \mathit{liftM}\ (C,)\ \mathit{pick} \end{array}$$

(where, for brevity, we have written $(A,)$ for the function $\lambda x \rightarrow (A, x)$). The remainder of the reasoning proceeds just as before, and the conclusion is still that the strategy *switch* wins two times in three, and *stick* only one time in three.

9. Tree relabelling

Finally, we turn our attention to the question that inspired our interest in reasoning about monadic programs in the first place. Hutton and Fulger [9] present a nice problem involving effectful computation with mutable state, concerning relabelling of trees. Given is a polymorphic datatype of trees,

$$\mathbf{data}\ \mathit{Tree}\ a = \mathit{Tip}\ a \mid \mathit{Bin}\ (\mathit{Tree}\ a)^2$$

(we continue to use the $(\text{-})^2$ shorthand for pairs from Section 6.1) and a type of symbols

$$\mathbf{newtype}\ \mathit{Symbol} = \ldots\ \mathbf{deriving}\ (\mathit{Eq})$$

with which to relabel. The problem is to prove that for some suitable definition of a function *relabel* that takes trees $t :: \mathit{Tree}\ a$ to relabelled trees $u :: \mathit{Tree}\ \mathit{Symbol}$, we have $\mathit{distinct}\ (\mathit{labels}\ u)$ for each such u, where

$$\begin{array}{l} \mathit{labels} :: \mathit{Tree}\ \mathit{Symbol} \rightarrow [\mathit{Symbol}] \\ \mathit{labels}\ (\mathit{Tip}\ a) = [a] \\ \mathit{labels}\ (\mathit{Bin}\ (t, u)) = \mathit{labels}\ t +\!\!+ \mathit{labels}\ u \\[1ex] \mathit{distinct} :: [\mathit{Symbol}] \rightarrow \mathit{Bool} \\ \mathit{distinct}\ [\,] \qquad = \mathit{True} \\ \mathit{distinct}\ (l : \mathit{ls}) = l \notin \mathit{ls} \wedge \mathit{distinct}\ \mathit{ls} \end{array}$$

For calculational convenience, in this section we will use uncurried versions of some familiar operators:

$$\begin{array}{l} \mathit{add} :: \mathit{Int}^2 \rightarrow \mathit{Int} \\ \mathit{add} = \mathit{uncurry}\ (+) \\[1ex] \mathit{cat} :: [a]^2 \rightarrow [a] \\ \mathit{cat} = \mathit{uncurry}\ (+\!\!+) \\[1ex] \mathit{disjoint} :: \mathit{Eq}\ a \Rightarrow [a]^2 \rightarrow \mathit{Bool} \\ \mathit{disjoint} = \mathit{null} \circ \mathit{uncurry}\ \mathit{intersect} \end{array}$$

We will also write simply '*M*' in place of *liftM* throughout Section 9, for brevity.

9.1 Fresh symbols

We'll assume a class of monads supporting fresh symbols:

$$\begin{array}{l} \mathbf{class}\ \mathit{Monad}\ m \Rightarrow \mathit{MonadFresh}\ m\ \mathbf{where} \\ \quad \mathit{fresh} :: m\ \mathit{Symbol} \end{array}$$

The operation *fresh* is not completely unconstrained; it has to generate symbols that are indeed fresh. We specify this by asserting that any sequence of fresh symbols will be distinct. That is, given an operation to generate a given number of fresh symbols:

$$\begin{array}{l} \mathit{symbols} :: \mathit{MonadFresh}\ m \Rightarrow \mathit{Int} \rightarrow m\ [\mathit{Symbol}] \\ \mathit{symbols}\ n = \mathit{sequence}\ (\mathit{replicate}\ n\ \mathit{fresh}) \end{array}$$

we require that

$$\mathit{assert}\ \mathit{distinct} \circ \mathit{symbols} = \mathit{symbols}$$

Note that we are again combining classes of effect, this time of *MonadFresh* and *MonadFail*: the two sides of the equation specifying *fresh* have the stronger type qualification *MonadFreshFail m*, where

$$\mathbf{class}\ (\mathit{MonadFresh}\ m, \mathit{MonadFail}\ m) \Rightarrow \mathit{MonadFreshFail}\ m$$

As with the combination of state and nondeterminism, to relate the two classes of effect we add the axiom that failure is a right zero of composition; that is, we again take a backtracking interpretation, and indeed, one might think of *MonadFresh* as modelling a kind of stateful computation (where the state is the store of fresh symbols).

As it turns out, the only property we will require of the predicate *distinct* is that it is *segment-closed*. Predicate p is segment-closed if

$$p\ (x +\!\!+ y) \Longrightarrow p\ x \wedge p\ y$$

The significance of this property is that *assert p* can be promoted through list concatenation: there is another predicate q on pairs of symbol lists such that

$$\mathit{assert}\ p \circ M\ \mathit{cat} \circ \mathit{pair} = M\ \mathit{cat} \circ \mathit{assert}\ q \circ \mathit{pair} \circ (\mathit{assert}\ p)^2$$

In particular, when $p = distinct$, then $q = disjoint$ suffices: the concatenation of two lists is all distinct if both lists are all distinct, and they are also disjoint.

For the remainder of the section, we will use only p and q, not *distinct* and *disjoint* themselves. Abstracting out the relevant properties of the predicate is helpful, because it means that the reasoning to follow can be generalized to other problems. For example, we might suppose that the *Symbol* type is not just an equality type, but an enumeration, and we want to prove that tree relabelling yields a contiguous segment of the enumeration of all symbols—informally, that no fresh symbols are wasted. Then the same condition on *symbols* suffices, but where the predicate p is 'is a contiguous segment of the enumeration'—this is segment closed, with q being the predicate on pairs 'are adjacent segments':

$$q\ (xs, ys) = null\ xs \lor null\ ys \lor (succ\ (last\ xs) == head\ ys)$$

9.2 Tree relabelling

Tree relabelling is a tree fold, using *fresh* at each tip. Given a fold combinator

$$\begin{aligned}
&foldt :: (a \to b) \to (b^2 \to b) \to Tree\ a \to b\\
&foldt\ f\ g\ (Tip\ a) \quad = f\ a\\
&foldt\ f\ g\ (Bin\ (t,u)) = g\ (foldt\ f\ g\ t, foldt\ f\ g\ u)
\end{aligned}$$

then we define

$$\begin{aligned}
&relabel :: MonadFresh\ m \Rightarrow Tree\ a \to m\ (Tree\ Symbol)\\
&relabel = foldt\ (M\ Tip \circ const\ fresh)\ (M\ Bin \circ pair)
\end{aligned}$$

Extracting the distinct symbol list from a tree is another fold, but this time within *MonadFail*:

$$\begin{aligned}
&dlabels :: MonadFail\ m \Rightarrow Tree\ Symbol \to m\ [Symbol]\\
&dlabels = foldt\ (return \circ wrap)\ (M\ cat \circ assert\ q \circ pair)
\end{aligned}$$

where $wrap\ a = [a]$ makes a singleton list.

Our claim is that the composition of *dlabels* and *relabel* never fails—the symbol list satisfies the predicate, and we always get a proper symbol list of the appropriate length:

$$dlabels \bullet relabel = symbols \circ size$$

where $m \bullet n = join \circ M\ m \circ n$ is Kleisli composition, and

$$\begin{aligned}
&size :: Tree\ a \to Int\\
&size = foldt\ (const\ 1)\ add
\end{aligned}$$

We justify that claim in the next section.

9.3 Verifying tree relabelling

First, we show that relabelling a tree and extracting its distinct symbols fuse to a single fold. We have

$$\begin{aligned}
&(dlabels \bullet relabel) \circ Tip\\
= &\quad [\![\text{ Kleisli composition }]\!]\\
&join \circ M\ dlabels \circ relabel \circ Tip\\
= &\quad [\![\text{ definition of } relabel \text{ as a fold }]\!]\\
&join \circ M\ dlabels \circ M\ Tip \circ const\ fresh\\
= &\quad [\![\text{ functors; definition of } dlabels \text{ as a fold }]\!]\\
&join \circ M\ (return \circ wrap) \circ const\ fresh\\
= &\quad [\![\text{ functors, monads }]\!]\\
&M\ wrap \circ const\ fresh
\end{aligned}$$

and

$$\begin{aligned}
&(dlabels \bullet relabel) \circ Bin\\
= &\quad [\![\text{ Kleisli composition }]\!]\\
&join \circ M\ dlabels \circ relabel \circ Bin\\
= &\quad [\![\text{ definition of } relabel \text{ as a fold }]\!]\\
&join \circ M\ dlabels \circ M\ Bin \circ pair \circ relabel^2\\
= &\quad [\![\text{ functors; definition of } dlabels \text{ as a fold }]\!]\\
&join \circ M\ (M\ cat \circ assert\ q \circ pair \circ dlabels^2) \circ pair \circ relabel^2\\
= &\quad [\![\text{ functors; naturality of } pair \text{ and } join \ ]\!]\\
&M\ cat \circ join \circ M\ (assert\ q \circ pair) \circ pair \circ (M\ dlabels \circ relabel)^2\\
= &\quad [\![\text{ commutativity of assertions—see below }]\!]\\
&M\ cat \circ assert\ q \circ join \circ M\ pair \circ pair \circ (M\ dlabels \circ relabel)^2\\
= &\quad [\![\text{ join and pairs—see below }]\!]\\
&M\ cat \circ assert\ q \circ pair \circ (join \circ M\ dlabels \circ relabel)^2\\
= &\quad [\![\text{ Kleisli composition }]\!]\\
&M\ cat \circ assert\ q \circ pair \circ (dlabels \bullet relabel)^2
\end{aligned}$$

and so, by the universal property of fold,

$$dlabels \bullet relabel = foldt\ drTip\ drBin$$

where

$$\begin{aligned}
&drTip = M\ wrap \circ const\ fresh\\
&drBin = M\ cat \circ assert\ q \circ pair
\end{aligned}$$

There are two non-trivial steps. The first is 'commutativity of assertions'

$$join \circ M\ (assert\ q) = assert\ q \circ join$$

which follows from guards commuting with anything. The second is the 'join and pairs' step

$$join \circ listM\ pair \circ pair = pair \circ join^2$$

This does not hold in general. It does hold for commutative monads; but our *MonadFreshFail* is not commutative. However, it also holds on pairs (mmx, mmy) in the special case that the inner computation in the mmx has effects only from *MonadFail*, because those effects commute with those of mmy. In our case, $mmx = M\ dlabels\ (relabel\ t)$, and indeed *dlabels* introduces only the possibility of failure, not any statefulness.

Now we show that $symbols \circ size$ is the same fold. We have

$$\begin{aligned}
&symbols \circ size \circ Tip\\
= &\quad [\![\text{ definition of } size \text{ as a fold }]\!]\\
&symbols \circ const\ 1\\
= &\quad [\![\text{ property of } symbols \ ]\!]\\
&M\ wrap \circ const\ fresh
\end{aligned}$$

and

$$\begin{aligned}
&symbols \circ size \circ Bin\\
= &\quad [\![\text{ specification of } symbols \ ]\!]\\
&assert\ p \circ symbols \circ size \circ Bin\\
= &\quad [\![\text{ definition of } size \ ]\!]\\
&assert\ p \circ symbols \circ add \circ size^2\\
= &\quad [\![\text{ properties of } symbols\text{; functors }]\!]\\
&assert\ p \circ M\ cat \circ pair \circ (symbols \circ size)^2\\
= &\quad [\![\ assert\ p \text{ distributes over concatenation }]\!]\\
&M\ cat \circ assert\ q \circ pair \circ (assert\ p \circ symbols \circ size)^2\\
= &\quad [\![\text{ specification of } symbols \ ]\!]\\
&M\ cat \circ assert\ q \circ pair \circ (symbols \circ size)^2
\end{aligned}$$

and so, again by the universal property of fold,

$$symbols \circ size = foldt\ drTip\ drBin$$

also. (The two 'properties of *symbols*' referred to are that

$$\begin{aligned}
&symbols \circ const\ 1 = M\ wrap \circ const\ fresh\\
&symbols \circ add \quad = M\ cat \circ pair \circ symbols^2
\end{aligned}$$

which follow easily from the definition of *symbols* by simple equational reasoning.)

10. Conclusions

10.1 Related work

We were inspired to write this paper by reading Hutton and Fulger on reasoning about effects [9]. We learned about the tree relabelling problem from them, although the same problem is also used as Example 4.4 in the APPSEM 2000 lecture notes on monads and effects by Benton, Hughes and Moggi [1]. That particular problem admits a number of different approaches—not only in abstracting from the specifics of the class of computational effects, as we have done here, but also in abstracting from the pattern of control, which we discuss in a related paper [4].

Hoare Type Theory [17] is a technique for introducing Hoare triples into a dependently typed language, allowing pre- and postconditions to be tracked by the type checker. It is based around a type constructor $\{P\}\ x{:}A\ \{Q\}$ of Hoare triples, denoting computations that, when run in a heap satisfying precondition P, will return a result x of type A and an updated heap that together satisfy postcondition Q. It has been embedded into the Coq proof system as an axiomatic extension called Ynot [18], and used as the basis for an implementation of separation logic [19]. Similarly, Schröder and Mossakowski [29] develop a *monad-independent Hoare logic* within the HASCASL algebraic specification language, and use this logic for reasoning about dynamic references. Either of these approaches makes a sound basis for certified development of effectful programs in the Hoare–Floyd style.

Like we do, Swierstra [31] also starts with Hutton and Fulger's tree relabelling problem, and with the observation that it is unfortunate to have to expand the definitions of return and bind for a particular monad in order to reason about a program using that monad. He uses these as a springboard for taking a lightweight approach to Hoare Type Theory, based on the state monad but not involving a heap. Roughly speaking, rather than a single monolithic type $\mathit{State}\ s\ a = (s \rightarrow (a,s))$ of state transformers (for fixed state type s and varying return type a), Swierstra introduces a family of types $\mathit{HoareState}\ p\ a\ q$ indexed by pre- and postconditions, such that the input must be a state satisfying the precondition p, and the output will a pair establishing the postcondition q. This allows him to conduct Hoare-Floyd-style reasoning for programs in the state monad, such as the tree relabelling problem; but the approach does not seem to be directly applicable to other monads.

Peyton Jones [21] discusses the 'awkward squad' of teletype I/O, concurrency, exceptions, and interfacing to foreign functions, all of which are effects wrapped up in the Haskell *IO* monad. He gives an operational semantics for the first three, but does not discuss reasoning about programs exploiting those classes of effect. Swierstra and Altenkirch [32] provide a simple functional implementation of teletype I/O, mutable state, and concurrency, using the free monad generated by the algebra of the operations supporting each class of effect—so in fact, taking an approach more closely aligned with algebraic theories, like we do. (Swierstra's doctoral thesis [30] extends this work to software transactional memory and distributed arrays too.)

10.2 Hoare-style reasoning

As we were developing the calculational approach to reasoning about effectful programs in this paper, we explored a technique owing more to Hoare triples than to algebraic specifications. In the end, we concluded that the Hoare-style technique was less convenient than the algebraic one exhibited in the rest of the paper, and (at least for all the examples we considered) unnecessary. Nevertheless, for completeness, we outline the technique here, and explain why we think it did not work so well.

The essence of the Hoare-style technique is the use of assertions, so for this section we work within *MonadFail*. For notational brevity, we will usually write '$p!$' for '$\mathit{guard}\ p$'. We'll also write '$mx\ \{p\}$' for the assertion that monadic computation mx establishes boolean postcondition p, a shorthand for

$$\mathbf{do}\ \{mx\,;p!\} = \mathbf{do}\ \{mx\}$$

in the simple case that mx returns unit. More generally, mx may return a meaningful result; more generally still, we might make an assertion $s_1\,;...\,;s_n\ \{p\}$ about a sequence of qualifiers. If these n statements $\mathit{stmts} = s_1\,;...\,;s_n$ contain m generators with patterns $u_1,...,u_m$, the returns should be of the m-tuple $\mathit{pats} = (u_1,...,u_m)$ of those patterns; so the assertion is a shorthand for the equality:

$$\mathbf{do}\ \{\mathit{stmts}\,;p!\,;\mathit{return}\ \mathit{pats}\} = \mathbf{do}\ \{\mathit{stmts}\,;\mathit{return}\ \mathit{pats}\}$$

(We assume for simplicity that no binding shadows any other, although this doesn't actually cause a problem. When there is just one generator, the return should be the value of that pattern; when there are no generators, the return should be the empty tuple. A similar construction is used by Erkök and Launchbury [2].)

Some monadic operations are particularly amenable to manipulation, because they are discardable, copyable, and relatively commutable; we call them *queries*. These characteristic properties of queries q,q' are expressed as follows:

$$\begin{aligned}
&\mathbf{do}\ \{_ \leftarrow q\,;\mathit{return}\ ()\} = \mathit{return}\ ()\\
&\mathbf{do}\ \{x \leftarrow q\,;y \leftarrow q\,;\mathit{return}\ (x,y)\} = \mathbf{do}\ \{x \leftarrow q\,;\mathit{return}\ (x,x)\}\\
&\mathbf{do}\ \{x \leftarrow q\,;y \leftarrow q'\,;\mathit{return}\ (x,y)\}\\
&\quad = \mathbf{do}\ \{y \leftarrow q'\,;x \leftarrow q\,;\mathit{return}\ (x,y)\}
\end{aligned}$$

For example, the *get* operation of the state monad is a query. But if we were to extend the *MonadCount* class in Section 3 with an operation *reset* to reset the counter, this would be copyable but not discardable; in a similar 'latch' monad, *set* and *reset* methods would be copyable but not relatively commutable; and the probabilistic operation *coin* in Section 8.2 is discardable but not copyable. (Schröder and Mossakowski [29] call queries 'pure'; however, in general, queries are not 'pure' in the sense of being instances of *return*.)

To illustrate the assertional style, recall the Towers of Hanoi problem from Section 3. We work here with an extended version of the *MonadCount* type class, offering also an operation to yield the current value of the counter:

$$\begin{aligned}
&\mathbf{class}\ \mathit{Monad}\ m \Rightarrow \mathit{MonadCount}\ m\ \mathbf{where}\\
&\quad \mathit{tick}\ \ ::m\ ()\\
&\quad \mathit{total}::m\ \mathit{Int}
\end{aligned}$$

Now we no longer intend the free interpretation of this interface; an implementation is constrained by the facts that *total* is a query, and that *tick* increments the total:

$$m \leftarrow \mathit{total}\,;\mathit{tick}\,;n \leftarrow \mathit{total}\ \{n = m+1\}$$

The operation *total* is intended a 'ghost variable', used only for reasoning and not for execution. We can therefore consider the same program as before:

$$\begin{aligned}
&\mathit{hanoi} :: \mathit{MonadCount}\ m \Rightarrow \mathit{Int} \rightarrow m\ ()\\
&\mathit{hanoi}\ 0 \qquad\ = \mathit{skip}\\
&\mathit{hanoi}\ (n+1) = \mathbf{do}\ \{\mathit{hanoi}\ n\,;\mathit{tick}\,;\mathit{hanoi}\ n\}
\end{aligned}$$

The 'correctness property' of *hanoi* is that

$$t \leftarrow \mathit{total}\,;\mathit{hanoi}\ n\,;u \leftarrow \mathit{total}\ \{u{-}t == 2^n - 1\}$$

The general approach to discharging such a proof obligation is to expand out definitions until the final assertion is evidently redundant and can be eliminated. The proof is by induction on n; the base case is straightforward:

$$\begin{aligned}
&\mathbf{do}\ \{t \leftarrow \mathit{total}\,;\mathit{hanoi}\ 0\,;u \leftarrow \mathit{total}\,;(u{-}t == 2^0 - 1)!\,;\\
&\qquad \mathit{return}\ (t,u)\}
\end{aligned}$$

$=$ ⟦ definition of *hanoi* ⟧
do $\{t \leftarrow total; skip; u \leftarrow total; (u-t == 2^0-1)!; return\ (t,u)\}$
$=$ ⟦ *skip* is a unit of composition ⟧
do $\{t \leftarrow total; u \leftarrow total; (u-t == 2^0-1)!; return\ (t,u)\}$
$=$ ⟦ *total* is a query ⟧
do $\{t \leftarrow total; (t-t == 2^0-1)!; return\ (t,t)\}$
$=$ ⟦ arithmetic; *True*! is just *skip* ⟧
do $\{t \leftarrow total; return\ (t,t)\}$
$=$ ⟦ reversing first three steps ⟧
do $\{t \leftarrow total; hanoi\ 0; u \leftarrow total; return\ (t,u)\}$

For the inductive step, we assume the statement for n, and calculate:

do $\{t \leftarrow total; hanoi\ (n+1); u \leftarrow total; (u-t == 2^{n+1}-1)!; return\ (t,u)\}$
$=$ ⟦ definition of *hanoi* ⟧
do $\{t \leftarrow total; hanoi\ n; tick; hanoi\ n; u \leftarrow total; (u-t == 2^{n+1}-1)!; return\ (t,u)\}$
$=$ ⟦ inserting some queries ⟧
do $\{t \leftarrow total; hanoi\ n; u' \leftarrow total; tick; t' \leftarrow total; hanoi\ n; u \leftarrow total; (u-t == 2^{n+1}-1)!; return\ (t,u)\}$
$=$ ⟦ inductive hypothesis; property of *tick* ⟧
do $\{t \leftarrow total; hanoi\ n; u' \leftarrow total; (u'-t = 2^n-1)!; tick; t' \leftarrow total; (t' = u'+1)!; hanoi\ n; u \leftarrow total; (u-t' = 2^n-1)!; (u-t == 2^{n+1}-1)!; return\ (t,u)\}$
$=$ ⟦ arithmetic: final guard follows from the others ⟧
do $\{t \leftarrow total; hanoi\ n; u' \leftarrow total; (u'-t = 2^n-1)!; tick; t' \leftarrow total; (t' = u'+1)!; hanoi\ n; u \leftarrow total; (u-t' = 2^n-1)!; return\ (t,u)\}$
$=$ ⟦ reversing first two steps ⟧
do $\{t \leftarrow total; hanoi\ (n+1); u \leftarrow total; return\ (t,u)\}$

This proof is significantly more verbose than the one in Section 3, because it phrased indirectly. Calculations tend to have a rightwards-pointing triangular ('▷') shape—definitions are expanded, the final assertion eliminated, and definitions contracted again—and the second half of each calculation is a mirror image of the first half.

Perhaps the reader feels that the Towers of Hanoi problem is too trivial to form the basis of any verdict. We felt so too, and although we could easily see the simpler solution for that problem, it took a long time to find the corresponding solution shown in Section 9 for the tree relabelling problem. As with the Towers of Hanoi, we extended the monad with a ghost operation:

class *Monad m* ⇒ *MonadFresh m* **where**
  $fresh :: m\ Symbol$
  $used :: m\ (Set\ Symbol)$

so that *used* is a query, returning the set of symbols used so far, and *fresh* returns and uses up some fresh symbols:

$x \leftarrow used; n \leftarrow fresh; y \leftarrow used\ \{x \subseteq y \wedge n \in y-x\}$

The problem is then to prove that for some suitable definition of a function

$relabel :: MonadFresh\ m \Rightarrow Tree\ a \rightarrow m\ (Tree\ Symbol)$

we have

$u \leftarrow relabel\ t\ \{distinct\ u\}$

for every t, where

$distinct :: Tree\ Symbol \rightarrow Bool$
$distinct\ (Tip\ a) = True$
$distinct\ (Bin\ (t,u)) = distinct\ t \wedge distinct\ u \wedge (labels\ t \cap labels\ u == \emptyset)$

and

$labels :: Tree\ Symbol \rightarrow Set\ Symbol$
$labels\ (Tip\ a) = \{a\}$
$labels\ (Bin\ (t,u)) = labels\ t \cup labels\ u$

As it happens, the correctness condition is too weak to support an inductive argument, and it has to be strengthened to

$x \leftarrow used; t' \leftarrow relabel\ t; y \leftarrow used$
$\{distinct\ t' \wedge x \subseteq y \wedge labels\ t' \subseteq y-x\}$

The resulting calculation was rather longwinded, and we much prefer the proof presented in Section 9.

As well as the verbosity of the Hoare-style approach, it seems a little odd that we used only postconditions and not preconditions. We might define the Hoare triple $\{p\}\ m\ \{q\}$ as a shorthand for the identity

do $\{p!; x \leftarrow m; q!; return\ x\} =$ **do** $\{p!; m\}$

But note that this is equivalent to the earlier notation for assertions, since

$\{p\}\ m\ \{q\} = p!; m\ \{q\}$

and in particular

$\{True\}\ m\ \{q\} = m\ \{q\}$

Others have come to the same conclusion; for example, Schröder and Mossakowski's monad-independent Hoare logic [29] similarly defines Hoare triples in terms of 'global evaluation formulae', which are analogous to our assertions.

10.3 Discussion

We have presented an approach to effectful functional programming that treats classes of effects as an abstract datatype, with an algebraic specification capturing its operations and equations. We didn't start out this way, but it turns out that the approach to which we have been led has less to do with monads as introduced into functional programming by Moggi [16] and Wadler [38], and more to do with so-called Lawvere theories [13].

Fundamentally, monads arise from adjunctions—classically, between algebraic constructions such as term algebras in one direction, and an underlying forgetful functor in the other direction. Lawvere theories arise more directly from equational theories of operations and their laws. Both were developed as categorical formulations of universal algebra [10], but Lawvere theories start off with the associated operations and their equational properties, whereas with monads these are a secondary notion. Indeed, the adjunction classically arising from the construction of the free model of an equational theory yields precisely the monad in Moggi's sense [24]; but the additional operations and equations to support a class of effects play little part in the story that starts with monads. Nevertheless, the monadic view makes a convenient interface for programming, and of course is embedded within the design of programming languages such as Haskell; so we do not wish to abandon it. (Power [10] points out that monads are in fact slightly more general than Lawvere theories: in particular, the monads for continuations and for partiality do not arise from operations and their equations in the same way as the other monads familiar to functional programmers.)

There is an intriguing duality in the Lawvere theory approach between algebraic operations and *effect handlers* [25]. For example, the *catch* operation of *MonadExcept* is an effect handler in this sense; technically it doesn't form an 'operation' of a Lawvere theory, because it doesn't have the right distributivity properties with respect to $\gg\!=$. Operations and handlers can be seen as 'effect constructors' and 'effect deconstructors', respectively; and the handlers can be defined as folds over the initial algebra induced by the free model of the algebraic operations [26]. Given the amenability of folds to equational reasoning, we feel that this development has consequences worthy of further investigation.

Acknowledgements

We gratefully acknowledge the many helpful comments from members of the *Algebra of Programming* research group at Oxford, especially Richard Bird, and from participants of the *IFIP WG 2.8* meeting in Marble Falls and the *European Workshop on Computational Effects* in Ljubljana, all of which have improved the presentation of this paper. This work was partially supported by UK Engineering and Physical Sciences Research Council grant EP/G034516/1 on *Reusability and Dependent Types*.

References

[1] N. Benton, J. Hughes, and E. Moggi. Monads and effects. In G. Barthe, P. Dybjer, L. Pinto, and J. Saraiva, editors, *APPSEM 2000*, volume 2395 of *LNCS*, pages 42–122. Springer, 2002.

[2] L. Erkök and J. Launchbury. Recursive monadic bindings. In *ICFP*, pages 174–185. ACM, September 2000.

[3] M. Erwig and S. Kollmansberger. Probabilistic functional programming in Haskell. *J. Funct. Prog.*, 16(1):21–34, 2006.

[4] J. Gibbons and R. Bird. Effective reasoning about effectful traversals. Work in progress, Mar. 2011.

[5] M. Giry. A categorical approach to probability theory. In *Categorical Aspects of Topology and Analysis*, volume 915 of *LNM*, pages 68–85. Springer, 1981.

[6] S. Goncharov, L. Schröder, and T. Mossakowski. Kleene monads: Handling iteration in a framework of generic effects. In *CALCO*, volume 5728 of *LNCS*, pages 18–33, 2009.

[7] R. Hinze. Prolog's control constructs in a functional setting: Axioms and implementation. *Intern. J. Found. Comput. Sci.*, 12(2):125–170, 2001.

[8] C. A. R. Hoare. A couple of novelties in the propositional calculus. *Z. Math. Logik Grundlag. Math.*, 31(2):173–178, 1985.

[9] G. Hutton and D. Fulger. Reasoning about effects: Seeing the wood through the trees. In *TFP*, May 2008.

[10] M. Hyland and J. Power. The category theoretic understanding of universal algebra: Lawvere theories and monads. *Electron. Notes Theoret. Comput. Sci.*, 172:437–458, 2007.

[11] C. Jones and G. Plotkin. A probabilistic powerdomain of evaluations. In *LICS*, pages 186–195, 1989.

[12] F. W. Lawvere. The category of probabilistic mappings. Preprint—we haven't managed to obtain a copy of this manuscript, 1962.

[13] F. W. Lawvere. *Functorial Semantics of Algebraic Theories*. PhD thesis, Columbia University, 1963. Also available with commentary as *Theory and Applications of Categories* Reprint 5.

[14] S. Mac Lane. *Categories for the Working Mathematician*. Springer-Verlag, 1971.

[15] A. McIver and C. Morgan. *Abstraction, Refinement and Proof for Probabilistic Systems*. Springer Verlag, 2005.

[16] E. Moggi. Notions of computation and monads. *Inform. & Comput.*, 93(1), 1991.

[17] A. Nanevski, G. Morrisett, and L. Birkedal. Hoare Type Theory, polymorphism and separation. *J. Funct. Prog.*, 18(5,6):865–911, 2008.

[18] A. Nanevski, G. Morrisett, A. Shinnar, P. Govereau, and L. Birkedal. Ynot: Dependent types for imperative programs. In *ICFP*, pages 229–240, 2008.

[19] P. W. O'Hearn, H. Yang, and J. C. Reynolds. Separation and information hiding. In *POPL*, pages 268–280, 2004.

[20] B. O'Sullivan, J. Goerzen, and D. Stewart. *Real World Haskell*. O'Reilly, 2008.

[21] S. Peyton Jones. Tackling the awkward squad: Monadic input/output, concurrency, exceptions, and foreign-language calls in Haskell. In T. Hoare, M. Broy, and R. Steinbrüggen, editors, *Engineering Theories of Software Construction*, volume 180 of *NATO Science Series*, pages 47–96. IOS Press, 2001.

[22] S. Peyton Jones. *Haskell 98 Language and Libraries: The Revised Report*. Cambridge University Press, 2003.

[23] S. Peyton Jones and P. Wadler. Imperative functional programming. In *POPL*, pages 71–84, 1993.

[24] G. Plotkin and J. Power. Notions of computation determine monads. In *FOSSACS*, volume 2303 of *LNCS*, pages 342–356, 2002.

[25] G. Plotkin and J. Power. Algebraic operations and generic effects. *Appl. Cat. Struct.*, 11(1):69–94, 2003.

[26] G. D. Plotkin and M. Pretnar. Handlers of algebraic effects. In *ESOP*, volume 5502 of *LNCS*, pages 80–94, 2009.

[27] N. Ramsey and A. Pfeffer. Stochastic lambda calculus and monads of probability distributions. In *POPL*, pages 154–165, 2002.

[28] J. Rosenhouse. *The Monty Hall Problem: The Remarkable Story of Math's Most Contentious Brain Teaser*. Oxford University Press, 2009.

[29] L. Schröder and T. Mossakowski. HASCASL: Integrated higher-order specification and program development. *Theoretical Comput. Sci.*, 410(12-13):1217–1260, 2009.

[30] W. Swierstra. *A Functional Specification of Effects*. PhD thesis, University of Nottingham, November 2008.

[31] W. Swierstra. A Hoare logic for the state monad. In *TPHOLs*, volume 5674 of *LNCS*, pages 440–451. Springer-Verlag, 2009.

[32] W. Swierstra and T. Altenkirch. Beauty in the beast. In *Haskell Workshop*, pages 25–36, 2007.

[33] R. Tix. *Continuous D-Cones: Convexity and Powerdomain Constructions*. PhD thesis, Technische Universität Darmstadt, 1999.

[34] D. Varacca and G. Winskel. Distributing probability over non-determinism. *Math. Struct. Comput. Sci.*, 16(1):87–113, 2006.

[35] M. Vos Savant. Ask Marilyn. *Parade Magazine*, 9th September 1990. See also `http://www.marilynvossavant.com/articles/gameshow.html`.

[36] P. Wadler. A critique of Abelson and Sussman: Why calculating is better than scheming. *SIGPLAN Not.*, 22(3):8, 1987.

[37] P. Wadler. Comprehending monads. *Math. Struct. Comput. Sci.*, 2(4):461–493, 1992.

[38] P. Wadler. Monads for functional programming. In M. Broy, editor, *Program Design Calculi: Proceedings of the Marktoberdorf Summer School*, 1992.

[39] A. Yakeley, *et al.* MonadPlus reform proposal. `http://www.haskell.org/haskellwiki/MonadPlus_reform_proposal`, Jan. 2006.

[40] W. Yi and K. G. Larsen. Testing probabilistic and nondeterministic processes. In *Protocol Specification, Testing and Verification XII*, pages 47–61, 1992.

Lightweight Monadic Programming in ML

Nikhil Swamy* Nataliya Guts† Daan Leijen* Michael Hicks†
*Microsoft Research, Redmond †University of Maryland, College Park

Abstract

Many useful programming constructions can be expressed as monads. Examples include probabilistic modeling, functional reactive programming, parsing, and information flow tracking, not to mention effectful functionality like state and I/O. In this paper, we present a type-based rewriting algorithm to make programming with arbitrary monads as easy as using ML's built-in support for state and I/O. Developers write programs using monadic values of type $m\ \tau$ as if they were of type τ, and our algorithm inserts the necessary binds, units, and monad-to-monad morphisms so that the program type checks. Our algorithm, based on Jones' qualified types, produces principal types. But principal types are sometimes problematic: the program's semantics could depend on the choice of instantiation when more than one instantiation is valid. In such situations we are able to simplify the types to remove any ambiguity but without adversely affecting typability; thus we can accept strictly more programs. Moreover, we have proved that this simplification is *efficient* (linear in the number of constraints) and *coherent*: while our algorithm induces a particular rewriting, all related rewritings will have the same semantics. We have implemented our approach for a core functional language and applied it successfully to simple examples from the domains listed above, which are used as illustrations throughout the paper.

Categories and Subject Descriptors D.3.2 [*Programming languages*]: Language Classifications—Applicative (functional) languages; F.3.3 [*Logics and Meanings of Programs*]: Studies of Program Constructs—Type structure

General Terms Languages,Theory

Keywords monad, type, rewriting, coherence, coercion

1. Introduction

The research literature abounds with useful programming constructions that can be expressed as monads, which consist of a type constructor m and two operations, *bind* and *unit*:[1]

$$\begin{array}{l} bind : \forall\alpha,\beta.\ m\ \alpha \to (\alpha \to m\ \beta) \to m\ \beta \\ unit : \forall\alpha.\ \alpha \to m\ \alpha \end{array}$$

Example monads include parsers [13], probabilistic computations [25], functional reactivity [3, 8], and information flow tracking [26]. In a monadic type system, if *values* are given type τ then *computations* are given type $m\ \tau$ for some monad constructor m. For example, an expression of type $IO\ \ \tau$ in Haskell represents a computation that will produce (if it terminates) a value of type τ but may perform effectful operations in the process. Haskell's `Monad` type class, which requires the `bind` and `unit` operations given above, is blessed with special syntax, the *do notation*, for programming with instances of this class.

Moggi [22], Filinksi [11], and others have noted that ML programs, which are impure and observe a deterministic, call-by-value evaluation order, are inherently monadic. For example, the value $\lambda x.e$ can be viewed as having type $\tau \to m\ \tau'$: the argument type τ is never monadic because x is always bound to a value in e, whereas the return type is monadic because the function, when applied, produces a computation. As such, call-by-value application and let-binding essentially employ monadic sequencing, but the monad constructor m and the `bind` and `unit` combinators for sequencing are implicit rather than explicit. In essence, the explicit IO monad in Haskell is implicit in ML.

While programming with I/O in ML is lightweight, programming with other monads is not. For example, suppose we are interested in programming *behaviors*, which are time-varying values, as in *functional reactive programs* [3, 8]. With the following notation we indicate that behaviors can be implemented as a monad: expressions of type $Beh\ \alpha$ represent values of type α that change with time, and `bindp` and `unitp` are its monadic operations:

$$\mathsf{Monad}(Beh, \texttt{bindb}, \texttt{unitb})$$

As a primitive, function `seconds` has type $unit \to Beh\ int$, its result representing the current time in seconds since the epoch. An ML program using Beh effectively has two monads: the implicit monad, which applies to normal ML computations, and the user-defined monad Beh. The former is handled primitively but the latter requires the programmer to explicitly use `bindb`, `unitb`, function composition, etc., as in the following example:

```
bindb (bindb (seconds()) (fun s-> unitb (is_even s)))
  (fun y-> unitb (if y then 1 else 2))
```

The type of this entire expression is $Beh\ \ int$: it is time-varying, oscillating between values 1 and 2 every second.

Instead of using tedious explicit syntax, we would like to overload the existing syntax so that monadic constructs are implicit, e.g., as in the following program (call it Q)

```
let y = is_even (seconds()) in
if y then 1 else 2
```

We can see that the programs are structurally related, with a bind corresponding to each let and application, and unit applied to the bound and final expressions.

While ML programming with one monad is tedious, programming with more than one is worse. Along with different binds and units for each monad, the programmer may have to insert calls to

[1] These operations must respect certain laws; cf. Wadler [29] for details.

ICFP'11, September 19–21, 2011, Tokyo, Japan.

morphisms, which are functions that lift one monad into another. For example, suppose that along with time-varying expressions like `seconds()` we allowed time-varying probability distributions expressed as a monad *BehPrb* α (we show an example of this in Section 2). Given a morphism from the first monad to the second, i.e., from a time-varying value to a time-varying probability distribution, the programmer must insert calls to it in the right places.

This paper presents an algorithm for automatically converting an ML program, like Q, which makes implicit use of monads, into one that, like P, makes explicit use of monads, with binds, units, and morphisms inserted where needed. Our algorithm operates as part of polymorphic type inference, following an approach similar to Jones [14], which is the foundation of Haskell's type class inference. We use the syntactic structure of the program to identify where binds, units, and morphisms may appear. Type inference introduces a fresh variable for the monad being used at these various points and, as in Jones, we produce qualified types of the form $\forall \bar{\nu}.P \Rightarrow \tau$, where $\bar{\nu}$ contains free type and monad variables, and P contains morphism constraints. We prove our algorithm produces principal types.

As it turns out, our basic scheme of inferring principal types could be encoded within Haskell's type class inference algorithm, e.g., one could define morphisms as instances of a `Morphism` type class and then rely on inference to insert them as necessary. However, this algorithm would reject many useful programs as potentially ambiguous, in particular, those whose types contain quantified variables that appear only in the constraints P but not in the type τ. In the general setting of Haskell, this is sensible, as different instantiations of these variables could produce programs with different semantics. By focusing our attention on monads we sidestep this problem. We can exploit laws governing the behavior of morphisms to ensure that all potential instantiations of such variables are *coherent*; i.e., the program semantics will not change with different instantiations. As such, our algorithm employs a linear-time strategy to eliminate such variables, thus simplifying the constraints P with no adverse effects on typability.

We have implemented our inference algorithm for a core functional language. We demonstrate its utility by applying it to example programs that use monads implementing behaviors, probabilistic computations, and parsers (cited above). We also develop an example using a family of monads for tracking information flows of high- and low-security data [7, 26]. We prove that our rewriting algorithm produces programs accepted by FlowCaml, a dialect of ML that performs information flow tracking [24], and thereby show that rewritten programs are secure (enjoy noninterference [12]).

In summary, this paper presents an extension to ML for monadic programming, providing the following benefits:

- Developers can define their own monads and program with them in a direct style, avoiding the tedium of introducing binds, units, and morphisms manually.
- Monadic operations are inserted automatically in conjunction with a novel type inference algorithm. Our algorithm produces qualified types which describe the monads and morphisms used by a piece of code, usefully revealing the monadic structure of the program to the developer. Exploiting the morphism laws, we efficiently infer general types and produce coherent rewritings.
- The system is quite flexible: we have shown, via our prototype implementation, that it supports many varieties of monads and their combination.

The next section presents an overview of our approach; our main technical results are contained in Sections 3–5; and applications and related work discussed in Sections 6 and 7, respectively.

2. Overview

This section presents an overview of our approach through the development of a few examples. We start by considering a single user-defined monad and see that this is relatively easy to handle. Then, we look at handling multiple monads, which require the use of morphisms. With these examples we illustrate our type inference and rewriting algorithm and discuss its key properties.

2.1 Programming with a single user-defined monad

As mentioned earlier, pure ML computations may be seen as already employing an implicit monad, e.g., covering partiality, state, exceptions, and I/O. We call this implicit monad *Bot*, since it is the bottom element of our monad hierarchy; in effect, its unit operator is the identity function, and bind is the reverse application. Our goal is to exploit the inherent monadic structure of ML to provide support for programming with multiple, user-defined monads with the same ease as programming, implicitly, with *Bot*. Of course, we aim to do this without breaking compatibility with ML.

Let us illustrate our idea on an example using the probability monad [25]. Expressions of type *Prb* α describe distributions over values of type α, with `bindp` and `unitp` as its bind and unit combinators, respectively:

$$\mathsf{Monad}(Prb, \texttt{bindp}, \texttt{unitp})$$

The probability monad can be used to define probabilistic models. The following program P, based on the classic example due to Pearl [23], is an example of model code we would like to write:

```
let rain = flip .5 in
let sprinkler = flip .3 in
let chance = flip .9 in
let grass_is_wet = (rain || sprinkler) && chance in
if grass_is_wet then rain else fail ()
```

This program uses two functions it does not define:

$$\begin{array}{lcl} \texttt{flip} & : & \mathit{float} \rightarrow \mathit{Prb}\ \mathit{bool} \\ \texttt{fail} & : & \forall \alpha.\mathit{unit} \rightarrow \mathit{Prb}\ \alpha \end{array}$$

The first introduces distributions: `flip`(p) is a distribution where `true` has probability p and `false` has probability $1 - p$. The second, `fail`, represents impossibility.

The first four lines of P define four random variables: `rain` is true when it is raining; `sprinkler` is true when the sprinkler is running; `chance` is explained below; and `grass_is_wet` is true when the grass is wet. The probability distribution for the last is dependent on the distributions of the first three: the grass is wet if either it is raining or the sprinkler is running, with an additional bit of uncertainty due to `chance`: e.g., even with rain, grass under a tree might be dry. The last line of P implements a conditional distribution; i.e., the probability that it is raining given that the grass is wet. Mathematically, this would be represented with notation Pr(`rain` | `grass_is_wet`).

Unfortunately, in ML we cannot write the above code directly because it is not type-correct. For example, the expression `rain || sprinkler` applies the `||` function, which has type $\mathit{bool} \rightarrow \mathit{bool} \rightarrow \mathit{bool}$, to `rain` and `sprinkler`, which each have type *Prb bool*. Fortunately, our system will automatically rewrite P so that it is type-correct, producing the code given below.

```
bindp (flip .5) (fun rain->
bindp (flip .3) (fun sprinkler->
bindp (flip .9) (fun chance->
bindp (unitp ((rain || sprinkler) && chance))
  (fun grass_is_wet->
if grass_is_wet then unitp rain else fail ()))))
```

When there is only one user-defined monad to consider, a rewriting such as this one is entirely syntactic. Roughly, each `let` is replaced by a `bindp` and each let-bound expression that is not already monadic is wrapped with `unitp`. By doing so, we keep to the monadic structure of sequencing implemented primitively by ML for its *Bot* monad, except we have now interposed the *Prb* monad. Although not shown above, function applications are handled similarly: we insert `bindp` on both the left- and right-hand sides, thereby echoing the call-by-value semantics of function application in ML.

Under this rewriting semantics, we can give a type to the original program even though it is not typable in ML—our algorithm infers the type *Prb bool* for the source program. The types we infer always have a particular structure that mirrors the monadic structure of ML. As in Moggi's computational lambda calculus, we note that inferred function types always have a monadic type in their co-domain and monadic types never appear to the left of arrows. This corresponds to the following intuition. Since values are always pure, under a call-by-value semantics, function arguments must always be effect free (hence, no monadic types to the left of arrows). Furthermore, since in ML functions can have arbitrary effects, their co-domains are always monadic.

2.2 Programming with multiple monads

Now suppose we wish to program with both probabilities and behaviors (introduced in Section 1). Perhaps we would like the probability of rain to change with time, e.g., according to the seasons. Then we can modify P (call it P') so that the argument to `flip` is a function `rainprb` of type $unit \rightarrow Beh\ float$:

```
let rain = flip (rainprb ()) in ...
```

Again, this program fragment is ill-typed, because `flip` expects a *float* but we have passed it a *Beh float*.

If our rewriting system is to be applied, what should be the type of `rain`? One might expect it to be $Beh\ (Prb\ bool)$, since it is a time-varying distribution. However, this type is nonsensical. Just as ML does not support data structures containing non-values (e.g., those having type $List\ (Bot\ \alpha)$) it does not support computations parameterized by non-values, e.g., expressions of type $Bot\ (Bot\ \alpha)$ and, for that matter, type $Beh\ (Prb\ \alpha)$. Therefore, a programmer must construct a combined monad, *BehPrb*, along with morphisms from the individual monads into the combined one, to ensure that the overall program's semantics makes sense. There are several standard techniques for combining monads [17]; here, we can combine them by defining objects of type $BehPrb\ \tau$ as a stream of distributions over τ, with the obvious morphisms.

$$\begin{array}{l}\mathsf{Monad}(BehPrb, \mathtt{bindbp}, \mathtt{unitbp})\\ \mathtt{p2bp} : Prb \rhd BehPrb\\ \mathtt{b2bp} : Beh \rhd BehPrb\end{array}$$

To allow automatic type-directed insertion of morphisms, we assume that there is at most one morphism between each pair of monads. In general, a morphism $f_{1,2} : m_1 \rhd m_2$ has the type $\forall \alpha.m_1\ \alpha \rightarrow m_2\ \alpha$.[2] (We implicitly consider the unit operation of monad m as the morphism $Bot \rhd m$.) Given the above morphisms, our system rewrites P' thus:

```
bindpb (bindpb (b2bp (rainprb ()))
         (fun v1-> p2bp (flip v1))) (fun rain->
  p2bp (bindp (flip .3) (fun sprinkler-> ...
```

where ... is identical to the corresponding part of the rewriting for P, and the final type is $BehPrb\ bool$. Here, the result of `rainprb()` is lifted into *BehPrb float* and then bound to the current value `v1`, which is passed to `flip` to generate a distribution. This value is in turn lifted into *BehPrb bool* and bound to boolean `rain` for the rest of the computation, whose result, of type *Prb bool*, is lifted into *BehPrb bool* by application of `p2bp`.

[2] Morphisms (just like the binds and units) are not part of the source program; as such, they are treated specially and not subject to the positivity condition on monadic types.

2.3 Properties of type inference and rewriting

Our examples so far have involved inserting known morphisms, binds, and units, producing monomorphic types. But our system is more general in that we can rewrite a function to abstract the monads and morphisms it uses. For such functions our algorithm infers *qualified* types of the form $\forall \bar{\nu}.P \Rightarrow \tau$, where P is a set of constraints $m_1 \rhd m_2$ where the m_i could be constant, known monads, like *Beh*, or abstracted, unknown monads μ that appear in the bound type variables $\bar{\nu}$ (along with the usual type variables α). For example, the type of

```
let compose f g x = f (g x)
```

inferred by our system is

$$\forall \alpha\beta\gamma\mu_1\mu_2\mu.\\ \quad (\mu_1 \rhd \mu, \mu_2 \rhd \mu) \Rightarrow (\beta \rightarrow \mu_2\ \gamma) \rightarrow (\alpha \rightarrow \mu_1\ \beta) \rightarrow \alpha \rightarrow \mu\gamma$$

(where two occurrences of *Bot* on arrow types have been elided for readability). The rewritten term will take as arguments a representation of the monads μ, μ_1, and μ_2, and two morphism functions corresponding to the two morphism constraints. Section 4 shows that our algorithm infers *principal types*, i.e. most general types.

By restricting the structure of inferred types (e.g., no monadic types to the left of arrows), and by providing only a limited form of subtyping, we obtain morphism constraints P that can be efficiently solved using a simple linear-time procedure. A solution of constraints allows us to instantiate the monadic operators and the morphisms in the elaborated term.

Last but not least, our algorithm enjoys *coherence*: any two rewritings of the same program are semantically equivalent. Said differently, choosing a particular solution does not affect the meaning of the program. Coherence allows us to accept programs that would otherwise be rejected as ambiguous by related systems that employ qualified types for type inference, e.g., Haskell's type-class mechanism. We achieve coherence by taking advantage of the following assumed properties of morphisms:

$$f_{1,2} \circ unit_1 = unit_2 \tag{1}$$

$$f_{1,2}\ (bind_1\ \mathsf{e}_1\ \mathsf{e}_2) = bind_2\ (f_{1,2}\ \mathsf{e}_1)\ (f_{1,2} \circ \mathsf{e}_2) \tag{2}$$

$$f_{2,3} \circ f_{1,2} = f_{1,3} \tag{3}$$

Properties (1–2) are the so-called *morphism laws*, and the third is the transitivity property.

For instance, the combination of *Beh*, *Prb*, and *BehPrb* in the example above leads to constraints that admit several valid solutions. One of these solutions, shown below, directly lifts all the let bindings to the *BehPrb* monad, instead of lifting parts of the computation to either the *Beh* or *Prb* monads.

```
bindbp (bindbp (b2bp (rainprb ()))
         (fun v1-> p2bp (flip v1))) (fun rain->
bindbp (p2bp (flip .3)) (fun sprinkler->
bindbp (p2bp (flip .9)) (fun chance->
bindbp (unitbp ((rain || sprinkler) && chance))
  (fun grass_is_wet->
bindpb (fail ()) (fun f->
unitpb (if_ grass_is_wet then rain else f))))))
```

Using the morphism laws, we can show that the two rewritings are equivalent. However we might argue that the first rewriting, produced by our algorithm, is more precise than this one; intuitively it applies morphisms "as late as possible" and uses the "simplest"

types	τ	$::=$	α	
		$\mid$	$T\ \tau_1 ... \tau_n$	($n \geqslant 0$ is the arity of T)
		$\mid$	$\tau_1 \to m\ \tau_2$	
monadic types	m	$::=$	$\mu \mid M$	
type variables	ν	$::=$	$\alpha \mid \mu$	
constraints	P	$::=$	$\pi_1, ..., \pi_n$	
constraint	π	$::=$	$m_1 \rhd m_2$	
type schemes	σ	$::=$	$\forall \bar{\nu}. P \Rightarrow \tau$	
environment	Γ	$::=$	$\cdot \mid \Gamma, c{:}\sigma \mid \Gamma, x{:}\sigma$	
values	v	$::=$	$x \mid c \mid \lambda x.e$	
expressions	e	$::=$	$v \mid e_1\ e_2 \mid \mathsf{let}\ x{=}e_1\ \mathsf{in}\ e_2$	

Figure 1. Core language syntax.

$$P \models m \rhd m \ \text{(M-Taut)} \qquad \frac{m_1 \rhd m_2 \in P}{P \models m_1 \rhd m_2}\ \text{(M-Hyp)}$$

$$\frac{P \models m_1 \rhd m_2 \qquad P \models m_2 \rhd m_3}{P \models m_1 \rhd m_3}\ \text{(M-Trans)}$$

$$\frac{P \vdash \pi_1\ ...\ P \vdash \pi_n}{P \vdash \pi_1, ..., \pi_n}\ \text{(M-Many)}$$

Figure 2. The constraint entailment relation.

$$\frac{\begin{array}{cc}\bar{\rho} = \overline{m}, \overline{\tau} & \theta = [\bar{\rho}/\overline{\nu_1}] \\ P, \pi_2 \models \theta\pi_1 & \bar{\nu}_2 \notin \mathsf{ftv}(\forall \bar{\nu}_1.\, \pi_1 \Rightarrow \tau)\end{array}}{P \vdash \forall \bar{\nu}_1.\, \pi_1 \Rightarrow \tau \geqslant \forall \bar{\nu}_2.\, \pi_2 \Rightarrow \theta\tau}\ \text{(Inst)}$$

Figure 3. The generic instance relation over type schemes.

monad as long as possible. As such, the types more precisely reveal the monads actually needed by a piece of code.

3. Qualified types for monadic programs

This section describes the formal type rules of our system. Figure 1 gives the syntax of types, constraints, environments, and expressions. Monotypes τ consist of type variables α, full applied type constructors $T\ \tau_1 ... \tau_n$, and function types $\tau_1 \to m\ \tau_2$. Function arrows can be seen as taking three arguments where the m is the monadic type. We could use a kind system to distinguish monadic types from regular types but, for simplicity, we distinguish them using different syntactic categories. Monadic types m are either monad constants M or monadic type variables μ.

Since types can be polymorphic over the actual monad (which is essential to principal types) we also have monadic constraints π of the form $m_1 \rhd m_2$, which states that a monad m_1 can be lifted to the monad m_2. Type schemes are the usual qualified types [14] where we can quantify over both regular and monadic type variables.

In the expression language, we distinguish between syntactic value expressions v, and regular expressions e. This is in order to impose the value restriction of ML where we can only generalize over let-bound values.

Figure 2 describes the structural rules of constraint entailment, where $P \models \pi$ states that the constraints in P entail the constraint π. The entailment relation is monotone (where $P' \subseteq P$ implies $P \models P'$), transitive, and closed under substitution. We also require that morphisms between the monads form a semi-lattice. This requirement is not essential for type inference but as shown in Section 5 it is necessary for a coherent evidence translation.

Using entailment, we define the generic instance relation $P \vdash \sigma_1 \geqslant \sigma_2$ in Figure 3. This is just the regular instance definition on type schemes where entailment is used over the constraints. In the common case where one instantiates to a monotype, the rule simplifies to:

$$\frac{\bar{\rho} = \overline{m}, \overline{\tau} \qquad \theta = [\bar{\rho}/\bar{\nu}] \qquad P \models \theta\bar{\pi}}{P \vdash \forall \bar{\nu}.\, \bar{\pi} \Rightarrow \tau \geqslant \theta\tau}\ \text{(Inst-Mono)}$$

3.1 Declarative type rules

Figure 4 describes the basic type rules of our system; we discuss rewriting in the next subsection. The rules come in two forms: the rule $P \mid \Gamma \vdash v : \sigma$ states that value expression v is well typed with a type σ, while the rule $P \mid \Gamma \vdash e : m\ \tau$ states that expression e is well-typed with a monadic type $m\ \tau$, in both cases assuming the constraints P and type environment Γ. The rule (TI-Bot) allows one to lift a regular type τ into a monadic type $Bot\ \tau$.

The rules for variables, constants, let-bound values, instantiation, and generalization are all standard. The rule for lambda expressions (TI-Lam) requires a monadic type in the premise to get well-formed function types. An expression like $\lambda x.x$ therefore gets type $\alpha \to Bot\ \alpha$ where the result is in the identity monad.

The application rule (TI-App) and let-rule (TI-Do) lift into an arbitrary result monad. The constraint $\forall i.\ P \models m_i \rhd m$ ensures that all the monads in the premise can be lifted to a common monad m, which allows a type-directed evidence translation to the underlying monadic program.

3.2 Type directed monadic translation

As described in Section 2, we rewrite a source program while performing type inference, inserting binds, units, and morphisms as needed. This translation can be elegantly described using a type directed evidence translation [14]. Since the translation is entirely standard, we elide the full rules, and only sketch how it is done. In Section 5 we do show the evidence translation for the type inference algorithm W since it is needed to show coherence.

Our elaborated target language is System F (but here we leave out type parameters for simplicity). For the declarative rules, we can define a judgment like $P \mid \Gamma \vdash e : m\ \tau \leadsto \mathsf{e}$ which proves that source term e is given monadic type $m\ \tau$ and elaborated to the well-typed output term e. Similarly, the entailment relation $P \models m_1 \rhd m_2 \leadsto f$ returns a morphism witness f with type $\forall \alpha.\, m_1\, \alpha \to m_2\, \alpha$.

As an example, consider the (TI-App) rule. The rule with a type directed translation is defined as:

$$\frac{\begin{array}{c}P \mid \Gamma \vdash e_1 : m_1\ (\tau_2 \to m_3\ \tau) \leadsto \mathsf{e}_1 \quad P \mid \Gamma \vdash e_2 : m_2\ \tau_2 \leadsto \mathsf{e}_2 \\ \forall i. P \models m_i \rhd m \leadsto f_i\end{array}}{\begin{array}{c}P \mid \Gamma \vdash e_1\ e_2 : m\ \tau \leadsto \\ bind_m\ (f_1\ \mathsf{e}_1)\ (\lambda \mathsf{x}{:}(\tau_2 \to m_3\ \tau).\, bind_m\ (f_2\, \mathsf{e}_2)\ (\lambda \mathsf{y}{:}\tau_2.\, f_3\ (\mathsf{x}\,\mathsf{y})))\end{array}}$$

The $bind_m$ evidence comes from the $\mathsf{Monad}(m, bind_m, unit_m)$ constraint. This constraint is left implicit in the type rules since it is always satisfied. Much of the time the morphisms are identity functions and the binding operations will be in the Bot monad which can all be optimized away. An optimizer can make further use of the monad laws to aggressively simplify the target terms.

3.3 Compatibility with ML

Figure 4 is backwards compatible with the ML type system: it accepts any program that is accepted by the standard Hindley-Milner typing rules [5] extended with the value restriction—we

$$\boxed{P \mid \Gamma \vdash v : \sigma \quad P \mid \Gamma \vdash e : m\ \tau} \qquad \frac{\Gamma(x) = \sigma}{P \mid \Gamma \vdash x : \sigma}\ \text{(TI-Var)} \qquad \frac{\Gamma(c) = \sigma}{P \mid \Gamma \vdash c : \sigma}\ \text{(TI-Const)} \qquad \frac{P \mid \Gamma, x{:}\tau_1 \vdash e : m\ \tau_2}{P \mid \Gamma \vdash \lambda x.e : \tau_1 \to m\ \tau_2}\ \text{(TI-Lam)}$$

$$\frac{P \mid \Gamma \vdash v : \tau}{P \mid \Gamma \vdash v : Bot\ \tau}\ \text{(TI-Bot)} \qquad \frac{P \mid \Gamma \vdash v : \sigma \quad P \vdash \sigma \geqslant \tau}{P \mid \Gamma \vdash v : \tau}\ \text{(TI-Inst)} \qquad \frac{P, \bar{\pi} \mid \Gamma \vdash v : \tau \quad \bar{\nu} \notin \mathsf{ftv}(\Gamma, P)}{P \mid \Gamma \vdash v : \forall \bar{\nu}.\ \bar{\pi} \Rightarrow \tau}\ \text{(TI-Gen)}$$

$$\frac{P \mid \Gamma \vdash e_1 : m_1\ (\tau_2 \to m_3\ \tau) \quad P \mid \Gamma \vdash e_2 : m_2\ \tau_2 \quad \forall i. P \models m_i \rhd m}{P \mid \Gamma \vdash e_1\ e_2 : m\ \tau}\ \text{(TI-App)}$$

$$\frac{P \mid \Gamma \vdash v : \sigma \quad P \mid \Gamma, x{:}\sigma \vdash e : m\ \tau}{P \mid \Gamma \vdash \mathsf{let}\ x{=}v\ \mathsf{in}\ e : m\ \tau}\ \text{(TI-Let)} \qquad \frac{P \mid \Gamma \vdash e_1 : m_1\ \tau_1 \quad P \mid \Gamma, x{:}\tau_1 \vdash e_2 : m_2\ \tau_2 \quad \forall i. P \models m_i \rhd m}{P \mid \Gamma \vdash \mathsf{let}\ x{=}e_1\ \mathsf{in}\ e_2 : m\ \tau_2}\ \text{(TI-Do)}$$

Figure 4. The basic declarative type rules.

$$\frac{P \mid \Gamma \vdash e : m\ \tau \quad P \models m \rhd m'}{P \mid \Gamma \vdash e : m'\ \tau}\ \text{(TI-Lift)}$$

Figure 5. The type rules extended with a lifting rule.

write an ML derivation as $\Gamma \vdash_{\text{ML}} e : \tau$. To compare the derivations in both systems, we need to translate regular ML function types to monadic function types, and we define $\langle\tau\rangle$ as:

$$\begin{array}{ll} \langle\alpha\rangle & = \alpha \\ \langle T\ \tau_1 \ldots \tau_n\rangle & = T\ \langle\tau_1\rangle \ldots \langle\tau_n\rangle \\ \langle\tau_1 \to \tau_2\rangle & = \langle\tau_1\rangle \to Bot\ \langle\tau_2\rangle \end{array}$$

We can state compatibility with ML formally as:

Theorem 1 (Compatibility with ML). *For any well-typed ML non-value expression e such that $\Gamma \vdash_{\text{ML}} e : \tau$, we also have a valid monadic derivation in the Bot monad of the form $\emptyset \mid \Gamma \vdash e : Bot\ \langle\tau\rangle$. For any well-typed value v where $\Gamma \vdash_{\text{ML}} v : \tau$, we have a monadic derivation of the form $\emptyset \mid \Gamma \vdash v : \langle\tau\rangle$.*

The proof is by straightforward induction over typing derivations. We observe that for a standard ML program, we only need the *Bot* monad which means we can always reason under an empty constraint set $\emptyset$. Assuming empty constraints, the instance relation and generalization rule coincide exactly with the Hindley-Milner rules. The other rules now also correspond directly. We show the case for the *App* rule as an example. By the induction hypothesis, we can assume the premise $\emptyset \mid \Gamma \vdash e_1 : Bot\ \langle\tau_2 \to \tau\rangle$ and the premise $\emptyset \mid \Gamma \vdash e_2 : Bot\ \langle\tau_2\rangle$. The first premise is equivalent to $\emptyset \mid \Gamma \vdash e_1 : Bot\ (\langle\tau_2\rangle \to Bot\ \langle\tau\rangle)$ by definition. Using the tautology rule of entailment, we can also conclude that $\emptyset \models Bot \rhd Bot$ and therefore we can apply rule (TI-App) to derive $\emptyset \mid \Gamma \vdash e_1\ e_2 : Bot\ \langle\tau\rangle$ which is the desired result.

3.4 Extensions

Unfortunately, the basic type rules are fragile with respect to η-expansion. For example, consider the following functions:

$$id\ = \lambda x.x$$

$$\begin{array}{l} iapp : (int \to Beh\ int) \to Beh\ int \quad \texttt{(* given *)} \\ iapp\ = \lambda f.f\ 1 \end{array}$$

The basic rules infer the type of id to be $\forall\alpha.\ \alpha \to Bot\ \alpha$, and we suppose the type of *iapp* is given by the programmer. With these types both the applications *iapp id* and *iapp* $(\lambda x.x)$ are rejected because *id* and $\lambda x.x$ have the type $\alpha \to Bot\ \alpha$ where the monadic type *Bot* doesn't match the expected monad *Beh*.

However, we can lift the monadic result type by using η-expansion and introducing an application node, e.g. the η-expanded expression *iapp* $(\lambda x.id\ x)$ is accepted since the application rule allows one to lift the result monad to the required *Beh* monad. Since the monadic types only occur on arrows, the programmer can always use a combination of applications and η-expansions to lift a monadic type anywhere in a type.

Fortunately, such manual η-expansion is rarely required: only when combining higher-order functions where automatic lifting is expected on the result type. The inferred types in the basic system are also often general enough to avoid need of it. For example, without annotation, the inferred principal type for *iapp* is $\forall\alpha\mu_1\mu_2.\ (\mu_1 \rhd \mu_2) \Rightarrow (int \to \mu_1\ \alpha) \to \mu_2\ \alpha$ where all the given applications are accepted as is without need for η-expansion.

Lifting

Nevertheless, it is possible to make the type rules more robust under η-expansion, where we extend the basic system with a general lifting rule (TI-Lift) given in Figure 5 which allows arbitrary lifting of monadic expressions. For example, the *id* function in this system has the inferred type $\forall\alpha\mu.\ \alpha \to \mu\ \alpha$. Using this new type, all the applications *iapp id*, *iapp* $(\lambda x.x)$, and *iapp* $(\lambda x.id\ x)$ are accepted. The good news is that extending the system with (TI-Lift) is benign: we can still do full type inference and constraint solving as shown in later sections. The bad news is that some inferred types become slightly more complicated. For example, the type for `compose` (given in Section 2.3) would be

$$\begin{array}{l} \forall\alpha\beta\gamma\mu_1\mu_2\mu_3\mu_4\mu.\ (\mu_1 \rhd \mu, \mu_2 \rhd \mu) \Rightarrow \\ \quad (\beta \to \mu_2\ \gamma) \to \mu_3\ ((\alpha \to \mu_1\ \beta) \to \mu_4\ (\alpha \to \mu\gamma)) \end{array}$$

Structural subtyping

To ensure robustness under η-expansion while retaining simple types we could introduce a structural subtyping rule. In particular, besides (TI-Lift) we could also introduce the rule:

$$\frac{P \mid \Gamma \vdash e : \tau \quad P \models \tau \rhd \tau'}{P \mid \Gamma \vdash e : \tau'}\ \text{(TI-Subsume)}$$

Note that the subsumption constraint is between *types* instead of between monads. The rules for subsumption are:

$$\frac{P \models \tau_1' \rhd \tau_1 \quad P \models \tau_2 \rhd \tau_2' \quad P \models m \rhd m'}{P \models \tau_1 \to m\ \tau_2 \rhd \tau_1' \to m'\ \tau_2'}\ \text{(S-Fun)}$$

$$P \models \tau \rhd \tau\ \text{(S-Taut)}$$

$$\boxed{P \mid \Gamma \vdash^\star v : \tau \quad P \mid \Gamma \vdash^\bullet e : m\ \tau}$$

$$\frac{\Gamma(x) = \sigma \qquad P \models \sigma \geqslant \tau}{P \mid \Gamma \vdash^\star x : \tau}\ \text{(TS-Var)} \qquad \frac{\Gamma(c) = \sigma \qquad P \models \sigma \geqslant \tau}{P \mid \Gamma \vdash^\star c : \tau}\ \text{(TS-Const)}$$

$$\frac{P \mid \Gamma \vdash^\star v : \tau}{P \mid \Gamma \vdash^\bullet v : \mathit{Bot}\ \tau}\ \text{(TS-Bot)} \qquad \frac{P \mid \Gamma \vdash^\bullet e_1 : m_1\ (\tau \to m_3\ \tau') \qquad P \mid \Gamma \vdash^\bullet e_2 : m_2\ \tau \qquad \forall i.\ P \models m_i \rhd m}{P \mid \Gamma \vdash^\bullet e_1\ e_2 : m\ \tau'}\ \text{(TS-App)}$$

$$\frac{P \mid \Gamma, x{:}\tau_1 \vdash^\bullet e : m\ \tau_2}{P \mid \Gamma \vdash^\star \lambda x.e : \tau_1 \to m\ \tau_2}\ \text{(TS-Lam)} \qquad \frac{P' \mid \Gamma \vdash^\star v : \tau' \qquad \sigma = \mathit{Gen}(\Gamma, P' \Rightarrow \tau') \qquad P \mid \Gamma, x{:}\sigma \vdash^\bullet e : m\ \tau}{P \mid \Gamma \vdash^\bullet \mathsf{let}\ x{=}v\ \mathsf{in}\ e : m\ \tau}\ \text{(TS-Let)}$$

$$\frac{e_1 \neq v \qquad P \mid \Gamma \vdash^\bullet e_1 : m_1\ \tau_1 \qquad P \mid \Gamma, x{:}\tau_1 \vdash^\bullet e_2 : m_2\ \tau_2 \qquad \forall i.\ P \models m_i \rhd m}{P \mid \Gamma \vdash^\bullet \mathsf{let}\ x{=}e_1\ \mathsf{in}\ e_2 : m\ \tau_2}\ \text{(TS-Do)}$$

Figure 6. The syntax-directed type rules. The generalization function is defined as: $\mathit{Gen}(\Gamma, \sigma) = \forall(\mathsf{ftv}(\sigma) \setminus \mathsf{ftv}(\Gamma)).\sigma$.

$$\frac{P \mid \Gamma \vdash^\star v : \tau}{P \mid \Gamma \vdash^\bullet v : m\ \tau}\ \text{(TS-Lift)}$$

Figure 7. The syntax directed type rules extended with a lifting rule which replaces the rule (TS-Bot).

These rules are structural over arrows using the usual co/contravariant typing.[3] With these rules we can give functions like id and $iapp$ fairly simple types:

$$id : \forall \alpha.\ \alpha \to \mathit{Bot}\ \alpha$$
$$iapp : \forall \mu.\ (\mathit{int} \to \mu\ \mathit{int}) \to \mu\ \mathit{int}$$

And under the subsumption rules we can show that this type for id, $\forall \alpha.\ \alpha \to \mathit{Bot}\ \alpha$, is as general as the type $\forall \alpha \mu.\ \alpha \to \mu\ \alpha$.

Unfortunately, it turns out that it is exceedingly difficult to solve constraints between arbitrary types, as opposed to constraints between just monadic types. Since the subsumption rules give rise to constraints between types, we cannot give a coherent constraint solving strategy that is still complete—we either need to reject certain reasonable programs or we need to solve such constraints too aggressively leading to an incomplete inference algorithm.

Thus, our implementation uses the simple strategy since neither lifting nor subsumption provide a satisfactory improvement.

3.5 Syntax-directed type inference

Figure 6 presents a syntax directed version of the declarative type rules. The rules come in two flavors, one for value expressions $P \mid \Gamma \vdash^\star v : \tau$, and one for general expressions $P \mid \Gamma \vdash^\bullet e : m\ \tau$. Since each flavor has a unique rule for each syntactical expression, the shape of the derivation tree is uniquely determined by the expression syntax. Just like the Hindley-Milner syntax directed rules, all instantiations occur at variable and constant introduction, while generalization is only applied at let-bound value expressions.

We can show that the syntax directed rules are sound and complete with respect to the declarative rules.

Theorem 2 (The syntax directed rules are sound and complete). ***Soundness**: For any derivation $P \mid \Gamma \vdash^\star v : \tau$ there exists a derivation $P \mid \Gamma \vdash v : \tau$, and similarly, for any $P \mid \Gamma \vdash^\bullet e : m\ \tau$ we have $P \mid \Gamma \vdash e : m\ \tau$.*
***Completeness**: For any derivation on a value expression $P \mid \Gamma \vdash v : \sigma$ there exists a derivation $P' \mid \Gamma \vdash^\star v : \tau$, such that $\Gamma \vdash (P' \mid \tau) \geqslant (P \mid \sigma)$. Similarly, for any derivation $P \mid \Gamma \vdash e : m\ \tau$, there exists a derivation $P' \mid \Gamma \vdash^\bullet e : m'\ \tau'$, such that $\Gamma \vdash (P' \mid m'\ \tau') \geqslant (P \mid m\ \tau)$.*

[3] Note that when a system has higher-kinds, we need to ensure that the arrow is not a first-class type constructor.

Both directions are proved by induction on the derivations. Following Jones [14], we use an extension of the instance relation in order to define an ordering of polymorphic type schemes and monadic types under some constraint set. We can define this formally as:

$$\frac{\sigma_1 = \forall \overline{\nu}.\ \overline{\pi} \Rightarrow \tau \qquad P_2 \vdash \mathit{Gen}(\Gamma, \forall \overline{\nu}.\ (P_1, \overline{\pi}) \Rightarrow \tau) \geqslant \sigma_2}{\Gamma \vdash (P_1 \mid \sigma_1) \geqslant (P_2 \mid \sigma_2)}$$

$$\frac{\begin{array}{cc}\bar{\alpha}, \bar{\mu} = \mathsf{ftv}(m_1, \tau_1, P_1) \setminus \mathsf{ftv}(\Gamma) & \theta = [\overline{m}/\bar{\mu}, \overline{\tau}/\bar{\alpha}] \\ P_2 \models \theta P_1 \qquad P_2 \models \theta m_1 \rhd m_2 & \theta \tau_1 = \tau_2\end{array}}{\Gamma \vdash (P_1 \mid m_1\ \tau_1) \geqslant (P_2 \mid m_2\ \tau_2)}$$

Besides extending the instance relation to monadic types, the definition of this qualified instance relation allows us specifically to relate derivations in the declarative system that can end in a type scheme σ, to derivations in the syntax directed system that always end in a monotype.

Finally, the syntax directed rules for the declarative type rules extended with the rule (TI-Lift) can be obtained by replacing the rule (TS-Bot) with the rule (TS-Lift) given in Figure 7. This extended system is also sound and complete with respect to the extended declarative rules.

4. Principal types

The standard next step in the development would be to define an algorithmic formulation of the system (including a rewriting to output terms) and then prove that the algorithm is sound and complete with respect to the syntactical rules, thereby establishing the principal types property. Interestingly, we can do this by translation. In particular, we can show that the syntactical rules in Figure 6 directly correspond to the syntactical rules of OML in the theory of qualified types [14]. In the next subsection we prove that for every derivation on an expression e in our syntactical system, there exists an equivalent derivation of an encoded term $[\![e]\!]$ in OML and the other way around. Since OML has a sound and complete type reconstruction algorithm, we could choose to reuse that as is, and thereby get sound and complete type inference (and as a consequence there exist principal derivations).

Unfortunately, the OML type reconstruction algorithm (essentially the Haskell type class inference algorithm) is not satisfactory, as it would reject many useful programs. Intuitively, this is because it conservatively rejects solutions to constraints that are reasonable in light of the morphism laws; since it is unaware of these laws it cannot take advantage of them. The next section develops an algorithm that takes advantage of the morphism laws to be both permissive and coherent.

4.1 Translation to OML

The translation between our system and OML is possible since we use the same instance and generalization relation as in the theory of qualified types. Moreover, it is easy to verify that our entailment relation over morphism constraints satisfies all the requirements of the theory, namely monotonicity, transitivity, and closure under substitution. The more difficult part is to find a direct encoding to OML terms. First, we are going to assume some primitive terms in OML that correspond to rules in our syntactical system:

$$\begin{aligned}
&\mathsf{bot} && : \forall \alpha.\, \alpha \to Bot\ \alpha \\
&\mathsf{do} && : \forall \alpha\beta\mu_1\mu_2\mu.\, (\mu_1 \rhd \mu, \mu_2 \rhd \mu) \\
& && \quad \Rightarrow \mu_1\ \alpha \to (\alpha \to \mu_2\ \beta) \to \mu\ \beta \\
&\mathsf{app} && : \forall \alpha\beta\mu_1\mu_2\mu_3\mu.\, (\mu_1 \rhd \mu, \mu_2 \rhd \mu, \mu_3 \rhd \mu) \\
& && \quad \Rightarrow \mu_1\ (\alpha \to \mu_3\ \beta) \to \mu_2\ \alpha \to \mu\ \beta
\end{aligned}$$

Using these primitives, we can give a syntactic encoding from our expressions into OML terms:

$$\begin{aligned}
&[\![x]\!]^\star && = x \\
&[\![c]\!]^\star && = c \\
&[\![\lambda x.e]\!]^\star && = \lambda x.[\![e]\!] \\
\\
&[\![v]\!] && = \mathsf{bot}\ [\![v]\!]^\star \\
&[\![e_1\ e_2]\!] && = \mathsf{app}\ [\![e_1]\!]\ [\![e_2]\!] \\
&[\![\mathsf{let}\ x = v\ \mathsf{in}\ e]\!] && = \mathsf{let}\ x = [\![v]\!]^\star\ \mathsf{in}\ [\![e]\!] \\
&[\![\mathsf{let}\ x = e_1\ \mathsf{in}\ e_2]\!] && = \mathsf{do}\ [\![e_1]\!]\ [\![\lambda x.e_2]\!]^\star \qquad (\text{with } e_1 \neq v)
\end{aligned}$$

We can now state soundness and completeness of our syntactic system with respect to encoded terms in OML, where we write $P \mid \Gamma \vdash_{\mathrm{OML}} e : \tau$ for a derivation in the syntax directed inference system of OML (cf. Jones [14], Fig. 4).

Theorem 3 (Elaboration to OML is sound and complete).
Soundness: *Whenever* $P \mid \Gamma \vdash^\star v : \tau$ *we can also derive* $P \mid \Gamma \vdash_{\mathrm{OML}} [\![v]\!]^\star : \tau$ *in OML. Similarly, when* $P \mid \Gamma \vdash^\bullet e : m\ \tau$ *we have* $P \mid \Gamma \vdash_{\mathrm{OML}} [\![e]\!] : m\ \tau$.
Completeness: *If we can derive* $P \mid \Gamma \vdash_{\mathrm{OML}} [\![v]\!]^\star : \tau$, *there also exists a derivation* $P \mid \Gamma \vdash^\star v : \tau$, *and similarly, whenever* $P \mid \Gamma \vdash_{\mathrm{OML}} [\![e]\!] : m\ \tau$, *we also have* $P \mid \Gamma \vdash^\bullet e : m\ \tau$.

The proof of both properties can be done by straightforward induction on terms. As a corollary, we can use the general type reconstruction algorithm W from the theory of qualified types which is shown sound and complete to the OML type rules. Furthermore, it means that our system is sound, and we can derive principal types.

Corollary 4. *The declarative and syntactic type rules admit principal types.*

Again, the same results hold for the extended type rules with the (TI-Lift) and (TS-Lift) rules. The only change needed is that the lifting primitive now needs to be polymorphic to reflect the (TS-Lift) rule, i.e. $\mathsf{bot} : \forall \alpha\mu.\, \alpha \to \mu\ \alpha$.

4.2 Ambiguous types

Following Theorem 3, we could encode our type inference algorithm using the type class facility of a language like Haskell, employing a morphism type class that provides morphisms between monads. In particular:

```
class Morph m n  where
  lift :: m a -> n a

app :: Morph m1 m, Morph m2 m, Morph m3 m, Monad m
        => m1 (a -> m2 b) -> m3 a -> m b
app mf mx = lift mf >>= \f ->
            lift mx >>= \x ->
            lift (f x)
...
```

Type checking could now be implemented using the syntactical encoding into a Haskell program and running the Haskell type checker. Unfortunately, this approach would not be very satisfactory: it turns out that our particular morphism constraints quickly lead to ambiguous types that cannot be solved by a generic system. In particular, Haskell rejects any types that have variables in the constraints that do not occur in the type (which we call free constraint variables).

Recall our function $iapp : (int \to Beh\ int) \to Beh\ int$. The expression $[\![iapp\ (\lambda x.\ id\ (id\ x))]\!]$ has the Haskell type $\forall \mu.(Morph\ \mu\ Beh) \Rightarrow Beh\ int$ where the type variable μ only occurs in the constraint but not in the body of the type. Any such type must be rejected in a system like Haskell. In general, there could exist multiple solutions for such free constraint variables where each solution gives rise to a different semantics. A common example in Haskell is the program $show$ [ ] with the type $\mathsf{Show}\ \alpha \Rightarrow string$. In this example, choosing to resolve α as $char$ results in the string "", while any other choice results in [ ].

We were initially discouraged by this situation until we realized that focusing only on morphism constraints confers an advantage: the monad morphism laws allow us to show that any solution for the free constraint variables leads to semantically equivalent programs; i.e., the evidence translations for each solution are coherent.

Moreover, there is an efficient and decidable algorithm for finding a particular "least" solution. At a high-level our algorithm works by requiring that the set of monad constants and morphisms between them form a semi-lattice, with Bot as the least element, where all morphisms satisfy the monad morphism laws. Another requirement that is fulfilled by careful design of the type system is that the only morphism constraints are between monadic type constants or monadic type variables, and never between arbitrary types. We can repeatedly simplify a given constraint graph by eagerly substituting free constraint variables μ with the least upper bound of their lower bounds when these lower bounds are constants. This simple strategy yields a linear-time decision procedure. The next section presents the algorithm in detail and proves coherence.

5. Constraint simplification and coherence

This section presents an algorithmic formulation (a variation on the Hindley-Milner algorithm W) of our syntax-directed type inference system. The previous section established that while the type reconstruction algorithm of Jones can infer principal types, these types are frequently ambiguous and hence programs with these types must be rejected. The contribution of this section is a simple (linear time) procedure that can eliminate some ambiguous variables in the constraints of a type in a *coherent* way. By performing constraint simplification, the types inferred by our algorithm are intentionally not the most general ones. However, simplification allows strictly more programs to be accepted. Moreover, we can show that simplification is *justified*, in that the typability of the program is not adversely effected by the simplified type.

Section 5.1 discusses the key algorithmic typing and rules and illustrates elaboration of source terms to System F target terms. Section 5.2 gives our constraint solving algorithm. Finally, Section 5.3 shows, by appealing to the morphism laws, that our solving algorithm is coherent and does not introduce ambiguity into the semantics of elaborated terms.

5.1 Algorithmic rewriting

The structure of our algorithm W closely follows Jones' algorithm for qualified types [14], and includes an elaboration into a calculus with first-class polymorphism. We formulate our algorithm in a stylized way to facilitate the proof of coherence. We think of the constraints generated by our system as forming a directed graph, with nodes corresponding to monad type constants and variables,

any type	t	::=	$m\ \tau \mid \tau$
constraint	π	::=	$\mathsf{Do}(m_1, m_2, m)$
		$\mid$	$\mathsf{App}(m_1, m_2, m_3, m)$
substitution	θ	::=	$\cdot \mid \alpha \mapsto \tau \mid \mu \mapsto m \mid \theta\theta'$
target types	t	::=	$\nu \mid \mathsf{t}_1\ \mathsf{t}_2 \mid \forall\nu.\mathsf{t} \mid \mathsf{t}_1 \rightarrow \mathsf{t}_2$
target terms	e	::=	$x \mid c \mid \lambda x{:}\mathsf{t}.\mathsf{e} \mid \mathsf{e}_1\ \mathsf{e}_2 \mid \Lambda\alpha.\mathsf{e} \mid \mathsf{e}\ [\mathsf{t}]$

Figure 8. Syntax of constraint bundles and a target language e.

and edges represented by the morphism relation $m \rhd m'$. However, instead of simply producing constraints of the form $m \rhd m'$ as in the syntax-directed system, our algorithm groups related constraints together in "bundles". Constraint bundles come in two flavors, corresponding to the fragments of the typing derivation (and hence bits of program syntax) that induced the constraints. The bundles allow us to reason that edges in constraint graph come in specific kinds of pairs or triples, thus syntactically restricting the shape of the graph and facilitating our coherence proof.

Figure 8 gives the syntax of target terms e and types t, and alters the syntax of constraints π to constraint bundles. As we will see shortly, the bundles arise from corresponding inference rules from Figure 9: $\mathsf{Do}(m_1, m_2, m)$ is induced by the monadic let-binding rule (W-Do) and $\mathsf{App}(m_1, m_2, m_3, m)$ by the (W-App) rule. Substitutions θ map type variables to types, and $\theta_1\theta_2$ denotes substitution composition.

Figure 9 shows the key rules in our algorithm W, expressed as a judgment $P \mid \Gamma \vdash^{\kappa} e : t; \theta \rightsquigarrow \mathsf{e}$ where the constraints P, type t, substitution θ, and target term e are synthesized. As shown in Figure 8, t is either τ or $m\ \tau$; as in the syntax-directed rules, κ denotes one of two modes, $\star$ and $\bullet$; and the target term e is explicitly typed. The substitution θ applies to the free type-level variables (α and μ) in Γ. An invariant of the rules is that $\theta(t) = t$, $\theta(P) = P$, and $\theta(\mathsf{e}) = \mathsf{e}$. For simplicity, we omit types on formal parameters and instantiation of type parameters in elaborated terms e. We also assume that a morphism from a monad m to m' is named $f_{m,m'}$; and the bind and unit of a monad m are $bind_m$ and $unit_m$. The omitted rules are unsurprising.

Rule (W-Bot) corresponds to the syntactic rule (TS-Bot). It switches modes from $\bullet$ to $\star$ in its premise, produces the monadic type $Bot\ \tau$, and elaborates the term by inserting the unit for Bot.

Rule (W-App) elaborates each sub-term in its first two premises, and in the fourth and fifth premises, computes the most-general unifier θ_3 of the formal parameter type of e_1 and the value type of e_2. We generate an App-constraint bundle which indicates that there is a morphism from each of $\theta_3\theta_2\mu_1$, $\theta_3\theta_1\mu_2$, and $\theta_3\mu'$ to the result monad μ. In the elaborated terms, $f_{\mu_i,\mu}$ stand for morphisms that will be abstracted (or solved) at the nearest enclosing let; similarly the $bind_\mu$ are the binds of the result monad. The rule for monadic let-bindings, (W-Do), is nearly identical to (W-App) except that there is one fewer monad variable.

Finally, rule (W-Let) implements generalization. We rewrite the let-bound value v in the first premise, and compute the variables $\bar{\nu}$ over which we can soundly generalize. In the third premise, we compute the variables $\bar{\mu}$ that appear in the constraints P_1 but are not free in the type τ—these variables are candidates for constraint simplification. The judgment $P_1 \overset{\mathrm{solve}(\bar{\mu})}{\longrightarrow} P_1'; \theta'$ simplifies constraints, eliminating the ambiguous type variables $\bar{\mu}$ coherently—this judgment is discussed in the next subsection. The last premise rewrites the body in a context in which x's type is generalized. In the conclusion, we translate to an explicitly typed application form, where the let-bound value is elaborated to generalize over both its constraints and the type variables $\bar{\nu}$.

5.2 Soundness and efficiency of constraint simplification

Intuitively, our algorithm views a constraint set P as a directed graph, where the nodes in the graph are the monad types, and the edges are introduced by the constraint bundles. For example, we view a bundle $\mathsf{Do}(m_1, m_2, m)$ as a graph with vertices for m_1, m_2 and m, and edges from m_1 to m and m_2 to m. In the discussion below, we informally use intuitions from this graphical view of P. For each edge between m and m' in the constraint graph, a solution to P must compute a specific morphism between m and m'.

We start our description of the algorithm with the definition of morphism-induced least-upper bounds. This definition is relative to an initial set of constraints P_0 that define the monad constants and primitive morphisms used to type a source program.

Definition 5 (Least-upper bound)**.** *With respect to an initial context P_0, given a set of monad constants $A = \{M_1, \ldots, M_n\}$, we write* $\mathrm{lub}(A) = M$ *to mean that M is the least upper bound of the monad constants in A, i.e., $\forall i.P_0 \models M_i \rhd M$; and for any M' such that $\forall i.P_0 \models M_i \rhd M'$, we have $P_0 \vdash M \rhd M'$. Although defined with regard to a particular initial context P_0, we write* $\mathrm{lub}(A)$ *for conciseness, leaving P_0 implicit.*

Our constraint simplification algorithm is straightforward. We limit our attention to cycle-free constraint graphs. Whenever a cycle is detected in the constraint graph, we require every variable and constant in the cycle to be identical—a constraint graph with a cycle containing more than one constant cannot be solved and the program is rejected.

Given a cycle-free graph we perform a topological sort and then proceed to simplify the graph starting from the leaves. We consider a variable μ only after all its children have been considered. All variables have lower bounds (in-edges), since variables are introduced by (W-Do) and (W-App) and have lower bounds by construction. Besides, the node corresponding to Bot has an out-edge to every other node. For each variable μ considered, if all its in-edges are from monad constants $A = \{M_1, \ldots, M_n\}$, and if μ has some out-edge (needed for coherence, and discussed in the next sub-section), we assign to μ the constant $lub(A)$, thus eliminating the variable and proceeding to consider the next variable, if any.

Figure 10 presents a set of inference rules that codifies this solving algorithm (omitting the cycle elimination phase, for simplicity). The judgment has the form $P \overset{\mathrm{solve}(\bar{\mu})}{\longrightarrow} P'; \theta$. It considers the free constraint variables $\bar{\mu}$ in P, replacing them with monad constants under certain conditions, returning the residual constraints P' that cannot be simplified further. This judgment ensures that $dom(\theta) \subseteq \bar{\mu}$ and $\theta P' = P'$. Thus, in the (W-Let) rule we apply θ' to the body of e_1 in the conclusion, in effect resolving any free morphism $f_{\mu,\mu'}$ to the specific morphism determined by θ'. Notice that since $dom(\theta) \subseteq \bar{\mu}$, the premises of (W-Let) ensure that we eliminate only those variables appearing in neither the final type nor the context.

The inference rules make use of a few auxiliary functions, defined to the right of Figure 10. First, for a constraint bundle π, function $up\text{-}bnd(\pi)$ is the type of the resulting monad. In contrast, $lo\text{-}bnd(\pi)$ is the set of types in a constraint bundle *from which* we require morphisms. Both of these are lifted to sets of constraints in the natural way. We also define $\mathsf{flowsTo}_\mu\ P$, the set of constraints in P that have μ as an upper bound; $\mathsf{flowsFrom}_\mu\ P$, the set of constraints that have μ as a lower bound.

We now explain the rules in detail. Rule (S-μ) is the workhorse of the algorithm. In the first two premises, it selects some constraint π whose upper bound μ is in the list of variables to be solved, $\bar{\mu}$. The third premise checks that μ has an upper bound; i.e., it is the lower bound of at least one constraint in P (for coherence). The fourth premise defines A, the set of all of μ's lower bounds, and the

$$\boxed{P \mid \Gamma \vdash^{\kappa} e : t; \theta \leadsto \mathsf{e}}$$

$$\frac{P \mid \Gamma \vdash^{\star} v : \tau; \theta \leadsto \mathsf{e}}{P, \pi \mid \Gamma \vdash^{\bullet} v : \mathit{Bot}\ \tau; \theta \leadsto (\mathit{unit}_{\mathit{Bot}}\ \mathsf{e})}\ \text{(W-Bot)}$$

$$\frac{\begin{array}{c} P_1 \mid \Gamma \vdash^{\bullet} e_1 : \mu_1\ \tau_1; \theta_1 \leadsto \mathsf{e}_1 \qquad P_2 \mid \Gamma \vdash^{\bullet} e_2 : \mu_2\ \tau_2; \theta_2 \leadsto \mathsf{e}_2 \qquad \mu, \mu', \alpha, \beta \text{ fresh} \\ \theta_2\tau_1 = \theta_3(\alpha \to \mu'\ \beta) \quad \theta_1\tau_2 = \theta_3\alpha \quad P = (\theta_3\theta_2 P_1), (\theta_3\theta_1 P_2), \mathsf{App}(\theta_3\theta_2\mu_1, \theta_3\theta_1\mu_2, \theta_3\mu', \mu) \quad \theta = \theta_1\theta_2\theta_3 \end{array}}{P \mid \Gamma \vdash^{\bullet} e_1\ e_2 : \theta_3(\mu\ \beta); \theta \leadsto \theta(\mathit{bind}_{\mu}\ (f_{\mu_1,\mu}\ \mathsf{e}_1)\ (\lambda x{:}\_.\mathit{bind}_{\mu}\ (f_{\mu_2,\mu}\mathsf{e}_2)\ \lambda y{:}\_.(f_{\mu',\mu}(x\ y))))}\ \text{(W-App)}$$

$$\frac{\begin{array}{c} e_1 \neq v \qquad P_1 \mid \Gamma \vdash^{\bullet} e_1 : \mu_1\ \tau_1; \theta_1 \leadsto \mathsf{e}_1 \qquad P_2 \mid \Gamma, x{:}\tau_1 \vdash^{\bullet} e_2 : \mu_2\ \tau_2; \theta_2 \leadsto \mathsf{e}_2 \qquad \mu, \alpha, \beta \text{ fresh} \\ \theta_2\tau_1 = \theta_3(\alpha) \quad \theta_1\tau_2 = \theta_3(\beta) \quad P = (\theta_3\theta_2 P_1), (\theta_3\theta_1 P_2), \mathsf{Do}(\theta_3\theta_2\mu_1, \theta_3\theta_1\mu_2, \mu) \quad \theta = \theta_1\theta_2\theta_3 \end{array}}{P \mid \Gamma \vdash^{\bullet} \mathsf{let}\ x{=}e_1\ \mathsf{in}\ e_2 : \theta_3(\mu\ \beta); \theta \leadsto \theta(\mathit{bind}_{\mu}\ (f_{\mu_1,\mu}\mathsf{e}_1)\ \lambda x{:}\alpha.(f_{\mu_2,\mu}\mathsf{e}_2))}\ \text{(W-Do)}$$

$$\frac{\begin{array}{c} P_1 \mid \Gamma \vdash^{\star} v : \tau; \theta_1 \leadsto \mathsf{e}_1 \qquad \bar{\nu} = \mathsf{ftv}(P_1 \Rightarrow \tau) \setminus \mathsf{ftv}(\Gamma) \qquad \bar{\mu} = (\mathsf{ftv}(P_1) \setminus \mathsf{ftv}(\tau)) \cap \bar{\nu} \\ P_1 \stackrel{\mathrm{solve}(\bar{\mu})}{\longrightarrow} P_1'; \theta' \quad \sigma = \forall \bar{\nu}.P_1' \Rightarrow \tau \quad P_2 \mid \Gamma, x{:}\sigma \vdash^{\bullet} e : m\ \tau; \theta_2 \leadsto \mathsf{e}_2 \quad \theta = \theta_1\theta_2 \end{array}}{P_2 \mid \Gamma \vdash^{\bullet} \mathsf{let}\ x{=}v\ \mathsf{in}\ e : \theta_1(m\ \tau); \theta \leadsto \theta((\lambda x{:}\_.\mathsf{e}_2)\ \Lambda\bar{\nu}.\mathsf{abstractConstraints}(P_1', \theta'\mathsf{e}_1))}\ \text{(W-Let)}$$

where

$$\begin{array}{lcl} \mathsf{abstractConstraints}((\pi, P), \mathsf{e}) & = & \mathsf{abstractConstraints}(\pi, \mathsf{abstractConstraints}(P, \mathsf{e})) \\ \mathsf{abstractConstraints}(\mathsf{Do}(m_1, m_2, m), \mathsf{e}) & = & \lambda \mathit{bind}_m{:}\_.\lambda f_{m_1,m}{:}\_.\lambda f_{m_2,m}{:}\_.\mathsf{e} \\ \mathsf{abstractConstraints}(\mathsf{App}(m_1, m_2, m_3, m), \mathsf{e}) & = & \lambda \mathit{bind}_m{:}\_.\lambda f_{m_1,m}{:}\_.\lambda f_{m_2,m}{:}\_.\lambda f_{m_3,m}{:}\_.\mathsf{e} \\ \mathsf{abstractConstraints}(\mathsf{Lift}(m), \mathsf{e}) & = & \lambda \mathit{unit}_m{:}\_.\mathsf{e} \end{array}$$

Figure 9. Selected algorithmic rules for elaboration into System F (with types in elaborated terms omitted for readability).

$$\frac{}{P \stackrel{\mathrm{solve}(\bar{\mu})}{\longrightarrow} P; \cdot} \qquad \frac{\pi, P \stackrel{\mathrm{solve}(\bar{\mu})}{\longrightarrow} P'; \theta}{\pi, \pi, P \stackrel{\mathrm{solve}(\bar{\mu})}{\longrightarrow} P'; \theta} \qquad \frac{P_2, P_1 \stackrel{\mathrm{solve}(\bar{\mu})}{\longrightarrow} P'; \theta}{P_1, P_2 \stackrel{\mathrm{solve}(\bar{\mu})}{\longrightarrow} P'; \theta}$$

$$\text{S-M}\ \frac{P_0 \models \mathit{lub}(\mathit{lo\text{-}bnds}(\pi)) \rhd \mathit{up\text{-}bnd}(\pi) \qquad P \stackrel{\mathrm{solve}(\bar{\mu})}{\longrightarrow} P'; \theta}{\pi, P \stackrel{\mathrm{solve}(\bar{\mu})}{\longrightarrow} P'; \theta}$$

$$\text{S-}\mu\ \frac{\begin{array}{c} \mathit{up\text{-}bnd}(\pi) = \mu \qquad \bar{\mu} = \mu, \bar{\mu}' \qquad \mathsf{flowsFrom}_{\mu}\ P \neq \{\} \\ A = \mathit{lo\text{-}bnds}(\pi, \mathsf{flowsTo}_{\mu}\ P) \quad \theta = (\mu \mapsto \mathit{lub}(A)) \quad \theta P \stackrel{\mathrm{solve}(\bar{\mu}')}{\longrightarrow} P'; \theta' \end{array}}{\pi, P \stackrel{\mathrm{solve}(\bar{\mu})}{\longrightarrow} P'; \theta\theta'}$$

where

$$\begin{array}{lcl} \mathit{up\text{-}bnd}(\mathsf{Lift}(m)) & = & m \\ \mathit{up\text{-}bnd}(\mathsf{App}(\cdot, \cdot, \cdot, m)) & = & m \\ \mathit{up\text{-}bnd}(\mathsf{Do}(\cdot, \cdot, m)) & = & m \\ \mathit{up\text{-}bnds}(P) & = & \bigcup_{\pi \in P}\{\mathit{up\text{-}bnd}(\pi)\} \\ & & \\ \mathit{lo\text{-}bnd}(\mathsf{Lift}(m)) & = & \mathit{Bot} \\ \mathit{lo\text{-}bnd}(\mathsf{App}(m_1, m_2, m_3, \cdot)) & = & \{m_1, m_2, m_3\} \\ \mathit{lo\text{-}bnd}(\mathsf{Do}(m_1, m_2, \cdot)) & = & \{m_1, m_2\} \\ \mathit{lo\text{-}bnds}(P) & = & \bigcup_{\pi \in P} \mathit{lo\text{-}bnd}(\pi) \end{array}$$

$$\begin{array}{lcl} \mathsf{flowsTo}_{\mu}\ P & = & \{\pi \mid \pi \in P\ \wedge\ \mu = \mathit{up\text{-}bnd}(\pi)\} \\ \mathsf{flowsFrom}_{\mu}\ P & = & \{\pi \mid \pi \in P\ \wedge\ \mu \in \mathit{lo\text{-}bnd}(\pi)\} \end{array}$$

Figure 10. $P \stackrel{\mathrm{solve}(\bar{\mu})}{\longrightarrow} P'; \theta$: Simplifying constraints using the *lub*-strategy.

fifth premise defines the substitution θ as mapping μ to the least upper bound of A. Recall again that *lub*is only defined on constant monads, so A must contain no variables μ'; this requirement essentially forces solving to proceed bottom up, with the leaves of the tree induced by P (following cycle elimination) solved first. Finally, the sixth premise applies the substitution to the constraints P and proceeds to solve them; the final substitution consists of the substitution θ' produced by this recursive step, composed with θ.

Rule (S-M) checks that constraints involving only constants (e.g., those whose μ have been completely substituted for) are consistent with the initial constraint set P_0, in which case they can be dropped. Finally, the first three rules help with bookkeeping, indicating that (1) constraints may remain unsimplified; (2) duplicate constraints may be dropped; and (3) constraints may be permuted. This last rule is non-deterministic, but it can be implemented easily using simple topological sort of a cycle-free constraint constraint graph.

The next definition and the following lemma establish that $P \stackrel{\mathrm{solve}(\bar{\mu})}{\longrightarrow} P'; \theta$ only produces sound solutions to a constraint set. The proof is straightforward.

Definition 6 (Sound solution)**.** *Given an initial context P_0 and a constraint set P, a solution θ to the constraints P is sound if and only if, for each μ in $dom(\theta)$, we have $\{M_1, \ldots, M_n\} = \mathit{lo\text{-}bnds}(\theta(\mathsf{flowsTo}_{\mu}\ P))$, and $\forall i. P_0 \models M_i \rhd \theta\mu$.*

Lemma 7 (Constraint simplification is sound)**.** *For all $P_0, P, \bar{\mu}, P', \theta$, if we have $P_0 \vdash P \stackrel{\mathrm{solve}(\bar{\mu})}{\longrightarrow} P'; \theta$, then θ is sound for P.* □

Theorem 8 (Constraint solving is linear time)**.** *Given a constraint set P and an initial context P_0, there exists a $O(|P|)$ algorithm to decide whether or not P is* fully solvable*, where a constraint set P is fully solvable iff $\bar{\mu} = \mathsf{ftv}(P)$ implies $P_0 \vdash P \stackrel{\mathrm{solve}(\bar{\mu})}{\longrightarrow} \cdot; \theta$.*

Proof. (sketch) The algorithm begins by detecting and eliminating cycles in the constraint graph. Doing so is linear in number of vertices and edges of the graph, i.e., $O(|V| + |E|)$, where $|V|$ and $|E|$ are each at most three times the number of $\mathsf{App}(m_1, m_2, m_3, m)$ constraints plus twice the number of $\mathsf{Do}(m_1, m_2, m)$ constraints.

Then the algorithm sorts the graph topologically (also linear).

Then it attempts to eliminate each constraint variable in sorted order. Eliminating a single constraint variable takes constant time. This is because elimination amounts to the cost of computing the *lub*for elements of a finite lattice in P_0 and all *lub*s can be precomputed on P_0 without dependence on P.

After eliminating all eligible constraint variables we are left with either a graph that has variables without upper bounds (in which case we answer "no") or we have a graph with only constants. Checking for upper bounds in a variable-free graph is again linear in the number of constraints, since each ordering can be answered in constant time (again, pre-computed on P_0). □

One would also like to show that our constraint solving algorithm does not solve constraints too aggressively. We define an *improvement* relation on type schemes (following the terminology of Jones [16]), as a lifting of the solving algorithm.

Definition 9 (Improvement of type schemes). *Given a type scheme* $\sigma = \forall\bar{\nu}.P_1 \Rightarrow \tau$ *and a set of type variables* $\bar{\mu} = (\mathsf{ftv}(P_1) \setminus \mathsf{ftv}(\tau)) \cap \bar{\nu}$. *If* $P_1 \xrightarrow{\text{solve}(\bar{\mu})} P_2;\theta$ *then we say* $\sigma' = \forall\bar{\nu}.P_2 \Rightarrow \tau$ *is an* improvement *of* σ.

We might conjecture at first that improvement of types is consistent with the type instantiation relation. That is, if σ' is an improvement of σ, then $P_0 \vdash \sigma' \geq \sigma$ and $P_0 \vdash \sigma \geq \sigma'$. However, by eliminating free constraint variables, our solving algorithm intentionally makes σ' less general than σ. For example, given $\sigma = \forall\mu.(M_1 \rhd \mu, \mu \rhd M_2) \Rightarrow \tau$, (where $\mu \notin \mathsf{ftv}(\tau)$) our algorithm could improve this to $\sigma' = M_1 \rhd M_2 \Rightarrow \tau$, and indeed further to τ, if $P_0 \models M_1 \rhd M_2$. However, for an arbitrary constant μ, it is not that case that $P_0 \models M_1 \rhd \mu, \mu \rhd M_2$, which is what is demanded by the instantiation relation.

Nevertheless, the type improvement scheme is still useful since improvement at generalization points does not impact the typability of the remainder of the program.

Theorem 10 (Improvement is justified). *For all* $P, \Gamma, x, \sigma, \sigma', e, m, \tau$, *if we have* $P \mid \Gamma, x{:}\sigma \vdash e : m\ \tau$, *and* σ' *is an improvement of* σ, *then* $P \mid \Gamma, x{:}\sigma' \vdash e : m\ \tau$.

Intuitively, we can see this theorem holds because the improvement of a type $\sigma = \forall\bar{\nu}.P_1 \Rightarrow \tau$ to $\forall\bar{\nu}.P_2 \Rightarrow \tau$ only effects the free constraint variables: the actual type τ is unchanged and if $P \models P_1$ we always have $P \models P_2$ too. At any instantiation of σ, we can always substitute the improved type since the type τ is the same and the improved constraints P_2 are also entailed if the original constraints P_1 were.

5.3 Coherence

The effectiveness of our constraint-solving strategy stems from our ability to eagerly substitute constraint variable μ with the least upper bound M of all the types that flow to it. Such a technique is not admissible in a setting with general purpose qualified type constraints, particularly when the evidence for constraints (in this case our morphisms, binds and units) has operational meaning. One may worry that by instantiating μ with some $M' \neq M$ where $M \rhd M'$, we may get an acceptable solution to the constraint graph but the meaning of the elaborated programs differs in each case. This section shows that when the monad morphisms satisfy the morphism laws our constraint improvement strategy is coherent, i.e., all admissible solutions to the constraints yield elaborations with the same semantics. So, any specific solution (including the one produced by the *lub*-strategy) can safely be chosen.

Our approach to showing coherence proceeds as follows:

1. Given a constraint set P and a derivation $P_0 \vdash P \xrightarrow{\text{solve}(\bar{\mu})} \cdot;\theta$, we call θ the *lub*-solution to P.
2. We can see all other solutions to P as being derived from the *lub*-solution by repeated *local modifications* to the *lub*-solution. A local modification involves picking a single variable μ such that $\theta = \theta'(\mu \mapsto M)$ and considering a solution to the constraint set $\theta' P$ that assigns some other solution $M' \neq M$ to μ; i.e., we have some solution $\theta_1 = \theta'(\mu \mapsto M')$. We can iterate this process, generating the solution θ_{i+1} from θ_i in this manner.
3. We enumerate the ways in which $\theta_i P$ can differ from $\theta_{i+1} P$, considering interactions between pairs of constraint bundles (App/App, Do/Do, Do/App, App/Do, etc.). In each case, since each kind of constraint bundle can be related to the abstract syntax of elaborated programs, we can reason about the differences in semantics that might arise from the θ_i and the θ_{i+1} solutions. We show that when all the morphisms satisfy the morphism laws, that the solutions are indeed equivalent.

Our result applies only to well-formed contexts, a notion defined below. In the definition, requirements (1) and (2) ensure that the monads and their morphisms are well-typed. Requirement (3) ensures that least-upper bounds are defined and that there is a Bot monad. Our notion of term equivalence, written $\mathsf{e}_1 \cong \mathsf{e}_2$, is extensional equality on well-typed, elaborated terms. Clauses (4) and (5) state that this equivalence is axiomatized by the transitivity property and the morphism laws.

Definition 11 (Well-formedness of a context). *The following conditions are required of well-formed contexts,* P_0, Γ*:*

1. *For any pair of monad constants* M *we have* $bind_M$ *and* $unit_M$ *bound as constants in* Γ, *with appropriate types.*
2. *For all* M_1, M_2, *if* $P_0 \models M_1 \rhd M_2$ *then* Γ *contains a constant* f_{M_1,M_2} *bound at the type* $\forall\alpha.M_1\ \alpha \to M_2\ \alpha$.
3. *For any set of monad constants* A, *there exists* M *such that* $\mathrm{lub}(A) = M$ *and* Bot *is a monad constant in* Γ *with* $P_0 \models Bot \rhd M$, *for all* M.
4. *We assume that for all* M_1, M_2, M_3, *if* $P_0 \models M_1 \rhd M_2$ *and* $P_0 \models M_2 \rhd M_3$, *then* $f_{M_2,M_3} \circ f_{M_1,M_2} \cong f_{M_1,M_3}$.
5. *We assume that for all* $M_1, M_2, \mathsf{e}_1, \mathsf{e}_2, \mathsf{t}_1, \mathsf{t}_2$, *such that* $P_0 \models M_1 \rhd M_2$ *and* $\mathsf{e}_1 : M_1\ \mathsf{t}_1$ *and* $\mathsf{e}_2 : M_2\ \mathsf{t}_2$, *we have* $f_{M_1,M_2}(bind_{M_1}\ \mathsf{e}_1\ \lambda x{:}\mathsf{t}_1.\mathsf{e}_2) \cong bind_{M_2}\ (f_{M_1,M_2}\ \mathsf{e}_1)\ \lambda x{:}\mathsf{t}_1.(f_{M_1,M_2}\ \mathsf{e}_2)$

The following lemma establishes that in well-formed contexts, our algorithm produces well-typed System F terms. The proof is a straightforward induction on the structure of the derivation, where by $\{\![\Gamma]\!\}$ we mean the translation of a source typing context to a System F context.

Lemma 12 (Well-typed elaborations). *Given* Γ *such that* P_0, Γ *is well-formed,* $e, t, \theta, \mathsf{e}, \kappa$, *such that* $P \mid \Gamma \vdash^{\kappa} e : t;\theta \rightsquigarrow \mathsf{e}$. *Then there exists* t *such that* $\{\![\theta\Gamma]\!\} \vdash_F \mathsf{abstractConstraints}(P, \mathsf{e}) : \mathsf{t}$.

Next, we formalize the notion of a local modification θ' of a valid solution θ to constraint set. Condition (1) identifies the variable μ which is the locus of the modification. Conditions (2) and (3) establish the range of admissible solutions to μ, and condition (4) asserts that the modified solution θ' picks a solution for μ that is different than θ, but still admissible.

Definition 13 (Local modification of a solution). *Given a solution* θ_1 *to a constraint set* (π, P), *a local modification to* θ_1 *is a solution* θ_2 *for which the following conditions are true:*

1. *There exists a variable* μ *and a constant* M *such that* $\mu = \textit{up-bnd}(\pi)$ *and* $\theta_1 = \theta_1'(\mu \mapsto M)$.
2. *There exists* $M^{lo} = \mathrm{lub}(\theta_1'(\textit{lo-bnds}(\mathsf{flowsTo}_\mu\ P))))$. M^{lo} *is a lower-bound for* μ.
3. *There exists* $\{M_1^{hi}, \ldots, M_n^{hi}\} = \theta_1'(\textit{up-bnds}(\mathsf{flowsFrom}_\mu\ P))$. *Each* M_i^{hi} *is an upper bound for* μ.
4. *There exists a monad constant* $M' \neq M$ *such that* $P_0 \vdash M^{lo} \rhd M'$ *and* $\forall i.P_0 \vdash M' \rhd M_i^{hi}$, *such that* $\theta_2 = \theta_1'(\mu \mapsto M')$

Finally, we state and sketch a representative case of the main result of this section: namely, that the *lub*-strategy is coherent when the morphisms form a semi-lattice and satisfy the morphism laws.

Theorem 14 (Coherence of constraint solving). *Given $P_0, \Gamma, P, e, t, \theta, \theta_1, \theta_2, \mathsf{e}, \kappa, \bar{\mu}$, such that*

1. P_0, Γ *is well-formed and* P *is cycle-free.*
2. *For all* $\mu \in \bar{\mu}$, *the set* $\mathsf{flowsFrom}_\mu\ P$ *is non-empty, i.e.,* μ *has an upper bound.*
3. $P \mid \Gamma \vdash^\kappa e : t; \theta \rightsquigarrow \mathsf{e}$.
4. *There exists* θ_1 *such that* $dom(\theta_1) \subseteq \bar{\mu}$ *and* θ_1 *is a sound solution for* P.
5. *There exists* θ_2, *a local modification of* θ_1.

Then, $\theta_1 \mathsf{e} \cong \theta_2 \mathsf{e}$.

Proof. (Sketch) Since θ_2 is a local modification, we have (from condition (1) of Definition 13) $\theta_1 = \theta_1'(\mu \mapsto M)$, for some μ, M, θ_1', and $P = \pi, P'$, where $\mu = \textit{up-bnd}(\pi)$ is the modified variable. We proceed by cases on the shape of π.

Case π is an App bundle: We have $\theta_1'\pi = \mathsf{App}(M_1^{lo}, M_2^{lo}, M_3^{lo}, \mu)$ (since from condition (2) of Definition 13, *lub* is only defined on monad constant). To identify the upper bounds of μ, we consider the constraints in $\theta_1'(\mathsf{flowsFrom}_\mu\ P')$, note that all the upper bounds must be constants (from condition (3)), and proceed by cases on the shape of each of the constraints π' in this set.

Sub-case π' is an App bundle: Without loss of generality on the specific position of μ, we have $\theta'\pi' = \mathsf{App}(m_1, \mu, m_3, M^{hi})$, where M^{hi} is an upper-bound of π'. From the shape of the constraints, we reason that we have a source term of the form $e\ (e_1\ e_2)$, that is elaborated to the term shown below, where $\mathsf{e}, \mathsf{e}_1, \mathsf{e}_2$ are the elaboration of the sub-terms.

1. $\textit{bind}_{M^{hi}}\ (f_{m_1,M^{hi}}\ \mathsf{e})\ (\lambda x{:}\_.\textit{bind}_{M^{hi}}$
2. $(f_{\mu,M^{hi}}(\textit{bind}_\mu\ (f_{M_1^{lo},\mu}\ \mathsf{e}_1)\ (\lambda x_1{:}\_.$
3. $\quad\textit{bind}_\mu\ (f_{M_2^{lo},\mu}\ \mathsf{e}_2)\ (\lambda x_2{:}\_.(f_{M_3^{lo},\mu}(x_1\ x_2))))))$
4. $(\lambda y{:}\_.f_{m_3,M^{hi}}\ (x\ y)))$

Under the solutions θ_1 and θ_2, the inner subterm at lines 2 and 3 (call it $\hat{\mathsf{e}}$) may differ syntactically, i.e., $\theta_1\hat{\mathsf{e}} \neq \theta_2\hat{\mathsf{e}}$. Specifically, the solution θ_1 chooses $\mu \mapsto M$ while θ_2 may choose $\mu \mapsto M'$, for $M \neq M'$. However, using two applications of the morphism laws, (condition (5) of Definition 11), we can show that the $\hat{\mathsf{e}}$ is extensionally equivalent to the term shown below.

2. $\textit{bind}_{M^{hi}}\ (f_{\mu,M^{hi}} \circ f_{M_1^{lo},\mu}\ \mathsf{e}_1)\ (\lambda x_1{:}\_.$
3. $\textit{bind}_{M^{hi}}\ (f_{\mu,M^{hi}} \circ f_{M_2^{lo},\mu}\ \mathsf{e}_2)\ (\lambda x_2{:}\_.$
   $(f_{\mu,M^{hi}} \circ f_{M_3^{lo},\mu}(x_1\ x_2))))$

Appealing to condition (4) of Definition 11, the transitivity property, we get that the term above is extensionally equivalent to the term below (call it $\hat{\mathsf{e}}'$).

2. $\textit{bind}_{M^{hi}}\ (f_{M_1^{lo},M^{hi}}\ \mathsf{e}_1)\ (\lambda x_1{:}\_.$
3. $\textit{bind}_{M^{hi}}\ (f_{M_2^{lo},M^{hi}}\ \mathsf{e}_2)\ (\lambda x_2{:}\_.(f_{M_3^{lo},M^{hi}}(x_1\ x_2))))$

We have $\hat{\mathsf{e}} \cong \hat{\mathsf{e}}'$ and hence $\theta_1\hat{\mathsf{e}} \cong \theta_1\hat{\mathsf{e}}'$. Since, $\mu \notin FV(\hat{\mathsf{e}}')$, we have $\theta_1\hat{\mathsf{e}}' \cong \theta_2\hat{\mathsf{e}}'$, and $\theta_2\hat{\mathsf{e}}' \cong \theta_2\hat{\mathsf{e}}$, thus establishing $\theta_1\hat{\mathsf{e}} = \theta_2\hat{\mathsf{e}}$, as required. □

5.4 Ambiguity and limitations of constraint solving

Our constraint solving procedure is effective in resolving many common cases of free constraint variables in types that would otherwise be rejected as ambiguous by Haskell. However, a limitation of our algorithm is that, for coherence of solving, we require free constraint variables to have some upper bound in the constraint set. (See condition (2) of Theorem 14.) A variable with no upper bound may admit several possible solutions, so the morphisms leading to these solutions differ and result in different program rewritings—our algorithm rejects such a program as ambiguous.

We argue that for typical programs our constraint solving strategy is still effective. Our experience shows that terms with an unbounded constraint variable either consist of 'dead' computations that are never executed, or constitute top-level expressions. In the next paragraph we discuss a particular example program with an ambiguous type, illustrating the former case. To deal with the latter case, top-level expressions should have type annotations. All the examples in this paper are deemed unambiguous by our algorithm provided a top-level annotation. Out of the 5 example programs, 3 programs have types with variables that do not appear in the final type. All of these types would be rejected by OML (or Haskell) as ambiguous but are accepted by our system since they all have constraint variables with several distinct lower bounds and an upper bound, so we can instantiate them with the lub of the lower bounds.

Consider the following example, with a state monad ST and a primitive function `read`: $int \to \mathsf{ST}\ char$:

```
let g = fun () ->
  let f = fun x -> fun y ->
    let z = read x in read y in
  let w = f 0 in ()
```

Here, the type inferred for `f` is $\forall\mu.(\mathsf{ST} \rhd \mu) \Rightarrow int \to Bot\ int \to \mu\ char$. Because of the partial application `f 0`, we must give `g` the type $\forall\mu,\mu'.(\mathsf{ST} \rhd \mu, Bot \rhd \mu') \Rightarrow unit \to \mu'\ unit$. Here, the constraint variable μ resulting from the partial application of `f` does not appear in the return type, while it appears in the constraints without an upper bound.

Picking an arbitrary solution for μ, say $\mu = \mathsf{ST}$ or $\mu = IO$, where $P_0 \models \mathsf{ST} \rhd IO$, causes the sub-term `w` to be given different types. This is a source of incoherence, since our extensional equality property is only defined on terms of the same type. However, pragmatically, the specific type chosen for `w` has no impact on the reduction of the program, and we conjecture that in all cases when this occurs, the unbounded constraint variable has no influence on the semantics of the program. As such, our implementation supports a "permissive" mode, so that despite it technically being ambiguous, we can accept the program `g`, and improve its type to $\forall\mu'.Bot \rhd \mu', \Rightarrow unit \to \mu'\ unit$, by solving $\mu = \mathsf{ST}$.

6. Implementation and applications

We have implemented our inference algorithm for the core language of Figure 1 extended with standard features, including conditionals and recursive functions. Our implementation is written in Objective Caml (v3.12) and is about 2000 lines of code. It follows our basic morphism insertion strategy (i.e., Figure 4), but also provides an alternative typing mode that uses the (TI-Lift) rule (Figure 5). All rewritings shown in this paper, modulo minor readability improvements, were produced with our implementation and run against matching monadic libraries.

In this section we present programs using two additional monads, to give further examples of the usefulness of our system: parsing and information flow tracking. For the latter, our technical report [27] further considers a source language extended with mutable references, which for tracking information flow requires *parameterized monads*. We can type rewritten programs using the FlowCaml security type system [24] and thereby prove they are secure.

6.1 Parsing example

A parser can be seen as a function taking an input string and returning its unconsumed remainder along with a result of type α. We can apply this idea directly by implementing a parser as a monad whose type $Par\ \ \alpha$ conveniently hides the input and output strings. Its bind and unit combinators have names `bindp` and `unitp`, respectively. The `token`: $char \rightarrow Par\ unit$ parser parses a particular character, while `choice`: $(unit \rightarrow Par\ \alpha) \rightarrow (unit \rightarrow Par\ \alpha) \rightarrow Par\ \alpha$ returns the result of the first (thunkified) parser if it is successful, and otherwise the result of the second parser.

As an example we shall write a parser that computes the maximum level of nested brackets in an input string:

```
(rec nesting. fun ()->
 let nonempty = fun ()->
   token '[';
   let n  = nesting() in
   token ']';
   let m  = nesting() in
   max (n + 1) m in
 let empty = fun () -> 0 in
 choice (fun ()-> nonempty()) (fun ()-> empty()))()
```

Interpreted as standard ML code, the above program is not type correct: the functions `max` and `+` are typed as $int \rightarrow int \rightarrow int$, which does not match with the type of `n` and `m` of type $Par\ \ int$.

In our system the example is well-typed where the term gets type $Par\ \ int$. The type directed translation automatically inserts the binds for sequencing and units to lift the final result into the parser monad. The actual translation produced by our implementation is:

```
(rec nesting. fun () ->
 let nonempty = (fun ()->
   bindp (token '[') (fun _ ->
   bindp (nesting()) (fun n ->
   bindp (token ']') (fun _ ->
   bindp (nesting()) (fun m ->
   unitp (max (n + 1) m)))))) in
 let empty = fun () -> 0 in
 choice (fun () -> nonempty())
        (fun () -> unitp (empty()))) ()
```

6.2 Information flow

We are interested in enforcing a confidentiality property by tracking information flow. Data may be labeled with a security level, and the target independence property, called noninterference [6, 12], ensures that low-security outputs do not depend on high-security inputs. Ever since Abadi et al. showed how to encode information flow tracking in a dependency calculus [1], a number of monadic encodings have been proposed [4, 7, 19, 26]. We focus on a variant of the `Sec` monad [26] that wraps data protected at some security level for a pure functional subset of ML. In the absence of side effects, we only have to ensure that data with a certain confidentiality level is not disclosed to lower-level adversaries (explicit flows).

Let us consider a simple security lattice $\{\bot \leq L \leq H \leq \top\}$. The information flow monad $SecH$ (resp., $SecL$) tracks data with confidentiality level H (resp., L) with monadic operators `bindh,unith` (resp., `bindl,unitl`). The may-flow relation is expressed via a morphism that permits public data at a protected level:

$$\texttt{labup}:\ SecL \rhd SecH$$

Thus data labeled L may be used in a context expecting data labeled H, but not vice versa.

The following small example computes the interest due for a savings account, and the date of the last payment. Primitive `savings` returns a secret, having type $unit \rightarrow SecH\ float$, `rate` returns a public input having type $unit \rightarrow SecL\ float$. `add_interest` is a pure function computing the new amount of the account after adding interest, having type $float \rightarrow float \rightarrow float$. Finally, `current_date` returns the current date, having type $unit \rightarrow int$.

```
add_interest (savings ()) (rate())
```

The rewriting lifts the low security `rate` to compute the high secrecy update for `savings`. The final type of the entire expression is $SecH\ float$.

```
bindh (savings ()) (fun y ->
bindh (labup (rate ())) (fun z ->
unith (add_interest y z)))}
```

Our extended technical report [27] gives a proof of soundness with respect to FlowCaml for an information flow state monad which subsumes the $Sec*$ monads; therefore they also soundly encode non-interference.

7. Related work

Our work builds on Jones' theory of qualified types [14–16], which ensures principal types and coherence of the type inference for OML and is used to infer Haskell type classes. We adapt this approach for a practical monadic setting. The key difference is that we make the solving procedure aware of morphism laws, in such a way that Jones' restriction on ambiguous types can be removed.

Filinski previously showed that any individual monadic effect can be synthesized from first-class (delimited) continuations and a storage cell [11], and thereby can be expressed in direct style without explicit use of bind and unit. Kiselyov and Shan [18] apply this representation to implement probabilistic programs as an extension to Objective Caml. While our system shares the same goals as these, it uses a different mechanism—type-directed rewriting—to insert monadic operators directly, rather than requiring them to be implemented in terms of continuations.

Filinski also showed how to implement monads in a composable way [9]: given implementations of individual monads, and an order in which they can be *layered* on top of each other, he gives a semantics to their compositions. However, Filinski's representation elides monadic types from terms, complicating program understanding. For example, the type of `seconds` in his system would be $unit \rightarrow int$, not $unit \rightarrow Beh\ int$. Our approach fully integrates monadic types with ML type inference and yields well-typed ML programs, therefore it is hopefully easy to understand by the programmers. Our approach can also be seen as orthogonal, since we leave the implementation of monads to the programmer, treating all monad operators as black boxes. The lattice induced by our morphism declarations corresponds to Filinski's layering structure between monads.

In his latest work on this topic [10], Filinski proposes an operational semantics for composing monads; he reflects monads in the types, as effects, and provides runtime guarantees for well-typed programs, by dynamically inserting the minimal number of binds and units, based on syntactic hints. Orthogonally, we perform type inference from unannotated source code. We make the monadic types, operators, and morphisms explicit in the rewritten program, which gives the programmer the option to review and assess the resulting program. Last but not least our approach supports polymorphism over monads, permitting us to abstract and generalize monads and morphisms. For example, the rewritten `compose` function, whose type is given in Section 2.3, would additionally take as arguments the monads and morphisms used by its body, akin to Haskell's dictionary-passing interpretation of type classes.

We can view our rewriting algorithm as a particular case of a more general strategy for *type-directed coercion insertion*, which supports automatic coercion of data from one type to another, without explicit intervention by the programmer. Most related to our approach is that of Luo [20, 21], which considers coercion insertion as part of polymorphic type inference. In Luo's system rewritings may be ambiguous: when more than one is possible, each may have different semantics. Also, the system does not include qualified types, so coercions may not be abstracted and generalized, hurting expressiveness. Our own prior work addressed the problem with ambiguity by carefully limiting the form and position of coercions [28]. However, we could not scale this approach to a setting with polymorphic type inference, as even the simplest combinations of coercions admitted (syntactic) ambiguity. Our restriction to monads in the present work addresses this issue: we can prove coherence by relying on the syntactic structure of the program to unambiguously identify where combinators should be inserted, and when the choice of combinators is unconstrained, the morphism laws allow us to prove that all choices are equivalent.

Benton and Kennedy developed MIL, the *monadic intermediate language*, as the basis of optimizations in their MLj compiler [2]. They observe, as we do, that ML terms can be viewed as having the structure of our types τ (Figure 1) where monads do not appear to the left of arrows. While our approach performs inference and translation together, their approach suggests an alternative: convert the source ML program into monadic form and then infer the binds, units, and morphisms. We know from our translation to Haskell that this approach can only work by informing the solver of monad morphisms.

8. Conclusions

Monads are a powerful idiom in that many useful programming disciplines can be encoded as monadic libraries. ML programs enjoy an inherent monadic structure, but the monad in question is hardwired to be the I/O monad. We set out to provide a way to exploit this structure so that ML programmers can program against monads of their choosing in a lightweight style.

The solution offered by this paper is a new way to infer monadic types for ML source programs and to elaborate these programs in a style that includes explicit calls into monadic libraries of the programmer's choice. A key consideration of our approach is to provide programmers with a way to reason about the semantics of elaborated programs. We achieve this in two ways. First, the types we infer are informative in that they explicitly indicate the monads involved. And, second, when our system accepts a program, we show that all possible elaborations of a program have the same meaning, i.e., our elaborations are coherent.

We implement our system in a prototype compiler, and evaluate it on a variety of domains. We find our system to be relatively simple, both to implement and to understand and use, and powerful in that it handles many applications of interest.

Acknowledgements The authors would like to thank Gavin Bierman and Matt McCutchen for their early contributions to this work, and to Gavin for comments on this draft. Hicks and Guts were both supported by NSF grant CNS-0905419.

References

[1] M. Abadi, A. Banerjee, N. Heintze, and J.G. Riecke. A core calculus of dependency. In *POPL*, volume 26, pages 147–160, 1999.

[2] Nick Benton and Andrew Kennedy. Monads, effects and transformations. In *Electronic Notes in Theoretical Computer Science*, 1999.

[3] Greg Cooper and Shriram Krishnamurthi. Embedding dynamic dataflow in a call-by-value language. In *ESOP*, 2006.

[4] K. Crary, A. Kliger, and F. Pfenning. A monadic analysis of information flow security with mutable state. *Journal of functional programming*, 15(02):249–291, 2005.

[5] L. Damas and R. Milner. Principal type-schemes for functional programs. In *POPL*, pages 207–212, 1982.

[6] D.E. Denning. A lattice model of secure information flow. *Communications of the ACM*, 19(5):236–243, 1976.

[7] D. Devriese and F. Piessens. Information flow enforcement in monadic libraries. In *TLDI*, pages 59–72, 2011.

[8] Conal Elliott and Paul Hudak. Functional reactive animation. In *ICFP*, pages 263–273, 1997.

[9] A. Filinski. Representing layered monads. In *POPL*, pages 175–188, 1999.

[10] A. Filinski. Monads in action. In *POPL*, pages 483–494, 2010.

[11] Andrzej Filinski. Representing monads. In *POPL*, 1994.

[12] J.A. Goguen and J. Meseguer. Security policy and security models. In *Symposium on Security and Privacy*, pages 11–20, 1982.

[13] Graham Hutton and Erik Meijer. Monadic Parsing in Haskell. *JFP*, 8(4), 1998.

[14] Mark P. Jones. A theory of qualified types. In *ESOP*, 1992.

[15] Mark P. Jones. Coherence for qualified types. Technical Report YALEU/DCS/RR-989, Yale University, September 1993.

[16] Mark P. Jones. Simplifying and Improving Qualified Types. Technical Report YALEU/DCS/RR-1040, Yale University, June 1994.

[17] Mark P. Jones and Luc Duponcheel. Composing monads. Technical Report YALEU/DCS/RR-1004, Yale University, 1993.

[18] Oleg Kiselyov and Chung chieh Shan. Embedded probabilistic programming. In *DSL*, 2009.

[19] P. Li and S. Zdancewic. Encoding information flow in Haskell. In *CSFW*, pages 16–27, 2006.

[20] Z. Luo. Coercions in a polymorphic type system. *MSCS*, 18(4), 2008.

[21] Z. Luo and R. Kießling. Coercions in Hindley-Milner systems. In *Proc. of Types*, 2004.

[22] Eugenio Moggi. Computational lambda-calculus and monads. In *LICS*, 1989.

[23] Judea Pearl. Embracing causality in default reasoning (research note). *Artificial Intelligence*, 35(2):259–271, 1988.

[24] F. Pottier and V. Simonet. Information flow inference for ML. *TOPLAS*, 25(1):117–158, 2003.

[25] Norman Ramsey and Avi Pfeffer. Stochastic lambda calculus and monads of probability distributions. In *POPL*, pages 154–165, 2002.

[26] Alejandro Russo, Koen Claessen, and John Hughes. A library for light-weight information-flow security in haskell. In *Haskell*, 2008.

[27] Nikhil Swamy, Nataliya Guts, Daan Leijen, and Michael Hicks. Lightweight monadic programming in ML. Technical Report MSR-TR-2011-039, Microsoft Research, May 2011.

[28] Nikhil Swamy, Michael Hicks, and Gavin M. Bierman. A theory of typed coercions and its applications. In *ICFP*, 2009.

[29] Philip Wadler. The essence of functional programming. In *POPL*, 1992.

Functional Programming through Deep Time: Modeling the first complex ecosystems on Earth

Experience Report

Emily G. Mitchell

University of Cambridge & British Antarctic Survey, Cambridge, UK

ek338@cam.ac.uk

Abstract

The ecology of Earth's first large organisms is an unsolved problem in palaeontology. This experience report discusses the determination of which ecosystems could have been feasible, by considering the biological feedbacks within them. Haskell was used to model the ecosystems for these first large organisms – the Ediacara biota. For verification of the results, the statistical language R was used. Neither Haskell nor R would have been sufficient for this work – Haskell's libraries for statistics are weak, while R lacks the structure for expressing algorithms in a maintainable manner. This work is the first to quantify all feedback loops in an ecosystem, and has generated considerable interest from both the ecological and palaeontological communities.

Categories and Subject Descriptors D.3 [*Software*]: Programming Languages

General Terms Languages, Experimentation

Keywords Haskell, R, Palaeontology, Ecology

1. Introduction

Complex life on Earth evolved 600 million years ago, after billions of years of simple microbial life. The first complex organisms were the Ediacara biota, which lasted only 30 million years – a blink of a geological eye. The Ediacara biota were shortly followed by the Cambrian Explosion, bringing with it the precursors to modern life, which have dominated the Earth ever since. Understanding why these Ediacara biota failed can give clues to how ecosystems function. These unsuccessful organisms are unlike anything else, so many traditional techniques from biology and palaeontology do not apply. Computer modelling can give us new insights by allowing us to test theories, including some that have been debated for over 40 years.

Rangeomorphs are a group of Ediacaran species, with a fractal branching structure, which maximizes surface area – see Figure 1. Organisms that maximize their surface area normally feed in one of three ways:

1. *Photosynthetic* - converting sunlight to energy [8].
2. *Suspension feeding* - filtering plankton from the water column [6].
3. *Osmotrophic* - absorbing organic carbon directly through their membrane walls [7].

We now know that most rangeomorphs lived in the deep ocean, so can't have been photosynthetic [15], but the debate rages on between the other two strategies. Using Haskell, I modelled potential Ediacaran ecosystem as graphs, with species as nodes and feeding relationships as edges [10]. From these graphs the feeding strategies corresponding to feasible ecosystems were determined. Most rangeomorphs were found to be osmotrophic.

How fossils are spatially distributed in the rock gives clues to their interactions in life. These distributions were used to validate my models by comparing feasible ecosystems to those suggested by the actual fossils. To extract a graph from spatial positions I used two approaches. Firstly, the programming language R [11] was used to compare the actual locations of fossils against a random layout (generated using Poisson processes). Monte Carlo simulation was used to quantify the significance of any variation. Secondly, Bayesian network inference was used on the spatial data to search for the most probable graph. To perform Bayesian network inference, a Haskell script was used which invokes Banjo, a program written in Java [13].

This experience report first discusses the use of computer programs in ecology and palaeontology in §2. The work is described in §3, then, since R is both the most commonly used language in ecology and the language this project was started in, R is compared to Haskell in §4. §5 describes how this work has been received by the wider ecological and palaeontological communities, and gives advice to colleagues choosing a programming language.

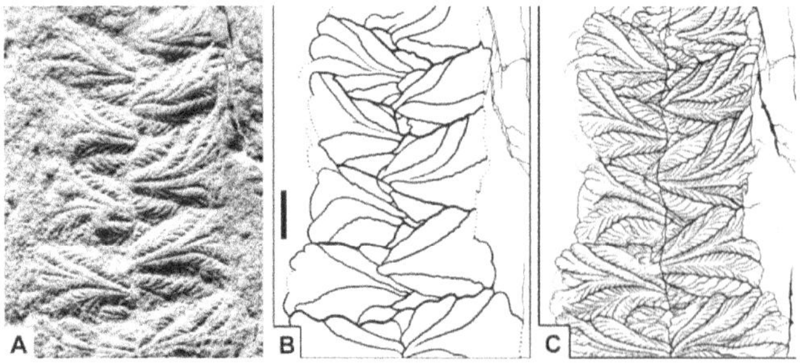

Figure 1. *Fractofusus misrai*, a type of Rangeomorph. A is a photo of the original fossil, B shows the primary branches and C shows the primary and secondary branches. The scale bar is 1cm. Taken from [2]

ICFP'11, September 19–21, 2011, Tokyo, Japan.

2. Language use in Ecology and Palaeontology

Ecology and palaeontology are both diverse subjects, ranging from qualitative descriptive work to theoretical work. Computer literacy varies greatly in both fields, from people who don't use computers even for word processing, to former computer scientists. Out of the two groups, ecologists tend to be more computer literate.

2.1 Ecologists

Computational and theoretical ecologists have the highest knowledge of computer science. These two areas require complex algorithms, and languages such as C/C++, Fortran and Perl are used. Ecology often requires statistical analysis, so most ecologists have experience using either a specialized GUI, or a programming language, typically R [11]. There are a number of reasons why R is preferred for statistics:

- There are many workshops and courses in R, from basic introductions to applying the latest statistical methods.
- Books on statistical ecology often give examples in R, and have R scripts available for download [5].
- Statisticians and computational ecologists often develop new techniques in R, resulting in a large number of specialist packages.
- Papers often reference R packages, documenting their applications and limitations.

2.2 Palaeontology

Palaeontology is often qualitative, so it is unusual for palaeontologists to have experience with programming languages, or even command line driven programs. Both quantitative and computational palaeontology are dominated by GUIs specifically written for palaeontologists [3] (apart from the small field of macroevolutionary modelling – which is dominated by C++). Additionally, Microsoft Excel is used for plots and regressions. As palaeontology starts to become more quantitative, there is a small but growing trend towards using R, with palaeontological R courses starting to be taught at masters level and above.

2.3 Choosing Haskell

Prior to entering the field of palaeontology, most of my previous research was in analytical mathematical physics. My main programming experience was in R, and I had also used some Matlab and C++. For my work in palaeontology, I initially used R.

I started considering alternative languages when I had trouble expressing more complex algorithms in R. I was aware of Haskell as my husband both works as a functional programmer and is active in the Haskell community. One motivation for choosing Haskell was to take advantage of his expertise. However, I found our programming styles surprisingly incompatible, and in practice programmed almost entirely independently.

My husband puts great emphasis on code that is "beautiful" – that is, economical, reusable, modular. This focus seems widespread in the Haskell community. In contrast, I am happy with code that works – once I have written a function, I rarely revisit it. I suspect that my style is widespread in scientific programming.

My primary resource when learning Haskell was Hutton [4], which I found to be clear, and had many suitable exercises. I read a variety of online Haskell tutorials (including Learn You a Haskell for Great Good), but did not find these particularly helpful – none had exercises which gradually increased in difficulty.

I wrote my Haskell code in TextPad on Windows XP, experimented on it using GHCi and compiled it using GHC [14]. I made light use of the built in GHC profiler. Once I had reached a basic level in my understanding of types, Hoogle [9] was useful for finding functions.

3. Haskell for Computational Palaeoecology

My work involves using biological interactions to understand the development of ancient ecosystems [1]. An ecosystem can be modelled as a graph, where species are represented as nodes, and interactions as edges. Feedback mechanisms are one way of analysing the structure of ecosystems, and these are represented by loops in the graph [10]. I first considered the relationship between feedback loops and stability for modern ecosystems, then applied the insights gained to Ediacaran ecosystems.

3.1 Technique Development

Properties of feedback loops have been shown to indicate ecosystem stability [10]. Previous work focused on "biologically interesting" feedback mechanisms, which account for less than 1% of the total number of loops. The natural extension to this work is to consider every type of loop. There is a R package which qualitatively finds all the loops in a graph (`LoopAnalyst`), however this package would have required significant adapting to be useful for my analysis. Therefore, I implemented a program in R that was able to quantitatively analyse all loops, and output the most significant.

Analysis of all loops revealed an unexpected result regarding ecosystem stability. To confirm this finding, variations on how the loops were computed and analysed needed to be explored. This exploration was problematic in R for two reasons, the program didn't run fast enough, and program modification was fiddly. Improvement of the algorithm in R would have made it more intricate, and thus even harder to modify. Writing a second version of the program in Haskell solved both these problems. A more advanced algorithm was used, but thanks to static typing and algebraic data types, modification was straightforward – the compiler did lots of the hard work. With a significantly improved algorithm, and with the advanced compilation techniques of GHC, the program ran over 10,000 times faster.

Using the Haskell program, possible relationships between loops and stability were investigated, which allowed confirmation of my initial results. Given my programming level, I would not have been able to get the same results using R, Matlab or C++. For this work, Haskell provided an easily modifiable language that ran quickly – I can't think of any improvements to Haskell which would have made it more suitable.

3.2 Application to Palaeontology

The Haskell program was used to investigate the plausibility of different feeding strategies of Ediacaran species. For each permutation of feeding strategy, an ecosystem graph was created, all loops found, and stability calculated. Using these stabilities, I showed that most of the early Ediacaran species must have been osmotrophic.

During this modelling work, the Haskell program was run hundreds of thousands of times, which would not have been feasible with the R program. For this type of work, seconds quickly add up, so a faster program is always better – but the Haskell program was fast enough. Finding Haskell packages to produce the right type of plot was hard, so the data was saved and viewed in R.

It is important to verify any conclusions drawn from modelling using statistical analysis of real data. I collected data from fossil sites in order to be able to statistically analyse the distributions of fossils on the rock face, allowing a network of fossil interactions to be built up. The book I used to learn the appropriate statistical techniques included examples in R, making it easy to use R for my analysis. I looked at the statistical packages available for Haskell, but the techniques I required were not supported (see §4.4). Switching back to R was the obvious choice.

4. Comparing Haskell and R

My work has used both Haskell and R, so this section is a comparison between them. R is a language designed for "statistical computing and graphics" [11]. R defers evaluation of function arguments, but is otherwise a strict language. R is impure and has no static typing; it has some functional aspects, but is typically used in an imperative manner. In contrast, Haskell is a lazy, pure, statically-typed functional language.

Writing simple programs in R is easy, but writing more complex programs can get messy. In contrast, writing simple programs in Haskell requires a greater understanding of the language (such as monads, types, etc.), but producing complicated programs is not much harder.

4.1 Syntax and Reasoning

I prefer the Haskell syntax because it is consistent, and has an obvious correspondence with mathematical concepts. This correspondence means that colleagues with no Haskell or functional programming experience can clearly understand my calculations. In comparison, the syntax for R is more verbose, and less consistent, but some statistical functions are written in a intuitive way – for example regressions are written `lm(`$z \sim x + y$`)`. Unfortunately, these syntactic shortcuts can be confusing in themselves, for example polynomial regressions are then written `lm(`$z \sim I(x^3) + y$`)`. The consistent syntax of Haskell means that when returning to Haskell after a break, getting back up to speed is quicker compared to returning to R.

Haskell's purity allows extensive use of equational reasoning – for example the code `if a then b else b` is equivalent to b (providing a terminates). In contrast, the equivalent R transformation is only true if a both terminates and does not produce side effects, which can be subtle, such as coercion changing a variable's underlying type. I have made such mistakes in R, which means it is harder to refactor my R code, and thus my Haskell code is cleaner. Similarly, when debugging Haskell I am able to deduce properties about my code using only local knowledge, whereas R requires a much more advanced understanding of both the program and the language.

The downside of purity is the requirement to use monadic IO. I found the descriptions of IO in tutorials obtuse, but found the reality to be significantly simpler. The only awkwardness is that switching between pure and monadic code feels like changing mode, the syntax is different and so are many of the functions (e.g. `map` vs. `mapM`).

4.2 Types

The static type system of Haskell is difficult to adjust to at first, but worth the struggle – the reduction in debugging time is significant. R has no static types, and makes significant use of coercions. If you try and use a string as a matrix, the string will be parsed as a matrix, which is particularly useful when reading data tables from a file. If you try and use a vector as a matrix, a matrix will be created by repeating the vector.

These coercions make debugging hard, and significantly reduce the confidence in numerical results. Many bugs that result in compile time type errors in Haskell, result in wrong (but plausible) results in R. Additionally, coercions can be handled somewhat inconsistently, e.g. a matrix produced by converting a list using `as.matrix` will cause a runtime type error when used with some matrix functions.

Static types are particularly helpful for beginners to find basic library functions, using Hoogle. For example, the type of the function to remove duplicates from a list is obvious (`Eq a => [a] -> [a]`), but it's name in Haskell is obscure (`nub`).

Sadly, Haskell packages do not always use consistent types – for example there are many different vectors/arrays, which makes using multiple packages painful. Some R packages also have different types, but these problems are entirely masked by coercions, meaning lots of R packages can be used together with ease.

4.3 Complex Code

Much of my work involves calling library functions, combining the results, and doing calculations which are mathematically taxing, but can be expressed fairly directly in any language. However, some of my work does require more careful thought about algorithms and more intricate structural manipulations. I find it significantly easier to write this complex code in Haskell, for three reasons:

Static types have an enormous impact on reliability, but for more complex code, they also provide a clear pattern for combining functions. Static types allow chunks of code to be combined like a jigsaw puzzle.

Algebraic data types allow me to accurately encode my data structures, and combined with the static type checking, make managing complexity much easier.

Higher-order functions allow detangling complex code, splitting out specific details from an algorithm. Both Haskell and R allow higher-order functions, but the lack of static type checking in R makes them much harder to use. In Haskell, using higher-order functions with algebraic data types, I was able to parameterize operations by the details I needed to tweak, making modifications straightforward.

4.4 Libraries

For the libraries I require, R has far better coverage than Haskell. The default installation of R has all the tools necessary for pre-university maths or statistics. In comparison, the standard Haskell installation (the Haskell Platform) includes advanced multithreading, but lacks a function to compute the mean. From the base installation, R can install new packages through the GUI, while Haskell requires the use of a command line tool, and far more background computer knowledge.

R has a huge range of specialist statistics packages available, including many cutting edge statistical techniques. In comparison, Haskell has nine statistics libraries, which have a reasonable amount of overlap, but skip things as basic as t-tests. One of the most important aspects of performing statistical tests is checking all the necessary assumptions are valid, something often overlooked in biological sciences [12]. Haskell packages provide normal distribution functions, but lack the Shapiro-Wilks Test which checks data for normality – a key assumption in most parametric tests.

R has a built in plotting environment, which easily produces a wide range of plots. Complex plots are provided in libraries, and most statistical packages integrate plotting functionality. In comparison, Haskell has a choice of many plotting libraries, all of which are significantly different, and none of which have the integration of R. In R a plot is only a simple function call away, and they are used continuously. In Haskell, a plot is significantly harder – I just export my data to R and plot it there.

As an example of the library issues discussed, the following R code plots the eigenvalues of a matrix read from disk:

```
plot(eigen(read.delim("matrix.txt"))$ values)
```

In Haskell finding eigenvalues involves installing `hmatrix` (which on Windows requires changing environment variables and setting Dll paths), reading a matrix requires parsing code, and plotting is never as simple as just calling `plot`. Performing this operation from a base install of R takes seconds, in Haskell it takes far more effort.

5. Evaluation

This section discusses how my work was received by the ecological and palaeontological communities, along with plans for my program and future use of Haskell. I conclude with advice on using Haskell for computational palaeoecology.

5.1 Reception

Ecologists are excited about my work. The work done by Neutel et al. [10] provoked much interest in loop analysis of ecological graphs, and because my program is quick and easy to use, people can now explore the importance of loops in much larger real and theoretical ecosystems.

My code is available on Hackage as `loopy`[1], but for my colleagues I provide a precompiled executable with an R wrapper script, which suits them well.

Palaeontologists are interested in my results, but not in my methods. Modelling ancient ecosystems as graphs is a new technique, and has yet to become mainstream. If I wanted palaeontologists to use my program, a GUI would probably be necessary, something I currently have no plans for.

5.2 Future Development

For huge graphs, it is infeasible to enumerate all loops (the number of loops can grow exponentially). I plan to explore approximations to allow larger graphs to be processed, which permit ecosystems to be modelled in finer detail. For this work, I will continue using Haskell, with R for any plotting or statistical analysis.

Haskell is my programming language of choice, and if it had adequate statistics libraries, I would rarely use anything else. If I ever need to run intensive statistical analysis on lots of large data sets, it would be worth writing the necessary libraries in Haskell.

Another language I am considering is F#. When I started this project, F# was a relatively new language, but now I think it could suit me quite well. F# provides access to the .NET libraries, which would provide much of the functionality missing in Haskell, while still keeping the benefits of functional programming and static typing.

5.3 Expansion of Haskell use in Ecology/Palaeoecology

Ecologists tend to use programming languages they have been taught at university, or languages already established in their research group. Once a language becomes dominant, it takes a long time to become unseated – Fortran is still being taught. Theoretical ecologists could find Haskell useful, because it's quicker to write complex code. However, the lack of simple integrated plots would be a severe obstacle. For statistical use, Haskell is unlikely to compete with R, which is deeply embedded in the community.

Computational palaeoecology is a new field – I am only aware of two other practitioners. Haskell is well suited for this domain, and if it became established, it would be unlikely for another language to take over. Whether it becomes established probably has more to do with the future career paths of existing computational palaeoecologists than with the language itself.

It would be difficult for Haskell to become the de facto language for scientific computing, due to its steep learning curve. Most undergraduate science degrees do not teach a separate programming course, instead teaching programming alongside a technique, such as statistics. Programming skills are gently built up in little steps, over several courses. Haskell could not be taught in this way, since static types and monads would need to be taught before getting to any technique, and this would probably be too much for one course.

Numerate disciplines like physics do have separate programming courses, where the choice of language depends on its usefulness post degree. If Haskell, or another functional language, became widely used commercially, universities would probably start to teach it outside the computer science department. These numerate disciplines could then write appropriate scientific libraries which could be used by less numerate sciences.

5.4 Conclusions

When colleagues ask which language they should use, I only recommend Haskell if they are an experienced programmer, and deal mostly with theoretical work. For everyone else, I recommend R. While I think Haskell is a superior language, it has a much steeper learning curve, and unless I was willing to teach them, R is a simpler choice. Within my department there is an R learning group, and various university run courses, which give useful support.

Haskell enabled me to get detailed results that I could not otherwise have found. I find functional programming and static typing powerful concepts, and other than R, would not consider using languages lacking these features.

Acknowledgments

Neil Mitchell for introducing me to Haskell, Mike Dodds for feedback on this paper and my supervisors Nicholas Butterfield and Anje Neutel. This work was funded by a NERC studentship.

References

[1] N. J. Butterfield. Macroevolution and macroecology through deep time. *Paleontology*, 50:41–55, 2007.

[2] J. Gehling and G. Narbonne. Spindle-shaped Ediacara fossils from the Mistaken Point assemblage, Avalon Zone, Newfoundland. *Canadian Journal of Earth Sciences*, 44(3):367–387, 2007.

[3] Ø. Hammer, D. Harper, and P. Ryan. PAST: Paleontological statistics software package for education and data analysis. *Palaeontologia Electronica*, 4(1), 2001.

[4] G. Hutton. *Programming in Haskell*. CUP, 2007.

[5] J. Illian. *Statistical analysis and modelling of spatial point patterns*.

[6] R. Jenkins and J. Gehling. *A review of the frond-like fossils of the Ediacara assemblage*. South Australian Museum, 1978.

[7] M. Laflamme, S. Xiao, and M. Kowalewski. Osmotrophy in modular Ediacara organisms. *Proceedings of the National Academy of Sciences*, 106(34):14438, 2009.

[8] M. McMenamin. The garden of Ediacara. *Palaios*, pages 178–182, 1986.

[9] N. Mitchell. Hoogle overview. *The Monad.Reader*, (12):27–35, November 2008.

[10] A. M. Neutel, J. A. P. Heesterbeek, J. van de Koppel, G. Hoenderboom, A. Vos, C. Kaldeway, F. Berendse, and P. C. de Ruiter. Reconciling complexity with stability in naturally assembling foodwebs. *Nature*, 449:559–602, 2007.

[11] R Development Core Team. *R: A Language and Environment for Statistical Computing*. R Foundation for Statistical Computing, Vienna, Austria, 2008.

[12] T. Siegfried. Odds are, it's wrong: Science fails to face the shortcomings of statistics. *Science News*, 177(7):26–29, 2010.

[13] V. Smith, J. Yu, T. Smulders, A. Hartemink, and E. Jarvis. Computational inference of neural information flow networks. *PLoS Computational Biology*, 2, 2006.

[14] The GHC Team. The GHC compiler, version 6.12.3. `http://www.haskell.org/ghc/`, 2010.

[15] D. Wood, R. Dalrymple, G. Narbonne, J. Gehling, and M. Clapham. Paleoenvironmental analysis of the late Neoproterozoic Mistaken Point and Trepassey formations, southeastern Newfoundland. *Canadian Journal of Earth Sciences*, 40(10):1375–1391, 2003.

[1] `http://hackage.haskell.org/package/loopy`

Monads, Zippers and Views

Virtualizing the Monad Stack

Tom Schrijvers
Department of Applied Mathematics and Computer Science, Universiteit Gent
tom.schrijvers@ugent.be

Bruno C. d. S. Oliveira
ROSAEC Center, Seoul National University
bruno@ropas.snu.ac.kr

Abstract

We make monadic components more reusable and robust to changes by employing two new techniques for *virtualizing* the monad stack: the *monad zipper* and *monad views*. The *monad zipper* is a higher-order monad transformer that creates *virtual* monad stacks by ignoring particular layers in a concrete stack. *Monad views* provide a general framework for monad stack virtualization: they take the monad zipper one step further and integrate it with a wide range of other virtualizations. For instance, particular views allow restricted access to monads in the stack. Furthermore, monad views provide components with a *call-by-reference*-like mechanism for accessing particular layers of the monad stack.

With our two new mechanisms, the monadic effects required by components no longer need to be literally reflected in the concrete monad stack. This makes these components more reusable and robust to changes.

Categories and Subject Descriptors D.3.3 [*Programming Languages*]: Language Classifications—Applicative (functional) languages

General Terms Design, Languages

Keywords Components with Side Effects, Modularity, Monad Transformers, Zipper

1. Introduction

Monads [15, 31] are a useful abstraction for encapsulating side-effects in purely functional languages like Haskell [18]. With monads different types of effects – such as state, non-determinism or exceptions – can be modeled with the same abstract interface.

Monads are composed via mechanisms such as monad transformers [13]. With monad transformers writing programs that use multiple effects is possible by stacking different transformers on top of each other to form a larger monad. Monads and monad transformers are interesting because they allow programmers to write realistic effectful programs that are still purely functional, thus enjoying reasoning principles such as *equational reasoning* and *parametricity* [21, 29]. Furthermore, because of these reasoning principles, monads and monad transformers also provide a good setting for studying modular effectful components, like Aspect-Oriented Programming (AOP) style advice [17] or models of Feature-Oriented Programming (FOP) [20].

Monad transformers come with a responsibility: it is necessary to manage the monad stack. In Haskell there are two existing approaches for this: *implicit liftings* and *explicit liftings*. Implicit liftings exploit type-directed overloading of methods, provided by type classes [32], to automatically route an effectful operation to the first layer of the right type in the monad stack. Explicit liftings offer more control to programmers, at the cost of automation, by allowing monadic components to directly refer to a monad layer at some position below the current layer using multiple invocations of the *lift* method (which moves from the current layer to the one immediately below).

However, there are two main problems with the current mechanisms for manipulating the monad stack:

1. **Inconvenience:** The first problem is that explicit lifting is simply "awkward" to use. Explicit lifting relies on a positional mechanism, similar to de Bruijn indices, to refer to particular layers of the monad stack. Because access to the *n*th layer below the current layer requires *n* calls to the *lift* method, code quickly becomes polluted with *lift* method invocations.
2. **Lack of robustness, limited expressiveness and reusability:** The second, and more fundamental, problem is that the current approach is not robust to changes and offers only limited expressiveness and reusability, specially when *higher-order components* (or *control flow* operators) are involved. Implicit lifting through overloaded methods is robust, but it is also quite limited in expressiveness since handling multiple monads of the same type is not possible. Explicit liftings are not robust to changes because the relative (positional) references impose a tight coupling between monadic components and the monad stack, which makes those components less adaptable. Furthermore, explicit lifting still has limited expressiveness because it only allows to refer to layers below the current layer, but not layers above.

The first problem is well-known in the Haskell community and there have been some proposals for solving it. Piponi [19] and Snyder & Alexander [25] suggested a solution by labeling monad transformers with (type-level) tags, allowing particular layers in a monad stack to be accessed by name rather than by position, eliminating the pollution arising from multiple calls to *lift*.

The second problem is a bit more subtle because it only shows up when monadic components are meant to be reused in different contexts with different monad stack layouts as, for example, in the modular effectful components studied by Prehofer [20] and Oliveira et al. [17]. For this to be possible, monadic components should abstract over the monad stack by keeping the type represent-

ICFP'11, September 19–21, 2011, Tokyo, Japan.

ing the monad stack polymorphic (though constrained). The use of names is also useful to solve this second problem because names are more robust to changes in the monad layout. However, existing tagged approaches [19, 25] are invasive, in the sense that monadic components have to be written specially with tagging in mind, and they still have reusability limitations (such as name clashes).

Contributions This paper proposes two new techniques for manipulating monad stacks: the *monad zipper* and *monad views*. The *monad zipper* is a monad transformer that allows ignoring particular layers in the concrete stack. *Monad views* abstract the concrete monad stack into a virtual monad stack, which presents itself with a more suitable interface to a particular component. Views also allow restricting access (in the sense of permissions) to particular layers of the monad. An important characteristic of both techniques is that they can be used non-invasively, by being applied externally and effectively providing the component with a tailored virtual monad stack. When there are conflicts that are local to a certain component, monad views can also be used invasively to provide a *call-by-reference* mechanism to refer to particular layers in the monad stack. By working with virtual stacks, requirements of components in terms of the monad stack shape no longer need to be literally reflected in the concrete monad stack, making these components more reusable and robust to changes.

We also briefly report on a non-trivial application of our techniques, developed by Schrijvers et al. [24], which shows that the techniques proposed by us scale well in terms of the number of monads in a monad stack. In that application 30 monadic components and equally as many monad transformers were used. We are not aware of any Haskell projects using as many transformers at the same time.

2. Overview

The presentation of our work will be made in Haskell, and we will assume knowledge of the language. Nevertheless, as discussed in more detail in Section 7.1, we believe that none of the main concepts presented by us (the monad zipper, views and masks) are Haskell-specific.

In this section we briefly introduce the Haskell monad transformer library (MTL), provide an overview of the current state-of-the-art in manipulating monad stacks and illustrate how the monad zipper and monad views improve upon that state-of-the-art by virtualizing the monad stack.

2.1 Quick Monad Transformers Reference

Our ideas and examples are formulated in terms of a variant of the MTL.[1] See Liang et al. [13] for a more in-depth introduction to MTL. Figure 1 summarizes the monad transformers, classes and operations that we use in the course of this paper. The transformers consist of pure computations ($\mathbb{I}_\mathrm{T}$, the identity monad transformer) and computations with a read-only environment ($\mathbb{R}_\mathrm{T}$), updateable state ($\mathbb{S}_\mathrm{T}$) and exceptions ($\mathbb{E}_\mathrm{T}$). These transformers are combined into different monad stacks with the identity monad ($\mathbb{I}$) at the bottom. The type classes (denoted with subscript M) constrain a monad stack to provide support for a particular effect, without assuming a particular stack configuration. Each class offers a number of primitive operations, such as *ask* to access the environment for $\mathbb{R}_\mathrm{M}$.

2.2 Monadic Components

An important distinction throughout this paper is between monadic *component* and *client* code. The main goal of this paper is to improve the robustness, reusability and convenience of use of the former. At first sight, it will seem that the client code pays the price for this improvement, because it is forced to make the necessary configuration choices for the more adaptable components. Fortunately, the complexity can be neatly hidden behind combinators.

Component code Component code is intended to be reused in different contexts. Typically such code resides in libraries, which are used by clients in various different applications. As two simple examples of monadic components, consider an incrementer and an assertion checker:

$$
\begin{aligned}
&inc :: \mathbb{S}_\mathrm{M}\ Int\ m \Rightarrow m\ Int\\
&inc = \mathbf{do}\ x \leftarrow get\\
&\qquad\qquad put\ (x+1)\\
&\qquad\qquad return\ (x+1)
\end{aligned}
$$

$$
\begin{aligned}
&assert :: \mathbb{E}_\mathrm{M}\ String\ m \Rightarrow Bool \rightarrow m\ ()\\
&assert\ test = \mathbf{if}\ test\\
&\qquad\qquad\qquad \mathbf{then}\ return\ ()\\
&\qquad\qquad\qquad \mathbf{else}\ throwError\ \texttt{"Assertion failed"}
\end{aligned}
$$

What is interesting about these components is that they can be adapted to work with different concrete monad stacks. This is possible because we use parametric polymorphism to abstract over the monad, imposing only the required restrictions on the layout by using (type-class) constraints. For example, what the signature of *inc* tells us is that it can be used by any client whose monad stack supports state.

Components can, of course, be combined into larger components. For example:

$$
\begin{aligned}
&comp :: (\mathbb{S}_\mathrm{M}\ Int\ m, \mathbb{E}_\mathrm{M}\ String\ m) \Rightarrow m\ ()\\
&comp = \mathbf{do}\ x \leftarrow inc\\
&\qquad\qquad\quad assert\ (x > 0)
\end{aligned}
$$

Client code Client code instantiates the monad stack, and is defined by the end-user when using the components to build particular applications. Different stack configurations may be possible:

$$
\begin{aligned}
&\mathbf{type}\ M_1 = \mathbb{S}_\mathrm{T}\ Int\ (\mathbb{E}_\mathrm{T}\ String\ \mathbb{I})\\
&\mathbf{type}\ M_2 = \mathbb{E}_\mathrm{T}\ String\ (\mathbb{S}_\mathrm{T}\ Int\ \mathbb{I})
\end{aligned}
$$

In general, different monad stack layouts have different semantics. Consider the following *run* functions for M_1 and M_2:

$$
\begin{aligned}
&runM_1 :: Int \rightarrow M_1\ a \rightarrow Either\ String\ (a, Int)\\
&runM_1\ n = run\mathbb{I} \circ run\mathbb{E}_\mathrm{T} \circ flip\ run\mathbb{S}_\mathrm{T}\ n
\end{aligned}
$$

$$
\begin{aligned}
&runM_2 :: Int \rightarrow M_2\ a \rightarrow (Either\ String\ a, Int)\\
&runM_2\ n = run\mathbb{I} \circ flip\ run\mathbb{S}_\mathrm{T}\ n \circ run\mathbb{E}_\mathrm{T}
\end{aligned}
$$

When we use these functions to instantiate the monad in *comp* we can observe the semantic differences between the two monad stacks:

$> runM_1\ (-1)\ comp$
$Left$ "Assertion failed"

$> runM_2\ (-1)\ comp$
$(Left$ "Assertion failed"$, 0)$

In the case of M_1 changes to the state are lost upon throwing an error, while this is not the case for M_2.

2.3 State-of-the-art Manipulation of the Monad Stack

Implicit lifting The monadic components presented in Section 2.2 use implicit lifting for accessing the right layer in the monad stack. Effectful operations like *get*, *put* or *throwError* are automatically routed to the first layer of the right type in the monad stack, by exploiting the type-based overloading mechanism of type classes. This approach is robust, because the routing automatically adapts to multiple layouts of the monad stack (such as M_1 or M_2).

[1] Section 7.2 discusses the differences.

-- identity transformer
newtype $\mathbb{I}_T\ m\ a$

$\mathbb{I}_T :: m\ a \rightarrow \mathbb{I}_T\ m\ a$
$run\mathbb{I}_T :: \mathbb{I}_T\ m\ a \rightarrow m\ a$

-- reader transformer
newtype $\mathbb{R}_T\ e\ m\ a$

$\mathbb{R}_T :: (e \rightarrow m\ a) \rightarrow \mathbb{R}_T\ e\ m\ a$
$run\mathbb{R}_T :: \mathbb{R}_T\ e\ m\ a \rightarrow e \rightarrow m\ a$

-- state transformer
newtype $\mathbb{S}_T\ s\ m\ a$

$\mathbb{S}_T :: (s \rightarrow m\ (a, s)) \rightarrow \mathbb{S}_T\ s\ m\ a$
$run\mathbb{S}_T :: \mathbb{S}_T\ s\ m\ a \rightarrow s \rightarrow m\ (a, s)$

-- exception transformer
newtype $\mathbb{E}_T\ x\ m\ a$

$\mathbb{E}_T :: m\ (Either\ x\ a) \rightarrow \mathbb{E}_T\ x\ m\ a$
$run\mathbb{E}_T :: \mathbb{E}_T\ x\ m\ a \rightarrow m\ (Either\ x\ a)$

-- identity monad
newtype $\mathbb{I}\ a$

$\mathbb{I} :: a \rightarrow \mathbb{I}\ a$
$run\mathbb{I} :: \mathbb{I}\ a \rightarrow a$

-- reader class
class $Monad\ m \Rightarrow \mathbb{R}_M\ e\ m \mid m \rightarrow e$

$ask :: \mathbb{R}_M\ e\ m \Rightarrow m\ e$

-- state class
class $Monad\ m \Rightarrow \mathbb{S}_M\ s\ m \mid m \rightarrow s$

$get :: \mathbb{S}_M\ s\ m \Rightarrow m\ s$
$put :: \mathbb{S}_M\ s\ m \Rightarrow s \rightarrow m\ ()$

-- exception class
class $Monad\ m \Rightarrow \mathbb{E}_M\ x\ m \mid m \rightarrow x$

$throwError :: \mathbb{E}_M\ x\ m \Rightarrow x \rightarrow m\ a$
$catchError :: \mathbb{E}_M\ x\ m \Rightarrow m\ a \rightarrow (x \rightarrow m\ a) \rightarrow m\ a$

Figure 1. MTL quick reference.

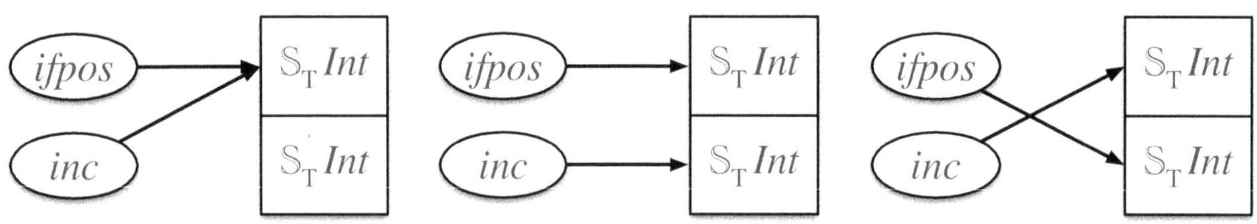

Figure 2. Three composition scenarios: *ifpos inc*, *ifpos* (*lift inc*) and $\uparrow$ (*ifpos* ($\downarrow$ *inc*)).

Implicit lifting has one big limitation: it is ineffective for combining multiple instances of the same effect because the automatic type-based selection of a monad layer always picks the first layer of the right type. If there is another layer of that type below that layer, implicit lifting cannot access it.

Explicit Lifting Explicit lifting addresses the limitation of implicit lifting to some extent because it allows moving down the monad stack into a lower layer. Therefore, by calling the effectful operations in lower layers, implicit liftings are routed to monad transformers that are not at the top of the stack.

The approach consists of using *lift* methods *explicitly* to disambiguate the targets of accesses to the monad stack. Suppose that we want to combine two instances of *inc* in such a way that they update different counters. Using explicit lifting we could write a component *doubleInc* that does the job:

$$doubleInc :: (\mathbb{S}_M\ Int\ (t\ m), \mathbb{S}_M\ Int\ m, MonadTrans\ t) \Rightarrow t\ m\ ()$$
$$doubleInc = inc \gg lift\ inc \gg return\ ()$$

The role of *lift* is to ensure that the second instance of *inc* updates a counter in the monad below the current layer (and not at the topmost layer). The use of *lift* is reflected in the constraints imposed on the stack. In this case, the requirement is that the top-level monad $t\ m$ must support state and the monad m below must also support state. If the monad stack is $\mathbb{S}_T\ Int\ (\mathbb{S}_T\ Int\ \mathbb{I})$, then *doubleInc* updates the two state layers. Hence, running *doubleInc* with the *run* function below yields the result $(((), 1), 6)$.

$$run\ c = run\mathbb{I}\ \$\ run\mathbb{S}_T\ (run\mathbb{S}_T\ c\ 0)\ 5$$

Explicit lifting is essentially, like de Bruijn indices, a *relative* reference mechanism: it allows moving n layers *below*[2] the current layer by using n calls to *lift*.

A clear limitation of this mechanism is that it is not possible to refer to layers *above* the current layer. Yet this functionality is particularly desirable to preserve modularity when *higher-order* components (also known as *control flow operators*) are involved. Some compositions of primitive monadic control flow operators (e.g. *catchError*) cannot be expressed with *lift* at all. Furthermore, components that use *lift* internally usually impose unnecessary restrictions on the layout of the monad stack, because they express relative orderings of layers.

In summary implicit liftings are quite robust to changes and are convenient to use, but have limited expressiveness; and, while explicit liftings address the limitations of implicit liftings to some extent, they too are still limited in expressiveness and there is a price to pay, in terms of a tighter coupling between component and monad stack.

[2] Note that there are two points of view for *lift m* in a certain calling context. From the calling context's point of view towards m the direction of movement is *downwards*, while, vice versa, the direction of movement from m's point of view towards the calling context is *upwards*. Usually, we adhere to the calling context's point of view, but occasionally we may have to use m's perspective; when that is the case, it should be clear from the context.

2.4 Virtualizing the Monad Stack

By presenting the component code with a virtual monad stack, components become decoupled from the client code's concrete monad stack. The monad stack virtualization is achieved by:

1. avoiding *lift* method invocations inside component code, which are responsible for the tight coupling; and
2. using the monad zipper and monad views to manage virtual monad stacks.

In this section we explain how the monad zipper and monad views are used to develop components free of *lift* invocations while, at the same time, allowing for additional expressiveness that is not possible with explicit lifting alone.

Note that, in the remainder of this section, the intention is just to demonstrate how the monad zipper, structural masks, nominal masks and views can be used from the user's point of view to solve various problems related to the manipulation of monad transformers. The reader is not expected to understand in detail how the examples work by the end of Section 2. Instead, the details of each mechanism will be explained in later sections: Section 3 describes how the monad zipper works, Section 4 presents views, and Section 5 presents the different flavors of masks.

The Monad Zipper With the monad zipper we derive a virtual stack from a concrete one, that ignores a prefix but does not forget it. For instance, M_3 is a virtual stack for $\mathbb{S}_T$ *Int* ($\mathbb{S}_T$ *Int* $\mathbb{I}$) that ignores, but does not forget, the topmost transformer:

type $M_3 = (\mathbb{S}_T\ \mathit{Int} \triangleright \mathbb{S}_T\ \mathit{Int})\ \mathbb{I}$

Ignoring a prefix enables an operation $\uparrow$ much like *lift*, while still enabling an inverse $\downarrow$ that has no counterpart in the explicit lifting approach. This is useful for adapting higher-order monadic components such as *ifpos*

$\mathit{ifpos} :: \mathbb{S}_M\ \mathit{Int}\ m \Rightarrow m\ \mathit{Int} \rightarrow m\ \mathit{Int}$
$\mathit{ifpos}\ c =$ **do** $x \leftarrow \mathit{get}$
  if $x > 0$
   then c
   else $\mathit{return}\ 0$

(which routes the flow of control to c when a state is positive) to monad layouts where the component c is supposed to access a monad *above* the current layer. With the monad zipper this problem is solved as follows:

$> \mathit{run}\ (\uparrow (\mathit{ifpos}\ (\downarrow \mathit{inc})))$
$((1, 1), 5)$

Without the monad zipper, the only way to achieve the same result is to invasively (non-modularly) modify *ifpos* such that the *get* method is lifted: explicit lifting alone is not enough to handle the scenario on the right of Figure 2. The zipper, on the other hand, allows *ifpos* to be reused without any invasive changes to the original code.

Structural Masks Masks take the monad zipper one step further and allow selectively ignoring stack layers at multiple arbitrary positions in the monad stack (not just prefixes). Consider for instance the monad stack

type $M = \mathbb{S}_T\ \mathit{Int}\ (\mathbb{S}_T\ \mathit{Int}\ (\mathbb{E}_T\ \mathit{String}\ (\mathbb{E}_T\ \mathit{String}\ \mathbb{I})))$

to which the two components *ifpos* and *comp* $>$ *get* have interleaved access in the composition

$\mathit{client} :: M\ \mathit{Int}$
$\mathit{client} = \mathit{from}\ m_1\ (\mathit{ifpos}\ (\mathit{to}\ m_1\ (\mathit{from}\ m_2\ (\mathit{comp} > \mathit{get}))))$
 where $m_1 = \blacksquare$
   $m_2 = \square ::: \blacksquare ::: \blacksquare ::: \square$

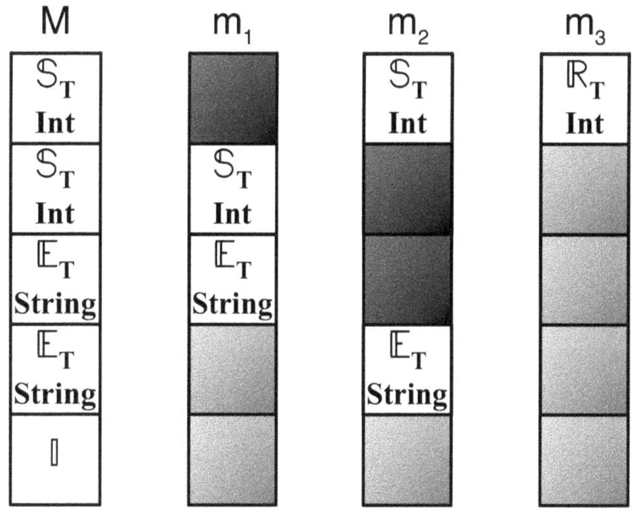

Figure 3. The monad stack M and the layers visible through masks m_1, m_2 and m_3: black layers are masked and gray layers are abstracted over.

Here, the mask $m_2 = \square ::: \blacksquare ::: \blacksquare ::: \square$ has a meaning similar to the bitvector 1001. When imposed on a monad stack, it ignores the second and third layers. The *from m* and *to m* functions, with m a mask, generalize $\uparrow$ and $\downarrow$. For instance, *from* m_2 *comp* gives *comp* access to the first and fourth layer in a monad stack. Similarly, m_1 provides *ifpos* with access to the second and third layers. See Figure 3 for a graphical depiction. Note that the layers in gray are not masked for the corresponding component, but nor is that component aware of their presence. This is either because a visible layer higher up in the monad stack blocks a similar layer lower down from view, or because the component's polymorphic type does not mention (i.e., abstracts away) the effect of a layer.

Masks with Restricted Views Masks are special instances of a more general mechanism called *views*. As such, masks can be freely combined with other types of views. For instance, the following example shows how to use masks in combination with a read-only view r_1, which provides a read-only view of a state monad.

$\mathit{client}' :: M\ \mathit{Int}$
$\mathit{client}' = \mathit{from}\ m_1\ (\mathit{ifpos}\ (\mathit{to}\ m_1\ (\mathit{from}\ m_2\ \mathit{comp} > \mathit{from}\ m_3\ \mathit{ask})))$
 where $m_1 = \blacksquare$
   $m_2 = \square ::: \blacksquare ::: \blacksquare ::: \square$
   $m_3 = r_1$

The *ask* component, whose type is $\mathbb{R}_M\ e\ m \Rightarrow m\ e$ (see also Figure 1), requires a reader monad, but the concrete monad M has no layer with a monad of that kind. However, we can *view* one of the state monads as a reader. The read-only view r_1, used in the mask m_3, does precisely this and allows the component *ask* to view the first state monad in M as a reader monad.

Nominal Masks Referring to layers in a structural fashion (with the monad zipper or bitvector-like masks) can be fragile when the layout of the monad stack is likely to change. With a nominal mask, the client code specifies the names (not the locations) of the layers to be used by a component. That component is then automatically matched up with the correspondingly named layers in the monad stack. For instance, with nominal masks the *client* example would be rewritten as:

$\mathit{client}'' = \mathit{ifpos}\ ((\mathit{comp} > \mathit{get})\ \text{`}\mathit{use}\text{`}\ (\mathit{Counter}_1\ \&\ \mathit{Err}_2))$

Here, $Counter_1$ and Err_2 are the names of respectively the first and fourth stack layer. The combinator *use* takes a list of names and makes the layers tagged with those names visible to the components. The list of names is assembled using the combinator & . The nominal masking infrastructure is built on top of structural masks. The big benefit of using the nominal approach instead is that it is much more robust: if the layers are rearranged, the nominal masks do not have to change at all.

Call-by-reference with Views A final application of views and masks is to allow for a call-by-reference programming style (that is discussed in Section 5.3) in which the view arguments act as references to particular layers in the monad stack.

$$\begin{aligned}
&add :: (Monad\ m, \mathbb{S}_{\mathrm{M}}\ Int\ n_1, \mathbb{S}_{\mathrm{M}}\ Int\ n_2) \\
&\quad \Rightarrow (n_1 \bowtie m) \rightarrow (n_2 \bowtie m) \rightarrow m\ () \\
&add\ xref\ yref = \mathbf{do}\ x \leftarrow get_v\ xref \\
&\qquad\qquad\qquad\qquad y \leftarrow get_v\ yref \\
&\qquad\qquad\qquad\qquad put_v\ xref\ (x + y)
\end{aligned}$$

In this example *xref* and *yref* are two view arguments and the get_v and put_v operations, which generalize the state monad *get* and *put* operations, use such views to access the right layer in the monad stack. This functionality is especially useful when a component employs multiple instances uses of the same effect. By using this call-by-reference style it is possible to avoid the pollution and the ordering constraints on the stack imposed by *lift* methods.

3. The Monad Zipper

This section presents the monad zipper: a monad transformer that is used to shift the focus of automatic lifting to the desired layer in the monad stack. In essence, the monad zipper allows us to ignore layers at the top of the stack while, at the same time, preserving these same layers, which allows shifting the focus back to the top when needed.

3.1 Stacks and Zippers

Sometimes type-level problems get easier when we move them to the term level. Let's reify the structure of the monad stack in a data type

$$\begin{aligned}
&\mathbf{data}\ Stack\ \ = Trans \cdot Stack \mid Bottom\ Monad \\
&\mathbf{data}\ Trans\ \ = T_1 \mid \ldots \mid T_n \\
&\mathbf{data}\ Monad = I
\end{aligned}$$

where the T_i represent the different transformers and I represents $\mathbb{I}$.

Huet [9] taught us how to shift the focus to any position in a data structure, with his *zipper*. Here is the *Zipper* for *Stack*:

$$\begin{aligned}
&\mathbf{data}\ Zipper = Zipper\ Path\ Trans\ Stack \\
&\mathbf{data}\ Path\ \ \ = Path \blacktriangleright Trans \mid Top
\end{aligned}$$

where $Zipper\ p\ l\ s$ denotes a stack with layer l in focus, remainder of the stack s and path p back to the top of the stack. The path is a reversed list, where the first element is closest to the layer in focus and the last element is the top of the stack. With a little syntactic sugar

$$(\triangleright) = Zipper$$

we obtain the self-explanatory notation $(Top \blacktriangleright T_1 \blacktriangleright T_2 \blacktriangleright T_3 \triangleright T_4)\ (T_5 \cdot I)$, where the triangles point towards the layer in focus T_4.

The *zipper* function turns a stack into a zipper with the first element in focus:

$$\begin{aligned}
&zipper :: Stack \rightarrow Zipper \\
&zipper\ (t \cdot s) = (Top \triangleright t)\ s
\end{aligned}$$

while the *up* and *down* functions allow shifting the focus one position up or down:

$$\begin{aligned}
&up, down :: Zipper \rightarrow Zipper \\
&up\ \ \ \ \ (Zipper\ (p \blacktriangleright t_1)\ t_2\ s) = (p \triangleright t_1)\ (t_2 \cdot s) \\
&down\ (Zipper\ p\ t_1\ (t_2 \cdot s))\ \ = (p \blacktriangleright t_1 \triangleright t_2)\ s
\end{aligned}$$

It's all well and good to zip around a reified form of the monad stack, but can we do it on the real thing too?

3.2 Monad Zipper

The answer is yes. Here is how the monad zipper $(\triangleright)$ is defined:

$$\mathbf{newtype}\ (t_1 \triangleright t_2)\ m\ a = \mathbb{Z}_{\mathrm{T}}\ \{run\mathbb{Z}_{\mathrm{T}} :: t_1\ (t_2\ m)\ a\}$$

where the type $(p \triangleright t)\ s$ has similar meaning to the reified data structure above. However, the monad zipper only changes the type representation: the **newtype** indicates that no actual structural change to the monad stack $t_1\ (t_2\ m)$ takes place. The only change takes place in the form of the type, which will enable us to select a different type class instance depending on the layer in focus. We will see more on this later, but first let us complete the analogy between types and terms.

Term-level stack composition $(\cdot)$, as in $T_1 \cdot M_1$, corresponds to type application, as in $t_1\ m_1$. As to $\blacktriangleright$, the type system will not allow terms of type *Zipper* to be used when terms of type *Stack* are expected. This segregation is not the case at the type level: the monad zipper type $(\triangleright)$ can appear as part of a monad stack. Indeed, we define $t_1 \triangleright t_2$ to be the *monad transformer composition* of t_1 and t_2:

$$\begin{aligned}
&\mathbf{instance}\ (MonadTrans\ t_1, MonadTrans\ t_2) \\
&\quad \Rightarrow MonadTrans\ (t_1 \triangleright t_2)\ \mathbf{where} \\
&\qquad lift = \mathbb{Z}_{\mathrm{T}} \circ lift \circ lift
\end{aligned}$$

Hence, at the type level, we simply use $\triangleright$ where $\blacktriangleright$ was needed at the term level. So, the monad stack representation $(t_1 \triangleright \cdots \triangleright t_i)\ (t_{i+1} \cdots m)$ denotes a monad stack with focus on t_i.

Finally, analogous to what the *zipper* function does with *Stack*, a monad transformer stack can be transformed into explicit zipper form by the following function:

$$\begin{aligned}
&zipper :: t\ m\ a \rightarrow (\mathbb{I}_{\mathrm{T}} \triangleright t)\ m\ a \\
&zipper = \mathbb{Z}_{\mathrm{T}} \circ \mathbb{I}_{\mathrm{T}}
\end{aligned}$$

where the identity monad transformer $\mathbb{I}_{\mathrm{T}}$ acts as the *Top* sentinel.

However, the $\mathbb{I}_{\mathrm{T}}$ sentinel is unnecessary, as the unadorned monad stack $t\ m\ a$ already expresses that the focus rests on t. There is no point in adding $\mathbb{I}_{\mathrm{T}}$ to subsequently ignore it again with $\mathbb{I}_{\mathrm{T}} \triangleright t$. In general, $t_1\ (t_2 \cdots (tn\ m))$ represents a monad stack with focus on t_1. So we will not actually use the above *zipper* function.

In summary, the term $(Top \blacktriangleright T_1 \blacktriangleright T_2 \blacktriangleright T_3 \triangleright T_4)\ (T_5 \cdot I)$ is the reified form of the type $(t_1 \triangleright t_2 \triangleright t_3 \triangleright t_4)\ (t_5\ \mathbb{I})$.

Relative Navigation Suppose we have a monad transformer stack $t_1\ (t_2 \cdots (t_n\ m))$. Then the focus lies by default on the top-most transformer t_1. The monad zipper becomes useful only when we shift the focus away from t_1 to t_2. The constructor $\mathbb{Z}_{\mathrm{T}}$ accomplishes that shift of focus, but how can we navigate further down, and back up?

Let us start with moving the focus one step further down:

$$\begin{aligned}
&step2to3 :: (t_1 \triangleright t_2)\ (t_3\ m)\ a \rightarrow (t_1 \triangleright t_2 \triangleright t_3)\ m\ a \\
&step2to3 = \mathbb{Z}_{\mathrm{T}}
\end{aligned}$$

A further step down:

$$\begin{aligned}
&step3to4 :: (t_1 \triangleright t_2 \triangleright t_3)\ (t_4\ m)\ a \rightarrow (t_1 \triangleright t_2 \triangleright t_3 \triangleright t_4)\ m\ a \\
&step3to4 = \mathbb{Z}_{\mathrm{T}}
\end{aligned}$$

The pattern should now be obvious. A single step down at any position in the stack is defined as:

$$\begin{aligned}
&\downarrow :: t_1\ (t_2\ m)\ a \rightarrow (t_1 \triangleright t_2)\ m\ a \\
&\downarrow = \mathbb{Z}_{\mathrm{T}}
\end{aligned}$$

Stepping back up is similar:

$$\uparrow :: (t_1 \triangleright t_2)\ m\ a \rightarrow t_1\ (t_2\ m)\ a$$
$$\uparrow = run\mathbb{Z}_T$$

Finally, note that $\downarrow \circ \uparrow \equiv id$ and $\uparrow \circ \downarrow \equiv id$ hold.

Focused Behavior So far, all we have seen is notation. The interesting *behavior* of $t_1 \triangleright t_2$, where it should deviate from a plain monad transformer composition, lies in the methods of the monad classes, e.g. *put* of $\mathbb{S}_M$. For looking up the method implementations it should ignore (look through) t_1 and only consider $t_2\ m$. This is achieved, e.g. for the state monad $\mathbb{S}_M$ defined in Figure 1, by lifting the operations through t_1:

instance $(MonadTrans\ t_1, MonadTrans\ t_2, Monad\ m, \mathbb{S}_M\ s\ (t_2\ m))$
$\quad \Rightarrow \mathbb{S}_M\ s\ ((t_1 \triangleright t_2)\ m)$ **where**
$\quad get = \mathbb{Z}_T\ \$\ lift\ \$\ get$
$\quad put = \mathbb{Z}_T \circ lift \circ put$

Contrast this with GHC's **newtype deriving** construct, that would adopt the same behavior for $(t_1 \triangleright t_2)\ m$ as for $t_1\ (t_2\ m)$, e.g., defining the former's *get* in terms of the latter's as $\mathbb{Z}_T\ get$.

In order to generally characterize the required behavior of monad subclass instances such as the above one for $\mathbb{S}_M$, we impose the following law.

LAW 1 (Lift Compatibility). *Given any monad subclass constraint* $\mathbb{C}_M$ *and any computation in this monad subclass* $x :: \forall\ m.\mathbb{C}_M\ m \Rightarrow m\ A$, *for any type A. Then we must have that*

$$\uparrow (x :: (T_1 \triangleright T_2)\ M\ A) \equiv lift\ (x :: T_2\ M\ A)$$

for any monad transformers T_1 *and* T_2, *and monad M such that* $\mathbb{C}_M\ (T_2\ M)$ *holds.*

Observe that this law holds for the above $\mathbb{S}_M$ instance.

As we have no space to provide the details of all monad transformer instances for the monad zipper, we refer the interested reader to our implementations using our variant of the MTL library[3] and the Monatron library [10].[4]

In summary, like explicit lifting, the monad zipper allows us to shift the focus to layers below the current focused layer via $\uparrow$. However, unlike explicit lifting, we can also shift the focus to layers above the focused layer with $\downarrow$. As we saw in Section 2.4 the extra expressiveness of the monad zipper allows for applications which are not possible with explicit liftings.

4. Views

The general problem we face when composing effectful components is that of incompatible assumptions about the monad stack. The solution is to work with one concrete monad stack, but to present each component with a suitable virtual monad stack. The correspondence between the concrete and virtual monad stack is captured in a view.[5] In Section 5 we will see how the views framework benefits from the monad zipper.

4.1 Virtual Views as Monad Morphisms

Semantically, a view corresponds to the categorical notion of a *monad morphism* (also called *monad transformation* in category theory, not to be confused with Haskell monad transformers that are a special case). Because we will be using different representations for monad morphisms, we capture the essential features in the *MonadCategory* type class.

[3] http://users.ugent.be/~tschrijv/Haskell/MTLzipper.tgz

[4] http://hackage.haskell.org/package/Monatron

[5] Not to be confused with Wadler's notion of *view* [28].

class $MonadCategory\ (\leadsto)$ **where**
$\quad id_M \quad :: (Monad\ m) \Rightarrow m \leadsto m$
$\quad (\bullet) \quad :: (Monad\ l, Monad\ m, Monad\ n)$
$\qquad \Rightarrow (m \leadsto n) \rightarrow (l \leadsto m) \rightarrow (l \leadsto n)$
$\quad hmap :: (Monad\ m, Monad\ n, MonadTrans\ t)$
$\qquad \Rightarrow (m \leadsto n) \rightarrow (t\ m \leadsto t\ n)$
$\quad from :: (Monad\ m, Monad\ n) \Rightarrow (n \leadsto m) \rightarrow n\ a \rightarrow m\ a$

The *MonadCategory* class describes a category with monads as objects and monad morphisms as arrows. The identity and composition of the category are id_M and $(\bullet)$, which satisfy the right and left identity, and associativity laws:

$$\begin{aligned} v \bullet id_M &\equiv v \\ id_M \bullet v &\equiv v \\ v_1 \bullet (v_2 \bullet v_3) &\equiv (v_1 \bullet v_2) \bullet v_3 \end{aligned}$$

A Haskell monad transformer t corresponds to an infinite number of monad morphisms in a particular representation $\leadsto$:

$$\{from^{-1} lift :: m \leadsto t\ m \mid m \in Monad\}$$

At the same time not all monad morphisms can be expressed by means of Haskell monad transformers. For instance, $\mathbb{R}_T\ \mathbb{I} \leadsto \mathbb{S}_T\ \mathbb{I}$ does not reflect the application of a monad transformer to a monad.

What characterizes Haskell monad transformers is that they are *functors* over monad morphisms, and *hmap* allows mapping a morphism through a monad transformer, which satisfies the functor laws:

$$\begin{aligned} hmap\ id_M &\equiv id_M \\ hmap\ (v_2 \bullet v_1) &\equiv hmap\ v_2 \bullet hmap\ v_1 \end{aligned}$$

The *from* function applies a monad morphism to a monadic computation. A monad morphism preserves the monad structure.

$$\begin{aligned} from\ v \circ return &\equiv return \\ from\ v\ (x \gg\!= f) &\equiv from\ v\ x \gg\!= from\ v \circ f \end{aligned}$$

4.2 Uni-directional Views

Uni-directional views constitute the obvious implementation of *MonadCategory*.

newtype $n \ltimes m = Uni\ (\forall a.n\ a \rightarrow m\ a)$
instance $MonadCategory\ (\ltimes)$ **where**
$\quad id_M \qquad = Uni\ id$
$\quad v_2 \bullet v_1 \quad = Uni\ \$\ from\ v_2 \circ from\ v_1$
$\quad hmap\ v \quad = Uni\ \$\ tmap\ (from\ v)$
$\quad from\ (Uni\ v) = v$

The above implementation is mostly straightforward, but we require a new operation *tmap* supported by all monad transformers to implement *hmap*. To avoid interrupting the flow, we continue with uni-directional views and refer to Section 7.2 for details on *tmap*.

The *lift* function is the most prominent example of a uni-directional view, which turns a monad transformer into the uni-directional view presentation:

$liftv :: (MonadTrans\ t, Monad\ m) \Rightarrow m \ltimes t\ m$
$liftv = Uni\ lift$

Uni-directional views for restricted access Uni-directional views are useful to restrict access to monadic layers that are shared by multiple components. For example, suppose we wanted to provide particular components only with read access to a shared state. The view r_1 can be used to achieve this.

$$r_1 :: (\mathit{MonadTrans}\ t, \mathit{Monad}\ m, \mathbb{S}_{\mathrm{M}}\ s\ (t\ m)) \Rightarrow \mathbb{R}_{\mathrm{T}}\ s\ m \ltimes t\ m$$
$$r_1 = \mathit{Uni}\ \$\ \lambda n \rightarrow \mathbf{do}\ s \leftarrow \mathit{get}$$
$$\qquad\qquad\qquad\qquad \mathit{lift}\ \$\ \mathit{run}\mathbb{R}_{\mathrm{T}}\ n\ s$$

In this case the monad transformer t can be any state monad transformer (in particular it can be $\mathbb{S}_{\mathrm{T}}\ s$).

4.3 Bi-Directional Views

Some views are invertible. An invertible view is a monad isomorphism, or bi-directional view. We capture bi-directional views in a separate datatype.

$$\mathbf{data}\ n \bowtie m = \mathit{Bi}\ \{\mathit{from}_{\bowtie} :: \forall a.n\ a \rightarrow m\ a$$
$$\qquad\qquad\qquad , \mathit{to}_{\bowtie} \ :: \forall a.m\ a \rightarrow n\ a\}$$

A bi-directional view is of course an instance of *MonadCategory*.

$$\begin{aligned}
&\mathbf{instance}\ \mathit{MonadCategory}\ (\bowtie)\ \mathbf{where}\\
&\quad \mathit{id}_M \quad = \mathit{Bi}\ \{\mathit{from}_{\bowtie} = \mathit{id}\\
&\qquad\qquad\quad , \mathit{to}_{\bowtie} \quad = \mathit{id}\}\\
&\quad v_2 \bullet v_1 \ = \mathit{Bi}\ \{\mathit{from}_{\bowtie} = \mathit{from}_{\bowtie}\ v_2 \circ \mathit{from}_{\bowtie}\ v_1\\
&\qquad\qquad\quad , \mathit{to}_{\bowtie} \quad = \mathit{to}_{\bowtie}\ v_1 \circ \mathit{to}_{\bowtie}\ v_2\}\\
&\quad \mathit{hmap}\ v = \mathit{Bi}\ \{\mathit{from}_{\bowtie} = \mathit{tmap}\ (\mathit{from}\ v)\\
&\qquad\qquad\quad , \mathit{to}_{\bowtie} \quad = \mathit{tmap}\ (\mathit{to}\ v)\}\\
&\quad \mathit{from}\ v \ = \mathit{from}_{\bowtie}\ v\\
&\mathit{to} :: (\mathit{Monad}\ n, \mathit{Monad}\ m) \Rightarrow n \bowtie m \rightarrow m\ a \rightarrow n\ a\\
&\mathit{to} = \mathit{to}_{\bowtie}\\
&\mathit{inverse} :: (\mathit{Monad}\ n, \mathit{Monad}\ m) \Rightarrow n \bowtie m \rightarrow m \bowtie n\\
&\mathit{inverse}\ (\mathit{Bi}\ \mathit{from}\ \mathit{to}) = \mathit{Bi}\ \mathit{to}\ \mathit{from}
\end{aligned}$$

where

$$v \bullet \mathit{inverse}\ v \equiv \mathit{id}_M \equiv \mathit{inverse}\ v \bullet v$$

Abstract view constructor To abstract from the *Uni* and *Bi* representations of bi-directional views, we provide an overloaded *view* constructor function.

$$\begin{aligned}
&\mathbf{class}\ \mathit{MonadCategory}\ (\leadsto) \Rightarrow \mathit{View}\ (\leadsto)\ \mathbf{where}\\
&\quad \mathit{view} :: (\forall a.n\ a \rightarrow m\ a) \rightarrow (\forall a.m\ a \rightarrow n\ a) \rightarrow n \leadsto m\\
&\mathbf{instance}\ \mathit{View}\ (\ltimes)\ \mathbf{where}\ \mathit{view}\ f\ f^{-1} = \mathit{Uni}\ f\\
&\mathbf{instance}\ \mathit{View}\ (\bowtie)\ \mathbf{where}\ \mathit{view}\ f\ f^{-1} = \mathit{Bi}\ f\ f^{-1}
\end{aligned}$$

Using this constructor has the advantage that we can build overloaded views that work not only as bi-directional views, but also as uni-directional views. This is useful to capture isomorphic views like:

$$\begin{aligned}
&\mathit{stateIso} :: (\mathit{Monad}\ m, \mathit{View}\ (\leadsto))\\
&\qquad \Rightarrow (s_2 \rightarrow s_1) \rightarrow (s_1 \rightarrow s_2) \rightarrow \mathbb{S}_{\mathrm{T}}\ s_2\ m \leadsto \mathbb{S}_{\mathrm{T}}\ s_1\ m\\
&\mathit{stateIso}\ f\ f^{-1} = \mathit{view}\ (\mathit{iso}\ f\ f^{-1})\ (\mathit{iso}\ f^{-1}\ f)\ \mathbf{where}\\
&\quad \mathit{iso}\ g\ h\ m = \mathbb{S}_{\mathrm{T}}\ \$\ \lambda s_2 \rightarrow \mathbf{do}\ (a, s_1) \leftarrow \mathit{run}\mathbb{S}_{\mathrm{T}}\ m\ (h\ s_2)\\
&\qquad\qquad\qquad\qquad\qquad\qquad \mathit{return}\ (a, g\ s_1)
\end{aligned}$$

without committing to bi-directional views in particular. In this case *stateIso* converts between $\mathbb{S}_{\mathrm{T}}\ s_1\ m$ and $\mathbb{S}_{\mathrm{T}}\ s_2\ m$ where s_1 and s_2 are isomorphic. This is useful, for instance, to share a state between components that expect values in different units, or to employ different character or data encodings.

Isomorphic Read-Only Views Consider how we can turn the uni-directional read-only view r_1 into a bi-directional one. For that purpose, the target type $\mathbb{R}_{\mathrm{T}}\ s\ m$ is unsuitable because it cannot keep track of updates. So we need to alter the target type for bi-directional read-only views. Fortunately, components are typically polymorphic in the monad stack and do not particularly care about a $\mathbb{R}_{\mathrm{T}}$ view; any instance of $\mathbb{R}_{\mathrm{M}}$ will do. We may put this freedom to good use by defining our own instance that is (trivially) isomorphic with any state monad.

$$\begin{aligned}
&\mathbf{newtype}\ \mathbb{S}_{\mathrm{M}}\mathbb{R}_{\mathrm{T}}\ s\ m\ a = \mathbb{S}_{\mathrm{M}}\mathbb{R}_{\mathrm{T}}\ \{\mathit{run}\mathbb{S}_{\mathrm{M}}\mathbb{R}_{\mathrm{T}} :: m\ a\}\\
&\mathbf{instance}\ \mathbb{S}_{\mathrm{M}}\ s\ m \Rightarrow \mathbb{R}_{\mathrm{M}}\ s\ (\mathbb{S}_{\mathrm{M}}\mathbb{R}_{\mathrm{T}}\ s\ m)\ \mathbf{where}\\
&\quad \mathit{ask} = \mathbb{S}_{\mathrm{M}}\mathbb{R}_{\mathrm{T}}\ \mathit{get}\\
&\mathbf{instance}\ \mathit{MonadTrans}\ (\mathbb{S}_{\mathrm{M}}\mathbb{R}_{\mathrm{T}}\ s)\\
&r :: (\mathbb{S}_{\mathrm{M}}\ s\ m, \mathit{View}\ (\leadsto)) \Rightarrow \mathbb{S}_{\mathrm{M}}\mathbb{R}_{\mathrm{T}}\ s\ m \leadsto m\\
&r = \mathit{view}\ \mathit{run}\mathbb{S}_{\mathrm{M}}\mathbb{R}_{\mathrm{T}}\ \mathbb{S}_{\mathrm{M}}\mathbb{R}_{\mathrm{T}}
\end{aligned}$$

5. Masks

The operations on views presented in Section 4 can be seen as the foundation for a masking language for monad transformers. Using this masking language it is possible to apply a mask to a particular monad stack to hide, restrict access or grant full access to the various layers in the monad stack.

5.1 Structural Masking

Consider again the example program of Section 2.4 where two components, *ifpos* and *comp* > *get*, access disjoint layers in the monad stack M.

$$\mathbf{type}\ M = \mathbb{S}_{\mathrm{T}}\ \mathit{Int}\ (\mathbb{S}_{\mathrm{T}}\ \mathit{Int}\ (\mathbb{E}_{\mathrm{T}}\ \mathit{String}\ (\mathbb{E}_{\mathrm{T}}\ \mathit{String}\ \mathbb{I})))$$

The former component accesses the second and third layer, while the latter component accesses the first and fourth layer. The snag is that the same state monad transformer type is used for the first and second layer, and the same error monad transformer for the third and fourth layer.

The repeated transformer types suggest to use the monad zipper, but there is a complication. So far we have used the monad zipper to create a *single focal point*, ignoring a prefix of the monad stack. What we need now are *multiple focal points*, ignoring arbitrary parts of the monad stack inbetween. We achieve this by composing multiple zippers into a single view. We call such a view a *structural mask*, a *mask* because it hides particular layers of the monad stack, and *structural* because the form of the mask follows the structure of the monad stack (we will see non-structural masks later).

To facilitate writing structural masks, we formulate them in terms of two primitive (1-layer or 1-bit) masks □ and ■, and one combinator (:::) that associates to the left.

The symbols □ and ■ denote respectively a transparent and an opaque mask, similar to role the bits 1 and 0 play in a bit mask. In our approach, □ means as much as "I want to see the current layer of the monad stack" and ■ means "I don't want to see the current layer". The (:::) combinator, that associates to the left, adds a 1-bit mask at the front of an n-bit mask, similar to the list cons operator (:).

The views framework of Section 4 provides the appropriate infrastructure to implement the mask primitives: The □ mask is nothing more than the identity isomorphism.

$$\square :: (\mathit{Monad}\ m, \mathit{View}\ (\leadsto)) \Rightarrow m \leadsto m$$
$$\square = \mathit{id}_M$$

The ■ mask captures another familiar isomorphism, that of the monad zipper.

$$\begin{aligned}
&\blacksquare :: \ (\mathit{MonadTrans}\ t_1, \mathit{MonadTrans}\ t_2, \mathit{Monad}\ m, \mathit{View}\ (\leadsto))\\
&\qquad \Rightarrow (t_1 \rhd t_2)\ m \leadsto t_1\ (t_2\ m)\\
&\blacksquare = \mathit{view} \uparrow \downarrow
\end{aligned}$$

Finally, the composition operator is:

$$\begin{aligned}
&(:::)\ ::\ (\mathit{Monad}\ m, \mathit{Monad}\ n\\
&\qquad\quad , \mathit{MonadTrans}\ t_1, \mathit{MonadTrans}\ t_2, \mathit{View}\ (\leadsto))\\
&\qquad \Rightarrow (t_1\ n \leadsto t_2\ n) \rightarrow (m \leadsto n) \rightarrow (t_1\ m \leadsto t_2\ n)\\
&v_1 ::: v_2 = v_1 \bullet \mathit{hmap}\ v_2
\end{aligned}$$

So a mask that hides the second and third layer is

$m_2 :: ... \Rightarrow t_1\ (((t_2 \rhd t_3) \rhd t_4)\ m) \rightsquigarrow t_1\ (t_2\ (t_3\ (t_4\ m)))$
$m_2 = \square ::: \blacksquare ::: \blacksquare ::: \square$

Similarly, we could write a mask that hides the first and fourth layer as $\blacksquare ::: \square ::: \square ::: \blacksquare$. However, the much shorter

$m_1 :: ... \Rightarrow (t_1 \rhd t_2)\ m \rightsquigarrow t_1\ (t_2\ m)$
$m_1 = \blacksquare$

has exactly the same effect in this example. In conclusion, the desired composition is

$client :: M\ Int$
$client = from\ m_1\ (ifpos\ (to\ m_1\ (from\ m_2\ (comp > get))))$

5.2 Nominal Masking

While the structural masking approach above resolves the issue of focusing on different layers, it can be awkward to use and maintain. Masking the stack requires global structural knowledge of the monad stack that is fragile with respect to changes. When the stack layout changes, all masks have to be adjusted accordingly.

As a remedy, we propose a *nominal* masking technique. A nominal mask specifies the names rather than the positions of the monad stack layers that a component may access. The layers in the monad stack are correspondingly tagged with these names. Using the names and the tagged stack structure, the appropriate structural masks are automatically derived. This makes the approach much more robust: when the stack layers are reorganized (e.g. to insert a new layer or to swap two layers), the structural masks are adjusted accordingly.

Tagged Monad Stack The $\mathbb{T}_T\ tag$ monad transformer labels a particular position in the monad stack with a type-level name *tag*.

newtype $\mathbb{T}_T\ tag\ m\ a = \mathbb{T}_T\ \{run\mathbb{T}_T :: m\ a\}$
instance $MonadTrans\ (\mathbb{T}_T\ tag)$ **where**
  $lift = \mathbb{T}_T$

which can be combined with other monad transformers, e.g. $\mathbb{S}_T$ to create tagged transformers.

type $\mathbb{TS}_T\ tag\ s\ m = \mathbb{T}_T\ tag\ (\mathbb{S}_T\ s\ m)$
$run\mathbb{TS}_T :: Monad\ m \Rightarrow tag \rightarrow s \rightarrow \mathbb{TS}_T\ tag\ s\ m\ a \rightarrow m\ (a, s)$
$run\mathbb{TS}_T\ t\ s\ m = run\mathbb{S}_T\ (run\mathbb{T}_T\ m)\ s$

Singleton types are used for tag names, e.g.

data $Counter_1 = Counter_1$
data $Counter_2 = Counter_2$

The type class $TWith\ tag\ n\ m$ relates a monad stack n with a particular mask m that puts the focus on the layer with name *tag*.

class $(Monad\ m, Monad\ n) \Rightarrow TWith\ tag\ n\ m$ **where**
  $structure :: View\ (\rightsquigarrow) \Rightarrow tag \rightarrow (n \rightsquigarrow m)$

We refer to Appendix A for the instances implementing *TWith*; these automatically derive the appropriate structural mask.

Two convenient additional combinators are

$use\ \ :: TWith\ tag\ n\ m \Rightarrow n\ a \rightarrow tag \rightarrow m\ a$
$c\ \text{`}use\text{`}\ name\ \ = from_{\bowtie}\ (structure\ name)\ c$
$expose :: TWith\ tag\ n\ m \Rightarrow m\ a \rightarrow tag \rightarrow n\ a$
$c\ \text{`}expose\text{`}\ name = to_{\bowtie}\ (structure\ name)\ c$

Hence, we may write

$c =$ **do** $inc\ \ \text{`}use\text{`}\ Counter_1$
  $(inc > inc)\ \text{`}use\text{`}\ Counter_2$
  $return\ ()$

to configure a number of incrementers. The stack layout is easily modified without requiring changes to the component configuration.

$> run\mathbb{I}\ \$\ run\mathbb{TS}_T\ Counter_2\ 5\ \$\ run\mathbb{TS}_T\ Counter_1\ 0\ \$\ c$
$(((), 1), 7)$
$> run\mathbb{I}\ \$\ run\mathbb{TS}_T\ Counter_1\ 0\ \$\ run\mathbb{TS}_T\ Counter_2\ 5\ \$\ c$
$(((), 7), 1)$

The above approach can be extended from masking with a single tag to masking with a type-level list of tags. For instance, $Counter_1\ \&\ Error_1$ represents a mask that views both layers $Counter_1$ and $Error_1$. Here, (&) is the constructor for non-empty type-level lists. We refer to the source code for all the necessary definitions.

Moreover, it nicely integrates with the other views. For instance, $stateIso\ f\ f^{-1} \bullet structure\ Counter$ selects the layer named *Counter* and applies a state isomorphism to it.

5.3 Formal Mask Parameters

So far, we have applied masks, and views in general, on components in a non-invasive fashion, from the *outside*. However, views as formal parameters within components also have an important use in disambiguating different instances of an effect. Obviously *externally* applied views are no solution to this problem that already manifests itself inside a component. The traditional solution to disambiguate two different states within a component is to use *lift*.

Consider again the *doubleInc* example in Section 2. To disambiguate the two states, we have used *lift*. Unfortunately, such internally motivated uses of *lift* impose unnecessary ordering constraints: in the monad stack one state transformer must appear above the other. Reversing the order of the two transformers is not possible; for that purpose we need to change the component implementation or write an alternate version.

Explicit view parameters allow us to abstract from the ordering, similarly to *tagged transformers* [19, 25] but with two advantages: *(i)* we get the full expressivity of views for adapting the concrete monad stack, and *(ii)* we get the full expressivity of bi-directional views for handling mutual embedding of components.

$doubleInc_2 :: (MonadCategory\ (\rightsquigarrow), \mathbb{S}_M\ Int\ n_1$
  $, \mathbb{S}_M\ Int\ n_2, Monad\ m)$
  $\Rightarrow (n_1 \rightsquigarrow m) \rightarrow (n_2 \rightsquigarrow m) \rightarrow m\ Int$
$doubleInc_2\ v_1\ v_2 =$ **do** $from\ v_1\ inc$
  $from\ v_2\ inc$

So $doubleInc_2\ \square\ \blacksquare$, $doubleInc_2\ \blacksquare\ \square$ and $doubleInc_2\ \square\ \square$ express both orderings of two disjoint states as well as a single shared state.

Call-by-reference Operations It is possible to create variants of effectful operations that take a view argument. For example, the get_v and put_v operations used in the *add* example in Section 2 are defined as:

$get_v\ v = from\ v\ \$\ get$
$put_v\ v = from\ v \circ put$

6. Case Study: Monadic Mixins

This section illustrates the uses of the monad zipper and monad views on monadic mixins. Because monadic mixins are higher-order components with non-trivial control flow patterns, traditional mechanisms to manipulate the monad stack do not provide adequate support. However, with the monad zipper and monad views, the complex control-flow patterns of monadic mixins do not pose a problem.

6.1 Monadic Mixin Components

Mixins We briefly summarize the notion of mixins, and refer the interested reader to previous literature on the topic for a more in-depth treatment [4]. A simple form of mixins can be easily implemented in Haskell as follows:

$$\textbf{type}\ \mathit{Mixin}\ s = s \rightarrow s$$
$$\mathit{fix} :: \mathit{Mixin}\ s \rightarrow s$$
$$\mathit{fix}\ a = a\ (\mathit{fix}\ a)$$

$$(\circledast) :: \mathit{Mixin}\ s \rightarrow \mathit{Mixin}\ s \rightarrow \mathit{Mixin}\ s$$
$$a_1 \circledast a_2 = \lambda \mathit{proceed} \rightarrow a_1\ (a_2\ \mathit{proceed})$$

The type $\mathit{Mixin}\ s$ is a synonym for a function with type $s \rightarrow s$ representing open recursion. The parameter of that function is called a *join point*, that is, the point in the component at which another component is added. The operation $\circledast$ defines component composition. The function *fix* is a fixpoint combinator used for closing, or sealing, an open and potentially composed component.

Combining monads with mixins When combined with monads, mixins allow us to model a simple form of AOP-like advice [17]. However, the control-flow patterns of programs using mixins are complex. For instance, consider the following memoization component and a monadic fibonacci function.

```
memo :: S_M (Map Int Int) m ⇒ Mixin (Int → m Int)
memo proceed x =
  do m ← get
     if member x m
       then return (m ! x)
       else do y ← proceed x
               m' ← get
               put (insert x y m')
               return y

fib :: Monad m ⇒ Mixin (Int → m Int)
fib proceed n =
  case n of
    0 → return 0
    1 → return 1
    _ → do y ← proceed (n − 1)
           x ← proceed (n − 2)
           return (x + y)
```

We can instantiate different monads, using the corresponding run functions of Figure 1, to recover variations of the fibonacci function. For example, the identity monad recovers the effect-free function while a fast fibonacci function is obtained by adding the memo advice and suitably instantiating the state monad:

```
slowfib :: Int → Int
slowfib = runI ∘ fix fib

fastfib :: Int → Int
fastfib = evalM empty ∘ fix (memo ⊛ fib)

evalM :: s → S_T s I a → a
evalM s m = runI $ runS_T m s >>= return ∘ fst
```

Another component for profiling is

```
prof :: S_M Int m ⇒ Mixin (a → m b)
prof proceed x = do c ← get
                    put (c + 1)
                    proceed x
```

which allows us to count the number of calls to the fibonacci function

```
proffib = evalM 0 ∘ fix (prof ⊛ fib)
```

Transformer Conflicts Of course, we would also like to profile the memoized fibonacci function to get an idea of how much more efficient it is.

```
profmemofib :: Int → S_T Int (S_T (Map Int Int) I) Int
profmemofib = fix (prof ⊛ memo ⊛ fib)
```

Unfortunately, the type checker complains that *Int* and *Map Int Int* are distinct types. The problem is that there are two uses of *get* in our components: one in *prof*; and another in *memo*. Due to automatic lifting, both *get* methods read the state from the same top-level $\mathbb{S}_T$, which happens to contain an *Int* value. This is the right thing to do for *prof*, but wrong for *memo* that expects a value of type *Map Int Int*.

6.2 Zipping Mixins

The problem above can be solved using the monad zipper to provide a new composition operator $\otimes$ for mixins.

```
(⊗) :: Mixin (a → t_1 (t_2 m) b)
     → Mixin (a → (t_1 ▷ t_2) m b)
     → Mixin (a → t_1 (t_2 m) b)
c_1 ⊗ c_2 = λproceed x → c_1 (↑ ∘ c_2 (↓ ∘ proceed)) x
```

This combinator associates the left-to-right order of components with a corresponding top-to-bottom order of monad layers. Here component c_1 focuses on the current layer, and c_2 looks one position down – that's why we have to bring *proceed* down (↓) to its level and shift the whole back up (↑) to the current level.

This combinator is very useful whenever we have a set of components that uses a disjoint set of monads (that is, each component will use different monads). No additional work is needed to make the two state transformers of *prof* and *memo* happily coexist.

```
profmemofib :: Int → S_T Int (S_T (Map Int Int) (I_T I)) Int
profmemofib = fix (prof ⊗ memo ⊗ fib)
```

Note that every component has its own transformer, notably $\mathbb{I}_T$ for *fib*, and we use the base monad $\mathbb{I}$ at the bottom of the stack.

6.3 Views and Masks

When using mixins we generally need the full power of bidirectional views to shift between two isomorphic monads. To make this shifting convenient we use the following combinator:

```
fmask :: (Monad m, Monad n)
      ⇒ (n ⋈ m) → Mixin (a → n b) → Mixin (a → m b)
fmask v mix proceed = from v ∘ mix (to v ∘ proceed)
mix `uses_m` names = fmask (structure names) mix
```

The *fmask* combinator takes a view v and applies it to a mixin *mix* executing the *to* function after proceeding and the *from* function after the mixin. Nominal views are applied with uses_m.

To demonstrate the application of masks and views on monadic mixin components, consider a simple assertion component that is used to check the output of a computation. We will show how this component is useful for checking whether the result of computing the fibonacci function has overflowed or not.

```
assertDump :: (E_M String m, R_M s m, Show a, Show b, Show s)
           ⇒ (b → Bool) → Mixin (a → m b)
```

The *assertDump* component applies an assertion (a function of type $b \rightarrow \mathit{Bool}$) to the output of *proceed*'s computation. If the assertion fails, an error is raised. The error message includes information on the state at the time of the error, to facilitate debugging.

This *assertDump* component allows the creation of another variant of the fibonacci program where, along with memoization and profiling, we also check for overflow and dump the memo table when overflow happens. Because we may be interested in recovering from the overflow (for example, by changing the representations of the inputs and outputs from *Int* to *Integer*) and continuing the computation, the exception layer should be at the top of the stack. Also, profiling works better if it is executed before memoization, so the profiler component should be in between *assertDump* and *memo*. However, *assertDump* requires access to the monadic layer with the memo table. In order to combine these components together we should make sure that all the constraints are satisfied.

Because there is no simple one-to-one correspondence between mixins and stack layers, we use the nominal approach. In addition, the *r* imposes a read-only view on the *Memo* state for *assertDump*.

$$
\begin{aligned}
&test :: Int \to ((Either\ String\ Int, Int), Map\ Int\ Int)\\
&test = myEval \circ\\
&\quad fix\ (\ assertDump\ (\geqslant 0)\ `fmask`\ r\ `uses_m`\ Err\ \&\ Memo\\
&\qquad \circledast\ prof \qquad\qquad `uses_m`\ Prof\\
&\qquad \circledast\ memo \qquad\quad `uses_m`\ Memo\\
&\qquad \circledast\ fib)\\
&myEval\ m = run\mathbb{I}\ \$\ run\mathbb{TS}_T\ Memo\ empty\\
&\qquad\qquad \$\ run\mathbb{TS}_T\ Prof\ 0\\
&\qquad\qquad \$\ run\mathbb{TE}_T\ Err\ \$\ m
\end{aligned}
$$

6.4 Monadic Mixins in Practice: Search Combinators

Schrijvers et al. [24] present a compelling application of the monadic mixins. They provide a Domain Specific Language (DSL) for expressing a complex search heuristic as a concise combination of primitive combinators. In their implementation, each primitive combinator corresponds to a monadic mixin component. The advantage and novelty is twofold: 1) *flexibility* because the user is able to combine combinators any way she wants, and 2) *extensibility* because the system developer is able to add new combinators without touching the existing ones.

To fit in with the Gecode C++ Constraint Programming library and for performance reasons, a staged approach is taken. The Haskell mixin components are code generators that collaborate to produce the C++ code for the overall search algorithm. For example, a search heuristic tailored to solving radiation therapy planning problems [1] of typical size consists of 20-30 monadic mixins, each with their own monad transformer, that collaborate to produce around 2000 lines of specialized C++ code. We are not aware of other Haskell projects with comparable monad stack sizes.

Effect Encapsulation Additionally to the techniques already introduced by us earlier in this section, the search combinators application employs a technique that facilitates the dynamic composition of many mixin components from a parsed specification string: each component encapsulates its own effect. Even statically this encapsulation makes sense. After all, the type of a monad stack with 20 layers is rather unwieldy.

The *Component* datatype below illustrates the encapsulation technique on the simple *Mixin* type.[6] The effect t_2 of the component is existentially quantified to hide it, and the included *run* function allows eliminating it.

$$
\begin{aligned}
&\textbf{data}\ Component\ a\ b = \forall\ t_2.MonadTrans\ t_2 \Rightarrow\\
&\quad Component\ \{behavior :: \forall\ t_1\ m.(MonadTrans\ t_1, Monad\ m)\\
&\qquad\qquad\qquad \Rightarrow Mixin\ (a \to (t_1 \rhd t_2)\ m\ b)\\
&\qquad\qquad ,run \quad :: \forall\ m\ x.Monad\ m \Rightarrow t_2\ m\ x \to m\ x\}
\end{aligned}
$$

While not all monad transformers support a *run* function of the above type, it is convenient and sufficient for our search combinators. For more details on the encapsulation technique and a more general form of *run* function, we refer to [22, Section 3.4].

[6] The mixin record type of search components is too elaborate to show here.

Performance Considerations We have not performed any systematic benchmarks yet, but do have a few observations on performance. Because it is defined as a `newtype`, wrapping and unwrapping the monad zipper does not add any space or runtime overhead. It does generate different type class dictionaries for the different components, and depending on the amount of inlining this either happens once (statically) or repeatedly for each invocation of a component (dynamically). The latter scenario notably arises when the effect types are existentially quantified. We have observed that this repeated creation of dictionaries puts compositions with around 60 monad transformers out of reach. In conclusion, gracefully and predictably scaling performance to monad stack sizes well beyond 30 layers is an open challenge.

7. Discussion and Related Work

7.1 The Haskell Setting

Our approach makes use of two key ingredients, monadic types and constrained polymorphism, which are both available in Haskell. The combination of these provides the necessary flexibility for effectful components to be adapted to many different settings.

One important advantage of using of Haskell is type-inference. In a setting like ours, where types can be relatively complex, type-inference is a blessing and allows most types to be inferred automatically. Indeed, although we have often used type annotations in our examples for documentation, those annotations are (for the most part) not necessary.

While Haskell provides the two necessary ingredients, there is potential for transferring the presented ideas to other settings. The monad zipper, views and structural masks have category theory interpretations and as such are of a more general nature. Indeed, they are relevant and adaptable to other settings that deal with explicit effects. Haskell-specific implementation aspects can find alternative counterparts in other languages. For instance, in Scala *implicits* can replace type classes [16]. The type-class tricks to look up names for nominal masks, popularized by Kiselyov [12], could be considerably simplified in a dependently typed language. Finally, a language design that natively supports the presented concepts is another option.

7.2 Effect Systems and Modular Monads

Effect systems (also known as type-and-effect systems) [14] form a popular non-monadic approach for making side effects explicit. However, they only describe (and do not define) programs that already have a meaning independent of the effect system. Hence, the effect annotations cannot adapt component behavior. Filinski's MultiMonadic MetaLanguage (M^3L) [7, 8] does embrace the monadic approach, but uses subtyping (or subeffecting) to combine the effects of different components. The subtyping relation is fixed at the program or language level, which does not provide the adaptability we achieve with constrained polymorphism.

Since Moggi [15] proposed monads to model side-effects, and Wadler [30] popularized them in the context of Haskell, various researchers (e.g., [11, 26]) have sought to modularize monads. Monad transformers emerged [3, 13] from this process, and in later years various alternative implementation designs, facilitating monad (transformer) implementations, have been proposed, such as Filinksi's layered monads [6] and Jaskelioff's Monatron [10].

In this paper, we rely on several of Monatron's techniques for implementing monad transformers. However, so as not to confuse the reader, we have incorporated the necessary techniques form Monatron in the familiar setting of the Monad Transformer Library[7] (MTL).

[7] which implements the original ideas of [13]

In our variant of the MTL, [8] monad transformers have to supply two additional operations, *tmap* and *mw*, which are inspired by Monatron:

$$
\begin{aligned}
&\textbf{class}\ \mathit{MonadTrans}\ t\ \textbf{where}\\
&\quad \mathit{lift}\ :: \mathit{Monad}\ m \Rightarrow m\ a \rightarrow t\ m\ a\\
&\quad \mathit{tmap} :: (\mathit{Monad}\ m, \mathit{Monad}\ n)\\
&\qquad \Rightarrow (\forall x.m\ x \rightarrow n\ x) \rightarrow t\ m\ a \rightarrow t\ n\ a\\
&\quad \mathit{mw}\ :: \mathit{Monad}\ m \Rightarrow \mathit{MonadWitness}\ t\ m
\end{aligned}
$$

Here, *tmap* allows transforming the monad underneath a transformer t. We have two uses for this additional operation:

- Our first use, just like in Monatron, is to lift control operators like *catchError* and *local* through other transformers; in the original MTL these operations could not be lifted. In our setting, it enables us to implement these control operators appropriately for the zipper ($\triangleright$).

  For instance, here is the zipper implementation of the *local* operator from the $\mathbb{R}_{\mathrm{M}}$ type class:

  $$\mathit{local}\ f\ m = \mathbb{Z}_{\mathrm{T}}\ \$\ \mathit{tmap}\ (\mathit{local}\ f)\ \$\ \mathit{run}\mathbb{Z}_{\mathrm{T}}\ m$$

- The second use, already covered in Section 4, is for the implementation of the *hmap* function of the *MonadCategory* type class.

The *mw* method encodes the property $\forall m.\mathit{Monad}\ m \Rightarrow \mathit{Monad}\ (t\ m)$ as a GADT witness.

$$
\begin{aligned}
&\textbf{data}\ \mathit{MonadWitness}\ t\ m\ \textbf{where}\\
&\quad \mathit{MW} :: \mathit{Monad}\ (t\ m) \Rightarrow \mathit{MonadWitness}\ t\ m
\end{aligned}
$$

In the original MTL, this property holds informally, but is neither enforced nor exploitable. We require this property to implement many of the zipper's operations. For instance, the *return* method for the zipper is defined as:

$$
\begin{aligned}
&\mathit{return}\ x = \textbf{case}\ (\mathit{mw} :: \mathit{MonadWitness}\ t_2\ m)\ \textbf{of}\\
&\quad \mathit{MW} \rightarrow \textbf{case}\ (\mathit{mw} :: \mathit{MonadWitness}\ t_1\ (t_2\ m))\ \textbf{of}\\
&\qquad \mathit{MW} \rightarrow \mathbb{Z}_{\mathrm{T}}\ \$\ \mathit{return}\ x
\end{aligned}
$$

In the Monatron design, the property is directly conveyed to the type checker in the form of a single type class instance:

$$\textbf{instance}\ (\mathit{Monad}\ m, \mathit{MonadTrans}\ t) \Rightarrow \mathit{Monad}\ (t\ m)\ \textbf{where}\ \ldots$$

However, this approach is not compatible with the MTL design. Hence, our GADT witness approach.

A limitation of *tmap*, both in Monatron and our MTL variant, is that it only works for covariant monad transformers. For instance, the contravariant continuation monad transformer cannot implement this operation.

7.3 Tag-indexed monads

It has been independently suggested by Snyder & Alexander [25] and Piponi [19] that indexing monad transformers with a type-level tag improves their convenience and robustness to changes. MTLX [25] is a monad transformer library that embodies this idea: automatic lifting ambiguities are resolved by tags. For example, consider the programs p_1 and p_2 written, respectively, in the MTL and MTLX.

$$
\begin{aligned}
&p_1 :: (\mathbb{S}_{\mathrm{M}}\ \mathit{Int}\ m, \mathbb{S}_{\mathrm{M}}\ \mathit{Bool}\ m) \Rightarrow m\ \mathit{Int}\\
&p_1 = \textbf{do}\ b \leftarrow \mathit{get}\\
&\qquad\quad x \leftarrow \mathit{get}\\
&\qquad\quad \mathit{return}\ (\textbf{if}\ b\ \textbf{then}\ x\ \textbf{else}\ 0)
\end{aligned}
$$

$$
\begin{aligned}
&p_2 :: (\mathbb{S}_{\mathrm{M}}\ \mathit{Ix}_1\ \mathit{Int}\ m, \mathbb{S}_{\mathrm{M}}\ \mathit{Ix}_2\ \mathit{Bool}\ m) \Rightarrow m\ \mathit{Int}\\
&p_2 = \textbf{do}\ b \leftarrow \mathit{get}\ \mathit{Ix}_1\\
&\qquad\quad x \leftarrow \mathit{get}\ \mathit{Ix}_2\\
&\qquad\quad \mathit{return}\ (\textbf{if}\ b\ \textbf{then}\ x\ \textbf{else}\ 0)
\end{aligned}
$$

The p_1 program does not type-check because the functional dependencies in the type class $\mathbb{S}_{\mathrm{M}}$ require that the state type is uniquely determined by m, but in this program two different state types are used. The program p_2, written for MTLX, solves this issue by using a $\mathbb{S}_{\mathrm{M}}$ class with a third type parameter, which is used to index the monad and determine the state type (along with the monad type), which avoids the conflict in p_1.

The main advantage of indexed monads is that they simplify the implementation of monadic components with multiple instances of the same effect. However tags commit to global names, which restricts reuse. If the lack of flexibility is not an objection, tags are a good solution. However, when the primary focus is flexibility and reusability, tags have important drawbacks compared to the monad zipper and monad views. In the MTLX approach, it is possible to abstract over the tag in order to be able to choose the monad layer later. For example:

$$
\begin{aligned}
&\mathit{inc} :: (\mathbb{S}_{\mathrm{M}}\ \mathit{ix}\ \mathit{Int}\ m) \Rightarrow \mathit{ix} \rightarrow m\ \mathit{Int}\\
&\mathit{inc}\ \mathit{ix} = \textbf{do}\ x \leftarrow \mathit{get}\ \mathit{ix}\\
&\qquad\qquad \mathit{put}\ \mathit{ix}\ (x+1)\\
&\qquad\qquad \mathit{return}\ (x+1)
\end{aligned}
$$

This value-level abstraction is more verbose than the monad zipper's type-level abstraction; it is an invasive approach that requires the component to be written with tags in mind. Moreover, for the price of value-level abstraction, we get a lot more expressivity from views: restricting access to layers is not possible with tags. Finally, a predefined set of tags is unsuitable when components are generated and composed dynamically, as in our search combinators application.

Ultimately, indexed monads and our techniques are useful for solving different problems and it is possible to get the benefits of both approaches by combining some of the techniques. For example, if we added monad views and the monad zipper to MTLX, we could use views to virtualize the tag names, by renaming or even removing the tags to suit the client's monad stack, and effectively acting as a scoping mechanism for the name tags.

7.4 Monadic Components

Many works have identified a need for reusable monadic components, but have not addressed the limitations related to monad stack management. Mixins were introduced by Cook [4] as a functional form of inheritance. Brown and Cook [2] first considered monadic mixins for memoization, while Oliveira et al. [17] model arbitrary AOP-style advice with them and show how to reason about interference between two components based on equational reasoning and parametricity. Our work should enable a generalization of the latter reasoning results to scenarios with arbitrarily many components. Prehofer [20] also considers a monadic model for FOP, which is not based on mixins.

The techniques presented in this paper can be used to improve the current state-of-the-art approaches to modular interpreters [5, 13, 27]. We describe a modular effectful interpreter case study, which uses the techniques presented in this paper, in a separate manuscript [23].

8. Conclusion

The current-state-of-the-art in monad stack management is too restrictive to effectively support reusable monadic components. The monad zipper provides the basic mechanism to lift these restrictions, and enables more powerful solutions such as structural and

[8] available at `http://users.ugent.be/~tschrijv/Haskell/MTLzipper.tgz`.

nominal masking. Views unite masks and other monad transformations in a single framework for adapting monadic components to a wide range of monad stacks.

Acknowledgments

We are grateful to the anonymous reviewers, Jeremy Gibbons, heisenbug, Mauro Jaskelioff, Wonchan Lee, Wouter Swierstra, Tarmo Uustalu, Phil Wadler, Stephanie Weirich and the members of IFIP WG 2.1 for their help and feedback.

Bruno Oliveira is supported by the Engineering Research Center of Excellence Program of Korea Ministry of Education, Science and Technology (MEST) / Korea Science and Engineering Foundation (KOSEF) grant R11-2008-007-01002-0 and the Mid-career Researcher Program (2010-0022061) through NRF grant funded by the MEST.

References

[1] D. Baatar, N. Boland, S. Brand, and P. Stuckey. CP and IP approaches to cancer radiotherapy delivery optimization. *Constraints*, 2011.

[2] D. Brown and W. R. Cook. Monadic memoization mixins. Technical Report TR-07-11, The University of Texas, 2007.

[3] P. Cenciarelli and E. Moggi. A syntactic approach to modularity in denotational semantics. In *CCTCS '93: Proceedings of the Conference on Category Theory and Computer Science*, 1993.

[4] W. R. Cook. *A Denotational Semantics of Inheritance*. PhD thesis, Brown University, 1989.

[5] L. Duponcheel. Writing modular interpreters using catamorphisms, subtypes and monad transformers. Technical report, Utrecht University, 1995.

[6] A. Filinski. Representing layered monads. In *Proceedings of the 26th ACM SIGPLAN-SIGACT symposium on Principles of programming languages*, POPL '99, pages 175–188, 1999.

[7] A. Filinski. On the relations between monadic semantics. *Theor. Comput. Sci.*, 375:41–75, April 2007.

[8] A. Filinski. Monads in action. In *Proceedings of the 37th annual ACM SIGPLAN-SIGACT symposium on Principles of programming languages*, POPL '10, pages 483–494, 2010.

[9] G. Huet. Functional Pearl: The Zipper. *Journal of Functional Programming*, 7(5):549–554, September 1997.

[10] M. Jaskelioff. Monatron: An extensible monad transformer library. In *IFL '08: Symposium on Implementation and Application of Functional Languages*, 2008.

[11] M. P. Jones and L. Duponcheel. Composing monads. Research Report YALEU/DCS/RR-1004, Yale University, New Haven, Connecticut, USA, December 1993.

[12] O. Kiselyov, R. Lämmel, and K. Schupke. Strongly typed heterogeneous collections. In *Haskell 04: Proceedings of the ACM SIGPLAN workshop on Haskell*, pages 96–107, 2004.

[13] S. Liang, P. Hudak, and M. Jones. Monad transformers and modular interpreters. In *POPL'95*, 1995.

[14] J. M. Lucassen and D. K. Gifford. Polymorphic effect systems. In *Proceedings of the 15th ACM SIGPLAN-SIGACT symposium on Principles of programming languages*, POPL '88, pages 47–57, 1988.

[15] E. Moggi. An abstract view of programming languages. Technical Report ECS-LFCS-90-113, Edinburgh University, Department of Computer Science, June 1989.

[16] B. C. d. S. Oliveira, A. Moors, and M. Odersky. Type classes as objects and implicits. In *OOPSLA '10:Proceedings of the ACM international conference on Object oriented programming systems languages and applications*, pages 341–360, 2010.

[17] B. C. d. S. Oliveira, T. Schrijvers, and W. R. Cook. Effectiveadvice: Disciplined advice with explicit effects. In *AOSD '10: ACM SIG Proceedings of the 9th International Conference on Aspect-Oriented Software Development*, 2010.

[18] S. Peyton Jones et al. The Haskell 98 language and libraries: The revised report. *Journal of Functional Programming*, 13(1):0–255, Jan 2003.

[19] D. Piponi. Tagging monad transformer layers, 2010. `http://blog.sigfpe.com/2010/02/tagging-monad-transformer-layers.html`.

[20] C. Prehofer. Flexible construction of software components: A feature oriented approach. Habilitation Thesis, Fakultät für Informatik der Technischen Universität München, 1999.

[21] J. C. Reynolds. Types, abstraction, and parametric polymorphism. *Information Processing*, 83:513–523, 1983.

[22] T. Schrijvers and B. C. d. S. Oliveira. Modular components with monadic effects. In *Preproceedings of the 22nd Symposium on Implementation and Application of Functional Languages (IFL 2010)*, number UU-CS-2010-020, pages 264–277, 2010.

[23] T. Schrijvers and B. C. d. S. Oliveira. The monad zipper. Report CW 595, Dept. of Computer Science, K.U.Leuven, 2010.

[24] T. Schrijvers, G. Tack, P. Wuille, H. Samulowitz, and P. Stuckey. Search combinators. In *Proceedings of the 17th International Conference on Principles and Practice of Constraint Programming*, 2011.

[25] M. Snyder and P. Alexander. Monad factory: Type-indexed monads. In *TFP 2010: Preproceedings of Trends in Functional Programming*, pages 106–120, 2010.

[26] G. L. Steele, Jr. Building interpreters by composing monads. In *POPL '94: Proceedings of the 21st ACM SIGPLAN-SIGACT symposium on Principles of programming languages*, pages 472–492, 1994.

[27] W. Swierstra. Data types à la carte. *J. Funct. Program.*, 18(4):423–436, 2008.

[28] P. Wadler. Views: a way for pattern matching to cohabit with data abstraction. In *POPL '87*, pages 307–313, 1987.

[29] P. Wadler. Theorems for free! In *Functional Programming Languages and Computer Architecture*, pages 347–359. 1989.

[30] P. Wadler. Monads for functional programming. In *Proceedings of the Marktoberdorf Summer School on Program Design Calculi*, August 1992.

[31] P. Wadler. The essence of functional programming. In *POPL '92: Principles of Programming Languages*, pages 1–14, 1992.

[32] P. Wadler and S. Blott. How to make ad-hoc polymorphism less ad hoc. In *POPL '89: Proceedings of the 16th ACM SIGPLAN-SIGACT symposium on Principles of programming languages*, pages 60–76, 1989.

A. TWith Instances

In this appendix, we provide the implementation of the overloaded *structure* function as a set of five overlapping instances for the *TWith* class. Three instances cover the three possible cases and two instances resolve overlaps between the three possible cases.

Although the implementation below may look daunting to the uninitiated, it relies only on folklore type-level programming techniques. Moreover, the user is never directly confronted with these instance implementations.

```
  -- [1] tag at the top
instance (Monad m, m~n) ⇒ TWith tag n (𝕋_T tag m) where
  structure _ = t

  -- auxiliary clause, to resolve overlap between [1] and [3]
instance (Monad m, m~t n, MonadTrans t)
    ⇒ TWith tag m (𝕋_T tag (t n)) where
      structure _ = t

  -- [2] tag in focus
instance (Monad m, Monad n, MonadTrans t, m~t n)
    ⇒ TWith tag m ((t ▷ 𝕋_T tag) n) where
```

```
    structure _ = case (mw :: MonadWitness t (𝕋_T tag n)) of
                    MW → ■⁻¹ • hmap t

  -- auxiliary clause, to resolve overlap between [2] and [3]
instance (Monad (t′ n), Monad m, Monad n, MonadTrans t,
          m~(((t ⊳ 𝕋_T tag) ⊳ t′) n), MonadTrans t′)
  ⇒ TWith tag m ((t ⊳ 𝕋_T tag) (t′ n)) where
    structure _ = case (mw :: MonadWitness t′ n) of
                    MW → ■

  -- [3] shift focus down
instance (Monad (t0 (t1 n)), Monad m, Monad n,
          TWith tag m ((t0 ⊳ t1) n), MonadTrans t0, MonadTrans t1)
  ⇒ TWith tag m (t0 (t1 n)) where
    structure tag =
      case (mw :: MonadWitness t1 n) of
        MW → case (mw :: MonadWitness t0 (t1 n)) of
          MW → ■ • structure tag
```

The above instances make use of the following auxiliary functions:

```
t :: View (⇝) ⇒ m ⇝ 𝕋_T tag m
t = view 𝕋_T run𝕋_T
■⁻¹ = view ↓ ↑
```

A Semantic Model for Graphical User Interfaces

Neelakantan R. Krishnaswami
Microsoft Research
<neelk@microsoft.com>

Nick Benton
Microsoft Research
<nick@microsoft.com>

Abstract

We give a denotational model for graphical user interface (GUI) programming using the Cartesian closed category of ultrametric spaces. The ultrametric structure enforces causality restrictions on reactive systems and allows well-founded recursive definitions by a generalization of guardedness. We capture the arbitrariness of user input (e.g., a user gets to *decide* the stream of clicks she sends to a program) by making use of the fact that the closed subsets of an ultrametric space themselves form an ultrametric space, allowing us to interpret nondeterminism with a "powerspace" monad.

Algebras for the powerspace monad yield a model of intuitionistic linear logic, which we exploit in the definition of a mixed linear/non-linear domain-specific language for writing GUI programs. The non-linear part of the language is used for writing reactive stream-processing functions whilst the linear sublanguage naturally captures the generativity and usage constraints on the various linear objects in GUIs, such as the elements of a DOM or scene graph.

We have implemented this DSL as an extension to OCaml, and give examples demonstrating that programs in this style can be short and readable.

Categories and Subject Descriptors D.3.3 [*Programming Languages*]: Language Constructs and Features

General Terms Languages, Theory, Design

Keywords denotational semantics, ultrametric spaces, functional reactive programming, guarded recursion, linear logic

1. Introduction

Graphical user interfaces (GUI) libraries are one of the most widely-used examples of higher-order programming; even languages such as Java or C$^{\#}$, in which programmers normally eschew higher-order style, offer user interface toolkits which expose higher-order interfaces. Unfortunately, these libraries are a poor advertisement for higher-order style; they are extremely imperative, difficult to extend, and understanding the behavior of client code requires deep familiarity with the internal implementation of the toolkit.

Since its introduction, functional reactive programming [12] has held great promise for simplifying the specification and interface to graphical user interface libraries. However, a persistent difficulty with modeling user interface toolkits with *functional* reactive programs is that certain basic abstractions, such as widgets, seem inherently effectful.

For example, creating two buttons differs from creating one button and accessing it twice, since creating two buttons creates two *distinct* streams of button clicks. That is, since the button abstraction uses its access to the outside world to generate a potentially arbitrary stream of clicks – indeed, this is the essence of the abstraction – it is difficult to explain it as a pure value.

In this paper, we extend our earlier work [17] on the semantics of functional reactive programming to account for this phenomenon. In that work, we used the category of ultrametric spaces to interpret higher-order functional reactive programs, and used Banach's theorem to interpret (guarded) feedback. This offers a simple, general semantics for functional reactive programming with an associated language that is essentially the simply-typed lambda calculus with a type constructor for streams and a 'next' modality.

Our primary observation is that the basic abstraction of reactive programming, the event stream, allows us to decouple the state changes arising from a stream taking on new values as time passes from the effects associated with opening new channels of communication with the user. We can model the creation of a new button, for example, as a nondeterministic choice over all possible streams of clicks that the user might generate.

The powerspace monad we use to interpret the nondeterminism associated with user interaction is rather well-behaved, allowing us to design a cleaner term language for GUI-manipulating code than would be possible for general imperative code. In particular, algebras for the powerspace monad form a model of intuitionistic linear logic, so we can use a linear lambda calculus syntax for GUI programming. Viewing the monadic effect as the composition of the free and forgetful functors, our DSL splits into two parts, a conventional nonlinear functional language (with an unconventional treatment of fixed points) in which programmers can write programs to control the *behavior* of their interface, and a linear one in which they can *construct* and compose widgets and other interactive components.

The linear treatment of widgets is a natural fit for interfacing our DSL to existing GUI toolkits. Most of these feature some global piece of state (variously called the DOM, the scene graph, the canvas, the widget hierarchy, etc.) representing the graphical interface. Modifications to this data structure change the graphical layout of the interface, and the components of this data structure typically[1] have a strong linearity constraint — a given node has a unique path from the root of the scene graph. By placing widget-manipulating operations in the linear part of our API, we can conveniently use this global mutable data structure, while still maintaining the relevant invariants and offering a purely functional specification.

To summarize, our contributions are:

[1] At the implementation level, this is typically a consequence of the fact that most GUI toolkits — including GTK, Win32, and the HTML/XML DOM — require that each node contain a pointer to its (unique) parent. The tree-shaped containment hierarchy is used for, amongst other things, routing events efficiently.

ICFP'11, September 19–21, 2011, Tokyo, Japan.

1. We build upon our earlier work on semantics of reactive systems to give a simple denotational semantics of GUI programs, including strikingly simple semantics for the arbitrariness of user interaction.
2. We give a type theory for this semantics, which integrates our recent work on type systems for guarded recursion with an adjoint calculus [1, 2] for mixed linear/nonlinear logic. Despite the presence of a fixed point operator fix $x : A.\ e$, this type theory has excellent proof-theoretic properties, including a simple normalization proof.
3. We illustrate our theoretical work with an implementation, demonstrating that it can lead to clean user code for GUI programs.

2. Programming Language and Model

In this section, we will describe the type structure and equational theory of our DSL. Our focus will be on conveying intuition about the programming model, as preparation for exploring an extended example. The denotational semantics and proof theory will come after that. In slogan form, we use an intuitionistic lambda calculus to give a language for higher-order reactive programming, and combine it with a linear lambda calculus to model the stateful nature of the display and user input.

Reactive programs are usually interpreted as *stream transformers*. A time-varying value of type X is a stream of Xs, and so a program that takes a time-varying X and produces a time-varying Y is then a function that takes a stream of Xs and produces a stream of Ys. In their original paper on functional reactive programming, Elliott and Hudak [12] proposed using general stream-processing functional programs to manipulate these dynamic values.

While stream programming is flexible, it suffers from a major difficulty: there are definable stream-processing programs which do not correspond to physically realistic stream transformers. If a stream of values represents a time-varying signal, then it follows that stream processors should be *causal*: the first n outputs of a program should only depend on the first n inputs. But there are common stream functions which are not causal; the simplest example of which is tail xs, whose n-th value is the $n+1$-st value of xs.

There have been several attempts to resolve this difficulty [18, 20], all of which build on the basic idea of using data abstraction to restrict the definable functions to the causal ones. In recent work [17], we have described a new solution to this problem which still blocks non-causal definitions, but does not surrender the flexibility of the original FRP model — in particular, its support for making free use of higher-order functions for building abstractions.

Our basic idea was to work in a lambda calculus with types not only for data, but also indexed by *time*. We introduced a type constructor $\bullet X$, pronounced "next X". If X is a type of values, then $\bullet X$ represents X at the next time step. Then, we can type infinite streams as follows:

$$\begin{array}{lcl} \mathsf{head} & : & S(X) \to X \\ \mathsf{tail} & : & S(X) \to \bullet S(X) \\ \mathsf{cons} & : & X \times \bullet S(X) \to S(X) \end{array}$$

Here, $S(X)$ is the type of streams of elements of X. The head operation has the usual type — it takes a stream and returns the first element, a value of type X. We diverge from the standard with the type of tail, which returns a value of type $\bullet S(X)$. So tail does not return a stream right away — it only returns a value of "stream tomorrow". As a result, it is impossible to take the head of the tail of a stream and perform a non-causal operation — typing rules out this possibility. Of course, given a value v of type X, and a stream tomorrow vs of type $\bullet S(X)$, we can construct a stream today, which will return v today, and then start producing the elements of vs tomorrow.

In Figure 1, we give the types of a small lambda typed calculus corresponding to this idea. The "nonlinear types" are the types just discussed, and are typed with a judgement $\Gamma \vdash e :_i X$. This can be read as saying "e is an expression of type X at time i, in context Γ". The context Γ also indexes all hypotheses with times, which controls when we can use variables — the UHYP rule says that a variable at time i can only be used at time i or later. The rules for the $\bullet X$ type internalize these time indices. The UDELAY rule tells us an expression of type X at time $i+1$ can be turned into a $\bullet X$ at time i, and conversely the UAWAIT rule tells us that a $\bullet X$ at time i can be used as an X at time $i+1$.

The last novelty in the nonlinear fragment is the UFIX rule. At first glance, it seems like an unrestricted fixed point, which is surprising in a calculus intended for defining well-founded stream programs. However, when we look at the time indices, it says that if we can create a value of type X at time i with a hypothesis at time $i+1$, then we can create a value at time i. The underlying intuition is best conveyed at the stream type. Suppose that we can build a stream, if only we had one tomorrow. Since we can't look at a stream tomorrow, this means that we can at least produce the head today — and so by turning today's output into tomorrow's input, we can tie the knot and construct a stream. (However, this works at *all* types, including functions and nested streams.)

The nonlinear language is sufficient for writing pure reactive programs, but cracks start to show if we try to bind it to GUI toolkits. The problem is best illustrated with an example. Suppose we had a function button : $1 \to S(\mathsf{bool})$, which created a button and returned a stream of booleans representing clicks. Now, consider the following two programs:

```
let bs = button() in   |   let bs = button() in
let bs' = button() in  |   map xor (zip bs bs)
map xor (zip bs bs')   |
```

On the left, we have a program which creates two buttons, and then returns the xor of their click streams. On the right, we have a program which creates a single button, and then a stream resulting from xor-ing the stream with itself. The program in the right will return a constantly-false stream, but there is no reason to expect that the same should happen for two *different* buttons. Were we to stay within our pure functional language, which satisfies all the usual CCC equations, we would have to identify these two programs, which is clearly wrong.

We will deal with the side-effects associated with changes to the widget hierarchy by assigning linear types to GUI expressions. (Though the behaviour associated with clicks and changes to, for example, the text displayed in widgets, are still dealt with functionally.) From a purely syntactic point of view, the linearity constraint means we cannot coalesce common subexpressions, and so typing blocks problematic examples like the above. We still need to say precisely what such a syntax should mean — a question whose answer we defer to the denotational semantics — but for now we keep in mind that any solution will have to account for the fact that users are free to click a button arbitrarily, whenever they choose.

So we add a linear sub-language, in the style of the LNL calculus [1], also known as the adjoint calculus [2]. We write A, B, C for the linear types, instead of the X, Y, Z we use for nonlinear types. Linear types include the tensor $A \otimes B$, the linear function space $A \multimap B$, and a type Window of GUI windows. We can give a small but representative set of constants for building GUIs with the following types:

$$\begin{array}{lcl} \mathsf{label} & : & F(S(\mathsf{string})) \multimap \mathsf{Window} \\ \mathsf{vstack} & : & \mathsf{Window} \otimes \mathsf{Window} \multimap \mathsf{Window} \\ \mathsf{hstack} & : & \mathsf{Window} \otimes \mathsf{Window} \multimap \mathsf{Window} \\ \mathsf{button} & : & F(S(\mathsf{string})) \multimap \mathsf{Window} \otimes F(S(\mathsf{bool})) \end{array}$$

The type constructor $F(X)$ embeds a *F*unctional type into the linear GUI sub-language (and dually the type $G(A)$ embeds a *G*UI type into the functional sub-language), and so the type of label says that if we supply a stream of strings (the time-varying message to display) we will receive a window as a return value. The vstack and hstack operations stack two windows vertically or horizontally, with the linearity constraint ensuring that a window cannot be packed on top of itself. The button function takes a stream of label messages, and then returns both a (linear) window, and a (nonlinear) stream of booleans representing the clicks from this button.

The typing judgment $\Gamma; \Delta \vdash t :_i A$ for linear types is a little more complicated than for nonlinear ones. There are two contexts, one for nonlinear variables, and a second for linear ones. The $\Gamma; \Delta \vdash t :_i A$ can be read as, "t is a term of type A at time i, which may freely use the variables in Γ, but must use the variables in Δ exactly once". The presence of the linear variables in Δ permits us to reason about imperative data structures such as windows in an apparently-functional way.

The $G(A)$ and $F(X)$ types serve to embed each language in the other. The UG rule says that we can treat a term of type A as a duplicable computation, when it uses no resources from the context. This rule is in the nonlinear part of the calculus, but its elimination rule LG lives in the linear sub-language, and says that any nonlinear $G(A)$ expression e can be run with the runG(e) expression to produce an A.

Conversely, the LFI rule says that we can embed any nonlinear term t into the linear language $F(t)$, without using any resources. Its elimination form let $F(x) = t$ in t' takes a term of type $F(X)$, and binds its result to the nonlinear variable x in the scope of t'. Now t' may use the result bound to x as often as it likes, even if constructing t originally needed some resources.

Finally, in Figure 2, we give the equational theory of our little language. Since our DSL is a total language, it supports all the β and η laws of the lambda calculus, for both the linear and nonlinear parts of the DSL. We also have $\beta\eta$-equalities for the adjoint type constructors and the delay type.

3. Example: A Stack-based Calculator

In this section, we illustrate our language by developing a small stack-based calculator program.

3.1 Implementation Description

Conceptually, the calculator consists of two parts. First, we implement the semantics of a calculator, making use of all the standard facilities of the host language of our DSL (in this case, Objective Caml). In the second part, we will use our DSL to turn the semantics into a reactive event processor, and to connect the event processor to a small GUI which lets a user interact with it.

3.1.1 Objective Caml Calculator Interpreter

In Figure 3, we give the Objective Caml code which implements the calculator's functionality. An RPN calculator acts on a stack, so on line 1 we define a type of stacks simply as a list of integers. On line 3-4 we define the logical events to which our calculator will react, including receiving a digit, an arithmetic operation, a push or pop instruction, or a no-op. Our type of events has no connection to the internal event-loop API of our GUI toolkit — it is just an ordinary Caml datatype representing the semantic events in terms of which we wish to program our calculator.

On lines 6-16, we give a step function which takes an event and a stack, and returns a new event. We process a digit event by adding it as the least significant digit of the topmost element of the stack (creating it if necessary). For example, if the topmost element of the stack is 7, then the sequence of digit operations `Digit` 1, `Digit` 2, `Digit` 3 will take the stack top from 7 to the number 7123.

$$
\begin{array}{llcl}
\text{Nonlinear} & X, Y & ::= & 1 \mid X \times Y \mid X \Rightarrow Y \mid S(X) \mid \bullet X \mid G(A) \\
\text{Linear} & A, B & ::= & \mathrm{I} \mid A \otimes B \mid A \multimap B \mid \mathsf{Window} \mid F(X)
\end{array}
$$

$$
\begin{array}{llcl}
\text{Terms} & e & ::= & () \mid (e,e) \mid \mathsf{fst}\ e \mid \mathsf{snd}\ e \mid \lambda x.\ t \mid t\ t' \mid G(t) \\
& & \mid & \bullet(e) \mid \mathsf{await}(e) \mid \mathsf{cons}(e,e') \mid \mathsf{head}\ e \mid \mathsf{tail}\ e \\
& & \mid & \mathsf{fix}\ x : A.\ e \mid x \\
& t & ::= & () \mid \mathsf{let}\ () = t\ \mathsf{in}\ t' \mid (t,t) \mid \mathsf{let}\ (u,v) = t\ \mathsf{in}\ t' \\
& & \mid & \lambda x.\ t \mid t\ t' \mid F(e) \mid \mathsf{let}\ F(x) = t\ \mathsf{in}\ t' \mid \mathsf{runG}(e) \mid x \\
\text{Contexts} & \Gamma & ::= & \cdot \mid \Gamma, x :_i X \\
& \Delta & ::= & \cdot \mid \Delta, x :_i A
\end{array}
$$

Nonlinear $\boxed{\Gamma \vdash e :_i X}$ Linear $\boxed{\Gamma; \Delta \vdash t :_i A}$

$$\frac{i \le j \quad x :_i A \in \Gamma}{\Gamma \vdash x :_j A}\ \textsc{UHyp} \qquad \frac{}{\Gamma \vdash () :_i 1}\ \textsc{UUnit}$$

$$\frac{\Gamma \vdash e :_i X \quad \Gamma \vdash e' :_i Y}{\Gamma \vdash (e, e') :_i X \times Y}\ \textsc{UPair} \qquad \frac{\Gamma \vdash e :_i X \times Y}{\Gamma \vdash \mathsf{fst}\ e :_i X}\ \textsc{UFst}$$

$$\frac{\Gamma \vdash e :_i X \times Y}{\Gamma \vdash \mathsf{snd}\ e :_i Y}\ \textsc{USnd} \qquad \frac{\Gamma, x :_i A \vdash e :_i B}{\Gamma \vdash \lambda x.\ e :_i A \Rightarrow B}\ \textsc{UFun}$$

$$\frac{\Gamma \vdash e :_i A \Rightarrow B \quad \Gamma \vdash e' :_i A}{\Gamma \vdash t\ t' :_i B}\ \textsc{UApp} \qquad \frac{\Gamma \vdash e :_{i+1} X}{\Gamma \vdash \bullet e :_i \bullet X}\ \textsc{UDelay}$$

$$\frac{\Gamma \vdash e :_i \bullet X}{\Gamma \vdash \mathsf{await}(e) :_{i+1} X}\ \textsc{UAwait}$$

$$\frac{\Gamma \vdash e :_i X \quad \Gamma \vdash e' :_{i+1} S(X)}{\Gamma \vdash \mathsf{cons}(e, e') :_i S(X)}\ \textsc{UCons}$$

$$\frac{\Gamma \vdash e :_i S(X)}{\Gamma \vdash \mathsf{head}\ e :_i X}\ \textsc{UHead} \qquad \frac{\Gamma \vdash e :_i S(X)}{\Gamma \vdash \mathsf{tail}\ e :_{i+1} S(X)}\ \textsc{UTail}$$

$$\frac{\Gamma, x :_{i+1} A \vdash e :_i A}{\Gamma \vdash \mathsf{fix}\ x : A.\ e :_i A}\ \textsc{UFix} \qquad \frac{\Gamma; \cdot \vdash t :_i A}{\Gamma \vdash G(t) :_i G(A)}\ \textsc{UG}$$

$$\frac{}{\Gamma; x :_i A \vdash x :_i A}\ \textsc{LHyp} \qquad \frac{}{\Gamma; \cdot \vdash () :_i \mathrm{I}}\ \textsc{LUnit}$$

$$\frac{\Gamma; \Delta \vdash t :_i \mathrm{I} \quad \Gamma; \Delta' \vdash t' :_i A}{\Gamma; \Delta, \Delta' \vdash \mathsf{let}\ () = t\ \mathsf{in}\ t' :_i A}\ \textsc{LUnitE}$$

$$\frac{\Gamma; \Delta \vdash t :_i A \quad \Gamma; \Delta' \vdash t' :_i B}{\Gamma; \Delta, \Delta' \vdash (t, t') :_i A \otimes B}\ \textsc{LPair}$$

$$\frac{\Gamma; \Delta \vdash t :_i A \otimes B \quad \Gamma; \Delta', x :_i A, y :_i B \vdash t' :_i C}{\Gamma; \Delta, \Delta' \vdash \mathsf{let}\ (x, y) = t\ \mathsf{in}\ t' :_i C}\ \textsc{LPairE}$$

$$\frac{\Gamma; \Delta, x :_i A \vdash t :_i B}{\Gamma; \Delta \vdash \lambda x.\ t :_i A \multimap B}\ \textsc{LFun}$$

$$\frac{\Gamma; \Delta \vdash t :_i A \multimap B \quad \Gamma; \Delta' \vdash t' :_i A}{\Gamma; \Delta, \Delta' \vdash t\ t' :_i B}\ \textsc{LApp}$$

$$\frac{\Gamma \vdash e :_i G(A)}{\Gamma; \cdot \vdash \mathsf{runG}(e) :_i A}\ \textsc{LG} \qquad \frac{\Gamma \vdash e :_i X}{\Gamma; \cdot \vdash F(e) :_i F(X)}\ \textsc{LFI}$$

$$\frac{\Gamma; \Delta \vdash t :_i F(X) \quad \Gamma, x :_i X; \Delta' \vdash t' :_i B}{\Gamma; \Delta, \Delta' \vdash \mathsf{let}\ F(x) = t\ \mathsf{in}\ t' :_i B}\ \textsc{LFE}$$

Figure 1. Types and Syntax

Type	Equation		
I	$\text{let } () = () \text{ in } t$	$=_\beta$	t
	$[t/a]t'$	$=_\eta$	$\text{let } () = t \text{ in } [()/a]t'$
$A \otimes B$	$\text{let } (a, b) = (t_1, t_2) \text{ in } t'$	$=_\beta$	$[t_1/a][t_2/b]t'$
	$[t/c]t'$	$=_\eta$	$\text{let } (a, b) = t \text{ in } [(a, b)/c]t'$
$A \multimap B$	$(\lambda a.\ t')\ t$	$=_\beta$	$[t/a]t'$
	t	$=_\beta$	$\lambda a.\ t\ a$
$F(X)$	$\text{let } F(x) = F(e) \text{ in } t$	$=_\beta$	$[e/x]t$
	$[t/a]t'$	$=_\eta$	$\text{let } F(x) = t \text{ in } [F(x)/a]t'$
1	e	$=_\eta$	$()$
$X \times Y$	$\text{fst } (e, e')$	$=_\beta$	e
	$\text{snd } (e, e')$	$=_\beta$	e'
	e	$=_\eta$	$(\text{fst } e, \text{snd } e)$
$X \Rightarrow Y$	$(\lambda x.\ e')\ e$	$=_\beta$	$[e/x]e'$
	e	$=_\eta$	$\lambda x.\ e\ x$
$S(X)$	$\text{head cons}(e, e')$	$=_\beta$	e
	$\text{tail cons}(e, e')$	$=_\beta$	e'
	e	$=_\beta$	$\text{cons}(\text{head } e, \text{tail } e)$
$\bullet A$	$\text{await}(\bullet e)$	$=_\beta$	e
	$\bullet(\text{await } e)$	$=_\eta$	e
$G(A)$	$\text{runG}(G(e))$	$=_\beta$	e
	t	$=_\eta$	$G(\text{runG}(t))$
X	$\text{fix } x : X.\ e$	$=$	$[\text{fix } x : X.\ e/x]e$

Figure 2. Equational Theory

As in other RPN-style calculators, we need a command to mark the end of a numeric input, which the `Push` event accomplishes by pushing 0 onto the top of the stack. Since digit operations only affect the topmost element, pushing 0 completes the entry of a number by making it the second element of the stack. The `Pop` operation deletes the topmost element from the stack, discarding it. The `Plus`, `Minus`, and `Times` operations each take the top two elements of the stack, and replace them with the result of performing the appropriate arithmetic operation on them (reducing the height of the stack by a net of one). The `Clear` operation simply sets the topmost element of the stack to 0.

Finally, we have a catchall clause which does nothing to the stack, which handles the `Nothing` event and also ensures that invalid operations (for instance `Plus` on a stack with 1 or 0 elements) do nothing.

On lines 18-22, we define a `display` function which takes a stack and returns a string of a comma-separated list of values. On lines 24-27, we define the `merge` function, which we will use to multiplex multiple streams of operations into a single stream. Since fair merge is inherently nondeterministic, we implement a simple biased choice operation. If its first argument is `Nothing`, then it returns its second argument — otherwise it returns its first argument. Finally, on lines 29-30 we define a function `bool_to_op op b` which returns `op` if `b` is true, and `Nothing` otherwise.

We reiterate that the code in Figure 3 is ordinary Ocaml code. Interpreters and symbolic computation is natural for functional languages, and we do not need any special additional features to implement this part. It is only when we need to write interactive code that programs in standard functional languages (and for that matter, OO languages) start to lose their appeal.

3.1.2 DSL Code for the User Interface

In Figure 4 we give the actual implementation of the user interface, as a program written in our domain-specific language. The ambient context of the code in this listing is on the functional side of the wall, making use of the $G(-)$ constructor to shift into the linear sublanguage as needed.

On lines 1-4, we have a function `stacks`, which takes an initial stack and a stream of operations, and turns it into a stream of stacks. It does this by taking the current operation and applies it to the current stack, to get the next stack, and recursively calls `stacks` on the next state and the tail of the stream of operations. Note that as a recursive definition (at a function type), the UFIX rule requires that any recursive calls to `stacks` must occur at a later time. In this definition, the only recursive call we make is inside the tail argument to cons, which according to the `UCons` rule occurs at a later time than the head argument. As a result, this is a safe recursive call which will pass typechecking.

Figure 4 contains *all* of the code we need to plug our state machine into the GUI event loop — there are no callbacks or anything like that. We just do familiar-looking functional programming with streams, with a type system that warns the user of any ill-founded definitions.

On lines 7-51, we actually build a GUI. On line 7, as an abbreviation we define the type of input builders $\texttt{input} = G(\text{Window} \otimes F(S(\text{op})))$. We can read this type as saying it is a GUI command which when executed builds a window yielding a stream of calculator operations. So this is the type we will use for user input GUI widgets in our calculator application.

On lines 9-12, we define the `calculator_button` widget. This function takes a string and an event, and returns a button labeled with the string argument, and which returns the event whenever the button is clicked. On line 11, we create a button, calling the button function with a constant stream of the message argument. This returns a window and a stream of clicks, and we map `bool_to_op` over that stream of clicks to generate a stream of events. (As an aside, we use a nested pattern matching syntax `let (w, F(bs)) = ...in ...` rather than splitting the term into the two bindings `let (w, fbs) = ...in let F(bs) = fbs in ...`. This is an easily desugared notational convenience.)

On lines 14-16, we use the `calculator_button` function to define the `numeric` function, which is the function we will use to create the number buttons of our calculator. It is just a call to `calculator_button` which converts its numeric argument to a string and a digit operation before calling `calculator_button`.

Despite its simplicity, this function illustrates a key feature of our library: defining new widgets is *easy*. We construct a new widget for no reason other than to avoid having to write calls like `calculator_button (string_of int 5) (Digit 5)`. This avoids a miniscule amount of redundancy, and yet defining new widget operations is lightweight enough that it is worth doing.

On lines 18-31, we define a function `pack`, which is a combinator for building new input widgets out of old ones. As arguments, it takes a stacking function `stack` to merge windows (which in this case will be hstack or vstack), and four inputs `(g1, g2, g3, g4)`, which it will coalesce into a new input widget. It does this by executing each of the `g`'s, and merging the returned windows `w1, w2, w3, w4` with `stack`, and merging the returned operation streams `es1, es2, es3, es4` with the `merge` operation.

The `pack` function shows off two strengths and one minor weakness of our DSL. The weakness is simply that we have not yet added lists to the type constructors of our DSL, and so `pack` is hard-coded to take a 4-tuple. The first strength is that `pack` is a higher-order function, parameterized in the packing order. This is something that a first-order embedded DSL, which did not supply its own interpretation of the function space, could not conveniently do, since the function space in question is a *linear* function space.

The second strength is the compositionality of functional programming. We have taken the type $G(\text{Window} \otimes F(S(\text{op})))$ to be the type of input widgets, and we are at liberty to construct new inhabitants of this type. Not only are individual buttons input widgets, but entire input panels are also input widgets. So in the definition of `input_panel` on lines 33-45, we are able to use the same `pack` function to lay out both the individual rows of buttons, and the stack

```
type stack = int list

type op = Push | Pop   | Digit of int
        | Plus | Minus | Times
        | Clear | Delete | Nothing

val step : op * stack → stack
let step = function
  | Digit n, m :: s     → (10 * m + n) :: s
  | Digit n, []         → [n]
  | Push,    s          → 0 :: s
  | Pop,     _ :: s     → s
  | Plus,    n :: m :: s → (n + m) :: s
  | Minus,   n :: m :: s → (n - m) :: s
  | Times,   n :: m :: s → (n * m) :: s
  | Clear,   n :: s     → 0 :: s
  | Delete,  n :: s     → s
  | _,       s          → s

val display : stack → string
let rec display = function
  | []     → "0"
  | [n]    → string_of_int n
  | n :: s → (string_of_int_n) ^ ", " ^ (display s)

val merge : op * op → op
let merge = function
  | Nothing, e → e
  | e, _       → e

val bool_to_op : op → bool → op
let bool_to_op op b = if b then op else Nothing
```

Figure 3. RPN Calculator Internals (in OCaml)

of rows, simply by varying the stacking parameter. Furthermore, since pack can do computation, it is able to act as a "smart constructor" which appropriately multiplexes the input signals of all its components. As a result, none of the wiring code is explicit in the code building the input panel — the code just follows the tree structure of the visual layout, like an HTML document, even though it also produces an output signal.

3.2 Comparison With Traditional Approaches

It is difficult to give a crisp, precise comparison with the traditional approach to GUI programming based on imperative callbacks and event loops, for two reasons. On the one hand, existing GUI libraries have few algebraic or equational properties, which makes theoretical comparisons difficult, and on the other, we have not yet written any large programs in our language, which makes practical comparisons difficult. Nevertheless, it is still possible to draw distinctions at the architectural level.

Traditional GUI toolkits (based on the model-view-controller pattern [15]) are logically structured as a collection of asynchronous event processors. Each GUI widget listens to events generated by some other widgets (and the main application/event loop), and generates events itself. The primary feature of this design is that widgets can generate events at different rates, and there is no guarantee of the order in which events are delivered to other widgets. (In practice, the order of delivery depends on the specific order in which callbacks were registered with a widget object.)

In contrast, our system is based on a *synchronous* model of time, such as used in languages such as Lustre [6] and Lucid Synchrone [21]. There is a global clock, which is respected by every event stream in the program — every stream generates one event each tick. Our primary motivation was that with a simpler deterministic semantics, it was possible to interpret higher-order

```
val stacks : stack × S(op) ⇒  S(stack)
let rec stacks (stack, ops) =
  let next_stack = step (head ops, stack) in
  cons(stack, stacks(next_stack, tail ops))


type input = G(Window ⊗ F(S(op)))

val calculator_button : string ⇒ op ⇒ input
let calculator_button msg op =
  G(let (window, F(bs)) = button F(constant msg) in
    (window, F(map (bool_to_op op) bs))

val numeric : int ⇒ input
let numeric n =
  calculator_button (string_of_int n) (Num n)

val pack : G(Window ⊗ Window ⊸ Window) ⇒
           (input × input × input × input) ⇒
           input
let pack stack (g1, g2, g3, g4) =
  G(let (w1, F(es1)) = runG g1 in
    let (w2, F(es2)) = runG g2 in
    let (w3, F(es3)) = runG g3 in
    let (w4, F(es4)) = runG g4 in
    let w = runG stack (runG stack (w1, w2),
                        runG stack (w2, w3)) in
    let es = F(merge(es1,
                 merge(es2,
                 merge(es3, es4)))) in
    (w, es))

val input_panel : input
let input_panel =
  pack G(vstack)
    (pack G(hstack) (numeric 7, numeric 8, numeric 9,
                     calculator_button "+" Plus),
     pack G(hstack) (numeric 4, numeric 5, numeric 6,
                     calculator_button "-" Minus),
     pack G(hstack) (numeric 1, numeric 2, numeric 3,
                     calculator_button "x" Times),
     pack G(hstack) (calculator_button "D" Delete,
                     numeric 0,
                     calculator_button "," Push,
                     calculator_button "C" Clear))

val calculator : G(Window)
let calculator =
  G(let (input, F(es)) = runG input_panel in
    let msgs = F(map display (stacks([], es))) in
    vstack(label msgs, input))
```

Figure 4. Code for Calculator (in embedded GUI DSL)

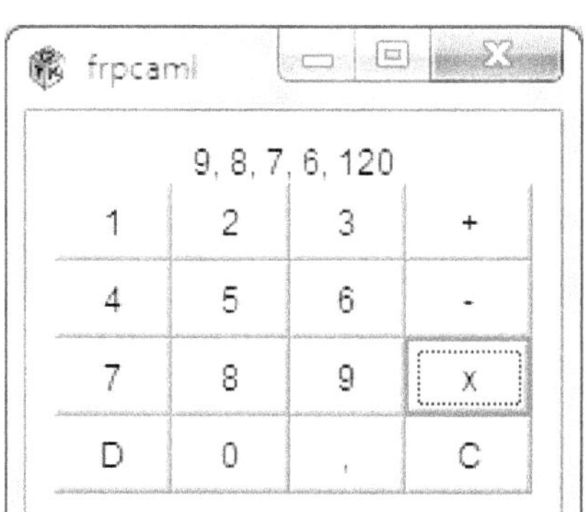

Figure 5. Screenshot of the RPN Calculator

constructions such as functions and streams of streams. We think that these constructions offer the same simplifications of reasoning that the lambda calculus offers over process calculi.

Under a strictly deterministic semantics, it is impossible to write certain programs, such as a fair merge of streams. In our calculator example, we have to explicitly write a function to multiplex events, as can be seen in the definition of `merge` on line 26-28 of Figure 3, and in its use in lines 28-31 of Figure 4. Here, we had to define a *biased* choice, which favors the left argument over the right. Even though fair merges are useful for specifying the behavior of GUIs, we think that it is a bad choice for implementation, since it makes debugging and reasoning about programs much harder than under a deterministic semantics.

Another tradeoff comes when trying to correlate events. As can be seen in the definition of the `op` datatype on line 3-5 of Figure 3, we need to explicitly include a `Nothing` constructor to indicate that no event happened on this tick. Under an asynchronous event semantics, no-ops do not need to be part of the event datatype, since the event source is never obligated to send a message.

However, this advantage is negated by the problems that arise when we need to correlate events from multiple sources. Since neither simultaneity nor order are guaranteed for event deliveries, clients have to build their own state machines to reconstruct event correlations (such as a view attempting to correlate events generated by the model and the controller). Building these state machines can get tricky, and programmers are often tempted to exploit details of the subject-observer implementation and register callbacks in a particular order to guarantee a certain order of event delivery. These tricks are fragile, and any errors lead to bugs which can be fiendishly difficult to diagnose.

4. Denotational Semantics

4.1 Intuition

Reactive programs are typically interpreted as *stream transformers*: functions which take a stream of inputs and generate a stream of outputs. However, not all functions on streams correspond to realistic reactive programs. For example, a stock trading program accepts a stream of price quotes and emits a sequence of buy and sell orders, but the set-theoretic function space $\mathsf{Price}^\omega \to \mathsf{Order}^\omega$ contains functions which produces orders that are a function of the *future* stock prices. These functions are, alas, not implementable.

The condition governing which stream functions are implementable is *causality*: the first n outputs may only depend on the first n inputs. Writing $\lfloor xs \rfloor_n$ for the n-element prefix of the stream xs, we can express causality as follows:

Definitition 1. *(Causality) A stream function $f : A^\omega \to B^\omega$ is* causal, *when for all n and all streams as and as', we have*

$$\lfloor as \rfloor_n = \lfloor as' \rfloor_n \implies \lfloor f\ as \rfloor_n = \lfloor f\ as' \rfloor_n$$

Causality is a very important idea, but it is defined in terms of stream functions, and for building programs we will need many more types than just the stream type. So we need to generalize causality to work at other types such as streams of streams, or even higher-order functions.

Furthermore, it is very common in reactive programming to define streams by feedback and recursion, such as in the following definition of the increasing sequence of naturals:

$$\mathsf{nats} = \mu(\lambda xs.\ 0 :: \mathsf{map\ succ}\ xs)$$

Intuitively, this fixed point is well-defined because the lambda-term can produce the first value of its output (that is, 0) before looking at its input. So we can imagine constructing the fixed point via a feedback process, in which we take the n-the output and feed it back to as the input at time $n+1$. So as long as we can generate *more* than n outputs from the first n inputs, we can find a fixed point.

Definitition 2. *(Guardedness) A function $f : A^\omega \to B^\omega$ is* guarded, *when there exists a $k > 0$ such that for all n and all streams as and as', we have*

$$\lfloor as \rfloor_n = \lfloor as' \rfloor_n \implies \lfloor f\ as \rfloor_{n+k} = \lfloor f\ as' \rfloor_{n+k}$$

Lemma 1. *(Fixed Points of Guarded Functions) Every guarded endofunction $g : A^\omega \to A^\omega$ has a unique fixed point.*

Just as with causality, the generalization to higher types seems both useful and unobvious. For example, we may which to define a recursive function to generate the Fibonacci numbers:

$$\mathsf{fib} = \mu(\lambda f.\ \lambda(j,k).\ j :: f(k, j+k))$$

The above definition of fib seems intuitively plausible, but goes beyond the stream-based definition of guardedness, since it involves taking a fixed point at function type.

To systematically answer these questions, we make use of the mathematics of metric spaces.

4.2 1-Bounded Complete Ultrametric Spaces

Definitition 3. *(Complete 1-bounded Ultrametric Spaces)* A complete 1-bounded ultrametric space *is a pair (X, d_X), where X is a set and $d_X \in X \times X \to [0,1]$ is a distance function, satisfying the following axioms:*

- $d_X(x,y) = 0$ *if and only if* $x = y$
- $d_X(x,y) = d_X(y,x)$
- $d_X(x,y) \leq \max(d_X(x,z), d_X(z,y))$
- *Every Cauchy sequence in X has a limit*

A sequence $\langle x_i \rangle$ is Cauchy if for any $\epsilon \in [0,1]$, there is an n such that for all $i > n$, $j > n$, $d(x_i, x_j) \leq \epsilon$. A limit is an x such that for all ϵ, there is an n such that for all $i > n$, $d(x, x_i) \leq \epsilon$.

The first three conditions axiomatize the properties of 1-bounded distance functions — that the distance between a point and itself is zero; that distances are symmetric, and the triangle inequality. Ultrametric spaces satisfy a stronger version of the triangle inequality than ordinary metric spaces, which only ask that $d(x,y)$ be less than or equal to $d_X(x,z) + d_X(z,y)$, rather than $\max(d_X(x,y), d_X(y,x'))$. We often just write X for (X, d_X). All the metric spaces we consider are *bisected*, meaning that the distance between any two points is 2^{-n} for some $n \in \mathbb{N}$.

We will often simply write X for a metric space, and d_X for its corresponding metric (or even d, if the expression is unambiguous).

Definitition 4. *(Nonexpansive maps) A function $f : X \to Y$ is* nonexpansive *when for all $a, a' \in X$, we have $d_Y(f\ a, f\ a') \leq d_X(a, a')$.*

Complete 1-bounded ultrametric spaces and nonexpansive maps form a category (which we will write Ult). The category Ult is bicartesian closed (ie, has sums, products and exponentials), and supports a number of other functors on it which we will use in our semantics. (Our semantics will only use nonempty spaces, even though we will perform our semantic constructions in the full category.)

1. Any set X (such as the natural numbers $\mathbb{N}$) forms a metric space under the discrete metric (i.e., $d(x,y) = 0$ if $x = y$, and 1 otherwise).
2. If (X, d_X) is an object of Ult, we can form causal streams $S(X)$ of the elements as follows:
   - $S(X) = (\{as \mid as \in \mathbb{N} \to X\}, d_{S(X)})$, where
   - $d_{S(X)}(xs, ys) = \sup\left\{2^{-n} \times d_X(xs_n, ys_n) \mid n \in N\right\}$

The intuition behind the stream metric is best conveyed by thinking of $S(\mathbb{N})$, the streams of natural numbers (a discrete space). In this case, the distance between two streams xs and ys is 2^{-n}, where n is the first position at which they disagree. So if xs and ys disagree immediately, at time 0, then their distance is 1. If they disagree at time 32, then their distance is 2^{-32}. If they never disagree, then their distance is $2^{-\infty} = 0$ — that is, they are the same stream.

It is a matter of unwinding definitions to establish that a non-expansive map $S(X) \to S(Y)$ (for discrete spaces X and Y) is equivalent to the definition of *causality* — that the first k outputs are determined by at most the first k inputs. In this sense, ultrametric spaces give a natural setting in which to interpret higher-order reactive programs [17], since we can interpret functions with the Cartesian closure and streams of arbitrary type with the stream functor, and nevertheless we can still rule out the definition of non-causal functions.

3. If (A, d_A) and (B, d_B) are objects of Ult, we have a Cartesian product
   - $(A, d_A) \times (B, d_B) \equiv (A \times B, d_{A\times B})$, where
   - $d_{A\times B}((a, b), (a', b')) = \max(d_A(a, a'), d_B(b, b'))$

   The elements of the product space are pairs of elements of the two underlying spaces, and the distance between two pairs is the maximum of the distances between the individual components.

4. If (A, d_A) and (B, d_B) are objects of Ult, we have an exponential defined as follows:
   - $(A, d_A) \Rightarrow (B, d_B) \equiv (\mathrm{Ult}(A, B), d_{A\Rightarrow B})$, where
   - $d_{A\Rightarrow B}(f, g) = \max\{d_B(f\ a, g\ a) \mid a \in A\}$

   The set of points for the function space is the set of nonexpansive functions from A to B (i.e., the hom-set for A and B), and the distance between two functions is the maximum distance between the results ranging over all arguments a. Intuitively, a function can be thought of as an A-indexed tuple of B's, and so the metric for the function space can be seen as a generalization of the metric for tuples.

5. If (A, d_A) and (B, d_B) are objects of Ult, we have a coproduct defined as follows:
   - $(A, d_A) + (B, d_B) \equiv (A + B, d_{A+B})$, where
   - $d_{A+B}(x, y) = \begin{cases} d_A(a, a') & \text{if } x = \mathsf{inl}(a), y = \mathsf{inl}(a') \\ d_B(b, b') & \text{if } x = \mathsf{inr}(b), y = \mathsf{inr}(b') \\ 1 & \text{otherwise} \end{cases}$

   The presence of coproducts in our semantic model means that it is possible to implement FRP-style "switching combinators" simply by performing a case analysis and returning different stream results, in the ordinary style of functional programming. (For space reasons, we did not include rules for sums in our calculus, though they can be added in the standard way.)

6. For each metric space, there is a contraction $\bullet(X)$ (pronounced "next-X") defined as follows:
   - $\bullet(X, d) = (X, d')$, where
   - $d'_{\bullet(X)}(a, a') = \frac{1}{2} d_X(a, a')$

   This functor is Cartesian closed. That is, there are isomorphisms $zip_\bullet : \bullet X \times \bullet Y \simeq \bullet(X \times Y)$ and $\epsilon : \bullet(X \Rightarrow Y) \simeq \bullet X \Rightarrow \bullet Y$.

   The $zip_\bullet$ isomorphism says that a delayed pair is the same as a pair of delayed values. A little more surprisingly, the ϵ isomorphism says that a delayed function is equivalent to a function which takes a delayed argument and returns a delayed result. These maps are all just the identity on points; the real content lies in the fact that these maps are nonexpansive. We will write ϵ for the left-to-right direction of the isomorphism, and write ϵ^{-1} for the right-to-left direction, and similarly for the other isomorphisms we make use of.

   We can also iterate these constructions, and will write ϵ_i for the isomorphism of type $\bullet^i(X \Rightarrow Y) \simeq \bullet^i X \Rightarrow \bullet^i Y$ (and again, similarly for the other isomorphisms). We give the explicit definitions of these isomorphisms in Figure 6.

   In addition, we have a natural transformation $\delta_X : X \to \bullet X$ (pronounced "delay") which embeds each space X into $\bullet X$ via the identity on points. Intuitively, this corresponds to taking a value and delaying using it until the tick of the clock.

   Theorem 1. *(Banach's Contraction Map Theorem) If $A \in$ Ult is a nonempty metric space, and $f : A \to A$ is a strictly contractive function, then f has a unique fixed point.*

   The utility of the delay functor is that it lets us concisely state Banach's contraction map theorem for any nonempty, bisected metric space X: Banach's theorem is equivalent (as our definable types are all nonempty) to the assertion that there is a fixed point operator $\mathit{fix} : (\bullet X \Rightarrow X) \to X$.

7. If X is an object of M, then we can construct the power space $\mathcal{P}_C(X)$ of its closed, nonempty subsets (a subset $S \subseteq X$ is closed if every Cauchy sequence of elements in S has a limit also in S):
   - $\mathcal{P}_C(X) = \{U \subseteq X \mid U \text{ is closed and nonempty}\}$
   - $d_{\mathcal{P}_C(X)}(U, V) = \max\begin{pmatrix} \sup_{x\in U} \inf_{y\in V} d_X(x, y), \\ \sup_{y\in V} \inf_{x\in U} d_X(x, y)) \end{pmatrix}$

   The metric $d_{\mathcal{P}_C X}$ is known as the *Hausdorff metric*. The functorial action of $\mathcal{P}_C(f) : \mathcal{P}_C(X) \to \mathcal{P}_C(Y)$ applies f pointwise to the elements of its argument, and takes the metric closure of that image. Explicitly, $\mathcal{P}_C(f) = \lambda X.\ \mathsf{cl}(\{f(x) \mid x \in X\})$.

   The functor $\mathcal{P}_C(-)$ gives rise to a strong, commutative monad [25]. We will write $\eta_X : X \to \mathcal{P}_C(X)$ and $\mu_X : \mathcal{P}^2_C(X) \to \mathcal{P}_C(X)$ for its unit and multiplication, and $\sigma_X : X \times \mathcal{P}_C(Y) \to \mathcal{P}_C(X \times Y)$ for its strength. Explicitly, the definition of the unit is $\eta(x) = \{x\}$, and the multiplication is $\mu(U) = \mathsf{cl}(\bigcup U)$.

   Furthermore, the contraction functor distributes over the powerspace; we have an isomorphism $\mathcal{P}^\bullet_C : \bullet\mathcal{P}_C(X) \simeq \mathcal{P}_C(\bullet\ X)$. (Again, this isomorphism is the identity on points, and following the pattern of Figure 6 we can iterate it to construct $\mathcal{P}^{\bullet i}_C : \bullet^i \mathcal{P}_C(X) \simeq \mathcal{P}_C(\bullet^i\ X)$.)

8. To interpret the Window type, we first take Pic to be the set of trees inductively generated from the following grammar (with s ranging over strings):

   $$p \quad ::= \quad \mathsf{Button}(s) \mid \mathsf{Label}(s) \mid \mathsf{Vert}(p, p) \mid \mathsf{Hor}(p, p)$$

   We turn this into a space by equipping it with the discrete metric, and then take Window to be streams of Pic.

4.3 The Eilenberg-Moore Category of $\mathcal{P}_C$

From Ult, we can construct its Eilenberg-Moore category $\mathrm{Ult}^{\mathcal{P}}$, whose objects are algebras $(A, \alpha : \mathcal{P}_C(A) \to A)$, where A is a nonempty 1-bounded ultrametric space, and α satisfies $\alpha \circ \mathcal{P}_C(\alpha) = \alpha \circ \mu$ and $\alpha \circ \eta = id_A$.

The morphisms from (A, α) to (B, β) are maps $A \to B$ in the category of ultrametric spaces which commute with the action (so that $f \circ \alpha = \beta \circ \mathcal{P}_C(f)$). Identity and composition are inherited from the underlying category Ult. (As a notational aid to keeping the categories distinct, we will use functional composition $f \circ g$

$$
\begin{array}{lcl}
zip^i_\bullet & : & \bullet^i(X) \times \bullet^i(Y) \to \bullet^i(X \times Y) \\
zip^0_\bullet & = & id_{X \times Y} \\
zip^{n+1}_\bullet & = & zip_\bullet \circ \bullet(zip^n_\bullet)
\end{array}
$$

$$
\begin{array}{lcl}
zip^i_\bullet & : & \bullet^i(X) \times \bullet^i(Y) \to \bullet^i(X \times Y) \\
zip^0_\bullet & = & id_{X \times Y} \\
zip^{n+1}_\bullet & = & \bullet(zip^n_\bullet) \circ zip_\bullet
\end{array}
$$

$$
\begin{array}{lcl}
\epsilon_i & : & \bullet^i(X \Rightarrow Y) \to \bullet^i(X) \Rightarrow \bullet^i(Y) \\
\epsilon_0 & = & id_{X \to Y} \\
\epsilon_{n+1} & = & \epsilon \circ \bullet(\epsilon_n)
\end{array}
$$

$$
\begin{array}{lcl}
\epsilon^{-1}_i & : & \bullet^i(X) \Rightarrow \bullet^i(Y) \to \bullet^i(X \Rightarrow Y) \\
\epsilon^{-1}_0 & = & id_{X \Rightarrow Y} \\
\epsilon^{-1}_{n+1} & = & \bullet(\epsilon_n) \circ \epsilon^{-1}
\end{array}
$$

$$
\begin{array}{lcl}
\delta_i & : & A \to \bullet^i(X) \\
\delta_0 & = & id_A \\
\delta_{n+1} & = & \delta \circ \delta_n
\end{array}
$$

Figure 6. Definition of Iterated Morphisms

when composing maps in Ult, and diagrammatic order $f; g$ when composing maps in $\text{Ult}^{\mathcal{P}}$.)

Because $\mathcal{P}_C$ is a commutative strong monad, Ult has equalizers and coequalizers [22], and $\text{Ult}^{\mathcal{P}}$ has coequalizers of reflexive pairs (since $\mathcal{P}_C$ preserves coequalizers of reflexive pairs), $\text{Ult}^{\mathcal{P}}$ is symmetric monoidal closed [2, 14, 16]. The tensor product is defined using a coequalizer and the exponential by an equalizer.

We can lift the distribution of the next modality through tensor products $\widehat{zip}_\bullet : \bullet A \otimes \bullet B \simeq \bullet(A \otimes B)$ and the monoidal exponential $\hat{\epsilon} : \bullet(A \multimap B) \simeq \bullet A \multimap \bullet B$, as well as the delay operator $\hat{\delta} : A \to \bullet A$. These operations simply inherit their structure from Ult, but for the operations to respect the algebra structure we need the isomorphism $\mathcal{P}^\bullet_C : \bullet\mathcal{P}_C(X) \simeq \mathcal{P}_C(\bullet\ X)$. This explains why we restricted $\mathcal{P}_C(X)$ to *nonempty* closed subsets of interpretation X — one leg of this isomorphism would fail to be nonexpansive in the presence of the empty set, which is distance 1 from any other subset.

We also iterate all of these morphisms following the pattern of Figure 6.

The free $F(X) = (\mathcal{P}_C(X), \mu)$ and forgetful $G(A, \alpha) = A$ functors give rise to an adjunction between Ult and $\text{Ult}^{\mathcal{P}}$, whose unit and counit we write $\eta_X : X \to G(F(X))$ and $\varepsilon_A : F(G(A, \alpha)) \to A$. The action of η as the unit of this adjunction is the same natural transformation as the unit of the monad $\mathcal{P}_C$, so no notational confusion can arise. The components of the counit ε are the algebra maps α of (A, α). This is a monoidal adjunction with a natural isomorphism $m : F(X) \otimes F(Y) \simeq F(X \times Y)$. This isomorphism lets us duplicate and discard F-typed values; we have maps $drop : F(X) \to \text{I}$ and $dup : F(X) \to F(X) \otimes F(X)$.

4.4 Interpretation of the Programming Language

In Figure 7, we give the interpretation of the syntactic types in terms of metric spaces. The interpretation follows the categorical constructions – in each category, products go to products, exponentials go to exponentials, and the F and G adjunctions interpret the modal operators connecting the *F*unctional and *G*raphical sub-languages.

In Figure 8, we give the semantic interpretation of the syntax of our language. A context $\Gamma = x :_i X, \ldots, z :_k Z$ is interpreted as a product $\bullet^i\llbracket X \rrbracket \times \ldots \bullet^k \llbracket Z \rrbracket$, and a term-in-context $\Gamma \vdash e :_i X$ is interpreted as a morphism $\llbracket \Gamma \rrbracket \to \bullet^i\llbracket X \rrbracket$. A context $\Delta = a :_i A, \ldots, b :_j B$ is interpreted by the tensor product $\bullet^i\llbracket A \rrbracket \otimes \ldots \bullet^j \llbracket B \rrbracket$. The pair of contexts $\Gamma; \Delta$ is interpreted by $F(\llbracket \Gamma \rrbracket) \otimes \llbracket \Delta \rrbracket$, and a linear term $\Gamma; \Delta \vdash t :_i A$ is interpreted as a morphism $F(\llbracket \Gamma \rrbracket) \otimes \llbracket \Delta \rrbracket \to \bullet^i\llbracket A \rrbracket$ in $\text{Ult}^{\mathcal{P}}$.

As an abuse of notation, we abbreviate $\llbracket \Gamma \vdash e :_i X \rrbracket$ as $\llbracket e \rrbracket$ when Γ, X and i are clear from context, and similarly we abbreviate $\llbracket \Gamma; \Delta \vdash t :_i A \rrbracket$ as $\llbracket t \rrbracket$.

Our semantics combines the interpretation of adjoint logic given in [1] with the guarded calculus given by Krishnaswami and Benton [17]. The main technical subtlety arose with the interpretation of the time indices. Concretely, consider the interpretation of $\Gamma \vdash G(t) :_i G(A)$, which we expect to be a map $\llbracket \Gamma \rrbracket \to \bullet^i\llbracket G(A) \rrbracket$, and contrast it with its subderivation $\Gamma; \cdot \vdash t :_i A$, whose interpretation (viewed as a map in Ult) is in $\llbracket \Gamma \rrbracket \to G(\bullet^i(A))$. To swap these constructors, we use the $\mathcal{P}^\bullet_C : \bullet\mathcal{P}_C(X) \simeq \mathcal{P}_C(\bullet\ X)$ isomorphism.

For readability, the semantics suppresses the associativity and commutativity maps needed to permute the context.

Theorem 2. *(Soundness of Substitution) Suppose $\Gamma \vdash e :_i X$ and $\Gamma; \Delta \vdash t :_i A$, and $i \leq j$. Then:*

- *If $\Gamma, x :_j X \vdash e' :_k Y$, then $\llbracket e' \rrbracket \circ \langle \Gamma, \delta^{j-i}_X \circ \llbracket e \rrbracket \rangle = \llbracket [e/x]e' \rrbracket$.*
- *If $\Gamma, x :_j X; \Delta \vdash t' :_k B$, then $F(\langle \Gamma, \delta^{j-i}_X \circ \llbracket e \rrbracket \rangle); \llbracket t \rrbracket = \llbracket [e/x]t' \rrbracket$.*
- *If $\Gamma; \Delta', a :_j A \vdash t' :_k B$, then $dup_{F(\Gamma)}; (F(\Gamma) \otimes \Delta' \otimes \llbracket t \rrbracket); \llbracket t' \rrbracket = \llbracket [t/a]t' \rrbracket$.*

Proof. The proof is a routine induction. □

Theorem 3. *(Soundness of Equality Rules) For well-typed terms, the equational rules in Figure 2 are sound with respect to the denotational semantics.*

Proof. The proof is a routine verification. □

4.5 Denotational Semantics of GUI Operations

We have left out the constructors from the syntax to keep from cluttering the proof theory. We give the semantics of a representative collection of GUI operations (including all of the ones used in the calculator example) below:

$$
\begin{array}{lcl}
\mathsf{label} & : & F(S(\mathsf{string})) \to \mathsf{Window} \\
\mathsf{label}\ X & = & \{\lambda n.\ \mathsf{Label}(xs_n) \mid xs \in X\} \\
\\
\mathsf{vstack} & : & \mathsf{Window} \otimes \mathsf{Window} \to \mathsf{Window} \\
\mathsf{vstack}(W, W') & = & \mathsf{cl}(\{\lambda n.\ \mathsf{Vert}(w_n, w'_n) \mid w \in W, w' \in W'\}) \\
\\
\mathsf{hstack} & : & \mathsf{Window} \otimes \mathsf{Window} \to \mathsf{Window} \\
\mathsf{hstack}(W, W') & = & \mathsf{cl}(\{\lambda n.\ \mathsf{Hor}(w_n, w'_n) \mid w \in W, w' \in W'\}) \\
\\
\mathsf{button} & : & F(S(\mathsf{string})) \to \mathsf{Window} \otimes F(S(\mathsf{bool})) \\
\mathsf{button}\ X & = & (\{\lambda n.\ \mathsf{Button}(xs_n) \mid xs \in X\}, S(\mathsf{bool})) \\
\\
\mathsf{delete} & : & \mathsf{Window} \to I \\
\mathsf{delete}\ W & = & ()
\end{array}
$$

Since the free functor F yields sets of possible values, we must define these constants so that they define appropriate outputs for all their possible inputs. The first label operation essentially just maps an operator over its input, and the two stacking operations take a Cartesian product to define the result for each pair of possibilities.

On the other hand, the button operation, which is an operation representing user input, does something a little more interesting. It returns a set of pairs of window values (constructed by mapping its input over the Button constructor), and a set of streams of booleans (denoting clicks). We define the windows values by mapping over the input, as with the other operations, but we return the full space of boolean streams as its second argument.

$$
\begin{array}{lcl}
1 & = & 1 \\
[\![X \times Y]\!] & = & [\![X]\!] \times [\![Y]\!] \\
[\![X \Rightarrow Y]\!] & = & [\![X]\!] \Rightarrow [\![Y]\!] \\
[\![S(X)]\!] & = & S([\![A]\!]) \\
[\![\bullet(X)]\!] & = & \bullet[\![X]\!] \\
[\![G(A)]\!] & = & G([\![A]\!]) \\
 & & \\
[\![I]\!] & = & 1 \\
[\![A \otimes B]\!] & = & [\![A]\!] \otimes [\![B]\!] \\
[\![A \multimap B]\!] & = & [\![A]\!] \multimap [\![B]\!] \\
[\![F(X)]\!] & = & F([\![X]\!]) \\
[\![\mathsf{Window}]\!] & = & F(S(\mathrm{Pic})) \\
 & & \\
F(X) & = & (\mathcal{P}_C(X), \mu) \\
G(A, \alpha) & = & A
\end{array}
$$

Figure 7. Interpretation of Types

Therefore, if we receive a fixed stream of string inputs xs, we may receive *any* stream of clicks as a possible return value. So the semantics of button captures the inherent nondeterminism of user actions in a simple way — we simply say that the user can click a button whenever he or she likes, and our semantics has to account for all of these possibilities.

Finally, the delete operation simply throws away its argument. Using the semantics of this command, it is possible to prove program equalities such as the following:

```
let (F(x), v) = button() in |  let (F(y), w) = button()
let (F(y), w) = button() in |  in w
let () = delete v           |
in w                        |
```

In this program, we create two buttons and throw the first of them away, which is equivalent to not creating it at all. The proof follows as easily from the semantics of programs as it ought.

One fact worth noting is that our semantics does not rule out the possibility of two different buttons both yielding a click event (ie, returning true) on the same time step. We see essentially two possibilities for ruling out such behavior, both of which we rejected for this work.

If we wish to retain a high-level semantics, where we specify the semantics of the API in terms of events like clicks, rather than primitive events such as mouse movements and keystrokes, then positing a collection of constraints (such as "two buttons are never simultaneously clicked") seems to require explicitly modeling a store of input channels and maintaining these constraints as an invariant on the store. This is a bit ugly, and more than a little technically complicated.

A better approach, in our view, would be to model layout and event synthesis explicitly. In our semantics, we model the display as a time-varying tree, much like an HTML document. If the display model actually specified what the graphic layout of a GUI program was, and supplied the primitive mouse movements, keystrokes, and clicks as an input, then the semantics could explicitly give the functions explaining how to interpret primitive events as high-level ones — for example, we might define a "click" to occur when the mouse is pressed down inside the button area, and subsequently released, while still inside the button area.

We think this level of precision is likely the right approach to take when building new GUI toolkits. However, if we wish to bind to existing toolkits, it is better to give a semantics imprecise enough to tolerate wide variation in precisely how it is implemented.

$$
\begin{array}{lcl}
[\![\Gamma \vdash \bullet e :_i \bullet A]\!] & = & [\![e]\!] \\
[\![\Gamma \vdash \mathsf{cons}(e, e') :_i S(A)]\!] & = & \bullet^i(cons) \circ zip^i_\bullet \circ \langle [\![e]\!], [\![e']\!] \rangle \\
[\![\Gamma \vdash \lambda x.\, e :_i A \to B]\!] & = & \epsilon^i \circ \lambda([\![\Gamma, x :_i A \vdash e :_i B]\!]) \\
[\![\Gamma \vdash x_n :_j A]\!] & = & \delta_A^{j-i} \circ \pi_n, \text{if } x_n :_i A \in \Gamma \\
[\![\Gamma \vdash \mathsf{await}(e) :_{i+1} A]\!] & = & [\![e]\!] \\
[\![\Gamma \vdash \mathsf{head}\ e :_i A]\!] & = & \bullet^i(hd) \circ [\![t]\!] \\
[\![\Gamma \vdash \mathsf{tail}\ e :_{i+1} S(A)]\!] & = & \bullet^i(tl) \circ [\![t]\!] \\
[\![\Gamma \vdash e\, e' :_i B]\!] & = & \bullet^i(eval) \circ zip^i_\bullet \circ \langle [\![e]\!], [\![e']\!] \rangle \\
[\![\Gamma \vdash G(t) :_i G(A)]\!] & = & \mathcal{P}_C^{\bullet i} \circ G([\![t]\!]) \circ \eta_\Gamma \\
[\![\Gamma \vdash \mathsf{fix}\ x : A.\, e :_i A]\!] & = & \bullet^i(\mathit{fix}_A) \circ \epsilon^i \circ \lambda([\![e]\!]) \\
 & & \\
[\![\Gamma; a :_i A \vdash a :_j A]\!] & = & drop; \hat{\delta}_{j-i} \\
[\![\Gamma; \cdot \vdash () :_i \mathrm{I}]\!] & = & drop; \hat{\delta}_i \\
[\![\Gamma; \Delta, \Delta' \vdash \mathsf{let}\ () = t\ \mathsf{in}\ t' :_i B]\!] & = & dup_{F(\Gamma)} \otimes \Delta \otimes \Delta'; [\![t]\!]; [\![t']\!] \\
[\![\Gamma; \Delta, \Delta' \vdash (t, t') :_i A \otimes B]\!] & = & dup_{F(\Gamma)} \otimes \Delta \otimes \Delta'; \\
 & & ([\![t]\!] \otimes [\![t']\!]); \widehat{zip}^i_\bullet \\
[\![\Gamma; \Delta, \Delta' \vdash \mathsf{let}\ (a, b) = t\ \mathsf{in}\ t' :_i C]\!] & = & dup_{F(\Gamma)} \otimes \Delta \otimes \Delta'; \\
 & & (F(\Gamma) \otimes \Delta' \otimes [\![t]\!]); [\![t']\!] \\
[\![\Gamma; \Delta \vdash \lambda a.\, t :_i A \multimap B]\!] & = & \lambda([\![\Gamma; \Delta, a :_i A \vdash t :_i B]\!]); \hat{\epsilon}^i \\
[\![\Gamma; \Delta, \Delta' \vdash t\, t' :_i B]\!] & = & dup_{F(\Gamma)} \otimes \Delta \otimes \Delta'; \\
 & & [\![t]\!] \otimes [\![t']\!]; \widehat{zip}^i_\bullet; eval \\
[\![\Gamma; \cdot \vdash \mathsf{runG}(e) :_i A]\!] & = & F(\mathcal{P}_C^{\bullet i} \circ [\![\Gamma \vdash e :_i G(A)]\!]); \varepsilon \\
[\![\Gamma; \cdot \vdash F(e) :_i F(X)]\!] & = & F([\![e]\!]) \\
[\![\Gamma; \Delta, \Delta' \vdash \mathsf{let}\ F(x) = t\ \mathsf{in}\ t' :_i C]\!] & = & dup_{F(\Gamma)} \otimes \Delta \otimes \Delta'; \\
 & & F(\Gamma) \otimes \Delta' \otimes [\![t]\!]; \\
 & & m \otimes \Delta'; [\![t']\!]
\end{array}
$$

Figure 8. Denotational Interpretation of Terms

5. Proof Theory

We have established denotationally that the β and η equalities are valid, but this does not make clear just how extraordinarily well-behaved this calculus is. We can prove a stratified normalization result, despite the fact that this language contains a recursion operator of the form $\mathsf{fix}\ x : A.\ e$.

To state the normalization theorem precisely, we must first say what the normal forms are. To see that this is not an entirely trivial question, consider the term $e \triangleq \mathsf{fix}\ xs : S(\mathbb{N}).\ \mathsf{cons}(0, x)$. The term e is equivalent to $\mathsf{cons}(0, e)$, and to $\mathsf{cons}(0, \mathsf{cons}(0, e))$ and so on for infinitely many unfoldings. So we have to ask, which of these unfoldings count as normal forms, and which do not?

In Figure 9, we give normal and atomic forms of the calculus. The normal and atomic forms are a sub-syntax of the full language with the property that only beta-normal terms are grammatically valid. In this syntax, we count fixed points as atomic forms, which means we still need to fix a policy for when to allow fixed points, and when not.

Next, we introduce the idea of a n-normal form, which are normal forms in which fixed point subterms $\mathsf{fix}\ x : A.\ e$ only occur at times of n or greater. So $e \triangleq \mathsf{fix}\ xs : S(\mathbb{N}).\ \mathsf{cons}(0, x)$ is itself a 0-normal form, and $\mathsf{cons}(0, e)$ is a 1-normal form, and $\mathsf{cons}(0, \mathsf{cons}(0, e))$ is a 2-normal form, and so on. To specify n-normal forms, we use the judgments $\Gamma \vdash_n e :_i X$ and $\Gamma; \Delta \vdash_n t :_i A$. These typing rules exactly mirror the existing typing rules, with the exception of the UFIX' rule (given in Figure 9), where we add a side-condition that a fixed point is permitted only when the time index i at which it is typechecked is at least as large as n. Hence an n-normal form is a normal form which passes the n-restricted typechecking rule for fixed points.

So our example $e \triangleq \mathsf{fix}\ xs : S(\mathbb{N}).\ \mathsf{cons}(0, x)$ is a 0-normal form but not a 1-normal form, since it has no redexes, but does have a fixed point at time 0. However, its unfolding $\mathsf{cons}(0, e)$ is a 1-normal form, since e occurs in the tail position of a cons, which is checked at a time index 1 greater than the cons expression.

Now, we can show that every term has a normal form (i.e., a weak normalization result) in the following manner. Given two n-normal terms, we can define a *hereditary substitution* [27] which combines substitution and computing a normal form. For our type system, an appropriate functions are given in Figures 10, 11, and 12.

In each of these figures, we define two of six mutually recursive procedures, one substituting a normal form into a normal form, and the other substituting a normal form into a atomic term. The normal-normal substitution returns a new normal form, and the normal-atomic substitution returns a pair of a term and optionally a type. If the result of the substitution is still an atomic term, then no type is returned, and if it is a normal form, the type of the substitutand is returned. Below, we write $A \sqsubseteq X$ to say that the type A is a subterm of the type X.

Theorem 4. *(Hereditary Substitution) Suppose* $\Gamma \vdash_n \hat{e} :_i X$ *and* $\Gamma; \Delta \vdash_n \hat{t} :_i A$ *and* $i \leq j$. *Then*

- *If* $\Gamma, x :_j X \vdash_n \hat{e}' :_k Y$ *then* $\Gamma \vdash_n \langle \hat{e}/x \rangle_X \hat{e}' :_k Y$
- *If* $\Gamma, x :_j X; \Delta \vdash_n \hat{t}' :_k B$ *then* $\Gamma; \Delta \vdash_n \langle \hat{e}/x \rangle_X \hat{t}' :_k B$
- *If* $\Gamma; \Delta', a :_j A \vdash_n \hat{t}' :_k B$ *then* $\Gamma; \Delta, \Delta' \vdash_n \langle \hat{t}/a \rangle_A \hat{t}' :_k B$
- *If* $\Gamma, x :_j X \vdash_n g :_k Y$ *then either*
  - $\langle \hat{e}/x \rangle_X g = (\hat{e}', Y)$ *and* $Y \sqsubseteq X$ *and* $\Gamma \vdash_n \hat{e}' :_k Y$
  - *or* $\langle \hat{e}/x \rangle_X g = (g', \mathsf{n/a})$ *and* $\Gamma \vdash_n g' :_k Y$
- *If* $\Gamma, x :_j X; \Delta \vdash_n u :_k B$ *then either*
  - $\langle \hat{e}/x \rangle_X u = (\hat{t}', B)$ *and* $B \sqsubseteq X$ *and* $\Gamma; \Delta \vdash_n \hat{t}' :_k B$
  - *or* $\langle \hat{e}/x \rangle_X u = (u', \mathsf{n/a})$ *and* $\Gamma; \Delta \vdash_n u' :_k B$
- *If* $\Gamma; \Delta', a :_j A \vdash_n u :_k B$ *then either*
  - $\langle \hat{t}/a \rangle_A u = (\hat{t}', B)$ *and* $B \sqsubseteq A$ *and* $\Gamma; \Delta, \Delta' \vdash_n \hat{t}' :_k B$
  - *or* $\langle \hat{t}/a \rangle_A u = (u', \mathsf{n/a})$ *and* $\Gamma; \Delta, \Delta' \vdash_n u' :_k B$

Furthermore, hereditary substitution is $\beta\eta$*-equivalent to ordinary substitution.*

The statement of the theorem is a bit complicated, since we have 6 cases, depending on which judgement and context we are substituting into, and whether we are substituting into a normal or atomic form. Luckily, the induction is straightforward, and the algorithm offers no surprises. The induction is lexicographically on the type of the term being substituted, together with the unordered product of the sizes of the two derivations of the substitutand and subtitutee.

Note that hereditary substitution never needs to unroll fixed points. By hypothesis, neither the substitutee nor the substitutand contain fixed point terms at an index less than n, and as a result, the process of substitution and normalization will never create a fixed point at the head of a term at time less than n.

As a result, we can prove an unrolling lemma separately, *without* any mutual recursion with the normalization algorithm. In Figure 13, we define an unfolding operation $\lceil e \rceil$ which unrolls all the fixed points in a term by one step, and prove the following theorem:

Theorem 5. *(Unrolling)*

- *If* $\Gamma \vdash_n e :_i X$, *then* $\Gamma \vdash_{n+1} \lceil e \rceil :_i X$
- *If* $\Gamma; \Delta \vdash_n t :_i X$, *then* $\Gamma; \Delta \vdash_{n+1} \lceil t \rceil :_i X$

Proof. The result follows by a routine induction on the derivation. □

Now we can combine these two theorems to prove a normalization theorem.

Theorem 6. *(Weak Normalization)*

- *Suppose* $\Gamma \vdash e :_i X$. *Then for any* m, *there is an* m*-normal form* e', *such that* $\Gamma \vdash_m e' :_i X$, *which is* $\beta\eta$*-equivalent to* e.

$$
\begin{array}{llcl}
\text{Normal Nonlinear} & \hat{e} & ::= & () \mid (\hat{e}, \hat{e}') \mid \lambda x.\, \hat{e} \\
 & & \mid & \mathsf{cons}(\hat{e}, \hat{e}') \mid G(\hat{t}) \mid \bullet(\hat{e}) \mid g \\
\text{Atomic Nonlinear} & g & ::= & x \mid g\ \hat{e} \mid \mathsf{fst}\ g \mid \mathsf{snd}\ g \mid \mathsf{await}(g) \\
 & & \mid & \mathsf{head}\ g \mid \mathsf{tail}\ g \mid \mathsf{fix}\ x : X.\, \hat{e} \\
\text{Normal Linear} & \hat{t} & ::= & () \mid (\hat{t}, \hat{t}') \mid \lambda x.\, \hat{t} \\
 & & \mid & \mathsf{let}\ () = u\ \mathsf{in}\ \hat{t} \mid \mathsf{let}\ (a, b) = u\ \mathsf{in}\ \hat{t} \\
 & & \mid & F(\hat{e}) \mid \mathsf{let}\ F(x) = u\ \mathsf{in}\ \hat{t} \mid u \\
\text{Atomic Linear} & u & ::= & a \mid u\ \hat{t} \mid \mathsf{runG}(g)
\end{array}
$$

$$\boxed{\Gamma \vdash_n e :_i X} \qquad \boxed{\Gamma; \Delta \vdash_n t :_i A}$$

$$\frac{\Gamma, x :_{i+1} X \vdash_n e :_i X \qquad i \geq n}{\Gamma \vdash_n \mathsf{fix}\ x : A.\, e :_i X}\ \text{UFIX'}$$

(all other rules unchanged except for the appearance of n)

Figure 9. Normal and Atomic Forms, and Leveled Fixed Points

$$
\begin{array}{lcl}
\langle \hat{e}/x \rangle_X\, () & = & () \\
\langle \hat{e}/x \rangle_X\, (\hat{e}', \hat{e}'') & = & (\langle \hat{e}/x \rangle_X\, \hat{e}', \langle \hat{e}/x \rangle_X\, \hat{e}'') \\
\langle \hat{e}/x \rangle_X\, \lambda y.\, \hat{e}' & = & \lambda y.\, \langle \hat{e}/x \rangle_X\, \hat{e}' \\
\langle \hat{e}/x \rangle_X\, \bullet\hat{e}' & = & \bullet(\langle \hat{e}/x \rangle_X\, \hat{e}') \\
\langle \hat{e}/x \rangle_X\, \mathsf{cons}(\hat{e}', \hat{e}'') & = & \mathsf{cons}(\langle \hat{e}/x \rangle_X\, \hat{e}', \langle \hat{e}/x \rangle_X\, \hat{e}'') \\
\langle \hat{e}/x \rangle_X\, G(t) & = & G(\langle \hat{e}/x \rangle_X\, t) \\
\langle \hat{e}/x \rangle_X\, g & = & \begin{cases} g' & \text{when } \langle \hat{e}/x \rangle_X\, g = (g', \mathsf{n/a}) \\ \hat{e}' & \text{when } \langle \hat{e}/x \rangle_X\, g = (\hat{e}', Y) \end{cases}
\end{array}
$$

$$
\begin{array}{lcl}
\langle \hat{e}/x \rangle_X\, x & = & (x, X) \\
\langle \hat{e}/x \rangle_X\, y & = & (y, \mathsf{n/a}) \\
\langle \hat{e}/x \rangle_X\, \mathsf{fix}\ y : Y.\, \hat{e}' & = & (\mathsf{fix}\ y : Y.\, (\langle \hat{e}/x \rangle_X\, \hat{e}'), Y) \\
\langle \hat{e}/x \rangle_X\, g_1\ \hat{e}_2 & = & \begin{array}{l} \mathsf{let}\ \hat{e}_2' = \langle \hat{e}/x \rangle_X\, \hat{e}_2\ \mathsf{in} \\ \mathsf{case}\ \langle \hat{e}/x \rangle_X\, g\ \mathsf{of} \\ \quad (g', \mathsf{n/a}) \to (g'\ \hat{e}_2', \mathsf{n/a}) \\ \quad (\lambda y.\, \hat{e}_1', Y \Rightarrow Z) \to \langle \hat{e}_2'/y \rangle_Y\, \hat{e}_1' \end{array} \\
\langle \hat{e}/x \rangle_X\, \mathsf{head}\ g & = & \begin{array}{l} \mathsf{case}\ \langle \hat{e}/x \rangle_X\, g\ \mathsf{of} \\ \quad (g', \mathsf{n/a}) \to (\mathsf{head}\ g', \mathsf{n/a}) \\ \quad (\mathsf{cons}(\hat{e}_1, \hat{e}_2), S(Y)) \to (\hat{e}_1, Y) \end{array} \\
\langle \hat{e}/x \rangle_X\, \mathsf{tail}\ g & = & \begin{array}{l} \mathsf{case}\ \langle \hat{e}/x \rangle_X\, g\ \mathsf{of} \\ \quad (g', \mathsf{n/a}) \to (\mathsf{tail}\ g', \mathsf{n/a}) \\ \quad (\mathsf{cons}(\hat{e}_1, \hat{e}_2), S(Y)) \to (\hat{e}_2, S(Y)) \end{array} \\
\langle \hat{e}/x \rangle_X\, \mathsf{fst}\ g & = & \begin{array}{l} \mathsf{case}\ \langle \hat{e}/x \rangle_X\, g\ \mathsf{of} \\ \quad (g', \mathsf{n/a}) \to (\mathsf{fst}\ g', \mathsf{n/a}) \\ \quad ((\hat{e}_1, \hat{e}_2), Y \times Z) \to (\hat{e}_2, Y) \end{array} \\
\langle \hat{e}/x \rangle_X\, \mathsf{snd}\ g & = & \begin{array}{l} \mathsf{case}\ \langle \hat{e}/x \rangle_X\, g\ \mathsf{of} \\ \quad (g', \mathsf{n/a}) \to (\mathsf{snd}\ g', \mathsf{n/a}) \\ \quad ((\hat{e}_1, \hat{e}_2), Y \times Z) \to (\hat{e}_2, Z) \end{array} \\
\langle \hat{e}/x \rangle_X\, \mathsf{await}(g) & = & \begin{array}{l} \mathsf{case}\ \langle \hat{e}/x \rangle_X\, g\ \mathsf{of} \\ \quad (g', \mathsf{n/a}) \to (\mathsf{await}(g'), \mathsf{n/a}) \\ \quad (\bullet\hat{e}', \bullet Y) \to (\hat{e}', Y) \end{array}
\end{array}
$$

Figure 10. Substituting Nonlinear Terms into Nonlinear Terms

- *Suppose* $\Gamma; \Delta \vdash t :_i A$. *Then for any* n, *there is an* n*-normal form* t', *such that* $\Gamma; \Delta \vdash_n t' :_i A$, *which is* $\beta\eta$*-equivalent to* t.

To prove this, note than any well-typed term satisfies the UFIX' rule for $n = 0$. Hence we can use the unfolding lemma n times to get a term which has no fixed points at times earlier than n. Then we can find a normal form, by inductively walking down the syntax and using hereditary substitution to eliminate reducible expressions.

$$
\begin{array}{lcl}
\langle \hat{e}/x \rangle_X \, () & = & () \\
\langle \hat{e}/x \rangle_X \, (t', t'') & = & (\langle \hat{e}/x \rangle_X \, t', \langle \hat{e}/x \rangle_X \, t'') \\
\langle \hat{e}/x \rangle_X \, \lambda y.\, t' & = & \lambda y.\, \langle \hat{e}/x \rangle_X \, t' \\
\langle \hat{e}/x \rangle_X \, F(\hat{e}') & = & F(\langle \hat{e}/x \rangle_X \, \hat{e}') \\
\langle \hat{e}/x \rangle_X \, \mathsf{let}\ () = u\ \mathsf{in}\ t & = & \begin{array}{l} \mathsf{case}\ \langle \hat{e}/x \rangle_X \, u\ \mathsf{of} \\ \quad (u', \mathsf{n/a}) \rightarrow \mathsf{let}\ () = u'\ \mathsf{in}\ \langle \hat{e}/x \rangle_X \, t \\ \quad ((), I) \quad\ \rightarrow \langle \hat{e}/x \rangle_X \, t \end{array} \\
\langle \hat{e}/x \rangle_X \, \mathsf{let}\ (a,b) = u\ \mathsf{in}\ t & = & \begin{array}{l} \mathsf{case}\ \langle \hat{e}/x \rangle_X \, u\ \mathsf{of} \\ \quad (u', \mathsf{n/a}) \rightarrow \\ \qquad \mathsf{let}\ (x,y) = u'\ \mathsf{in}\ \langle \hat{e}/x \rangle_X \, t \\ \quad ((t_1, t_2), A \otimes B) \rightarrow \\ \qquad \langle t_2/b \rangle_B \, (\langle t_1/a \rangle_A \, (\langle \hat{e}/x \rangle_X \, t)) \end{array} \\
\langle \hat{e}/x \rangle_X \, \mathsf{let}\ F(x) = u\ \mathsf{in}\ t & = & \begin{array}{l} \mathsf{case}\ \langle \hat{e}/x \rangle_X \, u\ \mathsf{of} \\ \quad (u', \mathsf{n/a}) \rightarrow \\ \qquad \mathsf{let}\ () = u'\ \mathsf{in}\ \langle \hat{e}/x \rangle_X \, t \\ \quad (F(\hat{e}'), F(Y)) \rightarrow \\ \qquad \langle \hat{e}'/y \rangle_Y \, (\langle \hat{e}/x \rangle_X \, t) \end{array} \\
\langle \hat{e}/x \rangle_X \, u & = & \left\{ \begin{array}{ll} u' & \text{when } \langle \hat{e}/x \rangle_X \, u = (u', \mathsf{n/a}) \\ t' & \text{when } \langle \hat{e}/x \rangle_X \, u = (t', A) \end{array} \right. \\
\langle \hat{e}/x \rangle_X \, a & = & (a, \mathsf{n/a}) \\
\langle \hat{e}/x \rangle_X \, \mathsf{runG}(g) & = & \begin{array}{l} \mathsf{case}\ \langle \hat{e}/x \rangle_X \, g\ \mathsf{of} \\ \quad (g', \mathsf{n/a}) \qquad \rightarrow (\mathsf{runG}(g'), \mathsf{n/a}) \\ \quad (G(t), G(A)) \rightarrow (t, A) \end{array} \\
\langle \hat{e}/x \rangle_X \, u_1\ t_2 & = & \begin{array}{l} \mathsf{let}\ t_2' = \langle \hat{e}/x \rangle_X \, t_2\ \mathsf{in} \\ \mathsf{case}\ \langle \hat{e}/x \rangle_X \, u_1\ \mathsf{of} \\ \quad (u_1', \mathsf{n/a}) \qquad\quad \rightarrow (u_1'\ \hat{e}_2', \mathsf{n/a}) \\ \quad (\lambda a.\, t_1', A \multimap B) \rightarrow \langle t_2'/a \rangle_A \, t_1' \end{array}
\end{array}
$$

Figure 11. Substituting Nonlinear Terms into Linear Terms

$$
\begin{array}{lcl}
\langle t/a \rangle_A \, () & = & () \\
\langle t/a \rangle_A \, (t', t'') & = & (\langle t/a \rangle_A \, t', \langle t/a \rangle_A \, t'') \\
\langle t/a \rangle_A \, \lambda y.\, t' & = & \lambda y.\, \langle t/a \rangle_A \, t' \\
\langle t/a \rangle_A \, F(\hat{e}') & = & F(\hat{e}') \\
\langle t/a \rangle_A \, \mathsf{let}\ () = u_1\ \mathsf{in}\ t_2 & = & \begin{array}{l} \mathsf{case}\ \langle t/a \rangle_A \, u_1\ \mathsf{of} \\ \quad (u_1', \mathsf{n/a}) \rightarrow \\ \qquad \mathsf{let}\ () = u_1'\ \mathsf{in}\ \langle t/a \rangle_A \, t_2 \\ \quad ((), I) \rightarrow \langle t/a \rangle_A \, t_2 \end{array} \\
\langle t/a \rangle_A \, \mathsf{let}\ (b,c) = u_1\ \mathsf{in}\ t_2 & = & \begin{array}{l} \mathsf{case}\ \langle t/a \rangle_A \, u_1\ \mathsf{of} \\ \quad (u_1', \mathsf{n/a}) \rightarrow \\ \qquad \mathsf{let}\ (x,y) = u_1'\ \mathsf{in}\ \langle t/a \rangle_A \, t_2 \\ \quad ((t_3, t_4), B \otimes C) \rightarrow \\ \qquad \langle t_4/c \rangle_C \, (\langle t_3/b \rangle_B \, (\langle t/a \rangle_A \, t_2)) \end{array} \\
\langle t/a \rangle_A \, \mathsf{let}\ F(x) = u_1\ \mathsf{in}\ t_2 & = & \begin{array}{l} \mathsf{case}\ \langle t/a \rangle_A \, u_1\ \mathsf{of} \\ \quad (u_1', \mathsf{n/a}) \rightarrow \\ \qquad \mathsf{let}\ () = u_1'\ \mathsf{in}\ \langle t/a \rangle_A \, t_2 \\ \quad (F(\hat{e}_1'), F(Y)) \rightarrow \\ \qquad \langle \hat{e}_1'/y \rangle_Y \, (\langle t/a \rangle_A \, t_2) \end{array} \\
\langle t/a \rangle_A \, u_1 & = & \left\{ \begin{array}{ll} u_1' & \text{when } \langle t/a \rangle_A \, u_1 = u_1' \\ t_1' & \text{when } \langle t/a \rangle_A \, u_1 = (t_1', B) \end{array} \right. \\
\langle t/a \rangle_A \, a & = & (t, A) \\
\langle t/a \rangle_A \, b & = & (b, \mathsf{n/a}) \\
\langle t/a \rangle_A \, \mathsf{runG}(g) & = & (\mathsf{runG}(g), \mathsf{n/a}) \\
\langle t/a \rangle_A \, u_1\ t_2 & = & \begin{array}{l} \mathsf{let}\ t_2' = \langle t/a \rangle_A \, t_2\ \mathsf{in} \\ \mathsf{case}\ \langle t/a \rangle_A \, u_1\ \mathsf{of} \\ \quad (u_1', \mathsf{n/a}) \qquad\quad \rightarrow (u_1'\ \hat{e}_2', \mathsf{n/a}) \\ \quad (\lambda b.\, t_1', B \multimap C) \rightarrow \langle t_2'/b \rangle_B \, t_1' \end{array}
\end{array}
$$

Figure 12. Substituting Linear Terms into Linear Terms

$$
\begin{array}{lcl}
\lceil () \rceil & = & \lceil () \rceil \\
\lceil (e, e') \rceil & = & (\lceil e \rceil, \lceil e' \rceil) \\
\lceil \lambda x.\, e \rceil & = & \lambda x.\, \lceil e \rceil \\
\lceil \mathsf{cons}(e, e') \rceil & = & \mathsf{cons}(\lceil e \rceil, \lceil e' \rceil) \\
\lceil \bullet(e) \rceil & = & \bullet(\lceil e \rceil) \\
\lceil G(t) \rceil & = & G(\lceil t \rceil) \\
\lceil x \rceil & = & x \\
\lceil e\ e' \rceil & = & \lceil e \rceil\ \lceil e' \rceil \\
\lceil \mathsf{fst}\ e \rceil & = & \mathsf{fst}\ \lceil e \rceil \\
\lceil \mathsf{snd}\ e \rceil & = & \mathsf{snd}\ \lceil e \rceil \\
\lceil \mathsf{head}\ e \rceil & = & \mathsf{head}\ \lceil e \rceil \\
\lceil \mathsf{tail}\ e \rceil & = & \mathsf{tail}\ \lceil e \rceil \\
\lceil \mathsf{await}(e) \rceil & = & \mathsf{await}(\lceil e \rceil) \\
\lceil \mathsf{fix}\ x : A.\ e \rceil & = & [\mathsf{fix}\ x : A.\ \lceil e \rceil / x]\ \lceil e \rceil \\
 & & \\
\lceil () \rceil & = & \lceil () \rceil \\
\lceil (t, t') \rceil & = & (\lceil t \rceil, \lceil t' \rceil) \\
\lceil \lambda a.\, t \rceil & = & \lambda a.\, \lceil t \rceil \\
\lceil F(e) \rceil & = & F(\lceil e \rceil) \\
\lceil a \rceil & = & a \\
\lceil t\ t' \rceil & = & \lceil t \rceil\ \lceil t' \rceil \\
\lceil \mathsf{let}\ () = t\ \mathsf{in}\ t' \rceil & = & \mathsf{let}\ () = \lceil t \rceil\ \mathsf{in}\ \lceil t' \rceil \\
\lceil \mathsf{let}\ (a, b) = t\ \mathsf{in}\ t' \rceil & = & \mathsf{let}\ (a, b) = \lceil t \rceil\ \mathsf{in}\ \lceil t' \rceil \\
\lceil \mathsf{let}\ F(x) = t\ \mathsf{in}\ t' \rceil & = & \mathsf{let}\ F(x) = \lceil t \rceil\ \mathsf{in}\ \lceil t' \rceil \\
\lceil \mathsf{runG}(e) \rceil & = & \mathsf{runG}(\lceil e \rceil)
\end{array}
$$

Figure 13. Unfolding

6. Implementation

The basic idea underlying our implementation is to represent a collection of streams with a dataflow graph. An imperative dataflow network is rather like a generalized spreadsheet. It has a collection of cells, each containing some code whose evaluation may read other cells. When a cell is read, the expression within the cell is evaluated, recursively triggering the evaluation of other cells as they are read by the program expression. Furthermore, each cell memoizes its expression, so that repeated reads of the same cell will not trigger re-evaluation.

Then, we implement reactive programs with a dataflow graph, which runs inside an event loop. Instead of representing streams as lazy sequences of elements, we represent our streams with mutable dataflow cells, which enumerate the values of the stream as they evolve over time. The event loop updates a clock cell to notify the cells in the graph that they may need to recompute themselves, so that each one reads the cells it depends on, doing the minimal amount of computation needed at each time step. The details of our implementation strategy are in our earlier paper [17], including a correctness proof for the purely functional fragment.

In this paper, we content ourselves with a brief informal discussion of how we extended that implementation to handle linear types. In our earlier paper, we implemented a family of abstract types representing the morphisms of the category of ultrametric spaces, and then wrote an Ocaml syntax extension which translated our DSL's lambda-calculus into calls to the procedures which called the combinators in question. We extend this implementation strategy continues to the adjoint calculus: now we have two families of abstract types, with one each for the nonlinear side and the linear side.

We represent the type of windows with widget objects from the GUI toolkit. As we mentioned in the introduction, we are exploiting linearity to double effect. At a low level, we use it to enforce the linear use of widgets in the scene graph, even though the high-level denotational semantics never mentions state, generativity or mutation at all – the semantics of windows is just a pure set of stream of Pic.

We have not yet done a correctness proof of the implementation, though this is an obvious next step. In our earlier correctness proof, we proved the adequacy of our denotational semantics with respect to an imperative implementation, by means of a Kripke logical relation which related the state of the dataflow graph to the meaning of the streams in the program. Our implementation was highly imperative to start with, and we expect that the Kripke structure should extend naturally to let us use imperative widget state to model the meanings of the widgets. Essentially, since we only ask the equations of the linear lambda calculus to hold, we ought to be able to realize Window values with mutable state.

On the other hand, specifying our contract with the GUI toolkit will be more challenging. The basic issue is to find a specification of the behavior of the toolkit precise enough to let us prove the correctness of the library, while still being abstract enough that we are not forced to verify large parts of the implementation of the underlying toolkit. A usable Hoare-style specification for an imperative toolkit API could well be a result of independent interest! It may involve ideas from process calculi, since low-level APIs such as Win32 or GTK are often designed with logically concurrent and asynchronous abstractions in mind (even though the actual implementations are usually sequential).

7. Discussion

In our earlier paper [17], we used ultrametric spaces to reinterpret the stream transformers familiar from the semantics of synchronous dataflow. In the special case of functions from streams to streams, causality and non-expansiveness precisely coincide, but complete ultrametric spaces are Cartesian closed, supporting function spaces at all orders, and a general notion of contractiveness for defining well-founded fixed points.

Metric methods entered semantics in the early 1980s, to simplify the denotational semantics of concurrency [10]. The applications to stream programming were recognized early, but not followed up on: in a surprisingly little-cited 1985 paper [9], de Bakker and Kok proposed an ultrametric semantics for a language of first-order stream programs over integers and wrote "We think there are no problems when we allow functions of higher order[. . .]".

Birkedal *et al.* [3] have recently given an ultrametric model of Nakano's [19] calculus for guarded recursion. Nakano's types are very similar to ours (though he supports full recursive types), making use of a delay type to guard recursive definition. However, his system includes both subtyping and rules (such as (•)) whose application does not affect the subject term, but which we wished to record for operational reasons. His correctness proof relied on a logical relation, whereas in this paper we have been able to prove normalization for a language including the recursion operator fix $x : X.\ e$ using only ordinary induction — as the proof of Banach's theorem hints we ought, since it only uses induction up to ω to find fixed points.

A suggestive paper of Escardo's [13] gives a metric model to PCF. He noticed that ultrametric spaces support a version of the lift monad from domain theory, and that the extra structure of metrics relative to domains means that the lift monad can be used to interpret timeouts. Since cancels and interrupt operations pervade interactive programs, this suggests a direction of investigation for learning how to support these operations without disturbing the reasoning principles of the language.

Recently, Birkedal et al. [4] have given an alternative model of guarded recursion, based on the topos of trees. Their construction forms a topos, and so many of the semantic constructions we performed with metric spaces can be replayed as set-theoretic operations within the internal language of their topos. In particular, we found the calculations involving powerspaces rather difficult, and so the possibility of working with ordinary powersets (albeit in a slightly different mathematical universe) seems quite attractive.

Pouzet and Caspi [5] extended synchronous dataflow programming to higher order with their co-iterative semantics. They illustrated how that this generated a Cartesian closed category (of size-preserving functions), which they used to interpret functions. Uustalu and Vene [24] subsequently observed that size-preserving functions could be understood more abstractly as the co-Kleisli category of streams. However, in both of these works, feedback was handled in a somewhat *ad hoc* fashion. The problem is that these categories contain too few global points (maps $S(1) \to S(\mathbb{N})$) to denote very many streams, including such basic ones such as $(1, 2, 3, 6, 24, \ldots)$.) Still, implicit lifting is a very attractive notation for simplifying writing stream programs, and there is an adjunction between the category of ultrametric spaces and the co-Kleisli category of the stream functor, which would makes it easy to return to Ult to take fixed points.

The original work on functional reactive programming [12] was based on writing reactive programs as unrestricted stream programs, but due to problems with causality, variations such as *arrowized FRP* [20] were introduced to give combinators restricting the definable stream transformers to the causal ones. The restriction to arrows is roughly equivalent to first-order functional programming, though Sculthorpe and Nilsson [23] introduced additional combinators to recover higher-order and dynamic behavior while using dependent types to retain causality. In contrast, Liu, Cheng and Hudak [18] showed how to exploit this first-order structure to develop a very efficient compilation scheme (reminiscent of the Bohm-Jacopini theorem) from arrow programs to single-loop code.

A distinctive feature of the original FRP work is its focus on continuous time. Though it does not yet do so, we hope our proof framework can extend to proving a sampling theorem, as in Wan and Hudak [26]. On the semantic side, we can easily model continuous behaviors as functions of type $\mathbb{R} \to A$, but relating it to an implementation delivering time deltas (instead of ticks, as presently) seems much more challenging.

Cooper and Krishnamurthi [7, 8], describe FrTime, an embedding of functional reactive programming into the PLT Scheme (now Racket) implementation. They integrate a language with full (i.e., non-commutative) effects, which rules out an adjoint-logic style as we have done here. However, it might be possible to use Egger *et al.*'s enriched effect calculus [11] to support both general effects and strong reasoning principles.

References

[1] N. Benton. A mixed linear and non-linear logic: Proofs, terms and models. In *Computer Science Logic*, volume 933 of *LNCS*, 1995.

[2] P. N. Benton and P. Wadler. Linear logic, monads and the lambda calculus. In *LICS*, pages 420–431, 1996.

[3] L. Birkedal, J. Schwinghammer, and K. Støvring. A metric model of guarded recursion. In *FICS*, 2010.

[4] L. Birkedal, R. E. Møgelberg, J. Schwinghammer, and K. Støvring. First steps in synthetic guarded domain theory: step-indexing in the topos of trees. In *LICS*, 2011.

[5] P. Caspi and M. Pouzet. A co-iterative characterization of synchronous stream functions. *Electr. Notes Theor. Comput. Sci.*, 11, 1998.

[6] P. Caspi, D. Pilaud, N. Halbwachs, and J. Plaice. LUSTRE: A declarative language for real-time programming. In *POPL*, 1987.

[7] G. Cooper. *Integrating dataflow evaluation into a practical higher-order call-by-value language*. PhD thesis, Brown University, 2008.

[8] G. Cooper and S. Krishnamurthi. Embedding dynamic dataflow in a call-by-value language. *Programming Languages and Systems*, pages 294–308, 2006.

[9] J. W. de Bakker and J. N. Kok. Towards a uniform topological treatment of streams and functions on streams. In *ICALP*, 1985.

[10] J. W. de Bakker and J. I. Zucker. Denotational semantics of concurrency. In *STOC*, pages 153–158. ACM, 1982.

[11] J. Egger, R. E. Møgelberg, and A. Simpson. Enriching an effect calculus with linear types. In E. Grädel and R. Kahle, editors, *CSL*, volume 5771 of *Lecture Notes in Computer Science*, pages 240–254. Springer, 2009. ISBN 978-3-642-04026-9.

[12] C. Elliott and P. Hudak. Functional reactive animation. In *ICFP*, 1997.

[13] M. Escardó. A metric model of PCF. In *Workshop on Realizability Semantics and Applications*, 1999.

[14] M. P. Fiore and G. D. Plotkin. An extension of models of axiomatic domain theory to models of synthetic domain theory. In *Proceedings of Computer Science Logic (CSL)*, volume 1258 of *Lecture Notes in Computer Science*. Springer, 1996.

[15] E. Gamma, R. Helm, R. Johnson, and J. Vlissides. *Design patterns: elements of reusable object-oriented software*. Addison-Wesley Longman Publishing Co., Inc. Boston, MA, USA, 1995.

[16] A. Kock. Closed categories generated by commutative monads. *Journal of the Australian Mathematical Society*, 12, 1971.

[17] N. Krishnaswami and N. Benton. Ultrametric semantics of reactive programs. In *LICS*. IEEE, 2011.

[18] H. Liu, E. Cheng, and P. Hudak. Causal commutative arrows and their optimization. In *ACM International Conference on Functional Programming*, 2009.

[19] H. Nakano. A modality for recursion. In *LICS*, pages 255–266, 2000.

[20] H. Nilsson, A. Courtney, and J. Peterson. Functional reactive programming, continued. In *ACM Haskell Workshop*, page 64. ACM, 2002.

[21] M. Pouzet. *Lucid Synchrone, version 3. Tutorial and reference manual*. Université Paris-Sud, LRI, 2006.

[22] J. J. M. M. Rutten. Elements of generalized ultrametric domain theory. *Theor. Comput. Sci.*, 170(1-2):349–381, 1996.

[23] N. Sculthorpe and H. Nilsson. Safe functional reactive programming through dependent types. In *ICFP*, 2009.

[24] T. Uustalu and V. Vene. The essence of dataflow programming. In *Central European Functional Programming School*, volume 4164 of *LNCS*, 2006.

[25] S. Vickers. Localic completion of generalized metric spaces II: Powerlocales. *Theory and Applications of Categories*, 14(15):328–356, 2005. ISSN 1201-561X.

[26] Z. Wan and P. Hudak. Functional reactive programming from first principles. In *PLDI*, pages 242–252, 2000.

[27] K. Watkins, I. Cervesato, F. Pfenning, , and D. Walker. A concurrent logical framework i: Judgments and properties. Technical Report CMU-CS-02-101, Carnegie Mellon University, 2002.

Modular Rollback through Control Logging

A Pair of Twin Functional Pearls

Olin Shivers
Northeastern University
shivers@ccs.neu.edu

Aaron Turon
Northeastern University
turon@ccs.neu.edu

Abstract

We present a technique, based on the use of first-class control operators, enabling programs to maintain and invoke rollback logs for sequences of reversible effects. Our technique is modular, in that it provides complete separation between some library of effectful operations, and a client, "driver" program which invokes and rolls back sequences of these operations. In particular, the checkpoint mechanism, which is entirely encapsulated within the effect library, logs not only the library's effects, but also the client's control state. Thus, logging and rollback can be almost completely transparent to the client code.

This separation of concerns manifests itself nicely when we must implement software with sophisticated error handling. We illustrate with two examples that exploit the architecture to disentangle some core parsing task from its error management. The parser code is completely separate from the error-correction code, although the two components are deeply intertwined at run time.

Categories and Subject Descriptors D.1.1 [*Applicative (Functional) Programming*]

General Terms Algorithms, Design, Languages

Keywords checkpoint, delimited control, error repair

Prologue

We all make mistakes. What counts is how we handle them.

There's little less pleasant in programming than watching beautiful code turn ugly. And nothing causes more contortion than catching and correcting input errors.

The problem is that error handling is not naturally modular: it is context-dependent, often relying on the details and current state of input processing. Extricating error checking into a separate prepass often entails duplicating some of the processing intended for correct input. For complicated artifacts like typecheckers, which are hard enough to get right in the first place, code to produce friendly error messages can obscure or even dwarf the code to check types [9]. When input is provided and processed interactively, checking and processing *must* be interleaved.

We tell a story in two parts, the moral of which is: error handling can be separable, even beautiful. The hero of our tale is `call/cc`, for to err is human, but to forgive requires first-class control.

ICFP'11, September 19–21, 2011, Tokyo, Japan.

Part one takes place in an "eager" Scheme REPL, which parses complete s-expressions as the user types a closing parenthesis, long before a carriage return. Yet, despite advancing the state of the parser, the user can interactively alter erroneous text by "backing up" with the delete key and re-entering corrected text. So here the error-handling is done, in part, by the user, but done in a way that's invisible to the input-processing code.

Part two retells the tale in ML, using a similar technique to automatically discover and repair the "true" source of a syntax error, perhaps far removed from the location where the parser got stuck. It's the functional programming equivalent to Burke-Fisher error repair [2]. Again, the key benefit is the complete separation between the parsing algorithm and the repair algorithm: you write a parser in any style you like, and send it through our `BurkeFisher` functor to get a new parser that intelligently repairs errors.

We use first-class control in two crucial ways:

- First, to provide rollback logging. We layer an interface on top of `call/cc`, constructed so that the very performance of a reversible side-effect has an additional effect: it logs the appropriate reversal. Control effects and other effects smoothly interleave, whether going forward or backward.
- Second, to provide modularity: we sneak checkpointing through an unsuspecting parser. Although parsing and error correction *functionality* is interleaved, the *code* is not. Parsing is done via standard recursive descent, with no concern for error correction; likewise, error correction needs only understand the structure of the input to the parser.

We hope that, while savoring the stories below, you will see that these two techniques transcend them.

1. Prompt reading and effect logging in Scheme

In our first example, we show how to recreate, with modern tools, a bit of "lost art" from classic Lisp input systems: how to intertwine input parsing with terminal-entry text editing without having to intertwine the code that carries out these separate tasks. As we do this, we'll discover a general technique for constructing "command" systems that allows us to transparently *log effects* in a way that permits them to be rolled back on demand, without having to compromise the simplicity of client code that issues sequences of these commands.

That's the big picture; let's begin by diving into the specifics of our example. S-expressions, the standard syntactic form for programs and data in Lisp and Scheme, have an interesting property: they are frequently self-delimiting. For example, we do not need to look past the terminating right parenthesis in the string "`(+ x y)`" to know that we have reached the end of the form. By way of contrast, this is not true of numerals: if an s-expression reader sees the string "`387`", it must look ahead one character to know if this string comprises an entire term, or if it is simply a prefix of a larger term. If the following character is a left parenthesis, then the string represents the integer three hundred eighty-seven (which happens to be followed by some list to be read at a later date); if the following character is another digit, then our string is simply the first three digits of some longer numeral.

Here is the breakdown for standard Scheme s-expressions, showing which kinds are self-terminating, and which aren't:

Self-terminating	Lists: `()`, `(+ x 3)`, ... Vectors: `#()`, `#(-2 7)`, ... Strings: `"fred"`, `"dog"`, ... Booleans: `#f`, `#t` Characters: `#\z`, `#\q`, ...
Not self-terminating	Symbols: `fred`, `dog`, ... Numerals: `387`, `0`, ...

The details vary across dialects of LISP and Scheme, but the general property remains.

Interactive systems that read commands or other structured input from a user frequently take their inputs in the form of an s-expression—the classic example is the LISP read-eval-print loop. In such a system, the human user enters some command, expression or definition at the terminal; the operating system passes this text to the LISP process, which parses it into an s-expression, and then computes the command, expression, definition, *etc.* that it describes.

It turns out that old, 1970's- and 1980's-era LISP systems (*e.g.*, Maclisp and Lisp Machine Lisp) took advantage of the self-delimiting property enjoyed by their s-expression-based interaction languages. When reading s-expressions, these interactive systems would read characters from the terminal eagerly—that is, they turned off the operating system's buffering machinery, so that each character was presented to the reader as soon as the user hit the key on the keyboard. Thus, the parse would complete the instant the terminating close-parenthesis was entered, without requiring the user to enter a redundant newline. It's a small but pleasant convenience that, in the post-Lisp-Machine age, has become lost from the text-interaction modality.

What makes providing this capability tricky is the task of error handling. Human typists make mistakes, which they'd like to correct as they enter their text. This is usually handled by the so-called "line discipline" code in the operating system's terminal device driver. This code buffers terminal input and provides a simple text editor for operating upon this buffered text: most characters are taken as input from the user, and echoed back to the terminal device, to make them visible on entry. A few keys, however, are reserved for this editing task. On a Unix system, for example:

- The delete key "backs up" one character: the OS removes the last character from the input buffer and outputs a backspace-space-backspace sequence to the terminal to erase it from the screen.
- The control-U character typically erases the entire line of text, erasing the entire buffer's worth of input.
- The characters control-C and control-Z direct the OS to send an asynchronous control signal to the reading process.
- Control-V turns off any special treatment of the following character.
- Control-D represents end-of-file.

The operating system does not release the buffered input to a process attempting to read from the terminal device until the user enters a newline character: this commits the input sequence.

Now, in order to provide eager reading, we have to turn this OS-provided machinery off: the user process must now be responsible for echoing input and implementing the interactive editing that humans use to back up through mistaken input and make corrections. This is not so terrible; we can encapsulate the editing code in a small library and be done with it.

What's tricky is that the parsing computation is now *interleaved* with the text-editing computation. Formerly, these things were split into distinct phases. First, we enter a string, with no parsing going on at all; during this phase, we can perform editing on each line as we enter it. Once we strike the newline key, the final version of that line is shipped off to the parser phase (*i.e.*, the interpreter), which consumes the text, produces a parse tree (that is, an s-expression), and proceeds with the requested task.

In our new (well, 1970's) world, the application is carrying out the parse as text is entered by the user. If we change our minds and wish to erase some of the text we've entered, as we back up through the input text, we also have to *rewind the parse computation*. For example, an s-expression reader is typically a little recursive-descent parser. When it is reading the elements of a nested list and it encounters a close-parenthesis character, it returns the accumulated list to its recursive caller. If we were to subsequently decide to *delete* that close parenthesis, we'd have to back the parse computation back down into that formerly completed call.

What we need is the ability to take "snapshots" of the computation at various points as we parse. Roughly speaking, every time the parser calls out to the "read character" routine, that routine should first checkpoint the parse computation and save the checkpoint away on a list. If the user tries to delete some previously entered characters, the input routine can pull the appropriate checkpoint from its saved history and reset the parse computation to that previous character-reading state.

By this point, it should be clear that the right tool for this job is the Scheme `call-with-current-continuation` (or, `call/cc`) procedure: creating computational checkpoints is its *raison d'être*.

The rubout port and the reset protocol

In Scheme, we do I/O on *ports*; our task is to construct a new kind of "rubout port" for reading from a terminal. We'll construct our rubout port using a low-level mechanism in Scheme48 [7]/scsh [12] that permits programmers to define their own input ports, which can be passed to the system input procedures like any other input port. To define one of our custom rubout ports, we provide the extended-port constructor two things. The first is a fixed suite of "port methods," described by a record whose fields are procedures the input system will use to read a character, "peek" at a character, close the port, and a few other less-important operations. We also provide a data value which encapsulates the port state; this value will be passed to the method procedures when operations are performed on the port. Here is the definition of the rubout port's data record:

```
(define-record rubout-port-data
  ttyin               ; input tty port
  ttyout              ; output tty port, for echoing
  (prev-tty-info #f)  ; tty's original echo state
  (peek-char     #f)  ; "lookahead" peek cache
  (checkpoint    #f)); most recent checkpoint
```

This piece of Scheme code defines a procedure

`(make-rubout-port-data` *ttyin ttyout*`)`

which constructs a record from a pair of ports connected to the terminal device; the other three fields of the record are initialised to false, `#f`. We also get field-accessor procedures, such as

`(rubout-port-data:ttyin` *rpd*`)`

`(rubout-port-data:ttyout` *rpd*`)`

and so forth, and some analogous field-assignment procedures with names like `(set-rubout-port-data:peek-char!` *rpd char*`)`.

Note the checkpoint field. Our intention is that every time application code does a (read-char *rp*) operation that causes the rubout-port to actually get a character from the terminal, before returning the character to the caller, the code will also grab a continuation with call/cc and stow it away in the port's checkpoint field. If, during a later attempt to read, the rubout-port code reads, say, a "delete" character and decides to undo the previous read, it will be able to do so by fetching this saved value from the checkpoint field of the rubout-port's data record and invoking it—this will reset the entire computation back to the previous read point.

The key piece of design we must pin down is the protocol used to invoke the checkpointed continuation. Specifically, a checkpoint is a Scheme continuation that must be applied to a single boolean argument: (checkpoint just-1?). If the just-1? argument is true, we wish to rewind the computation back just one step—that is, to the immediately prior read operation. If the argument is false, then we wish to rewind all the way back to the beginning of the entire read session.

The core effects: reading and echoing

We can now define the pair of low-level procedures that perform our system's two primitive side-effects: reading a character from the keyboard, and echoing an input character to the display. Since each of these procedures carries out an effect, it must log the effect as it performs it—that is, we must update the port's checkpoint to add a rollback handler that will undo the effect if we rewind back through this point in the computation. Here is the code for echoing:

```
(define (echo c pd)
  (let* ((oport (rubout-port-data:ttyout pd))
         (reset (rubout-port-data:checkpoint pd)))
    (write-char c oport)      ; 1: Echo the character.

    ;; 2: Set a checkpoint to undo the echo.
    (set-rubout-port-data:checkpoint pd
      (call/cc (λ (ret)
                 (let ((just-1? (call/cc ret)))
                   (print-rubout-sequence oport)
                   (reset just-1?)))))))

;;; Output backspace/space/backspace to the port.
(define (print-rubout-sequence oport)
  (write-string "\b \b" oport))
```

The rubout-port machinery calls echo whenever it needs to echo a character just read to the terminal. The procedure writes the character out on line 4, and then logs the effect in the last half of the procedure by updating the port's checkpoint. This is the first piece of serious continuation manipulation we've performed, so we will trace through its execution carefully. The first, outer call/cc creates a return point ret; applying ret to some value *cp* will cause *cp* to be installed as the port's new checkpoint. The second, inner call/cc creates the actual checkpoint continuation; call/cc passes this continuation to ret, so, just as we described, this continuation gets installed as the current checkpoint.

Now, consider what happens when this checkpoint is invoked at some later time, by fetching it from the rubout port's data record and applying it to some boolean argument. We'll reset the computation back to *now*: the inner call/cc will return the boolean value, so it will be bound by the let form to the variable just-1?. Then we'll proceed into the body of the let, which contains the rollback action: we write out a backspace/space/backspace character sequence to the terminal, which will erase the character we previously echoed back on line 4 of the code, then we'll pass the just-1? boolean on to *our* checkpoint. We do this because we are in the process of rewinding back to some prior input—the echo action is an output effect, not an input effect, so we need to continue rewinding the computation.

Our next procedure (which appears in Figure 1) is the primitive character-input procedure. When the rubout-port machinery needs to actually read a character, it applies %read-char to the port's data record. This code is, essentially, our "line discipline" driver code, written in Scheme. The procedure sits in a loop (the named-let function lp), which does an input operation on the actual terminal, binding the variable c to the character entered by the user. Then we perform a variety of actions, depending on the character. Inducing rollback is easy: if the character is the delete character, we apply the port's current checkpoint continuation rubout to true, which will abort what we're doing, and reset to the previous read (and also undo any echoing we might have logged in-between). That previous read will then be able to get a new character from the user and return it to the parser in place of the original character it had input back when it first ran. (We'll see the code that does this—the code at the target end of our reset-continuation's non-local jump—in just a moment.)

If the character is the line-kill character, control-U, then we apply the checkpoint to false; by the rules of the checkpoint invocation protocol, this will induce a rewind all the way back to the beginning of the entire parse session, clearing previously echoed characters from the display as we rewind.

If the user entered control-C or control-Z, the code sends the current process the appropriate OS signal, and then loops by tail-calling (lp), to continue trying to read a character. (The process signals itself in a context that resets the terminal's echoing and buffering state to its original settings, but this is a fine point we can skip.)

These first few cases describe the text-editing functionality of our "device driver," where characters input by the user are not intended as data to be passed on to the process, but are rather interpreted directly by the input-port system as requesting various actions. The final case (the else clause of the cond) is the actual-input case: we've read an ordinary character c (or we've encountered the end of file, or we've read the "knockdown" character, control-V, followed by any character at all). Since we can now be considered to have successfully accomplished an input side-effect, before we return c to our caller, we must first log the operation by updating the port's checkpoint. Just as with echo, this is done with a nested, double call/cc pattern. The first, outer call/cc simply captures the context we'll use to return c and proceed with the parse by returning from %read-char. The second, inner call/cc creates the checkpoint continuation, naming it ckpt. We then install ckpt into the port's data record, and apply ret to the character c, which will lead us to produce c as the return value of %read-char. What happens when, at some later time, the checkpoint continuation is invoked? What we want to accomplish, if this happens, is to rewind the computation back to *now*, then get a new character c' from the terminal and return that *instead* of the character c we just now produced.

That's exactly what happens. Suppose some future call to %read-char gets a delete character and so fetches the checkpoint continuation we just now created from the port's data record and applies it to true (*i.e.*, executes line 7 of the procedure). When the checkpoint continuation is applied to true, we'll rewind to "now," and the second, inner call/cc will return the true value—so it will be let-bound to the variable just-1?, and we'll proceed into the body of the let form, whose if conditional will jump back to the top of our original loop, lp, continuing our current read. Any character c' we get will be returned to our caller, so the net effect is that, after rewinding the computation to here, we'll proceed with c' instead of our originally-read character. In short, we undid the input effect and replaced it with a new one.

```
(define (%read-char port-data)
  (let ((rubout (rubout-port-data:checkpoint port-data))
        (iport  (rubout-port-data:ttyin port-data)))
    (let lp ()
      ;; Assert: (rubout-port-data:peek-data port-data) = #F.
      (let ((c (read-char iport))) ; real input!
        (cond ((rubout-char?   c)  (rubout #t)) ; DEL => rubout a char
              ((linekill-char? c)  (rubout #f)) ; ^U  => kill the whole sexp.

              ((interrupt-char? c) ; ^C => interrupt
               ;; Undo the tty's raw/no-echo modes before raising the signal.
               (with-rubout-port-restored port-data
                 (signal-process 0 signal/int))
               (lp)) ; The process survived the signal => keep reading.

              ((suspend-char? c) ; ^Z => suspend
               ;; Undo the tty's raw/no-echo modes before raising the signal.
               (with-rubout-port-restored port-data
                 (signal-process 0 signal/tstp))
               (lp))

              (else (let ((c (cond ((knockdown-char? c) ; ^V => turn off special handling.
                                     (read-char iport))
                                    ((eof-char? c) *eof-object*) ; ^D => EOF
                                    (else c))))                  ; Normal char

                      ;; Outstanding! We have read an actual character, C.
                      ;; Before returning it to the parser, set a new
                      ;; checkpoint, so that if we later wish to rub C out,
                      ;; we can come back here, get a new character, and resume.
                      (call/cc                             ; Therein lies the rubout.
                       (λ (ret)
                         (let ((just-1? (call/cc (λ (ckpt) ; Set the checkpoint & return C:
                                                   (set-rubout-port-data:checkpoint port-data ckpt)
                                                   (ret c)))))
                           ;; On rewind, we'll bind JUST-1? & come here.
                           (if just-1? (lp)           ; Either re-do the current read,
                               (rubout #f)))))))))))) ; or keep rewinding.
```

Figure 1. The checkpointing character reader

On the other hand, suppose at some point in the future the user enters the "line-kill" character, Control-U. Then the checkpoint continuation will be applied to false (by line 8 of that future invocation of `%read-char`). The computation will be reset to "now," and the inner `call/cc` will produce the false value, which will be let-bound to `just-1?`. So, instead of looping in our current read, we'll keep rewinding by applying *our* checkpoint to false, in the very last line of the procedure: `(rubout #f)`.

In other words, we don't have to keep an explicit stack of checkpoints. The "stack" is implicit in the *environment structure* of the various checkpoints: each checkpoint continuation has access to the next checkpoint back in the timeline: it is bound to the variable `rubout` in the current checkpoint's lexical scope. (Similarly, it is bound to the variable `reset`, in the checkpoint created by the echo procedure.)

Peeking and reading

All the heavy lifting in our system is accomplished by the echo and `%read-char` primitives. The rubout-port system calls them from its peek-character and read-character "method" procedures. Note a policy decision encoded in these procedures: a character is *not* echoed as soon as we get it from the keyboard: peeks don't count. This code doesn't echo a character to the display until the parser actually consumes it with a `read-char` operation.

```
(define (rubout-peek-char port-data)
  ;; A "subsequent" peek: don't checkpoint
  (or (rubout-port-data:peek-char port-data)
      ;; A "first" peek -- checkpoint it
      (let ((c (%read-char port-data)))
        ;; then set the peek cache:
        (set-rubout-port-data:peek-char port-data c)
        c))) ; then return the character.

(define (rubout-read-char port-data)
  ;; If the peek does input, it will be logged:
  (let ((c (rubout-peek-char port-data)))

    ;; If we echo, it will be logged:
    (if (not (eof-object? c)) (echo c port-data))

    ;; Clear the peek cache.
    (set-rubout-port-data:peek-char port-data #f)
    c))
```

Note also that these two higher-level procedures do not concern themselves with setting checkpoints or logging effects. One of the nice properties of our design is that the effect-logging code is tightly bound to the code that commits the effects. Thus, doing a side effect and logging its rollback handler are welded together.

Client code, like the two procedures above, or the application's parser, just commit side-effects at will; it's impossible for them to break the pairing of effects and rollbacks. (This nice property is only extended to the side-effects that we included in our design, of course. Parser clients must be aware that they cannot perform other side-effects and expect them to be undone during rollback.)

Failure is not an option

All that remains is to define `with-rubout-session*`, the procedure used to delimit a single parse session; it appears in Figure 2. We can perform a rubout-enabled parse with something like:

```
(with-rubout-session* rubout-port
  (λ () (read rubout-port)))
```

The central body of this procedure executes in a dynamic context, established by the R5RS Scheme `dynamic-wind` procedure, that saves and restores the rubout port's checkpoint if we should throw out and then back into the session's dynamic extent by invoking saved continuations. It also serves another purpose: the `dynamic-wind`'s exit thunk clears the checkpoint from the rubout port, which permits the checkpoint to be garbage collected even if the rubout port itself continues to remain alive.

Note that the rubout-session's thunk executes in an exception-handler context that treats parser-syntax errors in a clever way: we refuse to accept input from the terminal that triggers a syntax-error exception. If the user should enter a character that causes the parser to raise this error, the exception handler "rings the bell" (in a visual manner), then discards the bad character by invoking the rubout port's current checkpoint, passing it true for its `just-1?` parameter. This rewinds the parse computation back to the read operation where the user entered the offending character (erasing the character as we rewind, if it had been echoed); we then resume the parse by reading an alternate character from the user.

For example, if the user tries to type in an ill-formed dotted-pair that has two dots, *e.g.*, `(a . b . c)`, the parser will stubbornly refuse to accept the second dot, ringing the bell every time the user attempts to enter it to signal that we have departed from the syntactic straight and narrow. Note that this facility is completely independent of the grammar we are parsing, or the details of the parser: the parser is just a piece of code that raises an error exception as soon as it encounters an illegal character.

The final task the rubout-session procedure must perform before invoking the client's parser computation `thunk` is to set the rubout port's initial checkpoint. Again, we see the nested, double `call/cc` pattern. Tracing through the `restart` loop shows that each time we rewind back to the initial checkpoint, we recreate and reinstall it into the port, then begin the parse (that is, call `thunk`) all over again. Thus, invoking the initial checkpoint has the effect of restarting the whole parse.

Discussion

The big idea The first thing to note about this rubout-handler system is that the technique is not at all limited to interactive text entry. The general idea here is that we have a library of effectful (but reversible) operations. Some client performs a series of effects by issuing a sequence of these operations; as the client computes, the application may decide to rewind the driving computation to some previous operation and do something different—perhaps (as in our rubout-handler scenario) in response to error conditions.

The design pattern we propose here is to instrument the effectful operation library to construct a rollback log for the operations it performs. More specifically, *by constructing this rollback log from continuations, we capture not only the library's effects, but also the client's control state at each operation-invocation point.* This is what permits completely transparent rollback of the client computation: it's all due to the power of `call/cc` to package up a general control state.

Delimiting our checkpoints Let's motivate our next point by considering an extension to our rubout-handler system. Many text-input systems have some kind of "history" mechanism: they save previous lines of input, which the user can recall by entering some special control key that cycles through previous entries. Suppose we wished to provide this kind of functionality—and, of course, keep our rubout-handling capability. Unfortunately, the saved continuations that make up our checkpoints capture *too much control state:* they capture not only the parse computation, but also the computational state of the client that called the parser. If we were to reset to one of the checkpoints from a previous read in, *e.g.*, a Scheme interpreter's read-eval-print loop, we'd reset the entire interpreter back to that earlier state!

This is a problem that is exactly handled by delimited-control operators such as Felleisen's `prompt` [4, 13] or Danvy and Filinski's `shift` [3]. We need only delimit the parse computation carried out by the thunk passed to `with-rubout-session*` and we're set. We leave this modification to our code as a (fun) exercise for the interested reader.

The dark side of Church encodings Scheme provides continuations encoded as procedures: we perform a non-local control transfer to a captured continuation by applying it to some argument. This has been a long-standing source of subtle problems using Scheme's continuations. The central issue is that, if we want to call procedure `p`, with argument `a` and continuation `k`, we cannot do the following: `(k (p a))`. This goes wrong because `k`'s underlying continuation does not actually become the *current* continuation until `p` returns; the whole time `p` is executing, the continuation is an extension of the one extant when we began evaluating the entire `(k (p a))` expression. So if `p` raises an exception, we will resolve it using the exception handlers of that continuation, not `k`'s handlers. If we were hoping to reclaim the original continuation's stack by installing `k` as the current continuation, this won't happen while `p` is executing—if it happens to be some long-running thread (such as a web server), then the original continuation's stack will *never* become free, leading to a subtle space leak. These kinds of space leaks aren't just theoretical oddities; they actually occur when programmers build thread schedulers based on continuations [1].

The real problem here is that when we Church-encode a kind of data, we can only do one thing with the data: apply it to an argument—that is the only operation permitted on procedures. In the case of continuations, we need to do two things: perform a function call with the given continuation for the call, and compose an $\alpha \rightarrow \beta$ function onto the "end" of a β-accepting continuation, producing an α-accepting continuation. These two procedures provide the necessary interface:

```
(with-continuation cont thunk)
(compose-continuation β-cont α->β)
```

Scheme doesn't have this kind of continuation mechanism, so we have to code in awkward ways to work around the limitations of `call/cc`.

This problem rears its head in our rubout-handler system. Consider the subtle, double-`call/cc` code that creates the new checkpoint when we read a character in `%read-char`. Couldn't we eliminate the inner `call/cc` and just use a simple procedure, instead of an exotic continuation, with the following?

```
(define (with-rubout-session* rubout-port thunk)
  (let ((pd (extensible-input-port-local-data rubout-port))
        (suspended-checkpoint #f))

    (with-raw-mode-rubout-port pd        ; Turn off tty buffering & echoing.
      (dynamic-wind
        ;; Dynamic-wind pre:
        ;;   If we are throwing back into the parse, restore the checkpoint
        ;;   we saved away when we threw out.
        (λ () (set-rubout-port-data:checkpoint pd suspended-checkpoint))

        ;; Dynamic-wind body:
        (λ () (with-syntax-error-handler
                ;; Here's the error handler. If the parser raises a syntax error,
                ;; ring the bell, clear the peek-char cache, then trigger a 1-step
                ;; rewind to rubout the last char, which triggered the error.
                (λ (c) (visible-bell (rubout-port-data:ttyout pd))
                       (set-rubout-port-data:peek-char pd #f)
                       ((rubout-port-data:checkpoint pd) #t))

                ;; Set the initial checkpoint, which comes back here and
                ;; restarts the whole parse.
                (call/cc (λ (go-start-parse)
                           (let restart ()
                             (call/cc (λ (icp)
                                        (set-rubout-port-data:checkpoint pd icp)
                                        (go-start-parse)))
                             ;; Come here when initial checkpoint ICP is invoked:
                             (restart))))

                (thunk))) ; Do the parse.

        ;; Dynamic-wind post:
        ;;   When we're done, clear out the port's checkpoint, so the port
        ;;   won't keep the checkpoint from being gc'd. But... we might not be
        ;;   done. We might be throwing out and later throwing back in. So
        ;;   save away the current checkpoint in case we later throw back in.
        (λ () (set! suspended-checkpoint (rubout-port-data:checkpoint pd))
              (set-rubout-port-data:checkpoint pd #f))))))

(define (visible-bell oport)      ; A simple "visible bell:"
  (write-char #\! oport)          ;   print out a !,
  (sleep 1)                       ;   pause one second, then
  (print-rubout-sequence oport)); erase it.
```

Figure 2. Delimiting a rubout-handler session.

```
(call/cc (λ (ret)
           (set-rubout-port-data:checkpoint port-data
             (λ (just-1?) (if just-1?
                              (ret (lp))
                              (rubout #f))))
           c))
```

Unfortunately, no. If some future delete command applies this checkpoint to true, we will perform the (lp) retry *in that future context*; we won't throw back to the previous control state until the lp call returns to the Scheme-style Church-encoded continuation ret. All the time that (lp) is running, it is running with the wrong exception-handler context, the wrong dynamic-wind undo/redo handlers, and so forth. Furthermore, the run-time system can't reclaim the triggering read's stack and other control context until lp returns; we want to reclaim it when lp *starts*.

The double-call/cc pattern establishes the proper context, then captures it with the inner call/cc, so things work out properly.

It would have been easier and simpler to write this code if we'd had the alternate continuation functionality described above. Our checkpoint-setting code would then look like this:

```
(call/cc
 (λ (ret)
   (let ((ckpt (compose-continuation ret
                 (λ (just-1?)
                   (if just-1? (lp) (rubout #f))))))
     (set-rubout-port-data:checkpoint port-data ckpt))
   c))
```

An observant reader might similarly have wondered why we didn't use a simple procedure as the checkpoint for the echo procedure. This is why. As a matter of style, checkpoints in our rubout-handler system—that is, things stored in the checkpoint field of a rubout port's data record—are always and only continuations—that is, things created by call/cc.

This issue matters less in the case of echo's checkpoints. If we'd written the checkpoint code for echo with the simpler

```
(set-rubout-port-data:checkpoint pd
  (λ (just-1?)
    (print-rubout-sequence oport)
    (reset just-1?)))
```

then the only code that would run in the wrong context would be the (print-rubout-sequence oport) call, which is short and presumably terminates with no other control effects such as raising an exception. Still, we preferred to work with the discipline of *only* using continuations for checkpoints.

Backwards and forwards An observant reader might also be wondering: old LISP systems didn't have call/cc or general continuations. So how did these systems provide prompt reading with rubout handling?

The answer is rather ingenious [10]. These systems couldn't back up to prior checkpoints by invoking saved continuations. Instead, the port machinery would log all the characters read during a session. If the user requested a single-character delete, the rubout handler would raise an exception, which would be caught by an exception handler established at the beginning of the rubout-handling session. The exception handler would delete the last character from the log, and then *completely restart* the entire parse. During the new parse attempt, the port would be in a special "replay" mode: whenever the parser requested a character from the port, the port would get the next item from the log, instead of going to the terminal to read a new character. When the log was exhausted, the port would revert to doing actual input from the terminal. So, to delete a character, the rubout handler would simply reread and reparse everything *but* the deleted character. Instead of going one step back, the system would do a complete restart and then go $n-1$ steps forward.

Monads and dependent types The technique of using continuations to construct rollback logs for command sequences, where we wish to capture client control state as well, seems nicely suited for expressing in a Haskell monad that uses both continuations and state.

We should mention that Conor McBride was able to code up a functional equivalent to our rubout handler in a dependently-typed extension to Haskell. Although McBride was, of course, able to capture many system invariants by means of a rich static type system, we should point out that his implementation required almost sixty lines of code to achieve this feat.

Why call/cc***?*** Our final point is the following. Many programmers think of call/cc and delimited control operators as being the province of effete language theorists. To which we really must reply[1]: "*Au contraire!*" Continuations are rather tools for hearty, robust systems programmers: we've used them to write a line-discipline driver to replace the one provided by the Unix kernel, and we only needed about 200 lines of code... and our version provides more functionality.

2. The Burke-Fisher functor in SML

Enough s-expressions. Let's look at some *real* syntax:

$$
\begin{array}{lcl}
\langle exp \rangle & ::= & \langle exp \rangle \texttt{ + } \langle exp \rangle \\
 & | & \langle num \rangle \\
 & | & \langle id \rangle \\
 & | & \ldots \\
\langle decl \rangle & ::= & \texttt{val } \langle id \rangle \texttt{ = } \langle exp \rangle \texttt{ ;} \\
 & | & \texttt{fun } \langle id \rangle \texttt{ (} \langle id \rangle \texttt{) = } \langle exp \rangle \texttt{ ;}
\end{array}
$$

This is just enough grammar to get us into some interesting trouble.

[1] In a hearty, robust manner, that is.

Imagine for a moment being a novice programmer sitting at the REPL. You type

```
> val f(x) = x + 1;
```

expecting to define your first function. But, of course, you are instead greeted by

```
SYNTAX ERROR: at (1:6), got '(', expected '='
```

Being a novice, you probably haven't seen the grammar above, which anyway would be much larger in practice. From the error, you only know that the first five characters drove the parser into a state from which '=' is the only way out. If you also believe that val declarations are the sole way of creating bindings—or have forgotten whether it's fun, fn, proc or function—you're in for a long and frustrating REPL session.

A more helpful parser might instead respond with

```
> val f(x) = x + 1;
SYNTAX ERROR: at (1:1), did you mean 'fun'?
```

Startlingly, the *location* of the syntax error has changed in this interaction. The parser is recommending that val be replaced by fun, even though val is permitted by the grammar. This recommendation seems more helpful than replacing (with =, but why?

There is a general principle at work, one elucidated in a classic paper by Burke and Fisher [2]. The principle, loosely stated, is that

> *Syntax errors are usefully explained by finding minimal, nearby edits that allow the parser to substantially progress.*

Looking at our novice REPL session, we see

- If we replace (with =, the parser will encounter another syntax error almost immediately: the now-unbalanced closing parenthesis. To recover from *that* error, we would probably delete several tokens—the initial replacement leads us straight into a syntactic quagmire.
- If instead we replace val by fun, which requires *backing up* from the location where the error was detected, that single-token change results in a grammatically-correct input.

In short, the fun replacement is better because it explains more of the programmer's original input.

Burke and Fisher outline two requirements for "practicality":

1. Error handling should not substantially increase the space or time needed to parse *correct* input.
2. Error analysis and recovery should take constant time.

The technique outlined in their paper relies on the details of explicit-stack LL and LR parsing, and works by maintaining *two* parser states. The first parser state represents the "real" parser, and is used to detect syntax errors. The second parser state lags some fixed number k of tokens behind. When the real parser encounters an error, it can be repeatedly reverted to the state of the lagging parser as different modifications to the input are tried. The winning modification is, roughly, the smallest one yielding the greatest amount of progress beyond the original error.[2]

While ingenious, Burke-Fisher error repair is also a vivid example of too-tight coupling between error handling and core logic: the error-handling code relies on complete knowledge of the representation and algorithm of the underlying parser.

Using similar techniques to the eager REPL, we can liberate Burke-Fisher error repair from its assumptions about parsing, achieving clean separation between processing valid input and handling erroneous input.

[2] To work in constant time, a test of a repair should only venture some fixed number of tokens beyond the original error.

Plot summary

The basic trick is to slide in error correction between a parser and its source of input, a lexer. As with the eager REPL, we do this by feeding the parser an instrumented, checkpointing lexer. To keep things interesting, we switch to SML, where we can use the module system to be very clear about the separation of concerns. In the end, we write a single functor, BurkeFisher, that can add error repair to *any* module of signature PARSER.

We use two extensions to the language: delimited control and higher-order functors, both of which can be had in SML/NJ [5, 8]. Why? Read on.

Setting the scene: the signature of a parser

We start with the lexer:

```
signature LEXER =
sig
  type tok
  type tok_stream
  val lex : tok_stream -> (tok * tok_stream) option
end
```

The LEXER signature characterizes the source of input to a parser: a stream of tokens (type tok). We know nothing about the internal structure of token streams, but can observe the next token and remaining stream, if any, using lex.

A PARSER is parameterized by its LEXER:

```
signature PARSER =
sig
  type tok
  type result
  functor ForLexer(L : LEXER where type tok = tok):
  sig
    exception ParseError of L.tok_stream list
    val parse : L.tok_stream -> result
  end
end
```

Here is our first use of SML/NJ's higher-order module system: a module implementing PARSER must include a functor, ForLexer, which can be applied to token-compatible lexers. ForLexer in turn provides a parse function specialized to the token stream of the given lexer. Of course, all this could be replaced by an appropriate use of polymorphism, but then, so can SML's module system [11]. Explicit structuring via signatures, modules and functors allows us to *name* the separate concepts with which we wish to work.

Because result is defined outside the ForLexer functor, the result type of a parser cannot depend on its lexer.

On the other hand, the ParseError it raises on detecting a syntax error is parameterized by the token stream—in fact, it takes a *list* of token streams. This is the one concession a parser must make to error repair: it must signal the detection of an error by throwing an exception holding the stream just after the error was detected. If the parser performs backtracking choice, but every choice fails, it should throw the exception with a list containing *each* failure point.

A simple parser

The module DeclRecognizer in Figure 3 implements a recognizer for the ⟨*decl*⟩ grammar, providing an example realization of the PARSER signature. Being a recognizer, there are only two possible outcomes of parse: a unit value if successful, and an exception if not. The implementation of DeclParser uses a few parser combinators [6], which provide interaction with both the lexer and, ultimately, error repair.

The combinator want simply checks that the given token is the next one on the stream, returning an advanced stream if so and raising an exception if not:

```
fun want t = fn s =>
  case L.lex s
   of NONE => raise ParseError [s]
    | SOME (t', s') =>
        if t=t' then s'
        else raise ParseError [s']
               (* stream /after/ the error *)
```

Usually we compose recognizers sequentially, letting errors propagate:

```
infix >>
fun p >> q = fn s => q (p s)
```

To handle nonterminals like ⟨*decl*⟩, which have multiple productions, we use backtracking choice:

```
infix <|>
fun p <|> q = fn s =>
  p s handle ParseError ss =>
  q s handle ParseError ss' =>
  raise ParseError (ss @ ss')
```

With choice we see concretely the concession the parser must make to error repair: it must do a bit of work to bundle together the possible error locations.

Checkpointing a lexer

Parsers are conveniently parameterized over lexers, leaving the perfect loophole through which to checkpoint parser state. Unlike the eager REPL, we will employ *delimited* continuations for checkpointing. A delimited continuation captures the evaluation context only up to the most recent delimiter. Delimitation will allow us to tentatively run the rest of a parse with various repairs, searching for the best one, without going on to execute the rest of the program.

We use an implementation of delimited control [3], due to David Herman in an ICFP pearl [5], that is parameterized by a single *answer* type:

```
signature CONTROL =
sig
  type ans
  val shift : (('a -> ans) -> ans) -> 'a
  val reset : (unit -> ans) -> ans
end
```

Delimiters are inserted using reset, which expects an answer-producing thunk. On the other hand, shift aborts to the nearest delimiter, but reifies the evaluation context up to the delimiter as a reusable function. Thus,

```
> (reset (fn () => shift (fn k => 1) + 1)) * 2;
2
> (reset (fn () => shift (fn k => k (k 1)) + 1)) * 2;
6
```

In the first case, the captured context [ ] + 1 is simply discarded; the reset is replaced by the answer 1, which is then doubled. In the second case, the captured context [ ] + 1 is applied, as a function, twice; the reset is replaced by the answer 3, which is then doubled.

For our purposes, a single delimiter surrounding a parse will suffice. The checkpoints captured by the lexer will correspond to the remaining execution of the parser, starting from its request for a token at some point in the stream, and continuing to the point

```
structure DeclRecognizer =
struct
  datatype tok = VAL | FUN | LPAREN | RPAREN | ID | EQ | NUM | PLUS | SEMI
  type result = unit

  functor ForLexer (L : LEXER where type tok = tok) =
  struct
    exception ParseError of L.tok_stream list

    (* ... definition of combinators want, >> and <|> as given in text ... *)

    val wantExp  = (* ... *)
    val wantDecl =
         (want FUN >> want ID >> want LPAREN >> want ID >> want RPAREN >> want EQ >> wantExp >> want SEMI)
     <|> (want VAL >> want ID >> want EQ >> wantExp >> want SEMI)
    fun parse s = let val _ = wantDecl s in () end
  end
end
```

Figure 3. A combinator-style recognizer for ⟨*decl*⟩

```
fun lex (s, PASSTHRU) =
    (case L.lex s
      of NONE => NONE
       | SOME (t, s') => SOME (t, (s', PASSTHRU)))

  | lex (s, CHECKPOINT w) =
    (case L.lex s
      of NONE => NONE
       | SOME (t, s') => SOME (C.shift (fn k =>
           k (t, (s', CHECKPOINT (Window.push w                  (* first time through, yield t *)
                  (fn t' => k (t', (s', PASSTHRU)))))))) (* on checkpoint invocation, yield t' *)
```

Figure 4. The checkpointing lexer

where it produces a final answer. The type ans will be `P.result` for a parser `P`.

The checkpointing instrumentation is performed by a `LEXER`-transforming functor. Using SML/NJ's `funsig` form, we can give it the following signature:

```
funsig LEXER_WRAPPER (C : CONTROL) (L : LEXER) =
                      LEXER where type tok = L.tok
```

As the signature indicates, the instrumented lexer produces the same type of tokens as the original one, so it will be compatible with the same parsers. What changes is the internal representation of token streams, which includes a `wrapper` component:

```
functor WrappedLexer (C : CONTROL) (L : LEXER) =
struct
  type tok = L.tok
  type checkpoint = L.tok -> C.ans
  datatype wrapper
    = CHECKPOINT of checkpoint Window.window
    | PASSTHRU
  type tok_stream = L.tok_stream * wrapper

  fun lex (* ... see figure ... *)
end
```

An instrumented lexer can operate in one of two modes: checkpointing or passthrough. Checkpointing is used during initial parsing, until a syntax error is found. The last k checkpoints are maintained using a window, so that instrumentation imposes only a constant-bounded space overhead:

```
signature WINDOW =
sig
  type 'a window
  val empty : 'a window
  (* keeps only last k pushes *)
  val push  : 'a window -> 'a -> 'a window
  val list  : 'a window -> 'a list
end
```

Figure 4 shows the implementation of instrumented lexing. In passthrough mode, instrumentation has no effect. In checkpointing mode, the lexer uses `shift` to abort while capturing the continuation up to the end of parsing. The delimited continuation k is immediately invoked—effectively undoing the abort—yielding the same token `t` that the underlying lexer would. However, a checkpoint is pushed that, when invoked, re-runs the parser from the point of the `shift`, providing an alternative token `t'` and switching to passthrough mode.

An instrumented lexer provides `wrap` to inject an underlying lexer, `unwrap` to project the underlying lexer, and `checkpoints` to extract the last k checkpoints:

```
fun wrap s = (s, CHECKPOINT Window.empty)
fun unwrap (s, _) = s
fun checkpoints (_, CHECKPOINT w) = Window.list w
  | checkpoints (_, PASSTHRU)     = []
```

Putting it together: the Burke-Fisher functor

Nearly all the ingredients are now in place. However, to search for repairs, we'll need to know something about the available tokens:

```
signature TOK =
sig
  type tok
  val toks : tok list
  val toString : tok -> string
end
```

The list toks provides an instance of each token that should be used for replacement or insertion during error repair.

With that, we can specify the shape of functional Burke-Fisher error repair:

```
funsig BURKE_FISHER
        (T : TOK)
        (P : PARSER where type tok = T.tok) =
  PARSER where type tok = T.tok
```

Figure 5 gives an implementation—the BurkeFisher functor. To keep the presentation short, the functor is not quite true to the original algorithm:

- It only performs a single repair.
- It requires the repair to make the entire input valid, rather than choosing a repair that makes maximal (but bounded) progress. This means, in particular, that repair is not constant-time.
- It only attempts repairs of Hamming distance 1, that is, single-token replacements.

These limitations can be easily addressed by modifying the functor, without any change to the underlying parser.

When applied to a parser P, BurkeFisher produces a parser with result type P.result * string option. The string component is a description of the single repair (if any) performed.

Internally, the functor uses Herman's GreatEscape functor [5], which provides delimited control by using SML/NJ's call/cc facility. Crucially, this implementation of delimited control interacts properly with exceptions: delimited continuations captured by shift also capture exception handlers up to the delimiter—no more, no less. Thus, as Herman writes,

```
reset
  (fn _ =>
      (shift (fn k => (k 0)
                      handle Fail _ => 1))
    + (raise Fail "uncaught"))
handle Fail _ => 2
```

returns 1 rather than 2. Since we use exceptions to communicate parse failures, and thus exception handlers to institute repair, we rely on this behavior.

Once BurkeFisher is applied to a particular parser and lexer, it instantiates the parser with an instrumented version of the lexer, yielding a module UP (for "underlying parser"). To parse an underlying stream us, it wraps the stream and feeds it to the underlying parser—within a reset, which sets the delimiter for the checkpointing lexer. The result of the parse is paired with NONE, meaning no repair was necessary, which is returned if all goes well. But *outside* this pair (in particular, outside the reset), there is an exception handler that kicks off the repair process. Placing the handler outside the reset guarantees it won't be captured in the checkpoints.

AT LAST—when the underlying parser throws a syntax error, BurkeFisher catches it and its list of wrapped streams wss. Each wrapped stream represents a possible syntax error within a choice. Concatenating the checkpoints from each stream, the repairing parse uses tryCPs to attempt a repair at each checkpoint in turn. If successful, tryCPs returns a pair of the result from the underlying parser and the replacement token it used to get that successful parse. Otherwise tryCPs returns NONE, and parse re-raises the parse error using the underlying lexer streams.

Supposing we've written modules Tok and SimpleLexer (which represents streams as lists of tokens), we can sit down at the REPL and see

```
> structure RP  = BurkeFisher(Tok)(DeclRecognizer);
> structure RPP = RP.ForLexer(SimpleLexer);
> RPP.parse [VAL,ID,LPAREN,ID,RPAREN,EQ,
             NUM,PLUS,NUM,SEMI];
((), SOME "Did you mean 'fun'?")
```

A caveat: choice points are commit points

There's a subtlety regarding choice: if we factor out " = ⟨*exp*⟩ ; ", which is common to both forms of ⟨*decl*⟩, the repair no longer works.

The problem is this: once a choice has been successfully parsed, only the checkpoints of the taken branch are retained. The effective result is that repair checkpoints do not always have access to all possible branches.

We used exceptions carrying a list of streams to join together the checkpoints of an unsuccessful choice. To deal with successful choices, we need to maintain all checkpoints even when backtracking—we need the backtracking control structure to play nicely with the checkpointing control structure. An easy and fairly pleasing way to do this is to parameterize the underlying parser by an implementation of backtracking choice—which BurkeFisher can then provide—which also allows ParseError exceptions to carry just a single stream:

```
fun choose p q = fn (us, w) =>
  p s handle ParseError (us', w') =>
  q (us, w')
```

Discussion

The big idea As with the eager REPL, the key benefit of control operators is the ability to hook into—even manipulate—the computation of a parser, without any understanding of how that computation is structured.

There are also two significant differences from the eager REPL. First, we assume that parsing and lexing are free from observable side effects, so we do not use effect logging (and, in fact, avoid state—see below). Thus, we are *only* logging control state. Second, by having a modicum of knowledge about the structure of input to the parser (via the Tok signature), we are able to intelligently explore the space of input repairs, while keeping the computational structure of the parser abstract.

Look Ma, no refs! Contra the eager Scheme REPL, we haven't used mutable state in implementing Burke-Fisher repair. We were able to avoid it because the PARSER signature requires parsers to use their lexers *functionally*—in particular, to thread the token stream through the parsing processes. The downside to this approach is that checkpointing is sensitive to the way the parser threads the token stream, which as we noted can cause problems when the parser itself backtracks.

But, of course, an imperative interface is also workable, and it has the benefit that *every* use of the lexer is checkpointed, regard less of how the token stream is threaded. What's more, the token streams can be dropped from the ParseError exception, further shrinking the interface between the parser and the repair functor.

```
functor BurkeFisher (T : TOK)
                    (P : PARSER where
                         type tok = T.tok) =
struct
  type tok = T.tok
  type repair = string
  type result = P.result * string option

  (* Herman's delimited control from call/cc *)
  structure C = GreatEscape(type ans = P.result)

  functor ForLexer (L : LEXER
                    where type tok = tok) =
  struct
    exception ParseError of L.tok_stream list
    structure WL = WrappedLexer (C) (L)
    structure UP = P.ForLexer (WL)

    fun tryReps k []       = NONE
      | tryReps k (t::ts) = SOME (k t, t)
          handle UP.ParseError _ => tryReps k ts

    fun tryCPs []       = NONE
      | tryCPs (k::ks) = case tryReps k T.toks
                         of NONE    => tryCPs ks
                          | SOME rt => SOME rt

    fun parse us =
      (C.reset (fn () =>
         UP.parse (WL.wrap us)), NONE)
      handle UP.ParseError wss =>
        case tryCPs (List.concat
                      (map WL.checkpoints wss))
           of NONE =>
                raise ParseError (map WL.unwrap wss)
            | SOME (r, t) =>
                (r, SOME (concat ["Did you mean ",
                                  T.toString t,
                                  "?\n"]))
  end
end
```

Figure 5. The Burke-Fisher functor

To type-checking, and beyond Having generalized Burke-Fisher repair to arbitrary parsers, it's natural to wonder if we can go even farther. By encapsulating the notion of input streams and local repairs in a separate module taken as an extra parameter, the `BurkeFisher` functor could be pared down to handling just the checkpointing and error-catching process. We suspect, for example, that Lerner *et al.*'s SEMINAL tool [9], which attempts to explain type errors by searching for repairs, could be restructured to use Burke-Fisher-style local search—becoming just one more instantiation of the functor.

The real deal The `BurkeFisher` functor came out of work done building new lexing and parsing infrastructure for SML/NJ; it is in use in production code, and available with recent versions of the compiler.[3] The implementation includes the full suite of Burke-Fisher repairs, allows for multiple repairs, and judges goodness of repairs using a sophisticated metric.

[3] See `http://smlnj.org/`

Acknowledgements

This article reports on work supported by the Defense Advanced Research Projects Agency under Air Force Research Laboratory (AFRL/Rome) Contract No. FA8650-10-C-7090 and Cooperative Agreement No. FA8750-10-2-0233. The views expressed are those of the authors and do not reflect the official policy or position of the Department of Defense or the U.S. Government.

Turon is currently supported by a Microsoft fellowship, and was supported by NSF award CNS-0454136 while writing the ML-ANTLR parser at the University of Chicago.

John Reppy provided much guidance. Matthias Felleisen provided encouragement and insightful comments to Shivers while he was working out the rubout-handler system; Mark Feeley provided Shivers an early opportunity to air the design at a Scheme workshop. The quotation on line 31 of Figure 1 is due to a prince in Denmark. Kent Pitman and Dan Weinreb were fonts of wisdom concerning sophisticated details of classic LISP technology. Thanks go to Vincent St-Amour, Sam Tobin-Hochstadt, and Jesse Tov for feedback on a draft of the paper.

Shivers would like to dedicate this set of twin pearls to another such set: Olin and Avery.

References

[1] E. Biagioni, K. Cline, P. Lee, C. Okasaki, and C. Stone. Safe-for-space threads in Standard ML. *Higher Order and Symbolic Computation*, 11: 209–225, Sept. 1998.

[2] M. G. Burke and G. A. Fisher. A practical method for LR and LL syntactic error diagnosis and recovery. *ACM Transactions on Programming Languages and Systems*, 9(2):164–197, Mar. 1987.

[3] O. Danvy and A. Filinski. Abstracting control. In *Proceedings of the 1990 ACM Conference on LISP and Functional Programming (LFP'90)*, pages 151–160, 1990.

[4] M. Felleisen. The theory and practice of first-class prompts. In *Conference Record of POPL 1988: The Fifteenth ACM SIGPLAN-SIGACT Symposium on Principles of Programming Languages*, pages 180–190, 1988.

[5] D. Herman. Functional pearl: The great escape, or how to jump the border without getting caught. In *Proceedings of the Twelfth ACM SIGPLAN International Conference on Functional Programming (ICFP'07)*, 2007.

[6] G. Hutton and E. Meijer. Monadic parsing in Haskell. *Journal of Functional Programming*, 8(4):437–444, July 1998.

[7] R. Kelsey and J. Rees. The Scheme48 system. `http://s48.org`.

[8] G. Kuan. *A true higher-order module system*. PhD thesis, University of Chicago, 2011.

[9] B. S. Lerner, M. Flower, D. Grossman, and C. Chambers. Searching for type-error messages. In *Proceedings of the 2007 ACM SIGPLAN Conference on Programming Language Design and Implementation (PLDI'07)*, 2007.

[10] K. M. Pitman. Ambitious evaluation: a new reading of an old issue. *Lisp Pointers*, VIII(2), May 1995.

[11] A. Rossberg, C. Russo, and D. Dreyer. F-ing modules. In *Proceedings of the ACM SIGPLAN Workshop on Types in Language Design and Implementation (TLDI'10)*, 2010.

[12] O. Shivers, B. Carlstrom, M. Gasbichler, and M. Sperber. The scsh manual, release 0.6.6. `http://scsh.net`, Mar. 2004.

[13] D. Sitaram and M. Felleisen. Control delimiters and their hierarchies. *Lisp and Symbolic Computation*, 3:67–99, May 1990.

Pushdown Flow Analysis of First-Class Control

Dimitrios Vardoulakis Olin Shivers
Northeastern University
dimvar@ccs.neu.edu shivers@ccs.neu.edu

Abstract

Pushdown models are better than control-flow graphs for higher-order flow analysis. They faithfully model the call/return structure of a program, which results in fewer spurious flows and increased precision. However, pushdown models require that calls and returns in the analyzed program nest properly. As a result, they cannot be used to analyze language constructs that break call/return nesting such as generators, coroutines, `call/cc`, *etc.*

In this paper, we extend the CFA2 flow analysis to create the first pushdown flow analysis for languages with first-class control. We modify the abstract semantics of CFA2 to allow continuations to escape to, and be restored from, the heap. We then present a summarization algorithm that handles escaping continuations via a new kind of summary edge. We prove that the algorithm is sound with respect to the abstract semantics.

Categories and Subject Descriptors F.3.2 [*Semantics of Programming Languages*]: Program Analysis

General Terms Languages

Keywords pushdown flow analysis, first-class continuations, restricted continuation-passing style, summarization, higher-order functional language

1. Introduction

Function call and return is the fundamental control-flow mechanism in higher-order languages. Therefore, if a flow analysis is to model program behavior faithfully, it must handle call and return well. Pushdown models of programs [15, 17, 22] enable flow analyses with unbounded call/return matching. These analyses are more precise than analyses based on control-flow graphs.

Pushdown models require that calls and returns in the analyzed program nest properly. However, many control constructs, some of them in mainstream programming languages, break call/return nesting. *Generators* (*e.g.*, in Python [14] or JavaScript [8]) are functions that are usually called inside loops to produce a sequence of values one at a time. A generator executes until it reaches a `yield` statement, at which point it returns the value passed to `yield` to its calling context. When the generator is called again, execution resumes at the first instruction after the `yield`. *Coroutines* (*e.g.*, in Simula67 [3] or Lua [11]) can also suspend and resume their execution, but are more expressive than generators because they can specify where to pass control when they yield. *First-class continuations* reify the rest of the computation as a value. Continuations allow complex control flow, such as jumping back to functions that have already returned. Undelimited continuations (`call/cc` in Scheme [20] and SML/NJ [1]) capture the entire stack. Delimited continuations [4, 7], found in Scala [16] and some Schemes, capture part of the stack. Continuations can express generators and coroutines, as well as multi-threading [18, 25] and Prolog-style backtracking. All these operators provide a rich variety of control behaviors. Unfortunately, we cannot currently use pushdown models to analyze programs that use them.

We rectify this situation by extending the CFA2 flow analysis [22] to languages with first-class control. In this article, we make the following contributions.

- CFA2 is based on abstract interpretation of programs in continuation-passing style (*abbrev.* CPS). We present a CFA2-style abstract semantics for Restricted CPS, a variant of CPS that allows continuations to escape, but also permits effective reasoning about the stack [23]. When we detect a continuation that may escape, we copy the stack into the heap (sec. 4.3). We prove that the abstract semantics is a safe approximation of the actual run-time behavior of the program (sec. 4.4).
- In pushdown flow analysis, each state has a stack of unbounded size. Hence, the state space is infinite. Algorithms that explore the state space use a technique called *summarization*. First-class control causes the stack to be copied into the heap, so our analysis must also deal with infinitely many heaps. We show that it is not necessary to keep continuations in the heap during summarization; we handle escaping continuations using a new kind of summary edge (sec. 5.3).
- When calls and returns nest properly, execution paths satisfy a property called *unique decomposition:* for each state s in a path, we can uniquely identify another state s' as the entry of the procedure that contains s [17]. In the presence of first-class control, a state can belong to more than one procedure. We allow paths that are decomposable in multiple ways and prove that our analysis is sound (sec. 5.4).
- If continuations escape upward, a flow analysis cannot generally avoid including extra, spurious control flows that degrade precision. What about continuations that are only used downward, such as exception handlers or continuations captured by `call/cc` that never escape? We show that CFA2 can avoid spurious control flows for downward continuations (sec. 5.5).

2. Why pushdown models?

Finite-state flow analyses, such as k-CFA, approximate programs as graphs of abstract machine states. Each node in such a graph represents a program point plus some amount of abstracted environment and control context. Every path in the graph is considered a possible execution of the program. Thus, executions are strings in a *regular* language.

ICFP'11, September 19–21, 2011, Tokyo, Japan.

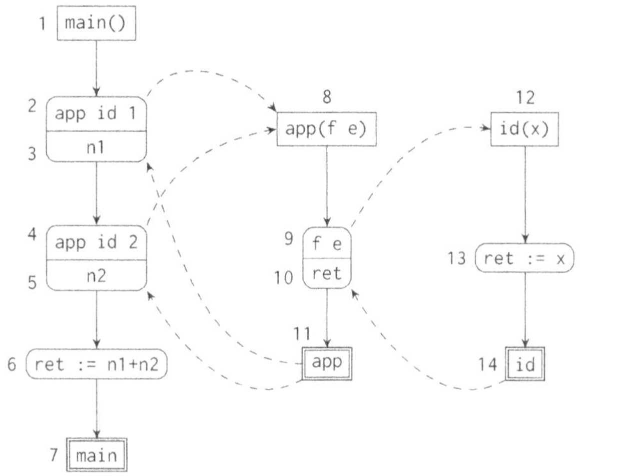

Figure 1. Control-flow graph for a simple program

Finite-state analyses do not handle call and return well. Remembering only a bounded number of pending calls, they must inevitably include spurious paths in which a function is called from one program point and returns to a different one.

Execution traces that match calls with returns are strings in a *context-free* language. Therefore, by abstracting a program to a pushdown automaton (or equivalent), we can use the stack to eliminate call/return mismatch. The following examples illustrate the advantages of pushdown models.

2.1 Data-flow information

The following Scheme program defines the apply and identity functions, then binds n1 to 1 and n2 to 2 and adds them. At program point (+ n1 n2), both variables are bound to constants; we would like a static analysis to be able to discover this.

```
(define app (λ (f e) (f e)))
(define id  (λ (x) x))

(let* ((n1 (app id 1))
       (n2 (app id 2)))
  (+ n1 n2))
```

Fig. 1 shows the control-flow graph for this program. In the graph, the top level of the program is presented as a function called main. Function entry and exit nodes are rectangles with sharp corners. Inner nodes are rectangles with rounded corners. Each call site is represented by a call node and a corresponding return node, which contains the variable to which the result of the call is assigned. Each function uses a local variable ret for its return value. Solid arrows are intraprocedural steps. Dashed arrows go from call sites to function entries and from function exits to return points. There is no edge between call and return nodes; a call reaches its corresponding return only if the callee terminates.

A monovariant analysis, such as 0CFA, considers all paths to be valid executions. Thus, we can bind n1 to 2 by calling app from 4 and returning to 3. Also, we can bind n2 to 1 by calling app from 2 and returning to 5. At point 6, 0CFA thinks that each variable can be bound to either 1 or 2. (For polyvariant analyses, we can create similar examples.) On the other hand, if we only consider paths that respect call/return matching, there is no spurious flow of data. At 6, n1 and n2 are bound to constants.

2.2 Stack-change calculation

Besides data-flow information, pushdown models also improve control-flow information. Hence, we can use them to accurately calculate stack changes between program points. With call/return matching, there is only one execution path in our example:

1 2 8 9 12 13 14 10 11 3 4 8 9 12 13 14 10 11 5 6 7

In contrast, 0CFA thinks that the program has a loop (there is a path from 4 to 3).

Many optimizations require accurate information about stack change. For instance:

- Most compound data are heap allocated in the general case. Examples include: closure environments, cons pairs, records, objects, *etc.* If we can show statically that such a piece of data is only passed downward, we can allocate it on the stack and reduce garbage-collection overhead.
- Continuations captured by call/cc may not escape upward. In this case, we do not need to copy the stack into the heap.
- In object-oriented languages, objects may have methods that are thread-safe by using locks. An escape analysis can eliminate unnecessary locking/unlocking in the methods of thread-private objects.

Such optimizations are better performed with pushdown models.

2.3 Fake rebinding

It is possible that two control-related references to the same variable are always bound in the same run-time environment. If a flow analysis cannot detect this, it will additionally consider execution traces in which the two references are bound to different abstract values. We call this phenomenon fake rebinding [22].

```
(define (compose-same f x) (f (f x)))
```

In compose-same, both references to f are always bound in the same environment (the top stack frame). However, if multiple closures flow to f, a finite-state analysis will consider traces that call one closure at the inner call site and a different closure at the outer call site. CFA2 forbids these paths because it knows that both references are bound in the top frame—it correctly relates *environment* and *control* structure.

2.4 Broadening the applicability of pushdown models

Pushdown-reachability algorithms use a dynamic-programming technique called summarization. Summarization relies on proper nesting of calls and returns. If we call function app from location 2 in our example, summarization knows that, if the call returns, it will return to location 3, *not* location 5.

What if the call to app is a tail call, in which case the return point is effectively in a different procedure from the call site? We can handle this by creating *cross-procedure* summaries [22].

In languages with exceptions, the return point may be deeper in the stack. We can transform this case into ordinary call/return nesting and handle it precisely with CFA2. Instead of thinking of an exception as a single jump deeper in the stack, we can return to the caller, which checks if it can handle the exception and if not, it passes it to its own caller and so on. Functions return a pair of values, one for normal return and one for exceptional return. The JavaScript implementation of CFA2 [5] uses this technique for exceptions.

But what if the return point has already been popped off the stack, as is the case when using first-class control constructs? Pushdown models cannot currently analyze such programs, so we have to fall back to a finite-state analysis and live with its limitations. In

$$
\begin{array}{rcl}
v \in \mathit{Var} & = & \mathit{UVar} + \mathit{CVar} \\
u \in \mathit{UVar} & = & \text{a set of identifiers} \\
k \in \mathit{CVar} & = & \text{a set of identifiers} \\
\psi \in \mathit{Lab} & = & \mathit{ULab} + \mathit{CLab} \\
l \in \mathit{ULab} & = & \text{a set of labels} \\
\gamma \in \mathit{CLab} & = & \text{a set of labels} \\
\mathit{lam} \in \mathit{Lam} & = & \mathit{ULam} + \mathit{CLam} \\
\mathit{ulam} \in \mathit{ULam} & ::= & (\lambda_l (u\, k)\ \mathit{call}) \\
\mathit{clam} \in \mathit{CLam} & ::= & (\lambda_\gamma (u)\ \mathit{call}) \\
\mathit{call} \in \mathit{Call} & = & \mathit{UCall} + \mathit{CCall} \\
\mathit{UCall} & ::= & (f\ e\ q)^l \\
\mathit{CCall} & ::= & (q\ e)^\gamma \\
g \in \mathit{Exp} & = & \mathit{UExp} + \mathit{CExp} \\
f, e \in \mathit{UExp} & = & \mathit{ULam} + \mathit{UVar} \\
q \in \mathit{CExp} & = & \mathit{CLam} + \mathit{CVar} \\
\mathit{pr} \in \mathit{Program} & = & \mathit{ULam}
\end{array}
$$

Figure 2. Partitioned CPS

the rest of this paper, we show how to generalize pushdown models to first-class control.

3. Restricted CPS

Preliminary definitions In this section we describe our CPS language. Compilers that use CPS [1, 10, 21] frequently partition the terms in a program into two disjoint sets, the *user* and the *continuation* set, and treat user terms differently from continuation terms. We adopt this partitioning here (Fig. 2). Variables, lambdas and calls get labels from ULab or CLab. Labels are pairwise distinct. User lambdas take a user argument and the current continuation; continuation lambdas take only a user argument.

We assume that all variables in a program have distinct names. Then, the defining lambda of a variable v, written $\mathit{def}_\lambda(v)$, is the lambda term that contains v in its list of formals. For any term g, $\mathit{iu}_\lambda(g)$ is the innermost user lambda that contains g. Concrete syntax enclosed in $[\![\cdot]\!]$ denotes an item of abstract syntax. Functions with a '?' subscript are predicates, *e.g.*, $\mathit{Var}_?(e)$ returns true if e is a variable and false otherwise.

We use two notations for tuples, $(e_1, \dots, e_n)$ and $\langle e_1, \dots, e_n \rangle$, to avoid confusion when tuples are deeply nested. We use the latter for lists as well; ambiguities will be resolved by the context. Lists are also described by a head-tail notation, *e.g.*, $3 :: \langle 1, 3, -47 \rangle$.

Handling first-class control In CPS, we can naturally express first-class control without using special primitives: when continuations are captured by user closures, they may escape.

Escaping continuations complicate reasoning about the stack. To enable reasoning about the stack in the presence of first-class control, we have previously proposed a syntactically-restricted variant of CPS, called Restricted CPS (*abbrev.* RCPS) [23].

Definition 1 (Restricted CPS). *A program is in Restricted CPS iff a continuation variable can appear free in a user lambda in operator position only.*

In RCPS, continuations escape in a well-behaved way: *after a continuation escapes, it can only be called*; it cannot be passed as an argument again. For example, the CPS-translation of `call/cc`, which is `(λ(f cc) (f (λ(v k) (cc v)) cc))`, is a valid RCPS term. Terms like `(λ(x k) (k (λ(y k2) (y 123 k))))` are not valid.

We can transform this term (and any CPS term) to a valid RCPS term by η-expanding to return the free reference to operator position: `(λ(x k) (k (λ(y k2) (y 123 (λ(u) (k u))))))`. Why do we distinguish these very similar terms? Because, according to the Orbit policy (*cf.* sec. 4.1), their stack behaviors differ. In the case of the first term, when execution reaches `(y 123 k)`, we must restore the environment of the continuation that flows to `k`, which may cause arbitrary change to the stack. In the second case, when execution reaches `(y 123 (λ(u) (k u)))`, a new continuation is born and no stack change is required. Thus, RCPS forces all exotic stack change to happen when calling an escaping continuation, not in other kinds of call sites.

Concrete semantics Execution in RCPS is guided by the semantics of Fig. 3. In the terminology of abstract interpretation [2], this semantics is called the *concrete* semantics. In order to find properties of a program at compile time, one needs to derive a computable approximation of the concrete semantics, called the *abstract* semantics (*cf.* sec. 4).

Execution traces alternate between Eval and Apply states. At an Eval state, we evaluate the subexpressions of a call site before performing a call. At an Apply, we perform the call.

The last component of each state is a *time*, which is a sequence of call sites. Eval-to-Apply transitions increment the time by recording the label of the corresponding call site. Apply-to-Eval transitions leave the time unchanged. Thus, the time t of a state reveals the call sites along the execution path to that state.

$$
\begin{array}{rcl}
\varsigma \in \mathit{State} & = & \mathit{Eval} + \mathit{Apply} \\
\mathit{Eval} & = & \mathit{UEval} + \mathit{CEval} \\
\mathit{UEval} & = & \mathit{UCall} \times \mathit{BEnv} \times \mathit{VEnv} \times \mathit{Time} \\
\mathit{CEval} & = & \mathit{CCall} \times \mathit{BEnv} \times \mathit{VEnv} \times \mathit{Time} \\
\mathit{Apply} & = & \mathit{UApply} + \mathit{CApply} \\
\mathit{UApply} & = & \mathit{UClos} \times \mathit{UClos} \times \mathit{CClos} \times \mathit{VEnv} \times \mathit{Time} \\
\mathit{CApply} & = & \mathit{CClos} \times \mathit{UClos} \times \mathit{VEnv} \times \mathit{Time} \\
\mathit{Clos} & = & \mathit{UClos} + \mathit{CClos} \\
d \in \mathit{UClos} & = & \mathit{ULam} \times \mathit{BEnv} \\
c \in \mathit{CClos} & = & (\mathit{CLam} \times \mathit{BEnv}) + \mathit{halt} \\
\beta \in \mathit{BEnv} & = & \mathit{Var} \rightharpoonup \mathit{Time} \\
\mathit{ve} \in \mathit{VEnv} & = & \mathit{Var} \times \mathit{Time} \rightharpoonup \mathit{Clos} \\
t \in \mathit{Time} & = & \mathit{Lab}^*
\end{array}
$$

(a) Concrete domains

$$
\mathcal{A}(g, \beta, \mathit{ve}) \triangleq \begin{cases} (g, \beta) & \mathit{Lam}_?(g) \\ \mathit{ve}(g, \beta(g)) & \mathit{Var}_?(g) \end{cases}
$$

$$
\begin{array}{ll}
[\text{UEA}] & ([\![(f\ e\ q)^l]\!], \beta, \mathit{ve}, t) \to (\mathit{proc}, d, c, \mathit{ve}, l :: t) \\
& \mathit{proc} = \mathcal{A}(f, \beta, \mathit{ve}) \\
& d = \mathcal{A}(e, \beta, \mathit{ve}) \\
& c = \mathcal{A}(q, \beta, \mathit{ve})
\end{array}
$$

$$
\begin{array}{ll}
[\text{UAE}] & (\mathit{proc}, d, c, \mathit{ve}, t) \to (\mathit{call}, \beta', \mathit{ve}', t) \\
& \mathit{proc} \equiv \langle [\![(\lambda_l (u\, k)\ \mathit{call})]\!], \beta \rangle \\
& \beta' = \beta[u \mapsto t][k \mapsto t] \\
& \mathit{ve}' = \mathit{ve}[(u, t) \mapsto d][(k, t) \mapsto c]
\end{array}
$$

$$
\begin{array}{ll}
[\text{CEA}] & ([\![(q\ e)^\gamma]\!], \beta, \mathit{ve}, t) \to (\mathit{proc}, d, \mathit{ve}, \gamma :: t) \\
& \mathit{proc} = \mathcal{A}(q, \beta, \mathit{ve}) \\
& d = \mathcal{A}(e, \beta, \mathit{ve})
\end{array}
$$

$$
\begin{array}{ll}
[\text{CAE}] & (\mathit{proc}, d, \mathit{ve}, t) \to (\mathit{call}, \beta', \mathit{ve}', t) \\
& \mathit{proc} = \langle [\![(\lambda_\gamma (u)\ \mathit{call})]\!], \beta \rangle \\
& \beta' = \beta[u \mapsto t] \\
& \mathit{ve}' = \mathit{ve}[(u, t) \mapsto d]
\end{array}
$$

(b) Concrete semantics

Figure 3. Concrete semantics and domains

Times indicate points in the execution when variables are bound. The binding environment β is a partial function that maps variables to their binding times. The variable environment ve maps variable/time pairs to values. To find the value of a variable v, we look up the time v was put in β, and use that to search for the actual value in ve. By pairing variables with times, we allow a single variable to have multiple bindings at run time.

Let's look at each transition individually. At a $UEval$ state over $[\![(f\ e\ q)^l]\!]$, we use the function $\mathcal{A}$ to evaluate the simple expressions f, e and q: lambdas are paired up with β to become closures, while variables are looked up in ve using β. We add the label l in front of the current time and transition to a $UApply$ state (rule [UEA]).

From $UApply$ to $Eval$, we bind the formals of a procedure $\langle[\![(\lambda_l(u\,k)\ call)]\!], \beta\rangle$ to the arguments and jump to its body. The new binding environment β' extends the procedure's environment, with u and k mapped to the current time. The new variable environment ve' maps (u, t) to the user argument d, and (k, t) to the continuation c (rule [UAE]).

The remaining two transitions are similar. We use $halt$ to denote the top-level continuation of a program pr. The initial state $\mathcal{I}(pr)$ is $((pr, \emptyset), \mathit{input}, \mathit{halt}, \emptyset, \langle\rangle)$, where input is a closure of the form $\langle[\![(\lambda_l(u\,k)\ call)]\!], \emptyset\rangle$. The initial time is the empty sequence of call sites.

4. The CFA2 abstraction

In this section, we'll extend the abstract semantics of CFA2 to handle first-class control. The semantics uses two binding environments, a stack and a heap; we also use the stack for return-point information.

We show the actual transition rules in section 4.3; the main difference from the previous semantics is that continuations can now be copied to, and restored from, the heap. Before that, we discuss how to manage the stack in RCPS (sec. 4.1) and how to decide whether a variable reference will be looked up in the stack or the heap (sec. 4.2). In section 4.4, we prove that the abstract semantics is an approximation of the concrete semantics.

The CFA2 abstraction only takes us halfway to a computable analysis: the abstract state space is infinite, so we cannot explore it by enumerating all states. We tackle this problem in section 5.

4.1 Stack-management policy

The Orbit compiler [9, 10] compiles a CPS intermediate representation to final code that uses a stack. Orbit views continuations as closures whose environment record is a stack frame. To decide when to push and pop the stack, we follow Orbit's policy. The main idea behind Orbit's policy is that *we can manage the stack for a CPS program in the same way that we would manage it for the original direct-style program:*

- For every call to a user function, we push a frame for the arguments.
- We pop a frame at function returns. In CPS, user functions "return" by calling the current continuation with a return value.
- We also pop a frame at tail calls. A $UCall$ call site is a tail call in CPS iff it was a tail call in the original direct-style program. In tail calls, the continuation argument is a variable.
- When a continuation is captured by a user closure, we copy the stack into the heap.
- When we call a continuation that has escaped, we restore its stack from the heap.

4.2 Stack/heap split

The stack in CFA2 is more than a control structure for return-point information; it is also an *environment* structure—it contains bindings. CFA2 has a novel approach to variable binding: *two references to the same variable need not be looked up in the same binding environment.* We split references into two categories: stack and heap references. In direct-style, if a reference appears at the same nesting level as its binder, then it is a stack reference, otherwise it is a heap reference. For example, `(λ1(x)(λ2(y)(x (x y))))` has a stack reference to `y` and two heap references to `x`.

Intuitively, only heap references may escape. When we call a user function, we push a frame for its arguments, so we know that stack references are always bound in the top frame. When control reaches a heap reference, its frame is either deeper in the stack, or it has been popped. We look up stack references in the top frame, and heap references in the heap. Stack lookups below the top frame never happen (Fig. 4b).

When a program p is CPS-converted to a program p', stack (*resp.* heap) references in p remain stack (*resp.* heap) references in p'. All references added by the transform are stack references.

We can give an equivalent definition of stack and heap references directly in CPS, without referring to the original direct-style program. Labels can be split into disjoint sets according to the innermost user lambda that contains them. For the CPS translation of the previous program,

```
(λ1(x k1)
   (k1 (λ2(y k2)
          (x y (λ3(u) (x u k2)⁴))⁵))⁶)
```

these sets are $\{1, 6\}$ and $\{2, 3, 4, 5\}$. The "label to variable" map $LV(\psi)$ returns all the variables bound by any lambdas that belong in the same set as ψ, *e.g.*, $LV(4) = \{\mathtt{y}, \mathtt{k2}, \mathtt{u}\}$ and $LV(6) = \{\mathtt{x}, \mathtt{k1}\}$. We use this map to model stack behavior, because all continuation lambdas that "belong" to a given user lambda λ_l get closed by extending λ_l's stack frame (*cf.* section 4.3). Notice that, for any ψ, $LV(\psi)$ contains exactly one continuation variable. Using LV, we give the following definition.

Definition 2 (Stack and heap references)**.**

- *Let ψ be a call site that refers to a variable v. The predicate $S_?(\psi, v)$ holds iff $v \in LV(\psi)$. We call v a* ***stack reference****.*
- *Let ψ be a call site that refers to a variable v. The predicate $H_?(\psi, v)$ holds iff $v \notin LV(\psi)$. We call v a* ***heap reference****.*
- *v is a* ***stack variable****, written $S_?(v)$, iff all its references satisfy $S_?$.*
- *v is a* ***heap variable****, written $H_?(v)$, iff some of its references satisfy $H_?$.*

For instance, $S_?(5, \mathtt{y})$ holds because $\mathtt{y} \in \{\mathtt{y}, \mathtt{k2}, \mathtt{u}\}$ and $H_?(5, \mathtt{x})$ holds because $\mathtt{x} \notin \{\mathtt{y}, \mathtt{k2}, \mathtt{u}\}$.

4.3 Abstract semantics

The CFA2 semantics is an abstract machine that executes a program in RCPS (Fig. 4). The abstract domains appear in Fig. 4a. An abstract user closure (member of the set $\widehat{UClos}$) is a set of user lambdas. An abstract continuation closure (member of $\widehat{CClos}$) is either a continuation lambda or $halt$. A frame is a map from variables to abstract values, and a stack is a sequence of frames. All stack operations except $push$ are defined for non-empty stacks only. A heap is a map from variables to abstract values. In contrast to the previous semantics of CFA2, the heap can contain continuation bindings.

Fig. 4c shows the transition rules. First-class control shows up in two of the rules, $[\widehat{\text{UAE}}]$ and $[\widehat{\text{CEA}}]$.

On transition from a $\widehat{UEval}$ state to a $\widehat{UApply}$ state (rule $[\widehat{\text{UEA}}]$), we first evaluate f, e and q. We evaluate atomic user

$$\hat{\varsigma} \in \widehat{UEval} = UCall \times Stack \times Heap$$
$$\hat{\varsigma} \in \widehat{UApply} = ULam \times \widehat{UClos} \times \widehat{CClos} \times Stack \times Heap$$
$$\hat{\varsigma} \in \widehat{CEval} = CCall \times Stack \times Heap$$
$$\hat{\varsigma} \in \widehat{CApply} = \widehat{CClos} \times \widehat{UClos} \times Stack \times Heap$$
$$\hat{d} \in \widehat{UClos} = Pow(ULam)$$
$$\hat{c} \in \widehat{CClos} = CLam + halt$$
$$fr, tf \in Frame = (UVar \rightharpoonup \widehat{UClos}) + (CVar \rightharpoonup \widehat{CClos})$$
$$st \in Stack = Frame^*$$
$$h \in Heap = (UVar \rightharpoonup \widehat{UClos}) + (CVar \rightharpoonup Pow(\widehat{CClos} \times Stack))$$

(a) Abstract domains

$$\begin{aligned} pop(tf :: st) &\triangleq st \\ push(fr, st) &\triangleq fr :: st \\ (tf :: st)(v) &\triangleq tf(v) \\ (tf :: st)[u \mapsto \hat{d}] &\triangleq tf[u \mapsto \hat{d}] :: st \end{aligned}$$

(b) Stack operations

$$\hat{\mathcal{A}}_u(e, \psi, st, h) \triangleq \begin{cases} \{e\} & Lam?(e) \\ st(e) & S?(\psi, e) \\ h(e) & H?(\psi, e) \end{cases}$$

$$[\widehat{UEA}]\ (\llbracket (f\ e\ q)^l \rrbracket, st, h) \rightsquigarrow (ulam, \hat{d}, \hat{c}, st', h)$$
$$ulam \in \hat{\mathcal{A}}_u(f, l, st, h)$$
$$\hat{d} = \hat{\mathcal{A}}_u(e, l, st, h)$$
$$\hat{c} = \begin{cases} st(q) & Var?(q) \\ q & Lam?(q) \end{cases}$$
$$st' = \begin{cases} pop(st) & Var?(q) \\ st & Lam?(q) \wedge (H?(l, f) \vee Lam?(f)) \\ st[f \mapsto \{ulam\}] & Lam?(q) \wedge S?(l, f) \end{cases}$$

$$[\widehat{UAE}]\ (\llbracket (\lambda_l (u\,k)\ call) \rrbracket, \hat{d}, \hat{c}, st, h) \rightsquigarrow (call, st', h')$$
$$st' = push([u \mapsto \hat{d}][k \mapsto \hat{c}], st)$$
$$h'(v) = \begin{cases} h(u) \cup \hat{d} & (v = u) \wedge H?(u) \\ h(k) \cup \{(\hat{c}, st)\} & (v = k) \wedge H?(k) \\ h(v) & o/w \end{cases}$$

$$[\widehat{CEA}]\ (\llbracket (q\ e)^\gamma \rrbracket, st, h) \rightsquigarrow (\hat{c}, \hat{d}, st', h)$$
$$\hat{d} = \hat{\mathcal{A}}_u(e, \gamma, st, h)$$
$$(\hat{c}, st') \in \begin{cases} \{(q, st)\} & Lam?(q) \\ \{(st(q), pop(st))\} & S?(\gamma, q) \\ h(q) & H?(\gamma, q) \end{cases}$$

$$[\widehat{CAE}]\ (\llbracket (\lambda_\gamma (u)\ call) \rrbracket, \hat{d}, st, h) \rightsquigarrow (call, st', h')$$
$$st' = st[u \mapsto \hat{d}]$$
$$h'(v) = \begin{cases} h(u) \cup \hat{d} & (v = u) \wedge H?(u) \\ h(v) & o/w \end{cases}$$

(c) Abstract semantics

Figure 4. Abstract semantics and relevant definitions

terms using $\hat{\mathcal{A}}_u$. We non-deterministically choose one of the lambdas that flow to f as the operator in the $\widehat{UApply}$ state.[1] The change to the stack depends on q and f. If q is a variable, the call is a tail call so we pop the stack (case 1). If q is a lambda, it evaluates to a new closure whose environment is the top frame, hence we do not pop the stack (cases 2, 3). Moreover, if f is a lambda or a heap reference then we leave the stack unchanged. However, if f is a stack reference, we set f's value in the top frame to $\{ulam\}$, possibly forgetting other lambdas that flow to f. The strong update to the stack prevents fake rebinding for stack references (*cf.* sec. 2.3): when we return to $\hat{c}$, we may reach more stack references of f. These references and the current one are bound at the same time. Therefore, they must also be bound to $ulam$.

In the $\widehat{UApply}$-to-$\widehat{Eval}$ transition (rule $[\widehat{UAE}]$), we push a frame for the procedure's arguments. If u is a heap variable, we update its binding in the heap with all lambdas in $\hat{d}$. If k is a heap variable, we have a possibly escaping continuation. We save $\hat{c}$ in the heap and also copy the stack, so that we can restore it if $\hat{c}$ gets called later.

In a $\widehat{CEval}$-to-$\widehat{CApply}$ transition (rule $[\widehat{CEA}]$), we are preparing for a call to a continuation so we must reset the stack to the stack of its birth. When q is a lambda, it is a newly created closure so the stack does not change. When q is a stack reference, the $\widehat{CEval}$ state is a function return and the continuation's environment is the second stack frame. Therefore, we pop a frame before calling $\hat{c}$. When q is a heap reference, we are calling a continuation that may have escaped. The stack change since the continuation capture can be arbitrary. We non-deterministically pick a pair $(\hat{c}, st')$ from $h(q)$, jump to $\hat{c}$ and restore st', which contains bindings for the stack references in $\hat{c}$.

In the $\widehat{CApply}$-to-$\widehat{Eval}$ transition (rule $[\widehat{CAE}]$), the top frame is the environment of $\llbracket (\lambda_\gamma (u)\ call) \rrbracket$; stack references in $call$ need this frame on the top of the stack. Hence, we do not push; we extend the top frame with the binding for the continuation's parameter u. If u is a heap variable, we also update the heap.

Example Let's see how the abstract semantics works on a program with `call/cc`. Consider the program

```
(call/cc (λ(c) (somefun (c 42))))
```

where *somefun* is an arbitrary function. We use `call/cc` to capture the top-level continuation and bind it to `c`. Then, *somefun* will never be called, because `(c 42)` will return to the top level with 42 as the result.

The CPS translation of `call/cc` is

```
(λ1(f cc) (f (λ2(x k2) (cc x)) cc))
```

The CPS translation of its argument is

```
(λ3(c k) (c 42 (λ4(u) (somefun_CPS u k))))
```

The initial state $\hat{\mathcal{I}}(pr) = (\lambda_1,\ \{\lambda_3\},\ halt,\ \langle\rangle,\ \emptyset)$ is a $\widehat{UApply}$. (We abbreviate lambdas by their labels.) We push a frame and jump to the body of λ_1. Since `cc` is a heap variable, we save the continuation and the stack in the heap, producing a heap h with a single element $[\texttt{cc} \mapsto \{(halt, \langle\rangle)\}]$, and $\widehat{UEval}$ state

$$(\llbracket (\texttt{f}\ \lambda_2\ \texttt{cc}) \rrbracket,\ \langle [\texttt{f} \mapsto \{\lambda_3\}][\texttt{cc} \mapsto halt] \rangle,\ h).$$

λ_2 is essentially a continuation reified as a user value. We tail call to λ_3, so we pop the stack, producing $\widehat{UApply}$ state

$$(\lambda_3,\ \{\lambda_2\},\ halt,\ \langle\rangle,\ h).$$

[1] An abstract execution explores one path, but the algorithm that searches the state space considers all possible executions.

$$|([\![(g_1 \ldots g_n)^{\psi}]\!], \beta, ve, t)|_{ca} = ([\![(g_1 \ldots g_n)^{\psi}]\!],\ toStack(LV(\psi), \beta, ve),\ |ve|_{ca})$$

$$|(\langle [\![(\lambda_l (u\,k)\ call)]\!], \beta\rangle, d, c, ve, t)|_{ca} = ([\![(\lambda_l (u\,k)\ call)]\!], |d|_{ca}, |c|_{ca}, st, |ve|_{ca})$$
$$\text{where } st = \begin{cases} \langle\rangle & c = halt \\ toStack(LV(\gamma), \beta', ve) & c = ([\![(\lambda_\gamma (u')call')]\!], \beta') \end{cases}$$

$$|(\langle [\![(\lambda_\gamma (u)\ call)]\!], \beta\rangle, d, ve, t)|_{ca} = ([\![(\lambda_\gamma (u)\ call)]\!],\ |d|_{ca}, toStack(LV(\gamma), \beta, ve),\ |ve|_{ca})$$

$$|(halt, d, ve, t)|_{ca} = (halt, |d|_{ca},\ \langle\rangle,\ |ve|_{ca})$$

$$|([\![(\lambda_l (u\,k)\ call)]\!], \beta)|_{ca} = \{[\![(\lambda_l (u\,k)\ call)]\!]\}$$

$$|([\![(\lambda_\gamma (u)\ call)]\!], \beta)|_{ca} = [\![(\lambda_\gamma (u)\ call)]\!]$$

$$|halt|_{ca} = halt$$

$$|ve|_{ca} = \{\, (u, \textstyle\bigcup_t |ve(u,t)|_{ca}) \ :\ (u \in UVar) \wedge H?(u)\} \cup \{\, (k, \textstyle\bigcup_t makecs(ve(k,t), ve)) \ :\ (k \in CVar) \wedge H?(k)\}$$
$$\text{where } makecs(c, ve) \triangleq \begin{cases} (halt, \langle\rangle) & c = halt \\ ([\![(\lambda_\gamma (u')call)]\!], toStack(LV(\gamma), \beta, ve)) & c = \langle [\![(\lambda_\gamma (u')call)]\!], \beta\rangle \end{cases}$$

$$toStack(\{u_1, \ldots, u_n, k\}, \beta, ve) \triangleq \begin{cases} \langle [\overline{u_i \mapsto \hat{d}_i}\,][k \mapsto halt]\rangle & ve(k, \beta(k)) = halt \\ [\overline{u_i \mapsto \hat{d}_i}\,][k \mapsto [\![(\lambda_\gamma (u)\ call)]\!]] :: st & ve(k, \beta(k)) = ([\![(\lambda_\gamma (u)\ call)]\!], \beta') \end{cases}$$
$$\text{where } \hat{d}_i = |ve(u_i, \beta(u_i))|_{ca} \text{ and } st = toStack(LV(\gamma), \beta', ve)$$

Figure 5. From concrete states to abstract states

$g \sqsubseteq g$ where $g \in (halt + Lam + Call)$

$\langle a_1, \ldots, a_n\rangle \sqsubseteq \langle b_1, \ldots, b_n\rangle$ iff for $1 \leqslant i \leqslant n,\ a_i \sqsubseteq b_i$

$\hat{d}_1 \sqsubseteq \hat{d}_2$ iff $\hat{d}_1 \subseteq \hat{d}_2$

$h_1 \sqsubseteq h_2$ iff $h_1(v) \sqsubseteq h_2(v)$ for each $v \in \text{dom}(h_1)$

$tf_1 :: st_1 \sqsubseteq tf_2 :: st_2$ iff $tf_1 \sqsubseteq tf_2 \wedge st_1 \sqsubseteq st_2$

$\langle\rangle \sqsubseteq \langle\rangle$

$tf_1 \sqsubseteq tf_2$ iff $tf_1(v) \sqsubseteq tf_2(v)$ for each $v \in \text{dom}(tf_1)$

Figure 6. The $\sqsubseteq$ relation on abstract states

We next push a frame and jump to the body of λ_3:

$$([\![(\texttt{c 42 } \lambda_4)]\!],\ \langle[\texttt{c} \mapsto \{\lambda_2\}][\texttt{k} \mapsto halt]\rangle,\ h).$$

This is a non-tail call, so we do not pop:

$$(\lambda_2,\ \{42\},\ \lambda_4,\ \langle[\texttt{c} \mapsto \{\lambda_2\}][\texttt{k} \mapsto halt]\rangle,\ h).$$

We push a frame and jump to the body of λ_2:

$$([\![(\texttt{cc x})]\!],\ \langle[\texttt{x} \mapsto \{42\}][\texttt{k2} \mapsto \lambda_4],\ [\texttt{c} \mapsto \{\lambda_2\}][\texttt{k} \mapsto halt]\rangle,\ h).$$

As cc is a heap reference, we ignore the current continuation and stack and restore $(halt, \langle\rangle)$ from the heap:

$$(halt,\ \{42\},\ \langle\rangle,\ h).$$

The program terminates with value $\{42\}$.

4.4 Correctness of the abstract semantics

In this section, we show that the abstract semantics *simulates* the concrete semantics, which means that the execution of a program under the abstract semantics is a safe approximation of its actual run-time behavior. First, we define a map $|\cdot|_{ca}$ from concrete to abstract states. Next, we show that if ς transitions to ς' in the concrete semantics, the abstract counterpart $|\varsigma|_{ca}$ of ς transitions to a state $\hat{\varsigma}'$ which approximates $|\varsigma'|_{ca}$. Therefore, each concrete execution, *i.e.*, sequence of states related by $\rightarrow$, has a corresponding abstract execution that computes an approximate answer.

The map $|\cdot|_{ca}$ appears in Fig. 5. The abstraction of an $Eval$ state ς of the form $([\![(g_1 \ldots g_n)^{\psi}]\!], \beta, ve, t)$ is an $\widehat{Eval}$ state $\hat{\varsigma}$ with the same call site. Since ς does not have a stack, we must expose stack-related information hidden in β and ve. Assume that λ_l is the innermost user lambda that contains ψ. To reach ψ, control passed from a $\widehat{UApply}$ state $\hat{\varsigma}'$ over λ_l. According to our stack policy, the top frame contains bindings for the formals of λ_l and any temporaries added along the path from $\hat{\varsigma}'$ to $\hat{\varsigma}$. Therefore, the domain of the top frame is a subset of $LV(l)$, *i.e.*, a subset of $LV(\psi)$. For each user variable $u_i \in (LV(\psi) \cap \text{dom}(\beta))$, the top frame contains $[u_i \mapsto |ve(u_i, \beta(u_i))|_{ca}]$. Let k be the sole continuation variable in $LV(\psi)$. If $ve(k, \beta(k))$ is $halt$ (the return continuation is the top-level continuation), the rest of the stack is empty. If $ve(k, \beta(k))$ is $([\![(\lambda_\gamma (u)\ call)]\!], \beta')$, the second frame is for the user lambda in which λ_γ was born, and so forth: proceeding through the stack, we add a frame for each live activation of a user lambda until we reach $halt$.

The abstraction of a $UApply$ state over $\langle [\![(\lambda_l (u\,k)\ call)]\!], \beta\rangle$ is a $\widehat{UApply}$ state $\hat{\varsigma}$ whose operator is $[\![(\lambda_l (u\,k)\ call)]\!]$. The stack of $\hat{\varsigma}$ represents the environment in which the continuation argument was created, and we compute it using $toStack$ as above.

Abstracting a $CApply$ is similar to the $UApply$ case, only now the top frame is the environment of the continuation operator. Note that the abstraction maps drop the time of the concrete states, since the abstract states do not use times.

The abstraction of a user closure is the singleton set with the corresponding lambda. The abstraction of a continuation closure is the corresponding lambda.

The abstraction $|ve|_{ca}$ of a variable environment is a heap, which contains bindings for the user and the continuation heap variables. Each heap user variable is bound to the set of lambdas of the closures that can flow to it. Each heap continuation variable k is bound to a set of continuation-stack pairs. For each closure that can flow to k, we create a pair with the lambda of that closure and the corresponding stack.

The relation $\hat{\varsigma}_1 \sqsubseteq \hat{\varsigma}_2$ is a partial order on abstract states and can be read as "$\hat{\varsigma}_1$ is more precise than $\hat{\varsigma}_2$" (Fig. 6). Tuples are ordered pointwise. Abstract user closures are ordered by inclusion. Two stacks are in $\sqsubseteq$ iff they have the same length and the corresponding frames are in $\sqsubseteq$.

We can now state the simulation theorem. The proof proceeds by case analysis on the concrete transition relation; full details can be found in the first author's forthcoming dissertation.

Theorem 3 (Simulation). *If $\varsigma \to \varsigma'$ and $|\varsigma|_{ca} \sqsubseteq \hat{\varsigma}$, then there exists $\hat{\varsigma}'$ such that $\hat{\varsigma} \leadsto \hat{\varsigma}'$ and $|\varsigma'|_{ca} \sqsubseteq \hat{\varsigma}'$.*

5. Exploring the infinite state space

Pushdown-reachability algorithms, including CFA2, deal with the unbounded stack size by using a dynamic-programming technique called *summarization*. These algorithms work on transition systems whose stack is unbounded, but the rest of the components are bounded. Due to escaping continuations, we also have to deal with infinitely many heaps.

5.1 Overview of summarization

We start with an informal overview of summarization. Assume that a program is executing and control reaches the entry of a procedure. We start computing inside the procedure. While doing so, we are visiting several program points inside the procedure and possibly calling (and returning from) other procedures. Sometime later, we reach the exit and are about to return to the caller with a result. The intuition behind summarization is that, during this computation, the return point was irrelevant; it influences reachability only after we return to the caller. Consequently, if from a program point n with an empty stack we can reach a point n' with stack s', then from n with stack s we can reach n' with stack *append*(s', s).

Let's use summarization to find which nodes of the graph of Fig. 1 are reachable from node 1. We find reachable nodes by recording *path edges, i.e.*, edges whose source is the entry of a procedure and target is some program point in the same procedure. Path edges should not be confused with the edges already present in the graph. They are artificial edges used by the analysis to represent intraprocedural paths, hence the name.

Node 1 goes to 2, so we record the edges $\langle 1, 1\rangle$ and $\langle 1, 2\rangle$. From 2 we call app, so we record the call $\langle 2, 8\rangle$ and jump to 8. In app, we find path edges $\langle 8, 8\rangle$ and $\langle 8, 9\rangle$. We find a new call $\langle 9, 12\rangle$ and jump to 12. Inside id, we discover the edges $\langle 12, 12\rangle$, $\langle 12, 13\rangle$ and $\langle 12, 14\rangle$. Edges that go from an entry to an exit, such as $\langle 12, 14\rangle$, are called *summary* edges. We have not been keeping track of the stack, so we use the recorded calls to find the return point. The only call to id is $\langle 9, 12\rangle$, so 14 returns to 10 and we find a new edge $\langle 8, 10\rangle$, which leads to $\langle 8, 11\rangle$. We record $\langle 8, 11\rangle$ as a summary also. From the call $\langle 2, 8\rangle$, we see that 11 returns to 3, so we record edges $\langle 1, 3\rangle$ and $\langle 1, 4\rangle$. Now, we have a new call to app. Reachability inside app does not depend on its calling context. From the summary $\langle 8, 11\rangle$, we know that 4 can reach 5, so we find $\langle 1, 5\rangle$. Subsequently, we find the last two path edges, which are $\langle 1, 6\rangle$ and $\langle 1, 7\rangle$.

During the search, we did two kinds of transitions. The first kind includes intraprocedural steps and calls; these transitions do not shrink the stack. The second is function returns, which shrink the stack. Since we are not keeping track of the stack, we find the target nodes of the second kind of transitions in an indirect way, by recording calls and summaries. We show a summarization-based algorithm for CFA2 in section 5.3. The next section describes the local semantics, which we use in the algorithm for transitions that do not shrink the stack.

$$
\begin{aligned}
\widetilde{Eval} &= Call \times \widetilde{Stack} \times \widetilde{Heap} \\
\widetilde{UApply} &= ULam \times \widetilde{UClos} \times \widetilde{Heap} \\
\widetilde{CApply} &= \widetilde{CClos} \times \widetilde{UClos} \times \widetilde{Stack} \times \widetilde{Heap} \\
\widetilde{Frame} &= UVar \rightharpoonup \widetilde{UClos} \\
\widetilde{Stack} &= \widetilde{Frame} \\
\widetilde{Heap} &= UVar \rightharpoonup \widetilde{UClos}
\end{aligned}
$$

(a) Local domains

$$
\begin{aligned}
&|(call, st, h)|_{al} = (call, |st|_{al}, |h|_{al}) \\
&|(ulam, \hat{d}, \hat{c}, st, h)|_{al} = (ulam, \hat{d}, |h|_{al}) \\
&|(\hat{c}, \hat{d}, st, h)|_{al} = (\hat{c}, \hat{d}, |st|_{al}, |h|_{al}) \\
&|st|_{al} = \begin{cases} \emptyset & st = \langle\rangle \\ tf \restriction UVar & st = tf :: st' \end{cases} \\
&|h|_{al} = h \restriction UVar
\end{aligned}
$$

(b) Abstract to local maps

$$
\tilde{\mathcal{A}}_u(e, \psi, tf, h) \triangleq \begin{cases} \{e\} & Lam_?(e) \\ tf(e) & S_?(\psi, e) \\ h(e) & H_?(\psi, e) \end{cases}
$$

$$
\begin{aligned}
&[\widetilde{\text{UEA}}]\quad ([\![(f\ e\ q)^l]\!], tf, h) \approx\!> (ulam, \hat{d}, h) \\
&\quad ulam \in \tilde{\mathcal{A}}_u(f, l, tf, h) \\
&\quad \hat{d} = \tilde{\mathcal{A}}_u(e, l, tf, h)
\end{aligned}
$$

$$
\begin{aligned}
&[\widetilde{\text{UAE}}]\quad ([\![(\lambda_l (u\ k)\ call)]\!], \hat{d}, h) \approx\!> (call, [u \mapsto \hat{d}], h') \\
&\quad h'(v) = \begin{cases} h(u) \cup \hat{d} & (v = u) \wedge H_?(u) \\ h(v) & o/w \end{cases}
\end{aligned}
$$

$$
\begin{aligned}
&[\widetilde{\text{CEA}}]\quad ([\![(clam\ e)^\gamma]\!], tf, h) \approx\!> (clam, \hat{d}, tf, h) \\
&\quad \hat{d} = \tilde{\mathcal{A}}_u(e, \gamma, tf, h)
\end{aligned}
$$

$$
\begin{aligned}
&[\widetilde{\text{CAE}}]\quad ([\![(\lambda_\gamma (u)\ call)]\!], \hat{d}, tf, h) \approx\!> (call, tf', h') \\
&\quad tf' = tf[u \mapsto \hat{d}] \\
&\quad h'(v) = \begin{cases} h(u) \cup \hat{d} & (v = u) \wedge H_?(u) \\ h(v) & o/w \end{cases}
\end{aligned}
$$

(c) Local semantics

Figure 7. Local semantics and relevant definitions

5.2 Local semantics

Summarization operates on a finite set of program points. Since the abstract state space is infinite, we cannot use abstract states as program points. For this reason, we introduce *local states* (Fig. 7a) and define a map $|\cdot|_{al}$ from abstract to local states (Fig. 7b).

The local semantics (Fig. 7) describes executions that do not touch the rest of the stack (*i.e.*, executions where functions do not return). A $\widetilde{CEval}$ state with call site $[\![(k\ e)^{\gamma}]\!]$ has no successor in this semantics. Since functions do not call their continuations, the local frames and heaps contain only user bindings. Local steps are otherwise similar to abstract steps. Note that there is no provision for first-class control in the local transitions; they are identical to the previous ones [22]. The metavariable $\tilde{\varsigma}$ ranges over local states. We define the map $|\cdot|_{cl}$ from concrete to local states to be $|\cdot|_{al} \circ |\cdot|_{ca}$.

Summarization distinguishes between different kinds of states: entries, exits, calls, returns and inner states. CPS lends itself naturally to such a categorization. The following definition works for all three state spaces: concrete, abstract and local.

Definition 4 (Classification of states).

- *A UApply state is an* ***Entry****—control is about to enter the body of a function.*
- *A CEval state is an* ***Exit-Ret*** *when the operator is a stack reference—a function is about to return a result to its context.*
- *A CEval state is an* ***Exit-Esc*** *when the operator is a heap reference—we are calling a continuation that may have escaped.*
- *A CEval state where the operator is a lambda is an* ***Inner*** *state.*
- *A UEval state is an* ***Exit-TC*** *when the continuation argument is a variable—at tail calls control does not return to the caller.*
- *A UEval state is a* ***Call*** *when the continuation argument is a lambda.*
- *A CApply state is a* ***Return*** *if its predecessor is an exit, or an* ***Inner*** *state if its predecessor is also an inner state. Our algorithm does not distinguish between the two kinds of CApplys; the difference is just conceptual.*

5.3 The CFA2 algorithm

The algorithm for CFA2 appears in Fig. 8. Its goal is to compute which local states are reachable from the initial state of a program.

For readers familiar with the previous algorithm: the main addition is the handling of Exit-Esc states (lines 25-33). Escaping continuations also require changes to the handling of entries and tail calls. Entries are now a separate case, instead of together with $\widetilde{CApply}$s and inner $\widetilde{CEval}$s. Last, the `Propagate` function takes an extra argument.

Structure of the algorithm The algorithm uses a workset W, which contains path edges and summaries to be examined. An edge $(\tilde{\varsigma}_1, \tilde{\varsigma}_2)$ is an ordered pair of local states. We call $\tilde{\varsigma}_1$ the *source* and $\tilde{\varsigma}_2$ the *target* of the edge. At every iteration, we remove an edge from W and process it, potentially adding new edges in W. We stop when W is empty.

An edge $(\tilde{\varsigma}_1, \tilde{\varsigma}_2)$ is a summary when $\tilde{\varsigma}_1$ is an entry and $\tilde{\varsigma}_2$ is either an Exit-Ret or an Exit-Esc, not necessarily in the same procedure. Summaries carry an important message: *each continuation that can be passed to* $\tilde{\varsigma}_1$ *can flow to the operator position of* $\tilde{\varsigma}_2$.

The algorithm maintains several sets. The results of the analysis are stored in the set $Seen$. It contains path edges (from a procedure entry to a state in the same procedure) and summary edges. The target of an edge in $Seen$ is reachable from the source and from the initial state. Summaries are also stored in $Summary$. $Escapes$ contains Exit-Esc states. If the continuation parameter of a user lambda is a heap variable, entries over that lambda are stored in $EntriesEsc$. $Final$ records final states, *i.e.*, $\widetilde{CApply}$s that call $halt$ with a return value for the whole program. $Callers$ contains triples $\langle\tilde{\varsigma}_1, \tilde{\varsigma}_2, \tilde{\varsigma}_3\rangle$, where $\tilde{\varsigma}_1$ is an entry, $\tilde{\varsigma}_2$ is a call in the same procedure and $\tilde{\varsigma}_3$ is the entry of the callee. $TCallers$ contains triples $\langle\tilde{\varsigma}_1, \tilde{\varsigma}_2, \tilde{\varsigma}_3\rangle$, where $\tilde{\varsigma}_1$ is an entry, $\tilde{\varsigma}_2$ is a tail call in the same procedure and $\tilde{\varsigma}_3$ is the entry of the callee. The initial state $\tilde{\mathcal{I}}(pr)$ is defined as $|\mathcal{I}(pr)|_{cl}$. The helper function $succ(\tilde{\varsigma})$ returns the successor(s) of $\tilde{\varsigma}$ according to the local semantics.

Summaries for first-class continuations Perhaps surprisingly, even though continuations can escape to the heap in the abstract semantics, we do not need continuations in the local heap. We can handle escaping continuations with summaries. Consider the example from section 4.3. When control reaches $[\![$`(cc x)`$]\!]$, we want to find which continuation flows to `cc`. We know that $def_\lambda($`cc`$)$ is λ_1. By looking at the single $\widehat{UApply}$ over λ_1, we find that $halt$ flows to `cc`. This suggests that, for escaping continuations, we need summaries of the form $(\tilde{\varsigma}_1, \tilde{\varsigma}_2)$ where $\tilde{\varsigma}_2$ is an Exit-Esc over a call site $[\![(k\ e)^{\gamma}]\!]$ and $\tilde{\varsigma}_1$ is an entry over $def_\lambda(k)$.

Edge processing Each edge $(\tilde{\varsigma}_1, \tilde{\varsigma}_2)$ is processed in one of six ways, depending on $\tilde{\varsigma}_2$. If $\tilde{\varsigma}_2$ is a return or an inner state (line 12), then its successor $\tilde{\varsigma}_3$ is a state in the same procedure. Since $\tilde{\varsigma}_2$ is reachable from $\tilde{\varsigma}_1$, $\tilde{\varsigma}_3$ is also reachable from $\tilde{\varsigma}_1$. If we have not already recorded the edge $(\tilde{\varsigma}_1, \tilde{\varsigma}_3)$, we do it now (line 44).

If $\tilde{\varsigma}_2$ is a call (line 14) then $\tilde{\varsigma}_3$ is the entry of the callee, so we propagate $(\tilde{\varsigma}_3, \tilde{\varsigma}_3)$ instead of $(\tilde{\varsigma}_1, \tilde{\varsigma}_3)$ (line 16). Also, we record the call in $Callers$. If an exit $\tilde{\varsigma}_4$ is reachable from $\tilde{\varsigma}_3$, it should return to the continuation born at $\tilde{\varsigma}_2$ (line 18). The function `Update` is responsible for computing the return state. We find the return value $\hat{d}$ by evaluating the expression e_4 passed to the continuation (lines 48-49). Since we are returning to λ_{γ_2}, we must restore the environment of its creation, which is tf_2 (possibly with stack filtering, line 50). The new state $\tilde{\varsigma}$ is the corresponding return of $\tilde{\varsigma}_2$, so we propagate $(\tilde{\varsigma}_1, \tilde{\varsigma})$ (lines 51-52).

If $\tilde{\varsigma}_2$ is an Exit-Ret and $\tilde{\varsigma}_1$ is the initial state (lines 19-20), then $\tilde{\varsigma}_2$'s successor is a final state (lines 53-54). If $\tilde{\varsigma}_1$ is some other entry, we record the edge in $Summary$ and pass the result of $\tilde{\varsigma}_2$ to the callers of $\tilde{\varsigma}_1$ (lines 22-23). Last, consider the case of a tail call $\tilde{\varsigma}_4$ to $\tilde{\varsigma}_1$ (line 24). No continuation is born at $\tilde{\varsigma}_4$. Thus, we must find where $\tilde{\varsigma}_3$ (the entry that led to the tail call) was called from. Then again, all calls to $\tilde{\varsigma}_3$ may be tail calls, in which case we keep searching further back in the call chain to find a return point. We do the backward search by transitively adding a cross-procedure summary from $\tilde{\varsigma}_3$ to $\tilde{\varsigma}_2$.

Let $\tilde{\varsigma}_2$ be an Exit-Esc over a call site $[\![(k\ e)^{\gamma}]\!]$ (line 25). Its predecessor $\tilde{\varsigma}'$ is an entry or a $\widetilde{CApply}$. To reach $\tilde{\varsigma}_2$, the algorithm must go through $\tilde{\varsigma}'$. Hence, the first time the algorithm sees $\tilde{\varsigma}_2$ is at line 7 or 13, which means that $\tilde{\varsigma}_1$ is an entry over $iu_\lambda([\![(k\ e)^{\gamma}]\!])$ and $(\tilde{\varsigma}_1, \tilde{\varsigma}_2)$ is not in $Summary$. Thus, the test at line 26 is true. We record $\tilde{\varsigma}_2$ in $Escapes$. We also create summaries from entries over $def_\lambda(k)$ to $\tilde{\varsigma}_2$, in order to find which continuations can flow to k. We make sure to put these summaries in $Summary$ (line 29), so that when they are examined, the test at line 26 is false.

When $\tilde{\varsigma}_2$ is examined again, this time $(\tilde{\varsigma}_1, \tilde{\varsigma}_2)$ is in $Summary$. If $\tilde{\varsigma}_1$ is the initial state, $\tilde{\varsigma}_2$ can call $halt$ and transition to a final state (line 30). Otherwise, we look for calls to $\tilde{\varsigma}_1$ to find continuations that can be called at $\tilde{\varsigma}_2$ (line 32). If there are tail calls to $\tilde{\varsigma}_1$, we propagate summaries transitively (line 33).

If $\tilde{\varsigma}_2$ is an entry over $[\![(\lambda_l\,(u\,k)\ call)]\!]$, its successor $\tilde{\varsigma}_3$ is a state in the same procedure, so we propagate $(\tilde{\varsigma}_1, \tilde{\varsigma}_3)$ (lines 6-7). If k is a heap variable (lines 8-9), we put $\tilde{\varsigma}_2$ in $EntriesEsc$ (so that it can be found from line 29). Also, if we have seen Exit-Esc states that call k, we create summaries from $\tilde{\varsigma}_2$ to those states (line 11).

If $\tilde{\varsigma}_2$ is a tail call (line 34), we find its successors and record the call in $TCallers$ (lines 35-37). If a successor of $\tilde{\varsigma}_2$ goes to an exit, we propagate a cross-procedure summary transitively (line 41). Moreover, if $\tilde{\varsigma}_4$ is an Exit-Esc, we want to make sure that $(\tilde{\varsigma}_1, \tilde{\varsigma}_4)$ is in $Summary$ when it is examined. We cannot call `Propagate` with `true` at line 41 because we would be mutating $Summary$ while iterating over it. Instead, we use a temporary set which we unite with $Summary$ after the loop (line 42).

```
Summary, Callers, TCallers, EntriesEsc, Escapes, Final ⟵ ∅
Seen, W ⟵ {(Ĩ(pr), Ĩ(pr))}
while W ≠ ∅
  remove (ς̃1, ς̃2) from W
  switch ς̃2
    case ς̃2 of Entry
      for the ς̃3 in succ(ς̃2), Propagate(ς̃1, ς̃3, false)
      ς̃2 of the form ([[(λl(u k) call)]], d̂, h)
      if H?(k) then
        insert ς̃2 in EntriesEsc
        for each ς̃3 in Escapes that calls k, Propagate(ς̃2, ς̃3, true)
    case ς̃2 of CApply, Inner-CEval
      for the ς̃3 in succ(ς̃2), Propagate(ς̃1, ς̃3, false)
    case ς̃2 of Call
      for each ς̃3 in succ(ς̃2)
        Propagate(ς̃3, ς̃3, false)
        insert (ς̃1, ς̃2, ς̃3) in Callers
        for each (ς̃3, ς̃4) in Summary, Update(ς̃1, ς̃2, ς̃3, ς̃4)
    case ς̃2 of Exit-Ret
      if ς̃1 = Ĩ(pr) then Final(ς̃2)
      else
        insert (ς̃1, ς̃2) in Summary
        for each (ς̃3, ς̃4, ς̃1) in Callers, Update(ς̃3, ς̃4, ς̃1, ς̃2)
        for each (ς̃3, ς̃4, ς̃1) in TCallers, Propagate(ς̃3, ς̃2, false)
    case ς̃2 of Exit-Esc
      if (ς̃1, ς̃2) not in Summary then
        insert ς̃2 in Escapes
        ς̃2 of the form ([[(k e)^γ]], tf, h)
        for each ς̃3 in EntriesEsc over def_λ(k), Propagate(ς̃3, ς̃2, true)
      else if ς̃1 = Ĩ(pr) then Final(ς̃2)
      else
        for each (ς̃3, ς̃4, ς̃1) in Callers, Update(ς̃3, ς̃4, ς̃1, ς̃2)
        for each (ς̃3, ς̃4, ς̃1) in TCallers, Propagate(ς̃3, ς̃2, true)
    case ς̃2 of Exit-TC
      for each ς̃3 in succ(ς̃2)
        Propagate(ς̃3, ς̃3, false)
        insert (ς̃1, ς̃2, ς̃3) in TCallers
        S ⟵ ∅
        for each (ς̃3, ς̃4) in Summary
          insert (ς̃1, ς̃4) in S
          Propagate(ς̃1, ς̃4, false)
        Summary ⟵ Summary ∪ S

Propagate(ς̃1, ς̃2, esc) ≜
  if esc then insert (ς̃1, ς̃2) in Summary
  if (ς̃1, ς̃2) not in Seen then insert (ς̃1, ς̃2) in Seen and W

Update(ς̃1, ς̃2, ς̃3, ς̃4) ≜
  ς̃1 of the form ([[(λl1(u1 k1) call1)]] , d̂1, h1)
  ς̃2 of the form ([[(f e2 (λγ2 (u2) call2))^l2]], tf2, h2)
  ς̃3 of the form ([[(λl3(u3 k3) call3)]] , d̂3, h2)
  ς̃4 of the form ([[(k4 e4)^γ4]], tf4, h4)
  d̂ ⟵ Ãu(e4, γ4, tf4, h4)
  tf ⟵ { tf2[f ↦ {[[(λl3(u3 k3) call3)]]}]   S?(l2, f)
       { tf2                                 H?(l2, f) ∨ Lam?(f)
  ς̃ ⟵ ([[(λγ2(u2) call2)]], d̂, tf, h4)
  Propagate(ς̃1, ς̃, false)

Final(ς̃) ≜
  ς̃ of the form ([[(k e)^γ]], tf, h)
  insert (halt, Ãu(e, γ, tf, h), ∅, h) in Final
```

Figure 8. CFA2 workset algorithm

5.4 Soundness

The local state space is finite, so there are finitely many path and summary edges. We record edges as seen when we insert them in W, which ensures that no edge is inserted in W twice. Therefore, the algorithm always terminates.

We obviously cannot visit an infinite number of abstract states. To establish soundness, we relate the results of the algorithm to the abstract semantics: we show that if a state $\hat{\varsigma}$ is reachable from $\hat{\mathcal{I}}(pr)$, then the algorithm visits $|\hat{\varsigma}|_{al}$ (*cf.* theorem 8).

First-class continuations create an intricate call/return structure, which complicates reasoning about soundness. When calls and returns nest properly, an execution path can be decomposed so that for each state $\hat{\varsigma}$, we can uniquely identify another state $\hat{\varsigma}'$ as the entry of the procedure that contains $\hat{\varsigma}$ [17]. When we add tail calls into the mix, unique decomposition is still possible [24].

However, in the presence of first-class control, a state can belong to *more than one* procedure. For instance, suppose we want to find the entry of the procedure containing $\hat{\varsigma}$ in the following path

$$\hat{\mathcal{I}}(pr) \rightsquigarrow^* \hat{\varsigma}_c \rightsquigarrow \hat{\varsigma}_e \rightsquigarrow^* \hat{\varsigma}'_c \rightsquigarrow \hat{\varsigma}'_e \rightsquigarrow^* \hat{\varsigma}' \rightsquigarrow \hat{\varsigma}$$

where $\hat{\varsigma}'$ is an Exit-Esc over $[\![(k\ e)^\gamma]\!]$, $\hat{\varsigma}_e$ and $\hat{\varsigma}'_e$ are entries over $def_\lambda(k)$, $\hat{\varsigma}_c$ and $\hat{\varsigma}'_c$ are calls. The two entries have the form

$$\hat{\varsigma}_e = (def_\lambda(k), \hat{d}, \hat{c}, st, h)$$
$$\hat{\varsigma}'_e = (def_\lambda(k), \hat{d}', \hat{c}', st', h')$$

Both $\hat{c}$ and $\hat{c}'$ can flow to k and we can call either at $\hat{\varsigma}'$. If we choose to restore $\hat{c}$ and st, then $\hat{\varsigma}$ is in the same procedure as $\hat{\varsigma}_c$. If we restore $\hat{c}'$ and st', $\hat{\varsigma}$ is in the same procedure as $\hat{\varsigma}'_c$. However, it is possible that $\hat{c} = \hat{c}'$ and $st = st'$, in which case $\hat{\varsigma}$ belongs to two procedures. Unique decomposition no longer holds.

For this reason, we now define a set of corresponding entries for each state, instead of a single entry [22].

Definition 5 (Corresponding Entries)**.**
Let $p \equiv \hat{\varsigma}_e \rightsquigarrow^* \hat{\varsigma}$ where $\hat{\varsigma}_e$ is an entry. We define $CE_p(\hat{\varsigma})$ to be the smallest set such that:

- *if $\hat{\varsigma}$ is an entry, $CE_p(\hat{\varsigma}) = \{\hat{\varsigma}\}$*
- *if $p \equiv \hat{\varsigma}_e \rightsquigarrow^* \hat{\varsigma}_1 \rightsquigarrow^+ \hat{\varsigma}$, $\hat{\varsigma}$ is an Exit-Esc over $[\![(k\ e)^\gamma]\!]$, $\hat{\varsigma}_1$ is an entry over $def_\lambda(k)$, then $\hat{\varsigma}_1 \in CE_p(\hat{\varsigma})$.*
- *if $p \equiv \hat{\varsigma}_e \rightsquigarrow^* \hat{\varsigma}_1 \rightsquigarrow \hat{\varsigma}$, $\hat{\varsigma}$ is neither an entry nor an Exit-Esc, $\hat{\varsigma}_1$ is neither an Exit-Ret nor an Exit-Esc, then $CE_p(\hat{\varsigma}) = CE_p(\hat{\varsigma}_1)$.*
- *if $p \equiv \hat{\varsigma}_e \rightsquigarrow^* \hat{\varsigma}_1 \rightsquigarrow \hat{\varsigma}_2 \rightsquigarrow^* \hat{\varsigma}_3 \rightsquigarrow^+ \hat{\varsigma}_4 \rightsquigarrow \hat{\varsigma}$, $\hat{\varsigma}$ is a $\widehat{CApply}$ of the form $(\hat{c}, \hat{d}, st, h)$, $\hat{\varsigma}_4$ is an Exit-Esc, $\hat{\varsigma}_3 \in CE_p(\hat{\varsigma}_4)$ and has the form $(ulam, \hat{d}', \hat{c}, st, h')$, $\hat{\varsigma}_2 \in CE^*_p(\hat{\varsigma}_3)$, $\hat{\varsigma}_1$ is a Call, then $CE_p(\hat{\varsigma}_1) \subseteq CE_p(\hat{\varsigma})$.*
- *if $p \equiv \hat{\varsigma}_e \rightsquigarrow^* \hat{\varsigma}_1 \rightsquigarrow \hat{\varsigma}_2 \rightsquigarrow^+ \hat{\varsigma}_3 \rightsquigarrow \hat{\varsigma}$, $\hat{\varsigma}$ is a $\widehat{CApply}$, $\hat{\varsigma}_3$ is an Exit-Ret, $\hat{\varsigma}_2 \in CE^*_p(\hat{\varsigma}_3)$, $\hat{\varsigma}_1$ is a Call, then $CE_p(\hat{\varsigma}_1) \subseteq CE_p(\hat{\varsigma})$.*

For each state $\hat{\varsigma}$, we also define $CE^*_p(\hat{\varsigma})$ to be the set of entries that can reach an entry in $CE_p(\hat{\varsigma})$ through tail calls.

Definition 6. *Let $p \equiv \hat{\varsigma}_e \rightsquigarrow^* \hat{\varsigma}$ where $\hat{\varsigma}_e$ is an entry. We define $CE^*_p(\hat{\varsigma})$ to be the smallest set such that:*

- *$CE_p(\hat{\varsigma}) \subseteq CE^*_p(\hat{\varsigma})$*
- *if $p \equiv \hat{\varsigma}_e \rightsquigarrow^* \hat{\varsigma}_1 \rightsquigarrow \hat{\varsigma}_2 \rightsquigarrow^* \hat{\varsigma}$, $\hat{\varsigma}_2 \in CE_p(\hat{\varsigma})$, $\hat{\varsigma}_1$ is a Tail Call, then $CE^*_p(\hat{\varsigma}_1) \subseteq CE^*_p(\hat{\varsigma})$.*

Note that if $\hat{\varsigma}$ is an Exit-Esc over $[\![(k\ e)^\gamma]\!]$, a procedure that contains $\hat{\varsigma}$ has an entry $\hat{\varsigma}'$ over $iu_\lambda([\![(k\ e)^\gamma]\!])$. Thus, $\hat{\varsigma}'$ is not in $CE_p(\hat{\varsigma})$ because $iu_\lambda([\![(k\ e)^\gamma]\!]) \neq def_\lambda(k)$. For all other states, $CE_p(\hat{\varsigma})$ is the set of entries of procedures that contain $\hat{\varsigma}$. The following lemma relates the stack of a state with the stacks of its corresponding entries.

Lemma 7. *Let $p \equiv \hat{\mathcal{I}}(pr) \rightsquigarrow^* \hat{\varsigma}$ where $\hat{\varsigma} \equiv (\ldots, st, h)$.*

1. *If $\hat{\varsigma}$ is a final state then $CE_p(\hat{\varsigma}) = \emptyset$.*
2. *If $\hat{\varsigma}$ is an entry then $CE_p(\hat{\varsigma}) \neq \emptyset$. (Thus, $CE^*_p(\hat{\varsigma}) \neq \emptyset$.)*
   Let $\hat{\varsigma}_e \in CE^*_p(\hat{\varsigma})$, of the form $(ulam, \hat{d}, \hat{c}, st_e, h_e)$. Then, $st = st_e$ and the continuation argument of $\hat{\varsigma}$ is $\hat{c}$.
3. *If $\hat{\varsigma}$ is an Exit-Esc then its stack is not empty and $CE_p(\hat{\varsigma}) \neq \emptyset$. (We do not assert anything about the stack change between a state in $CE^*_p(\hat{\varsigma})$ and $\hat{\varsigma}$; it can be arbitrary.)*
4. *If $\hat{\varsigma}$ is none of the above, then $CE_p(\hat{\varsigma}) \neq \emptyset$.*
   Let $\hat{\varsigma}_e = ([\![(\lambda_l(u\,k)\ call)]\!], \hat{d}, \hat{c}, st_e, h_e)$.
   If $\hat{\varsigma}_e \in (CE^*_p(\hat{\varsigma}) \setminus CE_p(\hat{\varsigma}))$ then
   - *there is a frame tf such that $st \equiv tf :: st_e$, and*
   - *there is a variable k' such that $tf(k') = \hat{c}$.*

   If $\hat{\varsigma}_e \in CE_p(\hat{\varsigma})$ then there is a frame tf such that $st \equiv tf :: st_e$, $\mathrm{dom}(tf) \subseteq LV(l)$, $tf(u) \sqsubseteq \hat{d}$, and $tf(k) = \hat{c}$.

The proof of lemma 7 proceeds by induction on the length of the path p. We now state the soundness theorem. Its proof and the proof of lemma 7 can be found in the first author's forthcoming dissertation.

Theorem 8 (Soundness)**.**
If $p \equiv \hat{\mathcal{I}}(pr) \rightsquigarrow^* \hat{\varsigma}$ then, after summarization:

- *If $\hat{\varsigma}$ is a final state, then $|\hat{\varsigma}|_{al} \in Final$.*
- *If $\hat{\varsigma}$ is not final and $\hat{\varsigma}' \in CE_p(\hat{\varsigma})$, then $(|\hat{\varsigma}'|_{al}, |\hat{\varsigma}|_{al}) \in Seen$.*
- *If $\hat{\varsigma}$ is an Exit-Ret or Exit-Esc and $\hat{\varsigma}' \in CE^*_p(\hat{\varsigma})$, then $(|\hat{\varsigma}'|_{al}, |\hat{\varsigma}|_{al}) \in Seen$.*

CFA2 without first-class control is complete, which means that there is no loss in precision when going from abstract to local states [24]. The algorithm of Fig. 8 is not complete; it may compute flows that never happen in the abstract semantics. Consider the code:

```
(define esc (λ(f cc) (f (λ(x k) (cc x)) cc)))

(esc (λ1(v1 k1) (v1 "foo" k1))
     (λ(a) (halt a)))

(esc (λ2(v2 k2) (k2 "bar"))
     (λ(b) (halt b)))
```

In this program, `esc` is the CPS translation of `call/cc`. The two user functions λ_1 and λ_2 expect a reified continuation as their first argument; λ_1 uses that continuation and λ_2 does not. The abstract semantics finds that `{"foo"}` flows to `a` and `{"bar"}` flows to `b`.

However, the workset algorithm thinks that `{"foo","bar"}` flows to `b`. At the second call to `esc`, it connects the entry to the Exit-Esc state over $[\![$`(cc x)`$]\!]$ at line 11, which is a spurious flow.

5.5 Various approaches to downward continuations

In RCPS, the general form of a user lambda that binds a heap continuation variable is

```
(λ1(u k) (. . . (λ2(u2 k2) (. . . (k e)γ . . .)) . . .))
```

where λ_1 contains a user lambda λ_2, which in turn contains a heap reference to `k` in operator position.

During execution, if a closure over λ_2 escapes upward, merging of continuations at $[\![$`(k e)`$^\gamma]\!]$ is unavoidable. However, when λ_2 is not passed upward, the abstract semantics still merges at $[\![$`(k e)`$^\gamma]\!]$. A natural question to ask is how precise can CFA2 be for downward continuations, such as exception handlers or continuations captured by `call/cc` that never escape. In both cases, we can avoid merging.

In section 2.4, we described how the JavaScript implementation of CFA2 handles exception throws precisely. Another way to achieve this is by uniformly passing two continuations to each user function, the current continuation and an exception handler [1]. Consider a user lambda $[\![$`(λ(u k1 k2) (... (k2 e)`$^\gamma$ `...))`$]\!]$ where $S_?(\gamma, \texttt{k2})$ holds. Every Exit-Ret over $[\![$`(k2 e)`$^\gamma]\!]$ is an exception throw. The handler continuation lives somewhere on the stack. To find it, we propagate transitive summaries for calls, as we do for tail calls. When the algorithm finds an edge $(\tilde{\varsigma}_1, \tilde{\varsigma}_2)$ where $\tilde{\varsigma}_2$ is an Exit-Ret over $[\![$`(k2 e)`$^\gamma]\!]$, it searches in *Callers* for a triple $(\tilde{\varsigma}_3, \tilde{\varsigma}_4, \tilde{\varsigma}_1)$. If the second continuation argument of $\tilde{\varsigma}_4$ is a lambda, we have found a handler. If not, we propagate a summary $(\tilde{\varsigma}_3, \tilde{\varsigma}_2)$, which has the effect of looking for a handler deeper in the stack. Note that the algorithm must keep these new summaries separate from the other summaries, so as not to confuse exceptional with ordinary control flow.

For continuations captured by `call/cc` that are only used downward, we can avoid merging by combining flow analysis and escape analysis. Consider the lambda at the beginning of this subsection. During flow analysis, we track if any closure over λ_2 escapes upward. We do this by checking for summaries $(\tilde{\varsigma}_1, \tilde{\varsigma}_2)$, where $\tilde{\varsigma}_1$ is an entry over λ_1. If λ_2 is contained in a binding reachable from $\tilde{\varsigma}_2$ [12, sec. 4.4.2], then λ_2 is passed upward and we use the heap to look up k at $[\![$`(k e)`$^\gamma]\!]$. Otherwise, we can assume that λ_2 does not escape. Hence, when we see an edge $(\tilde{\varsigma}_1, \tilde{\varsigma}_2)$ where $\tilde{\varsigma}_1$ is an entry over λ_2 and $\tilde{\varsigma}_2$ is an Exit-Esc over $[\![$`(k e)`$^\gamma]\!]$, we treat it as an exception throw. We use the new transitive summaries to search deeper in the stack for a live activation of λ_1, which tells us what flows to k.

6. Related work

The CFA2 workset algorithm is influenced by the functional approach of Sharir and Pnueli [17] and the tabulation algorithm of Reps *et al.* [15]. CFA2 extends these algorithms to first-class functions, introduces the stack/heap split and applies to control constructs that break call/return nesting. Traditional summary edges describe intraprocedural entry-to-exit flows. We have created several kinds of cross-procedure summaries for the various control patterns. Summaries for tail calls describe flows that do not grow the stack. Summaries for exceptions describe flows that grow the stack; the source of the summary may be deeper in the stack than the target. Finally, summaries for first-class control describe flows with arbitrary stack change. The four different kinds of summaries can be conceptually unified because they serve a common purpose: *they connect a continuation passed to a user function with the state that calls it.*

Earl *et al.* have proposed a pushdown higher-order flow analysis that does not use frames [6]. Instead, their analysis allocates all bindings in the heap with context, in the style of k-CFA. For $k = 0$, their analysis runs in time $O(n^6)$, where n is the size of the program. Like all pushdown-reachability algorithms, Earl *et al.*'s analysis records pairs of states $(\varsigma_1, \varsigma_2)$ where ς_2 is same-context reachable from ς_1. However, their algorithm does not classify states as entries, exits, calls, *etc.* This has two drawbacks compared to the tabulation algorithm. First, they do not distinguish between path and summary edges. Thus, they have to search the whole set of edges when they look for return points, even though only summaries can contribute to the search. More importantly, path edges are only a small subset of the set S of all edges between same-context reachable states. By not classifying states, their algorithm maintains the whole set S, not just the path edges. In other words, it records edges whose source is not an entry. In the graph of Fig. 1, some of these edges are $\langle 2,3\rangle$, $\langle 2,6\rangle$, $\langle 5,7\rangle$. Such edges slow down the analysis and do not contribute to call/return matching, because they cannot evolve into summary edges. In CFA2, it is possible to disable the use of frames by classifying each reference as a heap reference. The resulting analysis has similar precision to Earl *et al.*'s analysis for $k = 0$. We conjecture that this variant is not a viable alternative in practice, because of the significant loss in precision.

While there is extensive literature on finite-state higher-order flow analysis, little progress has been made in taming the power of `call/cc` and general continuations. Might and Shivers's ΔCFA [12, 13] introduced a notion of "frame strings" to track stack motion; these strings provide a notational vocabulary for describing and distinguishing various sorts of control transfer: recursive call, tail call, return, primitive application, as well as the more exotic control acts that are constructed with first-class control operators. However, the expressiveness of this device is brought low by its eventual regular-expression-based abstraction. Once abstracted, it loses much of its ability to reason about unusual patterns of control flow. We suspect that the infinite-state analytic framework provided by CFA2 could be the missing piece that would enable a ΔCFA-based analysis to be computed without requiring precision-destroying abstractions.

Shivers and Might have also shown how functional coroutines can be constructed with continuations, and then exploited to fuse pipelines of online transducers together into efficient, optimized code [19]. Being able to apply the power of pushdown models such as CFA2 to the transducer-fusion task raises interesting new possibilities. For example, suppose we had a coroutine generator with a recursive control structure—one that walks a binary tree producing the elements at the leaves. We wish to connect this tree-walking generator to a simple iterative coroutine that adds up all the items it receives. Is a pushdown flow analysis powerful enough to fuse the composition of these two coroutines into a single, recursive tree traversal, instead of an awkward, heavyweight implementation that ping-pongs back and forth between two independent stacks?

7. Conclusions

In this paper, we generalize the CFA2 flow analysis to first-class control. We propose an abstract semantics that allows stacks to be copied to the heap, and a summarization algorithm that handles the infinitely many heaps with a new kind of summary edges. With these additions, CFA2 becomes the first pushdown model that analyzes first-class control constructs. Moreover, CFA2 can now analyze the same language features as k-CFA, and do it more accurately. Thus, implementors of higher-order languages can use CFA2 as a drop-in replacement of k-CFA.

We also revisit the idea of path decomposition to accommodate states that belong to multiple procedures and prove our analysis sound. We show a program for which the abstract semantics gives a different result from the local semantics and conclude that our new summarization algorithm is not complete. We are not certain that first-class control unavoidably leads to incompleteness; we plan to investigate if changes to the algorithm can make it complete. However, it is possible that the abstract semantics describes a machine strictly more expressive than pushdown systems, and that reachability for this machine is not decidable.

Acknowledgements

This article reports on work supported by the Mozilla Foundation, and by the Defense Advanced Research Projects Agency under Air Force Research Laboratory (AFRL/Rome) Contract No. FA8650-10-C-7090 and Cooperative Agreement No. FA8750-10-2-0233. The views expressed are those of the authors and do not reflect the official policy or position of the Department of Defense or the U.S. Government.

References

[1] A. W. Appel. *Compiling with Continuations*. Cambridge University Press, 1992.

[2] P. Cousot and R. Cousot. Abstract interpretation: a unified lattice model for static analysis of programs by construction or approximation of fixpoints. In *Proceedings of the Fourth Annual ACM Symposium on Principles of Programming Languages*, pages 238–252, Jan. 1977.

[3] O.-J. Dahl and K. Nygaard. SIMULA—an ALGOL-based simulation language. *Communications of the ACM*, 9(9):671–678, 1966.

[4] O. Danvy and A. Filinski. A functional abstraction of typed contexts. Technical Report 89/12, University of Copenhagen, 1989.

[5] Doctor JS: A set of static-analysis tools for JavaScript. `https://github.com/mozilla/doctorjs`.

[6] C. Earl, M. Might, and D. Van Horn. Pushdown control-flow analysis of higher-order programs. In *Proceedings of the 2010 Workshop on Scheme and Functional Programming*, 2010.

[7] M. Felleisen. The theory and practice of first-class prompts. In *Proceedings of the Fifteenth Annual ACM Symposium on Principles of Programming Languages*, pages 180–190, 1988.

[8] JavaScript generators. `https://developer.mozilla.org/en/JavaScript/New_in_JavaScript/1.7`.

[9] D. Kranz. *ORBIT: An Optimizing Compiler for Scheme*. PhD thesis, Yale University, 1988.

[10] D. Kranz, R. Kelsey, J. Rees, P. Hudak, J. Philbin, and N. Adams. Orbit: an optimizing compiler for Scheme. In *Proceedings of the 1986 SIGPLAN Symposium on Compiler Construction*, pages 219–233, 1986.

[11] The Lua programming language. `http://www.lua.org`.

[12] M. Might. *Environment Analysis of Higher-Order Languages*. PhD thesis, Georgia Institute of Technology, 2007.

[13] M. Might and O. Shivers. Analyzing the environment structure of higher-order languages using frame strings. *Theoretical Computer Science*, 375(1–3):137–168, May 2007.

[14] Python generators. `http://www.python.org/dev/peps/pep-0255`.

[15] T. W. Reps, S. Horwitz, and S. Sagiv. Precise interprocedural dataflow analysis via graph reachability. In *Proceedings of the Twenty-Second Annual ACM Symposium on Principles of Programming Languages*, pages 49–61, 1995.

[16] T. Rompf, I. Maier, and M. Odersky. Implementing first-class polymorphic delimited continuations by a type-directed selective CPS-transform. In *Proceeding of the 14th ACM SIGPLAN International Conference on Functional Programming*, pages 317–328, 2009.

[17] M. Sharir and A. Pnueli. Two approaches to interprocedural dataflow analysis. In S. Muchnick and N. Jones, editors, *Program Flow Analysis: Theory and Applications*. Prentice Hall, 1981.

[18] O. Shivers. Continuations and threads: Expressing machine concurrency directly in advanced languages. In O. Danvy, editor, *Proceedings of the Second ACM SIGPLAN Workshop on Continuations (CW 1997)*, Technical report BRICS-NS-96-13, University of Århus, pages 2:1–15, Paris, France, Jan. 1997.

[19] O. Shivers and M. Might. Continuations and transducer composition. In *Proceedings of the 2006 ACM SIGPLAN Conference on Programming Language Design and Implementation (PLDI 2006)*, pages 295–307, Ottawa, Canada, June 2006.

[20] M. Sperber, R. K. Dybvig, M. Flatt, A. van Straaten, R. Findler, and J. Matthews, editors. *Revised^6 Report on the Algorithmic Language Scheme*. Cambridge University Press, 2010.

[21] G. L. Steele. Rabbit: A Compiler for Scheme. Master's thesis, MIT, 1978.

[22] D. Vardoulakis and O. Shivers. CFA2: A context-free approach to control-flow analysis. In *Proceedings of the 19th European Symposium on Programming (ESOP 2010)*, volume 6012 of *Lecture Notes in Computer Science*, pages 570–589, Paphos, Cyprus, Mar. 2010. Springer.

[23] D. Vardoulakis and O. Shivers. Ordering multiple continuations on the stack. In *Proceedings of the 2011 ACM SIGPLAN Workshop on Partial Evaluation and Program Manipulation (PEPM 2011)*, pages 13–22, Austin, Texas, Jan. 2011.

[24] D. Vardoulakis and O. Shivers. CFA2: A context-free approach to control-flow analysis. *Logical Methods in Computer Science*, 7(2:3): 1–39, May 2011.

[25] M. Wand. Continuation-based multiprocessing. In *Conference Record of the 1980 LISP Conference*, pages 19–28, Stanford, 1980.

Subtyping Delimited Continuations

Marek Materzok
Institute of Computer Science
University of Wrocław
Wrocław, Poland
tilk@tilk.eu

Dariusz Biernacki
Institute of Computer Science
University of Wrocław
Wrocław, Poland
dabi@cs.uni.wroc.pl

Abstract

We present a type system with subtyping for first-class delimited continuations that generalizes Danvy and Filinski's type system for *shift* and *reset* by maintaining explicit information about the types of contexts in the metacontext. We exploit this generalization by considering the control operators known as *shift*$_0$ and *reset*$_0$ that can access arbitrary contexts in the metacontext. We use subtyping to control the level of information about the metacontext the expression actually requires and in particular to coerce pure expressions into effectful ones. For this type system we prove strong type soundness and termination of evaluation and we present a provably correct type reconstruction algorithm. We also introduce two CPS translations for *shift*$_0$ and *reset*$_0$: one targeting the untyped lambda calculus, and another—type-directed—targeting the simply-typed lambda calculus. The latter translation preserves typability and is selective in that it keeps pure expressions in direct style.

Categories and Subject Descriptors D.3.3 [*Programming Languages*]: Language Constructs and Features—Control structures; F.3.3 [*Logics and Meanings of Programs*]: Studies of Program Constructs

General Terms Languages, Theory

Keywords Delimited Continuation, Continuation-Passing Style, Type System, Subtyping

1. Introduction

Control operators for first-class delimited continuations, introduced independently by Felleisen [17] and by Danvy and Filinski [13, 14], serve to abstract control in functional programming languages by reifying the current continuation as a first-class value. However, in contrast to the well-known abortive control operator *call/cc* present in Scheme [23] and SML/NJ [20], delimited-control operators model composition of delimited (partial) continuations rather than jumps to undelimited continuations. In particular, while *call/cc* offers the programmer the power of the continuation-passing style (CPS) in direct style, Danvy and Filinski's *shift* and *reset* offer the power of the continuation-composing style (CCS) characteristic of the success-failure continuation model of backtracking [14]. It has been shown by Filinski that *shift* and *reset* play an important role among the most fundamental concepts in the landscape of functional programming—a language equipped with *shift* and *reset* is monadically complete, i.e., any computational monad can be represented in direct style with the aid of these control operators [18, 19]. A long list of non-trivial applications of delimited continuations includes normalization by evaluation and partial evaluation [3, 12, 15], mobile computing [33], linguistics [4], and operating systems [25] to name but a few.

The intuitive semantics of delimited-control operators such as *shift* ($\mathcal{S}$) and *reset* ($\langle\rangle$) can be explained as follows. When the expression $\mathcal{S}k.e$ is evaluated, the current—delimited by the nearest dynamically-enclosing reset—continuation is captured, i.e., it is removed and the variable k is bound to it. When later k is applied to a value, the then-current continuation is composed with the captured continuation. For example, the following expression (where ++ is string concatenation):

$$\begin{array}{l}\text{"}\mathit{Alice}\text{"} \mathbin{++} \langle \text{"}\mathit{\ has\ }\text{"} \mathbin{++} \\ (\mathcal{S}k.(k\ \text{"}\mathit{a\ dog\ }\text{"}) \mathbin{++} \text{"}\mathit{and\ the\ dog}\text{"} \mathbin{++} (k\ \text{"}\mathit{a\ cat.}\text{"}))\rangle\end{array}$$

evaluates to the string *"Alice has a dog and the dog has a cat."*

In their first article on delimited continuations [13], Danvy and Filinski briefly described a variant of *shift* and *reset*, known as *shift*$_0$ ($\mathcal{S}_0$) and *reset*$_0$, where the operational semantics of the control delimiter *reset*$_0$ coincides with that of *reset*, but *shift*$_0$, when capturing a continuation, instead of resetting it, replaces it with the inner-most delimited continuation pending on the metacontinuation. In other words, in contrast to *shift*, *shift*$_0$ removes the control delimiter along with the captured continuation, which makes it possible to use *shift*$_0$ to access continuations arbitrarily deep in the metacontinuation by repeatedly shifting continuations. For example, the following expression:

$$\langle \text{"}\mathit{Alice}\text{"} \mathbin{++} \langle \text{"}\mathit{\ has\ }\text{"} \mathbin{++} (\mathcal{S}_0 k_1.\mathcal{S}_0 k_2.\text{"}\mathit{A\ cat}\text{"} \mathbin{++} (k_1 (k_2\ \text{"}.\text{"})))\rangle\rangle$$

evaluates to the string *"A cat has Alice."*, since the second shifting has access to the continuation that prepends the string *"Alice"* to a given string. The ability to access arbitrary contexts (a first-order representation of continuations [9]) in the metacontext (a first order representation of the metacontinuation [9])) makes $\mathcal{S}_0$ a particularly interesting and powerful control operator.

In the untyped setting, *shift*$_0$ and *reset*$_0$ have been investigated by Shan [32], who presented a CPS translation for *shift*$_0$ and *reset*$_0$ that conservatively extends Plotkin's call-by-value CPS translation [28] and that leads to a simulation of *shift*$_0$ and *reset*$_0$ in terms of *shift* and *reset*. This CPS translation and simulation hinge on the requirement that the continuations be represented by recursive functions taking a list of continuations as one of their arguments. (The converse simulation is trivial—one simply resets the body of each *shift*$_0$ expression.)

In a typed setting, Kiselyov and Shan [26] introduced a substructural type system for *shift*$_0$ and *reset*$_0$ that abstractly interprets

ICFP'11, September 19–21, 2011, Tokyo, Japan.

(in the sense of abstract interpretation of Cousot and Cousot [11]) small-step reduction semantics of the language. Their type system allows for continuation answer type modifications and, in a sense, extends Danvy and Filinski's type system which is the most expressive of the known monomorphic type systems for *shift* and *reset*. Judgments in Danvy and Filinski's type system have the form $\Gamma; B \vdash e : A; C$, with the interpretation that expression e can be plugged into a context expecting a value of type A and producing a value of type B, and a metacontext expecting a value of type C, where B and C can be different types. Hence, expressions are allowed to change the answer type of the context in which they are embedded. For example, the expression $\langle 1 + \mathcal{S}k.\ \mathit{true}\rangle$ is well typed in this type system. The typing rules of Danvy and Filinski's type system have been derived from a left-to-right call-by-value evaluator in continuation-passing style [13].

In this article we present a new type-and-effect system for shift_0 and reset_0 that generalizes Danvy and Filinski's original type system for *shift* and *reset*. To this end, we first introduce a new CPS translation for shift_0 and reset_0 which conservatively extends Plotkin's call-by-value CPS translation and which turns out to be close to a curried version of Shan's CPS translation [32]. From this CPS translation, we derive an abstract machine and a type-and-effect system à la Danvy and Filinski which we refine by allowing for subtyping of types and effect annotations. We show that the type system with subtyping we present satisfies several crucial properties such as strong type soundness and termination of evaluation, and we describe and prove correct a type inference algorithm for this type system. Compared to Kiselyov and Shan's type system [26], the one presented here is more conventional, it corresponds directly to the CPS translation it has been obtained from, and it heavily relies on subtyping built in the system. Furthermore, we take advantage of the fact that our type system distinguishes between pure and effectful expressions and we present a selective type-directed CPS translation from the language with shift_0 and reset_0 to the simply-typed λ-calculus that transforms to CPS only effectful expressions, leaving pure ones in direct style. We also show that Danvy and Filinski's original type system for *shift* and *reset* can naturally be embedded into our type system, and that when restricted, our type system gives rise to a type system à la Danvy and Filinski with subtyping for *shift* and *reset*. Similarly, the CPS translations for shift_0 and reset_0 that we present induce new CPS translations for *shift* and *reset*.

It is worth stressing that the subtyping mechanism of our type system addresses one of the subtle limitations of Danvy and Filinski's type system concerning the typing rules for *shift* and λ-abstraction:

$$\frac{\Gamma, f : A\,{}_F \!\to_F B; E \vdash e : E; C}{\Gamma; B \vdash \mathcal{S}f.e : B; C}$$

$$\frac{\Gamma, x : A; C \vdash e : B; D}{\Gamma; B \vdash \lambda x.e : A\,{}_C \!\to_D B; C}$$

According to the above rule for *shift*, the type system assigns the captured continuation a functional type with a single, chosen upfront answer type (F), which prevents it from being resumed in contexts with a different answer type. But the continuations captured by *shift* do not modify the context of their resumption, and therefore they should be applicable in any context. One way to deal with this shortcoming is to introduce polymorphism into the language, as in Asai and Kameyama's work [2]. In their type system, the continuation captured by *shift* is assigned a functional type with polymorphic answer type. Another approach is to distinguish between continuations and functions in such a way that a captured continuation is given a type which does not mention the answer type [6]. In this approach, additional syntactic construct—a continuation application, distinct from function application—has to be added to the language. Unfortunately, in this type system, functions without control effects (when C and D are the same arbitrary type in the rule for λ-abstraction) still have an answer type chosen upfront and are subject to the same restrictions as described above.

In a way, one can treat the continuation types from [6] as more general than function types—continuations can be applied in any context, whereas functions can only be applied in contexts with matching answer types. The type system of this article removes the syntactic distinction between continuations and functions by the means of subtyping of effect annotations. The subtyping relation allows functions to be called when more is known about the types of the contexts in the metacontext than the function actually requires. In particular, a pure function, possibly representing a captured continuation, can be arbitrarily coerced into an effectful one.

The rest of this article is structured as follows. In Section 2.1, we introduce the syntax and reduction semantics for the call-by-value λ-calculus with shift_0 and reset_0. In Section 2.2, we present a CPS translation for the language and we relate it to the reduction semantics. In Section 2.3, we derive a type-and-effect system à la Danvy and Filinski from the CPS. In Sections 3.1 and 3.2, we introduce subtyping to the type system and we prove several standard properties for the system, including strong type soundness. In Section 3.3, we use a context-based method of reducibility predicates to prove termination of evaluation of well-typed programs. In Section 3.4, we present and prove correct a type inference algorithm for our type system. In Section 3.5, we present a selective type-directed CPS translation for the language. In Section 4, we consider some practical applications of the presented language. In Section 5, we show how the type system for shift_0 and reset_0 can be restricted to Danvy and Filinski's type system for *shift* and *reset*, and we discuss the CPS translations for *shift* and *reset* induced by the presented CPS translations for shift_0 and reset_0. In Sections 6 and 7, we discuss related and future work and we conclude in Section 8.

The article is accompanied by a Haskell implementation of the presented programming language and by a Twelf formalization of its metatheory, both available at `http://www.tilk.eu/shift0/`.

2. The language $\lambda^{\mathcal{S}_0}$

2.1 Syntax and semantics

In this subsection, we define the language we will be working with. The language, which we call $\lambda^{\mathcal{S}_0}$, is the call-by-value λ-calculus extended with the two control operators shift_0 ($\mathcal{S}_0$) and reset_0 ($\langle\cdot\rangle$).

We introduce three syntactic categories of terms, evaluation contexts and trails (i.e., stacks of evaluation contexts):

$$\begin{array}{llll} \textit{values} & v & ::= & \lambda x.e \mid x \\ \textit{terms} & e & ::= & v \mid e\,e \mid \langle e \rangle \mid \mathcal{S}_0 f.e \\ \textit{contexts} & K & ::= & \bullet \mid K\,e \mid v\,K \\ \textit{trails} & T & ::= & \Box \mid K \cdot T \end{array}$$

We use the notation $T \cdot T'$ for trail concatenation, defined as follows:

$$\Box \cdot T \;=\; T \qquad (K \cdot T) \cdot T' \;=\; K \cdot (T \cdot T')$$

Contexts and trails are represented inside-out, which is formalized by the following definition of the plugging of a term inside a context:

$$\begin{array}{rclrcl} \bullet[e] & = & e & \Box[e] & = & e \\ (K\,e')[e] & = & K[e\,e'] & (K \cdot T)[e] & = & T[\langle K[e] \rangle] \\ (v\,K)[e] & = & K[v\,e] & & & \end{array}$$

$$
\begin{array}{rl}
\text{Environments:} & \rho ::= \rho_{\text{init}} \mid \rho[x \mapsto v] \\
\text{Values:} & v ::= [x, e, \rho] \mid k \\
\text{Contexts:} & k ::= \text{End} \mid \text{Arg}(e, \rho, k) \mid \text{Fun}(v, k) \\
\text{Metacontexts:} & mk ::= [\,] \mid k : mk \\
\\
\text{Initial configurations:} & \langle e, \rho_{\text{init}}, \text{End} : [\,] \rangle_{\text{eval}} \\
\text{Final configurations:} & \langle \text{End}, v, [\,] \rangle_{\text{cont}}
\end{array}
$$

$$
\begin{array}{rcl}
\langle x, \rho, k : mk \rangle_{\text{eval}} & \Rightarrow & \langle k, \rho(x), mk \rangle_{\text{cont}} \\
\langle \lambda x.e, \rho, k : mk \rangle_{\text{eval}} & \Rightarrow & \langle k, [x, e, \rho], mk \rangle_{\text{cont}} \\
\langle e_1 e_2, \rho, k : mk \rangle_{\text{eval}} & \Rightarrow & \langle e_1, \rho, \text{Arg}(e_2, \rho, k) : mk \rangle_{\text{eval}} \\
\langle \mathcal{S}_0 f.e, \rho, k : mk \rangle_{\text{eval}} & \Rightarrow & \langle e, \rho[f \mapsto k], mk \rangle_{\text{eval}} \\
\langle \langle e \rangle, \rho, mk \rangle_{\text{eval}} & \Rightarrow & \langle e, \rho, \text{End} : mk \rangle_{\text{eval}} \\
\langle \text{End}, v, k : mk \rangle_{\text{cont}} & \Rightarrow & \langle k, v, mk \rangle_{\text{cont}} \\
\langle \text{Arg}(e, \rho, k), v, mk \rangle_{\text{cont}} & \Rightarrow & \langle e, \rho, \text{Fun}(v, k) : mk \rangle_{\text{eval}} \\
\langle \text{Fun}(k', k), v, mk \rangle_{\text{cont}} & \Rightarrow & \langle k', v, k : mk \rangle_{\text{cont}} \\
\langle \text{Fun}([x, e, \rho], k), v, mk \rangle_{\text{cont}} & \Rightarrow & \langle e, \rho[x \mapsto v], k : mk \rangle_{\text{eval}}
\end{array}
$$

Figure 1. Abstract machine for $\lambda^{\mathcal{S}_0}$

$$
\begin{array}{rcl}
[\![x]\!] & = & \lambda k.k\,x \\
[\![\lambda x.e]\!] & = & \lambda k.k\,(\lambda x.[\![e]\!]) \\
[\![e_1 e_2]\!] & = & \lambda k.[\![e_1]\!](\lambda f.[\![e_2]\!](\lambda x.f\,x\,k)) \\
[\![\langle e \rangle]\!] & = & [\![e]\!](\lambda x.\lambda k.k\,x) \\
[\![\mathcal{S}_0 f.e]\!] & = & \lambda f.[\![e]\!]
\end{array}
$$

Figure 2. Untyped CPS translation for $\lambda^{\mathcal{S}_0}$

$$
\begin{array}{rcl}
[\![x]\!]^{@} & = & \lambda^l(k : ks).k\,x \mathbin{@} ks \\
[\![\lambda x.e]\!]^{@} & = & \lambda^l(k : ks).k\,(\lambda x.[\![e]\!]^{@}) \mathbin{@} ks \\
[\![e_1 e_2]\!]^{@} & = & \lambda^l(k : ks).[\![e_1]\!]^{@} \mathbin{@} ((\lambda f.\lambda^l ks'.[\![e_2]\!]^{@} \mathbin{@} \\
& & ((\lambda x.\lambda^l ks''.f\,x \mathbin{@} (k : ks'')) : ks')) : ks) \\
[\![\langle e \rangle]\!]^{@} & = & \lambda^l ks.[\![e]\!]^{@} \mathbin{@} ((\lambda x.\lambda^l(k : ks').k\,x \mathbin{@} ks') : ks) \\
[\![\mathcal{S}_0 f.e]\!]^{@} & = & \lambda^l(f : ks).[\![e]\!]^{@} \mathbin{@} ks
\end{array}
$$

Figure 3. Untyped uncurried CPS translation for $\lambda^{\mathcal{S}_0}$

There are three contraction rules:

$$
\begin{array}{rcl}
(\lambda x.e)v & \rightsquigarrow & e[x/v] \\
\langle v \rangle & \rightsquigarrow & v \\
\langle K[\mathcal{S}_0 f.e] \rangle & \rightsquigarrow & e[f/\lambda x.\langle K[x] \rangle]
\end{array}
$$

where $e[x/e']$ stands for the usual capture-avoiding substitution of e' for x in e. A term matching the left-hand side of a contraction rule is called a redex.

The reduction rule for *shift*$_0$ differs from the rule for *shift*

$$\langle K[\mathcal{S} f.e] \rangle \rightsquigarrow \langle e[f/\lambda x.\langle K[x] \rangle] \rangle$$

in that it removes the *reset*$_0$ at the root of the redex. This small difference enables the *shift*$_0$ operator to inspect the entire context stack, where *shift* has access only to the topmost context. This feature has a big impact on the type systems that we present later in the article.

Finally, we define the reduction relation on terms representing programs (i.e., triples $\langle e, T, K \rangle$):

$$K[T[e]] \to K[T[e']] \text{ if } e \rightsquigarrow e'$$

where any closed non-value term can be uniquely represented as $K[T[e]]$. The context K (at the bottom of the stack) is the only one not delimited by a *reset*$_0$. As we shall see later, having this last context distinguished from the others is important from the viewpoint of the type system, because it can be assigned a simpler type than the other contexts. A trail T along with the distinguished evaluation context K will be called a metacontext.

2.2 CPS translation

The *shift*$_0$ control operator allows access to every context in the trail. What is more, unlike with *shift*, control effects in a captured context are not isolated—the captured context, when applied, can capture contexts present at the invocation site. This ability must be reflected in the CPS translation for the *shift*$_0$ operator. In the translation presented by Shan [32], the trail is represented explicitly as a list of contexts which must be passed to every continuation. In our approach, the contexts below the current one are captured by additional lambda abstractions. The translation for the *shift*$_0$ operator captures a context using a lambda abstraction, and the translation for *reset*$_0$ introduces a new context represented by the CPS-translated identity continuation. Hence, just like in Shan's work, our CPS accounting for *shift*$_0$ relies on continuations accepting continuations as parameters. The entire CPS translation is shown in Figure 2. Evaluating a well-delimited (i.e., with no dangling *shift*$_0$'s) CPS-translated program requires an initial continuation $\lambda x.x$. The translation preserves the semantics:

Theorem 1. *If* $e_1 \to^* e_2$ *in* $\lambda^{\mathcal{S}_0}$, *then* $[\![e_1]\!] =_{\beta\eta} [\![e_2]\!]$ *in* $\lambda_{\to}$.

For reference, and to make it possible for the reader to compare the evaluation model encoded in our initial CPS translation with the existing ones [10, 16, 32], we briefly discuss possible modifications of the CPS translation. First of all, the translation can be modified so that every translated term takes all its continuation parameters in one list parameter. Figure 3 presents such an uncurried CPS translation that targets the untyped lambda-calculus extended with a separate syntactic category of lists and two new kinds of expressions: list abstraction λ^l and list application @. The translation underlies a continuation-passing style interpreter that, when defunctionalized [1, 29], gives rise to the abstract machine of Figure 1. This abstract machine can be seen to be equivalent with the abstract machine for *shift*$_0$/*reset*$_0$ described by Biernacki et al. [10]. (An alternative way to obtain an abstract machine for the language we consider would be to follow Biernacka and Danvy's syntactic correspondence between context-based reduction semantics with explicit substitutions and abstract machines [7, 8].) Had we decided to translate terms in such a way that the head and tail of the continuation list are passed as separate arguments, we would have obtained a CPS translation that coincides with Shan's [32] and which corresponds exactly to the abstract machine of Biernacki et al. [10].

2.3 From CPS translation to a type system

With the CPS translation defined, one can use the approach of Danvy and Filinski [13] and build a type system based on this translation. Let us thus limit our attention to those terms of $\lambda^{\mathcal{S}_0}$, whose translations are well-typed terms in $\lambda_{\to}$. One can then easily see that the types for variables, lambda abstractions and application must have the same form as in the type system of Danvy and

$$\frac{}{\Gamma, x : \tau_x \vdash x : \tau_x \, [\tau \, \sigma] \, \tau \, \sigma} \text{ VAR} \qquad \frac{\Gamma, x : \tau_1 \vdash e : \tau_2 \, \sigma}{\Gamma \vdash \lambda x.e : \tau_1 \xrightarrow{\sigma} \tau_2 \, [\tau \, \sigma'] \, \tau \, \sigma'} \text{ ABS}$$

$$\frac{\Gamma \vdash f : \tau_1 \xrightarrow{[\tau_1' \, \sigma_1] \, \tau_3' \, \sigma_3} \tau_2 \, [\tau_4' \, \sigma_4] \, \tau_2' \, \sigma_2 \qquad \Gamma \vdash e : \tau_1 \, [\tau_3' \, \sigma_3] \, \tau_4' \, \sigma_4}{\Gamma \vdash f e : \tau_2 \, [\tau_1' \, \sigma_1] \, \tau_2' \, \sigma_2} \text{ APP}$$

$$\frac{\Gamma, f : \tau_1 \xrightarrow{\sigma_1} \tau_2 \vdash e : \tau_3 \, \sigma_2}{\Gamma \vdash \mathcal{S}_0 f.e : \tau_1 \, [\tau_2 \, \sigma_1] \, \tau_3 \, \sigma_2} \text{ SHIFT0} \qquad \frac{\Gamma \vdash e : \tau' \, [\tau' \, [\tau'' \, \sigma''] \, \tau'' \, \sigma''] \, \tau \, \sigma}{\Gamma \vdash \langle e \rangle : \tau \, \sigma} \text{ RESET0}$$

Figure 4. Type system for $\lambda^{\mathcal{S}_0}$ without subtyping

Filinski. And what types should we assign to *shift*$_0$ and *reset*$_0$? Suppose that $[\![e]\!]$ has type τ, then $[\![\mathcal{S}_0 f.e]\!] = \lambda f.[\![e]\!]$ must have the type $\tau' \to \tau$, where τ' is the type of the captured continuation. For *reset*$_0$, for $[\![\langle e \rangle]\!] = [\![e]\!] \, (\lambda x.\lambda k.kx)$ to have type τ, $[\![e]\!]$ has to have a type of the form $(\tau' \to (\tau' \to \tau'') \to \tau'') \to \tau$. Thus every use of *shift*$_0$ introduces a new function arrow into the type, and every use of *reset*$_0$ removes one. This leads us to a recursive definition of effect annotations, which in a sense "remembers" the number of nested uses of *shift*$_0$ inside a term.

We now introduce the syntactic categories of types and effect annotations:

$$\begin{array}{lccl} \textit{types} & \tau & ::= & \alpha \mid \tau \xrightarrow{\sigma} \tau \\ \textit{annotations} & \sigma & ::= & \epsilon \mid [\tau \, \sigma] \, \tau \, \sigma \end{array}$$

The resulting type system for $\lambda^{\mathcal{S}_0}$ is shown in Figure 4.

The type annotations require some explanation. Their meaning is best understood together with types they annotate. The typing judgment $\Gamma \vdash e : \tau_1' \, [\tau_1 \, \sigma_1] \, \tau_2' \ldots [\tau_n \, \sigma_n] \, \tau$ (we omit ϵ for brevity) can be read as follows: "the term e in a typing context Γ may evaluate to a value of type τ when plugged in a trail of contexts of types $\tau_1' \xrightarrow{\sigma_1} \tau_1, \ldots, \tau_n' \xrightarrow{\sigma_n} \tau_n$". As a special case, $\Gamma \vdash e : \tau$ means: "the term e in a typing context Γ may evaluate to a value of type τ without observable control effects." Function types also have effect annotations, which can be thought to be associated with the return type.

This type system preserves types as stated in Theorem 2 below, where translations on types and annotated types are defined as follows:

$$\begin{array}{rcl} [\![\alpha]\!] & = & \alpha \\ [\![\tau_1 \xrightarrow{\sigma} \tau_2]\!] & = & [\![\tau_1]\!] \to [\![\tau_2 \, \sigma]\!] \\ [\![\tau \, \epsilon]\!] & = & \tau \\ [\![\tau \, [\tau_1 \, \sigma_1] \, \tau_2 \, \sigma_2]\!] & = & ([\![\tau]\!] \to [\![\tau_1 \, \sigma_1]\!]) \to [\![\tau_2 \, \sigma_2]\!] \end{array}$$

Theorem 2. *If* $\Gamma \vdash e : \tau \, \sigma$, *then* $[\![\Gamma]\!] \vdash [\![e]\!] : [\![\tau \, \sigma]\!]$ *in* $\lambda_{\to}$.

While interesting, this type system is very restrictive. For example, the term $\lambda x.\mathcal{S}_0 f.f \, \langle f \, x \rangle$ is translated (with administrative redexes reduced for clarity) to

$$\lambda k.k \, (\lambda x.\lambda f.\lambda k.(\lambda k.f \, x \, k)(\lambda x.\lambda k.k \, x)(\lambda x.f \, x \, k))$$

This term cannot be given a type in the simply typed lambda calculus. The reason is that the type of functions restricts their use to only those locations in a term, where the number and types of contexts match exactly. This is an unnecessary restriction—a function which requires the top k contexts to be of some type can obviously be run safely when more contexts are present, if the other contexts can be composed together and accept the function's return value. This observation leads us to another, much more expressive type system, which we present in the next section.

3. The type system with subtyping

3.1 The type system $\lambda_{\leq}^{\mathcal{S}_0}$

The type system with subtyping for $\lambda^{\mathcal{S}_0}$, called $\lambda_{\leq}^{\mathcal{S}_0}$, is shown in Figure 5. In this type system, the term $\lambda x.\mathcal{S}_0 f.f \, \langle f \, x \rangle$, which could not be typed before, is well typed and can be assigned the type $\alpha \xrightarrow{[\alpha] \, \alpha} \alpha$.

We define three subtyping relations: one defined on types, one on effect annotations, and (for convenience) one on pairs of types and effect annotations.

Lemma 1. *The subtyping relations are partial orders—they are reflexive, transitive and weakly antisymmetric.*

All subtyping rules are rather straightforward, except the rule for $\epsilon \leq [\tau \, \sigma] \, \tau \, \sigma$, which seems non-intuitive. To get some understanding of what this rule means, let us consider an effect-annotated type where the contexts are effect-free: $\tau_1 \, [\tau_1'] \, \tau_2 \ldots \tau_n \, [\tau_n'] \, \tau_f$. For a pure τ to be a subtype of this type, it is required by the rule for $\epsilon \leq [\tau \, \sigma] \, \tau \, \sigma$ that $\tau_k' \leq \tau_{k+1}$ for all k; in other words, that the contexts can be composed.

The type system has two distinct rules for function application: one for pure expressions (i.e., those without control effects), and one for impure expressions. The rule for pure application seems not strictly necessary, but its removal reduces the expressiveness of the type system—for example, the following term

$$(\lambda f.\lambda y.(\lambda z.\langle(\lambda v.\lambda w.y) \, (f \, y)\rangle) \, \langle f \, y \rangle) \, (\lambda x.(\lambda x.x) \, x)$$

can no longer be typed without this rule. The reason is that the function application inside the subterm $\lambda x.(\lambda x.x) \, x$ would then force it into "impure" typing, which makes the typing fail in the left part of the term because of answer type incompatibility.

Theorem 3 (Subject reduction). *If* $\vdash e : \tau \, \sigma$ *and* $e \to e'$ *for some* e', *then* $\vdash e' : \tau \, \sigma$.

Theorem 4 (Progress). *If* $\vdash e : \tau \, \sigma$, *then* e *is a value,* $e \to e'$ *for some* e', *or* $e = K[\mathcal{S}_0 f.e]$. *If* $\sigma = \epsilon$, *the third case cannot occur.*

Theorem 5 (Unique decomposition). *If* $\vdash e : \tau$ *and* $e \to e'$ *for some* e', *then* $e = K[T[r]]$ *for exactly one context* K, *trail* T *and redex* r.

3.2 Typing contexts and trails

Even though it is not strictly necessary, it is useful to have separate typing rules for contexts and trails as a proof device and for improving the understanding of the system.

We first have to introduce a different way of looking at the types of expressions. In the type system shown in Figure 5, we put emphasis on the argument type of the first context on the trail (or of the bottom context, if the trail is empty). In the current, alternative approach, the final answer type will be emphasized.

$$\frac{}{\epsilon \leq \epsilon} \qquad \frac{\tau\,\sigma \leq \tau'\,\sigma'}{\epsilon \leq [\tau\,\sigma]\,\tau'\,\sigma'} \qquad \frac{\tau_2\,\sigma_2 \leq \tau_1\,\sigma_1 \qquad \tau_1'\,\sigma_1' \leq \tau_2'\,\sigma_2'}{[\tau_1\,\sigma_1]\,\tau_1'\,\sigma_1' \leq [\tau_2\,\sigma_2]\,\tau_2'\,\sigma_2'}$$

$$\frac{\tau \leq \tau' \qquad \sigma \leq \sigma'}{\tau\,\sigma \leq \tau'\,\sigma'} \qquad \frac{}{\alpha \leq \alpha} \qquad \frac{\tau_2' \leq \tau_1' \qquad \tau_1\,\sigma_1 \leq \tau_2\,\sigma_2}{\tau_1' \xrightarrow{\sigma_1} \tau_1 \leq \tau_2' \xrightarrow{\sigma_2} \tau_2}$$

$$\frac{}{\Gamma, x : \tau \vdash x : \tau}\ \text{VAR} \qquad \frac{\Gamma \vdash e : \tau\,\sigma \qquad \tau\,\sigma \leq \tau'\,\sigma'}{\Gamma \vdash e : \tau'\,\sigma'}\ \text{SUB}$$

$$\frac{\Gamma, x : \tau_1 \vdash e : \tau_2\,\sigma}{\Gamma \vdash \lambda x.e : \tau_1 \xrightarrow{\sigma} \tau_2}\ \text{ABS} \qquad \frac{\Gamma \vdash f : \tau_1 \to \tau_2 \qquad \Gamma \vdash e : \tau_1}{\Gamma \vdash fe : \tau_2}\ \text{APP-PURE}$$

$$\frac{\Gamma \vdash f : \tau_1 \xrightarrow{[\tau_1'\,\sigma_1]\,\tau_3'\,\sigma_3} \tau_2\,[\tau_4'\,\sigma_4]\,\tau_2'\,\sigma_2 \qquad \Gamma \vdash e : \tau_1\,[\tau_3'\,\sigma_3]\,\tau_4'\,\sigma_4}{\Gamma \vdash fe : \tau_2\,[\tau_1'\,\sigma_1]\,\tau_2'\,\sigma_2}\ \text{APP}$$

$$\frac{\Gamma, f : \tau_1 \xrightarrow{\sigma_1} \tau_2 \vdash e : \tau_3\,\sigma_2}{\Gamma \vdash \mathcal{S}_0 f.e : \tau_1\,[\tau_2\,\sigma_1]\,\tau_3\,\sigma_2}\ \text{SHIFT0} \qquad \frac{\Gamma \vdash e : \tau'\,[\tau']\,\tau\,\sigma}{\Gamma \vdash \langle e \rangle : \tau\,\sigma}\ \text{RESET0}$$

Figure 5. Type system for $\lambda^{\mathcal{S}_0}$ with subtyping ($\lambda^{\mathcal{S}_0}_{\leq}$)

Let us introduce the syntactic category of trail types (which are just sequences of function types):

$$\pi ::= (\tau \xrightarrow{\sigma} \tau)^*$$

We use ι to denote the empty trail type, and we use juxtaposition for trail type concatenation.

We define three functions: $\overrightarrow{\tau\,\sigma}$, which extracts the trail type, $\downarrow(\tau\,\sigma)$ which extracts the answer type, and the composition $\pi(\tau\sigma)$, which appends a trail type to an effect-annotated type. These functions are defined as follows:

$$\begin{aligned}
\overrightarrow{\tau} &= \iota \\
\overrightarrow{\tau_1'\,[\tau_1\,\sigma_1]\,\tau\,\sigma} &= (\tau_1' \xrightarrow{\sigma_1} \tau_1)\,\overrightarrow{\tau\sigma} \\
\downarrow\tau &= \tau \\
\downarrow(\tau_1'\,[\tau_1\,\sigma_1]\,\tau\,\sigma) &= \downarrow(\tau\,\sigma) \\
\iota\,(\tau\,\sigma) &= \tau\,\sigma \\
\pi\,(\tau_1' \xrightarrow{\sigma_1} \tau_1)\,(\tau\,\sigma) &= \pi\,(\tau_1'\,[\tau_1\,\sigma_1]\,\tau\,\sigma)
\end{aligned}$$

We will omit the parentheses when there is no confusion about the meaning of the given expression.

Property 1. *For any τ and σ, we have $\tau\,\sigma = \overrightarrow{\tau\,\sigma}\downarrow\tau\,\sigma$.*

Property 2. *For any π, π', τ and σ we have $(\pi'\pi)\tau\sigma = \pi'(\pi\tau\sigma)$.*

The typing rules for contexts and trails are shown in Figure 6. Contexts are assigned function types, and the types of trails are just lists of context types. We can relate these typings to the typing relation for terms:

Lemma 2 (Typing contexts). $\Gamma \vdash K : \tau' \xrightarrow{\sigma} \tau$ *if and only if* $\Gamma \vdash \lambda x.\langle K[x] \rangle : \tau' \xrightarrow{\sigma} \tau$.

Lemma 3 (Typing trails). $\Gamma \vdash T : \pi$ *is derivable if and only if for every e, τ, σ such that* $\Gamma \vdash e : \pi\,\tau\,\sigma$ *one can derive* $\Gamma \vdash T[e] : \tau\,\sigma$.

Additionally, we introduce the notion of pure contexts, which are not allowed to have occurrences of the *shift*$_0$ operator not surrounded by a *reset*$_0$. For this typing relation the following lemma holds:

Lemma 4 (Typing pure contexts). $\Gamma \vdash_P K : \tau' \to \tau$ *if and only if* $\Gamma \vdash \lambda x.K[x] : \tau' \to \tau$.

Pure typing of contexts is a restricted version of the impure typing, in the sense that even when considering only contexts with a pure type (i.e., of the form $\tau \to \tau'$), there are strictly fewer pure contexts than impure ones. For example, we have

$$y : \alpha \vdash \lambda x.\langle x\,(\mathcal{S}_0 f.y) \rangle : (\alpha \xrightarrow{[\alpha]\,\alpha} \alpha) \to \alpha$$

but it is not a valid typing for $\lambda x.x\,(\mathcal{S}_0 f.y)$.

However, every pure context is an impure one:

Lemma 5 (Impure typing of pure contexts). *If* $\Gamma \vdash_P K : \tau' \to \tau$, *then* $\Gamma \vdash K : \tau' \to \tau$.

We can now introduce the typing relation for programs. As witnessed by the unique-decomposition theorem, we can view a program as composed of three parts: an expression, a trail, and a pure context at the bottom. The following theorem establishes the correctness of the rule PROG:

Lemma 6 (Typing programs). $\Gamma \vdash \langle e, T, K \rangle : \tau$ *if and only if* $\Gamma \vdash K[T[e]] : \tau$.

Next, we formally introduce the notion of metacontexts, which will play a role in proving termination. A metacontext in our system is a pair of a trail T_M, typed $\Gamma \vdash T_M : \pi$ for some π, and a pure context K, typed $\Gamma \vdash_P K : \tau'' \to \tau'$ for some τ' and τ'', and where for some τ we have $\tau \leq \pi\,\tau''$. The intuitive meaning of this restriction is that the contexts in the trail cannot access contexts outside of it and they can be composed, so that when given a value of type τ, they produce a value of type τ'', which can be put into the pure context at the bottom.

Lemma 7 (Typing metacontexts). $\Gamma \vdash \langle T_M, K \rangle : \tau \to \tau'$ *if and only if* $\Gamma, x : \tau \vdash K[T_M[x]] : \tau'$.

Finally, we introduce a different notion of program decomposition. In a well-typed program, the trail can be split into two parts: the top part, which is accessible by the expression inside, and the bottom part, which is guaranteed by the type of the expression to be inaccessible. This bottom part of the trail, together with the pure context at the very bottom, form a metacontext. This is made formal by the following theorem:

Contexts

$$\frac{}{\Gamma \vdash \bullet : \tau \to \tau}\ \text{EMPTY} \qquad \frac{\Gamma \vdash K : \tau \xrightarrow{\sigma_1} \tau_1 \qquad \Gamma \vdash e : \tau' \,[\tau_2\, \sigma_2]\, \tau_3\, \sigma_3}{\Gamma \vdash Ke : (\tau' \xrightarrow{[\tau_1\, \sigma_1]\, \tau_2\, \sigma_2} \tau) \xrightarrow{\sigma_3} \tau_3}\ \text{APPL}$$

$$\frac{\Gamma \vdash K : \tau \xrightarrow{\sigma_1} \tau_1 \qquad \Gamma \vdash v : \tau' \xrightarrow{[\tau_1\, \sigma_1]\, \tau_2\, \sigma_2} \tau}{\Gamma \vdash vK : \tau' \xrightarrow{\sigma_2} \tau_2}\ \text{APPR} \qquad \frac{\Gamma \vdash K : \tau_1 \xrightarrow{\sigma} \tau_2 \qquad \tau_1' \leq \tau_1 \qquad \tau_2\, \sigma \leq \tau_2'\, \sigma'}{\Gamma \vdash K : \tau_1' \xrightarrow{\sigma'} \tau_2'}\ \text{SUB}$$

Pure contexts

$$\frac{}{\Gamma \vdash_P \bullet : \tau \to \tau}\ \text{EMPTY} \qquad \frac{\Gamma \vdash_P K : \tau_1 \to \tau_2 \qquad \Gamma \vdash e : \tau_3}{\Gamma \vdash_P Ke : (\tau_3 \to \tau_1) \to \tau_2}\ \text{APPL}$$

$$\frac{\Gamma \vdash_P K : \tau_1 \to \tau_2 \qquad \Gamma \vdash v : \tau_3 \to \tau_1}{\Gamma \vdash_P vK : \tau_3 \to \tau_2}\ \text{APPR} \qquad \frac{\Gamma \vdash_P K : \tau_1 \to \tau_2 \qquad \tau_1' \leq \tau_1 \qquad \tau_2 \leq \tau_2'}{\Gamma \vdash_P K : \tau_1' \to \tau_2'}\ \text{SUB}$$

Trails

$$\frac{}{\Gamma \vdash \Box : \iota}\ \text{EMPTY} \qquad \frac{\Gamma \vdash K : \tau' \xrightarrow{\sigma} \tau \qquad \Gamma \vdash M : \pi}{\Gamma \vdash K \cdot M : \tau' \xrightarrow{\sigma} \tau\, \pi}\ \text{CONS}$$

Subtyping for trail types

$$\frac{}{\iota \leq \iota} \qquad \frac{\tau_1 \xrightarrow{\sigma} \tau_2 \leq \tau_1' \xrightarrow{\sigma'} \tau_2' \qquad \pi \leq \pi'}{\tau_1 \xrightarrow{\sigma} \tau_2\, \pi \leq \tau_1' \xrightarrow{\sigma'} \tau_2'\, \pi'}$$

Metacontexts, programs

$$\frac{\Gamma \vdash T_M : \pi \qquad \Gamma \vdash_P K : \tau'' \to \tau' \qquad \tau \leq \pi\, \tau''}{\Gamma \vdash \langle T_M, K \rangle : \tau \to \tau'}\ \text{META} \qquad \frac{\Gamma \vdash e : \tau\, \sigma \qquad \Gamma \vdash T : \overrightarrow{\tau\, \sigma} \qquad \Gamma \vdash_P K : \downarrow\!\tau\, \sigma \to \tau'}{\Gamma \vdash \langle e, T, K \rangle : \tau'}\ \text{PROG}$$

Figure 6. Typing rules for contexts and trails in $\lambda_{\leq}^{\mathcal{S}_0}$

Theorem 6. *If $\Gamma \vdash e : \tau\, \sigma$ and $\Gamma \vdash \langle e, T, K \rangle : \tau'$, then there exist T_1 and T_M such that $T = T_1 \cdot T_M$, $\Gamma \vdash T_1 : \overrightarrow{\tau\, \sigma}$, and $\Gamma \vdash \langle T_M, K \rangle : \downarrow\!\tau\, \sigma \to \tau'$.*

3.3 Termination

We now prove termination of evaluation of closed well-typed expressions using a variant of the method described in [5, 6]. We believe that it is instructive to see the proof in full detail. First, the proof reveals otherwise hidden nuances of how the reduction semantics and the type system interact. Second, it contains explicit information on how well-typed terms in our language are evaluated: each case of the proof of Lemma 12 corresponds exactly to a clause of an evaluator which can be extracted from this proof [5, 6].

Let us start by defining three families of mutually inductive predicates. The families are defined by induction on types: $\mathcal{R}_\tau$ is defined on well-typed values and is indexed by their types, $\mathcal{T}_\pi$ is defined on well-typed trails and is indexed by trail types, and finally $\mathcal{M}_\tau$ is defined on metacontexts and is indexed by their argument types. We also define a predicate $\mathcal{N}(e, T, K)$ defined on well-typed programs, which means that the evaluation of this program terminates, i.e., that $K[T[e]] \to^* v$ for some value v.

$$\begin{aligned}
\mathcal{R}_\alpha(v) &:= \top \\
\mathcal{R}_{\tau' \xrightarrow{\sigma} \tau}(v) &:= \forall v', T, T_M, K.\mathcal{R}_{\tau'}(v') \Rightarrow \mathcal{T}_{\overrightarrow{\tau\,\sigma}}(T) \\
&\qquad \Rightarrow \mathcal{M}_{\downarrow\tau\,\sigma}(T_M, K) \\
&\qquad \Rightarrow \mathcal{N}(v\, v', T \cdot T_M, K) \\
\\
\mathcal{T}_\iota() &:= \top \\
\mathcal{T}_{\tau' \xrightarrow{\sigma} \tau\, \pi}(K \cdot T) &:= \mathcal{R}_{\tau' \xrightarrow{\sigma} \tau}(\lambda x.\langle K[x]\rangle) \wedge \mathcal{T}_\pi(T) \\
\mathcal{M}_\tau(T_M, K) &:= \forall v.\mathcal{R}_\tau(v) \Rightarrow \mathcal{N}(v, T_M, K)
\end{aligned}$$

For the proof, we need several lemmas about the subtyping relation and its connection to the typing rules and the above predicates.

Lemma 8. *If $\tau \leq \pi\, \tau_1$, $\Gamma \vdash T : \pi$, $\Gamma \vdash \langle T_M, K \rangle : \tau_1 \to \tau_2$, then $\Gamma \vdash \langle T \cdot T_M, K \rangle : \tau \to \tau_2$.*

Proof. From $\Gamma \vdash \langle T_M, K \rangle : \tau_1 \to \tau_2$ for some τ', π' we have $\Gamma \vdash T_M : \pi'$, $\Gamma \vdash_P K : \tau' \to \tau_2$ and $\tau_1 \leq \pi'\, \tau'$. So $\Gamma \vdash T \cdot T_M : \pi\, \pi'$. From $\tau_1 \leq \pi'\, \tau'$ we have $\pi\, \tau_1 \leq \pi\, \pi'\, \tau'$, by transitivity from the assumption $\tau \leq \pi\, \tau_1$ we have $\tau \leq \pi\, \pi'\, \tau'$. □

Lemma 9. *1. The predicates respect the subtyping relations:*

R. If $\tau \leq \tau'$ and $\mathcal{R}_\tau(v)$, then $\mathcal{R}_{\tau'}(v)$.

T. If $\pi \leq \pi'$ and $\mathcal{T}_\pi(T)$, then $\mathcal{T}_{\pi'}(T)$.

M. If $\tau' \leq \tau$ and $\mathcal{M}_\tau(T_M, K)$, then $\mathcal{M}_{\tau'}(T_M, K)$.

2. If $\tau'\, \sigma' \leq \tau\, \sigma$, $\mathcal{T}_{\overrightarrow{\tau\,\sigma}}(T)$ and $\mathcal{M}_{\downarrow\tau\,\sigma}(T_M, K)$, then for some T', T_M' we have $\mathcal{T}_{\overrightarrow{\tau'\,\sigma'}}(T')$, $\mathcal{M}_{\downarrow\tau'\,\sigma'}(T_M', K)$ and $T \cdot T_M = T' \cdot T_M'$.

Proof. Proof by simultaneous induction. The proofs refer to other cases of the lemma with smaller subtyping derivations. The only exception is a reference from (1M) to (1R), but since it does not introduce a cycle, the induction is justified.

1R. $\tau = \tau_1 \xrightarrow{\sigma} \tau_2$, $\tau' = \tau_1' \xrightarrow{\sigma'} \tau_2'$. We have $\tau_1' \leq \tau_1$ and $\tau_2\, \sigma \leq \tau_2'\, \sigma'$. Let v, T, T_M, K be such that $\mathcal{R}_{\tau_1'}(v)$, $\mathcal{T}_{\overrightarrow{\tau_2'\,\sigma'}}(T)$, $\mathcal{M}_{\downarrow\tau_2'\,\sigma'}(T_M, K)$. By induction hypothesis for case (2) we have T' and T_M' such that $\mathcal{T}_{\overrightarrow{\tau_2\,\sigma}}(T')$, $\mathcal{M}_{\downarrow\tau_2\,\sigma}(T_M', K)$ and $T \cdot T_M = T' \cdot T_M'$. Thus from the assumption $\mathcal{R}_\tau(v)$ follows the thesis.

1T. The case $\pi = \pi' = \iota$ is trivial. Let $\pi = \tau_1 \xrightarrow{\sigma} \tau_2\, \pi_1$ and $\pi' = \tau_1' \xrightarrow{\sigma'} \tau_2' \pi_1'$. Then we have $\tau_1 \xrightarrow{\sigma} \tau_2 \leq \tau_1' \xrightarrow{\sigma'} \tau_2'$, $\pi_1 \leq \pi_1'$, $T = K \cdot T_1$, $\mathcal{R}_{\tau_1 \xrightarrow{\sigma} \tau_2}(\lambda x.\langle K[x]\rangle)$ and $\mathcal{T}_{\pi_1}(T_1)$. By induction hypothesis for case (1R) and (1T) we get $\mathcal{R}_{\tau_1' \xrightarrow{\sigma'} \tau_2'}(\lambda x.\langle K[x]\rangle)$ and $\mathcal{T}_{\pi_1'}(T_1)$, which give us the thesis.

1M. Let v be such that $\mathcal{R}_{\tau'}(v)$. By case (1R) we have $\mathcal{R}_{\tau}(v)$, with $\mathcal{M}_{\tau}(T_M, K)$ this gives us $\mathcal{N}(v, T_M, K)$.

2. Induction on the subtyping derivation.
   - $\sigma' = \epsilon$, $\sigma = \epsilon$. Then $T = \Box$, $\tau' \leq \tau$, $\mathcal{M}_{\tau}(T_M, K)$. Let $T' = \Box$, $T'_M = T_M$. We thus need to show that $\mathcal{M}_{\tau'}(T_M, K)$, but that follows from case (1M).
   - $\sigma' = \epsilon, \sigma = [\tau_1\,\sigma_1]\,\tau_2\,\sigma_2$. Then $\tau' \leq \tau, \tau_1\,\sigma_1 \leq \tau_2\sigma_2, T = K_1 \cdot T'$, $\mathcal{T}_{\tau \xrightarrow{\sigma_1} \tau_1}(K_1)$, $\mathcal{T}_{\overrightarrow{\tau_2\,\sigma_2}}(T')$, $\mathcal{M}_{\downarrow \tau_2\,\sigma_2}(T_M, K)$. Let $T' = \Box$, $T'_M = T \cdot T_M$. Trivially we have $\mathcal{T}_{\iota}(\Box)$, we need to show that $\mathcal{M}_{\tau'}(T \cdot T_M, K)$. The metacontext $\langle T \cdot T_M, K\rangle$ is well-typed by Lemma 8. Let v be such that $\mathcal{R}_{\tau'}(v)$, I will show that $\mathcal{N}(v, T \cdot T_M, K)$. From case (1T) we have $\mathcal{T}_{\tau' \xrightarrow{\sigma_2} \tau_2}(K_1)$, by definition of $\mathcal{T}_{\tau' \xrightarrow{\sigma_2} \tau_2}$ we have $\mathcal{R}_{\tau' \xrightarrow{\sigma_2} \tau_2}(\lambda x.\langle K_1[x]\rangle)$. With $\mathcal{R}_{\tau'}(v)$, $\mathcal{T}_{\overrightarrow{\tau_2\,\sigma_2}}(T')$ and $\mathcal{M}_{\downarrow \tau_2\,\sigma_2}(T_M, K)$ we have $\mathcal{N}((\lambda x.\langle K_1[x]\rangle)\,v, T' \cdot T_M, K)$. Because $(\lambda x.\langle K_1[x]\rangle)\,v$ reduces in single step to $\langle K_1[v]\rangle$, we have $\mathcal{N}(\langle K_1[v]\rangle, T' \cdot T_M, K)$, which is equivalent to $\mathcal{N}(v, K_1 \cdot T' \cdot T_M, K)$, which we wanted to prove.
   - $\sigma' = [\tau'_1\;\sigma'_1]\;\tau'_2\;\sigma'_2$, $\sigma = [\tau_1\;\sigma_1]\;\tau_2\;\sigma_2$. Then $T = K_1 \cdot T_1$, $\mathcal{T}_{\tau \xrightarrow{\sigma_1} \tau_1}(K_1)$, $\mathcal{T}_{\overrightarrow{\tau_2\,\sigma_2}}(T_1)$, $\mathcal{M}_{\downarrow \tau_2\,\sigma_2}(T_M, K)$, $\tau' \leq \tau$ and $\tau'_2\;\sigma'_2 \leq \tau_2\;\sigma_2$. By induction hypothesis we have T'_1, T'_M such that $\mathcal{T}_{\overrightarrow{\tau'_2\,\sigma'_2}}(T'_1)$, $\mathcal{M}_{\downarrow \tau'_2\,\sigma'_2}(T'_M, K)$ and $T_1 \cdot T_M = T'_1 \cdot T'_M$. From $\mathcal{M}_{\downarrow \tau'_2\,\sigma'_2}(T'_M, K)$ we have $\mathcal{M}_{\downarrow \tau'\,\sigma'}(T'_M, , K)$. Let $T' = K_1 \cdot T'_1$. From $\tau_1\,\sigma_1 \leq \tau'_1\,\sigma'_1$, $\tau' \leq \tau$, $\mathcal{T}_{\tau \xrightarrow{\sigma_1} \tau_1}(K_1)$ and the induction hypothesis for case (1T) we have $\mathcal{T}_{\tau' \xrightarrow{\sigma'_1} \tau'_1}(K_1)$. With $\mathcal{T}_{\overrightarrow{\tau'_2\,\sigma'_2}}(T'_1)$ we have $\mathcal{T}_{\overrightarrow{\tau'\,\sigma'}}(K_1 \cdot T'_1)$.

□

Lemma 10. *For every type τ, $\mathcal{T}_{\tau \to \tau}(\bullet)$ holds.*

Proof. By the definition of $\mathcal{T}_{\tau \to \tau}$ it is sufficient to prove that $\mathcal{R}_{\tau \to \tau}(\lambda x.\langle x\rangle)$. Let v, T_M, and K be such that $\mathcal{R}_{\tau}(v)$ and $\mathcal{M}_{\tau}(T_M, K)$. We have to show that $\mathcal{N}((\lambda x.\langle x\rangle)\,v, T_M, K)$. The expression $(\lambda x.\langle x\rangle)\,v$ reduces in two steps to v, so it suffices to prove $\mathcal{N}(v, T_M, K)$, which follows from $\mathcal{R}_{\tau}(v)$. □

Lemma 11. *For every type τ, $\mathcal{M}_{\tau}(\Box, \bullet)$ holds.*

Proof. Let v be a value of type τ, then $\mathcal{N}(v, \Box, \bullet)$ is trivially true. □

We now state the main lemma:

Lemma 12. *Let $\Gamma \vdash e : \tau\;\sigma$, where $\Gamma = x_1 : \tau_1, \ldots, x_n : \tau_n$. Assume that $\vec{v}$ is a sequence of values of length n such that for every i, $\mathcal{R}_{\tau_i}(v_i)$ holds. Then for every trail T such that $\mathcal{T}_{\overrightarrow{\tau\,\sigma}}(T)$ holds, and for every metacontext $\langle T_M, K\rangle$ such that $\mathcal{M}_{\downarrow \tau\,\sigma}(T_M, K,)$ holds, $\mathcal{N}(e\{\vec{x}/\vec{v}\}, T \cdot T_M, K)$ holds.*

Proof. Induction on the structure of the typing derivation D of e.

- $D = \text{SUB}(D', \tau'\,\sigma' \leq \tau\,\sigma)$. From Lemma 9 we have T', T'_M such that $\mathcal{T}_{\overrightarrow{\tau'\,\sigma'}}(T')$, $\mathcal{M}_{\downarrow \tau'\,\sigma'}(T'_M, K)$ and $T \cdot T_M = T' \cdot T'_M$. The conclusion follows from the induction hypothesis.
- $D = \text{VAR}$, $e = x_i$. So we have $e\{\vec{x}/\vec{v}\} = v_i$, $\tau = \tau_i$, $\sigma = \epsilon$,$T = \Box$, $\mathcal{M}_{\tau_i}(T_M, K)$. By assumption $\mathcal{R}_{\tau_i}(v_i)$ and the definition of $\mathcal{M}_{\tau_i}$ we have $\mathcal{N}(v_i, T_M, K)$.
- $D = \text{ABS}(D')$, $e = \lambda x.e'$. So $\tau = \tau'' \to \sigma'\tau'$, $\sigma = \epsilon$, $T = \Box$, $\mathcal{M}_{\tau}(T_M, K)$. As in the previous case, to show that $\mathcal{N}((\lambda x.e')\{\vec{x}/\vec{v}\}, T_M, K)$ we need $\mathcal{R}_{\tau}(\lambda x.e'\{\vec{x}/\vec{v}\})$.
  Let v, T, T_M, K be such that we have $\mathcal{R}_{\tau''}(v)$, $\mathcal{T}_{\overrightarrow{\tau'\,\sigma'}}(T)$ and $\mathcal{M}_{\downarrow \tau'\,\sigma'}(T_M, K)$. We need to show that $\mathcal{N}((\lambda x.e'\{\vec{x}/\vec{v}\})\,v, T \cdot T_M, K)$. Because $(\lambda x.e'\{\vec{x}/\vec{v}\})\,v$ reduces in one step to $e'\{\vec{x}/\vec{v}\}\{x/v\}$, it suffices to show $\mathcal{N}(e'\{\vec{x}/\vec{v}\}\{x/v\}, T \cdot T_M, K)$, which follows from the induction hypothesis.
- $D = \text{APP}(D_1, D_2)$, $e = e_1\,e_2$. Then $\sigma = [\tau_A\;\sigma_A]\;\tau_D\;\sigma_D$, $T = K_1 \cdot T'$, $\mathcal{T}_{\tau \xrightarrow{\sigma_A} \tau_A}(K_1)$, $\mathcal{T}_{\overrightarrow{\tau_B\,\sigma_B}}(T')$, $\Gamma \vdash e_1 : \tau' \xrightarrow{[\tau_A\,\sigma_A]\,\tau_B\,\sigma_B} \tau\,[\tau_C\,\sigma_C]\,\tau_D\,\sigma_D$, $\Gamma \vdash e_2 : \tau'\,[\tau_B\,\sigma_B]\,\tau_C\,\sigma_C$. Let $e'_1 = e_1\{\vec{x}/\vec{v}\}$ and $e'_2 = \{\vec{x}/\vec{v}\}$. To show that $\mathcal{N}(e'_1\,e'_2, K_1 \cdot T' \cdot T_M, K)$, we can show instead that $\mathcal{N}(e'_1, K_1\,e'_2 \cdot T' \cdot T_M, K)$ using the induction hypothesis for D_1, providing that $\mathcal{T}_{(\tau' \xrightarrow{[\tau_A\,\sigma_A]\,\tau_B\,\sigma_B} \tau) \xrightarrow{\sigma_C} \tau_C}(K_1\,e'_2)$. To show that, let us unfold the definitions. Let v_L, T_L, T_{KL} and M_L satisfy the appropriate predicates, i.e., $\mathcal{R}_{\tau' \xrightarrow{[\tau_A\,\sigma_A]\,\tau_B\,\sigma_B} \tau}(v_L)$, $\mathcal{T}_{\overrightarrow{\tau_C\,\sigma_C}}(T_L)$ and $\mathcal{M}_{\downarrow \tau_C\,\sigma_C}(T_{KL}, M_L)$. Then we have to show that $\mathcal{N}((\lambda x.\langle K_1[x\,e_2]\rangle)\,v_L, T_L \cdot T_{KL}, M_L)$. Because $(\lambda x.\langle K_1[x\,e_2]\rangle)\,v_L$ reduces in one step to $\langle K_1[v_L\,e_2]\rangle$, we can show instead that $\mathcal{N}(\langle K_1[v_L\,e_2]\rangle, T_L \cdot T_{KL}, M_L)$. We will show instead that $\mathcal{N}(e_2, v_L\,K_1 \cdot T_L \cdot T_{KL}, M_L)$. This follows for the induction hypothesis for D_2, providing that $\mathcal{T}_{\tau' \xrightarrow{\sigma_B} \tau_B}(v_L\,K_1)$. To show that, let us unfold the definitions again. Let v_R, T_R, T_{KR} and M_R be such that $\mathcal{R}_{\tau'}(v_R)$, $\mathcal{T}_{\overrightarrow{\tau_B\,\sigma_B}}(T_R)$ and $\mathcal{M}_{\downarrow \tau_B\,\sigma_B}(T_{KR}, M_R)$. We have to show that $\mathcal{N}((\lambda x.\langle K_1[v_L\,x]\rangle)\,v_R, T_R \cdot T_{KR}, M_R)$. Using analogous reasoning as before, it is sufficient to show that $\mathcal{N}(v_L\,v_R, K_1 \cdot T_R \cdot T_{KR}, M_R)$, which follows from $\mathcal{R}_{\tau' \xrightarrow{[\tau_A\,\sigma_A]\,\tau_B\,\sigma_B} \tau}(v_L)$.
- $D = \text{APP-PURE}(D_1, D_2)$, $e = e_1\,e_2$. The proof is similar to the case for APP.
- $D = \text{SHIFT0}(D')$, $e = \mathcal{S}_0 f.e'$. So $\sigma = [\tau'\sigma']\tau''\sigma''$, $T = K_1 \cdot T'$, $\mathcal{R}_{\tau \xrightarrow{\sigma'} \tau'}(\lambda x.\langle K_1[x]\rangle)$, $\mathcal{T}_{\overrightarrow{\tau''\sigma''}}(T')$ and $\mathcal{M}_{\downarrow \tau''\sigma''}(T_M, K)$. We want to show $\mathcal{N}(\mathcal{S}_0 f.e\{\vec{x}/\vec{v}\}, K_1 \cdot T' \cdot T_M, K)$, which is equivalent to $\mathcal{N}(\langle K_1[\mathcal{S}_0 f.e\{\vec{x}/\vec{v}\}]\rangle, T' \cdot T_M, K)$. Because $\langle K_1[\mathcal{S}_0 f.e\{\vec{x}/\vec{v}\}]\rangle$ reduces to $e\{\vec{x}/\vec{v}\}\{f/\lambda x.\langle K[x]\}$, it suffices to show that $\mathcal{N}(e\{\vec{x}/\vec{v}\}\{f/\lambda x.\langle K[x]\}, T' \cdot T_M, K)$, which follows from the induction hypothesis.
- $D = \text{RESET0}(D')$, $e = \langle e'\rangle$. Then for some τ' we have $\Gamma \vdash e' : \tau'\;[\tau']\;\tau\;\sigma$. From Lemma 10 have $\mathcal{T}_{\tau' \to \tau'}(\bullet)$, and thus $\mathcal{T}_{\overrightarrow{\tau'\,[\tau']\,\tau\,\sigma}}(\bullet \cdot T)$. The induction hypothesis gives us $\mathcal{N}(e'\{\vec{x}/\vec{v}\}, \bullet \cdot T \cdot T_M, K)$, which is equivalent to the thesis, $\mathcal{N}(\langle e'\rangle\{\vec{x}/\vec{v}\}, \cdot T \cdot T_M, K)$.

□

Theorem 7 (Termination). *If $\vdash e : \tau$, then the evaluation of e terminates, i.e., $\mathcal{N}(e, \Box, \bullet)$ holds.*

Proof. We have $\mathcal{T}_{\iota}(\Box)$ and from Lemma 11 we have $\mathcal{M}_{\tau}(\Box, \bullet)$, thus the theorem follows from Lemma 12. □

3.4 Type inference

Type inference in $\lambda^{\mathcal{S}_0}_{\leq}$ is decidable. For the purpose of type inference, we replace the rules APP and APP-IND with the following (equivalent) rule:

$$\frac{\Gamma \vdash f : \tau' \xrightarrow{\sigma_3} \tau\,\sigma_1 \qquad \Gamma \vdash e : \tau'\,\sigma_2 \qquad \sigma \ll \sigma_1\,\sigma_2\,\sigma_3}{\Gamma \vdash f e : \tau\,\sigma}\ \text{APP-COMP},$$

where the relation $\ll$ is defined as follows:

$$\frac{}{\epsilon \ll} \qquad \frac{}{[\tau\,\sigma]\,\tau\,\sigma \ll}$$

$$\frac{\epsilon \ll \vec{\sigma}}{\epsilon \ll \epsilon\,\vec{\sigma}} \qquad \frac{[\tau_f\,\sigma_f]\,\tau_2\,\sigma_2 \ll \vec{\sigma}}{[\tau_f\,\sigma_f]\,\tau_1\,\sigma_1 \ll [\tau_2\,\sigma_2]\,\tau_1\,\sigma_1\,\vec{\sigma}}$$

Expressions of the form $\sigma \leq^{?} \sigma$ will be called *subtyping constraints*, and expressions of the form $\sigma \ll^{?} \vec{\sigma}$ will be called

$$
\begin{array}{rcl}
[\![\alpha]\!] & = & \alpha \\
[\![\tau_1 \xrightarrow{\sigma} \tau_2]\!] & = & [\![\tau_1]\!] \rightarrow [\![\tau_2\ \sigma]\!] \\
[\![\tau\ \epsilon]\!] & = & [\![\tau]\!] \\
[\![\tau\ [\tau_1\ \sigma_1]\ \tau_2\ \sigma_2]\!] & = & ([\![\tau]\!] \rightarrow [\![\tau_1\ \sigma_1]\!]) \rightarrow [\![\tau_2\ \sigma_2]\!] \\
[\![\alpha \leq \alpha]\!] & = & \lambda x.x \\
[\![\tau_1' \xrightarrow{\sigma_1} \tau_1 \leq \tau_2' \xrightarrow{\sigma_2} \tau_2]\!] & = & \lambda f.\lambda x.[\![\tau_1\ \sigma_1 \leq \tau_2\ \sigma_2]\!](f([\![\tau_2' \leq \tau_1']\!]x)) \\
[\![\tau\ \epsilon \leq \tau'\ \epsilon]\!] & = & [\![\tau \leq \tau']\!] \\
[\![\tau\ \epsilon \leq \tau'\ [\tau_1\ \sigma_1]\ \tau_2\ \sigma_2]\!] & = & \lambda x.\lambda f.[\![\tau_1\ \sigma_1 \leq \tau_2\ \sigma_2]\!](f([\![\tau \leq \tau']\!]x)) \\
[\![\tau\ [\tau_1\ \sigma_1]\ \tau_1'\ \sigma_1' \leq \tau'\ [\tau_2\ \sigma_2]\ \tau_2'\ \sigma_2']\!] & = & \lambda f.\lambda g.[\![\tau_1'\ \sigma_1' \leq \tau_2'\ \sigma_2']\!](f(\lambda x.[\![\tau_2\ \sigma_2 \leq \tau_1\ \sigma_1]\!](g([\![\tau \leq \tau']\!]x)))) \\
[\![x]\!]_{\text{VAR}} & = & x \\
[\![e]\!]_{\text{SUB}(D,\tau\ \sigma \leq \tau'\ \sigma')} & = & [\![\tau\ \sigma \leq \tau'\ \sigma']\!][\![e]\!]_D \\
[\![\lambda x.e]\!]_{\text{ABS}(D)} & = & \lambda x.[\![e]\!]_D \\
[\![fe]\!]_{\text{APP-PURE}(D_1,D_2)} & = & [\![f]\!]_{D_1}[\![e]\!]_{D_2} \\
[\![fe]\!]_{\text{APP}(D_1,D_2)} & = & \lambda k.[\![f]\!]_{D_1}(\lambda f.[\![e]\!]_{D_2}(\lambda e.fek)) \\
[\![\mathcal{S}_0 f.e]\!]_{\text{SHIFT0}(D)} & = & \lambda f.[\![e]\!]_D \\
[\![\langle e\rangle]\!]_{\text{RESET0}(D)} & = & [\![e]\!]_D(\lambda x.x)
\end{array}
$$

Figure 7. Type-directed CPS translation for $\lambda_{\leq}^{\mathcal{S}_0}$

composition constraints. Inside the constraints, the syntax of effect annotations is extended by annotation variables δ.

We will be using substitutions defined on both the type variables and annotation variables. We call a substitution σ-grounding, if its values do not contain any annotation variables. We say that a substitution s solves a constraint $\sigma_1 \leq^? \sigma_2$ ($\sigma_1 \ll^? \vec{\sigma}$) if and only if $s(\sigma_1) \leq s(\sigma_2)$ ($s(\sigma_1) \ll s(\vec{\sigma})$) is derivable.

Theorem 8 (Principal types). *For every term e and typing environment Γ there exist: α, δ, a set of $\tau\sigma$-subtyping constraints S, and a set of composition constraints C, such that:*

1. *For every σ-grounding substitution s which solves S and C we have $\Gamma \vdash e : s(\alpha)\ s(\delta)$.*
2. *For every τ, σ satisfying $\Gamma \vdash e : \tau\ \sigma$ there exists a σ-grounding substitution s such that $s(\alpha) = \tau$, $s(\delta) = \sigma$ and s solves S and C.*

The type inference algorithm finds the principal type (along with the unsolved constraints) in polynomial time and it also generates a typing derivation skeleton, where subtyping derivations have to be filled in. In order to check if the term is actually well-typed (and to obtain a concrete typing derivation), one has to find a σ-grounding substitution which solves the inequalities.

3.5 Type-directed CPS translation

Having extended the type system with subtyping, we can derive from it a type-directed CPS translation, which takes into account the additional information given by the subtyping. This translation, defined in Figure 7, targets the simply-typed lambda calculus, and as the CPS translation of Figure 2, it preserves types:

Theorem 9 (Type preservation). *If D is a typing derivation of $\Gamma \vdash e : \tau\ \sigma$ in $\lambda_{\leq}^{\mathcal{S}_0}$, then $[\![\Gamma]\!] \vdash [\![e]\!]_D : [\![\tau\ \sigma]\!]$ in $\lambda_{\rightarrow}$.*

The derivations of the subtyping relation are translated to coercion functions, which are typed as expected:

Lemma 13. *If $\tau\ \sigma \leq \tau'\ \sigma'$, then $\vdash [\![\tau\ \sigma \leq \tau'\ \sigma']\!] : [\![\tau\ \sigma]\!] \rightarrow [\![\tau'\ \sigma']\!]$ in $\lambda_{\rightarrow}$. If $\tau \leq \tau'$, then $\vdash [\![\tau \leq \tau']\!] : [\![\tau]\!] \rightarrow [\![\tau']\!]$ in $\lambda_{\rightarrow}$.*

Another interesting property of the translation is that it keeps terms annotated as pure in direct style. This is similar to the selective translations presented in [24], [27], and recently in [31], which also use effect annotations to distinguish pure terms from effectful ones. The property suggests that the translation presented here may be useful in implementing *shift*$_0$/*reset*$_0$ in functional programming languages.

Unfortunately, the translation does not preserve reductions. For example, let us consider the term $\langle \mathcal{S}_0 f.f\rangle$. We have $\vdash \langle \mathcal{S}_0 f.f\rangle : \tau \rightarrow \tau$ and $\langle \mathcal{S}_0 f.f\rangle \rightarrow \lambda x.\langle x\rangle$. For the simplest derivation D, we have

$$[\![\langle \mathcal{S}_0 f.f\rangle]\!]_D = (\lambda f.f)\ (\lambda x.x)$$

and for the simplest derivation D', we have

$$[\![\lambda x.\langle x\rangle]\!]_{D'} = \lambda x.(\lambda x.\lambda k.(\lambda x.x)\ (k\ ((\lambda x.x)\ x)))\ x\ (\lambda x.x).$$

So we cannot β-reduce $[\![\langle \mathcal{S}_0 f.f\rangle]\!]_D$ to $[\![\lambda x.\langle x\rangle]\!]_{D'}$, although they are β-equal. For this reason, this CPS translation could not be used as-is for proving termination of evaluation of well-typed terms in $\lambda_{\leq}^{\mathcal{S}_0}$.

4. Programming examples

4.1 Prototype implementation

In order to study the applications of the type system $\lambda_{\leq}^{\mathcal{S}_0}$ to practical programming, we have developed its prototype implementation. The implementation adds some standard syntactic sugar to the language and extends it with integers, algebraic data types and recursion.

We extend the syntax as follows:

$$
\begin{array}{rl}
e ::= & \ldots \mid \text{true} \mid \text{false} \mid \text{if } e \text{ then } e \text{ else } e \\
 & \mid \text{nil} \mid \text{cons}(e, e) \mid \text{case } e\ \{\text{nil} \rightarrow e; \text{cons}(x_1, x_2) \rightarrow e\} \\
 & \mid k \mid e \oplus e \mid e \gtreqless e \mid \text{fix}x.e \\
\tau ::= & \ldots \mid \text{int} \mid \text{bool} \mid \text{list}(\tau)
\end{array}
$$

The typing rules for new expressions introduced above are given in Figure 8.

In the implementation language, the string `@f.e` means $\mathcal{S}_0 f.e$, and `<e>` means $\langle e\rangle$. The rest of the syntax used is ML-like.

$$\frac{}{\Gamma \vdash \text{true} : \text{bool}}\ \text{TRUE} \qquad \frac{}{\Gamma \vdash \text{false} : \text{bool}}\ \text{FALSE}$$

$$\frac{\Gamma \vdash b : \text{bool}\ \sigma_1 \qquad \Gamma \vdash e_1 : \tau\ \sigma_2 \qquad \Gamma \vdash e_2 : \tau\ \sigma_2 \qquad \sigma \ll \sigma_1\ \sigma_2}{\Gamma \vdash \text{if } b \text{ then } e_1 \text{ else } e_2 : \tau\ \sigma}\ \text{IF}$$

$$\frac{}{\Gamma \vdash k : \text{int}}\ \text{INT}$$

$$\frac{\Gamma \vdash k_1 : \text{int}\ \sigma_1 \qquad \Gamma \vdash k_2 : \text{int}\ \sigma_2 \qquad \sigma \ll \sigma_1\ \sigma_2}{\Gamma \vdash k_1 \oplus k_2 : \text{int}\ \sigma}\ \text{ARITH}$$

$$\frac{\Gamma \vdash k_1 : \text{int}\ \sigma_1 \qquad \Gamma \vdash k_2 : \text{int}\ \sigma_2 \qquad \sigma \ll \sigma_1\ \sigma_2}{\Gamma \vdash k_1 \gtreqless k_2 : \text{bool}\ \sigma}\ \text{REL}$$

$$\frac{}{\Gamma \vdash \text{nil} : \text{list}(\tau)}\ \text{NIL}$$

$$\frac{\Gamma \vdash h : \tau\ \sigma_1 \qquad \Gamma \vdash t : \text{list}(\tau)\ \sigma_2 \qquad \sigma \ll \sigma_1\ \sigma_2}{\Gamma \vdash \text{cons}(h, t) : \text{list}(\tau)\ \sigma}\ \text{CONS}$$

$$\frac{\Gamma \vdash e : \text{list}(\tau_l)\ \sigma_1 \qquad \Gamma \vdash e_1 : \tau\ \sigma_2 \qquad \Gamma, h : \tau_l, t : \text{list}(\tau_l) \vdash e_2 : \tau\ \sigma_2 \qquad \sigma \ll \sigma_1\ \sigma_2}{\Gamma \vdash \text{case } e\{\text{nil} \to e_1; \text{cons}(h, t) \to e_2\} : \tau\ \sigma}\ \text{CASE}$$

$$\frac{\Gamma, x : \tau \vdash e : \tau}{\Gamma \vdash \text{fix } x.e : \tau}\ \text{FIX}$$

Figure 8. Typing rules for booleans, integers, lists and recursion

4.2 Example—*prefixes*

The *prefixes* example shown in Figure 9 has been considered in [2] and in [6]. The function `prefixes` lists prefixes of a given list, e.g., `prefixes [1,2,3]` yields `[[1],[1,2],[1,2,3]]`. This example cannot be typed in the original type system of Danvy and Filinski, because the captured continuation is applied in contexts with different answer types. In our type system, this problem is taken care of by the subtyping relation. In the first occurrence (`k []`) the continuation is simply given the pure type $\text{list(int)} \to \text{list(int)}$. In the second (`k (w xs)`), it is given a more complex type $\text{list(int)} \xrightarrow{[\text{list(int)}]\ \text{list(int)}} \text{list(int)}$.

4.3 Example—*partition*

The *prefixes* example does not take advantage of the semantics of *shift*$_0$, because it can be typed with flat effect annotations. This is not the case for *partition*, shown in Figure 10. This program partitions a list of integers into three parts: the ones less than, equal, and greater than a number given as a parameter, maintaining the original order between the integers in each group, e.g., `partition 3 [4,1,3,5,2,3]` yields `[1,2,3,3,4,5]`. The idea behind this example is that the two *reset*$_0$'s are used as "markers" for the positions in the result where we insert new elements, and *shift*$_0$ is used to reach those markers.

The inner function `part` is given the following type:

$$\text{list(int)} \xrightarrow{[\text{list(int)}]\ \text{list(int)}\ [\text{list(int)}]\ \text{list(int)}} \text{list(int)}$$

Hence, it requires two contexts, both of the type $\text{list(int)} \to \text{list(int)}$, and returns a final value of type list(int). These contexts are the "accumulators" for the elements less than and equal to the given value.

```
let prefixes xs =
   let w l = case l {
      Nil -> @k. Nil
    | Cons(x, xs) ->
         Cons(x, @k. <Cons(k [], <k (w xs)>)>)
   } in <w xs>
```

Figure 9. Example program—*prefixes*

```
let partition a l =
   let part l = case l {
      Nil -> []
    | Cons(h,t) ->
         if h > a
         then Cons(h, part t)
         else if h == a
            then @f. Cons(h, <f (part t)>)
            else @f g. Cons(h, <g <f (part t)>>)
   } in <<part l>>
```

Figure 10. Example program—*partition*

The subtyping relation is crucial for typing this example. In particular, in the non-recursive `Nil` case, the following subtyping is used:

$$\text{list(int)} \leq \text{list(int)}\ [\text{list(int)}]\ \text{list(int)}\ [\text{list(int)}]\ \text{list(int)},$$

where the subtyping derivation for the effect annotations is as follows:

$$\frac{\frac{}{\text{list(int)} \leq \text{list(int)}} \qquad \frac{\frac{}{\text{list(int)} \leq \text{list(int)}} \qquad \frac{}{\epsilon \leq \epsilon}}{\epsilon \leq [\text{list(int)}]\ \text{list(int)}}}{\epsilon \leq [\text{list(int)}]\ \text{list(int)}\ [\text{list(int)}]\ \text{list(int)}}$$

Using the translation from Figure 7 we obtain the following coercion function (reduced to normal form for clarity):

$$\lambda x.\lambda k_1.\lambda k_2.k_2\ (k_1\ x)$$

We can see that in the translated term the composition of the "accumulator" contexts after traversing the entire input list is done by the coercion function.

5. Relation to shift/reset

The *shift* operator can be defined with *shift*$_0$ and *reset*$_0$ by putting a *reset*$_0$ inside a *shift*$_0$: $\mathcal{S}f.e = \mathcal{S}_0 f.\langle e\rangle$; *reset*$_0$ then behaves just like *reset*. Using this definition, one can check how the type system presented here relates to the type system for *shift/reset* introduced by Danvy and Filinski [14] (let us call their system $\lambda^{\mathcal{S}}_{\rightarrow}$). First, we define a translation from $\lambda^{\mathcal{S}}_{\rightarrow}$ to $\lambda^{\mathcal{S}_0}_{\leq}$ on terms and types (the syntactic forms not mentioned below translate homomorphically):

$$\begin{aligned} \overline{\tau} &= \tau \\ \overline{\tau_1\ {}_{\tau_3}\!\!\to_{\tau_4} \tau_2} &= \overline{\tau_1} \xrightarrow{[\overline{\tau_3}]\ \overline{\tau_4}} \overline{\tau_2} \\ \overline{\mathcal{S}f.e} &= \mathcal{S}_0 f.\langle \overline{e} \rangle \end{aligned}$$

The translation on typing derivations is shown in Figure 11. Using this translation, one can prove the following result:

Theorem 10. *If* $\Gamma; \tau_1 \vdash e : \tau; \tau_2$ *in* $\lambda^{\mathcal{S}}_{\rightarrow}$, *then* $\overline{\Gamma} \vdash \overline{e} : \overline{\tau}\ [\overline{\tau_1}]\ \overline{\tau_2}$ *in* $\lambda^{\mathcal{S}_0}_{\leq}$.

One can also consider the CPS translations in both systems $\lambda^{\mathcal{S}}_{\rightarrow}$ and $\lambda^{\mathcal{S}_0}_{\leq}$. First, we notice that the CPS translations of the typing derivations resulting from the translation in Figure 11 are β-equal

$$\frac{}{\Gamma, x : \tau; \tau' \vdash x : \tau; \tau'}\ \textsc{var} \qquad \frac{\dfrac{}{\Gamma, x : \tau \vdash x : \tau}\ \textsc{var} \qquad \dfrac{\cdots}{\tau \leq \tau\,[\tau']\,\tau'}}{\Gamma, x : \tau \vdash x : \tau\,[\tau']\,\tau'}\ \textsc{sub}$$

$$\frac{\Gamma, x : \tau; \tau_1 \vdash e : \tau'; \tau_2}{\Gamma; \tau'' \vdash \lambda x.e : (\tau\ {}_{\tau_1}\!\!\rightarrow_{\tau_2} \tau'); \tau''}\ \textsc{abs} \qquad \frac{\dfrac{\Gamma, x : \tau \vdash e : \tau'\,[\tau_1]\,\tau_2}{\Gamma \vdash \lambda x.e : \tau \xrightarrow{[\tau_1]\,\tau_2} \tau'}\ \textsc{abs} \qquad \dfrac{\cdots}{\tau \xrightarrow{[\tau_1]\,\tau_2} \tau' \leq \tau \xrightarrow{[\tau_1]\,\tau_2} \tau'[\tau'']\,\tau''}}{\Gamma \vdash \lambda x.e : \tau \xrightarrow{[\tau_1]\,\tau_2} \tau'\,[\tau'']\,\tau''}\ \textsc{sub}$$

$$\frac{\Gamma; \tau_4' \vdash f : (\tau_1\ {}_{\tau_1'}\!\!\rightarrow_{\tau_3'} \tau_2); \tau_2' \qquad \Gamma; \tau_3' \vdash e : \tau_2; \tau_4'}{\Gamma; \tau_1' \vdash fe : \tau_2; \tau_2'}\ \textsc{app} \qquad \frac{\Gamma \vdash f : \tau_1 \xrightarrow{[\tau_1']\,\tau_3'} \tau_2\,[\tau_4']\,\tau_2' \qquad \Gamma \vdash e : \tau_1\,[\tau_3']\,\tau_4'}{\Gamma \vdash fe : \tau_2\,[\tau_1']\,\tau_2'}\ \textsc{app}$$

$$\frac{\Gamma, f : (\tau\ {}_{\tau'}\!\!\rightarrow_{\tau'} \tau_1); \tau_3 \vdash e : \tau_3; \tau_2}{\Gamma; \tau_1 \vdash \mathcal{S}f.e : \tau; \tau_2}\ \textsc{shift} \qquad \frac{\dfrac{\dfrac{\Gamma, f : \tau \xrightarrow{[\tau']\,\tau'} \tau_1 \vdash e : \tau_3\,[\tau_3]\,\tau_2}{\Gamma, f : \tau \xrightarrow{[\tau']\,\tau'} \tau_1 \vdash \langle e \rangle : \tau_2}\ \textsc{reset0}}{\Gamma \vdash \mathcal{S}_0 f.\langle e \rangle : \tau\,[\tau_1\,[\tau']\,\tau']\,\tau_2}\ \textsc{shift0} \qquad \dfrac{\cdots}{\tau\,[\tau_1\,[\tau']\,\tau']\,\tau_2 \leq \tau\,[\tau_1]\,\tau_2}}{\Gamma \vdash \mathcal{S}_0 f.\langle e \rangle : \tau\,[\tau_1]\,\tau_2}\ \textsc{sub}$$

$$\frac{\Gamma; \tau_1 \vdash e : \tau_1; \tau}{\Gamma; \tau' \vdash \langle e \rangle : \tau; \tau'}\ \textsc{reset} \qquad \frac{\dfrac{\Gamma \vdash e : \tau_1\,[\tau_1]\,\tau}{\Gamma \vdash \langle e \rangle : \tau}\ \textsc{reset0} \qquad \dfrac{\cdots}{\tau \leq \tau\,[\tau']\,\tau'}}{\Gamma \vdash \langle e \rangle : \tau\,[\tau']\,\tau'}\ \textsc{sub}$$

Figure 11. Embedding of Danvy and Filinski's type system $\lambda^{\mathcal{S}}_{\rightarrow}$ into $\lambda^{\mathcal{S}_0}_{\leq}$

to the standard CPS translations [14]. In order to formalize this observation we introduce the following notation. If D is a typing derivation in $\lambda^{\mathcal{S}}_{\rightarrow}$, then $\overline{D}$ is the corresponding typing derivation in $\lambda^{\mathcal{S}_0}_{\leq}$, obtained using the translation inductively defined in Figure 11.

Lemma 14. *Let D_e be a typing derivation for the term e in $\lambda^{\mathcal{S}}_{\rightarrow}$. Then the following equalities hold:*

- $[\![\overline{\mathcal{S}f.e}]\!]_{\overline{D_{\mathcal{S}f.e}}} =_\beta \lambda k.[\![\overline{e}]\!]_{\overline{D_e}}\{f/\lambda x.\lambda k'.k'\,(k\,x)\}(\lambda x.x)$
- $[\![\overline{\langle e \rangle}]\!]_{\overline{D_{\langle e \rangle}}} =_\beta \lambda k.k([\![\overline{e}]\!]_{\overline{D_e}}(\lambda x.x))$

As a corollary, we can prove the following theorem by straightforward induction:

Theorem 11. *Let e be a well-typed term in $\lambda^{\mathcal{S}}_{\rightarrow}$, and let D be its typing derivation. Then $[\![e]\!] =_\beta [\![\overline{e}]\!]_{\overline{D}}$.*

The untyped CPS translations of Section 2.2 also induce a CPS translation for *shift* and *reset*. For instance, the curried CPS translation of Figure 2 yields:

$$\begin{aligned} [\![\mathcal{S}f.e]\!] &= \lambda f.[\![e]\!]\,(\lambda x.\lambda k.k\,x) \\ [\![\langle e \rangle]\!] &= [\![e]\!](\lambda x.\lambda k.k\,x) \end{aligned}$$

It is interesting to observe that although this CPS translation validates the standard reduction semantics of *shift* and *reset*:

$$\begin{aligned} \langle v \rangle &\rightsquigarrow v \\ \langle K[\mathcal{S}f.e] \rangle &\rightsquigarrow \langle e[f/\lambda x.\langle K[x] \rangle] \rangle \end{aligned}$$

it generates a different equational theory than the one of the standard CPS translation for *shift* and *reset* [22]. For example, the equation

$$\langle \langle e \rangle \rangle = \langle e \rangle$$

is not sound with respect to the presented CPS translation. So in a sense, by using the CPS translation for *shift*$_0$ and *reset*$_0$ we have obtained a variant of *shift* and *reset*. However, when considered in the type system with subtyping, *shift*$_0$ and *reset*$_0$ give rise to the standard *shift* and *reset*, as demonstrated by Lemma 14.

Each of the CPS translations of Section 2.2 determines a definition of *shift*$_0$ and *reset*$_0$ in the corresponding continuation monad. Since we can represent arbitrary computational monads in direct style using *shift* and *reset* [18], we obtain two static simulations of *shift*$_0$ and *reset*$_0$. The simulation obtained from the uncurried translation of Figure 3 is similar to the one presented by Shan [32], but the one obtained from the translation of Figure 2 is novel:

$$\begin{aligned} \mathcal{S}_0 f.e &:= \mathcal{S}k.\lambda c.(\lambda f.\langle(\lambda x.\lambda k.k\,x)\,e\rangle) \\ &\qquad (\lambda x.\mathcal{S}k'.\lambda c'.k\,x\,c\,(\lambda x'.k'\,x'\,c')) \\ \langle e \rangle_0 &:= \mathcal{S}k.\lambda c.\langle(\lambda x.\lambda k.k\,x)\,e\rangle\,(\lambda x.\lambda k.k\,x)\,(\lambda x.k\,x\,c) \\ \mathrm{run}\mathcal{S}_0\,e &:= \langle(\lambda x.\lambda k.k\,x)\,e\rangle\,(\lambda x.x) \end{aligned}$$

We can also consider the type system of [6], which we call $\lambda^{\mathcal{S}}_{\triangleright}$. Again, we first define a translation on terms, types and context types (as before, syntactic forms not mentioned below are translated homomorphically):

$$\begin{aligned} \overline{b} &= \tau_b \\ \overline{\tau_1\ {}_{\tau_3}\!\!\rightarrow_{\tau_4} \tau_2} &= \overline{\tau_1} \xrightarrow{[\overline{\tau_3}]\,\overline{\tau_4}} \overline{\tau_2} \\ \overline{\tau_1 \triangleright \tau_2} &= \overline{\tau_1} \rightarrow \overline{\tau_2} \\ \overline{k \hookleftarrow e} &= k\,\overline{e} \\ \overline{\mathcal{S}k.e} &= \mathcal{S}_0 k.\langle \overline{e} \rangle \end{aligned}$$

Next, we can write a translation on typing derivations, which satisfies the following theorem:

Theorem 12. *If $\Gamma, \Delta; \tau_1 \vdash e : \tau; \tau_2$ in $\lambda^{\mathcal{S}}_{\triangleright}$, then $\overline{\Gamma} \cup \overline{\Delta} \vdash \overline{e} : \overline{\tau}\,[\overline{\tau_1}]\,\overline{\tau_2}$ in $\lambda^{\mathcal{S}_0}_{\leq}$.*

For both type systems for *shift* considered here, there exist terms which are not well-typed in those systems, but their translation to $\lambda^{\mathcal{S}_0}_{\leq}$ is well-typed. In particular, the following term:

$$(\lambda f.\lambda y.(\lambda z.\langle(\lambda v.\lambda w.y)\,(f\,y)\rangle)\,\langle f\,y\rangle)\,(\lambda x.x)$$

is a valid term and cannot be typed in neither of the two systems. However, it translates without changes to $\lambda^{\mathcal{S}_0}_{\leq}$, where it is well

$$\frac{}{\epsilon \leq \epsilon} \qquad \frac{\tau \leq \tau'}{\epsilon \leq [\tau]\,\tau'} \qquad \frac{\tau_2 \leq \tau_1 \qquad \tau_1' \leq \tau_2'}{[\tau_1]\,\tau_1' \leq [\tau_2]\,\tau_2'}$$

$$\frac{\tau \leq \tau' \qquad \sigma \leq \sigma'}{\tau\,\sigma \leq \tau'\,\sigma'} \qquad \frac{}{\alpha \leq \alpha} \qquad \frac{\tau_2' \leq \tau_1' \qquad \tau_1\,\sigma_1 \leq \tau_2\,\sigma_2}{\tau_1' \xrightarrow{\sigma_1} \tau_1 \leq \tau_2' \xrightarrow{\sigma_2} \tau_2}$$

$$\frac{}{\Gamma, x : \tau \vdash x : \tau}\ \text{VAR} \qquad \frac{\Gamma \vdash e : \tau\,\sigma \qquad \tau\,\sigma \leq \tau'\,\sigma'}{\Gamma \vdash e : \tau'\,\sigma'}\ \text{SUB}$$

$$\frac{\Gamma, x : \tau_1 \vdash e : \tau_2\,\sigma}{\Gamma \vdash \lambda x.e : \tau_1 \xrightarrow{\sigma} \tau_2}\ \text{ABS} \qquad \frac{\Gamma \vdash f : \tau_1 \rightarrow \tau_2 \qquad \Gamma \vdash e : \tau_1}{\Gamma \vdash fe : \tau_2}\ \text{APP-PURE}$$

$$\frac{\Gamma \vdash f : \tau_1 \xrightarrow{[\tau_1']\,\tau_3'} \tau_2\,[\tau_4']\,\tau_2' \qquad \Gamma \vdash e : \tau_1\,[\tau_3']\,\tau_4'}{\Gamma \vdash fe : \tau_2\,[\tau_1']\,\tau_2'}\ \text{APP}$$

$$\frac{\Gamma, f : \tau_1 \rightarrow \tau_2 \vdash e : \tau_3}{\Gamma \vdash \mathcal{S}_0 f.e : \tau_1\,[\tau_2]\,\tau_3}\ \text{SHIFT0} \qquad \frac{\Gamma \vdash e : \tau'\,[\tau']\,\tau}{\Gamma \vdash \langle e \rangle : \tau}\ \text{RESET0}$$

Figure 12. Type system for $\lambda^{\mathcal{S}_0}$ with flat effect annotations ($\lambda^{\mathcal{S}}_{\leq}$)

typed (for example, it can be assigned the type $\alpha \rightarrow (\beta \rightarrow \alpha)$). In this sense, the type system presented here is strictly more expressive than the other systems.

An interesting feature of both translations is that a non-empty type annotation never occurs inside another type annotation—the annotations are "flat." Thus one can consider a variant of the $\lambda^{\mathcal{S}_0}_{\leq}$ type system, which enforces this restriction syntactically:

$$\begin{array}{rcl} \tau & ::= & \alpha \mid \tau \xrightarrow{\sigma} \tau \\ \sigma & ::= & \epsilon \mid [\tau]\,\tau \end{array}$$

The typing rules for this system (called $\lambda^{\mathcal{S}}_{\leq}$) are shown in Figure 12.

In this type system *shift*$_0$ is forbidden from being used inside another *shift*$_0$ without a corresponding control delimiter and, therefore, only the top context of the stack can be accessed by control operations. It follows that in this type system *shift*$_0$ has the semantics of *shift*. We can thus view this type system as an exotic type system for the *shift* operator (that is why we call it $\lambda^{\mathcal{S}}_{\leq}$).

6. Related work

6.1 Relation to the Scala implementation

The type system and the selective CPS-translation presented here resemble strongly those presented by Rompf et al. in [31] for the programming language Scala. The presentation in [31] is based on Scala and is somewhat informal, so the exact comparison is not possible, but still one can see the following similarities:

- Our annotations (from the type system $\lambda^{\mathcal{S}}_{\leq}$) correspond to `@cps` annotations. For example, our type $\alpha\,[\beta]\,\gamma$ corresponds to `A @cps[B, C]` in Scala.
- The type system of Scala distinguishes pure and impure expressions as our type system does. In particular, as in our restricted system with flat annotations, the expression inside a *shift* must have a pure type, the entire expression has an impure type, and the captured continuation has a pure function type.
- Scala's `Shift` class used for implementing delimited control, which implements the continuation monad, is constructed by *shift* and consumed by *reset*, in the same way that in our translation *shift*$_0$ introduces a lambda abstraction and *reset*$_0$ eliminates it.
- Our annotation composition relation $\ll$ introduced in Section 3.4 corresponds to the *comp* control effect composition operation.

The type system in [31] does not allow *shift* to be used inside another *shift*—it has to be put inside a new *reset*. This is what happens with the *shift*$_0$ operator with flat effect annotations in our type system. This reinforces our opinion that Scala implements the restricted *shift*$_0$/*reset*$_0$ operators, which only happen to coincide with *shift*/*reset*.

6.2 Substructural type system of Kiselyov and Shan

The type system for *shift*$_0$/*reset*$_0$ introduced by Kiselyov and Shan [26] shares many properties with the type system presented in this work—in particular, strong type soundness and termination. In their work, expressions and evaluation contexts are treated as structure in linear logic, where structural rules play a vital role. Moreover, their type system abstractly interprets (in the sense of abstract interpretation of Cousot and Cousot [11]) small-step reduction semantics of the language and it does not require effect annotations in judgments and arrow types. Instead these annotations occur in types and cotypes assigned to terms and coterms, respectively. In terms of presentation, our system is very close to the well-known type system by Danvy and Filinski and seems more conventional than Kiselyov and Shan's. Both type systems allow for answer type modifications and for exploring the stack of contexts beyond the nearest control delimiter. While in our type system subtyping is built in and plays a major role, leading to a clever CPS translation, in Kiselyov and Shan's work it is just an entailment of the type system.

Our type system can be embedded in the type system of Kiselyov and Shan. A converse translation appears to be impossible because their language is richer: it includes an operator \$, which is a generalization of *reset*$_0$ and, in a sense, the inverse of the *shift*$_0$ operator. Because our language does not differentiate between functions and contexts, it is currently not clear how to include this operator in it, so the subject requires further study.

7. Future work

The type system presented here is monomorphic. We are planning to explore how adding polymorphism (*let*-polymorphism, system F-like explicit polymorphism) affects the system. We expect that, as in the polymorphic type system of Asai and Kameyama presented in [2], it should be safe to generalize the types of pure terms. Also, because of the presence of subtyping, we will need to store constraints about generalized variables in the polymorphic types, as in [21].

Because of the similarities of the system presented here to the Scala implementation of delimited continuations [31], we are going to investigate whether it would be possible to implement our system in Scala. Our type annotations translate to Scala by nesting the `@cps` annotations already used by the current implementation of delimited control. For example, the effect-annotated type $\alpha\,[\alpha]\,\alpha\,[\alpha]\,\alpha$ would translate to Scala's type `A @cps[A, A @cps[A, A]]`.

Another important aspect of this work that has not been researched yet are equational theories of *shift*$_0$ and *reset*$_0$ in the untyped and typed settings as well as of the variant of *shift* and *reset* in the untyped setting, described in Section 5. In particular, it seems vital to understand the role of the subtyping relation in the equational theories of the typed control operators.

8. Conclusion

We have presented a new type system for the delimited-control operators *shift*$_0$ and *reset*$_0$ that has been derived from a CPS translation for these control operators and that generalizes Danvy and Filinski's type system for *shift* and *reset*. The type system is equipped with two subtyping relations: one on types and the other one on effect annotations describing a stack of contexts in which a given expression can be embedded. The subtyping mechanism makes it possible to coerce pure expressions into effectful ones.

The effect annotations and the corresponding subtyping relation are used to guide a selective CPS translation that precisely takes into account the information about the contexts surrounding a translated expression. In particular, it leaves pure expressions in direct style. Such a translation seems promising, if one would like to implement full-fledged *shift*$_0$ and *reset*$_0$, e.g., in Scala (instead of their flat version that accidentally coincides with *shift* and *reset* [31]). As shown in Section 4, the full power of *shift*$_0$ and *reset*$_0$ can be very useful and we believe that there are other interesting applications of these operators waiting to be discovered.

The present article also demonstrates the effectiveness of the context-based method of reducibility predicates [5, 6] that has turned out to be the right way to tackle the non-trivial problem of termination of evaluation for the case of the type-and-effect system with subtyping considered here. It can be observed (and remains to be verified, e.g., in Coq) that the computational content of this constructive proof takes the form of a type-directed evaluator in CPS that corresponds to the type-directed CPS translation presented in this work.

Acknowledgments

First of all, we would like to thank Małgorzata Biernacka for numerous comments on the presentation of this work as well as for helping us to get the proof of termination of evaluation under control. We also thank the anonymous referees and the PC members of ICFP'11 for their valuable comments on the presentation and contents of this article. Hugo Herbelin made the observation about the difference between the standard equational theory for *shift* and *reset* and the one induced by the untyped CPS translation of Section 2.2.

This work has been partially supported by the MNiSW grant number N N206 357436, 2009-2011.

References

[1] M. S. Ager, D. Biernacki, O. Danvy, and J. Midtgaard. A functional correspondence between evaluators and abstract machines. In D. Miller, editor, *Proceedings of the Fifth ACM-SIGPLAN International Conference on Principles and Practice of Declarative Programming (PPDP'03)*, pages 8–19, Uppsala, Sweden, Aug. 2003. ACM Press.

[2] K. Asai and Y. Kameyama. Polymorphic delimited continuations. In *Proceedings of the Fifth Asian symposium on Programming Languages and Systems, APLAS'07*, number 4807 in Lecture Notes in Computer Science, pages 239–254, Singapore, Dec. 2007.

[3] V. Balat and O. Danvy. Memoization in type-directed partial evaluation. In D. Batory, C. Consel, and W. Taha, editors, *Proceedings of the 2002 ACM SIGPLAN/SIGSOFT Conference on Generative Programming and Component Engineering, GPCE 2002*, number 2487 in Lecture Notes in Computer Science, pages 78–92, Pittsburgh, Pennsylvania, Oct. 2002. Springer-Verlag.

[4] C. Barker. Continuations in natural language. In H. Thielecke, editor, *Proceedings of the Fourth ACM SIGPLAN Workshop on Continuations (CW'04)*, Technical report CSR-04-1, Department of Computer Science, Queen Mary's College, pages 1–11, Venice, Italy, Jan. 2004.

[5] M. Biernacka and D. Biernacki. A context-based approach to proving termination of evaluation. In *Proceedings of the 25th Annual Conference on Mathematical Foundations of Programming Semantics(MFPS XXV)*, Oxford, UK, Apr. 2009.

[6] M. Biernacka and D. Biernacki. Context-based proofs of termination for typed delimited-control operators. In F. J. López-Fraguas, editor, *Proceedings of the 11th ACM-SIGPLAN International Conference on Principles and Practice of Declarative Programming (PPDP'09)*, Coimbra, Portugal, Sept. 2009. ACM Press.

[7] M. Biernacka and O. Danvy. A syntactic correspondence between context-sensitive calculi and abstract machines. *Theoretical Computer Science*, 375(1-3):76–108, 2007.

[8] M. Biernacka and O. Danvy. A concrete framework for environment machines. *ACM Transactions on Computational Logic*, 9(1):1–30, 2007.

[9] M. Biernacka, D. Biernacki, and O. Danvy. An operational foundation for delimited continuations in the CPS hierarchy. *Logical Methods in Computer Science*, 1(2:5):1–39, Nov. 2005. A preliminary version was presented at the Fourth ACM SIGPLAN Workshop on Continuations (CW'04).

[10] D. Biernacki, O. Danvy, and K. Millikin. A dynamic continuation-passing style for dynamic delimited continuations. Technical Report BRICS RS-05-16, DAIMI, Department of Computer Science, Aarhus University, Aarhus, Denmark, May 2005.

[11] P. Cousot and R. Cousot. Abstract interpretation: a unified lattice model for static analysis of programs by construction or approximation of fixpoints. In R. Sethi, editor, *Proceedings of the Fourth Annual ACM Symposium on Principles of Programming Languages*, pages 238–252, Los Angeles, California, Jan. 1977. ACM Press.

[12] O. Danvy. Type-directed partial evaluation. In G. L. Steele Jr., editor, *Proceedings of the Twenty-Third Annual ACM Symposium on Principles of Programming Languages*, pages 242–257, St. Petersburg Beach, Florida, Jan. 1996. ACM Press.

[13] O. Danvy and A. Filinski. A functional abstraction of typed contexts. DIKU Rapport 89/12, DIKU, Computer Science Department, University of Copenhagen, Copenhagen, Denmark, July 1989.

[14] O. Danvy and A. Filinski. Abstracting control. In M. Wand, editor, *Proceedings of the 1990 ACM Conference on Lisp and Functional Programming*, pages 151–160, Nice, France, June 1990. ACM Press.

[15] P. Dybjer and A. Filinski. Normalization and partial evaluation. In G. Barthe, P. Dybjer, L. Pinto, and J. Saraiva, editors, *Applied Semantics – Advanced Lectures*, number 2395 in Lecture Notes in Computer Science, pages 137–192, Caminha, Portugal, Sept. 2000. Springer-Verlag.

[16] R. K. Dybvig, S. Peyton-Jones, and A. Sabry. A monadic framework for delimited continuations. *Journal of Functional Programming*, 17 (6):687–730, 2007.

[17] M. Felleisen. The theory and practice of first-class prompts. In J. Ferrante and P. Mager, editors, *Proceedings of the Fifteenth Annual ACM Symposium on Principles of Programming Languages*, pages 180–190, San Diego, California, Jan. 1988. ACM Press.

[18] A. Filinski. Representing monads. In H.-J. Boehm, editor, *Proceedings of the Twenty-First Annual ACM Symposium on Principles of Programming Languages*, pages 446–457, Portland, Oregon, Jan. 1994. ACM Press.

[19] A. Filinski. Representing layered monads. In A. Aiken, editor, *Proceedings of the Twenty-Sixth Annual ACM Symposium on Principles of Programming Languages*, pages 175–188, San Antonio, Texas, Jan. 1999. ACM Press.

[20] R. Harper, B. F. Duba, and D. MacQueen. Typing first-class continuations in ML. *Journal of Functional Programming*, 3(4):465–484, Oct. 1993. A preliminary version was presented at the Eighteenth Annual ACM Symposium on Principles of Programming Languages (POPL 1991).

[21] F. Henglein. Syntactic properties of polymorphic subtyping. Technical Report Semantics Report D-293, DIKU, Computer Science Department, University of Copenhagen, May 1996.

[22] Y. Kameyama and M. Hasegawa. A sound and complete axiomatization of delimited continuations. In O. Shivers, editor, *Proceedings of the 2003 ACM SIGPLAN International Conference on Functional Programming (ICFP'03)*, SIGPLAN Notices, Vol. 38, No. 9, pages 177–188, Uppsala, Sweden, Aug. 2003. ACM Press.

[23] R. Kelsey, W. Clinger, and J. Rees, editors. Revised^5 report on the algorithmic language Scheme. *Higher-Order and Symbolic Computation*, 11(1):7–105, 1998.

[24] J. Kim, K. Yi, and O. Danvy. Assessing the overhead of ML exceptions by selective CPS transformation. In G. Morrisett, editor, *Record of the 1998 ACM SIGPLAN Workshop on ML and its Applications*, Baltimore, Maryland, Sept. 1998.

[25] O. Kiselyov and C. Shan. Delimited continuations in operating systems. In B. Kokinov, D. C. Richardson, T. R. Roth-Berghofer, and L. Vieu, editors, *Modeling and Using Context, 6th International and Interdisciplinary Conference, CONTEXT 2007*, number 4635 in Lecture Notes in Artificial Intelligence, pages 291–302, Roskilde, Denmark, Aug. 2007. Springer.

[26] O. Kiselyov and C. Shan. A substructural type system for delimited continuations. In S. R. D. Rocca, editor, *Typed Lambda Calculi and Applications, 8th International Conference, TLCA 2007*, number 4583 in Lecture Notes in Computer Science, pages 223–239, Paris, France, June 2007. Springer-Verlag.

[27] L. R. Nielsen. A selective CPS transformation. In S. Brookes and M. Mislove, editors, *Proceedings of the 17th Annual Conference on Mathematical Foundations of Programming Semantics*, volume 45 of *Electronic Notes in Theoretical Computer Science*, pages 201–222, Aarhus, Denmark, May 2001. Elsevier Science Publishers.

[28] G. D. Plotkin. Call-by-name, call-by-value and the λ-calculus. *Theoretical Computer Science*, 1:125–159, 1975.

[29] J. C. Reynolds. Definitional interpreters for higher-order programming languages. In *Proceedings of 25th ACM National Conference*, pages 717–740, Boston, Massachusetts, 1972. Reprinted in Higher-Order and Symbolic Computation 11(4):363–397, 1998, with a foreword [30].

[30] J. C. Reynolds. Definitional interpreters revisited. *Higher-Order and Symbolic Computation*, 11(4):355–361, 1998.

[31] T. Rompf, I. Maier, and M. Odersky. Implementing first-class polymorphic delimited continuations by a type-directed selective cps-transform. In A. Tolmach, editor, *Proceedings of the 2009 ACM SIGPLAN International Conference on Functional Programming (ICFP'09)*, pages 317–328, Edinburgh, UK, Aug. 2009. ACM Press.

[32] C. Shan. A static simulation of dynamic delimited control. *Higher-Order and Symbolic Computation*, 20(4):371–401, 2007.

[33] E. Sumii. An implementation of transparent migration on standard Scheme. In M. Felleisen, editor, *Proceedings of the Workshop on Scheme and Functional Programming*, Technical Report 00-368, Rice University, pages 61–64, Montréal, Canada, Sept. 2000.

Set-theoretic Foundation of Parametric Polymorphism and Subtyping

Giuseppe Castagna[1] Zhiwu Xu[1,2] *

[1]CNRS, Laboratoire Preuves, Programmes et Systèmes, Univ Paris Diderot, Sorbonne Paris Cité, Paris, France.
[2]State Key Laboratory of Computer Science, Institute of Software, Chinese Academy of Science, Beijing, China

Abstract. We define and study parametric polymorphism for a type system with recursive, product, union, intersection, negation, and function types. We first recall why the definition of such a system was considered hard—when not impossible—and then present the main ideas at the basis of our solution. In particular, we introduce the notion of "convexity" on which our solution is built up and discuss its connections with parametricity as defined by Reynolds to whose study our work sheds new light.

Categories and Subject Descriptors D.3.3 [*Programming Languages*]: Language Constructs and Features—Polymorphism; Data types and structure; F.3.3 [*Logics and Meanings of Programs*]: Studies of Program Constructs—type structure

General Terms Theory, Languages

Keywords Types, subtyping, polymorphism, parametricity, XML

1. Introduction

The standard approach to defining subtyping is to define a collection of syntax-driven subtyping rules that relate types with similar syntactic structure. However the presence of logical operators, such as unions and intersections, makes a syntactic characterization difficult, which is why a semantic approach is used instead: type t is a subtype of type s if the set of values denoted by t is a subset of the set of values denoted by s. The goal of this study is to extend this approach to parametric types. Since such type systems are at the heart of functional languages manipulating XML data, our study directly applies to them. Parametric polymorphism has repeatedly been requested to and discussed in various working groups of standards (*eg*, RELAX NG [5] and XQuery [6]) since it would bring not only the well-known advantages already demonstrated in existing functional languages, but also new usages peculiar to XML. A typical example is SOAP [21] that provides XML "envelopes" to wrap generic content. Functions manipulating SOAP envelopes are thus working on polymorphically typed objects encapsulated in XML structures. Polymorphic higher-order functions are also needed, as shown by our practice of Ocsigen [1], a framework to develop dynamic web sites where web-site paths (uri) are associated to functions that take the uri parameters —the so-called "query strings"[7]— and return a Xhtml page. The core of the dynamic part of Ocsigen system is the function `register_new_service` whose (moral) type is:

$$\forall X{<:}\texttt{Params}.(\texttt{Path} \times (X \to \texttt{Xhtml})) \to \texttt{unit}$$

That is, it is a function that registers the association of its two parameters: a path in the site hierarchy and a function that fed with a query string that matches the description X (`Params` being the XML type of all possible query strings) returns an Xhtml page. Unfortunately, this kind of polymorphism is not available and the current implementation of `register_new_service` must bypass the type system (of OCaml, OCamlDuce [9], and/or CDuce [2]), losing all the advantages of static verification.

So why despite all this interest and motivations does no satisfactory solution exist yet? The crux of the problem is that, despite several efforts (*eg*, [15, 20]), it was not known how to define —and *a fortiori* how to decide— the subtyping relation for XML types in the presence of type variables. Actually, a purely semantic subtyping approach to polymorphism was believed to be impossible.

In this paper we focus on this problem and —though, henceforth we will seldom mention XML— solve it. The solution — which is more broadly applicable than just to an XML processing setting— is based on some strong intuitions and a lot of technical work. We follow this dichotomy for our presentation and organize it in two parts: an informal description of the main ideas and intuitions underlying the approach and the formal description of the technical development. More precisely, in Section 2 we first examine why this problem is deemed unfeasible or unpractical and simple solutions do not work (§2.1-2.3). Then we present the intuition underlying our solution (§2.4) and outline, in an informal way, the main properties that make the definition of subtyping possible (§2.5) as well as the key technical details of the algorithm that decides it (§2.6). We conclude this first part by giving some examples of the subtyping relation (§2.7) and discussing related work (§2.8). In Section 3 we present the key steps of the formal treatment to support the claims of Section 2 in particular the soundness and completeness of the algorithm and the decidability of the subtyping relation. We conclude our presentation with Section 4 where we discuss at length the connections between parametricity and our solution, as well as the new perspectives of research that our work opens. It may seem odd that we focus on a subtyping relation without defining any calculus to use it. Defining the polymorphic subtyping relation and defining a polymorphic calculus are distinct problems (though the latter depends on the former), and there is no doubt that the former is the very harder one. Once the subtyping relation is defined, it can be immediately applied to simple polymorphic calculi (*eg*, an extension with higher-order functions of the

* This author was partially supported by the National Natural Science Foundation of China under Grant No. 61070038 and by a joint training program by CNRS and the Chinese Academy of Science.

ICFP'11, September 19–21, 2011, Tokyo, Japan.

language in [15]) but the definition of calculi that fully exploit the expressiveness of these types and of algorithms that (even partially) infer type annotations are different and very difficult problems that we leave for future work.

2. The key ideas

2.1 Regular types

XML types are essentially regular tree languages: an XML type is the set of all XML documents that match the type. As such they can be encoded by product types (for concatenation), union types (for regexp unions) and recursive types (for Kleene's star). To type higher order functions we need arrow types and we also need intersection and negation types since in the presence of arrows they can no longer be encoded. Therefore, studying polymorphism for XML types is equivalent to studying it for the types that are coinductively (for recursion) produced by the following grammar:

$$t ::= b \mid t \times t \mid t \to t \mid t \vee t \mid t \wedge t \mid \neg t \mid \mathbb{0} \mid \mathbb{1}$$

where b ranges over basic types (*eg*, `Bool`, `Real`, `Int`, ...), and $\mathbb{0}$ and $\mathbb{1}$ respectively denote the empty (*ie*, that contains no value) and top (*ie*, that contains all values) types. In other terms, types are nothing but a propositional logic (with standard logical connectives: $\wedge, \vee, \neg$) whose atoms are $\mathbb{0}$, $\mathbb{1}$, basic, product, and arrow types. We use $\mathcal{T}$ to denote the set of all types.

In order to preserve the semantics of XML types as sets of documents (but also to give programmers a very intuitive interpretation of types) it is advisable to interpret a type as the set of all values that have that type. Accordingly, `Int` is interpreted as the set that contains the values `0`, `1`, `-1`, `2`, ...; `Bool` is interpreted as the set the contains the values `true` and `false`; and so on. In particular, then, unions, intersections, and negations (*ie*, type *connectives*) must have a set-theoretic semantics. Formally, this corresponds to define an interpretation function from types to the sets of some domain $\mathcal{D}$ (for simplicity the reader can think of $\mathcal{D}$ as the set of all values of the language), that is $[\![\_]\!] : \mathcal{T} \to \mathscr{P}(\mathcal{D})$, such that (*i*) $[\![t_1 \vee t_2]\!] = [\![t_1]\!] \cup [\![t_2]\!]$, (*ii*) $[\![t_1 \wedge t_2]\!] = [\![t_1]\!] \cap [\![t_2]\!]$, (*iii*) $[\![\neg t]\!] = \mathcal{D} \setminus [\![t]\!]$, (*iv*) $[\![\mathbb{0}]\!] = \varnothing$, and (*v*) $[\![\mathbb{1}]\!] = \mathcal{D}$. Once we have defined such an interpretation, then the subtyping relation is naturally defined in terms of it:

$$t_1 \leq t_2 \overset{\text{def}}{\iff} [\![t_1]\!] \subseteq [\![t_2]\!]$$

which, restricted to XML types, corresponds to the usual interpretation of subtyping as language containment.

2.2 Higher-order functions

All definitions above run quite smoothly as long as basic and product types are the only atoms we consider (*ie*, the setting studied by Hosoya and Pierce [16]). But as soon as we add higher-order functions, that is, arrow types, the definitions above no longer work:

1. If we take as $\mathcal{D}$ the set of all values, then this must include also λ-abstractions. Therefore, to define the semantic interpretation of types we need to define the type of λ-abstractions (in particular of the applications that may occur in their bodies) which needs the subtyping relation, which needs the semantic interpretation. We fall on a circularity.
2. If we take as $\mathcal{D}$ some mathematical domain, then we must interpret $t_1 \to t_2$ as the set of functions from $[\![t_1]\!]$ to $[\![t_2]\!]$. For instance if we consider functions as binary relations, then $[\![t_1 \to t_2]\!]$ could be the set
$$\{ f \subseteq \mathcal{D}^2 \mid (d_1, d_2) \in f \text{ and } d_1 \in [\![t_1]\!] \text{ implies } d_2 \in [\![t_2]\!] \} \quad (1)$$
or, compactly, $\mathscr{P}(\overline{[\![t_1]\!] \times \overline{[\![t_2]\!]}})$, where the $\overline{S}$ denotes the complement of the set S within the appropriate universe (in words, these are the sets of pairs in which it is *not* true that the first projection belongs to $[\![t_1]\!]$ and the second does not belong to $[\![t_2]\!]$). But here the problem is not circularity but cardinality, since this would require $\mathcal{D}$ to contain $\mathscr{P}(\mathcal{D}^2)$, which is impossible.

The solution to *both* problems is given by the theory of semantic subtyping [10], and relies on the observation that in order to use types in a programming language we do not need to know what types are, but just how they are related (by subtyping). In other terms, we do not require the semantic interpretation to map arrow types into the set in (1), but just to map them into sets that induce the same subtyping relation as (1) do. Roughly speaking, this turns out to require that for all s_1, s_2, t_1, t_2, the function $[\![.]\!]$ satisfies the property:

$$[\![s_1 \to s_2]\!] \subseteq [\![t_1 \to t_2]\!] \iff \mathscr{P}(\overline{[\![s_1]\!] \times \overline{[\![s_2]\!]}}) \subseteq \mathscr{P}(\overline{[\![t_1]\!] \times \overline{[\![t_2]\!]}}) \quad (2)$$

whatever the sets denoted by $s_1 \to s_2$ and $t_1 \to t_2$ are. Equation (2) above covers only the case in which we compare two single arrow types. But, of course, a similar restriction must be imposed also when comparing arbitrary Boolean combinations of arrows. Formally, this can be enforced as follows. Let $[\![.]\!]$ be a mapping from $\mathcal{T}$ to $\mathscr{P}(\mathcal{D})$, we define a new mapping $\mathbb{E}_{[\![.]\!]}$ as follows (henceforth we omit the $[\![.]\!]$ subscript from $\mathbb{E}_{[\![.]\!]}$):

$$\begin{array}{ll} \mathbb{E}(\mathbb{0}) = \varnothing & \mathbb{E}(\mathbb{1}) = \mathcal{D} \\ \mathbb{E}(\neg t) = \mathcal{D} \setminus \mathbb{E}(t) & \mathbb{E}(b) = [\![b]\!] \\ \mathbb{E}(t_1 \vee t_2) = \mathbb{E}(t_1) \cup \mathbb{E}(t_2) & \mathbb{E}(t_1 \times t_2) = [\![t_1]\!] \times [\![t_2]\!] \\ \mathbb{E}(t_1 \wedge t_2) = \mathbb{E}(t_1) \cap \mathbb{E}(t_2) & \mathbb{E}(t_1 \to t_2) = \mathscr{P}(\overline{[\![t_1]\!] \times \overline{[\![t_2]\!]}}) \end{array}$$

Then $[\![.]\!]$ and $\mathcal{D}$ form a set-theoretic *model* of types if, besides the properties (*i-v*) for the type connectives we stated in §2.1, the function $[\![.]\!]$ also satisfies the following property:

$$[\![t_1]\!] \subseteq [\![t_2]\!] \iff \mathbb{E}(t_1) \subseteq \mathbb{E}(t_2) \quad (3)$$

which clearly implies (2). All these definitions yield a subtyping relation with all the desired properties: type connectives (*ie*, unions, intersections, and negations) have a set-theoretic semantics, type constructors (*ie*, products and arrows) behave as set-theoretic products and function spaces, and (with some care in defining the language and its typing relation) a type can be interpreted as the set of values that have that type. All that remains to do is:

1. show that a model exists[1] (easy) and
2. show how to decide the subtyping relation (difficult).

Both points are solved in [10] and the resulting type system is at the core of the programming language $\mathbb{C}$Duce [2].

2.3 The problem and a naive (wrong) solution

The problem we want to solve in this paper is how to extend the approach described above when we add type variables (in bold):

$$t ::= \boldsymbol{\alpha} \mid b \mid t \times t \mid t \to t \mid t \vee t \mid t \wedge t \mid \neg t \mid \mathbb{0} \mid \mathbb{1}$$

where α ranges over a countable set of type variables $\mathcal{V}$. We did not include any explicit quantification for type variables: in this work (as well as, all works in the domain we are aware of, foremost [15, 20]) we focus on prenex parametric polymorphism where type quantification is meta-theoretic. Once more, the crux of the problem is how to *define* the subtyping relation between two types that contain type variables. Since we know how to subtype closed types (*ie*, types without variables), then a naive solution is to reuse this relation by considering all possible ground instances of types with variables. Let σ denote a *ground substitution*, that is

[1] We do not need to look for a particular model, since all models induce essentially the same subtyping relation: see [8] for details.

a substitution from type variables to closed types. Then according to our naive definition two types are in subtyping relation if so are their ground instances:

$$t_1 \leq t_2 \quad \overset{\text{def}}{\iff} \quad \forall\sigma.\ [\![t_1\sigma]\!] \subseteq [\![t_2\sigma]\!] \qquad (4)$$

(provided that the domain of σ contains all the variables occurring in t_1 and t_2). This closely matches the syntactic intuition of subtyping for prenex polymorphism according to which the statement $t_1 \leq t_2$ is to be intended as $\forall\alpha_1...\alpha_n(t_1 \leq t_2)$, where $\alpha_1...\alpha_n$ are all the variables occurring in t_1 or t_2. Clearly, the containment on the right hand side of (4) is a *necessary* condition for subtyping. Unfortunately, considering it also as *necessary* and, thus, using (4) to define subtyping yields a subtyping relation that suffers too many problems to be useful.

The first obstacle is that, as conjectured by Hosoya in [15], if the subtyping relation defined by (4) is decidable (which is an open problem), then deciding it is at least as hard as the satisfiability problem for set constraint systems with *negative constraints*, which is NEXPTIME-complete and for which, so far, no practical algorithm is known.

But even if the subtyping relation defined by (4) were decidable and Hosoya's conjecture wrong, definition (4) yields a subtyping relation that misses the intuitiveness of the relation on ground types. This can be shown by an example drawn from [15]. For the sake of the example, imagine that our system includes singleton types, that is types that contain just one value, for every value of the language, and consider the following subtyping statement:

$$t \times \alpha \quad \leq \quad (t \times \neg t) \vee (\alpha \times t) \qquad (5)$$

where t is a closed type.
According to (4) the statement holds if and only if $t \times s \leq (t \times \neg t) \vee (s \times t)$ holds for every closed type s. It is easy to see that the latter holds if and only if t is a singleton type. This follows from the set theoretic property that if S is a singleton, then for every set X, either $S \subseteq X$ or $X \subseteq \overline{S}$. By using this property on the singleton type t, we deduce that for every ground substitution of α either $\alpha \leq \neg t$ (therefore $t{\times}\alpha \leq t{\times}\neg t$, whence (5) follows) or $t \leq \alpha$ (therefore $t \times \alpha = (t \times \alpha \backslash t) \vee (t \times t)$ and the latter is contained component-wise in $(t \times \neg t) \vee (\alpha \times t)$, whence (5) holds again). Vice versa, if t contains at least two values, then substituting α by any singleton containing a value of t disproves the containment.

More generally, (5) holds if and only if t is an *indivisible* type, that is, a non-empty type whose only proper subtype is the empty type. Singleton types are just an example of indivisible types, but in the absence of singleton types, basic types that are pairwise disjoint are indivisible as well. Therefore, while the case of singleton types is evocative, the same problem occurs in a language with just the `Int` type, too.

Equation (5) is pivotal in our work. It gives us two reasons to think that the subtyping relation defined by (4) is unfit to be used in practice. First, it tells us that in such a system deciding subtyping is at least as difficult as deciding the indivisibility of a type. This is a very hard problem (see [3] for an instance of this problem in a simpler setting) that makes us believe more in the undecidability of the relation, than in its decidability. Second, and much worse, it completely breaks parametricity yielding a completely non-intuitive subtyping relation. Indeed notice that in the two types in (5) the type variable α occurs on the right of a product in one type and on the left of a product in the other. The idea of parametricity is that a function cannot explore arguments whose type is a type variable, it can just discard them, pass them to another function or copy them into the result. Now if (4) holds it means that by a simple subsumption a function that is parametric in its second argument can be considered parametric in its first argument instead. Understanding the intuition underlying this subtyping relation for type variables (where the same type variable may appear in unrelated positions in two related types) seems out of reach of even theoretically-oriented programmers. This is why a semantic approach for subtyping polymorphic types has been deemed unfeasible and discarded in favor of partial or syntactic solutions (see related works in §2.8).

2.4 Ideas for a solution

Although the problems we pointed out in [15] are substantial, they do not preclude a semantic approach to parametric polymorphism. Furthermore the shortcomings caused by the absence of this approach make the study well worth of trying. Here we show that—paraphrasing a famous article by John Reynolds [19]—subtyping of polymorphism *is* set-theoretic.

The conjecture that we have been following since we discovered the problem of [15], and that is at the basis of all this work, is that *the loss of parametricity is only due to the behavior of indivisible types*, all the rest works (more or less) smoothly. The crux of the problem is that for an indivisible type t the validity of the formula

$$t \leq \alpha \quad \text{or} \quad \alpha \leq \neg t \qquad (6)$$

can *stutter* from one subformula to the other (according to the assignment of α) losing in this way the uniformity typical of parametricity. If we can give a *semantic* characterization of models in which *stuttering* is absent, we believed this would have yielded a subtyping relation that is (i) semantic, (ii) intuitive for the programmer,[2] and (iii) decidable. The problem with indivisible types is that they are either completely inside or completely outside any other type. What we need, then, is to make indivisible types "splittable", so that type variables can range over strict subsets of any type, indivisible ones included. Since this is impossible at a syntactic level, we shall do it at a semantic level. First, we replace ground substitutions with semantic (set) assignments of type variables, $\eta : \mathcal{V} \to \mathscr{P}(\mathcal{D})$, and add to interpretation functions a semantic assignment as a further parameter (as is customary in denotational semantics):

$$[\![.]\!] : \mathcal{T} \to \mathscr{P}(\mathcal{D})^{\mathcal{V}} \to \mathscr{P}(\mathcal{D})$$

Such an interpretation (actually, the pair $([\![.]\!], \mathcal{D})$) is then a *set-theoretic model* if and only if for all assignments η it satisfies the following conditions (in bold the condition that shows the role of the assignment parameter η):

$$\begin{array}{rclrcl}
\boldsymbol{[\![\alpha]\!]\eta} & \boldsymbol{=} & \boldsymbol{\eta(\alpha)} & [\![\neg t]\!]\eta & = & \mathcal{D}\backslash[\![t]\!]\eta \\
[\![\mathbb{0}]\!]\eta & = & \varnothing & [\![t_1 \vee t_2]\!]\eta & = & [\![t_1]\!]\eta \cup [\![t_2]\!]\eta \\
[\![\mathbb{1}]\!]\eta & = & \mathcal{D} & [\![t_1 \wedge t_2]\!]\eta & = & [\![t_1]\!]\eta \cap [\![t_2]\!]\eta
\end{array}$$
$$[\![t_1]\!]\eta \subseteq [\![t_2]\!]\eta \iff \mathbb{E}(t_1)\eta \subseteq \mathbb{E}(t_2)\eta$$

(where $\mathbb{E}()$ is extended in the obvious way to cope with semantic assignments). Then the subtyping relation is defined as follows:

$$t_1 \leq t_2 \overset{\text{def}}{\iff} \forall\eta{\in}\mathscr{P}(\mathcal{D})^{\mathcal{V}}.\ [\![t_1]\!]\eta \subseteq [\![t_2]\!]\eta \qquad (7)$$

In this setting, every type t that denotes a set of at least two elements of $\mathcal{D}$ can be split by an assignment. That is, it is possible to define an assignment for which a type variable α denotes a subset of $\mathcal{D}$ that is neither completely inside nor completely outside the interpretation of t. Therefore for such a type t, neither equation (6) nor, *a fortiori*, equation (5) hold. It is then clear that the stuttering of (6) is absent in every set-theoretic model in which all non-empty types—indivisible types included—denote *infinite* subsets of $\mathcal{D}$. Infinite denotations for non-empty types look as a possible, though

[2] For instance, type variables can only be subsumed to themselves and according to whether they occur in a covariant or contravariant position, to $\mathbb{1}$ and to unions in which they explicitly appear or to $\mathbb{0}$ and intersections in which they explicitly appear, respectively. De Morgan's laws can be used to reduce other cases to one of these.

specific, solution to the problem of indivisible types. But what we are looking for is not a particular solution. We are looking for a semantic characterization of the "uniformity" that characterizes parametricity, in order to define a subtyping relation that is, we repeat, semantic, intuitive, and decidable.

This characterization is provided by the property of *convexity*.

2.5 Convexity

A set theoretic model $([\![.]\!], \mathcal{D})$ is *convex* if and only if for every finite set of types $t_1, \ldots, t_n$ it satisfies the following property:

$$\begin{array}{c}\forall\eta.([\![t_1]\!]\eta{=}\varnothing \text{ or } \cdots \text{ or } [\![t_n]\!]\eta{=}\varnothing)\\ \Longleftrightarrow \\ (\forall\eta.[\![t_1]\!]\eta{=}\varnothing) \text{ or } \cdots \text{ or } (\forall\eta.[\![t_n]\!]\eta{=}\varnothing)\end{array} \tag{8}$$

This property is the cornerstone of our approach. As such it deserves detailed comments. It states that, given any finite set of types, if every assignment makes some of these types empty, then it is so because there exists one particular type that is empty for all possible assignments.[3] Therefore convexity forces the interpretation function to behave uniformly on its zeros (*ie*, on types whose interpretation is the empty set). Now, the zeros of the interpretation function play a crucial role in the theory of semantic subtyping, since they completely characterize the subtyping relation. Indeed $s \leq t \Leftrightarrow [\![s]\!] \subseteq [\![t]\!] \Leftrightarrow [\![s]\!] \cap \overline{[\![t]\!]} \subseteq \varnothing \Leftrightarrow [\![s \wedge \neg t]\!] = \varnothing$. Consequently, checking whether $s \leq t$ is equivalent to checking whether the type $s \wedge \neg t$ is empty; likewise, equation (3) in §2.2 is equivalent to requiring that for all t it satisfies $[\![t]\!] = \varnothing \iff \mathbb{E}(t) = \varnothing$. We deduce that convexity forces the subtyping relation to have a uniform behavior and, ergo, rules out non-intuitive relations such as the one in (5). This is so because convexity prevents stuttering, insofar as in every convex model $([\![t\wedge\neg\alpha]\!]\eta{=}\varnothing \text{ or } [\![t\wedge\alpha]\!]\eta{=}\varnothing)$ holds for all assignments η if and only if t is empty.

Convexity is the property we seek. The resulting subtyping relation is semantically defined and preserves the set-theoretic semantics of type connectives (union, intersection, negation) and the containment behavior of set-theoretic interpretations of type constructors (set-theoretic products for product types and set-theoretic function spaces for arrow types). Furthermore, the subtyping relation is not only semantic but also intuitive. First, it excludes non-intuitive relations by imposing a uniform behavior distinctive of the parametricity *à la* Reynolds: as we discuss at length in the conclusion, we push the analogy much farther since we believe that parametricity and convexity are connected, despite the fact that the former is defined in terms of *transformations* of related terms while the latter deals only with (subtyping) relations. Second, it is very easy to explain the intuition of type variables to a programmer:

> For what concerns subtyping, a type variable can be considered as a special new user-defined basic type that is unrelated to any other atom but $\mathbb{0}$ and $\mathbb{1}$ and itself.[4] Type variables are special because their intersection with any ground type may be non-empty, whatever this type is.

Of course, neither in the theoretical development nor in the subtyping algorithm type variables are dealt with as basic types. They need very subtle and elaborated techniques that form the core of our work. But this complexity is completely transparent to the programmer which can thus rely on a very simple intuition.

All that remains to do is (i) to prove the convexity property is not too restrictive, that is, that there exists at least one convex set-theoretic model and (ii) to show an algorithm that checks the subtyping relation. Contrary to the ground case, *both* problems are difficult. While their solutions require a lot of technical results (see Section 3), the intuition underlying them is relatively simple. For what concerns the existence of a convex set-theoretic model, the intuition can be grasped by considering just the logical fragment of our types, that is, the types in which $\mathbb{0}$ and $\mathbb{1}$ are the only atoms. This corresponds to the (classical) propositional logic where the two atoms represent, respectively, `false` and `true`. Next, consider the instance of the convexity property given for just two types, t_1 and t_2. It is possible to prove that every non-degenerate Boolean algebra (*ie*, every Boolean algebra with more than two elements) satisfies it. Reasoning by induction it is possible to prove that convexity for n types is satisfied by any Boolean algebra containing at least $n + 1!$ elements and from there deduce that all infinite Boolean algebras satisfy convexity. It is then possible to extend the proof to the case that includes basic, product, and arrow types and deduce the following result:

> Every set-theoretic model of closed types in which non-empty types denote infinite sets is a convex set-theoretic model for the polymorphic types.

Therefore, not only do we have a large class of convex models, but also we recover our initial intuition that models with infinite denotations was the way to go.

All that remains to explain is the subtype checking algorithm. We do it in the next section, but before we want to address the possible doubts of a reader about what the denotation of a "finite" type like `Bool` is in such models. In particular, since this denotation contains not only (the denotations of) `true` and `false` but infinitely many other elements, then the reader can rightly wonder what these other elements are and whether they carry any intuitive meaning. In order to explain this point, let us first reexamine what convexity does for infinite types. Convexity is a condition that makes the interpretation of subtyping in some sense independent from the particular syntax of types. Imagine that the syntax of types includes just one basic type: `Int`. Then `Int` is an indivisible type and therefore there exist non-convex models in which the following relation (which is an instance of equation (5) of Section 2.3) holds.

$$\texttt{Int} \times \alpha \quad \leq \quad (\texttt{Int} \times \neg\texttt{Int}) \vee (\alpha \times \texttt{Int}) \tag{9}$$

(*eg*, a model where `Int` is interpreted by a singleton set: in a non-convex model nothing prevents such an interpretation). Now imagine to add the type `Odd`, subtype of `Int`, to the type system: then (9) no longer holds (precisely, the interpretation at issue no longer is a model) since the substitution of α by `Odd` disproves it. Should the presence of `Odd` change the containment relation between `Int` and the other types? Semantically this should not happen. A relation as (9) should have the same meaning independently from whether `Odd` is included in the syntax of types or not. In other terms we want the addition of `Odd` to yield a conservative extension of the subtyping relation. Therefore, all models in which (9) is valid must be discarded. Convexity does it.

The point is that convexity pushes this idea to all types, so that their interpretation is independent from the possible syntactic subtypes they may have. It is as if the interpretation of subtyping assumed that every type has at least one (actually, infinitely many) stricter non empty subtype(s). So what could the denotation of type

---

[3] We dubbed this property *convexity* after convex formulas: a formula is convex if whenever it entails a disjunction of formulas, then it entails one of them. The $\Rightarrow$ direction of (8) (the other direction is trivial) states the convexity of assignments with respect to emptiness: $\eta \in \mathscr{P}(\mathcal{D})^{\mathcal{V}} \Rightarrow \bigvee_{i\in I}[\![t_i]\!]\eta = \varnothing$ implies that there exists $h \in I$ such that $\eta \in \mathscr{P}(\mathcal{D})^{\mathcal{V}} \Rightarrow [\![t_h]\!]\eta = \varnothing$.

[4] This holds true even for languages with bounded quantification which, as it is well known, defines the subtyping relation for type variables. Bounded quantification does not require any modification to our system, since it can be encoded by intersections: a type variable α bounded by a type t can be encoded by a fresh (unbounded) variable β by replacing $\beta\wedge t$ for every occurrence of α. We can do even more, since by using intersections we can impose different bounds to different occurrences of the same variable.

Bool be in such a model, then? A possible choice is to interpret Bool into a set containing labeled versions of `true` and `false`, where labels are drawn from an infinite set of labels (a similar interpretation was first introduced by Gesbert *et al.* [14]: see Section 2.8 on related work). Here the singleton type {`true`} is interpreted as an infinite set containing differently labeled versions of the single element `true`. Does this labeling carry any intuitive meaning? One can think of it as representing name subtyping: these labels are the names of subtypes of the singleton type {`true`} for which the subtyping relation is defined by name subtyping. As we do not want the subtyping relation for `Int` to change (non conservatively) when adding to the system the type `Odd`, so for the same reason we do not want the subtyping relation for singleton types to change when adding by name subtyping new subtypes, even when these subtypes are subtypes of a singleton type. So convexity makes the subtyping relation insensitive to possible extensions by name subtyping.

2.6 Subtyping algorithm

The subtyping algorithm for the relation induced by convex models can be decomposed in 6 elementary steps. Let us explain the intuition underlying each of them: all missing details can be found in Section 3.

First of all, we already said that deciding $t_1 \leq t_2$—*ie*, whether for all η, $[\![t_1]\!]\eta \subseteq [\![t_2]\!]\eta$—is equivalent to decide the emptiness of the type $t_1 \wedge \neg t_2$—*ie*, whether for all η, $[\![t_1 \wedge \neg t_2]\!]\eta = \varnothing$—. So the first step of the algorithm is to transform the problem $t_1 \leq t_2$ into the problem $t_1 \wedge \neg t_2 \leq \mathbb{0}$:

Step 1: *transform the subtyping problem into an emptiness decision problem.*

Our types are just a propositional logic whose atoms are type variables, $\mathbb{0}$, $\mathbb{1}$, basic, product, and arrow types. We use a to range over atoms and, following the logic nomenclature, call *literal*, ranged over by ℓ, an atom or its negation:

$$a ::= b \mid t \times t \mid t \rightarrow t \mid \mathbb{0} \mid \mathbb{1} \mid \alpha \qquad\qquad \ell ::= a \mid \neg a$$

By using the laws of propositional logic we can transform every type into a disjunctive normal form, that is, into a union of intersections of literals:

$$\bigvee_{i \in I} \bigwedge_{j \in J} \ell_{ij}$$

Since the interpretation function preserves the set-theoretic semantics of type connectives, then every type is empty if and only if its disjunctive normal form is empty. So the second step of our algorithm consists of transforming the type $t_1 \wedge \neg t_2$ whose emptiness was to be checked, into a disjunctive normal form:

Step 2: *put the type whose emptiness is to be decided in a disjunctive normal form.*

Next, we have to decide when a normal form, that is, a union of intersections, is empty. A union is empty if and only if every member of the union is empty. Therefore the problem reduces to deciding emptiness of an intersection of literals: $\bigwedge_{i \in I} \ell_i$. Intersections of literals can be straightforwardly simplified. Every occurrence of the literal $\mathbb{1}$ can be erased since it does not change the result of the intersection. If either any of the literals is $\mathbb{0}$ or two literals are a variable and its negation, then we do not have to perform further checks since the intersection is surely empty. An intersection can be simplified also when two literals with different constructors occur in it: if in the intersections there are two atoms of different constructors, say, $t_1 \times t_2$ and $t_1 \rightarrow t_2$, then their intersection is empty and so is the whole intersection; if one of the two atoms is negated, say, $t_1 \times t_2$ and $\neg(t_1 \rightarrow t_2)$, then it can be eliminated since it contains the one that is not negated; if both atoms are negated, then the intersection can also be simplified (with some more work: *cf.* the formal development in Section 3). Therefore the third step of the algorithm is to perform these simplifications so that the problem is reduced to deciding emptiness of intersections that are formed by literals that are (possible negations of) either type variables or atoms all of the same constructor (all basic, all product, or all arrow types):

Step 3: *simplify mixed intersections.*

At this stage we have to decide emptiness of intersections of the form $\bigwedge_{i \in I} a_i \wedge \bigwedge_{j \in J} \neg a'_j \wedge \bigwedge_{h \in H} \alpha_h \wedge \bigwedge_{k \in K} \neg \beta_k$ where all the a_i's and a'_j's are atoms with the same constructor, and where $\{\alpha_h\}_{h \in H}$ and $\{\beta_k\}_{k \in K}$ are disjoint sets of type variables: we just reordered literals so that negated variables and the other negated atoms are grouped together. In this step we want to get rid of the rightmost group in the intersection, that is, the one with negated type variables. In other terms, we want to reduce our problem to deciding the emptiness of an intersections as the above, but where all top-level occurrences of type variables are positive. This is quite easy, and stems from the observation that if a type with a type variable α is empty for every possible assignment of α, then it will be empty also if one replaces $\neg\alpha$ for α in it: exactly the same checks will be performed since the denotation of the first type for $\alpha \mapsto S \subseteq \mathcal{D}$ will be equal to the denotation of the second type for $\alpha \mapsto \overline{S} \subseteq \mathcal{D}$. That is to say, $\forall \eta.[\![t]\!]\eta = \varnothing$ if and only if $\forall \eta.[\![t\{\neg\alpha/_\alpha\}]\!]\eta = \varnothing$ (where $t\{t'/_\alpha\}$ denotes the substitution in t of t' for α). So all the negations of the group of toplevel negated variables can be eliminated by substituting $\neg\beta_k$ for β_k in the a_i's and a'_j's:

Step 4: *eliminate toplevel negative variables.*

Next comes what probably is the trickiest step of the algorithm. We have to prove emptiness of intersections of atoms a_i and negated atoms a'_j all on the same constructors and of positive variables α_k. To lighten the presentation let us consider just the case in which atoms are all product types (the case for arrow types is similar though trickier, while the case for basic types is trivial since it reduces to the case for basic types without variables). By using De Morgan's laws we can move negated atoms on the right hand-side of the relation so that we have to check the following containment

$$\bigwedge_{t_1 \times t_2 \in P} t_1 \times t_2 \wedge \bigwedge_{h \in H} \alpha_h \quad \leq \quad \bigvee_{t'_1 \times t'_2 \in N} t'_1 \times t'_2 \tag{10}$$

where P and N respectively denote the sets of positive and negative atoms. Our goal is to eliminate all top-level occurrences of variables (the α_h's) so that the problem is reduced to checking emptiness of product literals. To that end observe that each α_h is intersected with other products. Therefore whatever the interpretation of α_h is, the only part of its denotation that matters is the one that intersects $\mathcal{D}^2$. Ergo, it is useless, at least at top-level, to check all possible assignments for α_h, since those contained in $\mathcal{D}^2$ will suffice. These can be checked by replacing $\gamma_h^1 \times \gamma_h^2$ for α_h, where γ_h^1, γ_h^2 are fresh type variables. Of course the above reasoning holds for the top-level variables, but nothing tells us that the non top-level occurrences of α_h will intersect any product. So replacing them with just $\gamma_h^1 \times \gamma_h^2$ would yield a sound but incomplete check. We rather replace every non toplevel occurrence of α_h by $(\gamma_h^1 \times \gamma_h^2) \vee \alpha_h$. This still is a sound substitution since if (10) holds, then it must also hold for the case where $(\gamma_h^1 \times \gamma_h^2) \vee \alpha_h$ is substituted for α_h (with the $\vee\alpha_h$ part useless for toplevel occurrences). Rather surprisingly, at least at first sight, this substitution is also complete, that is (10) holds if and only if the following holds:

$$\bigwedge_{t_1 \times t_2 \in P} t_1\theta \times t_2\theta \wedge \bigwedge_{h \in H} \gamma_h^1 \times \gamma_h^2 \quad \leq \quad \bigvee_{t'_1 \times t'_2 \in N} t'_1\theta \times t'_2\theta$$

where θ is the substitution $\{(\gamma_h^1\times\gamma_h^2)\vee\alpha_h/_{\alpha_h}\}_{h\in H}$.[5] As an aside, we signal that this transformation holds only because α_h's are positive: the application of *Step 4* is thus a necessary precondition to the application of this one. We thus succeeded to eliminate all toplevel occurrences of type variables and, thus, we reduced the initial problem to the problem of deciding emptiness of intersections in which all literals are products or negations of products (and similarly for arrows):

Step 5: *eliminate toplevel variables.*

The final step of our algorithm must decompose the type constructors occurring at toplevel in order to recurse or stop. To that end it will use set-theoretic properties to deconstruct atom types and, above all, the convexity property to decompose the emptiness problem into a set of emptiness subproblems (this is where convexity plays an irreplaceable role: without convexity the definition of an algorithm seems to be out of our reach). Let us continue with our example with products. At this stage all it remains to solve is to decide a containment of the following form (we included the products of fresh variables into P):

$$\bigwedge_{t_1\times t_2\in P} t_1\times t_2 \;\leq\; \bigvee_{t'_1\times t'_2\in N} t'_1\times t'_2 \tag{11}$$

Using the set-theoretic properties of the interpretation function and our definition of subtyping, we can prove (see Lemma 6.4 in [10] for details) that (11) holds if and only if for all $N'\subseteq N$,

$$\forall\eta.\left(\llbracket \bigwedge_{t_1\times t_2\in P} t_1 \wedge \bigwedge_{t'_1\times t'_2\in N'} \neg t'_1\rrbracket\eta=\varnothing \;\text{ or }\; \llbracket \bigwedge_{t_1\times t_2\in P} t_2 \wedge \bigwedge_{t'_1\times t'_2\in N\setminus N'} \neg t'_2\rrbracket\eta=\varnothing\right)$$

We can now apply the convexity property and distribute the quantification on η on each subformula of the or. This is equivalent to state that we have to check the emptiness for each type that occurs as argument of the interpretation function. Playing a little more with De Morgan's laws and applying the definition of subtyping we can thus prove that (11) holds if and only if

$$\forall N'\subseteq N.\left(\bigwedge_{t_1\times t_2\in P} t_1 \leq \bigvee_{t'_1\times t'_2\in N'} t'_1\right) \text{ or } \left(\bigwedge_{t_1\times t_2\in P} t_2 \leq \bigvee_{t'_1\times t'_2\in N\setminus N'} t'_2\right)$$

To understand the rationale of this transformation the reader can consider the case in which both P and N contain just one atom, namely, the case for $t_1\times t_2 \leq t'_1\times t'_2$. There are just two cases to check ($N'=\varnothing$ and $N'=N$) and it is not difficult to see that the condition above becomes: $(t_1\leq\mathbb{0})$ or $(t_2\leq\mathbb{0})$ or $(t_1\leq t'_1$ and $t_2\leq t'_2)$, as expected.

The important point however is that we were able to express the problem of (11) in terms of subproblems that rest on strict subterms (there is a similar decomposition rule for arrow types). Remember that our types are possibly infinite trees since they were *coinductively* generated by the grammar in §2.1. We do not consider every possible coinductively generated tree, but only those that are regular (*ie*, that have a finite number of distinct subtrees) and in which every infinite branch contains infinitely many occurrences of type constructors (ie, products and arrows). The last condition rules out meaningless terms (such as $t = \neg t$) as well as infinite unions and intersections. It also provides a well-founded order that allows us to use recursion. Therefore, we memoize the relation in (11) and recursively call the algorithm from *Step 1* on the subterms we obtained from decomposing the toplevel constructors:

[5] Note that the result of this substitution is equivalent to using the substitution $\{(\gamma_h^1\times\gamma_h^2)\vee\gamma_h^3/_{\alpha_h}\}_{h\in H}$ where γ_h^3 is also a fresh variable: we just spare a new variable by reusing α_h which would be no longer used (actually this artifice makes proofs much easier).

Step 6: *eliminate toplevel constructors, memoize, and recurse.*

The algorithm is sound and complete with respect to the subtyping relation defined by (7) and terminates on all types (which implies the decidability of the subtyping relation).

2.7 Examples

The purpose of this subsection is twofold: first, we want to give some examples to convey the idea that the subtyping relation is intuitive; second we present some cases that justify the subtler and more technical aspects of the subtyping algorithm we exposed in the previous subsection. All the examples below can be tested in our prototype subtype-checker.

In what follows we will use x, y, z to range over recursion variables and the notation $\mu x.t$ to denote recursive types. This should suffice to avoid confusion with free type variables that are ranged over by α, β, and γ.

As a first example we show how to use type variables to internalize meta-properties. For instance, for all ground types t_1, t_2, and t_3 the relation $(t_1\to t_3)\wedge(t_2\to t_3)\leq(t_1\vee t_2)\to t_3$ and its converse hold. This meta-theoretic property can be expressed in our type system since the following relation holds:

$$(\alpha\to\gamma)\wedge(\beta\to\gamma) \;\sim\; (\alpha\vee\beta)\to\gamma$$

(where $\sim$ denotes that both $\leq$ and $\geq$ hold). Of course we can apply this generalization to any relation that holds for generic types. For instance, we can prove common distributive laws such as

$$((\alpha\vee\beta)\times\gamma) \;\sim\; (\alpha\times\gamma)\vee(\beta\times\gamma) \tag{12}$$

and combine it with the previous relation and the covariance of arrow on codomains to deduce

$$(\alpha\times\gamma\to\delta_1)\wedge(\beta\times\gamma\to\delta_2) \;\leq\; ((\alpha\vee\beta)\times\gamma)\to\delta_1\vee\delta_2$$

Similarly we can prove that the set of lists whose elements have type α, that is, α list $=\mu x.(\alpha\times x)\vee$ nil, contains both the α-lists with an even number of elements

$$\mu x.(\alpha\times(\alpha\times x))\vee\mathsf{nil} \;\leq\; \mu x.(\alpha\times x)\vee\mathsf{nil}$$

(where nil denotes the singleton type containing just the value nil) and the α-lists with an odd number of elements

$$\mu x.(\alpha\times(\alpha\times x))\vee(\alpha\times\mathsf{nil}) \;\leq\; \mu x.(\alpha\times x)\vee\mathsf{nil}$$

and it is itself contained in the union of the two, that is:

$$\alpha\ \mathsf{list} \;\sim\; (\mu x.(\alpha\times(\alpha\times x))\vee\mathsf{nil})\vee(\mu x.(\alpha\times(\alpha\times x))\vee(\alpha\times\mathsf{nil}))$$

We said that the intuition for subtyping type variables is to consider them as basic types. But type variables are *not* basic types. As an example, if t is a non-empty type, then we have that:

$$\alpha\wedge(\alpha\times t) \;\not\leq\; t_1\to t_2$$

which implies that $\alpha\wedge(\alpha\times t)$ is not empty. This is correct because if for instance we substitute the type $t\vee(t\times t)$ for α, then (by the distributivity law stated in (12)) the intersection is equal to $(t\times t)$, which is non-empty. However, note that if α were a basic type, then the intersection $\alpha\wedge(\alpha\times t)$ would be empty. Furthermore, since the following relation holds

$$\alpha\wedge(\alpha\times t) \;\leq\; \alpha$$

then, this last containment is an example of non-trivial containment (in the sense that the left hand-side is not empty) involving type variables. For an example of non-trivial containment involving arrows the reader can check

$$\mathbb{1}\to\mathbb{0} \;\leq\; \alpha\to\beta \;\leq\mathbb{0}\to\mathbb{1}$$

which states that $\mathbb{1}\to\mathbb{0}$, the set of all functions that diverge on all arguments, is contained in all arrow types $\alpha\to\beta$ (whatever types

α and β are) and that the latter are contained in $\mathbb{0} \to \mathbb{1}$, which is the set of all function values.

Type connectives implement classic proposition logic. If we use $\alpha \Rightarrow \beta$ to denote $\neg\alpha \vee \beta$, that is logical implication, then the following subtyping relation is a proof of Pierce's law:

$$\mathbb{1} \leq ((\alpha \Rightarrow \beta) \Rightarrow \alpha) \Rightarrow \alpha$$

since being a supertype of $\mathbb{1}$ logically corresponds to being equivalent to `true` (note that arrow types do not represent logical implication; for instance, $\mathbb{0}\to\mathbb{1}$ is not empty: it contains all function values). Similarly, the system captures the fundamental property that for all non-empty sets β the set $(\beta\wedge\alpha) \vee (\beta\wedge\neg\alpha)$ is never empty:

$$(\beta \wedge \alpha) \vee (\beta \wedge \neg\alpha) \sim \beta$$

from which we can derive

$$\mathbb{1} \leq (((\beta\wedge\alpha) \vee (\beta\wedge\neg\alpha)) \Rightarrow \mathbb{0}) \Rightarrow (\beta \Rightarrow \mathbb{0})$$

This last relation can be read as follows: if $(\beta\wedge\alpha) \vee (\beta\wedge\neg\alpha)$ is empty, then β is empty.

But the property above will never show a stuttering validity since the algorithm returns false when asked to prove

$$\mathsf{nil} \times \alpha \quad \leq \quad (\mathsf{nil} \times \neg\mathsf{nil}) \vee (\alpha \times \mathsf{nil})$$

even for a singleton type as nil.

The subtyping relation has some simple form of introspection since $t_1 \leq t_2$ if and only if $\mathbb{1} \leq t_1 \Rightarrow t_2$ (*ie*, by negating both types and reversing the subtyping relation, $t_1\wedge\neg t_2 \leq \mathbb{0}$). However, the introspection capability is very limited insofar as it is possible to state interesting properties only when atoms are type variables: although we can characterize the subtyping relation $\leq$, we have no idea about how to characterize its negation $\not\leq$. [6]

The necessity for the tricky substitution $\alpha \mapsto (\gamma_1\times\gamma_2)\vee\alpha$ performed at *Step 5* of the algorithm can be understood by considering the following example where t is any non-empty type:

$$(\alpha \times t) \wedge \alpha \leq ((\mathbb{1} \times \mathbb{1}) \times t).$$

If in order to check the relation above we substituted just $\gamma_1 \times \gamma_2$ for α, then this would yield a positive result, which is wrong: if we replace α by $b \vee (b\times t)$, where b is any basic type, then the intersection on the left becomes $(b\times t)$ and b is neither contained in $\mathbb{1} \times \mathbb{1}$ nor empty. Our algorithm correctly disproves the containment, since it checks also the substitution of $(\gamma_1 \times \gamma_2) \vee \alpha$ for the first occurrence of α, which captures the above counterexample.

Finally, the system also proves subtler relations whose meaning is not clear at first sight, such as:

$$\alpha_1 \to \beta_1 \leq ((\alpha_1\wedge\alpha_2)\to(\beta_1\wedge\beta_2)) \vee \neg(\alpha_2\to(\beta_2\wedge\neg\beta_1)) \quad (13)$$

In order to prove it, the subtyping algorithm first moves the occurrence of $\alpha_2 \to (\beta_2\wedge\neg\beta_1)$ from the right of the subtyping relation to its left: $(\alpha_1\to\beta_1)\wedge(\alpha_2\to(\beta_2\wedge\neg\beta_1)) \leq ((\alpha_1\wedge\alpha_2)\to(\beta_1\wedge\beta_2))$; then following the decomposition rules for arrows the algorithm checks the four following cases (Step 6 of the algorithm), which hold straightforwardly:

$$\begin{cases} \alpha_1\wedge\alpha_2 \leq \mathbb{0} \text{ or } \beta_1 \wedge (\beta_2 \wedge \neg\beta_1) \leq \beta_1 \wedge \beta_2 \\ \alpha_1\wedge\alpha_2 \leq \alpha_1 \text{ or } (\beta_2 \wedge \neg\beta_1) \leq \beta_1 \wedge \beta_2 \\ \alpha_1\wedge\alpha_2 \leq \alpha_2 \text{ or } \beta_1 \leq \beta_1 \wedge \beta_2 \\ \alpha_1\wedge\alpha_2 \leq \alpha_1 \vee \alpha_2 \end{cases}$$

[6] For instance, it would be nice to prove something like:

$$(\neg\beta_1 \vee ((\beta_1\Rightarrow\alpha_1) \wedge (\alpha_2\Rightarrow\beta_2))) \sim (\alpha_1\to\alpha_2 \Rightarrow \beta_1\to\beta_2)$$

since it seems to provide a complete characterization of the subtyping relation between two arrow types. Unfortunately the equivalence is false since $\beta_1 \not\leq \alpha_1$ does not imply $\beta_1 \wedge \neg\alpha_1 \geq \mathbb{1}$ but just $\beta_1 \wedge \neg\alpha_1 \not\leq \mathbb{0}$. This property can be stated only at meta level, that is: $\alpha_1\to\alpha_2 \leq \beta_1\to\beta_2$ if and only if $(\beta_1 \leq \mathbb{0}$ or $(\beta_1\leq\alpha_1$ and $\alpha_2\leq\beta_2))$.

Notice that relation (13) is quite subtle insofar as neither $\alpha_1 \to \beta_1 \leq (\alpha_1\wedge\alpha_2) \to (\beta_1\wedge\beta_2)$ nor $\alpha_1 \to \beta_1 \leq \neg(\alpha_2 \to (\beta_2\wedge\neg\beta_1))$ hold: the type on left hand-side of (13) is contained in the union of the two types on the right hand-side of (13) without being completely contained in either of them.

2.8 Related work

This work extends the work on semantic subtyping [10], as such the two works share the same approach and common developments. Since convex models of our theory can be derived from the models of [10], then several techniques we used in our subtyping algorithm (in particular the decomposition of toplevel type constructors) are directly issued from the research in [10]. This work starts precisely from where [10] stopped, that is the monomorphic case, and adds prenex parametric polymorphism to it.

The most advanced work on polymorphism for XML types, thus far, is the Hosoya, Frisch, and Castagna's approach described in [15], whose extended abstract was first presented at POPL '05. Together with [10], the paper by Hosoya, Frisch, and Castagna constitutes the starting point of this work. A starting point that, so far, was rather considered to establish a (negative) final point. As a matter of fact, although the polymorphic system in [15] is the one used to define the polymorphic extension of XDuce [16] (incorporated from version 0.5.0 of the language), the three authors of [15] agree that the main interest of their work does not reside in its type system, but rather in the negative results that motivate it. In particular, the pivotal example of our work, equation (5), was first presented in [15], and used there to corroborate the idea that a purely semantic approach for polymorphism of regular tree types was an hopeless quest. At that time, this seemed so more hopeless that the equation (5) did not involve arrow types: a semantically defined polymorphic subtyping looked out of reach even in the restrictive setting of Hosoya and Pierce seminal work [16], which did not account for higher-order functions. This is why [15] falls back on a syntactic approach that, even if it retains some flavors of semantic subtyping, it cannot be extended to higher-order functions (a lack that nevertheless fits XDuce). Our works shows that the negative results of [15] were not so insurmountable as it had been thought.

Hitherto, the only work that blends polymorphic regular types and arrow types is Jérôme Vouillon's work that was presented at POPL '06 [20]. His approach, however, is very different from ours insofar as it is intrinsically syntactic. Vouillon starts from a particular language (actually, a peculiar pattern algebra) and coinductively builds up on it the subtyping relation by a set of inference rules. The type algebra includes only the union connective (negation and intersection are missing) and a semantic interpretation of subtyping is given *a posteriori* by showing that a pattern (types are special cases of patterns) can be considered as the set of values that match the pattern. Nevertheless, this interpretation is still syntactic in nature since it relies on the definition of matching and containment, yielding a system tailored for the peculiar language of the paper. This allows Vouillon to state impressive and elegant results such as the translation of the calculus into a non-explicitly-typed one, or the interpretation of open types containment as in our equation (4) (according to Vouillon this last result is made possible in his system by the absence of intersection types, although the critical example in (5) does not involve any intersection). But the price to pay is a system that lacks naturalness (*eg*, the wild-card pattern has different meanings according to whether it occurs in the right or in left type of a subtyping relation) and, even more, it lacks the generality of our approach (we did not state our subtype system for any specific language while Vouillon's system is inherently tied to a particular language whose semantics it completely relies on). The semantics of Vouillon's patterns is so different from ours that typing Vouillon's language with our types seems quite difficult.

Other works less related to ours are those in which XML and polymorphism are loosely coupled. This is the case of OCamlDuce [9] where ML-polymorphism and XML types and patterns are merged together without mixing: the main limitation of this approach is that it does not allow parametric polymorphism for XML types, which is the whole point of our (and Vouillon's) work(s). A similar remark can be done for Xtatic [11] that merges C# name subtyping with the XDuce set-theoretic subtyping and for XHaskell [17] whose main focus is to implement XML subtyping using Haskell's type-classes. A more thorough comparison of these approaches can be found in [9, 15].

Polymorphism can be attained by adopting the so-called data-binding approach which consists in encoding XML types and values into the structures of an existing polymorphic programming language. This is the approach followed by HaXML [23]. While the polymorphism is inherited from the target language, the rigid encoding of XML data into fixed structures loses all flexibility of the XML type equivalences so as, for instance, $(t{\times}s_1) \vee (t{\times}s_2)$ and $(t{\times}s_1{\vee}s_2)$ are different (and even unrelated) types.

Our work already has a follow-up. In a paper included in these same proceedings [14] Gesbert, Genevès, and Layaïda use the framework we define here to give a different decision procedure for our subtyping relation. More precisely, they take a specific model for the monomorphic type system (*ie*, the model defined by Frisch *et al.* [10] and used by the language ℂDuce), they encode the subtyping relation induced by this model into a tree logic, and use a satisfiability solver to efficiently decide it. Next, they extend the type system with type variables and they obtain a convex model by interpreting non-empty types as infinite sets using a labeling technique similar to the one we outlined at the end of Section 2.5: they label values by (finite sets of) type variables and every non empty ground type is, thus, interpreted as an infinite set containing the infinitely many labelings of its values. Again the satisfiability solver provides a decision procedure for the subtyping relation. Their technique is interesting in several respects. First it provides a very elegant solution to the problem of deciding our subtyping relation, solution that is completely different from the one given here. Second, their technique shows that the decision problem is EXPTIME, (while here we only prove the decidability of the problem by showing the termination of our algorithm). Finally, their logical encoding paves the way to extending types (and subtyping) with more expressive logical constraints representable by their tree logic. In contrast, our algorithm is interesting for quite different reasons: first, it is defined for generic interpretations rather than for a fixed model; second, it shows how convexity is used in practice (see in particular ***Step 6*** of the algorithm); and, finally, our algorithm is a straightforward modification of the algorithm used in ℂDuce and, as such, can benefit of the technology and optimizations used there.[7] We expect the integration of this subtyping relation in the ℂDuce to be available in the near future.

Finally, we signal the work on polymorphic iterators for XML presented in [4]. It introduces a very simple strongly normalizing calculus fashioned to define tree iterators. These iterators are lightly checked at the moment of their definition: the compiler does not complain unless they are irremediably flawed. This optimistic typing, combined with the relatively limited expressive power of the calculus, makes it possible to type iterator applications in a very precise way (essentially, by performing an abstract execution of the iterator on the types) yielding a kind of polymorphism that is out of reach of parametric or subtype polymorphism (for instance it can precisely type the reverse function applied to *heterogeneous* lists and thus deduce that the application of reverse to a list of type, say, `[ Int Bool* Char+ ]` yields a result of type `[ Char+ Bool* Int ]`). As such it is orthogonal to the kind of polymorphism presented here, and both can and should coexist in a same language.

[7] Alain Frisch's PhD. thesis [8] describes two algorithms that improve over the simple saturation-based strategy described in Section 3.4. They are used both in ℂDuce compiler and in the prototype we implemented to check the subtyping relation presented in this work.

3. Formal development

In this section we describe the technical development that supports the results we exposed in the previous section. We (strongly) suggest readers to skip this section on first reading and directly jump to the conclusions in Section 4. For space reasons all proofs are omitted. They can be found in the extended version available from the first author's web page together with a link to the source code of our subtype checker prototype. The prose is reduced to the strict necessary, and limited to explain points that were not dealt with in the previous section.

3.1 Types

Definition 3.1. (Types) *Consider a countable set of type variables $\mathcal{V}$ ranged over by α and a finite set of basic (or constant) types ranged over by b. A* type *is a regular tree coinductively produced by the following grammar*

$$t ::= \alpha \mid b \mid t \times t \mid t \to t \mid t \vee t \mid \neg t \mid \mathbb{0}$$

*and in which every infinite branch contains infinitely many occurrences of atoms (*ie*, either a type variable or the immediate application of a type constructor: basic, product, arrow)*

We write $t_1{\setminus}t_2$, $t_1{\wedge}t_2$, and $\mathbb{1}$ respectively as abbreviation for $t_1{\wedge}\neg t_2$, $\neg(\neg t_1{\vee}\neg t_2)$, and $\neg\mathbb{0}$.

The condition on infinite branches bars out ill-formed types such as $t = t \vee t$ (which does not carry any information about the set denoted by the type) or $t = \neg t$ (which cannot represent any set). It also ensures that the binary relation $\rhd \subseteq \mathcal{T}^2$ defined by $t_1 \vee t_2 \rhd t_i$, $\neg t \rhd t$ is Noetherian (that is, strongly normalizing). This gives an induction principle on $\mathcal{T}$ that we will use without any further explicit reference to the relation.

Notation. *Let t be a type. We use $\mathsf{var}(t)$ to denote the set of type variables occurring in t and by $\mathsf{tlv}(t)$ (toplevel variables) all the variables of t that have at least one occurrence not under a constructor, that is: $\mathsf{tlv}(\alpha) = \{\alpha\}$, $\mathsf{tlv}(\neg t) = \mathsf{tlv}(t)$, $\mathsf{tlv}(t \vee s) = \mathsf{tlv}(t) \cup \mathsf{tlv}(s)$, and $\mathsf{tlv}(t) = \varnothing$ otherwise. We say that t is* ground *or* closed *if and only if $\mathsf{var}(t)$ is empty.*

3.2 Subtyping

Definition 3.2 (Set-Theoretic Interpretation). *A* set-theoretic interpretation *of $\mathcal{T}$ is given by a set $\mathcal{D}$ and a function $[\![\_]\!] : \mathcal{T} \to \mathscr{P}(\mathcal{D})^{\mathcal{V}} \to \mathscr{P}(\mathcal{D})$ such that, for all $t_1, t_2, t \in \mathcal{T}$, $\alpha \in \mathcal{V}$ and $\eta \in \mathscr{P}(\mathcal{D})^{\mathcal{V}}$: $[\![t_1 \vee t_2]\!]\eta = [\![t_1]\!]\eta \cup [\![t_2]\!]\eta$, $[\![\neg t]\!]\eta = \mathcal{D} \setminus [\![t]\!]\eta$, $[\![\alpha]\!]\eta = \eta(\alpha)$, and $[\![\mathbb{0}]\!]\eta = \varnothing$.*

Definition 3.3. (Subtyping Relation) *Let $[\![\_]\!] : \mathcal{T} \to \mathscr{P}(\mathcal{D})^{\mathcal{V}} \to \mathscr{P}(\mathcal{D})$ be a set-theoretic interpretation. We define the* subtyping relation *$\leq_{[\![\,]\!]} \subseteq \mathcal{T}^2$ as follows:*

$$t \leq_{[\![\,]\!]} s \Leftrightarrow \forall \eta \in \mathscr{P}(\mathcal{D})^{\mathcal{V}} \;.\; [\![t]\!]\eta \subseteq [\![s]\!]\eta$$

We write $t \leq s$ when the interpretation $[\![\_]\!]$ is clear from the context.

For each basic type b, we assume there is a fixed set of constants $\mathbb{B}(b) \subseteq \mathscr{C}$ whose elements are called constants of type b. For two basic types b_1, b_2, the sets $\mathbb{B}(b_i)$ can have a non-empty intersection.

If, as suggested in Section 2, we interpret extensionally an arrow $t_1{\to}t_2$ as $\mathscr{P}([\![t_1]\!]{\times}\overline{[\![t_2]\!]})$ (precisely as $\mathscr{P}(\mathcal{D}^2{\setminus}([\![t_1]\!]{\times}(\mathcal{D}{\setminus}[\![t_2]\!])))$, then every function type is a subtype of $\mathbb{1}\to\mathbb{1}$. We do not want such a property to hold because, otherwise, we could subsume every function to a function that accepts every value and, therefore, every application of a well-typed function to a well-typed argument would be well-typed, independently from the types of the function and of the argument. For example, if, say, succ: Int→Int, then we could deduce succ: $\mathbb{1}\to\mathbb{1}$ and then succ(true) would have type $\mathbb{1}$. To avoid this problem we introduce an explicit type error Ω and use it to define function spaces:

Definition 3.4. *If D is a set and X, Y are subsets of D, we write D_Ω for $D + \{\Omega\}$ and define $X \to Y$ as:*

$$X \to Y \stackrel{\text{def}}{=} \{f \subseteq D \times D_\Omega \mid \forall (d, d') \in f.\, d \in X \Rightarrow d' \in Y\}$$

This is used in the definition of the extensional interpretation:

Definition 3.5 (Extensional Interpretation). *Let $[\![\_]\!] : \mathcal{T} \to \mathscr{P}(\mathcal{D})^{\mathcal{V}} \to \mathscr{P}(\mathcal{D})$ be a set-theoretic interpretation. Its associated* extensional interpretation *is the unique function $\mathbb{E}(\_) : \mathcal{T} \to \mathscr{P}(\mathcal{D})^{\mathcal{V}} \to \mathscr{P}(\mathbb{E}\mathcal{D})$ where $\mathbb{E}\mathcal{D} = \mathcal{D} + \mathcal{D}^2 + \mathscr{P}(\mathcal{D} \times \mathcal{D}_\Omega)$, defined as follows:*

$$\begin{aligned}
\mathbb{E}(\alpha)\eta &= \eta(\alpha) \subseteq \mathcal{D}\\
\mathbb{E}(b)\eta &= \mathbb{B}(b) \subseteq \mathcal{D}\\
\mathbb{E}(t_1 \times t_2)\eta &= [\![t_1]\!]\eta \times [\![t_2]\!]\eta \subseteq \mathcal{D}^2\\
\mathbb{E}(t_1 \to t_2)\eta &= [\![t_1]\!]\eta \to [\![t_2]\!]\eta \subseteq \mathscr{P}(\mathcal{D} \times \mathcal{D}_\Omega)\\
\mathbb{E}(\mathbb{0})\eta &= \varnothing\\
\mathbb{E}(t_1 \vee t_2)\eta &= \mathbb{E}(t_1)\eta \cup \mathbb{E}(t_2)\eta\\
\mathbb{E}(\neg t)\eta &= \mathbb{E}\mathcal{D} \setminus \mathbb{E}(t)\eta
\end{aligned}$$

The definition of set-theoretic model is then as expected:

Definition 3.6 (Foundation, Convexity, and Models). *Let $[\![\_]\!] : \mathcal{T} \to \mathscr{P}(\mathcal{D})^{\mathcal{V}} \to \mathscr{P}(\mathcal{D})$ be a set-theoretic interpretation. It is*

1. convex *if it satisfies equation (8) for all finite choices of types $t_1, ..., t_n$;*
2. structural *if $\mathcal{D}^2 \subseteq \mathcal{D}$, $[\![t_1 \times t_2]\!]\eta = [\![t_1]\!]\eta \times [\![t_2]\!]\eta$ and the relation on $\mathcal{D}$ induced by $(d_1, d_2) \blacktriangleright d_i$ is Noetherian;*
3. *a* model *if it induces the same subtyping relation as its associated extensional interpretation, that is: $\forall t \in \mathcal{T}\,.\, \forall \eta \in \mathscr{P}(\mathcal{D})^{\mathcal{V}}\,.\, [\![t]\!]\eta = \varnothing \iff \mathbb{E}(t)\eta = \varnothing$. A model is* convex *if its set-theoretic interpretation is convex; it is* well-founded *if it induces the same subtyping relation as a structural set-theoretic interpretation.*

From now on we consider only *well-founded convex* models. We already explained the necessity of the notion of convexity we introduced in §2.5. The notion of well-founded model was introduced in §4.3 of [10]. Intuitively, well-founded models are models that contain only values that are finite (*eg*, in a well-founded model the type $\mu x.(x \times x)$—*ie*, the type that "should" contain all and only infinite binary trees—is empty). This fits the practical motivations of this paper, since XML documents—*ie*, values—are *finite* trees.

3.3 Properties of the subtyping relation

We write $\mathscr{A}_{\text{fun}}$ for atoms of the form $t_1 \to t_2$, $\mathscr{A}_{\text{prod}}$ for atoms of the form $t_1 \times t_2$, $\mathscr{A}_{\text{basic}}$ for basic types, and $\mathscr{A}$ for $\mathscr{A}_{\text{fun}} \cup \mathscr{A}_{\text{prod}} \cup \mathscr{A}_{\text{basic}}$. Therefore $\mathcal{V} \cup \mathscr{A} \cup \{\mathbb{0}, \mathbb{1}\}$ denotes the set of all atoms. Henceforth, we will disregard the atoms $\mathbb{0}$ and $\mathbb{1}$ since they can be straightforwardly eliminated during the algorithmic treatment of subtyping.

Definition 3.7. (Normal Form) *A (disjunctive)* normal form *τ is a finite set of pairs of finite sets of atoms, that is, an element of $\mathscr{P}_f(\mathscr{P}_f(\mathscr{A} \cup \mathcal{V}) \times \mathscr{P}_f(\mathscr{A} \cup \mathcal{V}))$ (where $\mathscr{P}_f(.)$ denotes the finite powerset). Moreover, we call an element of $\mathscr{P}_f(\mathscr{A} \cup \mathcal{V}) \times \mathscr{P}_f(\mathscr{A} \cup \mathcal{V})$ a single normal form. If $[\![\_]\!] : \mathcal{T} \to \mathscr{P}(\mathcal{D})^{\mathcal{V}} \to \mathscr{P}(\mathcal{D})$ is an arbitrary set-theoretic interpretation, τ a normal form and η an assignment, we define $[\![\tau]\!]\eta$ as:*

$$[\![\tau]\!]\eta = \bigcup_{(P,N)\in\tau} \bigcap_{a\in P} [\![a]\!]\eta \cap \bigcap_{a\in N} (\mathcal{D} \setminus [\![a]\!]\eta)$$

(with the convention that an intersection over an empty set is taken to be $\mathcal{D}$).

For every type t there exists a normal form $\mathcal{N}(t)$ that has the same interpretation, and vice versa. For instance, consider the type $t = a_1 \wedge (a_3 \vee \neg a_2)$ where a_1, a_2, and a_3 are any atoms. Then $\mathcal{N}(t) = \{(\{a_1, a_3\}, \varnothing), (\{a_1\}, \{a_2\})\}$. This corresponds to the fact that for every set-theoretic interpretation and semantic assignment $\mathcal{N}(t)$, t, and $(a_1 \wedge a_3) \vee (a_1 \wedge \neg a_2)$ have the same denotation.

For these reasons henceforth we will often confound the notions of types and normal forms, and often speak of the "type" τ, taking the latter as a canonical representation of all the types in $\mathcal{N}^{-1}(\tau)$.

Let $[\![\_]\!]$ be a set-theoretic interpretation. Given a normal form τ, we are interested in comparing the assertions $\forall \eta \in \mathscr{P}(\mathcal{D})^{\mathcal{V}}.\, \mathbb{E}(\tau)\eta = \varnothing$ and $\forall \eta \in \mathscr{P}(\mathcal{D})^{\mathcal{V}}.\, [\![\tau]\!]\eta = \varnothing$. Clearly, the equation $\forall \eta \in \mathscr{P}(\mathcal{D})^{\mathcal{V}}.\, \mathbb{E}(\tau)\eta = \varnothing$ is equivalent to:

$$\forall \eta \in \mathscr{P}(\mathcal{D})^{\mathcal{V}}\,.\, \forall (P, N) \in \tau\,.\, \bigcap_{a\in P} \mathbb{E}(a)\eta \subseteq \bigcup_{a\in N} \mathbb{E}(a)\eta \quad (14)$$

Let us write $\mathbb{E}^{\text{basic}}\mathcal{D} = \mathcal{D}$, $\mathbb{E}^{\text{prod}}\mathcal{D} = \mathcal{D}^2$ and $\mathbb{E}^{\text{fun}}\mathcal{D} = \mathscr{P}(\mathcal{D} \times \mathcal{D}_\Omega)$. Then we have $\mathbb{E}\mathcal{D} = \bigcup_{u\in U} \mathbb{E}^u\mathcal{D}$ where $U = \{\text{basic}, \text{prod}, \text{fun}\}$. Thus we can rewrite Inequality (14) as:

$$\begin{aligned}
&\forall \eta \in \mathscr{P}(\mathcal{D})^{\mathcal{V}}\,.\, \forall u \in U\,.\, \forall (P, N) \in \tau\,.\\
&\qquad \bigcap_{a\in P} (\mathbb{E}(a)\eta \cap \mathbb{E}^u\mathcal{D}) \subseteq \bigcup_{a\in N} (\mathbb{E}(a)\eta \cap \mathbb{E}^u\mathcal{D})
\end{aligned} \quad (15)$$

For an atom $a \in \mathscr{A}$, we have $\mathbb{E}(a)\eta \cap \mathbb{E}^u\mathcal{D} = \varnothing$ if $a \notin \mathscr{A}_u$ and $\mathbb{E}(a)\eta \cap \mathbb{E}^u\mathcal{D} = \mathbb{E}(a)\eta$ if $a \in \mathscr{A}_u$. Then we can rewrite Inequality (15) as:

$$\begin{aligned}
&\forall \eta \in \mathscr{P}(\mathcal{D})^{\mathcal{V}}.\, \forall u \in U.\, \forall (P, N) \in \tau.\, (P \subseteq \mathscr{A}_u \cup \mathcal{V}) \Rightarrow\\
&\quad \bigcap_{a\in P\cap\mathscr{A}_u} \mathbb{E}(a)\eta \cap \bigcap_{\alpha\in P\cap\mathcal{V}} (\eta(\alpha) \cap \mathbb{E}^u\mathcal{D}) \subseteq\\
&\qquad \bigcup_{a\in N\cap\mathscr{A}_u} \mathbb{E}(a)\eta \cup \bigcup_{\alpha\in N\cap\mathcal{V}} (\eta(\alpha) \cap \mathbb{E}^u\mathcal{D})
\end{aligned} \quad (16)$$

(where the intersection is taken to be $\mathbb{E}\mathcal{D}$ when $P = \varnothing$). Furthermore, if the same variable occurs both in P and in N, then (16) is trivially satisfied. So we can suppose that $P \cap N \cap \mathcal{V} = \varnothing$. This justifies the simplifications made in *Step 3* of the subtyping algorithm, that is the simplification of mixed single normal forms.

Step 4, the elimination of negated toplevel variables, is justified by the following lemma:

Lemma 3.8. *Let P, N be two finite subsets of atoms and α an arbitrary type variable, then we have*

$$\begin{aligned}
&\forall \eta \in \mathscr{P}(\mathcal{D})^{\mathcal{V}}\,.\, \bigcap_{a\in P} \mathbb{E}(a)\eta \subseteq \bigcup_{a\in N} \mathbb{E}(a)\eta \cup \eta(\alpha) \Leftrightarrow\\
&\forall \eta \in \mathscr{P}(\mathcal{D})^{\mathcal{V}}\,.\, \bigcap_{a\in P} \mathbb{E}(\theta_\alpha^{\neg\beta}(a))\eta \cap \eta(\beta) \subseteq \bigcup_{a\in N} \mathbb{E}(\theta_\alpha^{\neg\beta}(a))\eta
\end{aligned}$$

where β is a fresh variable and $\theta_\alpha^{\neg\beta}(a) = a\{^{\neg\beta}/_{\alpha}\}$

Note that Lemma 3.8 only deals with one type variable, but it is trivial to generalize this lemma to multiple type variables (the same holds for Lemmas 3.9 and 3.10).

Using Lemma 3.8, we can rewrite Inequality (16) as:

$$\forall \eta \in \mathscr{P}(\mathcal{D})^{\mathcal{V}} . \forall u \in U . \forall (P,N) \in \tau . (P \subseteq \mathscr{A}_u \cup \mathcal{V}) \Rightarrow \bigcap_{a \in P \cap \mathscr{A}_u} \mathbb{E}(a)\eta \cap \bigcap_{\alpha \in P \cap \mathcal{V}} (\eta(\alpha) \cap \mathbb{E}^u \mathcal{D}) \subseteq \bigcup_{a \in N \cap \mathscr{A}_u} \mathbb{E}(a)\eta \quad (17)$$

since we can assume $N \cap \mathcal{V} = \varnothing$.

Next, we justify *Step 5* of the algorithm, that is the elimination of the toplevel variables. In (17) this corresponds to eliminating the variables in $P \cap \mathcal{V}$. When $u =$ basic this can be easily done since all variables (which can appear only at top-level) can be straightforwardly removed. Indeed, notice that if s and t are closed types then $s \wedge \alpha \leq t$ if and only if $s \leq t$.

The justification of *Step 5* for $u =$ prod is given by Lemma 3.9.

Lemma 3.9. *Let $(\mathcal{D}, [\![.]\!])$ be a well-founded model, P, N two finite subsets of $\mathscr{A}_{\mathsf{prod}}$ and α an arbitrary type variable.*

$$\forall \eta \in \mathscr{P}(\mathcal{D})^{\mathcal{V}} . \bigcap_{a \in P} \mathbb{E}(a)\eta \cap (\eta(\alpha) \cap \mathbb{E}^{\mathsf{prod}} \mathcal{D}) \subseteq \bigcup_{a \in N} \mathbb{E}(a)\eta \Leftrightarrow$$

$$\forall \eta \in \mathscr{P}(\mathcal{D})^{\mathcal{V}} . \bigcap_{a \in P} \mathbb{E}(\theta_\alpha^\times(a))\eta \cap \mathbb{E}(\alpha_1 \times \alpha_2)\eta \subseteq \bigcup_{a \in N} \mathbb{E}(\theta_\alpha^\times(a))\eta$$

where $\theta_\alpha^\times(a) = a\{(\alpha_1 \times \alpha_2) \vee \alpha/_\alpha\}$ and α_1, α_2 are fresh variables.

The case for $u =$ fun is trickier because $\mathbb{1} \to \mathbb{0}$ is contained in every arrow type, and therefore sets of arrows that do not contain it must be explicitly checked. If, analogously to $u =$ prod, we used just $\{(\alpha_1 \to \alpha_2) \vee \alpha/_\alpha\}$, then the subtypes of $\mathbb{0} \to \mathbb{1}$ that do not contain $\mathbb{1} \to \mathbb{0}$ would never be assigned to α by the algorithm and, thus, never checked. Therefore, $\{((\alpha_1 \to \alpha_2) \setminus (\mathbb{1} \to \mathbb{0})) \vee \alpha/_\alpha\}$ must be checked, as well.

Lemma 3.10. *Let $(\mathcal{D}, [\![.]\!])$ be a well-founded model, P, N two finite subsets of $\mathscr{A}_{\mathsf{fun}}$ and α an arbitrary type variable. Then*

$$\forall \eta \in \mathscr{P}(\mathcal{D})^{\mathcal{V}} . \bigcap_{a \in P} \mathbb{E}(a)\eta \cap (\eta(\alpha) \cap \mathbb{E}^{\mathsf{fun}} \mathcal{D}) \subseteq \bigcup_{a \in N} \mathbb{E}(a)\eta \Leftrightarrow$$

$$\forall \eta \in \mathscr{P}(\mathcal{D})^{\mathcal{V}} . \bigcap_{a \in P} \mathbb{E}(\theta_\alpha^\to(a))\eta \cap \mathbb{E}(\alpha_1 \to \alpha_2)\eta \subseteq \bigcup_{a \in N} \mathbb{E}(\theta_\alpha^\to(a))\eta$$

$$\text{and} \quad \forall \eta \in \mathscr{P}(\mathcal{D})^{\mathcal{V}} . \bigcap_{a \in P} \mathbb{E}(\theta_\alpha^{\not\to}(a))\eta \cap \mathbb{E}((\alpha_1 \to \alpha_2) \setminus (\mathbb{1} \to \mathbb{0}))\eta \subseteq \bigcup_{a \in N} \mathbb{E}(\theta_\alpha^{\not\to}(a))\eta$$

where α_1, α_2 are fresh variables, $\theta_\alpha^\to(a) = a\{(\alpha_1 \to \alpha_2) \vee \alpha/_\alpha\}$, and $\theta_\alpha^{\not\to}(a) = a\{((\alpha_1 \to \alpha_2) \setminus (\mathbb{1} \to \mathbb{0})) \vee \alpha/_\alpha\}$.

As an aside notice that both lemmas above would not hold if the variable α in their statements occurred negated at toplevel, whence the necessity of *Step 4*.

Finally, *Step 6* is justified by the two following lemmas in whose proofs the hypothesis of convexity plays a crucial role:

Lemma 3.11. *Let $(\mathcal{D}, [\![.]\!])$ be a convex set-theoretic interpretation and P, N two finite subsets of $\mathscr{A}_{\mathsf{prod}}$. Then:*

$$\forall \eta . \bigcap_{a \in P} \mathbb{E}(a)\eta \subseteq \bigcup_{a \in N} \mathbb{E}(a)\eta \Leftrightarrow$$

$$\forall N' \subseteq N . \begin{cases} \forall \eta . [\![\bigwedge_{t_1 \times t_2 \in P} t_1 \wedge \bigwedge_{t_1 \times t_2 \in N'} \neg t_1]\!]\eta = \varnothing \\ \vee \\ \forall \eta . [\![\bigwedge_{t_1 \times t_2 \in P} t_2 \wedge \bigwedge_{t_1 \times t_2 \in N \setminus N'} \neg t_2]\!]\eta = \varnothing \end{cases}$$

(with the convention $\bigcap_{a \in \varnothing} \mathbb{E}(a)\eta = \mathbb{E}^{\mathsf{prod}}\mathcal{D}$).

Lemma 3.12. *Let $(\mathcal{D}, [\![.]\!])$ be a convex set-theoretic interpretation and P, N be two finite subsets of $\mathscr{A}_{\mathsf{fun}}$. Then:*

$$\forall \eta . \bigcap_{a \in P} \mathbb{E}(a)\eta \subseteq \bigcup_{a \in N} \mathbb{E}(a)\eta \Leftrightarrow$$

$$\exists (t_0 \to s_0) \in N . \forall P' \subseteq P . \begin{cases} \forall \eta . [\![t_0 \setminus (\bigvee_{t \to s \in P'} t)]\!]\eta = \varnothing \\ \vee \\ \begin{cases} P \neq P' \\ \wedge \\ \forall \eta . [\![(\bigwedge_{t \to s \in P \setminus P'} s) \setminus s_0]\!]\eta = \varnothing \end{cases} \end{cases}$$

(with the convention $\bigcap_{a \in \varnothing} \mathbb{E}(a)\eta = \mathbb{E}^{\mathsf{fun}}\mathcal{D}$)

3.4 Algorithm

The formalization of the subtyping algorithm is done via notion of *simulation* that we borrow from [10] and extend to account for type variables and type instantiation. We use θ to range over (syntactic) substitutions, that is, partial functions from $\mathcal{V}$ to $\mathcal{T}$ (we reserve the meta-variable σ we introduced in Section 2 for ground substitutions). The application of a substitution to a type is straightforwardly homomorphically defined (notice that there is no binder). This definition is naturally extended to normal forms by applying the substitution to each type in the sets that form the normal form. It is then used to define the set of instances of a type.

Definition 3.13 (Instances). *Given a type $t \in \mathcal{T}$, we define $[t]_\approx$, the* set of instances *of t as:*

$$[t]_\approx \stackrel{\text{def}}{=} \{s \mid \exists \theta : \mathcal{V} \to \mathcal{T} . t\theta = s\}$$

Definition 3.14 (Simulation). *Let $\mathscr{S}$ be an arbitrary set of normal forms. We define another set of normal forms $\mathbb{E}\mathscr{S}$ as*

$$\{\tau \mid \forall s \in [\tau]_\approx . \forall u \in U . \forall (P,N) \in \mathcal{N}(s) . (P \subseteq \mathscr{A}_u \Rightarrow C_u^{P, N \cap \mathscr{A}_u})\}$$

where:

$$C_{\mathsf{basic}}^{P,N} \stackrel{\text{def}}{=} \bigcap_{b \in P} \mathbb{B}(b) \subseteq \bigcup_{b \in N \cap \mathscr{A}_{\mathsf{basic}}} \mathbb{B}(b)$$

$$C_{\mathsf{prod}}^{P,N} \stackrel{\text{def}}{=} \forall N' \subseteq N . \begin{cases} \mathcal{N}(\bigwedge_{t_1 \times t_2 \in P} t_1 \wedge \bigwedge_{t_1 \times t_2 \in N'} \neg t_1) \in \mathscr{S} \\ \vee \\ \mathcal{N}(\bigwedge_{t_1 \times t_2 \in P} t_2 \wedge \bigwedge_{t_1 \times t_2 \in N \setminus N'} \neg t_2) \in \mathscr{S} \end{cases}$$

$$C_{\mathsf{fun}}^{P,N} \stackrel{\text{def}}{=} \exists t_0 \to s_0 \in N . \forall P' \subseteq P . \begin{cases} \mathcal{N}(t_0 \wedge \bigwedge_{t \to s \in P'} \neg t) \in \mathscr{S} \\ \vee \\ \begin{cases} P \neq P' \\ \wedge \\ \mathcal{N}((\neg s_0) \wedge \bigwedge_{t \to s \in P \setminus P'} s) \in \mathscr{S} \end{cases} \end{cases}$$

We say that $\mathscr{S}$ is a simulation *if:*

$$\mathscr{S} \subseteq \mathbb{E}\mathscr{S}$$

The notion of simulation is at the basis of our subtyping algorithm. In what follows we show that simulations soundly and completely characterize the set of empty types of a well-founded convex model. More precisely, we show that every type in a simulation is empty (soundness) and that the set of all empty types is a simulation (completeness), actually, the largest simulation.

Lemma 3.15. *Let $[\![\_]\!] : \mathcal{T} \to \mathscr{P}(\mathcal{D})^{\mathcal{V}} \to \mathscr{P}(\mathcal{D})$ be a set-theoretic interpretation and t a type. If $\forall \eta \in \mathscr{P}(\mathcal{D})^{\mathcal{V}} . [\![t]\!]\eta = \varnothing$, then $\forall \theta : \mathcal{V} \to \mathcal{T} . \forall \eta \in \mathscr{P}(\mathcal{D})^{\mathcal{V}} . [\![t\theta]\!]\eta = \varnothing$*

Lemma 3.15 shows that if a type is empty, then all its syntactic instances are empty. In particular if a type is empty we can rename all its type variables without changing any property. So when working with empty types or, equivalently, with subtyping relations, types can be considered equivalent modulo α-renaming (*ie*, the renaming of type variables).

The first result we prove is that every simulation contains only empty types.

Theorem 3.16 (Soundness). *Let* $[\![\_]\!] : \mathcal{T} \to \mathscr{P}(\mathcal{D})^{\mathcal{V}} \to \mathscr{P}(\mathcal{D})$ *be a convex structural interpretation and* $\mathscr{S}$ *a simulation. Then for all* $\tau \in \mathscr{S}$, *we have* $\forall \eta \in \mathscr{P}(\mathcal{D})^{\mathcal{V}} . [\![\tau]\!]\eta = \varnothing$

The intuition of the simulation is that if we consider the statements of Lemmas 3.11 and 3.12 as if they were rewriting rules (from right to left), then $\mathbb{E}\mathscr{S}$ contains all the types that we can deduce to be empty in one step reduction when we suppose that the types in $\mathscr{S}$ are empty. A simulation is thus a set that is already saturated with respect to such a rewriting. In particular, if we consider the statements of Lemmas 3.11 and 3.12 as inference rules for determining when a type is equal to $\mathbb{0}$, then $\mathbb{E}\mathscr{S}$ is the set of immediate consequences of $\mathscr{S}$, and a simulation is a *self-justifying* set, that is a co-inductive proof of the fact that all its elements are equal to $\mathbb{0}$.

Completeness derives straightforwardly from the construction of simulation and the lemmas we proved about it.

Theorem 3.17. *Let* $[\![\_]\!] : \mathcal{T} \to \mathscr{P}(\mathcal{D})^{\mathcal{V}} \to \mathscr{P}(\mathcal{D})$ *be a convex set-theoretic interpretation. We define a set of normal forms* $\mathscr{S}$ *by:*

$$\mathscr{S} \stackrel{\text{def}}{=} \{\tau \mid \forall \eta \in \mathscr{P}(\mathcal{D})^{\mathcal{V}} . [\![\tau]\!]\eta = \varnothing\}$$

Then:

$$\mathbb{E}\mathscr{S} = \{\tau \mid \forall \eta \in \mathscr{P}(\mathcal{D})^{\mathcal{V}} . \mathbb{E}(\tau)\eta = \varnothing\}$$

Corollary 3.18. *Let* $[\![\_]\!] : \mathcal{T} \to \mathscr{P}(\mathcal{D})^{\mathcal{V}} \to \mathscr{P}(\mathcal{D})$ *be a convex structural interpretation. Define as above* $\mathscr{S} = \{\tau \mid \forall \eta \in \mathscr{P}(\mathcal{D})^{\mathcal{V}} . \mathbb{E}(\tau)\eta = \varnothing\}$. *Then* $[\![\_]\!]$ *is a model if and only if* $\mathscr{S} = \mathbb{E}\mathscr{S}$.

This corollary has two implications: first, that the condition for a set-theoretic interpretation to be a model depends only on the subtyping relation it induces; second, that the simulation that contains all the empty types is the largest simulation. In particular this second implication entails the following corollary.

Corollary 3.19 (Completeness). *Let* $[\![\_]\!] : \mathcal{T} \to \mathscr{P}(\mathcal{D})^{\mathcal{V}} \to \mathscr{P}(\mathcal{D})$ *be a well-formed convex model and* s *and* t *two types. Then* $s \leq t$ *if and only if there exists a simulation* $\mathscr{S}$ *such that* $\mathcal{N}(s \wedge \neg t) \in \mathscr{S}$.

The corollary states that to check whether $s \leq t$ we have to check whether there exists a simulation that contains the normal form, denoted by τ_0, of $s \wedge \neg t$. Thus a simple subtyping algorithm is to use Definition 3.14 as a set of saturation rules: we start from τ_0 and try to saturate it. At each step of saturation we add just the normal forms in which we eliminated top-level variables according to Lemmas 3.8, 3.9, and 3.10. Because of the presence of "or" in the definition, the algorithm follows different branches until it reaches a simulation (in which case it stops with success) or it adds a non-empty type (in which case the whole branch is abandoned).

All results we stated so far have never used the regularity of types. The theory holds also for non regular types and the algorithm described above is a sound and complete procedure to check their inclusion. The only result that needs regularity is decidability.

3.5 Decidability

As anticipated in the related work section, the subtyping relation on polymorphic regular types is decidable in EXPTIME. We prove decidability but the result on complexity is due to Gesbert *et al.* [14] who, as we already hinted, gave a linear encoding of the relation presented here in their variant of the μ-calculus, for which they have an EXPTIME solver [13], thus obtaining a subtyping decision algorithm that is EXPTIME [8] (in doing so they also spotted a subtle error in the original definition of our subtyping algorithm).

To prove decidability we just prove that our algorithm terminates. We do so by first showing that it terminates on finite trees (which is the crux of the problem since the only potential source of loop are the substitutions of free variables performed in ***Step 5***) and then show that when we switch to regular trees the algorithm always ends up on memoized terms (see the extended version).

3.6 Convex Models

The last step of our development is to prove that there exists at least one set-theoretical model that is convex. From a practical point of view this step is not necessary since one can always take the work we did so far as a syntactic definition of the subtyping relation. However, the mathematical support makes our theory general and applicable to several different domains (*eg*, Gesbert *et al*'s starting point and early attempts relied on this result), so finding a model is not done just for the sake of the theory. As it turns out, there actually exist a lot of convex models since every model for ground types with infinite denotations is convex. So to define a convex model it just suffices to take any model defined in [10] and straightforwardly modify the interpretation of basic and singleton types (more generally, of all indivisible types[9]) so they have infinite denotations.

Definition 3.20 (Infinite support). *A model* $(\mathcal{D}, [\![]\!])$ *is* with infinite support *if for every ground type* t *and assignment* η, *if* $[\![t]\!]\eta \neq \varnothing$, *then* $[\![t]\!]\eta$ *is an infinite set.*

What we want to prove then is the following theorem.

Theorem 3.21. *Every well-founded model with infinite support is convex.*

The proof of this theorem is quite technical—it is the proof that required us most effort—and proceeds in three logical steps. First, we prove that the theorem holds when all types at issue do not contain any product or arrow type. In other words, we prove that equation (8) holds for $[\![.]\!]$ with infinite support and where all t_i's are Boolean combinations of type variables and basic types. This is the key step in which we use the hypothesis of infinite support, since in the proof—done by contradiction—we need to pick an unbounded number of elements from our basic types in order to build a counterexample that proves the result. Second, we extend the previous proof to any type t_i that contains finitely many applications of the product constructor. In other terms, we prove the result for any (possibly infinite) type, provided that recursion traverses just arrow types, but not product types. As in the first case, the proof builds some particular elements of the domain. In the presence of type constructors the elements are built inductively. This is possible since products are not recursive, while for arrows it is always possible to pick a fresh appropriate element that resides in that arrow since every arrow type contains the (indivisible) closed type $\mathbb{1} \to \mathbb{0}$. Third, and last, we use the previous result and the well-foundedness of the model to show that the result holds for all types, that is, also for types in which recursion traverses a product type. More precisely, we prove that if we assume that the result

[8] This is also a lower bound for the complexity since the subtyping problem for ground regular types (without arrows) is known to be EXPTIME-complete.

[9] Our system has a very peculiar indivisible type: $\mathbb{1} \to \mathbb{0}$, the type of the functions that diverge on all arguments. This can be handled by adding a fixed infinite set of fresh elements of the domain to the interpretation of every arrow type (*cf.* the proof of Corollary 3.26 in the extended version).

does not hold for some infinite product type then it is possible to build a finite product type (actually, a finite expansion of the infinite type) that disproves equation (8), contradicting what is stated in our second step. Well-foundedness of the model allows us to build this finite type by induction on the elements denoted by the infinite one.

More precisely, we proceed as follows.

Definition 3.22. *We use* $\mathcal{T}^{\mathsf{fp}}$ *to denote the set of* types with finite products, *that is, the set of all types in which every infinite branch contains a finite number of occurrences of the* $\times$ *constructor.*

The first two steps of our proof are proved simultaneously in the following lemma.

Lemma 3.23. *Let* $(\mathcal{D}, [\![\_]\!])$ *be a model with infinite support, and* $t_i \in \mathcal{T}^{\mathsf{fp}}$ *for* $i \in [1..n]$. *Then*

$$\forall\eta\,.\,[\![t_1]\!]\eta = \varnothing \vee \ldots \vee [\![t_n]\!]\eta = \varnothing \Leftrightarrow$$
$$\forall\eta\,.\,[\![t_1]\!]\eta = \varnothing \vee \ldots \vee \forall\eta\,.\,[\![t_n]\!]\eta = \varnothing$$

Finally, it just remains to prove Theorem 3.21, that is to say, that Lemma 3.23 above holds also for t_i's with recursive products. This result requires the following preliminary lemma.

Lemma 3.24. *Let* $[\![\_]\!]$ *be a well-founded model with infinite support and* t *a type (which may thus contain infinite product types). If there exists a value* d *and an assignment* $\overline{\eta}$ *such that* $d \in [\![t]\!]\overline{\eta}$, *then there exists a type* $t^{\mathsf{fp}} \in \mathcal{T}^{\mathsf{fp}}$ *such that* $d \in [\![t^{\mathsf{fp}}]\!]\overline{\eta}$ *and for all assignment* η *if* $[\![t]\!]\eta = \varnothing$, *then* $[\![t^{\mathsf{fp}}]\!]\eta = \varnothing$.

While the statement of the previous lemma may, at first sight, seem obscure, its meaning is rather obvious. It states that in a well-founded model (*ie*, a model in which all the values are finite) whenever a recursive (product) type contains some value, then we can find a *finite* expansion of this type that contains the same value; furthermore, if the recursive type is empty in a given assignment, then also its finite expansion is empty in that assignment. This immediately yields our final result.

Lemma 3.25. *Let* $(\mathcal{D}, [\![\_]\!])$ *be a well-founded model with infinite support, and* t_i *for* $i \in [1..n]$. *Then*

$$\forall\eta\,.\,[\![t_1]\!]\eta = \varnothing \vee \ldots \vee [\![t_n]\!]\eta = \varnothing \Leftrightarrow$$
$$\forall\eta\,.\,[\![t_1]\!]\eta = \varnothing \vee \ldots \vee \forall\eta\,.\,[\![t_n]\!]\eta = \varnothing$$

Corollary 3.26 (Convex model). *There exists a convex model.*

4. Conclusion

This work constitutes the first solution to the problem of defining a semantic subtyping relation for a polymorphic extension of regular tree types. This problem, despite its important practical interest and potential fallouts, has been somehow neglected by most recent research since it was considered untreatable or unfeasible. Our solution not only has immediate application to the definition of programming languages for XML, but also opens several new research directions that we briefly discuss below.

The first direction concerns the definition of extensions of the type system itself. Among the possible extensions the most interesting (and difficult) one seems to be the extension of types with explicit second order quantifications. Currently, we consider prenex polymorphism, thus quantification on types is performed only at meta-level. But since this work proved the feasibility of a semantic subtyping approach for polymorphic types, we are eager to check whether it can be further extended to impredicative second order types, by adding explicit type quantification. This would be interesting not only from a programming language perspective, but also from a logic viewpoint since it would remove some of the limitations to the introspection capabilities we pointed out in Section 2.7. This may move our type system closer to being an expressive logic for subtyping. On the model side, it would be interesting to check whether the infinite support property (Definition 3.20) is not only a sufficient but also a necessary condition for convexity. This seems likely to the extent that the result holds for the type system restricted to basic type constructors (*ie*, without products and arrows). However, this is just a weak conjecture since the proof of sufficiency heavily relies (in the case for product types) on the well-foundedness property. Therefore, there may even exist non-well-founded models (non-well-founded models exist in the ground case: see [8, 10]) that are with infinite support but not convex. Nevertheless, an equivalent characterization of convexity—whether it were infinite support or some other characterization—would provide us a different angle of attack to study the connections between convexity and parametricity (see later on).

The second direction is to explore the definition of new languages to take advantage of the new capabilities of our system. A first natural test will be to see how to add overloaded (typed by intersection types) and higher-order (typed by arrow types) functions to the language defined in [15]. This already looks as quite a challenging problem since it needs local type inference for both subtyping and instantiation,[10] and we are actively working on it. But the overall design space for a programming language that can exploit the advanced features of our types is rather large since a lot of possible variations can be considered (*eg*, the use of type variables in pattern matching) and even more features can be encoded (*eg*, as explained in Footnote 4, bounded quantification can not only be encoded via intersection types but, thanks to them, also made more general since intersections allow the programmer to specify bounds on a per-occurrence basis). While exploring this design space it will be interesting to check whether our polymorphic union types can encode advanced type features such as polymorphic variants [12] and GADTs [24].

In our opinion, the definition of convexity is the most important and promising contribution of our work especially in view of its potential implications on the study of parametricity. As a matter of fact, there are strong connections between parametricity and convexity. We have already seen that convexity removes the stuttering behavior that clashes with parametricity, as equation (5) clearly illustrates. More generally, both convexity and parametricity describe or enforce uniformity of behavior. Parametricity imposes to functions a uniform behavior on parameters typed by type variables, since the latter cannot be deconstructed. This allows Wadler to deduce "theorems for free": the uniformity imposed by parametricity (actually, imposed by the property of being definable in second order λ-calculus) dramatically restricts the choice of possible behaviors of parametric functions to a point that it is easy to deduce theorems about a function just by considering its type [22]. In a similar way convexity imposes a uniform behavior to the zeros of the semantic interpretation, which is equivalent to imposing uniformity to the subtyping relation. An example of this uniformity is given by product types: in our framework a product $(t_1 \times \ldots \times t_n)$ is empty (*ie*, it is empty for every possible assignment of its variables) if and only if there exists a particular t_i that is empty (for

[10] To have some flavor of the problem, consider an overloaded function `even` for the domain $\mathbb{1}$ that when applied to an integer returns whether it is even or not, while it returns arguments of any other type unchanged. Its type is $(\texttt{Int} \to \texttt{Bool}) \wedge (\alpha\backslash\texttt{Int} \to \alpha\backslash\texttt{Int})$. If we apply a currified $\texttt{map} : (\beta \to \gamma) \to \beta* \to \gamma*$ to odd, then we want to deduce `map(even)`: $(\texttt{Int}* \to \texttt{Bool}*) \wedge ((\alpha\backslash\texttt{Int})* \to (\alpha\backslash\texttt{Int})*) \wedge ((\alpha \vee \texttt{Int})* \to ((\alpha\backslash\texttt{Int}) \vee \texttt{Bool})*)$. That is, when we apply `map(even)` to a list of integers it returns a list of booleans; when we apply it to a list that does not contain integers, then it returns a list of the same type; when the list contains some integers (*eg*, a list of reals), then it replaces integer elements by boolean ones. This is not an instance of the output type of `map`.

all possible assignments). We recover a property typical of closed types.

We conjecture the connection to be much deeper than described above. This can be clearly perceived by rereading the original Reynolds paper on parametricity [18] in the light of our results. Reynolds tries to characterize parametricity—or *abstraction* in Reynolds terminology—in a set-theoretic setting since, in Reynolds words, "if types denote specific subsets of a universe then their unions and intersections are well defined", which in Reynolds opinion is the very idea of abstraction. This can be rephrased as the fact that the operations for some types are well defined independently from the representation used for each type (Reynolds speaks of abstraction and representation since he sees the abstraction property as a result about change of representation). The underlying idea of parametricity according to Reynolds is that "meanings of an expression in 'related' environments will be 'related' " [18]. But as he points out few lines later "while the relation for each type variable is arbitrary, the relation for compound type expressions [*ie*, type constructors] must be induced in a specified way. We must specify how an assignment of relations to type variables is extended to type expressions" [18]. Reynolds formalizes this extension by defining a "relation semantics" for type constructors and, as Wadler brilliantly explains [22], this corresponds to regard types as relations. In particular pairs are related if their corresponding components are related and functions are related if they take related arguments into related results: there is a precise correspondence with the extensional interpretation of type constructors we gave in Definition 3.5 and, more generally, between the framework used to state parametricity and the one in our work.

Parametricity holds for terms written in the Girard/Reynolds second order typed lambda calculus (also known as pure polymorphic lambda calculus or System F). The property of being definable in the second-order typed lambda-calculus is *the* condition that harnesses expressions and forces them to behave uniformly. Convexity, instead, does not require any definability property. It *semantically* harnesses the denotations of expressions and forces them to behave uniformly. Therefore all seems to suggest that convexity may be a semantic characterization of what in Reynolds approach is the definability in the second-order typed lambda-calculus, which is a syntactic property. Or, to put it otherwise, convexity states parametricity for (or transposes it to) models rather than languages.

Although we have this strong intuition about the connection between convexity and parametricity, we do not know how to express this connection in a formal way, yet. We believe that the answer may come from the study of the calculus associated to our subtyping relation. We do not speak here of some language that can take advantage of our subtyping relation and whose design space we discussed earlier in this conclusion. What we are speaking of is every calculus whose model of values (*ie*, the model obtained by associating each type to the set of values that have that type) induces the same subtyping relation as the one devised here. Indeed, as parametricity leaves little freedom to the definition of transformations, so the semantic subtyping framework leaves little freedom to the definition of a language whose model of values induces the same subtyping relation as the relation used to type its values. If we could prove that every such language must automatically satisfy Reynolds abstraction theorem (and, even more, prove also the converse), then we would have a formal and strong connection between convexity and parametricity, the former being a purely semantic (in the sense that it does not rely on any language or calculus) characterization of the latter. But this is a long term and ambitious goal that goes well beyond the scope of the present work.

Acknowledgments. We were given a decisive help by Nino Salibra, who showed us how to prove that all powersets of infinite sets are convex models of the propositional logic. Pietro Abate implemented an early version of our prototype subtype checker. Bow-Yaw Wang drew our attention to the connection with convex theories. Claude Benzaken pointed out several useful results in combinatorics to us. Nils Gesbert spotted a subtle mistake in our subtyping algorithm. Many persons discussed the contents of this work with us and gave precious suggestions. Among them we are particularly grateful to Véronique Benzaken, Mariangiola Dezani-Ciancaglini, Kim Nguyen, Daniele Varacca, and Philip Wadler.

References

[1] V. Balat, J. Vouillon, and B. Yakobowski. Experience report: Ocsigen, a web programming framework. In *ICFP '09*. ACM Press, 2009.

[2] V. Benzaken, G. Castagna, and A. Frisch. CDuce: an XML-friendly general purpose language. In *ICFP '03*. ACM Press, 2003.

[3] G. Castagna, R. De Nicola, and D. Varacca. Semantic subtyping for the π-calculus. *Theor. Comput. Sci.*, 398(1-3):217–242, 2008.

[4] G. Castagna and K. Nguyen. Typed iterators for XML. In *ICFP '08*, pages 15–26. ACM Press, 2008.

[5] J. Clark and M. Murata. Relax-NG, 2001. `www.relaxng.org`.

[6] D. Draper et al. XQuery 1.0 and XPath 2.0 Formal Semantics, 2007. `http://www.w3.org/TR/query-semantics/`.

[7] T. Berners-Lee et al. *Uniform Resource Identifier*, January 2005. RFC 3986, STD 66.

[8] A. Frisch. *Théorie, conception et réalisation d'un langage de programmation fonctionnel adapté à XML*. PhD thesis, Université Paris 7, December 2004.

[9] A. Frisch. OCaml + XDuce. In *ICFP '06*. ACM Press, 2006.

[10] A. Frisch, G. Castagna, and V. Benzaken. Semantic subtyping: dealing set-theoretically with function, union, intersection, and negation types. *The Journal of ACM*, 55(4):1–64, 2008.

[11] V. Gapeyev, M.Y. Levin, B.C. Pierce, and A. Schmitt. The Xtatic compiler and runtime system, 2005. `http://www.cis.upenn.edu/~bcpierce/xtatic`.

[12] J. Garrigue. Programming with polymorphic variants. In *Proc. of ML Workshop*, 1998.

[13] P. Genevès, N. Layaïda, and A. Schmitt. Efficient static analysis of XML paths and types. In *PLDI '07*. ACM Press, 2007.

[14] N. Gesbert, P. Genevès, and N. Layaïda. Parametric Polymorphism and Semantic Subtyping: the Logical Connection. In *ICFP '11*, 2011.

[15] H. Hosoya, A. Frisch, and G. Castagna. Parametric polymorphism for XML. *ACM TOPLAS*, 32(1):1–56, 2009.

[16] H. Hosoya and B. Pierce. XDuce: A statically typed XML processing language. *ACM TOIT*, 3(2):117–148, 2003.

[17] K. Zhuo Ming Lu and M. Sulzmann. An implementation of subtyping among regular expression types. In *Proc. of APLAS'04*, volume 3302 of *LNCS*, pages 57–73. Springer, 2004.

[18] J.C. Reynolds. Types, abstraction and parametric polymorphism. In *Information Processing*, pages 513–523. Elsevier, 1983.

[19] J.C. Reynolds. Polymorphism is not set-theoretic. In *Semantics of Data Types*, volume 173 of *LNCS*, pages 145–156. Springer, 1984.

[20] J. Vouillon. Polymorphic regular tree types and patterns. In *POPL '06*, pages 103–114, 2006.

[21] W3C. *SOAP Version 1.2*. `http://www.w3.org/TR/soap`.

[22] P. Wadler. Theorems for free! In *Functional Programming Languages and Computer Architecture*, pages 347–359. ACM Press, 1989.

[23] C. Wallace and C. Runciman. Haskell and XML: Generic combinators or type based translation? In *ICFP '99*, pages 148–159, 1999.

[24] H. Xi, C. Chen, and G. Chen. Guarded recursive datatype constructors. In *POPL '03*, pages 224–235. ACM Press, 2003.

Parametric Polymorphism and Semantic Subtyping: the Logical Connection

Nils Gesbert
INRIA
nils.gesbert@inria.fr

Pierre Genevès
CNRS
pierre.geneves@inria.fr

Nabil Layaïda
INRIA
nabil.layaida@inria.fr

Abstract

We consider a type algebra equipped with recursive, product, function, intersection, union, and complement types together with type variables and implicit universal quantification over them. We consider the subtyping relation recently defined by Castagna and Xu over such type expressions and show how this relation can be decided in EXPTIME, answering an open question. The novelty, originality and strength of our solution reside in introducing a logical modeling for the semantic subtyping framework. We model semantic subtyping in a tree logic and use a satisfiability-testing algorithm in order to decide subtyping. We report on practical experiments made with a full implementation of the system. This provides a powerful polymorphic type system aiming at maintaining full static type-safety of functional programs that manipulate trees, even with higher-order functions, which is particularly useful in the context of XML.

Categories and Subject Descriptors D.3.3 [*Programming Languages*]: Language Constructs and Features—Polymorphism; F.3.3 [*Logics and Meanings of Programs*]: Studies of Program Constructs—Type structure

General Terms Algorithms, Design, Languages, Theory, Verification

Keywords Type-system, Polymorphism, subtyping

1. Introduction

This paper studies parametric polymorphism for type systems aiming at maintaining full static type-safety of functional programs that manipulate linked structures such as trees, potentially with higher-order functions. We consider a type algebra equipped with recursive, product, function (arrow), intersection, union, and complement types. We first show how the subtyping relation between such type expressions can be decided through a logical approach. Our main result solves an open problem: we prove the decidability of the subtyping relation when this type algebra is extended with type variables. This provides a powerful polymorphic type system (using ML-style prenex polymorphism, where variables are implicitly universally quantified at toplevel), for which defining the subtyping relation is not obvious, as pointed out in [5] and discussed in Section 5.1, and for which no candidate definition of subtyping had been proved decidable before. The novelty, originality and strength of our solution reside in introducing a logical modeling for the semantic subtyping framework. Specifically, we model semantic subtyping in a mu-calculus over finite trees and rely on a satisfiability solver in order to decide subtyping in practice. We obtain an EXPTIME complexity bound as well as an efficient implementation in practice.

1.1 The Need for Polymorphism and Subtyping

Subtyping makes it possible to prove that term substitution in a program source code preserves type-safety. For example, let us consider a simple property relating polymorphic types of functions that manipulate lists. We consider a type α, and denote by $[\alpha]$ the type of α-lists (lists whose elements are of type α). The type τ of functions that process an α-list and return a boolean is written as follows:

$$\tau = [\alpha] \to \texttt{Bool}$$

where $\texttt{Bool} = \{\texttt{true}, \texttt{false}\}$ is the type containing only the two values `true` and `false` Now let us consider functions that distinguish α-lists of even length from α-lists of odd length: such a function returns `true` for lists with an even number of elements of type α, and returns `false` for lists with an odd number of elements of type α. One may represent the set of these functions by a type τ' written as follows:

$$\begin{array}{ll} & \text{even}[\alpha] \quad \to \{\texttt{true}\} \\ \wedge & \text{odd}[\alpha] \quad \to \{\texttt{false}\} \end{array}$$

where `{true}` and `{false}` are singleton types (containing just one value). If we make explicit the parametric types even$[\alpha]$ and odd$[\alpha]$, τ' becomes:

$$\begin{array}{lll} \tau' = & \mu v.(\alpha \times (\alpha \times v)) \vee \text{nil} & \to \{\texttt{true}\} \\ \wedge & \mu v.(\alpha \times (\alpha \times v)) \vee (\alpha \times \text{nil}) & \to \{\texttt{false}\} \end{array}$$

where $\times$ denotes the cartesian product, μ binds the variable v for denoting a recursive type, and nil is a singleton type.

Obviously, a particular function of type τ' can also be seen as a less-specific function of type τ. In other terms, from a practical point of view, a function of type τ can be replaced by a more specific function of type τ' while preserving type-safety (however the converse is not true). This is further formalized by the notion of subtyping; in that case we write:

$$\tau' \leqslant \tau \qquad (1)$$

where $\leqslant$ denotes a subtyping relation that can be defined in two fundamentally different ways in the literature: either syntactically or semantically. In this paper, we define $\leqslant$ as a semantic subtyping relation by adopting a set-theoretic interpretation in the manner of [9], in contrast with more traditional subtyping through direct

ICFP'11, September 19–21, 2011, Tokyo, Japan.

syntactic rules. As a main contribution, we show how to decide this relation.

This work is motivated by a growing need for polymorphic type systems for programming languages that manipulate XML data. For instance, XQuery [4] is the standard query and functional language designed for querying collections of XML data. The support of higher-order functions, currently missing from XQuery, appears in the requirements for the forthcoming XQuery 3.0 language [8]. This results in an increasing demand in algorithms for proving or disproving statements such as the one of the example (1) with polymorphic types, but also with types of higher-order functions (like the traditional `map` and `fold` functions), or more generally, statements involving the subtyping relation over a type algebra with recursive, product, function, intersection, union, and complement types together with type variables and universal quantification over them.

1.2 Semantic Subtyping with Logical Solvers

During the last few years, a growing interest has been seen in the use of logical solvers such as satisfiability solver and satisfiability-modulo solvers in the context of functional programming and static type checking [1, 3]. In particular, solvers for tree logics [7, 10] are used as basic building blocks for type systems for XQuery.

The main idea in this paper is a type-checking algorithm for polymorphic types based on deciding subtyping through a logical solver. To decide whether τ is a subtype of type τ', we first construct equivalent logical formulas φ_τ and $\varphi_{\tau'}$ and then check the validity of the formula $\psi = \varphi_\tau \Rightarrow \varphi_{\tau'}$ by testing the unsatisfiability of $\neg\psi$ using the satisfiability-testing solver. This technique corresponds to semantic subtyping [9] since the underlying logic is inherently tied to a set-theoretic interpretation. Semantic subtyping has been applied to a wide variety of types including refinement types [3] and types for XML such as regular tree types [12], function types [2], and XPath [6] expressions [10].

This fruitful connection between logics, their decision procedures, and programming languages permitted to equip the latter with rich type systems for sophisticated programming constructs such as expressive pattern-matching and querying techniques. The potential benefits of this interconnection crucially depend on the expressivity of the underlying logics. Therefore, there is an increasing demand for more and more expressiveness. For example, in the context of XML:

- SMT solvers like [7] offer an expressive power that corresponds to a fragment of first-order logic in order to solve the intersection problem between two queries [1];
- full first-order logic solvers over finite trees [10] solve containment and equivalence of XPath expressions;
- monadic second-order logic solvers over trees, and – equivalent yet much more effective – satisfiability-solvers for μ-calculus over trees [10] are used to solve query containment problems in the presence of type constraints.

1.3 Contributions of the Paper

To the best of our knowledge, novelty of our work is threefold. It is the first work that:

- proves the decidability of semantic subtyping for polymorphic types with function, product, intersection, union, and complement types, as defined by Castagna and Xu [5], and gives a precise complexity upper-bound: $2^{\mathcal{O}(n)}$, where n is the size of types being checked. Decidability was only conjectured by Castagna and Xu before our result, although they have now proved it independently; our result on complexity is still the only one. In addition, we provide an effective implementation of the decision procedure.
- produces counterexamples whenever subtyping does not hold. These counterexamples are valuable for programmers as they represent evidence that the relation does not hold.
- pushes the integration between programming languages and logical solvers to a very high level. The logic in use is not only capable to range over higher order functions, but it is also capable of expressing values from semantic domains that correspond to monadic second-order logic such as XML tree types [10]. This shows that such solvers can become the core of XML-centric functional languages type-checkers such as those used in CDuce [2] or XDuce [11].

1.4 Structure of the Paper

We introduce the semantic subtyping framework in Section 2 where we start with the monomorphic type algebra (without type variables). We present the tree logic in which we model semantic subtyping in Section 3. We detail the logical encoding of types in Section 4. Then, in Section 5 we extend the type algebra with type variables, and state the main result of the paper: we show how to decide the subtyping relation for the polymorphic case in exponential time. We report on practical experiments using the implementation in Section 6. Finally, we discuss related work in Section 7 before concluding in Section 8.

2. Semantic Subtyping Framework

In this section, we present the type algebra we consider: we introduce its syntax and define its semantics in terms of semantic domains. This framework is the one described at length in [9]; we do not discuss its properties here but just give the necessary definitions, that we will then extend with type variables in Section 5.

2.1 Types

Type terms are defined using the following grammar:

$$
\begin{array}{lcll}
\tau & ::= & & \\
 & & b & \text{basic type} \\
 & | & \tau \times \tau & \text{product type} \\
 & | & \tau \to \tau & \text{function type} \\
 & | & \tau \vee \tau & \text{union type} \\
 & | & \neg\tau & \text{complement type} \\
 & | & \mathbf{0} & \text{empty type} \\
 & | & v & \text{recursion variable} \\
 & | & \mu v.\tau & \text{recursive type}
\end{array}
$$

We consider μ as a binder and define the notions of free and bound variables and closed terms as standard. A type is a closed type term which is *well-formed* in the sense that:

- the negation operator only occurs in front of *closed* types;
- every occurrence of a recursion variable is separated from its binder by at least one occurrence of the product or arrow constructor.

So, for example, $\mu v.\mathbf{0} \vee v$ is not well-formed, nor is $\mu v.\mathbf{0} \to \neg v$.

Additionally, the following abbreviations are defined:

$$\tau_1 \wedge \tau_2 \stackrel{\text{def}}{=} \neg(\neg\tau_1 \vee \neg\tau_2)$$

and

$$\mathbf{1} = \neg\mathbf{0}$$

2.2 Semantic domain

Consider an arbitrary set $\mathcal{C}$ of constants. From it, we define the semantic domain $\mathcal{D}$ as the set of ds generated by the following grammar, where c ranges over constants in $\mathcal{C}$:

d	$::=$		domain element
		c	base constant
	$\mid$	(d, d)	pair
	$\mid$	$\{(d, d'), \ldots, (d, d')\}$	function
d'	$::=$		extended domain element
		d	
	$\mid$	Ω	error

The function terms are *finite* sets of pairs representing nondeterministic partial functions from $\mathcal{D}$ to $\mathcal{D} \cup \{\Omega\}$: each pair (d, d') in the set means that, when given d as an argument, the function *may* yield d' as a result. If d does not appear as the first element of any pair, the operational interpretation is that the function can still accept d as an argument but will not yield a result: this represents a computation which does not terminate. A pair of the form (d, Ω) is used to represent a function rejecting d as an argument: when given d, it yields an error.

This grammar is only able to represent functions which diverge but on a finite number of possible arguments. However it is shown in [9] (Lemma 6.32) that considering only those functions does not affect the subtyping relation.

2.3 Interpretation

We suppose we have an interpretation $\mathbb{B}[\![\cdot]\!]$ of basic types b as subsets of $\mathcal{C}$.

The predicate $(d' : \tau)$ where d' is an element of $\mathcal{D}$ or Ω and τ is a type is defined recursively in the following way:

$$\begin{aligned}
(\Omega : \tau) &= \mathsf{false} \\
(c : b) &= c \in \mathbb{B}[\![b]\!] \\
((d_1, d_2) : \tau_1 \times \tau_2) &= (d_1 : \tau_1) \wedge (d_2 : \tau_2) \\
(\{(d_1, d_1'), \ldots, (d_n, d_n')\} : \tau_1 \rightarrow \tau_2) &= \forall i, (d_i : \tau_1) \Rightarrow (d_i' : \tau_2) \\
(d : \tau_1 \vee \tau_2) &= (d : \tau_1) \vee (d : \tau_2) \\
(d : \neg\tau) &= \neg(d : \tau) \\
(d : \mu v.\tau) &= (d : \tau\{^{\mu v.\tau}/_v\}) \\
(d : \tau) &= \mathsf{false} \text{ in any other case}
\end{aligned}$$

To prove this definition is well-founded, we first define the shallow depth of a type term as the longest path, in its syntactic tree, starting from the root and consisting only of μ, $\vee$, and $\neg$ nodes. We then use the following ordering on pairs (d', t) :

- $d_1' \leqslant d_2'$ if d_1' is a subterm of d_2'
- $\tau_1 \leqslant \tau_2$ if the shallow depth of τ_1 is less than the shallow depth of τ_2
- pairs are ordered lexicographically, i. e. $(d_1', \tau_1) \leqslant (d_2', \tau_2)$ if either $d_1' < d_2'$ or $d_1' = d_2'$ and $\tau_1 \leqslant \tau_2$.

Now we can see that all occurrences of the predicate on the right-hand side of the definition are for pairs strictly smaller than the one on the left (in the case of $\mu v.\tau$, this is due to the well-formedness constraint: the variable being substituted can only appear below a $\times$ or $\rightarrow$ node). Because all terms and types are finite, this makes the definition well-founded.

The interpretation of types as parts of $\mathcal{D}$ is then defined as $[\![\tau]\!] = \{d \mid (d : \tau)\}$. Note that Ω is not part of any type, as expected.

In this framework, we consider XML types as regular tree languages. An XML tree type is interpreted as the set of documents that match the type.

2.4 Subtyping

The subtyping relation is defined as $\tau_1 \leqslant \tau_2 \Leftrightarrow [\![\tau_1]\!] \subset [\![\tau_2]\!]$, or, equivalently, $[\![\tau_1 \wedge \neg\tau_2]\!] = \emptyset$.

3. Tree logic framework

In this section we introduce the logic in which we model the semantic subtyping framework. This logic is a subset of the one proposed in [10]: a variant of μ-calculus whose models are finite trees. We first introduce below the syntax and semantics of the logic, before tuning it for representing types.

3.1 Formulas

Formulas are defined thus:

φ, ψ	$::=$		formula
		$\top$	true
	$\mid$	$\sigma \mid \neg\sigma$	atomic proposition (negated)
	$\mid$	X	variable
	$\mid$	$\varphi \vee \psi$	disjunction
	$\mid$	$\varphi \wedge \psi$	conjunction
	$\mid$	$\langle a \rangle \varphi \mid \neg \langle a \rangle \top$	existential (negated)
	$\mid$	$\mu(X_i = \varphi_i)_{i \in I}$ in ψ	(least) n-ary fixpoint

where $a \in \{1, 2\}$ are *programs*, and I is a finite set. Atomic propositions σ correspond to labels from a countable set Σ. Additionnally, we use the abbreviation $\mu X.\varphi$ for $\mu(X = \varphi)$ in φ.

3.2 Semantic domain

The semantic domain is the set $\mathcal{F}$ of focused trees defined by the following syntax, where we have an alphabet Σ of labels, ranged over by σ:

t	$::=$	$\sigma[tl]$	tree
tl	$::=$		list of trees
		ϵ	empty list
	$\mid$	$t :: tl$	cons cell
c	$::=$		context
		(tl, Top, tl)	root of the tree
	$\mid$	$(tl, c[\sigma], tl)$	context node
f	$::=$	(t, c)	focused tree

A focused tree (t, c) is a pair consisting of a tree t and its context c. The context $(tl, c[\sigma], tl)$ comprises three components: a list of trees at the left of the current tree in reverse order (the first element of the list is the tree immediately to the left of the current tree), the context above the tree, and a list of trees at the right of the current tree. The context above the tree may be Top if the current tree is at the root, otherwise it is of the form $c[\sigma]$ where σ is the label of the enclosing element and c is the context in which the enclosing element occurs.

The *name* of a focused tree is defined as $\mathtt{nm}(\sigma[tl], c) = \sigma$.

We now describe how to navigate focused trees, in binary style. There are four directions, or *modalities*, that can be followed: for a focused tree f, $f\langle 1 \rangle$ changes the focus to the first child of the current tree, $f\langle 2 \rangle$ changes the focus to the next sibling of the current tree, $f\langle \bar{1} \rangle$ changes the focus to the parent of the tree *if the current tree is a leftmost sibling*, and $f\langle \bar{2} \rangle$ changes the focus to the previous sibling.

Formally, we have:

$$\begin{aligned}
(\sigma[t :: tl], c)\langle 1 \rangle &\stackrel{\text{def}}{=} (t, (\epsilon, c[\sigma], tl)) \\
(t, (tl_l, c[\sigma], t' :: tl_r))\langle 2 \rangle &\stackrel{\text{def}}{=} (t', (t :: tl_l, c[\sigma], tl_r)) \\
(t, (\epsilon, c[\sigma], tl))\langle \bar{1} \rangle &\stackrel{\text{def}}{=} (\sigma[t :: tl], c) \\
(t', (t :: tl_l, c[\sigma], tl_r))\langle \bar{2} \rangle &\stackrel{\text{def}}{=} (t, (tl_l, c[\sigma], t' :: tl_r))
\end{aligned}$$

When the focused tree does not have the required shape, these operations are not defined.

3.3 Interpretation

Formulas are interpreted as subsets of $\mathcal{F}$ in the following way, where V is a mapping from variables to formulas:

$$[\![\top]\!]_V \stackrel{\text{def}}{=} \mathcal{F} \qquad [\![\sigma]\!]_V \stackrel{\text{def}}{=} \{f \mid \mathtt{nm}(f) = \sigma\}$$

$$[\![X]\!]_V \stackrel{\text{def}}{=} V(X) \qquad [\![\neg\sigma]\!]_V \stackrel{\text{def}}{=} \{f \mid \mathtt{nm}(f) \neq \sigma\}$$

$$[\![\varphi \vee \psi]\!]_V \stackrel{\text{def}}{=} [\![\varphi]\!]_V \cup [\![\psi]\!]_V \qquad [\![\varphi \wedge \psi]\!]_V \stackrel{\text{def}}{=} [\![\varphi]\!]_V \cap [\![\psi]\!]_V$$

$$[\![\langle a \rangle\, \varphi]\!]_V \stackrel{\text{def}}{=} \{f \langle \overline{a} \rangle \mid f \in [\![\varphi]\!]_V \wedge f \langle \overline{a} \rangle \text{ defined}\}$$

$$[\![\neg \langle a \rangle \top]\!]_V \stackrel{\text{def}}{=} \{f \mid f \langle a \rangle \text{ undefined}\}$$

$$\begin{aligned}&[\![\mu(X_i = \varphi_i)_{i \in I} \text{ in } \psi]\!]_V \stackrel{\text{def}}{=}\\ &\quad \text{let } S = \{(T_i) \in \mathcal{P}(\mathcal{F})^I \mid \forall j \in I, [\![\varphi_j]\!]_{V[\overline{T_i/X_i}]} \subseteq T_j\} \quad \text{in}\\ &\quad \text{let } (U_j) = \left(\textstyle\bigcap_{(T_i) \in S} T_j\right)_{j \in I} \quad \text{in} \quad [\![\psi]\!]_{V[\overline{U_i/X_i}]}\end{aligned}$$

where $V[\overline{T_i/X_i}](X) = V(X)$ if $X \notin \{X_i\}$ and T_i if $X = X_i$.

The lemma 4.2 of [10] says that the interpretation of a fixpoint formula is equal to the union of the interpretations of all its finite unfoldings (where unfolding is defined as usual). A consequence (detailed in [10]) is that the logic is closed under negation, i. e. for any closed φ, $\neg\varphi$ can be expressed in the syntax using De Morgan's relations and this definition:

$$\neg \langle a \rangle\, \varphi \stackrel{\text{def}}{=} \neg \langle a \rangle \top \vee \langle a \rangle \neg\varphi$$

$$\neg\mu(X_i = \varphi_i) \text{ in } \psi \stackrel{\text{def}}{=} \mu(X_i = \neg\varphi_i\{\overline{^{X_i}/_{\neg X_i}}\}) \text{ in } \neg\psi\{\overline{^{X_i}/_{\neg X_i}}\}$$

In the following, we consider only closed formulas and write $[\![\varphi]\!]$ for $[\![\varphi]\!]_\emptyset$.

4. Logical Encoding

In the context of the present paper, we want finite tree models of the logic to correspond to types introduced in section 2. Thus, we first extend the alphabet of node labels to be able to reason with type constructors. Then, we present the translation of a type into a logical formula.

4.1 Representation of domain elements

Let $\mathcal{T}$ be the set of (unfocused) trees. Set $\mathcal{C} = \{\mathbb{B}[tl] \mid tl \in \mathcal{T}^*\}$, where $\mathbb{B}$ is a label **not in** Σ : the set of trees with a distinguished root $\mathbb{B}$. Let $\mathcal{T}_{ext}$ be the set of trees obtained by extending Σ with the four extra labels $(\rightarrow), (\times), \mathbb{B}$ and Ω. Then $\mathcal{D}_\Omega$ can straightforwardly be embedded into $\mathcal{T}_{ext}$ in the following way:

$$\begin{aligned}\mathsf{tree}(c) &= c\\ \mathsf{tree}(\Omega) &= \Omega[\epsilon]\\ \mathsf{tree}(d, d') &= (\times)[\mathsf{tree}(d) :: \mathsf{tree}(d') :: \epsilon]\\ \mathsf{tree}(\{(d_1, d_1'), \ldots, (d_n, d_n')\}) &=\\ &(\rightarrow)[\mathsf{tree}(d_1, d_1') :: \ldots :: \mathsf{tree}(d_n, d_n') :: \epsilon]\end{aligned}$$

In the following we consider this embedding implicitly done, so $\mathcal{D}_\Omega \subset \mathcal{T}_{ext}$.

4.2 Translation of types

First of all, we can define basic types b, which are to represent sets of trees with no special nodes but the distinguished root $\mathbb{B}$, as the (closed) base formulas of the logic. The full interpretation of formulas uses sets of focused trees, but note that a toplevel formula cannot contain any constraint on what is above or to the left of the node at focus, so it can be considered as describing just a list of trees. The interpretation of a base type will then be a $\mathbb{B}$ root whose list of children is described by the formula. Formally:

$$\mathbb{B}[\![\varphi]\!] \stackrel{\text{def}}{=} \{\mathbb{B}[t :: tl_2] \mid (t, (tl_1, c[\sigma], tl_2)) \in [\![\varphi]\!]\}$$

Note how the only part of the context taken into account in defining the semantics is the list of following siblings of the current node.

Then, we translate the types into *extended* formulas obtained (as for extended trees) by adding to Σ the labels $(\times), (\rightarrow), \Omega$ and $\mathbb{B}$. Straightforwardly these formulas denote lists of trees in $\mathcal{T}_{ext}$.

First define the following formulas:

$$\begin{aligned}\mathsf{isbase} &= \mu X.((\neg \langle 1 \rangle \top \vee \langle 1 \rangle X) \wedge (\neg \langle 2 \rangle \top \vee \langle 2 \rangle X)\\ &\qquad \wedge \neg\mathbb{B} \wedge \neg(\rightarrow) \wedge \neg(\times) \wedge \neg\Omega)\\ \mathsf{error} &= \Omega \wedge \neg \langle 1 \rangle \top\\ \mathsf{isd} &= \mu X.(\\ &\quad (\mathbb{B} \wedge \langle 1 \rangle\, \mathsf{isbase}) \vee\\ &\quad ((\times) \wedge \langle 1 \rangle\, (X \wedge \langle 2 \rangle\, (X \wedge \neg \langle 2 \rangle \top))) \vee\\ &\quad ((\rightarrow) \wedge (\neg \langle 1 \rangle \top \vee\\ &\qquad \langle 1 \rangle\, \mu Y.((\neg \langle 2 \rangle \top \vee \langle 2 \rangle\, Y) \wedge\\ &\qquad\quad (\times) \wedge \langle 1 \rangle\, (X \wedge \langle 2 \rangle\, ((X \vee \mathsf{error}) \wedge \neg \langle 2 \rangle \top))\\ &\quad))))\end{aligned}$$

isbase selects all tree lists which do not contain any of the special labels (the fixpoint is for selecting all the nodes). error is straightforward. isd selects all elements of $\mathcal{D}$ (actually, all tree lists whose first element is in $\mathcal{D}$): either they are a constant (a $\mathbb{B}$ node with a base list as children), or a pair (a $(\times)$ node with exactly two children each of which is itself in $\mathcal{D}$), or a function: a $(\rightarrow)$ node with either no children at all or a list of children (described by Y) all of which are pairs whose second element may be error.

We now associate to every type τ the formula $\mathsf{fullform}(\tau) = \mathsf{isd} \wedge \mathsf{form}(\tau)$, with $\mathsf{form}(\tau)$ defined as follows, where X_v is a different variable for every v and is also different from X:

$$\begin{aligned}\mathsf{form}(b) &= \mathbb{B} \wedge \langle 1 \rangle\, b\\ \mathsf{form}(\tau_1 \times \tau_2) &= (\times) \wedge \langle 1 \rangle\, (\mathsf{form}(\tau_1) \wedge \langle 2 \rangle\, \mathsf{form}(\tau_2))\\ \mathsf{form}(\tau_1 \rightarrow \tau_2) &= (\rightarrow) \wedge (\neg \langle 1 \rangle \top \vee\\ &\qquad \langle 1 \rangle\, \mu X.((\neg \langle 2 \rangle \top \vee \langle 2 \rangle\, X)\\ &\qquad\quad \wedge \langle 1 \rangle\, (\neg\mathsf{form}(\tau_1) \vee \langle 2 \rangle\, \mathsf{form}(\tau_2)))\\ &\quad)\\ \mathsf{form}(\tau_1 \vee \tau_2) &= \mathsf{form}(\tau_1) \vee \mathsf{form}(\tau_2)\\ \mathsf{form}(\neg\tau) &= \neg\mathsf{form}(\tau)\\ \mathsf{form}(\mathbf{0}) &= \neg\top\\ \mathsf{form}(v) &= X_v\\ \mathsf{form}(\mu v.\tau) &= \mu X_v.\mathsf{form}(\tau)\end{aligned}$$

Recall that basic types b are themselves formulas, but that their interpretation as a type is different from their interpretation as a formula (see the first paragraph of Section 4.2 and the definition of $\mathbb{B}[\![\varphi]\!]$, the interpretation as a type, in terms of $[\![\varphi]\!]$, the interpretation as a formula). This explains why the translation of b contains b itself. The translation of product types is simple: it describes a $(\times)$ node whose first child is described by $\mathsf{form}(\tau_1)$ and has a following sibling described by $\mathsf{form}(\tau_2)$. The translation of arrow types has a structure similar to what appeared in isd: it describes a $(\rightarrow)$ node with either no children or a list of children recursively described by X (each node has either no following sibling or a following sibling itself described by X). Each of these nodes must have a first child which either is not of type τ_1 or has a next sibling of type τ_2 — this means that these nodes represent pairs (d_i, d_i') such that

$(d_i : \tau_1) \Rightarrow (d'_i : \tau_2)$. The attentive reader may notice that the formula $\mathsf{form}(\tau_1 \rightarrow \tau_2)$ does not enforce in itself that all children of the $(\rightarrow)$ node are actually pairs; the reason for that is that isd already enforces it.

We can see that the formulas in the translation do not contain any $\langle 2 \rangle$ at toplevel (i. e. not under $\langle 1 \rangle$), nor does isd. This means they describe a single tree (they say nothing on its siblings), or in other words that in their interpretation as focused trees, the context is completely arbitrary, as it is not constrained in any way. Formally, we thus define the restricted interpretation of extended formulas as follows:

$$\mathbb{F}[\![\varphi]\!] \stackrel{\text{def}}{=} \{t \mid (t, c) \in [\![\varphi]\!]\}$$

That is, we drop the context completely.

Then we have $\mathbb{F}[\![\mathsf{fullform}(\tau)]\!] = [\![\tau]\!]$. This is a particular case of the property for polymorphic types which will be proved in the following section.

The main consequence of this property is that a type τ is empty if and only if the interpretation of the corresponding formula is empty — which is equivalent to the formula being unsatisfiable. Because their exists a satisfiability-checking algorithm for this tree logic [10], this means this translation gives an alternative way to decide the classical semantic subtyping relation as defined in [9]. More interestingly, it yields a decision procedure for the subtyping relation *in the polymorphic case as well*, as we will explain in the next section.

5. Polymorphism: Supporting Type Variables

So far we have described a new, logic-based approach to a question — semantic subtyping in the presence of intersection, negation and arrow types — which had already been studied. We now show how this new approach allows us, in a very natural way, to encompass the latest work by adding polymorphism to the types along the lines of [5].

We add to the syntax of types *variables*, α, β, γ taken from a countable set $\mathcal{V}$. If τ is a polymorphic type, we write $\mathsf{var}(\tau)$ the set of variables it contains and call *ground type* a type with no variable. We sometimes write $\tau(\overline{\alpha})$ to indicate that $\mathsf{var}(\tau)$ is included in $\overline{\alpha}$.

5.1 Subtyping in the polymorphic case: a problem of definition

The intuition of subtyping in the presence of type variables is that $\tau_1(\overline{\alpha}) \leqslant \tau_2(\overline{\alpha})$ should hold true whenever, *independently of the variables* $\overline{\alpha}$, any value of type τ_1 has type τ_2 as well. However the correct definition of 'independently' is not obvious. It should look like this:

$$\forall \overline{\alpha}, [\![\tau_1(\overline{\alpha})]\!] \subset [\![\tau_2(\overline{\alpha})]\!]$$

but because variables are abstractions, it is not completely clear over what to quantify them. As mentioned in [13], a candidate — naive — definition would use *ground substitutions*, that is, if the inclusion of interpretations always holds when variables are replaced with ground types, then the subtyping relation holds:

$$\tau_1(\overline{\alpha}) \leqslant \tau_2(\overline{\alpha}) \Leftrightarrow \forall \overline{\tau} \text{ ground types}, [\![\tau_1(\overline{\tau}/_{\overline{\alpha}})]\!] \subset [\![\tau_2(\overline{\tau}/_{\overline{\alpha}})]\!] \quad (2)$$

Obviously the condition on the right must be *necessary* for subtyping to hold. But deciding that it is *sufficient* as well makes the relation unsatisfactory and somehow counterintuitive, as remarked in [13]. Indeed, suppose int is an *indivisible* type, that is, that it has no subtype beside **0** and itself. Then the following would hold:

$$\mathsf{int} \times \alpha \leqslant (\mathsf{int} \times \neg\mathsf{int}) \vee (\alpha \times \mathsf{int}) \quad (3)$$

This relation abuses the definition by taking advantage of the fact that for any ground type τ, either $[\![\mathsf{int}]\!] \subset [\![\tau]\!]$ or $[\![\tau]\!] \subset [\![\neg\mathsf{int}]\!]$. In the first case, because $[\![\tau]\!] \subset ([\![\neg\mathsf{int}]\!] \cup [\![\mathsf{int}]\!])$, we have $[\![\mathsf{int} \times \tau]\!] \subset [\![\mathsf{int} \times \neg\mathsf{int}]\!] \cup [\![\mathsf{int} \times \mathsf{int}]\!]$ and then the second member of the union is included in $[\![\tau \times \mathsf{int}]\!]$. In the second case, we directly have $[\![\mathsf{int} \times \tau]\!] \subset [\![\mathsf{int} \times \neg\mathsf{int}]\!]$.

This trick, which only works with indivisible ground types, not only shows that candidate definition (2) yields bizarre relations where a variable occurs in unrelated positions on both sides. It also means the candidate definition is very sensitive to the precise semantics of base types, since it distinguishes indivisible types from others. More precisely, it means that refining the collection of base types, for example by adding types even and odd, can break subtyping relations which held true without these new types — this is simply due to the fact that it increases the set over which $\overline{\tau}$ is quantified in (2), making the relation stricter. This could hardly be considered a nice feature of the subtyping relation.

The conclusion is thus that the types in (3) should be considered related *by chance* rather than by necessity, hence not in the subtyping relation, and that quantifying over all possible ground types is not enough; in other words, candidate definition (2) is too weak and does not properly reflect the intuition of 'independently of the variables'. Indeed, (3) is in fact dependent on the variable as we saw, the point being that there are only two cases and that the convoluted right-hand type is crafted so that the relation holds in both of them, though for different reasons.

In order to restrict the definition of subtyping, [13], which concentrates on XML types, uses a notion of *marking*: some parts of a value can be marked (using paths) as corresponding to a variable, and the relation 'a value has a type' is changed into 'a marked value matches a type', so the semantics of a type is not a set of values but of pairs of a value and a marking. This is designed so that it integrates well in the XDuce language, which has pattern-matching but no higher-order functions (hence no arrow types), so their system is tied to the operational semantics of matching and provides only a partial solution.

The question of finding the correct definition of semantic subtyping in the polymorphic case was finally settled very recently by Castagna and Xu [5]. Their definition does, in the same way as (2), follow the idea of a universal quantification over possible *meanings* of variables but solves the problem raised by (3) by using a much larger set of possible meanings — thus yielding a stricter relation. More precisely, variables are allowed to represent not just ground types but any arbitrary part of the semantic domain; furthermore, the semantic domain itself must be large enough, which is embodied by the notion of *convexity*. We refer the reader to [5] for a detailed discussion of this property and its relation to the notion of *parametricity* studied by Reynolds in [14]; we will here limit ourselves to introducing the definitions strictly necessary for the discussion at hand.

In this work, we do not use this definition with its universal quantification directly. Rather, we retain from [13] the idea of tagging (pieces of) values which correspond to variables, but do so in a more abstract way, by extending the semantic domain, and define a *fixed* interpretation of polymorphic types in this extended domain as a straightforward extension of the monomorphic framework. We then show how to build a set-theoretic model of polymorphic types, in the sense of [5], based on this domain, and prove that the inclusion relation on fixed interpretations is equivalent to the full subtyping relation induced by this model. Finally, we explain briefly the notion of convexity and show that this model is convex, implying that this relation is, in fact, the semantic subtyping relation on polymorphic types, as defined in [5]. These steps are formally detailed in the following section.

5.2 Interpretation of polymorphic types

Let Λ be an infinite set of optional labels, and ι an injective function from $\mathcal{V}$ to Λ. (It would be possible to set $\Lambda = \mathcal{V}$, but for clarity we prefer to distinguish *labels* which tag elements of the semantic domain from *variables* which occur in types.) We extend the grammar of (extended) trees by allowing any node to bear, in addition to its single σ label from $\Sigma \cup \{(\rightarrow), (\times), \mathbb{B}, \Omega\}$, any (finite) number of labels from Λ. We write it $\sigma_L[tl]$ where L is a finite part of Λ. We extend $\mathcal{C}$ and $\mathcal{D}$ accordingly. When using the non-tree form of types, for instance (d_1, d_2), we indicate the set of root labels on the bottom right like this: $(d_1, d_2)_L$ (here L is the set of labels borne by the $(\times)$ node constituting the root of the pair tree).

We then extend the predicate defining the interpretation of types given in Section 2.3 with the following additional case:

$$(\sigma_L[tl] : \alpha) = \iota(\alpha) \in L$$

In other words, the interpretation of a type variable is the set of all trees whose root bears the label corresponding to that variable. The other cases are unchanged, except that the semantic domain is now much larger. This means that the same definition leads to larger interpretations; in particular, the interpretation of a (nonempty) ground type is always an infinite set which contains all possible labellings for each of its trees.

Subtyping over polymorphic types is then defined, as before, as set inclusion between interpretations:

$$\tau_1(\overline{\alpha}) \leqslant \tau_2(\overline{\alpha}) \Leftrightarrow [\![\tau_1(\overline{\alpha})]\!] \subset [\![\tau_2(\overline{\alpha})]\!] \qquad (4)$$

It may seem strange to give type *variables* a *fixed* interpretation, and on the other hand it may seem surprising that this definition of subtyping does not actually contain any quantification and is nevertheless stronger than (2) which contains one. The keypoint is that a form of universal quantification is implicit in the extension of the semantic domain: in some sense, the interpretation of a variable represents all possible values of the variable *at once*. Indeed, for any variable α and any tree d in the domain, there always exist both an infinity of copies of d which are in the interpretation of α and another infinity of copies which are not. From the point of view of logical satisfiability, this makes the domain big enough to contain all possible cases.

In order to show that, despite the appearances, Definition (4) accurately represents a relation that holds *independently of the variables*, we rely, as discussed above, on the formal framework developed by Castagna and Xu [5]. For this, we first introduce *assignments* η: functions from $\mathcal{V}$ to $\mathcal{P}(\mathcal{D})$ (where $\mathcal{D}$ is the extended semantic domain with labels). Thus an assignment attributes to each variable an arbitrary set of elements from the semantic domain.

We then define the interpretation of a type *relative to an assignment* in the following way: the predicate $(d' :_\eta \tau)$ is defined inductively in the same way as the $(d' : \tau)$ of Section 2.3 but with the additional clause:

$$(d :_\eta \alpha) = d \in \eta(\alpha).$$

The interpretation of the polymorphic type τ relative to the assignment η is then $[\![\tau]\!]\eta = \{d \mid (d :_\eta \tau)\}$. This defines an infinity of possible interpretations for a type, depending on the actual values assigned to the variables, and constitutes a set-theoretic model of types in the sense of [5]. The subtyping relation induced by this model is the following:

$$\tau_1(\overline{\alpha}) \leqslant \tau_2(\overline{\alpha}) \Leftrightarrow \forall \eta \in \mathcal{P}(\mathcal{D})^{\mathcal{V}}, [\![\tau_1(\overline{\alpha})]\!]\eta \subset [\![\tau_2(\overline{\alpha})]\!]\eta \qquad (5)$$

which we can more easily compare to the candidate definition (2): it does in the same way quantify over possible meanings of the variables but uses a much larger set of possible meanings, yielding a stricter relation. We will now prove that this relation is, for our particular model, actually equivalent to (4).

For this, let us first define the *canonical assignment* η_ι as follows:

$$\eta_\iota(\alpha) \stackrel{\text{def}}{=} \{\sigma_L[tl] \in \mathcal{D} \mid \iota(\alpha) \in L\}.$$

Then it is easily seen that the fixed interpretation $[\![\tau]\!]$ of a polymorphic type is the same as its interpretation relative to the canonical assignment, $[\![\tau]\!]\eta_\iota$. What we would like to prove is that the canonical assignment is somehow representative of all possible assignments, making the fixed interpretation sufficient for the purpose of defining subtyping. This is done by the following lemma and corollary.

LEMMA 5.1. *Let V be a finite part of $\mathcal{V}$. Let η be an assignment. Let T be the set of all types τ such that* $\mathsf{var}(\tau) \subset V$. *Then there exists a function $F_V^\eta : \mathcal{D} \to \mathcal{D}$ such that: $\forall \tau \in T, \forall d \in \mathcal{D}, d \in [\![\tau]\!]\eta \Leftrightarrow F_V^\eta(d) \in [\![\tau]\!]\eta_\iota$.*

Proof: For d in $\mathcal{D}$, let $L(d) = \{\iota(\alpha) \mid \alpha \in V \wedge d \in \eta(\alpha)\}$. Since V is finite, $L(d)$ is finite as well. We define $F_V^\eta(d)$ inductively as follows:

- if $d = \mathbb{B}_L[tl]$ then $F_V^\eta(d) = \mathbb{B}_{L(d)}[tl]$
- if $d = (d_1, d_2)_L$ then $F_V^\eta(d) = (F_V^\eta(d_1), F_V^\eta(d_2))_{L(d)}$
- $F_V^\eta(\Omega) = \Omega$
- if $d = \{(d_1, d_1'), \ldots, (d_n, d_n')\}_L$ then $F_V^\eta(d) = \{(F_V^\eta(d_1), F_V^\eta(d_1')), \ldots, (F_V^\eta(d_n), F_V^\eta(d_n'))\}_{L(d)}$

So F_V^η preserves the structure but changes the labels so that the root node of $F_V^\eta(d)$ is labelled with $L(d)$ and so on inductively for its subterms.

Let $\mathcal{P}(d, \tau) = d \in [\![\tau]\!]\eta \Leftrightarrow F_V^\eta(d) \in [\![\tau]\!]\eta_\iota$. We prove that it holds for all pairs (d, τ) such that τ is in T by induction on those pairs, using the ordering relation on them defined in Section 2.3, noticing that $\tau \in T$ implies that all subterms (and unfoldings) of τ are in T as well. The base cases are:

- if τ is a variable. Then it is in V by hypothesis and $\mathcal{P}(d, \tau)$ is true by definition of $L(d)$.
- if it is a base type. Then $\mathcal{P}(d, \tau)$ is true because the interpretation of τ is independent of assignments and labellings.

For the inductive cases, we suppose the property true for all strictly smaller pairs (d, τ) such that τ is in T.

- For the arrow and product cases, the inductive definition of F_V^η makes the result straightforward.
- For the negation and disjunction cases, the result is immediate from the induction hypothesis.
- For $\mu v.\tau$, recall that the well-formedness constraint on types implies that the type's unfolding has a strictly smaller shallow depth than the original type, hence we can use the induction hypothesis on the unfolding and conclude.

COROLLARY 5.2. *Let τ be a type. $\bigcup_{\eta \in \mathcal{P}(\mathcal{D})^{\mathcal{V}}} [\![\tau]\!]\eta = \emptyset$ if and only if $[\![\tau]\!]\eta_\iota = \emptyset$.*

Proof: If the union is not empty, there exists η and d such that $d \in [\![\tau]\!]\eta$. From the previous lemma we then have $F_{\mathsf{var}(\tau)}^\eta(d) \in [\![\tau]\!]\eta_\iota$.

This corollary shows that the canonical assignment is representative of all possible assignments and implies that the subtyping relation defined by (4) is equivalent to the one defined by (5).

Convexity of the model. Definition (5) corresponds to semantic subtyping as defined in [5], but only on the condition that the underlying model of types be *convex*. Indeed, we can see that this definition is dependent on the set of possible assignments, which itself depends on the chosen (abstract) semantic domain, so it is reasonable to think that increasing the semantic domain could restrict the relation further. In other words, for the definition to be correct, the domain must be large enough to cover all cases. Castagna and Xu's *convexity* characterises this notion of 'large enough'. The property is the following: a set-theoretic model of types is *convex* if, whenever a finite collection of types τ_1 to τ_n each possess a nonempty interpretation relative to some assignment, then there exists a common assignment making all interpretations nonempty at once. This reflects the idea that there are enough elements in the domain to witness all the cases.

In our case, it comes as no surprise that the extended model of types is convex since any nonempty ground type has an infinite interpretation, which, as proved in [5], is a sufficient condition. But we need not even rely on this result since Corollary 5.2 proves a property even stronger than convexity: having a nonempty interpretation relative to *some* assignment is the same as having a nonempty interpretation relative to *the* common canonical assignment. This stronger property makes the apparently weaker relation defined by (4) equivalent, in our particular model, to the full semantic subtyping relation Castagna and Xu defined. This allows us to reduce the problem of deciding their relation to a question of inclusion between fixed interpretations, making the addition of polymorphism a mostly straightforward extension to the logical encoding we presented for the monomorphic case.

Interestingly, in [5] the authors suggest that convexity constrains the relation enough that it should allow reasoning on types, similarly to the way parametricity allowed Wadler [16] to deduce 'theorems for free' from typing information. The fact that our logical reasoning approach very naturally has this convexity property — indeed, it is difficult to think of a logical representation of variables which would not have it — seems to corroborate their intuition, although reasoning on types beyond deciding subtyping is currently left as future work.

We now show how this extension of the type system is encoded in our logic.

5.3 Logical encoding of variables

We extend the logic with atomic propositions α which behave similarly as σ except they are not mutually exclusive. The interpretation of these propositions is defined as:

$$[\![\alpha]\!] = \{(\sigma_L[tl], c) \mid \iota(\alpha) \in L\}$$

$$[\![\neg\alpha]\!] = \{(\sigma_L[tl], c) \mid \iota(\alpha) \notin L\}$$

The translation $\mathsf{form}(\tau)$ of types into formulas is extended in the obvious way by $\mathsf{form}(\alpha) = \alpha$.

THEOREM 5.3. *With these extended definitions,* $\mathbb{F}[\![\mathsf{fullform}(\tau)]\!] = [\![\tau]\!]$.

Proof (sketch): Preliminary remark: whenever φ does not contain any $\langle 2\rangle$ at toplevel (which is the case of the formulas representing types), then $[\![\varphi]\!] = \mathbb{F}[\![\varphi]\!] \times \mathbf{C}$ where $\mathbf{C}$ is the set of all possible contexts. Hence, when considering such formulas, set-theoretic relations between full interpretations are equivalent to the same relations between first components.

First we check that $\mathbb{F}[\![\mathsf{isd}]\!] = \mathcal{D}$ and reformulate the statement as $\mathcal{D} \cap \mathbb{F}[\![\mathsf{form}(\tau)]\!] = [\![\tau]\!]$.

We make the embedding function tree explicit for greater clarity. What we have to show is that, for any d in $\mathcal{D}$, we have $(d : \tau)$ if and only if $(\mathsf{tree}(d), c)$ is in $[\![\mathsf{form}(\tau)]\!]$ for some (or, equivalently, for any) c.

The property is proved by induction on the pair (d, τ), following the definition of the predicate:

- for $(c : b)$ it holds by definition.
- for $((d_1, d_2)_L : \tau_1 \times \tau_2)$, let $f = (\mathsf{tree}((d_1, d_2)_L), c)$. f is in $[\![\mathsf{form}(\tau_1 \times \tau_2)]\!]$ if and only if $f\langle 1\rangle$ is in $[\![\mathsf{form}(\tau_1)]\!]$ and $f\langle 1\rangle\langle 2\rangle$ is in $[\![\mathsf{form}(\tau_2)]\!]$. (We already know that the node name is $(\times)$ by the structure of d.) Just see that the tree rooted at $f\langle 1\rangle$ is $\mathsf{tree}(d_1)$ and the one at $f\langle 1\rangle\langle 2\rangle$ is $\mathsf{tree}(d_2)$.
- for functions, use the finite unfolding property and the fact the set of pairs is finite, then see, similarly as above, that the correct properties are enforced when navigating the tree.
- for union, negation and empty types, use the preliminary remark.
- for $(d : \alpha)$, just see that $d \in \iota(\alpha)$ and $d \in \mathbb{F}[\![\alpha]\!]$ both mean that the root node of d, which is the node at focus in the formula, bears the label $\iota(\alpha)$.
- for $(d : \mu v.\tau)$, use the property that the interpretation of a fixpoint formula and its unfolding are the same (lemma 4.2 of [10]).

COROLLARY 5.4. $\tau_1 \leqslant \tau_2$ *holds if and only if* $\mathsf{fullform}(\tau_1 \wedge \neg\tau_2)$, *or alternatively* $\mathsf{isd} \wedge \mathsf{form}(\tau_1) \wedge \neg\mathsf{form}(\tau_2)$, *is unsatisfiable.*

5.4 Complexity

LEMMA 5.5. *Provided two types* τ_1 *and* τ_2, *the subtyping relation* $\tau_1 \leqslant \tau_2$ *can be decided in time* $2^{\mathcal{O}(|\tau_1|+|\tau_2|)}$ *where* $|\tau_i|$ *is the size of* τ_i.

Proof (sketch): The logical translation of types performed by the function $\mathsf{form}(\cdot)$ does not involve duplication of subformulas of variable size, therefore $\mathsf{form}(\tau)$ is of linear size with respect to $|\tau|$. Since isd has constant size, the whole translation $\mathsf{fullform}(\tau)$ is linear in terms of $|\tau|$. For testing satisfiability of the logical formula, we use the satisfiability-checking algorithm presented in [10] whose time complexity is $2^{\mathcal{O}(n)}$ in terms of the formula size n.

6. Practical Experiments

In this section we report on some interesting lessons learned from practical experiments with the implementation of the system in order to prove relations in the type algebra.

6.1 Implementation

The algorithm for deciding the subtyping relation has been fully implemented on top of the satisfiability solver introduced in [10]. Our implementation is publicly available. Interaction with the system is offered through a user interface in a web browser. The system is available online at:

`http://wam.inrialpes.fr/websolver/`

A screenshot of the interface is given in Figure 1. The user can either enter a formula through area (1) of Figure 1 or select from pre-loaded analysis tasks offered in area (4) of Figure 1. The level of details displayed by the solver can be adjusted in area (2) of Figure 1 and makes it possible to inspect logical translations and statistics on problem size and the different operation costs. The results of the analysis are displayed in area (3) of Figure 1 together with counter-examples.

In the polymorphic setting, a counter-example, that is, a model satisfying a formula, is in principle, according to the extended semantics, a labelled tree. However, as mentioned in Section 5.2, whenever a formula is satisfiable there always exists an infinity of possible labellings which satisfy it. Therefore, rather than proposing just one labelled tree, the solver gives a minimal tree together with *labelling constraints* representing all labellings which make that particular tree a counter-example. Namely, for each variable α, every node will be labelled with α to indicate that it *must* be labelled with α for the formula to be satisfied, with $\neg\alpha$ to indicate that it *must not* be, or with nothing if label α is irrelevant for that particular node. This allows an easier interpretation of the counter-example in terms of assignments: the subtyping relation fails whenever the assignment for each variable α contains all the trees whose root is marked with α and none of those whose root is marked with $\neg\alpha$.

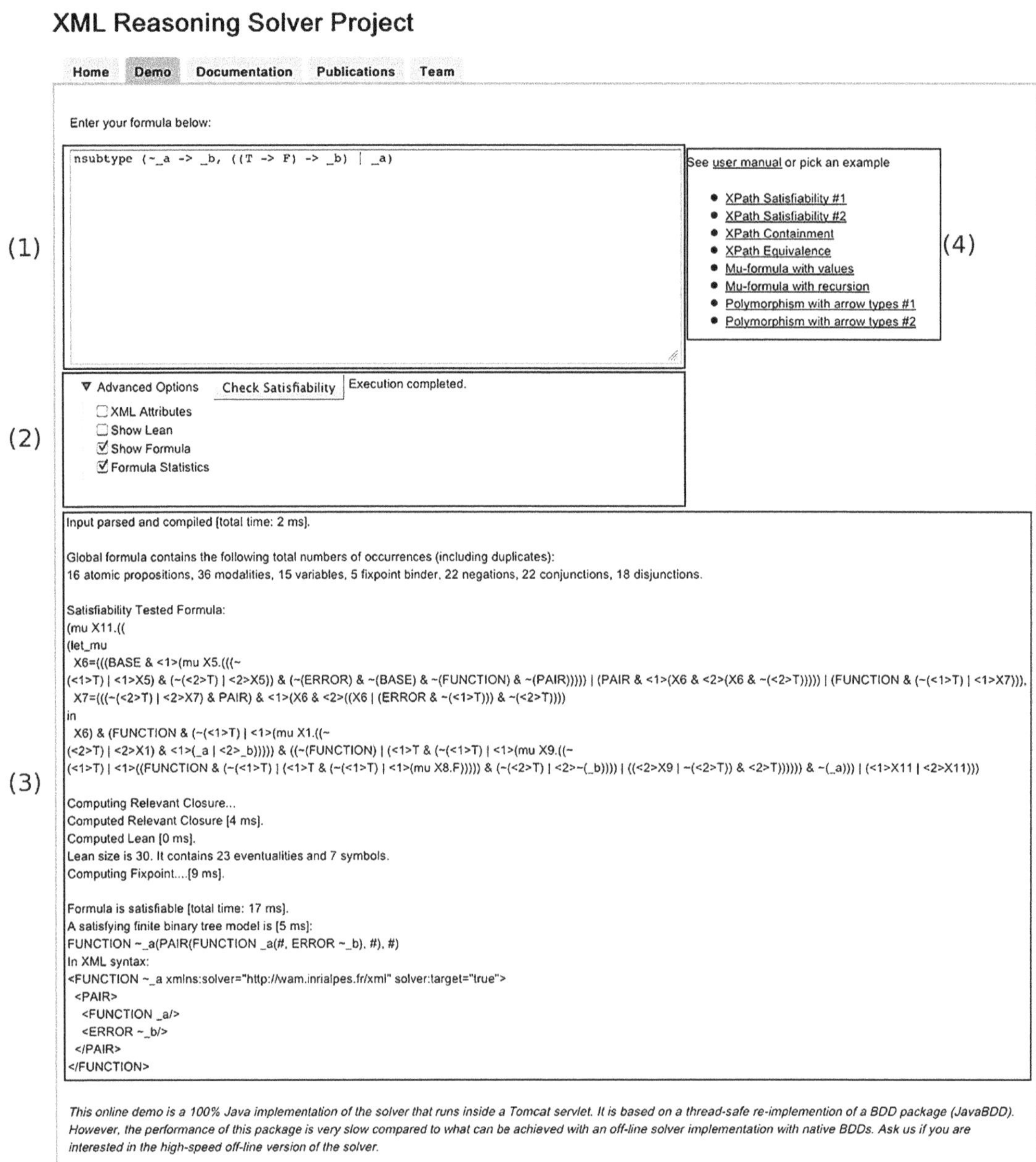

Figure 1. Screenshot of the Interface.

6.2 Concrete Syntax for Type Algebra

All the examples in the subsection that follows can be tested in our online prototype. For this purpose, the following table gives the correspondence between the syntax used in the paper and the syntax that must be used in the implementation. Additionally, the embedding of a base formula of the logic into a base type is provided by curly braces: $\{\varphi\}$ is an abbreviation for isbase$\wedge\langle 1\rangle\,\varphi$.

	Paper Syntax	Implementation Syntax
Type variables	α, β, γ	`_a, _b, _g`
Type constructors	$\times, \to$	`*, ->`
Recursive types	$\mu v.\tau$	`let $v = t in $v`
Basic types	$\mathbf{0}, \mathbf{1}$	`F, T`
Logical connectives	$\wedge, \vee, \neg, \Rightarrow$	`&, |, ~, =>`
Subtyping	$\neg(\tau_1 \leqslant \tau_2)$	`nsubtype(t1,t2)`

6.3 Examples and Discussion

The goal of this subsection is to illustrate through some examples how our logical setting is natural and intuitive for proving subtyping relations. For example, one can prove simple properties such as the one below:

$$(\alpha \to \gamma) \wedge (\beta \to \gamma) \leqslant (\alpha \vee \beta) \to \gamma \tag{6}$$

This is formulated as follows:

```
nsubtype((_a -> _g) & (_b -> _g), (_a | _b) -> _g)
```

which is automatically compiled into the logical formula shown on Figure 2 and given to the satisfiability solver that returns:

```
Formula is unsatisfiable [16 ms].
```

which means that no satisfying tree was found for the formula, or, in other terms, that the negation of the formula is valid. The

```
(mu X8.(((
(let_mu
  X5=(((BASE & <1>(mu X4.(((~(<1>T) | <1>X4) & (~(<2>T) | <2>X4))
     & (~(ERROR) & ~(BASE) & ~(FUNCTION) & ~(PAIR)))))
       | (PAIR & <1>(X5 & <2>(X5 & ~(<2>T))))) | (FUNCTION & (~(<1>T) | <1>X6))),
  X6=(((~(<2>T) | <2>X6) & PAIR) & <1>(X5 & <2>((X5 | (ERROR & ~(<1>T))) & ~(<2>T))))
in
  X5) & ((FUNCTION & (~(<1>T) | <1>(mu X1.((~(<2>T) | <2>X1) & <1>(~(_a) | <2>_g)))))
      & (FUNCTION & (~(<1>T) | <1>(mu X2.((~(<2>T) | <2>X2) & <1>(~(_b) | <2>_g))))))
       & (~(FUNCTION) | (<1>T & (~(<1>T) | <1>(mu X7.((<2>T & (~(<2>T) | <2>X7))
        | (~(<1>T) | <1>((_a | _b) & (~(<2>T) | <2>~(_g)))))))))) | (<1>X8 | <2>X8)))
```

Figure 2. Logical translation tested for satisfiability.

satisfiability solver is seen as a theorem prover since its run built a formal proof that property (6) holds.

Jerôme Vouillon [15] uses simple examples with lists to illustrate polymorphism with recursive types. For instance, consider the type of lists of elements of type α:

$$\tau_{\text{list}} = \mu v.(\alpha \times v) \vee \text{nil}$$

where "nil" is a singleton type. The type of lists of an even number of such elements can be written as:

$$\tau_{\text{even}} = \mu v.(\alpha \times (\alpha \times v)) \vee \text{nil}$$

By giving the following formula to the solver :

```
nsubtype(let $v = (_a * _a * $v) | {nil} in $v,
         let $w= (_a * $w) | {nil} in $w )
```

which is found unsatisfiable, we prove that

$$\tau_{\text{even}} \leqslant \tau_{\text{list}}$$

If we now consider the type of lists of an odd number of elements of type α:

$$\tau_{\text{odd}} = \mu v.(\alpha \times (\alpha \times v)) \vee (\alpha \times \text{nil})$$

we can check additional properties in a similar manner, like:

$$(\tau_{\text{even}} \vee \tau_{\text{odd}} \leqslant \tau_{\text{list}}) \wedge (\tau_{\text{list}} \leqslant \tau_{\text{even}} \vee \tau_{\text{odd}})$$

The following formula corresponds to the example (1) of the introduction:

```
bool() = {true|false};
list() = let $l = (_a * $l) | {nil} in $l;
odd()  = let $o = (_a * _a * $o) | (_a * {nil}) in $o;
even() = let $e = (_a * _a * $e) | {nil} in $e;

nsubtype ( (odd() -> {true}) & (even() -> {false}),
           list() -> bool() )
```

This formula is found unsatisfiable by the solver, which proves the validity of the subtyping statement (1).

Giuseppe Castagna (see section 2.7 of [5]) gives some examples of non-trivial relations that hold in the type algebra. For instance, the reader can check that the types $\mathbf{1} \to \mathbf{0}$ and $\mathbf{0} \to \mathbf{1}$ can be seen as extrema among the function types:

$$\mathbf{1} \to \mathbf{0} \leqslant \alpha \to \beta \quad \text{and} \quad \alpha \to \beta \leqslant \mathbf{0} \to \mathbf{1}$$

Our system also permitted to detect an error in [5] and provided some helpful information to the authors of [5] in order to find the origin of the error and make corrections. Specifically, in a former version of [5], the following relation was considered:

$$(\neg\alpha \to \beta) \leqslant ((\mathbf{1} \to \mathbf{0}) \to \beta) \vee \alpha \qquad (7)$$

Authors explained how this relation was proved by their algorithm. However, by encoding the relation in our system we found that this relation actually does not hold. Specifically, this is formulated as follows in our system:

```
nsubtype (~_a -> _b, ((T -> F) -> _b) | _a)
```

The satisfiability solver, when fed this formula, returns the following counter-example:

```
FUNCTION ~_a (PAIR(FUNCTION _a (#,  ~_b ERROR), #), #)
```

`FUNCTION` represents $(\to)$ and `PAIR` represents $(\times)$. This is a binary tree representation of the n-ary tree

$$(\to)_{\neg\alpha}[(\times)[(\to)_{\alpha}[\epsilon] :: \Omega :: \epsilon] :: \epsilon]$$

which corresponds to the domain element

$$\{(\{\}_{\alpha}, \Omega)\}_{\neg\alpha}.$$

The inner $(\to)$ node has no children and thus represents the function which always diverges: $\{\}$. More precisely, it represents *a* copy f of this function that belongs to the interpretation of α. The root $(\to)$ node then represents a function which is *not* in $[\![\alpha]\!]$ and which to f associates an error, while diverging on any other input.

Now, why is it a counter-example to (7)? As the function diverges but on one input f and that input is in $[\![\alpha]\!]$, it is vacuously true that on all inputs in $[\![\neg\alpha]\!]$ for which it returns a result, this result is in $[\![\beta]\!]$. Thus it does have the type on the left-hand side. However, it does not have type α, nor does it have type $((\mathbf{1} \to \mathbf{0}) \to \beta)$. Indeed, f does have type $\mathbf{1} \to \mathbf{0}$ and our counter-example function associates to it an error, which is not in $[\![\beta]\!]$.

7. Related Work

We review below related works while recalling how the introduction of XML progressively renewed the interests in parametric polymorphism.

The seminal work by Hosoya, Vouillon and Pierce on a type system for XML [12] applied the theory of regular expression types and finite tree automata in the context of XML. The resulting language XDuce [11] is a strongly typed language featuring recursive, product, intersection, union, and complement types. The subtyping relation is decided through a reduction to containment of finite tree automata, which is known to be in EXPTIME. This work does not support function types nor polymorphism, but provided a ground for further research.

In particular, Frisch, Castagna and Benzaken provide a gentle introduction to semantic subtyping in [9]. Semantic subtyping focuses on a set-theoretic interpretation, as opposed to traditional subtyping through direct syntactic rules. Our logical modeling presented in Section 4 naturally follows the semantic subtyping approach as the underlying logic has a set-theoretic semantics. Frisch, Castagna and Benzaken added function types to the semantic subtyping performed by XDuce's type system. This notably resulted in the CDuce language [2]. However, CDuce does not support type variables and thus lacks polymorphism.

Vouillon studied polymorphism in the context of regular types with arrow types in [15]. Specifically, he introduced a pattern algebra and a subtyping relation defined by a set of syntactic inference rules. A semantic interpretation of subtyping is given by ground substitution of variables in patterns. The type algebra has the union connective but lacks negation and intersection. The resulting type system is thus less general than ours.

Polymorphism was also the focus of the later work found in [13]. In [5], it is explained that at that time a semantically defined polymorphic subtyping looked out of reach, even in the restrictive setting of [11], which did not account for higher-order functions. This is why [13] fell back on a somewhat syntactic approach linked to pattern-matching that seemed difficult to extend to higher-order functions. Our work shows however that such an extension was possible using similar basic ideas, only slightly more abstract.

The most closely related work is the one found in [5], in the same proceedings as the current paper, which solves the problem of defining subtyping semantically in the polymorphic case for the first time, and addresses the problem of its decision through an ad-hoc and multi-step algorithm, which was only recently proved to terminate in all cases. Our approach also addresses the problem of deciding their subtyping relation and solves it through a more direct, generic, natural and extensible approach since our solution relies on a modeling into a well-known modal logic (the μ-calculus) and on using a satisfiability solver such as the one proposed in [10]. This logical connection also opens the way for extending polymorphic types with several features found in modal logics.

The work of [3] follows the same spirit than ours: typechecking is subcontracted to an external logical solver. An SMT-solver is used to extend a type-checker for the language Dminor (a core dialect for M) with refinement type and type-tests. The type-checking relies on a semantic subtyping interpretation but neither function types nor polymorphism are considered. Therefore, their work is incomparable to ours.

The present work heavily relies on the work presented in [10] since we repurpose the satisfiability-checking algorithm of [10] for deciding the subtyping relation. The goal pursued in [10] was very different in spirit: the goal was to decide containment of XPath queries in the presence of regular tree types. To this end, the decidability of a logic with converse for finite ordered trees is proved in a time complexity which is a simple exponential of the size of the formula. The present work builds on these results for solving semantic subtyping in the polymorphic case.

8. Conclusion

The main contribution of this paper is to define a logical encoding of the subtyping relation defined in [5], yielding a decision algorithm for it. We prove that this relation is decidable with an upper-bound time complexity of $2^{(n)}$, where n is the size of types being checked. In addition, we provide an effective implementation of the decision procedure that works well in practice.

This work illustrates a tight integration between a functional language type-checker and a logical solver. The type-checker uses the logical solver for deciding subtyping, which in turn provides counter-examples (whenever subtyping does not hold) to the type-checker. These counterexamples are valuable for programmers as they represent evidence that the relation does not hold. As a result, our solver represents a very attractive back-end for functional programming languages type-checkers.

This result pushes the integration between programming languages and logical solvers to an advanced level. The proposed logical approach is not only capable of modeling higher order functions, but it is also capable of expressing values from semantic domains that correspond to monadic second-order logics such as XML tree types. This shows that such logical solvers can become the core of XML-centric functional languages type-checkers such as those used in CDuce or XDuce.

Acknowledgments. We are thankful to Giuseppe Castagna for bringing our attention to the problem of subtyping with arrow types in the polymorphic case. He gave us precious insights for the precise formulation of the problem, that he also addressed in a paper published in the current proceedings. Several people also discussed or exchanged with us about subtyping and polymorphism: Zhiwu Xu, Véronique Benzaken and Kim Nguyen.

References

[1] M. Benedikt and J. Cheney. Destabilizers and independence of XML updates. *Proceedings of the VLDB Endowment*, 3(1):906–917, 2010.

[2] V. Benzaken, G. Castagna, and A. Frisch. CDuce: an XML-centric general-purpose language. In *Proceedings of the 8th international conference on functional programming (ICFP '03)*, pages 51–63, Upsala, Sweden, 2003. `http://doi.acm.org/10.1145/944705.944711`.

[3] G. M. Bierman, A. D. Gordon, C. Hriţcu, and D. Langworthy. Semantic subtyping with an SMT solver. In *Proceedings of the 15th international conference on functional programming (ICFP '10)*, pages 105–116, Baltimore, MD, USA, 2010. `http://doi.acm.org/10.1145/1863543.1863560`.

[4] S. Boag, D. Chamberlin, M. F. Fernández, D. Florescu, J. Robie, and J. Siméon. XQuery 1.0: An XML query language, W3C recommendation, 2007.

[5] G. Castagna and Z. Xu. Set-theoretic foundation of parametric polymorphism and subtyping. In *Proceedings of the 16th international conference on functional programming (ICFP '11)*, Tokyo, 2011.

[6] J. Clark and S. DeRose. XML path language (XPath) version 1.0, W3C recommendation, 1999. `http://www.w3.org/TR/1999/REC-xpath-19991116`.

[7] L. M. de Moura and N. Bjørner. Z3: An efficient SMT solver. In *Proceedings of the 14th international conference on tools and algorithms for the construction and analysis of systems (TACAS '08)*, pages 337–340, Budapest, 2008. `http://dx.doi.org/10.1007/978-3-540-78800-3_24`.

[8] D. Engovatov and J. Robie. XQuery 3.0 requirements, W3C working draft, 2010. `http://www.w3.org/TR/xquery-30-requirements`

[9] A. Frisch, G. Castagna, and V. Benzaken. Semantic subtyping: dealing set-theoretically with function, union, intersection, and negation types. *Journal of the ACM*, 55(4):1–64, 2008.

[10] P. Genevès, N. Layaïda, and A. Schmitt. Efficient static analysis of XML paths and types. In *Proceedings of the 28th conference on programming language design and implementation (PLDI '07)*, pages 342–351, San Diego, CA, USA, 2007. `http://doi.acm.org/10.1145/1250734.1250773`.

[11] H. Hosoya and B. C. Pierce. XDuce: A statically typed XML processing language. *ACM Transactions on Internet Technology*, 3(2):117–148, 2003. `http://doi.acm.org/10.1145/767193.767195`.

[12] H. Hosoya, J. Vouillon, and B. C. Pierce. Regular expression types for XML. *ACM Transactions on Programming Languages and Systems*, 27:46–90, 2005. `http://doi.acm.org/10.1145/1053468.1053470`.

[13] H. Hosoya, A. Frisch, and G. Castagna. Parametric polymorphism for XML. *ACM Transactions on Programming Languages and Systems*, 32(1):1–56, 2009.

[14] J. C. Reynolds. Types, abstraction and parametric polymorphism. In *IFIP Congress*, pages 513–523, 1983.

[15] J. Vouillon. Polymorphic regular tree types and patterns. In *Proceedings of the 33rd symposium on principles of programming languages (POPL '06)*, pages 103–114, Charleston, SC, USA, 2006. `http://doi.acm.org/10.1145/1111037.1111047`.

[16] P. Wadler. Theorems for free! In *Proceedings of the 4th international conference on functional programming languages and computer architecture (FPCA '89)*, pages 347–359, London, 1989. `http://doi.acm.org/10.1145/99370.99404`.

Balanced Trees Inhabiting Functional Parallel Programming

Akimasa Morihata
Tohoku University
morihata@riec.tohoku.ac.jp

Kiminori Matsuzaki
Kochi University of Technology
matsuzaki.kiminori@kochi-tech.ac.jp

Abstract

Divide-and-conquer is an important technique in parallel programming. However, algebraic data structures do not fit divide-and-conquer parallelism. For example, the usual pointer-based implementation of lists cannot efficiently be divided at their middle, which prevents us from developing list-iterating divide-and-conquer parallel programs. Tree-iterating programs possibly face a similar problem, because trees might be ill-balanced and list-like shapes. This paper examines parallel programming based on balanced trees: we consider balanced-tree structures and develop recursive functions on them. By virtue of their balancing nature, either bottom-up or top-down recursive functions exploit divide-and-conquer parallelism. Our main contribution is to demonstrate the promise of this approach. We propose a way of systematically developing balanced trees from parallel algorithms, and then, we show that efficient parallel programs on them can be developed by equational reasoning powered by Reynolds' relational parametricity. We consider functions that operate either lists or binary trees, and show that our methods can uniformly deal with both cases. The developed parallel programs are purely functional, correct by construction, and sometimes even simpler than known algorithms.

Categories and Subject Descriptors D.1. [*Programming Techniques*]: Concurrent Programming—Parallel Programming; D.1.1 [*Programming Techniques*]: Applicative (Functional) Programming; E.1 [*Data Structures*]: Trees

General Terms Theory, Algorithms

Keywords Balanced Tree, Divide-and-conquer Parallelism, Equational Reasoning, Parametric Polymorphism

1. Introduction

Parallel programming is an important concept now. Efficient parallel programs are necessary to better utilize modern multi-core and multi-CPU machines. However, efficient parallel programs are difficult to develop. There are several reasons for this, but one is that our favorite data structures and programming idioms, namely linear lists, *foldr* and *foldl*, are *not* suitable for parallelism. They are inherently sequential. Parallel programming therefore requires other data structures and idioms.

To see the gap between standard programs and those suitable for parallel evaluation, let us consider calculating the total sum of list elements.

$$\begin{aligned} sum_{\mathsf{List}}\ [\,] &= 0 \\ sum_{\mathsf{List}}\ (a : x) &= a + sum_{\mathsf{List}}\ x \end{aligned}$$

Regrettably, this accustomed program is not a parallel program. There are no expressions that can be evaluated in parallel. To achieve good parallelism, we may think of the divide-and-conquer summation.

$$\begin{aligned} sum_{\mathsf{List}}\ [\,] &= 0 \\ sum_{\mathsf{List}}\ [a] &= a \\ sum_{\mathsf{List}}\ (x +\!\!+\ y) &= sum_{\mathsf{List}}\ x + sum_{\mathsf{List}}\ y \end{aligned}$$

We borrow $+\!\!+$ from Haskell to denote list concatenation. The intended meaning of this pseudoprogram is "If the input consists of more than one element, we split it in the middle, simultaneously compute the summations of sublists, and then merge the two results." However, it is not a real program because conventional functional programming languages do not support pattern-matching by $+\!\!+$. An "actual" program should be something like the following:

$$\begin{aligned} sum_{\mathsf{List}}\ [\,] &= 0 \\ sum_{\mathsf{List}}\ [a] &= a \\ sum_{\mathsf{List}}\ z &= \mathbf{let}\ (x, y) = splitAt\ (div\ (length\ z)\ 2)\ z \\ &\quad\ \mathbf{in}\ sum_{\mathsf{List}}\ x + sum_{\mathsf{List}}\ y \end{aligned}$$

Here, we split the input list in the middle by using *splitAt*. Now this definition brings an opportunity for parallel evaluation—we can calculate $sum\ x$ and $sum\ y$ in parallel. However, this is not satisfactory. *splitAt* will form a bottleneck because its calculation cannot be parallelized.

Note that we might face a similar problem even when we are manipulating trees. Consider the summation on binary trees.

$$\begin{aligned} sum_{\mathsf{Tree}}\ (\mathsf{Tip}\ a) &= a \\ sum_{\mathsf{Tree}}\ (\mathsf{Bin}\ l\ a\ r) &= sum_{\mathsf{Tree}}\ l + a + sum_{\mathsf{Tree}}\ r \end{aligned}$$

This appears to be a good parallel program because we can simultaneously evaluate $sum_{\mathsf{Tree}}\ l$ and $sum_{\mathsf{Tree}}\ r$, but it is not efficient in general. The program cannot achieve parallel speedups when the input is a list-like tree whose left subtrees are all leaves.

As seen, there are gaps between standard functional programs and parallel programs. One of the most critical gaps involves data structures. The usual pointer-based structures such as lists are not suitable for parallel programming. They do not provide an efficient way of dividing themselves, and therefore, computations on them cannot be efficiently divided into a reasonably sized tasks that can be evaluated in parallel.

To resolve this problem, we focus on balanced trees. We adopt balanced trees as abstract data structures that encapsulate divide-and-conquer parallelism, and develop recursive functions on them as basic components for functional parallel programming. Intuitively, this approach regards $+\!\!+$ as a constructor. Then, sum_{List} defined by using $+\!\!+$ is a conventional structural recursion on the tree, and the flexibility of splitting the input to the sublists (as $x +\!\!+\ y$) enables us to let the tree balanced.

ICFP'11, September 19–21, 2011, Tokyo, Japan.

This approach, considering recursive functions on balanced trees, has several strong points. First of all, it isolates parallel algorithmic issues from the program description. The balanced trees implicitly guarantees parallel speedups with respect to the number of processors, and we do not need to worry about parallelism when developing programs. Moreover, we may be able to implement balanced trees by known self-balancing trees, and then their dynamic rebalancing enables us to add elements to or remove elements from them without seriously affecting parallel speedups.

Note that recognizing $+\!\!+$ as a constructor is not very new. This view has been taken by Hu et al. [1998, 2002] for formalizing functional parallel programming patterns, and a balanced-tree representation of lists is also employed in an implementation of a parallel functional programming language [Fluet et al. 2008]. However, it has not been clarified whether this approach scales up. There are several questions that have not been resolved yet, such as whether it can deal with functions on structures other than lists, whether it can encapsulate complicated parallel algorithms, and whether we can effectively utilize them.

In this paper, we describe an experiment carried out to demonstrate the promise of this approach. We propose a method of systematically developing balanced tree structures and parallel programs on them. The method primarily consists of the following two parts.

- We propose a systematic way of relating parallel algorithms to balanced trees. Given a parallel algorithm and its input, we relate them to a tree structure on which the parallel algorithm forms a structural recursion. Its height is guaranteed to be less than the number of parallel steps of performing the computation; therefore, it is balanced if the original algorithm exploits much parallelism. Moreover, flexibility in parallel algorithms, such as flexibility in dividing the underlying structure, brings rebalancing of the derived balanced trees. For instance, we show that a parallel tree contraction algorithm by Abrahamson et al. [1989], which has been well studied as a basis of developing efficient parallel tree operations, derives a variant of the directed topology tree [Frederickson 1997], which is a self-balancing tree structure for retaining binary trees.
- We demonstrate systematic development of parallel programs on the balanced trees. Our vehicle is equational reasoning powered by Reynolds' relational parametricity [Reynolds 1983; Wadler 1989]. It enables us to systematically develop parallel programs that are correct by construction. Most notably, we develop new efficient, purely functional implementations of the parallel tree accumulations by Gibbons et al. [1994], whose original implementations are involved intricate pointer manipulations.

The most characteristic feature is that our method does not rely on certain structures of computations or data. We demonstrate that it can uniformly deal with computations on both of lists (Section 3) and binary trees (Sections 4 and 5).

2. Preliminary

We consider typed, purely functional programs with the Hindley-Milner type system. We assume all computations terminate without raising any errors regardless of their reduction orders.

We use Haskell [Peyton Jones 2003] to describe programs. We use Greek letters, $\alpha, \beta, \ldots$, for type variables, and capital English letters, $A, B, \ldots$, for meta variables ranging over types. $id :: \forall \alpha.\, \alpha \to \alpha$ denotes the identity function. Operator $(\circ) :: \forall \alpha, \beta, \gamma.\, (\beta \to \gamma) \to (\alpha \to \beta) \to \alpha \to \gamma$ denotes the function composition, i.e., $(f \circ g)\ x = f\ (g\ x)$. An underline, $\_$, denotes a "don't care" pattern that matches any value and provides no binding.

We adopt EREW PRAM (exclusive-read exclusive-write parallel random access machines) as our parallel computation model. Unless otherwise stated, P denotes the number of processors.

3. Balanced Trees for Parallel List Operations

First, let us consider parallel evaluation of list operations. We extract the computation structure of divide-and-conquer summations (Section 3.1), develop a balanced-tree structure from it (Section 3.2), confirm that the structure supports efficient dynamic rebalancing (Section 3.3), and develop parallel programs on it (Section 3.4). This section might appear to be rather trivial. In the next two sections, we will consider tree operations and see that this method scales up to a more complicated case.

3.1 List-homomorphism Scheme

Our starting point is the divide-and-conquer summation. We ignore the empty list for simplicity.

$$\begin{array}{lcl} sum_{\mathsf{List}}\ [a] & = & a \\ sum_{\mathsf{List}}\ (x +\!\!+ y) & = & sum_{\mathsf{List}}\ x + sum_{\mathsf{List}}\ y \end{array}$$

Usually, a function calculates values by aggregating information in the input structure. We focus on this aggregation structure. sum_{List} just extracts the element from each singleton list, and merges the results of independent sublists by addition. By abstracting out the concrete computations, we obtain the following "skeleton", known as list homomorphisms [Bird 1987].

$$\begin{array}{lcl} hom :: \forall \alpha, \beta.\, (\beta \to \beta \to \beta) \to (\alpha \to \beta) \to [\alpha] \to \beta \\ hom\ (\oplus)\ f\ [a] & = & f\ a \\ hom\ (\oplus)\ f\ (x +\!\!+ y) & = & hom\ (\oplus)\ f\ x \oplus hom\ (\oplus)\ f\ y \end{array}$$

We assume associativity of $\oplus$ so as to make the latter equation meaningful.

Note that a list homomorphism does not specify any strategy for dividing the input list. It is natural to split the list in the middle. However, other strategies are worth considering in general, for example when computational units are heterogeneous. In short, a list homomorphism represents a set of functions.

Let us formally specify functions that correspond to list homomorphisms. Apparently, each of these functions, say h, should have the following polymorphic type[1]:

$$h :: \forall \beta.\, (\beta \to \beta \to \beta) \to (A \to \beta) \to [A] \to \beta.$$

This polymorphic type is not sufficient to characterize list homomorphisms. For example, the following h_{Bad} could have this polymorphic type but $h_{\mathrm{Bad}}\ (+)\ id \neq hom\ (+)\ id = sum_{\mathsf{List}}$.

$$\begin{array}{lcl} h_{\mathrm{Bad}}\ (\oplus)\ f\ [a] & = & f\ a \\ h_{\mathrm{Bad}}\ (\oplus)\ f\ (a : x) & = & f\ a \oplus (f\ a \oplus h_{\mathrm{Bad}}\ x) \end{array}$$

Therefore, we should impose some restrictions. A natural idea is to exclude those that duplicate, discard, or disorder elements. In other words, as the following equation describes, the function should be able to put back the original list if no computation is performed.

$$h\ (+\!\!+)\ (\lambda a \to [a])\ x = x$$

This requirement is actually sufficient. Reynolds' relational parametricity [Reynolds 1983; Wadler 1989] explains that h satisfies

[1] Functions that have more generic types are also acceptable. Note that A does not need to be polymorphic. Specializing h to A could be worthwhile because we may change the strategy of splitting the input according to A. For example, if A consists of structures such as trees, we may take account of their sizes.

the following property from its type.

$$g\ (l \oplus r) = g\ l \otimes g\ r\ \Rightarrow\ g\ (h\ (\oplus)\ f\ x) = h\ (\otimes)\ (g\ \circ f)\ x$$

Then, it is straightforward to prove $h\ (+)\ id = sum_{\mathsf{List}}$.

$$\begin{array}{l} h\ (+)\ id\ x = sum_{\mathsf{List}}\ x \\ \quad \Leftrightarrow\ \{ \text{the requirement} \} \\ \quad\quad h\ (+)\ id\ x = sum_{\mathsf{List}}\ (h\ (+\!\!+)\ (\lambda a \rightarrow [a])\ x) \\ \quad \Leftarrow\ \{ \text{parametricity} \} \\ \quad\quad sum_{\mathsf{List}}\ (l +\!\!+ r) = sum_{\mathsf{List}}\ l + sum_{\mathsf{List}}\ r \\ \quad\quad\ \wedge\ sum_{\mathsf{List}} \circ (\lambda a \rightarrow [a]) = id \\ \quad \Leftrightarrow\ \{ \text{definition of } sum_{\mathsf{List}} \} \\ \quad\quad \text{True} \end{array}$$

We have successfully characterized list homomorphisms by using a set of functions. We call them *list-homomorphism schemes.*

DEFINITION 3.1. *Polymorphic function*

$$h :: \forall \beta.\ (\beta \rightarrow \beta \rightarrow \beta) \rightarrow (A \rightarrow \beta) \rightarrow [A] \rightarrow \beta$$

is said to be a list-homomorphism scheme *if it satisfies*

$$h\ (+\!\!+)\ (\lambda a \rightarrow [a])\ x = x$$

for any list x. □

3.2 Join Lists

Next, we derive a balanced tree structure. This is easy; supplying constructors to list-homomorphism schemes is sufficient. This tree structure is called *join (or append) lists* [Hu et al. 1998, 2002].

$$\textbf{data}\ \mathsf{JList}\ \alpha = \mathsf{Single}\ \alpha\ \mid\ \mathsf{Join}\ (\mathsf{JList}\ \alpha)\ (\mathsf{JList}\ \alpha)$$

Given a list, say x, we construct its join list representation as h Join Single x by using a list-homomorphism scheme, h. We can restore the original list from its join-list representation.

$$\begin{array}{l} j2l :: \forall \alpha.\ \mathsf{JList}\ \alpha \rightarrow [\alpha] \\ j2l\ (\mathsf{Single}\ a)\ =\ [a] \\ j2l\ (\mathsf{Join}\ l\ r)\ \ =\ j2l\ l +\!\!+ j2l\ r \end{array}$$

Interestingly, $j2l$ provides an exact characterization of list-homomorphism schemes. This fact may justify their definition.

THEOREM 3.2. *Polymorphic function*

$$h :: \forall \beta.\ (\beta \rightarrow \beta \rightarrow \beta) \rightarrow (A \rightarrow \beta) \rightarrow [A] \rightarrow \beta$$

is a list-homomorphism scheme if and only if the following equation holds for any list x.

$$j2l\ (h\ \mathsf{Join}\ \mathsf{Single}\ x) = x$$

PROOF. Note that it is sufficient to prove the following equation.

$$h\ (+\!\!+)\ (\lambda a \rightarrow [a])\ x = j2l\ (h\ \mathsf{Join}\ \mathsf{Single}\ x)$$

It can be proved from the parametricity.

$$\begin{array}{l} h\ (+\!\!+)\ (\lambda a \rightarrow [a])\ x = j2l\ (h\ \mathsf{Join}\ \mathsf{Single}\ x) \\ \quad \Leftarrow\ \{ \text{parametricity} \} \\ \quad\quad j2l\ (\mathsf{Join}\ l\ r) = j2l\ l +\!\!+ j2l\ r\ \wedge\ j2l\ (\mathsf{Single}\ a) = [a] \\ \quad \Leftrightarrow\ \{ \text{definition of } j2l \} \\ \quad\quad \text{True} \end{array}$$

□

Theorem 3.2 implies another view of join lists: Single and Join are the *frozen representations* [Kühnemann et al. 2001; Voigtländer 2002] of $(+\!\!+)$ and $(\lambda a \rightarrow [a])$, respectively, and $j2l$ is the *thawing* function for them. Join lists crystallize the computational structure of a list-homomorphism scheme.

It is worth noting that there are equivalent join lists that represent the same list, i.e., thy result in the same list by $j2l$. For example, both of the following two join lists

$$\begin{array}{l} \mathsf{Join}\ (\mathsf{Join}\ (\mathsf{Single}\ 1)\ (\mathsf{Single}\ 2))\ (\mathsf{Single}\ 3) \\ \mathsf{Join}\ (\mathsf{Single}\ 1)\ (\mathsf{Join}\ (\mathsf{Single}\ 2)\ (\mathsf{Single}\ 3)) \end{array}$$

represent $[1, 2, 3]$ and are thus equivalent. This flexibility corresponds to the possibility of choosing a list-homomorphism scheme. In fact, this flexibility is the key to efficient parallel computations. We can use divide-and-conquer parallelism by taking a balanced representation from among those that are equivalent.

3.3 Balancing Join Lists

It is not difficult to obtain a balanced join-list representation of a list. Given a list homomorphism scheme that finishes its computation in k parallel steps, we can obtain a join list whose height is k. Therefore, the following theorem holds.

THEOREM 3.3. *Given a list of length* N *implemented by an array, we can obtain its join list representation whose height is* $\lceil \log_2 \mathrm{N} \rceil$ *in time* $\mathrm{O}(\mathrm{N}/\mathrm{P} + \log \mathrm{P})$. □

Actually, we can do more—we can efficiently modify the structure while maintaining its balance. It is apparent from the definition of $j2l$ and Theorem 3.2 that join lists are only sensitive to the order of leaves. Therefore, we can implement join lists by self-balancing binary search trees. For example, by using biased search trees [Bent et al. 1985], we can prove the following theorem.

THEOREM 3.4. *Given a list of length* N, *there exists its join list representation whose height is* $\mathrm{O}(\log \mathrm{N})$ *and that can both remove its sublist and append another list in time* $\mathrm{O}(\log \mathrm{N})$, *which results in a join list representation of height* $\mathrm{O}(\mathrm{N})$. □

Note that the time complexity of rebalancing, $\mathrm{O}(\log \mathrm{N})$, is adequate even though it is not a parallel algorithm. Even if computations on join lists finish in time $\mathrm{O}(\mathrm{N}/\mathrm{P})$, which is really ideal, the rebalancing cost is not dominant if $\mathrm{P} \in \mathrm{O}(\mathrm{N}/\log \mathrm{N})$.

Another balanced tree structure called a rope [Boehm et al. 1995] is adopted in a functional parallel programming language, Manticore [Fluet et al. 2008]. Compared to biased search trees, ropes have smaller hidden constants and support more efficient concatenation, while their rebalancing is more costly.

3.4 Developing Programs on Join Lists

Because we can keep join lists balanced, either bottom-up or top-down recursive functions on them will achieve good parallel speedups. However, we should not use arbitrary recursive functions. If functions do not respect the balancing operations, we cannot take advantage of the balancing nature. In other words, we require that each function should result in the same value for all equivalent join lists.

We propose implementing join lists as an abstract datatype that possesses several higher-order functions that form a safe interface. It forces us to respect the equivalence on join lists. An additional benefit is that it conceals the concrete structure of the tree and thus, can implicitly balance itself.

The main issue is the interface design. Here we refer to *algorithmic skeletons* [Cole 1989], which are well-designed parallel programming patterns. Standard list-operating skeletons include *map*, *filter*, *foldr*, and *scanr*. We develop their implementations on join lists as follows. Given function $g :: [A] \rightarrow B$, we would like to obtain its join-list version $g_{\mathrm{J}} :: \mathsf{JList}\ A \rightarrow B$ that simulates the computation of g on join lists.

$$g_{\mathrm{J}} = g \circ j2l$$

From this characteristic equation, we work out a recursive definition of g_{J} by equational reasoning. Note that g_{J} developed in this manner results in the same value for all equivalent join lists.

It is worth noting that our derivations are routine for fusion (also known as deforestation) transformation based on the classic unfolding-folding method [Burstall and Darlington 1977; Wadler

1990]: we unfold function definitions so as to distribute their computations and then try to match the expression to the characteristic equation so as to obtain a recursive definition. There are no parallel programming issues.

3.4.1 List Homomorphisms

Several skeletons, for example *map* and *filter*, are instances of list homomorphisms. It is easy to implement list homomorphisms on join lists. From the strategy above, we can immediately obtain the following join-list version.

$$\begin{aligned} hom_{\mathsf{J}}\ (\oplus)\ f\ (\mathsf{Single}\ a) &= f\ a \\ hom_{\mathsf{J}}\ (\oplus)\ f\ (\mathsf{Join}\ x\ y) &= hom_{\mathsf{J}}\ (\oplus)\ f\ x \oplus hom_{\mathsf{J}}\ (\oplus)\ f\ y \end{aligned}$$

3.4.2 *foldr*

A more nontrivial example is *foldr*.

$$\begin{aligned} foldr\ f\ e\ [a] &= f\ a\ e \\ foldr\ f\ e\ (a : x) &= f\ a\ (foldr\ f\ e\ x) \end{aligned}$$

foldr is not always suitable for evaluation on join lists. We derive a sufficient condition by working out its join-list version.

$$\begin{aligned} foldr_{\mathsf{J}}\ f\ e\ (\mathsf{Single}\ a) &= \{\ \text{definition of } foldr_{\mathsf{J}}\ \} \\ &\quad\ foldr\ f\ e\ (j2l\ (\mathsf{Single}\ a)) \\ &= \{\ \text{definitions of } j2l \text{ and } foldr\ \} \\ &\quad\ f\ a\ e \end{aligned}$$

$$\begin{aligned} & foldr_{\mathsf{J}}\ f\ e\ (\mathsf{Join}\ l\ r) \\ &= \{\ \text{definition of } foldr_{\mathsf{J}}\ \} \\ &\quad foldr\ f\ e\ (j2l\ (\mathsf{Join}\ l\ r)) \\ &= \{\ \text{definition of } j2l\ \} \\ &\quad foldr\ f\ e\ (j2l\ l +\!\!+\ j2l\ r) \\ &= \{\ \text{claim: } foldr\ f\ e\ (x +\!\!+\ y) = foldr\ f\ (foldr\ f\ e\ y)\ x\ \} \\ &\quad foldr\ f\ (foldr\ f\ e\ (j2l\ r))\ (j2l\ l) \\ &= \{\ \text{let } foldr'_{\mathsf{J}}\ f\ x\ e = foldr_{\mathsf{J}}\ f\ e\ x\ \} \\ &\quad (foldr'_{\mathsf{J}}\ f\ l \circ foldr'_{\mathsf{J}}\ f\ r)\ e \end{aligned}$$

Confirming the claim is straightforward. Now the reasoning shows that $foldr'_{\mathsf{J}}$ rather than $foldr_{\mathsf{J}}$ is more suitable for bottom-up parallel evaluation on join lists. $foldr_{\mathsf{J}}$ can be evaluated in a bottom-up manner if we can efficiently implement the function composition operation.

THEOREM 3.5 (Context preservation thereom [Chin et al. 1998; Morihata and Matsuzaki 2010]). *$foldr_{\mathsf{J}}\ f\ e$ can be computed by a bottom-up divide-and-conquer parallel algorithm provided that there exists a set of constant-time functions $\mathcal{F}$ such that $f_1, f_2 \in \mathcal{F}$ implies $f_1 \circ f_2 \in \mathcal{F}$.* □

3.4.3 *scanr*

So far, we have considered bottom-up computations on join lists. As the last example, we consider *scanr* and demonstrate that it results in a more interesting parallel program that includes a top-down sweep on join lists.

$$\begin{aligned} scanr\ f\ e\ [\_] &= [e] \\ scanr\ f\ e\ (\_ : x) &= [foldr\ f\ e\ x] : scanr\ f\ e\ x \end{aligned}$$

We may consider developing $scanr_{\mathsf{J}}$ such that $scanr_{\mathsf{J}}\ f\ e = scanr\ f\ e \circ j2l$. Yet, it seems more useful if $scanr_{\mathsf{J}}$ returns join lists. Thus, we define $scanr_{\mathsf{J}}$ as follows.

$$j2l \circ scanr_{\mathsf{J}}\ f\ e = scanr\ f\ e \circ j2l$$

Let us now work out $scanr_{\mathsf{J}}$.

$$\begin{aligned} j2l\ (scanr_{\mathsf{J}}\ f\ e\ (\mathsf{Single}\ \_)) &= \{\ \text{definition of } scanr_{\mathsf{J}}\ \} \\ &\quad\ scanr\ f\ e\ (j2l\ (\mathsf{Single}\ \_)) \\ &= \{\ \text{definitions of } j2l \text{ and } foldr\ \} \\ &\quad\ [e] \end{aligned}$$

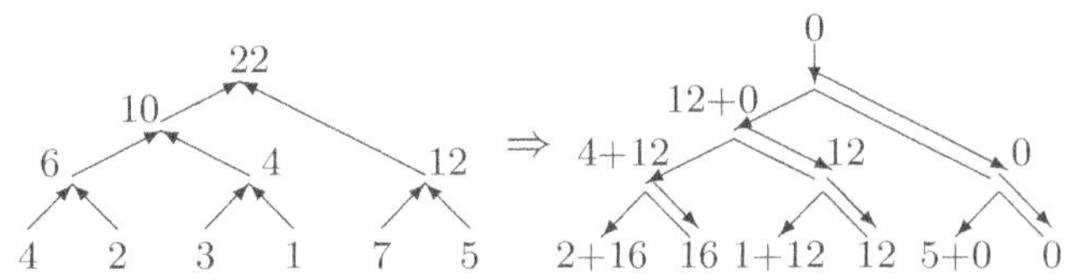

Figure 1. Parallel evaluation of $scanr_{\mathsf{J}}\ (+)\ 0$ on a join-list representation of $[4, 2, 3, 1, 7, 5]$: a bottom-up calculation of $foldr'_{\mathsf{J}}\ (+)$ (the left picture) is followed by a top-down distribution (the right picture) of the calculated values.

$$\begin{aligned} & j2l\ (scanr_{\mathsf{J}}\ f\ e\ (\mathsf{Join}\ l\ r)) \\ &= \{\ \text{definition of } scanr_{\mathsf{J}}\ \} \\ &\quad scanr\ f\ e\ (j2l\ (\mathsf{Join}\ l\ r)) \\ &= \{\ \text{definition of } j2l\ \} \\ &\quad scanr\ f\ e\ (j2l\ l +\!\!+\ j2l\ r) \\ &= \{\ \text{claim (described below)}\ \} \\ &\quad scanr\ f\ (foldr\ f\ e\ (j2l\ r))\ (j2l\ l) +\!\!+\ scanr\ f\ e\ (j2l\ r) \\ &= \{\ \text{definition of } foldr'_{\mathsf{J}}\ \} \\ &\quad scanr\ f\ (foldr'_{\mathsf{J}}\ f\ r\ e)\ (j2l\ l) +\!\!+\ scanr\ f\ e\ (j2l\ r) \\ &= \{\ \text{definition of } scanr_{\mathsf{J}}\ \} \\ &\quad j2l\ (scanr_{\mathsf{J}}\ f\ (foldr'_{\mathsf{J}}\ f\ r\ e)\ l) +\!\!+\ j2l\ (scanr_{\mathsf{J}}\ f\ e\ r) \\ &= \{\ \text{definition of } j2l\ \} \\ &\quad j2l\ (\mathsf{Join}\ (scanr_{\mathsf{J}}\ f\ (foldr'_{\mathsf{J}}\ f\ r\ e)\ l)\ (scanr_{\mathsf{J}}\ f\ e\ r)) \end{aligned}$$

The claim is

$$scanr\ f\ e\ (x +\!\!+\ y) = scanr\ f\ (foldr\ f\ e\ y)\ x +\!\!+\ scanr\ f\ e\ y,$$

and can be easily proved. In summary, we obtain the following recursive definition.

$$\begin{aligned} & scanr_{\mathsf{J}}\ f\ e\ (\mathsf{Single}\ \_) = \mathsf{Single}\ e \\ & scanr_{\mathsf{J}}\ f\ e\ (\mathsf{Join}\ l\ r) \\ &\quad = \mathsf{Join}\ (scanr_{\mathsf{J}}\ f\ (foldr'_{\mathsf{J}}\ f\ r\ e)\ l)\ (scanr_{\mathsf{J}}\ f\ e\ r) \end{aligned}$$

The program suggests the following parallel evaluation of $scanr_{\mathsf{J}}$. We first calculate $foldr'_{\mathsf{J}}\ f$ for each subtree in a bottom-up manner. To carry out this calculation, we assume the premise of Theorem 3.5. Then, we distribute the calculated value in the top-down manner: we pass those from the parent and the right subtree to the right and left subtrees, respectively. Finally, we update the leaf values. Figure 1 depicts the procedure. It finishes parallel steps proportionally to the height of the join lists.

4. Balanced Trees for Parallel Tree Operations

Next, we show that our method scales up to binary trees.

$$\textbf{data}\ \mathsf{Tree}\ \alpha\ \beta = \mathsf{Tip}\ \alpha \mid \mathsf{Bin}\ (\mathsf{Tree}\ \alpha\ \beta)\ \beta\ (\mathsf{Tree}\ \alpha\ \beta)$$

As briefly discussed in the introduction, the naive divide-and-conquer evaluation, namely processing each subtrees in parallel, is not generally effective. It requires $\Omega(h)$ parallel steps where h is the height of the input. In other words, when the input is monadic like lists, it shows little parallel speedups. List-like trees often appear in practice. For instance, syntax trees and XMLs are usually list-like.

We would like to develop a balanced tree structure that retains (possibly list-like) binary trees so as to exploit more parallelism. We focus on *parallel tree contraction algorithms* [Abrahamson et al. 1989; Miller and Reif 1985; Reif 1993], which we review in Section 4.1. Parallel tree contraction algorithms provide a scheduling for processing a tree of size N in $\mathrm{O}(\log \mathrm{N})$ parallel steps regardless of the shape of the tree. Therefore they could be a good starting point for developing a balanced tree structure.

We formalize a parallel tree contraction algorithm using a family of polymorphic functions (Section 4.2), derive a balanced tree structure (Section 4.3), and see that existing self-balancing trees

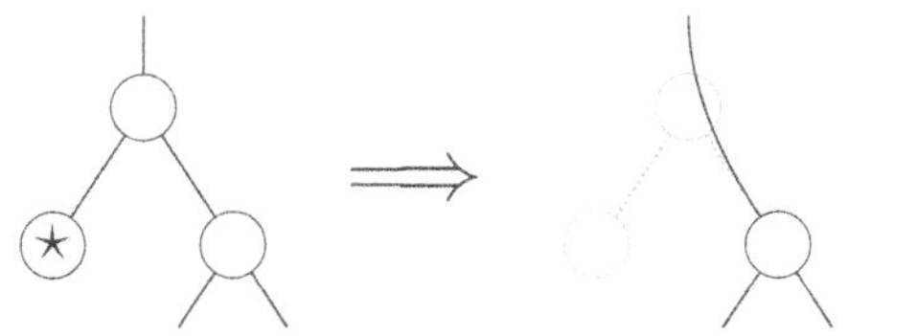

Figure 2. A Shunt operation applied to the star-marked leaf.

can implement the derived tree structure (Section 4.4). We develop implementations of algorithmic skeletons on this balanced tree structure in the next section.

4.1 Parallel Tree Contraction

Parallel tree contraction algorithms [Miller and Reif 1985; Reif 1993] collapse a tree, namely to reduce a tree to a leaf, through simultaneous applications of primitive contraction operations. The Shunt contraction algorithm [Abrahamson et al. 1989; Kosaraju and Delcher 1988; Reif 1993] is one that uses *Shunt* as the primitive contraction operation. Figure 2 describes the Shunt operation applied to the star-marked leaf. Shunt is an operation to a leaf, in which the leaf and its parent is removed. In order to keep the whole structure as a tree, the node remaining after the contraction is connected to its grandparent. The following is a functional description of a Shunt operation.

$$\begin{aligned} &shunt :: \forall\alpha,\beta.\ \mathsf{Tree}\ \alpha\ \beta \to \mathsf{Tree}\ \alpha\ \beta \\ &shunt\ (\mathsf{Bin}\ t\ \_\ (\mathsf{Tip}\ \_)) = t \\ &shunt\ (\mathsf{Bin}\ (\mathsf{Tip}\ \_)\ \_\ t) = t \end{aligned}$$

The Shunt contraction algorithm provides a good scheduling for processing trees.

THEOREM 4.1 ([Abrahamson et al. 1989; Kosaraju and Delcher 1988]). *We can completely collapse a tree of size* N *using Shunt operations in time* $O(N/P + \log P)$. □

A parallel tree contraction algorithm can implement many computations on trees by aggregating information in trees according to contraction operations [Abrahamson et al. 1989; Gibbons et al. 1994; Matsuzaki 2007; Matsuzaki et al. 2006a,b; Miller and Reif 1985; Reif 1993]. For example, by using the following add_S instead of $shunt$, we can calculate the total sum of the values in the tree in parallel.

$$\begin{aligned} &add_S :: \mathsf{Tree\ Int\ Int} \to \mathsf{Tree\ Int\ Int} \\ &add_S\ (\mathsf{Bin}\ (\mathsf{Bin}\ t_1\ b\ t_2)\ a\ (\mathsf{Tip}\ c)) = \mathsf{Bin}\ t_1\ (b+a+c)\ t_2 \\ &add_S\ (\mathsf{Bin}\ (\mathsf{Tip}\ b)\ a\ (\mathsf{Bin}\ t_1\ c\ t_2)) = \mathsf{Bin}\ t_1\ (b+a+c)\ t_2 \\ &add_S\ (\mathsf{Bin}\ (\mathsf{Tip}\ b)\ a\ (\mathsf{Tip}\ c)) = \mathsf{Tip}\ (b+a+c) \end{aligned}$$

We do not present the concrete procedures of parallel tree contraction algorithms here; other sources such as [Reif 1993] can be consulted for details. We note that they are based on intensive use of arrays and pointers, and moreover, they completely destroy the input tree as a side effect; therefore, it seems disadvantageous to implement them in purely functional settings.

4.2 Shunt Contraction Scheme

Now, let us formalize Shunt-based programs in terms of a family of polymorphic functions. Recall that each Shunt operation aggregates information from three nodes. As seen in add_S, there are three cases: the left child is an internal node; the right is an internal node; and none of the children are internal nodes. Therefore, we specify aggregating operations by the following record type, where α and β respectively denote the types of values of leaves and internal nodes.

$$\begin{aligned} \mathbf{data}\ \mathsf{Shunt}\ \alpha\ \beta = \mathsf{Shunt}\ \{ &left :: \beta \to \beta \to \alpha \to \beta, \\ &right :: \alpha \to \beta \to \beta \to \beta, \\ &none :: \alpha \to \beta \to \alpha \to \alpha \} \end{aligned}$$

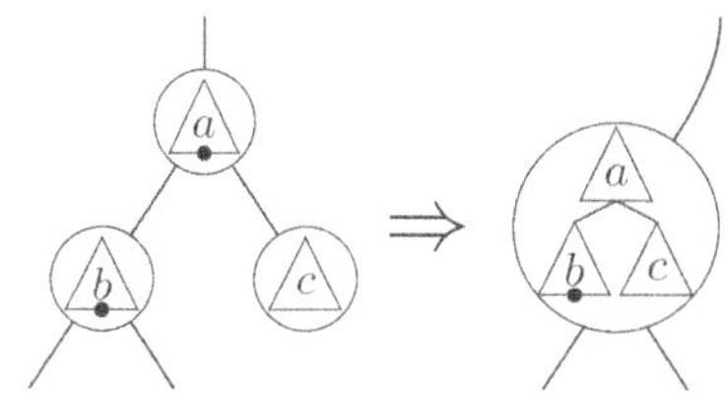

Figure 3. The computation of $connect_L$: A Shunt operation is applied to the right leaf that retains a tree c. a and b are contexts retained in the parent and the left sibling. The contraction yields a larger context.

We write $(\![\psi_L, \psi_R, \psi_N]\!)$ as a shorthand of $\mathsf{Shunt}\ \{left = \psi_L, right = \psi_R, none = \psi_N\}$.

We intend to capture the Shunt contraction by functions that have the following polymorphic type.

$$\begin{aligned} scs :: \forall\alpha,\beta.\ (A \to \alpha) \to (B \to \beta) \to \mathsf{Shunt}\ \alpha\ \beta \\ \to \mathsf{Tree}\ A\ B \to \alpha \end{aligned} \qquad (1)$$

Function scs prepares initial values for leaves and internal nodes using the first and second parameters, respectively, and then, it aggregates the values using the third parameter. The result type is α because parallel tree contraction results in a leaf.

For example, we intend to implement the summation on trees, say sum_{Tree}, as follows:

$$sum_{\mathsf{Tree}} = scs\ id\ id\ (\![add3, add3, add3]\!),$$

where $add3\ b\ a\ c = b + a + c$. Indeed, following $scsBU$, which corresponds to the naive bottom-up computation, have the polymorphic type (1) and $scsBU\ id\ id\ (\![add3, add3, add3]\!)$ calculates the total sum.

$$\begin{aligned} &scsBU\ f\ g\ (\![\psi_L,\psi_R,\psi_N]\!)\ (\mathsf{Tip}\ a) = f\ a \\ &scsBU\ f\ g\ (\![\psi_L,\psi_R,\psi_N]\!)\ (\mathsf{Bin}\ l\ a\ r) = \psi_N\ b\ (g\ a)\ c \\ &\quad \mathbf{where}\ b = scsBU\ f\ g\ (\![\psi_L,\psi_R,\psi_N]\!)\ l \\ &\quad\qquad\quad c = scsBU\ f\ g\ (\![\psi_L,\psi_R,\psi_N]\!)\ r \end{aligned}$$

Merging occurs only when both children become leaves, and hence it uses only ψ_N.

Yet, the polymorphic type (1) is not sufficient. We would like to forbid discarding, duplicating, and shuffling subtrees. To express this requirement, we consider reconstructing the input tree.

$$scs\ \mathsf{Tip}\ hole\ connect\ t = t$$

The arguments, *hole* and *connect*, are defined as follows. *hole* prepares a context, i.e., a tree with a hole, and *connect* constructs a larger context or tree by combining smaller contexts and trees.

$$\begin{aligned} &\mathbf{type}\ \mathsf{Context}\ \alpha\ \beta = (\mathsf{Tree}\ \alpha\ \beta, \mathsf{Tree}\ \alpha\ \beta) \to \mathsf{Tree}\ \alpha\ \beta \\ &hole :: \forall\alpha,\beta.\ \beta \to \mathsf{Context}\ \alpha\ \beta \\ &hole\ a = \lambda(l,r) \to \mathsf{Bin}\ l\ a\ r \\ &connect :: \forall\alpha,\beta.\ \mathsf{Shunt}\ (\mathsf{Tree}\ \alpha\ \beta)\ (\mathsf{Context}\ \alpha\ \beta) \\ &connect = (\![connect_L, connect_R, connect_N]\!) \\ &\quad \mathbf{where}\ connect_L\ b\ a\ c = \lambda t \to a\ (b\ t, c) \\ &\qquad\qquad connect_R\ b\ a\ c = \lambda t \to a\ (b, c\ t) \\ &\qquad\qquad connect_N\ b\ a\ c = a\ (b, c) \end{aligned}$$

Figure 3 shows the behavior of $connect_L$. It connects two contexts, a and b, and tree c, which are respectively retained in the parent, the left child, and the right child.

To summarize, we formalize the Shunt contraction as follows.

DEFINITION 4.2 (Shunt-contraction scheme). *A function scs of the polymorphic type (1) is said to be a* Shunt-contraction scheme *if*

$$scs\ \mathsf{Tip}\ hole\ connect\ t = t$$

holds for any tree t. □

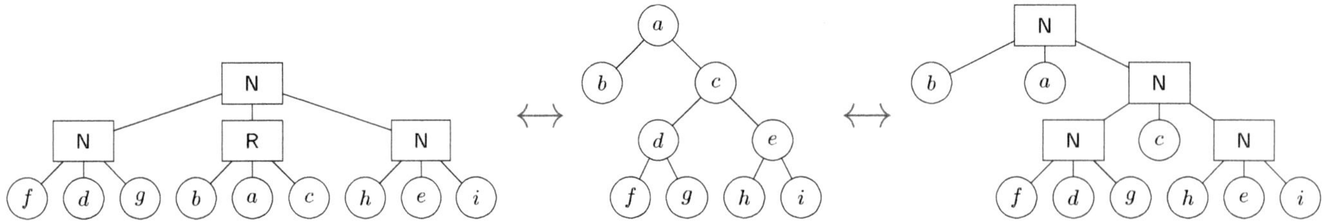

Figure 4. Two equivalent Shunt trees. We omit T and $\mathsf{H}_\bullet$; a, c, d, and e are wrapped by $\mathsf{H}_\bullet$, while b, f, g, h, and i are by T.

The following lemma follows from the relational parametricity.

LEMMA 4.3. *Given function h, assume that there exists h' such that the following three equations hold.*

$$\begin{aligned} h'\ (\psi_{\mathsf{L}}\ b\ a\ c) &= \psi'_{\mathsf{L}}\ (h'\ b)\ (h'\ a)\ (h\ c) \\ h'\ (\psi_{\mathsf{R}}\ b\ a\ c) &= \psi'_{\mathsf{R}}\ (h\ b)\ (h'\ a)\ (h'\ c) \\ h\ (\psi_{\mathsf{N}}\ b\ a\ c) &= \psi'_{\mathsf{N}}\ (h\ b)\ (h'\ a)\ (h\ c) \end{aligned}$$

Then the following equation holds for any function scs of the polymorphic type (1).

$$h \circ scs\ f\ g\ (\!|\psi_{\mathsf{L}}, \psi_{\mathsf{R}}, \psi_{\mathsf{N}}|\!) = scs\ (h \circ f)\ (h' \circ g)\ (\!|\psi'_{\mathsf{L}}, \psi'_{\mathsf{R}}, \psi'_{\mathsf{N}}|\!) \Box$$

Lemma 4.3 is useful for reasoning about Shunt-based parallel programs. For example, $sum_{\mathsf{Tree}} = scs\ id\ id\ (\!|add3, add3, add3|\!)$ follows for any Shunt-contraction scheme scs.

$$\begin{aligned}
& sum_{\mathsf{Tree}} = scs\ id\ id\ (\!|add3, add3, add3|\!) \\
\Leftrightarrow\ & \{\ scs \text{ is a Shunt-contraction scheme }\} \\
& \quad sum_{\mathsf{Tree}} \circ scs\ \mathsf{Tip}\ hole\ connect \\
& \qquad = scs\ id\ id\ (\!|add3, add3, add3|\!) \\
\Leftarrow\ & \{\ \text{Lemma 4.3 with letting } h'\ t = sum_{\mathsf{Tree}}\ (t\ (\mathsf{Tip}\ 0, \mathsf{Tip}\ 0))\ \} \\
& \quad sum_{\mathsf{Tree}} \circ \mathsf{Tip} = id \wedge h' \circ hole = id \wedge \\
& \quad h'\ (connect_{\mathsf{L}}\ b\ a\ c) = add3\ (h'\ b)\ (h'\ a)\ (sum_{\mathsf{Tree}}\ c) \wedge \\
& \quad h'\ (connect_{\mathsf{R}}\ b\ a\ c) = add3\ (sum_{\mathsf{Tree}}\ b)\ (h'\ a)\ (h'\ c) \wedge \\
& \quad sum_{\mathsf{Tree}}\ (connect_{\mathsf{N}}\ b\ a\ c) \\
& \qquad = add3\ (sum_{\mathsf{Tree}}\ b)\ (h'\ a)\ (sum_{\mathsf{Tree}}\ c) \\
\Leftrightarrow\ & \{\ \text{unfolding definitions (note } \mathsf{Tip}\ 0 \text{ does not affect the sum)}\ \} \\
& \quad sum_{\mathsf{Tree}}\ (a\ (b, c)) \\
& \qquad = sum_{\mathsf{Tree}}\ c + sum_{\mathsf{Tree}}\ (a\ (\mathsf{Tip}\ 0, \mathsf{Tip}\ 0)) + sum_{\mathsf{Tree}}\ b
\end{aligned}$$

The obtained equation can be read as follows: the total sum of a large tree, $a\ (b, c)$, can be calculated in a "divide at the middle and conquer" manner, namely adding the total sums of the upper part, a, and subtrees b and c. This evidently holds.

4.3 Shunt Trees

Next, we derive a balanced tree structure from Shunt-contraction schemes. We name it a *Shunt tree* and define as follows[2].

$$\begin{aligned}
\mathbf{data}\ \mathsf{ST}\ \alpha\ \beta &= \mathsf{T}\ \alpha \\
&\mid\ \mathsf{N}\ (\mathsf{ST}\ \alpha\ \beta)\ \ (\mathsf{ST}_\bullet\ \alpha\ \beta)\ (\mathsf{ST}\ \alpha\ \beta) \\
\mathbf{data}\ \mathsf{ST}_\bullet\ \alpha\ \beta &= \mathsf{H}_\bullet\ \beta \\
&\mid\ \mathsf{L}_\bullet\ (\mathsf{ST}_\bullet\ \alpha\ \beta)\ (\mathsf{ST}_\bullet\ \alpha\ \beta)\ (\mathsf{ST}\ \alpha\ \beta) \\
&\mid\ \mathsf{R}_\bullet\ (\mathsf{ST}\ \alpha\ \beta)\ \ (\mathsf{ST}_\bullet\ \alpha\ \beta)\ (\mathsf{ST}_\bullet\ \alpha\ \beta)
\end{aligned}$$

Shunt trees consist of two mutually-defined datatypes. ST represents a binary tree, while $\mathsf{ST}_\bullet$ represents a context. The following functions, $s2t$ and $s2c$, provide the meaning of Shunt trees.

$$\begin{aligned}
& s2t :: \forall\alpha, \beta.\ \mathsf{ST}\ \alpha\ \beta \to \mathsf{Tree}\ \alpha\ \beta \\
& s2t\ (\mathsf{T}\ a) \quad\ \ = \mathsf{Tip}\ a \\
& s2t\ (\mathsf{N}\ b\ a\ c) = connect_{\mathsf{N}}\ (s2t\ b)\ (s2c\ a)\ (s2t\ c)
\end{aligned}$$

$$\begin{aligned}
& s2c :: \forall\alpha, \beta.\ \mathsf{ST}_\bullet\ \alpha\ \beta \to \mathsf{Context}\ \alpha\ \beta \\
& s2c\ (\mathsf{H}_\bullet\ a) \qquad = hole\ a \\
& s2c\ (\mathsf{L}_\bullet\ b\ a\ c) = connect_{\mathsf{L}}\ (s2c\ b)\ (s2c\ a)\ (s2t\ c) \\
& s2c\ (\mathsf{R}_\bullet\ b\ a\ c) = connect_{\mathsf{R}}\ (s2t\ b)\ (s2c\ a)\ (s2c\ c)
\end{aligned}$$

By using the constructors and a Shunt-contraction scheme scs, we can transform a tree t to its Shunt-tree representation as follows.

$$scs\ \mathsf{T}\ \mathsf{H}_\bullet\ (\!|\mathsf{L}_\bullet, \mathsf{R}_\bullet, \mathsf{N}|\!)\ t$$

The following theorem justifies the construction of Shunt trees.

THEOREM 4.4. *Function scs of the polymorphic type (1) is a Shunt-contraction scheme if and only if the following equation holds for any tree t.*

$$s2t\ (scs\ \mathsf{T}\ \mathsf{H}_\bullet\ (\!|\mathsf{L}_\bullet, \mathsf{R}_\bullet, \mathsf{N}|\!)\ t) = t$$

PROOF. It is sufficient to confirm the following equation.

$$s2t\ (scs\ \mathsf{T}\ \mathsf{H}_\bullet\ (\!|\mathsf{L}_\bullet, \mathsf{R}_\bullet, \mathsf{N}|\!)\ t) = scs\ \mathsf{Tip}\ hole\ connect\ t$$

It is evident from the definition of $s2t$ and Lemma 4.3. $\Box$

A Shunt tree crystallizes a Shunt contraction scheme. Given a Shunt-contraction scheme scs and a binary tree t, the Shunt tree $scs\ \mathsf{T}\ \mathsf{H}_\bullet\ (\!|\mathsf{L}_\bullet, \mathsf{R}_\bullet, \mathsf{N}|\!)\ t$ describes how scs will process t. The constructors denote what operations we should apply.

As the case of join lists, there are many Shunt trees that are equivalent in the sense that they correspond to the same binary tree. Figure 4 shows an example. The left and the right Shunt trees are equivalent and correspond to the middle binary tree.

4.4 Balancing Shunt trees

To fully exploit divide-and-conquer parallelism, we would like to find a balanced Shunt tree among the equivalent ones.

One way to obtain a balanced Shunt tree is to use the Shunt contraction algorithm. It calculate a balanced Shunt tree in parallel.

THEOREM 4.5. *Given a tree of N nodes, we can find its Shunt tree representation whose height is at most $2\lceil\log \mathrm{N}\rceil$ in time $O(\mathrm{N}/\mathrm{P} + \log \mathrm{N})$.*

PROOF SKETCH. Use the Shunt contraction scheme that corresponds to the known algorithm [Abrahamson et al. 1989; Kosaraju and Delcher 1988]. The complexity and the height are evident from the algorithm. $\Box$

Moreover, it is possible to support dynamic rebalancing. Here we use directed topology trees [Frederickson 1997]. Directed topology trees provide self-balancing representations of binary trees.

LEMMA 4.6 ([Frederickson 1997]). *The height of each directed topology tree of N nodes is $O(\log \mathrm{N})$.* $\Box$

LEMMA 4.7 ([Frederickson 1997]). *Given directed topology trees of N nodes, their* link *(merging two trees by adding an edge) and* cut *(removing an edge and thereby obtaining two trees) can be performed in time $O(\log \mathrm{N})$.* $\Box$

[2] T, H, L, R, and N respectively abbreviate "Tip," "Hole," "Left," "Right," and "None." The $\bullet$ stands for the hole.

$$
\begin{array}{l}
map_{\mathsf{Tree}} :: \forall \alpha, \alpha', \beta, \beta'. (\alpha \to \alpha') \to (\beta \to \beta') \to \mathsf{Tree}\ \alpha\ \beta \to \mathsf{Tree}\ \alpha'\ \beta' \\
map_{\mathsf{Tree}}\ f\ g\ (\mathsf{Tip}\ a) \quad = \mathsf{Tip}\ (f\ a) \\
map_{\mathsf{Tree}}\ f\ g\ (\mathsf{Bin}\ t_1\ a\ t_2) = \mathsf{Bin}\ (map_{\mathsf{Tree}}\ f\ g\ t_1)\ (g\ a)\ (map_{\mathsf{Tree}}\ f\ g\ t_1) \\
zip_{\mathsf{Tree}} :: \forall \alpha, \alpha', \beta, \beta'. \mathsf{Tree}\ \alpha\ \beta \to \mathsf{Tree}\ \alpha'\ \beta' \to \mathsf{Tree}\ (\alpha, \alpha')\ (\beta, \beta') \\
zip_{\mathsf{Tree}}\ (\mathsf{Tip}\ a)\ (\mathsf{Tip}\ b) \quad = \mathsf{Tip}\ (a, b) \\
zip_{\mathsf{Tree}}\ (\mathsf{Bin}\ t_1\ a\ t_2)\ (\mathsf{Bin}\ u_1\ b\ u_2) = \mathsf{Bin}\ (zip_{\mathsf{Tree}}\ t_1\ u_1)\ (a, b)\ (zip_{\mathsf{Tree}}\ t_2\ u_2) \\
reduce :: \forall \alpha, \beta, \gamma. (\alpha \to \gamma) \to (\gamma \to \beta \to \gamma \to \gamma) \to \mathsf{Tree}\ \alpha\ \beta \to \gamma \\
reduce\ f\ g\ (\mathsf{Tip}\ a) \quad = f\ a \\
reduce\ f\ g\ (\mathsf{Bin}\ t_1\ a\ t_2) = g\ (reduce\ f\ g\ t_1)\ a\ (reduce\ f\ g\ t_1) \\
uAcc :: \forall \alpha, \beta, \gamma. (\alpha \to \gamma) \to (\gamma \to \beta \to \gamma \to \gamma) \to \mathsf{Tree}\ \alpha\ \beta \to \mathsf{Tree}\ \gamma\ \gamma \\
uAcc\ f\ g\ (\mathsf{Tip}\ a) \quad = \mathsf{Tip}\ (f\ a) \\
uAcc\ f\ g\ (\mathsf{Bin}\ t_1\ a\ t_2) = \mathsf{Bin}\ (uAcc\ f\ g\ t_1)\ (reduce\ f\ g\ (\mathsf{Bin}\ t_1\ a\ t_2))\ (uAcc\ f\ g\ t_2) \\
dAcc :: \forall \alpha, \beta, \gamma. (\gamma \to \beta \to \gamma) \to (\gamma \to \beta \to \gamma) \to \mathsf{Tree}\ \alpha\ \beta \to \gamma \to \mathsf{Tree}\ \gamma\ \gamma \\
dAcc\ f_L\ f_R\ (\mathsf{Tip}\ \_)\ e \quad = \mathsf{Tip}\ e \\
dAcc\ f_L\ f_R\ (\mathsf{Bin}\ t_1\ a\ t_2)\ e = \mathsf{Bin}\ (dAcc\ f_L\ f_R\ t_1\ (f_L\ e\ a))\ e\ (dAcc\ f_L\ f_R\ t_2\ (f_R\ e\ a))
\end{array}
$$

Figure 5. Definitions of tree skeletons.

Shunt trees can be implemented by using directed topology trees. Here we just show consequences, and will give a detailed explanation in Appendix A.

THEOREM 4.8. *We can implement a Shunt tree by a directed topology tree so that its height is* $O(\log N)$ *and link and cut operations for it take time* $O(\log N)$, *where* N *is the number of its nodes.* □

5. Developing Parallel Programs on Shunt Trees

We have developed balanced Shunt trees. As their interfaces, we employ algorithmic skeletons that operate trees [Gibbons et al. 1994; Skillicorn 1996], called tree skeletons, and develop their Shunt-tree versions by equational reasoning.

Figure 5 summarizes the definitions of tree skeletons. map_{Tree} and zip_{Tree} are tree versions of the well-known list operations. $reduce$ is similar to $foldr$, and aggregates values in the tree. $uAcc$ is similar to $scanr$, and puts the intermediate result of $reduce$ on each node. $dAcc$ update node values while traversing a tree from its root to leaves. Their usefulness has been demonstrated through several examples [Matsuzaki et al. 2006b; Skillicorn 1997, 1996], including dynamic programming and XML processing.

Implementations of map_{Tree} and zip_{Tree} are apparent. We consider the others.

5.1 Shunt-based Programs

Before considering tree skeletons, we show that our approach is not less expressive than a Shunt-contraction-based approach.

THEOREM 5.1. *Given function* h, $h = scs\ \psi_{\mathsf{T}}\ \psi_{\mathsf{H}}\ (\!|\psi_{\mathsf{L}}, \psi_{\mathsf{R}}, \psi_{\mathsf{N}}|\!)$ *holds for any Shunt contraction scheme* scs *if and only if* $h_S = h \circ s2t$ *holds for function* h_S *defined as follows.*

$$
\begin{array}{l}
h_S\ (\mathsf{T}\ a) \quad = \psi_{\mathsf{T}}\ a \\
h_S\ (\mathsf{N}\ b\ a\ c) = \psi_{\mathsf{N}}\ (h_S\ b)\ (h'_S\ a)\ (h_S\ c) \\
h'_S\ (\mathsf{H}_\bullet\ a) \quad = \psi_{\mathsf{H}}\ a \\
h'_S\ (\mathsf{L}_\bullet\ b\ a\ c) = \psi_{\mathsf{L}}\ (h'_S\ b)\ (h'_S\ a)\ (h_S\ c) \\
h'_S\ (\mathsf{R}_\bullet\ b\ a\ c) = \psi_{\mathsf{R}}\ (h_S\ b)\ (h'_S\ a)\ (h'_S\ c)
\end{array}
$$

PROOF. We prove this theorem as follows.

$$
\begin{array}{l}
h = scs\ \psi_{\mathsf{T}}\ \psi_{\mathsf{H}}\ (\!|\psi_{\mathsf{L}}, \psi_{\mathsf{R}}, \psi_{\mathsf{N}}|\!) \\
\Leftrightarrow \{ \text{claim 1 (explained below)} \} \\
\quad h = h_S \circ scs\ \mathsf{T}\ \mathsf{H}_\bullet\ (\!|\mathsf{L}_\bullet, \mathsf{R}_\bullet, \mathsf{N}|\!) \\
\Leftrightarrow \{ \text{Theorem 4.4} \} \\
\quad h \circ s2t \circ scs\ \mathsf{T}\ \mathsf{H}_\bullet\ (\!|\mathsf{L}_\bullet, \mathsf{R}_\bullet, \mathsf{N}|\!) = h_S \circ scs\ \mathsf{T}\ \mathsf{H}_\bullet\ (\!|\mathsf{L}_\bullet, \mathsf{R}_\bullet, \mathsf{N}|\!) \\
\Leftrightarrow \{ \text{claim 2 (explained below)} \} \\
\quad h \circ s2t = h_S
\end{array}
$$

The first claim is straightforward from Lemma 4.3. The second claim holds because any Shunt trees can be generated by $scs\ \mathsf{T}\ \mathsf{H}_\bullet\ (\!|\mathsf{L}_\bullet, \mathsf{R}_\bullet, \mathsf{N}|\!)\ t$ with appropriate scs and t. □

This theorem states that Shunt-contraction-based program h can be implemented on Shunt trees by h_S and h'_S. Since they are bottom-up recursive programs, their parallel evaluation is easy.

5.2 Tree Reduction

As the first skeleton, let us consider the tree reduction, $reduce$. We would like to develop its Shunt-tree version, $reduce_S$.

$$
\begin{array}{l}
reduce_S :: \forall \alpha, \beta, \gamma. (\alpha \to \gamma) \to (\gamma \to \beta \to \gamma \to \gamma) \\
\qquad\qquad \to \mathsf{ST}\ \alpha\ \beta \to \gamma \\
reduce_S\ f\ g\ s = reduce\ f\ g\ (s2t\ s)
\end{array}
$$

Since Shunt trees include $\mathsf{ST}_\bullet$, we also need to develop the $\mathsf{ST}_\bullet$ version, say $reduce'_S$. It calculates the tree reduction from the context and the value of the missing subtree.

$$
\begin{array}{l}
reduce'_S :: \forall \alpha, \beta, \gamma. (\alpha \to \gamma) \to (\gamma \to \beta \to \gamma \to \gamma) \\
\qquad\qquad \to \mathsf{ST}_\bullet\ \alpha\ \beta \to (\gamma, \gamma) \to \gamma \\
reduce'_S\ f\ g\ s\ (reduce\ f\ g\ l, reduce\ f\ g\ r) \\
\quad = reduce\ f\ g\ (s2c\ s\ (l, r))
\end{array}
$$

Let us develop recursive definitions of $reduce_S$ and $reduce'_S$.

$$
\begin{array}{l}
reduce_S\ f\ g\ (\mathsf{T}\ a) = \{ \text{definition of } reduce_S \} \\
\qquad reduce\ f\ g\ (s2t\ (\mathsf{T}\ a)) \\
\quad = \{ \text{definitions of } s2t \text{ and } reduce \} \\
\qquad f\ a \\
reduce_S\ f\ g\ (\mathsf{N}\ b\ a\ c) \\
\quad = \{ \text{definition of } reduce_S \} \\
\qquad reduce\ f\ g\ (s2t\ (\mathsf{N}\ b\ a\ c)) \\
\quad = \{ \text{definition of } s2t \} \\
\qquad reduce\ f\ g\ (s2c\ a\ (s2t\ b, s2t\ c)) \\
\quad = \{ \text{definition of } reduce'_S \} \\
\qquad reduce'_S\ f\ g\ a\ (reduce\ f\ g\ (s2t\ b), reduce\ f\ g\ (s2t\ c)) \\
\quad = \{ \text{definition of } reduce_S \} \\
\qquad reduce'_S\ f\ g\ a\ (reduce_S\ f\ g\ b, reduce_S\ f\ g\ c) \\
\quad = \{ \text{abstraction} \} \\
\qquad \textbf{let}\ a' = reduce'_S\ f\ g\ a \\
\qquad\quad\ \ b' = reduce_S\ f\ g\ b \\
\qquad\quad\ \ c' = reduce_S\ f\ g\ c \\
\qquad \textbf{in}\ a'\ (b', c')
\end{array}
$$

We introduced the last step so as to make our attention to the divide-and-conquer parallelism explicit.

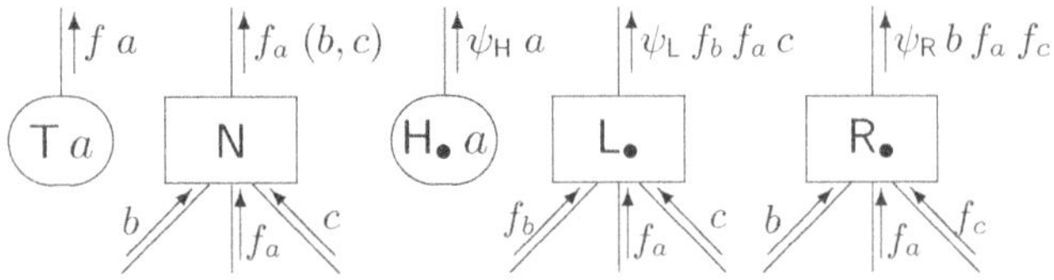

Figure 6. Implementation of *reduce* f g on Shunt trees: from the values given from its children, the value of the node is calculated and is sent to its parent; the variables used here correspond to those in Theorem 5.2.

Next, we deal with $reduce'_S$. In the following, we use l_{red} and r_{red} to denote *reduce* $f\ g\ l$ and *reduce* $f\ g\ r$, respectively.

$$
\begin{aligned}
& reduce'_S\ f\ g\ (l_{red}, r_{red})\ (\mathsf{H}_\bullet\ a) \\
&\quad = \{ \text{definition of } reduce'_S \} \\
&\quad\quad reduce\ f\ g\ (s2c\ (\mathsf{H}_\bullet\ a)\ (l, r)) \\
&\quad = \{ \text{definition of } s2c \} \\
&\quad\quad reduce\ f\ g\ (\mathsf{Bin}\ l\ a\ r) \\
&\quad = \{ \text{definition of } reduce \} \\
&\quad\quad g\ l_{red}\ a\ r_{red}
\end{aligned}
$$

$$
\begin{aligned}
& reduce'_S\ f\ g\ (l_{red}, r_{red})\ (\mathsf{L}_\bullet\ b\ a\ c) \\
& = \{ \text{definition of } reduce'_S \} \\
&\quad reduce\ f\ g\ (s2c\ (\mathsf{L}_\bullet\ b\ a\ c)\ (l, r)) \\
& = \{ \text{definition of } s2c \} \\
&\quad reduce\ f\ g\ (s2c\ a\ (s2c\ b\ (l, r), s2t\ c)) \\
& = \{ \text{definition of } reduce'_S \} \\
&\quad reduce'_S\ f\ g\ a\ (reduce\ f\ g\ (s2c\ b\ (l, r)), reduce\ f\ g\ (s2t\ c)) \\
& = \{ \text{definition of } reduce'_S \text{ and } reduce_S \} \\
&\quad reduce'_S\ f\ g\ a\ (reduce'_S\ f\ g\ b\ (l_{red}, r_{red}), reduce_S\ f\ g\ c) \\
& = \{ \text{abstraction} \} \\
&\quad \mathbf{let}\ a' = reduce'_S\ f\ g\ a \\
&\quad\quad\ \ b' = reduce'_S\ f\ g\ b \\
&\quad\quad\ \ c' = reduce_S\ f\ g\ c \\
&\quad \mathbf{in}\ (\lambda h \to a'\ (b'\ h, c'))\ (l_{red}, r_{red})
\end{aligned}
$$

$$
\begin{aligned}
& reduce'_S\ f\ g\ (l_{red}, r_{red})\ (\mathsf{R}_\bullet\ b\ a\ c) \\
&\quad = \{ \text{similar to the case of } \mathsf{L}_\bullet \} \\
&\quad\quad \mathbf{let}\ a' = reduce'_S\ f\ g\ a \\
&\quad\quad\quad\ \ b' = reduce_S\ f\ g\ b \\
&\quad\quad\quad\ \ c' = reduce'_S\ f\ g\ c \\
&\quad\quad \mathbf{in}\ (\lambda h \to a'\ (b', c'\ h))\ (l_{red}, r_{red})
\end{aligned}
$$

The recursive definition implies a sufficient condition for its divide-and-conquer evaluation. The condition is in spirit very similar to that for Theorem 3.5: We can achieve efficient parallel computation if we can efficiently merge and evaluate closures.

THEOREM 5.2. *$reduce_S\ f\ g :: \mathsf{ST}\ A\ B \to C$ can be computed by a bottom-up divide-and-conquer parallel algorithm provided that there exist a set of constant-time functions $\mathcal{F} \subseteq ((C, C) \to C)$ and three constant-time functions $\psi_\mathsf{H} :: B \to \mathcal{F}$, $\psi_\mathsf{L} :: \mathcal{F} \to \mathcal{F} \to C \to \mathcal{F}$, $\psi_\mathsf{R} :: \mathcal{F} \to C \to \mathcal{F} \to \mathcal{F}$ defined as follows.*

$$
\begin{aligned}
\psi_\mathsf{H}\ a &= \lambda(b, c) \to g\ b\ a\ c \\
\psi_\mathsf{L}\ f_b\ f_a\ c &= \lambda h \to f_a\ (f_b\ h, c) \\
\psi_\mathsf{R}\ b\ f_a\ f_c &= \lambda h \to f_a\ (b, f_c\ h)
\end{aligned}
\qquad \square
$$

In Theorem 5.2, each function in $\mathcal{F}$ represents a closure raised by $reduce'_S$. We depict the implementation in Figure 6.

The premise of Theorem 5.2, namely existence set of constant-time functions $\mathcal{F}$, may appears to be artificial. In fact, similar notions have been used as a basis for developing efficient parallel algorithms. A classic application is parallel evaluation of an arithmetic expression that consists of $+$, $-$, $\times$, and $/$, where $\mathcal{F} = \{(\lambda x\ y.\ (a \times (x \oplus y) + b)/(c \times (x \oplus y) + d)) \mid a, b, c, d \in \mathbb{R} \wedge \oplus \in \{+, -, \times, /\}\}$ [Brent 1974]. Abrahamson et al. [1989] considered essentially the same condition as a sufficient condition for implementing tree operations by using the Shunt contraction algorithm. Matsuzaki et al. [2006a] discussed more involved applications including dynamic programming and XML querying by using matrices to encode $\mathcal{F}$.

5.3 Upward Accumulation

Next, let us consider the upward accumulation skeleton, $uAcc$, proposed by Gibbons et al. [1994]. We derive a parallel implementation of $uAcc$ by developing $uAcc_S$ and $uAcc'_S$, characterized as follows.

$$
\begin{aligned}
& s2t\ (uAcc_S\ f\ g\ s) = uAcc\ f\ g\ (s2t\ s) \\
& s2c\ (uAcc'_S\ f\ g\ s\ (reduce\ f\ g\ l, reduce\ f\ g\ r)) \\
&\quad (uAcc\ f\ g\ l, uAcc\ f\ g\ r) = uAcc\ f\ g\ (s2c\ s\ (l, r))
\end{aligned}
$$

Since $uAcc$ relies on *reduce*, $uAcc'_S$ takes the *reduce* values of the missing subtrees as arguments.

We will calculate their recursive definitions. We use some shorthand notations in the following derivation: we omit function parameters f and g; we abbreviate *reduce* to *red*; we let $l_{red} = red\ f\ g\ l$, $r_{red} = red\ f\ g\ r$, $l_{uA} = uAcc\ f\ g\ l$, and $r_{uA} = uAcc\ f\ g\ r$; we omit the case of $\mathsf{R}_\bullet$.

$$
\begin{aligned}
s2t\ (uAcc_S\ (\mathsf{T}\ a)) &= \{ \text{definitions of } uAcc_S, s2t, \text{and } uAcc \} \\
&\quad\ \mathsf{Tip}\ (f\ a) \\
&= \{ \text{definition of } s2t \} \\
&\quad\ s2t\ (\mathsf{T}\ (f\ a))
\end{aligned}
$$

$$
\begin{aligned}
& s2t\ (uAcc_S\ (\mathsf{N}\ b\ a\ c)) \\
&\quad = \{ \text{definitions of } uAcc_S \text{ and } s2t \} \\
&\quad\quad uAcc\ (s2c\ a\ (s2t\ b, s2t\ c)) \\
&\quad = \{ \text{definitions of } uAcc_S, uAcc'_S, \text{and } red_S \} \\
&\quad\quad s2c\ (uAcc'_S\ a\ (red_S\ b, red_S\ c)) \\
&\quad\quad\quad (s2t\ (uAcc_S\ b), s2t\ (uAcc_S\ c)) \\
&\quad = \{ \text{definition of } connect_\mathsf{N} \} \\
&\quad\quad connect_\mathsf{N}\ (s2t\ (uAcc_S\ b)) \\
&\quad\quad\quad (s2c\ (uAcc'_S\ a\ (red_S\ b, red_S\ c))) \\
&\quad\quad\quad (s2t\ (uAcc_S\ c)) \\
&\quad = \{ \text{definition of } s2t \} \\
&\quad\quad s2t\ (\mathsf{N}\ (uAcc_S\ b)\ (uAcc'_S\ a\ (red_S\ b, red_S\ c))\ (uAcc_S\ c))
\end{aligned}
$$

$$
\begin{aligned}
& s2c\ (uAcc'_S\ (\mathsf{H}_\bullet\ a)\ (l_{red}, r_{red}))\ (l_{uA}, r_{uA}) \\
&\quad = \{ \text{definitions of } uAcc'_S, s2c, \text{and } uAcc \} \\
&\quad\quad \mathsf{Bin}\ l_{uA}\ (g\ l_{red}\ a\ r_{red})\ r_{uA} \\
&\quad = \{ \text{definition of } s2c \} \\
&\quad\quad s2c\ (\mathsf{H}_\bullet\ (g\ l_{red}\ a\ r_{red}))\ (l_{uA}, r_{uA})
\end{aligned}
$$

$$
\begin{aligned}
& s2c\ (uAcc'_S\ (\mathsf{L}_\bullet\ b\ a\ c)\ (l_{red}, r_{red}))\ (l_{uA}, r_{uA}) \\
&\quad = \{ \text{definitions of } uAcc'_S \text{ and } s2c \} \\
&\quad\quad uAcc\ (s2c\ a\ (s2c\ b\ (l, r), s2t\ c)) \\
&\quad = \{ \text{definitions of } uAcc_S, uAcc'_S, red_S \text{ and } red'_S \} \\
&\quad\quad s2c\ (uAcc'_S\ a\ (red'_S\ b\ (l_{red}, r_{red}), red_S\ c)) \\
&\quad\quad\quad (s2c\ (uAcc'_S\ b\ (l_{red}, r_{red}))\ (l_{uA}, r_{uA}), s2t\ (uAcc_S\ c)) \\
&\quad = \{ \text{definition of } connect_\mathsf{L} \} \\
&\quad\quad connect_\mathsf{L}\ (s2c\ (uAcc'_S\ b\ (l_{red}, r_{red}))) \\
&\quad\quad\quad (s2c\ (uAcc'_S\ a\ (red'_S\ b\ (l_{red}, r_{red}), red_S\ c))) \\
&\quad\quad\quad (s2t\ (uAcc_S\ c))\ (l_{uA}, r_{uA}) \\
&\quad = \{ \text{definition of } s2c \} \\
&\quad\quad s2c\ (\mathsf{L}_\bullet\ (uAcc'_S\ b\ (l_{red}, r_{red})) \\
&\quad\quad\quad (uAcc'_S\ a\ (red'_S\ b\ (l_{red}, r_{red}), red_S\ c)) \\
&\quad\quad\quad (uAcc_S\ c))\ (l_{uA}, r_{uA})
\end{aligned}
$$

We have developed the following recursive definitions.

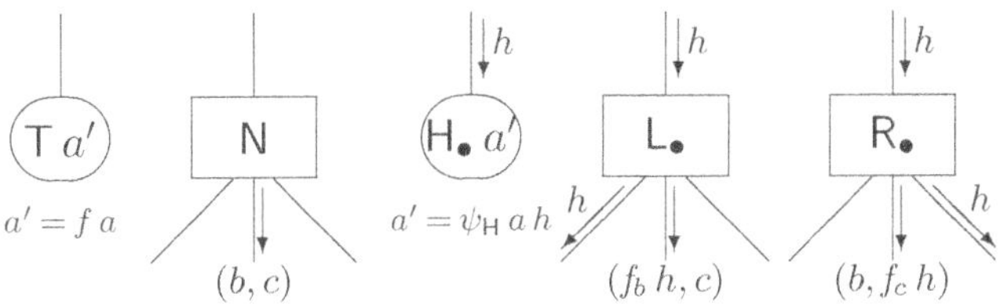

Figure 7. Implementation of $uAcc\ f\ g$ on Shunt trees: given the value h from its parent, values are sent to its children; note that this must follow $reduce\ f\ g$ depicted in Figure 6, and a, b, c, f_b and f_c are those in that figure.

$$
\begin{aligned}
& uAcc_S\ f\ g\ (\mathsf{T}\ a) = \mathsf{T}\ (f\ a) \\
& uAcc_S\ f\ g\ (\mathsf{N}\ b\ a\ c) \\
& \quad = \mathsf{N}\ (uAcc_S\ f\ g\ b) \\
& \qquad\quad (uAcc'_S\ f\ g\ a\ (reduce_S\ f\ g\ b, reduce_S\ f\ g\ c)) \\
& \qquad\quad (uAcc_S\ f\ g\ c) \\
& uAcc'_S\ f\ g\ (\mathsf{H}_\bullet\ a)\ (l_{red}, r_{red}) = \mathsf{H}_\bullet\ (g\ l_{red}\ a\ r_{red}) \\
& uAcc'_S\ f\ g\ (\mathsf{L}_\bullet\ b\ a\ c)\ h \\
& \quad = \mathsf{L}_\bullet\ (uAcc'_S\ f\ g\ b\ h) \\
& \qquad\quad (uAcc'_S\ f\ g\ a\ (reduce'_S\ f\ g\ b\ h, reduce_S\ f\ g\ c)) \\
& \qquad\quad (uAcc_S\ f\ g\ c) \\
& uAcc'_S\ f\ g\ (\mathsf{R}_\bullet\ b\ a\ c)\ h \\
& \quad = \mathsf{R}_\bullet\ (uAcc_S\ f\ g\ b) \\
& \qquad\quad (uAcc'_S\ f\ g\ a\ (reduce_S\ f\ g\ b, reduce'_S\ f\ g\ c\ h)) \\
& \qquad\quad (uAcc'_S\ f\ g\ c\ h)
\end{aligned}
$$

These recursive definitions show that we can perform $uAcc_S$ in a divide-and-conquer manner if $reduce_S$ can. Moreover, they suggest an implementation similar to *scanr*: we first calculate $reduce_S$ in a bottom-up manner, as in Figure 6, and then distribute the calculated values by a top-down sweep, as in Figure 7.

THEOREM 5.3. *There exists a two-sweeps divide-and-conquer parallel algorithm for $uAcc_S\ f\ g$, provided that the premises of Theorem 5.2 hold.* □

It is worth noting that, in contrast to *reduce*, it is nontrivial to implement *uAcc* with the Shunt contraction, because it is hard to capture the top-down sweep by Shunt contraction schemes.

5.4 Downward Accumulation

Gibbons et al. [1994] also introduced another skeleton, called downward accumulations, *dAcc*. We can derive its Shunt-tree version as being similar to *uAcc*. The derivation is routine and therefore we show it in Appendix B. The following is the developed program.

$$
\begin{aligned}
& dAcc_S\ f_L\ f_R\ e\ (\mathsf{T}\ \_) = \mathsf{T}\ e \\
& dAcc_S\ f_L\ f_R\ e\ (\mathsf{N}\ b\ a\ c) \\
& \quad = \mathsf{N}\ (dAcc_S\ f_L\ f_R\ e_L\ b)\ a'\ (dAcc_S\ f_L\ f_R\ e_R\ c) \\
& \qquad \mathbf{where}\ (a', (e_L, e_R)) = dAcc'_S\ f_L\ f_R\ e\ a \\
& dAcc'_S\ f_L\ f_R\ e\ (\mathsf{H}_\bullet\ a) = (\mathsf{H}_\bullet\ e, (f_L\ e\ a, f_R\ e\ a)) \\
& dAcc'_S\ f_L\ f_R\ e\ (\mathsf{L}_\bullet\ b\ a\ c) \\
& \quad = (\mathsf{L}_\bullet\ b'\ a'\ (dAcc_S\ f\ g\ e_R\ c), (e'_L, e'_R)) \\
& \qquad \mathbf{where}\ (a', (e_L, e_R)) = dAcc'_S\ f_L\ f_R\ e\ a \\
& \qquad\qquad\ \ (b', (e'_L, e'_R)) = dAcc'_S\ f_L\ f_R\ e_L\ b \\
& dAcc'_S\ f_L\ f_R\ e\ (\mathsf{R}_\bullet\ b\ a\ c) \\
& \quad = (\mathsf{R}_\bullet\ (dAcc_S\ f\ g\ e_L\ b)\ a'\ c', (e'_L, e'_R)) \\
& \qquad \mathbf{where}\ (a', (e_L, e_R)) = dAcc'_S\ f_L\ f_R\ e\ a \\
& \qquad\qquad\ \ (c', (e'_L, e'_R)) = dAcc'_S\ f_L\ f_R\ e_R\ c
\end{aligned}
$$

Note that the implementation on $\mathsf{ST}_\bullet$, namely $dAcc'_S$, returns two additional values that are accumulation parameters for processing missing subtrees. As similar to the case of *uAcc*, the whole computation can be performed in parallel if these accumulation parameters can be calculated in a bottom-up sweep.

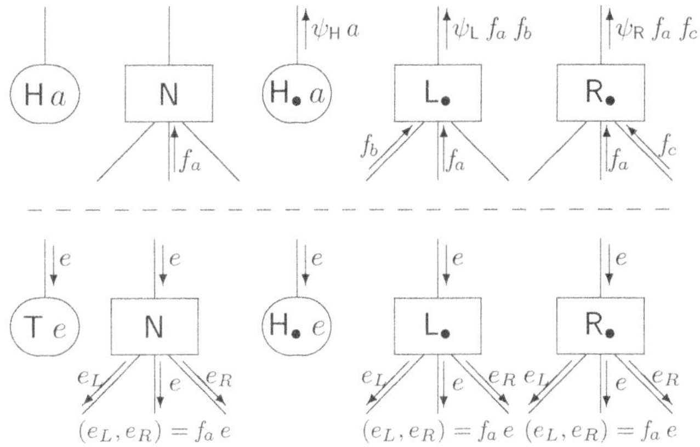

Figure 8. Implementation of $dAcc\ f_L\ f_R$ on Shunt trees: the top-down phase (the lower picture) follows after the the bottom-up phase (the upper picture); in each phase, each node receives values from either its parent or its children and sends calculated values to others; the variables used here correspond to those in Theorem 5.4.

THEOREM 5.4. *There is a two-sweep divide-and-conquer parallel algorithm for $dAcc_S\ f_L\ f_R :: \mathsf{ST}\ A\ B \to \mathsf{ST}\ C\ C$, provided that there exist a set of constant-time functions $\mathcal{F} \subseteq (C \to (C, C))$ and three constant-time functions $\psi_\mathsf{H} :: B \to \mathcal{F}$, $\psi_\mathsf{L} :: \mathcal{F} \to \mathcal{F} \to \mathcal{F}$, and $\psi_\mathsf{R} :: \mathcal{F} \to \mathcal{F} \to \mathcal{F}$, defined as follows.*

$$
\begin{aligned}
& \psi_\mathsf{H}\ a = \lambda e \to (f_L\ e\ a, f_R\ e\ a) \\
& \psi_\mathsf{L}\ f_a\ f_b = \lambda e \to \mathbf{let}\ (e'_L, e'_R) = f_a\ e\ \mathbf{in}\ f_b\ e_L \\
& \psi_\mathsf{R}\ f_a\ f_c = \lambda e \to \mathbf{let}\ (e'_L, e'_R) = f_a\ e\ \mathbf{in}\ f_c\ e_R
\end{aligned}
\qquad \square
$$

We depict the implementation in Figure 8. We first prepare the accumulation parameters and then perform a top-down sweep so as to distribute them and thereby update the node values.

6. Conclusion, Related Work, and Future Work

We have discussed developments and applications of balanced tree structures in purely functional parallel programming. We have developed balanced trees by extracting and then freezing the computational structures of parallel computations. The balanced trees enable us to naturally implement rather complicated parallel algorithms. Moreover, the balanced trees are in fact variants of known self-balancing tree structures, and hence, we can efficiently obtain well-balanced ones. Although we have considered only programs that operate lists and binary trees, our method should be able to cope with those on non-binary trees by following the study of Morihata et al. [2009]. Furthermore, since our method does not use any tree-specific properties, we believe that it can be extended to other parallel algorithms.

Because balanced trees suggest strategies for distributing the input tree to each processor, their use would be effective on distributed-memory environments. We are developing balanced-tree-based implementations of developed parallel programs so as to confirm their effectiveness.

6.1 Functional Parallel Programming and Algorithmic Skeletons

Our initial objective was to formalize and to provide purely functional implementations to algorithmic skeletons, especially data parallel skeletons. Data parallel skeletons simultaneously perform the same operations on each element of large data. All skeletons we have considered are data parallel skeletons. Other examples of data parallel skeletons include list comprehension operations in NESL [Blelloch et al. 1994] and Google's MapReduce [Dean and Ghemawat 2004]. The effectiveness of data parallel skeletons, especially those for lists or arrays (called list skeletons), are well recognized, and most of the modern parallel functional programming languages support list skeletons [Fluet et al. 2008; Keller et al. 2010; Peyton Jones et al. 2008].

An unresolved issue is the implementation of the underlying data. As discussed in the introduction, the usual implementation of lists and trees can hardly support efficient parallel computations, and therefore, data parallel skeletons are usually implemented on a special data structure. Designing of the data structure is a crucial task. It will determine what kind of skeletons and operations we can support and what parallel computational environments we can use.

List skeletons are usually implemented based on arrays; however, this implementation cannot support efficient structural modifications. Manticore [Fluet et al. 2008] adopts a balanced tree called a rope. Tree skeletons, which are usually implemented on parallel tree contraction algorithms [Gibbons et al. 1994; Matsuzaki 2007; Matsuzaki et al. 2006b; Skillicorn 1996], have a similar difficulty. The original Shunt contraction algorithm [Abrahamson et al. 1989; Kosaraju and Delcher 1988] uses pointer-based implementation of trees; however, this prohibits us from using the algorithm on distributed-memory environments. Matsuzaki [2007] used the m-bridge technique [Gazit et al. 1987; Reif 1993] so as to implement tree skeletons on distributed-memory environments; however, this implementation cannot support efficient structural modifications.

Our method provides a systematic way of developing implementations of both underlying data structures and skeletons on them. To the best of our knowledge, it is the first method of systematically developing skeletons. Our derivations result in balanced trees, which are suitable for most of the parallel computation environments and which support efficient structural updates. Our implementations of skeletons are correct by construction. Moreover, our two-sweep algorithms for $uAcc$ and $dAcc$ are simpler than the existing ones [Gibbons et al. 1994; Matsuzaki 2007].

6.2 Parallel Tree Contractions and Balanced Trees

From parallel tree contraction algorithms, we have developed Shunt trees, which are a variant of directed topology trees. Some researches have also pointed out the relationship between self-balancing trees and parallel tree contractions.

Frederickson [1997] proposed directed topology trees. He compared them with parallel tree contraction, and included the following explanation. Note that "rake" and "compress" are primitive contraction operations used in the original parallel tree contraction by Miller and Reif [1985].

> Since the rake-and-compress operations cited here were not designed to handle dynamic situations, there is no flexibility in choosing which operations to apply. Thus there is only one tree that can result from applying the operations to a given tree during one iteration. This lack of flexibility would cause global restructuring after an update, and thus would be quite inefficient.

Indeed, we have introduced flexibility of applying contraction operations. The key to the flexibility is the introduction of a set of polymorphic functions that are observationally characterized.

Acar et al. [2004] introduced a machine model that supports incremental evaluation based on computational traces. They applied their method to a randomized variant of the parallel tree contraction algorithm by Miller and Reif [1985], and obtained a self-balancing tree structure they named RC trees. Their method is very interesting because they discovered a new self-balancing tree structure, while we have mainly focused on reasoning and development of parallel programs and have used existing structures for making our balanced trees self-balanced. A combination of the two methods could be fruitful, though we did not use the RC trees because they do not guarantee the worst-case time.

6.3 Formalization of Parallel Algorithms

We have formalized parallel algorithms using a family of polymorphic functions, i.e., list homomorphism schemes and Shunt contraction schemes. This was inspired from those who formalize domain-specific procedures using polymorphic functions. Day et al. [1999] pointed out that Knuth's 0-1 principle [Knuth 1998] can be rephrased in terms of Reynolds' relational parametricity. Voigtländer [2008, 2009] demonstrated several applications of parametricity. Here we have added another application, namely the development of parallel programs.

We have developed balanced trees from these schemes. The underlying idea is a hylomorphism [Meijer et al. 1991]. A hylomorphism is a function expressed by a composition of two functions: an anamorphism, which is a structural corecursion that generates an intermediate structure, and a catamorphism, which is a structural recursion that consumes the intermediate structure. By virtue of induction/coinduction on the intermediate structure, hylomorphisms are suitable for reasoning and manipulation [Hu et al. 1996, 1997; Takano and Meijer 1995]. Usually, the intermediate data structures of hylomorphisms are algebraic data structures. Here, we have used balanced trees, which are abstract data structures, as the intermediate data structures and showed that parametricity enables us to reason about such hylomorphisms.

Acknowledgments

The authors are grateful for Zhenjiang Hu for his collaborating discussions, and Tachio Terauchi and Takeshi Tsukada for their encouragements. The authors are also grateful for anonymous reviewers of ICFP'11, POPL'10, and SPAA'09 for their helpful comments. In particular, a similarity between Shunt trees and known self-balancing trees was originally suggested by reviewers of SPAA'09. The second author is supported by the JSPS Grant-in-Aid for Young Scientists (B) 22700037.

References

K. R. Abrahamson, N. Dadoun, D. G. Kirkpatrick, and T. M. Przytycka. A simple parallel tree contraction algorithm. *J. Algorithms*, 10(2):287–302, 1989.

U. A. Acar, G. E. Blelloch, R. Harper, J. L. Vittes, and S. L. M. Woo. Dynamizing static algorithms, with applications to dynamic trees and history independence. In *Proc. the Fifteenth Annual ACM-SIAM Symposium on Discrete Algorithms, SODA 2004*, pages 531–540. SIAM, 2004.

R. P. Brent. The parallel evaluation of general arithmetic expressions. *J. ACM*, 21(2):201–206, 1974.

S. W. Bent, D. D. Sleator, and R. E. Tarjan. Biased search trees. *SIAM J. Comput.*, 14(3):545–568, 1985.

R. S. Bird. An Introduction to the Theory of Lists. In *Logic of Programming and Calculi of Discrete Design*, volume 36 of *NATO ASI Series F*, pages 3–42. Springer-Verlag, 1987.

G. E. Blelloch, J. C. Hardwick, J. Sipelstein, M. Zagha, and S. Chatterjee. Implementation of a portable nested data-parallel language. *J. Parallel Distrib. Comput.*, 21(1):4–14, 1994.

H.-J. Boehm, R. R. Atkinson, and M. F. Plass. Ropes: An alternative to strings. *Softw., Pract. Exper.* 25(12): 1315–1330, 1995.

R. M. Burstall and J. Darlington. A transformation system for developing recursive programs. *J. ACM*, 24(1):44–67, 1977.

W.-N. Chin, A. Takano, and Z. Hu. Parallelization via context preservation. In *Proc. the 1998 International Conference on Computer Languages, ICCL '98*, pages 153–162. IEEE Computer Society, 1998.

M. I. Cole. *Algorithmic Skeletons: Structural Management of Parallel Computation*. MIT Press, 1989.

N. A. Day, J. Launchbury, and J. Lewis. Logical abstractions in Haskell. In *Proc. the 1999 Haskell Workshop*. Utrecht University Department of Computer Science, Technical Report UU-CS-1999-28, October 1999.

J. Dean and S. Ghemawat. MapReduce: Simplified data processing on large clusters. In *Proc. 6th Symposium on Operating System Design and Implementation (OSDI 2004)*, pages 137–150. USENIX, 2004.

M. Fluet, M. Rainey, J. H. Reppy, and A. Shaw Implicitly-threaded parallelism in Manticore. In *Proc. the 13th ACM SIGPLAN International Conference on Functional Programming, ICFP 2008*, pages 119–130. ACM, 2008.

G. N. Frederickson. A data structure for dynamically maintaining rooted trees. *J. Algorithms*, 24(1):37–65, 1997.

H. Gazit, G. L. Miller, and S.-H. Teng. Optimal tree contraction in the EREW model. In *Proc. the Princeton Workshop on Algorithms, Architectures, and Technology Issues for Models of Concurrent Computation*, pages 139–156. Plenum Press, 1987.

J. Gibbons, W. Cai, and D. B. Skillicorn. Efficient parallel algorithms for tree accumulations. *Sci. Comput. Program.*, 23(1):1–18, 1994.

Z. Hu, H. Iwasaki, and M. Takeichi. Deriving structural hylomorphisms from recursive definitions. In *Proc. the 1st ACM SIGPLAN International Conference on Functional Programming, ICFP'96*, pages 73–82. ACM, 1996.

Z. Hu, H. Iwasaki, M. Takeichi, and A. Takano. Tupling calculation eliminates multiple data traversals. In *Proc. the 2nd ACM SIGPLAN International Conference on Functional Programming, ICFP'97*, pages 164–175. ACM, 1997.

Z. Hu, M. Takeichi, and W.-N. Chin. Parallelization in calculational forms. In *POPL '98: Proc. the 25th ACM SIGPLAN-SIGACT Symposium on Principles of Programming Languages*, pages 316–328. ACM, 1998.

Z. Hu, H. Iwasaki, and M. Takeichi. An accumulative parallel skeleton for all. In *Programming Languages and Systems, 11th European Symposium on Programming, ESOP 2002, Proceedings*, volume 2305 of *Lecture Notes in Computer Science*, pages 83–97. Springer, 2002.

G. Keller, M. M. T. Chakravarty, R. Leshchinskiy, S. L. P. Jones, and B. Lippmeier. Regular, shape-polymorphic, parallel arrays in haskell. In *Proc. the 15th ACM SIGPLAN International Conference on Functional Programming, ICFP 2010*, pages 261–272. ACM, 2010.

D. Knuth. *The Art of Computer Programming*, volume 3. Addison Wesley Longman, second edition edition, 1998.

S. R. Kosaraju and A. L. Delcher. Optimal parallel evaluation of tree-structured computations by raking. In *VLSI Algorithms and Architectures, 3rd Aegean Workshop on Computing, AWOC 88, Proceedings*, volume 319 of *Lecture Notes in Computer Science*, pages 101–110. Springer, 1988.

A. Kühnemann, R. Glück, and K. Kakehi. Relating accumulative and non-accumulative functional programs. In *Rewriting Techniques and Applications, 12th International Conference, RTA 2001, Proceedings*, volume 2051 of *Lecture Notes in Computer Science*, pages 154–168. Springer, 2001.

K. Matsuzaki. Efficient implementation of tree accumulations on distributed-memory parallel computers. In *Computational Science - ICCS 2007, 7th International Conference, Proceedings, Part II*, volume 4488 of *Lecture Notes in Computer Science*, pages 609–616. Springer, 2007.

K. Matsuzaki, Z. Hu, and M. Takeichi. Towards automatic parallelization of tree reductions in dynamic programming. In *SPAA 2006: Proc. the 18th Annual ACM Symposium on Parallel Algorithms and Architectures*, pages 39–48. ACM, 2006a.

K. Matsuzaki, Z. Hu, and M. Takeichi. Parallel skeletons for manipulating general trees. *Parallel Comput.*, 32(7-8):590–603, 2006b.

E. Meijer, M. M. Fokkinga, and R. Paterson. Functional programming with bananas, lenses, envelopes and barbed wire. In *Functional Programming Languages and Computer Architecture, 5th ACM Conference, Proceedings*, volume 523 of *Lecture Notes in Computer Science*, pages 124–144. Springer, 1991.

G. L. Miller and J. H. Reif. Parallel tree contraction and its application. In *26th Annual Symposium on Foundations of Computer Science*, pages 478–489. IEEE, 1985.

A. Morihata and K. Matsuzaki. Automatic parallelization of recursive functions using quantifier elimination. In *Functional and Logic Programming, 10th International Symposium, FLOPS 2010, Proceedings*, volume 6009 of *Lecture Notes in Computer Science*, pages 321–336. Springer, 2010.

A. Morihata, K. Matsuzaki, Z. Hu, and M. Takeichi. The third homomorphism theorem on trees: Downward & upward lead to divide-and-conquer. In *Proc. the 36th ACM SIGPLAN-SIGACT Symposium on Principles of Programming Languages, POPL 2009*, pages 177–185. ACM, 2009.

S. Peyton Jones, editor. *Haskell 98 Language and Libraries: The Revised Report*. Cambridge University Press, Cambridge, UK, 2003.

S. L. Peyton Jones, R. Leshchinskiy, G. Keller, and M. M. T. Chakravarty. Harnessing the multicores: Nested data parallelism in haskell. In *IARCS Annual Conference on Foundations of Software Technology and Theoretical Computer Science, FSTTCS 2008*, volume 08004 of *Dagstuhl Seminar Proceedings*. Internationales Begegnungs-und Forschungszentrum fuer Informatik (IBFI), 2008.

J. H. Reif, editor. *Synthesis of Parallel Algorithms*. Morgan Kaufmann Publishers, 1993.

J. C. Reynolds. Types, abstraction and parametric polymorphism. *Inf. Process.*, 83:513–523, 1983.

D. B. Skillicorn. Structured parallel parallel computation in structured documents. *J. UCS*, 3(1):42–68, 1997.

D. B. Skillicorn. Parallel implementation of tree skeletons. *J. Parallel Distrib. Comput.*, 39(2):115–125, 1996.

A. Takano and E. Meijer. Shortcut deforestation in calculational form. In *Conference Record of FPCA'95: SIGPLAN-SIGARCH-WG2.8 Conference on Functional Programming Languages and Computer Architecture*, pages 306–313. ACM, 1995.

J. Voigtländer. Concatenate, reverse and map vanish for free. In *Proc. the Seventh ACM SIGPLAN International Conference on Functional Programming (ICFP'02)*, pages 14–25, 2002.

J. Voigtländer. Much ado about two (pearl): a pearl on parallel prefix computation. In *Proc. the 35th ACM SIGPLAN-SIGACT Symposium on Principles of Programming Languages, POPL 2008*, pages 29–35. ACM, 2008.

J. Voigtländer. Bidirectionalization for free! (pearl). In *Proc. the 36th ACM SIGPLAN-SIGACT Symposium on Principles of Programming Languages, POPL 2009*, pages 165–176. ACM, 2009.

P. Wadler. Theorems for free! In *FPCA'89 Conference on Functional Programming Languages and Computer Architecture*, pages 347–359. ACM, 1989.

P. Wadler. Deforestation: Transforming programs to eliminate trees. *Theor. Comput. Sci.*, 73(2):231–248, 1990.

A. Implementing Shunt Tree by Directed Topology Tree

We first review directed topology trees proposed by Frederickson [1997]. The following is the datatype of directed topology trees that represent binary trees, Tree $\alpha\ \beta$.

$$
\begin{aligned}
\textbf{data}\ \mathsf{DTT}\ \alpha\ \beta\ &=\ \mathsf{Leaf}\ \alpha \\
&\ \ \mid\ \mathsf{Rake}\ (\mathsf{DTT}_\bullet\ \alpha\ \beta)\ (\mathsf{DTT}\ \alpha\ \beta) \\
\textbf{data}\ \mathsf{DTT}_\bullet\ \alpha\ \beta\ &=\ \mathsf{Rake\_L}_\bullet\ \beta\ (\mathsf{DTT}\ \alpha\ \beta) \\
&\ \ \mid\ \mathsf{Rake\_R}_\bullet\ (\mathsf{DTT}\ \alpha\ \beta)\ \beta \\
&\ \ \mid\ \mathsf{Compress}\ (\mathsf{DTT}_\bullet\ \alpha\ \beta)\ (\mathsf{DTT}_\bullet\ \alpha\ \beta)
\end{aligned}
$$

Given a binary tree, a directed topology tree is a binary tree that retains recursive merging of the given tree. DTT and $\mathsf{DTT}_\bullet$ respectively represent a tree and a cluster one of whose subtrees are missing. Rake, $\mathsf{Rake\_L}_\bullet$, and $\mathsf{Rake\_R}_\bullet$ merge a tree to its parent cluster. Compress merges two adjunct clusters each of which has a unique child cluster. Note that the names of the merging operations are different from those given by Frederickson [1997]. We borrow these names from the tree contraction algorithm by Miller and Reif [1985] so as to explicitly show the relationship between directed topology trees and the tree contraction.

The following function $d2t$ converts directed topology trees to binary trees.

$$\begin{array}{lll}
d2t :: \mathsf{DTT}\ \alpha\ \beta \to \mathsf{Tree}\ \alpha\ \beta & & \\
d2t\ (\mathsf{Leaf}\ a) & = & \mathsf{Tip}\ a \\
d2t\ (\mathsf{Rake}\ d_\bullet\ d) & = & d2t_\bullet\ d_\bullet\ (d2t\ d) \\
d2t_\bullet :: \mathsf{DTT}_\bullet\ \alpha\ \beta \to \mathsf{Tree}\ \alpha\ \beta \to \mathsf{Tree}\ \alpha\ \beta & & \\
d2t_\bullet\ (\mathsf{Rake_L}_\bullet\ b\ d) & = & \lambda t \to \mathsf{Bin}\ t\ b\ (d2t\ d) \\
d2t_\bullet\ (\mathsf{Rake_R}_\bullet\ d\ b) & = & \lambda t \to \mathsf{Bin}\ (d2t\ d)\ b\ t \\
d2t_\bullet\ (\mathsf{Compress}\ d^1_\bullet\ d^2_\bullet) & = & d2t_\bullet\ d^1_\bullet \circ d2t_\bullet\ d^2_\bullet
\end{array}$$

Directed topology trees must satisfy some structural properties. Here we omit them because they are important only for guaranteeing height and efficient updating and thus do not affect our discussion.

Th following function $d2s$ establishes a relationship between directed topology trees and Shunt trees.

$$\begin{array}{lll}
d2s :: \mathsf{DTT}\ \alpha\ \beta \to \mathsf{ST}\ \alpha\ \beta & & \\
d2s\ (\mathsf{Leaf}\ a) & = & \mathsf{T}\ a \\
d2s\ (\mathsf{Rake}\ d_\bullet\ d) & = & \mathsf{case}\ d2s_\bullet\ d_\bullet\ \mathsf{of} \\
 & & \quad (c, \mathsf{Left}\ s) \to \mathsf{N}\ (d2s\ d)\ c\ s \\
 & & \quad (c, \mathsf{Right}\ s) \to \mathsf{N}\ s\ c\ (d2s\ d) \\
d2s_\bullet :: \mathsf{DTT}_\bullet\ \alpha\ \beta \to (\mathsf{ST}_\bullet\ \alpha\ \beta, \mathsf{Either}\ (\mathsf{ST}\ \alpha\ \beta)\ (\mathsf{ST}\ \alpha\ \beta)) & & \\
d2s_\bullet\ (\mathsf{Rake_L}_\bullet\ b\ d) & = & (\mathsf{H}_\bullet\ b, \mathsf{Left}\ (d2s\ d)) \\
d2s_\bullet\ (\mathsf{Rake_R}_\bullet\ d\ b) & = & (\mathsf{H}_\bullet\ b, \mathsf{Right}\ (d2s\ d)) \\
d2s_\bullet\ (\mathsf{Compress}\ d^1_\bullet\ d^2_\bullet) & = & \mathsf{let}\ (c_2, s_2) = d2s_\bullet\ d^2_\bullet \\
 & & \mathsf{in\ case}\ d2s_\bullet\ d^1_\bullet\ \mathsf{of} \\
 & & \quad (c_1, \mathsf{Left}\ s_1) \to (\mathsf{L}\ c_2\ c_1\ s_1, s_2) \\
 & & \quad (c_1, \mathsf{Right}\ s_1) \to (\mathsf{R}\ s_1\ c_1\ c_2, s_2)
\end{array}$$

It is not difficult to see $s2t \circ d2s = d2t$; moreover, we can effectively retain Shunt trees by directed topology trees because local modifications of directed topology trees are translated to local modification of Shunt trees. These observations justify Theorem 4.8.

B. Developing Shunt-tree Version of $dAcc$

We consider the Shunt-tree version of $dAcc$ characterized as follows. Note that $dAcc'_{\mathsf{S}}$ returns accumulation parameters so as to process the missing subtrees.

$$\begin{array}{l}
s2t\ (dAcc_{\mathsf{S}}\ f_L\ f_R\ e\ s) = dAcc\ f_L\ f_R\ e\ (s2t\ s) \\
\mathbf{let}\ (s', (e_L, e_R)) = dAcc'_{\mathsf{S}}\ f_L\ f_R\ e\ s \\
\mathbf{in}\ s2c\ s'\ (dAcc\ f_L\ f_R\ e_L\ l, dAcc\ f_L\ f_R\ e_R\ r) \\
\qquad = dAcc\ f_L\ f_R\ e\ (s2c\ s\ (l, r))
\end{array}$$

We develop their definitions as follows, where we omit the function parameters and the case of $\mathsf{R}_\bullet$.

$$\begin{array}{lll}
s2t\ (dAcc_{\mathsf{S}}\ e\ (\mathsf{T}\ _)) & = & \{\text{ definitions of } dAcc_{\mathsf{S}} \text{ and } s2t\ \} \\
 & & dAcc\ e\ (\mathsf{Tip}\ _) \\
 & = & \{\text{ definitions of } dAcc \text{ and } s2t\ \} \\
 & & s2t\ (\mathsf{T}\ e)
\end{array}$$

$$\begin{array}{ll}
\multicolumn{2}{l}{s2t\ (dAcc_{\mathsf{S}}\ e\ (\mathsf{N}\ b\ a\ c))} \\
= & \{\text{ definitions of } dAcc_{\mathsf{S}} \text{ and } s2t\ \} \\
 & dAcc\ e\ (s2c\ a\ (s2t\ b, s2t\ c)) \\
= & \{\text{ definitions of } dAcc_{\mathsf{S}} \text{ and } dAcc'_{\mathsf{S}}\ \} \\
 & \mathbf{let}\ (a', (e_L, e_R)) = dAcc'_{\mathsf{S}}\ e\ a \\
 & \mathbf{in}\ s2c\ a'\ (s2t\ (dAcc_{\mathsf{S}}\ e_L\ b), s2t\ (dAcc_{\mathsf{S}}\ e_R\ c)) \\
= & \{\text{ definition of } s2t\ \} \\
 & \mathbf{let}\ (a', (e_L, e_R)) = dAcc'_{\mathsf{S}}\ e\ a \\
 & \mathbf{in}\ s2t\ (\mathsf{N}\ (dAcc_{\mathsf{S}}\ e_L\ b)\ a'\ (dAcc_{\mathsf{S}}\ e_R\ c))
\end{array}$$

$$\begin{array}{ll}
\multicolumn{2}{l}{\mathbf{let}\ (s', (e_L, e_R)) = dAcc'_{\mathsf{S}}\ e\ (\mathsf{H}_\bullet\ a)} \\
\multicolumn{2}{l}{\mathbf{in}\ s2c\ s'\ (dAcc\ e_L\ l, dAcc\ e_R\ r)} \\
= & \{\text{ definitions of } dAcc'_{\mathsf{S}} \text{ and } s2c\ \} \\
 & dAcc\ e\ (\mathsf{Bin}\ l\ a\ r) \\
= & \{\text{ definition of } dAcc\ \} \\
 & \mathsf{Bin}\ (dAcc\ (f_L\ e\ a)\ l)\ e\ (dAcc\ (f_R\ e\ a)\ r) \\
= & \{\text{ definition of } s2c\ \} \\
 & s2c\ (\mathsf{H}_\bullet\ e)\ (dAcc\ (f_L\ e\ a)\ l, dAcc\ (f_R\ e\ a)\ r)
\end{array}$$

$$\begin{array}{ll}
\multicolumn{2}{l}{\mathbf{let}\ (s', (e_L, e_R)) = dAcc'_{\mathsf{S}}\ e\ (\mathsf{L}_\bullet\ b\ a\ c)} \\
\multicolumn{2}{l}{\mathbf{in}\ s2c\ s'\ (dAcc\ e_L\ l, dAcc\ e_R\ r)} \\
= & \{\text{ definitions of } dAcc'_{\mathsf{S}} \text{ and } s2c\ \} \\
 & dAcc\ e\ (s2c\ a\ (s2c\ l\ (l, r), s2t\ r)) \\
= & \{\text{ definitions of } dAcc'_{\mathsf{S}} \text{ and } dAcc_{\mathsf{S}}\ \} \\
 & \mathbf{let}\ (a', (e'_L, e'_R)) = dAcc'_{\mathsf{S}}\ e\ a \\
 & \qquad (b', (e''_L, e''_R)) = dAcc'_{\mathsf{S}}\ e'_L\ b \\
 & \mathbf{in}\ s2c\ a'\ (s2c\ b'\ (dAcc\ e''_L\ l, dAcc\ e''_R\ r), s2t\ (dAcc_{\mathsf{S}}\ e'_R\ c)) \\
= & \{\text{ definition of } s2c\ \} \\
 & \mathbf{let}\ (a', (e'_L, e'_R)) = dAcc'_{\mathsf{S}}\ e\ a \\
 & \qquad (b', (e''_L, e''_R)) = dAcc'_{\mathsf{S}}\ e'_L\ b \\
 & \mathbf{in}\ s2c\ (\mathsf{L}_\bullet\ b'\ a'\ (dAcc_{\mathsf{S}}\ e'_R\ c))\ (dAcc\ e''_L\ l, dAcc\ e''_R\ r)
\end{array}$$

Implicit Self-Adjusting Computation for Purely Functional Programs

Yan Chen Joshua Dunfield Matthew A. Hammer Umut A. Acar

Max Planck Institute for Software Systems

{chenyan, joshua, hammer, umut}@mpi-sws.org

Abstract

Computational problems that involve dynamic data, such as physics simulations and program development environments, have been an important subject of study in programming languages. Building on this work, recent advances in self-adjusting computation have developed techniques that enable programs to respond automatically and efficiently to dynamic changes in their inputs. Self-adjusting programs have been shown to be efficient for a reasonably broad range of problems but the approach still requires an explicit programming style, where the programmer must use specific monadic types and primitives to identify, create and operate on data that can change over time.

We describe techniques for automatically translating purely functional programs into self-adjusting programs. In this implicit approach, the programmer need only annotate the (top-level) input types of the programs to be translated. Type inference finds all other types, and a type-directed translation rewrites the source program into an explicitly self-adjusting target program. The type system is related to information-flow type systems and enjoys decidable type inference via constraint solving. We prove that the translation outputs well-typed self-adjusting programs and preserves the source program's input-output behavior, guaranteeing that translated programs respond correctly to all changes to their data. Using a cost semantics, we also prove that the translation preserves the asymptotic complexity of the source program.

Categories and Subject Descriptors D.1.1 [*Programming Techniques*]: Applicative (Functional) Programming; F.3.3 [*Logics and Meanings of Programs*]: Studies of Program Constructs

General Terms Algorithms, Languages, Performance

1. Introduction

Dynamic changes are pervasive in computational problems: physics simulations often involve moving objects; robots interact with dynamic environments; compilers must respond to slight modifications in their input programs. Such dynamic changes are often small, or *incremental*, and result in only slightly different output, so computations can often respond to them asymptotically faster than performing a complete re-computation. Such asymptotic improvements can lead to massive speedup in practice but traditionally require careful algorithm design and analysis (e.g., Chiang and Tamassia [1992]; Guibas [2004]; Demetrescu et al. [2005]), which can be challenging even for seemingly simple problems.

Motivated by this problem, researchers have developed language-based techniques that enable computations to respond to dynamic data changes automatically and efficiently (see Ramalingam and Reps [1993] for a survey). This line of research, traditionally known as *incremental computation*, aims to reduce dynamic problems to static (conventional or batch) problems by developing compilers that automatically generate code for dynamic responses. This is challenging, because the compiler-generated code aims to handle changes asymptotically faster than the source code. Early proposals [Demers et al. 1981; Pugh and Teitelbaum 1989; Field and Teitelbaum 1990] were limited to certain classes of applications (e.g., attribute grammars), allowed limited forms of data changes, and/or yielded suboptimal efficiency. Some of these approaches, however, had the important advantage of being *implicit*: they required little or no change to the program code to support dynamic change—conventional programs could be compiled to executables that respond automatically to dynamic changes.

Recent work based on *self-adjusting computation* made progress towards achieving efficient incremental computation by providing algorithmic language abstractions to express computations that respond automatically to changes to their data [Ley-Wild et al. 2008; Acar et al. 2009]. Self-adjusting computation can deliver asymptotically efficient updates in a reasonably broad range of problem domains [Acar et al. 2007, 2010a], and have even helped solve challenging open problems [Acar et al. 2010b]. Existing self-adjusting computation techniques, however, require the programmer to program *explicitly* by using a certain set of primitives [Carlsson 2002; Ley-Wild et al. 2008; Acar et al. 2009]. Specifically the programmer must manually distinguish *stable data*, which remains the same, from *changeable data*, which can change over time, and operate on changeable data via a special set of primitives. As a result, rewriting a conventional program into a self-adjusting program requires extensive changes to the code. For example, a purely functional program will need to be rewritten in imperative style using write-once, monadic references.

In this paper, we present techniques for *implicit* self-adjusting computation that allow conventional programs to be translated automatically into efficient self-adjusting programs. Our approach consists of a type system for inferring self-adjusting computation types from purely functional programs and a type-guided translation algorithm that rewrites purely functional programs into self-adjusting programs.

The type system hinges on a key observation connecting self-adjusting computation to information flow [Pottier and Simonet 2003; Sabelfeld and Myers 2003]: both involve tracking data dependencies (of changeable data and sensitive data, respectively) as well as dependencies between expressions and data. Specifi-

ICFP'11, September 19–21, 2011, Tokyo, Japan.

cally, we show that a type system that encodes the changeability of data and expressions in self-adjusting computation as secrecy of information suffices to statically enforce the invariants needed by self-adjusting computation. The type system uses polymorphism to capture stable and changeable uses of the same data or expression. Our type system admits a constraint-based formulation where the constraints are a strict subset of those needed by traditional information-flow type systems. Consequently, as with information flow, our type system admits an HM(X) inference algorithm [Odersky et al. 1999] that can infer all type annotations from top-level type specifications on the input of a program.

For this work, determination of types via type inference is not an end unto itself but a means for translating purely functional programs into self-adjusting programs. To achieve this, we first present a set of compositional, non-deterministic transformation rules. Guided by the types, the rules identify the set of all changeable expressions that operate on changeable data and rewrite them into the self-adjusting target language. We then present a deterministic translation algorithm that applies the compositional rules judiciously, considering the type and context (enclosing expressions) of each translated subexpression, to generate a well-typed self-adjusting target program.

Taken together, the type system, its inference algorithm, and the translation algorithm enable translating purely functional source programs to self-adjusting target programs using top-level type annotations on the input type of the source program. These top-level type annotations simply mark what part of the input data is subject to change. Figure 1 illustrates how source programs written in Level ML, a purely functional subset of ML with *level types*, can be translated to self-adjusting programs in the target language AFL, a language for self-adjusting computation with explicit primitives [Acar et al. 2006]. We prove three critical properties of the approach.

- **Type soundness.** On source code of a given type, the translation algorithm produces well-typed self-adjusting code of a corresponding target type (Theorem 6.1).
- **Observational equivalence.** The translated self-adjusting program, when evaluated, produces the same value as the source program (Theorem 6.5).
- **Asymptotic complexity.** The time to evaluate the translated program is asymptotically the same as the time to evaluate the source program (Theorem 6.9).

Type soundness and observational equivalence together imply a critical consistency property: that self-adjusting programs respond correctly to changing data (via the consistency of the target self-adjusting language [Acar et al. 2006]). The third property shows that the translated program takes asymptotically as long to evaluate (from scratch) as the corresponding source program. In addition, it places a worst-case bound on the time taken to self-adjust via change propagation, which can and often does take significantly less time when data changes are small. To prove this complexity result, we use a cost semantics [Sands 1990; Sansom and Peyton Jones 1995] that enables precise reasoning about the complexity of the evaluation time. We do not, however, prove tighter bounds on the complexity of self-adjustments; this would be beyond the scope of this paper.

We intend to complete an implementation of our approach as an extension of Standard ML and the MLton compiler [MLton]. However, we expect the proposed approach could be implemented in other languages such as Haskell, where self-adjusting libraries also exist [Carlsson 2002]. In general, since our approach simply generates target code, it is agnostic to implementation details of the explicit self-adjusting-computation mechanisms employed in the target language and thus can be applied broadly.

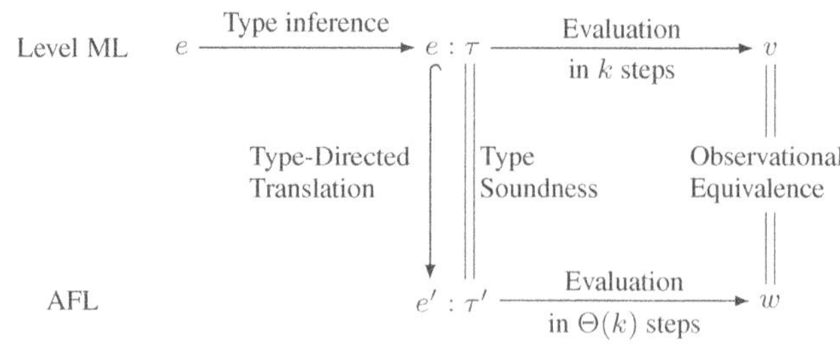

Figure 1. Visualizing the translation between the source language Level ML and the target language AFL, and related properties.

Paper guide. We find it better to give an overview of the proposed approach by focusing on the translation problem and working back to the type system in a "top-down" manner (Section 2). The details of the translation algorithm and our theorems, however, rely on the type system. We therefore take a more "bottom-up" approach in the rest of the paper: we first present the static semantics (the syntax and the type system) (Sections 3 and 4), and then describe the target language AFL (Section 5) and the translation (Section 6). Finally, we discuss related work (Section 7) and conclude. Due to space restrictions, we include all the proofs in the appendix [Chen et al. 2011].

2. Overview

We present an informal overview of our approach via examples. First we briefly describe explicit self-adjusting computation, as laid out in previous work, and which we use as a target language. Then we outline our proposed approach.

2.1 Explicit Self-Adjusting Computation

The key concept behind explicit approaches is the notion of a *modifiable (reference)*, which stores *changeable* values that can change over time [Acar et al. 2006]. The programmer operates on modifiables with **mod**, **read**, and **write** constructs to create, read from, and write into modifiables. The run-time system of a self-adjusting language uses these constructs to represent the execution as a graph, enabling efficient *change propagation* when the data changes in small amounts.

As an example, consider a trivial program that computes $x^2 + y$:

```
squareplus: int * int → int
fun squareplus (x, y) =
  let x2 = x * x in
    let r = x2 + y in
      r
```

To make this program self-adjusting with respect to changes in y, while leaving x unchanging or *stable*, we assign y the type int **mod** (of modifiables containing integers) and **read** the contents of the modifiable. The body of the **read** is a *changeable expression* ending with a **write**. This function has a changeable arrow type $\xrightarrow[\mathbb{C}]{}$:

```
squareplus_SC: int * int mod →C int
fun squareplus_SC (x, y) =
  let x2 = x * x in
    read y as y' in
      let r = x2 + y' in
        write(r)
```

The read operation delineates the code that depends on the changeable value y, and the changeable arrow type ensures a critical consistency property: $\xrightarrow[\mathbb{C}]{}$-functions can only be called within the context of a changeable expression. If we change the value of y, change propagation can update the result, re-executing only the read and its body, reusing the computation of the square x2.

Suppose we wish to make x changeable while leaving y stable. We need to read x and place x2 into a modifiable (because we can only read within the context of a changeable expression), and immediately read back x2 and finish by writing the sum. (To avoid creating this modifiable would require further structural changes to the code.)

```
squareplus_CS: int mod * int →C int
fun squareplus_CS (x, y) =
  let x2 = mod (read x as x' in write(x' * x')) in
    read x2 as x2' in
      let r = x2' + y in
        write(r)
```

As this example shows, rewriting even a trivial program can require modifications to the code, and different choices about what is or is not changeable lead to different code. Moreover, if we need squareplus_SC *and* squareplus_CS—for instance, if we want to pass squareplus to various higher-order functions—we must write, and maintain, both versions.

Conservatively treating all data as changeable would require writing just one version, but treating all data as modifiable can introduce unacceptably high overhead. At the other extreme, making everything stable requires no rewriting, but forgoes the benefits of change propagation. Instead, we take an approach where data is modifiable only where necessary.

2.2 Implicit Self-Adjusting Computation

To make self-adjusting computation implicit, we use type information to insert **read**s, **write**s, and **mod**s automatically. The user annotates the input type of the program; we infer types for all expressions, and use this information to guide a translation algorithm. The translation algorithm returns well-typed self-adjusting target programs. The translation requires no expression-level annotations. For the example function squareplus above, we can automatically derive squareplus_SC and squareplus_CS from just the type of the function (expressed in a slightly different form, as we discuss next).

Level types. To uniformly describe source functions (more generally, expressions) that differ only in their "changeability", we need a more general type system than that of the target language. This type system refines types with *levels* $\mathbb{S}$ (stable) and $\mathbb{C}$ (changeable). The type $\mathbf{int}^{\delta}$ is an integer whose level is δ; for example, to get squaresum_CS we can annotate squaresum's argument with the type $\mathbf{int}^{\mathbb{C}} \times \mathbf{int}^{\mathbb{S}}$.

Level types are an important connection between information-flow types [Pottier and Simonet 2003] and those needed for our translation: high-security secret data (level H) behaves like changeable data (level $\mathbb{C}$), and low-security public data (level L) behaves like stable data (level $\mathbb{S}$). In information flow, data that depends on secret data must be secret; in self-adjusting computation, data that depends on changeable data must be changeable. Building on this connection, we develop a type system with several features and mechanisms similar to information flow. Among these is level polymorphism; our type system assigns level-polymorphic types to expressions that accommodate various "changeabilities". (As with ML's polymorphism over types, our level polymorphism is prenex.) Another similarity is evident in our constraint-based type inference system, where the constraints are a strict subset of those in Pottier and Simonet [2003]. As a corollary, our system admits a constraint-based type inference algorithm [Odersky et al. 1999].

Translation. The main purpose of our type system is to support translation. Given a source expression and its type, translation inserts the appropriate mod, read, and write primitives and restructures the code to produce an expression that is well-typed in the target language. The type system of the target language, which is explicitly self-adjusting, is monomorphic in the levels or changeability, while the implicitly self-adjusting source language is polymorphic over levels. Consequently, translation also needs to monomorphize the source code. Our translation generates code that is well-typed, has the same input-output behavior as the source program, and is, at worst, a constant factor slower than the source program. Since the source and target languages differ, proving these properties is nontrivial; in fact, the proofs critically guided our formulation of the type system and translation algorithm.

```
datatype α list = nil | cons of α * α list

inc : int → int
fun inc (x) = x+1

map : (α → β) → α list → β list
fun map f l =
  case l of
    nil ⇒ nil
  | cons(h,t) ⇒ cons(f h, map f t)

mapPair : (int list * int list) → (int list * int list)
fun mapPair (l,a) = (map inc l, map inc a)
```

Figure 2. Function mapPair in ML

```
datatype α list^δ = nil | cons of α * (α list^δ)

mapPair : ((int^S list^C) * (int^C list^S))
        →S ((int^S list^C) * (int^C list^S))

...  (* inc, map, mapPair same as in Figure 1. *)
```

Figure 3. Function mapPair in Level ML, with level types

A more detailed example: *mapPair*. To illustrate how our translation works, consider a function mapPair that takes two integer lists and increments the elements in both lists. This function can be written by applying the standard higher-order map over lists. Figure 2 shows the purely functional code in an ML-like language for an implementation of mapPair, with a datatype α list, an increment function inc, and a polymorphic map function. Type signatures give the types of functions.

To obtain a self-adjusting mapPair, we first decide how we wish to allow the input to change. Suppose that we want to allow insertion and deletion of elements in the first list, but we expect the length of the second list to remain constant, with only its elements changing. We can express this with the versions of the list type with different changeability:

- α $\mathtt{list}^{\mathbb{C}}$ for lists of α with changeable tails;
- α $\mathtt{list}^{\mathbb{S}}$ for lists of α with stable tails.

Then a list of integers allowing insertion and deletion has type $\mathbf{int}^{\mathbb{S}}$ $\mathtt{list}^{\mathbb{C}}$, and one with unchanging length has type $\mathbf{int}^{\mathbb{C}}$ $\mathtt{list}^{\mathbb{S}}$. Now we can write the type annotation on mapPair shown in Figure 3. Given only that annotation, type inference can find appropriate types for inc and map and our translation algorithm generates self-adjusting code from these annotations. Note that to obtain a self-adjusting program, we only had to provide types for the function. We call this language with level types Level ML.

Target code for *mapPair*. Translating the code in Figure 3 produces the self-adjusting target code in Figure 4. Note that inc and map have *level-polymorphic* types. In map inc l we increment sta-

```
datatype α list_S = nil | cons of α * α list_S
datatype α list_C = nil | cons of α * (α list_C) mod

inc_S : int →𝕊 int        (* 'inc' specialized for stable data *)
fun𝕊 inc_S (x) = x+1

inc_C : int →ℂ int        (* 'inc' specialized for changeable data *)
funℂ inc_C (x) = read x as x' in write (x'+1)

inc : ∀δ. intᵟ →δ intᵟ
val inc = select {δ=𝕊 ⇒ inc_S
                 | δ=ℂ ⇒ inc_C}

map_SC : (α →𝕊 β) →𝕊 (α list_C) mod →𝕊 (β list_C) mod
fun𝕊 map_SC f l =     (* 'map' for stable heads, changeable tails *)
  mod (read l as x in
        case x of
          nil ⇒ write nil
        | cons(h,t) ⇒ write (cons(f h, map_SC f t)))

map_CS : (α →ℂ β) →𝕊 (α list_S) →𝕊 (β list_S)
fun𝕊 map_CS f l =     (* 'map' for changeable heads, stable tails *)
  case l of
    nil ⇒ nil
  | cons(h,t) ⇒ let val h' = mod (f h)
                in cons(h', map_CS f t)

map : ∀δh, δt. (α →δh β) →𝕊 α list^δt →𝕊 β list^δt
val map = select {δh=𝕊, δt=ℂ ⇒ map_SC
                 | δh=ℂ, δt=𝕊 ⇒ map_CS}

mapPair :  ((int list_C) mod * (int mod) list_S)
        →𝕊 ((int list_C) mod * (int mod) list_S)
fun𝕊 mapPair (l, a) = (map[δh=𝕊,δt=ℂ] inc[δ=𝕊] l,
                       map[δh=ℂ,δt=𝕊] inc[δ=ℂ] a)
```

Figure 4. Translated mapPair with **mod** types and explicit level polymorphism.

ble integers, and in `map inc a` we increment changeable integers, so the type inferred for inc must be generic: $\forall\delta.\ \mathbf{int}^{\delta} \underset{\delta}{\rightarrow} \mathbf{int}^{\delta}$. Our translation produces two implementations of inc, one per instantiation (δ=$\mathbb{S}$ and δ=$\mathbb{C}$): inc_S and inc_C (in Figure 4). Sine we want to use inc with the higher-order function map, we need to generate a "selector" function that takes an instantiation and picks out the appropriate implementation:

```
inc : ∀δ. intᵟ →δ intᵟ
val inc = select {δ=𝕊 ⇒ inc_S
                 | δ=ℂ ⇒ inc_C}
```

In mapPair itself, we pass a level instantiation to the selector: inc[δ=$\mathbb{S}$]. (This instantiation is known statically, so it could be replaced with inc_S at compile time.)

Observe how the single annotation on mapPair led to duplication of the two functions it uses. While inc_S is the same as the original inc, the changeable version inc_C adds a **read** and a **write**. Note also that the two generated versions of map are both different from the original.

The interplay of type inference and translation. Given user annotations on the input, type inference finds a satisfying type assignment, which then guides our translation algorithm to produce self-adjusting code. In many cases, multiple type assignments could satisfy the annotations; for example, subsumption allows any stable type to be promoted to a changeable type. Translation yields target code that satisfies the crucial type soundness, operational equivalence, and complexity properties under any satisfying assignment.

Levels	$\delta, \varepsilon ::= \mathbb{S} \mid \mathbb{C} \mid \alpha$
Types	$\tau ::= \mathbf{int}^{\delta} \mid (\tau_1 \times \tau_2)^{\delta} \mid (\tau_1 + \tau_2)^{\delta} \mid (\tau_1 \underset{\varepsilon}{\rightarrow} \tau_2)^{\delta}$
Constraints	$C, D ::= \mathbf{true} \mid \mathbf{false} \mid \exists\vec{\alpha}.C \mid C \wedge D \mid \alpha = \beta \mid \alpha \leq \beta \mid \delta \lhd \tau$
Type schemes	$\sigma ::= \tau \mid \forall\vec{\alpha}[D].\ \tau$

Figure 5. Levels, constraints, types, and type schemes

But some type assignments are preferable, especially when one considers constant factors. Choosing $\mathbb{C}$ levels whenever possible is always a viable strategy, but treating all data as changeable results in more overhead. As in information flow, where we want to consider data secret only when absolutely necessary, inference yields principal typings that are minimally changeable, always preferring $\mathbb{S}$ over $\mathbb{C}$.

3. From Information Flow Types to SAC

Self-adjusting computation separates the computation and data into two parts: stable and changeable. Changeable data refers to data that can change over time; all non-changeable data is stable. Similarly, changeable expressions refers to expressions that operate (via elimination forms) on changeable data; all non-changeable expressions are stable. Evaluation of changeable expressions (that is, changeable computations) can change as the data that they operate on changes: changes in data cause changes in control flow. These distinctions are critical to effective self-adjustment: previous work shows that it suffices to track and remember changeable data and evaluations of changeable expressions because stable data and evaluations of stable expressions remain invariant over time. Previous work therefore presents languages that enable the programmer to separate stable and changeable data, and type systems that enforce the correct usage of these constructs.

In this section, we describe the self-adjusting computation types that we infer for purely functional programs. A key insight behind our approach is that in information-flow type systems, secret (high-security) data is infectious: any data that depends on secret data itself must be secret. This corresponds to self-adjusting computation: data that depends on changeable data must itself be changeable. In addition, self-adjusting computation requires expressions that inspect changeable data—elimination forms—to be changeable. To encode this invariant, we extend function types with a *mode*, which is either stable or changeable; only changeable functions can inspect changeable data. This additional structure preserves the spirit of information flow-based type systems, and, moreover, supports constraint-based type inference in a similar style.

The starting point for our formulation is Pottier and Simonet [2003]. Our types include two *(security) levels*, stable and changeable. We generally follow their approach and notation. The two key differences are that (1) since Level ML is purely functional, we need no "program counter" level "*pc*"; (2) we need a mode ε on function types.

Levels. The *levels* $\mathbb{S}$ (*stable*) and $\mathbb{C}$ (*changeable*) have a total order:

$$\overline{\mathbb{S} \leq \mathbb{S}} \qquad \overline{\mathbb{C} \leq \mathbb{C}} \qquad \overline{\mathbb{S} \leq \mathbb{C}}$$

To support polymorphism and enable type inference, we allow *level variables* α, β to appear in types.

Types. Types consist of integers tagged with their level, products[1] and sums with an associated level, and arrow (function) types. Function types $(\tau_1 \underset{\varepsilon}{\rightarrow} \tau_2)^{\delta}$ carry two level annotations ε and δ.

[1] In Pottier and Simonet [2003], product types are low-security (stable) because pairing adds no extra information. In our setting, changeable products give more control over the granularity of change propagation.

$$\frac{\delta \leq \delta'}{\mathbf{int}^{\delta} <: \mathbf{int}^{\delta'}}\ (\text{subInt}) \qquad \frac{\tau_1 <: \tau_1' \quad \tau_2 <: \tau_2' \quad \delta \leq \delta'}{(\tau_1 \times \tau_2)^{\delta} <: (\tau_1' \times \tau_2')^{\delta'}}\ (\text{subProd})$$

$$\frac{\tau_1 <: \tau_1' \qquad \tau_2 <: \tau_2' \qquad \delta \leq \delta'}{(\tau_1 + \tau_2)^{\delta} <: (\tau_1' + \tau_2')^{\delta'}}\ (\text{subSum})$$

$$\frac{\varepsilon = \varepsilon' \qquad \delta \leq \delta' \qquad \tau_1' <: \tau_1 \qquad \tau_2 <: \tau_2'}{(\tau_1 \xrightarrow[\varepsilon]{} \tau_2)^{\delta} <: (\tau_1' \xrightarrow[\varepsilon']{} \tau_2')^{\delta'}}\ (\text{subArrow})$$

Figure 6. Subtyping

$$\frac{\delta \leq \delta'}{\delta \lhd \mathbf{int}^{\delta'}}\ (\lhd\text{-Int}) \qquad \frac{\delta \leq \delta'}{\delta \lhd (\tau_1 \times \tau_2)^{\delta'}}\ (\lhd\text{-Prod})$$

$$\frac{\delta \leq \delta'}{\delta \lhd (\tau_1 \xrightarrow[\varepsilon]{} \tau_2)^{\delta'}}\ (\lhd\text{-Arrow}) \qquad \frac{\delta \leq \delta'}{\delta \lhd (\tau_1 + \tau_2)^{\delta'}}\ (\lhd\text{-Sum})$$

Figure 7. Lower bound of a type

$$\overline{\mathbf{int}^{\mathbb{S}}\ \mathsf{O.S.}} \quad \overline{(\tau_1 \xrightarrow[\varepsilon]{} \tau_2)^{\mathbb{S}}\ \mathsf{O.S.}} \quad \overline{(\tau_1 \times \tau_2)^{\mathbb{S}}\ \mathsf{O.S.}} \quad \overline{(\tau_1 + \tau_2)^{\mathbb{S}}\ \mathsf{O.S.}}$$

$$\overline{\mathbf{int}^{\mathbb{C}}\ \mathsf{O.C.}} \quad \overline{(\tau_1 \xrightarrow[\varepsilon]{} \tau_2)^{\mathbb{C}}\ \mathsf{O.C.}} \quad \overline{(\tau_1 \times \tau_2)^{\mathbb{C}}\ \mathsf{O.C.}} \quad \overline{(\tau_1 + \tau_2)^{\mathbb{C}}\ \mathsf{O.C.}}$$

$$\mathbf{int}^{\delta_1} \doteq \mathbf{int}^{\delta_2} \qquad (\tau_1 + \tau_2)^{\delta_1} \doteq (\tau_1 + \tau_2)^{\delta_2}$$
$$(\tau_1 \times \tau_2)^{\delta_1} \doteq (\tau_1 \times \tau_2)^{\delta_2} \qquad (\tau_1 \xrightarrow[\varepsilon]{} \tau_2)^{\delta_1} \doteq (\tau_1 \xrightarrow[\varepsilon]{} \tau_2)^{\delta_2}$$

Figure 8. Outer-stable and outer-changeable types, and equality up to outer levels

The *mode* ε is the level of the computation encapsulated by the function. This mode determines how a function can manipulate changeable values: a function in stable mode cannot directly manipulate changeable values; it can only pass them around. By contrast, a changeable-mode function can directly manipulate changeable values. The outer level δ is the level of the function itself, as a value. We say that a type is *ground* if it contains no level variables.

Subtyping. Figure 6 shows the subtyping relation $\tau <: \tau'$, which is standard except for the levels. It requires that the outer level of the subtype is smaller than the outer level of the supertype and that the modes match in the case of functions: a stable-mode function is never a subtype or supertype of a changeable-mode function. (It would be sound to make stable-mode functions subtypes of changeable-mode functions, but changeable mode functions are more expensive; silent coercion would make performance less predictable.)

Levels and types. We rely on several relations between levels and types to ascertain various invariants. A type τ is *higher than* δ, written $\delta \lhd \tau$, if the outer level of the type is at least δ. In other words, δ is a lower bound of the outer level(s) of τ. Figure 7 defines this relation. We distinguish between outer-stable and outer-changeable types (Figure 8). We write τ O.S. if the outer level of τ is $\mathbb{S}$. Similarly, we write τ O.C. if the outer level of τ is $\mathbb{C}$. Finally, two types τ_1 and τ_2 are *equal up to their outer levels*, written $\tau_1 \doteq \tau_2$, if $\tau_1 = \tau_2$ or they differ only in their outer levels.

Constraints. To perform type inference, we extend levels with level variables α and β, and use a constraint solver to find solutions for the variables. Our constraints C, D include level-variable comparisons $\leq$ and level-type comparisons $\delta \lhd \tau$, which type inference composes into conjunctions of satisfiability predicates $\exists\vec{\alpha}.C$.

The subtyping and lower bound relations defined in Figures 6 and 7 consider closed types only. For type inference, we can extend these with a constraint to allow non-closed types.

A *(ground) assignment*, written ϕ, substitutes concrete levels $\mathbb{S}$ and $\mathbb{C}$ for level variables. An assignment ϕ satisfies a constraint C, written $\phi \vdash C$, if and only if C holds true after the substitution of variables to ground types as specified by ϕ. We say that C *entails* D, written $C \Vdash D$, if and only if every assignment ϕ that satisfies C also satisfies D. We write $\phi(\alpha)$ for the solution of α in ϕ, and $[\phi]\tau$ for the usual substitution operation on types. For example, if $\phi(\alpha) = \mathbb{S}$ then $[\phi]\left((\mathbf{int}^{\alpha} + \mathbf{int}^{\mathbb{C}})^{\alpha}\right) = (\mathbf{int}^{\mathbb{S}} + \mathbf{int}^{\mathbb{C}})^{\mathbb{S}}$.

Type schemes. A *type scheme* σ is a type with universally quantified level variables: $\sigma = \forall\vec{\alpha}[D].\,\tau$. We say that the variables $\vec{\alpha}$ are bound by σ. The type scheme is bounded by the constraint D, which specifies the conditions that must hold on the variables. As usual, we consider type schemes equivalent under capture-avoiding renaming of their bound variables. Ground types can be written as type schemes, e.g. $\mathbf{int}^{\mathbb{C}}$ as $\forall\emptyset[\mathbf{true}].\,\mathbf{int}^{\mathbb{C}}$.

$$\begin{array}{llcl} \textit{Values} & v & ::= & n \mid x \mid (v_1, v_2) \mid \mathbf{inl}\ v \mid \mathbf{inr}\ v \mid \mathbf{fun}\ f(x) = e \\ \textit{Expr.'s} & e & ::= & v \mid \oplus(x_1, x_2) \mid \mathbf{fst}\ x \mid \mathbf{snd}\ x \mid \\ & & & \mathbf{case}\ x\ \mathbf{of}\ \{x_1 \Rightarrow e_1\ ,\ x_2 \Rightarrow e_2\} \mid \\ & & & \mathbf{apply}(x_1, x_2) \mid \mathbf{let}\ x = e_1\ \mathbf{in}\ e_2 \end{array}$$

Figure 9. Abstract syntax of the source language Level ML

4. Source Language

4.1 Static Semantics

Syntax. Figure 9 shows the syntax for our source language Level ML, a purely functional language with integers (as base types), products, and sums. The expressions consist of values (integers, pairs, tagged values, recursive functions), projections, case expressions, function applications, and let bindings. For convenience, we consider only expressions in A-normal form, which names intermediate results. A-normal form simplifies some technical issues, while maintaining expressiveness.

Constraint-based type system. We could define types as

$$\tau\ ::=\ \mathbf{int} \mid \tau_1 \times \tau_2 \mid \tau_1 + \tau_2 \mid \tau_1 \to \tau_2$$

Such a type system would be completely standard. Instead, we use a richer type system that allows us to directly translate Level ML programs into self-adjusting programs in AFL. This constraint-based type system has the level-decorated types, constraints, and type schemes in Figure 5 and described in Section 3. After discussing the rules themselves, we will look at type inference (Section 4.2).

Typing takes place in the context of a constraint formula C and a typing environment Γ that maps variables to type schemes: $\Gamma\ ::=\ \cdot \mid \Gamma, x : \sigma$. The typing judgment $C; \Gamma \vdash_{\varepsilon} e : \tau$ has a constraint C and typing environment Γ, and infers type τ for expression e in mode ε. Beyond the usual typing concerns, there are three important aspects of the typing rules: the determination of modes and levels, level polymorphism, and constraints. To help separate concerns, we discuss constraints later in the section—at this time, the reader can ignore the constraints in the rules and read $C; \Gamma \vdash_{\varepsilon} e : \tau$ as $\Gamma \vdash_{\varepsilon} e : \tau$, read $C \Vdash \delta \lhd \tau_2$ as $\delta \lhd \tau_2$, and so on.

The mode of each typing judgment affects the types that can be used "directly" by the expression being typed. Specifically, the mode discipline prevents the elimination forms from being applied

$$\boxed{C;\Gamma \vdash_\varepsilon e : \tau}$$ Under constraint C and source typing environment Γ, source expression e has type τ

$$\frac{}{C;\Gamma \vdash_\varepsilon n : \mathbf{int}^{\mathbb{S}}}\ \text{(SInt)} \qquad \frac{\Gamma(x) = \forall\vec{\alpha}[D].\,\tau \quad C \Vdash \exists\vec{\beta}.[\vec{\beta}/\vec{\alpha}]D}{C \wedge [\vec{\beta}/\vec{\alpha}]D;\Gamma \vdash_\varepsilon x : [\vec{\beta}/\vec{\alpha}]\tau}\ \text{(SVar)}$$

$$\frac{C;\Gamma \vdash_\varepsilon v_1 : \tau_1 \qquad C;\Gamma \vdash_\varepsilon v_2 : \tau_2}{C;\Gamma \vdash_\varepsilon (v_1, v_2) : (\tau_1 \times \tau_2)^{\mathbb{S}}}\ \text{(SPair)}$$

$$\frac{C;\Gamma \vdash_\varepsilon v : \tau_1}{C;\Gamma \vdash_\varepsilon \mathbf{inl}\ v : (\tau_1 + \tau_2)^{\mathbb{S}}}\ \text{(SSum)}$$

$$\frac{C;\Gamma, x : \tau_1, f : (\tau_1 \underset{\varepsilon}{\rightarrow} \tau_2)^{\mathbb{S}} \vdash_\varepsilon e : \tau_2 \qquad C \Vdash \varepsilon \lhd \tau_2}{C;\Gamma \vdash_{\varepsilon'} (\mathbf{fun}\ f(x) = e) : (\tau_1 \underset{\varepsilon}{\rightarrow} \tau_2)^{\mathbb{S}}}\ \text{(SFun)}$$

$$\frac{\begin{array}{l} C;\Gamma \vdash_{\mathbb{S}} x_1 : \mathbf{int}^{\delta_1} \quad C \Vdash \delta_1 = \delta_2 \\ C;\Gamma \vdash_{\mathbb{S}} x_2 : \mathbf{int}^{\delta_2} \quad C \Vdash \delta_1 \le \varepsilon \quad \oplus : \mathbf{int} \times \mathbf{int} \to \mathbf{int} \end{array}}{C;\Gamma \vdash_\varepsilon \oplus(x_1, x_2) : \mathbf{int}^{\delta_1}}\ \text{(SPrim)}$$

$$\frac{C;\Gamma \vdash_{\mathbb{S}} x : (\tau_1 \times \tau_2)^{\delta} \qquad C \Vdash \delta \le \varepsilon}{C;\Gamma \vdash_\varepsilon \mathbf{fst}\ x : \tau_1}\ \text{(SFst)}$$

$$\frac{\begin{array}{ll} C;\Gamma \vdash_{\varepsilon'} e_1 : \tau' & C;\Gamma, x : \tau'' \vdash_\varepsilon e_2 : \tau \\ C \Vdash \tau' <: \tau'' & C \Vdash \tau' \doteq \tau'' \end{array}}{C;\Gamma \vdash_\varepsilon \mathbf{let}\ x = e_1\ \mathbf{in}\ e_2 : \tau}\ \text{(SLetE)}$$

$$\frac{\begin{array}{lll} C \wedge D;\Gamma \vdash_{\mathbb{S}} v_1 : \tau' & \multicolumn{2}{l}{C;\Gamma, x : \forall\vec{\alpha}[D].\,\tau'' \vdash_\varepsilon e_2 : \tau} \\ \vec{\alpha} \cap FV(C,\Gamma) = \emptyset & C \Vdash \tau' <: \tau'' & C \Vdash \tau' \doteq \tau'' \end{array}}{C \wedge \exists\vec{\alpha}.D;\Gamma \vdash_\varepsilon \mathbf{let}\ x = v_1\ \mathbf{in}\ e_2 : \tau}\ \text{(SLetV)}$$

$$\frac{\begin{array}{ll} C;\Gamma \vdash_{\mathbb{S}} x_1 : (\tau_1 \underset{\varepsilon'}{\rightarrow} \tau_2)^{\delta} & C \Vdash \varepsilon' = \varepsilon \\ C;\Gamma \vdash_{\mathbb{S}} x_2 : \tau_1 & C \Vdash \delta \lhd \tau_2 \end{array}}{C;\Gamma \vdash_\varepsilon \mathbf{apply}(x_1, x_2) : \tau_2}\ \text{(SApp)}$$

$$\frac{\begin{array}{lll} C;\Gamma \vdash_{\mathbb{S}} x : (\tau_1 + \tau_2)^{\delta} & & C;\Gamma, x_1 : \tau_1 \vdash_\varepsilon e_1 : \tau \\ C \Vdash \delta \le \varepsilon & C \Vdash \delta \lhd \tau & C;\Gamma, x_2 : \tau_2 \vdash_\varepsilon e_2 : \tau \end{array}}{C;\Gamma \vdash_\varepsilon \mathbf{case}\ x\ \mathbf{of}\ \{x_1 \Rightarrow e_1\ ,\ x_2 \Rightarrow e_2\} : \tau}\ \text{(SCase)}$$

Figure 10. Typing rules for Level ML

to changeable values in the stable mode. This is a key principle of the type system.

No computation happens in values, so they can be typed in either mode. The typing rules for variables (SVar), integers (SInt), pairs (SPair), and sums (SSum) are otherwise standard (we omit the symmetric judgment **inr** v). Rule (SVar) instantiates a variable's polymorphic type. For clarity, we also make explicit the renaming of the quantified type variables $\vec{\alpha}$ to some fresh $\vec{\beta}$ (which will be instantiated later by constraint solving). To type a function (SFun), we type the body in the mode ε specified by the function type $(\tau_1 \underset{\varepsilon}{\rightarrow} \tau_2)^{\delta}$, and require the result type τ_2 to be higher than the mode, $\varepsilon \lhd \tau_2$. As a result, a changeable-mode function must have a changeable return type. This captures the idea that a changeable-mode function is a computation that depends on changeable data, and thus its result must accommodate changes to that data. Primitive operators $\oplus$ take two stable integers and return a stable integer result.

As is common in Damas-Milner-style systems, when typing **let** we can generalize variables in types (in our system, level variables) to yield a polymorphic value only when the bound expression is a value. This *value restriction* is not essential because Level ML is pure, but facilitates adding side effects at a later date. In the first case (SLetE), the expression bound may be a non-value, so we do not generalize and simply type the body in the same mode as the whole **let**, assuming that the bound expression has the specified type in any mode ε'.[2] We allow subsumption only when the subtype and supertype are equal up to their outer levels, e.g. from a bound expression e_1 of subtype $\mathbf{int}^{\mathbb{S}}$ to an assumption $x : \mathbf{int}^{\mathbb{C}}$. This simplifies the translation, with no loss of expressiveness: to handle "deep" subsumption, such as $(\mathbf{int}^{\mathbb{S}} \underset{\mathbb{S}}{\rightarrow} \mathbf{int}^{\mathbb{S}})^{\mathbb{S}} <: (\mathbf{int}^{\mathbb{S}} \underset{\mathbb{S}}{\rightarrow} \mathbf{int}^{\mathbb{C}})^{\mathbb{C}}$, we can insert *coercions* into the source program before typing it with these rules. (This process could easily be automated.)

In the second case (SLetV), when the expression bound is a value, we type the let expression in mode ε by typing the body in the same mode ε, assuming that the value bound is typed in the stable mode (the mode is ignored in the rules typing values). As in (SLetE), we allow subsumption on the bound value only when the types are equal up to their outer level. Because we are binding a value, we generalize its type by quantifying over the type's free level variables.

Function application, $\oplus$, **fst**, and **case** are the forms that eliminate values of changeable type. An application is typed in the mode ε' of the function being applied because changeable functions can operate on changeable values; the typing mode must match ($\varepsilon' = \varepsilon$). Furthermore, the result of the function must be higher than the function's level: if a function is itself changeable, $(\tau_1 \underset{\varepsilon}{\rightarrow} \tau_2)^{\mathbb{C}}$, then it could be replaced by another function and thus the result of this application must be changeable. (Due to **let**-subsumption, checking this in (SFun) alone is not enough.)

The rule (SCase) types a case expression, in either mode ε, by typing each branch in ε. The mode ε must be higher than the level δ of the scrutinee to ensure that a changeable sum type is not inspected at the stable mode. Furthermore, the level of the result τ must also be higher than δ: if the scrutinee changes, we may take the other branch, requiring a changeable result.

Rule (SFst) enforces a condition, similar to (SCase), that we can project out of a changeable tuple of type $(\tau_1 \times \tau_2)^{\mathbb{C}}$ only in changeable mode. We omit the symmetric rule for **snd**.

Our premises on variables, such as the scrutinee of (SCase), are stable-mode ($\vdash_{\mathbb{S}}$), but this was an arbitrary decision; since (SVar) is the only rule that can derive such premises, their mode is irrelevant.

4.2 Constraints and Type Inference

Many of the rules simply pass around the constraint C. An implementation of rules with constraint-based premises, such as (SFun), implicitly adds those premises to the constraint, so that $C = \ldots \wedge (\varepsilon \lhd \tau_2)$. Rule (SLetV) generalizes level variables instead of type variables, with the "occurs check" $\vec{\alpha} \cap FV(C,\Gamma) = \emptyset$.

Standard techniques in the tradition of Damas and Milner [1982] can infer types for Level ML. In particular, our rules and constraints fall within the HM(X) framework [Odersky et al. 1999], permitting inference of principal types via constraint solving. As always, we cannot infer the types of polymorphically recursive functions.

Using a constraint solver that, given the choice between assigning $\mathbb{S}$ or $\mathbb{C}$ to some level variable, prefers $\mathbb{S}$, inference finds principal typings that are *minimally* changeable. Thus, data and computations will only be made changeable—and incur tracking overhead—where necessary to satisfy the programmer's annotation. This corresponds to preferring a lower security level in information flow [Pottier and Simonet 2003].

[2] In the target language, bound expressions must be stable-mode, but the translation puts changeable bound expressions inside a **mod**, yielding a stable-mode bound expression.

Levels	δ, ε	$::=$	$\mathbb{S} \mid \mathbb{C}$
Types	$\underline{\tau}$	$::=$	$\mathbf{int} \mid \underline{\tau}\ \mathbf{mod} \mid \underline{\tau}_1 \times \underline{\tau}_2 \mid \underline{\tau}_1 + \underline{\tau}_2 \mid \underline{\tau}_1 \underset{\varepsilon}{\rightarrow} \underline{\tau}_2$
Type schemes	$\underline{\sigma}$	$::=$	$\Pi\vec{\alpha}[D].\,\tau$
Typing environments	Γ	$::=$	$\cdot \mid \Gamma, x : \underline{\sigma} \mid \Gamma, x : \underline{\tau}$
Variables	$\underline{x}$	$::=$	$x \mid x[\vec{\alpha} = \vec{\delta}]$
Values	v	$::=$	$n \mid \underline{x} \mid \ell \mid (v_1, v_2) \mid \mathbf{inl}\ v \mid \mathbf{inr}\ v \mid \mathbf{fun}^{\mathbb{S}}\ f(x) = e^{\mathbb{S}} \mid \mathbf{fun}^{\mathbb{C}}\ f(x) = e^{\mathbb{C}} \mid \mathbf{select}\ \{(\vec{\alpha_i} = \vec{\delta_i}) \Rightarrow e_i\}_i$
Expressions	e	$::=$	$e^{\mathbb{S}} \mid e^{\mathbb{C}}$
Stable expressions	$e^{\mathbb{S}}$	$::=$	$v \mid \oplus(\underline{x_1}, \underline{x_2}) \mid \mathbf{fst}\ \underline{x} \mid \mathbf{snd}\ \underline{x} \mid \mathbf{apply}^{\mathbb{S}}(\underline{x_1}, \underline{x_2}) \mid \mathbf{let}\ x = e^{\mathbb{S}}\ \mathbf{in}\ e^{\mathbb{S}} \mid \mathbf{case}\ \underline{x}\ \mathbf{of}\ \{x_1 \Rightarrow e^{\mathbb{S}}\ ,\ x_2 \Rightarrow e^{\mathbb{S}}\} \mid \mathbf{mod}\ e^{\mathbb{C}}$
Changeable expressions	$e^{\mathbb{C}}$	$::=$	$\mathbf{apply}^{\mathbb{C}}(\underline{x_1}, \underline{x_2}) \mid \mathbf{let}\ x = e^{\mathbb{S}}\ \mathbf{in}\ e^{\mathbb{C}} \mid \mathbf{case}\ \underline{x}\ \mathbf{of}\ \{x_1 \Rightarrow e^{\mathbb{C}}\ ,\ x_2 \Rightarrow e^{\mathbb{C}}\} \mid \mathbf{read}\ \underline{x}\ \mathbf{as}\ y\ \mathbf{in}\ e^{\mathbb{C}} \mid \mathbf{write}(\underline{x})$

Figure 11. Types and expressions in the target language AFL

4.3 Dynamic Semantics

The call-by-value semantics of source programs is defined by a big-step judgment $e \Downarrow v$, read "e evaluates to value v". Our rules in Figure 13 are standard; we write $[v/x]e$ for capture-avoiding substitution of v for the variable x in e.

5. Target Language

The target language AFL (Figure 11) is a self-adjusting language with modifiables. In addition to integers, products, and sums, the target type system makes a modal distinction between ordinary types (e.g. **int**) and modifiable types (e.g. **int mod**). It also distinguishes stable-mode and changeable-mode functions. Level polymorphism is supported through an explicit **select** construct and an explicit polymorphic instantiation. In Section 6, we describe how polymorphic source expressions become **select**s in AFL.

The values of the language are integers, variables, polymorphic variable instantiation $x[\vec{\alpha} = \vec{\delta}]$, locations ℓ (which appear only at runtime), pairs, tagged values, stable and changeable functions, and the **select** construct, which acts as a function and case expression on levels: if x is bound to **select** $\{(\alpha = \mathbb{S}) \Rightarrow e_1 \mid (\alpha = \mathbb{C}) \Rightarrow e_2\}$ then $x[\alpha = \mathbb{S}]$ yields e_1. The symbol $\underline{x}$ stands for a bare variable x or an instantiation $x[\vec{\alpha} = \vec{\delta}]$.

We distinguish stable expressions $e^{\mathbb{S}}$ from changeable expressions $e^{\mathbb{C}}$. Stable expressions create purely functional values; **apply**$^{\mathbb{S}}$ applies a stable-mode function. The **mod** construct evaluates a changeable expression and writes the output value to a modifiable, yielding a location, which is a stable expression. Changeable expressions are computations that end in a **write** of a pure value. Changeable-mode application **apply**$^{\mathbb{C}}$ applies a changeable-mode function.

The **let** construct is either stable or changeable according to its body. When the body is a changeable expression, **let** enables a changeable computation to evaluate a stable expression and bind its result to a variable. The **case** expression is likewise stable or changeable, according to its case arms. The **read** expression binds the contents of a modifiable $\underline{x}$ to a variable y and evaluates the body of the **read**.

The typing rules in Figure 12 follow the structure of the expressions. Rule (TSelect) checks that each monomorphized expression e_i in a **select** has type $\|[\vec{\delta}/\vec{\alpha}]\tau\|$, where $[\vec{\delta}/\vec{\alpha}]\tau$ is a source-level

$\boxed{\Lambda; \Gamma \vdash_{\varepsilon} v : \underline{\sigma}}$ Under store typing Λ and target typing environment Γ, target value v has type scheme $\underline{\sigma}$

$$\frac{\text{for all } \vec{\delta_i} \text{ such that } \vec{\alpha} = \vec{\delta_i} \Vdash D \qquad \Lambda; \Gamma \vdash_{\mathbb{S}} e_i : \|[\vec{\delta_i}/\vec{\alpha}]\tau\|}{\Lambda; \Gamma \vdash_{\mathbb{S}} \mathbf{select}\ \{\vec{\delta_i} \Rightarrow e_i\}_i : \Pi\vec{\alpha}[D].\,\tau}\ \text{(TSelect)}$$

$\boxed{\Lambda; \Gamma \vdash_{\varepsilon} e^{\varepsilon} : \underline{\tau}}$ Under store typing Λ and target typing environment Γ, target expression e^{ε} has target type $\underline{\tau}$

$$\frac{\Lambda(\ell) = \underline{\tau}}{\Lambda; \Gamma \vdash_{\mathbb{S}} \ell : \underline{\tau}}\ \text{(TLoc)} \qquad \frac{}{\Lambda; \Gamma \vdash_{\mathbb{S}} n : \mathbf{int}}\ \text{(TInt)}$$

$$\frac{\Gamma(x) = \underline{\tau}}{\Lambda; \Gamma \vdash_{\mathbb{S}} x : \underline{\tau}}\ \text{(TPVar)} \qquad \frac{\Gamma(x) = \Pi\vec{\alpha}[D].\,\tau}{\Lambda; \Gamma \vdash_{\mathbb{S}} x[\vec{\alpha} = \vec{\delta}] : \|[\vec{\delta}/\vec{\alpha}]\tau\|}\ \text{(TVar)}$$

$$\frac{\Lambda; \Gamma \vdash_{\mathbb{S}} v_1 : \underline{\tau}_1 \qquad \Lambda; \Gamma \vdash_{\mathbb{S}} v_2 : \underline{\tau}_2}{\Lambda; \Gamma \vdash_{\mathbb{S}} (v_1, v_2) : \underline{\tau}_1 \times \underline{\tau}_2}\ \text{(TPair)}$$

$$\frac{\Lambda; \Gamma, x : \underline{\tau}_1, f : (\underline{\tau}_1 \underset{\varepsilon}{\rightarrow} \underline{\tau}_2) \vdash_{\varepsilon} e : \underline{\tau}_2}{\Lambda; \Gamma \vdash_{\mathbb{S}} \mathbf{fun}^{\varepsilon}\ f(x) = e : (\underline{\tau}_1 \underset{\varepsilon}{\rightarrow} \underline{\tau}_2)}\ \text{(TFun)}$$

$$\frac{\Lambda; \Gamma \vdash_{\mathbb{S}} v : \underline{\tau}_1}{\Lambda; \Gamma \vdash_{\mathbb{S}} \mathbf{inl}\ v : \underline{\tau}_1 + \underline{\tau}_2}\ \text{(TSum)} \qquad \frac{\Lambda; \Gamma \vdash_{\mathbb{S}} \underline{x} : \underline{\tau}_1 \times \underline{\tau}_2}{\Lambda; \Gamma \vdash_{\mathbb{S}} \mathbf{fst}\ \underline{x} : \underline{\tau}_1}\ \text{(TFst)}$$

$$\frac{\Lambda; \Gamma \vdash_{\mathbb{S}} \underline{x_1} : \mathbf{int} \qquad \Lambda; \Gamma \vdash_{\mathbb{S}} \underline{x_2} : \mathbf{int} \qquad \vdash \oplus : \mathbf{int} \times \mathbf{int} \rightarrow \mathbf{int}}{\Lambda; \Gamma \vdash_{\mathbb{S}} \oplus(\underline{x_1}, \underline{x_2}) : \mathbf{int}}\ \text{(TPrim)}$$

$$\frac{\Lambda; \Gamma \vdash_{\mathbb{S}} e_1^{\mathbb{S}} : \underline{\sigma} \qquad \Lambda; \Gamma, x : \underline{\sigma} \vdash_{\varepsilon} e_2 : \underline{\tau}'}{\Lambda; \Gamma \vdash_{\varepsilon} \mathbf{let}\ x = e_1^{\mathbb{S}}\ \mathbf{in}\ e_2 : \underline{\tau}'}\ \text{(TLet)}$$

$$\frac{\Lambda; \Gamma \vdash_{\mathbb{S}} \underline{x_1} : (\underline{\tau}_1 \underset{\varepsilon}{\rightarrow} \underline{\tau}_2) \qquad \Lambda; \Gamma \vdash_{\mathbb{S}} \underline{x_2} : \underline{\tau}_1}{\Lambda; \Gamma \vdash_{\varepsilon} \mathbf{apply}^{\varepsilon}(\underline{x_1}, \underline{x_2}) : \underline{\tau}_2}\ \text{(TApp)}$$

$$\frac{\Lambda; \Gamma \vdash_{\mathbb{S}} \underline{x} : \underline{\tau}_1 + \underline{\tau}_2 \qquad \Lambda; \Gamma, x_1 : \underline{\tau}_1 \vdash_{\varepsilon} e_1 : \underline{\tau} \qquad \Lambda; \Gamma, x_2 : \underline{\tau}_2 \vdash_{\varepsilon} e_2 : \underline{\tau}}{\Lambda; \Gamma \vdash_{\varepsilon} \mathbf{case}\ \underline{x}\ \mathbf{of}\ \{x_1 \Rightarrow e_1\ ,\ x_2 \Rightarrow e_2\} : \underline{\tau}}\ \text{(TCase)}$$

$$\frac{\Lambda; \Gamma \vdash_{\mathbb{C}} e : \underline{\tau}}{\Lambda; \Gamma \vdash_{\mathbb{S}} \mathbf{mod}\ e : \underline{\tau}\ \mathbf{mod}}\ \text{(TMod)} \qquad \frac{\Lambda; \Gamma \vdash_{\mathbb{S}} \underline{x} : \underline{\tau}}{\Lambda; \Gamma \vdash_{\mathbb{C}} \mathbf{write}(\underline{x}) : \underline{\tau}}\ \text{(TWrite)}$$

$$\frac{\Lambda; \Gamma \vdash_{\mathbb{S}} \underline{x_1} : \underline{\tau}_1\ \mathbf{mod} \qquad \Lambda; \Gamma, x : \underline{\tau}_1 \vdash_{\mathbb{C}} e_2 : \underline{\tau}_2}{\Lambda; \Gamma \vdash_{\mathbb{C}} \mathbf{read}\ \underline{x_1}\ \mathbf{as}\ x\ \mathbf{in}\ e_2 : \underline{\tau}_2}\ \text{(TRead)}$$

Figure 12. Typing rules of the target language AFL

polymorphic type with the levels $\vec{\delta}$ substituted for the variables $\vec{\alpha}$, and $\|-\|$ translates source types to target types (see Section 6.1). Rule (TPVar) is a standard rule for variables of monomorphic type, but rule (TVar) gives the instantiation $x[\vec{\alpha} = \vec{\delta}]$, of a variable x of polymorphic type, the type $\|[\vec{\delta}/\vec{\alpha}]\tau\|$—matching the monomorphic expression from the **select** to which x is bound.

5.1 Dynamic Semantics

For the source language, our big-step evaluation rules (Figure 13) are standard. In the target language AFL, our rules (Figure 14) model the evaluation of a first run of the program: modifiables are created, written to (once), and read from (any number of times), but never updated to reflect changes to the program input. Both sets of rules permit expressions that are not in A-normal form, enabling

$\boxed{e \Downarrow v}$ Source expression e evaluates to v

$$\frac{}{v \Downarrow v}\ (\text{SEvValue}) \qquad \frac{e_1 \Downarrow v_1 \quad e_2 \Downarrow v_2}{(e_1, e_2) \Downarrow (v_1, v_2)}\ (\text{SEvPair})$$

$$\frac{e \Downarrow v}{\mathbf{inl}\ e \Downarrow \mathbf{inl}\ v}\ (\text{SEvSum}) \qquad \frac{\begin{array}{l} e_1 \Downarrow v_1 \\ e_2 \Downarrow v_2 \quad \oplus(v_1, v_2) = v' \end{array}}{\oplus(e_1, e_2) \Downarrow v'}\ (\text{SEvPrimop})$$

$$\frac{e \Downarrow (v_1, v_2)}{\mathbf{fst}\ e \Downarrow v_1}\ (\text{SEvFst}) \qquad \frac{e_1 \Downarrow v_1 \quad [v_1/x]e_2 \Downarrow v_2}{\mathbf{let}\ x = e_1\ \mathbf{in}\ e_2 \Downarrow v_2}\ (\text{SEvLet})$$

$$\frac{e \Downarrow \mathbf{inl}\ v_1 \quad [v_1/x_1]e_1 \Downarrow v}{\mathbf{case}\ e\ \mathbf{of}\ \{x_1 \Rightarrow e_1\ ,\ x_2 \Rightarrow e_2\} \Downarrow v}\ (\text{SEvCaseLeft})$$

$$\frac{\begin{array}{l} e_1 \Downarrow \mathbf{fun}\ f(x) = e \\ e_2 \Downarrow v_2 \qquad [(\mathbf{fun}\ f(x) = e)/f][v_2/x]e \Downarrow v \end{array}}{\mathbf{apply}(e_1, e_2) \Downarrow v}\ (\text{SEvApply})$$

Figure 13. Dynamic semantics of source Level ML programs

standard capture-avoiding substitution. To simplify the translation, we call instantiations $x[\vec{\alpha} = \vec{\delta}]$ values, even though $x[\vec{\alpha} = \vec{\delta}]$ does not evaluate to itself. So we distinguish *machine values* w—which do evaluate to themselves—from values v. The only difference is that machine values do not include $x[\vec{\alpha} = \vec{\delta}]$.

Machine values $w ::= n \mid x \mid \ell \mid (w, w) \mid \mathbf{inl}\ w \mid \mathbf{inr}\ w \mid \mathbf{fun}^{\varepsilon}\ f(x) = e^{\varepsilon} \mid \mathbf{select}\ \{(\vec{\alpha_i} = \vec{\delta_i}) \Rightarrow e_i\}_i$

6. Translation

We specify the translation from Level ML to the target language AFL by a set of a rules. Because AFL is a modal language that distinguishes stable and changeable expressions, with a corresponding type system (Section 5), the translation is also modal: the translation in the stable mode $\underset{\mathbb{S}}{\hookrightarrow}$ produces a stable AFL expression $e^{\mathbb{S}}$, and the translation in the changeable mode $\underset{\mathbb{C}}{\hookrightarrow}$ produces a changeable expression $e^{\mathbb{C}}$.

It is not enough to generate AFL expressions of the right syntactic form; they must also have the right type. To achieve this, the rules are type-directed: we translate a source expression e *at type* τ. But we are transforming expressions from one language to another, where each language has its own type system; translating some $e : \tau$ cannot produce some $e' : \tau$, but some $e' : \underline{\tau}'$ where $\underline{\tau}'$ is a target type that *corresponds to* τ. To express this vital property, we need to translate types, as well as expressions. We developed the translation of expressions and types together (along with the proof that the property holds); the translation of types was instrumental in getting the translation of expressions right. To understand how to translate expressions, it is helpful to first understand how we translate types.

6.1 Translating Types

Figure 15 defines the translation of types via two mutually recursive functions from Level ML types to AFL types. The first function, $\|\tau\|$, tells us what type the target expression $e^{\mathbb{S}}$ should have when we translate e in the stable mode, $e : \tau \underset{\mathbb{S}}{\hookrightarrow} e^{\mathbb{S}}$. We also use it to translate the types in the environment Γ. The second function, $\|\tau\|^{\to\mathbb{C}}$, makes sense in two related situations: translating the type τ of an expression e in the changeable mode ($e : \tau \underset{\mathbb{C}}{\hookrightarrow} e^{\mathbb{C}}$) and translating the codomain of changeable functions.

In the stable mode, values of stable type can be used and created directly, so the "stable" translation $\|\mathbf{int}^{\mathbb{S}}\|$ of a stable integer is

$\boxed{\rho \vdash e \Downarrow (\rho' \vdash w)}$ In the store ρ, target expression e evaluates to w with updated store ρ'

$$\frac{}{\rho \vdash w \Downarrow (\rho \vdash w)}\ (\text{TEvMachineValue})$$

$$\frac{\rho \vdash e_1 \Downarrow (\rho_1 \vdash w_1) \qquad \rho_1 \vdash e_2 \Downarrow (\rho_2 \vdash w_2)}{\rho \vdash (e_1, e_2) \Downarrow (\rho_2 \vdash (w_1, w_2))}\ (\text{TEvPair})$$

$$\frac{\rho \vdash e \Downarrow (\rho' \vdash w)}{\rho \vdash \mathbf{inl}\ e \Downarrow (\rho' \vdash \mathbf{inl}\ w)}\ (\text{TEvSum})$$

$$\frac{\begin{array}{l} \rho \vdash e_1 \Downarrow (\rho_1 \vdash w_1) \\ \rho_1 \vdash e_2 \Downarrow (\rho_2 \vdash w_2) \qquad \oplus(w_1, w_2) = w' \end{array}}{\rho \vdash \oplus(e_1, e_2) \Downarrow (\rho_2 \vdash w')}\ (\text{TEvPrimop})$$

$$\frac{\rho \vdash e \Downarrow (\rho' \vdash (w_1, w_2))}{\rho \vdash \mathbf{fst}\ e \Downarrow (\rho' \vdash w_1)}\ (\text{TEvFst})$$

$$\frac{\rho \vdash e_1 \Downarrow (\rho_1 \vdash w_1) \qquad \rho_1 \vdash [w_1/x]e_2 \Downarrow (\rho_2 \vdash w_2)}{\rho \vdash \mathbf{let}\ x = e_1\ \mathbf{in}\ e_2 \Downarrow (\rho_2 \vdash w_2)}\ (\text{TEvLet})$$

$$\frac{\begin{array}{c} \rho \vdash e \Downarrow (\rho_1 \vdash \mathbf{inl}\ w_1) \\ \rho_1 \vdash [w_1/x_1]e_1 \Downarrow (\rho_2 \vdash w) \end{array}}{\rho \vdash \mathbf{case}\ e\ \mathbf{of}\ \{x_1 \Rightarrow e_1\ ,\ x_2 \Rightarrow e_2\} \Downarrow (\rho_2 \vdash w)}\ (\text{TEvCaseLeft})$$

$$\frac{\begin{array}{l} \rho \vdash e_1^{\varepsilon} \Downarrow (\rho_1 \vdash \mathbf{fun}^{\varepsilon}\ f(x) = e^{\varepsilon}) \\ \rho_1 \vdash e_2^{\varepsilon} \Downarrow (\rho_2 \vdash w_2) \\ \rho_2 \vdash [(\mathbf{fun}^{\varepsilon}\ f(x) = e^{\varepsilon})/f][w_2/x]e^{\varepsilon} \Downarrow (\rho_3 \vdash w) \end{array}}{\rho \vdash \mathbf{apply}^{\varepsilon}(e_1^{\varepsilon}, e_2^{\varepsilon}) \Downarrow (\rho_3 \vdash w)}\ (\text{TEvApply})$$

$$\frac{\rho \vdash e \Downarrow (\rho' \vdash w)}{\rho \vdash \mathbf{write}(e) \Downarrow (\rho' \vdash w)}\ (\text{TEvWrite})$$

$$\frac{\rho \vdash e_1 \Downarrow (\rho_1 \vdash \ell) \qquad \rho_1 \vdash [\rho_1(\ell)/x']e^{\mathbb{C}} \Downarrow (\rho_2 \vdash w)}{\rho \vdash \mathbf{read}\ e_1\ \mathbf{as}\ x'\ \mathbf{in}\ e^{\mathbb{C}} \Downarrow (\rho_2 \vdash w)}\ (\text{TEvRead})$$

$$\frac{\rho_1 \vdash e_1 \Downarrow (\rho' \vdash w)}{\rho \vdash (\mathbf{select}\ \{\ldots, \vec{\delta} \Rightarrow e_1, \ldots\})[\vec{\alpha} = \vec{\delta}] \Downarrow (\rho' \vdash w)}\ (\text{TEvSelectE})$$

$$\frac{\rho \vdash e^{\mathbb{C}} \Downarrow (\rho' \vdash w)}{\rho \vdash \mathbf{mod}\ e^{\mathbb{C}} \Downarrow ((\rho', \ell \mapsto w) \vdash \ell)}\ (\text{TEvMod})$$

Figure 14. Dynamic semantics for first runs of AFL programs

just **int**. In contrast, a changeable integer cannot be inspected or directly created in stable mode, but must be placed into a modifiable: $\|\mathbf{int}^{\mathbb{C}}\| = \mathbf{int\ mod}$. The remaining parts of the definition follow this pattern: the target type is wrapped with **mod** if and only if the outer level of the source type is $\mathbb{C}$. When we translate a changeable-mode function type (with $\mathbb{C}$ below the arrow), its codomain is translated "output-changeable": $\|(\tau_1 \underset{\mathbb{C}}{\to} \tau_2)^{\mathbb{S}}\| = \|\tau_1\| \underset{\mathbb{C}}{\to} \|\tau_2\|^{\to\mathbb{C}}$. The reason is that a changeable-mode function can only be applied in the changeable mode; the function result is not placed into a modifiable until we return to the stable mode, so putting a **mod** on the codomain would not match the dynamic semantics of AFL.

The second function $\|\tau\|^{\to\mathbb{C}}$ defines the type of a changeable expression e that writes to a modifiable containing τ, yielding a changeable target expression $e^{\mathbb{C}}$. The source type has an outer $\mathbb{C}$, so when the value is written, it will be placed into a modifiable and have **mod** type. But while evaluating $e^{\mathbb{C}}$, there is no outer **mod**. Thus the translation $\|\tau\|^{\to\mathbb{C}}$ ignores the outer level (using the function $|-|^{\mathbb{S}}$, which replaces an outer level $\mathbb{C}$ with $\mathbb{S}$), and never

$$
\begin{aligned}
\left|\mathbf{int}^{\mathbb{C}}\right|^{\mathbb{S}} &= \mathbf{int}^{\mathbb{S}} \\
\left|(\tau_1 \times \tau_2)^{\mathbb{C}}\right|^{\mathbb{S}} &= (\tau_1 \times \tau_2)^{\mathbb{S}} \\
\left|(\tau_1 + \tau_2)^{\mathbb{C}}\right|^{\mathbb{S}} &= (\tau_1 + \tau_2)^{\mathbb{S}} \\
\left|(\tau_1 \underset{\varepsilon}{\to} \tau_2)^{\mathbb{C}}\right|^{\mathbb{S}} &= (\tau_1 \underset{\varepsilon}{\to} \tau_2)^{\mathbb{S}}
\end{aligned}
$$

$$
\begin{aligned}
\|\mathbf{int}^{\mathbb{S}}\| &= \mathbf{int} \\
\|\mathbf{int}^{\mathbb{C}}\| &= \mathbf{int\ mod} \\
\|(\tau_1 \underset{\mathbb{S}}{\to} \tau_2)^{\mathbb{S}}\| &= \|\tau_1\| \underset{\mathbb{S}}{\to} \|\tau_2\| \\
\|(\tau_1 \underset{\mathbb{S}}{\to} \tau_2)^{\mathbb{C}}\| &= \left(\|\tau_1\| \underset{\mathbb{S}}{\to} \|\tau_2\|\right) \mathbf{mod} \\
\|(\tau_1 \underset{\mathbb{C}}{\to} \tau_2)^{\mathbb{S}}\| &= \|\tau_1\| \underset{\mathbb{C}}{\to} \|\tau_2\|^{\to\mathbb{C}} \\
\|(\tau_1 \underset{\mathbb{C}}{\to} \tau_2)^{\mathbb{C}}\| &= \left(\|\tau_1\| \underset{\mathbb{C}}{\to} \|\tau_2\|^{\to\mathbb{C}}\right) \mathbf{mod} \\
\|(\tau_1 \times \tau_2)^{\mathbb{S}}\| &= \|\tau_1\| \times \|\tau_2\| \\
\|(\tau_1 \times \tau_2)^{\mathbb{C}}\| &= (\|\tau_1\| \times \|\tau_2\|)\ \mathbf{mod} \\
\|(\tau_1 + \tau_2)^{\mathbb{S}}\| &= \|\tau_1\| + \|\tau_2\| \\
\|(\tau_1 + \tau_2)^{\mathbb{C}}\| &= (\|\tau_1\| + \|\tau_2\|)\ \mathbf{mod}
\end{aligned}
$$

$$
\|\tau\|^{\to\mathbb{C}} = \begin{cases} \|\left|\tau\right|^{\mathbb{S}}\| & \text{if } \tau \text{ O.C.} \\ \|\tau\| & \text{if } \tau \text{ O.S.} \end{cases}
$$

$$
\begin{aligned}
\|\cdot\| &= \cdot & \|\tau\|_{\phi} &= \|[\phi]\tau\| \\
\|\Gamma, x : \forall\emptyset[\mathsf{true}].\,\tau\| &= \|\Gamma\|, x : \|\tau\| & \|\tau\|_{\phi}^{\to\mathbb{C}} &= \|[\phi]\tau\|^{\to\mathbb{C}} \\
\|\Gamma, x : \forall\vec{\alpha}[D].\,\tau\| &= \|\Gamma\|, x : \Pi\vec{\alpha}[D].\,\tau & \|\Gamma\|_{\phi} &= \|[\phi]\Gamma\|
\end{aligned}
$$

Figure 15. Stabilization of types $\left|\tau\right|^{\mathbb{S}}$; translations $\|\tau\|$ and $\|\tau\|^{\to\mathbb{C}}$ of types; translation of typing environments $\|\Gamma\|$

returns a type of the form $(\cdots$ **mod**$)$. However, since the value being returned may contain subexpressions that will be placed into modifiables, we use $\|-\|$ for the inner types. For instance, $\|(\tau_1 + \tau_2)^{\delta}\|^{\to\mathbb{C}} = \|\tau_1\| + \|\tau_2\|$.

These functions are defined on closed types—types with no free level variables. Before applying one of these functions to a type found by the constraint typing rules, we always need to apply the satisfying assignment ϕ to the type, so for convenience we write $\|\tau\|_{\phi}$ for $\|[\phi]\tau\|$, and so on. Because the translation only makes sense for closed types, type schemes $\forall\vec{\alpha}[D].\,\tau$ cannot be translated. The translation $\|\Gamma\|$ therefore translates only monomorphic types τ; type schemes are left alone (except for replacing the symbol $\forall$ with Π) until instantiation. Once instantiated, the type scheme is an ordinary closed source type, and can be translated by rule (TVar).

6.2 Translating Expressions

We define the translation of expressions as a set of type-directed rules. Given (1) a derivation of $C; \Gamma \vdash_{\varepsilon} e : \tau$ in the constraint-based typing system and (2) a satisfying assignment ϕ for C, it is always possible to produce a correctly typed stable target expression $e^{\mathbb{S}}$ *and* a correctly typed changeable target expression $e^{\mathbb{C}}$ (see Theorem 6.1 below). The environment Γ in the translation rules is a source typing environment, but must have no free level variables. Given an environment Γ from the constraint typing, we apply the satisfying assignment ϕ to eliminate its free level variables before using it for the translation: $[\phi]\Gamma$. With the environment closed, we need not refer to C.

Many of the rules in Figure 17 are purely syntax-directed and are similar to the constraint-based rules. One exception is the (Var) rule, which needs the source type to know how to instantiate the level variables in the type scheme. For example, given the polymorphic $x : \forall\alpha[\mathsf{true}].\,(\mathbf{int}^{\alpha} \underset{\alpha}{\to} \mathbf{int}^{\alpha})^{\mathbb{S}}$, we need the type from $C; \Gamma \vdash_{\varepsilon} x : (\mathbf{int}^{\mathbb{C}} \underset{\mathbb{C}}{\to} \mathbf{int}^{\mathbb{C}})^{\mathbb{S}}$ so we can instantiate α in the translated term $x[\alpha = \mathbb{C}]$.

$$
\boxed{\Gamma \vdash e \rightsquigarrow (x \gg x' : \tau \vdash e')}
$$

Under source typing Γ, renaming the "head" x in e to $x' : \tau$ yields expression e'

$$
\frac{\Gamma \vdash x_1 : \tau}{\Gamma \vdash \oplus(x_1, x_2) \rightsquigarrow (x_1 \gg x_1' : \tau \vdash \oplus(x_1', x_2))}\ \text{(LPrimop1)}
$$

$$
\frac{\Gamma \vdash x_2 : \tau}{\Gamma \vdash \oplus(x_1, x_2) \rightsquigarrow (x_2 \gg x_2' : \tau \vdash \oplus(x_1, x_2'))}\ \text{(LPrimop2)}
$$

$$
\frac{\Gamma \vdash x : \tau}{\Gamma \vdash \mathbf{fst}\, x \rightsquigarrow (x \gg x' : \tau \vdash \mathbf{fst}\, x')}\ \text{(LFst)}
$$

$$
\frac{\Gamma \vdash x_1 : \tau}{\Gamma \vdash \mathbf{apply}(x_1, x_2) \rightsquigarrow (x_1 \gg x' : \tau \vdash \mathbf{apply}(x', x_2))}\ \text{(LApply)}
$$

$$
\frac{\Gamma \vdash x : \tau}{\begin{array}{l}\Gamma \vdash \mathbf{case}\, x\, \mathbf{of}\, \{x_1 \Rightarrow e_1\,,\, x_2 \Rightarrow e_2\} \\ \quad \rightsquigarrow (x \gg x' : \tau \vdash \mathbf{case}\, x'\, \mathbf{of}\, \{x_1 \Rightarrow e_1\,,\, x_2 \Rightarrow e_2\})\end{array}}\ \text{(LCase)}
$$

Figure 16. Renaming the variable to be read (elimination forms)

Our rules are nondeterministic, avoiding the need to "decorate" them with context-sensitive details. Our algorithm in Section 6.3 resolves the nondeterminism through type information.

Stable rules. The rules (Int), (Var), (Pair), (Fun), (Sum), (Fst) and (Prim) can only translate in the stable mode. To translate to a changeable expression, use a rule that shifts to changeable mode.

Shifting to changeable mode. Given a translation of e in the stable mode to some $e^{\mathbb{S}}$, the rules (Write) and (ReadWrite) at the bottom of Figure 17 translate e in the changeable mode, producing an $e^{\mathbb{C}}$. If the expression's type τ is outer stable (say, $\mathbf{int}^{\mathbb{S}}$), the (Write) rule simply binds it to a variable and then writes that variable. If τ is outer changeable (say, $\mathbf{int}^{\mathbb{C}}$) it will be in a modifiable at runtime, so we read it into r' and then write it. (The let-bindings merely satisfy the requirements of A-normal form.)

Shifting to stable mode. To generate a stable expression $e^{\mathbb{S}}$ based on a changeable expression $e^{\mathbb{C}}$, we have the (Lift) and (Mod) rules. These rules require the source type τ to be outer changeable: in (Lift), the premise $\left|\tau\right|^{\mathbb{S}} = \underline{\tau}'$ requires that $\left|\tau\right|^{\mathbb{S}}$ is defined, and it is defined only for outer changeable τ; in (Mod), the requirement is explicit: $\vdash \tau$ O.C.

(Mod) is the simpler of the two: if e translates to $e^{\mathbb{C}}$ at type τ, then e translates to the stable expression **mod** $e^{\mathbb{C}}$ at type τ. In (Lift), the expression is translated not at the given type τ but at its *stabilized* $\left|\tau\right|^{\mathbb{S}}$, capturing the "shallow subsumption" in the constraint typing rules (SLetE) and (SLetV): a bound expression of type $\tau_0^{\mathbb{S}}$ can be translated at type $\tau_0^{\mathbb{S}}$ to $e^{\mathbb{S}}$, and then "promoted" to type $\tau_0^{\mathbb{C}}$ by placing it inside a **mod**.

Reading from changeable data. To use an expression of changeable type in a context where a stable value is needed—such as passing some $x : \mathbf{int}^{\mathbb{C}}$ to a function expecting $\mathbf{int}^{\mathbb{S}}$—the (Read) rule generates a target expression that reads the value out of $x : \mathbf{int}^{\mathbb{C}}$ into a variable $x' : \mathbf{int}^{\mathbb{S}}$. The variable-renaming judgment $\Gamma \vdash e \rightsquigarrow (x \gg x' : \tau \vdash e')$ takes the expression e, finds a variable x about to be used, and yields an expression e' with that occurrence replaced by x'. For example, $\Gamma \vdash \mathbf{case}\, x\, \mathbf{of} \ldots \rightsquigarrow (x \gg x' : \tau \vdash \mathbf{case}\, x'\, \mathbf{of} \ldots)$. This judgment is derivable only for **apply**, **case**, **fst**, and $\oplus$, because these are the elimination forms for outer-changeable data. For $\oplus(x_1, x_2)$, we need to read both variables, so we have one rule for each. The rules are given in Figure 16.

$$\boxed{\Gamma \vdash e : \tau \underset{\varepsilon}{\hookrightarrow} e^{\varepsilon}}$$

Under closed source typing environment Γ, source expression e is translated at type τ in mode ε to target expression e^{ε}

$$\frac{}{\Gamma \vdash n : \mathbf{int}^{\delta} \underset{\mathbb{S}}{\hookrightarrow} n}\ (\text{Int}) \qquad \frac{\Gamma(x) = \forall\vec{\alpha}[D].\,\tau}{\Gamma \vdash x : [\vec{\delta}/\vec{\alpha}]\tau \underset{\mathbb{S}}{\hookrightarrow} x[\vec{\alpha} = \vec{\delta}]}\ (\text{Var})$$

$$\frac{\Gamma \vdash v_1 : \tau_1 \underset{\mathbb{S}}{\hookrightarrow} v_1' \qquad \Gamma \vdash v_2 : \tau_2 \underset{\mathbb{S}}{\hookrightarrow} v_2'}{\Gamma \vdash (v_1, v_2) : (\tau_1 \times \tau_2)^{\mathbb{S}} \underset{\mathbb{S}}{\hookrightarrow} (v_1', v_2')}\ (\text{Pair})$$

$$\frac{\Gamma, x : \tau_1, f : (\tau_1 \underset{\varepsilon}{\rightarrow} \tau_2)^{\mathbb{S}} \vdash e : \tau_2 \underset{\varepsilon}{\hookrightarrow} e^{\varepsilon}}{\Gamma \vdash \mathbf{fun}\ f(x) = e : (\tau_1 \underset{\varepsilon}{\rightarrow} \tau_2)^{\mathbb{S}} \underset{\mathbb{S}}{\hookrightarrow} \mathbf{fun}^{\varepsilon}\ f(x) = e^{\varepsilon}}\ (\text{Fun})$$

$$\frac{\Gamma \vdash v : \tau_1 \underset{\mathbb{S}}{\hookrightarrow} v'}{\Gamma \vdash \mathbf{inl}\ v : (\tau_1 + \tau_2)^{\mathbb{S}} \underset{\mathbb{S}}{\hookrightarrow} \mathbf{inl}\ v'}\ (\text{Sum})$$

$$\frac{\Gamma \vdash x : (\tau_1 \times \tau_2)^{\mathbb{S}} \underset{\mathbb{S}}{\hookrightarrow} \underline{x}}{\Gamma \vdash \mathbf{fst}\ x : \tau_1 \underset{\mathbb{S}}{\hookrightarrow} \mathbf{fst}\ \underline{x}}\ (\text{Fst})$$

$$\frac{\Gamma \vdash x_1 : \mathbf{int}^{\mathbb{S}} \underset{\mathbb{S}}{\hookrightarrow} \underline{x_1} \qquad \Gamma \vdash x_2 : \mathbf{int}^{\mathbb{S}} \underset{\mathbb{S}}{\hookrightarrow} \underline{x_2}}{\Gamma \vdash \oplus(x_1, x_2) : \mathbf{int}^{\delta} \underset{\mathbb{S}}{\hookrightarrow} \oplus(\underline{x_1}, \underline{x_2})}\ (\text{Prim})$$

$$\frac{\Gamma \vdash x_1 : (\tau_1 \underset{\varepsilon}{\rightarrow} \tau_2)^{\mathbb{S}} \underset{\mathbb{S}}{\hookrightarrow} \underline{x_1} \qquad \Gamma \vdash x_2 : \tau_1 \underset{\mathbb{S}}{\hookrightarrow} \underline{x_2}}{\Gamma \vdash \mathbf{apply}(x_1, x_2) : \tau_2 \underset{\varepsilon}{\hookrightarrow} \mathbf{apply}^{\varepsilon}(\underline{x_1}, \underline{x_2})}\ (\text{App})$$

$$\frac{\Gamma \vdash x : (\tau_1 + \tau_2)^{\mathbb{S}} \underset{\mathbb{S}}{\hookrightarrow} \underline{x} \qquad \begin{array}{l}\Gamma, x_1 : \tau_1 \vdash e_1 : \tau \underset{\varepsilon}{\hookrightarrow} e_1' \\ \Gamma, x_2 : \tau_2 \vdash e_2 : \tau \underset{\varepsilon}{\hookrightarrow} e_2'\end{array}}{\begin{array}{l}\Gamma \vdash \quad \mathbf{case}\ x\ \mathbf{of}\ \{x_1 \Rightarrow e_1\ ,\ x_2 \Rightarrow e_2\} : \tau \\ \quad \underset{\varepsilon}{\hookrightarrow} \mathbf{case}\ \underline{x}\ \mathbf{of}\ \{x_1 \Rightarrow e_1'\ ,\ x_2 \Rightarrow e_2'\}\end{array}}\ (\text{Case})$$

$$\frac{\Gamma \vdash e : \tau' \underset{\mathbb{C}}{\hookrightarrow} e^{\mathbb{C}} \qquad |\tau|^{\mathbb{S}} = \tau'}{\Gamma \vdash e : \tau \underset{\mathbb{S}}{\hookrightarrow} \mathbf{mod}\ e^{\mathbb{C}}}\ (\text{Lift}) \qquad \frac{\Gamma \vdash e : \tau \underset{\mathbb{C}}{\hookrightarrow} e^{\mathbb{C}} \qquad \tau\ \mathsf{O.C.}}{\Gamma \vdash e : \tau \underset{\mathbb{S}}{\hookrightarrow} \mathbf{mod}\ e^{\mathbb{C}}}\ (\text{Mod})$$

$$\frac{\Gamma \vdash e_1 : \tau' \underset{\mathbb{S}}{\hookrightarrow} e^{\mathbb{S}} \qquad \Gamma, x : \tau' \vdash e_2 : \tau \underset{\varepsilon}{\hookrightarrow} e_2'}{\Gamma \vdash \mathbf{let}\ x = e_1\ \mathbf{in}\ e_2 : \tau \underset{\varepsilon}{\hookrightarrow} \mathbf{let}\ x = e^{\mathbb{S}}\ \mathbf{in}\ e_2'}\ (\text{LetE})$$

$$\frac{\Gamma, x : \forall\vec{\alpha}[D].\,\tau' \vdash e : \tau \underset{\varepsilon}{\hookrightarrow} e' \qquad \begin{array}{r}\text{For all } \vec{\delta_i} \text{ s.t. } \vec{\alpha} = \vec{\delta_i} \Vdash D, \\ \Gamma \vdash v : [\vec{\delta_i}/\vec{\alpha}]\tau' \underset{\mathbb{S}}{\hookrightarrow} e_i'\end{array}}{\Gamma \vdash \mathbf{let}\ x = v\ \mathbf{in}\ e : \tau \underset{\varepsilon}{\hookrightarrow} \mathbf{let}\ x = \mathbf{select}\ \{(\vec{\alpha}{=}\vec{\delta_i}) \Rightarrow e_i'\}_i\ \mathbf{in}\ e'}\ (\text{LetV})$$

$$\frac{\begin{array}{ll}\Gamma \vdash e \rightsquigarrow (x \gg x' : \tau' \vdash e') & \tau'\ \mathsf{O.C.} \\ \Gamma, x' : |\tau'|^{\mathbb{S}} \vdash e' : \tau \underset{\mathbb{C}}{\hookrightarrow} e^{\mathbb{C}} & \Gamma \vdash x : \tau' \underset{\mathbb{S}}{\hookrightarrow} \underline{x}\end{array}}{\Gamma \vdash e : \tau \underset{\mathbb{C}}{\hookrightarrow} \mathbf{read}\ \underline{x}\ \mathbf{as}\ x'\ \mathbf{in}\ e^{\mathbb{C}}}\ (\text{Read})$$

$$\frac{\Gamma \vdash e : \tau \underset{\mathbb{S}}{\hookrightarrow} e^{\mathbb{S}} \qquad \tau\ \mathsf{O.S.}}{\Gamma \vdash e : \tau \underset{\mathbb{C}}{\hookrightarrow} \mathbf{let}\ r = e^{\mathbb{S}}\ \mathbf{in}\ \mathbf{write}(r)}\ (\text{Write})$$

$$\frac{\Gamma \vdash e : \tau \underset{\mathbb{S}}{\hookrightarrow} e^{\mathbb{S}} \qquad \tau\ \mathsf{O.C.}}{\Gamma \vdash e : \tau \underset{\mathbb{C}}{\hookrightarrow} \mathbf{let}\ r = e^{\mathbb{S}}\ \mathbf{in}\ \mathbf{read}\ r\ \mathbf{as}\ r'\ \mathbf{in}\ \mathbf{write}(r')}\ (\text{ReadWrite})$$

Figure 17. Monomorphizing translation

Monomorphization. A polymorphic source expression has no directly corresponding target expression: the `map` function from Section 2 corresponds to the two functions `map_SC` and `map_CS`. Given a polymorphic source value $v : \forall\vec{\alpha}[D].\,\tau'$, the (LetV) rule translates v once for each instantiation $\vec{\delta_i}$ that satisfies the constraint D (each $\vec{\delta_i}$ such that $\vec{\alpha} = \vec{\delta_i} \Vdash D$). That is, we translate the value at source type $[\vec{\delta_i}/\vec{\alpha}]\tau'$. This yields a sequence of source expressions $e_1, \ldots, e_n$ for the n possible instances. For example, given $\forall\alpha[\mathsf{true}].\,\tau'$, we translate the value at type $[\mathbb{S}/\alpha]\tau'$ yielding e_1 and at type $[\mathbb{C}/\alpha]\tau'$ yielding e_2. Finally, the rule produces a **select** expression, which acts as a function that takes the desired instance $\vec{\delta_i}$ and returns the appropriate e_i.

Since (LetV) generates one function for each satisfying $\vec{\delta_i}$, it can create up to 2^n instances for n variables. However, dead-code elimination can remove functions that are not used. Moreover, the functions that *are* used would have been handwritten in an explicit setting, so while the code size is exponential in the worst case, the saved effort is as well.

6.3 Algorithm

The system of translation rules in Figure 17 is not deterministic. In fact, if the wrong choices are made it can produce painfully inefficient code. Suppose we have $2 : \mathbf{int}^{\mathbb{C}}$, and want to translate it to a stable target expression. Choosing rule (Int) yields the target expression 2. But we could use (Int), then (ReadWrite)—which generates an $e^{\mathbb{C}}$ with a **let**, a **read** and a **write**—then (Mod), which wraps that $e^{\mathbb{C}}$ in a **mod**. Clearly, we should have stopped with (Int).

To resolve this nondeterminism in the rules would complicate them further. Instead, we give the algorithm in Figure 18, which examines the source expression e and, using type information, applies the rules necessary to produce an expression of mode ε.

6.4 Properties

Given a constraint-based source typing derivation and assignment ϕ for some term e, there are translations from e to (1) a stable $e^{\mathbb{S}}$ and (2) a changeable $e^{\mathbb{C}}$, with appropriate target types:

Theorem 6.1 (Translation Type Soundness).
If $C; \Gamma \vdash_{\varepsilon} e : \tau$ and ϕ is a satisfying assignment for C then
(1) there exists $e^{\mathbb{S}}$ such that $[\phi]\Gamma \vdash e : [\phi]\tau \underset{\mathbb{S}}{\hookrightarrow} e^{\mathbb{S}}$ and $\cdot; \|\Gamma\|_{\phi} \vdash_{\mathbb{S}} e^{\mathbb{S}} : \|\tau\|_{\phi}$ and, if e is a value, then $e^{\mathbb{S}}$ is a value;
(2) there exists $e^{\mathbb{C}}$ such that $[\phi]\Gamma \vdash e : [\phi]\tau \underset{\mathbb{C}}{\hookrightarrow} e^{\mathbb{C}}$ and $\cdot; \|\Gamma\|_{\phi} \vdash_{\mathbb{C}} e^{\mathbb{C}} : \|\tau\|_{\phi}^{\rightarrow\mathbb{C}}$.

The proof (in the appendix [Chen et al. 2011]) is by induction on the height of the given derivation of $C; \Gamma \vdash_{\varepsilon} e : \tau$. If the concluding rule was (SLetE), we use a substitution property (Lemma A.2) for each $\vec{\delta_i}$ to get a monomorphic constraint typing derivation; that derivation is not larger than the input derivation, so we can apply the induction hypothesis to get a translated e_i'. The proof constructs the same translation derivations as the algorithm in Figure 18 (in fact, we extracted the algorithm from the proof).

We also prove that running a translated program gives the same result as running the source program. Theorem 6.5 states that in an initially empty store $\cdot$, if evaluating the translated program e' yields v' with new store ρ', then e evaluates to v where v corresponds to $[\rho']v'$ (the result of substituting values in the store ρ' for locations appearing in v').

To define this correspondence, we use a device somewhat similar to logical relations: a relation $\looparrowright$ on source and target expressions, allowing us to show that if $e : \tau \looparrowright e' : \underline{\tau}'$ then $v : \tau \looparrowright [\rho]v' : \underline{\tau}'$. Both e and e' must be closed. Our definition is weaker than the equivalence relations used in logical relations proofs: $\mathbf{apply}(\mathrm{id}, 4) \not\looparrowright 4$, for example. It does not attempt to equate all programs that have the same meaning, but only particu-

```
function trans (e, ε) = case (e, ε) of
 | (n, 𝕊) ⇒ Int
 | (x, 𝕊) ⇒ Var
 | ((v₁,v₂), 𝕊) ⇒ Pair(trans(v₁, 𝕊), trans(v₂, 𝕊))
 | (fun f(x) = e′ : (τ₁ →_ε′ τ₂)^𝕊, 𝕊) ⇒ Fun(trans(e′, ε′))
 | (inl v, 𝕊) ⇒ Sum(trans(v, 𝕊))
 | (fst (x : (τ₁ × τ₂)^δ, ε) ⇒ case (δ, ε) of
     | (𝕊,𝕊) ⇒ Fst(trans(x, 𝕊))
     | (𝕊,ℂ) ⇒ if τ₁ O.S. then Write(trans(e, 𝕊))
                 else ReadWrite(trans(e, 𝕊)))
     | (ℂ,ℂ) ⇒ Read(LFst, trans(fst (x′:(τ₁×τ₂)^𝕊), ℂ),
                     trans(x, 𝕊))

 | (⊕(x₁ : int^𝕊, x₂ : int^𝕊), 𝕊) ⇒
     Prim(trans(x₁, 𝕊), trans(x₂, 𝕊))
 | (⊕(x₁ : int^𝕊, x₂ : int^𝕊), ℂ) ⇒ Write(trans(e, 𝕊))))
 | (⊕(x₁ : int^ℂ, x₂ : int^ℂ), ℂ) ⇒
     Read(LPrimop1,
          Read(LPrimop2, Write(trans(⊕(x′₁,x′₂), 𝕊))))

 | (let x : τ″ = e₁ : τ′ in e₂, ε) ⇒
     LetE(if τ″ O.S. then trans(e₁, 𝕊)
          else (if τ′ = τ″ then Mod(trans(e₁, ℂ))
                else Lift(trans(e₁, ℂ))),
          trans(e₂, ε))

 | (let x : ∀α⃗[D]. τ″ = v₁ : τ′ in e₂, ε) ⇒
     let variants = all δ⃗ᵢ such that α⃗ = δ⃗ᵢ ⊩ D in
     let f = λs. if τ″ O.S. then trans(v₁, 𝕊)
                 else (if τ′ = τ″ then Mod(trans(v₁, ℂ))
                       else Lift(trans(v₁, ℂ))) in
       LetV(map f variants, trans(e₂, ε))

 | (apply(x₁ : (τ₁ →_ε′ τ₂)^δ, x₂), ε) ⇒ case (ε′, δ, ε) of
     | (𝕊,𝕊,𝕊) ⇒ App(trans(x₁, 𝕊), trans(x₂, 𝕊))
     | (ℂ,𝕊,ℂ) ⇒ App(trans(x₁, 𝕊), trans(x₂, 𝕊))
     | (𝕊,𝕊,ℂ) ⇒ if τ₂ O.S. then Write(trans(e, 𝕊))
                   else ReadWrite(trans(e, 𝕊))
     | (ε′,ℂ,ℂ) ⇒ Read(LApply,
                        trans(apply(x′:(τ₁ →_ε′ τ₂)^𝕊, x₂), ℂ),
                        trans(x₁, 𝕊))
     | (ℂ,𝕊,𝕊) ⇒ Mod(trans(e, ℂ))
     | (ε′,ℂ,𝕊) ⇒ Mod(trans(e, ℂ))

 | (case x : τ of {x₁⇒e₁ , x₂⇒e₂}, ε) ⇒
     if τ O.S. then
       Case(trans(x, 𝕊), trans(e₁, ε), trans(e₂, ε))
     else Read(LCase,
               trans(case x′ : |τ|^𝕊 of {x₁⇒e₁ , x₂⇒e₂}, ℂ),
               trans(x, 𝕊))

 | (x : τ, ℂ) ⇒ if τ O.S. then Write(trans(e, 𝕊))
                else ReadWrite(trans(e, 𝕊))
 | (fun f(x) = e′, ℂ) | (inl v, ℂ)
 | (n, ℂ) | ((v₁, v₂), ℂ) ⇒ Write(trans(e, 𝕊))
```

Figure 18. Translation algorithm

lar Level ML terms to AFL terms that are similarly structured, but have overhead (**mod**, write, etc.). Thus, integers are related to integers, pairs are related if their components are related, and so forth. The definition essentially ignores **mod** and **write** and ignores the mode in $\textbf{apply}^{\varepsilon}$. Since translated programs can have "extra" **read** and **let** expressions, these are "substituted out" in the relation, so that $3 \looparrowright \textbf{let}\ x = 3\ \textbf{in}\ x$. Functions are related if, given related arguments, they produce related results. Note that we will not induct over this relation; neither the term, nor the type, gets smaller.

We also relate substitutions: a source substitution s and a target substitution $\underline{s}$,

$$s = v_1/x_1, \ldots, v_n/x_n$$
$$\underline{s} = w_1/x_1, \ldots, w_n/x_n$$

are related at their environments $\Gamma = x_1 : \tau_1, \ldots, x_n : \tau_n$ and $\Gamma' = x_1 : \underline{\tau}'_1, \ldots, x_n : \underline{\tau}'_n$, written

$$(v_1/x_1, \ldots, v_n/x_n) : (x_1 : \tau_1, \ldots, x_n : \tau_n)$$
$$\looparrowright (w_1/x_1, \ldots, w_n/x_n) : (x_1 : \underline{\tau}'_1, \ldots, x_n : \underline{\tau}'_n)$$

if, for all k from 1 to n, we have $v_k : \tau_k \looparrowright w_k : \underline{\tau}_k$.

The key lemma (Lemma 6.3) is that if $e \underset{\varepsilon}{\hookrightarrow} e'$, the target program e' is related to e. Combined with Theorem 6.4, which shows that related programs evaluate to related values, this means that the translated program e' evaluates to the same value that e does. (Actually, e' is a value *related to* that value; only at $\textbf{int}^{\delta}/\textbf{int}$, and products thereof, are they identical.)

We begin by defining a *store substitution* operation:

Definition 6.2. The *store substitution* $[\rho]e$ is defined as an ordinary substitution, except for $e = \ell$, in which case $[\rho]\ell = [\rho](\textbf{mod}\ \rho(\ell))$.

For example, $[\ell_1 \mapsto 1, \ell_2 \mapsto 2](\ell_1, \ell_2) = (\textbf{mod}\ 1, \textbf{mod}\ 2)$.

Proofs and several other lemmas can be found in the appendix [Chen et al. 2011].

Lemma 6.3 (Relation of Translation). *If* $\Gamma \vdash e : \tau \underset{\varepsilon}{\hookrightarrow} e'$ *and* $\cdot \vdash s : \Gamma$ *and* $\cdot \vdash \underline{s} : \|\Gamma\|$ *and* $s : \Gamma \looparrowright \underline{s} : \|\Gamma\|$ *then*

$$[s]e : \tau \looparrowright [\underline{s}]e' : \underline{\tau}'$$

where $\underline{\tau}' = \|\tau\|$ *if* $\varepsilon = \mathbb{S}$, *and* $\underline{\tau}' = \|\tau\|^{\to\mathbb{C}}$ *if* $\varepsilon = \mathbb{C}$.

Theorem 6.4 (Generalized Translation Soundness).
If $e : \sigma \looparrowright [\rho]e' : \underline{\sigma}'$ *and* $\mathcal{D} :: \rho \vdash e' \Downarrow (\rho' \vdash w)$
then $\mathcal{D}' :: e \Downarrow v$ *where* $v : \sigma \looparrowright [\rho']w : \underline{\sigma}'$.

Translation soundness now follows from Lemma 6.3 and Theorem 6.4:

Theorem 6.5 (Translation Soundness). *If* $\cdot \vdash e : \tau \underset{\varepsilon}{\hookrightarrow} e'$ *and* $\cdot \vdash e' \Downarrow (\rho' \vdash w)$, *then* $e \Downarrow v$ *where* $v : \tau \looparrowright [\rho']w : \underline{\tau}'$.

Finally, we extend Theorem 6.5 to further show that the size $W(\mathcal{D})$ of the derivation of the target-language evaluation is within a constant factor of the size $W(\mathcal{D}')$ of the derivation of $e \Downarrow v$. We need a few definitions and intermediate results, which can be found in the appendix. The proof hinges on classifying the keywords added by the translation, such as **write**, as "dirty": a dirty keyword will lead to applications of the dirty rule (TEvWrite) in the evaluation derivation; such applications have no equivalent in the source-language evaluation.

We then define the "head cost" *HC* of terms and derivations, which counts the number of dirty rules applied near the root of the term, or the root of the derivation, without passing through clean parts of the term or derivation. Just counting *all* the dirty keywords in a term would not rule out a β-reduction duplicating a particularly dirty part of the term. By defining head cost and proving that the translation generates terms with bounded head cost—including for all subterms—we ensure that *no* part of the term is too dirty; consequently, substituting a subterm during evaluation yields terms that are not too dirty.

Definition 6.6. A term e is shallowly k-bounded if $HC(e) \leq k$. A term e is deeply k-bounded if every subterm of e (including e itself) is shallowly k-bounded. Similarly, a derivation $\mathcal{D}$ is shallowly k-bounded if $HC(\mathcal{D}) \leq k$, and deeply k-bounded if all its subderivations are shallowly k-bounded.

Theorem 6.7. *If* trans $(e, \varepsilon) = e'$ *then* e' *is deeply* 6*-bounded.*

$e : \sigma \looparrowright e' : \underline{\sigma}'$ Source expression e at type [schema] σ is related to target expression e' at type [schema] $\underline{\sigma}'$

$$
\begin{array}{rcll}
n : \mathbf{int}^{\delta} & \looparrowright & n : \mathbf{int} & \\
(e_1, e_2) : (\tau_1 \times \tau_2)^{\delta} & \looparrowright & (e'_1, e'_2) : \underline{\tau}'_1 \times \underline{\tau}'_2 & \text{if } e_1 : \tau_1 \looparrowright e'_1 : \underline{\tau}'_1 \text{ and } e_2 : \tau_2 \looparrowright e'_2 : \underline{\tau}'_2 \\
(\mathbf{inl}\ e) : (\tau_1 + \tau_2)^{\delta} & \looparrowright & (\mathbf{inl}\ e') : \underline{\tau}'_1 + \underline{\tau}'_2 & \text{if } e : \tau_1 \looparrowright e' : \underline{\tau}'_1 \\
(\mathbf{fst}\ e) : \tau & \looparrowright & (\mathbf{fst}\ e') : \underline{\tau}' & \text{if } e : (\tau \times \tau_2)^{\delta} \looparrowright e' : \underline{\tau}' \times \underline{\tau}'_2 \\
\oplus(e_1, e_2) : \tau & \looparrowright & \oplus(e'_1, e'_2) : \underline{\tau}' & \text{if } e_1 : \tau_1 \looparrowright e'_1 : \underline{\tau}'_1 \text{ and } e_2 : \tau_2 \looparrowright e'_2 : \underline{\tau}'_2 \\
e : \tau & \looparrowright & (\mathbf{mod}\ e^{\mathbb{C}}) : \underline{\tau}'\ \mathbf{mod} & \text{if } e : \tau \looparrowright e^{\mathbb{C}} : \underline{\tau}' \\
e : \tau & \looparrowright & (\mathbf{write}(e^{\mathbb{S}})) : \underline{\tau}' & \text{if } e : \tau \looparrowright e^{\mathbb{S}} : \underline{\tau}' \\
[e_1/x]e : \tau_2 & \looparrowright & (\mathbf{read}\ e^{\mathbb{S}}\ \mathbf{as}\ x\ \mathbf{in}\ e^{\mathbb{C}}) : \underline{\tau}'_2 & \text{if } e_1 : \tau_1 \looparrowright e^{\mathbb{S}} : \underline{\tau}'_1\ \mathbf{mod} \text{ and for all } v : \tau_1 \looparrowright w : \underline{\tau}'_1, \\
 & & & \quad \text{we have } [v/x]e : \tau_2 \looparrowright [w/x]e^{\mathbb{C}} : \underline{\tau}'_2 \\
\mathbf{apply}(e_1, e_2) : \tau_2 & \looparrowright & \mathbf{apply}^{\varepsilon}(e'_1, e'_2) : \underline{\tau}'_2 & \text{if } e_1 : (\tau_1 \underset{\varepsilon}{\rightarrow} \tau_2)^{\delta} \looparrowright e'_1 : \underline{\tau}'_1 \underset{\varepsilon}{\rightarrow} \underline{\tau}'_2 \text{ and } e_2 : \tau_1 \looparrowright e'_2 : \underline{\tau}'_1 \\
e : [\vec{\delta}/\vec{\alpha}]\tau & \looparrowright & e'[\vec{\alpha} = \vec{\delta}] : \|[\vec{\delta}/\vec{\alpha}]\tau\| & \text{if } e : \forall\vec{\alpha}[D].\,\tau \looparrowright e' : \Pi\vec{\alpha}[D].\,\tau \\
v : \forall\vec{\alpha}[D].\,\tau & \looparrowright & \mathbf{select}\ \{\vec{\delta_i} \Rightarrow e_i\}_i : \Pi\vec{\alpha}[D].\,\tau & \text{if for all } i \text{ we have } v : [\vec{\delta}/\vec{\alpha}]\tau \looparrowright e_i : \|[\vec{\delta}/\vec{\alpha}]\tau\| \\
(\mathbf{fun}\ f(x) = e) : (\tau_1 \underset{\varepsilon}{\rightarrow} \tau_2)^{\delta} & \looparrowright & (\mathbf{fun}^{\varepsilon}\ f(x) = e^{\varepsilon}) : \underline{\tau}'_1 \underset{\varepsilon}{\rightarrow} \underline{\tau}'_2 & \text{if for all } v : \tau_1 \looparrowright w : \underline{\tau}'_1, \\
 & & & \quad ([(\mathbf{fun}\ f(x) = e)/f][v/x]e) : \tau_2 \\
 & & & \quad \looparrowright ([(\mathbf{fun}^{\varepsilon}\ f(x) = e^{\varepsilon})/f][w/x]e^{\varepsilon}) : \underline{\tau}'_2 \\
(\mathbf{let}\ x = e_1\ \mathbf{in}\ e_2) : \tau_2 & \looparrowright & (\mathbf{let}\ x = e'_1\ \mathbf{in}\ e'_2) : \underline{\tau}'_2 & \text{if } e_1 : \tau_1 \looparrowright e'_1 : \underline{\tau}'_1 \text{ and} \\
 & & & \text{for all } v : \tau_1 \looparrowright w : \underline{\tau}'_1,\ [v/x]e_2 : \tau_2 \looparrowright [w/x]e'_2 : \underline{\tau}'_2 \\
[e_1/x]e_2 : \tau_2 & \looparrowright & (\mathbf{let}\ x = e'_1\ \mathbf{in}\ e'_2) : \underline{\tau}'_2 & \text{if } e_1 : \tau_1 \looparrowright e'_1 : \underline{\tau}'_1 \text{ and} \\
 & & & \text{for all } v : \tau_1 \looparrowright w : \underline{\tau}'_1,\ [v/x]e_2 : \tau_2 \looparrowright [w/x]e'_2 : \underline{\tau}'_2 \\
(\mathbf{case}\ e\ \mathbf{of}\ \{x_1 \Rightarrow e_1\ ,\ x_2 \Rightarrow e_2\}) : \tau & \looparrowright & (\mathbf{case}\ e'\ \mathbf{of}\ \{x_1 \Rightarrow e'_1\ ,\ x_2 \Rightarrow e'_2\}) : \underline{\tau}' & \text{if } e : (\tau_1 + \tau_2)^{\delta} \looparrowright e' : \underline{\tau}'_1 + \underline{\tau}'_2 \text{ and} \\
 & & & \text{for all } v : \tau_k \looparrowright w : \underline{\tau}'_k, \\
 & & & [v/x_k]e_k : \tau \looparrowright [w/x_k]e'_k : \underline{\tau}' \text{ for } k \in \{1, 2\}
\end{array}
$$

Figure 19. Correspondence of source and target expressions, used in Theorem 6.5 and other results

Theorem 6.8 (Cost Result). *Given $\mathcal{D} :: \rho \vdash e' \Downarrow (\rho' \vdash w)$ where for every subderivation $\mathcal{D}^* :: \rho_1^* \vdash e^* \Downarrow (\rho_2^* \vdash w^*)$ of $\mathcal{D}$ (including $\mathcal{D}$), $HC(\mathcal{D}^*) \leq k$, then the number of dirty rule applications in $\mathcal{D}$ is at most $\frac{k}{k+1} W(\mathcal{D})$.*

The cost theorem follows from Theorem C.5 (in the appendix)—a generalization of Theorem 6.4—and Theorem 6.8:

Theorem 6.9. *If $\mathcal{D}$ derives $\cdot \vdash \mathtt{trans}\ (e, \varepsilon) \Downarrow (\rho' \vdash w)$ then $\mathcal{D}'$ derives $e \Downarrow v$ where $v : \tau \looparrowright [\rho']w : \underline{\tau}'$ and $W(\mathcal{D}) \leq 7W(\mathcal{D}')$.*

Acar et al. [2006] proved that given a well-typed AFL program, change propagation updates the output consistently with an initial run. Using Theorems 6.1 and 6.5, this implies that change propagation is consistent with an initial run of the source program.

7. Related Work

Incremental computation. Self-adjusting computation provides an approach to incremental computation, which has been studied extensively [Ramalingam and Reps 1993; Demers et al. 1981; Pugh and Teitelbaum 1989; Abadi et al. 1996]. Key techniques behind self-adjusting computation include dynamic dependence graphs, which allows a fully general change propagation mechanism [Acar et al. 2006], and a form of memoization that allows inexact computations to be reused via memoized computations that are (recursively) self-adjusting [Acar et al. 2009]. Programming-language features allow writing self-adjusting programs but these require syntactically separating stable and changeable data, as well as code that operates on such data [Acar et al. 2006, 2009; Ley-Wild et al. 2008; Hammer et al. 2009]. DITTO [Shankar and Bodik 2007] shows the benefits of eliminating user annotations. By customizing dependency tracking for invariant checking programs, DITTO provides a fully automatic incremental invariant checker. The approach, however, is domain-specific and only works for certain programs (e.g., functions cannot return arbitrary values): it is unsound in general.

Information flow and constraint-based type inference. A number of information flow type systems have been developed to check security properties, including the SLam calculus [Heintze and Riecke 1998], JFlow [Myers 1999] and a monadic system [Crary et al. 2005]. Our type system uses many ideas from Pottier and Simonet [2003], including a form of constraint-based type inference [Odersky et al. 1999], and is also broadly similar to other systems that use subtyping constraints [Simonet 2003; Foster et al. 2006].

Cost semantics. To prove that our translation yields efficient self-adjusting target programs, we use a simple cost semantics. The idea of instrumenting evaluations with cost information goes back to the early '90s [Sands 1990]. Cost semantics is particularly important in lazy [Sands 1990; Sansom and Peyton Jones 1995]) and parallel languages [Spoonhower et al. 2008] where it is especially difficult to relate execution time to the source code, as well as in self-adjusting computation [Ley-Wild et al. 2009].

8. Conclusion

This paper presents techniques for translating purely functional programs to programs that can automatically self-adjust in response to dynamic changes to their data. Our contributions include a constraint-based type system for inferring self-adjusting-computation types from purely functional programs, a type-directed translation algorithm that rewrites purely functional programs into self-adjusting programs, and proofs of critical properties of the translation: type soundness and observational equivalence, as well as the intrinsic property of time complexity. Perhaps unsurprisingly, the theorems and their proofs were critical to the determination of the type systems and the translation algorithm: many of our initial attempts at the problem resulted in target programs that were not type sound, that did not ensure observational equivalence, or were asymptotically slower than the source.

These results take an important step towards the development of languages and compilers that can generate code that can respond automatically to dynamically changing data correctly and asymptotically optimally, without substantial programming effort. Remaining open problems include generalization to imperative programs with references, techniques and proofs to determine or improve the asymptotic complexity of dynamic responses, and a complete and careful implementation and its evaluation.

Acknowledgments

We thank the anonymous ICFP reviewers, as well as Arthur Charguéraud, for their useful comments on the submitted version of this paper.

References

M. Abadi, B. W. Lampson, and J.-J. Lévy. Analysis and caching of dependencies. In *International Conference on Functional Programming*, pages 83–91, 1996.

U. A. Acar, G. E. Blelloch, and R. Harper. Adaptive functional programming. *ACM Trans. Prog. Lang. Sys.*, 28(6):990–1034, 2006.

U. A. Acar, A. Ihler, R. Mettu, and O. Sümer. Adaptive Bayesian inference. In *Neural Information Processing Systems (NIPS)*, 2007.

U. A. Acar, G. E. Blelloch, M. Blume, R. Harper, and K. Tangwongsan. An experimental analysis of self-adjusting computation. *ACM Trans. Prog. Lang. Sys.*, 32(1):3:1–3:53, 2009.

U. A. Acar, G. E. Blelloch, R. Ley-Wild, K. Tangwongsan, and D. Türkoğlu. Traceable data types for self-adjusting computation. In *Programming Language Design and Implementation*, 2010a.

U. A. Acar, A. Cotter, B. Hudson, and D. Türkoğlu. Dynamic well-spaced point sets. In *Symposium on Computational Geometry*, 2010b.

M. Carlsson. Monads for incremental computing. In *International Conference on Functional Programming*, pages 26–35, 2002.

Y. Chen, J. Dunfield, M. A. Hammer, and U. A. Acar. Online appendix to *Implicit Self-Adjusting Computation for Purely Functional Programs*, 2011. `http://www.mpi-sws.org/~joshua/Chen11appendix.pdf`.

Y.-J. Chiang and R. Tamassia. Dynamic algorithms in computational geometry. *Proceedings of the IEEE*, 80(9):1412–1434, 1992.

K. Crary, A. Kliger, and F. Pfenning. A monadic analysis of information flow security with mutable state. *Journal of Functional Programming*, 15(2):249–291, Mar. 2005.

L. Damas and R. Milner. Principal type-schemes for functional programs. In *Principles of Programming Languages*, pages 207–212. ACM, 1982.

A. Demers, T. Reps, and T. Teitelbaum. Incremental evaluation of attribute grammars with application to syntax-directed editors. In *Principles of Programming Languages*, pages 105–116, 1981.

C. Demetrescu, I. Finocchi, and G. Italiano. *Handbook on Data Structures and Applications*, chapter 36: Dynamic Graphs. CRC Press, 2005.

J. Field and T. Teitelbaum. Incremental reduction in the lambda calculus. In *ACM Conf. LISP and Functional Programming*, pages 307–322, 1990.

J. S. Foster, R. Johnson, J. Kodumal, and A. Aiken. Flow-insensitive type qualifiers. *ACM Trans. Prog. Lang. Sys.*, 28: 1035–1087, 2006.

L. Guibas. Modeling motion. In J. Goodman and J. O'Rourke, editors, *Handbook of Discrete and Computational Geometry*, pages 1117–1134. Chapman and Hall/CRC, 2nd edition, 2004.

M. A. Hammer, U. A. Acar, and Y. Chen. CEAL: a C-based language for self-adjusting computation. In *Proceedings of the 2009 ACM SIGPLAN Conference on Programming Language Design and Implementation*, June 2009.

N. Heintze and J. G. Riecke. The SLam calculus: programming with secrecy and integrity. In *Principles of Programming Languages (POPL '98)*, pages 365–377, 1998.

R. Ley-Wild, M. Fluet, and U. A. Acar. Compiling self-adjusting programs with continuations. In *Proceedings of the International Conference on Functional Programming*, 2008.

R. Ley-Wild, U. A. Acar, and M. Fluet. A cost semantics for self-adjusting computation. In *Proceedings of the 26th Annual ACM Symposium on Principles of Programming Languages*, 2009.

MLton. MLton web site. `http://www.mlton.org`.

A. C. Myers. JFlow: practical mostly-static information flow control. In *Principles of Programming Languages*, pages 228–241, 1999.

M. Odersky, M. Sulzmann, and M. Wehr. Type inference with constrained types. *Theory and Practice of Object Systems*, 5 (1):35–55, 1999.

F. Pottier and V. Simonet. Information flow inference for ML. *ACM Trans. Prog. Lang. Sys.*, 25(1):117–158, Jan. 2003.

W. Pugh and T. Teitelbaum. Incremental computation via function caching. In *Principles of Programming Languages*, pages 315–328, 1989.

G. Ramalingam and T. Reps. A categorized bibliography on incremental computation. In *Principles of Programming Languages*, pages 502–510, 1993.

A. Sabelfeld and A. C. Myers. Language-based information-flow security. *IEEE J. Selected Areas in Communications*, 21(1), 2003.

D. Sands. *Calculi for Time Analysis of Functional Programs*. PhD thesis, University of London, Imperial College, September 1990.

P. M. Sansom and S. L. Peyton Jones. Time and space profiling for non-strict, higher-order functional languages. In *Principles of Programming Languages*, pages 355–366, 1995.

A. Shankar and R. Bodik. DITTO: Automatic incrementalization of data structure invariant checks (in Java). In *Programming Language Design and Implementation*, 2007.

V. Simonet. Type inference with structural subtyping: A faithful formalization of an efficient constraint solver. In *APLAS*, pages 283–302, 2003.

D. Spoonhower, G. E. Blelloch, R. Harper, and P. B. Gibbons. Space profiling for parallel functional programs. In *International Conference on Functional Programming*, 2008.

Invited Talk

Programming Assurance Cases in Agda

Makoto Takeyama
Information Technology Research Institute,
National Institute of Advanced Industrial Science and Technology (AIST)
3-11-46 Nakoji, Amagasaki, Hyogo, 661-0974 Japan
makoto.takeyama@aist.go.jp

Abstract

Agda is a modern functional programming language equipped with an interactive proof assistant as its developing environment. Its features include dependent types, type universe, inductive and coinductive families of types, pattern matching, records, and nested parameterized modules. Based on the "propositions as types, proofs as programs" correspondence in Martin-Löf's Type Theory, Agda lets users to construct, verify, and execute a smooth mixture of programs and proofs.

Using Agda is similar to using an editor in a modern IDE. Users have more direct control over how programs / proofs are written than in automation-oriented systems using command-scripts for proof construction. Agda thus encourages users to express their ideas with more sophisticated dependently typed programming and less logical proofs. Programming techniques for readability and maintainability now translate to techniques for writing verified documents for human communication.

Agda has been developed at Chalmers University of Technology by Ulf Norell and others. A growing international community of developers and users applies it in research, education, and industry. At AIST in Japan, we aim to introduce its merits to construction, verification, maintenance, and run-time evaluation of "assurance cases", which are documented bodies of systems assurance arguments used as the hub for assurance- and risk-communication among stakeholders.

The talk gives an overview of Agda and presents our current effort on programming assurance cases in Agda.

Categories & Subject Descriptors: D.1.1 [**Programming Techniques**]: Applicative (functional) programming; F.3.1 [**Logics and Meanings of Programs**]: Specifying and Verifying and Reasoning about Programs---Mechanical verification, Logics of programs, Specification techniques; D.2.6 [**Software Engineering**]: Programming Environments---Interactive environment; D.2.9 [**Software Engineering**]: Management---Software quality assurance; I.7.2 [**Document and Text Processing**]: Document Preparation---Languages and system; D.2.4 [**Software Engineering**]: Software/Program Verification---Formal methods

General Terms: Languages, Verification, Documentation, Management

Keywords: Dependent types, Type theory, Agda, Assurance cases

Bio

The speaker is a research scientist at National Institute of Advanced Industrial Science and Technology (AIST) in Japan. He received his Ph.D. in Computer Science from the University of Edinburgh. He previously worked at Queen's University in Canada and Chalmers University of Technology in Sweden. His primary technical interest is in practical applications of formal methods, including Type Theory, combination of interactive and automatic proving, and standardization. He has also worked in the area of categorical semantics of programming languages.

ICFP'11, September 19–21, 2011, Tokyo, Japan.
ACM 978-1-4503-0865-6/11/09.

On the Bright Side of Type Classes: Instance Arguments in Agda

Dominique Devriese   Frank Piessens

KULeuven

{dominique.devriese,frank.piessens}@cs.kuleuven.be

Abstract

We present instance arguments: an alternative to type classes and related features in the dependently typed, purely functional programming language/proof assistant Agda. They are a new, general type of function arguments, resolved from call-site scope in a type-directed way. The mechanism is inspired by both Scala's implicits and Agda's existing implicit arguments, but differs from both in important ways. Our mechanism is designed and implemented for Agda, but our design choices can be applied to other programming languages as well.

Like Scala's implicits, we do not provide a separate structure for type classes and their instances, but instead rely on Agda's standard dependently typed records, so that standard language mechanisms provide features that are missing or expensive in other proposals. Like Scala, we support the equivalent of local instances. Unlike Scala, functions taking our new arguments are first-class citizens and can be abstracted over and manipulated in standard ways. Compared to other proposals, we avoid the pitfall of introducing a separate type-level computational model through the instance search mechanism. All values in scope are automatically candidates for instance resolution. A final novelty of our approach is that existing Agda libraries using records gain the benefits of type classes without any modification.

We discuss our implementation in Agda (to be part of Agda 2.2.12) and we use monads as an example to show how it allows existing concepts in the Agda standard library to be used in a similar way as corresponding Haskell code using type classes. We also demonstrate and discuss equivalents and alternatives to some advanced type class-related patterns from the literature and some new patterns specific to our system.

Categories and Subject Descriptors D.3.3 [*Programming Languages*]: Language Constructs and Features

General Terms Languages

Keywords Agda, instance arguments, type classes, ad hoc polymorphism

ICFP'11, September 19–21, 2011, Tokyo, Japan.

1. Introduction

1.1 Type Classes

In 1998, a group of scholars on the Haskell Committee were facing the problem of fixing the types of the numeric and equality operators in the emerging Haskell programming language [8]. These operators feature a natural requirement for overloading or "ad hoc" polymorphism. For example, the == operator, of type t → t → Bool, should only be defined for certain types t (e.g. Bool, Integer) and not for others (e.g. function types). Additionally, different implementations are required for different types t.

The committee at the time recognized the issue as an instance of a more general problem in need of a general solution and adopted Wadler's proposal for what is now known as the Haskell type class system. For the == operator, the solution is based on a type class Eq t, with instances for appropriate types t. To avoid troubling this section with notations for infix operators, we write equal for ==.

```
class Eq t where equal :: t → t → Bool
instance Eq Bool where equal = primEqBool
instance Eq Integer where equal = primEqInteger
neq :: Eq t ⇒ t → t → Bool
neq a b = not (equal a b)
test :: Bool
test = equal (5 :: Integer) 5
```

Subclasses can also be defined:

```
data Ordering = LT | EQ | GT
class Eq t ⇒ Ord t where
  compare :: t → t → Ordering
```

An essential requirement for type classes to work is that functions like neq which use the equal operator for an abstract type t declare this in their type. The compiler can then check that the required instances are defined when t is instantiated to a concrete type: when equal is called on two Integer values in the definition of test, it looks for an Integer instance of the type class in scope and uses that instance's implementation of the equal operator.

Before we continue, we want to make it clear that when talking about Haskell, we will amalgamate the type class concept in Haskell proper with common and uncontroversial extensions like FlexibleContexts, FlexibleInstances, MultiParamTypeClasses, TypeFamilies and RankNTypes.

Note also that when we mention ad hoc polymorphism, we mean *open* ad hoc polymorphism. This means that additional instances of abstract concepts can be added independently by users of functions that require the concept. If openness is not required, Agda supports other solutions based on the definition of a universe representing the complete set of types that satisfy the concept.

1.2 The downsides of an extra structuring concept

A disadvantage of Haskell's type class system is that classes and instances form a separate, special-purpose structuring concept, in addition to the more standard algebraic data types (ADTs). Because of this duplication of functionality, many of the features that have in the past been introduced as extensions of type classes duplicate features that already existed for ADTs. Constraint families [18] (allowing classes to have abstract constraints on type class parameters) and associated type families [23] (allowing classes to specify abstract types) both roughly correspond to how generalized algebraic data type [21] values can carry types or type functors that are not parameters of the data type. In the area of generic programming, succesful techniques existed for ADTs [19], but these have had to be adapted for type classes [12, 27].

Another example is how higher-rank types [22] have long allowed ADTs to be abstracted over. However, in a paper about a datatype-generic programming technique [12], Lämmel and Peyton Jones note that this is not possible for type classes. In the following pseudo-code, they wanted to abstract over a type class cxt (the meaning of these type classes is not important here):

```
-- Pseudo-Haskell
class (Typeable a, cxt a) ⇒ Data cxt a where
  gmapQ :: (forall b.Data cxt b ⇒ b → r) → a → [r]
instance Data Size t ⇒ Size t where
  gsize t = 1 + sum (gmapQ gsize t)
```

This pseudo-code is not legal Haskell so Lämmel and Peyton Jones provide a solution based on a "generic" type class Sat parameterised by the type of a dictionary record that it should carry:

```
class Sat a where dict :: a
```

We find this a clever solution, but it amounts to replacing a type class with an ADT for which the desired feature (abstracting over one) is available.

1.3 Dictionary Translation

A well-known model of type classes using standard ADTs is known as *dictionary translation* [26]. This translation is often used as an implementation strategy, but also gives an accurate semantic model of the type class concept. A type class is modelled as a dictionary record type, with the type class operations as record fields. Instances become record values with as fields the definitions in the instance. The above code translates to the following:

```
data Eq t = EqDict {equal :: t → t → Bool}
data Ord t = OrdDict {eqDict :: Eq t
                     , compare :: t → t → Ordering}

boolEq :: Eq Bool
boolEq = EqDict primEqBool

intEq :: Eq Integer
intEq = EqDict primEqInteger

neq :: Eq t → t → t → Bool
neq dict a b = not (equal dict a b)

test :: Bool
test = equal intEq 5 5
```

Striking about this translation is that the resulting code is not actually that far from the original. Apart from the additional naming of instances (which has also been proposed for Haskell [10]), the translation only produces extra verbiage in the implementation of functions that use the type class's operations. In the neq function, the dictionary of type Eq t is now passed around explicitly where this was implicitly done for us before. Additionally, in the definition of test, we need to explicitly specify the intEq dictionary as an extra parameter whereas it was inferred by the compiler before.

Apart from the automatic inference of instances, the dictionary model has many advantages over the standard type class system. All the power of normal language record mechanisms is available, and they can be defined, manipulated and abstracted over in standard ways.

1.4 Instance search

An aspect of type classes we have not yet touched upon is instance search. Haskell allows instance definitions like the following:

```
instance Eq a ⇒ Eq [a] where
  equal [] [] = True
  equal (a : as) (b : bs) = equal a b ∧ equal as bs
  equal _ _ = False
```

With this instance, Haskell will resolve constraints of the form Eq [a] by recursively resolving the constraint Eq a and then using the above definition of equal. This mechanism makes the instance search algorithm a lot more powerful and complex and a set of restrictions is enforced on the structure of the types involved in instance contexts to ensure that the instance search remains decidable. Two widely used Haskell extensions (associated type families [23] and functional dependencies [9]) introduce further complexity by adding what are essentially decidable type-level computation primitives, which can be triggered during the instance search process. As a reviewer notes, these extensions effectively expose an interpreter for a simple logic programming language (no backtracking) which can reason about Haskell types.

In a non-dependently typed language like Haskell, type-level computation is not directly available in the base language. Therefore, the type-level computation primitives provided by these primitives fill a certain gap in the language and various people have demonstrated the surprising amount of power that these extensions offer [11, 14]. However, the computational model for these primitives differs strongly from the standard Haskell model: a form of structural recursion is used instead of non-structural (although many compilers provide an option to change this), pattern matching is open instead of closed and the syntactic order of pattern matching and recursive calls is reversed.

1.5 Scala Implicits

The Scala programming language features an alternative feature to type classes called implicits that avoids the introduction of a new structuring mechanism [2, 17]. Powerful mechanisms like existential types [17, §3.2.10] and abstract type declarations [17, §4.3] can be used to model features that would have to be specifically defined and implemented for type classes. Our running equal example can be encoded in Scala as follows:

```
trait Eq [A] {def equal (x: A, y: A) : Boolean}
def equal [A] (x: A, y: A) (implicit eqA : Eq [A]) =
  eqA.equal (x, y)
implicit object boolEq extends Eq [Boolean] {
  def equal (x: Boolean, y: Boolean) : Boolean =
    x == y}
implicit object intEq extends Eq [Int] {
  def equal (x: Int, y: Int) : Boolean = x == y}
def neq [A] (x:A, y: A) (implicit eqA : Eq [A]) =
  ! equal (x, y)
val test = equal (1, 3) ∨ equal (true, false)
```

The type class Eq is modelled as a dictionary trait Eq [A]. Traits are a general object-oriented structuring concept provided by

Scala, similar (for our purposes) to records. Two dictionary objects intEq and boolEq are introduced and annotated with the **implicit** modifier. The equal function is defined to accept an argument eqA of type Eq A that is marked as **implicit**, with the effect that when the function is called, and the implicit arguments are not explicitly provided, values are inferred. Candidate values are searched from a precisely defined set of candidates, which includes all definitions that were annotated with the **implicit** modifier and are either accessible at the call-site without a prefix, or were defined in companion modules of the implicit argument's type or its components. A function can accept several implicit arguments, but they have to come after all other function arguments.

Unfortunately, functions with implicit arguments are not first-class citizens in Scala, mostly due to syntax-technical problems. Some important features of Scala's standard functions (currying, partial application, lambda expressions) either require non-trivial encodings or are not available for implicits.

More concretely, Scala implicits have the following restrictions. In the first place, implicit arguments are restricted to occur after all the other arguments. Abstracting over functions taking implicit arguments is not syntactically possible but requires such functions to be encoded as objects with an apply method taking an implicit argument or first converted by the caller to normal functions. There is no user syntax for the type of a function accepting implicit arguments. Anonymous functions cannot accept implicit arguments[1]. Full and tight control on the insertion of implicit arguments does not seem to be available and it does not seem possible to partially apply a given function with implicit arguments to any chosen subset of its (implicit and ordinary) arguments (while keeping the implicit arguments implicit).

Scala also uses a certain search algorithm to infer a value for implicit arguments that are not explicitly provided. This algorithm is similar to Haskell's instance search. To resolve an implicit argument of type T, Scala will consider candidate values that have been marked "implicit" and which are *accessible* (can be named without a prefix) or in the *implicit scope* of type T (defined in a module related in a specific way [17, §7.2 pp. 104–107] to type T). It will consider values of type T, but also functions that themselves take only implicit arguments and return a value of type T. This makes the instance search recursive, like Haskell's instance search. To ensure decidability of the search, Scala keeps track of the "call stack" of instance searches and detects infinite loops using a certain criterion [17, §7.2 p. 106].

Like Haskell's instance search, Scala's implicit search can also be exploited as a type-level computation primitive. Oliveira et al. demonstrate [2] an encoding of session types, an arity-polymorphic zipWith function and a form of generalized constraints. However, this computation primitive presents a computational model like Haskell's instance search, different from Scala's standard model.

1.6 Agda implicit function arguments

A final language feature we want to present before introducing our proposal, can be found in our target language itself: Agda's *implicit* or *hidden arguments* [15]. Agda allows function arguments to be marked as "implicit", indicating that they do not need to be provided explicitly at the call site. For example, an Agda polymorphic identity function can be defined as follows.

```
id : {A : Set} → A → A
id v = v
```

When type checking the expression id true, Agda silently inserts a meta-variable (as if the expression was id {_} true), and Agda's unifier will instantiate this meta-variable to Bool. The argument can optionally be specified explicitly, by writing id {Bool} true. Implicit arguments are pervasive in most Agda code, and Agda would arguably be nearly unusable without it.

Unfortunately, Agda's implicit arguments are of no help for passing around and inferring type class dictionaries in the background. This is because Agda will only infer implicit arguments if it can statically decide that only a single value[2] exists of the required type. This makes the feature unsuitable for passing our type class dictionaries, because for a type t, many values of type Eq t can typically be defined. For example, even for a simple type like Bool, we can define a trivial equality operator equal _ _ = true in addition to the standard one.

However, unlike for Scala's implicit arguments, functions taking an implicit argument in Agda are first-class citizens. They can be abstracted over, their types can be spelled out, anonymous functions with hidden arguments are no problem and syntax is available to keep a tight control over whether or not implicit arguments are inferred or not. In some cases this requires writing for example λ {A} → id {A} instead of id to make sure that Agda does not try to infer the hidden argument.

1.7 Contributions

In this paper, we propose and study *instance arguments*: a new language feature that is an alternative to type classes, with an implementation in Agda. Our proposal is inspired by Scala's and Agda's implicit argument mechanisms. It does not introduce a separate structuring concept, but our ad hoc polymorphic functions are first-class citizens. Our proposal can work with less or more powerful types of instance resolution, but we choose a simple one that avoids the introduction of a separate computational model.

To the best of our knowledge, no other proposal in the literature offers equivalents to *all* of the following features: associated type families and constraint families, multi-parameter type classes, local instances, abstraction over type classes and first-class ad hoc polymorphic functions (although Coq, Haskell and Scala each have almost all of them). No other proposal has explored an alternative to type classes without introducing a separate computational model in the language. No other proposal did not require "instances" to be somehow marked eligible for implicit resolution. Finally, no other proposal has an equivalent to the way that we automatically bring the benefits of type classes to unmodified records.

We formally define the workings of our feature, and discuss our design choices. We demonstrate the use of monads and present (often simpler) encodings of some type class based patterns from the literature. We also present some novel patterns of our own.

2. Instance arguments

The feature we propose in this text is inspired by both Agda's implicit arguments and Scala's implicits. It is a new kind of function arguments, which we call *instance arguments*. These arguments can be inferred by the compiler even if multiple possible values exist with the expected type, provided only a single definition of such a value is in scope at the call site (more details in section A.3). We do not require values to be marked in a specific way to be eligible for this resolution. Like for Agda's existing implicit arguments, functions with the new arguments are first class citizens and there are no limitations on the location of the implicit arguments. We take care to limit the computational power of our instance search algorithm so that we do not unwantedly introduce an alternative computational model.

[1] The Scala syntax (**implicit** x ⇒ x) defines an anonymous function that takes a *normal* argument x, but makes x eligible for implicit resolution in the function body [17, §6.23].

[2] In a dependently typed language like Agda, types are values too.

2.1 By example

Let us consider our running example equal, and define a standard Agda record called Eq representing the Eq type class dictionary, and "instances" for the ℕ and Bool type from the Agda standard library [3]. These two types correspond (for our purposes) to Haskell's Integer and Bool.

```
record Eq (t : Set) : Set where
  field equal : t → t → Bool
eqBool : Eq Bool
eqBool = record {equal = primEqBool}
eqNat : Eq ℕ
eqNat = record {equal = primEqNat}
```

All of this is standard Agda code. Our modified version of Agda allows us to define the following:

```
equal : {t : Set} → {{eqT : Eq t}} → t → t → Bool
```

This type signature says that the function equal takes a Set (type) as its first (standard) implicit argument t. The double braces mark the function's second argument eqT of type Eq t as an instance argument. Next, the function takes two standard arguments of type t and returns a Bool. In equal's definition, we simply take the implicitly passed dictionary and return the equal function contained in it:

```
equal {{eqT}} = Eq.equal eqT
```

With this type signature, we can now use equal as if it were defined in a Haskell type class. The following definition for example, normalises to the expected value false (assuming standard definitions of primEqBool and primEqNat).

```
test = equal 5 3 ∨ equal true false
```

What happens underneath, for example for the application equal 5 3, is that the Agda type-checker notices that in order to pass the non-hidden argument 5 to function equal, it first needs to infer the two implicit arguments (t and eqT). It will assign a new meta-variable [16] to both, but for the second argument, a constraint will additionally be registered indicating that that meta-variable needs to be resolved as an instance argument. The argument 5 will then be passed to equal as the third argument, and Agda will unify the first meta-variable with value ℕ. Agda will now notice that there is *only one value of type Eq ℕ in scope* (eqNat) and assign it to the second metavariable.

Like for implicit arguments, it is also possible to provide the instance arguments explicitly, should this be necessary:

```
test2 = equal {{eqNat}} 5 3 ∨ equal {{eqBool}} true false
```

Our version of neq looks nice: like equal, it accepts a dictionary of type Eq t as an instance argument:

```
neq : ∀ {t} → {{eqT : Eq t}} → t → t → Bool
neq {{eqT}} a b = ¬ (equal {{eqT}} a b)
```

In the definition, we explicitly accept the dictionary argument and pass it to the equal function, but in fact this is not necessary. If we leave out the dictionaries in the definition, Agda will silently insert an unnamed instance argument in the left-hand side and will silently infer equal's instance argument to that unnamed value:

```
neq a b = ¬ (equal a b)
```

Notice how the mechanism is strikingly similar to Agda's existing implicit arguments in many respects. Only the resolution of the instance value is different.

2.2 Native support code for records

An important and novel feature of our proposed system is that we can automatically bring its benefits to unmodified libraries that use standard dependently-typed records. In the above example, it is the function equal of type

```
equal : ∀ {t} → {{eqT : Eq t}} → t → t → Bool
```

which allows us to use the Eq record in a more convenient, type-class-like way. The similarity to the standard projection operator Eq.equal which Agda generates in the background [15, 4.3 pp.82–83] is striking:

```
Eq.equal : ∀ {t} → (eqT : Eq t) → t → t → Bool
```

From this observation, it is not a big leap to automatically generate new versions of the projection functions which (like our equal) take the record as an instance argument instead of as a standard one. In fact, it is even easier and more powerful to generate an Agda module application like the following:

```
module EqInst {t} {{eqT : Eq t}} = Eq eqT
```

Module applications are part of Agda's module system. They allow to manipulate in certain ways the contents of a module. This module application will create a new module EqInst containing all the definitions in the right-hand-side module Eq, abstracted on the left-hand-side arguments {t} and {{eqT : Eq t}} and applied to the right-hand-side argument eqT. This makes not only the projection functions available in the new module, but also other functions defined in the scope of the record (more details in section 2.4). For the above example, we could have omitted the definition of function equal, instead just importing equal from a new type of module application, written Eq {{...}}:

```
open Eq {{...}} using (equal)
```

The function equal in these modules is identical to our custom definition above. Our monads case study in section 3 demonstrate that these definitions expose an interface that is very similar to the equivalent with type classes.

2.3 Subclasses

In dictionary models of type classes, a subclass dictionary typically carries a superclass dictionary as one of its fields. The Agda standard library for example uses such a model. In the context of a dependently typed language, there is actually another possible model for subclasses, known as Pebble-style structuring, which is recommended by Sozeau et al. [24, §4.1]. In this style, subclass dictionaries carry superclass dictionaries as parameters instead of fields.

Both models can be expressed with our system. Each has some specific advantages, e.g. a requirement to explicitly bring in scope superclass dictionaries or the need for an extra implicit superclass dictionary parameter in functions with a subclass constraint. In this section, we demonstrate a Pebble-style model of an Ord subclass of our previously defined Eq:

```
record Ord {A : Set} (eqA : Eq A) : Set where
  field _<_ : A → A → Bool
```

Let's now suppose that we have values of type Eq ℕ, Ord ℕ and Eq Bool in scope, but no instance of type Ord Bool. We can then still open the Eq {{...}} and Ord {{...}} modules and use the appropriate methods on ℕ and Bools, with the correct dictionaries being resolved in the background.

```
open Ord {{...}}
open Eq {{...}}
test₁ = 5 < 3
```

$$\mathsf{test}_2 = \mathsf{eq}\ 5\ 3$$
$$\mathsf{test}_3 = \mathsf{eq\ true\ false}$$

An ad-hoc polymorphic function $\_\leqslant\_$ now looks as follows:

$$\_\leqslant\_ : \{A : \mathsf{Set}\} \rightarrow \{\mathsf{eqA} : \mathsf{Eq}\ A\} \rightarrow \{\!\{\mathsf{ordA} : \mathsf{Ord\ eqA}\}\!\} \rightarrow A \rightarrow A \rightarrow \mathsf{Bool}$$
$$a \leqslant b = a < b \vee \mathsf{eq}\ a\ b$$

Note how the Pebble-style subclass model requires us to explicitly mention a superclass constraint in the type signature of $\_\leqslant\_$. This argument $\mathsf{eqA} : \mathsf{Eq}\ A$ is accepted as an implicit argument, not an instance, because it can typically be inferred from the parameters of the chosen ordA parameter. Because we require the superclass dictionary as an argument, it is automatically in scope for resolution inside the method.

The above shows that our mechanism does not impose a choice as to how subclasses are to be modelled by the programmer. We think this demonstrates that our instance arguments are a fundamental mechanism, giving the programmer the freedom to make his or her own design choices.

2.4 Native support code for records

A novel feature of our instance arguments is the fact that we can automatically bring its benefits to existing record based code, as demonstrated in the introduction. Let us assume we have a dependently-typed record definition of the following form:

$$
\begin{array}{l}
\textbf{record}\ R\ \Delta\ :\ \mathsf{Set}\ \textbf{where}\\
\quad \textbf{field}\\
\qquad x_1 : A_1\\
\qquad x_2 : A_2\ [x_1]\\
\qquad \ldots\\
\qquad x_n : A_n\ [x_1 \cdots x_{n-1}]\\
\quad y_1 : B_1\ [x_1 \cdots x_n]\\
\quad y_1 = v_1\ [x_1 \cdots x_n]\\
\quad \ldots\\
\quad y_n : B_1\ [x_1 \cdots x_n, y_1 \cdots y_{n-1}]\\
\quad y_n = v_n\ [x_1 \cdots x_n, y_1 \cdots y_{n-1}]
\end{array}
$$

Agda will automatically generate a module of the following form:

$$
\begin{array}{l}
\textbf{module}\ R\ \{\Delta\}\ (r : R\ \Delta)\ \textbf{where}\\
\quad x_1 : A_1\\
\quad x_1 = \cdots\\
\quad \ldots\\
\quad x_n : A_n\ [x_1 \cdots x_{n-1}]\\
\quad x_n = \cdots\\
\quad y_1 : B_1\ [x_1 \cdots x_n]\\
\quad y_1 = v_1\ [x_1 \cdots x_n]\\
\quad \ldots\\
\quad y_n : B\ [x_1 \cdots x_n, y_1 \cdots y_{n-1}]\\
\quad y_n = v_n\ [x_1 \cdots x_n, y_1 \cdots y_{n-1}]
\end{array}
$$

This module is parameterised on a record value r, and the functions in the module are implemented using its field values. We now allow a new form of module application:

$$\textbf{open}\ R\ \{\!\{\ldots\}\!\}$$

Like for Agda's standard module applications, the modifiers **public**, **using**, **renaming** and **hiding** can be used to control precisely what is imported. This new module application is equivalent to the following older-style notation (except that it doesn't name the RInst module):

$$\textbf{open module}\ \mathsf{RInst}\ \{\Delta\}\ \{\!\{r : R\ \Delta\}\!\} = R\ \{\Delta\}\ r$$

In this new module, all the definitions from module R, including the field projections $x_1 \cdots x_n$ and additional declarations $y_1 \cdots y_n$, are available in a form that accepts the record value r as a instance argument. As we have demonstrated in the introduction, these definitions allow them to be used in a *type-class-like* way.

Technically, this new type of section applications can in fact be applied to any module taking at least one argument, turning the last (normal or hidden) argument into an instance argument. This allows the mechanism to also be used for situations like in section 3, where the Agda standard library's monad concept is not defined as a record directly, but as a special case of an indexed monad.

2.5 Considerations for instance arguments in other languages

An important question about our proposed instance arguments is how Agda-specific they are. We believe that the mechanism is widely applicable, and that many variations on our design choices are possible.

Let us consider the different modifications that we have made. A first step is the introduction of a new, specially annotated type of arguments to functions, which is likely unproblematic in many programming languages. Clearly, in non-dependently typed languages, the arguments' type must be restricted to not depend on earlier non-type arguments' values, but this reflects the rules for normal arguments in those languages. However, care must be taken that functions with the new type of arguments are fully first-class on the one hand and that the programmer can tightly control the introduction of values for implicit arguments on the other hand.

To the best of our knowledge, Agda was the first language to demonstrate that these two requirements can be combined with a natural syntax through a careful balancing in the type checking rules which govern function applications, lambda expressions, and the implicit insertion of implicit lambda's. The rules in section A.1 and A.2 for our instance arguments are simply adaptations of the corresponding rules for Agda's existing implicit arguments [15]. We think that a similar type of function arguments and similar rules can be introduced for any language which has some form of partial function application and lambda expressions.

The choice of the algorithm by which not explicitly provided instance arguments are inferred is in fact orthogonal to the rest of our design. We clearly choose a relatively low-power one (more explanation in section 4), but we think that other choices can also be combined with the rest of our design, ranging from our relatively low-power inference (see section 4) to a full-power automated proof-search like Coq's [24]. An advantage of our algorithm is that we do not require values in scope to be specially annotated to be eligible for this inference, but an annotation similar to Scala implicit annotations can be used to limit the complexity of a more powerful inference. Another advantage of our low-power inference algorithm is that it does not introduce a separate type-level computational model in the language.

2.6 Formal Developments

In appendix A, we formally develop instance arguments, based on the formalism that Norell uses to present the Agda language [15]. We formally define functions with instance arguments, how values for them are type-checked, when values for instance arguments are inferred and the rules for this resolution. We discuss various technical points and present a soundness result.

2.7 Implementation

We have implemented the above proposal in Agda. Our implementation is surprisingly cheap, with a non-context-diff of about 750 lines. It's hard to compare line-counts between different programming languages (Agda is implemented in Haskell, Coq in OCaml), but for what it's worth: the initial diff of Sozeau's Coq type classes [24] was ~2k lines long. Our implementation has been incorporated in the development version of Agda[3], and will be part of Agda 2.2.12 when it is released.

3. Monads case study

Our instance arguments provide an alternative for type classes. They lift some of the limitations of type classes but our inference algorithm is less powerful than Haskell's. To demonstrate that our mechanism is at least powerful enough for many common use cases of type classes, we take a look at a typical type class example: monads. In this section, we demonstrate that with our instance arguments, we can use the Agda standard library's RawMonad's in similar ways to Haskell's monads.

The closest equivalent of Haskell's Monad type class in Agda's standard library is the RawMonad concept in the Category.Monad module. Unlike its Haskell relative, it is defined as a special kind of indexed monad, a concept that is defined as RawIMonad in module Category.Monad.Indexed[4]. We copy the most important parts of the definitions here:

```
RawMonad : ∀ {f} → (Set f → Set f) → Set _
RawMonad M = RawIMonad {I = ⊤} (λ _ _ → M)
record RawIMonad {i f} {I : Set i} (M : IFun I f) :
  Set (i ⊔ suc f) where
  infixl 1 _≫=_ _≫_
  field
    return : forall {i A} → A → M i i A
    _≫=_ : forall {i j k A B} → M i j A →
      (A → M j k B) → M i k B
  _≫_ : ∀ {i j k A B} →
      M i j A → M j k B → M i k B
  m₁ ≫ m₂ = m₁ ≫= λ _ → m₂
```

We see that RawMonad is defined as an indexed monad which just ignores its indices. An indexed monad contains the essential monadic operators return and _≫=_ as fields and provides the _≫_ operation. In order to highlight correspondence with Haskell's monads, we slightly modify the RawIMonad record module to additionally include a syntax definition (a form of restricted macro) for a form of do-notation. This addition is orthogonal to the use of instance arguments.

```
bind : ∀ {i j k A B} →
  M i j A → (A → M j k B) → M i k B
bind {i} {j} {k} {A} {B} =
  _≫=_ {i} {j} {k} {A} {B}
syntax bind m (λ x → c) = do x ← m then c
```

We can bring in scope some monad "instances" from the Agda standard library. We bring in scope a state monad with mutable state variable of fixed type ℕ, a partiality monad (defining a form of partial or possibly non-terminating computations) and the list monad (defining monadic operations over the List type constructor):

```
open import Category.Monad.State using (StateMonad)
stateMonad = StateMonad ℕ
open import Category.Monad.Partiality using ()
  renaming (monad to partialityMonad)
pmonad = partialityMonad
open import Data.List using (List; _∷_; [])
  renaming (monad to listMonad)
lmonad = listMonad
```

There is a technical reason, related to the universe polymorphism of these monad instances, why we need to provide the apparently trivial definitions of pmonad and lmonad. We will come back to this in section 4.

In current Agda, the most convenient way to use these monad "instances", is to apply the RawMonad module to the correct monad instance at the location where it is used.

```
test1 : ℕ → ℕ ⊥
test1 k = let open RawMonad partialityMonad in
          do x ← return k then
          if (equal x 4) then return 10 else never
```

This code does not look too bad actually. Opening a monad instance's module brings in scope just the definitions of the monadic operations we need. However, it becomes more difficult if we decide that we need to use for example the monadic bind operator on a list, requiring monadic operations from two different monad "instances". In this case, current Agda requires us to rename one:

```
postulate nToList : ℕ → List ℕ
test₂ : ℕ → (List ℕ) ⊥
test₂ k =
  let open RawMonad partialityMonad
      open RawMonad lmonad using ()
        renaming (_≫=_ to _≫=ₗ_) in
  do x ← return [k] then
  if (equal k 4) then return (x ≫=ₗ nToList) else never
```

We can improve upon this situation using instance arguments. First, we bring the definitions from the RawMonad {{ ... }} module application in scope. We have to define it ourselves because RawMonad is not directly defined as a record, but it is general and could be added to Agda's standard library. We can then define our examples in a simpler way and let Agda infer the correct values for the instance arguments.

```
open RawMonad {{...}}
test₁ : ℕ → ℕ ⊥
test₁ k = do x ← return k then
          if (equal x 4) then return 10 else never
test₂ : ℕ → (List ℕ) ⊥
test₂ k =
  do x ← return [k] then
  if (equal k 4) then return (x ≫= nToList) else never
```

In the case of test₁, one could argue that we don't actually gain all that much. Agda now automatically chooses the correct monad "instance" from the values in scope instead of requiring the programmer to make this choice. However, the second example shows that in a case where we use monadic operations from different monad "instances", instance arguments effectively spare us some uninteresting bookkeeping, by inferring appropriate "instances" in the background.

4. No automated proof search

Our resolution algorithm is only a restricted analog to Haskell's instance search. The mechanism is designed so that only one type-directed scope-based resolution will be done per not explicitly provided instance argument in the program (see section A.3). This limitation is a deliberate choice, intended to avoid introducing a separate computational model through the instance search mechanism, as for Scala implicits or Haskell and Coq type classes. However,

[3] Use the command `darcs get http://code.haskell.org/Agda` to download the latest source code.

[4] The definitions are called *raw* because they do not contain proofs of the monad laws.

this decision does unavoidably limit the functionality of our mechanism. For example, for the Eq type introduced in section 2, we could have a definition like the following:

```
listEq : {A : Set} → Eq A → Eq (List A)
listEq {A} eqA = record {equal = eq'} where
  eq' : List A → List A → Bool
  eq' [] [] = true
  eq' (a :: as) (b :: bs) = and (equal eqA a b) (eq' as bs)
  eq' _ _ = false
```

Now, with the eqBool value from section 2 in scope, you might expect an instance of Eq (List Bool) to be automatically inferred as listEq eqBool. However, in our system, this is not the case: in such a situation, we require the user to explicitly construct a value of the correct type himself. It suffices to bring this value in scope at the call site, for example by placing it in a local **where** block.

```
test = equal (true :: false :: true :: []) (true :: false :: [])
  where listBoolEq = listEq eqBool
```

We encountered another interesting case of this problem in the previous section, where we had to provide seemingly "trivial" definitions for values pmonad and lmonad. The reason that these were needed is that the definitions were not actually trivial. The types of the values involved are as follows:

```
partialityMonad : {l : Level} → RawMonad (_⊥ {l})
pmonad : RawMonad (_⊥ {_})
listMonad : {l : Level} → RawMonad (List {l})
lmonad : RawMonad (List {_})
```

This is an example of Agda's universe polymorphism. The value _⊥ is not a functor of type Set → Set, but instead, for any *level* l, _⊥{*l*} is a functor of type Set l → Set l. This means that partial computations can be defined producing values (Set 0), types (Set 1), kinds (Set 2), and for each of these types of partial computations, a monad "instance" is provided as partialityMonad {l}.

The monadic computations and lists we used before all produced or contained values, so our pmonad and lmonad are defined as monad instances for resp. partial computations and lists working with values. Note that we did not need to specify level 0 explicitly for this. Because we just omit the level argument, Agda inserts an underscore implicitly and infers its value when it resolves pmonad and lmonad as values for the instance arguments.

4.1 But why not?

So, in both of the above examples, our resolution search was not smart enough to automatically infer certain instance arguments that one might expect it to. In both cases, help from the programmer is required to make it find the correct value. The extra information is limited (placing the required value in scope) and does not require explicitly passing the instance arguments everywhere they are used.

We actually believe that a smarter resolution algorithm can be defined for our mechanism. Extensions can be imagined where functions like listEq are annotated somehow to make the resolution consider them. Such an extension would be largely orthogonal to the rest of our design. However, introducing such an extension makes the instance search recursive. Even if it can still be kept decidable with restrictions on the functions considered, it would inevitably expose an additional computational model, similar to Haskell's, Scala's or Coq's instance search.

Because our implementation is in Agda, we are extra sensitive to this point. Any instance search that can automatically infer for example the value of listBoolEq above, must somehow perform a reasonably powerful automated proof search. This is an area where up to now, the Agda language designers have taken a very principled approach. Agda does provide such a mechanism (dubbed auto), but only in the interactive proving/programming environment, not in the language. Agda has also refrained from introducing an equivalent to Coq's untyped, imperative meta-programming facility (Coq "tactics"), instead developing a more principled mechanism through the quoteGoal construct. This construct is intended to allow Agda to function in a sense as "its own tactic language", although it is currently still limited because no access to the context or scope is available to the meta-programs. We believe that Agda's approach in this area is very promising, and the limited power of our inference algorithm avoids compromising Agda's principled design choices in these areas by introducing a parallel computational model which could be exploited as a meta-programming construct, as has happened in other languages.

4.2 Advantages

Note also that our simple resolution scheme has some advantages of its own. We have used it for all of the examples in section 3 and 5 and the resolution has proven practical, predictable, intuitive and sufficient. Also, we do not need to limit resolution complexity by requiring candidate values to be annotated specially, instead considering all values in scope. This lowers the impact of our feature on users' code and makes for example the ellipsis in section 5 more widely usable. Its intuitive meaning also changes from "Fill in this value from an *annotated* value in scope" to "Fill in this value from the scope", which feels more natural to us.

Note that because the entire scope is considered for resolution, it is up to the programmer to make sure that only a single value of a correct type is in scope. Instance arguments should only be used on types which are informative enough so that they typically identify values uniquely. If there still is a conflict, existing features in Agda's module system (e.g. **hiding** and **using** modifiers) can be used to control the scope. Note also that values that are not directly in scope but via a named module are not considered for instance resolution, but they can still be accessed explicitly. In our experiments, we find that instance arguments provide a solution (ad hoc overloading) for many of the name conflicts that arise in typical use of Agda's standard library (e.g. $\_\stackrel{?}{=}\_$ in Data.Nat, Data.Bool etc.) and that type conflicts for reasonably typed instance arguments occur seldom.

5. Some advanced patterns

It turns out that our relatively simple extension of Agda can support analogs or variants of many features which have required important implementation efforts in Haskell, as well as some new patterns of its own. In this section, we discuss a selection of such topics.

5.1 Standing on the shoulders of records

We discussed in the introduction how modelling type classes using an existing powerful record mechanism such as Agda's dependently typed records makes certain features available "for free" that require separate extensions for Haskell type classes. Sozeau et al. and Oliveira et al. have previously demonstrated this observation for Coq type classes (which are Coq dependently typed records underneath [24]) and Scala implicits (where type classes are typically modelled as Scala traits [2]).

One such feature is the equivalent of Haskell's associated type families [23]. An associated type family is essentially a type class member that is a type or type functor. Using a dictionary model of a type class in a dependently typed language, there is nothing special about records with members that are not just values and we essentially get associated type families for free.

Another feature which we get "for free" is known as constraint families for Haskell [18]. A constraint (synonym) family in Haskell is a member of a type class that represents a class constraint on a type class's parameters and/or other types. Using a dictionary model of type classes, this concept actually reduces to type families. Orchard and Schrijvers' example of constrained functors (positive type functors whose fmap function is restricted to types in a certain type class) can be modelled as follows:

```
record ConstrainedFunctor (F : Set → Set) : Set where
  field Constraint : Set → Set
        fmap : ∀ {A B : Set} → Constraint A →
          Constraint B → (A → B) → F A → F B
listConstrainedFunctor : ConstrainedFunctor List
listConstrainedFunctor = record {
   Constraint = λ _ → ⊤
  , fmap = λ _ _ → List.map}
setConstrainedFunctor : ConstrainedFunctor Set
setConstraintedFunctor = record {
   Constraint = Ord, fmap = Set.map}
```

5.2 Multi-parameter type classes and functional dependencies

A multi-parameter type class in Haskell is (obviously) a type class with more than one parameter. The equivalent in our approach would be instance arguments of a record type with more than one parameter, and this is clearly allowed in our system. Functional dependencies in a multi-parameter type class are annotations which indicate that certain parameters of a type class can be deduced from (a subset of) the others [9]. Such an annotation cannot directly be provided in our framework. However, in this section, we highlight certain behaviour of our system, which is reminiscent of functional dependencies, even though it works differently under the hood.

Consider the following code, which uses the IsDecEquivalence record from module Relation.Binary in the Agda standard library. We use explicit **using** declarations to avoid certain name clashes, but also to make it more clear what is happening under the hood.

```
open import Relation.Binary using (module DecSetoid;
  module IsDecEquivalence)
open import Data.Bool using (false; true; decSetoid)
open DecSetoid decSetoid using (isDecEquivalence)

open IsDecEquivalence {{...}} using (_≟_)

test = false ≟ true
```

The IsDecEquivalence t _≈_ record is semantically a more developed version of the record Eq from the introduction, containing essentially an equality decision procedure _≟_ for a binary predicate _≈_ on type t (as well as proof that _≈_ is an equivalence relation). The field _≟_ has the following type:

$$\_\stackrel{?}{=}\_ : (a : t) \to (b : t) \to \mathsf{Dec}\ (a \approx b)$$

A value of type Dec $(a \approx b)$ contains either a proof that $a \approx b$ or a proof that $a \not\approx b$. We can bring a value of type IsDecEquivalence Bool _≡_ in scope by importing Data.Bool and opening the decSetoid record (this would be more convenient if isEquivalence were exported directly by the Data.Bool module). Finally, we bring the new record field projection operator (taking the record as a instance argument) into scope by importing it from the IsDecEquivalence {{...}} module application (see section 2.4). From that point on, we can transparently use the function _≟_ on Bools, as demonstrated in the definition of test.

A first thing to note is that the IsDecEquivalence record takes two arguments, making it the equivalent of a multi-parameter type class. It is interesting to consider what happens when type-checking the definition of test. The function _≟_ has the following type (ignoring universe polymorphism):

```
_≟_ : {A : Set} → {_≈_ : A → A → Set} →
      {{isDE : IsDecEquivalence A _≈_}} →
      (a : A) → (b : B) → Dec (a ≈ b)
```

When false ≟ true is type checked, Agda infers that A = Bool from the arguments of _≟_. It then infers the instance argument isDE from the local scope. The only candidate value in scope is isEquivalence, typed IsDecEquivalence Bool _≡_. From unifying the type of this value with the expected type of isDE, Agda infers that the implicit argument _≈_ must be the binary predicate _≡_.

In this case, we see that one argument of the IsDecEquivalence type constructor already uniquely determines the value to be used from the scope. Its other arguments can then be inferred from this value, producing an effect similar to a hypothetical situation where IsDecEquivalence were a multi-parameter type class with a functional dependency from type A to binary predicate _≈_.

Nevertheless, our mechanism works very differently from Haskell type classes with functional dependencies. First of all, nowhere have we declared any functional dependencies between arguments of the IsDecEquivalence record type, and these dependencies were not checked when we brought values of type IsDecEquivalence into scope. Only when we actually needed to infer an instance argument, it was checked that only a single suitably-typed value was in scope.

Semantically, declaring the equivalent of a functional dependency on the arguments of the IsDecEquivalence record type corresponds to an assertion that only one decidable equality predicate can exist for any given type A. This assertion is semantically wrong here and can cause problems in scenarios where multiple such predicates are used together. Our system manages to infer the value of the _≈_ predicate without such a dependency, because only one value of type IsDecEquivalence Bool _≈_ is *in scope* at the call site of _≟_, which is semantically a much weaker requirement.

Note finally that it is a value, not a type, that is being inferred in a functional dependencies-like way. In fact, our mechanism does not make any fundamental distinction between types or values, as one might expect in a dependently-typed language like Agda. The mechanism will even happily infer types from values, which is not possible in Haskell.

5.3 Implicit Configurations

One pattern implemented in the context of type classes which is rendered almost trivial in the context of our proposal is Kiselyov and Shan's implicit configurations [11]. The authors discuss a solution to what they call the *configurations problem*: propagating run-time preferences throughout a program, allowing multiple concurrent configuration sets to coexist safely under statically guaranteed separation. Their main example concerns modular arithmetic: they want to be able to build expressions in modular arithmetic which are parameterised over a concrete modulus but without the need to pass the modulus around explicitly. They also want static assurance that the same modulus is used for all operations in such an expression.

Kiselyov and Shan's solution is based on a mix of phantom types, type classes and type-level computation. We demonstrate that a simpler encoding is possible in our system, and that we can even fully avoid one of the main difficulties in their work: the reflection at type-level of run-time values. Let us suppose that we have a signature like the following: we assume an Integral dictionary record and add, mul and obj operations taking such a dictionary as a instance argument. We also assume we have a type

N containing values zero, one, two and three and a dictionary nInt of type Integral N.

```
postulate
  Integral : Set → Set
  add : ∀ {A} {{intA : Integral A}} → A → A → A
  mul : ∀ {A} {{intA : Integral A}} → A → A → A
  mod : ∀ {A} {{intA : Integral A}} → A → A → A
  N : Set
  zero one two three : N
  nInt : Integral N
```

Like Kiselyov and Shan, we define a wrapper data type M s A parameterised by phantom token s (in our case not a type but a value of opaque type Token) and type A. This wrapper represents a value of type A that is being considered under an unspecified modulus. We also define a dictionary record Modulus s A (also parameterised by a token s and type A).

```
private postulate Token : Set
record Modulus (s : Token) (A : Set) : Set where
  field modulus : A
data M (s : Token) (A : Set) : Set where
  MkM : A → M s A
unMkM : ∀ {s A} → M s A → A
unMkM (MkM a) = a
```

Our withModulus function is simpler than Kiselyov and Shan's because we don't have to bother with constructing a type for which the Modulus instance returns a certain value, but instead just pass the desired dictionary explicitly.

```
private postulate theOnlyToken : Token
withModulus :
  ∀ {A} → {{intA : Integral A}} → (modulus : A) →
  (∀ {s} → {{mod : Modulus s A}} → M s A) → A
withModulus modulus f = unMkM $
  f {theOnlyToken} {{record {modulus = modulus}}}
```

Our addition and multiplication become pretty similar to Kiselyov and Shan's version:

```
normalize : ∀ {s A} {{intA : Integral A}}
            {{mod : Modulus s A}} → A → M s A
normalize a = MkM $ mod modulus a
_+_ : ∀ {s A} {{intA : Integral A}}
  {{mod : Modulus s A}} → M s A → M s A → M s A
(MkM a) + (MkM b) = normalize $ add a b
_*_ : ∀ {s A} {{intA : Integral A}}
  {{mod : Modulus s A}} → M s A → M s A → M s A
(MkM a) * (MkM b) = normalize $ mul a b
```

These operators are used similarly to Kiselyov and Shan's:

```
test₁ : N
test₁ = withModulus two $
        let o = MkM one in (o + o) * (o + o)
testExpr : ∀ {s} → {{mod : Modulus s N}} → M s N
testExpr = let o = MkM one; t = MkM two
           in (o + t) * t
test₂ : N
test₂ = withModulus three testExpr
```

With this, our encoding of Kiselyov and Shan's implicit configurations is done. We believe that we achieve the same goals as Kiselyov and Shan, but we avoid their threading of values into types (through an involved type-level reflection of values) and back again (through a form of type-level computation), which seems unneeded, very complex and possibly inefficient (depending on what optimisations the compiler can perform). Interestingly, the fact that we don't need to reflect values at the type level is not (as one might expect) a consequence of Agda's dependently typed nature. Instead, it is the value-level representation of dictionaries which allows this greater simplicity. More concretely, in the definition of withModulus above, we can construct the dictionary as a value and pass it explicitly to the computation, whereas Kiselyov and Shan need to jump through a lot of hoops to construct a type for which the correct instance will be inferred. Kiselyov and Shan instead proposed adding a form of local instances to Haskell, of which we also support an equivalent (see section 5.5).

5.4 Implicit Proof Obligations

In the context of Agda, we believe that instance arguments are useful for a pattern which is (to the best of our knowledge) novel: implicit proof obligations. Consider the integer division operator in module Data.Nat.DivMod in Agda's standard library:

```
_div_ : (dividend divisor : ℕ)
          {≢0 : False (divisor ≟ 0)} → ℕ
```

This division operator requires a guarantee that the provided divisor is non-zero. However, instead of requiring a normal argument of type divisor $\not\equiv$ 0, the _div_ operator cleverly accepts a value of type False (divisor $\stackrel{?}{=}$ 0). This type contains a single value if and only if divisor is non-zero, but additionally, this value can be automatically inferred if Agda knows that divisor is of the form suc n for some n. For example, if we write 5 div 3, then Agda will infer the non-zeroness proof obligation. This pattern has been described by Norell [15, 3.7.1 p.71], and critically depends on the fact that the property in question (non-zeroness) can be decided. Proof obligations modelled using this pattern are not passed on implicitly to other methods that require it. Finally, the _div_ operator becomes somewhat clumsy to use in a situation where only a normal proof divisor $\not\equiv$ 0 is available.

We propose an additional operator _div'_ which takes the proof obligation as an instance argument (we omit the definition in terms of the above _div_). This operator does not have the limitations of the _div_ operator discussed above, but does have some limitations of its own: for example in the call 5 div' 3, Agda can only infer the implicit argument of our operator if a value of type 3 $\not\equiv$ 0 is in scope.

```
_divMod'_ : (dividend divisor : ℕ)
            {{≢0 : divisor ≢ 0}} → ℕ × ℕ
_divMod'_ = -- omitted
_div'_ : (dividend divisor : ℕ) {{≢0 : divisor ≢ 0}} → ℕ
a div' b with a divMod' b
a div' b | (q, _) = q
postulate
  d : ℕ
  d≢0 : d ≢ 0
test : ℕ
test = 5 div' d
```

Note how in the definition of _div'_, the proof obligation is implicitly passed on to the _divMod'_ function, which also requires it. We believe that this example shows that our proposed instance arguments have uses that go beyond those of type classes. Not only dictionary records can be usefully passed around implicitly but also other values which are uniquely identified by their type in call-site scopes. In a dependently typed language like Agda, implicit proof obligations are a clear example of such values.

5.5 Local instances

A feature that is not supported by Haskell type classes are local type class instances. Consider the following two equality functions on Strings: the first represents standard equality and the second only compares the strings' lengths. The first definition uses the standard string equality decision procedure and the second applies the EqInst.eq operator after first applying a string length function to its two arguments. Note that we assume a single, standard value of type Eq $\mathbb{N}$ in scope.

$$\begin{aligned}&\mathsf{eqString}_1 : \mathsf{String} \to \mathsf{String} \to \mathsf{Bool}\\&\mathsf{eqString}_1\ s_1\ s_2 = \lfloor s_1 \stackrel{?}{=} s_2 \rfloor\\&\mathsf{eqString}_2 : \mathsf{String} \to \mathsf{String} \to \mathsf{Bool}\\&\mathsf{eqString}_2 = \mathsf{eq\ on\ length}\end{aligned}$$

Now suppose that we have a function whose behaviour depends on a configuration argument, determining which type of equality it should use throughout a series of calculations. We can support this by defining the equivalent of a *local instance* eqLocal of the Eq *type class*, which uses the correct string equality operator, depending on the configuration parameter.

```
test : Bool → Bool
test lengthEq = if eq "abcd" "dcba" then ... else ...
  where eqLocal = record {eq =
    if lengthEq then eqString₂ else eqString₁ }
```

The value eqLocal functions as a local type class instance, something which is also supported by Scala implicits, but not by Haskell or Coq type classes, where type class instances are always global.

5.6 Two final examples

As a small encore in this section, we can't resist discussing two code snippets using instance arguments. The first is an example of a function abstracting over functions with implicit arguments. It demonstrates the first-class nature of our new type of arguments: functions with instance arguments can be abstracted over, their types can be written out etc.

```
explicitize : ∀ {A : Set} {B : A → Set} →
   ({{x : A}} → B x) → (x : A) → B x
explicitize f x = f {{x}}
```

Our final example is small, but very useful: it is an analog of Agda's standard underscore construct for instance arguments, similar to Scala's implicitly or ?. Like in Scala, we don't need to introduce special syntax for this: the following definition suffices. This ellipsis can be used as a shorthand in any situation where only a single type-correct value is in scope. Because our resolution algorithm does not require candidates to be specially annotated to be eligible, our ellipsis is more generally useful than Scala's implicitly.

```
··· : {A : Set} → {{a : A}} → A
··· {{a}} = a
```

6. Related Work

There exists a lot of literature about type classes, extensions of them and alternatives to them [2, 5, 6, 9, 10, 18, 20, 23, 24, 26, 27]. We have already discussed Haskell type classes and Scala implicits in the introduction and we do not repeat this here.

We do not further discuss implicit parameters as implemented in Hugs and GHC [13], as these use a name-based resolution, instead of the type-based resolution of our design and are thus not suited for our use cases.

6.1 Coq Type Classes

Sozeau and Oury have recently presented Coq type classes [24]. Coq is a dependently typed, purely functional programming language/proof assistant like Agda, with a longer history and a larger user base. Unlike Agda, it has a very principled core language and associated type-checker. On top of that, there is a variety of arguably less principled language features and meta-programming/proof automation facilities.

The authors introduce type classes as essentially a new way to define dependently typed record types. If a function has an implicit argument of such a record type, and its value cannot be inferred through Coq's standard unification, then Coq will try to infer a value through an instance search. This instance search is implemented as an automated proof search using a special-purpose port of the `eauto` tactic. It performs a bounded breadth- or depth-first search using the type class's instances as lemma's. This can include both direct instances (objects of the record type) and parameterized instances (functions which take certain arguments and return such an object).

Sozeau and Oury go on to discuss some superficial syntax extensions and relatively straightforward models of superclasses and substructures and then provide a discussion of various aspects of their system, most importantly their instance search tactic. They think their current instance search tactic is not sufficient in the context of multi-parameter type classes and arbitrary instances (which their system currently allows). They state the algorithm's non-determinism and impredictability as problems which they hope to address in the future by restricting the shape of allowed instances and using a more predictable algorithm.

In addition to these problems, we believe that Sozeau et al.'s instance search procedure is currently at least as powerful as Haskell's or Scala's instance/implicit search and exposes the same kind of separate computational model (see section 4). Also, if we understand Sozeau and Oury's text correctly, a given implicit function argument can sometimes behave as a type class constraint and sometimes as a normal implicit argument, if its type depends on the value of previous arguments. Our resolution algorithm is less powerful than Sozeau et al.'s, but it is predictable, deterministic and does not expose an alternate computational model.

Sozeau and Oury's mechanism is limited to *record types* that were *defined as a type class*, so existing libraries need to be adapted to benefit from it. Type class instances can be defined locally (see section 5.5), but it seems that the local instance will not be considered for automatic resolution.

6.2 Coq Canonical Structures

Coq features another type system concept which can be exploited as an alternative to type classes: *canonical structures* [1, 25]. This feature allows certain values of a record type to be marked as *canonical structures*. Such values are then automatically considered when the Coq type inferencer tries to infer a value of the record type from the value of one of its fields. Canonical structures have existed for some time in Coq, but have recently attracted the attention of authors looking to provide easy to use libraries of complex concepts, exploiting canonical structures as a powerful meta-programming feature that can be implicitly triggered to resolve values in the background. There are some similarities in the design to ours, as it does not introduce a separate type of structure and does a form of implicit resolution from call-site scope. However, because the resolution is keyed on values instead of types, the idea is not suitable for non-dependently typed languages, where we can only reason about types at compile time.

However, the entire design of the feature seems very pragmatic. We have not been able to find a detailed (formal?) description of the exact workings of the system. From what we understand, it is deeply coupled to Coq's type inference engine and uses certain syntactic criteria, behaving differently for semantically equivalent values. There seems to be a certain interaction with a form of backtracking in Coq's type inference engine, which can be exploited for encoding backtracking in the specification of how values should be inferred. All of this leads to a meta-programming model that seems even more powerful than Haskell's instance resolution, hard to understand and strongly different from Coq's standard computational model(s).

6.3 Explicit Haskell

In an unpublished technical report, Dijkstra and Swierstra describe an implicit arguments system which they have implemented in a Haskell variant called *Explicit Haskell* [4]. Their main motivation is that Haskell does not provide a way to override the automatic resolution of instances (dictionaries) for functions with a type class constraint. They extend Haskell with named instances, local instances, and a way to explicitly provide an instance to a function with a type class constraint, either by naming the instance or by lifting a value of a record type corresponding to the type class. They also allow type class constraints to appear anywhere in a type, not just at the beginning. For resolving type class constraints, they use a resolution close to Haskell's. The only difference is that instances can be annotated to not take part in this resolution (in which case they can only be used by name). In the same text, Dijkstra and Swierstra discuss a system for partial type signatures, which seems to have independent value. The system allows the user to partially specify types for values and leave the rest to be inferred.

This design has many similarities to our system. Their extensions to the concept of type class constraints effectively transforms them into a special form of function arguments similar to our instance arguments. Their design offers some of the same benefits as ours (e.g. local instances, named instances), and they discuss some of the same examples as we do in section 5.

However, they make some different choices than we do: their constraints remain limited to arguments whose type was defined as a type class instance and their resolution is similar to Haskell's. They do not fully unify type classes with their associated record types, so that some of the advantages we can offer are not available (e.g. abstracting over a type class).

6.4 Modular Type Classes

Dreyer et al. discuss an alternative to type classes in the context of ML [5]. They share our view that Haskell type classes duplicate functionality by introducing a separate structuring concept, and they argue that ML modules already provide functionality akin to associated type families and type class inheritance (like we do for ADT's). They propose to model single-parameter type classes as *class signatures*: module signatures with a single abstract type named t. Instances become modules and functors. Their primitive **overload** fun **from** sig returns a version of function fun from class signature sig that will resolve the appropriate module implementing sig from call-site scope. Another primitive canon (sig) resolves and returns this module.

Resolution of such a module takes into account modules and functors that have been annotated in the current scope with a **using** declaration. Since functors are considered, the instance search is recursive, and can likely be exploited as a type-level programming primitive similar to Haskell's instance search, even though Dreyer et al do not discuss this. Their proposal does not support the equivalent of multi-parameter type classes. It is not clear to us if and how their type class modules can be abstracted over.

Acknowledgments

This research is partially funded by the Interuniversity Attraction Poles Programme Belgian State, Belgian Science Policy, and by the Research Fund K.U.Leuven. Dominique Devriese holds a Ph. D. fellowship of the Research Foundation - Flanders (FWO). The authors thank Adriaan Moors (EPFL) for providing valuable feedback on a draft of this text, as well as clarifying various points about Scala implicits. We thank the anonymous reviewers for many valuable comments and PC Chair Olivier Danvy for suggesting the final title.

References

[1] Y. Bertot, G. Gonthier, S. Ould Biha, and I. Pasca. Canonical big operators. In *TPHOLs*, 2008.

[2] B. C. d. S. Oliveira, A. Moors, and M. Odersky. Type classes as objects and implicits. In *OOPSLA*, 2010.

[3] N. Danielsson, U. Norell, S. Mu, S. Bronson, D. Doel, P. Jansson, and L. Chen. The Agda standard library, 2009.

[4] A. Dijkstra and S. D. Swierstra. Making implicit parameters explicit. Technical Report UU-CS-2005-032, Dept. ICS, Utrecht University, 2005.

[5] D. Dreyer, R. Harper, M. M. T. Chakravarty, and G. Keller. Modular type classes. In *POPL*, 2007.

[6] D. Duggan and J. Ophel. Type-checking multi-parameter type classes. *Journal of Functional Programming*, 12(02):133–158, 2002.

[7] B. Heeren, J. Hage, and S. Swierstra. Scripting the type inference process. In *ACM SIGPLAN Notices*, volume 38, 2003.

[8] P. Hudak, J. Hughes, S. Peyton Jones, and P. Wadler. A history of haskell: being lazy with class. In *History of Programming Languages*, 2007.

[9] M. Jones. Type classes with functional dependencies. *PLAS*, pages 230–244, 2003.

[10] W. Kahl and J. Scheffczyk. Named instances for Haskell type classes. In *HASKELL*, 2001.

[11] O. Kiselyov and C.-c. Shan. Functional pearl: Implicit configurations. In *HASKELL*, 2004.

[12] R. Lämmel and S. Peyton Jones. Scrap your boilerplate with class: extensible generic functions. In *ICFP*, pages 204–215, 2005.

[13] J. Lewis, J. Launchbury, E. Meijer, and M. Shields. Implicit parameters: Dynamic scoping with static types. In *POPL*, pages 108–118, 2000.

[14] C. McBride. Faking it: Simulating dependent types in haskell. *Journal of Functional Programming*, 12(4&5), 2002.

[15] U. Norell. *Towards a practical programming language based on dependent type theory*. PhD thesis, Chalmers University of Technology, 2007.

[16] U. Norell and C. Coquand. Type checking in the presence of meta-variables. Unpublished draft., 2007. URL `http://www.cse.chalmers.se/~ulfn/papers/meta-variables.html`.

[17] M. Odersky. The Scala language specification, version 2.8. online, 2010. URL `http://www.scala-lang.org/docu/files/ScalaReference.pdf`.

[18] D. Orchard and T. Schrijvers. Haskell type constraints unleashed. In *FLOPS*, 2010.

[19] S. Peyton Jones and R. Lämmel. Scrap your boilerplate. In *APLAS*, page 357, 2003.

[20] S. Peyton Jones, M. Jones, and E. Meijer. Type classes: an exploration of the design space. In *HASKELL*, 1997.

[21] S. Peyton Jones, D. Vytiniotis, S. Weirich, and G. Washburn. Simple unification-based type inference for GADTs. In *ICFP*, 2006.

[22] S. Peyton Jones, D. Vytiniotis, S. Weirich, and M. Shields. Practical type inference for arbitrary-rank types. *Journal of Functional Programming*, 17(1), 2007.

[23] T. Schrijvers, S. Peyton Jones, M. Chakravarty, and M. Sulzmann. Type checking with open type functions. In *ICFP*, 2008.

[24] M. Sozeau and N. Oury. First-class type classes. In *TPHOLs*, 2008.

[25] The Coq development team. The Coq reference manual. online, 2010. URL `http://coq.inria.fr/refman/`. v8.3.

[26] P. Wadler and S. Blott. How to make ad-hoc polymorphism less ad hoc. In *POPL*, 1989.

[27] S. Weirich. Replib: a library for derivable type classes. In *HASKELL*, 2006.

A. Under the hood

In this appendix, we discuss the precise changes we make in more detail. The definitions in this section are extensions and adaptations of Norell's rules for current Agda type-checking and standard implicit arguments [15, 3.5 pp. 69–70, 5.1.5 pp. 99–100]. They should be read in the context of Norell's developments and may not be fully clear without them.

A.1 Implicit lambdas

We add another implicit function space {{ x : A }} → B in addition to the existing { x : A } → B and (x : A) → B. Like the existing implicit functions, the new functions are semantically equivalent to the corresponding ordinary functions. Values of type {{ x : A }} → B can be introduced as (typed or untyped) lambda values λ {{ x }} → e or λ {{ x : A }} → e or they can be defined as constants (at the top-level or in where-clauses).

For type-checking values of this type, we extend the rules for Agda's standard implicit arguments [15, 3.5 pp. 69–70] as follows. If a value does not explicitly mention an instance argument from the type it is checked against, rule (2) infers implicit lambda's, like for normal implicit arguments.

$$\frac{\Gamma, x : A \vdash e \uparrow B \leadsto s}{\Gamma \vdash \lambda\{\{x\}\}.e \uparrow \{\{x : A\}\} \to B \leadsto \lambda\{\{x\}\}.s} \quad (1)$$

$$\frac{\Gamma, x : A \vdash e \uparrow B \leadsto s \qquad e \neq \lambda\{\{x\}\}.e'}{\Gamma \vdash e \uparrow \{\{x : A\}\} \to B \leadsto \lambda\{\{x\}\}.s} \quad (2)$$

A.2 Instance arguments

Next, we need to determine when instance arguments of a function are not provided explicitly and should be inferred. This mechanism is governed by the inference rules for argument checking judgements of the form $\Gamma \vdash A \mathbin{@} \bar{e} \downarrow B \leadsto \bar{s}$. Such a judgement means that the values $\bar{e}$ can be passed as arguments to a value of type A, producing a value of type B. The full list of arguments to be applied to the function (including implicitly inserted ones) is "returned" in $\bar{s}$.

We extend the corresponding rules for implicit arguments [15, 3.5 p. 70] as follows. For a non-provided instance argument, we do not just insert a meta-variable α, but we additionally add a constraint $\mathrm{FindInScope}\,\alpha$. This is a special kind of constraint that indicates that α should be resolved as an instance argument. To do this, we need to extend the form of argument checking judgements to additionally return a set of constraints $\mathcal{C}$: $\Gamma \vdash A \mathbin{@} \bar{e} \downarrow B \leadsto \bar{s}, \mathcal{C}$. This adapted form actually corresponds more closely to Agda's existing implementation of the rules. Existing rules in the old form of the judgement should now be read as simply producing no constraints or simply pass generated constraints through if they recurse.

$$\frac{\Gamma \vdash e \uparrow A \leadsto s \qquad \Gamma \vdash B[x := s] \mathbin{@} \bar{e} \downarrow B' \leadsto \bar{s}, \mathcal{C}}{\Gamma \vdash \{\{x : A\}\} \to B \mathbin{@} \{\{e\}\}; \bar{e} \downarrow B' \leadsto s; \bar{s}, \mathcal{C}} \quad (3)$$

$$\frac{\mathrm{AddMeta}(\alpha : \Gamma \to A) \qquad \bar{e} \neq \{\{e\}\}; \bar{e}' \\ \Gamma \vdash \{\{x : A\}\} \to B \mathbin{@} \{\{\alpha\}\}; \bar{e} \downarrow B' \leadsto \bar{s}, \mathcal{C}}{\Gamma \vdash \{\{x : A\}\} \to B \mathbin{@} \bar{e} \downarrow B' \leadsto \bar{s}, \mathcal{C} \cup \{\mathrm{FindInScope}\,\alpha\}} \quad (4)$$

We change the last rule on [15, p. 70] to the following:

$$\frac{A \neq \{\{x : A_1\}\} \to A_2 \qquad A \neq \{x : A_1\} \to A_2}{\Gamma \vdash A \mathbin{@} \epsilon \downarrow A \leadsto \epsilon, \{\}} \quad (5)$$

A somewhat technical point here is that at the moment, we do not allow meta-variables introduced for instance arguments to be η-expanded, as this is done for Agda's normal implicit arguments. We take a conservative approach because we currently do not have a good understanding of possible interactions between η-expansion and instance resolution. During our experiments, we have established that all of them (see section 3 and 5) have worked well without η-expansion. It is future work to get a better understanding of the issues involved.

A.3 Resolution algorithm

The resolution of a constraint $\mathrm{FindInScope}\,\alpha$ in context Γ and scope S with $\Gamma \vdash \alpha : A$ tries to infer a value from either the values in the current context Γ or the constants in scope S. If only one candidate is found in both sets, it is selected. If there is more than one candidate, resolution of the constraint is postponed in the hope that more type information will become available further on, reducing the set of candidates further. If the constraint is not resolved when type checking finishes, this is reported to the user. If there are no candidates, then the constraint cannot be solved and this is also reported.

To formalise these rules, we need some extra information about meta variables introduced through inference rule (4) above: the context and scopes at the point where they were defined. We do not make this change explicit because the context is actually already implicitly being maintained throughout Norell's development [15], and because both the scope and the context are already being kept in the Agda implementation. For a meta variable α, we write $\mathrm{MScp}\,\alpha$ and $\mathrm{MCtx}\,\alpha$ for the scope resp. the context in which a meta variable α was introduced.

With these nuances, we can formally define how we solve constraints $\mathrm{FindInScope}\,\alpha$ as follows:

$$\frac{\mathrm{Lookup}(\alpha : A) \\ \mathrm{Candidates}(\mathrm{MCtx}(\alpha), \mathrm{MScp}(\alpha), \alpha, A) = \{(n, A_n)\} \\ \Gamma \vdash A \simeq A_n \leadsto \mathcal{C} \qquad \alpha := n}{\Gamma \vdash \mathrm{FindInScope}\,\alpha \leadsto \mathcal{C}} \quad (6)$$

This definition says that if we have a meta-variable α typed A, that is to be inferred as an instance argument, then it is resolved if there is a unique solution. In this case, we require convertibility of the types and assign the value to the meta-variable. The set of candidates in context Γ and scope S, for meta-variable α, of type A is defined by predicate Candidates:

$$\mathrm{Candidates}(\Gamma, S, \alpha, A) = \\ \{(n, A_n) \mid \mathrm{Cand}(\Gamma, S, n, A_n) \text{ and } \mathrm{ValidCand}(\alpha, A, n, A_n)\} \quad (7)$$

The candidates are those terms n, of type A_n, that are potential candidates in the current context and scope (predicate Cand below) and are valid with respect to the current meta-variable and its type. This last property is defined by the ValidCand predicate.

$$\frac{\langle\Sigma\rangle\ \mathrm{CheckCand}(\alpha, A, n', A') \leadsto \mathcal{C} \Longrightarrow \langle\Sigma'\rangle}{\langle\Sigma\rangle\ \mathrm{ValidCand}(\alpha, A, n', A') \Longrightarrow \langle\Sigma\rangle} \quad (8)$$

In the definition of this predicate, we perform a check, but if this check makes changes to the current signature, we do not yet carry them through here. This is formalised using the explicit notation of the signatures in the judgements [15, 3.3.1 p. 54].

$$\frac{\Gamma \vdash A \simeq A' \rightsquigarrow \mathcal{C} \quad \alpha := n \quad \mathrm{CurrentConstraints}(\mathcal{C}) \qquad \forall C \in \mathcal{C} : C \neq \mathrm{FindInScope}\,\alpha' \Rightarrow \neg(\nvdash C \rightsquigarrow \mathcal{C}')}{\mathrm{CheckCand}(\alpha, A, n', A') \rightsquigarrow \mathcal{C}} \tag{9}$$

The check that a certain term is valid for a certain meta-variable consists of two parts. First, the term's type must be convertible to the required type. Second, if we assign the value to the meta-variable, no other constraint must be immediately invalidated. For this last check, we do not recursively consider other FindInScope constraints, since this would introduce recursion in the instance search. This check is necessarily incomplete: in Norell's words, the type checker will give one of three answers [15, Note p. 65]: "yes it is type correct", "no it is not correct" or "it might be correct if the metavariables are instantiated properly". Only if we get the second answer, we reject the candidate under scrutiny.

Rule (9) strikes a fine balance. On the one hand, the resolution algorithm needs to be powerful enough to be usable, but we avoid making it too powerful (see discussion in section 4). The intuition behind the criterion above is that we consider any value that is type-correct in the sense that it has the correct type, but also in the sense that it does not immediately invalidate constraints. The criterion has proven sufficient for all use cases discussed in this text, but also necessary: without the check for invalidated constraints, monad instances for example are often not resolved. Note that we have used a new CurrentConstraints operation, which works on the signature that is implicit in the typing judgements:

$$\langle\Sigma\rangle\ \mathrm{CurrentConstraints}(\mathcal{C}) \Longrightarrow \langle\Sigma\rangle \text{ where } \mathcal{C} = \{C \mid C \in \Sigma\} \tag{10}$$

We still need to define the potential candidates in a given context and scope. The Cand property formalises this:

$$\frac{\Gamma = \Gamma_1; n : A; \Gamma_2}{\mathrm{Cand}(\Gamma, S, n, A)} \tag{11}$$

$$\frac{\mathrm{Visible}_{\mathsf{pri}}(n, S) \quad \mathrm{Lookup}(n : A)}{\mathrm{Cand}(\Gamma, S, n, A)} \tag{12}$$

The somewhat technical predicate $\mathrm{Visible}_p(n, S)$ asserts that name n is publicly or privately (defined by p) in scope S:

$$\frac{\mathrm{Visible}_{\mathsf{pub}}(n, S)}{\mathrm{Visible}_\alpha(n, S \blacktriangleright \sigma)} \tag{13}$$

$$\frac{\mathrm{VisibleNS}_\alpha(n, \sigma) \vee \mathrm{VisibleNS}_{\mathsf{pub}}(n, \sigma)}{\mathrm{Visible}_\alpha(n, S \blacktriangleright \sigma)} \tag{14}$$

$$\frac{n \in ns_\alpha(cn)}{\mathrm{VisibleNS}_\alpha(n, \langle M, ns_{\mathsf{pub}}, ns_{\mathsf{pri}}\rangle)} \tag{15}$$

From rules (6) and (9) above, it is clear that resolution of constraints $\mathrm{FindInScope}\,\alpha$ only compares types that have already been type checked, and does not trigger extra type checking. Therefore, only one constraint $\mathrm{FindInScope}\,\alpha$ will be resolved per occurence in the user's code of a function taking an instance argument without a value being provided explicitly. This means that, contrary to other proposals, the computational power of our resolution algorithm is fundamentally limited, in the sense that it does not allow any form of recursion, looping or backtracking. It therefore does not introduce a separate computational model in the language (see section 4).

A.4 Soundness

Intuitively, soundness of the rules above is easily guaranteed, because all we do is assign terms of the correct type to meta-variables.

The following lemma reflects this intuition, supplementing Norell's Lemma 3.5.13:

Lemma 1 (Instance resolution preserves consistency). *If* $\Gamma \vdash_{|\Sigma|}$ **valid**, Σ *is consistent and*

$$\langle\Sigma\rangle\ \Gamma \vdash \mathrm{FindInScope}\,\alpha \Longrightarrow \langle\Sigma'\rangle$$

then Σ' *is consistent.*

Proof. A consequence of Norell's Lemma 3.5.12 (Refinement preserves consistent signatures), together with the observation that rule (6) will only ever perform a type correct assignment of a meta-variable (a signature refinement). □

This lemma suffices to establish that Norell's Lemma 3.5.14 (Constraint solving is sound) stays valid in the context of our new kind of constraints, as well as the main result, Theorem 3.5.18 (Soundness of type checking).

Like Norell for normal implicit arguments, we provide formal rules for the insertion of instance arguments and the insertion of instance lambda's, but do not prove any formal results about them.

Some of the rules above may give the impression that this resolution algorithm is sensitive to the order in which type-checking is interleaved with constraint solving. However, this sensitivity actually only exists for error reporting. Remember that during type-checking, constraints will only be added and solved (after a correct meta-variable assignment), but they cannot otherwise be removed. As a consequence of this, the candidates set for a given instance argument meta-variable α, defined by rule (7) above, form a descending series during type-checking: later sets are subsets of previous ones. Furthermore, if a value in scope can be assigned to α such that the entire Agda expression succesfully type checks, then this value will be contained in all of these candidate sets. All non-valid candidates will eventually be removed. Therefore, if no other valid candidates are available, the valid value will inevitably be chosen.

For erroneous programs, the order of constraint solving may determine the kind of error message that is generated. Depending on whether a constraint C is registered after a certain instance argument is already resolved, or before, an error will be reported for the FindInScope constraint or the constraint C. This influence of type-checking on error reporting also exists for standard Hindley-Milner type inferencing [7], so we consider it acceptable.

One extension of the current resolution scheme that we have considered in detail is based on a prioritisation of candidates, e.g. by giving precedence to values defined closer to the call site. However, contrary to our current resolution algorithm, such a prioritisation does make the result of instance resolution depend on the order of constraint resolution. Suppose there is a value in the highest priority set which is valid except for a constraint produced late during type checking and suppose this is the only candidate at the highest priority, but a lower priority candidate is also valid, and does not invalidate the late constraint. Since we don't know upfront which constraints will be produced during the rest of type-checking, we have to decide at some point which value to use. If the late constraint has then not yet been produced, the highest priority candidate will be selected and a type error will be reported when the late constraint is finally encountered. However, if the resolution occurs after the production of the late constraint, the valid low-priority candidate is chosen instead of the invalid high-priority one, and all goes well.

We currently do not see a solution for this problem, so we keep the introduction of a prioritised resolution algorithm as future work. Our experiments (see section 3 and 5) show that the current non-prioritised resolution scheme suffices for real use.

Functional Modelling of Musical Harmony

An experience report

José Pedro Magalhães W. Bas de Haas

Department of Information and Computing Sciences, Utrecht University, P.O. Box 80.089, 3508 TB Utrecht, The Netherlands

{jpm,bash}@cs.uu.nl

Abstract

Music theory has been essential in composing and performing music for centuries. Within Western tonal music, from the early Baroque on to modern-day jazz and pop music, the function of chords within a chord sequence can be explained by harmony theory. Although Western tonal harmony theory is a thoroughly studied area, formalising this theory is a hard problem.

We present a formalisation of the rules of tonal harmony as a Haskell (generalized) algebraic datatype. Given a sequence of chord labels, the harmonic function of a chord in its tonal context is automatically derived. For this, we use several advanced functional programming techniques, such as type-level computations, datatype-generic programming, and error-correcting parsers. As a detailed example, we show how our model can be used to improve content-based retrieval of jazz songs.

We explain why Haskell is the perfect match for these tasks, and compare our implementation to an earlier solution in Java. We also point out shortcomings of the language and libraries that limit our work, and discuss future developments which may ameliorate our solution.

Categories and Subject Descriptors D.1.1 [*Programming Techniques*]: Functional Programming; H.5.5 [*Information Interfaces and Presentation*]: Sound and Music Computing—Modelling

General Terms Experimentation, Languages

1. Introduction

> [Tonality is] the art of combining tones in such successions and such harmonies or successions of harmonies, that the relation of all events to a fundamental tone is made possible.
>
> Arnold Schoenberg, in *Problems of Harmony*

The deep connection between mathematics and music has been known at least since the times of Plato (Mountford 1923). In the realm of tonal harmony in particular, when studying the relationships between sequential chords, we notice order and regularity; some combinations sound pleasing while others sound peculiar. These observations led music theorists to develop ways to analyse the function of a chord in its tonal context (e.g. Riemann 1893). Among the first to formalize these theories were Lerdahl and Jackendoff (1983), who gave an encompasing account on how experienced listeners hierarchically organise tonal music. More formally, Steedman (1984) proposes a generative grammar for twelve-bar blues chord progressions, and Rohrmeier (2007, 2011) describes the core of tonal harmony as a formal grammar. This grammar was implemented by De Haas et al. (2009) and used for modelling harmonic similarity. Models of tonal harmony are useful because they explain the role or function that a musical chord has within a piece of music. For instance, the same musical chord often has different functions depending on the context in which it occurs.

We present HARMTRACE (Harmony Analysis and Retrieval of Music with Type-level Representations of Abstract Chords Entities), an adaptation and extension of the Java approach of De Haas et al. to a functional setting. Exploring the connection between a context-free grammar and an algebraic datatype, we represent different musical harmonies as values of a datatype. Unlike in previous work, we encode all the musical restrictions in the type itself; strong static typing guarantees that well-typed values represent harmonical sequences. Furthermore, a strongly-typed model gives us higher expressiveness and results in simpler code: through techniques such as datatype-generic programming and type-level computation, most of the code is automatically derived from the types. In a way, *the types are the code*: most of the code (that would otherwise have to be written manually) follows directly from the types.

A formal model of musical harmony can be used to improve many other typical music processing tasks. Content-based Music Information Retrieval (MIR, Downie 2003), for instance, is a rapidly expanding area within multimedia research which aims at keeping large repositories of digital music maintainable and accessible. Within MIR the notion of *similarity* is crucial: songs that are similar in one or more features to a given relevant song are likely to be relevant as well. The majority of approaches to notation-based music retrieval focus on melodic similarity. Using our harmony model, we present a method that allows the retrieval of music based on harmonic similarity. We compare harmonic analyses in a tree form (which explains the functions of chords within a sequence) using a generic edit-distance function, and show that this comparison predicts harmonic similarity better than an edit-distance between the original textual sequences of chords. Chord labels which do not "fit" in our model are automatically corrected at the parsing stage, allowing comparison to proceed.

Contribution In this paper we present a new functional model of Western tonal harmony and explain why Haskell is particularly well-suited for modelling harmony. We show how our model can be used to perform automatic harmony analysis of sequences of textual chord labels, and that such an analysis improves the task of retrieving harmonically similar pieces. Along the way, we explain how several features of Haskell, such as type-level computations,

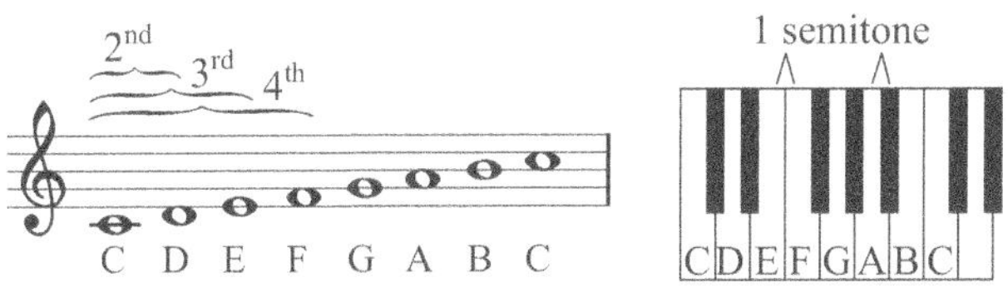

Figure 1. On the left: the C major scale with the names of the notes at the bottom and three example intervals above the notes. On the right: a schematic piano keyboard containing note names and highlighting the semitone interval.

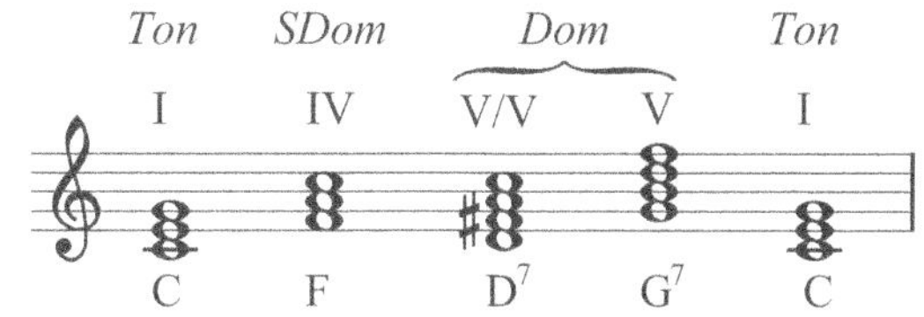

Figure 2. An often occurring chord sequence. The chord labels are printed below the score, and the scale degrees and functional analysis above the score.

error-correcting parsers, and generic programming, are essential to our approach. All the code of HARMTRACE is available on Hackage (package `HarmTrace-0.4`).

The rest of this report is structured as follows: we first introduce basic concepts of harmony in Section 2, and then explain how we encode them in Haskell in Section 3. In Section 4 we show applications of our model, which we evaluate in Section 5. We conclude in Section 6, discussing the limitations of our system and pointing out directions for future development.

2. Harmony

The French-American composer Edgard Varèse once defined music as "organised sound". In this section we present a very brief introduction of how tonal harmony organises sound in Western music; for a thorough approach, we refer the reader to Piston and DeVoto (1991).

We start with the most basic element in music: a *tone*. A tone is a sound with a fixed frequency or *pitch* which can be described in musical notation with a *note*. All notes have a name, e.g. C, D, E, etc., and represent tones of a specific pitch (Figure 1 on the left). The distance between two notes is called an *interval* and is measured in *semitones*, which is the smallest interval in Western tonal music. A semitone is also the distance between a black and a white key (or two adjacent white keys) on a piano (Figure 1 on the right). *Harmony* arises when two or more tones sound at the same time. Simultaneously sounding notes form chords, which can in turn be used to form chord sequences. A *chord* is a group of tones sounding at the same time, and separated by intervals of roughly the same size. The two most important factors that characterize a chord are its structure, which determined by the intervals between the notes of the chord, and the chord *root*. The root is the note on which the chord is built. Chords can be labelled by describing their root and the relative interval structure of the tones in the chord.

Figure 2 displays a frequently occurring chord sequence, in the C major key. The *key* of a piece of music is the tonal center of the piece. It specifies the *tonic*, which is perceived as the most stable tone in that piece. Often pieces begin and end with chords rooted on the tonic of the key. Moreover, the key specifies the *scale*, which is the set of pitches that occur most frequently in the piece and that sound reasonably well together. For instance, the key of C major only contains the white keys of a piano keyboard.

The same chord sounds differently in pieces of different keys. On the other hand, a chord sequence that is transposed to a different key, by moving all notes up or down by a fixed interval, sounds very similar to the original sequence. *Scale degrees* are used to abstract from key and absolute pitch. A scale degree represents the relative interval between a tone and the tonic of the piece. They are typically denoted with Roman numerals, as seen in Figure 2.

In music, building up and releasing tension is crucial. In the development of harmonic tension, three functional roles can generally be discerned: tonic, dominant, and subdominant. The dominant induces maximal tension, the subdominant prepares a dominant by building up tension, and the tonic releases tension. Hence, every scale degree can be categorized by having a dominant, subdominant, or tonic role. Similarly to the preparation of a tonic by a dominant, or a dominant by a subdominant, any scale degree can be recursively preceded by the scale degree seven semitones (or a fifth) up, e.g. the D^7 preceding G^7 in Figure 2. This allow the creation of chains of scale degrees, so-called *secondary dominants*.

We have presented an extremely condensed view on harmony theory. Nevertheless, it is clear that within a sequence not every chord is equally important. Some chords can easily be removed leaving the global structure of the piece intact, whereas other chords cannot be removed without altering the way the piece is perceived. For instance, the D^7 in Figure 2 can be removed leaving the general harmony structure intact, while removing the G^7 or the C at the end would change the harmony structure. This suggests that the rules of tonal harmony can be formalized hierarchically, analogically to linguistics. This is what we do in the next section, building on ideas of Rohrmeier (2007, 2011) and the previous formalisation as a context-free grammar by De Haas et al. (2009). However, it is important to stress that formal modelling of tonal harmony is a difficult task, since the rules of harmony are highly ambiguous and often formulated imprecisely.

3. Encoding harmony as a datatype

We now discuss how we formalize general harmony theory as a datatype. Throughout the rest of the paper we elide most of the musical details and concentrate on a small but representative subset of the rules. The general idea is that we convert an input sequence of chord labels, such as `"C:maj F:maj D:7 G:7 C:maj"` (also shown in Figure 2), into a value of a Haskell datatype which captures the function of chords within the sequence. Since we want to abstract from specific keys, we first translate every chord label into a scale degree. For this to be possible, we assume we know the key of every input song. For instance, our previous example is in C major, so it translates to `"I:maj IV:maj II:7 V:7 I:maj"`.

3.1 Naive approach

Using standard algebraic datatypes, we can encode alternatives as constructors, sequences as arguments to a constructor, and repetitions as lists. A first (and very simplified) approach could be the following:

```
data Piece  = Piece [Phrase]
data Phrase = PT Ton | PD Dom
data Ton    = T_IMaj Degree
data Dom    = D_VMaj Degree | D_SD,D SDom Dom
data SDom   = S_IVMaj Degree
```

We see a piece as a list of phrases. A phrase is either a tonic or a dominant. A tonic is simply the first scale degree, while a dominant might branch into a subdominant and a dominant, or simply be the fifth degree.

The leaves of our tree are the input labelled scale degrees, which consist of a root degree (an integer between 1 and 7) together with a chord class:

$$\textbf{data}\ \mathsf{Degree} = \mathit{Deg}\ \mathsf{Int}\ \mathsf{Class}$$

$$\textbf{data}\ \mathsf{Class}\ \ = \mathit{Maj} \mid \mathit{Min} \mid \mathit{Dom}^7 \mid \ldots$$

The chord class is used to group chords into a small number of categories based on their internal interval structure. All major chords, which tend to be perceived as sounding joyfully, are grouped under *Maj*. Similarly, *Min* groups all minor chords, which are generally perceived as sounding darker than major chords, and Dom^7 groups chords that have an interval structure that induces tension.

We can now encode harmonic sequences as values of type Piece:

$$\begin{aligned}
&\mathit{goodPiece}, \mathit{badPiece} :: \mathsf{Piece}\\
&\mathit{goodPiece} = \mathit{Piece}\ [\mathit{PT}\ (T_{IMaj}\ (\mathit{Deg}\ 1\ \mathit{Maj}))]\\
&\mathit{badPiece}\ \ = \mathit{Piece}\ [\mathit{PT}\ (T_{IMaj}\ (\mathit{Deg}\ 2\ \mathit{Maj}))]
\end{aligned}$$

The problem with this representation is evident: non-sensical sequences such as *badPiece* are allowed by the type-checker. We know that a Tonic can never be the second scale degree: it must be the first degree. However, since we do not constrain the Degree argument in T_{IMaj}, we have to make sure at the value-level that we only accept *Deg* 1 *Maj* as an argument. To guarantee that the model never deals with invalid sequences we would need a separate proof of code correctness.

3.2 More type information

Fortunately, we can make our model "more typed" simply by using phantom types to encode degrees and chord classes at the type level:

$$\begin{aligned}
&\textbf{data}\ \mathsf{Ton}\ \ \ \ = T_{IMaj}\ (\mathsf{Degree}\ \mathsf{I}\ \ \ \mathsf{Maj})\\
&\textbf{data}\ \mathsf{Dom}\ \ \ = D_{VMaj}\ (\mathsf{Degree}\ \mathsf{V}\ \ \mathsf{Maj}) \mid D_{SD,D}\ \mathsf{SDom}\ \mathsf{Dom}\\
&\textbf{data}\ \mathsf{SDom} = S_{IVMaj}\ (\mathsf{Degree}\ \mathsf{IV}\ \mathsf{Maj})
\end{aligned}$$

$$\textbf{data}\ \mathsf{Degree}\ \delta\ \gamma = \mathit{Deg}\ \mathsf{Int}\ \mathsf{Class}$$

Now we detail precisely the root and class of the scale degree expected by each of the constructors. We need type-level scale degrees and classes to use as arguments to the new Degree type:

$$\textbf{data}\ \mathsf{I}; \textbf{data}\ \mathsf{II}; \textbf{data}\ \mathsf{III}; \textbf{data}\ \mathsf{IV}; \textbf{data}\ \mathsf{V}; \textbf{data}\ \mathsf{VI}; \textbf{data}\ \mathsf{VII};$$

$$\textbf{data}\ \mathsf{Maj}; \textbf{data}\ \mathsf{Dom}^7; \ldots$$

It only remains to guarantee that Degrees are built correctly. An easy way to achieve this is to have a type class mediating type-to-value conversions, and a function to build degrees:

$$\begin{aligned}
&\textbf{class}\ \ \ \ \ \ \ \mathsf{ToRoot}\ \delta\ \textbf{where}\ \mathit{toRoot} :: \delta \to \mathsf{Int}\\
&\textbf{instance}\ \mathsf{ToRoot}\ \mathsf{I}\ \ \textbf{where}\ \mathit{toRoot}\ _ = 1\\
&\ldots\\
&\textbf{class}\ \ \ \ \ \ \ \mathsf{ToClass}\ \gamma\ \ \ \ \textbf{where}\ \mathit{toClass} :: \gamma \to \mathsf{Class}\\
&\textbf{instance}\ \mathsf{ToClass}\ \mathsf{Maj}\ \textbf{where}\ \mathit{toClass}\ _ = \mathit{Maj}\\
&\ldots\\
&\mathit{deg} :: (\mathsf{ToRoot}\ \delta, \mathsf{ToClass}\ \gamma) \Rightarrow \delta \to \gamma \to \mathsf{Degree}\ \delta\ \gamma\\
&\mathit{deg}\ r\ c = \mathit{Deg}\ (\mathit{toRoot}\ r)\ (\mathit{toClass}\ c)
\end{aligned}$$

If we also make sure that the constructor *Deg* is not exported, we can be certain that our value-level Degrees correctly reflect their type. Sequences like *badPiece* above are no longer possible, since the term $T_{IMaj}\ (\mathit{deg}\ (\bot :: \mathsf{II})\ (\bot :: \mathsf{Maj}))$ is not well-typed.

3.3 Secondary dominants

So far we have seen how to encode simple harmonic rules and guaranteed that well-typed pieces make "sense". However, we also need to encode harmonic rules that account for secondary dominants. According to harmony theory, every scale degree can be preceded by the scale degree of the dominant class a fifth interval (seven semitones) up. To encode this notion we need to compute transpositions on scale degrees. Since we encode the degree at the type-level this means we need type-level computations. For this we use GADTs (Peyton Jones et al. 2006) and type families (Schrijvers et al. 2008). GADTs allow us to conveniently restrict the chord root and class for certain constructors, while type families perform the necessary transpositions for relative degrees. To support chains of secondary dominants we change the Degree type as follows:

$$\begin{aligned}
&\textbf{data}\ \mathsf{Degree_n}\ \delta\ \gamma\ \eta\ \textbf{where}\\
&\quad \mathit{Base}_{Deg} :: \mathsf{Degree_{Final}}\ \delta\ \gamma \to \mathsf{Degree_n}\ \delta\ \gamma\ (\mathsf{Su}\ \eta)\\
&\quad \mathit{Cons}_V\ \ \ :: \mathsf{Degree_n}\ (\mathsf{V}/\ \delta)\ \mathsf{Dom}^7\ \eta \to \mathsf{Degree_{Final}}\ \delta\ \gamma\\
&\qquad\qquad \to \mathsf{Degree_n}\ \delta\ \gamma\ (\mathsf{Su}\ \eta)\\
&\textbf{data}\ \mathsf{Degree_{Final}}\ \delta\ \gamma = \mathit{Deg}\ \mathsf{Int}\ \mathsf{Class}
\end{aligned}$$

We now have two constructors for $\mathsf{Degree_n}$: Base_{Deg} is the base case, which stores a Root and a Class as before. In Cons_V we encode the relative dominants. Its type says we can produce a $\mathsf{Degree_n}$ for any root δ and class γ by having a $\mathsf{Degree_{Final}}$ for that root and class preceded by a $\mathsf{Degree_n}$ of root $\mathsf{V}/\ \delta$ of the dominant class. The type family $\mathsf{V}/$ transposes its argument degree a fifth up:

$$\begin{aligned}
&\textbf{type family}\ \ \ \mathsf{V}/\ \delta\\
&\textbf{type instance}\ \mathsf{V}/\ \mathsf{I}\ \ = \mathsf{V}\\
&\textbf{type instance}\ \mathsf{V}/\ \mathsf{V} = \mathsf{II}\\
&\ldots
\end{aligned}$$

To avoid infinite recursion in the parser (Section 4.1) we use a type-level natural number in $\mathsf{Degree_n}$. This parameter also serves to control the number of allowed secondary dominants:

$$\begin{aligned}
&\textbf{data}\ \mathsf{Su}\ \eta\\
&\textbf{data}\ \mathsf{Ze}
\end{aligned}$$

$$\textbf{type}\ \mathsf{Degree}\ \delta\ \gamma = \mathsf{Degree_n}\ \delta\ \gamma\ (\mathsf{Su}\ (\mathsf{Su}\ (\mathsf{Su}\ (\mathsf{Su}\ \mathsf{Ze}))))$$

Typically we use values between 4 and 7 for η. Its value greatly affects compilation time; see the discussion in Section 6.1.

3.4 Examples

We have shown a very simplified description of our model of musical harmony as a Haskell datatype. In reality, our model is larger and more detailed, albeit still far simpler than the hundreds of pages of Piston and DeVoto (1991), for instance. To provide an idea of the kind of structure our datatype models, we show the chord sequence of Figure 2 as a pretty-printed tree in Figure 3. Every chord is classified as being part of a dominant, subdominant, or tonic structure, and the `D:7` is classified as a secondary dominant of the `G:7` (V/V).

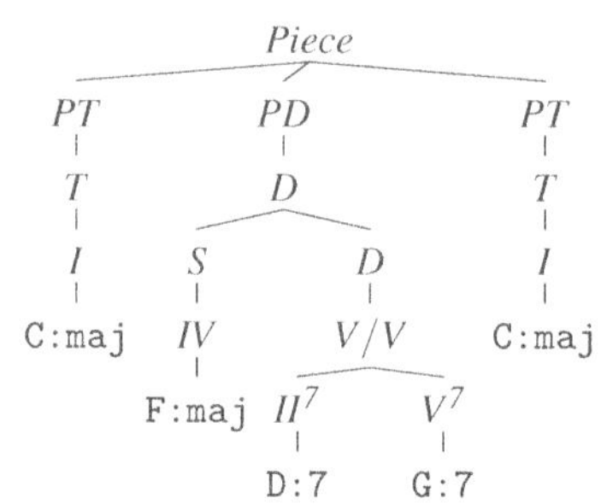

Figure 3. The parse tree for the chord sequence shown in Figure 2. *PT* and *PD* represent phrase nodes. *T*, *D*, and *S* denote tonic, dominant, and subdominant, respectively, and the secondary dominant is denoted by V/V.

Another example piece is displayed in Figure 4. Within this short piece, the `IV:maj` and `G:7` are preceded by their secondary dominants. Because the model expects the first `C:7` to resolve to an `F:maj`, the parser inserts the expected scale degree *IV* (see Section 4.1.2). Note that although `C:7` sounds similar to `C:maj`, their harmonic functions in Figure 4 are distinct.

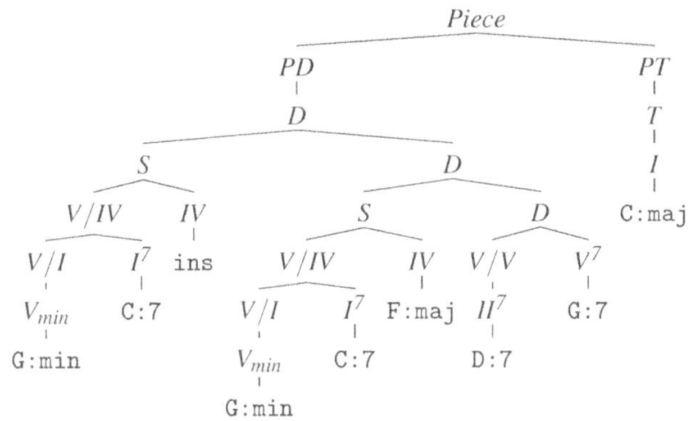

Figure 4. The pretty-printed parse tree generated for the chord sequence `"G:min C:7 G:min C:7 F:maj D:7 G:7 C:maj"`.

4. From chord labels to harmonic structure

We have seen how to put Haskell's advanced type system features to good use in the definition of a model of tonal harmony. In this section we further exploit the advantages of a well-typed model while defining a generic parser from labelled scale degrees (e.g. `"I:maj IV:maj II:7 V:7 I:maj"`) to our datatype. We also show other operations on the model, like pretty-printing and diffing.

4.1 Parsing

From the high-level musical structure (e.g. the Ton and Dom datatypes of Section 3.2) we can easily build a parser in applicative style mimicking the structure of the types:

```
data Parser α  -- abstract
class Parse α where parse :: Parser α
instance Parse Ton where
  parse = T_IMaj <$> parse
instance Parse Dom where
  parse = D_VMaj <$> parse
      <|> D_SD,D <$> parse <*> parse
```

For the purposes of this paper we keep Parser abstract; in our implementation we use the `uu-parsinglib` package (Swierstra 2009). We prefer `uu-parsinglib` over, say, `parsec` because our grammar is highly ambiguous and we can put error correction to good use, as we explain in Section 4.1.2.

The instances of Parse for Ton and Dom are trivial because they follow directly from the structure of the datatypes. They can even be obtained by syntactic manipulation of the datatype declaration: replace | by <|>, add <$> after the constructor name, separate constructor arguments by <*> and replace each argument by *parse*. The code is tedious to write, and since we have several similar datatypes it becomes repetitive and long.

To compound the problem, the rules of harmony are naturally ambiguous, and we often change the model in search of the best solution. Even more importantly, different musical styles can have significantly different harmony rules (e.g. baroque harmony versus jazz), so our solution should support multiple models. We solve all these problems by *not* writing instances like the one above. Instead, we use *datatype-generic programming* to derive a parser automatically in a type-safe way. We use the `instant-generics` package, which implements a library similar to that initially described by Chakravarty et al. (2009). Due to length considerations we cannot explain how generic programming works in this paper, but our generic parser is entirely trivial. The order of the constructors and their arguments determines the order of the alternatives and sequences; in particular, we avoid left-recursion in our datatypes, since we do not implement a grammar analysis like Devriese and Piessens (2011).

4.1.1 Adhoc parsers

The only truly non-generic parser is that for $\mathsf{Degree}_{\mathsf{Final}}$, which is also the only parser that consumes any input. It uses the type classes ToRoot and ToClass as described in Section 3.2.

Unfortunately, we are also forced to write the parser instances for GADTs such as $\mathsf{Degree}_{\mathsf{n}}$, since `instant-generics` does not support GADTs. Although the code remains entirely trivial, the instance heads become more complicated, since they have to reflect the type equalities introduced by the GADT. As an example, we show the parser code for $\mathsf{Degree}_{\mathsf{n}}$:

```
instance ( Parse (Degree_Final δ γ)
         , Parse (Degree_n (V/ δ) Dom^7 η       ))
        ⇒ Parse (Degree_n δ         γ   (Su η)) where
  parse = Base_Deg <$> parse
      <|> Cons_V   <$> parse <*> parse
```

The context of the instance reflects the type of the constructors of $\mathsf{Degree}_{\mathsf{n}}$: $Base_{Deg}$ introduces the Parse ($\mathsf{Degree}_{\mathsf{Final}}\ \delta\ \gamma$) constraint, whereas $Cons_V$ requires Parse ($\mathsf{Degree}_{\mathsf{n}}$ (V/ δ) $\mathsf{Dom}^7\ \eta$)) too.

The need for type-level natural numbers becomes evident here; the instance above is "undecidable" for GHC, meaning that the rules for instance contexts become relaxed. Normally there are constraints on what can be written in the context to guarantee termination of type-checking. Undecidable instances lift these restrictions, with the side-effect that type-checking becomes undecidable in general. However, we are certain that type-checking will always terminate since we recursively decrease the type-level natural number η. This means we also need a "base case instance" where we use the *empty* parser which always fails; this is acceptable because it is never used.

```
instance Parse (Degree_n δ γ Ze) where parse = empty
```

Note how useful the type class resolution mechanism becomes: it recursively builds a parser for all possible alternatives, driven by the type argument η. This also means potentially long type-checking times; fortunately our current implementation remains compilable under a minute. We discuss parser performance issues in more detail in Section 6.2.

4.1.2 Error correction

We cannot hope to be able to model all valid harmonic relations in our datatype. Furthermore, songs often contain mistakes or mistyped chords, or sequences of dubious harmonic validity. However, these things are often a localized problem, and most of the song still makes sense. In our solution we rely on error correction while parsing: chords that do not fit the structure are automatically deleted or preceded by inserted chords, according to heuristics computed from the grammar structure. We keep track of the number of corrections, since the ratio of corrections to number of input chords provides a measure of meaningfulness of the parse tree. For most songs, parsing proceeds with none or very few corrections. Songs with a very high error ratio denote bad input or wrong key assignment, which results in meaningless scale degrees.

4.2 Visualising harmonic relations

In a way similar to the generic parser of Section 4.1, we also have a generic pretty-printer, which produces output suitable for generation of graphical representations such as that of Figure 4. Similar issues with adhoc instances for GADTs arise, which we solve in the exact same way as described in Section 4.1.1.

4.3 Generic diff

A practical application of our tonal harmony model is estimating the harmonic similarity of two songs. An easy way to obtain a measure of similarity between two Pieces is to use a generic diff algorithm. Just like the parser and the pretty-printer, our generic diff is derived from the structure of the datatypes, and adapts automatically to any change. We have implemented it in the style of Lempsink et al. (2009) for the `instant-generics` library. This diff is based on four primitive generic functions: *children*, which returns a (heterogenously-typed) list of all children of a term, *build*, which rebuilds a term given a list of new children, *eqCon*, which computes equality of terms based only on their top-level constructor, and *typeOf*, which returns a unique representation for the type of a term. For performance reasons we use *typeOf* from the standard `Data.Typeable` library, while the other functions are easily implemented in `instant-generics`. However, the generic diff is rather slow; we discuss this problem in detail in Section 6.3.

5. Evaluation

In this section we evaluate the parsing results of our system and compare the retrieval performance of the `gdiff` similarity measure with a simple baseline `diff` on the input tokens.

5.1 Datasets

We have performed our experiment with two datasets: the dataset of De Haas et al. (2009, which we call `small`) and a larger dataset (`large`). Both datasets consist of textual chord sequences extracted from user-generated Band-in-a-Box files that were collected from the Internet. Band-in-a-Box is a software package that generates accompaniment given a chord sequence provided by the user. The `small` dataset contains a selection of pieces that "harmonically make sense", while the `large` dataset includes many songs that are harmonically atypical. This is because the files are user-generated, and contain peculiar and unfinished pieces, wrong key assignments and other errors; it can therefore be considered "real life" data. Within both datasets there are different chord sequences that describe the same piece in different ways; these can be used to do a retrieval experiment.

We summarize the statistics of each dataset in Table 1. The last column shows the average number of chord labels per song on the dataset, and the clusters are the number of songs that are similar. For instance, in the `small` dataset, 35 songs have no similar songs, 11 songs have one other similar song, and 5 songs have two other similar songs (for a total of $35 + 11 * 2 + 5 * 3 = 72$ songs). The `large` dataset contains about 11 times more songs than `small` (854 songs), and the songs are also longer on average. Note also that songs with no similar songs are akin to noise for the retrieval task (see Section 5.3).

Dataset	Clusters	Avg. labels/song
`small`	35 11 5	41.70
`large`	485 71 27 21 7 2 1 1	54.73

Table 1. Cluster size distribution and average number of chord labels per song. The `small` dataset has cluster sizes ranging from 1 to 3, and the `large` dataset has cluster sizes ranging from 1 to 8.

5.2 Parsing results

The parsing results are shown in Table 2. For each dataset, we show the average time taken to parse a song and the average error ratio. The error ratio is a measure of how many corrections the parser performed. We define it as a ratio between the number of correction steps and the number of chord labels, but we remove sequences of duplicate chord labels from the input first. A ratio of 0.2, for instance, means that 20% of the significant labels of the sequence have been altered. Note that a single chord that doesn't match the specification might cause multiple corrections, e.g. one deletion followed by one insertion. Lower ratios indicate that the song fits our harmony model better.

Dataset	Error ratio	Time taken (ms)
`small`	0.067	23.833
`large`	0.200	381.837

Table 2. Error ratio and parsing runtime averaged over all songs

On the `small` dataset, which consists of "harmonically correct" chord sequences, our model performs very well. The songs are parsed quickly and with average error ratio below 0.07. The `large` dataset is more problematic. The parsing time increases considerably, mostly because the ambiguity of our model can make the error-correction process rather expensive. The error ratio also increases considerably, but in no way does the parser crash or refuse to produce a valid output. A higher error ratio is also expected, since this dataset has many noisy or meaningless songs.

5.3 Matching results

To test `gdiff` as a similarity measure for musical harmony, we have performed a retrieval experiment. In this experiment, the task is to retrieve the similar (but not identical) songs based on the edit distance of the `gdiff` algorithm. The distance between all pairs of songs is calculated, and for every song a ranking is constructed by sorting all other songs on the basis of their distance. To place the performance of the `gdiff` algorithm and the difficulty of the task in perspective, we compare with a baseline algorithm. This method uses no harmony information whatsoever; we simply tokenize the input string into a list of Degrees and perform a standard `diff` on that list (using the `diff` package). We use this method to provide a baseline case; the generic `diff`, having all the harmony information available, has to perform better than this. We call this simple algorithm `baseline`, while the generic `diff` of Section 4.3 is named `gdiff`.

For our datasets we know all the clusters of similar songs. We can therefore analyse the rankings by calculating the Mean Average Precision (MAP). The MAP is a single-figure measure between 0 and 1 quantifying the precision of the retrieved results at all recall levels (Manning et al. 2008, Chap. 8, p. 160); a higher MAP value indicates a better ranking. For the `small` dataset, `gdiff` has a MAP of 0.853, while `baseline` scores 0.475. In the `large` dataset the difference is smaller, but `gdiff` still outperforms `baseline` with a score of 0.510 against 0.395, respectively.

We tested whether the difference in MAP is significant by performing a Wilcoxon Signed-rank test[1]. We chose the Wilcoxon Signed-rank test because the underlying distribution of the average precision over the queries is unknown, and this Signed-ranks test does not require the distribution to be normally distributed. The differences between `baseline` and `gdiff` were statistically significant, with $W = 1058.5, p < 0.0001$ on the `small` dataset, and also on the `large` dataset, with $W = 80352, p < 0.0001$.

[1] All statistical tests were performed with the R language.

5.4 Comparison with previous work

There are considerable differences between our HARMTRACE system and the context-free grammar approach of De Haas et al. (2009, hereafter referred to as ISMIR09).

5.4.1 Error-correcting parsers

One of the drawbacks of ISMIR09 is that a sequence of chords that does not match the context-free specification precisely will be rejected. For instance, appending one nonsensical chord to an otherwise grammatically correct sequence of symbols will still force the parser to reject the complete sequence, not returning any partial information about what it has parsed. HARMTRACE solves this rejection problem by using error correcting parsers (Swierstra 2009). This allows us to formalize the rules of tonal harmony that we are certain of, and leave the borderline cases to the parser.

5.4.2 Ambiguity control

Music, and harmony in particular, is intrinsically ambiguous. Hence, certain chords can have multiple meanings within a tonal context. This is reflected in both ISMIR09 and HARMTRACE. A major drawback of ISMIR09 is that it is very limited in ways of controlling the ambiguity of the grammar. ISMIR09 uses weighting to order the grammar rules by adding low weights to rules that explain rare phenomena. However, controlling conditional execution would require some form of high-level grammar generation system, since all rules are replicated for each scale degree and chord class. On the other hand, HARMTRACE supports more flexible conditional execution, through the use of GADTs and type families. An example is the restriction of secondary dominants to chords of the Dom^7 class (Section 3.3).

5.4.3 Parsing performance

There are considerable differences in the parsing performance of HARMTRACE compared to ISMIR09 on both datasets. HARMTRACE takes 1.65s to parse the `small` dataset, while ISMIR09 takes more than 9m. When we compare parsing performance on the `large` dataset the differences become even more prominent: ISMIR09 rejects 89.7% of the 854 pieces and 3.9% of the dataset had to be excluded because the parsing process would not terminate (due to unconstrained ambiguities). The remaining pieces parse in 84m13s, while HARMTRACE parses the entire dataset in 5m14s. All measurements were done on the same Intel Core 2 duo E6600, 2.4 GHz machine using GHC 7.0.2 and Java SE 1.6.0_17.

5.4.4 Retrieval effectiveness

Both HARMTRACE as well as ISMIR09 have been evaluated on the `small` dataset. When we compare the retrieval effectiveness of the `gdiff` approach with the best performing variant of ISMIR09 (MAP of 0.859), we conclude that there is no statistically significant difference ($W = 685, p = 1.00$, using the same test procedure as in Section 5.3). Because ISMIR09 rejects 89.7 percent of the pieces, no sensible comparison between the two approaches on the `large` data set can be performed.

5.4.5 Grammar simplicity

In ISMIR09 all context-free rules were written by hand, which is not only a tedious and error-prone enterprise, but can also result in very large grammars. By using Haskell's GADTs to represent the rules of tonal harmony, we gain more expressive power, and the grammar becomes shorter and easier to maintain. For instance, GADTs allow us to write rules that hold for every Maj chord. In ISMIR09 this is expressed by having one rule for major `I`, `II`, `III`, etc.

5.4.6 Code repetition

Our Haskell system is more concise than the Java implementation of ISMIR09. An analysis of the number of significant source lines of code[2] reveals that ISMIR09 has 5545 lines, while HARMTRACE has 1311, less than one quarter.

6. Discussion and conclusion

We have shown how Haskell can be used to implement a model of musical harmony. Our solution outperforms a previous Java approach in terms of speed, functionality, and elegance. However, the current implementation has a number of limitations, which we now describe in detail.

6.1 Type-checker performance

As mentioned in Section 4.1.1, it is easy to make the type-checker take very long to compile our code. We managed to keep the type-checking time acceptably low, but this is only because we are "helping" it. We minimized the number of type families used (four in total, all similar to V/), and we (automatically) place each instance declaration in a separate module, since this speeds up compilation considerably. Furthermore, we represent each scale degree as an independent type; type-level computations, such as transposition, are then indexed over each type. A more concise way of representing scale degrees would be to use type-level naturals. Transposition is then simply summing modulo the total number of scale degrees. Unfortunately this makes the compilation time unacceptably high. We hope that native type-level naturals are added to GHC soon[3] so that we can simplify our type-level computations without a performance penalty.

6.2 Parser performance

The higher average parsing time per song on the `large` dataset shown in Table 2 is caused mostly by a few songs taking very long. In this dataset, only about 6% of the songs take longer than one second to parse. The three slowest songs take 41s, 24s, and 15s to parse. They are long songs, and either contain chord sequences which our model does not account for or are harmonically atypical. In these pathological cases the parser combinators take very long to compute the possible corrections. This is somewhat understandable, since our grammar is highly ambiguous and there are multiple non-trivial possible corrections. However, such long parsing times are undesirable; perhaps the number of steps to lookahead in the parser could be dynamically adjusted based on the number of possible alternatives. This would hopefully lead to shorter parsing times, albeit at the cost of potentially worse corrections.

6.3 Matching performance

The generic diff is a powerful tool that solves the matching problem almost "for free" (Section 5.3). However, to use it we need new generic functions to be derived for every datatype. This means longer compilation times, but also more adhoc instances, since there is no suitable generic programming library supporting GADTs. These instances amount to over 200 lines of repetitive and error-prone code. Worse, this code runs very slowly; our implementation uses type-safe runtime casts, which prevents fusion of the generic representations (Magalhães et al. 2010). This prevents us from using the generic diff on datasets with thousands of songs.

Besides addressing the limitations pointed out above, we also plan to add new functionality to our system.

[2] Using `http://cloc.sourceforge.net/`.

[3] `http://hackage.haskell.org/trac/ghc/ticket/4385`

6.4 Mode and key

In Section 3 we only discussed the rules for pieces in a major key. However, many songs are written in a minor key; this affects the expected scale degrees at the leaves, invalidates some alternatives, and creates others. Nevertheless, a large number of rules hold for both pieces in a major and a minor key. Currently we handle this using a similar model for pieces in a minor key:

$$\textbf{data}\ \mathsf{Piece} = \mathit{Piece}_{Maj}\ [\mathsf{Phrase}_{\mathsf{Maj}}] \mid \mathit{Piece}_{Min}\ [\mathsf{Phrase}_{\mathsf{Min}}]$$

However, this leads to unnecessary code duplication, since most of the harmony rules are independent of mode. A better alternative would be to index pieces by their mode:

$$\textbf{data}\ \mathsf{Maj}_{\mathsf{Mode}}; \textbf{data}\ \mathsf{Min}_{\mathsf{Mode}};$$
$$\textbf{data}\ \mathsf{Piece}\ \mu = \mathit{Piece}\ [\mathsf{Phrase}\ \mu]$$

The type variable μ would then be indexed with either $\mathsf{Maj}_{\mathsf{Mode}}$ or $\mathsf{Min}_{\mathsf{Mode}}$, similarly to δ for degrees and γ for chord classes. We think this would be an elegant way of expressing mode in the model.

Additionally, we currently restrict ourselves to songs in a single key, but often songs change the key throughout their development. This means that scale degree I no longer maps to chord C, but to F, for instance. Indexing the model over the key, and introducing rules for modulation which would change this key, would be a good way of encoding key changes.

Such changes would make the entire model indexed over one or more type variables. We plan to see if the extensions to `instant-generics` reported by Magalhães and Jeuring (2011) allow us to continue using generic programming for our model.

6.5 Other applications

We show how to use our model for improving music retrieval, but we believe other tasks can be improved similarly. For instance, algorithms for computing chord labels from audio or images (scores) often recognize a set of possible chords at each step, with different probabilities. Our model could be used to check which chords are harmonically valid at each step, therefore introducing harmony knowledge into the algorithm. Another interesting development would be to implement a (generic) enumerator over our datatypes; this would correspond to a generator of harmonically valid sequences of chords.

6.6 Dependently-typed implementation

It would be interesting to see if we could easily port our system to a dependently-typed setting. We plan to use Agda (Norell 2009), due to its proximity to Haskell, or Idris (Brady 2011), since it has efficient type-level naturals. We expect that deriving the parser automatically will not be as easy, since generic programming support in dependently-typed languages is more primitive than in Haskell. However, we believe the model can benefit from a more expressive type language. Having no barriers between values and types would reduce code duplication and simplify the model. At the same time, we expect that the increased expressiveness can be used to model more complex harmonic relations.

Overall, we are convinced that strong static typing and generic programming are essential tools in modelling musical harmony. We hope that our approach paves the way for future functional approaches to musical modelling and processing.

Acknowledgments

This work has been partially funded by the Portuguese Foundation for Science and Technology (FCT) via the SFRH/BD/35999/2007 grant, and by the Dutch ICES/KIS III Bsik project MultimediaN. We thank Jurriaan Hage, Johan Jeuring, Andres Löh, Frans Wiering, and the anonymous reviewers for their helpful comments, and Doaitse Swierstra for his exhaustive technical support in using his parser combinators.

References

E. Brady. Idris—systems programming meets full dependent yypes. In *PLPV'11*, pages 43–54, 2011.

M. M. T. Chakravarty, G. C. Ditu, and R. Leshchinskiy. Instant generics: Fast and easy, 2009. Draft version.

D. Devriese and F. Piessens. Explicitly recursive grammar combinators—a better model for shallow parser DSLs. In *PADL'11*, pages 84–98. Springer, 2011.

J. Stephen Downie. Music information retrieval. *Annual Review of Information Science and Technology*, 37(1):295–340, 2003.

W. B. de Haas, M. Rohrmeier, R. C. Veltkamp, and F. Wiering. Modeling harmonic similarity using a generative grammar of tonal harmony. In *Proceedings of the Tenth International Conference on Music Information Retrieval (ISMIR'09)*, pages 549–554, 2009.

E. Lempsink, S. Leather, and A. Löh. Type-safe diff for families of datatypes. In *WGP'09*, pages 61–72. ACM, 2009.

F. Lerdahl and R. Jackendoff. *A Generative Theory of Tonal Music*. The MIT Press, 1983. ISBN 0-262-62107-X.

J. P. Magalhães and J. Jeuring. Generic programming for indexed datatypes. Technical Report UU-CS-2011-021, Department of Information and Computing Sciences, Utrecht University, 2011.

J. P. Magalhães, S. Holdermans, J. Jeuring, and A. Löh. Optimizing generics is easy! In *PEPM'10*, pages 33–42. ACM, 2010.

C. D. Manning, P. Raghavan, and H. Schütze. *Introduction to Information Retrieval*. Cambridge University Press, 2008.

J. F. Mountford. The musical scales of Plato's Republic. *The Classical Quarterly*, 17(3/4):125–136, 1923.

U. Norell. Dependently typed programming in agda. In *AFP'08*, volume 5832 of *LNCS*, pages 230–266. Springer, 2009.

S. Peyton Jones, D. Vytiniotis, S. Weirich, and G. Washburn. Simple unification-based type inference for GADTs. In *ICFP'06*, pages 50–61. ACM, 2006.

W. Piston and M. DeVoto. *Harmony*. Victor Gollancz, 1991.

H. Riemann. *Vereinfachte Harmonielehre; oder, die Lehre von den tonalen Funktionen der Akkorde*. Augener, 1893.

M. Rohrmeier. A generative grammar approach to diatonic harmonic structure. In *Proceedings of the 4th Sound and Music Computing Conference*, pages 97–100, 2007.

M. Rohrmeier. Towards a generative syntax of tonal harmony. *Journal of Mathematics and Music*, 5(1):35–53, 2011.

R. Schrijvers, S. Peyton Jones, M. M. T. Chakravarty, and M. Sulzmann. Type checking with open type functions. In *ICFP'08*, pages 51–62. ACM, 2008.

M. J. Steedman. A generative grammar for jazz chord sequences. *Music Perception*, 2(1):52–77, 1984.

S. Doaitse Swierstra. *Combinator Parsing: A Short Tutorial*, pages 252–300. Springer-Verlag, 2009.

How to Make Ad Hoc Proof Automation Less Ad Hoc

Georges Gonthier
Microsoft Research
gonthier@microsoft.com

Beta Ziliani
MPI-SWS
beta@mpi-sws.org

Aleksandar Nanevski
IMDEA Software Institute
aleks.nanevski@imdea.org

Derek Dreyer
MPI-SWS
dreyer@mpi-sws.org

Abstract

Most interactive theorem provers provide support for some form of user-customizable proof automation. In a number of popular systems, such as Coq and Isabelle, this automation is achieved primarily through *tactics*, which are programmed in a separate language from that of the prover's base logic. While tactics are clearly useful in practice, they can be difficult to maintain and compose because, unlike lemmas, their behavior cannot be specified within the expressive type system of the prover itself.

We propose a novel approach to proof automation in Coq that allows the user to specify the behavior of custom automated routines in terms of Coq's own type system. Our approach involves a sophisticated application of Coq's *canonical structures*, which generalize Haskell type classes and facilitate a flexible style of dependently-typed logic programming. Specifically, just as Haskell type classes are used to infer the canonical implementation of an overloaded term at a given type, canonical structures can be used to infer the canonical *proof* of an overloaded *lemma* for a given instantiation of its parameters. We present a series of design patterns for canonical structure programming that enable one to carefully and predictably coax Coq's type inference engine into triggering the execution of user-supplied algorithms during unification, and we illustrate these patterns through several realistic examples drawn from Hoare Type Theory. We assume no prior knowledge of Coq and describe the relevant aspects of Coq type inference from first principles.

Categories and Subject Descriptors D.3.3 [*Programming Languages*]: Language Constructs and Features—Data types and structures; F.3.1 [*Logics and Meanings of Programs*]: Specifying and Verifying and Reasoning about Programs—Mechanical verification; F.4.1 [*Mathematical Logic and Formal Languages*]: Mathematical Logic—Logic and constraint programming

General Terms Languages, Design, Theory, Verification

Keywords Interactive theorem proving, custom proof automation, Coq, canonical structures, type classes, tactics, Hoare Type Theory

This research has been partially supported by Spanish MICINN Project TIN2010-20639 Paran10; AMAROUT grant PCOFUND-GA-2008-229599; and Ramon y Cajal grant RYC-2010-0743.

ICFP'11, September 19–21, 2011, Tokyo, Japan.

1. Introduction

In recent years, interactive theorem proving has been successfully applied to the verification of important mathematical theorems and substantial software code bases. Some of the most significant examples are the proof of the Four Color Theorem [8] (in Coq), the verification of the optimizing compiler CompCert [17] (also in Coq), and the verification of the operating system microkernel seL4 [16] (in Isabelle). The abovementioned proof assistants employ higher-order logics and type systems in order to maximize expressiveness and generality, but also to facilitate modularity and reuse of verification effort. However, despite the expressiveness of these theorem provers, effective solutions to some verification problems can often only be achieved by going outside of the provers' base logics.

To illustrate, consider the following Coq lemma, which naturally arises when reasoning about heaps and pointer aliasing:

$$\mathsf{noalias} : \forall h{:}\mathsf{heap}.\, \forall x_1 x_2{:}\mathsf{ptr}.\, \forall v_1{:}A_1.\, \forall v_2{:}A_2.\\ \mathsf{def}\,(x_1 \mapsto v_1 \bullet x_2 \mapsto v_2 \bullet h) \to x_1 \;\texttt{!=}\; x_2$$

Here, the type heap classifies finite maps from pointers of type ptr to values, $h_1 \bullet h_2$ is the disjoint union of h_1 and h_2, and $x \mapsto v$ is a singleton heap consisting solely of the pointer x, storing the value v. The disjoint union may be undefined if h_1 and h_2 overlap, so we need a predicate def h, declaring that h is not undefined. Consequently, def $(h_1 \bullet h_2)$ holds iff h_1 and h_2 are disjoint heaps. Finally, the conclusion $x_1 \;\texttt{!=}\; x_2$ is in fact a *term* of type bool, which Coq implicitly coerces to the *proposition* $(x_1 \;\texttt{!=}\; x_2) = \mathsf{true}$. The noalias lemma states that x_1 and x_2 are not aliased, if they are known to belong to disjoint singleton heaps.

Now suppose we want to prove a goal consisting of a number of no-aliasing facts, *e.g.,*

$$(x_1 \;\texttt{!=}\; x_2) \;\&\&\; (x_2 \;\texttt{!=}\; x_3) \;\&\&\; (x_3 \;\texttt{!=}\; x_1),$$

under the following hypothesis:

$$D : \mathsf{def}\,(i_1 \bullet (x_1 \mapsto v_1 \bullet x_2 \mapsto v_2) \bullet (i_2 \bullet x_3 \mapsto v_3)).$$

Before noalias can be applied to prove, say, $x_2 \;\texttt{!=}\; x_3$, the disjoint union in D will have to be rearranged, so that the pointers x_2 and x_3 appear at the top of the union, as in:

$$D' : \mathsf{def}\,(x_2 \mapsto v_2 \bullet x_3 \mapsto v_3 \bullet i_1 \bullet i_2 \bullet x_1 \mapsto v_1)$$

Otherwise, the noalias lemma will not apply. Because $\bullet$ is commutative and associative, the rearrangement is sound, but it is tedious to perform by hand, and it is not very robust under adaptation. Indeed, if the user goes back and changes the input heap in D, a new rearrangement is necessary. Furthermore, the tedium is exacerbated by the need for different rearrangements in proving $x_1 \;\texttt{!=}\; x_2$ and $x_3 \;\texttt{!=}\; x_1$.

The most effective solution would be for the type checker to somehow automatically recognize that the heap expression from D is in fact equivalent to some form required by noalias. Unfortunately, none of the proof assistants that we are aware of provide such automatic reasoning primitively. Instead, they typically provide a separate language for writing *tactics*, which are customized procedures for solving a class of proof obligations. For example, one can write an auto_noalias tactic to solve a goal like x_2 != x_3 by automatically converting the assumption D into D' and then applying the noalias lemma. However, while tactics have been deployed successfully (and with impressive dexterity) in a variety of scenarios [6, 7], they are beset by certain fundamental limitations.

The primary drawback of tactics is that they lack the precise typing of the theorem prover's base logic (and in the case of Coq, they are essentially untyped). This can make them much more difficult to maintain than lemmas, as changes in basic definitions do not necessarily raise type errors in the code of the tactics affected by the changes. Rather, type checking is performed on the goals obtained during tactic execution, resulting in potentially obscure error messages and unpredictable proof states in the case of failure. Moreover, the behavior of a tactic typically cannot be specified, nor can it be verified against a specification.

Due to their lack of precise typing, tactics suffer a second-class status, in the sense that they may not be used as flexibly as lemmas. For example, suppose the pointer (in-)equalities we want to resolve are embedded in a larger context, *e.g.*,

$$G : \text{if } (x_2 \texttt{ == } x_3) \;\&\&\; (x_1 \texttt{ != } x_2) \text{ then } E_1 \text{ else } E_2$$

In this situation, we cannot apply the auto_noalias tactic directly to reduce (x_2 == x_3) and (x_1 != x_2) to false and true, respectively, since those (in-)equalities are not the top-level goal. Coq's rewrite primitive is designed precisely for this situation—it enables one to reduce all (in-)equalities within G that match the conclusion of a particular lemma—but it is not applicable to tactics (like auto_noalias).

Thus, with the auto_noalias tactic, we are left with essentially two options: (1) use it to prove a bespoke lemma about one specific inequality (say, x_1 != x_2), perform a rewrite using that lemma, and repeat for other (in-)equalities of interest, or (2) implement another custom tactic that crawls over the goal G searching for any and all (in-)equalities that auto_noalias might resolve. The former option sacrifices the benefits of automation, while the latter option redundantly duplicates the functionality of rewrite.

Ideally, we would prefer instead to have a way of writing auto_noalias as a *lemma* rather than a tactic. Had we such a lemma, we could give it a precisely typed specification, we could rewrite the goal G with it directly, and we could also compose it with other lemmas. For instance, we could use ordinary function composition to compose it with the standard lemma

$$\text{negbTE} : \forall b{:}\text{bool}.\, !b = \text{true} \rightarrow b = \text{false},$$

thus transforming auto_noalias into a rewrite rule for positive facts of the form (x_2 == x_3) = false. Consequently, we could apply rewrite (negbTE (auto_noalias D)) to the goal G, thereby reducing it to E_2.

The question of how to support automation, while remaining within the first-class world of lemmas, is the subject of this paper.

1.1 Contributions

We propose a novel and powerful approach to proof automation in Coq, which avoids the aforementioned problems with tactics by allowing one to program custom automated routines within the expressive dependent type system of Coq itself. In particular, we will be able to rephrase the noalias lemma so that it can automatically analyze its heap-definedness hypothesis D in order to derive whatever valid pointer inequalities are needed, without any manual intervention from the user. Our proposal is much more general, however, and we will illustrate it on a variety of different and significantly more involved examples than just noalias.

Our approach involves a sophisticated application of Coq's *canonical structures*, which have existed in Coq for quite some time [23], but with sparse documentation and (perhaps as a consequence) relatively little use. At a high level, canonical structures may be viewed as a generalization of Haskell's *type classes* [28, 13], in the sense that they provide a principled way to construct default dictionaries of values and methods—and hence support overloading and implicit program construction—as part of the type inference process.

However, unlike in Haskell, where the construction of canonical instances is keyed solely on the *type* belonging to a certain type class, instance construction in Coq may be keyed on *terms* as well. This, together with Coq's support for backtracking during type inference, enables a very flexible style of dependently-typed logic programming.[1] Furthermore, since canonical structures can embed *proofs* of interesting invariants about the instance fields being computed, one can use them to implement custom algorithms (in logic-programming style) *together with* proofs of their (partial) correctness. Thus, just as Haskell type classes are used to infer the canonical implementation of an overloaded term at a given type, canonical structures can be used to infer the canonical *proof* of an overloaded *lemma* for a given instantiation of its parameters. We feel this constitutes a beautiful application of the Curry-Howard correspondence between proofs and programs in Coq.

Intuitively, our approach works as follows. Suppose we want to write a lemma whose application may need to trigger an automated solution to some subproblem (*e.g.*, in the case of noalias, the problem of testing whether two pointers x_1 and x_2 appear in disjoint subheaps of the heap characterized by the heap-definedness hypothesis D). In this case, we define a *structure* (like a type class) to encapsulate the problem whose solution we wish to automate, and we encode the algorithm for solving that problem—along with its proof of correctness—in the canonical instances of the structure. Then, when the lemma is applied to a particular goal, unification of the goal with the conclusion of the lemma will trigger the construction of a canonical instance of our structure that solves the automation problem for that goal. For example, if auto_noalias is the overloaded version of noalias, and we try to apply (auto_noalias D) to the goal of proving x_2 != x_3, type inference will trigger construction of a canonical instance proving that the heap characterized by D contains bindings for x_2 and x_3 in two disjoint subheaps. (This is analogous to how the application of an overloaded function in Haskell triggers the construction of a canonical dictionary that solves the appropriate instantiation of its type class constraints.) Although we have described the approach here in terms of backward reasoning, one may also apply overloaded lemmas using forward reasoning, as we will see in Section 5.

Key to the success of our whole approach is the Coq type inference engine's use of *syntactic* pattern-matching in determining which canonical instances to apply when solving automation problems. Distinguishing between syntactically distinct (yet semantically equivalent) terms and types is essential if one wishes to simulate the automation power of tactics. However, it is also an aspect of our approach that Coq's type system cannot account for because it does not observe such syntactic distinctions. Fortunately, our reliance on Coq's unification algorithm for analysis of syntax is the *only* aspect of our approach that resides outside of Coq's type system, unlike tactics, which are wholly extra-linguistic.

Perhaps the greatest challenge in making our approach fly is in developing effective and reliable ways of circumventing certain

[1] It is folklore that one can simulate logic programming to some extent using Haskell's multi-parameter classes with functional dependencies [15] or with associated types [5], but Haskell's lack of support for backtracking during type inference limits what kinds of logic programming idioms are possible.

inherent restrictions of Coq's canonical structures, which were not designed with our ambitious application in mind. In particular, in order to implement various useful forms of automation using canonical structures, it is critically important to be able to write *overlapping instances*, but also to control the order in which they are considered and the order in which unification subproblems are solved. None of these features are supported primitively, but they are encodable using a series of simple "design patterns", which form the core technical contribution of this paper.

We illustrate these patterns through several realistic examples involving reasoning about heaps, pointers and aliasing. All of these examples have been implemented and tested in the context of Hoare Type Theory (HTT) [19], where they have replaced often-used tactics. The code in this paper and HTT itself is built on top of Ssreflect [10], which is a recent extension of Coq providing a very robust language of proofs, as well as libraries for reflection-based reasoning. However, in the current paper, we assume no prior knowledge of Coq, Ssreflect, or canonical structures themselves. We will remain close, but not adhere strictly, to the Coq notation and syntax. All of our sources are available on the web at `http://www.mpi-sws.org/~beta/lessadhoc`.

2. Basics of Canonical Structures

In this section, we provide a quick introduction to the basics of canonical structure programming, leading up to our first important "design pattern"—*tagging*—which is critical for supporting ordering of overlapping instance declarations.

2.1 "Type Class" Programming

In the literature and everyday use of Coq, the word "structure" is used interchangeably (and confusingly) to mean both dependent records *and* the types they inhabit. To disambiguate, in this paper we use *structure* for the type, *instance* for the value, and *canonical instance* for a canonical value of a certain type. We will use the term *canonical structures* only when referring generally to the use of all of these mechanisms in tandem.

The following definition is a simplified example from a structure (*i.e.*, type) taken from the standard Ssreflect library [10]:

$$\underline{\mathsf{structure}}\ \mathsf{eqType} := \mathsf{EqType}\ \{\mathsf{sort} : \mathsf{Type};\ \mathsf{equal} : \mathsf{sort} \to \mathsf{sort} \to \mathsf{bool};\ \_ : \forall x\ y : \mathsf{sort}.\ \mathsf{equal}\ x\ y \leftrightarrow x = y\}$$

The definition makes eqType a record type, with EqType as its constructor, taking three arguments: a type sort, a boolean binary operation equal on sort, and a proof that equal decides the equality on sort. For example, one possible eqType *instance* for the type bool, may be

$$\mathsf{eqType\_bool} := \mathsf{EqType\ bool\ eq\_bool\ pf\_bool}$$

where $\mathsf{eq\_bool}\ x\ y := (x\ \&\&\ y)\ ||\ (!x\ \&\&\ !y)$, and pf_bool is a proof, omitted here, that $\forall x\ y : \mathsf{bool}.\ \mathsf{eq\_bool}\ x\ y \leftrightarrow x = y$.

The labels for the record fields serve as projections out of the record, so the definition of eqType also introduces the constants:

$$\begin{array}{lll} \mathsf{sort} & : & \mathsf{eqType} \to \mathsf{Type} \\ \mathsf{equal} & : & \forall T{:}\mathsf{eqType}.\ \mathsf{sort}\ T \to \mathsf{sort}\ T \to \mathsf{bool} \end{array}$$

We do not care to project out the proof component of the record, so we declare it anonymous by naming it with an underscore.

Notational Convention 1. We will usually omit the argument T of equal, and write equal $x\ y$ instead of equal $T\ x\ y$, as T can be inferred from the types of x and y. We use the same convention for other functions as well, and make implicit such arguments that can be inferred from the types of other arguments. This is a standard notational convention in Coq.

It is also very useful to define *generic* instances. For example, consider the eqType instance for the pair type $A \times B$, where A and B are themselves instances of eqType:

$$\begin{array}{l} \mathsf{eqType\_pair}\ (A\ B : \mathsf{eqType}) := \\ \quad \mathsf{EqType}\ (\mathsf{sort}\ A \times \mathsf{sort}\ B)\ (\mathsf{eq\_pair}\ A\ B)\ (\mathsf{pf\_pair}\ A\ B) \end{array}$$

where

$$\begin{array}{l} \mathsf{eq\_pair}\ (A\ B : \mathsf{eqType})\ (u\ v : \mathsf{sort}\ A \times \mathsf{sort}\ B) := \\ \quad \mathsf{equal}\ (\pi_1\ u)\ (\pi_1\ v)\ \&\&\ \mathsf{equal}\ (\pi_2\ u)\ (\pi_2\ v) \end{array}$$

and pf_pair is omitted as before.

Declaring both eqType_bool and eqType_pair now as *canonical instances*—using Coq's canonical keyword—will have the following effect: whenever the type checker is asked to type a term like equal $(b_1, b_2)\ (c_1, c_2)$, where b_1, b_2, c_1 and c_2 are of type bool, it will generate a unification problem of the form

$$\mathsf{sort}\ ?T \mathrel{\hat{=}} \mathsf{bool} \times \mathsf{bool}$$

for some unification variable $?T$, generated implicitly at the application of equal. It will then try to solve this problem using the canonical instance eqType_pair, resulting in two new unification subproblems, for fresh unification variables $?A$ and $?B$:

$$\mathsf{sort}\ ?A \mathrel{\hat{=}} \mathsf{bool} \qquad \mathsf{sort}\ ?B \mathrel{\hat{=}} \mathsf{bool}$$

Next, it will choose $?A \mathrel{\hat{=}} \mathsf{eqType\_bool}$ and $?B \mathrel{\hat{=}} \mathsf{eqType\_bool}$, with the final result that equal $(b_1, b_2)\ (c_1, c_2)$ reduces implicitly to eq_bool $b_1\ c_1$ && eq_bool $b_2\ c_2$, as one would expect.

In this manner, canonical instances can be used for *overloading*, similar to the way type classes are used in Haskell [28, 13].[2] We can declare a number of canonical eqType instances, for various primitive types, as well as generic instances for type constructors (like the pair example above). Then we can uniformly write equal $x\ y$, and the typechecker will compute the canonical implementation of equality at the types of x and y by solving for equal's implicit argument T.

Generalizing from eqType to arbitrary structures S, the declaration of an instance $V : S$ as canonical instructs the typechecker that *for each* projection proj of the structure S, and c the *head symbol* of proj V, the unknown X in the unification equation

$$\mathsf{proj}\ X \mathrel{\hat{=}} c\, x_1 \ldots x_n \qquad (*)$$

should by default be solved by unifying $X \mathrel{\hat{=}} V$. For instance, in the case of eqType_pair, the projector proj is sort, the head constant c is $(\cdot \times \cdot)$, and the head constant arguments $x_1 \ldots x_n$ are bool and bool. We emphasize that: (1) to control the number of such default facts, we will frequently anonymize the projections if they are not important for the application, as in the case of the proof in eqType above; and (2) there can only be one specified default solution for any given proj and c (*i.e.*, overlapping canonical instances are not permitted). As we will see shortly, however, there is a simple design pattern that will allow us to circumvent this limitation.

2.2 "Logic" Programming

Although the eqType example is typical of how canonical structures are used in much existing Coq code, it is not actually representative of the style of canonical structure programming that we explore in this paper. Our idiomatic style is closer in flavor to logic programming and relies on the fact that, unlike in Haskell, the construction of canonical instances in Coq can be guided not only by the structure of types (such as the sort projection of eqType) but by the structure of *terms* as well.

[2] It is worth noting that Coq also provides a built-in *type class* mechanism, but this feature is independent of canonical structures. We discuss Coq type classes more in Section 7.

To make matters concrete, let's consider a simple automation task, one which we will employ gainfully in Section 3 when we present our first "overloaded lemma". We will first present a naïve approach to solving the task, which *almost* works; the manner in which it fails will motivate our first "design pattern" (Section 2.3).

The task is as follows: search for a pointer x in a heap h. If the search is successful, that is, if h is of the form

$$\cdots \bullet (\cdots \bullet x \mapsto v \bullet \cdots) \bullet \cdots,$$

then return a proof that $x \in \mathsf{dom}\ h$. To solve this task using canonical structures, we will first define a structure find:

$$\underline{\mathsf{structure}}\ \mathsf{find}\ x := \mathsf{Find}\ \{\mathsf{heap\_of} : \mathsf{heap};\ \_ : \mathsf{invariant}\ x\ \mathsf{heap\_of}\}$$

where invariant is defined as

$$\mathsf{invariant}\ x\ h := \mathsf{def}\ h \to x \in \mathsf{dom}\ h$$

The first thing to note here is that the structure find is *parameterized* by the pointer x (causing the constructor Find to be implicitly parameterized by x as well). This is a common idiom in canonical structure programming—and we will see that structure parameters can be used for various different purposes—but here x may be viewed simply as an "input" to the automation task. The second thing to note here is that the structure has no type component, only a heap_of projection, together with a proof that $x \in \mathsf{dom}$ heap_of (under the assumption that heap_of is well-defined).

The search task will commence when some input heap h gets unified with heap_of X for an unknown X : find x, at which point Coq's unification algorithm will recursively deconstruct h in order to search for a canonical implementation of X such that heap_of $X = h$. If that search is successful, the last field of X will be a proof of invariant $x\ h$, which we can apply to a proof of def h to obtain a proof of $x \in \mathsf{dom}\ h$, as desired. (By way of analogy, this is similar to what we previously used for eqType_pair. The construction of a canonical equality operator at a given type A will commence when A is unified with sort T for an unknown T : eqType, and the unification algorithm will proceed to solve for T by recursively deconstructing A and composing the relevant canonical instances.)

The structure find provides a formal specification of what a successful completion of the search task will produce, but now we need to actually implement the search. We do that by defining several canonical instances of find corresponding to the different cases of the recursive search, and relying on Coq's unification algorithm to actually implement the recursion:

$$\underline{\mathsf{canonical}}\ \mathsf{found\_struct}\ A\ x\ (v : A) := \mathsf{Find}\ x\ (x \mapsto v)\ (\mathsf{found\_pf}\ A\ x\ v)$$

$$\underline{\mathsf{canonical}}\ \mathsf{left\_struct}\ x\ h\ (f : \mathsf{find}\ x) := \mathsf{Find}\ x\ ((\mathsf{heap\_of}\ f) \bullet h)\ (\mathsf{left\_pf}\ x\ h\ f)$$

$$\underline{\mathsf{canonical}}\ \mathsf{right\_struct}\ x\ h\ (f : \mathsf{find}\ x) := \mathsf{Find}\ x\ (h \bullet (\mathsf{heap\_of}\ f))\ (\mathsf{right\_pf}\ x\ h\ f)$$

Note that the first argument to the constructor Find in these instances is the parameter x of the find structure.

The first instance, found_struct, corresponds to the case where the heap_of projection is a singleton heap whose domain contains precisely the x we're searching for. (If the heap is $y \mapsto v$ for $y \neq x$, then unification fails.) The second and third instances, left_struct and right_struct, handle the cases where the heap_of projection is of the form $h_1 \bullet h_2$, and x is in the domain of h_1 or h_2, respectively. Note that the recursive nature of the search is implicit in the fact that the latter two instances are parameterized by instances f : find x whose heap_of projections are unified with the subheaps h_1 or h_2 of the original heap_of projection.

Notational Convention 2. In the declarations above, found_pf, left_pf and right_pf are proofs, witnessing that invariant relates x and the appropriate heap expression. We omit the proofs here, but they are available in our source files. From now on, we omit writing such explicit proofs in instances, and simply replace them with "...", as in: Find x ((heap_of f) $\bullet$ h) ...

Unfortunately, this set of canonical instances does not quite work. The trouble is that left_struct and right_struct are overlapping instances since both match against the same head symbol (namely, $\bullet$), and overlapping instances are not permitted in Coq. Moreover, even if overlapping instances were permitted, we would still need some way to tell Coq that it should try one instance first and then, if that fails, to backtrack and try another. Consequently, we need some way to deterministically specify the order in which overlapping instances are to be considered. For this, we introduce our first design pattern.

2.3 Tagging: A Technique for Ordering Canonical Instances

Our approach to ordering canonical instances is, in programming terms, remarkably simple. However, understanding why it actually works is quite tricky because its success relies critically on an aspect of Coq's unification algorithm that diverges significantly from how unification works in, say, Haskell. We will thus first illustrate the pattern concretely in terms of our find example, and then explain afterwards how it solves the problem.

The Pattern First, we define a "tagged" version of the type of thing we're recursively analyzing—in this case, the heap type:

$$\underline{\mathsf{structure}}\ \mathsf{tagged\_heap} := \mathsf{Tag}\ \{\mathsf{untag} : \mathsf{heap}\}$$

This structure declaration also introduces two functions witnessing the isomorphism between heap and tagged_heap:

$$\begin{array}{lcl} \mathsf{Tag} & : & \mathsf{heap} \to \mathsf{tagged\_heap} \\ \mathsf{untag} & : & \mathsf{tagged\_heap} \to \mathsf{heap} \end{array}$$

Then, we modify the find structure to carry a tagged_heap instead of a plain heap, *i.e.*, we declare

$$\mathsf{invariant}\ x\ (h : \mathsf{tagged\_heap}) := \mathsf{def}\ (\mathsf{untag}\ h) \to x \in \mathsf{dom}\ (\mathsf{untag}\ h)$$

$$\underline{\mathsf{structure}}\ \mathsf{find}\ x := \mathsf{Find}\ \{\mathsf{heap\_of} : \mathsf{tagged\_heap};\ \_ : \mathsf{invariant}\ x\ \mathsf{heap\_of}\}$$

Next, we define a sequence of *synonyms* for Tag, one for each canonical instance of find. Importantly, we define the tag synonyms in the *reverse* order in which we want the canonical instances to be considered during unification, and we make the *last* tag synonym in the sequence be *the* canonical instance of the tagged_heap structure itself. (The order doesn't matter much in this particular example, but it does in other examples in the paper.)

$$\begin{array}{l} \mathsf{right\_tag}\ h := \mathsf{Tag}\ h \\ \mathsf{left\_tag}\ h := \mathsf{right\_tag}\ h \\ \underline{\mathsf{canonical}}\ \mathsf{found\_tag}\ h := \mathsf{left\_tag}\ h \end{array}$$

Finally, we modify each canonical instance so that its heap_of projection is wrapped with the corresponding tag synonym.

$$\underline{\mathsf{canonical}}\ \mathsf{found\_struct}\ A\ x\ (v : A) := \mathsf{Find}\ x\ (\mathsf{found\_tag}\ (x \mapsto v))\ \ldots$$

$$\underline{\mathsf{canonical}}\ \mathsf{left\_struct}\ x\ h\ (f : \mathsf{find}\ x) := \mathsf{Find}\ x\ (\mathsf{left\_tag}\ ((\mathsf{untag}\ (\mathsf{heap\_of}\ f)) \bullet h))\ \ldots$$

$$\underline{\mathsf{canonical}}\ \mathsf{right\_struct}\ x\ h\ (f : \mathsf{find}\ x) := \mathsf{Find}\ x\ (\mathsf{right\_tag}\ (h \bullet (\mathsf{untag}\ (\mathsf{heap\_of}\ f))))\ \ldots$$

The Explanation The key to the tagging pattern is that, by employing different tags for each of the canonical instance declarations, we are able to syntactically differentiate the head constants of the heap_of projections, thereby circumventing the need for overlapping instances. But the reader is probably wondering: (1) how can semantically equivalent tag synonyms differentiate anything? and (2) what's the deal with defining them in the reverse order?

The answer to (1) is that Coq does *not* unfold *all* definitions automatically during unification—it only unfolds the definition of a term like found_tag h automatically if that term is unified with something else and the unification fails (see the next paragraph). This stands in contrast to Haskell type inference, which implicitly expands all (type) synonyms right away. Thus, even though found_tag, left_tag, and right_tag are all semantically equivalent to Tag, the unification algorithm can distinguish between them, rendering the three canonical instances of find non-overlapping.

The answer to (2) is as follows. By making the last tag synonym found_tag the sole canonical instance of tagged_heap, we guarantee that unification always pattern-matches against the found_struct case of the search algorithm first before any other. To see this, observe that the execution of the search for x in h will get triggered when a unification problem arises of the form

$$\mathsf{untag}\ (\mathsf{heap\_of}\ ?f) \mathrel{\hat{=}} h,$$

for some unknown $?f$: find x. Since found_tag is canonical, the problem will be reduced to unifying

$$\mathsf{heap\_of}\ ?f \mathrel{\hat{=}} \mathsf{found\_tag}\ h.$$

As found_struct is the only canonical instance of find whose heap_of projection has found_tag as its head constant, Coq will first attempt to unify $?f$ with some instantiation of found_struct. If h is a singleton heap containing x, then the unification will succeed. Otherwise, Coq will backtrack and try unfolding the definition of found_tag h instead, resulting in the new unification problem

$$\mathsf{heap\_of}\ ?f \mathrel{\hat{=}} \mathsf{left\_tag}\ h,$$

which will in turn cause Coq to try unifying $?f$ with some instantiation of left_struct. Again, if that fails, left_tag h will be unfolded to right_tag h and Coq will try right_struct. If in the end that fails as well, then it means that the search has failed to find x in h, and Coq will correctly flag the original unification problem as unsolvable.

3. A Simple Overloaded Lemma

Let us now attempt our first example of lemma overloading, which makes immediate use of the find structure that we developed in the previous section. First, here is the *un*-overloaded version:

$$\begin{aligned}\mathsf{indom} \ :\ & \forall x{:}\mathsf{ptr}.\, \forall v{:}A.\, \forall h{:}\mathsf{heap}.\\ & \mathsf{def}\ (x \mapsto v \bullet h) \to x \in \mathsf{dom}\ (x \mapsto v \bullet h)\end{aligned}$$

The indom lemma is somewhat simpler than noalias from Section 1, but the problems in applying them are the same—neither lemma is applicable unless its heap expressions are of a special syntactic form, with the relevant pointer(s) at the top of the heap.

To lift this restriction, we will rephrase the lemma into the following form:

$$\begin{aligned}\mathsf{indomR} \ :\ & \forall x{:}\mathsf{ptr}.\, \forall f{:}\mathsf{find}\ x.\\ & \mathsf{def}\ (\mathsf{untag}\ (\mathsf{heap\_of}\ f)) \to\\ & \quad x \in \mathsf{dom}\ (\mathsf{untag}\ (\mathsf{heap\_of}\ f))\end{aligned}$$

The lemma is now parameterized over an instance f of structure find x, which we know—just according to the definition of find alone—contains within it a heap h = untag (heap_of f), together with a proof of def $h \to x \in$ dom h. Based on this, it should come as no surprise that the proof of indomR is trivial (it's a half-line long in Ssreflect). In fact, the lemma is really just the projection function corresponding to the unnamed invariant component from the find structure, much as the overloaded equal function from Section 2.1 is a projection function from the eqType structure.

To demonstrate the automated nature of indomR on a concrete example, we will walk in detail through the "trace" of Coq type inference when indomR is applied to prove the goal

$$z \in \mathsf{dom}\ h$$

in a context where $x\ y\ z$: ptr, $u\ v\ w$: A, h : heap := $x \mapsto u \bullet y \mapsto v \bullet z \mapsto w$, and D : def h. When indomR is applied, its formal parameters are turned into unification variables $?x$ and $?f$: find $?x$, which will be constrained by the unification process. (Hereafter, we will use ? to denote unification variables, with previously unused $?x$'s denoting fresh unification variables.)

As a first step, the system tries to unify

$$?x \in \mathsf{dom}\ (\mathsf{untag}\ (\mathsf{heap\_of}\ ?f)) \mathrel{\hat{=}} z \in \mathsf{dom}\ h$$

getting $?x = z$, and, then

$$\mathsf{untag}\ (\mathsf{heap\_of}\ ?f) \mathrel{\hat{=}} h$$

By canonicity of found_tag, we need to solve

$$\mathsf{heap\_of}\ ?f \mathrel{\hat{=}} \mathsf{found\_tag}\ h$$

Unification tries to instantiate $?f$ with found_struct, but for that it must unify the entire heap h with $z \mapsto ?v$, which fails. Before giving up, the system realizes it can unfold the definitions of h and of found_tag, yielding, as $\bullet$ is left-associative,

$$\mathsf{heap\_of}\ ?f \mathrel{\hat{=}} \mathsf{left\_tag}\ ((x \mapsto u \bullet y \mapsto v) \bullet z \mapsto w) \quad (1)$$

Now, left_struct can be used for $?f$, and the following unification problems eventually arise:

$$\begin{aligned}\mathsf{untag}\ (\mathsf{heap\_of}\ ?f_2) &\mathrel{\hat{=}} x \mapsto u \bullet y \mapsto v\\ ?h &\mathrel{\hat{=}} z \mapsto w\\ ?f &\mathrel{\hat{=}} \mathsf{left\_struct}\ z\ ?h\ ?f_2\end{aligned}$$

Attempting to solve the first equation, the system again applies found_tag and found_struct. As before, it fails, unfolds found_tag to get left_tag, then attempts left_struct to get

$$\mathsf{untag}\ (\mathsf{heap\_of}\ ?f_3) \mathrel{\hat{=}} x \mapsto u,$$

It can now apply found_tag and found_struct to finally fail, because z does not match x. Rolling back, it unfolds left_tag to right_tag, matches z with y, fails again, and rolls back to the equation (1). At this point it unfolds left_tag to right_tag, resulting in

$$\mathsf{heap\_of}\ ?f \mathrel{\hat{=}} \mathsf{right\_tag}\ (x \mapsto u \bullet y \mapsto v \bullet z \mapsto w),$$

then chooses right_struct to eventually obtain

$$\begin{aligned}?h' &\mathrel{\hat{=}} x \mapsto u \bullet y \mapsto v\\ \mathsf{untag}\ (\mathsf{heap\_of}\ ?f_2') &\mathrel{\hat{=}} z \mapsto w\\ ?f &\mathrel{\hat{=}} \mathsf{right\_struct}\ z\ ?h'\ ?f_2'\end{aligned}$$

The first equation unifies immediately, after which the second one is solved by applying found_tag and choosing found_struct for $?f_2'$. After that, the third equation also unifies right away.

4. Reflection: Turning Semantics into Syntax

As canonical structures are closely coupled with the type checker, it is possible to fruitfully combine the logic-programming idiom afforded by canonical structures together with ordinary functional programming in Coq. In this section, we illustrate the combination by developing a thoroughly worked example of an overloaded lemma for performing cancellation on heap equations. In our implementation of Hoare Type Theory, this lemma is designed to replace an often used, but rather complicated and brittle, tactic.

Mathematically, cancellation merely involves removing common terms from disjoint unions on the two sides of a heap equation. For example, if we are given an equation

$$x \mapsto v_1 \bullet (h_3 \bullet h_4) = h_4 \bullet x \mapsto v_2$$

and we know that the heaps are disjoint (*i.e.*, the unions are defined), then we can extract the implied equations

$$v_1 = v_2 \wedge h_3 = \mathsf{empty}$$

We will implement the lemma in two stages. The first stage is a canonical structure program, which *reflects* the equation, that is, turns the equation on heap expressions into an abstract syntax tree (or abstract syntax *list*, as it will turn out). Then the second stage is a functional program, which cancels common terms from the syntax tree. Notice that the functional program from the second stage cannot work directly on the heap equation for two reasons: (1) it needs to compare heap and pointer variable names, and (2) it needs to pattern match on function names, since in HTT heaps are really partial maps from locations to values, and $\mapsto$ and $\bullet$ are merely convenient functions for constructing them. As neither of these is possible within Coq's base logic, the equation has to be reflected into syntax in the first stage. The main challenge then is in implementing reflection, so that the various occurrences of one and the same heap variable or pointer variable in the equation are ascribed the same syntactic representation.

Cancellation Since the second stage is simpler, we explain it first. For the purposes of presentation, we restrict our pointers to only store values of some predetermined type T (although the actual implementation in our source files is more general). The data type that we use for syntactic representation of heap expressions is then the following:

$$\begin{aligned} \mathsf{elem} &:= \mathsf{Var\ of\ nat} \mid \mathsf{Pts\ of\ nat} \,\&\, T \\ \mathsf{term} &:= \mathsf{seq\ elem} \end{aligned}$$

An *element* of type elem identifies a heap component as being either a heap variable or a points-to clause $x \mapsto v$. In the first case, the component is represented as Var n, where n is a number identifying the *heap* variable in the style of de Bruijn indices; that is, as an index into some environment (to be explained below). In the second case, the component is represented as Pts m v, where m is a number identifying the *pointer* variable in an environment. We do not perform any reflection on v, as it is not necessary for the cancellation algorithm. A heap expression is then represented via term as a list (seq) of elements. We could have represented the original heap expression more faithfully as a tree, but since $\bullet$ is commutative and associative, lists suffice for our purposes.

We will require two kinds of environments, which we package into the type of *contexts*:

$$\mathsf{ctx} := \mathsf{seq\ heap} \times \mathsf{seq\ ptr}$$

The first component of a context is a list of heaps. In a term reflecting a heap expression, the element Var n stands for the n-th element of this list. Similarly, the second component is a list of pointers, and in the element Pts m v, the number m stands for the m-th pointer in the list.

Because we will need to verify that our syntactic manipulation preserves the semantics of heap operations, we need a function that *interprets* syntax back into semantics. Assuming lookup functions hlook and plook which search for an index in a context of a heap or pointer, respectively, the interpretation function crawls over the syntactic term, replacing each number index with its value from the context (and returning an undefined heap, if the index is out of bounds). The function is implemented as follows:

```
interp (i : ctx) (t : term) : heap :=
  match t with
    Var n :: t' ⇒ if hlook i n is Some h then  h • interp i t'
                  else Undef
  | Pts m v :: t' ⇒
       if plook i m is Some x then x ↦ v • interp i t'
       else Undef
  | nil ⇒ empty
  end
```

For example, if the context i is $([h_3, h_4], [x])$, then

$$\begin{aligned} \mathsf{interp}\ i\ [\mathsf{Pts}\ 0\ v_1, \mathsf{Var}\ 0, \mathsf{Var}\ 1] &= x \mapsto v_1 \bullet (h_3 \bullet (h_4 \bullet \mathsf{empty})) \\ \mathsf{interp}\ i\ [\mathsf{Var}\ 1, \mathsf{Pts}\ 0\ v_2] &= h_4 \bullet (x \mapsto v_2 \bullet \mathsf{empty}) \end{aligned}$$

```
cancel (i : ctx) (t1 t2 r : term) : Prop :=
  match t1 with
    nil ⇒ interp i r = interp i t2
  | Pts m v :: t1' ⇒
      if premove m t2 is Some (v', t2') then
         cancel i t1' t2' r ∧ v = v'
      else cancel i t1' t2 (Pts m v :: r)
  | Var n :: t1' ⇒
      if hremove n t2 is Some t2' then cancel i t1' t2' r
      else cancel i t1' t2 (Var n :: r)
  end
```

Figure 1. Heap cancellation algorithm.

Given this definition of term, we can now encode the cancellation algorithm as a predicate (*i.e.*, a function into Prop) in Coq (Figure 1). The predicate essentially constructs a conjunction of the residual equations obtained as a consequence of cancellation. Referring to Figure 1, the algorithm works as follows. It looks at the head element of the left term t_1, and tries to find it in the right term t_2 (keying on the deBruijn index of the element). If the element is found, it is removed from both sides, before recursing over the rest of t_1. When removing a Pts element keyed on a pointer x, the values v and v' stored into x in t_1 and t_2 must be equal. Thus, the proposition computed by cancel should contain an equation between these values as a conjunct. If the element is not found in t_2, it is shuffled to the accumulator r, before recursing. When the term t_1 is exhausted, *i.e.*, it becomes the empty list, then the accumulator stores the elements from t_1 that were not cancelled by anything in t_2. The equation between the interpretations of r and t_2 is a semantic consequence of the original equation, so cancel immediately returns it (our actual implementation performs some additional optimization before returning). The helper function premove m t_2 searches for the occurrences of the pointer index m in the term t_2, and if found, returns the value stored into the pointer, as well as the term t_2' obtained after removing m from t_2. Similarly, hremove n t_2 searches for Var n in t_2 and if found, returns t_2' obtained from t_2 after removal of n.

Soundness of cancel is established by the following lemma which shows that the facts computed by cancel indeed do follow from the input equation between heaps, when cancel is started with the empty accumulator.

$$\begin{aligned} &\mathsf{cancel\_sound} : \forall i : \mathsf{ctx}.\ \forall t_1\ t_2 : \mathsf{term}. \\ &\quad \mathsf{def}\ (\mathsf{interp}\ i\ t_1) \to \mathsf{interp}\ i\ t_1 = \mathsf{interp}\ i\ t_2 \to \\ &\quad \mathsf{cancel}\ i\ t_1\ t_2\ \mathsf{nil}. \end{aligned}$$

The proof of cancel_sound is rather involved so we omit it here, but it can be found in our source files. We could have proved the converse direction as well, to obtain a completeness result, but this was not necessary for our purposes.

The related work on proofs by reflection usually implements the cancellation phase in a manner similar to above (see for example the work of Grégoire et al. [12]). Where we differ from the related work is the implementation of the reflection phase. This phase is usually implemented by a tactic, but here we show that it can be implemented with canonical structures instead.

Reflection via Canonical Structures Intuitively, the reflection algorithm traverses a heap expression, and produces the corresponding syntactic term. In our overloaded lemma, presented further below, we will invoke this algorithm twice, to reflect both sides of the equation. To facilitate cancellation, we need to ensure that identical variables on the two equation sides, call them E_1 and E_2, are represented by identical syntactic elements. Therefore, reflection of E_1 has to produce a context of newly encountered elements and their syntactic equivalents, which is then fed as an input to the reflection of E_2. If reflection of E_2 encounters an expression which is already in the context, the expression is reflected with the syntactic element provided by the context.

Notational Convention 3. Hereafter, projections out of an instance are considered *implicit coercions*, and we will typically omit them from our syntax. For example, in Figure 2 (described below), the canonical instance union_struct says union_tag($f_1 \bullet f_2$) instead of union_tag((untag (heap_of f_1))$\bullet$(untag (heap_of f_2))), which is significantly more verbose. This is a standard technique in Coq.

The reflection algorithm is encoded using the structure ast from Figure 2. The inputs to each traversal are the initial context i of ast, and the initial heap in the heap_of projection. The output is the (potentially extended) context j and the syntactic term t that reflects the initial heap. One invariant of the structure is precisely that the term t, when interpreted under the output heap j, reflects the input heap:

$$\text{interp } j\ t = \text{heap\_of}$$

There are additional invariants too, which are necessary to carry out the proofs, but we omit them here for brevity; they can be found in our source files.

There are several cases to consider during a traversal, as shown by the canonical instances in Figure 2. We first check if the input heap is a union, as can be seen from the (as usual, reverse) ordering of tag synonyms. In this case, the canonical instance is union_struct. The instance specifies that we recurse over both subheaps, by unifying the left subheap with f_1 and the right subheap with f_2.

The types of f_1 and f_2 show that the two recursive calls work as follows. First the call to f_1 starts with the input context i and computes the output context j and term t_1. Then the call to f_2 proceeds with input context j, and computes outputs k and t_2. The output context of the whole union is k, and the output reflected term is the list-concatenation of t_1 and t_2.

When reflecting the empty heap, the instance is empty_struct. In this case, the input context i is simply passed as output, and the reflected term is the empty list.

When reflecting a singleton heap $x \mapsto v$, the corresponding instance is ptr_struct. In this case, we first have to check if x is a pointer that already appears in the pointer part xs_1 of the input context. If so, we should obtain the index m at which x appears in xs_1. This is the number representing x, and the returned reflected elem is Pts m v. On the other hand, if x does not appear in xs_1, we need to add it. We compute a new context xs_2 which appends x at the end of xs_1, and this is the output pointer context for ptr_struct. The number m representing x in xs_2 now equals the size of xs_2, and returned reflected elem is again Pts m v. Similar considerations apply in the case when we are reflecting a heap variable h. The instance is then var_struct and we search in the heap portion of the context hs_1, producing a new heap portion hs_2.

In both cases, the task of searching and extending the context is performed by the polymorphic structure xfind (Figure 3), which recurses over the context lists in search of an element, relying on unification to make syntactic comparisons between expressions. The inputs to the structure are the parameter s which is the sequence to search in, and the field elem_of, which is the (tagged) element to search for. The output sequence r equals s if elem_of is not in s, or extends s with elem_of otherwise. The output parameter i is the position at which the elem_of is found *in* r.

```
var_tag h := Tag h
pts_tag h := var_tag h
empty_tag h := pts_tag h
canonical union_tag h := empty_tag h

structure ast (i j : ctx) (t : term) :=
  Ast {heap_of : tagged_heap;
       _ : interp j t = heap_of ∧ ...}

canonical union_struct (i j k : ctx) (t1 t2 : term)
                       (f1 : ast i j t1)(f2 : ast j k t2) :=
  Ast i k (append t1 t2) (union_tag (f1 • f2)) ...

canonical empty_struct (i : ctx) :=
  Ast i i nil (empty_tag empty) ...

canonical pts_struct (hs : seq heap) (xs1 xs2 : seq ptr)
                     (m : nat) (v : A) (f : xfind xs1 xs2 m) :=
  Ast (hs, xs1) (hs, xs2) [Pts m v] (pts_tag (f ↦ v)) ...

canonical var_struct (hs1 hs2 : seq heap) (xs : seq ptr)
                     (n : nat) (f : xfind hs1 hs2 n) :=
  Ast (hs1, xs) (hs2, xs) [Var n] (var_tag f) ...
```

Figure 2. Structure ast for reflecting a heap.

```
structure xtagged A := XTag {xuntag : A}

extend_tag A (x : A) := XTag x
recurse_tag A (x : A) := extend_tag x
canonical found_tag A (x : A) := recurse_tag x

structure xfind A (s r : seq A) (i : nat) :=
  XFind {elem_of : xtagged A;
         _ : index r i = elem_of ∧ ...}

canonical found_struct A (x : A) (s : seq A) :=
  XFind (x :: s) (x :: s) 0 (found_tag x) ...

canonical recurse_struct (i : nat) (y : A) (s r : seq A)
                         (f : xfind s r i) :=
  XFind (y :: s) (y :: r) (i + 1) (recurse_tag f) ...

canonical extend_struct A (x : A) :=
  XFind nil [x] 0 (extend_tag x) ...
```

Figure 3. Structure xfind for searching for an element in a list; appending the element at the end if not found.

If the searched element x appears at the head of the list, the selected instance is found_struct and the index $i = 0$. Otherwise, we recurse using recurse_struct. Ultimately, if s is empty, the returned r is the singleton $[x]$, via the instance extend_struct.

It may be interesting to notice here that while xfind is in principle similar to find from Section 2.3, it is keyed on the element being searched for, rather than on the list (or in the case of find, the heap) in which the search is being performed. This exemplifies that there are many ways in which canonical structures of similar functionality can be organized. In particular, which term one keys on (*i.e.*, which term one unifies with the projection from the structure) may in general depend on when a certain computation needs to be triggered. If we reorganized xfind to match find in this respect, then the structure ast would have to be reorganized too. Specifically, ast would have to recursively invoke xfind by unifying it against the contexts xs_1 and hs_1 in the instances pts_struct and var_struct, respectively. As we will argue in Section 6, such unification leads to incorrect results, if done directly, but we will be able to perform it *indirectly*, using a new design pattern.

Now we can present the overloaded lemma cancelR.

$$\begin{aligned}\mathsf{cancelR} : \forall j\ k : \mathsf{ctx}. \forall t_1\ t_2 : \mathsf{term}.\\ \forall f_1 : \mathsf{ast\ nil}\ j\ t_1. \forall f_2 : \mathsf{ast}\ j\ k\ t_2.\\ \mathsf{def\ (untag\ (heap\_of}\ f_1)) \to\\ \mathsf{untag\ (heap\_of}\ f_1) = \mathsf{untag\ (heap\_of}\ f_2) \to\\ \mathsf{cancel}\ k\ t_1\ t_2\ \mathsf{nil}\end{aligned}$$

Assuming we have a hypothesis

$$H : \overbrace{x \mapsto v_1 \bullet (h_3 \bullet h_4)}^{h_1} = \overbrace{h_4 \bullet x \mapsto v_2}^{h_2}$$

and a hypothesis $D : \mathsf{def}\ \ h_1$, we can apply

$$\mathsf{move/(cancelR}\ D) : H.$$

This will make Coq fire the following unification problems:

1. $\mathsf{def\ (untag\ (heap\_of}\ ?f_1)) \mathrel{\hat{=}} \mathsf{def}\ h_1$
2. $\mathsf{untag\ (heap\_of}\ ?f_1)) \mathrel{\hat{=}} h_1$
3. $\mathsf{untag\ (heap\_of}\ ?f_2)) \mathrel{\hat{=}} h_2$

Because f_1 and f_2 are variable instances of the structure ast, Coq will construct canonical values for them, thus reflecting the heaps into terms t_1 and t_2, respectively. The reflection of h_1 will start with the empty context, while the reflection of h_2 will start with the output context of f_1, which in this case is $([h_3, h_4], [x])$.

Finally, the lemma will perform cancel on t_1 and t_2 to produce $v_1 = v_2 \land h_3 = \mathsf{empty} \land \mathsf{empty} = \mathsf{empty}$. The trailing empty = empty can ultimately be removed with a few simple optimizations of cancel, which we omitted to simplify the presentation.

5. Solving for Functional Instances

Previous sections described examples that search for a pointer in a heap expression or for an element in a list. The pattern we show in this section requires a more complicated "search and replace" functionality, and we describe it in the context of our higher-order implementation of separation logic [22] in Coq. Interestingly, this *search-and-replace* pattern can also be described as higher-order, as it crucially relies on the typechecker's ability to manipulate first-class functions and solve unification problems involving functions.

To set the stage, the formalization of separation logic that we use centers on the predicate

$$\mathsf{verify} : \mathsf{prog}\ A \to \mathsf{heap} \to (A \to \mathsf{heap} \to \mathsf{Prop}) \to \mathsf{Prop}.$$

The exact definition of verify is not important for our purposes here, but it suffices to say that it encodes a form of Hoare-style triples. Given a program e : prog A returning values of type A, an input heap i : heap, and a postcondition $q : A \to \mathsf{heap} \to \mathsf{Prop}$ over A-values and heaps, the predicate

$$\mathsf{verify}\ e\ i\ q$$

holds if executing e in heap i is memory-safe, and either diverges or terminates with a value y and heap m, such that $q\ y\ m$ holds.

Programs can perform the basic heap operations: reading and writing a heap location, allocation, and deallocation. In this section, we focus on the writing primitive; given x : ptr and $v : A$, the program write $x\ v$: prog unit stores v into x and terminates. We also require the operation for sequential composition, which takes the form of monadic bind:

$$\mathsf{bind} : \mathsf{prog}\ A \to (A \to \mathsf{prog}\ B) \to \mathsf{prog}\ B.$$

We next consider the following provable lemma, which serves as a Floyd-style rule for symbolic evaluation of write.

$$\begin{aligned}\mathsf{bnd\_write} : \mathsf{verify}\ (e\ ())\ (x \mapsto v \bullet h)\ q \to\\ \mathsf{verify\ (bind\ (write}\ x\ v)\ e)\ (x \mapsto w \bullet h)\ q\end{aligned}$$

To verify write $x\ v$ in a heap $x \mapsto w \bullet h$, it suffices to change the contents of x to v, and proceed to verify the continuation e.

In practice, bnd_write suffers from the same problem as indom and noalias, as each application requires bringing the pointer x to the top of the heap. We would like to devise an automated version bnd_writeR, but, unlike indomR, application of bnd_writeR cannot merely check if a pointer x is in the heap. It needs to remember the heap from the goal, and reproduce it in the premise, only with the contents of x changed from w to v.

For example, applying bnd_writeR to the goal

$$\begin{aligned}G_1 : \mathsf{verify\ (bind\ (write}\ x_2\ 4)\ e)\\ (i_1 \bullet (x_1 \mapsto 1 \bullet x_2 \mapsto 2) \bullet (i_2 \bullet x_3 \mapsto 3))\\ q\end{aligned}$$

should return a subgoal which changes x_2 in place, as in:

$$G_2 : \mathsf{verify}\ (e\ ())\ (i_1 \bullet (x_1 \mapsto 1 \bullet x_2 \mapsto 4) \bullet (i_2 \bullet x_3 \mapsto 3))\ q.$$

The Pattern Here is where functions come in. The bnd_writeR lemma should attempt to infer a function f which represents a heap with a "hole", so that filling the hole with $x \mapsto w$ (i.e., computing $f\ (x \mapsto w)$), obtains the heap from the goal. Then replacing w with v is computed as $f\ (x \mapsto v)$.

For example, in G_1 we want to "fill the hole" with $x \mapsto 2$, while in G_2, we want to fill it with $x \mapsto 4$. Hence, in this case, the inferred function f should, intuitively, be:

$$\mathsf{fun}\ k. i_1 \bullet (x_1 \mapsto 1 \bullet k) \bullet (i_2 \bullet x_3 \mapsto 3).$$

The function f therefore takes an input heap k, but it should not merely produce an output heap. Instead, we want f's range to be a structure, called here partition $k\ r$ (Figure 4). A projection heap_of out of this structure will be used to trigger the search for the subheap that should be replaced with a hole.

For technical reasons, partition has an additional heap parameter r, whose role will be explained later. Because the range of f depends on the input k, f must have a *dependent function type*, and the bnd_writeR lemma looks as below. For clarity, we use Π to distinguish a function, even when Coq does not make that distinction.

$$\begin{aligned}\mathsf{bnd\_writeR} : \forall r : \mathsf{heap}. \forall f : (\Pi k : \mathsf{heap.\ partition}\ k\ r).\\ \mathsf{verify}\ (e\ ())\ (f\ (x \mapsto v))\ q \to\\ \mathsf{verify\ (bind\ (write}\ x\ v)\ e)\ (f\ (x \mapsto w))\ q\end{aligned}$$

We have omitted the projections and written $f\ (x \mapsto w)$ instead of untag (heap_of $(f\ (x \mapsto w))$), and similarly in the case of $x \mapsto v$.

When the bnd_writeR lemma is applied to a verify goal with a heap h, the type checker attempts to unify

$$\mathsf{untag\ (heap\_of}\ (?f\ (x \mapsto w))) \mathrel{\hat{=}} h.$$

$\underline{\text{structure}}$ tagged_heap := Tag {untag : heap}

right_tag (h : heap) := Tag h
left_tag h := right_tag h
$\underline{\text{canonical}}$ found_tag h := left_tag h

$\underline{\text{structure}}$ partition (k r : heap) :=
  Partition {heap_of : tagged_heap;
    _ : heap_of $= k \bullet r$}

$\underline{\text{canonical}}$ found_struct k :=
  Partition k empty (found_tag k) . . .

$\underline{\text{canonical}}$ left_struct h r (f : Πk. partition k r) k :=
  Partition k ($r \bullet h$) (left_tag (f $k \bullet h$)) . . .

$\underline{\text{canonical}}$ right_struct h r (f : Πk. partition k r) k :=
  Partition k ($h \bullet r$) (right_tag ($h \bullet f$ k)) . . .

Figure 4. Structure partition for partitioning a heap into two parts: the part matching k, and "the rest" (r).

The instances in Figure 4 are designed so that the canonical solution f will have the property that the heap component of f $(x \mapsto w)$ *syntactically* equals h, matching exactly the order and the parenthesization of the summands in h. We have three instance selectors: one for the case where we found the heap we are looking for, and two to recurse over each side of the $\bullet$.

The reader may wonder why all the instances of partition take the k parameter *last*, thus forcing the f parameter in the latter two instances to be itself abstracted over k as well. The reason is simple. The last step in solving the above unification goal will be to unify $?f$ $(x \mapsto w)$ with whatever canonical structure is ultimately computed. For example, if $h = h_0 \bullet x \mapsto w$, then the last step of unification will resolve the following goal:

$$?f\ (x \mapsto w) \ \hat{=}\ \text{right\_struct}\ h_0\ \text{empty}\ \text{found\_struct}\ (x \mapsto w).$$

Coq's unification will reduce to subgoals involving the structural components of the applications:

$$?f \ \hat{=}\ \text{right\_struct}\ h_0\ \text{empty}\ \text{found\_struct}$$

and

$$x \mapsto w \ \hat{=}\ x \mapsto w,$$

which are solved immediately. However, this only works because the k parameter of right_struct comes last, thus making it possible to structurally match the occurrences of $x \mapsto w$ on the two sides of the equation. If k came earlier, the unification would simply fail.

We have described how to construct the canonical solution f, but the mere construction is not sufficient to carry out the proof of bnd_writeR. For the proof, we further require an explicit invariant that f $(x \mapsto v)$ produces a heap in which the contents of x is changed to v, but *everything else is unchanged* when compared to f $(x \mapsto w)$.

This is the role of the parameter r, which is constrained by the invariant in the definition of partition to equal the "rest of the heap", that is

$$h = k \bullet r.$$

With this invariant in place, we can vary the parameter k from $x \mapsto w$ in the conclusion of bnd_writeR to $x \mapsto v$ in the premise. However, r remains fixed by the type of f, providing the guarantee that the only change to the heap was in the contents of x.

It may be interesting to note that, while our code computes an f that syntactically matches the parentheses and the order of summands in h (as this is important for using the lemma in practice), the above invariant on h, k and r is in fact a *semantic*, not a syntactic, equality. In particular, it doesn't guarantee that h and $k \bullet r$ are constructed from the same exact applications of $\mapsto$ and $\bullet$, since in HTT those are defined functions, not primitive constructors. Rather, it captures only equality up to commutativity, associativity and other semantic properties of heaps as partial maps. This suffices to prove bnd_writeR, but more to the point: the syntactic property, while true, cannot even be expressed in Coq's logic, precisely because it concerns the syntax and not the semantics of heap expressions.

To conclude the section, notice that the premise and conclusion of bnd_writeR both contain projections out of f. Therefore, the lemma may be used both in forward reasoning (out of hypotheses) and in backward reasoning (for discharging a given goal). For example, we can prove the goal

$$\text{verify (bind (write } x_2\ 4)\ e)\ (i_1 \bullet (x_1 \mapsto 1 \bullet x_2 \mapsto 2))\ q$$

under hypothesis

$$H\ :\ \text{verify}\ (e\ ())\ (i_1 \bullet (x_1 \mapsto 1 \bullet x_2 \mapsto 4))\ q$$

in two ways:

- *Backward*: By applying bnd_writeR to the goal. The goal will therefore be changed to exactly match H.
- *Forward*: By applying bnd_writeR $(x := x_2)$ $(w := 2)$ to the hypothesis H, thus obtaining the goal. Note how in this case we need to explicitly provide the instantiations of the parameters x and w because they cannot be gleaned just from looking at H.

This kind of versatility is yet another advantage that lemmas based on canonical instances exhibit when compared to tactics. The latter, it seems, must be specialized to either forward or backward mode, and we have not managed to encode a tactic equivalent of bnd_writeR that is usable in both directions.

6. Reordering Unification Subproblems

In this section we design an overloaded version of our original noalias lemma from Section 1. The main challenge, as it turns out, is ensuring that the unification constraints generated during canonical structure inference are resolved in the intended order. This is important because the postponing of a certain constraint may underspecify certain variables, leading the system to choose a wrong intermediate value that will eventually fail to satisfy the postponed constraint. In the case of noalias, the problem is that a naïve implementation will result in the triggering of a search for a pointer in a heap before we know what pointer we're searching for. Fortunately, it is possible to handle this problem very easily using an extremely simple design pattern we call *hoisting*.

Before we come to explain the details of the problem and the pattern, let us first present the search structures that form the core of the automation for noalias and are shown in Figures 5–7. Given a heap h, and two pointers x and y, the algorithm for noalias proceeds in three steps: (1) scan h to compute the list of pointers s appearing in it, which must by well-definedness of h be a list of *distinct* pointers; (2) search through s until we find either x or y; (3) once we find one of the pointers, continue searching through the remainder of s for the other one.

Step (1) is implemented by the scan structure in Figure 5. Like the ast structure from Section 4, scan returns its output using its *parameter* (here, s). It also outputs a proof that the pointers in s are all distinct (*i.e.,* uniq s) and that they are all in the domain of the input heap, assuming it was well-defined.

Step (2) is implemented by the search2 structure (named so because it is searches for *two* pointers, both taken as parameters to the structure). It produces a proof that x and y are both distinct members of the input list s, which will be passed in through unification

```
structure tagged_heap := Tag {untag : heap}
default_tag (h : heap) := Tag h
ptr_tag h := default_tag h
canonical union_tag h := ptr_tag h

structure scan (s : seq ptr) :=
  Scan {heap_of : tagged_heap;
       _ : def heap_of →
             uniq s ∧ ∀x. x ∈ s → x ∈ dom heap_of}

canonical union_struct s1 s2 (f1 : scan s1) (f2 : scan s2) :=
  Scan (append s1 s2) (union_tag (f1 • f2)) ...

canonical ptr_struct A x (v : A) :=
  Scan (x :: nil) (ptr_tag (x ↦ v)) ...

canonical default_struct h := Scan nil (default_tag h) ...
```

Figure 5. Structure scan for computing a list of pointers syntactically appearing in a heap.

```
structure tagged_seq2 := Tag2 {untag2 : seq ptr}
foundz (s : seq ptr) := Tag2 s
foundy s := foundz s
canonical foundx s := foundy s

structure search2 (x y : ptr) :=
  Search2 {seq2_of : tagged_seq2;
           _ : x ∈ seq2_of ∧ y ∈ seq2_of
               ∧(uniq seq2_of → x != y)}

canonical x_struct x y (s1 : search1 y) :=
  Search2 x y (foundx (x :: s1)) ...

canonical y_struct x y (s1 : search1 x) :=
  Search2 x y (foundy (y :: s1)) ...

canonical z_struct x y z (s2 : search2 x y) :=
  Search2 x y (foundz (z :: s2)) ...
```

Figure 6. Structure search2 for finding two pointers in a list.

```
structure tagged_seq1 := Tag1 {untag1 : seq ptr}
recurse_tag (s : seq ptr) := Tag1 s
canonical found_tag s := recurse_tag s

structure search1 (x : ptr) := Search1 {seq1_of : tagged_seq1;
                                        _ : x ∈ seq1_of}

canonical found_struct (x : ptr) (s : seq ptr) :=
  Search1 x (found_tag (x :: s)) ...

canonical recurse_struct (x y : ptr) (f : search1 x) :=
  Seach1 x (recurse_tag (y :: f)) ...
```

Figure 7. Structure search1 for finding a pointer in a list.

with the seq2_of projection. The search proceeds until either x or y is found, at which point the search1 structure (next paragraph) is invoked with the other pointer.

Step (3) is implemented by the search1 structure, which searches for a single pointer x in the remaining piece of s, returning a proof of x's membership in s if it succeeds. Its implementation is quite similar to that of the find structure from Section 2.3.

With our core automated machinery in hand, we are ready for our first (failed) attempt at an overloaded version of noalias:

```
noaliasR_wrong :
  ∀x : ptr. ∀s : seq ptr. ∀f : scan s. ∀g : check x s.
    def (untag (heap_of f)) → x != unpack (y_of g)
```

The intuition behind the reformulation can be explained in programming terms. When the lemma is applied to a hypothesis D of type def h, the heap h will be unified with the projection untag (heap_of f). This will trigger an inference problem in which the system solves for the canonical implementation of f by executing the scan algorithm, thus producing as output the pointer list s. For example, if

$$h = i_1 \bullet (x_1 \mapsto v_1 \bullet x_2 \mapsto v_2) \bullet (i_2 \bullet x_3 \mapsto v_3),$$

then s will get unified with $[x_1, x_2, x_3]$, so it can serve as a well-defined input to the search steps that follow.

When the lemma is subsequently applied in order to solve a goal of the form x' != y', we need some way to get the unification with the conclusion of the lemma to trigger the automated search for x' and y' in the list s. Toward this end, we can use the unification with either x' or y' as the trigger for the search, and here we choose the latter. Specifically, we define a structure check, whose construction is keyed on a projection y_of that will be unified with y':[3]

```
structure packed_ptr := Pack {unpack : ptr}

canonical pack (z : ptr) := Pack z

structure check (x : ptr) (s : seq ptr) :=
  Check {y_of : packed_ptr;
         _ : uniq s → x != unpack y_of}

canonical start x y (s2 : search2 x y) :=
  Check x (untag2 (seq2_of s2)) (pack y) ...
```

The sole purpose of the canonical instance start for the check structure is to take x' and s, passed in as parameters, and y', passed in through unification with the y_of projection, and repackage them appropriately in the form that the search2 structure expects. In particular, recall that search2 expects the two pointers to be passed in as parameters, and s to be unified with its seq2_of projection.

Unfortunately, the linking structure we've defined here doesn't quite work. The trouble has to do with the way in which Coq orders the subproblems that arise during canonical instance unification. Although a fully detailed presentation of the Coq unification algorithm is beyond the scope of this paper, the rule of thumb is that when matching against a canonical instance, Coq solves the unification subproblems in a *left-to-right* order—that is, it first solves the unification subproblems corresponding to each of the structure parameters (in the case of check, the x and s parameters) and only then unifies the structure projections (like y_of in this case).

Thus, when matching against the start instance, what happens is the following. First, fresh unification variables are generated for the instance parameters $?x$, $?y$ and $?s_2$. Then, three new unification subproblems are generated and solved in the following order,

[3] The astute reader may notice that it is not actually necessary to tag (or in this case, pack) the y_of projection of the check structure since we are only defining one canonical instance for the structure. We tag y_of simply to minimize the delta required when we describe the hoisting pattern below.

corresponding to the arguments of Check:

$$?x \mathrel{\widehat{=}} x'$$
$$\text{untag2(seq2\_of } ?s_2) \mathrel{\widehat{=}} s$$
$$?y \mathrel{\widehat{=}} y'$$

The problem is that the solution to the second equation will fire the search for a canonical solution for $?s_2$ of type search2 x' $?y$—thus triggering the search for x' and $?y$ in s—*before* the third equation has unified $?y$ with y'. So we will end up searching s for an unknown $?y$, leading to the wrong behavior in most cases.

The Pattern In order to fix our check structure, we need a way to arrange for $?y$ to be unified with y' before the search algorithm gets triggered on the pointer list s. The trick to doing this is to give check an extra parameter y, which will appear earlier than (*i.e.*, to the left of) s in the parameter list, thus ensuring higher priority in the unification order. But we will also constrain that parameter y to be equal to the y_of projection from the structure by (effectively) giving the projection a singleton type. We call this *hoisting*.

To illustrate, here is how to change the packed_ptr and check structures (and their instances) according to the hoisting pattern:

```
structure equals_ptr (z : ptr) := Pack {unpack : ptr}

canonical equate (z : ptr) := Pack z z

structure check (x y : ptr) (s : seq ptr) :=
  Check {y_of : equals_ptr y;
    _ : uniq s → x != unpack y_of}

canonical start x y (s2 : search2 x y) :=
  Check x y (untag2 (seq2_of s2)) (equate y) ...
```

The key here is the new version of packed_ptr, which (for clarity) we call equals_ptr, and which is now explicitly parameterized over a pointer z. The instance equate guarantees that the canonical value of type equals_ptr z is a package containing z itself. We rely on this guarantee in the check structure, whose y_of projection now has type equals_ptr y, thus constraining it to be equal to check's new parameter y.

We can now revise our statement of the overloaded noaliasR lemma ever so slightly to mention the new parameter y:

```
noaliasR :
  ∀x y : ptr. ∀s : seq ptr. ∀f : scan s. ∀g : check x y s.
    def (untag (heap_of f)) → x != unpack (y_of g)
```

As above, suppose that noaliasR has already been applied to a hypothesis D of type def h, so that the lemma's parameter s has already been solved for. Then, when noaliasR is applied to a goal x' != y', the unification engine will unify x' with the argument $?x$ of noaliasR, and proceed to unify

$$\text{unpack (y\_of } ?g) \mathrel{\widehat{=}} y'$$

in a context where $?g$: check x' $?y$ s. Note that, although we have elided it, unpack here really takes as its first (implicit) argument the unknown pointer $?y$ that is implied by equals_ptr $?y$ (the type of y_of $?g$). Thus, by canonicity, the equation will be resolved with equate, and two new equations will be generated (in this order):

$$?y \mathrel{\widehat{=}} y'$$
$$\text{y\_of } ?g \mathrel{\widehat{=}} \text{equate } y'$$

The first unification is the essential one that needs to happen prior to triggering of the search procedure, so that all inputs to the search are known; the rest of unification then works as expected.

Intuitively, the reason the equation between $?y$ and y' is generated first is because it arises from unifying the *types* of y_of $?g$ and equate y', which is necessary before one can unify the terms themselves. For a more formal explanation of canonical instance resolution, we refer the reader to our online appendix [11].

Finally, note the y that is shared between the parameter (y) and the projection (equate y) of the start instance. By hoisting y so that it appears before s in the argument list of Check, we have ensured that it will be unified with the y' from the goal before the search through s begins.

Applying the Lemma The overloaded noaliasR lemma supports a number of modes of use: it can be applied, used as a rewrite rule, or composed with other lemmas. For example, assume that we have a hypothesis specifying a disjointness of a number of heaps in a union:

$$D : \text{def } (i_1 \bullet (x_1 \mapsto v_1 \bullet x_2 \mapsto v_2) \bullet (i_2 \bullet x_3 \mapsto v_3)).$$

Assume further that the arguments x, y, s, f and g of noaliasR are implicit, so that we can write simply (noaliasR D) when we want to partially instantiate the lemma with the hypothesis D. Then the following are some example goals, and proofs to discharge them, illustrating the flexibility of use. As can be seen, no tedious reordering of heap expressions by commutativity and associativity is needed.

1. The lemma can be used in backward reasoning. The type checker picks up x_1 and x_2 from the goal, and confirms they appear in D.

   Goal : x_1 != x_2
   Proof : by apply : (noaliasR D).

2. The lemma can be used in iterated rewriting (notice the modifier "!"). The lemma is partially instantiated with D. It performs the initial scan of D once, but is then used three times to reduce each conjunct to true. There is no need *in the proof* to specify the input pointers to be checked for aliasing. The type checker can pick them up from the goal, in the order in which they appear in the conjunction.

   Goal : (x_1 != x_2) && (x_2 != x_3) && (x_3 != x_1)
   Proof : by rewrite !(noaliasR D).

3. The lemma can be composed with other lemmas, to form new rewrite rules. Again, there is no need to provide the input pointers in the proofs. For example, given the standard library lemma negbTE : ∀b:bool. !b = true → b = false, we have:

   Goal : if (x_2 == x_3) && (x_1 != x_2) then false else true
   Proof : by rewrite (negbTE (noaliasR D)).

4. That said, we can provide the input pointers in several ways, if we wanted to, which would correspond to forward reasoning. We can use the term selection feature of rewrite to reduce only the specified conjunct in the goal.

   Goal : ((x_1 != x_2) && (x_2 != x_3)) = (x_1 != x_2)
   Proof : by rewrite [x_2 != x_3](noaliasR D) andbT.

   Here a rewrite by andbT : ∀b. b && true = b is used to remove the true left in the goal after rewriting by noaliasR.

5. Or, we can supply one (or both) of the pointer arguments directly to noaliasR.

   Goal : ((x_1 != x_2) && (x_2 != x_3)) = (x_1 != x_2)
   Proof : by rewrite (noaliasR (x := x_2) D) andbT.

   Goal : ((x_1 != x_2) && (x_2 != x_3)) = (x_1 != x_2)
   Proof : by rewrite (noaliasR (y := x_3) D) andbT.

7. Related Work

Expressive Type Systems for Proof Automation A number of recent languages consider specifying tactics via very expressive dependent types. Examples include VeriML [26] for automating proofs in Coq, and Delphin [21] and Beluga [20] for proofs in Twelf. Their starting point is the higher-order abstract syntax (HOAS) style of term representation; consequently, one of their main concerns is using types to track the variable contexts of subgoals generated during tactic execution. In contrast, we do not build a separate language on top of Coq, but rather customize Coq's unification algorithm. This is much more lightweight, as we do not need to track variable contexts in types, but it also comes with limitations. For example, our automations are pure logic programs, whereas the other proposals may freely use imperative features. On the other hand, as we have demonstrated, canonical structures can benefit from freely mixing with Coq's primitives for higher-order computation. The mixing would not have been possible had the automation and the base language been kept separated, as is the case in other proposals. Another benefit of the tight integration is that canonical structures can be used to automate not only proofs, but also more general aspects of type inference (*e.g.*, overloading).

In this paper, we have not considered HOAS representations, but we have successfully made first steps in that direction. The interested reader can find in our source files an implementation of the motivating example from VeriML, which considers a simple automation tactic for a logic with quantifiers.

Canonical Structures One important application of canonical structures is described by Bertot et al. [3], where the ability to key on terms, rather than just types, is used for encoding iterated versions of classes of algebraic operators.

Gonthier [9] describes a library for matrix algebra in Coq, which introduces a variant of the tagging pattern, but briefly, and as a relatively small part of a larger mathematical development. In contrast, in the current paper, we give a more abstract and detailed presentation of the general tagging pattern and explain its operation with a careful trace. We also present several other novel design patterns for canonical structures, and explore their use in reasoning about heap-manipulating programs.

Asperti et al. [1] present unification hints, which generalize Coq's canonical structures by allowing that a canonical solution be declared for any class of unification equations, not only for equations involving a projection out of a structure. Hints are shown to support applications similar to our reflection pattern from Section 4. However, they come with limitations; for example, the authors comment that hints cannot support backtracking. Thus, we believe that the design patterns that we have developed in the current paper are not obviated by the additional generality of hints, and would be useful in that framework as well.

Type Classes Sozeau and Oury [24] present type classes for Coq, which are similar to canonical structures, but differ in a few important respects. The most salient difference is that inference for type class instances is not performed by unification, but by general proof search. This proof search is triggered after unification, and it is possible to give a weight to each instance to prioritize the search. This leads to somewhat simpler code, since no tagging nor hoisting is needed, but, on the other hand, it seems less expressive. For instance, we were not able to implement the search-and-replace pattern of Section 5 using Coq type classes, due to the lack of connection between proof search and unification. We *were* able to derive a different solution for bnd_writeR using type classes, but the solution was more involved (requiring two specialized classes to differentiate the operations such as write which perform updates to specific heaps, from the operations which merely inspect pointers without performing updates). More importantly, we were not able to scale this solution to more advanced lemmas from our implementation of higher-order separation logic. In contrast, canonical structures did scale, and we provide the overloaded code for these lemmas in our source files [11].

In the end, we managed to implement all the examples in this paper using Coq type classes, demonstrating that lemma overloading is a useful high-level concept and is not tied specifically to canonical structures. (The implementations using type classes are included in our source files as well [11].) Nevertheless, unlike for canonical structures, we have not yet arrived at a full understanding of how Coq type classes perform instance resolution. In addition, the preliminary performance results are mixed, with type classes sometimes beating canonical structures (in terms of speed) and sometimes vice versa. Ultimately, it may turn out that the two formalisms are interchangeable in practice, but we need more experience with type classes to confirm this.

Spitters and van der Weegen [25] present a reflection algorithm using Coq type classes based on the example of Asperti et al. discussed above. In addition, they consider the use of type classes for overloading and inheritance when defining abstract mathematical structures such as rings and fields. They do not, however, consider lemma overloading more generally as a means of proof automation, as we have presented here.

Finally, in the context of Haskell, Morris and Jones [18] propose an alternative design for a type class system, called `ilab`, which is based on the concept of *instance chains*. Essentially, instance chains avoid the need for overlapping instances by allowing the programmer to control the order in which instances are considered during constraint resolution and to place conditions on when they may be considered. Our tagging pattern (Section 2.3) can be seen as a way of coding up a restricted form of instance chains directly in existing Coq, instead of as a language extension, by relying on knowledge of how the Coq unification algorithm works. `ilab` also supports *failure clauses*, which enable one to write instances that can only be applied if some constraint fails to hold. Our approach does not support anything directly analogous, although (as Morris and Jones mention) failure clauses can be encoded to some extent in terms of more heavyweight type class machinery.

Dependent Types Modulo Theories Several recent works have considered enriching the term equality of a dependently typed system to natively admit inference modulo theories. One example is Strub et al.'s CoqMT [27, 2], which extends Coq's typechecker with *first-order equational* theories. Another is Jia et al.'s language $\lambda^{\cong}$ (pronounced "lambda-eek") [14], which can be instantiated with various abstract term-equivalence relations, with the goal of studying how the theoretical properties (*e.g.*, the theory of contextual equivalence) vary with instantiations. Also related are Braibant et al.'s AAC tactics for rewriting modulo associativity and commutativity in Coq [4].

In our paper, we do not change the term equality of Coq. Instead, we allow user-supplied algorithms to be executed when desired, rather than by default whenever two terms have to be checked for equality. Moreover, these algorithms do not have to be only decision procedures, but can implement general-purpose computations.

8. Conclusions and Future Work

The most common approach to proof automation in interactive provers is via tactics, which are powerful but suffer from several practical and theoretical limitations. In this paper, we propose an alternative, specifically for Coq, which we believe puts the problem of interactive proof automation on a stronger foundational footing.

The approach is rooted in the recognition that the type checker and inference engines are already automation tools, and can be coerced via Coq's canonical structures into executing user-supplied code. Automating proofs in this style is analogous to program overloading via type classes in Haskell. In analogy with the Curry-Howard isomorphism, the automated lemmas are nothing but overloaded programs. In the course of resolving the overloading, the type checker performs the proof automation.

We have illustrated the flexibility and generality of the approach by applying it to a diverse set of lemmas about heaps and pointer aliasing, which naturally arise in verification of stateful programs. Overloading these lemmas required developing a number of design patterns which we used to guide the different aspects of Coq's unification towards automatically inferring the requisite proofs.

Of course, beyond this, much remains to be done, regarding both the theoretical and pragmatic aspects of our approach. From the theoretical standpoint, we believe it is very important that Coq's unification algorithm, as well as the algorithm for inference of canonical structures, be presented in a formal, declarative fashion, which is currently not the case. To somewhat remedy the situation, and help the reader interested in developing their own overloaded lemmas, we include in our online appendix [11] a brief description of the order in which canonical instances are resolved in Coq. This is essentially a specification of the "operational semantics" of canonical instance resolution, and we have found it invaluable, but it has been obtained by a diligent study of the source code of Coq's unification algorithm.

The study of the unification algorithm is also important from the pragmatic standpoint, as in our experience, the current implementation suffers from a number of peculiar performance problems. For example, we have observed that the time to perform a simple assignment to a unification variable is quadratic in the number of variables in the context, and linear in the size of the term being assigned. In contrast, in Ltac, or in type classes, variable assignment is essentially constant-time.

Thus, even though the proof terms produced by application of our overloaded lemmas are usually much shorter than the proofs generated by corresponding tactics, they often take somewhat longer to generate and type check, and scale much worse. This complexity has so far not been too problematic in practice, as interactive proofs tend to keep variable contexts short, for readability. However, it is a serious concern, and one which is not inherent to overloading or to canonical structures; if addressed by an optimization of Coq's kernel functionality, it will likely improve many other aspects of the system.

Acknowledgments

We would like to thank Cyril Cohen and Matthieu Sozeau for very helpful discussions.

References

[1] Andrea Asperti, Wilmer Ricciotti, Claudio Sacerdoti Coen, and Enrico Tassi. Hints in unification. In *TPHOLs*, volume 5674 of *LNCS*, pages 84–98, 2009.

[2] Bruno Barras, Jean-Pierre Jouannaud, Pierre-Yves Strub, and Qian Wang. CoqMTU: a higher-order type theory with a predicative hierarchy of universes parametrized by a decidable first-order theory. In *LICS*, pages 143–151, 2011.

[3] Yves Bertot, Georges Gonthier, Sidi Ould Biha, and Ioana Pasca. Canonical big operators. In *TPHOLs*, volume 5170 of *LNCS*, pages 86–101, 2008.

[4] Thomas Braibant and Damien Pous. Rewriting modulo associativity and commutativity in Coq. In *Second Coq workshop*, 2010.

[5] Manuel M. T. Chakravarty, Gabriele Keller, and Simon Peyton Jones. Associated type synonyms. In *ICFP*, pages 241–253, 2005.

[6] Adam Chlipala. Certified programming with dependent types. URL: `http://adam.chlipala.net/cpdt`, 2008.

[7] Adam Chlipala. Mostly-automated verification of low-level programs in computational separation logic. In *PLDI*, 2011.

[8] Georges Gonthier. Formal proof — the four-color theorem. *Notices of the AMS*, 55(11):1382–93, 2008.

[9] Georges Gonthier. Point-free, set-free concrete linear algebra. In *ITP*, 2011.

[10] Georges Gonthier and Assia Mahboubi. An introduction to small scale reflection in Coq. *Journal of Formalized Reasoning*, 3(2):95–152, 2010.

[11] Georges Gonthier, Beta Ziliani, Aleksandar Nanevski, and Derek Dreyer. How to make ad hoc proof automation less ad hoc, 2011. Code + appendix: `http://www.mpi-sws.org/~beta/lessadhoc`.

[12] Benjamin Grégoire and Assia Mahboubi. Proving equalities in a commutative ring done right in Coq. In *TPHOLs*, pages 98–113, 2005.

[13] Cordelia Hall, Kevin Hammond, Simon Peyton Jones, and Philip Wadler. Type classes in Haskell. *TOPLAS*, 18:241–256, 1996.

[14] Limin Jia, Jianzhou Zhao, Vilhelm Sjöberg, and Stephanie Weirich. Dependent types and program equivalence. In *POPL*, pages 275–286, 2010.

[15] Mark P. Jones. Type classes with functional dependencies. In *ESOP*, pages 230–244, 2000.

[16] Gerwin Klein, June Andronick, Kevin Elphinstone, Gernot Heiser, David Cock, Philip Derrin, Dhammika Elkaduwe, Kai Engelhardt, Rafal Kolanski, Michael Norrish, Thomas Sewell, Harvey Tuch, and Simon Winwood. seL4: formal verification of an operating-system kernel. *CACM*, 53(6):107–115, 2010.

[17] Xavier Leroy. Formal verification of a realistic compiler. *CACM*, 52:107–115, July 2009.

[18] J. Garrett Morris and Mark P. Jones. Instance chains: Type class programming without overlapping instances. In *ICFP*, pages 375–386, 2010.

[19] Aleksandar Nanevski, Viktor Vafeiadis, and Josh Berdine. Structuring the verification of heap-manipulating programs. In *POPL*, pages 261–274, 2010.

[20] Brigitte Pientka and Joshua Dunfield. Programming with proofs and explicit contexts. In *PPDP*, pages 163–173, 2008.

[21] Adam Poswolsky and Carsten Schürmann. System description: Delphin – a functional programming language for deductive systems. *ENTCS*, 228:113–120, 2009.

[22] John C. Reynolds. Separation logic: a logic for shared mutable data structures. In *LICS*, 2002.

[23] Amokrane Saïbi. Typing algorithm in type theory with inheritance. In *POPL*, pages 292–301, 1997.

[24] Matthieu Sozeau and Nicolas Oury. First-class type classes. In *TPHOLs*, volume 5170 of *LNCS*, pages 278–293, 2008.

[25] Bas Spitters and Eelis van der Weegen. Type classes for mathematics in type theory. *MSCS, Special issue on 'Interactive theorem proving and the formalization of mathematics'*, 21:1–31, 2011.

[26] Antonis Stampoulis and Zhong Shao. VeriML: Typed computation of logical terms inside a language with effects. In *ICFP*, pages 333–344, 2010.

[27] Pierre-Yves Strub. Coq modulo theory. In *CSL*, pages 529–543, 2010.

[28] Philip Wadler and Stephen Blott. How to make ad-hoc polymorphism less ad hoc. In *POPL*, pages 60–76, 1989.

Temporal Higher-Order Contracts

Tim Disney
University of California, Santa Cruz

Cormac Flanagan
University of California, Santa Cruz

Jay McCarthy
Brigham Young University

Abstract

Behavioral contracts are embraced by software engineers because they document module interfaces, detect interface violations, and help identify faulty modules (packages, classes, functions, etc). This paper extends prior higher-order contract systems to also express and enforce temporal properties, which are common in software systems with imperative state, but which are mostly left implicit or are at best informally specified. The paper presents both a programmatic contract API as well as a temporal contract language, and reports on experience and performance results from implementing these contracts in Racket.

Our development formalizes module behavior as a trace of events such as function calls and returns. Our contract system provides both non-interference (where contracts cannot influence correct executions) and also a notion of completeness (where contracts can enforce any decidable, prefix-closed predicate on event traces).

Categories and Subject Descriptors D.3.1 [*Formal Definitions and Theory*]: Semantics; D.3.3 [*Language Constructs and Features*]: Constraints

General Terms Languages, Reliability, Security, Verification.

Keywords Higher-order Programming, Temporal Contracts

1. Contract Expressiveness

Large software systems typically consist of many modules (e.g., packages, classes, functions) produced by different development teams. When the system fails, an initial difficulty is *fault localization*: identifying the module that failed to perform as expected. Undocumented module interfaces are problematic for various reasons, not least because they lead to disagreements about which module is considered "at fault" and should be fixed.

Software engineers embrace behavioral contracts because they address many of these problems. In particular, behavioral contracts provide a mechanism to explicitly document each module's assumptions and guarantees; to dynamically detect contract violations; and to identify faulty modules. Behavioral contracts are widely used in procedural, object-oriented, and functional languages, including Eiffel [36], C [42], C# [32], Haskell [26], Java [28], Python [44], Scheme [19, 15, 22], and Smalltalk [10].

Existing contract systems can express a range of interface specifications. Below, we consider a range of possible specifications for a `sort` routine, not all of which are supported by existing contract systems.

1. *The* `sort` *function takes two arguments, an array of positive integers and a comparison function* `cmp`.

   This standard, first-order precondition constrains *how* `sort` should be called, that is, what arguments are valid. These kinds of basic first-order contracts are supported by most contract systems, for example, Eiffel [36].

2. *The argument function* `cmp` *in turn requires two arguments, both positive integers.*

   This higher-order precondition constrains how the `sort` module can call the function argument `cmp`, and so is a guarantee provided by `sort` rather than an obligation on the client. Higher-order contract systems [19, 15, 22, 24, 45] support such preconditions by wrapping the `cmp` argument to enforce this property dynamically.

3. *The* `sort` *function is not re-entrant–it can only be called after all previous* `sort` *invocations have completed.*

   Unlike the previous contracts that constrain how functions may be called, this temporal contract constrains *when* `sort` can be called [12, 13]. This constraint implies that `sort` must be used carefully in a multithreaded setting. Moreover, it also imposes restrictions in a sequential setting, since for example, `cmp` is not allowed to call `sort`. A variety of prior systems support such first-order temporal contracts: for example, MOP [33], Tracematches [39], PathExplorer [25], Eagle [6], RuleR [7], and others.

4. `sort` *is granted a capability to call the* `cmp` *function only until* `sort` *returns.*

   This last contract is a *higher-order temporal contract* in that it combines both higher-order and temporal aspects. It expresses a temporal constraint, not on `sort` itself, but on its higher-order interaction with the `cmp` argument it was passed.

   To enforce this contract, it is not sufficient to instrument all `cmp` functions passed to `sort`, since these may legally be called from other call sites after `sort` returns. It is also insufficient to instrument only calls to `cmp` within `sort`, since `sort` might pass a reference to `cmp` to a third party, who in turn could call `cmp` after `sort` returns.

Our study of a widely-used standard library (see Section 8) indicates that higher-order temporal constraints are common in software systems with imperative state, but are mostly left implicit or are at best informally specified. In this paper, we study how to express and enforce such higher-order temporal contracts. Our development leverages and combines techniques from prior higher-order contract systems [19, 15, 22] and from first-order temporal contract systems [33, 39, 25, 6, 7]. We also address blame assignment in a temporal setting. For the example considered above where `sort`

ICFP'11, September 19–21, 2011, Tokyo, Japan.

passes cmp to a third party that later calls cmp, our temporal contract system immediately detects the error, halts execution, and correctly blames the sort module, even though it is neither the caller (the third party) nor the callee (cmp) of the erroneous function call.

In a very general sense, contracts provide a means to specify and restrict the *behavior of a module*. In a higher-order imperative setting, this notion of a module's behavior is quite complex, as it can involve higher-order callbacks, mutual recursion, and sharing of imperative state between modules. Understanding the temporal and higher-order aspects of module behavior is a prerequisite to developing expressive contracts for constraining this behavior.

The first step in our investigation is to formalize the behavior of each module as a sequence of *events*, namely remote procedure calls to other modules and matching returns, etc. We start with an operational abstract machine that extends a control-store machine [16, 17] with a remote procedure call mechanism. This abstract machine then generates structural and scoping constraints on event sequences, and so "bootstraps" the game semantics. Module *linking* involves running abstract machines in parallel and appropriately routing events between them.

In this setting, the observable behavior of a module is captured by the set of possible event sequences it can generate. Consequently, the most general notion of a *contract* is a predicate describing permitted event sequences (that is, permitted observable behaviors of the module). We require that the set of event sequences permitted by a contract is prefix-closed, so that errors are detected as soon as they occur. We also require that contracts are computable predicates.

Based on this formalism, we provide a *monitor interface* whereby programmers can express arbitrary contracts as predicates over event sequences. This monitor interface provides:

1. *non-interference*, since the monitor code does not gain references (a.k.a. capabilities [37]) to mutable data or to functions, and so the monitor cannot perturb correct program executions, but can only halt erroneous executions;[1] and
2. a notion of completeness that we call *trace completeness*, meaning that a monitor can impose any computable prefix-closed predicate on a module's event trace (i.e., on its observable behavior).

It is straightforward to achieve one of non-interference or trace completeness; achieving both simultaneously requires a more subtle design since we need to provide monitors with all information about the observed trace (to achieve trace completeness) without giving it access to function references or to mutable state (in order to ensure non-interference).

In addition to this programmatic monitor interface, we also provide a *declarative contract language* for expressing both structural and temporal specifications of a module's behavior. The structural specifications expresses constraints on function arguments and results, and also names each function (including function arguments such as cmp above). The temporal specifications is a regular grammar[2] over calls and returns of functions named in the structural component, and includes *dependent sequences* to express, for example, that a call to release(x) must be preceded by a call to acquire(x), for any resource x. Each constraint in this language is compiled into a monitor, and thus leverages the monitor interface to provide non-interference and blame assignment.

[1] Earlier work on higher-order contracts [20] also proposed non-interference as a design goal, but did not achieve a notion of completeness.

[2] We focus on checking safety but not liveness properties, and so do not need the additional expressiveness of temporal logics such as LTL [40].

Contributions The main contributions of this paper are:

- We formalize the behavior of imperative higher-order modules as event sequences, using an operational semantics (section 3).
- We formalize a *contract* as a computable, prefix-closed predicate on event sequences (section 4).
- We present a *monitor interface* that satisfies the twin design goals of non-interference and trace completeness (section 5).
- We show how to track and assign blame for complex temporal contracts (section 6).
- We present a declarative contract language for expressing mixed structural and temporal contracts (section 7).
- We describe a Racket [22][3] implementation of both the monitor interface and the contract language, and include preliminary performance and usability results (section 8).[4]

2. Motivating Examples

We first illustrate how our proposed contract language succinctly captures important structural and temporal constraints of software interfaces.

To start, the following formal contract captures all four of the desired constraints for sort informally outlined above:

```
SortContract =
  sort : (List Pos)                                    // 1
         (cmp : Pos → Pos → Bool)                      // 2
      → (List Pos)
  where not ... call(sort,_) !ret(sort,_)*
                call(sort,_)                           // 3
    and not ... ret(sort,_)  ... call(cmp,_)           // 4
```

By convention, we use Initial Capitals to denote contract names such as Bool and Pos (for positive numbers) and SortContract. The notation "*name* : *Dom* → *Rng*" describes a function contract where the argument and result values should satisfy contracts *Dom* and *Rng* respectively. The optional "*name* :" prefix associates a name with each function, which can then be referenced in the where clause. This clause expresses a regular constraint over the sequence of *events* (calls and returns of these named functions). The pattern "..." matches any sequence of events, and the not operator has low precedence, so its argument extends to the end of the where clause. The pattern "_" matches any argument in a call or any return value in a ret. The prefix "!" denotes the negation of a single event (unlike "not", which negates a pattern), and the postfix "*" denotes a sequence matching the preceding pattern. Thus, "!ret(sort,_)*" denotes any sequence of events that does not include a return from sort. Whereas, "not ret(sort,_)*" matches any traces that are not only returns from sort, such as traces that start with a return from sort, a call to something else, then any other events.

Constraint (3) declares sort to be non-reentrant; it cannot be called a second time before the first call returns. Constraint (4) is a little more complex in that it is a higher-order temporal contract. Each call of sort introduces a binding for cmp in the above contract, and so cmp denotes not just one function, but any comparison function ever passed to sort. Each such comparison function has an associated sort invocation, and constraint (4) explicates that the comparison function cannot be called after the associated sort invocation returns.

[3] Formerly known as PLT Scheme.

[4] The implementation is available in the core Racket distribution as of July 2011 in the "unstable" collection.

As a simpler example, an implicit property of many library functions is that they are expected to return immediately after being called, with no intervening callbacks to client code. We document this *atomicity* property with the following contract, which detects an error if a call to `f` is not immediately followed by a matching return.

```
AtomicContract =
  f : Any → Any
  where not ... call(f,_) !ret(f,_)
```

Since internal calls within `f` are not externally visible, this contract still permits arbitrary internal computation, but forbids callbacks to outside code. Note that this atomicity guarantee is useful even in a sequential setting.

The following interface describes a file system whose `open` method returns a `File` object corresponding to the given file name. Each `File` object contains methods for reading, writing, and closing that file, with the temporal constraint that once the file is closed these methods should not be called. Note that this temporal constraint is scoped to its enclosing `File` object: calling `close` on one file does not influence the ability to access other open files. Put differently, the alphabet of close events is unbounded.

```
FileSystemContract =
  open : String → FileContract

FileContract =
  Record read  : Unit → String
         write : String → Unit
         close : Unit → Unit
  where not
    ... ret(close,_) ...
    (call(close,_) | call(read,_) | call(write,_))
```

Finally, consider the following contract that documents a standard `alloc/free` interface on some resource, where each resource instance has an associated integer handle z. After a resource handle z has been freed, it should not be freed again until after it has been re-allocated. The pattern "?z" binds a variable z to an argument/result, allowing z to be referenced later in the grammar.

```
AllocFreeContract =
  Record alloc : Unit → Int
         free  : Int  → Unit
  where not
    ...  call(free,?z) !ret(alloc,z)* call(free,z)
```

We now proceed to investigate a contract system that can express these kinds of mixed structural and temporal constraints.

3. A Model of Module Interactions

The starting point for our investigation of contract expressiveness is an imperative higher-order language, namely the untyped imperative lambda calculus with constants (c) and mutable reference cells.

$$e \;::=\; x \mid \lambda x.\, e \mid e\; e \mid c \mid \texttt{ref}\; e$$

To simplify our presentation, we use standard lambda-calculus encodings of `let` expressions, sequencing, n-ary function definitions and calls, pairs (with accessors `fst` and `snd`), n-ary records, sums, booleans, conditionals, recursive definitions, and assertions. Thus, despite its simplicity, this language is sufficient to model many aspects of modern languages, including encapsulated behavior (via λ-expressions) and both encapsulated and shared imperative state (via `ref`).[5]

[5] The language does not support concurrency, whose interaction with temporal higher-order contracts remains an important topic for future work.

To facilitate our technical development, we take an "interface-oriented" view to reference cells, as proposed by Reynolds [41], whereby `ref` e returns a pair of getter and setter functions for reading and updating the newly created reference cell. This representation allows calls to getter/setter functions to also model operations on shared mutable data, and so all inter-module interaction is modeled by function calls and returns.

A module generally denotes a syntactic construct such as a package, class, function, etc. In the setting of the λ-calculus, we take a *module* to simply mean a closed expression e. Two modules e_1 and e_2 can be *linked* via function application ($e_1\; e_2$).

As an example, consider the following module *twice* with an associated test harness H:

$$\begin{aligned} \mathit{twice} &\stackrel{\text{def}}{=} (\lambda f.\, \lambda x.\, f\,(f\; x)) \\ H &\stackrel{\text{def}}{=} (\lambda t.\, t\,(\lambda x.\, x{+}1)\; 4) \end{aligned}$$

The linked program (H *twice*) passes the result of *twice* into H, which then calls *twice* with appropriate arguments ($\lambda x.\, x{+}1$) and 4. The module *twice* in turn calls back into the ($\lambda x.\, x{+}1$) function provided by H. Thus, despite its simplicity, the imperative lambda calculus permits rich patterns of module interaction and callbacks. The goal of this paper is to formalize (and subsequently constrain, via contracts) these interactions.

3.1 Semantics of Modules

We formalize the semantics of a module using the operational abstract machine called the CSI machine defined in Figure 1. This machine includes both code (C) and a store (S), and so in part functions much like Felleisen's $\langle C, S\rangle$ machine [16, 17]. The [CALL] rule performs standard β-reduction within an evaluation context $\mathcal{E}$. The rule [PRIM] leverages an auxiliary δ function to define the semantics of primitives. For example, $\delta(\texttt{constant?}, 4) = \texttt{true}$. The rule [REF] for ($\texttt{ref}\; v$) creates a new reference cell by extending the store S with a triple "$(x, y) \mapsto v$", where v is the initial value of the cell, and x and y are binding occurrences for functions that read and write the value of this cell via the [GET] and [SET] rules, respectively.

The last four rules of the CSI machine add inter-module interactions, in a manner analogous to remote procedure calls. Specifically, the code term C may contain free variables not bound in the store S; these free variables are external references to functions defined by other modules. The CSI machine communicates with these other modules via an event stream.

The CSI machine does not transmit λ-expressions themselves; instead, each transmitted value is first translated into a *handle*, which is either a constant or a fresh variable. The following operation $I[h \rhd v]$ performs the appropriate translation of a value v into a handle h, and returns an appropriately updated interface component. Constants c are transmitted by-value, and functions ($\lambda y.\, e$) and imported variables y are transmitted by exporting a fresh variable z that is bound by I to that value. As usual, $I[z \mapsto v]$ denotes a function that is identical to I except that it maps z to v.

$$\begin{aligned} I[c \rhd c] &\stackrel{\text{def}}{=} I \\ I[z \rhd (\lambda y.\, e)] &\stackrel{\text{def}}{=} I[z \mapsto \lambda y.\, e] \quad z \text{ fresh} \\ I[z \rhd y] &\stackrel{\text{def}}{=} I[z \mapsto y] \quad z \text{ fresh} \end{aligned}$$

In a function application $\mathcal{E}[x\; v]$ where x is externally defined, the rule [SEND-CALL] first translates the argument value v into an external handle h via the operation $I[h \rhd v]$, and then transmits the event $\texttt{send.call}(x, h)$.

After transmitting the event $\texttt{send.call}(x, h)$, the module becomes inactive or *quiescent*, with code $\mathcal{E}[\texttt{send.call}_x\; \bot]$ indicating that the module is waiting for a matching return $\texttt{rcv.ret}(x, h')$, after which evaluation continues with $\mathcal{E}[h']$: see [RCV-RET].

Figure 1: CSI Machine

Domains

State	CSI	$\in$	$Code \times Store \times Interface$
Code	C	$::=$	$\mathcal{E}[e] \mid \mathcal{Q}[\bot]$
Store	S	$\in$	$\mathcal{P}(Var \times Var \times Value)$
Interface	I	$\in$	$Var \rightarrow Value$

Evaluation context	$\mathcal{E}$	$::=$	$\mathcal{E}[\bullet\ e] \mid \mathcal{E}[v\ \bullet] \mid \mathcal{E}[\texttt{ref}\ \bullet] \mid \mathcal{Q}[\texttt{rcv.call}_x\ \bullet]$
Quiescent context	$\mathcal{Q}$	$::=$	$\bullet \mid \mathcal{E}[\texttt{send.call}_x\ \bullet]$
Value	v	$::=$	$c \mid x \mid \lambda y.\, e$
Handle	h	$::=$	$c \mid x$
Event	a	$::=$	$\rho.\texttt{ret}(x,h) \mid \rho.\texttt{call}(x,h)$
Direction	ρ	$::=$	$\texttt{send} \mid \texttt{rcv}$
Trace	t	$::=$	$\vec{a}$

Transition relation $(\rightarrow)\ \subseteq\ State \times Event_{\bot} \times State$

$\langle\ \mathcal{E}[(\lambda x.\, e)\ v],\quad S,\quad I\ \rangle$	$\rightarrow$	$\langle\ \mathcal{E}[e[x := v]],$	$S,$	$I\ \rangle$		[CALL]
$\langle\ \mathcal{E}[c\ v],\quad S,\quad I\ \rangle$	$\rightarrow$	$\langle\ \mathcal{E}[v'],$	$S,$	$I\ \rangle$	$v' = \delta(c,v)$	[PRIM]
$\langle\ \mathcal{E}[\texttt{ref}\ v],\quad S,\quad I\ \rangle$	$\rightarrow$	$\langle\ \mathcal{E}[\texttt{pair}\ x\ y],$	$S[(x,y) \mapsto v],$	$I\ \rangle$	x, y fresh	[REF]
$\langle\ \mathcal{E}[x\ v],\quad S[(x,y) \mapsto v'],\quad I\ \rangle$	$\rightarrow$	$\langle\ \mathcal{E}[v'],$	$S[(x,y) \mapsto v'],$	$I\ \rangle$		[GET]
$\langle\ \mathcal{E}[y\ v],\quad S[(x,y) \mapsto v'],\quad I\ \rangle$	$\rightarrow$	$\langle\ \mathcal{E}[v],$	$S[(x,y) \mapsto v],$	$I\ \rangle$		[SET]
$\langle\ \mathcal{E}[x\ v],\quad S,\quad I\ \rangle$	$\rightarrow^{\texttt{send.call}(x,h)}$	$\langle\ \mathcal{E}[\texttt{send.call}_x\ \bot],$	$S,$	$I[h \rhd v]\ \rangle$	$x \notin BV(S)$	[SEND-CALL]
$\langle \mathcal{E}[\texttt{send.call}_x\ \bot],\quad S,\quad I\ \rangle$	$\rightarrow^{\texttt{rcv.ret}(x,h)}$	$\langle\ \mathcal{E}[h],$	$S,$	$I\ \rangle$		[RCV-RET]
$\langle\ \mathcal{Q}[\bot],\quad S,\quad I\ \rangle$	$\rightarrow^{\texttt{rcv.call}(x,h)}$	$\langle \mathcal{Q}[\texttt{rcv.call}_x\ (v\ h)],$	$S,$	$I\ \rangle$	$I(x) = v$	[RCV-CALL]
$\langle\ \mathcal{Q}[\texttt{rcv.call}_x\ v],\quad S,\quad I\ \rangle$	$\rightarrow^{\texttt{send.ret}(x,h)}$	$\langle\ \mathcal{Q}[\bot],$	$S,$	$I[h \rhd v]\ \rangle$		[SEND-RET]

Figure 2: Example of Linking and Running Two CSI Machines Concurrently

The two CSI machines shown below cooperate to evaluate $linkRun([\![H]\!], [\![twice]\!])$. After the initial bootstrapping, `send` events of one machine match `rcv` events of the other and vice-versa. The final $\texttt{send.ret}(y, 6)$ event reports the result of the execution is 6.

Evaluation of $H = (\lambda t.\, t\ (\lambda x.\, x{+}1)\ 4)$
$I_1 = [y \mapsto (\lambda t.\, t\ (\lambda x.\, x{+}1)\ 4)]$
$J_1 = [y \mapsto (\lambda t.\, t\ (\lambda x.\, x{+}1)\ 4),\ f \mapsto (\lambda x.\, x{+}1)]$

$\langle\,\texttt{rcv.call}_{start}\ (\lambda t.\, t\ (\lambda x.\, x{+}1)\ 4),$	$\emptyset, \emptyset\ \rangle$	$\rightarrow^{\texttt{send.ret}(start,y)}$
$\langle\,\bot,$	$\emptyset, I_1\ \rangle$	$\rightarrow^{\texttt{rcv.call}(y,t)}$
$\langle\,\texttt{rcv.call}_y\ ((\lambda t.\, t\ (\lambda x.\, x{+}1)\ 4)\ t),$	$\emptyset, I_1\ \rangle$	$\rightarrow$
$\langle\,\texttt{rcv.call}_y\ ((t\ (\lambda x.\, x{+}1))\ 4),$	$\emptyset, I_1\ \rangle$	$\rightarrow^{\texttt{send.call}(t,f)}$
$\langle\,\texttt{rcv.call}_y\ (\texttt{send.call}_t\ \bot)\ 4),$	$\emptyset, J_1\ \rangle$	
		$\rightarrow^{\texttt{rcv.ret}(t,g)}$
$\langle\,\texttt{rcv.call}_y\ (g\ 4),$	$\emptyset, J_1\ \rangle$	$\rightarrow^{\texttt{send.call}(g,4)}$
$\langle\,\texttt{rcv.call}_y\ (\texttt{send.call}_g\ \bot),$	$\emptyset, J_1\ \rangle$	
		$\rightarrow^{\texttt{rcv.call}(f,4)}$
$\langle\,\texttt{rcv.call}_y\ (\texttt{send.call}_g\ (\texttt{rcv.call}_f\ ((\lambda x.\, x{+}1)\ 4))),$	$\emptyset, J_1\ \rangle$	$\rightarrow^2$
$\langle\,\texttt{rcv.call}_y\ (\texttt{send.call}_g\ (\texttt{rcv.call}_f\ 5)),$	$\emptyset, J_1\ \rangle$	$\rightarrow^{\texttt{send.ret}(f,5)}$
$\langle\,\texttt{rcv.call}_y\ (\texttt{send.call}_g\ \bot),$	$\emptyset, J_1\ \rangle$	$\rightarrow^{\texttt{rcv.call}(f,5)}$
$\langle\,\texttt{rcv.call}_y\ (\texttt{send.call}_g\ (\texttt{rcv.call}_f\ ((\lambda x.\, x{+}1)\ 5))),$	$\emptyset, J_1\ \rangle$	$\rightarrow^2$
$\langle\,\texttt{rcv.call}_y\ (\texttt{send.call}_g\ (\texttt{rcv.call}_f\ 6)),$	$\emptyset, J_1\ \rangle$	$\rightarrow^{\texttt{send.ret}(f,6)}$
$\langle\,\texttt{rcv.call}_y\ (\texttt{send.call}_g\ \bot),$	$\emptyset, J_1\ \rangle$	$\rightarrow^{\texttt{rcv.ret}(g,6)}$
$\langle\,\texttt{rcv.call}_y\ 6,$	$\emptyset, J_1\ \rangle$	$\rightarrow^{\texttt{send.ret}(y,6)}$
$\langle\,\bot,$	$\emptyset, J_1\ \rangle$	

Evaluation of $twice = (\lambda f.\, \lambda x.\, f\ (f\ x))$
$I_2 = [t \mapsto (\lambda f.\, \lambda x.\, f\ (f\ x))]$
$J_2 = [t \mapsto (\lambda f.\, \lambda x.\, f\ (f\ x)),\ g \mapsto (\lambda x.\, f\ (f\ x))]$

	$\langle\,\texttt{rcv.call}_{start}\ (\lambda f.\, \lambda x.\, f\ (f\ x)),$	$\emptyset, \emptyset\ \rangle$
$\rightarrow^{\texttt{send.ret}(start,t)}$	$\langle\,\bot,$	$\emptyset, I_2\ \rangle$
$\rightarrow^{\texttt{rcv.call}(t,f)}$	$\langle\,\texttt{rcv.call}_t\ ((\lambda f.\, \lambda x.\, f\ (f\ x))\ f),$	$\emptyset, I_2\ \rangle$
$\rightarrow$	$\langle\,\texttt{rcv.call}_t\ (\lambda x.\, f\ (f\ x)),$	$\emptyset, I_2\ \rangle$
$\rightarrow^{\texttt{send.ret}(t,g)}$	$\langle\,\bot,$	$\emptyset, J_2\ \rangle$
$\rightarrow^{\texttt{rcv.call}(g,4)}$	$\langle\,\texttt{rcv.call}_g\ ((\lambda x.\, f\ (f\ x))\ 4),$	$\emptyset, J_2\ \rangle$
$\rightarrow$	$\langle\,\texttt{rcv.call}_g\ (f\ (f\ 4)),$	$\emptyset, J_2\ \rangle$
$\rightarrow^{\texttt{send.call}(f,4)}$	$\langle\,\texttt{rcv.call}_g\ (\texttt{send.call}_f\ (f\ \bot)),$	$\emptyset, J_2\ \rangle$
$\rightarrow^{\texttt{rcv.ret}(f,5)}$	$\langle\,\texttt{rcv.call}_g\ (f\ 5),$	$\emptyset, J_2\ \rangle$
$\rightarrow^{\texttt{send.call}(f,5)}$	$\langle\,\texttt{rcv.call}_g\ (\texttt{send.call}_f\ \bot),$	$\emptyset, J_2\ \rangle$
$\rightarrow^{\texttt{rcv.ret}(f,6)}$	$\langle\,\texttt{rcv.call}_g\ 6,$	$\emptyset, J_2\ \rangle$
$\rightarrow^{\texttt{send.ret}(g,6)}$	$\langle\,\bot,$	$\emptyset, J_2\ \rangle$

Since the code component encodes both active and quiescent states, we define both standard evaluation contexts $\mathcal{E}$ and *quiescent contexts* $\mathcal{Q}$. A code component of $\mathcal{Q}[\bot]$ means that control is external to the module, but the module can still receive external calls via a $\texttt{rcv.call}(x, h)$ event. Here, x should be some previously exported function whose definition v is defined by I, and evaluation continues with $\mathcal{Q}[\texttt{rcv.call}_x\ (v\ h)]$, as described by [RCV-CALL]. Once $(v\ h)$ reduces to a value v', the $\texttt{rcv.call}_x$ marker indicates that control should return to the caller module via [SEND-RET].

For a module e, we initialize its execution with the code $(\texttt{rcv.call}_{start}\ e)$, where *start* is an artificial variable name denoting the initial evaluation of a module. Once the evaluation of e terminates, it will return $\texttt{send.ret}(start, h)$ and wait for incoming events. The *meaning* of a module e is then the set of all possible event sequences $\vec{a}$ that e can generate under the CSI machine:

$$\begin{array}{rcl} [\![-]\!] & : & Module \to \mathcal{P}(Trace) \\ [\![e]\!] & = & \{\vec{a} \mid \langle \texttt{rcv.call}_{start}\ e, \emptyset, \emptyset\rangle \to^{\vec{a}} CSI\ \} \end{array}$$

We use t to range over traces or finite event sequences $\vec{a}$; we use T to range over sets of traces; and $t \cdot t'$ to denote trace concatenation. The *exported variables* (EV) and *imported variables* (IV) in a CSI machine state, and the *bound variables* (BV) of a store S, are:

$$\begin{array}{rcl} EV(\ C, S, I\ ) & \stackrel{\text{def}}{=} & dom(I) \\ IV(\ C, S, I\ ) & \stackrel{\text{def}}{=} & (FV(C) \cup FV(rng(S)) \cup\ FV(rng(I))) \\ & & \setminus BV(S) \\ BV(S) & \stackrel{\text{def}}{=} & \{x, y \mid S \text{ contains } (x, y) \mapsto v\} \end{array}$$

Thus, the initial state $\langle \texttt{rcv.call}_{start}\ e, \emptyset, \emptyset\rangle$ of a module's computation has no imported variables or *capabilities* [37]; they must be passed explicitly as arguments to functions defined by the module.

3.2 Running a Single Module

Suppose a program consists of a single module e, which performs some computation and then returns a final result, with no subsequent interactions. We assume that the result is first-order data (*i.e.*, a constant) since a function result would be opaque and thus meaningless. The following function $run(T)$ extracts from the trace set $T = [\![e]\!]$ the result of running the program e, which is simply the constant it returns.

$$run(T) \stackrel{\text{def}}{=} \{c \mid \texttt{send.ret}(start, c) \in T\}$$

Thus, we run a program e by starting the CSI machine in state $\langle \texttt{rcv.call}_{start}\ e, \emptyset, \emptyset\rangle$ and run its computation until it emits a $\texttt{send.ret}(start, c)$ event containing the result of that computation.

3.3 Linking Two Modules

More generally, a program may consist of multiple (reactive) modules that must be linked before running. For simplicity, we consider the case where the program consists of just two modules e_1 and e_2, where the module e_1 is a function that expects the result of e_2 as an argument. Subsequently, the two modules may continue to interact by communicating events, where every send event of e_2 becomes a rcv event by e_1, and vice versa. More generally, every event a of e_2 must match a dual event $\overline{a}$ of e_1, where the *dual* operation $\overline{\rho}$ on directions swaps sends and receives, and this dual operation extends in a compatible manner to events and to event sequences:

$$\overline{\texttt{send}} \stackrel{\text{def}}{=} \texttt{rcv} \qquad\qquad \overline{\texttt{rcv}} \stackrel{\text{def}}{=} \texttt{send}$$

Based on this dual operation, we formalize the notion of linking and running two trace sets T_1 and T_2 (where $T_i = [\![e_i]\!]$) as follows:

$$\begin{array}{l} linkRun(T_1, T_2) \stackrel{\text{def}}{=} \\ \{c \mid \texttt{send.ret}(start, h) \cdot t_2 \in T_2 \\ \quad \texttt{send.ret}(start, x) \cdot \texttt{rcv.call}(x, h) \cdot \overline{t_2} \cdot \texttt{send.ret}(x, c) \in T_1\} \end{array}$$

Here, trace set T_2 (for the function argument) starts by returning a handle h. Trace set T_1 returns a function x that is then immediately applied to handle h from T_2. Subsequent events from the two trace sets must then correspond, with each send event from T_1 matching a receive event from T_2, and vice versa. Eventually, after the function x completes its computation and its interaction with its argument h, trace set T_1 finally returns a result c. We assume that this result is first-order data (*i.e.*, a constant) since a function result would be opaque and thus meaningless.

3.4 Example

To illustrate module linking, Figure 2 revisits the $(H\ twice)$ example to show how each module can run on a separate CSI machine, using the function *linkRun* to link up the event traces from these two machines. In particular, the handle t returned by the evaluation of $twice$ is passed as the argument to the function y produced by the evaluation of H. Subsequent events from the two modules must match exactly, with each send event from one module matching a corresponding rcv event from the other module. Finally, the H module returns the constant 6 as the result of applying y to $twice$; thus 6 is the final result of running this program.

For this test harness, the module $twice$ produces the trace shown in the right column of Figure 2. However, $twice$ can generate many additional traces if linked with other modules. The trace set $[\![twice]\!]$ captures the set of all possible traces generated by the CSI machine when executing $twice$.

3.5 Semantic Equivalence

We now have two notions of module linking. We can link two modules e_1 and e_2 via function application, and run the resulting expression $(e_1\ e_2)$ on a single CSI machine according to *run*. Alternatively, we can run e_1 and e_2 on separate CSI machines that communicate according to *linkRun*. The following theorem proves that these two notions coincide, which implies that *linkRun* correctly captures our notion of module composition as function application:

THEOREM 1 (Module Transparency). *For any closed expressions e_1 and e_2, $linkRun([\![e_1]\!], [\![e_2]\!]) = run([\![e_1\ e_2]\!])$.*

PROOF: By proving a bisimulation relation between the CSI machine state of *run* and the *CSI state pairs* of *linkRun*. □

3.6 Well-Formed Traces

An inspection of the CSI machine reveals that it generates traces satisfying the following structural and scoping properties; we refer to such traces as being *well-formed*.

1. Traces consist of alternating send events, which produce a quiescent state, and receive events, which re-initiate computation.
2. Every $\texttt{send.ret}(x, h)$ matches a preceding $\texttt{rcv.call}(x, h')$, and every $\texttt{rcv.ret}(x, h)$ matches a preceding $\texttt{send.call}(x, h')$, so these events form "balanced bracket pairs", with the exception of the initial $\texttt{send.ret}(start, h)$ that starts each trace.
3. Exporting a variable x via $\texttt{send.call}(y, x)$ or $\texttt{send.ret}(y, x)$ adds x to the interface I, where it is in scope for subsequent $\texttt{rcv.call}(x, h)$ events.

4. Importing a variable x via $\texttt{rcv.call}(y, x)$ or $\texttt{rcv.ret}(y, x)$ means that x occurs free in the CSI machine and can be used in subsequent $\texttt{send.call}(x, h)$ events.

Properties 3 and 4 provide an implicit notion of variable scoping, where the second variable in each event is a binding occurrence, and the first argument must be a bound occurrence. We consider two traces to be α-equivalent if they are identical modulo consistent renaming of bound variables, and we implicitly perform α-conversion to avoid name collisions.

The set T of traces generated by the CSI machine also satisfies the following properties:

1. It is prefix-closed.
2. It is *input-enabled*, in that whenever it can receive one event it is willing to receive any well-formed event: if $t.a \in T$, a and a' are both receive events, and $t.a'$ is well-formed then $t.a' \in T$.
3. It is *output-deterministic*, in that at most one send event is possible at any point. Thus, if $t.a \in T$, $t.a' \in T$, and a and a' are both send events, then $a = a'$.

4. Contracts as Trace Predicates

The CSI machine semantics exposes each module's behavior as a trace set. We now use this formalism to study contract enforcement.

Consider a module e whose behavior is the set of traces $[\![e]\!]$. Each trace represents a behavior that could be observed on a particular execution. A contract is a mechanism for restricting the set of observable behaviors to those satisfying some safety predicate.

Formally, a *contract* is a set of traces $K \subseteq \mathit{Trace}$ that is prefix-closed, computable, and that contains only well-formed traces. The execution of e under contract K should only generate traces in the intersection $K \cap [\![e]\!]$. Since K restricts both `rcv` and `send` events, it explicates e's assumptions and guarantees.

For a contract K, we want to implement a function e_K that takes as argument the module e. The function e_K then observes all of e's behaviors and halts program execution if any of those behaviors violate K. Thus, e_K should satisfy a requirement like $[\![e_K\ e]\!] = K \cap [\![e]\!]$. However, $[\![e_K\ e]\!]$ must be input-enabled but K (and hence $K \cap [\![e]\!]$) may not be input-enabled, so more precisely $[\![e_K\ e]\!]$ should be the *input-enabled closure* of $K \cap [\![e]\!]$, that is, the smallest superset of $K \cap [\![e]\!]$ that is input-enabled. Intuitively, $[\![e_K\ e]\!]$ has to receive "bad" events from its enclosing context but can block them from being sent on to e.

4.1 The Universal Contract

The identity function $(\lambda x.\, x)$ behaves like a universal contract, in that $((\lambda x.\, x)\ e)$ exposes all the behaviors of module e. We start by studying the semantics $[\![\lambda x.\, x]\!]$ of this universal contract.

Consider the possible executions of the CSI machine starting from the initial state $S_0 = \langle \texttt{rcv.call}_{start}\ (\lambda x.\, x), \emptyset, \emptyset \rangle$. Whenever the machine imports a variable y via [RCV-CALL] or [RCV-RET], it immediately exports a fresh name, say $\widehat{y}$, for that variable, via [SEND-CALL] or [SEND-RET]. Here, the hat $(\widehat{\cdot})$ operator maps between imported and exported variable names, and is an involution (its own inverse). We extend this hat operator to handles by defining $\hat{c} = c$. The set of identity function traces $[\![\lambda x.\, x]\!]$ is then the well-formed subset of the prefix-closure of the following regular grammar. Note that the last two productions essentially copy events from one side of the identity function to the other, renaming variables appropriately.

$$
\begin{array}{rcl}
T_{id} & ::= & \texttt{send.ret}(\mathit{start}, f) \\
& | & T_{id} \cdot \texttt{rcv.call}(f, h) \cdot \texttt{send.ret}\ (f, \widehat{h}) \\
& | & T_{id} \cdot \texttt{rcv.call}(y, h) \cdot \texttt{send.call}(\widehat{y}, \widehat{h}) \\
& | & T_{id} \cdot \texttt{rcv.ret}\ (y, h) \cdot \texttt{send.ret}\ (\widehat{y}, \widehat{h})
\end{array}
$$

4.2 Copycat Traces

We next consider contracts that are more restrictive than the identity function. Suppose the target module e generates the trace:

$$t = \texttt{send.ret}(\mathit{start}, h) \cdot a_1 \cdot \ldots \cdot a_n$$

If the contract K permits this trace then $[\![e_K]\!]$ should include:

$$
\begin{array}{l}
\mathit{copycat}(t) \stackrel{\text{def}}{=} \\
\quad \texttt{send.ret}(\mathit{start}, f) \cdot \texttt{rcv.call}(f, h) \cdot \texttt{send.ret}(f, \widehat{h}) \cdot \\
\quad \mathit{copy}(a_1) \cdot \ldots \cdot \mathit{copy}(a_n)
\end{array}
$$

This trace returns a function f that is applied to the handle h produced by t. It then returns a renamed handle $\widehat{h}$, and subsequently copies every event a_i from one side of e_K to the other via the following event copying function $\mathit{copy}(a)$:

$$
\begin{array}{rcl}
\mathit{copy}(\texttt{send.call}(y, h)) & = & \texttt{rcv.call}(y, h) \cdot \texttt{send.call}(\widehat{y}, \widehat{h}) \\
\mathit{copy}(\texttt{send.ret}\ (y, h)) & = & \texttt{rcv.ret}\ (y, h) \cdot \texttt{send.ret}\ (\widehat{y}, \widehat{h}) \\
\mathit{copy}(\texttt{rcv.call}(y, h)) & = & \texttt{rcv.call}(\widehat{y}, \widehat{h}) \cdot \texttt{send.call}(y, h) \\
\mathit{copy}(\texttt{rcv.ret}\ (y, h)) & = & \texttt{rcv.ret}\ (\widehat{y}, \widehat{h}) \cdot \texttt{send.ret}\ (y, h)
\end{array}
$$

We extend $\mathit{copycat}$ from traces to trace sets in a pointwise fashion:

$$\mathit{copycat}(K) \stackrel{\text{def}}{=} \{\mathit{copycat}(t) \mid t \in K\}$$

This $\mathit{copycat}$ function allows us to formalize the relationship between the permissible traces K and the contract implementation e_K. We require that e_K copies only K-traces:

$[\![e_K]\!]$ is the prefix and input-enabled closure of $\mathit{copycat}(K)$

5. The Programmatic Monitor Interface

Based on the above specification, it is possible to hand-code an implementation e_K for each contract K, but these implementations are difficult to read and write, and can violate non-interference.

Instead, we propose to express e_K as a pair of a *guard* and a *monitor*. The predefined **guard** function performs the necessary copycat behavior on event streams and guarantees non-interference. It also encodes the observed event stream and communicates it to the monitor M, which detects errors and reports them to the guard, which then halts execution. Thus, we implement e_K as:

$$e_K \stackrel{\text{def}}{=} (\textbf{guard}\ M)$$

Traces contain scope and binding information, which is tricky to communicate to the monitor M. Our chosen encoding is that, when an event such as $\texttt{rcv.call}(\cdot, x)$ introduces a new variable x, the monitor M creates two new sub-monitors, say M_{call} and M_{ret}, which handle events $\rho.\texttt{call}(x, \_)$ and $\rho.\texttt{ret}(x, \_)$, respectively. This encoding avoids passing function references (or getters/setters for mutable reference cells) to M, which helps ensure non-interference. We also require that the monitor M is closed, so that it does not gain accesses to function references through its environment.

Based on this discussion, the type τ of the monitor M is:

$$\tau = (\mathit{Constant} \rightarrow \mathit{Bool}) \times (\mathit{Unit} \rightarrow (\mathit{False} + (\tau \times \tau)))$$

When an event transmits a constant, the first component of M is called to decide if that event is permitted. That function can use mutable internal state to track and enforce temporal properties. Thus, temporal properties of the contracts are implemented via imperative state in the monitor.

When an event transmits a function x, the second component of M is called, which again has the opportunity to halt execution by retuning `false`. Otherwise, the function should return a pair of monitors for handling `call` and `ret` events on the function x.

The function guard below then converts its monitor argument M into an appropriate contract implementation that queries M to verify that each transmitted event is permitted:

```
guard M =
 λx. if (constant? x) then
        assert ((fst M) x) != false
        x
     else
        let MM = (snd M)()
        assert MM != false
        λy. (guard (snd MM) (x (guard (fst MM) y)))
```

5.1 Example Monitors

Using the monitor interface, it is straightforward to implement a universal monitor Any that permits all communication:

```
rec Any = pair (λx. true) (λ. pair Any Any)
```

As a more interesting example, the following code shows how to implement *revokable membranes* [37]. In this code, `ref true` returns a pair of `get` and `set` methods. As long as `get()` returns `true`, the monitor M behaves like the universal contract. Calling `revoke` puts `false` into the reference cell, after which all further communication is prohibited. The top-level `membrane` function returns a pair of the membrane monitor and its revoke function.

```
membrane =
  λ. let (get,set) = ref true
     let revoke    = λ. set false
     letrec M      = pair (λx. get())
                          (λ . if (get())
                                then (pair M M)
                                else false)
     in pair M revoke
```

Note that M is not strictly speaking a monitor, since it calls a free variable `get`, which could (in theory, but not in this case) interfere with the enclosing program.

5.2 Deep Tracing

A particularly interesting monitor is `deepTrace`, which performs "deep" or higher-order tracing. The code `((guard deepTrace) g)` prints all calls and returns of g. Additionally, if g takes or returns functions, then those functions are also traced. Thus, deep tracing reports both first-order and higher-order interactions between the module g and the rest of the program.

Revisiting the example *twice* from Section 3.4, the program

$(H$ `((guard deepTrace)` $twice))$

prints out the event sequence shown in the right half of Figure 2 (modulo naming of bound variables). Alternatively, the program

`(((guard deepTrace)` $H)$ $twice)$

prints out the event sequence shown in the left half of that figure. In this manner, deep tracing allows the programmer to observe the trace semantics of a module as explored during a particular run.

The implementation of `deepTrace` uses an auxiliary function `helper` to generate the appropriate monitor. The `helper` function takes four arguments: the first two indicate whether this monitor is observing send or receive events; the third whether it is receiving `ret` or `call` events; and the fourth argument is a function name. Every function that passes through the guard is assigned a new name via `gensym`, and the generated monitor then prints each event.

```
deepTrace = (helper "send" "rcv" "ret" "start")

helper send rcv op fn =
  pair (λx. print (send+"."+op+"("+fn+","+x+")")
            true)
       (λ.  let name = gensym()
            print (send+"."+op+"("+fn+","+name+")")
            pair (helper rcv send "call" name)
                 (helper send rcv "ret"  name))
```

5.3 Non-Interference and Trace Completeness

We now revisit the design goals of non-interference and trace completeness, to show how they are achieved by the guard/monitor architecture.

First, for any monitor M, the function (guard M) satisfies non-interference, in that it behaves like the identity function except that it may abruptly halt certain (erroneous) executions. Thus, guard behaves like an "information diode", in that information can flow into the monitor M but can never flow back out to the program. In a richer language with exceptions, guard would need to appropriately catch any thrown exceptions to ensure that they do not constitute an additional information channel between the monitor and the enclosing program.

THEOREM 2 (Non-Interference). *For any closed expression M,*

$$[\![\texttt{guard}\ M]\!] \subseteq [\![\lambda x.\, x]\!]$$

PROOF: By showing that the trace set $[\![\lambda x.\, x]\!]$ from section 4.1 is a superset of $[\![\texttt{guard}\ M]\!]$. The behavior of M is irrelevant, since non-interference is guaranteed entirely by guard. □

Our argument for trace completeness is based on showing that the monitor observes all events that cross the contract boundary. Specifically, consider the semantics of an arbitrary module e under the `deepTrace` monitor, *i.e.*,

$$[\![(\texttt{guard deepTrace})\ e]\!]$$

An investigation of the reachable states of the corresponding CSI machine shows that this module prints each `send` event before transmitting it, and prints each `rcv` event right after receiving it. Instead of printing these events, `deepTrace` could feed them into an algorithm that decides a computable contract K over event traces, and could halt execution once that algorithm detects a trace that violates K. Consequently, any computable predicate over traces could be implemented using the monitor interface.

5.4 Dependent Contracts

Dependent contracts allow a function's range contract R to depend on the function's argument x. If the argument x is itself a function, then R could violate non-interference by calling x.

Our guard/monitor architecture avoids this difficulty by only allowing dependency when the argument x is a first-order value (that is, a constant). Essentially, the argument x is saved on a stack by the domain contract, and is then popped by the matching range contract. The following monitor illustrates how to implement such dependent contracts. It specifies a function contract where the integer result should be greater than the integer argument. The monitor accepts only functions, where the function's argument x must be an integer constant that is pushed on a stack that records the arguments of currently active calls, and the function's result y must be an integer that is greater than the argument.

```
increasingMonitor =
  let (push,pop) = newStack()
  pair (λx. false) // no constants allowed
       (λ. pair (pair (λx. (push x); (integer? x))
                      (λ.  false))
                (pair (λy. (integer? y) && y > pop())
                      (λ.  false)))
```

This explicit stack design also avoids subtle difficulties with blame assignment in traditional dependent contracts [15].

6. Blame Assignment

The discussion so far has focused on detecting contract violations; we next address how to assign blame for these violations. In particular, we show that *blame assignment*, previously studied in higher-order contract systems [19], extends in a consistent fashion to the more general setting of temporal higher-order contracts.

Suppose the program consists of two modules e_1 and e_2, with corresponding trace sets $T_i = [\![e_i]\!]$ for $i \in 1, 2$, and suppose that K is a contract on e_2. The semantics of correct executions is defined as:

$$linkRun(T_1, K \cap T_2)$$

This formula links together the modules e_1 and e_2, with the requirement that all interaction between the two modules must be permitted by K.

We now extend that semantics to assign blame, via the function $linkMonitorRun(T_1, K, T_2)$ shown below. The first case in this definition is analogous to the function *linkRun* defined earlier, with the additional requirement that the trace $\texttt{send.ret}(start, h) \cdot t_2$ in T_2 must be permitted by K. The second case deals with assigning blame, where T_1 and T_2 want to exchange a message a that is not permitted by K, but where the prefix of a is accepted by all parties. In this situation, the module i sending that message is blamed.

$$
\begin{array}{l}
linkMonitorRun(T_1, K, T_2) \stackrel{\text{def}}{=} \\
\{c \mid \texttt{send.ret}(start, h) \cdot t_2 \in K \cap T_2 \\
\quad \texttt{send.ret}(start, x) \cdot \texttt{rcv.call}(x, h) \cdot \overline{t_2} \cdot \texttt{send.ret}(x, c) \in T_1\} \\
\cup \{blame_i \mid \texttt{send.ret}(start, h) \cdot t_2 \cdot a \in T_2 \\
\qquad \texttt{send.ret}(start, x) \cdot \texttt{rcv.call}(x, h) \cdot \overline{t_2} \cdot \overline{a} \in T_1 \\
\qquad \texttt{send.ret}(start, h) \cdot t_2 \in K \\
\qquad \texttt{send.ret}(start, h) \cdot t_2 \cdot a \notin K \\
\qquad \texttt{if } |t_2| \ odd \ \texttt{then } i = 1 \ \texttt{else } i = 2 \quad \}
\end{array}
$$

Thus $linkMonitorRun(T_1, K, T_2)$ extends $linkRun(T_1, K \cap T_2)$ to return a blame label in situations where *linkRun* would fail silently.

To incorporate blame assignment into the guard implementation, we introduce additional arguments to track the module and enclosing context of each monitor, where these two arguments are swapped for contravariant domain checks (as in [19]). We assume a primitive `blame` for reporting blame, and an appropriate representation for module labels (e.g., strings).

```
guard module context M =
 λx. if (constant? x) then
       if ((fst M) x) == false then blame module
       x
     else
       let MM = (snd M)()
       if MM == false then blame module
       λy. (guard module context (snd MM)
             (x (guard context module (fst MM) y)))
```

Figure 3: Declarative HOT Contracts

M	$::=$	S `where` R	HOT contract
S	$::=$	$\mathit{flat}(e) \mid n{:}S_1 \mapsto S_2$	Structural contract
R	$::=$	$A \mid !A \mid RR \mid R^* \mid \texttt{not}\ R \mid R \cup R$	Temporal contract
	$\mid$	$\ldots \mid \texttt{call}(n, ?x)\ R \mid \texttt{ret}(n, ?x)\ R$	
A	$::=$	$\texttt{call}(n, p) \mid \texttt{ret}(n, p)$	Event patterns
p	$::=$	$\_ \mid x \mid c$	Value patterns
n	$\in$	$Name$	Function names

7. The Declarative Contract Language

The programmatic monitor interface provides trace completeness, non-interference, and blame assignment. We now leverage that interface to develop a declarative contract language for writing mixed higher-order temporal (HOT) contracts. Our declarative language sacrifices trace completeness for ease-of-expression, but still interoperates with the monitor interface for situations where additional expressiveness is required.

Figure 3 summarizes the contract syntax. A *HOT contract*

$$S \ \texttt{where} \ R$$

contains both a structural component (S) that binds function names (n), and a temporal component (R) that imposes constraints on when those functions can be called or return.

The flat structural contract $\mathit{flat}(e)$ describes the set of constants c that satisfy the predicate e. The higher-order structural contract $(n : S_1 \mapsto S_2)$ describes functions where S_1 and S_2 specify the function's domain and range contracts, respectively, and n provides a *name* for this function that can be referenced in the temporal component.

In the temporal component, event patterns $\texttt{call}(n, p)$ and $\texttt{ret}(n, p)$ denote calls and returns of the function named n, where the argument or result matches pattern p. Patterns include constants, variables x, and "_", which matches any argument.

Temporal contracts (R) include events (A), negated events ($!A$), concatentation (RR), Kleene closure (R^*), negation of trace sets ($\texttt{not}\ R$), union ($R \cup R$), and the universal temporal contract ("$\ldots$"), which matches any trace. Temporal contracts also include *dependent sequencing* patterns such as $\texttt{call}(n, ?x)\ R$, where the argument from the first event is bound to x, and can be referred to from within R. Dependent sequencing captures common constraints on function arguments and returns, for example, that the argument passed to `free` must previously have been returned from `alloc`.

7.1 Semantics of HOT Contracts

To formalize the semantics of a structural contract S, we define an abstract machine called the EF machine that describes what traces S permits.

This EF machine contains an environment E and a stack F. The environment E associates each variable x with a direction ρ (describing whether x was sent or received) and a structural contract S (describing permitted uses of x). The stack F contains the variable names of inter-module calls (or stack frames).

$$
\begin{array}{lcl}
E & ::= & \epsilon \mid E, x : \rho S \\
F & ::= & Variable^*
\end{array}
$$

The EF machine generates traces according to the following transition relation $EF \Rightarrow^a EF'$. The stack length $|F|$ indicates whether the contracted module is active or quescient, so if $|F|$ is odd we require that $\rho = \texttt{send}$, and otherwise that $\rho = \texttt{rcv}$, in both of these rules.

$$\langle E, F\rangle \quad \Rightarrow^{\rho.\mathtt{call}(x,h)} \quad \langle E \oplus (h : \rho S_1), F.x\rangle \quad \text{[S-CALL]}$$
$$\text{where } E(x) = \overline{\rho}(n : S_1 \mapsto S_2)$$

$$\langle E, F.x\rangle \quad \Rightarrow^{\rho.\mathtt{ret}(x,h)} \quad \langle E \oplus (h : \rho S_2), F\rangle \quad \text{[S-RET]}$$
$$\text{where } E(x) = \rho(n : S_1 \mapsto S_2)$$

Assuming $\rho = \mathtt{send}$, the rule [S-CALL] generates a call event $\mathtt{send.call}(x, h)$, provided x was previously received and has a function contract. (If $\rho = \mathtt{rcv}$ then the dual situation applies.) The [S-RET] rule generates a return event that must return to the top variable on the stack F.

The operation $E \oplus (h : \rho S_1)$ checks if a sent handle h is compatible with the argument contract S_1, and extends the environment E appropriately. Note that the check $run([\![e\ c]\!]) = \mathtt{true}$ ensures that the constant c satisfies the structural contract $\mathit{flat}(e)$.

$$\begin{array}{lcll} E \oplus (c : \rho\, \mathit{flat}(e)) & = & E & \text{provided } run([\![e\ c]\!]) = \mathtt{true} \\ E \oplus (x : \rho S) & = & E, x : \rho S & \end{array}$$

The meaning of a structural contract S is then defined as the set of all traces that first return a handle satisfying S, and where subsequent interactions satisfy the requirements of the EF machine:

$$[\![S]\!] \quad = \quad \{\ \mathtt{send.ret}(\mathit{start}, h).t \mid \langle E_0, \mathit{start}\rangle \Rightarrow^t \langle E, F\rangle\ \}$$
$$\text{where } E_0 = \emptyset \oplus (h : \mathtt{send}\ S)$$

The meaning of a temporal contract R is defined with respect to the environment E that is produced by the EF machine, where E is used to map each variable x in the trace to a name n that is referenced in the temporal contract. The relation $p \sim h$ defines when a pattern p matches a handle h. Constants match constants ($c \sim c$), and the pattern "_" matches any handle ($\_ \sim h$).

$$\begin{array}{rcl} [\![\bullet]\!]_\bullet : R \times E & \rightarrow & \mathcal{P}(\mathit{Trace}) \\ [\![\mathtt{call}(n,p)]\!]_E & = & \{\rho.\mathtt{call}(y,h) \mid E(y) = n : \ldots \text{ and } p \sim h\} \\ [\![\mathtt{ret}(n,p)]\!]_E & = & \{\rho.\mathtt{ret}(y,h) \mid E(y) = n : \ldots \text{ and } p \sim h\} \\ [\![!A]\!]_E & = & \mathit{Event} \setminus [\![A]\!]_E \\ [\![R_1 R_2]\!]_E & = & [\![R_1]\!]_E \cdot [\![R_2]\!]_E \\ [\![R^*]\!]_E & = & [\![R]\!]_E^* \\ [\![\mathtt{not}\ R]\!]_E & = & \text{any trace} \setminus [\![R]\!]_E \\ [\![R_1 \cup R_2]\!]_E & = & [\![R_1]\!]_E \cup [\![R_2]\!]_E \\ [\![\ \ldots\ ]\!]_E & = & \text{any trace} \\ [\![\mathtt{call}(n, ?x)\ R]\!]_E & = & \{\rho.\mathtt{call}(y,c) \cdot t \mid E(y) = n : .., \ t \in [\![R[x := c]]\!]_E\} \\ [\![\mathtt{ret}(n, ?x)\ R]\!]_E & = & \{\rho.\mathtt{ret}(y,c) \cdot t \mid E(y) = n : .., \ t \in [\![R[x := c]]\!]_E\} \end{array}$$

Finally, the meaning of a contract (S `where` R) is defined as any trace that satisfies S, providing a resulting environment E, and where the trace also satisfies R with respect to E. The function $\mathit{prefixes}$ performs prefix-closure on a set of traces.

$$\begin{array}{l} [\![S\ \mathtt{where}\ R]\!] \\ \stackrel{\text{def}}{=} \{\ (\mathtt{send.ret}(\mathit{start}, h) \cdot t) \in \mathit{prefixes}([\![R]\!]_E) \mid \\ \quad \langle E_0, \mathit{start}\rangle \Rightarrow^t \langle E, F\rangle \text{ and } E_0 = \emptyset \oplus (h : \mathtt{send}\ S)\ \} \end{array}$$

Thus, a module e under contract S `where` R yields the trace set:

$$[\![e]\!] \cap [\![S\ \mathtt{where}\ R]\!]$$

7.2 Compiling HOT Contracts

We enforce each contract (S `where` R) by compiling it into an appropriate monitor. We convert the temporal component R into a finite state automaton, where `s` ranges over the state space of the automaton, s_0 denotes the initial state, and the handlers $\mathtt{call}_n$ and $\mathtt{ret}_n$ for each function name n imperatively update `s` appropriately and return `true` if the automaton is in an accepting state and `false` otherwise. The code is roughly:

$$\begin{array}{lcl} \mathtt{let\ s} & = & s_0 \\ \quad \mathtt{call}_n & = & \lambda i. \cdots \text{check and update } \mathtt{s} \text{ appropriately } \cdots \\ \quad \ldots & & \ldots \\ \quad \mathtt{ret}_n & = & \lambda o. \cdots \text{check and update } \mathtt{s} \text{ appropriately } \cdots \\ \quad \ldots & & \ldots \\ \mathtt{in}\ \mathit{compile}(\lambda \mathtt{x.true}, S) & & \end{array}$$

The function $\mathit{compile}(f, S)$ generates a monitor that ensures that the trace satisfies S, and which is parameterized over a number of $\mathtt{call}_n$ and $\mathtt{ret}_n$ functions that communicate to the temporal code above. The additional argument

$$f : (\mathit{Constant} \cup \{\lambda \mathtt{x.x}\} \mapsto \mathit{Bool})$$

is an "observer function" that is called and can signal an error whenever a value passes through this S boundary; it is used in the following recursive definition of $\mathit{compile}$.

$$\mathit{compile} : (\mathit{Constant} \cup \{\lambda \mathtt{x.x}\} \mapsto \mathit{Bool}) \times S \mapsto \mathit{Monitor}$$

```
compile(f, flat(e)) ≝
  pair (λx. (e x) && (f x))
       (λ.  false)
compile(f, n:S1 ↦ S2) ≝
  pair (λx. false)
       (λ.  (f (λx.x)) && (pair compile(call_n, S1)
                                compile(ret_n,  S2)))
compile(f, y) ≝
  let (chkconst,chkfn) = y
  pair (λx. (f x)       && (chkconst x))
       (λ.  (f (λx.x)) && (chkfn()))
```

For the contract $\mathit{flat}(e)$, the generated monitor accepts only constants; it checks that the constant satisfies both the observer function f and the predicate e. For the function contract $n : S_1 \mapsto S_2$, the generated monitor accepts only functions. It immediately notifies the observer that a function is passing through this contract, and then returns a pair of monitors that monitor calls and returns of this function, in each case notifying $\mathtt{call}_n$ or $\mathtt{ret}_n$ and enforcing the sub-contracts S_1 or S_2, as appropriate.

Our implementation extends the structural contract language to include variable references (y) for referring to predefined monitors such as the `Any` monitor defined in section 5.1. The compilation of such monitor references extends the referenced monitor to call the observer function f appropriately.

Compilation Correctness The $\mathit{compile}$ function compiles a structural contract S into a monitor in a manner than respects the intended meaning $[\![S]\!]$ of the structural contract.

THEOREM 3 (Compilation Correctness). *For any structural contract* S, $[\![S]\!] = [\![\mathtt{guard}\ \mathit{compile}(\lambda \mathtt{x.true}, S)]\!]$.

PROOF SKETCH: We proceed by structural induction on S.

In the case that $S = \mathit{flat}(e)$: we substitute into the theorem, then focus on the right-hand side. We expand the definition of $\mathit{compile}$ and do beta reduction. The application of `(`f `x)` in the definition reduces to true with the given f, so we remove it and the *and*-expression. This and an application of eta produces the right-hand side: $[\![\mathtt{guard}\ (\mathtt{pair}\ e\ (\lambda.\mathtt{false}))]\!]$. If we expand this application of guard, it only succeeds if the value sent to the contract is a constant, c, such that $(e\ c)$ evaluates to true. We now focus on the left-hand side. By expanding the definition of $[\![S]\!]$ and $\oplus$, we get the condition that $run([\![e\ c]\!]) = \texttt{true}$ where c is the constant sent to the contract. Clearly these two constraints are the same, so this case is completed.

In the case that $S = n : S_1 \mapsto S_2$, we use the inductive hypothesis twice. However, getting to that point requires a few subtle steps. First, we assume that $\texttt{call}_n$ and $\texttt{ret}_n$ are $\lambda\texttt{x.true}$ for all n, since we are only considering structural contracts, so there are no temporal properties to enforce. Next, we consider the behavior of both sides after it has been applied. Only the case where it is actually a function is relevant, because if it is a constant, both trivially reject any subsequent events. After assuming we've received a function, we then assume that the function is called and returns. The contracts S_1 and S_2 protect the call and return through the S-CALL and S-RET rules on the left and through the recursive calls to guard on the right—and the inductive hypothesis ensures that these have identical semantics. □

Compiling Dependent Sequences For dependent sequences, we follow the same general approach, except we cannot compile to a finite state automaton. For example, the constraint

```
not ... call(free,?z) !ret(alloc,z)* call(free,z)
```

requires unbound storage to record all freed locations z. Instead, we compile to a lazily constructed infinite automaton. Each automaton is a function from an event (call or return) to a next automaton—as well as a boolean to encode acceptance. Event patterns are functions that return the epsilon automaton on matching and a null (rejecting) automaton otherwise. In contrast, dependent sequences return a new automaton representing the rest of the trace, and which includes an appropriate binding for the dependent variable z.

Each of the regular grammar operators (sequencing, complement, etc) is implemented as an explicit automaton that simulates the operator using the automaton functions representing its pieces. These implementations correspond precisely to the intuitive explanations of regular operator closure properties found in any textbook on automata theory. Since Kleene star and sequencing may invoke their arguments multiple times, dependent sequences embedded in them will be duplicated for each successful match of the pattern. This approach is similar to regular expression derivatives [9, 38].

7.3 Examples

Section 2 presented a variety of examples of structural/temporal contracts, whose meaning and compilation can now be understood based on the formalism of this section. In particular, the contract combinator "Pair S_1 S_2" abbreviates the contract for Church-encoded pairs "$(S_1 \to S_2 \to \texttt{Any}) \to \texttt{Any}$", and generalizes to a Record combinator that supports n-ary tuples.

The specification of temporal properties involves some subtleties, which we illustrate by considering various contracts for a lock object with acquire and release methods. Our initial contract states that acquire and release are atomic, and calls must alternate between these functions, with acquire being called first.

```
LockContract =
  Record acquire : Unit → Unit
         release : Unit → Unit
  where ( call(acquire,_) ret(acquire,_)
          call(release,_) ret(release,_) )*
```

This contract states the "good" behavior of this module. This kind of specification is not *stable under extension*, since adding and calling other methods from this module would violate this contract.

It is often safer to enumerate "bad" behavior, so that all unmentioned good behavior is allowed—including good behavior not yet implemented. The following contract reads, "Do not call acquire twice without an interleaving release, and do not call release twice without an interleaving acquire."

```
where not ... call(acquire,_)
              !call(release,_)* call(acquire,_)
  and not ... call(release,_)
              !call(acquire,_)* call(release,_)
```

We must include the initial "..." in the negations, because otherwise we are only disallowing traces that *start* with the illegal sequence.

Unfortunately, this contract does not specify that acquire must be called first. We rephrase the property as "After calling acquire, you may not call it again until you call release, after which you may not call release and so on.":

```
where ( call(acquire,_) !call(acquire,_)*
        call(release,_) !call(release,_)* )*
```

This version is extensible, because our use of event negation matches functions that have yet to be written. Unfortunately, it constrains future versions of the module so that acquire must be the first call. If we simply rotate the sequence, we avoid that problem:

```
where ( !call(release,_)*  call(acquire,_)
        !call(acquire,_)*  call(release,_) )*
```

This version reads, "It is illegal to call release until you acquire, and you may not call acquire twice before calling release." Note that this specification constrains only the client, not the lock object itself. We conjoin the following atomicity requirement to complete our specification.

```
and not ... call(acquire,_) !ret(acquire,_)
and not ... call(release,_) !ret(release,_)
```

8. Implementation

Our presentation so far addresses an idealized language. To evaluate this approach in practice, we have extended and implemented this design for the Racket programing language [22]. Our implementation includes both the programmatic monitor interface from Section 5 and the declarative HOT contract language of Section 7.

Guard/Monitor Implementation Racket already provide a higher-order contract system with a variety of contract combinators that have been widely used to document Racket's libraries, but which do not support temporal properties directly.

Racket also provides a programmatic make-contract interface, which creates a contract from a user-provided *projection function* e_{proj} that is expected to satisfy the requirement $[\![e_{proj}]\!] \subseteq [\![\lambda x.\, x]\!]$ (ignoring blame issues for simplicity). Since make-contract does not check that e_{proj} is actually a projection, it cannot guarantee non-interference.

Our implementation uses this make-contract interface as a foundation on which to implement our guard/monitor architecture. This design allows monitors to interoperate with the Racket language and to annotate module boundaries, while also guaranteeing non-interference.

Our implementation addresses a number of additional issues not considered in the λ-caculus model. For example, the presence of first-class continuations allows functions to return multiple times, or never return, and so the resulting event traces do not satisfy the well-bracketed property. In order to properly match calls and returns, call events include a unique label, which is then repeated in each matching return event. The implementation works seamlessly with mutation, allowing monitors to interpose between accesses and updates to mutable structures—which are just differently-labeled events in the trace grammar. The implementation's monitors are safe with respect to concurrent interaction via a kill-safe manager thread [21].

Declarative Contract Implementation Our HOT contract language and implementation are almost exactly as described in section 7.2, although the implementation is more general. In particular, as well as the structural contract forms of section 7.2, it also accepts Racket's previous non-temporal contract language (where these contracts do not produce events for the temporal portion).

We also provide a facility for defining macros to abbreviate common temporal constraints, such as the following atomic and transient macros. A function is *atomic* if it returns immediately after it is called, with no intermediate interactions that are visible to the contract; meaning no interactions to explicitly labeled functions, since we do not do deep-tracing by default:

$$\texttt{atomic(f)} \stackrel{\text{def}}{=} \texttt{not ... call(f,\_) !ret(f,\_)}$$

A higher-order argument `g` is *transient* when passed to a function `f` if `g` can only be called before `f` returns—that is, `f` does not get a permanent capability to call `g`, but only a transient capability.

$$\texttt{transient(g,f)} \stackrel{\text{def}}{=} \texttt{not ... ret(f,\_) ... call(g,\_)}$$

The syntax $R_1 \cap R_2$ is introduced via a macro that expands to $\texttt{not}\,(\texttt{not}\,R_1) \cup (\texttt{not}\,R_2)$. Other macros including optional events, bounded-length sequences, etc.

Performance Evaluation The performance overhead of contracts depends critically on the amount of work performed by the application within a contract boundary. To avoid this application dependence, we compared the performance of temporal contracts with Racket's current contract system using the following microbenchmark. We applied a contract to the identity function that checks for integer arguments and results. The following results measure the time to call the resulting function 10^6 times, under three different contract implementations:

- 870ms for Racket's current contract system.
- 877ms for the new monitor interface.
- 854ms for the HOT contract language.

The results demonstrate that, when the additional expressiveness of temporal contracts is not used, our proposed contract system provides equivalent performance to Racket's current non-temporal contract implementation. Furthermore, both the programmatic monitor interface and the HOT contract language provide equivalent performance.

We investigated the overhead of temporal constraints by extending the contract to check that the called function is atomic. The resulting performance numbers are:

- 931ms for the new monitor interface when enforcing atomicity.
- 1435ms for the HOT contract language when enforcing atomicity, using an optimized implementation that does not support dependent sequencing.
- 2371ms for the HOT contract language when enforcing atomicity, using a more general implementation that supports dependent sequencing.

These results indicate that the monitor architecture provides an efficient mechanism for enforcing simple temporal properties with little additional overhead.

Our current implementation of temporal automata for the HOT contract language is quite general and so a little slow. Restricting temporal constraints to disallow dependent sequences improves performance significantly, and we conjecture that other plausible optimizations could achieve performance comparable to the monitor-based implementation. In theory, it should be possible to optimize HOT contract patterns to the equivalent hand-coded monitor, at least for common specifications such as atomicity, but this remains for future work.

Monitoring Filesystem Accesses Experience with Racket's current contract system indicate its overhead is quite adequate for monitoring the vast majority of APIs, where the work inside the contract boundary dominates the contract overhead, and so contracts have little impact on performance. We conjecture that many temporal contracts would similarly have no performance impact. To evaluate this hypothesis, we modified a GUI text editor to use a temporal contract to monitor its filesystem accesses. As expected, we found no change in the user experience – in particular, the difference in overall application runtime was unmeasurable in benchmarking runs.

Temporal Contracts for the Standard Library We conducted a study of 600 functions in the Racket standard library to determine how many of these function could benefit from temporal contracts. We found that:

- 519 functions in the standard library are intended to be atomic. For example, the `number?` predicate may be passed a function argument, but it is not permitted to call this argument; instead it should immediately return a boolean result.
- 51 library function are passed *transient* function arguments that the library may call, but only before the library function returns. Examples include `map`, `build-list`, `filter`. None of these library functions are allowed to retain a reference to the argument function after the library function returns.
- 17 library function exhibit the opposite behavior, where they are passed function arguments that should *not* be called *until* the library function returns. These are `in-port`, `in-producer`, `stop-before`, `stop-after`, `make-do-sequence`, `make-custom-hash`, `make-immutable-custom-hash`, `make-weak-custom-hash`, `compose`, `procedure-rename`, `procedure->method`, `procedure-reduce-arity`, `make-keyword-procedure`, `procedure-reduce-keyword-arity`, `negate`, `curry`, `curryr`.
- The remaining 13 library functions have quite unconstrained behavior. Examples include `apply`, `keyword-apply`, and 11 "sequence" functions that may cause additional function calls (because inspecting a sequence can cause lazy code evaluation across a module boundary.)

Note that the issue of *when* a function is called, that is addressed in these temporal specifications, is much more critical in a language with imperative state and reactive behavior than in a purely function language, and our work proposes a means to specify and enforce these temporal aspects of behavior.

Adversarial Defense The contract examples presented so far are useful for identifying and localizing defects in well-intentioned but perhaps buggy code. Contracts are also valuable for enforcing properties at trust boundaries between modules written by different principals.

As an example, we developed an implementation of Tic-tac-toe with adversarial players, where each player provides a function

$$\texttt{turn} : \texttt{Board} \rightarrow \texttt{Board}$$

Here, `Board` is an abstract data type that provides `board-get` and `board-set` methods, and each player's `turn` function is supposed to update the Board by placing an additional mark. The core of the game places complete confidence in the players to follow the rules—namely that they must only take one move and they cannot place their mark over the other player's mark—and this assumption greatly simplifies the implementation of the game core.

Of course, this confidence in each player's code may be misplaced, due to unintentional bugs as well as intentional violations of the game rules. To make each untrusted turn function trustworthy, it is monitored by a temporal contract. For example, the following contract states that a turn may not contain two calls to board-set.

```
not ... call(board-set,_,_,_,_) !ret(turn,_,_,_)*
        call(board-set,_,_,_,_)
```

Additionally, the board should not observe the same row and column of the board being set twice (by either player) during a game.[6]

```
not ... call(board-set,_,?r,?c,_) !ret(game,_)*
        call(board-set,_, r, c,_)
```

To evaluate this architecture, we wrote a collection of player functions, including textual and graphical interactive players, non-cheating AI players, and cheating AI players. In all cases, the contracts behave as expected—they catch all cheaters, both human and AI.

Note that the game core consists entirely of calls to contracted functions. To evaluate the performance overhead, we measured the time to play a 7 move game between two deterministic non-cheating AI players, both with and without the temporal contracts. The average running time of 100 runs is:

- 247ms for the version without contracts, and
- 255ms for the version with contracts.

This example demonstrates a key software engineering benefit of HOT contracts: the game model can be decoupled from the security policy, simplifying both in the process, while imposing minimal performance overhead in this case study.

9. Related Work

Temporal Constraints Temporal constraints are widely understood to be important aspects on a module's behavior, and prior work has eloquently argued for modeling software modules as players in a formal game [12, 13]. Our event sequences are analogous to the *interface automata* of prior work, and extend those ideas to handle higher-order languages by introducing the notions of variable binding and scope in event sequences. It also addresses dynamic enforcement rather than static verification.

Runtime Verification Much prior work has addressed runtime monitoring of system behaviors. The MOP Framework [33] provides a general runtime monitoring framework that supports multiple languages and logics. Aspect-Oriented Programming [29] is a technique for *weaving* into an existing program additional functionality, including contract checks on module boundaries. AOP has been used in tools that enforce temporal properties specified in LTL, such as Tracematches [39] and J-LO [8]. In other approaches, runtime monitors are synthesized from formal specifications, for example in PathExplorer [25], Eagle [6], and RuleR [7]. Program Trace Query Language (PTQL) [23] expresses temporal properties as SQL-like queries over program traces. Generally speaking, these approaches focus on temporal properties and do not provide explicit support for higher-order functions.

[6] Alternatively, this property could be enforced by a contract that calls board-get instead of keeping history information, but that specification does not guarantee non-interference.

Behavioral Contracts Meyer [34, 35, 36] introduced contracts with Eiffel and its contract-oriented design approach. Since then contracts have been used to extend static checking [14, 5] and for runtime monitoring of higher-order programs [18]. These investigations have progressed towards more expressive *dependent contracts* [18, 31, 24, 15]. In contrast, our work moves contract expressiveness in a different—orthogonal—direction where contracts enforce temporal properties.

Our work explicitly enforces that contracts can only observe, but not influence, execution (apart from stopping execution on contract violations). Prior work on dependent contracts has been more lax in this regard, including allowing dependent function contracts to observe the argument value, and even call that value in cases where it is a function [18, 31]. This interpretation of "contracts as code" eventually requires that each contract is considered an additional module in the system, with its own blame label [15].

Our usage of the flexibility of Racket contracts to enforce temporal constraints is unique[7], except in one case: Tov and Pucella [43] implement a contract for affine functions. Of course, affine-ness—allowing at most a single call—is a temporal property that is trivially encoded in our DSL. Their implementation approach is neceassarily similar to ours, although it is clearly limited to a single temporal property.

Game Semantics Much prior work has studied the denotational semantics of higher-order languages, often with the goal of developing fully abstract denotational semantics in which observable equivalence implies denotational equivalence. Game semantics has emerged as an appealing foundation for developing fully abstract denotational models. For example, fully abstract game semantics have been developed for PCF [3, 27] or for languages with features such as call-by-value [4], general references [2], and exceptions [11, 30], to name just a few. Compositional game semantics also facilitate compositional verification [1]. Our work draws deeply on game semantics as a tool to study contract systems and module behavior, but follows a different development that starts with the CSI machine, which provides a connection between operational semantics and game semantics.

10. Discussion and Future Work

We have presented a programmatic monitor architecture for contracts that satisfies the twin goals of trace completeness (all computable, prefix-closed contracts are expressible) and non-interference (contracts cannot influence correct executions). The architecture also provides precise blame assignment, even for complex temporal properties.

Additionally, we presented a declarative contract language that can express a variety of temporal constraints on module behavior that are common in software systems with imperative state, but they are often left undocumented. Our contract language provides a convenient declarative means for explicating these temporal aspects of library interfaces.

We have formalized our ideas in the context of an untyped language that supports rich interactions between modules, including mutual recursion, higher-order functions and callbacks, and both encapsulated and shared imperative state. Extending these ideas to additional language features is an important topic for future work. For compound data structures such as lists or arrays, contracts could be enforced eagerly (as with constants) or lazily (as with functions). In this work, compound data structures are Church-encoded as functions and so checked lazily, but eager checking is an interesting alternative. Other topics for future work include the de-

[7] Based on a search on the publically available Racket code: the core distribution and an online package repository.

velopment of temporal contracts for typed languages and the study of temporal higher-order contracts in a concurrent setting.

Acknowledgements We thank Shriram Krishnamurthi and Michael Greenberg for valuable comments on an earlier draft of this paper, Robby Findler for helpful discussions on temporal contracts, and Matthias Felleisen for exploring temporal contracts for game policy enforcement. We are also grateful to the anonymous reviewers of ICFP 2011 for their constructive feedback. This material is based upon work supported by the National Science Foundation under Grants 1016334 and 0905650.

References

[1] Samson Abramsky, Dan R. Ghica, Andrzej S. Murawski, and C.-H. Luke Ong. Applying game semantics to compositional software modeling and verification. In *TACAS*, pages 421–435, 2004.

[2] Samson Abramsky, Kohei Honda, and Guy McCusker. A fully abstract game semantics for general references. In *LICS*, pages 334–344, 1998.

[3] Samson Abramsky, Radha Jagadeesan, and Pasquale Malacaria. Full abstraction for PCF. *Information and Computation*, 163:409–470, 1996.

[4] Samson Abramsky and Guy McCusker. Call-by-value games. In *CSL*, pages 1–17, 1997.

[5] Mike Barnett, K. Rustan M. Leino, and Wolfram Schulte. The Spec# programming system: An overview. In *Construction and Analysis of Safe, Secure and Interoperable Smart Devices*, pages 49–69, 2004.

[6] Howard Barringer, Allen Goldberg, Klaus Havelund, and Koushik Sen. Rule-based runtime verification. In *VMCAI*, pages 44–57, 2004.

[7] Howard Barringer, David Rydeheard, and Klaus Havelund. Rule Systems for Run-time Monitoring: from EAGLE to RULER. *J Logic Computation*, November 2008.

[8] Eric Bodden. J-LO - A tool for runtime-checking temporal assertions. Diploma thesis, RWTH Aachen University, November 2005.

[9] Janusz A. Brzozowski. Derivatives of regular expressions. *J. ACM*, 11:481–494, October 1964.

[10] Manuela Carrillo-Castellon, Jesús García Molina, Ernesto Pimentel, and Israel Repiso. Design by contract in smalltalk. *JOOP*, 9(7):23–28, 1996.

[11] Robert Cartwright, Pierre-Louis Curien, and Matthias Felleisen. Fully abstract semantics for observably sequential languages. *Inf. Comput.*, 111(2):297–401, 1994.

[12] Luca de Alfaro and Thomas A. Henzinger. Interface automata. In *Foundations of Software Engineering*, pages 109–120, 2001.

[13] Luca de Alfaro and Mariëlle Stoelinga. Interfaces: A game-theoretic framework for reasoning about component-based systems. *Electr. Notes Theor. Comput. Sci.*, 97:3–23, 2004.

[14] David L. Detlefs, K. Rustan M. Leino, Greg Nelson, and James B. Saxe. Extended static checking. Research Report 159, Compaq Systems Research Center, December 1998.

[15] C. Dimoulas, R. Findler, C. Flanagan, and M. Felleisen. Correct blame for contracts: No more scapegoating. In *POPL*, 2011.

[16] Matthias Felleisen, Robert Bruce Findler, and Matthew Flatt. *Semantics Engineering with PLT Redex*. The MIT Press, 1st edition, 2009.

[17] Matthias Felleisen and Daniel P. Friedman. A calculus for assignments in higher-order languages. In *POPL*, pages 314–325, 1987.

[18] R. Findler and M. Felleisen. Contracts for higher-order functions. In *ICFP*, 2002.

[19] Robert Findler and Matthias Blume. Contracts as pairs of projections. *Functional and Logic Programming*, pages 226–241, 2006.

[20] Robert Bruce Findler, Matthias Blume, and Matthias Felleisen. An investigation of contracts as projections. Technical report, University of Chicago, 2004.

[21] Matthew Flatt and Robert Bruce Findler. Kill-safe synchronization abstractions. In *Programming Language Design and Implementation*, pages 47–58, 2004.

[22] Matthew Flatt and PLT. Reference: Racket. Technical Report PLT-TR-2010-1, PLT Inc., 2010. `http://racket-lang.org/tr1/`.

[23] Simon F. Goldsmith, Robert O'Callahan, and Alex Aiken. Relational queries over program traces. OOPSLA, pages 385–402, 2005.

[24] Michael Greenberg, Benjamin C. Pierce, and Stephanie Weirich. Contracts made manifest. In *POPL*, 2010.

[25] Klaus Havelund and Grigore Rosu. An overview of the runtime verification tool Java PathExplorer. In *Formal Methods in System Design*, 2003.

[26] Ralf Hinze, Johan Jeuring, and Andres Löh. Typed contracts for functional programming. In *Functional and Logic Programming (FLOPS)*, pages 208–225. Springer-Verlag, 2006.

[27] J. M. E. Hyland and C.-H. Luke Ong. On full abstraction for PCF: I, II, and III. *Inf. Comput.*, 163(2):285–408, 2000.

[28] Murat Karaorman, Urs Hölzle, and John Bruno. jContractor: A reflective Java library to support design by contract, 1998.

[29] Gregor Kiczales, John Lamping, Anurag Mendhekar, Chris Maeda, Cristina Lopes, Jean-Marc Loingtier, and John Irwin. Aspect-oriented programming. In *ECOOP*, chapter 10, pages 220–242. 1997.

[30] J. Laird. A fully abstract game semantics of local exceptions. In *Logic in Computer Science*, Washington, DC, USA, 2001.

[31] Blume Matthias and David McAllester. Sound and complete models of contracts. *J. Funct. Program.*, 16:375–414, July 2006.

[32] K McFarlane. Design by contract framework.

[33] Patrick O'Neil Meredith, Dongyun Jin, Dennis Griffith, Feng Chen, and Grigore Roşu. An overview of the MOP runtime verification framework. *International Journal on Software Techniques for Technology Transfer*, 2011. to appear.

[34] B. Meyer. *Object-oriented Software Construction*. Prentice-Hall, 1988.

[35] B. Meyer. Design by contract. In *Advances in Object-Oriented Software Engineering*, pages 1–50. Prentice-Hall, 1991.

[36] B. Meyer. *Eiffel: The Language*. Prentice-Hall, 1992.

[37] Mark Samuel Miller. *Robust composition: towards a unified approach to access control and concurrency control*. PhD thesis, Johns Hopkins University, Baltimore, MD, USA, 2006.

[38] Scott Owens, John Reppy, and Aaron Turon. Regular-expression derivatives re-examined. *J. Funct. Program.*, 19:173–190, March 2009.

[39] Chris Allan Pavel, Chris Allan, Pavel Avgustinov, Aske Simon Christensen, Laurie Hendren, Sascha Kuzins, Oege De Moor, Damien Sereni, Ganesh Sittampalam, and Julian Tibble. Adding trace matching with free variables to AspectJ. In *OOPSLA*, pages 345–364. ACM Press, 2005.

[40] Amir Pnueli. The temporal logic of programs. In *Foundations of Computer Science*, pages 46–57, 1977.

[41] John C. Reynolds. *The essence of ALGOL*, pages 67–88. Birkhauser Boston Inc., Cambridge, MA, USA, 1997.

[42] David S. Rosenblum. A practical approach to programming with assertions. *IEEE Transactions on Software Engineering*, 21, 1995.

[43] Jesse Tov and Riccardo Pucella. Stateful contracts for affine types. *Programming Languages and Systems*, pages 550–569, 2010.

[44] T. Tuglular, C. A. Muftuoglu, F. Belli, and M. Linschulte. Event-based input validation using design-by-contract patterns. In *Software Reliability Engineering*, pages 195–204, 2009.

[45] Dana N. Xu, Simon L. Peyton Jones, and Koen Claessen. Static contract checking for Haskell. In *POPL*, pages 41–52, 2009.

Parsing with Derivatives

A Functional Pearl

Matthew Might David Darais
University of Utah
might@cs.utah.edu, david.darais@gmail.com

Daniel Spiewak
University of Wisconsin, Milwaukee
dspiewak@uwm.edu

Abstract

We present a functional approach to parsing unrestricted context-free grammars based on Brzozowski's derivative of regular expressions. If we consider context-free grammars as recursive regular expressions, Brzozowski's equational theory extends without modification to context-free grammars (and it generalizes to parser combinators). The supporting actors in this story are three concepts familiar to functional programmers—laziness, memoization and fixed points; these allow Brzozowski's original equations to be transliterated into purely functional code in about 30 lines spread over three functions.

Yet, this almost impossibly brief implementation has a drawback: its performance is sour—in both theory *and* practice. The culprit? Each derivative can *double* the size of a grammar, and with it, the cost of the next derivative.

Fortunately, much of the new structure inflicted by the derivative is either dead on arrival, or it dies after the very next derivative. To eliminate it, we once again exploit laziness and memoization to transliterate an equational theory that prunes such debris into working code. Thanks to this compaction, parsing times become reasonable in practice.

We equip the functional programmer with two equational theories that, when combined, make for an abbreviated understanding and implementation of a system for parsing context-free languages.

Categories and Subject Descriptors F.4.3 [*Formal Languages*]: Operations on languages

General Terms Algorithms, Languages, Theory

Keywords formal languages, parsing, derivative, regular expressions, context-free grammar, parser combinator

1. Introduction

It is easy to lose sight of the essence of parsing in the minutiae of forbidden grammars, shift-reduce conflicts and opaque action tables. To the extent that understanding in computer science comes from implementation, a deeper appreciation of parsing often seems out of reach. Brzozowski's derivative upsets this calculus of effort and understanding to make the construction of parsing systems accessible to the common functional programmer.

ICFP'11, September 19–21, 2011, Tokyo, Japan.

The derivative of regular expressions [1], if gently tempered with laziness, memoization and fixed points, acts immediately as a pure, functional technique for generating parse forests from arbitrary context-free grammars. Despite—even because of—its simplicity, the derivative transparently handles ambiguity, left-recursion, right-recursion, ill-founded recursion or any combination thereof.

1.1 Outline

- After a review of formal languages, we introduce Brzozowski's derivative for regular languages. A brief implementation highlights its rugged elegance.
- As our implementation of the derivative engages context-free languages, non-termination emerges as a problem.
- Three small, surgical modifications to the implementation (but not the theory)—laziness, memoization and fixed points—guarantee termination. Termination means the derivative can recognize arbitrary context-free languages.
- We generalize the derivative to parsers and parser combinators through an equational theory for generating parse forests.
- We find poor performance in both theory and practice. The root cause is vestigial structure left in the grammar by earlier derivatives; this structure is malignant: though it no longer serves a purpose, it still grows in size with each derivative.
- We develop an optimization—compaction—that collapses grammars by excising this mass. Compaction, like the derivative, comes from a clean, equational theory that exploits laziness and memoization in its transliteration to working code.

In this article, we provide code in Racket, but it should adapt readily to any Lisp. All code and test cases within or referenced from this article (plus additional implementations in Haskell and Scala) are available from:

`http://www.ucombinator.org/projects/parsing/`

2. Preliminary: Formal languages

A language L is a set of strings. A string w is a sequence of characters from an alphabet A. (From the parser's perspective, a "character" might be a token/terminal.)

Two atomic languages arise often in formal languages: the empty language and the null (or empty-string) language:

- The empty language $\emptyset$ contains no strings at all:
$$\emptyset = \{\}.$$
- The null language ϵ contains only the length-zero "null" string:
$$\epsilon = \{w\} \text{ where } \mathit{length}(w) = 0.$$

Or, using C notation for strings, $\epsilon = \{""\}$. For convenience, we may use the symbol ϵ to refer to both the null language and the null string.

Given an alphabet A, there is a singleton language for every character c in that alphabet. Where it is clear from context, we use the character itself to denote that language; that is:

$$c \equiv \{c\}.$$

2.1 Operations on languages

Because languages are sets, set operations like union apply:

$$\{\texttt{foo}\} \cup \{\texttt{bar}, \texttt{baz}\} = \{\texttt{foo}, \texttt{bar}, \texttt{baz}\}.$$

Concatenation ($\circ$) appends the product of the two languages:

$$L_1 \circ L_2 = \{w_1 w_2 : w_1 \in L_1 \text{ and } w_2 \in L_2\}.$$

The nth power of a language is the set of strings of n consecutive words from that language:

$$L^n = \{w_1 w_2 \ldots w_n : w_i \in L \text{ for } 1 \le i \le n\}.$$

And, the non-empty repetition of a language (its Kleene star) is the infinite union of all its powers:

$$L^\star = \bigcup_{i=0}^{\infty} L^i.$$

2.2 Regular languages and context-free languages

If a language is non-recursively definable from atomic sets using only union, concatenation and repetition, that language is regular.

If we allow mutually recursive definitions, then the set of describable languages is exactly the set of context-free languages. (Even without Kleene star, the resulting set of languages is context-free.) We assume, of course, a least-fixed-point interpretation of such recursive structure. For instance, given the language L:

$$L = (\{\texttt{x}\} \circ L) \cup \epsilon.$$

The least-fixed-point interpretation of L is a set containing a finite string of every length (plus the null string). Every string contains only the character x. [The greatest-fixed-point interpretation of L adds an infinite string of x's.]

2.3 Encoding languages

To represent the atomic and complex languages in code, there is a `struct` for each kind of language:

```
(define-struct empty {})          ; ∅
(define-struct eps   {})          ; ϵ
(define-struct char  {value})

(define-struct cat {left right}) ; left ∘ right
(define-struct alt {this that})  ; this ∪ that
(define-struct rep {lang})       ; lang⋆
```

Example In code, the language:

$$L_{ab} = L_{ab} \circ \{\texttt{a}, \texttt{b}\}$$
$$\cup\, \epsilon,$$

becomes:

```
(define L (alt (cat L (alt (char 'a) (char 'b)))
               (eps)))
```

3. Brzozowski's derivative

Brzozowski defined the derivative of regular expressions in his work on the recognition of regular languages [1]. The derivative of a language L with respect to a character c is a new language that has been "filtered" and "chopped"—$D_c(L)$:

1. First, retain only the strings that start with the character c.
2. Second, chop that first character off every string.

Formally:

$$D_c(L) = \{w : cw \in L\}.$$

Examples

$$D_{\texttt{b}}\{\texttt{foo}, \texttt{bar}, \texttt{baz}\} = \{\texttt{ar}, \texttt{az}\}$$
$$D_{\texttt{f}}\{\texttt{foo}, \texttt{bar}, \texttt{baz}\} = \{\texttt{oo}\}$$
$$D_{\texttt{a}}\{\texttt{foo}, \texttt{bar}, \texttt{baz}\} = \emptyset.$$

3.1 Recognition with the derivative

The simplicity of the derivative's definition masks its power. If one can compute successive derivatives of a language, it is straightforward to determine the membership of a string within a language, thanks to the following property:

$$cw \in L \text{ iff } w \in D_c(L).$$

To determine membership, derive a language with respect to each character, and check if the final language contains the null string: if yes, the original string was in; if not, it wasn't.

3.2 A recursive definition of the derivative

Brzozowski noted that the derivative is closed over regular languages, and admits a recursive implementation:

- For the atomic languages:

$$D_c(\emptyset) = \emptyset$$
$$D_c(\epsilon) = \emptyset$$
$$D_c(c) = \epsilon$$
$$D_c(c') = \emptyset \text{ if } c \neq c'.$$

- For the derivative over union:

$$D_c(L_1 \cup L_2) = D_c(L_1) \cup D_c(L_2).$$

- The derivative over Kleene star peels off a copy of the language:

$$D_c(L^\star) = D_c(L) \circ L^\star.$$

- For the derivative of concatenation, we must consider the possibility that the first language could be null:

$$D_c(L_1 \circ L_2) = D_c(L_1) \circ L_2 \text{ if } \epsilon \notin L_1$$
$$D_c(L_1 \circ L_2) = (D_c(L_1) \circ L_2) \cup D_c(L_2) \text{ if } \epsilon \in L_1$$

We can express concatenation without a conditional through the nullability function: δ. This function returns the null language if its input language contains the null string, and the empty set otherwise:

$$\delta(L) = \emptyset \text{ if } \epsilon \notin L$$
$$\delta(L) = \epsilon \text{ if } \epsilon \in L.$$

Thus, we can equivalently define concatenation:

$$D_c(L_1 \circ L_2) = (D_c(L_1) \circ L_2) \cup (\delta(L_1) \circ D_c(L_2)).$$

3.3 Nullability of regular languages

Conveniently, nullability may also be computed using structural recursion on regular languages:

$$\begin{aligned}
\delta(\emptyset) &= \emptyset \\
\delta(\epsilon) &= \epsilon \\
\delta(c) &= \emptyset \\
\delta(L_1 \cup L_2) &= \delta(L_1) \cup \delta(L_2) \\
\delta(L_1 \circ L_2) &= \delta(L_1) \circ \delta(L_2) \\
\delta(L^{\star}) &= \epsilon.
\end{aligned}$$

A recursive implementation of the Boolean variant of the nullability function is straightforward:

```
(define (δ L)
  (match L
    [(empty)       #f]
    [(eps)         #t]
    [(char _)      #f]

    [(rep _)       #t]
    [(alt L1 L2)   (or  (δ L1) (δ L2))]
    [(cat L1 L2)   (and (δ L1) (δ L2))]))
```

Examples A couple examples illustrate the derivative on regular languages:

$$D_{\texttt{f}}\,\{\texttt{foo},\texttt{bar}\}^{\star} = \{\texttt{oo}\} \circ \{\texttt{foo},\texttt{bar}\}^{\star}$$

$$D_{\texttt{f}}\,\{\texttt{foo},\texttt{bar}\}^{\star} \circ \{\texttt{frak}\} = \{\texttt{oo}\} \circ \{\texttt{foo},\texttt{bar}\}^{\star} \circ \{\texttt{frak}\} \cup \{\texttt{rak}\}.$$

3.4 An implementation of the derivative

As the description of a regular language is not recursive, it is straightforward to transliterate the derivative into working code:

```
(define (D c L)
  (match L
    [(empty)       (empty)]
    [(eps)         (empty)]
    [(char a)      (if (equal? c a)
                       (eps)
                       (empty))]

    [(alt L1 L2)   (alt (D c L1)
                        (D c L2))]
    [(cat (and (? δ) L1) L2)
                   (alt (D c L2)
                        (cat (D c L1) L2))]
    [(cat L1 L2)   (cat (D c L1) L2)]
    [(rep L1)      (cat (D c L1) L)]))
```

Matching a regular language `L` against a `consed` list of characters `w` is straightforward:

```
(define (matches? w L)
  (if (null? w)
      (δ L)
      (matches? (cdr w) (D (car w) L))))
```

4. Derivatives of context-free languages

Since a context-free language is a recursive regular language, it is tempting to use the same code for computing the derivative. From the perspective of parsing, this has two chief drawbacks:

1. It doesn't work.
2. It wouldn't produce a parse forest even if it did.

The first problem comes from the recursive implementation of the derivative running into the recursive nature of context-free grammars. It leads to non-termination.

The second comes from the fact that our regular implementation *recognizes* whether a string is in a language rather than parsing the string. We tackle the termination problem in this section, and the parsing problem in the next.

Example Consider the following left-recursive language:

$$\begin{aligned}
L &= L \circ \{\texttt{x}\} \\
&\cup \epsilon.
\end{aligned}$$

If we take the derivative of L, we get a new language:

$$\begin{aligned}
D_{\texttt{x}}L &= D_{\texttt{x}}L \circ \{\texttt{x}\} \\
&\cup \epsilon.
\end{aligned}$$

Mathematically, this is sensible. Computationally, it is not. The code from the previous section recurs forever as it attempts to compute the derivative of the language L.

4.1 Step 1: Laziness

Preventing the implementation of the derivative from making an infinite descent on a recursive grammar requires targeted laziness. Specifically, it requires making the fields of the structs `cat`, `alt` and `rep` by-need.[1] With by-need fields, the computation of any (potentially self-referential) derivatives in those fields gets suspended until the values in those fields are required.

4.2 Step 2: Memoization

With laziness, we can compute the derivative until it requires nullability (as in concatenation or testing membership). Nullability eagerly walks the structure of the entire language. Thus, nullability fails to terminate on a derived language such as the one above. We need the derivative to return a finite (if lazily explored) graph. By memoizing the derivative, it "ties the knot" when it re-encounters a language it has already seen:

```
(define/memoize (D c L)
  #:order ([L #:eq] [c #:equal])
  (match L
    [(empty)       (empty)]
    [(eps)         (empty)]
    [(char a)      (if (equal? a c)
                       (eps)
                       (empty))]

    [(alt L1 L2)   (alt (D c L1)
                        (D c L2))]
    [(cat (and (? δ) L1) L2)
                   (alt (D c L2)
    [(cat L1 L2)   (cat (D c L1) L2)]
    [(rep L1)      (cat (D c L1) L)]))
```

The `define/memoize` form above defines a derivative function `D` that memoizes first by pointer equality on the language and then by value equality on the character.

4.3 Step 3: Fixed points

The computation of nullability is more challenging than the computation of the derivative because it isn't looking for a structure; it's looking for a single answer: "Yes, it's nullable," or "No, it's

[1] Lisp implementations that do not support lazy fields have to provide them transparently with macros, `delay` and `force`.

not." As such, laziness and memoization can't help side-step self-dependencies the way they did for the derivative. Consider the nullability of the left-recursive language L:

$$\delta(L) = (\delta(L) \circ \emptyset) \cup \epsilon.$$

To know the nullability of L requires knowing the nullability of L. For decades, this problem has been solved by interpreting the nullability of L as the least fixed point of the nullability equations.

To bare only the essence of nullability, we can hide the computation of a least fixed point behind a purely functional abstraction: `define/fix`. The `define/fix` form uses Kleene's theorem to compute the least fixed point of a monotonic recursive definition, and it allows the prior definition of nullability to be used with little change:

```
(define/fix (δ L)
  #:bottom #f
  (match L
    [(empty)        #f]
    [(eps)          #t]
    [(char _)       #f]

    [(rep _)        #t]
    [(alt L1 L2)    (or  (δ L1) (δ L2))]
    [(cat L1 L2)    (and (δ L1) (δ L2))]))
```

The `#:bottom` keyword indicates from where to begin the iterative ascent toward the least fixed point.

The `define/fix` form defines a function mapping nodes in a graph (V, E) to values in a lattice X, so that given an instance:

`(define/fix (f v) #:bottom` $\perp_X$ *body*`)`

After this definition, the function $f : V \to X$ is a least fixed point:

$$f = \text{lfp}(\lambda f.\lambda v.\mathit{body}),$$

which is easily computed with straightforward iteration:

$$\text{lfp}(F) = F^n(\perp_{V \to X}) \text{ for some finite } n.$$

4.4 Recognizing context-free languages

No special modification is required for the `matches?` function. It works as-is for recognizing context-free languages.

With access to laziness, memoization and a facility for computing fixed points, we were able to construct a system for recognizing any context-free language in less than 30 lines of code.

5. Parsers and parser combinators

Using standard techniques from functional programming, we lifted the derivative from regular languages to context-free languages. If *recognition* of strings in context-free languages were our goal, we would be done.

But, our goal is parsing. So, our next step is to generalize the derivative to parsers. This section reviews parsers and parser combinators. (For a more detailed treatment, we refer the reader to [15, 16].) In the next section, we explore their derivative.

A partial parser p is a function that consumes a string and produces "partial" parses of that string. A partial parse is a pair containing the remaining unparsed input, and a parse tree for the prefix. The set $\mathbb{P}(A, T)$ contains the partial parsers over alphabet A that produce parse trees in the set T:

$$\mathbb{P}(A, T) \subseteq A^* \to \mathcal{P}(T \times A^*).$$

A (full) parser p consumes a string and produces all possible parses of the full string. The set $\lfloor\mathbb{P}\rfloor(A, T)$ contains the full parsers over alphabet A that produce parse trees in the set T:

$$\lfloor\mathbb{P}\rfloor(A, T) \subseteq A^* \to \mathcal{P}(T).$$

Of course, we can treat a partial parser $p \in \mathbb{P}(A, T)$ as a full parser:

$$\lfloor p\rfloor(w) = \{t : (t, \epsilon) \in p(w)\},$$

by discarding any partial parse that did not exhaust the input.

5.1 Simple parsers

Simple languages can be implicitly promoted to partial parsers:

- A character c converts into a partial parser for exactly itself:

$$c \equiv \lambda w. \begin{cases} \{(c, w')\} & w = cw' \\ \emptyset & \text{otherwise.} \end{cases}$$

- The null string becomes the consume-nothing parser:

$$\epsilon \equiv \lambda w. \{(\epsilon, w)\}.$$

- The empty set becomes the reject-everything parser:

$$\emptyset \equiv \lambda w. \{\}.$$

5.2 Combining parsers

Parsers combine in the same fashion as languages:

- The union of two parsers, $p, q \in \mathbb{P}(A, X)$, combines all parse trees together, so that $p \cup q \in \mathbb{P}(A, X)$:

$$p \cup q = \lambda w.p(w) \cup q(w).$$

- The concatenation of two parsers, $p \in \mathbb{P}(A, X)$ and $q \in \mathbb{Q}(A, Y)$, produces a parser that pairs the parse trees of the individual parsers together, so that $p \circ q \in \mathbb{P}(A, X \times Y)$:

$$p \circ q = \lambda w.\{((x, y), w'') : (x, w') \in p(w), (y, w'') \in q(w')\}$$

  In effect, the first parser consumes a prefix of the input and produces a parse tree. It passes the remainder of that input to the second parser, which produces another parse tree. The result is the left-over input paired with both of those parse trees.

- A reduction by function $f : X \to Y$ over a parser $p \in \mathbb{P}(A, X)$ creates a new partial parser, $p \to f \in \mathbb{P}(A, Y)$:

$$p \to f = \lambda w.\{((f(x), w') : (x, w') \in p(w)\}$$

  A reduction parser maps trees from X into trees from Y.

  In code, a new struct represents reduction parsers:

```
(define-struct red {lang f})
```

  Once again, the field `lang` should be lazy.

5.3 The nullability combinator

A special nullability combinator, δ, simplifies the definition of the derivative over parsers. It becomes a reject-everything parser if the language cannot parse empty, and the null parser if it can:

$$\delta(p) = \lambda w. \{(t, w) : t \in \lfloor p\rfloor(\epsilon)\}.$$

We can add a new kind of language node to represent these:

```
(define-struct δ {lang})
```

Once again, the field `lang` is lazy. (Please note that δ is no longer the *function* from the previous section.)

5.4 The null reduction parser

To implement the derivative of parsers for single characters: the null reduction partial parser, $\epsilon \downarrow S$, is handy. This parser can only parse the null string; it returns a set of parse trees stored within:

$$\epsilon \downarrow S \equiv \lambda w. \{(t, w) : t \in S\}.$$

A new struct provides null-reduction nodes:

```
(define-struct eps* {trees})
```

5.5 The repetition combinator

It is easiest to define the Kleene star of a partial parser $p \in \mathbb{P}(A, T)$ in terms of concatenation, union and reduction, so that $p^\star \in \mathbb{P}(A, T^*)$:

$$p^\star = (p \circ p^\star) \to \lambda(head, tail).head : tail$$
$$\cup\, \epsilon \downarrow \{\langle\rangle\}.$$

The colon operator (:) is the sequence constructor, and $\langle\rangle$ is the empty sequence.

6. Derivatives of parser combinators

If we can generalize the derivative *to* parsers and *over* parser combinators, then we can construct parse forests using derivatives. But first, we must consider the question:

"What *is* the derivative of a parser?"

Intuitively, the derivative of a parser with respect to the character c should be a new parser. It should have the same type as the original parser; that is, if the original parser consumed the alphabet A to construct parse trees of type X, then the new parser should do the same. Formally:

$$D_c : \mathbb{P}(A, T) \to \mathbb{P}(A, T).$$

But, how should the derived parser behave?

It should act as though the character c has been consumed, so that if the string w is supplied, it returns parses for the string cw. However, it also needs to strip away any null parses that come back. If it didn't strip these, then null parses containing cw would return when trying to parse w with the derived parser. It is nonsensical for a partial parser to expand its input. Thus:

$$D_c(p) = \lambda w.p(cw) - (\lfloor p \rfloor(\epsilon) \times \{cw\}).$$

To arrive at a framework for parsing, we can solve this equation for the partial parser p in terms of the derivative:

$$D_c(p) = \lambda w.p(cw) - (\lfloor p \rfloor(\epsilon) \times \{cw\})$$
$$\text{iff } D_c(p)(w) = p(cw) - (\lfloor p \rfloor(\epsilon) \times \{cw\})$$
$$\text{iff } p(cw) = D_c(p)(w) \cup (\lfloor p \rfloor(\epsilon) \times \{cw\}).$$

Fortunately, we'll never have to deal with the "left-over" null parses in practice. With a full parser, these null parses are discarded:

$$\lfloor p \rfloor(cw) = \lfloor D_c(p) \rfloor(w).$$

Given their similarity, it should not surprise that the derivative of a partial parser resembles the derivative of a language:

- The derivative of the empty parser is empty:

$$D_c(\emptyset) = \emptyset.$$

- The derivative of the null parser is also empty:

$$D_c(\epsilon) = \emptyset.$$

- The derivative of the nullability combinator must be empty, since it at most parses the empty string:

$$D_c(\delta(L)) = \emptyset.$$

- The derivative of a single-character parser is either the null reduction parser or the empty parser:

$$D_c(c') = \begin{cases} \epsilon \downarrow \{c\} & c = c' \\ \emptyset & \text{otherwise.} \end{cases}$$

This rule is important: it allows the derived parser to retain fragments of the input string within itself. Over time, as successive derivatives are taken, the parser is steadily transforming itself into a parse forest with nodes like this.

- The derivative of the union is the union of the derivative:

$$D_c(p \cup q) = D_c(p) \cup D_c(q).$$

- The derivative of a reduction is the reduction of the derivative:

$$D_c(p \to f) = D_c(p) \to f.$$

- The derivative of concatenation requires nullability, in case the first parser doesn't consume any input:

$$D_c(p \circ q) = (D_c(p) \circ q) \cup (\delta(p) \circ D_c(q)).$$

- The derivative of Kleene star peels off a copy of the parser:

$$D_c(p^\star) = (D_c(p) \circ p^\star) \to \lambda(h, t).h : t$$

The rules are so similar to the derivative for languages that we can modify the implementation of the derivative for languages to arrive at a derivative suitable for parsers:

```
(define/memoize (D c L)
  #:order ([L #:eq] [c #:equal])
  (match L
    [(empty)        (empty)]
    [(eps* T)       (empty)]
    [(δ _)          (empty)]
    [(char a)       (if (equal? a c)
                        (eps* (set c))
                        (empty))]

    [(alt L1 L2)    (alt (D c L1) (D c L2))]
    [(cat L1 L2)    (alt (cat (D c L1) L2))
                         (cat (δ L1) (D c L2))]
    [(rep L1)       (cat (D c L1) L)]
    [(red L f)      (red (D c L) f)]))
```

(Because pairing and list-building in Lisps both use `cons`, there is no reduction around the derivative of repetition.)

6.1 Parsing with derivatives

Parsing with derivatives is straightforward—until the last character has been consumed. To parse, compute successive derivatives of the top-level parser with respect to each character in a string. When the string is depleted, supply the null string to the final parser. In code, the `parse` function has the same structure as `matches?`:

```
(define (parse w p)
  (if (null? w)
      (parse-null p)
      (parse (cdr w) (D (car w) p))))
```

The question of interest is how to define `parse-null`, which produces a parse forest for the null parses of its input.

Yet again, an equational theory guides:

$$\lfloor \emptyset \rfloor(\epsilon) = \{\}$$
$$\lfloor \epsilon \downarrow T \rfloor(\epsilon) = T$$
$$\lfloor \delta(p) \rfloor = \lfloor p \rfloor(\epsilon)$$
$$\lfloor p \cup q \rfloor(\epsilon) = \lfloor p \rfloor(\epsilon) \cup \lfloor q \rfloor(\epsilon)$$
$$\lfloor p \circ q \rfloor(\epsilon) = \lfloor p \rfloor(\epsilon) \times \lfloor q \rfloor(\epsilon)$$
$$\lfloor p \to f \rfloor(\epsilon) = \{f(t_1), \ldots, f(t_n)\}$$
$$\text{where } \{t_1, \ldots, t_n\} = \lfloor p \rfloor(\epsilon)$$
$$\lfloor p^\star \rfloor(\epsilon) = (\lfloor p \rfloor(\epsilon))^*$$

A note on repetition The rule for repetition can mislead. If the interior parser can parse null, then there are an infinite number of parse trees to return. However, in terms of descriptiveness, one gains nothing by allowing the interior of a Kleene star operation to parse null—Kleene star already parses null by definition. So, in practice, we can replace that last rule by:

$$\lfloor p^\star \rfloor(\epsilon) = \begin{cases} \{\langle\rangle\} & p \text{ cannot parse null} \\ \textit{undefined} & \text{otherwise.} \end{cases}$$

What we have at this point are mutually recursive set constraint equations that mimic the structure of the nullability function for languages. Once again, the least fixed point is a sensible way of interpreting these equations. Thus, Kleene's fixed-point theorem, via `define/fix`, returns the set of full null parses:

```
(define/fix (parse-null p)
  #:bottom (set)
  (match l
    [(empty)      (set)]
    [(eps* T)     T]
    [(δ L)        (parse-null L)]
    [(char _)     (set)]

    [(alt p1 p2)  (set-union (parse-null p1)
                             (parse-null p2))]
    [(cat p1 p2)  (for*/set ([t1 (parse-null p1)]
                             [t2 (parse-null p2)])
                            (cons t1 t2))]
    [(red p1 f)   (for/set ([t (parse-null p1)])
                           (f t))]
    [(rep _)      (set '())]))
```

It assumes that the null parse of each node is initially empty.

7. Performance and complexity

The implementation is brief. The code is pure. The theory is elegant. So, how does this perform in practice? In brief, it is awful.

We constructed a parser for Python 3.1. On one-line examples, it returns interactively. Yet, it takes just under three *minutes* to parse a (syntactically valid) 31-line input. The culprit? The size of the grammar within the parser can grow exponentially with the number of derivatives. (The rule for concatenation is to blame.) Specifically, the grammar can double in size under the derivative. The cost model for parsing with derivatives is:

number of derivatives
$\times$ cost of derivative
$+$ cost of fixed point at the end.

The cost of the derivative is proportional to the size of the current grammar. The cost of the fixed point is quadratic in the size of the grammar for unambiguous parses in the worst case. Thus, the worst-case complexity of parsing a grammar of size G over an input of length n is:

$$O(n2^nG + (2^nG)^2) = O(2^{2n}G^2).$$

Considering this complexity, it is remarkable that our example finished at all. That it finished in three minutes is astonishing.

7.1 Example: Growth in the grammar

A glance at run-time behavior on the left-recursive list grammar exposes the nature of the problem. The image on the left represents the grammar at the start; the image on the right represents the grammar after ten derivatives:

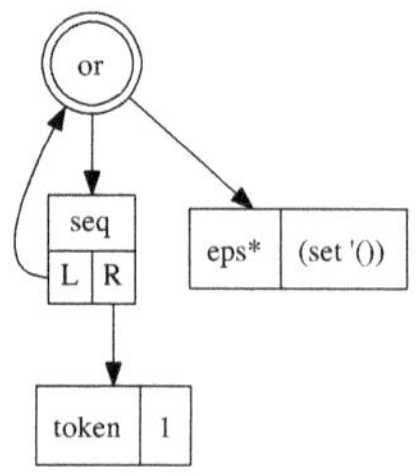

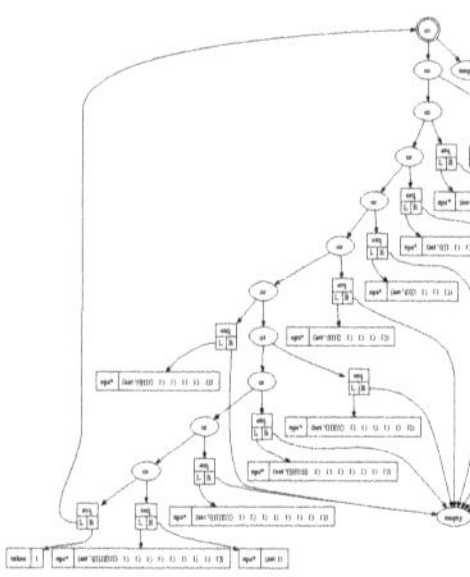

If one were to zoom in on image on the right, the node on the bottom right is `(empty)`. All of the inbound edges are from concatenation nodes—all of these nodes can be discarded.

8. Compaction

Another equational theory shows how to eliminate unnecessary structure. The empty parser is an annihilator under concatenation and the identity under union; a null parser is the identity under concatenation.

It is possible to aggressively perform reductions as pieces of parse trees emerge. Our implementation utilizes the following simplifications; we use $(\Rightarrow)$ in lieu of $(=)$ to emphasize direction:

$$\begin{aligned}
\emptyset \circ p = p \circ \emptyset &\Rightarrow \emptyset \\
\emptyset \cup p = p \cup \emptyset &\Rightarrow p \\
(\epsilon \downarrow \{t_1\}) \circ p &\Rightarrow p \rightarrow \lambda t_2.(t_1, t_2) \\
p \circ (\epsilon \downarrow \{t_2\}) &\Rightarrow p \rightarrow \lambda t_1.(t_1, t_2) \\
(\epsilon \downarrow \{t_1, \ldots, t_n\}) \rightarrow f &\Rightarrow \epsilon \downarrow \{f(t_1), \ldots, f(t_n)\} \\
((\epsilon \downarrow \{t_1\}) \circ p) \rightarrow f &\Rightarrow p \rightarrow \lambda t_2.(t_1, t_2) \\
(p \rightarrow f) \rightarrow g &\Rightarrow p \rightarrow (g \circ f) \\
\emptyset^\star &\Rightarrow \epsilon \downarrow \{\langle\rangle\}.
\end{aligned}$$

We can implement these simplification rules in a memoized, recursive simplification function. When simplification is deeply recursive and memoized, we term it *compaction*. If the algorithm compacts after every derivative, then the time to parse the 31-line Python file drops from three *minutes* to two *seconds*. A graph of the size of the residual Python grammar with respect to each derivative hints as to why:

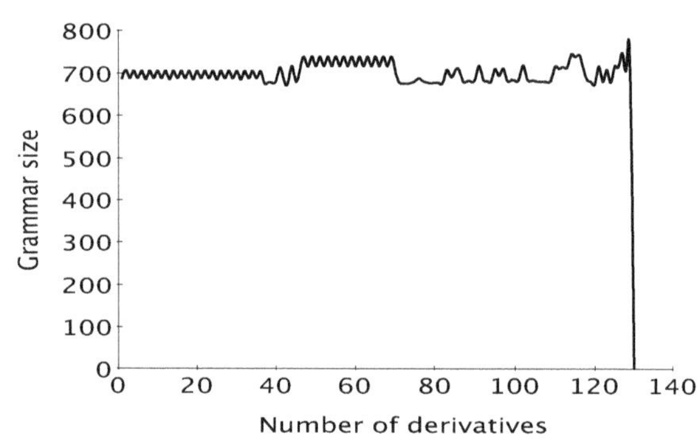

The size of the grammar (and the cost of each derivative) stays constant.

Warning With mere top-level simplification in lieu of memoization and deep recursive simplification, the grammar still grows with each derivative, and the cost of parsing the 31-line example explodes from two seconds to one minute.

8.1 Complexity

The worst-case complexity is unchanged: it is still exponential. However, we can hypothesize about its average performance given the observation that the grammar tends to stay roughly constant in size (until collapsing into a parse forest at the very end). The cost of each derivative remains proportional to the size of the original grammar. The cost of the fixed point at the end is negligible because the grammar has collapsed under compaction. Thus, we conjecture with reason that the cost of parsing with derivatives is $O(nG)$ in practice (for unambiguous grammars), where n is the size of the string, and G is the size of the grammar. Even for the ambiguous expression grammar, *recognition* appears to be $O(nG)$ (while producing all parse trees is exponential).

9. Related work

There has been a revival of interest in Brzozowski's derivative, itself a specialization of the well-known left quotient operation on languages. Owens, Reppy and Turon re-examined the derivative in light of lexer construction [13], and Danielsson [5] used it to prove the totality of parser combinators.

The literature on parsing is vast; there are dozens of methods for parsing, including but not limited to abstract interpretation [3, 4], operator-precedence parsing [9, 14], simple precedence parsing [7], parser combinators [15, 16], LALR parsing [6], LR(k) parsing [12], GLR parsing [17], CYK parsing [11, 20, 2], Earley parsing [8], LL(k) parsing, and recursive descent parsing [19]. packrat/PEG parsing [10, 18]. Derivative-based parsing shares full coverage of all context-free grammars with GLR, CYK and Earley.

Derivative-based parsing is not easy to classify as a top-down or bottom-up method. In personal correspondence, Stuart Kurtz pointed out that when the grammar is in Greibach Normal Form (GNF), the algorithm acquires a "parallel" top-down flavor. For grammars outside GNF, while watching the algorithm evolve under compaction, one sees what appears to be a pushdown stack emerge inside the grammar. (Pushes and pops appear as the jagged edges in the graph to the left.)

The most directly related work is Danielsson's work on total parser combinators [5]. His work computes residual parsers similar to our own, but does not detail a simplification operation. According to our correspondence with Danielsson, simplification does exist in the implementation. Yet, because it is unable to memoize the simplification operation (turning it into compaction), the implementation exhibits exponential complexity even in practice.

Acknowledgements We are grateful for the thousands of comments on reddit, hackernews, Lambda the Ultimate and elsewhere that thoroughly dissected and improved an earlier draft of this work. We also thank the ICFP 2011 and the ESOP 2010 reviewers for their thoughtful and detailed feedback. This research is partly supported by the National Science Foundation under Grant No. 1035658, by the DARPA CRASH project "GnoSys: Raising the level of discourse in systems program," and by the National Nuclear Security Administration under the "Accelerating Development of Retorfitable CO2 Capture Technologies through Predictivity" project through DOE Cooperative Agreement DE-NA0000740.

10. Conclusion

Our goal was a means to abbreviate the understanding and implementation of parsing. Brzozowski's derivative met the challenge: its theory is equational, its implementation is functional and, with an orthogonal optimization, its performance is not unreasonable.

References

[1] Brzozowski, J. A. Derivatives of regular expressions. *Journal of the ACM 11*, 4 (Oct. 1964), 481–494.

[2] Cocke, J., and Schwartz, J. T. Programming languages and their compilers: Preliminary notes. Tech. rep., Courant Institute of Mathematical Sciences, New York University, New York, NY, 1970.

[3] Cousot, P., and Cousot, R. Parsing as abstract interpretation of grammar semantics. *Theoretical Computer Science 290* (2003), 531–544.

[4] Cousot, P., and Cousot, R. Grammar analysis and parsing by abstract interpretation, invited chapter. In *Program Analysis and Compilation, Theory and Practice: Essays dedicated to Reinhard Wilhelm*, T. Reps, M. Sagiv, and J. Bauer, Eds., LNCS 4444. Springer discretionary--Verlag, Dec. 2006, pp. 178–203.

[5] Danielsson, N. A. Total parser combinators. In *Proceedings of the 15th ACM SIGPLAN international conference on Functional programming* (New York, NY, USA, 2010), ICFP '10, ACM, pp. 285–296.

[6] DeRemer, F. L. Practical translators for LR(k) languages. Tech. rep., Cambridge, MA, USA, 1969.

[7] Dijkstra, E. W. *Selected Writings on Computing: A Personal Perspective*. Springer, Oct. 1982.

[8] Earley, J. An efficient context-free parsing algorithm. *Communications of the ACM 13*, 2 (Feb. 1970), 94–102.

[9] Floyd, R. W. Syntactic analysis and operator precedence. *Journal of the ACM 10*, 3 (July 1963), 316–333.

[10] Ford, B. Packrat parsing: Simple, powerful, lazy, linear time. In *Proceedings of the 2002 International Conference on Functional Programming* (Oct. 2002).

[11] Kasami, T. An efficient recognition and syntax-analysis algorithm for context-free languages. Tech. rep., Air Force Cambridge Research Lab, Bedford, MA, 1965.

[12] Knuth, D. On the translation of languages from left to right. *Information and Control 8* (1965), 607–639.

[13] Owens, S., Reppy, J., and Turon, A. Regular-expression derivatives re-examined. *Journal of Functional Programming 19*, 02 (2009), 173–190.

[14] Pratt, V. R. Top down operator precedence. In *POPL '73: Proceedings of the 1st annual ACM SIGACT-SIGPLAN Symposium on Principles of Programming Languages* (New York, NY, USA, 1973), POPL '73, ACM, pp. 41–51.

[15] Swierstra, D. S., Pablo, and Sariava, J. Designing and implementing combinator languages. In *Advanced Functional Programming* (1998), pp. 150–206.

[16] Swierstra, S. Combinator parsing: A short tutorial. In *Language Engineering and Rigorous Software Development*, A. Bove, L. Barbosa, A. Pardo, and J. Pinto, Eds., vol. 5520 of *Lecture Notes in Computer Science*. Springer Berlin / Heidelberg, Berlin, Heidelberg, 2009, ch. 6, pp. 252–300.

[17] Tomita, M. LR parsers for natural languages. In *ACL-22: Proceedings of the 10th International Conference on Computational Linguistics and 22nd annual meeting on Association for Computational Linguistics* (Morristown, NJ, USA, 1984), Association for Computational Linguistics, pp. 354–357.

[18] Warth, A., Douglass, J. R., and Millstein, T. Packrat parsers can support left recursion. In *PEPM '08: Proceedings of the 2008 ACM SIGPLAN Symposium on Partial Evaluation and Semantics-based Program Manipulation* (New York, NY, USA, 2008), ACM, pp. 103–110.

[19] Wirth, N. *Compiler Construction (International Computer Science Series)*, pap/dsk ed. Addison Wesley Pub (Sd).

[20] Younger, D. H. Recognition and parsing of context-free languages in time n3. *Information and Control 10*, 2 (1967), 189–208.

An Efficient Non-Moving Garbage Collector for Functional Languages

Katsuhiro Ueno Atsushi Ohori Toshiaki Otomo *

Research Institute of Electrical Communication
Tohoku University
{katsu, ohori, o-toshi}@riec.tohoku.ac.jp

Abstract

Motivated by developing a memory management system that allows functional languages to seamlessly inter-operate with C, we propose an efficient non-moving garbage collection algorithm based on bitmap marking and report its implementation and performance evaluation.

In our method, the heap consists of sub-heaps $\{H_i \mid c \leq i \leq B\}$ of exponentially increasing allocation sizes (H_i for 2^i bytes) and a special sub-heap for exceptionally large objects. Actual space for each sub-heap is dynamically allocated and reclaimed from a pool of fixed size allocation segments. In each allocation segment, the algorithm maintains a bitmap representing the set of live objects. Allocation is done by searching for the next free bit in the bitmap. By adding meta-level bitmaps that summarize the contents of bitmaps hierarchically and maintaining the current bit position in the bitmap hierarchy, the next free bit can be found in a small constant time for most cases, and in $\log_{32}(segmentSize)$ time in the worst case on a 32-bit architecture. The collection is done by clearing the bitmaps and tracing live objects. The algorithm can be extended to generational GC by maintaining multiple bitmaps for the same heap space. The proposed method does not require compaction and objects are not moved at all. This property is significant for a functional language to inter-operate with C, and it should also be beneficial in supporting multiple native threads.

The proposed method has been implemented in a full-scale Standard ML compiler. Our benchmark tests show that our non-moving collector performs as efficiently as a generational copying collector designed for functional languages.

Categories and Subject Descriptors D.3.4 [*Programming Languages*]: Processors—memory management (garbage collection)

General Terms Algorithms, Languages, Performance

Keywords Non-moving Garbage Collection, Bitmap Marking, Generational Collectors, SML#

* The third author's current affiliation: Hitachi Advanced Digital, Inc.

ICFP'11, September 19–21, 2011, Tokyo, Japan.

1. Introduction

The general motivation of this research is to develop a memory management system for a functional language that supports seamless interoperability with the C language. We have partially achieved this goal through type-directed compilation for *natural data representations* in ML [25]. Under this scheme, ML records and arrays as well as atomic types such as `int` and `real` have the same representation as in C and are therefore directly read or updated by a C program without any data representation conversion. This has been embodied in our SML# compiler [33]. In this implementation, one can directly import a C function and call it with data structures such as records, mutable arrays, and function closures (for call-backs) created in SML#. The following code is a fragment of a demo program distributed with SML#.

```
val glNormal3dv =
    dlsym (libgl, "glNormal3dv")
    : _import (real * real * real) -> unit
...
  map (fn (vec, ...) => (glNormal3dv vec; ...))
      [((1.0, 0.0, 0.0), ...), ...]
```

This code dynamically links `glNormal3dv` function in the OpenGL library as an ML function of type `real * real * real -> unit` and uses it with other SML# code. SML# compiles `(1.0, 0.0, 0.0)` to a pointer to a heap block containing 3 double precision floating point numbers. Since this record has the same representation as a `double` array of C, `glNormal3dv` works correctly. In addition to this natural data representation, each SML# heap object has a header containing object layout information indicating whether each field is a pointer or not. This information is used by the SML# garbage collector (GC) to exactly trace live objects. By adopting the strategy that the SML# GC only traces and collects SML# objects and leaves management of C allocated objects to C code, we should be able to achieve seamless interoperability between SML# and C.

The solution so far is however only partial in that data structures that are passed to foreign functions must be allocated in a special non-moving area. SML# compiler, as well as most other functional language compilers, has used copying garbage collection (GC) based on the commonly accepted belief being that, for functional programs requiring large amount of short-lived data, the Cheney's copying collector [8] would be the most efficient for their minor collection. However, any (precise) copying GC requires that the runtime system must be able to locate and update all the pointers to each heap allocated data. This prohibits functional programs from inter-operating with foreign functions or any programs that use local memory space not accessible from the garbage collector. To side-step this problem, the programmer must explicitly request GC not to move those data that are passed to external code. This "object pinning" approach is not only cumbersome but also dangerous. This problem should be painfully familiar to anyone who has tried to write a functional program that interacts with a foreign library that requires callbacks or locally stores object pointers passed from the caller. For a language with rather limited interoperability, "object pinning" might be performed automatically, but for an ML-style language that provides seamless interoperability, automatic "object pinning" is difficult, if not impossible. To see the problem, suppose a C function is called with an array and a call-back function. Since both the C function and the call-back function can freely mutate the array, the runtime system can only safely estimate that the set of reachable objects from the array passed to the C function to be the set of all the live objects in the entire heap, including even those that may be created later by the call-back function.

To solve this problem, we would like to develop a *non-moving* garbage collection algorithm suitable for functional languages. Since functional programs rely heavily on efficient allocation and collection, a new non-moving GC algorithm should ideally be as efficient as currently widely used copying GC with generational extension [21, 35]. The purpose of this paper is to develop such a garbage collection algorithm, to implement it for a full-scale ML compiler, and to evaluate its performance through extensive benchmarks to verify the feasibility of the algorithm.

An obvious non-moving candidate is mark and sweep GC [24]. Compared with copying GC, however, simple mark and sweep GC tends to exhibit the following general weaknesses.

- *Fragmentation and slow allocation.* Functional programs require objects of various sizes with various life time. Due to this property, the heap space becomes fragmented very quickly, resulting in slow allocation and reclamation. To avoid this problem, practical variant of mark-and-sweep GC algorithms sometimes perform costly compaction at sweep phase. In contrast, copying GC automatically performs compaction and yields a very fast allocator, which has only to check the heap boundary and to advance the allocation pointer.
- *High sweep cost.* Mark and sweep GC requires to sweep the heap, which takes time proportional to the size of the heap. Again this is in contrast with copying GC whose collection cost is proportional to the amount of live data.
- *Difficulty in developing efficient generational GC.* While it is straightforward to combine mark and sweep GC with other GC to form a generational GC, developing generational mark and sweep GC requires certain amount of additional machinery, which would result in slower GC time [10].

Perhaps due to these problems, mark and sweep GC seems to be considered not suitable for primary GC (e.g. minor GC in generational GC) of functional programs, which produces large amount of short-lived data of varied size very rapidly.

The main new technical contribution of this paper is to develop a variant of mark and sweep GC that is as efficient as Cheney's copying GC and its generational extensions, and to demonstrate its feasibility for functional languages thorough implementation and evaluation. Our basic strategy is well known *bitmap marking* (see [37] and [17] for a survey.) We associate a heap with bitmaps that represent the set of live objects. This structure alone does not yield an efficient allocation and collection. We have developed a series of new data structures and algorithms that overcome the weakness of mark and sweep GC mentioned above. The following is a summary of the features of our GC algorithm.

1. *A fragmentation-avoided and compaction-free heap.* Fragmentation occurs when objects have varied sizes; if all the objects were of the same size, then the heap could be a fixed size array that can be managed by a bitmap without incurring fragmentation. An extreme idea is to set up a separate heap for each object size. Of course we cannot prepare sufficiently large separate heaps for all possible object sizes, so we prepare a series of sub-heaps $\{H_i \mid c \leq i\}$ of exponentially increasing allocation block sizes, i.e. each H_i consists of allocation blocks of 2^i bytes. Actual allocation space of H_i is dynamically maintained as a list of fixed-size *segments*. Each segment contains an array of 2^i-byte blocks. 2^c is the minimum allocation block size in bytes. In SML#, the minimum size of non-empty objects is 8 (2^3) byte, so we fix c to be 3 in this paper.

   These structures eliminate the fragmentation problem associated with mark and sweep collection. Since a segment is a fixed size array, it is efficiently maintained by a bitmap where each bit corresponds to one block. Moreover, size of each H_i is dynamically adjusted through allocation and reclamation of segments.

   In our scheme, an allocation block in H_i in general contains an object smaller than 2^i bytes, and some amount of memory is unused. Our observation is that, we can avoid costly compaction at the expense of locally wasting space in each allocation block, and that this cost is quite acceptable in practice. Our evaluation shows that the space usage is better than that of copying GC in most cases.

   Since we cannot prepare H_i for unbounded i, we set a bound B of i and allocate exceptionally large objects of size more than 2^B to a special sub-heap $\mathcal{M}$. B can be as large as the size of one segment. According to our experimentation, $B = 12$ (i.e. at most 4096 bytes) appears to be sufficient for functional programs (e.g. covers most of allocation requests.) Hence, in our system, the heap consists of 10 sub-heaps, $H_3, \ldots H_{12}$. Since the special sub-heap $\mathcal{M}$ occupies a very small portion of the entire heap and can be managed by any non-copying GC method, we do not consider this further.

2. *Efficient allocation.* A bitmap can be used not only for marking but also for allocation by searching for a free bit in a bitmap. Simple search for a free bit in a bitmap takes, in the worst case, the time proportional to the number of busy bits. Perhaps due to this problem, most of bitmap based GC algorithms use some form of free list for allocation. We solve this problem by adding meta-level bitmaps that summarize the contents of bitmaps. The set of all bitmaps form a hierarchically organized tree. The sequence of bits at the leaf level in the tree is the ordinary bitmap representing liveness of the set of allocation blocks, and the sequence of bits at an intermediate level summarizes the bitmap one level below. On this bitmap tree, we maintain a data structure representing both the next bit position to be examined and the corresponding block address. This structure corresponds to the allocation pointer of copying GC, so we call it an *allocation pointer*. The whole organization is depicted in Figure 2 whose details will be explained in Section 2. By constructing a series of optimized searching algorithms on this data structure, the next free bit can be found in a small constant time for most cases, and in $\log_{32}(segmentSize)$ time in the worst case.

3. *Small GC cost.* Sweeping is done by clearing bitmaps. The total collection cost of a bitmap making GC is the sum of the costs for clearing bitmaps, tracing live objects, and setting the bits in the bitmaps. Among them, the bitmap clearing requires $N/32$ steps where N is the total number of allocation blocks. Our extensive evaluation shows that bitmap clear time is negligible (about 1% of the GC time), and therefore, in practice, the total cost of our GC is dominated by the tracing and marking cost. So in practice our GC algorithm behaves similarly to that of copying GC. In most of the benchmark tests we performed, the

total GC cost was smaller than those of simple copying collector and generational copying collector.

4. *Non-moving generational GC.* By adapting the idea of *partial collection* proposed by Demers et.al. [10], our bitmap marking GC scales up to generational GC without moving objects. This is based on our observation that a bitmap represents a subset of the set of objects in a heap. Generational GC can be realized by maintaining a separate bitmap for each generation. The partial collection with "sticky bit" technique presented in [10] coincides with a special case where tenuring threshold is 1 and the number of generations is 2. Pointers to younger generations from older generations are tracked using a *write barrier* and a *remembered set*. In the above special case, the remembered set can be allocated in the collector's trace stack due to the property that the remembered set can be flushed after minor collection. The resulting implementation of the special case does not require any additional memory space other than those used in the non-generational version.

We have implemented the data structures and algorithms in a Standard ML compiler, and have done extensive benchmark tests. We have evaluated and compared them against a simple Cheney's copying GC, and a generational copying GC for functional languages described in [29], and have obtained the following results: (i) segment-based dynamic sub-heap size adjustment automatically achieves optimal hand-tuned sub-heap size assignment, (ii) the bitmap marking GC is as efficient as Cheney's copying GC, and (iii) the generational extension outperforms the non-generational bitmap GC, and shows comparable or better performance results compared to generational copying GC. These results demonstrate that our development have achieved the goal of developing a non-moving GC method for functional language.

The proposed method has additional advantage of supporting multiple native threads without much additional machinery. Our segment-based heap organization allows each concurrent thread to allocate objects in a shared global heap without any locking. The detailed implementation and evaluation for multithread extension is out of the scope of the present paper, but our preliminary implementation of multithread extension shows promising result.

All the implementation is done in our SML# compiler, which compiles the full set of Standard ML language (with the (mostly) seamless interoperability with C) into x86 native code. SML# version 0.40 or later includes the GC algorithms reported in this paper, and they are available and enabled by default in x86 native compilation mode.

The rest of the paper is organized as follows. Section 2 presents the bitmap marking GC algorithm. Section 3 extends the GC method to generational GC. Section 4 reports implementation and performance evaluation. Section 5 compares the contribution with related works. Section 6 concludes the paper.

2. The bitmap marking GC

This section describes the details of the data structures and algorithms for the bitmap marking GC. This description involves low-level bit manipulation. To achieve efficient allocation with bitmaps, we found it essential to design data structures and algorithms in detail. Accurately reporting them requires us to present them in details, sometimes referring to bit-level manipulation. For this reason, we use C like syntax in describing the algorithms.

2.1 The GC-mutator interface

Our GC is an exact tracing GC for functional languages. It can be used with any compiler that produces objects with their layout information and maintains an exact root set. In order to make accurate comparison with other GC algorithms, we design our GC algorithm with a uniform interface to a compiler. For this purpose, the implementation of our GC provides a function for the mutator to register a *root set enumerator*, which takes a function on a heap object pointer of the following type `void trace_fn(void **);` and applies this function to each object in a root set. At the beginning of each GC, the collector calls all the registered root set enumerators with an appropriate `trace_fn` function. In the case of Cheney collector, for example, this would be a function to move an object from one semi-space to the other; in our GC, this is a function that marks the bit corresponding to an object.

An allocation operation is designed as a function which takes a request size in bytes and returns a pointer to a newly allocated object. This is the most general style of allocator required for natural data representation. Since the size of natural data representation is different according to their types, the size of some records in a polymorphic function can only be determined at runtime. For example, consider a function of type `'a -> 'a * 'a`. This function returns a 8 byte record for an `int` argument and a 16 byte record for an `real` argument. Of course, for monomorphic cases, where sizes are statically known, we can inline-expand the allocation function to mutator code to produce an optimized allocation code. For the inline-expansion, however, compiler requires detailed knowledge of the allocation function, which may vary according to GC algorithms. To make the compiler independent of GC methods, in this paper, we turn off the inlining.

2.2 The structure of the heap space and allocation strategy

In what follows, we assume that one machine word is 32-bit long. This is not a restriction; any other word size can equally be used.

We use a given allocation space as a pool of fixed size allocation areas, called *segments*, and set up the entire heap as follows.

$$heap = (\mathcal{M}, \mathcal{S}, (H_3, \ldots, H_{12}))$$

$\mathcal{M}$ is a special sub-heap for large objects explained earlier. $\mathcal{S}$ is a free segment pool, i.e. set of unused segments. Each H_i is a sub-heap for 2^i byte allocation blocks. Each sub-heap has the following structure.

$$H_i = (SegList_i, P_i)$$

$SegList_i$ is a list of segments currently belonging to H_i. P_i is an allocation pointer for sub-heap H_i whose structure is defined in subsection 2.4.

A segment S_i initialized for H_i has the following structure.

$$S_i = (Count_i, Blks_i, BitMap_i, Twork_i)$$

where $Count_i$ is the number of already allocated blocks in this segment, $Blks_i$ is an array of 2^i byte allocation blocks, $BitMap_i$ is a bitmap tree, and $Twork_i$ is the working area used for tracing live objects. The number of allocation blocks in a segment is derived from the segment size, which is statically fixed. We write $Size_i$ for the number of allocation blocks in S_i. We assume that every segment is aligned to power-of-2 boundary for fast bit-level address computation.

We write $Blks_i(k)$ for the k-th block in $Blks_i$. Let $L_i = \lceil \log_{32}(Size_i) \rceil$. This determines the height of the bitmap tree in a segment S_i. The bitmap tree has the following structure

$$BitMap_i = (BM_i^0, \ldots, BM_i^{L_i-1})$$

where BM_i^j is the j-th level bitmap which is a sequence of bits organized as an array of 32 bit words. We write $BM_i^j(k)$ to denote the k-th bit and $BM_i^j[k]$ the k-th word in the j-th level bitmap. The least significant bit in $BM_i^j[k]$ is the bit $BM_i^j(32 \times k + 0)$ and its most significant bit is $BM_i^j(32 \times k + 31)$. The leaf-level bitmap

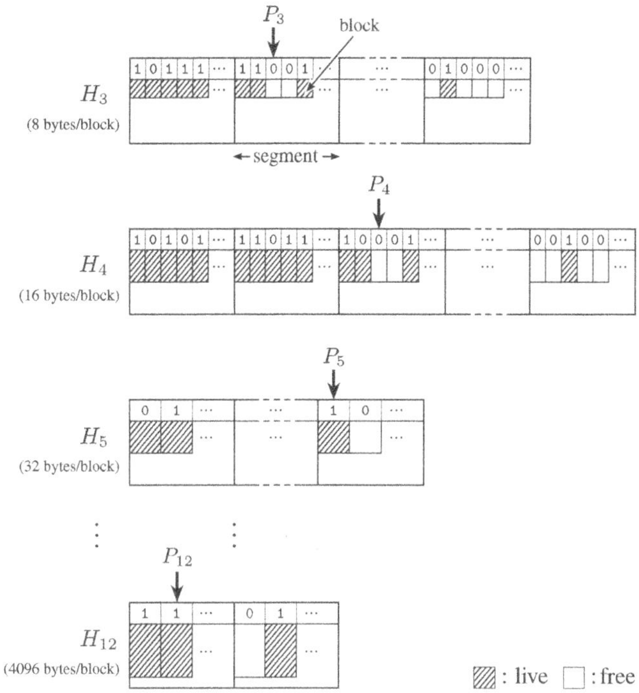

Figure 1. Heap structure

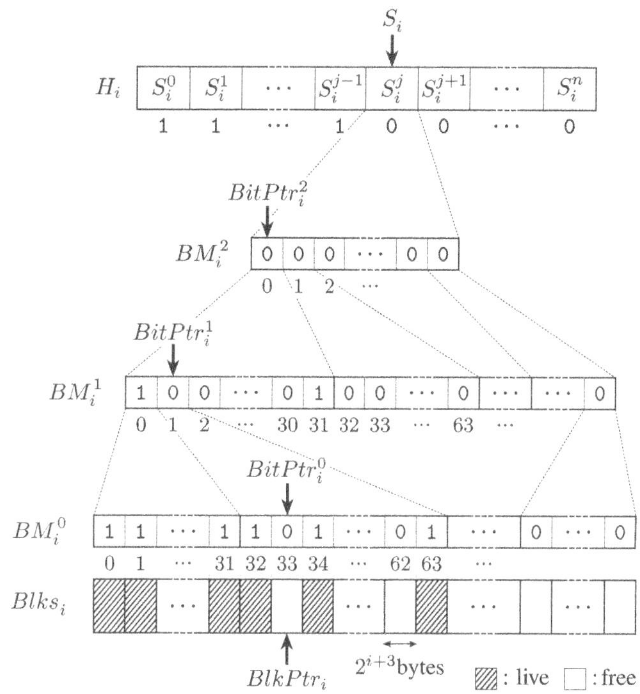

Figure 2. Segment structure

BM_i^0 represents the liveness of $Blks_i$, namely,

$$BM_i^0(k) = \begin{cases} 1 & Blks_i(k) \text{ is live,} \\ 0 & Blks_i(k) \text{ is free.} \end{cases}$$

As we shall explain below, meanings of 1 and 0 are chosen in such a way that free bit search can be implemented efficiently. The $j+1$-th level bitmap BM_i^{j+1} represents whether each word in BM_i^j has free entry or not, namely,

$$BM_i^{j+1}(k) = \begin{cases} 1 & \text{all bits in } BM_i^j[k] \text{ are } 1, \\ 0 & \text{otherwise.} \end{cases}$$

So for example if all the bits of the top-level bitmap $BM_i^{L_i-1}$ is 1 then all the blocks in $Blks_i$ are live, and there is no space left.

2.3 The allocation strategy

With the above structure, $SegList_i$ in H_i forms a single allocation area managed by one (virtual) hierarchically organized tree of bitmaps. The list itself is regarded as the root bitmap of the entire bitmap tree where each bit indicates whether each segment is full or not, and each segment in the list is regarded as an immediate sub-tree of the root bitmap. This structure guarantees that the next free block in H_i can be found in $\log_{32}(Size_i)$ time in the worst case.

In addition, we need to make average allocation as efficient as possible so that it can be comparable to "bump allocation" in Cheney GC. To this end, we observe that in most cases the block array $Blks_i$ is very sparsely used after GC. So we adopt the following strategy.

1. We sequentially allocate the next free block in H_i.
2. To make the typical case of allocation fast, we maintain a position information of the next candidate of allocation block. If this block is free then the allocator simply returns this next block and advances the position information.
3. If the next block is live, then the allocator searches for the next free bit using the bitmap tree. To perform this search efficiently, we maintain the next bit position information for higher-level bitmaps.

The allocation pointer P_i in H_i introduced in the previous subsection is for this purpose, whose structure is given below.

$$\begin{aligned} P_i &= (S_i, BitPtrs_i, BlkPtr_i) \\ BitPtrs_i &= (BitPtr_i^0, \ldots, BitPtr_i^{L_i-1}) \end{aligned}$$

S_i is a pointer to the *active* segment in H_i, i.e. the segment in which blocks are being allocated. $BitPtrs_i$ are *bit pointers* indicating the next bit positions in S_i to be examined. $BitPtr_i^0$ indicates the next bit position to be tested in the leaf-level bitmap BM_i^0. For each $0 \leq j \leq L_i - 2$, $BitPtr_i^{j+1}$ points to the parent bit representing the bitmap word that includes the bit pointed by $BitPtr_i^j$. $BlkPtr_i$ is a *block pointer* indicating the block address corresponding to the bit pointed by $BitPtr_i^0$. Using these pointers, allocation is done as fast as "bump allocation" when the next block is free.

Figure 1 and 2 shows the structures of the set of sub-heaps and a segment, respectively.

2.4 The allocation algorithm

In writing algorithms below, we simply write $SegList_i$ instead of a more verbose notation such as $H_i.SegList$, to indicate that this is the segment list belonging to H_i. Similar notations are used for all the other elements including $BitMap_i$, BM_i^j etc.

The structure of the allocation algorithm is given in Figure 3. `alloc(`n`)` first locates the sub-heap H_i by `findSubHeapBySize` function. If the target CPU has a native instruction counting trailing 0 bits of an integer (such as `BSR` instruction of x86 machine), this function can be implemented by a sequence of a few instructions. In general cases, this is implemented through a decision tree designed according to allocation ratio of blocks of various sizes. Our benchmark tests show the following average allocation ratio (in number of requests) of first 4 sizes.

```
alloc(n) {
  H_i = findSubHeapBySize(n);
  temp = tryAlloc(H_i);
  if (temp == Fail) {
    bitmapMarkingGC();
    temp = tryAlloc(H_i); }
  return temp;
}

tryAlloc(H_i) {
  if (isMarked(P_i)) {
    if (findNextFreeBlock(P_i) == Fail) {
      if (nextSegment(SegList_i, P_i) == Fail) {
        if (newSegment(H_i) == Fail) {
          return Fail; } }
      findNextFreeBlock(P_i); } }
  temp = BlkPtr_i;
  inc(P_i);
  return temp;
}

newSegment(H_i) {
  S = allocSegment(i);
  if (S == Fail) return Fail;
  append S to SegList_i;
  P_i = firstBlockOfLastSegment(SegList_i);
  return Success;
}

inc(P_i) {
  incBlkPtr(BlkPtr_i);
  incBitPtr(BitPtr_i^0);
}
```

Figure 3. Allocation algorithm (top-level)

H_i	H_0	H_1	H_2	H_3
alloc %	11.6	51.3	31.4	4.5

From them, we coded `findSubHeapBySize(`n`)` so that it determines H_i for about 93% of allocation requests by 2 comparisons. The algorithm then tries to allocate a block in H_i using `tryAlloc(`H_i`)`. If it fails then it invokes the bitmap marking garbage collector. `tryAlloc(`H_i`)` first checks whether the block pointed by P_i is marked. If not, then it simply returns the block address stored in P_i and increment P_i by `inc` function. If the next block is already marked, then it searches for the next free bit in the active segment. If the search fails then it advances P_i to the first block of the next segment in the $SegList_i$. If there is no next segment then it tries to dynamically allocate a new segment from the free segment pool by `newSegment` function. Then it tries to search a free bit in the next or new segment. The collection algorithm described later organizes $SegList_i$ so that the search in the next segment never fails. We note that under our strategy of sequentially allocating blocks in H_i, it is not needed to set any bit at allocation. The auxiliary functions used in Figure 3 such as `nextSegment` should be clear from their names.

The remaining thing is to define `findNextFreeBlock` as efficient as possible. For this purpose, we have examined and experimented a number of algorithms in detail. The following is the one that we found the fastest.

We implement $BlkPtr_i$ as a machine address of a block, similar to the allocation pointer in copying GC. So `incBlkPtr` just increments the address. $BitPtr_i^j$ is an abstract data structure whose implementation is the following two word data

$$BitPtr_i^j = (Idx_i^j, Mask_i^j)$$

where

- Idx_i^j is an index into the bitmap array BM_i^j, and
- $Mask_i^j$ is a 32 bit word in which only one bit is set, indicating the bit position.

For example, if $BitPtr_i^0 = (1, 8)$ (in decimal notation) then it denotes the 3rd bit in the second bitmap word, and corresponds to the 35th block. For bit pointers, we define the following primitives.

- `incBitPtr(`$BitPtr_i^j$`)` increments $BitPtr_i^j$.
- `indexToBitptr(`x`)` converts a bit index x to a bit pointer.
- `bitptrToIndex(`$BitPtr_i^j$`)` converts a bit pointer to a bit index.
- `isMarked(`$BitPtr_i^j$`)` tests whether the bit in BM_i^j at $BitPtr_i^j$ is 1.
- `blockAddress(`$BitPtr_i^0$`)` converts a bit pointer to the corresponding block address.

The last two are used in the context of some particular S_i. These primitives can be implemented through efficient bit manipulation (e.g. see [36] for bit manipulation techniques.) Similar primitives are defined for P_i, which contains $BitPtr_i^0$. In Figure 3 and the following, we also use these primitives for P_i as well as for $BitPtr_i^j$.

We implement `findNextFreeBlock` by using the bit pointers and their primitives. This function finds the next free bit in the bitmap tree of a segment and adjust $BitPtrs_i$ by performing the following steps.

1. Search for a 0 bit in the current bitmap word after $BitPtr_i^0$. If one is found then advance $BitPtr_i^0$ by setting its $Mask_i^0$ accordingly, and return. Otherwise, perform the following two steps.
2. Compute the next free bitmap word index k after Idx_i^0 at level 0 by traversing the bitmap trees at level 1 and above. Set Idx_i^0 to k and $Mask_i^0$ to 1.
3. Set $Mask_i^0$ to the position of the first 0 bit in $BM_i^0[Idx_i^0]$. This always succeeds and yields the new mask.

The second step may in turn require to compute the free bitmap word indexes and the masks at level 1 and above. So we define the above operation as a procedure `forwardBitPtr(`j`)` that recursively computes the bit pointer of level j using the bitmaps of level $j+1$ and above. Then the step 2 above can be implemented as follows.

2.1 Calculate the $j+1$ level bit pointer $BitPtr_i^{j+1}$ that points to the bit corresponding to the Idx_i^j-th word in the j level bitmap BM_i^j.

2.2 Call `forwardBitPtr(`$j+1$`)` to advance $BitPtr_i^{j+1}$ to the next free bit position.

2.3 Set $BitPtr_i^j$ to the first 0 bit in the bitmap word $BM_i^j[k]$ where $k =$ `bitptrToIndex(`$BitPtr_i^{j+1}$`)`.

Figure 4 shows the structure of the bit search algorithm, which uses the following operation.

- `nextMask(`$BitPtr_i^j$`)` returns a bit mask $Mask$ such that a bit pointer $(Idx_i^j, Mask)$ points to the next free bit of $BitPtr_i^j$ in the same word. If no free bit is found, it returns `Fail`. This operation is used in the context of some particular S_i.

This operation can be implemented efficiently through bit manipulations as well as bit pointer primitives defined earlier.

```
findNextFreeBlock(P_i) {
  Mask_i^0 = nextMask(BitPtr_i^0);
  if (Mask_i^0 == Fail) {
    if (forwardBitPtr(P_i,0) == Fail) {
      return Fail; } }
  BlkPtr_i = blockAddress(S_i, BitPtr_i^0);
  return Success;
}

forwardBitPtr(P_i,j) {
  if (j+1 >= L_i) return Fail;
  BitPtr_i^{j+1} = indexToBitptr(Idx_i^j);
  Mask_i^{j+1} = nextMask(BitPtr_i^{j+1});
  if (Mask_i^{j+1} == Fail) {
    if (forwardBitPtr(P_i,j+1) == Fail) {
      return Fail; } }
  Idx_i^j = bitptrToIndex(BitPtr_i^{j+1});
  Mask_i^j = 1;
  Mask_i^j = nextMask(BitPtr_i^j);
  return Success;
}
```

Figure 4. Free bit search algorithm

2.5 The bitmap marking GC algorithm

When `tryAlloc` fails to allocate a block in certain H_i, the garbage collector is invoked. In addition to standard marking collection, after marking phase, the collector rearranges the newly marked $SegList_i$ in such a way that every segment after the position P_i has at least one free block. This operation ensures that searching a free block in successive segments of the allocation pointer never fail. This arrangement also effectively performs *compacting* the bitmap tree in very low cost by moving all the filled sub-trees to the left of the allocation pointer.

Figure 5 shows the bitmap marking collection algorithm. It performs the following.

1. For each H_i, clear all the bitmaps in all the segments by writing 0 to each word of in their bitmap trees. This corresponds to sweeping the entire heap area.
2. For each object in the root set, mark the object, increment the live object count $Count_i$, and record it to the trace stack. The trace stack is implemented as a linked list using $Twork$ work areas.
3. While the trace stack is not empty, pop the trace stack. For each object reference stored in a field of the popped object, mark and push the referenced object to the trace stack, and increment the count.
4. When the marking is complete, then the algorithm reclaims empty segments, and reconstructs $SegList$ by rearranging the remaining non-empty segment. The allocation pointer is put at the beginning of the first segment which has at least one free block.

Marking an object involves the following operations.

1. Find the bit position corresponding to the object.
2. Check whether the bit has already been set. If not, set the bit and propagate this change to upper levels in the bitmap tree.

It uses the following auxiliary function.

- `findBitptr(`O`)` finds the segment S_i in which O is allocated and the bit pointer corresponding to O as follows. Let $addr(X)$ be the starting address of X. First, it computes $addr(S_i)$ by bit-level computation from $addr(O)$. Since every segment is aligned to power-of-2 boundary, this is done by masking lower bits of $addr(O)$ to 0. Second, it computes the block index k of O in the block array $Blks_i$ of S_i by address arithmetic. `indexToBitptr(`k`)` is the desired bit pointer.

```
bitmapMarkingGC() {
  for each H_i { clearAllBitmapsAndCount(H_i); }
  traceLiveObjects();
  for each H_i { rearrangeSegList(H_i); }
}

traceLiveObjects() {
  for each O in rootSet { markAndPush(O); }
  while (stackIsNotEmpty()) {
    O = pop();
    for each O' in PointerFields(O) {
      markAndPush(O'); } }
}

markAndPush(O) {
  S_i, BitPtr_i^0 = findBitptr(O);
  if (not isMarked(BitPtr_i^0)) {
    setBit(P_i,0);
    incrementSegmentCount(S_i);
    push(O); }
}

rearrangeSegList(H_i) {
  empty = {S_i^j | S_i^j ∈ SegList_i, Count_i^j = 0}
  filled = {S_i^j | S_i^j ∈ SegList_i, Count_i^j = Size_i}
  unfilled = {S_i^j | S_i^j ∈ SegList_i, 0 < Count_i^j < Size_i}
  reclaim all segments in empty;
  SegList_i = concatSegList(filled, unfilled);
  set P_i to the first S_i^j in SegList_i such that Count_i^j < Size_i;
}

setBit(P_i,j) {
  BM_i^j[Idx_i^j] = BM_i^j[Idx_i^j] | Mask_i^j;
  if (j+1 < L_i and BM_i^j[Idx_i^j] == 0xFFFFFFFF) {
    BitPtr_i^{j+1} = indexToBitptr(Idx_i^j);
    setBit(P_i,j+1); }
}
```

Figure 5. Bitmap marking GC algorithm

Any other auxiliary functions used in Figure 5 should be clear from their names.

3. Generational extension

In order for our non-moving bitmap marking GC to become a practical and truly better alternative to copying GC, we would like to extend it to generational GC. It is of course straightforward to combine our bitmap marking GC with any other GC to form a generational GC by moving objects between two heaps managed by two separate GC, but the resulting system loses the non-moving property. Our goal is to develop a new method that achieves the desired effect of generational GC without actually moving objects. This section presents one such general method.

3.1 General strategy

Demers et.al. [10] observed that generational GC is a partial GC that collects some subset of objects, and presented two variants of generational mark and sweep GC. This general idea can be adapted to develop a generational extension of our bitmap marking GC. Our strategy is to maintain *multiple bitmap trees for the same sub-heap*: one for each generation.

In an abstract view, generational GC manages the set of live objects in H_i as n disjoint sets $\mathcal{G}_i^1, \ldots, \mathcal{G}_i^n$, called generations. We note that a bitmap tree $BitMap_i$ of H_i can represent any subset of the set of all blocks in H_i, and therefore that each generation $\mathcal{G}_i^k$ can be represented by a separate bitmap tree $BitMap_i^k$ of H_i. These observations yield the following strategy. We use n bitmap trees $BitMap_i^1, BitMap_i^2, \ldots, BitMap_i^n$ for the same sub-heap H_i. Let $[\![BitMap_i^k]\!]$ be the set of objects represented by $BitMap_i^k$. The GC algorithm maintains the following invariant for each k:

$$[\![BitMap_i^k]\!] = \mathcal{G}_i^k \cup \mathcal{G}_i^{k+1} \cup \cdots \cup \mathcal{G}_i^n$$

or equivalently, $\mathcal{G}_i^k = [\![BitMap_i^k]\!] \setminus [\![BitMap_i^{k+1}]\!]$. The generational GC algorithm can then be realized as follows.

1. Every object is assigned a generation number k and a "tenure" counter indicating the number of minor collections it survived.
2. The mutator allocates an object in $\mathcal{G}_i^1$ with its tenure counter initialized to 0.
3. Reclamation of $\mathcal{G}_i^k$ is done by performing the following steps. If $k = n$, then the algorithm clears all the bitmap trees for H_i. If $k < n$ then it overrides $BitMap_i^k$ with $BitMap_i^{k+1}$. This corresponds to sweeping $\mathcal{G}_i^k$ by clearing the bits of objects in $\mathcal{G}_i^k$. The algorithm then traces the set of live objects. If it finds an unmarked live object, it marks the object in $BitMap_i^k$ and increments its tenure counter. If the tenure counter reaches the tenuring threshold, *tenureAge*, then the algorithm also marks it in $BitMap_i^{k+1}$. This corresponds to promoting the object to $\mathcal{G}_i^{k+1}$. When the tracing completes, the algorithm resets $BitMap_i^j$ to $BitMap_i^k$ for all j smaller than k.
4. Reclamation of $\mathcal{G}_i^1$ (minor GC) is invoked at some interval determined by a GC policy. When $\mathcal{G}_i^1$ is filled up to some predefined level, the algorithm estimates the oldest generation $\mathcal{G}_i^k$ that needs to be collected, and invokes the collection of $\mathcal{G}_i^k$.

3.2 The GC algorithm

In this paper we restrict the number of generations to 2. Then GC is either minor collection of $\mathcal{G}_i^1$ or major collection of $\mathcal{G}_i^2$. For this simple case, the major tuning parameters are the effective "size of minor heap" and the frequency of minor collections. In our segment based bitmap GC, these two can be controlled by the following two parameters.

- *minorSize*: the number of segments which can be allocated before the minor collection.
- *fillLimit*: the percentage limit to which each segment can continue to be filled after minor GC. Segments that are filled beyond this limit are regarded as full and will not be used for further allocation.

Each segment S_i is extended with $oldBitMap_i$ corresponding to $BitMap_i^2$. A generational GC algorithm is obtained by extending the `tryAlloc` function and defining a new procedure `minorGC` for minor collection. Figure 6 defines these functions. The algorithm for the major collection is the same as `bitmapMarkingGC` defined before. The allocation function `alloc` is also the same as before, except that it uses the new `tryAlloc`. The `traceLiveObjects` is also the same, except that it uses the new `markAndPush` that manages the tenure counter and promotion. The underlined part in the figure 6 is required refinement to the non-generational version. The `setBit` is extended so that it can mark bits in $oldBitMap_i$.

```
tryAlloc(H_i) {
  if (isMarked(P_i)) {
    if (findNextFreeBlock(P_i) == Fail) {
      increment the minor GC counter;
      if (minor GC counter >= minorSize_i) minorGC();
      if (findNextFreeBlock(P_i) == Fail) {
        if (nextSegment(SegList_i, P_i) == Fail) {
          if (newSegment(H_i) == Fail) {
            return Fail; } }
        findNextFreeBlock(P_i); } } }
  temp = BlkPtr_i;
  inc(P_i);
  return temp;
}

minorGC() {
  for each H_i {
    for each S_i^j in Sub(SegList_i, P_i, minorSize) {
      overwrite BitMap_i^j with oldBitMap_i^j; } }
  traceLiveObjects();
  for each H_i { rearrangeSegListMinor(H_i); }
  reset the minor GC counter;
}

markAndPush(O) {
  S_i, BitPtr_i^0 = findBitptr(O);
  if (not isMarked(BitPtr_i^0)) {
    setBit(P_i);
    incrementSegmentCount(P_i);
    push(O);
    increment the tenure counter of O;
    if (the tenure counter of O >= tenureAge) {
      reset the tenure counter of O;
      setBit(P_i) in oldBitMap_i; } }
}

rearrangeSegListMinor(H_i) {
  filled = {S_i^j | S_i^j ∈ Sub(SegList_i, P_i, minorSize),
                    Count_i^j >= fillLimit × Size_i}
  unfilled = {S_i^j | S_i^j ∈ Sub(SegList_i, P_i, minorSize),
                    Count_i^j < fillLimit × Size_i}
  list = concatSegList(filled, unfilled);
  replace Sub(SegList_i, P_i, minorSize) with list;
  set P_i to the first S_i^j in SegList_i
      such that Count_i^j < fillLimit × Size_i;
}
```

Figure 6. Generational bitmap marking GC algorithm

`Sub`$(SegList_i, P_i, n)$ is a reference to the sub-list of $SegList_i$ consisting of n segments immediately preceding P_i in the list.

If we further restrict *tenureAge* to 1, a particularly simple variant exists. As we noted earlier, allocation only advances the bit pointer without setting the bits corresponding to newly allocated blocks. This means that $BitMap_i$ is unchanged during allocation. Since *tenureAge* is 1, $BitMap_i$ after minor GC is the new contents of $oldBitMap_i$. So we do not actually need $oldBitMap_i$. The simple variant is obtained from the algorithm in Figure 6 by eliminating the bitmap overriding operation in `minorGC`, and using the same `markAndPush` function as non-generational GC defined in Section 2.5. The resulting algorithm coincides with the collection algorithm using "sticky mark bits" described in [10]. This simplified generational GC algorithm can be implemented with the same data structure and the support functions as the non-generational version.

4. Implementation and Evaluation

We have implemented the bitmap marking GC algorithm presented in Section 2 and its generational extension presented in Section 3. For comparison purpose, we have also implemented a plain Cheney copying collector, and a generational copying GC algorithm for Standard ML described in [29]. In this section, we outline our implementation and show the detailed evaluation results.

4.1 Implementation

Our implementation of non-generational GC takes the segment size and the total usable memory size as parameters, allocates the specified memory using `mmap` system call, and sets up the free segment pool and the 10 sub-heaps. The special sub-heap $\mathcal{M}$ for large objects is implemented as a mark and sweep GC, whose allocation area is dynamically obtained and freed using C library functions `malloc` and `free`. Since the usage of this special heap is very low in our benchmark tests, this special heap does not affect much on performance results. So we will not include performance data of this heap.

The free segment pool $\mathcal{S}$ is implemented as a free list of segments.

In addition to the above standard implementation, we have also implemented a special version of non-generational bitmap-marking GC. In this special version, instead of managing the allocation space as a collection of segments, each sub-heap H_i consists of a single large segment whose size is statically determined. This special implementation first reads an environment variable that holds 10 numbers $R_3, \ldots, R_{12}$ representing percentage ratio of the sizes of sub-heaps $H_3, \ldots, H_{12}$, and sets up the single segment for each H_i. As we shall report in the next subsection, this version is used to evaluate performance of sub-heap size adjustment through segment-based dynamic allocation and reclamation.

In what follows, we refer to the standard implementation of our non-generational bitmap marking GC as **bitmap** (or **bm**), and the special version as **bitmap(static)**.

We have implemented the simplified version of generational GC with 2 generations and $tenureAge = 1$, described in Section 3.2, by extending the standard implementation **bitmap**. The only major addition is a mechanism for a *write barrier* and a *remembered set* to keep track of pointers to young objects from outside. Since $tenureAge$ is 1 and any object survived a minor collection is promoted to the old generation, the remembered set can be flushed after minor GC. Taking advantage of this fact, we allocate a remembered set in the collector's trace stack. As mentioned before, our trace stack is implemented as a linked list using $Twork$ work areas. This is done by assigning a unique pointer slot in $Twork$ to each object. This implementation allows us to determine whether a given object is already in the list or not by checking whether the pointer is non-null. This automatically eliminates duplication in the remembered set. A write barrier can then be incorporated in the generational collector as follows. A write barrier code takes a young object that is to be referred from the old generation due to mutation, and marks it and pushes it to the trace stack. Minor collector simply traces objects using the trace stack whose initial contents is the remembered set. In what follows this implementation is referred to as **bitmap(gen)** (or **bm(gen)**).

Our implementation of Cheney collector uses the given memory as their two semi-spaces. In addition, we modified the standard Cheney algorithm so that it also uses the special sub-heap $\mathcal{M}$ for large objects, just the same way as in **bitmap**, **bitmap(static)** and **bitmap(gen)**. We have carefully tuned and optimized the allocation and collection functions of the Cheney collector, consulting the generated x86 assembly code, to make the Cheney collector performs the best as itself for x86 machine. We note that our change of including a special sub-heap for large objects makes the Cheney GC slightly faster in most cases, especially for those programs that use large objects. So this change is in favor of the Cheney collector. We also note that this change adds two x86 machine instructions to the optimized Cheney allocator, which should have increased allocation overhead by very small amount. According to our evaluation, this overhead is below margin of error. We refer to this implementation as **cheney** (or **cp**).

Our implementation of a generational copying GC for Standard ML mostly follows [29], which is one of standard generational GC algorithm for functional languages, except that it uses a fixed heap layout instead of dynamically allocating to-spaces, and that our implementation uses exact remembered set instead of card-marking. As in [29], the tenuring threshold is fixed to 1. The number of generations can be set to a number given as a parameter. The default number of generations used in Standard ML of New Jersey compiler is 5, and our GC only have 2 generations. So we have compared our GC against this copying GC with 2 generations and 5 generations. We refer to them as **copy(2g)** (or **cp(2g)**) and **copy(5g)** (or **cp(5g)**) respectively.

4.2 Performance Evaluation

We evaluate performance of our algorithms using publicly available benchmark programs for Standard ML, omitting benchmarks such as `fib, tak, ntakl` whose memory usage is very small. The evaluation has been done on an Intel Xeon 5150 2.66GHz processor with 8GB memory running SUSE Linux Enterprise Server 10. Execution time is measured by the system timer.

We organize our performance evaluation using the following general parameters and measures.

- *Heap size*. The entire heap size allocated by the runtime system except for special sub-heap $\mathcal{M}$. This size includes the allocation area as well as all the administrative data for GC. For the Cheney collector, this is the size of the sum of "to" and "from" spaces. For our GC, this is the size of the sum of allocation blocks, bitmap trees, and a trace stack combined.
- *Live object ratio*. The average percentage ratio of the total size of live objects after GC against the heap size.
- *Memory occupancy ratio*. The average percentage ratio of the amount of memory actually used for objects just before GC against the entire heap size. In the case of the Cheney GC, this is 50% at best. Since the allocator aligns each objects to double word boundary, the actual occupancy ratio is lower than 50%. The ratio of our GC depends on the sub-heap configuration.
- *Total time*. The *user* time (in seconds) spent for the program to run.
- *GC time*. The time (in seconds) spent in GC.

In our method, sweeping is done by clearing bitmaps, which is proportional to the heap size with very small constant factor. According to all the results, the bitmap clear time is in the range of 2.4% – 0.06% of the GC time, and in most cases they are less than 1% of the GC time. So we can safely conclude that bitmap clear time is negligible. We omit the detailed data.

Through preliminary evaluations and comparisons, we found that performance depends on the live object ratio, and that the set of benchmarks can be roughly grouped into the following three categories.

- Group I of those that only produce very short-lived data, and show very low live object ratio.

Group	benchmark	size (MB)	bitmap(static)			bitmap			cheney		
			time	live	occ.	time	live	occ.	time	live	occ.
I	count_graphs	2	15.27	6.01	67.8	15.15	6.02	55.44	15.77	6.02	48.7
	cpstak	2	1.33	5.52	64.2	1.26	5.56	51.63	1.43	5.55	48.9
II	knuth_bendix	12	0.74	10.01	63.4	0.76	10.45	61.1	0.75	10.17	46.1
	ratio_regions	20	37.82	12.21	54.0	37.24	11.97	62.3	38.21	11.95	47.4
III	gcbench	65	3.39	9.80	64.6	3.49	10.61	65.9	3.87	10.25	42.9
	perm9	190	3.03	14.20	53.2	3.32	22.36	57.6	3.49	16.91	41.6

Table 1. Performance of segment-based sub-heap size adjustment

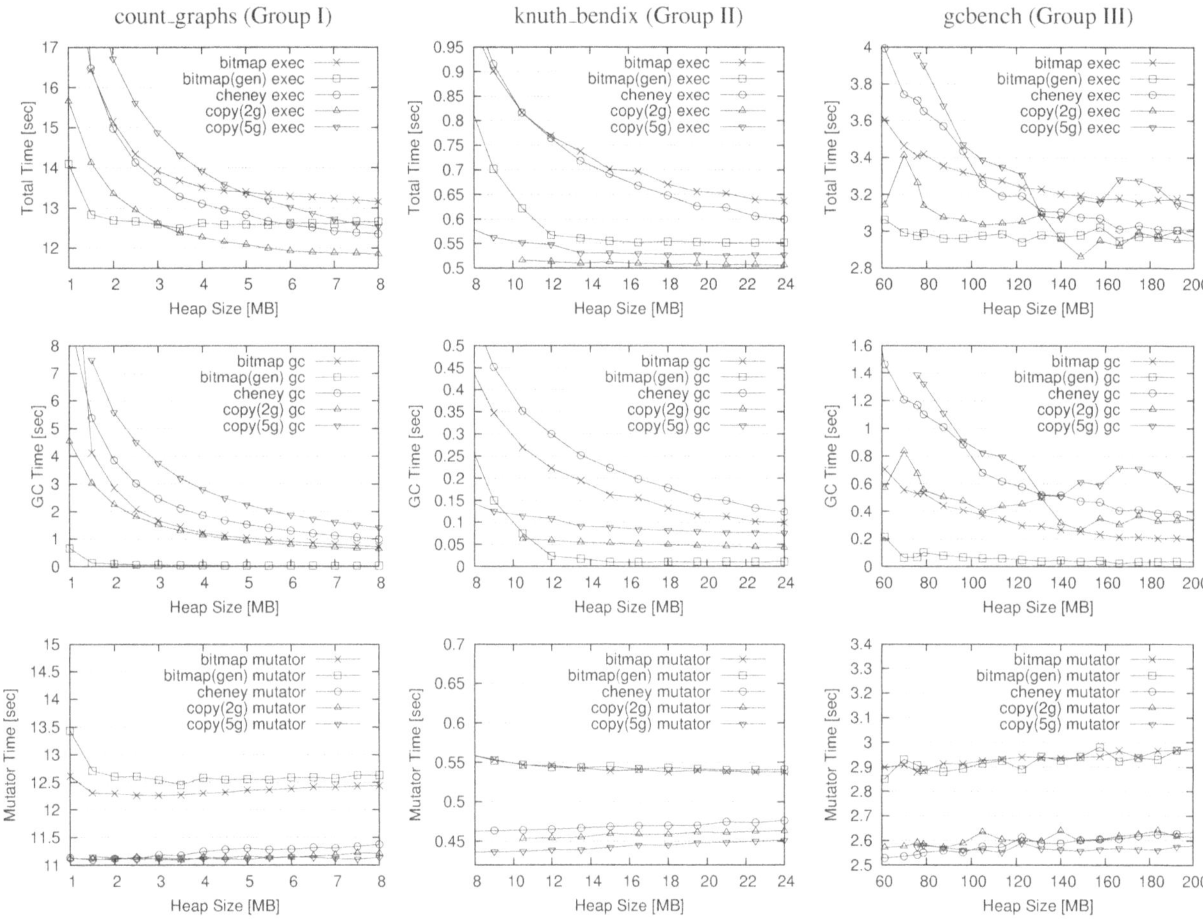

Figure 7. Performance of **bitmap(gen)** on typical benchmarks

- Group III of those that require some amount of memory and show high live object ratio.
- Group II is in between Group I and Group III.

We sometimes use these groups in evaluation and comparison.

Our first evaluation is the performance of automatic sub-heap size adjustment through dynamic segment allocation and reclamation. Our claim of fragmentation-avoided heap depends on this performance. If sub-heap size adjustment is not optimal in our GC then large amount of memory would have been wasted. To evaluate this, we have first estimated the best possible sub-heap size configuration for each benchmark using our **bitmap(static)** implementation; we have run each benchmark test on **bitmap(static)** a number of times (30 – 80 times) with different sub-heap size configurations by changing the environment variable we mentioned above. For each benchmark, we have selected the sub-heap size configuration that shows the best performance as our estimate of the optimal sub-heap size configuration for **bitmap(static)**. We have then compared performance of this hand-tuned **bitmap(static)** against **bitmap** and **cheney**. We omit the details of the result and only show a summary of overall performance of two typical benchmarks in each group in Table 1. We witnessed that all the others show similar behavior. The results show the following.

- The hand-tuned **bitmap(static)** performs better than **cheney** in most cases. The GC time is always shorter, and the total time is slightly better in most cases.
- The hand-tuned **bitmap(static)** shows significantly better memory usage for almost all the cases.
- Performance of the standard **bitmap** is as good as the best hand-tuned **bitmap(static)** in memory usage, GC time and the execution time.

These results verify that the dynamic segment allocation mechanism we have developed and implemented performs as efficiently as the best possible sub-heap size assignment obtained through hand-tuning. We thus conclude that this mechanism achieves almost optimal heap size adjustment automatically and dynamically.

Prior to overall performance evaluation, we searched for optimal values of the tuning parameters for the standard version **bitmap** and the generational version **bitmap(gen)**.

The segment size is a tuning parameter common to **bitmap** and **bitmap(gen)**. We have evaluated the performance of **bitmap** with various segment sizes from 32KB to 512KB. The results show that GC performance is not sensitive to segment size except for the cases where the total heap size is rather small compared to segment size. We omit the detailed data, and only state our conclusion that the segment size of 128KB is generally acceptable for all the benchmarks we used. All the data of **bitmap** and **bitmap(gen)** in this section are taken with 128KB segments.

For **bitmap(gen)**, we need to set its tuning parameters $fillLimit$ and $minorSize$. To determine the optimal values for $fillLimit$, we have evaluated the benchmarks against values of $0.2, 0.3, \ldots, 0.9$. According to the results, which we omit here, both the GC time and the total time of the most of benchmarks are not sensitive to this parameter, and 0.5 is reasonable for all the cases. So we set $fillLimit$ to 0.5. To determine the optimal value of $minorSize$, we have evaluated the benchmarks with different $minorSize$ values from 1 to the total number of segments. The benchmark test results, which we omit, indicate that larger $minorSize$ value is generally favorable. So we set $minorSize$ to be unlimited.

With these parameters, we have evaluated our generational GC **bitmap(gen)** and compared the results with those of the copying collectors **copy(2g)** and **copy(5g)**. For this purpose, we have run each of the benchmark programs with various heap sizes, ranging from the minimum runnable size to sufficiently large size.

Figure 7 shows the results of a typical benchmark of each of the three groups. It shows the total execution time (exec), the GC time (gc), and the mutator time (mutator) i.e. the difference of exec and gc against various heap sizes. From these sample results, we observe the following properties.

- For both generational and non-generational versions, the GC time of bitmap marking GC methods is shorter than that of copying GC methods. In particular, the GC time of **bitmap(gen)** is the shortest in most cases. Among the copying GC methods, **copy(2g)** is the shortest in GC time.
- The mutator time of bitmap GCs is longer than that of copying GCs, as expected. This difference should be due to the overhead of bitmap searching against bump pointer allocation. The difference of mutator time between non-generational and generational versions is very small.
- The total execution time of **bitmap(gen)** is shorter than that of **bitmap**. This shows that our generational GC scheme has the expected advantage for mark and sweep GC. Among copying GC methods, **copy(2g)** is the shortest in the total time.
- We cannot draw any definite conclusion on the relative strength of **bitmap(gen)** against **copy(2g)**; sometimes **bitmap(gen)** outperforms **copy(2g)** and conversely depending on benchmarks and heap size.

In addition to those 3 benchmarks shown in Figure 7, we evaluated the other benchmarks against varying heap sizes. We analyze these evaluation results and try to extract general property of our bitmap GC method, in particular, the relative strength of **bitmap(gen)** against **copy(2g)**.

To make a proper analysis of the benchmark data, we normalize them according to the relative heap size against the minimum runnable heap size. For most of the benchmarks, the minimal heap size of a bitmap marking GC is smaller than the corresponding copying GCs in both simple and general version. So we take the minimal heap size of each benchmark as the minimal heap with which **bitmap(gen)** can run. To eliminate anomalous or singular results due to too small or large heap, we sample the benchmark results with heap sizes from 2 to 6 times of this minimum heap size unit. Table 2 shows the summary of the average execution time over varying heap sizes for each benchmark. This table shows the following.

Group	benchmark	min	**bm**	**bm(gen)**	**cp**	**cp(2g)**	**cp(5g)**
I	barnes_hut	1	1.24	1.17	1.20	1.13	1.29
	count_graphs	1	13.75	12.60	13.32	12.40	14.25
	cpstak	1	1.09	0.89	1.06	0.92	1.16
	diviter	1	3.40	3.15	3.36	3.22	3.53
	divrec	1	4.03	3.75	3.80	3.64	3.94
	fft	2	1.61	1.52	1.55	1.49	1.57
	life	1	0.59	0.57	0.56	0.55	0.58
	logic	1	2.26	2.09	2.22	2.16	2.65
	mandelbrot	1	1.05	0.97	1.00	0.97	1.03
	nucleic	1	0.13	0.12	0.13	0.12	0.14
	puzzle	2	27.40	24.99	26.62	24.04	25.08
	ray	1	0.95	0.84	0.91	0.84	0.95
	simple	2	1.82	1.69	1.73	1.64	1.76
II	boyer	5	0.09	0.09	0.10	0.09	0.10
	knuth_bendix	6	0.65	0.55	0.62	0.51	0.52
	lexgen	8	1.21	1.12	1.06	0.99	1.01
	mlyacc	9	0.20	0.19	0.18	0.17	0.17
	ratio_regions	13	35.47	38.16	33.60	33.05	36.55
	smlboyer	5	0.75	0.73	0.77	0.80	0.85
	tsp	7	0.51	0.52	0.51	0.61	0.66
	vliw	2	1.81	1.37	1.52	1.30	1.54
III	gcbench	35	3.25	2.98	3.23	3.03	3.33
	perm9	95	2.95	2.99	3.07	3.58	4.29

(min: minimum heap size in MB for **bm(gen)**. **bm**, **bm(gen)**, **cp**, and **cp(ng)**: average total execution time with each GC method in seconds.)

Table 2. Performance summary

- **bitmap(gen)** outperform **bitmap** in almost all cases, as expected.
- **copy(2g)** shows the best performance among the copying GC methods in most cases.

Figure 8 shows the ratio of total execution time of **bitmap(gen)** against that of **copy(2g)** (smaller is better) under 2, 4, and 6 times of the minimum heap size. These results show that, for smaller heap size, **bitmap(gen)** outperforms **copy(2g)**. While the performance of **bitmap(gen)** is getting slightly worse than that of **copy(2g)** when the heap size increases, the ratios are around 1 in most of benchmarks. From these data, we can conclude that the performance of **bitmap(gen)** is comparable to that of **copy(2g)**.

These results are quite satisfactory; they show that our non-moving generational GC is a viable alternative to generational copying GC for functional languages.

5. Related works

This section compares our approach with some more related works that are not mentioned in Section 1.

Supporting efficient GC is essential for any optimizing functional language compilers. The current state-of-the-art in this field appears to be a generational GC whose minor (younger) collector is a variant of Cheney copying collector. OCaml, MLton, and old version of Haskell use a hybrid of copying GC with mark-compact GC [7, 31]. SML/NJ [29], Chez Scheme [14], and the latest Glasgow Haskell Compiler [23] use generational copying GC. In all

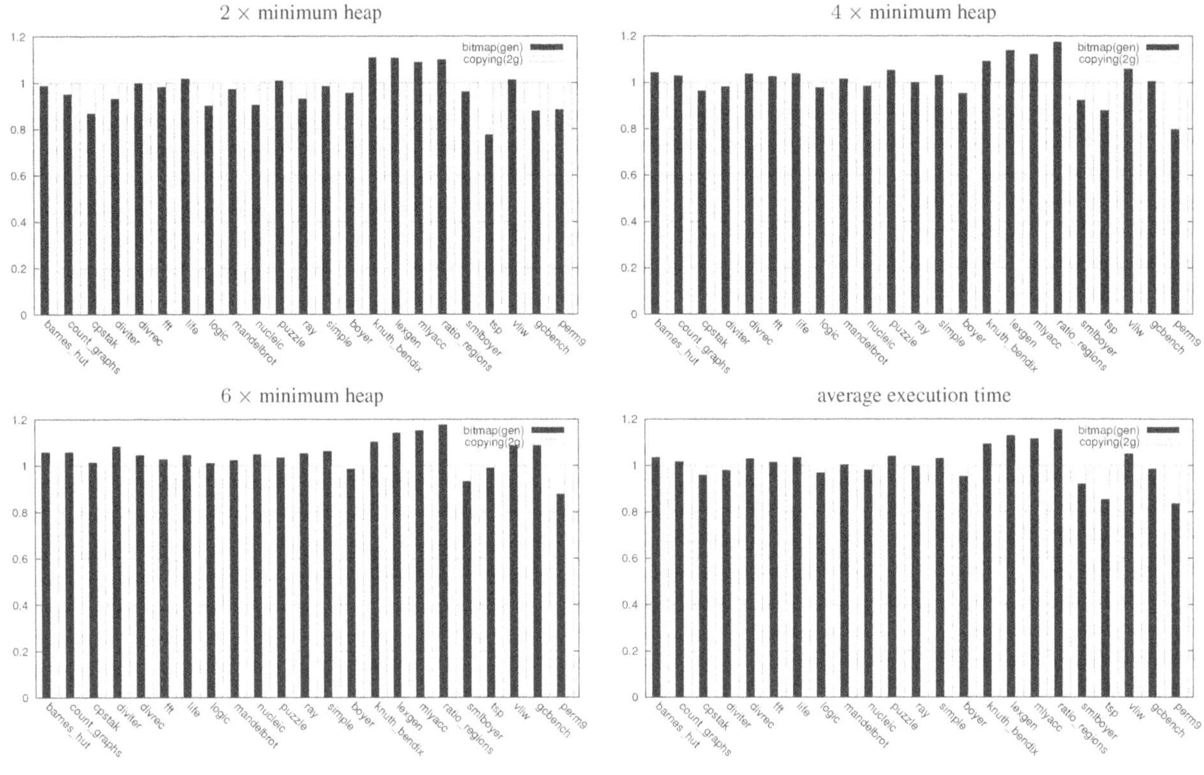

Figure 8. bitmap(gen) vs. **copy(2g)**

these systems, the Cheney's copying collector is used for minor GC and object-moving is inevitable, which makes inter-operation with other languages cumbersome and error-prone. A new contribution of our work is to present a non-moving alternative. Our benchmark tests including those that generate large amount of short-lived data such as `cpstak` show the feasibility of our approach.

Mark and sweep GC has also been extensively studied. Major issues have been efficient data structure for live objects, efficient allocation, avoiding fragmentation through compaction, and efficient sweeping.

The idea of using separate bitmaps to represent live objects is well known. Examples include bitwise sweep [12], bitmapped fits [37], and mark-and-deferred-sweep [38] based on lazy sweeping [16]. The main focuses of these works and others are on reducing the GC time and the cost for free list construction by avoiding scanning the entire heap. In contrast, our GC method uses bitmaps not only for representing live objects but also for allocation. Allocation is done using bitmaps without any other data structure.

Reducing sweep cost has been one of central issue, and a number of approaches have been proposed and implemented. Examples include mark during sweep [28], Treadmill [1], lazy sweeping [5, 16, 38], and selective sweeping [9]. Mark and split [30] eliminates subsequent sweep operations. In the context of sweeping, we can say that our approach eliminates the need of complex algorithms and data structures for sweeping and compaction, and yet achieves very fast sweeping; sweep is done simply by clearing bitmaps, whose cost is shown to be negligible in our benchmark tests.

One approach for efficient allocation, widely used in many GC methods [4, 6, 11, 15, 22, 29, 34], is to divide the heap into multiple areas of different size and manage those areas as a pool of *Big Bag of Pages* (BiBoP) [18] and some form of segregated free list such as [20]. In general perspective, our method of dividing the heap into sub-heaps of fixed size segment shares the same motivation with these previous works. In particular, obtaining a bit pointer from an object address mentioned in Subsection 2.5 can be regarded as an instance of encoding object meta-data in BiBoP. Our major new contribution is to prepare a sequence of sub-heaps of exponentially increasing block sizes. With this configuration, we avoid costly compaction at a reasonable expense of locally wasting space in each allocation block.

The problem of fragmentation and efficient compaction have also been extensively investigated. Example of recent works include [2, 4, 19, 26]. However, in most of the proposed approaches, possibility of fragmentation remains and for long running program, object-moving compaction is inevitable. SCHISM/CMR [27] attempts to eliminate fragmentation by fixing the size of an allocation unit, and decomposing objects into multiple units. Although this eliminates fragmentation in the main heap, it needs to introduce a separate copying heap for meta-level data to represent object structures. In contrast, our GC does not require any other structure than the heap itself, and still does not create fragmentation. So compaction is not needed by construction. Our observation is that our sub-heap organization achieves satisfactory compaction-free heaps at the acceptable expense of locally wasting allocation space.

Our goal is to develop an efficient non-moving collector. A pioneering work on this area is Boehm-Weiser conservative GC [6] developed for C. Since it is not possible to locate all the pointers of objects allocated by C programs, object-moving GC is impossible. Our non-moving constraint has the same origin: to inter-operate with C, we cannot move objects that are accessed from C programs. The problem domain is however rather different. Our aim is not to collect objects allocated in the C heap, but to collect only objects that are allocated in the functional-language heap. We hope that this opens up a new possibility of using GC technologies developed for functional languages to develop a new method satisfying non-moving constraint. Precise relationship between our GC method and those of conservative GC and its variants including mostly-copying GC [3, 32] is a topic for further investigation.

6. Conclusions and further development

Motivated by developing a memory management system that allows functional languages to seamlessly inter-operate with C, we have proposed a new garbage collection algorithm based on bitmap marking and have reported its implementation and performance evaluation. The proposed method realizes *a fragmentation-avoided heap* through a family of sub-heaps for objects of 2^i bytes ($3 \leq i \leq 12$), and *efficient allocation* through hierarchically organized bitmaps. This method can be extended to non-moving generational GC by maintaining separate bitmaps for the same allocation segments. In our extensive benchmark tests, our method is comparable to simple and generational copying GC in most cases. These results achieves our goal of developing a non-moving GC method that is as efficient as copying GC currently used in functional languages.

This is our first step towards a satisfactory memory management system suitable for functional languages that support various practical features including interoperability with C. A number of further issues remain to be investigated, including:

1. complete implementation and evaluation of generational GC,
2. further efficient allocation techniques such as bunched allocations, and
3. efficient multithreading support for modern shared memory multi-core processors.

The first and second one can be implemented without much difficulty. The last one is more challenging and requires new data structures and algorithms. We have already done preliminary design and implementation of multithreading extension of our GC method. Its detailed development and evaluation is outside of the scope of the present paper. In what follows, we briefly described the extension, focusing on the advantage offered by our new GC method.

There are a number of issues in developing efficient allocation and GC method that support multithreading on a modern shared memory multi-core architecture. Here we focus on the reduction of synchronizations overhead at allocation time. Obtaining a lock at each allocation time would be prohibitively expensive. An existing proposal for a functional language [13] is to use thread-local heaps. However, introduction of thread local heaps in an ML-style imperative functional language complicates the algorithms and would incur overhead in both allocation and collection due to the need of maintaining the invariant that there should be no pointer from a global heap to a local heap. In contrast, our GC method allows each thread to allocate a block in a global heap directly without any locking for most of the cases. As described in section 2, our allocation algorithm searches for a free block within the current active segment using an allocation pointer and a bitmap for that segment. A multithread extension can then be obtained simply by giving each thread its own active segment. Since the allocation pointer and the bitmap in each segment is local to that segment, each thread can allocate objects without any locking at all until the active segment becomes full. When the current active segment for a thread becomes full, the thread acquires exclusive lock on the sub-heap and attempts to obtain a new segment for the active allocation segment of the thread. If the free segment pool is empty, GC is invoked. The simple strategy to extend our GC to support multithreading is stop-the-world: suspending all threads before starting the bitmap marking GC. We have already experimentally implemented this approach and obtained preliminary evaluation result showing that it achieves expected efficient allocation in a multithreaded program running on a multi-core processor.

We expect that non-moving property should also be beneficial in developing concurrent GC, and that the combination of the above approach with concurrent and parallel GC mechanisms (see [17] for survey) would yield a satisfactory non-moving concurrent GC for functional languages, which can work with native threads.

References

[1] H. G. Baker. The treadmill: real-time garbage collection without motion sickness. *SIGPLAN Notices*, 27(3):66–70, 1992.

[2] K. Barabash, O. B.-Yitzhak, I. Goft, E. K. Kolodner, V. Leikehman, Y. Ossia, A. Owshanko, and E. Petrank. A parallel, incremental, mostly concurrent garbage collector for servers. *ACM Transactions on Programming Languages and Systems*, 27:1097–1146, 2005.

[3] J. F. Bartlett. Compacting garbage collection with ambiguous roots. *SIGPLAN Lisp Pointers*, 1(6):3–12, 1988.

[4] S. M. Blackburn and K. S. McKinley. Immix: a mark-region garbage collector with space efficiency, fast collection, and mutator performance. In *Proceedings of the ACM SIGPLAN Conference on Programming Language Design and Implementation*, pages 22–32, 2008.

[5] H.-J. Boehm. Reducing garbage collector cache misses. In *Proceedings of the International Symposium on Memory management*, pages 59–64, 2000.

[6] H.-J. Boehm and M. Weiser. Garbage collection in an uncooperative environment. *Software Practice and Experience*, 18(9):807–820, 1988.

[7] E. Chailloux, P. Manoury, and B. Pagano. *Developing applications with Objective Caml.* O'Reilly, April 2000. French version.

[8] C. J. Cheney. A nonrecursive list compacting algorithm. *Communications of the ACM*, 13(11), 1970.

[9] Y. C. Chung, S.-M. Moon, K. Ebcioğlu, and D. Sahlin. Selective sweeping. *Software Practice and Experience*, 35(1):15–26, 2005.

[10] A. Demers, M. Weiser, B. Hayes, H. Boehm, D. Bobrow, and S. Shenker. Combining generational and conservative garbage collection: framework and implementations. In *Proceedings of the ACM SIGPLAN-SIGACT Symposium on Principles of Programming Languages*, pages 261–269, 1990.

[11] D. Detlefs, C. Flood, S. Heller, and T. Printezis. Garbage-first garbage collection. In *Proceedings of the International Symposium on Memory Management*, pages 37–48, 2004.

[12] R. Dimpsey, R. Arora, and K. Kuiper. Java server performance: a case study of building efficient, scalable Jvms. *IBM Systems Journal*, 39(1):151–174, 2000.

[13] D. Doligez and X. Leroy. A concurrent, generational garbage collector for a multithreaded implementation of ML. In *Proceedings of the ACM SIGPLAN-SIGACT Symposium on Principles of Programming Languages*, pages 113–123, 1993.

[14] R. K. Dybvig. The development of Chez Scheme. In *Proceedings of the ACM International Conference on Functional Programming*, pages 1–12, 2006.

[15] R. K. Dybvig, D. Eby, and C. Bruggeman. Don't stop the BIBOP: Flexible and efficient storage management for dynamically-typed languages. Technical report, Indiana University, 1994.

[16] R. J. M. Hughes. A semi-incremental garbage collection algorithm. *Software Practice and Experience*, 12(11):1081–1082, 1982.

[17] R. Jones and R. Lins. *Garbage collection: algorithms for automatic dynamic memory management.* John Wiley & Sons, Inc., 1996.

[18] G. L. Steele Jr. Data representation in PDP-10 MACLISP. *MIT AI Memo 421*, September 1977.

[19] H. Kermany and E. Petrank. The Compressor: concurrent, incremental, and parallel compaction. In *Proceedings of the ACM SIGPLAN Conference on Programming Language Design and Implementation*, pages 354–363, 2006.

[20] D. Lea. A memory allocator. http://gee.cs.oswego.edu/dl/html/malloc.html.

[21] H. Lieberman and C. Hewitt. A real-time garbage collector based on the lifetimes of objects. *Communications of the ACM*, 26(6):419–429, 1983.

[22] S. Marlow, T. Harris, R. P. James, and S. P. Jones. Parallel generational-copying garbage collection with a block-structured heap. In *Proceedings of the International Symposium on Memory Management*, pages 11–20, 2008.

[23] S. Marlow, S. P. Jones, and S. Singh. Runtime support for multicore Haskell. In *Proceedings of the ACM SIGPLAN International Conference on Functional Programming*, pages 65–78, 2009.

[24] J. McCarthy. Recursive functions of symbolic expressions and their computation by machine, Part I. *Communications of the ACM*, 3(4):184–195, April 1960.

[25] H.-D. Nguyen and A. Ohori. Compiling ML polymporphism with explicit layout bitmap. In *Proceedings of the ACM SIGPLAN International Conference on Principles and Practice of Declarative Programming*, pages 237–248, 2006.

[26] F. Pizlo, D. Frampton, E. Petrank, and B. Steensgaard. Stopless: a real-time garbage collector for multiprocessors. In *Proceedings of the International Symposium on Memory management*, pages 159–172, 2007.

[27] F. Pizlo, L. Ziarek, P. Maj, A. L. Hosking, E. Blanton, and J. Vitek. Schism: fragmentation-tolerant real-time garbage collection. In *Proceedings of the ACM SIGPLAN Conference on Programming Language Design and Implementation*, pages 146–159, 2010.

[28] C. Queinnec, B. Beaudoing, and J.-P. Queille. Mark during sweep rather than mark then sweep. In *Proceedings of the Parallel Architectures and Languages Europe, Volume I: Parallel Architectures*, pages 224–237, 1989.

[29] J. H. Reppy. A high-performance garbage collector for Standard ML. Technical report, AT&T Bell Laboratories Technical Memo, 1994.

[30] K. Sagonas and J. Wilhelmsson. Mark and split. In *Proceedings of the International Symposium on Memory Management*, pages 29–39, 2006.

[31] P. M. Sansom and S. L. P. Jones. Generational garbage collection for Haskell. In *Proceedings of the Conference on Functional Programming Languages and Computer Architecture*, pages 106–116, 1993.

[32] F. Smith and G. Morrisett. Comparing mostly-copying and mark-sweep conservative collection. In *Proceedings of the International Symposium on Memory Management*, pages 68–78, 1998.

[33] SML# compiler. http://www.pllab.riec.tohoku.ac.jp/smlsharp/.

[34] D. Spoonhower, G. Blelloch, and R. Harper. Using page residency to balance tradeoffs in tracing garbage collection. In *Proceedings of the ACM/USENIX International Conference on Virtual Execution Environments*, pages 57–67, 2005.

[35] D. Ungar. Generation scavenging: A non-disruptive high performance storage reclamation algorithm. In *Proceedings of the ACM SIGSOFT/SIGPLAN Software Engineering Symposium on Practical Software Development Environments*, pages 157–167, 1984.

[36] H. S. Warren. *Hacker's Delight*. Addison-Wesley Longman Publishing Co., Inc., 2002.

[37] P. R. Wilson, M. S. Johnstone, M. Neely, and D. Boles. Dynamic storage allocation: A survey and critical review. In *Proceedings of the International Workshop on Memory Management*, pages 1–116, 1995.

[38] B. Zorn. Comparing mark-and-sweep and stop-and-copy garbage collection. In *Proceedings of the ACM Conference on LISP and Functional Programming*, pages 87–98, 1990.

Deriving an Efficient FPGA Implementation of a Low Density Parity Check Forward Error Corrector

Andy Gill   Andrew Farmer

The University of Kansas

{andygill,afarmer}@ittc.ku.edu

Abstract

Creating correct hardware is hard. Though there is much talk of using formal and semi-formal methods to develop designs and implementations, in practice most implementations are written without the support of any formal or semi-formal methodology. Having such a methodology brings many benefits, including improved likelihood of a correct implementation, lowering the cost of design exploration and lowering the cost of certification. In this paper, we introduce a semi-formal methodology for connecting executable specifications written in the functional language Haskell to efficient VHDL implementations. The connection is performed by manual edits, using semi-formal equational reasoning facilitated by the worker/wrapper transformation, and directed using commutable functors. We explain our methodology on a full-scale example, an efficient Low-Density Parity Check forward error correcting code, which has been implemented on a Virtex-5 FPGA.

Categories and Subject Descriptors D.3.2 [*Programming Languages*]: Language Classifications—Applicative (functional) languages

General Terms Design, Performance, Reliability, Verification

Keywords Lava, DSL, Error Correction, LDPC

1. Introduction

Connecting a clear description of an algorithm to an efficient, hardware based implementation brings many benefits. Real implementations contain many compromises, for example in the dimensions of performance, latency, power consumption, or capacity. In this paper, we discuss in detail a full-scale derivation from a specification of the Low Density Parity Check (LDPC) Forward Error Corrector to an efficient and deployable implementation, paying attention to these compromises.

We use the functional language Haskell both as our specification language and our implementation language. Our specification of the LDPC is a short and direct executable description of the algorithm, transliterated from the standard reference on error correcting codes (Moon 2005). Our implementation is expressed in a Haskell library called Kansas Lava (Gill et al. 2010). Kansas Lava takes idiomatic Haskell expressions that resemble hardware descriptions of component connectivity, and generates VHDL that can be synthesized using standard tools like Xilinx's ISE.

This paper presents a case study of taking the Haskell description of the LDPC and refining it into a Kansas Lava implementation. Having both the specification and implementation in the same host language allows a number of well-understood transformations to be used inside the common framework of Haskell refinement. We make extensive use of basic equational reasoning, Burstall-Darlington style fold/unfold (Burstall and Darlington 1977), and most critically, the recently formalized worker/wrapper meta-transformation (Gill and Hutton 2009).

ICFP'11, September 19–21, 2011, Tokyo, Japan.

2. Haskell, Architectures and Hardware

Consider a Haskell implementation of the well-known Game of Life, as described in (Hutton 2007). The game models a trivial cellular system, played on a 2-dimensional board.

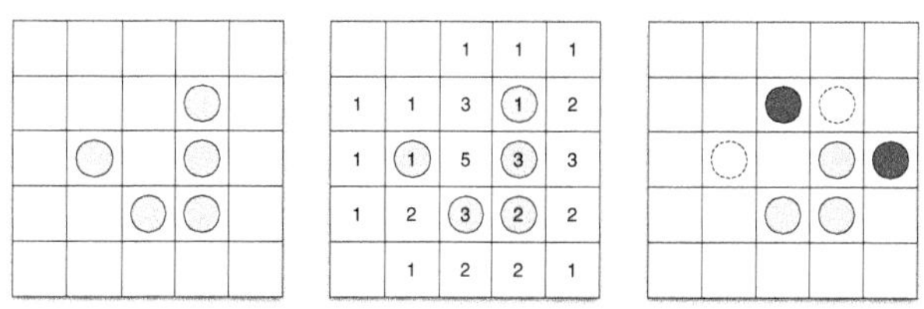

(a) (b) (c)

Each square in the board (a) either contains a living cell, marked here with a filled-in circle, or is empty. Each step consists of counting your eight neighbors (b). If you are alive and have two or three living neighbors, then you survive to the next generation (c), otherwise you die (c; dotted circles). Empty squares with three living neighbors spawn a new cell (c; darker circles).

Hutton describes the world of the game using a list of coordinates of living cells.

```
type Board = [(Int,Int)]
```

Hutton then defines a function that finds survivors and another that finds births, and uses them to define a stepper function, called **nextgen**.

```
surviors, births :: Board -> [(Int,Int)]

nextgen :: Board -> Board
nextgen b = survivors b ++ births b
```

This is a classic example of using big-step computation to cleanly capture the behavior of a system, something Haskell excels at. The pertinent question for this paper is can this Haskell implementation inform the *architecture* and *implementation* of a hardware rendition of the Game of Life in a meaningful way?

In making any transition to hardware, decisions about the layout of computation, or architecture, are critical. This architecture takes into consideration what will be computed where, and what components will communicate, without taking into consideration exact timing and clocking issues. For instance, in our Game of Life, we can imagine each box in the 5x5 grid using the values communicated directly from its neighbors to compute its liveness for the next generation.

Assuming we use the common idiom of streams to represent values that change over time, with each time step being a generation, one possible implementation of an architecture takes a list of streams from all the neighbors and returns a stream representing the liveness of the cell over time.

```
box :: Bool -> [Stream Bool] -> Stream Bool
box init nss = res
  where
     res = init : zipWith step (transpose nss) res

step :: [Bool] -> Bool -> Bool
step ns live
   | live     && neighbors == 2 = True
   | live     && neighbors == 3 = True
   | not live && neighbors == 3 = True
   | otherwise                  = False
  where
     neighbors = length (filter id ns)
```

Again, Haskell is a useful descriptive tool, this time for architectural concerns. The type of box implies that this architecture takes inputs from its neighbors, using a single boolean result from each one on each conceptual cycle. No commitment has been made about the specific implementation or timing of this communication channel.

Finally, we can consider a hardware description of box. The obvious implementation in this example would mirror the architecture, having the 8 neighborly values communicated directly. For illustration purposes, we encode this using an 8-tuple. So, given a nominal data-type Signal, which represents a wire that encodes a clocked signal, the type of one possible implementation uses an initial boolean value and an 8-tuple of neighbor signals to generate a boolean output signal.

```
type Tuple8 a = (a,a,a,a,a,a,a,a)

box_impl :: Bool
         -> Tuple8 (Maybe (Signal Bool))
         -> Signal Bool
```

Of course, for this example there are other alternative implementations, but working with and coding around implementation specific restrictions is completely typical for reaching efficient implementations. This brings out the critical contribution of the step between the architecture and the implementation, namely the elaboration of the decision of how to communicate between computational blocks. Pictorially, the relationship between the arguments of box and box_impl can be representing using:

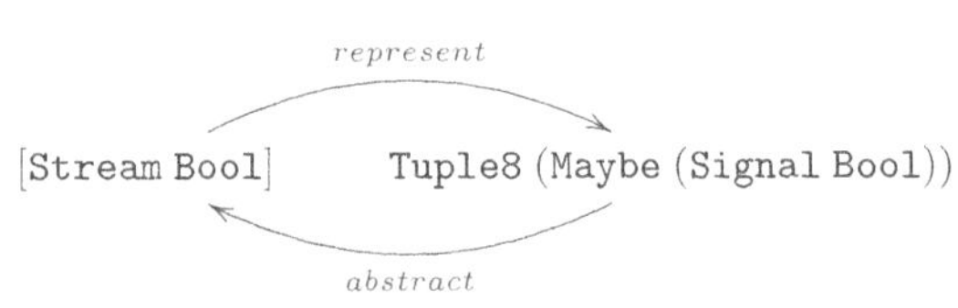

From a refinement perspective, there is an interesting relationship between these two types, and encoding this relationship is the central task of any refinement from architecture to implementation.

If we consider all three versions of the Game of Life, there is a pattern of refinement that can be observed. In Hutton's example, a big-step computation is being performed on the entire state for each new generation. In the architectural description, the computation has been partitioned and state transitions happen locally. In the final example, both computation and communication have been refined into an efficient, hardware-centric implementation.

This paper contains a case study that follows this specification to architecture to implementation pattern. We first introduce the general worker/wrapper transformation, our main refinement weapon in our derivation (§3). We then introduce the notion of commutable functors, which we use to direct our use of worker/wrapper when performing refinements (§4). Next, we introduce Kansas Lava, our Haskell library for expressing hardware (§5), and our target algorithm, the Low Density Parity Check forward error correcting algorithm, and its executable specification in Haskell (§6). We take this specification and refine it into our LDPC architecture by making decisions about computational layout (§7). Finally, we take the architecture and refine it into our LDPC implementation in Kansas Lava, which executes on an FPGA (§8). We close with performance results, discussions of related work, and our conclusion.

In this paper, we make the following contributions.

- This case study is the first example of the new formalization of the worker/wrapper transformation being used in anger on a large example. The case study also demonstrates the viability and usefulness of worker/wrapper as an informal refinement tool, even without a mechanized implementation.
- We give the intermediate steps of our refinement in detail, as well as the challenges faced and decisions made. The intent is that this study be a prelude to adding some automation to our refinement processes, and knowing useful non-trivial examples helps in the design of our (future) refinement engines.
- Finally, we illustrate the utility of using functors to model and implement communication channels, and the refinement possibilities this opens up. Specifically, commutable functors play a pivotal role in allowing us to plot a course through a derivation and show that following this course gives, as a side effect, a list of proof obligations and other useful artifacts.

3. The Worker/Wrapper Transformation

The worker/wrapper transformation (Gill and Hutton 2009; Peyton Jones and Launchbury 1991) changes how a (typically recursive) function operates using only locally verifiable assumptions. The transformation is a general form of data-refinement (Hoare 1972). As a local transformation that acts on a single function, the worker/wrapper transformation can achieve a global influence on a program by pushing specially crafted coercion *wrappers* in a systematic way from definition site to call sites. Worker/wrapper has been used as a mechanism to implement strictness analysis optimizations (Jones and Partain 1993), argument transposition (Launchbury and Sheard 1995), constructor specialization (Jones 2007), and in the worker/wrapper journal article memoization (Michie 1968) and CPS translation (Appel 1992; Sussman and Steele 1975) are also performed. The transformation is straightforward and remarkably general. For these reasons, the worker/wrapper transformation is an ideal candidate for a meta-refinement in our methodology. Specifically, we will use the ability to change the type over which functions operate to perform a number of type-directed hops from our specification to implementation.

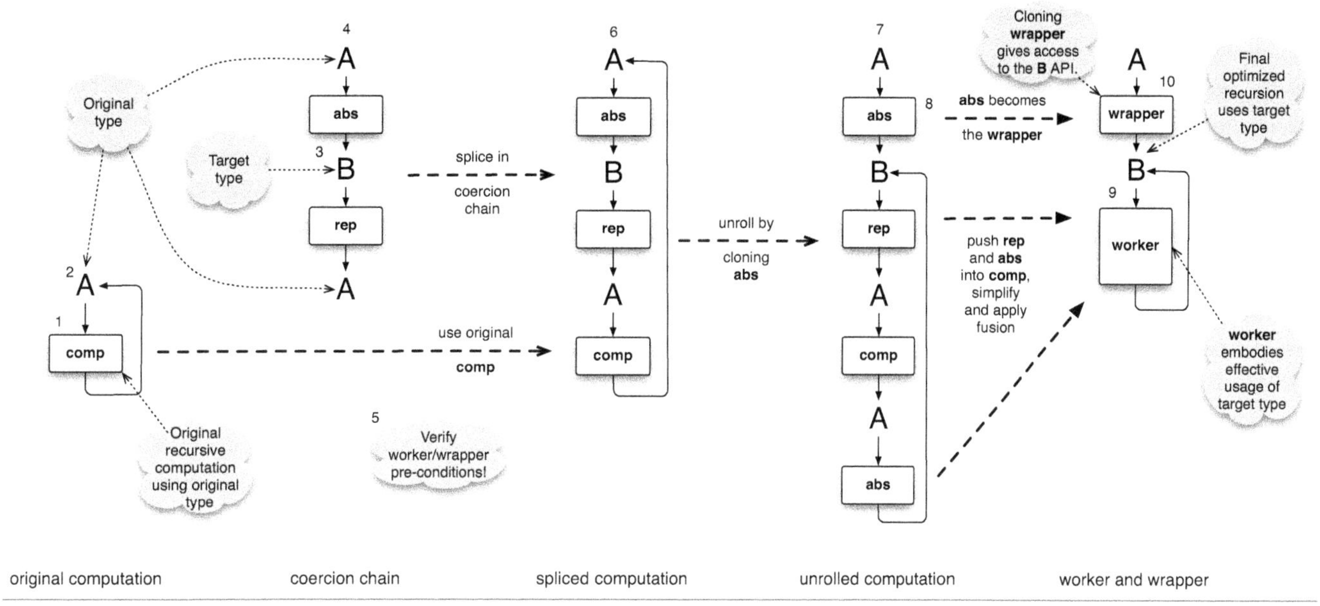

Figure 1. The Worker/Wrapper Transformation

The worker/wrapper transformation is illustrated in Figure 1. Solid arrows signify function calls, and dashed arrows signify the application of specified refinements. The boxes are computations that have a type, given as an incoming arrow, and require the use of a second computation, given as an outgoing arrow. As such, these computational boxes can be considered as representing functions with higher-order arguments. **A** and **B** should be read as the type of a computation or service.

The **original computation**[1] is a recursive function, notated with an arrow back to the type of the computation, **A**[2]. (Superscripts in this section refer to Figure 1.) The worker/wrapper transformation operates as follows: A target type[3] for the recursion is selected, here called **B**. A **coercion chain**[4] is constructed from two higher-order functions, that coerce from **A** to **B**, and back to **A**, using the standard data-refinement terminology of **abs** and **rep** (Hoare 1972). The worker/wrapper local preconditions are verified[5]; one example is when **abs** and **rep** form an identity over **A**. The coercion-chain can now be spliced into the original recursion back-edge[6], replacing the original computation. The **abs** definition can now be unrolled a single step[7], which exposes **abs** as a non-recursive component of the overall computation[8]. This new formulation can be transformed and optimized using local, well understood algebraic transformations and fusion rules into an efficient *worker*[9] that operates over **B**, and a *wrapper*[10] that allows original users of the **A** API to call the new function.

3.1 Worker/Wrapper Pre-Conditions

Three possible pre-conditions for worker/wrapper are:

- $\mathbf{abs} \circ \mathbf{rep} = \mathbf{id}_\mathbf{A}$; or
- $\mathbf{abs} \circ \mathbf{rep} \circ \mathbf{comp} = \mathbf{comp}$; or
- $\mathbf{fix}(\mathbf{abs} \circ \mathbf{rep} \circ \mathbf{comp}) = \mathbf{fix}\ \mathbf{comp}$.

All three follow from the formalization, with each pre-condition directly implying the subsequent, weaker pre-condition. The third pre-condition can actually be observed inside Figure 1, where the splicing is a use of this final rule. The intuition behind all the pre-conditions is that they ensure, specifically for the function `comp`, that the alternative type **B** can safely be used.

3.2 Example of Worker/Wrapper

To give a short example of worker/wrapper in use, we transform the naïve Haskell definition of `reverse` into an efficient implementation.

```
reverse :: [a] -> [a]
reverse xs = comp xs
   where comp []     = []
         comp (x:xs) = reverse xs ++ [x]
```

- `reverse` is defined as a computation (`comp`) that takes a list `[a]` and returns the reverse of the list, also of type `[a]`[1]. As such, the initial type **A** is `[a] -> [a]`[2].
- We choose the type `[a] -> H a` for **B**, where `H a` is a data structure that acts like a list, but efficiently implements appending to the end of the list[3]. There are a number of possible such implementations (Hughes 1986; Okasaki 1998).
- Our higher-order functions **abs** and **rep** (not given) contain the functions `absH` and `repH`:

```
-- converting an H list into a regular list
absH :: H a -> [a]
-- converting a regular list into an H list
repH :: [a] -> H a
```

- It can be shown that our **abs** and **rep** satisfy $\mathbf{abs} \circ \mathbf{rep} = id_\mathbf{A}$[4], meeting one of the worker/wrapper pre-conditions[5].

Wrap the computation in `absH` and `repH` functions, which form an identity[6].

```
reverse :: [a] -> [a]
reverse xs = absH (repH (comp xs))
   where comp []     = []
         comp (x:xs) = reverse xs ++ [x]
```

Note that `reverse` and `comp` are mutually recursive. Unroll the recursive call to `reverse` once, so `comp` calls itself[7].

```
reverse :: [a] -> [a]
reverse xs = absH (repH (comp xs))
   where comp []     = []
         comp (x:xs) = absH (repH (comp xs)) ++ [x]
```

Create a new worker function, which is the expression contained in the outer absH, namely: repH (comp xs). After this, reverse is a *wrapper*[8] that calls worker.

```
reverse :: [a] -> [a]
reverse xs = absH (worker xs)

worker :: [a] -> H a
worker xs = repH (comp xs)
    where comp []     = []
          comp (x:xs) = absH (worker xs) ++ [x]
```

Now the optimization of the worker can begin in earnest[9]. We do not repeat the wrapper reverse again, because it remains unchanged. After some well-understood transformations, we reach:

```
worker :: [a] -> H a
worker []     = repH []
worker (x:xs) = snocH (repH (absH (worker xs))) x
```

In this specific case, repH can fuse with absH, and we can reach the optimized solution, reaching:

```
worker :: [a] -> H a
worker []     = repH []
worker (x:xs) = snocH (worker xs) x
```

The whole definition of worker now operates using the new type H a, and we have successfully translated a computation over **A** into a computation over **B**[10]. Note that the wrapper (here, reverse) is no longer recursive, and its body can be cloned and inlined at all call sites.

This example was presented in a first order, syntactical style, but the transformation itself is higher-order. Exactly the same framework can be used to change the argument types, or even the number of arguments. Indeed, as long as **A** and **B** can be used as alternative representations of the same underlying computation, worker/wrapper can be applied. Furthermore, the transformation can be repeated, changing to yet another type. We are going to use this chaining ability to help perform the key step of turning an executable specification of LDPC into an efficient implementation.

4. Functors are our Friends

Given the ability to perform type-directed transformation using worker/wrapper, we now present a small set of types that model different components of computation and storage that will be used as our alphabet for both the executable specification and the implementation. These components are all modeled after a mathematical structure called a **functor**. Formally, a functor is mapping between categories in category theory, and we use the term functor in this paper in the more general sense than the specific Haskell class Functor.

In Haskell the class Functor provides an implementation for a function fmap, a mnemonic for functor-map, which obeys two properties.

```
class Functor f where
  -- law: fmap id = id
  -- law: fmap f . fmap g = fmap (f. g)
  fmap :: (a -> b) -> f a -> f b
```

There are many Haskell data-structures that are functors, for example Haskell lists and Maybe. Take as a concrete example streams. A Stream and its Functor instance can be defined as:

```
data Stream a = Cons a (Stream a)

instance Functor Stream where
   fmap (Cons x xs) = Cons (f x) (fmap f xs)
```

It is straightforward to show that this implementation satisfies the two laws.

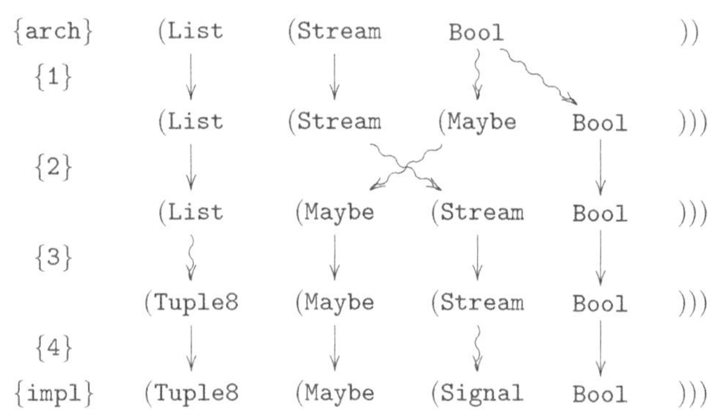

Figure 2. Refining the Game of Life: Architecture to Implementation

4.1 The Big Idea

A functor often represents a container, like a list, that contains zero or more items of a given type. Functors can also be used to represent computation models, like an infinite stream of data. Our thesis is that functor-like structures can be effectively used to represent structures that describe real-world communication inside architectural descriptions and hardware solutions. As such, these functor chains become guideposts to performing larger refinement.

Reconsidering the example from Section 2, we refine from an architecture of a list of streams of booleans, and reach a fixed-sized tuple of optional signals of boolean. Figure 2 illustrates the steps taken in this example, from architecture to implementation. For symmetry, we will write the list type using List, and not "[]", for the remainder of the paper. In the example, we are performing three possible translations: adding a functor (step 1); commuting functors (step 2); replacing one functor with another (steps 3 and 4). Each translation has its respective proof obligation. This type-level explanation can be used to explain the stepwise thinking of the implementation refinement.

Lifting the Bool

We choose to implement the Game of Life where the edges *do not* wrap back on each other. As such, neighbors that would be outside the boundary wall are always zero. We want to optimize the code generated for the edges. Though in this example this optimization makes little difference, we intend to implement operations acting on a sparse matrix in our large case study, and in that case, the ability to generate no code for zeros is critical to reaching an efficient implementation. The Maybe functor is used to represent the case of being always zero because the neighbor is out-of-bounds.

Rather than jump straight to the the type Maybe (Signal Bool), we lift the type of Bool to Maybe Bool. The reason for this intermediate step is to be explicit about what Maybe actually represents. By first using Nothing to represent *always zero* on operations that use the innermost type (Bool), we separate the optimization from the meaning of zero in this circuit. Using the abs and rep terminology, we have the following implementation of the coercions.

```
rep1 True = Just True
rep1 False = Just False

abs1 Nothing = False
abs1 (Just True) = True
abs1 (Just False) = False
```

Worker/wrapper can therefore be used to translate box into a worker with the type following the first step in Figure 2.

Commute Maybe and Stream

We now want to commute the Functors `Stream` and `Maybe`. There is a significant difference between a stream of optional values, and an optional stream of values. If we try define an `abs` and `rep`, these differences are reflected in the preconditions.

```
abs2 :: Maybe (Stream a) -> Stream (Maybe a)
abs2 Nothing    = repeat Nothing
abs2 (Just xs) = fmap Just xs

rep2 :: Stream (Maybe a) -> Maybe (Stream a)
rep2 = ????
```

`abs` is straightforward to write, but `rep` cannot be written; there are too many possible input shapes to represent. However, if we restrict the use of the `Stream (Maybe a)` space to streams where *all* the values are Nothing or all the values are just Just, then we can write `rep`.

```
-- Pre-condition: Stream in canonical form
rep2 (Cons Nothing _) = Nothing
rep2 ss               = Just (fmap fromJust ss)
```

The external condition, that the `Stream (Maybe a)` be one of two specific canonical forms, *could* be captured formally as a context-sensitive extension of the worker/wrapper transformation. We remain however intentionally informal here; this is exactly the type of refactoring refinement that programmers routinely do without appealing to semi-formal reasoning, and we want to support this while capturing proof obligations that could be filled in later. A reasonable question to ask is if by allowing this informality, we have watered down the methodology too far from its formal roots. We do not believe so, because it is the use of chains of functors that provides the major engineering value, allowing documentation and design exploration that traditional refactoring techniques find challenging. We will, however, revisit this specific point when we have better tool support for these ideas and refinements.

Commuting `Stream` and `Maybe` is the step that yields our key optimization. By taking out-of-bounds streams that were always `Nothing` values and eliminating them altogether, we avoid generating unnecessary hardware. This concept is key to our later LDPC example. More generally, this is an example of a commutable functor pair. Under certain well-defined conditions, specific functors can be safely transposed, and when used with the worker/wrapper transformation, this transposition gives a new program that is one step closer to an implementation.

Replacing List with Tuple8

The next step is to replace the list (which we knew was always 8 elements long) with an 8-tuple. There are a number of pragmatic reasons why we want to generate hardware components with fixed sized inputs. First, this makes reification into hardware possible (Gill 2009). Second, using a fixed shape can encourage sharing of components when generating FPGA bitstreams, potentially speeding up bitstream generation. The `abs` and `rep` are trivial.

```
abs3 :: Tuple8 a -> List a
abs3 (a,b,c,d,e,f,g,h) = [a,b,c,d,e,f,g,h]

rep3 :: List a -> Tuple8 a
rep3 [a,b,c,d,e,f,g,h] = (a,b,c,d,e,f,g,h)
```

Here, the pre-condition is that the code that uses `box` only generates lists with eight elements. This assumption would be easy to verify, once again using a context-aware pre-condition.

Replacing Stream with Signal

The final step in this example is replacing `Stream` with `Signal`. In this case, the two are used with a trivial isomorphism, where both are clocked using an implicit clock at the same speed, resulting in a one to one mapping. This mapping is not always this trivial. For example, a stream could be sampled using control logic when being translated into a signal. Given the trivial translation however, we can use coercion functions to and from `Signal`.

```
abs4 :: Signal a -> Stream a
abs4 = fromSignal

rep4 :: Stream a -> Signal a
rep4 = toSignal
```

4.2 Discussion

We have (informally) translated an architectural description into an efficient implementation, using functors as our guides. Each step involved demonstrating, in some sense, that the two types represent the same communication within the problem domain.

There are many alternative ways of doing this derivation, even using the same methodology. For example, a more direct approach to optimizing the walls would have been to explicitly build in support for lists up to 8 long, with the walls not contributing elements to the argument list. Another approach would be to just generate a constant `False` for the walls. The overarching point is that tradeoffs in the implementation are reflected in the choice of functors and how these functors are translated.

Finally, the `box` function is not recursive. The worker/wrapper transformation provides a useful framework for semi-formal reasoning, even in this case. We will return to using worker/wrapper on a recursively defined architectural description shortly.

5. Kansas Lava

We target Kansas Lava because it is a subset of Haskell from which we can generate synthesizable VHDL. We will take executable specifications in Haskell, which use Haskell functors, and transform them via worker/wrapper into hardware implementations in Kansas Lava, which use Kansas Lava functors. Targeting Kansas Lava in this way dramatically narrows the gap between Haskell specification and hardware realization.

Kansas Lava is a Haskell-hosted Embedded Domain Specific Language (EDSL) for hardware description and synthesis. Based on the idea of directly specifying circuits as functions, as in the original Lava (Bjesse et al. 1998), Kansas Lava seeks to be a modern and scalable implementation of the Lava paradigm.

Kansas Lava is based around two functor-like structures: `Comb`, for combinationally generated values, and `Seq`, for sequentially generated values. `Comb`-centric circuits can be lifted into sequential circuits, using a small set of built-in lift functions:

```
liftS0 :: Comb a
       -> Seq a
liftS1 :: (Comb a -> Comb b)
       -> Seq a
       -> Seq b
liftS2 :: (Comb a -> Comb b -> Comb c)
       -> Seq a
       -> Seq b
       -> Seq c
```

Kansas Lava simultaneously maintains both a shallow and a deep embedding of a circuit, so a Lava circuit can be executed directly (the shallow embedding), or can be reified into VHDL for use on an FPGA (using the deep embedding). The ability to execute a partially refined Lava circuit allows for faster design iteration.

On top of Comb and Seq, Kansas Lava makes use of other structures to express common idioms. Two important structures we use are Enabled and Write.

```
type Enabled a = Maybe a
type Write a b = Enabled (a,b)
```

Enabled represents an optional value being passed over a wire, typically using an extra boolean signal to express validity. Write represents an optional index-value pair, and is used to express element-wise updates to mutable state, as well as multiplex larger values over time.

Kansas Lava also has a complete implementation of sized types, rendered using associated type functions (Chakravarty et al. 2005), and uses them to implement sized matrices, and sized signed and unsigned bit vectors. Our size types, by notation, start with X.

```
-- Size types
data X1 = ...
data X2 = ...
data X3 = ...
...
data X256 = ...
```

We use the names Matrix, Signed and Unsigned to denote our sized structures, where the x (phantom) type parameter is the size type.

```
-- Matrix, and Sized Signed and Unsigned
data Matrix x a = ... array of a, sized x ...
data Signed x = ... signed number of width x ...
data Unsigned x = ... unsigned number of width x ...
```

We define Matrix x as an instance of Functor. Matrix X8, for example, replaces the use of Tuple8. In addition, we have a number of useful synonyms built on these sized types. One we will be using is U_n, an unsigned n-bit number.

```
type U1 = Unsigned X1
type U2 = Unsigned X2
type U3 = Unsigned X3
...
```

Apart from these idioms, we also support an fmap style lifting over Seq (and Comb, using overloading). The key lift function works by enumerating all inputs and recording all outputs, which are stored on a ROM, which is a Seq to Seq function.

```
funMap :: (Rep a, Rep b) => (a -> b) -> Seq a -> Seq b
```

Rep is a class that encodes construction and deconstruction of the bitwise representation, allowing enumeration of all inputs.

In addition to the signal types, Kansas Lava makes extensive use of associated type families to permit the flexible handling of groups of signals. This is implemented via a type class and a type function Unpacked. (Both Comb and Seq are instances of Signal.)

```
class (Signal sig) => Pack sig a where
    type Unpacked sig a
    pack :: Unpacked sig a -> sig a
    unpack :: sig a -> Unpacked sig a
```

pack and unpack allow us to effortlessly commute between packed and unpacked signals. This commuting groups of signals with pack and unpack turns out to be exactly the same shape as the data transformations we are performing in this paper, and have turned out to be Really Useful in practice.

To give an example of an actual Kansas Lava program, Figure 3 provides the implementation of the box circuit reached by refinement at the end of Section 2, but using the new types and functions we have just introduced. The definition of n encodes the decision that missing streams (corresponding to out-of-bounds neighbors) will be represented by a stream of zeros. We also convert each

```
box_impl :: Bool -> Matrix X8 (Maybe (Seq Bool)) -> Seq Bool
box_impl init ns = res
    where
          n :: Seq U3
          n = foldr (\ a b ->
                         case a of
                           Just v -> unsigned v + b
                           Nothing -> b)
                     0
             $ M.toList ns

          res :: Seq Bool
          res = register init
              $ funMap life (pack (n,res))

          life :: (U3,Bool) -> Maybe Bool

          -- stay alive if 2 or 3 neighbors are alive
          life (2,True)  = return True
          life (3,True)  = return True

          -- spawn if 3 neighbors are alive
          life (3,False) = return True

          -- otherwise die
          life _         = return False
```

Figure 3. Kansas Lava Implementation of box

```
entity box is
  port(rst : in std_logic;
       clk : in std_logic;
       clk_en : in std_logic;
       i0 : in std_logic;
       i1 : in std_logic;
       i2 : in std_logic;
       o0 : out std_logic);
end entity box;
architecture str of box is
  signal sig_2_o0 : std_logic := '1';
  signal sig_3_o0 : std_logic;
  ...
  type sig_4_o0_memory_type is array (15 downto 0)
                of std_logic_vector(0 downto 0);
  signal sig_4_o0 : sig_4_o0_memory_type:=
                ("0","0","0","0","1","1","0","0",
                 "0","0","0","0","1","0","0","0");
begin
  ...
  sig_6_o0 <= std_logic_vector((unsigned(sig_7_o0)
                                + unsigned(sig_8_o0)));
  ....
  sig_7_o0 <= "00" & i0;
  ...
end architecture box;
```

Figure 4. Kansas Lava Generated VHDL

boolean signal into a signal of three-bit unsigned numbers, and add them together, giving the number of live neighbors. It should be observed that this is a regular foldr over the Matrix content.

We then use funMap to lift the regular Haskell function life over a stream containing the number of live neighbors and this cell's status. Since the domain of life is limited by the size type, every possible input can be enumerated and a ROM can be generated to implement this function as a lookup.

Figure 4 lists the VHDL generated for the top-left hand box only. There are three inputs (neighbors), and one output, as well as clocking and control signals. We can see, for example, the two-bit unsigned extend in the signal assignment to sig_7_o0.

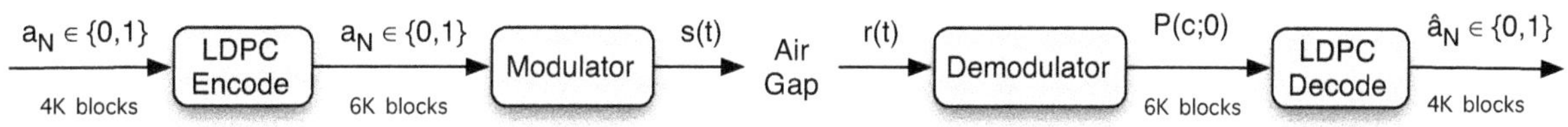

Figure 5. Using a 2/3-rate 4K LDPC

6. LDPC

A Low Density Parity Check (LDPC) code is a Forward Error Correcting (FEC) code that uses parity bits to support the recovery of data transmitted over a noisy link (Moon 2005). The LDPC algorithm uses Belief Propagation to attempt to find the original message inside a received signal, and can be constructed in a way that is arbitrarily close to the channel capacity, or the Shannon Limit. Though invented in the 60's by Gallager (Gallager 1962), it remained until the mid-90's a theoretical curiosity due to the computational cost of any implementation. Advances in LDPC code construction have resulted in codes that can be decoded in real time (Andrews et al. 2007). Our lab was tasked with implementing one such code, on an FPGA fabric, and investigating the properties of the final implementation.

Figure 5 illustrates how parity is used to provide recovery of a signal over a noisy medium. A signal is transmitted in discrete packets, with extra parity information, and the LDPC algorithm is used to extract the original message, finding an answer that meets a parity check. The encoder is trivial to construct, being a simple bitwise matrix multiply. The decoder, and the subject of this refinement case study, is more challenging.

The decode specification is concise, and can be given by three equations. Using the notation from the standard reference on error correcting codes (Moon 2005), and starting with the matrix $\eta^{[0]} = 0$, and a received signal $\lambda^{[0]}$, we have:

For each (m, n) where $A(m, n) = 1$:

$$\eta^{[l]}_{m,n} = -2\tanh^{-1}\left(\prod_{j\in\mathcal{N}_{m,n}} \tanh\left(\tfrac{1}{2}\left(\eta^{[l-1]}_{m,j} - \lambda^{[l-1]}_{j}\right)\right)\right)$$

For each n:

$$\lambda^{[l]}_{n} = \lambda^{[0]}_{n} + \sum_{m\in\mathcal{M}_n} \eta^{[l]}_{m,n}$$

For each n:

$$\hat{c}^{[l]}_{n} = 1, \text{if} \lambda^{[l]}_{n} > 0, \text{otherwise} = 0.$$

Each of $\eta^{[l]}, \lambda^{[l]}, \hat{c}^{[l]}$ is computed, starting from iteration 1. This algorithm terminates with the result $\hat{c}^{[l]}$ if parity is achieved ($A\hat{c}^{[l]} = 0$), or alternatively an iteration threshold is reached, in which case, then $\hat{c}^{[0]}_{n}$ is returned. The input, $\lambda^{[0]}$ is a soft input, being a representation of likelihood of a symbol, with zero representing unknown. Finally, $\mathcal{M}_n$ represents $\{m : A_{m,n} = 1\}$, and $\mathcal{N}_{m,n}$ represents $\{n : A_{m,n} = 1\} \setminus n$.

A is a sparse binary matrix that forms a parity checking property for messages that have parity added using the encoding matrix. The details of how to invent these two matrices, jointly called a code, are not important here; in our case we were required to use a specific code invented by JPL (Consultive Committee for Space Data Systems (CCSDS) 2007). The JPL code we are using is a 4K 2/3-rate code, which takes 4096 bits, and transmits 2048 additional parity bits. The decoder actually operates on 7K bits, the last 1K being extra untransmitted parity bits.

Each row of the sparse matrix A represents an individual parity check between a small number of bits. When multiplying A with a symbolized received packet (normalized to the binary symbols 0 and 1), if every value in the result is zero, then the received packet is, with extremely high probability, without error. The challenge of LDPC is finding a variant of the received noisy signal that achieves parity. The algorithm works by having each (non-zero) element of η contain a small delta that attempts to allow its specific row to reach parity.

Performing tanh and $\tanh^{-1}$ is pervasive in the algorithm, but expensive in hardware, so the following compromise is often taken:

For each (m, n) where $A(m, n) = 1$:

$$\eta^{[l]}_{m,n} = -\tfrac{3}{4}\, \texttt{fold}\, \min^{\dagger}\, [\eta^{[l-1]}_{m,j} - \lambda^{[l-1]}_{j} | j \in \mathcal{N}_{m,n}]$$

$$\min^{\dagger}(x, y) = sign(x) * sign(y) * min(|x|, |y|)$$

The intuition behind this modification of the algorithm is that the Belief Propagation was dominated by the *smallest* value, because of the use of the product of the log likelihoods. This compromise results in a slight loss of decoding quality, around 0.2dB, in return for an algorithm that is much easier to map onto FPGAs. In the FPGA literature (Andrews et al. 2007) this function is a known simplified variant of the `min*` function. From an algebraic point of view, we observe that `min`† is associative and commutative, so any `fold` (left, right or balanced) can be used. We also observe that `min`† is also bit-accurately associative and commutative, even when used on quantized fixed-precision values.

It is straightforward to transliterate this mathematical description into a Haskell-based executable specification, as given in Figure 6. This is actually an optimized Haskell program, using three different representations of matrices, that ran fast enough to use on real test vectors. (In this paper, as much as possible, we present original code, but for presentation purposes and due to space considerations we have performed some minor α-conversions, and other small changes, like omitting the debugging parameterization. None of the changes affect the thesis of this paper.)

```
loop :: forall x y a
      . (Fractional a, Ord a, Size x, Size y)
     => Options
     -> Int
     -> A y x
     -> SM.Matrix (y,x) a
     -> Matrix x a
     -> Matrix x a
     -> IO (Maybe (Matrix x U1,Int))
loop options n a@(A a_rref aRows aCols) ne lam orig_lam
  | cardinality ans == 0    = return $ Just (c_hat,n)
  | n > iterations options  = return Nothing
  | otherwise = loop options (n+1) a ne' lam' orig_lam
  where
    c_hat :: Matrix x U1
    c_hat = fmap (\ c -> if c > 0 then 1 else 0) lam

    ans :: BitMatrix (y, X1)
    ans = a_rref `mult` fromMatrix (unitColumn c_hat)

    ne' :: SM.Matrix (y,x) a
    ne' = SM.fromAssocList 0
       [ ((m,n), - 0.75 * (foldr1 metric
             [ (ne SM.! (m,j)) - (lam ! j)
             | j <- toList (aRows ! m), j /= n]
          ))
       | (m,n) <- BitMatrix.toList a_rref ]

    lam' :: Matrix x a
    lam' = forAll $ \ n -> (orig_lam ! n)
         + sum [ ne' SM.! (m,n) | m <- toList (aCols ! n) ]
```

Figure 6. Haskell Description of LDPC

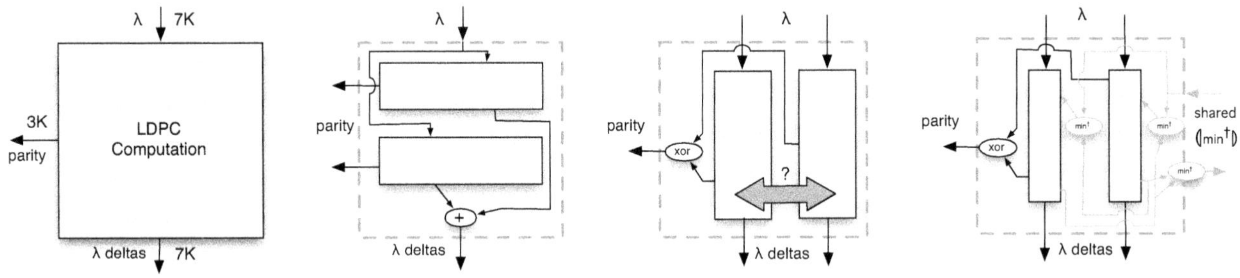

(a) Basic LDPC Fabric (b) Fabric Split Horizontally (c) Fabric Split Vertically (d) Refined Vertical Split

Figure 7. Abstract Computational Fabrics

7. From Specification to Architecture

We start our implementation with a requirement to handle a 4 Mbps stream of data, transmitted over a 70MHz carrier frequency. This is inside the performance range of existing implementations on Virtex-4 technologies (Andrews et al. 2007), but still requires careful performance engineering. The first stage of our derivation is to *choose* our architecture. That is, a Haskell program that represents the way we choose to lay out computation on a hardware fabric, without being specific about details like clocking or control. Most existing hardware implementations of LDPC use a crossbar architecture to communicate between different segments of λ, via intermediate nodes that represent individual rows of η. Values are passed from λ nodes to η nodes, and back, through this crossbar, and this communication dominates the cost of computing each iteration. Much of the recent research into LDPC implementation efficiency has focused on optimizing this aspect through creative scheduling.

When looking at the sparse A matrix, which drives the mathematical "shape" of the computation, we were curious if there was a way to layout the FPGA based on the A matrix directly. The overarching code-generation design pattern is to divide the layout into two parts, call a function to generate the sub-components based on the computations driven by the sub-matrices, and generate logic to wire the two sub-components to make the whole solution. This is classical divide and conquer, and we can re-apply it recursively many times, down to a suitable level of granularity. In this way, we can partially automate the tradeoffs between communication costs and parallelism opportunities; because generally, more sub-division leads to more parallelism and more communication overhead between blocks.

Figure 7 illustrates the sub-division of the computation, based on this thinking. Figure 7(a) shows a complete computation block, where 7K of informational datums are sent in and 7K of informational datums are sent out, as well as parity results. Figure 7(b) shows the conceptual breakup into "cells" of computation. Dividing the fabric horizontally is trivial. The same λ is passed in both the top and bottom, and the λ deltas can be computed for each column using a simple addition. The parity is delivered as two separate channels. After analysis of the communications required, splitting the fabric horizontally resulted in a fabric with communications costs proportional to the *perimeter* of the fabric, and therefore amicable for use on an FPGA.

Dividing the fabric vertically, as shown in Figure 7(c), is more challenging. This is because, assuming an identity element for $\min^\dagger$ notated using θ, each non-zero element in η is being computed using

$$\texttt{fold}\ \min^\dagger\ \theta\ [(\eta_{m,j}^{[l-1]} - \lambda_j^{[l-1]}) \mid j \in \mathcal{N}_{m,n}],$$

that is, every η value of a row depends on every other (non-zero) η value in the same row. This means that splitting the fabric vertically unfortunately results in a communication overhead that is no longer proportional to the *perimeter* of the fabric and instead depends on the number of contributing values in each row of η.

We can use the associativity and commutability of $\min^\dagger$ to minimize communication costs. Specially, it is straightforward to demonstrate that, for any associative and commutative f that has an identity element z, and any total predicate p, the following holds.

$$\forall xs.\ \text{fold}\ f\ z\ xs \equiv \begin{array}{l} f(\text{fold}\ f\ z\ [x \mid x \in xs, p\ x]) \\ \quad (\text{fold}\ f\ z\ [x \mid x \in xs, \neg p\ x]) \end{array}$$

Given this, we can rework our row-based computations.

For each row m, and partition predicate p, where $p\ n$ is $true$:

$$\texttt{fold}\ \min^\dagger\ \theta\ [(\eta_{m,j}^{[l-1]} - \lambda_j^{[l-1]}) \mid j \in \mathcal{N}_{m,n}]$$

$\{$Expand out explicitly the $\neq n, \mathcal{N}_m$ represents $\{n : A_{m,n} = 1\}\}$

$$\equiv\ \texttt{fold}\ \min^\dagger\ \theta\ [(\eta_{m,j}^{[l-1]} - \lambda_j^{[l-1]}) \mid j \in \mathcal{N}_m, j \neq n]$$

$\{$For $\min^\dagger$, we can factor our `fold` into two `folds`$\}$

$$\equiv\ \begin{array}{l} \min^\dagger(\texttt{fold}\ \min^\dagger\ \theta\ [(\eta_{m,j}^{[l-1]} - \lambda_j^{[l-1]}) \mid j \in \mathcal{N}_m, j \neq n, p\ j]) \\ \quad (\texttt{fold}\ \min^\dagger\ \theta\ [(\eta_{m,j}^{[l-1]} - \lambda_j^{[l-1]}) \mid j \in \mathcal{N}_m, j \neq n, \neg p\ j]]) \end{array}$$

$\{\ p\ n = true \wedge \neg p\ j\ \Rightarrow\ j \neq n\ \}$

$$\equiv\ \begin{array}{l} \min^\dagger(\texttt{fold}\ \min^\dagger\ \theta\ [(\eta_{m,j}^{[l-1]} - \lambda_j^{[l-1]}) \mid j \in \mathcal{N}_m, j \neq n, p\ j]) \\ \quad (\texttt{fold}\ \min^\dagger\ \theta\ [(\eta_{m,j}^{[l-1]} - \lambda_j^{[l-1]}) \mid j \in \mathcal{N}_m, \neg p\ j]]) \end{array}$$

This derivation means that we can combine *all* the values outside our (arbitrary) partitioning once, and use this external result as part of the answer for each sub-computation, inside the partition. This trick of splitting folded values is used at the (arbitrary) vertical boundary of our computation fabric. Figure 7(d) illustrates this formulation. The left and right sides both use each others' row summary as well as any external row summary, and the resultant row summary for the larger box is the $\min^\dagger$ of the two row summaries.

Armed with the ability to split the computation fabric in two different directions, we need to choose a suitable sized "cell". Reducing to single 1x1 cells results in optimal parallelism, but unmanageable communication, and would not fit on any current FPGA. When we examine the JPL LDPC decode matrix A, we find a by-construction curiosity that unlocks our architectural choice. Specifically, the decode matrix is constructed entirely of fixed-sized cells of either an empty matrix, an identity matrix, or of a cyclically shifted identity matrix. This property holds by design for the JPL codes, and in the case of the 4K code, we have a matrix of 28 columns by 12 rows, containing cells of 256x256.

Assuming we render each of these 256x256 cells as individual hardware components in our architecture, we can (1) invent the type for our cells, (2) define a mechanism for routing data between cells, and (3) refine our specification into a Haskell program that implements (1) and (2). The aspect of these cells that draws us to this design is that each cell contains only 256 individual intermediate η values, but implements a sub-matrix of the η matrix sized 256^2, a wonderful property!

We can now target a specific abstracted architecture that reflects our choices. Figure 8 gives the type and pseudo-code for our main architecture function. Rather than write this by hand, we used by-hand refinement from the specification. We set up adjacent Haskell modules with the same API, and imported them `qualified`, allowing the main driver to pick and choose of set of possible implementations to execute using tests vectors, and compare results. In this way, each new refinement step could be tested against its previous step. The steps taken were as follows.

- A purely functional `solve` function is extracted from the `loop` function, which explicitly takes and returns the two pieces of state (the η and λ).

```
solve :: forall x y a . (Size x, Size y, Fractional a, Ord a)
      => A y x
      -> (SM.Matrix (y,x) a, Matrix x a)
      -> (SM.Matrix (y,x) a, Matrix x a)
```

  `SM.Matrix` is our sparse representation of a matrix.

- From this solve function, a first version of `operate` is extracted, which takes and returns unsized Haskell arrays.

```
operate0 :: (Ord b, Fractional b, Num b, x ~ Int, y ~ Int)
         => Array (x,y) U1       -- A
         -> Array (x,y) b        -- eta
         -> Array y b            -- lambda
         -> Array x (Maybe b)    -- Global partial
         -> ( Array (x,y) b      -- new eta
            , Array x (Maybe b)  -- Local partial
            , Array y b )        -- new lambda *delta*
```

- The `operate` function is factored to act using `Stream`, rather than take and return state.

```
operate1 :: (Ord b, Fractional b, Num b, x ~ Int, y ~ Int)
    => Array (x,y) U1                   -- A
    -> Stream (Array y b)               -- lambda
    -> Stream (Array x (Maybe b))       -- Global partial
    -> ( Stream (Array x (Maybe b)) -- Local partial
       , Stream (Array y b) )           -- new lambda delta
```

- The ability to handle splitting, both vertically and horizontally, was added into `operate`, as well as spotting zero matrices. This makes no difference to the type, but relies on the splitting function actually implementing the LDPC by correctly chaining together vertical and horizontal components.

- We finally added the ability to represent the optimized zeros, giving the type in Figure 8. This final step was actually performed using a by-hand execution of the worker/wrapper transformation.

8. From Architecture to Implementation

We now have our working executable architecture model of LDPC, expressed in terms of arguments with chains of functors. We now apply the same approach as in Section 4.1, to get from our architecture to our implementation. Of course, this real implementation example is more involved. The steps we took to translation from architecture to (efficient) implementation were as follows.

```
operate2
  :: forall b x y
   . (Ord b, Fractional b, Num b, x ~ Int, y ~ Int)
  => Array (x,y) U1
  -> Stream (Array y b)            -- lambda
  -> Stream (Array x (Maybe b))    -- Global partial
  -> ( Stream (Array x (Maybe b)) -- Local partial
     , Stream (Array y (Maybe b))-- new lambda *delta*
     )
operate2 a lam glob
   | if-should divide vertically
   = let (l_A,r_A)            = splitV a
         (l_lam,r_lam)        = splitV lam
         l_glob               = liftA2 minD glob l_shared
         r_glob               = liftA2 minD glob r_shared
         (l_shared,l_delta) = operate2 l_A l_lam l_glob
         (r_shared,r_delta) = operate2 r_A r_lam r_glob
     in
         ( liftA2 minD l_shared r_shared
         , l_delta `append` r_delta
         )

   | if-should divide horizontally
   = let (t_A,b_A)            = splitH a
         (t_glob,b_glob)      = splitH glob
         (t_shared,t_delta) = operate2 t_A lam t_glob
         (b_shared,b_delta) = operate2 b_A lam b_glob
     in
         ( t_shared `append` b_shared
         , liftA2 add t_delta b_delta
         )

   | if A matrix all zeros
   = return $ constStream
            $ constArray Nothing (.. range of x ..)

   | otherwise
   = generic implementation of LDPC
```

Figure 8. Haskell LDPC Architecture Description

- We switched to using a generic representation of the large sparse array `A` using worker/wrapper. This was more an artifact of the way we were using the model, rather than strictly necessary.

- Next, we use worker/wrapper to change `Stream` of `Array` into List of Stream of (fixed-size) Matrix. This step also committed to the fixed cell size SZ.

```
operate3
  :: forall b x y
   . (Ord b, Fractional b, Num b, Real b, x ~ Int, y ~ Int)
  => A (x,y)         -- A
  -> List (Stream (Matrix SZ b))
  -> List (Stream (Matrix SZ (Maybe b)))
  -> ( List (Stream (Matrix SZ (Maybe b)))
     , List (Stream (Matrix SZ (Maybe b))))
```

- We then commuted the `Maybe` functor outwards, giving:

```
operate4
  :: forall b x y
   . (Ord b, Fractional b, Num b, Real b, x ~ Int, y ~ Int)
  => A (x,y)         -- A
  -> List (Stream (Matrix SZ b))
  -> List (Maybe (Stream (Matrix SZ b)))
  -> ( List (Maybe (Stream (Matrix SZ b)))
     , List (Maybe (Stream (Matrix SZ b))))
```

  This is an extension of the transformation performed when commuting `Maybe` and `Stream`, in § 4.1.

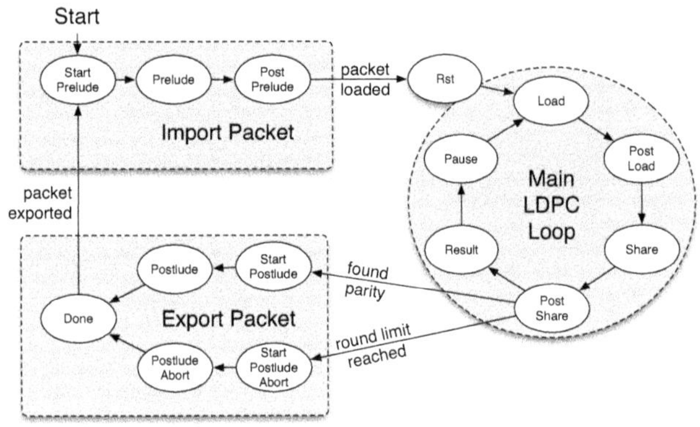

Figure 9. LDPC Control Logic State Machine

- Next, we added a control logic argument, and use of the `Write` tuple based on this logic. We also specialize our implementation to our target quantized type of FLOAT, an 8-bit fixed precision representation.

  This step gives timing to the computation cell, with a stream of matrices of values replaced by a `Seq` of `Write` commands, which can are optional index-value pairs. Figure 9 gives the state machine for our control logic. The control logic, which was developed concurrently to the derivation, was built using a Haskell state-to-state function, and lifted into a ROM using the `mapFun` function discussed in Section 5.

```
operate5
  :: forall b x y
   . (Ord b, Fractional b, Num b, Real b, x ~ Int, y ~ Int)
  -> A (x,y)          -- A
  -> Seq DecodeCntrl
  -> List (Seq (Write SZ FLOAT))
  -> List (Maybe (Seq (Write SZ FLOAT)))
  -> ( List (Maybe (Seq (Write SZ FLOAT)))
     , List (Maybe (Seq (Write SZ FLOAT)))
     )
```

- We now piece together these cells, to give a larger computation "block", which is composed of `N` by `M` cells. The `Bool` output is a partial computation of parity, looking for the termination condition. Figure 10 gives the type of this function.

The circuit in Figure 10 can be directly reified into a VHDL program. Around this implementation, we added FIFO support for input and output and control logic support that loads the memories, detects when the LDPC is complete (or run out of time quota), and outputs the result. This extra logic could have been written in either VHDL or Lava, but we choose to write it in Lava.

9. Onwards to Hardware

The final step is taking our working and cycle-accurate VHDL generated by Kansas Lava, and executing it on our hardware. Techniques for *programming* an FPGA board are well documented, and there are many online examples and other resources to draw from. Our first place-and-routed version of LDPC came back with unrealistic path delays. The circuit clocked at around 14Mhz, which is unfortunately too slow to run on our board, which requires at least 40MHz.

In Kansas Lava, the internal graph structure of all nodes is a first class data-structure. It was straightforward to add an option for annotating code with path length comments, making finding critical paths at the Kansas Lava-level straightforward. The depth (distance from a register output, excluding trivial wiring) also appeared as comments in our generated VHDL. The ability to start within

```
generateVHDL
 :: (Index x ~ Int, Index y ~ Int, Size x, Size y)
 => A (x,y)                                    -- A
 -> Rst                                -- The reset signal
 -> Seq DecodeCntrl                    -- the control signals
 -> Seq ( Matrix N_SZ (Write SZ FLOAT) ) -- lambda
 -> Seq ( Matrix N_SZ (Write SZ FLOAT)    -- lambda *delta*
        , Matrix M_SZ (Write SZ Bool)     -- parity
        )
```

Figure 10. Haskell LDPC Implementation Type Signature

the high level description language yet also achieve instant cycle accurate simulation allows for quick exploration of designs.

Using the depth data from these comments, we again refine the type of `operate`. One place there was a depth issue was the tree of min†, caused by the recursive code-generating solution. The obvious solution was to place a register after every min†, but there is no guarantee in this design that all sub-trees of min† have the same depth. This would result in the stream of values becoming out of sync, and the wrong values being operated on.

Our generative code approach offers another alternative. The type we are communicating with internally is:

```
... (Maybe (Seq (Write SZ FLOAT))) ...
```

taken from the second-to-last step in Section 8. We refine this (using worker/wrapper) into:

```
... (Maybe (Delay (Seq (Write SZ FLOAT)))) ...
```

```
-- definition of Delay
type Delay a = (Int,a)
```

The `Int` in `Delay` represents the number of cycles the index-value `Write` datum has been statically delayed, using the `Delay` functor definition.

We then lifted min† function, over the delay.

```
liftDelay :: (Rep a, Rep b, Rep c)
          => (Comb a -> Comb b -> Comb c)
          -> Delay (Seq a)
          -> Delay (Seq b)
          -> Delay (Seq c)
liftDelay f (n,a) (m,b) = ( max n m + 1
                          , liftS2 f a' b'
                          )
  where
        a' = delays (max n m - n) a
        b' = delays (max n m - m) b
```

This lifting, and an extra pause of a few cycles added to the state "Post Share" in Figure 9 allowed for the min† function to be automatically retimed with the correctly aligned data arriving for merging in the same cycle. This automated the addition of a set of strategic registers between components. After making the necessary changes to the control logic to accommodate this, we reached a more respectable clock rate of 92.5Mhz and more scope for optimization remains. Table 1 gives a summary of the current device utilization, including the communication driver, for the 8-bit quantized version of LDPC.

Table 1. Device Utilization on the XC5VLX110T

Number of RAMB18X2s	122 out of 148	82%
Number of Slice Registers	10214 out of 69120	14%
Number of Slice LUTS	19902 out of 69120	28%
Number of Slice LUT-Flip Flop pairs	22035 out of 69120	31%

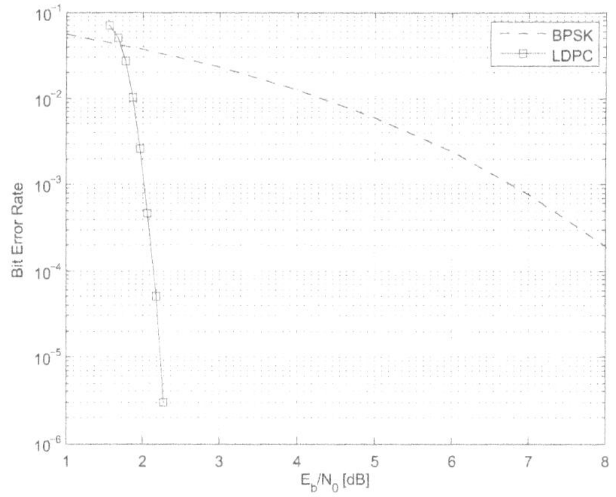

Figure 11. Bit Error Rates for the 4096/6144 LDPC Code

10. Results on FPGA

Figure 11 shows the result of running the 8-bit quantized LDPC circuit, on the FPGA, performing forward error correction.

- BPSK is the a trivial decode with no parity checking, and is our baseline.
- LDPC is our forward error correction decoder in action.

LDPC requires extra parity bits be transmitted, and therefore the LPDC results can be worse than BPSK when low signal to noise causes LDPC to fail frequently. However, under normal operating conditions, the LDPC is known to allow for around 8dB of forward error correction, allowing for lower power transmitters and/or operation in noisier environments.

The next stages in the project include:

- Testing our circuit with real noise over an air gap, rather than additive white Gaussian noise. This will involve connecting the LDPC to our existing implementation of a demodulator, and building a transmitter. Both are project requirements.
- Accurately verifying the maximum possible rate from this circuit.
- Experimenting with new control logic to transfer multiple `FLOAT` values per cycle, increasing the throughput further. We think that the use of functors for refinement will make this possible to explore.
- By using the `min`†, we took a small compromise over an implementation based on tan, and we would like to attempt to build a $tanh$ version of the LDPC for FPGAs.

How competitive is our implementation of LDPC? Our current implementation is well within data rate for the original specification (4 Mbps). Figure 11 shows LDPC running a maximum of 200 iterations of Belief Propagation on each 6K frame. Under normal conditions an average of 25 iterations are required. Given our current timing of approximately 800 cycles per iteration, we can theoretically handle a data rate around 16 Mbps. This appears comparable with other implementations (Andrews et al. 2007), though accurate comparisons are challenging, because published results for LDPC are often given in terms of best case, rather than actual throughput speed. As already mentioned, we have not by any means exhausted our optimization opportunities, and we have a realtime decoder. Of course, if we want a faster circuit, we chain up our functors, and start refining again.

11. Related Work

Functional programming has a long and rich history of program refinement. It is taught in undergraduate textbooks (Hutton 2007), and some members of the functional programming community have made this into an art form (Bird 2010). What was attempted in this paper was of a slightly different nature; the refinement was a guide for a semi-formal method, but as when refactoring programs in the wild, we were prepared to take leaps of faith with correctness. The difference here is that, as a consequence of the use of worker/wrapper in many places, we have an audit trail of (currently unsatisfied) proof obligations.

The worker/wrapper transformation was initially used to exploit strictness information to unbox integer computations in the Glasgow Haskell Compiler (Jones and Partain 1993) and was more recently formalized (Gill and Hutton 2009). We believe there is tremendous untapped potential for systematic refinement, and the work described in this paper is a prelude to future refinement and automation; we now know where the shoe pinches!

We make critical use of the ability to generate VHDL provided by Kansas Lava, and the Xilinx XST toolkit to generate bit files for FPGA reprogramming. Gill et al. (2011) presents the FPGA-specific details of deploying our generated LDPC implementation, including board-specific challenges and data transportation issues. Given the common LDPC artifact, there is overlap between Gill et al. (2011) and this paper. Specifically, the generic description of the LDPC algorithm in Section 6, and the high-level description of our fabric partitioning aspect at the start of Section 7 were both adapted from the descriptions in the earlier paper. The earlier paper alluded to but is not specific about the existence of a refinement methodology (Section 5, final paragraph). Apart from this reference, the earlier published work assumes that we implement the LDPC algorithm in Kansas Lava directly to facilitate generation of the VHDL LDPC; this paper discusses in detail how we instead reached our implementation using refinement techniques.

The original ideas for Lava (Bjesse et al. 1998) can be traced back to the Ruby hardware description language (Jones and Sheeran 1990) and prior to that, μFP (Sheeran 1984). Kansas Lava, like other Lavas, is a modeling language. Kansas Lava models communicating processes, via synchronous or hand-shaken signals. There are several other modeling languages that share a similar basic computational basis, for example Esterel (Berry 1999). Finally, there are many other models for communicating processes, and each model family has many language-based implementations. The overview paper written by Jantsch, et. al. (Jantsch and Sander 2005) gives a good summary.

12. Conclusion

We have developed a toolkit called Kansas Lava for expressing FPGA-level concerns, following in the tradition of previous Lava implementations while also leveraging modern features like associated type families. On top of this toolkit, we have a functor-based semi-formal methodology for deriving circuits from executable specifications. We have completed one full-scale derivation by hand, and are preparing to undertake more derivations and automate some of the mundane details.

While Kansas Lava is a subset of Haskell, there are important restrictions on the types available, as they must be representable in hardware if we are to realize a VHDL or FPGA-based implementation. As such, there is a gap between the executable specification in Haskell and the version that operates only on the available Kansas Lava types. We extensively use the worker/wrapper meta-transformation to bridge this gap. With worker/wrapper, we systematically transform the type of our computation to achieve a viable implementation from an executable specification.

Functors play a crucial role in this implementation derivation. The type of our architectural description is given as a chain of functors, which we transform by adding, commuting, or replacing functors in the chain until the type is fully realizable in hardware. The fact that Kansas Lava signal types are functors within the restrictions of the preconditions makes this transformation possible.

By expressing intermediate computations using chains of functors, and performing refinement transformations by hand, we have developed an efficient LDPC decoder than runs in real time. This implementation of LDPC meets all the project's performance, correctness, and resource utilization goals.

The major weakness of commutable functors and worker/wrapper for deriving hardware circuits, as used in this paper, is that everything is done by hand. This leads to proof obligations being notes in a derivation chain, not formally captured, and means that architecture exploration is challenging, especially if an earlier stage needs revisited. At one point in the derivation, we backtracked to change a representation, resulting in changing several stages of implementations of LDPC, not just one, which was burdensome.

The next steps are two-fold. The derivation was a free-for-all, with approximate directions being provided by the architecture, and the human deriver figuring out how to twist the functors to hit the target. We want to develop a more rigorous methodology, based on functors and using worker/wrapper, that provides more guidance. Simultaneously, we want to start automating many of the transformations we are using.

Acknowledgments

The authors would like to thank the Test Resource Management Center (TRMC) Test and Evaluation/Science and Technology (T&E/S&T) Program for their support. This work was funded in part by the T&E/S&T Program through the Army PEO STRI Contracting Office, contract number W900KK-09-C-0018 for High-Rate High-Speed Forward Error Correction Architectures for Aeronautical Telemetry (HFEC). The authors would also like to thank Xilinx University Program for their donation of FPGA equipment. Finally, the authors would like to thank the members of the CSDL lab at ITTC, and the EECS 800 Advanced Functional Programming class, for many fruitful discussions about using functional languages for hardware description and other applications.

References

K. S. Andrews, D. Divsalar, S. Dolinar, J. Hamkins, C. R. Jones, and F. Pollara. The development of turbo and LDPC codes for deep-space applications. *Proc. IEEE*, 95(11):2142–2156, Nov. 2007.

A. W. Appel. *Compiling with Continuations*. Cambridge University Press, 1992.

G. Berry. The constructive semantics of pure Esterel. http://www-sop.inria.fr/esterel.org/files/, 1999.

R. Bird. *Pearls of Functional Algorithm Design*. Cambridge University Press, 2010. ISBN 9780521513388. URL `http://www.cambridge.org/gb/knowledge/isbn/item5600469`.

P. Bjesse, K. Claessen, M. Sheeran, and S. Singh. Lava: Hardware design in Haskell. In *International Conference on Functional Programming*, pages 174–184, 1998.

R. Burstall and J. Darlington. A transformation system for developing recursive programs. *Journal of the ACM*, 24(1), January 1977.

M. M. T. Chakravarty, G. Keller, and S. P. Jones. Associated type synonyms. In *ICFP '05: Proceedings of the Tenth ACM SIGPLAN International Conference on Functional Programming*, pages 241–253, New York, NY, USA, 2005. ACM. ISBN 1-59593-064-7.

Consultive Committee for Space Data Systems (CCSDS). Low density parity check codes for use in near-Earth and deep space applications (131.1-O-2 Orange Book), Sep. 2007.

R. G. Gallager. Low density parity check codes. *Transactions of the IRE Professional Group on Information Theory*, IT-8:21–28, January 1962.

A. Gill. Type-safe observable sharing in Haskell. In *Proceedings of the 2009 ACM SIGPLAN Haskell Symposium*, Sep 2009.

A. Gill and G. Hutton. The worker/wrapper transformation. *Journal of Functional Programming*, 19(2):227–251, March 2009.

A. Gill, T. Bull, A. Farmer, G. Kimmell, and E. Komp. Types and type families for hardware simulation and synthesis: The internals and externals of Kansas Lava. In *Proceedings of Trends in Functional Programming*, May 2010.

A. Gill, T. Bull, D. DePardo, A. Farmer, E. Komp, and E. Perrins. Using functional programming to generate an LDPC forward error corrector. In *IEEE Symposium on Field-Programmable Custom Computing Machines*, May 2011.

C. A. R. Hoare. Proof of correctness of data representations. *Acta Informatica*, 1:271–281, 1972. ISSN 0001-5903. URL `http://dx.doi.org/10.1007/BF00289507`. 10.1007/BF00289507.

R. J. M. Hughes. A novel representation of lists and its application to the function "reverse". *Information Processing Letters*, 22(3):141 – 144, 1986. ISSN 0020-0190. doi: DOI:10.1016/0020-0190(86)90059-1. URL `http://www.sciencedirect.com/science/article/B6V0F-482YK2S-3X/2/a570cfef125ec3167fe6bda9571e095f`.

G. Hutton. *Programming in Haskell*. Cambridge University Press, Jan. 2007.

A. Jantsch and I. Sander. Models of computation and languages for embedded system design. *IEE Proceedings on Computers and Digital Techniques*, 152(2):114–129, March 2005. URL `http://www.imit.kth.se/~axel/papers/2005/IEE-Proceedings.pdf`. Special issue on Embedded Microelectronic Systems.

G. Jones and M. Sheeran. Circuit design in ruby. In Staunstrup, editor, *Formal Methods for VLSI Design*. Elsevier Science Publications, 1990.

S. P. Jones and W. Partain. Measuring the effectiveness of a simple strictness analyser. In Hammond and O'Donnell, editors, *Functional Programming*, Springer Verlag Workshops in Computing, pages 201–220, 1993.

J. Launchbury and T. Sheard. Warm fusion: deriving build-catas from recursive definitions. In *FPCA '95: Proceedings of the 7th international conference on Functional programming languages and computer architecture*, pages 314–323. ACM Press, 1995.

D. Michie. Memo Functions and Machine Learning. *Nature*, 218:19–22, 1968.

T. K. Moon. *Error correction coding : mathematical methods and algorithms*. Wiley-Interscience, Hoboken, N.J., 2005. ISBN 0471648000 (cloth). URL `http://www.loc.gov/catdir/toc/ecip055/2004031019.html`.

C. Okasaki. *Purely Functional Data Structures*. Cambridge University Press, 1998.

S. P. Jones. Call-pattern specialisation for Haskell programs. In *Proceedings of the 12th ACM SIGPLAN international conference on Functional programming*, ICFP '07, pages 327–337, New York, NY, USA, 2007. ACM. ISBN 978-1-59593-815-2. doi: http://doi.acm.org/10.1145/1291151.1291200. URL `http://doi.acm.org/10.1145/1291151.1291200`.

S. L. Peyton Jones and J. Launchbury. Unboxed values as first class citizens in a non-strict functional language. In *Proceedings of the 5th ACM conference on Functional programming languages and computer architecture*, pages 636–666, New York, NY, USA, 1991. Springer-Verlag New York, Inc. ISBN 0-387-54396-1.

M. Sheeran. mufp, a language for vlsi design. In *LFP '84: Proceedings of the 1984 ACM Symposium on LISP and functional programming*, pages 104–112, New York, NY, USA, 1984. ACM. ISBN 0-89791-142-3. doi: http://doi.acm.org/10.1145/800055.802026.

G. J. Sussman and G. L. Steele, Jr. An interpreter for extended lambda calculus. Technical report, Cambridge, MA, USA, 1975.

Geometry of Synthesis IV

Compiling Affine Recursion into Static Hardware

Dan R. Ghica
University of Birmingham
d.r.ghica@cs.bham.ac.uk

Alex Smith
University of Birmingham
ais523@cs.bham.ac.uk

Satnam Singh
Microsoft Research
satnams@microsoft.com

Abstract

Abramsky's Geometry of Interaction interpretation (GoI) is a logical-directed way to reconcile the process and functional views of computation, and can lead to a dataflow-style semantics of programming languages that is both operational (i.e. effective) and denotational (i.e. inductive on the language syntax). The key idea of Ghica's Geometry of Synthesis (GoS) approach is that for certain programming languages (namely Reynolds's affine Syntactic Control of Interference–SCI) the GoI processes-like interpretation of the language can be given a finitary representation, for both internal state and tokens. A physical realisation of this representation becomes a semantics-directed compiler for SCI into hardware. In this paper we examine the issue of compiling affine recursive programs into hardware using the GoS method. We give syntax and compilation techniques for unfolding recursive computation in space or in time and we illustrate it with simple benchmark-style examples. We examine the performance of the benchmarks against conventional CPU-based execution models.

Categories and Subject Descriptors B.5.2 [*Hardware*]: Design Aids—Automatic Synthesis

General Terms Languages, Theory, Design

1. Introduction

Why compile recursive functions into FPGA hardware? A few years ago the case for compiling recursive functions into FPGA circuits was less compelling because these chips had limited computational resources and no specialized on-chip memory, so a stack would have to be made using precious flip-flops. Modern FPGAs can implement million-gate circuits and can contain thousands of independent dual-port memory blocks (e.g. block-RAMs on Xilinx FPGAs which are around 36 Kbits in size) which are ideal for implementing stacks and other local computational state. Since there are many independent memories it is possible to have many circuit sub-components executing in parallel without one single stack acting as a memory bottle-neck.

So now that we have effective elements for implementing recursive computations on FPGAs are there any applications that actually need recursive descriptions? Certainly. As FPGAs have grown in capacity there has been an increasing desire to map computations that were previously implemented in software for execution on a regular processor onto FPGAs instead, in order to improve performance or reduce energy consumption. Recently FPGAs have gained the capability to access large amounts of external memory using multiple memory controllers and this allows us to manipulate dynamic data-structures like trees with FPGA gates and exploit the thousands of on-chip independent memories as caches. With dynamic data-structures one naturally has the desire to express computations with recursive algorithms (e.g. balancing trees and inserting and removing nodes). Example applications include line-speed network packet processing which may require building up auxiliary dynamic data structures (e.g. trees) which are used to help classify and route packets, such as Netezza's data warehousing project[1] or IBM's DataPower accelerated XML parser[2].

Recursive procedures, functions and methods have been used to describe the behaviour of digital circuits in a variety of programming languages ranging from mainstream hardware description languages like VHDL to experimental embedded domain specific languages like Lava [BCSS98] for many years. Most systems typically implement recursion by inlining it at compile time to produce descriptions that are unfolded in space. These descriptions assume the depth of the recursion to be determinable at compile time. A specific example of such a recursive function is one that adds the elements of an array by using a recursive divide and conquer strategy yielding an adder-tree implementation. At compile time the size of the array has to be known but not the value of the array elements.

Our goal is to allow recursive descriptions of circuits which unfold in time and space where the depth of recursion is not known at compile time. This in turn allows us to describe recursive functions that can operate over dynamic data structures. We aim to research and develop techniques for translating a sub-set of recursive functions into circuits where the depth of recursion is dependent on the dynamic values.

Domain specific hardware description langauges sometimes offer limited support for recursion. For example, Contessa [TL07] is used for finance applications but only supports tail recursion. There has also been considerable interest in describing hardware using *embedded* domain specific langauges i.e. by designing a library that captures important aspects of circuit design. For example, the JHDL system [BH98] provided a system coded in Java for performing structural hardware design. The Lava system provides a combinator library that makes it easier to descibe circuit layout and behaviour [HD08]. All of these systems allow recursive descriptions but they all require the descriptions to be in-lined. Even Bluespec [Nik04] which is a modern hardware description language based on functional programming concepts allows the specification

ICFP'11 September 19–21, 2011, Tokyo, Japan.

[1] `http://www.netezza.com/data-warehouse-appliance-products/`

[2] `http://www-01.ibm.com/software/integration/datapower/`

of recursive functions but does not support the synthesis of dynamic recursion.

Sklyarov describes a mechanism for compiling recursive C++ descriptions into FPGA circuits [Skl04] using hierarchical finite state machines which have been applied to the design of Huffman encoder circuits and sorting networks. Sklyarov's technique has the advantage of dealing with general recursion but it has the drawback of requring centralized control and it produces rather slow circuits running at only 25 MHz. Our approach is more modular, does not require centralized control and produces faster circuits. The knapsack and Kinght's Tour problems were described as recursive hardware algorithms by Maruyama, Takagi and Hoshino [MTH99] although this technique is limited to loop unrolling and pipeling and the use of a stack to hold state information.

Ferizis and Gindy show how recursive functions can be implemented by using dynamic reconfiguration [FG06] to unroll recursive function calls at run-time which avoids the need for a stack. However, this approach is very limited because it replicates the body of the recursive function, which is likely to quickly exhuast the available FPGA resources, and it also relies on immature dynamic reconfiguration technology.

Contribution. This paper gives the most general method to date for compiling recursive programs into static hardware. The main language-level restriction we impose, the use of an affine type system, is unavoidable because of computational reasons—non-affine functions do not have a finite state model. We describe a compiler to sequential circuits and we illustrate it with a typical benchmark for recursive programs, computing Fibonacci numbers.

2. Geometry of Synthesis

2.1 Objectives, methodology, motivation

Higher-level synthesis (HLS) is the production of gate-level description of circuits from behavioural descriptions given in higher-level programming languages.

Current HLS tools and techniques have significant limitations. One specific limitation is the weak treatment of function calls, which are typically implemented by inlining. This restriction is limiting the more general application of high level synthesis technology to a wider class of algorithms than benefit from dynamic procedure calls and recursion.

By inlining function calls at source-code level, which in hardware corresponds to replication of circuitry, current tools generate code which is often inefficient. Also, ordinary programming languages interface via function calls with libraries and with run-time services. Lack of support for proper function calls makes such interoperability impossible, which means that the entire system must be developed in one single programming language. Separate compilation, foreign function interfaces and application binary interfaces, standard facilities in modern compilers, cannot be supported without a proper function mechanism.

The Geometry of Synthesis (GoS) approach [Ghi07, GS10, GS11] enables full and proper implementation of ordinary programming languages, with an emphasis on correct and effective handling of function calls. Through static analysis the compiler can decide whether the circuit for a particular function must be re-instantiated or can be reused, depending on the desired trade-offs between area/power and latency/throughput. More importantly, code can be compiled without requiring all definitions of all functions to be available at compile time. Appropriate hardware interfaces are generated for the missing functions so that a complete functional circuit can be synthesised later, in a linking stage. This means that pre-compiled libraries can be created, distributed and commercialised with better protection for intellectual property. Finally, code written in one language can interact with code written in other languages so long as certain interface protocols are respected by the components. Moreover, these protocols can be enforced via the type system at the level of the programming language. Designs developed directly in conventional hardware description languages, subject to respecting the interface protocols, can also be used from the programming language via function calls. This allows the reuse of a vast existing portfolio of specialised, high-performance designs. Run-time services: certain circuits, which manage physical resources such as memory, network interface, video or audio interface, etc., cannot be meaningfully replicated as the resource itself cannot be replicated. Such services can also be used from ordinary programming languages via function calls.

Note the technology fully supports so-called higher-order functions, i.e. functions which operate on functions as argument or result. Such functions play an important role in the design of highly efficient parallel algorithms, such as Map-Reduce. These methodological considerations are discussed at length elsewhere [Ghi11].

2.2 Theoretical background

Abramsky's Geometry of Interaction (GoI) interpretation is a logical-directed way to reconcile the process and and functional views of computation, and can lead to a dataflow-style semantics of programming languages that is both operational (i.e. effective) and denotational (i.e. inductive on the language syntax) [AJ92]. These ideas have already been exploited in devising optimal compilation strategies for the lambda calculus, a technique called *Geometry of Implementation* [Mac94, Mac95].

The key idea of the *Geometry of Synthesis* (GoS) approach is that for certain programming languages, of which Reynolds's affine version of Idealized Algol (called *Syntactic Control of Interference* [Rey78, Rey89]) is a typical representative, the process-like interpretation given by the GoI can be represented in a finite way. This finitary representation applies both to the internal state of the token machine and the tokens themselves.

Subsequent developments in *game semantics* (see [Ghi09] for a survey) made it possible to give interpretations of a large variety of computational features (state, control, names, etc.) in an interactive way which is compatible with the GoI framework. Such computational features often have themselves a finite-state representation, as noted in [GM00].

A physical realisation of the finite-state representation of a GoI-style semantics then becomes a semantics-directed compiler for suitable languages, such as SCI, directly into hardware [Ghi07]. The hardware itself can be synchronous or asynchronous [GS10]. Subsequent work also showed how programs of more expressive type systems, such as full Idealized Algol, can be systematically represented into SCI as an intermediary language via type inference and *serialization* [GS11].

As a final observation, the somewhat surprising way in which higher order abstraction and application are compiled into circuits is best understood via the connection between GoI and monoidal categories, especially compact-closed categories [KL80], since such categories are an ideal formal setting for diagrammatic representation [Sel09].

3. Syntactic Control of Interference

Reynolds's Idealized Algol (IA) is a compact language which combines the fundamental features of imperative languages with a full higher-order procedural mechanism [Rey81]. This combination makes the language very expressive, for example allowing the encoding of classes and objects. Because of its expressiveness and elegance, IA has attracted a great deal of attention from theoreticians [OT81].

The typing system *(Basic) Syntactic Control of Interference (SCI)* is an affine version of IA in which contraction is disallowed over function application and parallel execution. SCI was initially proposed by Reynolds as a programming language which would facilitate Hoare-style correctness reasoning because covert interference between terms is disallowed [Rey78, Rey89]. SCI turned out to be semantically interesting and it was studied extensively [Red96, OPTT99, McC07, McC10]. The restriction on contraction in SCI makes it particularly well suited for hardware compilation because any term in the language has a finite-state model and can therefore be compiled as a static circuit [Ghi07, GS10].

The primitive types of the language are commands, memory cells, and bounded-integer expressions $\sigma ::= \mathsf{com} \mid \mathsf{var} \mid \mathsf{exp}$. The type constructors are product and function: $\theta ::= \theta \times \theta \mid \theta \to \theta \mid \sigma$. Terms are described by typing judgements of the form $x_1 : \theta_1, \ldots, x_k : \theta_k \vdash M : \theta$, where we denote the list of identifier type assignments on the left by Γ. By convention, if we write Γ, Γ' it assumes that the two type assignments have disjoint sets of identifiers.

The term formation rules of the language are those of the affine lambda calculus:

$$\frac{}{x : \theta \vdash x : \theta}\ \text{Identity}$$

$$\frac{\Gamma \vdash M : \theta'}{x : \theta, \Gamma \vdash M : \theta'}\ \text{Weakening}$$

$$\frac{\Gamma, x : \theta, x' : \theta', \Gamma' \vdash M : \theta''}{\Gamma, x' : \theta', x : \theta, \Gamma' \vdash M : \theta''}\ \text{Commutativity}$$

$$\frac{\Gamma, x : \theta' \vdash M : \theta}{\Gamma \vdash \lambda x.M : \theta' \to \theta}\ \text{Abstraction}$$

$$\frac{\Gamma \vdash M : \theta \to \theta' \qquad \Delta \vdash N : \theta}{\Gamma, \Delta \vdash MN : \theta'}\ \text{Application}$$

$$\frac{\Gamma \vdash M_i : \theta_i}{\Gamma \vdash \langle M_1, M_2 \rangle : \theta_1 \times \theta_2}\ \text{Product}$$

Importantly, contraction (identifier reuse) is allowed in product formation but not in function application.

The constants of the language are described below:

n : exp are the integer constants;

skip : com is the only command constant ("no-op");

asg : var $\times$ exp $\to$ com is assignment to memory cell, denoted by ":=" when used in infix notation;

der : var $\to$ exp is dereferencing of memory cell, also denoted by "!";

seq : com $\times\ \sigma \to \sigma$ is command sequencing, denoted by ";" when used in infix notation – if $\sigma \neq$ com then the resulting expression is said to have side-effects;

op : exp $\times$ exp $\to$ exp stands for arithmetic and logic operators;

if : exp $\times$ com $\times$ com $\to$ com is branching;

while : exp $\times$ com $\to$ com is iteration;

newvar : (var $\to \sigma) \to \sigma$ is local variable declaration in block command or block expression.

Local variable binding is presented with a quantifier-style type in order to avoid introducing new variable binders in the language. Local variable declaration can be sugared into a more familiar syntax as $\mathsf{newvar}(\lambda x.M) \equiv \mathsf{newvar}\ x$ in M.

We can reuse identifiers in products, so conventional imperative program terms such as x:=!x+1 or c;c can be written as $\mathsf{asg}\langle x, \mathsf{add}\langle \mathsf{der}(x), 1\rangle\rangle$ and $\mathsf{seq}\langle c, c\rangle$ respectively. One immediate consequence of the affine-type restriction is that nested application is no longer possible, i.e. terms such as $f : \mathsf{com} \to \mathsf{com} \vdash f(f(\mathsf{skip}))$ are illegal, so the usual operational unfolding of recursion no longer preserves typing. Therefore, the rec_θ operator in its most general formulation must be also eliminated. An appropriately adapted recursion operator will be presented in the next section.

Despite its restrictions SCI is still expressive enough to allow many interesting programs. Its finite state model makes it perfectly suited for hardware compilation [Ghi07, GS10]. The operational semantics of SCI is essentially the same as that of IA, which is standard. In this paper we are interested in compiling SCI to *sequential hardware*; the GoS method relies essentially on the existence of a game-semantic model for the programming language. The existing game [Wal04] and game-like [McC10] models of SCI are *asynchronous*, and using them to create *synchronous* hardware raises some technical challenges, which are addressed in previous work on *round abstraction* [GM10, GM11].

The compiler is defined inductively on the syntax of the language. Each type corresponds to a circuit interface, defined as a list of ports, each defined by data bit-width and a polarity. Every port has a default one-bit control component. For example we write an interface with n-bit input and n-bit output as $I = (+n, -n)$. More complex interfaces can be defined from simpler ones using concatenation $I_1 @ I_2$ and polarity reversal $I^- = \mathsf{map}\,(\lambda x.-x)I$. If a port has only control and no data we write it as $+0$ or -0, depending of polarity. Note that obviously $+0 \neq -0$ in this notation!

An interface for type θ is written as $[\![\theta]\!]$, defined as follows:

$$[\![\mathsf{com}]\!] = (+0, -0) \qquad [\![\mathsf{exp}]\!] = (+0, -n)$$
$$[\![\mathsf{var}]\!] = (+n, -0, +0, -n)$$
$$[\![\theta \times \theta']\!] = [\![\theta]\!] @ [\![\theta']\!] \qquad [\![\theta \to \theta']\!] = [\![\theta]\!]^- @ [\![\theta']\!].$$

The interface for com has two control ports, an input for starting execution and an output for reporting termination. The interface for exp has an input control for starting evaluation and data output for reporting the value. Variables var have data input for a write request and control output for acknowledgment, and control input for a read request along with data output for the value.

Tensor and arrow types are given interpretations which should be quite intuitive to the reader familiar with compact-closed categories [KL80]. The tensor is a disjoint sum of the ports on the two interfaces while the arrow is the tensor along with a polarity-reversal of the ports in the contravariant position. Reversal of polarities gives the dual object in the compact closed category.

Diagrammatically, a list will correspond to ports read from left-to-right and from top-to-bottom. We indicate ports of zero width (only the control bit) by a thin line and ports of width n by an additional thicker line (the data part). For example a circuit of interface $[\![\mathsf{com} \to \mathsf{com}]\!] = (-0, +0, +0, -0)$ can be written in any of these two ways:

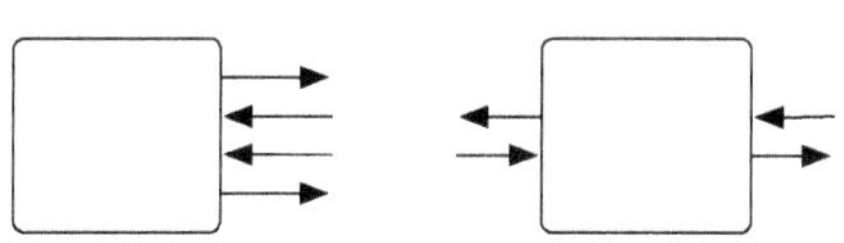

The unit-width ports are used to transmit *events*, represented as the value of the port being held high for one clock cycle. The n-width ports correspond to data lines. The data on the line is only considered to be meaningful while there is an event on the control line.

Below, for each language constant we will give the asynchronous game-semantic interpretation and its low-latency synchronous representation [GM11] and the (obvious) circuit implementation. For the purpose of giving the game-semantics and its representation, the circuit interface will correspond to the *set of moves*; the semantics is a set of traces over the possible moves. We denote a move/event on port k of interface $I = (p_1, \ldots, p_m)$ by

n_k, where n is the data value; if the data-width is 0 we write $*_k$. We use $\langle m, m \rangle$ to indicate the simultaneity of move/event m and m'. We use $m \cdot m'$ to indicate concatenation, i.e. move/event m' happens *after* m, but not necessarily in the very next clock cycle. We define $m \bullet m' = \{\langle m, m' \rangle, m \cdot m'\}$. We define the game semantic interpretation by $[\![-]\!]_g$ and the synchronous representation by $[\![-]\!]_s$. The notation $pc-$ applied to a set means closure under prefix-taking.

Skip

$$\mathsf{skip} : \mathsf{com}, [\![\mathsf{com}]\!] = (+0, -0)$$
$$[\![\mathsf{skip}]\!]_g = pc\{*_1 \cdot *_2\}$$
$$[\![\mathsf{skip}]\!]_s = pc\{\langle *_1, *_2 \rangle\}.$$

The circuit representation is:

SKIP

Intuitively the input port of a command is a request to run the command and the output port is the acknowledgment of successful completion. In the case of skip the acknowledgment is immediate.

Integer constant

$$\mathsf{k} : \mathsf{exp}, [\![\mathsf{exp}]\!] = (+1, -n)$$
$$[\![\mathsf{k}]\!]_g = pc\{*_1 \cdot k_2\}$$
$$[\![\mathsf{k}]\!]_s = pc\{\langle *_1, k_2 \rangle\}.$$

The circuit representation is:

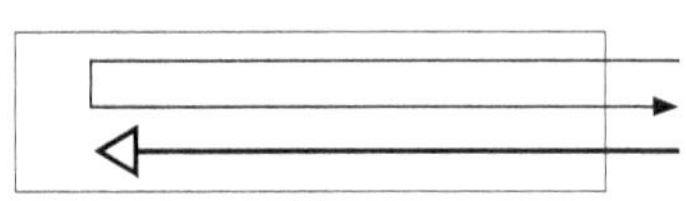

N

Intuitively the input port of an expression is a request to evaluate the expression and the output port is the data result and a control signal indicating successful evaluation. In the case of a constant n the acknowledgment is immediate and the data is connected to a fixed bit pattern.

Sequential composition

$$\mathsf{seq} : \mathsf{com} \times \mathsf{exp} \to \mathsf{exp}$$
$$[\![\mathsf{com} \times \mathsf{exp} \to \mathsf{exp}]\!] = (-0, +0, -0, +n, +0, -n)$$
$$[\![\mathsf{seq}]\!]_g = pc\{*_5 \cdot *_1 \cdot *_2 \cdot *_3 \cdot k_4 \cdot k_6 \mid k \in Z\}$$
$$[\![\mathsf{seq}]\!]_s = pc\{\langle *_5, *_1 \rangle \bullet *_2 \cdot *_3 \bullet \langle k_4 \cdot k_6 \rangle \mid k \in Z\}.$$

The circuit representation is:

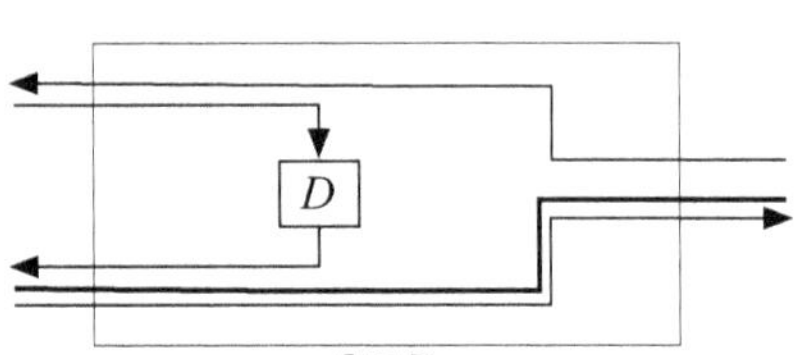

SEQ

Above, D denotes a one-clock delay (D-flip-flop). A sequencer SEQ propagates the request to evaluate a command in sequence with an expression by first sending an execute request to the command, then to the expression upon receiving the acknowledgment from the command. The result of the expression is propagated to the calling context. Note the unit delay placed between the command acknowledgment and the expression request. Its presence is a necessary artifact of correctly representing asynchronous processes synchronously and cannot be optimised away [GM11].

Assignment and dereferencing

$$\mathsf{asg} : \mathsf{var} \times \mathsf{exp} \to \mathsf{com}$$
$$[\![\mathsf{var} \times \mathsf{exp} \to \mathsf{com}]\!] = (-n, +0, -0, +n, -0, +n, +0, -n)$$
$$[\![\mathsf{asg}]\!]_g = pc\{*_7 \cdot *_5 \cdot k_6 \cdot k_1 \cdot *_2 \cdot *_8 \mid k \in Z\}$$
$$[\![\mathsf{asg}]\!]_s = pc\{\langle *_7, *_5 \rangle \bullet k_6 \cdot k_1 \bullet \langle *_2, *_8 \rangle \mid k \in Z\}.$$

$$\mathsf{der} : \mathsf{var} \to \mathsf{exp}, [\![\mathsf{var} \to \mathsf{exp} = (-n, +0, -0, +n, +0, -n)]\!]$$
$$[\![\mathsf{der}]\!]_g = pc\{*_5 \cdot *_3 \cdot k_4 \cdot k_6 \mid k \in Z\}$$
$$[\![\mathsf{der}]\!]_s = pc\{\langle *_5, *_3 \rangle \bullet \langle k_4, k_6 \rangle \mid k \in Z\}$$

The circuit representations are, respectively:

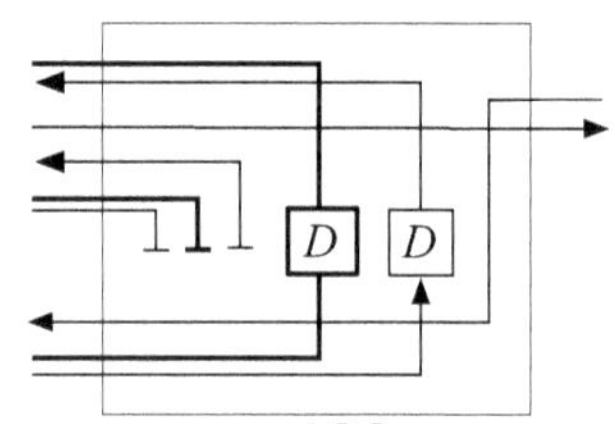

ASG

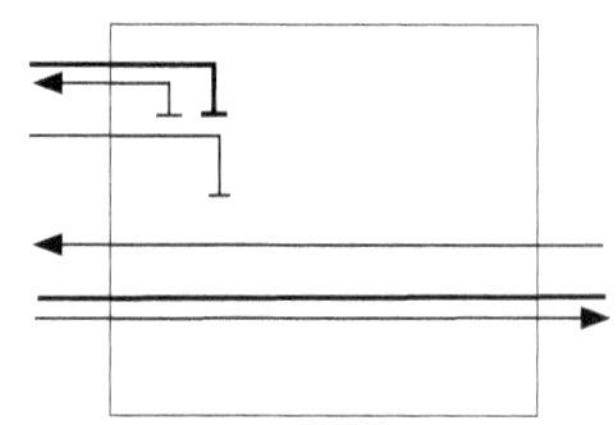

DER

The variable type has four ports: writing data (n bits), acknowledging a write (0 bits), requesting a read (0 bits) and providing data (n bits). Assignment is a sequencing of an evaluation of the integer argument with a write request to the variable; the unused variable ports are grounded. Dereferencing is simply a projection of a variable interface onto an expression interface by propagating the read-part of the interface and blocking the write part.

Operators

$$\mathsf{op} : \mathsf{exp} \times \mathsf{exp} \to \mathsf{exp}$$
$$[\![\mathsf{exp} \times \mathsf{exp} \to \mathsf{exp}]\!] = (-0, +n, -0, +n, +0, -n)$$
$$[\![\mathsf{op}]\!]_g = pc\{*_5 \cdot *_1 \cdot k_2 \cdot *_3 \cdot k'_4 \cdot k''_6 \mid op(k, k') = k'' \in Z\}$$
$$[\![\mathsf{op}]\!]_s = pc\{\langle *_5, *_1 \rangle \bullet k_2 \cdot *_3 \bullet \langle k'_4 \cdot k_6 \rangle \mid k'' \in Z\}.$$

The circuit representation is:

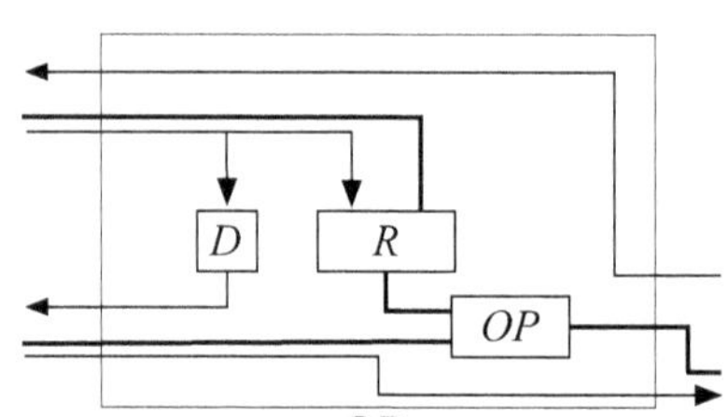

OP

R above is a register. The input control of port 2 is connected to the *load* pin of the register. The (combinatorial) circuit OP implements the operation. Note that the value of the first operator is saved in the register because expressions can change their value in time due to side-effects.

Branching

$$\text{if} : \text{exp} \times \text{exp} \times \text{exp} \rightarrow \text{exp}$$

$$\llbracket \text{exp} \times \text{exp} \times \text{exp} \rightarrow \text{exp} \rrbracket = (-0, +n, -0, +n, -0, +n, +0, -n)$$

$$\llbracket \text{if} \rrbracket_g = pc\{*_7 \cdot *_1 \cdot 0_2 \cdot *_5 \cdot k_6 \cdot k_8, *_7 \cdot *_1 \cdot k'_2 \cdot *_3 \cdot k_4 \cdot k_8 \mid k' \neq 0, k \in Z\}$$

$$\llbracket \text{if} \rrbracket_s = pc\{\langle *_7, *_1 \rangle \bullet 0_2 \cdot *_5 \bullet \langle k_6, k_8 \rangle, \langle *_7, *_1 \rangle \bullet k'_2 \cdot *_3 \bullet \langle k_4, k_8 \rangle \mid k' \neq 0, k \in Z\}$$

The corresponding circuit is:

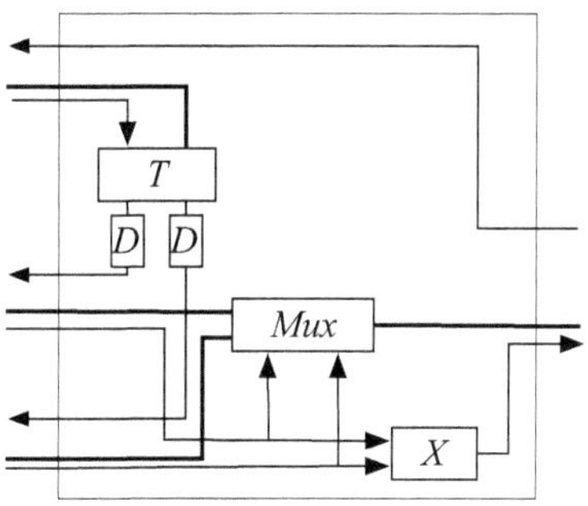

IF

Above, *Mux* is a (combinatorial) n-bit multiplexer which selects one data path or the other depending on the control signal. X is a merge of two control signals (*or* or *exclusive-or*) and T is a demultiplexer which propagates the input control signal to the first or second output, depending on whether the data value is zero or nonzero. As before, the delay D is necessary for correctness considerations.

Iteration

$$\llbracket \text{while} : \text{exp} \times \text{com} \rightarrow \text{com} \rrbracket$$

$$\llbracket \text{exp} \times \text{com} \rightarrow \text{com} \rrbracket = (-0, +n, -0, +0, +0, -0)$$

$$\llbracket \text{while} \rrbracket_g = pc\{*_5 \cdot (*_1 \cdot 0_2 \cdot *_3 \cdot *_4)^* \cdot *_1 \cdot k_2 \cdot *_6 \mid k \in Z \setminus \{0\}\}$$

$$\llbracket \text{while} \rrbracket_s = pc\{\langle *_5, *_1 \rangle \bullet 0_2 \cdot *_3 \bullet *_4 \cdot (*_1 \bullet 0_2 \cdot *_3 \bullet *_4)^* \cdot *_1 \bullet k_2 \cdot *_6, \langle *_5, *_1 \rangle \bullet k_2 \cdot *_6 \mid k \in Z \setminus \{0\}\}$$

The circuit is:

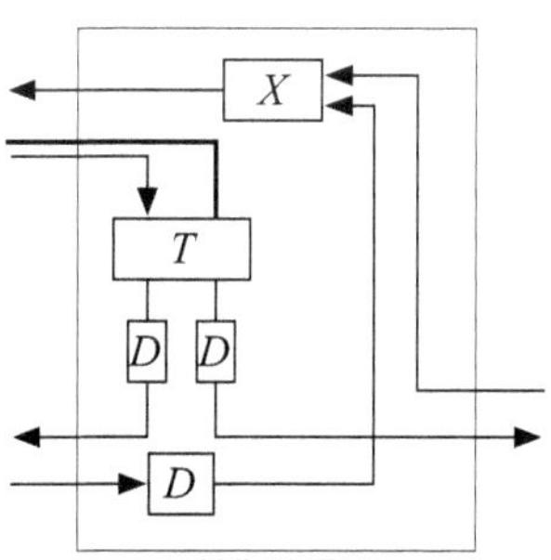

WHILE

The iterator will keep executing the second argument as long as the first argument is zero.

State The local variable binder is a higher-order constant.

$$\text{newvar} : (\text{var} \rightarrow \text{com}) \rightarrow \text{com}$$

$$\llbracket (\text{var} \rightarrow \text{com}) \rightarrow \text{com} \rrbracket = (+n, -0, +0, -n, -0, +0, +0, -0)$$

$$\llbracket \text{newvar} \rrbracket_g = pc\{*_7 \cdot *_5 \cdot v \cdot *_6 \cdot *_8 \mid v \in \big(\sum_{k \in Z} k_1 \cdot *_2 \cdot (*_3 \cdot k_4)^*\big)^*\}$$

$$\llbracket \text{newvar} \rrbracket_s = pc\{\langle *_7, *_5 \rangle \bullet v \bullet \langle *_6, *_8 \rangle \mid v \in \big(\sum_{k \in Z} \langle k_1, *_2 \rangle \bullet \langle *_3, k_4 \rangle^*\big)^*\}$$

The circuit with this behaviour is basically just a register:

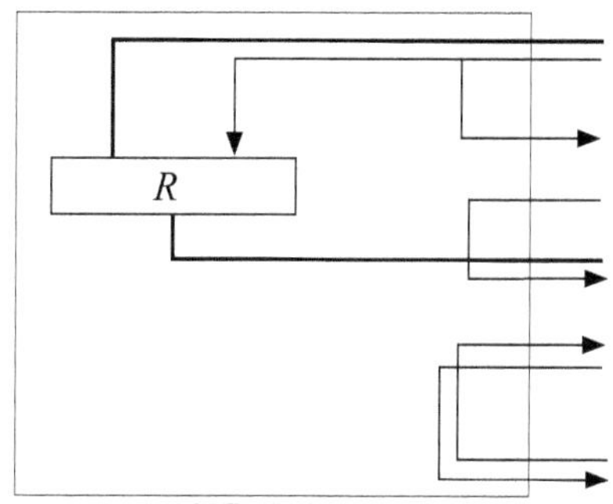

NEWVAR

In addition to the constants of the language we also interpret structural rules (abstraction, application, product formation) as constructions on circuits. In diagrams we represent bunches of wires (*buses*) as thick lines. When we connect two interfaces by a bus we assume that the two interfaces match in number and kind of port perfectly.

In general a term of signature $x_1 : \theta_1, \ldots, x_k : \theta_k \vdash M : \theta$ will be interpreted as a circuit of interface $\llbracket \theta_1 \times \cdots \times \theta_k \rightarrow \theta \rrbracket$.

Abstraction Semantically, in both the original game semantics and the synchronous representation the abstraction $\Gamma \vdash \lambda x : \theta.M : \theta'$ is interpreted by the currying isomorphism. Similarly, in circuits the two interfaces for this circuit and $\Gamma, x : \theta \vdash M : \theta'$ are isomorphic.

Application To apply a function of type $\Gamma \vdash F : \theta \rightarrow \theta'$ to an argument $\Delta \vdash M : \theta$ we simply connect the ports in $\llbracket \theta \rrbracket$ from the two circuits:

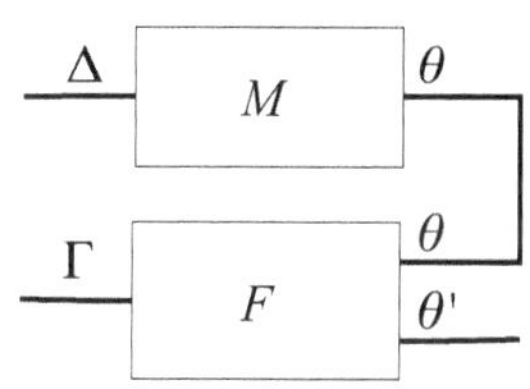

Product formation Unlike application, in product formation we allow the sharing of identifiers. This is realised through special circuitry implementing the *diagonal* function $\lambda x.\langle x, x \rangle$ for any type θ. Diagrammatically, the product of terms $\Gamma \vdash M_i : \theta_i$ is:

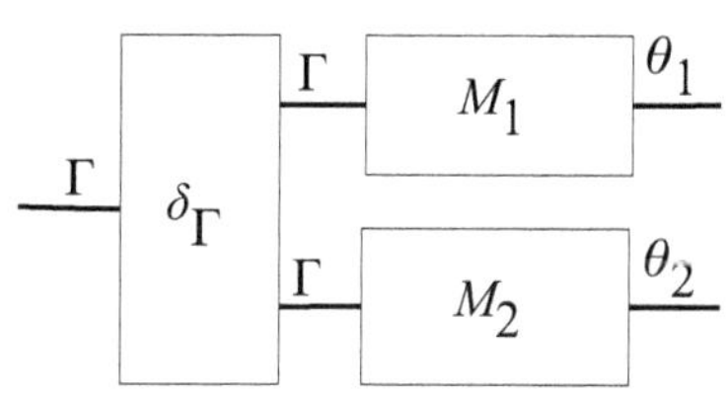

The diagonal circuit is behaviourally similar to a stateful multiplexer-demultiplexer. It routes an input signal from the interfaces on the right to the shared interface on the left while storing the source of the signal in a *set-reset* register. From the semantic model we know that any output signal in the shared interface is followed by an input signal in the same interface, which is routed to the originating component using the demultiplexer T. SR registers are needed for all initial questions and T blocks use the registers for the matching question.

In the simplest case, for δ_{com} the circuit looks like this:

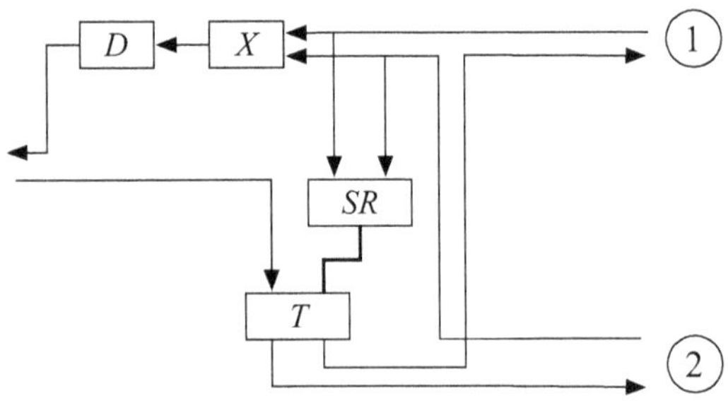

Note that this diagonal introduces a unit delay, which is not strictly necessary for correctness. A lower-latency diagonal that correctly handles instant feedback without the delay D can be implemented, but is more complex.

Structural rules Finally, we give constructions for commutativity, weakening and identity. They are represented by the circuits below:

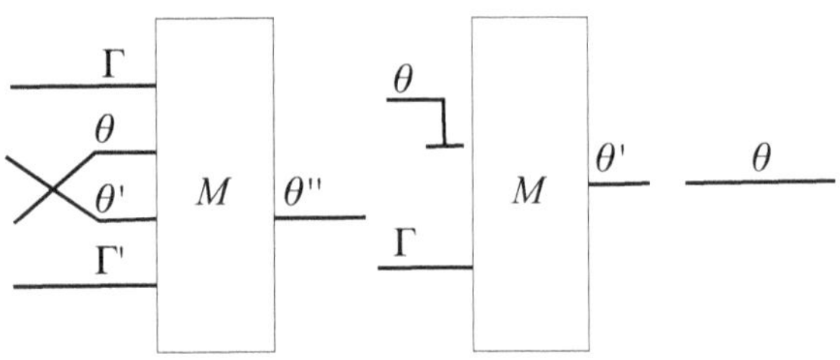

Commutativity is rearranging ports in the interface, weakening is the addition of dummy ports and identities are typed buses.

Example. The GoS approach allows the compilation of higher-order, open terms. Consider for example a program that executes in-place map on a data structure equipped with an iterator: $\lambda f : \mathsf{exp} \to \mathsf{exp}.\mathsf{init}; \mathsf{while}(\mathsf{more})(\mathsf{curr} := \mathsf{f}(!\mathsf{curr}); \mathsf{next}) : \mathsf{com}$, where $\mathsf{init} : \mathsf{com}, \mathsf{curr} : \mathsf{var}, \mathsf{next} : \mathsf{com}, \mathsf{more} : \mathsf{exp}$. The interface of the iterator consists of an initialiser, access to the current element, advance to the next element and test if there are more elements in the store. Since SCI is call-by-name all free identifiers are thunks. The block diagram of the circuit is given in Fig. 1: The full schematic of the circuit for in-place map is also given in Fig. 1; for clarity we have identified what ports correspond to what identifiers. The ports on the right correspond to the term type com. Note that we can optimise away the diagonal for variable identifier curr because the first instance is used for writing while the second one for reading.

4. Unfolding finite recursion in space

In its simplest instance recursion can be seen simply as an unfolding of a circuit definition. Such recursive definitions can only apply to well-founded definitions as infinite unfoldings cannot be synthesised. To support finite recursion via unfolding we augment the SCI type system with a rudimentary form of dependent typing.

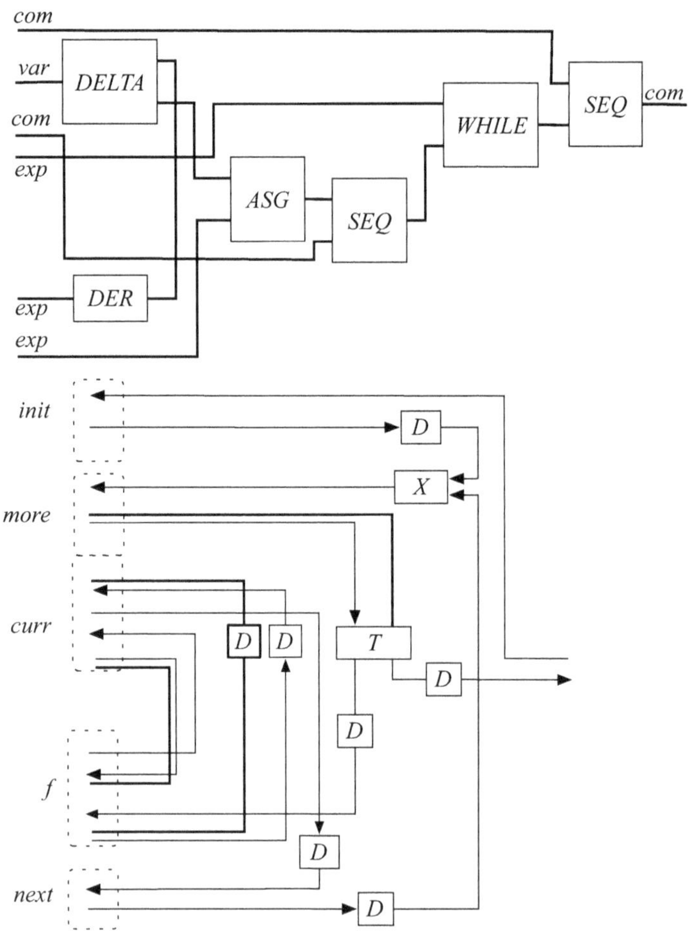

Figure 1. In-place map schematic and implementation

First, it is convenient to add linear product (tensor) explicitly to the type system:

$$\frac{\Gamma \vdash M : \theta \qquad \Gamma' \vdash M' : \theta'}{\Gamma, \Gamma' \vdash M \otimes M' : \theta \otimes \theta'}$$

We also add a very simple form of dependent types, $\theta\{N\}$ which is defined as

$$\theta\{0\} = \mathbf{1}, \qquad \theta\{N\} = \theta \otimes \theta\{N-1\},$$

where $\mathbf{1}$ is the unit type (the empty interface).

The language of indices N consists of natural number constants, subtraction and division (over natural numbers). This will guarantee that recursive definitions have finite unfoldings. Note that since $\otimes$ is adjoint to $\to$ in the type system, the following three types are isomorphic:

$$\theta \otimes \cdots \otimes \theta \to \theta' \simeq \theta \to \cdots \to \theta \to \theta' \simeq \theta\{N\} \to \theta'.$$

For example, an N-ary parallel execution operator can be recursively defined, for example, as:

$$\begin{aligned}\mathsf{par}\{1\} &= \lambda x : \mathsf{com}.x : \mathsf{com} \to \mathsf{com}\\ \mathsf{par}\{N\} &= \lambda x : \mathsf{com}.(x \mid\mid \mathsf{par}\{N-1\})\\ &\quad : \mathsf{com} \to \mathsf{com}\{N-1\} \to \mathsf{com} \simeq \mathsf{com}\{N\} \to \mathsf{com}.\end{aligned}$$

Recursive definitions in this dependent-type metalanguage are elaborated first into SCI by unfolding the definitions until all indices $\{N\}$ are reduced, after which the normal compilation process applies.

Although this approach is technically very simple it is surprisingly effective. For example, it allows the definition of sorting networks using programming language syntax so that the elaborated SCI programs synthesise precisely into the desired sorting network.

4.1 Batcher's Bitonic Sort

Bitonic Sort [Bat68] is a well known algorithm for generating optimal sorting networks. The definition of the algorithm is *structural*, i.e. it describes how the network is constructed from subcomponents, rather than *behavioural*, i.e. indicating the way input data is processed into output data, as is the case with most "software" algorithms. As a consequence, mapping Batcher's description of a sorting network into a parallelisable program usually needs to change the point of view from the network to the individual element. This is quite subtle and it renders the algorithm unrecognisable[3].

The computational element of a sorting network is a compare-and-swap circuit

$$CS(m,n) = \begin{cases} (m,n) & \text{if } m \leq n \\ (n,m) & \text{if } m > n. \end{cases}$$

A *sorting network* is a circuit formed exclusively from CS circuits. A simple, but inefficient, sorting network is the odd-even transposition network, which for 4 elements is:

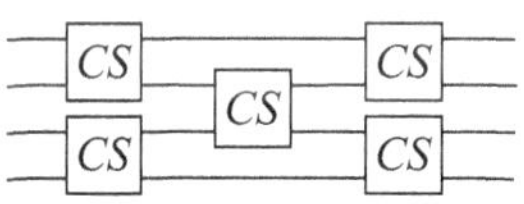

In SCI the CS box can be implemented as

$$CS \stackrel{def}{=} \lambda m{:}\mathsf{exp}.\lambda n{:}\mathsf{exp}.\mathsf{if}\ m < n\ \mathsf{then}\ m \otimes n\ \mathsf{else}\ n \otimes m$$

With $CS : \mathsf{exp} \to \mathsf{exp} \to \mathsf{exp} \otimes \mathsf{exp} \simeq \mathsf{exp} \otimes \mathsf{exp} \to \mathsf{exp} \otimes \mathsf{exp}$. Let SC be the converse circuit:

$$SC \stackrel{def}{=} \lambda m{:}\mathsf{exp}.\lambda n{:}\mathsf{exp}.\mathsf{if}\ m > n\ \mathsf{then}\ m \otimes n\ \mathsf{else}\ n \otimes m.$$

Note that the type system allows the $<$ operator to be given a parallel implementation; we can also use the special CS circuit, packaged like this so that it conforms to the type signature:

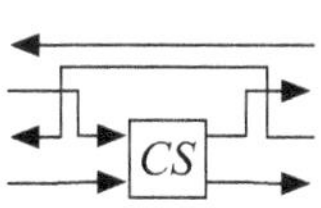

The standard definition of Batcher's algorithm as a recursively specified sorting network is this:

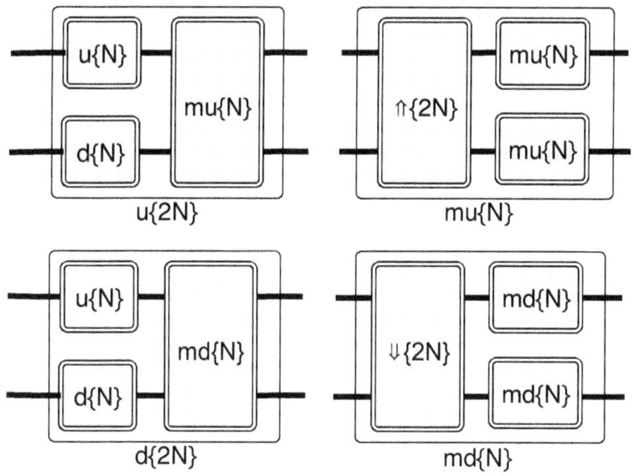

The circuit $\Uparrow\{2N\}$ compares-and-swaps the k-th element in the array against the $N+k$-th element, merging two bitonic sequences; for $N = 4$ is:

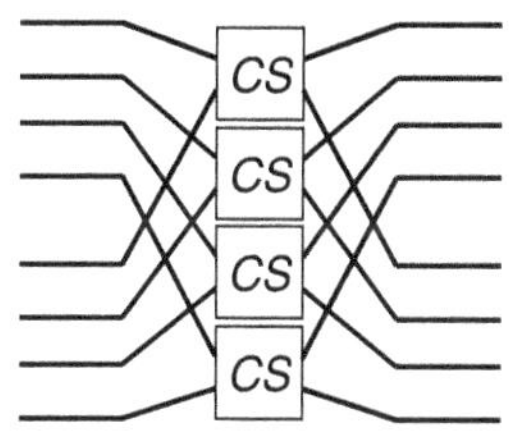

$\Downarrow\{2N\}$ is the "upside-down" $\Uparrow\{N\}$ circuit. The other circuits involved in the recursive definition are: u (up-sort), d (down-sort), mu (merge-up) and md (merge-down).

First let us introduce syntactic sugar for function composition, $f \circ g = \lambda x : \theta.f(g(x))$. In SCI the Batcher's bitonic sorting network is defined by the following program:

$$\begin{aligned}
\mathrm{u}\{1\} &= \mathrm{d}\{1\} = \lambda x{:}\mathsf{exp}.x \\
\mathrm{mu}\{1\} &= \mathrm{md}\{1\} = \lambda x{:}\mathsf{exp}.x \\
\mathrm{u}\{N\} &= \mathrm{mu}\{N\} \circ (\mathrm{u}\{N/2\} \otimes \mathrm{d}\{N/2\}) \\
\mathrm{d}\{N\} &= \mathrm{md}\{N\} \circ (\mathrm{u}\{N/2\} \otimes \mathrm{d}\{N/2\}) \\
\mathrm{mu}\{N\} &= (\mathrm{mu}\{N/2\} \otimes \mathrm{mu}\{N/2\}) \circ \mathrm{up}\{N\} \\
\mathrm{md}\{N\} &= (\mathrm{md}\{N/2\} \otimes \mathrm{md}\{N/2\}) \circ \mathrm{down}\{N\} \\
\mathrm{up}\{N\} &= (\lambda x{:}\mathsf{exp}\{N/2{-}1\}.\lambda z{:}\mathsf{exp}\{N/2{-}1\}.\lambda y{:}\mathsf{exp}.\lambda u{:}\mathsf{exp}. \\
&\qquad x \otimes y \otimes z \otimes u) \\
&\quad \circ (CS \otimes \mathrm{up}\{N/2-2\}) \\
&\quad \circ (\lambda x{:}\mathsf{exp}.\lambda y{:}\mathsf{exp}\{N/2{-}1\}.\lambda z{:}\mathsf{exp}.\lambda u{:}\mathsf{exp}\{N/2{-}1\}. \\
&\qquad x \otimes z \otimes y \otimes u) \\
\mathrm{down}\{N\} &= (\lambda x{:}\mathsf{exp}\{N/2{-}1\}.\lambda z{:}\mathsf{exp}\{N/2{-}1\}.\lambda y{:}\mathsf{exp}.\lambda u{:}\mathsf{exp}. \\
&\qquad x \otimes y \otimes z \otimes u) \\
&\quad \circ (SC \otimes \mathrm{up}\{N/2-2\}) \\
&\quad \circ (\lambda x{:}\mathsf{exp}.\lambda y{:}\mathsf{exp}\{N/2{-}1\}.\lambda z{:}\mathsf{exp}.\lambda u{:}\mathsf{exp}\{N/2{-}1\}. \\
&\qquad x \otimes z \otimes y \otimes u)
\end{aligned}$$

Note that above the $\circ$ operator needs to be elaborated with the proper type, which is a trivial exercise in type inference. A bitonic sorter is $\mathrm{u}\{N\}$ for N a power of 2.

This program elaborates to a SCI program which then synthesises to the standard bitonic sorting network. Note that this approach is very similar to the approach that structural functional

[3] See `http://www.tools-of-computing.com/tc/CS/Sorts/bitonic_sort.htm` and the CUDA implementation at `http://developer.download.nvidia.com/compute/cuda/sdk/website/samples.html`.

hardware description languages such as Lava[4]. However, because our syntax is based on compact-closed combinators they match conventional programming language syntax based on abstraction and application. In the case of Lava, the underlying syntax is set (albeit not explicitly) in a traced-monoidal framework which is somewhat more rigid [JSV96].

5. Unfolding affine recursion in time

Sometimes a recursive unfolding of a circuit is not desired or not possible and we may wish to have genuine run-time recursive behaviour.

First note that unrestricted recursion in SCI is not possible as the unfolding of the recursive calls can violate the typing rule requiring disjointness of free identifiers between a function and its argument, as in $\mathsf{fix}(F) \longrightarrow F(\mathsf{fix}(F))$. Therefore fix-point can only be applied to closed terms:

$$\frac{\vdash F : \theta \to \theta}{\vdash \mathsf{fix}(F) : \theta} \text{ fix-point}$$

The recursive unfolding of the fix-point combinator suggests that the circuit representation of the fix-point circuit should be equivalent to the following infinite circuit:

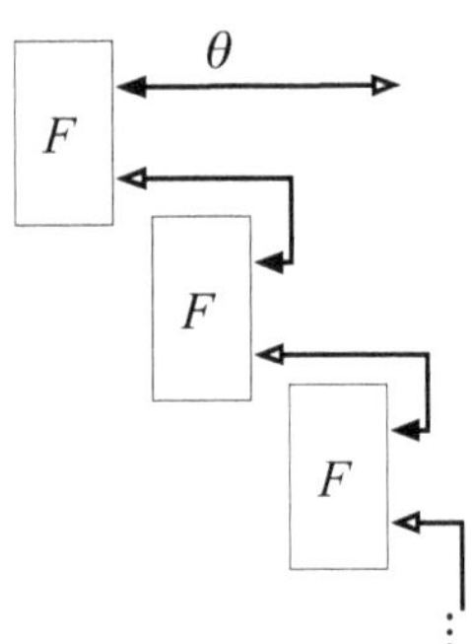

The solid/hollow arrows indicate the change of polarity of the bus $[\![\theta]\!]$. Obviously, what we would like is something like this:

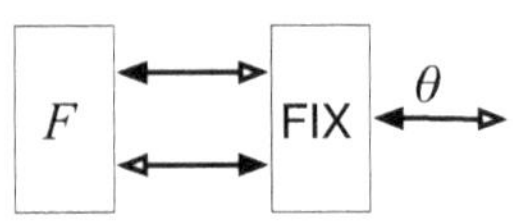

A tempting idea is to fold the circuit for $[\![F]\!]$ onto itself by using a FIX circuit very similar to the diagonal. However, this is not possible: some of the constituent circuits of $[\![F]\!]$ are stateful and their states can be different in different instances of F. The relevant stateful circuits are:

R used in the implementation of operators and local variables.

SR used in the implementation of the diagonal.

The other stateful circuit is D, but while the FIX block is executing, its state is the same for all instances of $[\![F]\!]$.

As a first step towards implementing recursion we replace all occurrences of registers R and SR with *indexed* versions Ri and SRi:

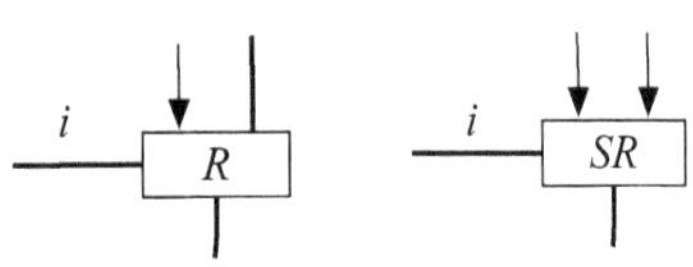

[4] See `http://raintown.org/lava/` for a Bitonic sort implementation.

Ri is implemented as follows:

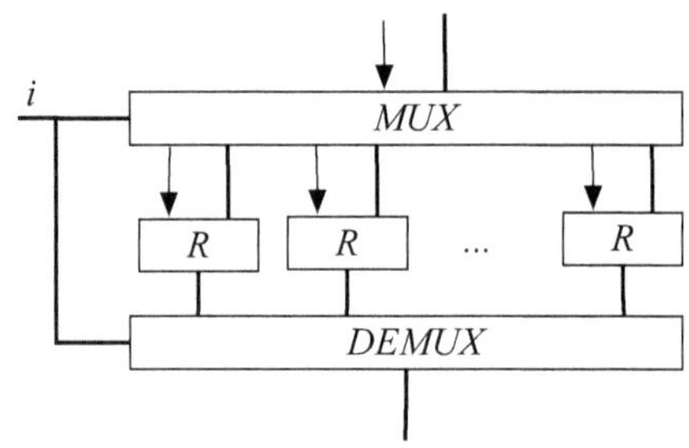

and SRi analogously. The registers must be replaced with small addressable memory elements.

Now we can rewrite our infinite unfolding of the fix-point like this:

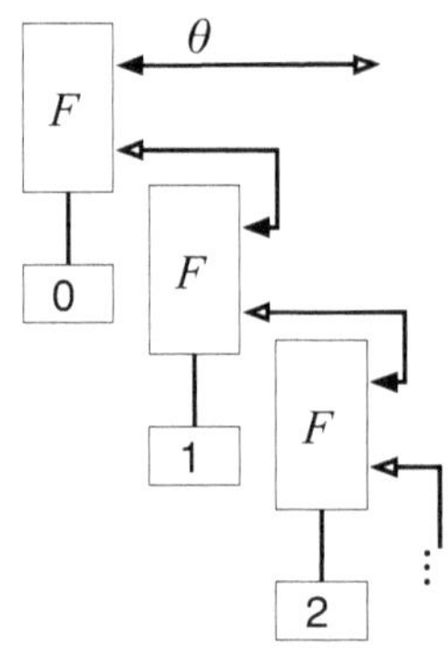

Every instance of $[\![F]\!]$ now uses a different index, but is otherwise identical. This means that we can replace the fixed indices with a counter and fold all the instances into one single instance, indexed by the counter. The value of the counter will indicate what "virtual" instance of $[\![F]\!]$ is active and will be used as an index into the registers.

The fix-point circuit will increase this global counter whenever a recursive call is made and decrease it when a recursive return is made. When the counter is 0 the recursive return will be to the environment.

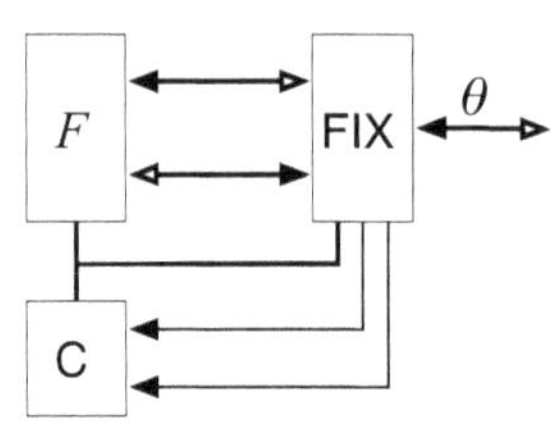

Circuit C is an up-down counter.

For example, for $\mathsf{exp} \to \mathsf{exp}$ the fix-point combinator which can be applied to function $\lambda f : \mathsf{exp} \to \mathsf{exp}.\lambda n : \mathsf{exp}.M$ is (data lines not shown):

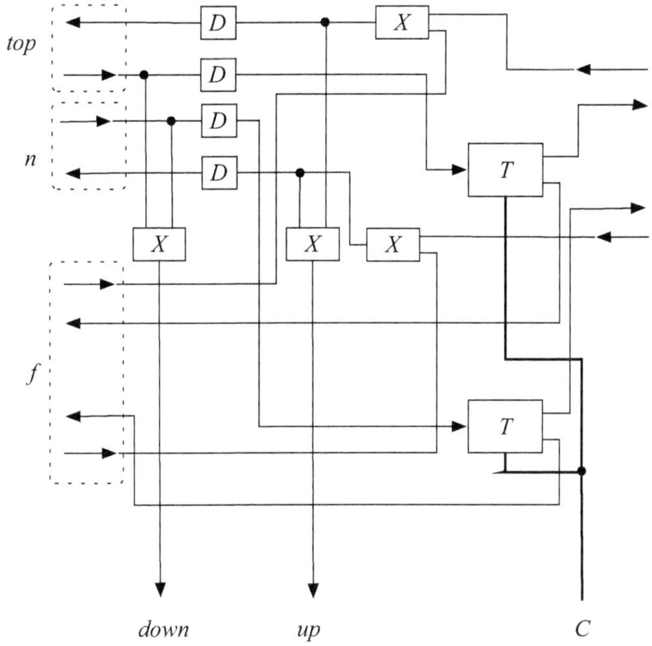

In the general case, for an arbitrary θ, the FIX_θ combinator is a replication of the circuit below

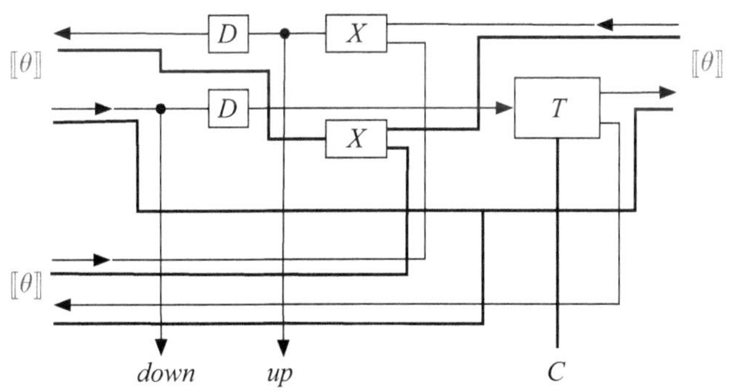

for each input and output port in θ. If the port is pure control then the data line can be omitted.

Correctness and limitations. Except for recursion, the implementation of the compiler is a hardware instantiation of the synchronous representation of the game semantics and is correct by construction as explained in a series of papers [McC02, GM10, GM11]. The detailed proof of correctness of the fix-point constructor is beyond the scope of this paper, but the step-by-step construction given in this section mirrors the structure of the proof of correctness. There are two limitations which play an important role in the correct implementation of fix-point:

Concurrency. The SCI type system allows concurrency in general, but concurrency inside the term to which the fix-point constructor is applied must be disallowed. It is crucial for the correctness of the implementation that only one "virtual" instance of the recursive function, as indicated by the recursion depth counter, is active at any one moment in time. If the recursive call is used in a concurrent context this can no longer be guaranteed. Note that recursively implemented functions can run in a parallel environment, only internally parallelism is disallowed. For simplicity we disallow all parallelism, but a more careful analysis which only bans the use of the recursive call in a parallel context is possible.

Nested recursion. For simplicity we assume that recursive definitions do not contain other recursive definitions. This is technically possible, by applying the same methodology and transforming the recursion counter into an indexed array of recursion counters.

5.1 Overflow detection

Recursive calls assume an idealized machine model with no bound on resources. In physical machines that cannot be the case so recursion calls that run too deep can overflow resources. On a conventional CPU-based architecture this leads to an abnormal termination of the program, triggered either by the run-time environment (memory management modules or the operating system). A synthesised program, in contrast, runs in isolation and runtime errors cannot be detected or processed. In our implementation, overflow would manifest simply by the counter rolling over, which would lead to active instances of the recursive functions being misidentified. This is problematic because it will not give an error but will produce the wrong result (similar to integer overflow in C).

It is important therefore to build into the language an error detection and handling mechanisms by providing the fix-point operator with an overflow handler. The syntax is

$$\frac{\vdash F : \theta \to \theta \qquad \Gamma \vdash M : \mathsf{com}}{\Gamma \vdash \mathsf{fix}\, F\, \mathsf{with}\, M : \theta}$$

The implementation:

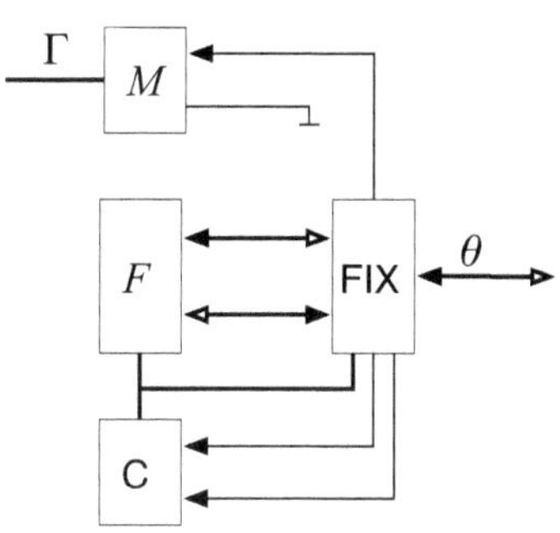

The fix-point operator is, by design, aware of the maximum size of the counter. When a recursive call is about to increase beyond the maximum size, instead of propagating the signal back to $[\![F]\!]$ it will issue a special error signal to command $[\![M]\!]$ which is the error handler. The control output of $[\![M]\!]$ is either ignored (grounded) or connected to a special global error port.

5.2 Tail recursion

Iteration (while) is included in the recursion-free fragment of SCI and it can be readily generalised to a higher-order tail-recursion operator. Because tail-recursive calls do not need to percolate back through each instance of the function the counter C and the instance-management apparatus are no longer necessary. The tail-recursive operator TAIL_θ becomes simply:

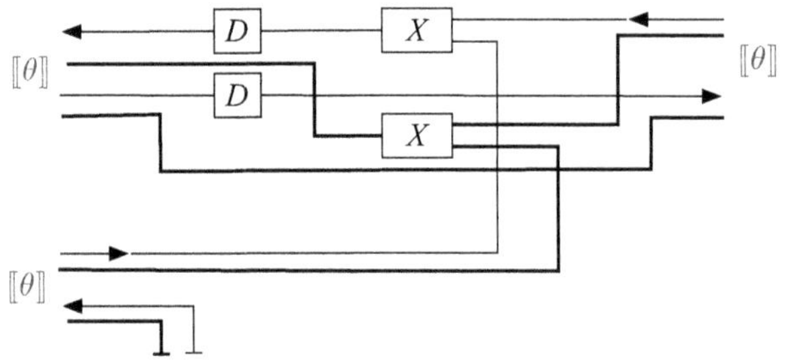

Note that the return from the recursive call is immediately propagated to the calling environment.

Also, there is no need for the tail recursion operation to be applied to closed terms, as the tail unfolding is sequential rather than nested application:

$$\frac{\Gamma \vdash F : \theta \to \theta}{\Gamma \vdash \mathsf{tail}_\theta F : \theta}$$

6. Performance and benchmarks

At this early stage our research is mainly qualitative, demonstrating the possibility of compiling recursive functions in static hardware.

We will give two benchmark-style examples to show that even in the absence of any compiler optimisations the performance is promising. We choose a naive Fibonacci number calculation as a farily common benchmark of recursion performance and we examine the call-by-name and the call-by-value versions. This is not a realistic efficient implementation but is an excellent contrived example for creating a large number of recursive calls in an arbitrarily nested pattern.

As this is the first, to our knowledge, attempt to give a general method for synthesising recursion in time (recursion in space has been explored thoroughly by Lava) we are forced to compare against execution on a conventional CPU-based architecture. It is difficult to abstract away from the fact that we use not only different devices (CPU versus FPGA) but also different compilers and run-time environments.

CPU We use an Intel Core 2 Duo processor running at 2.4 GHz on a machine with the Mac OS X 10.5 operating system, the Marst[5] Algol 60 compiler and the gcc 4.0.1 C compiler.

FPGA We use a Altera Stratix III EPSL150 device, programmed using Quartus 10.0, set on a Terasic DE3 board, operating at a default 50 MHz. We compute the maximum safe clock frequency using the TimeQuest timing constraint tool, part of the `Quartus` tool-set, and we scale execution time accordingly.

In order to normalise the performance comparison we will consider two main metrics:

Relative throughput We measure the relative throughput between the two devices computing from exactly the same source code. We take into account execution time and resource utilisation, which indicate the amount of parallelism that the device can support. Note that on the FPGA parallel execution has no additional overhead or contention over resources, even in the case of recursive functions, as no global stack is used in the implementation.

Relative throughput per transistor We further normalise the relative throughput of the two computations relative to the transistor count, in order to obtain a fairer measure of performance.

On both these measures the circuits we synthesise perform better than CPU-based execution.

[5] `http://www.gnu.org/software/marst/`

6.1 Fibonacci, call-by-name

We use the simple-minded implementation of Fibonacci numbers in order to generate a very large number of recursive calls from small and simple code. This is appropriate as we do want to focus our benchmarking on the effectiveness of the implementation of recursion.

In traditional Algol60 syntax the program is:

```
integer procedure fib(n);
  integer n;
  begin
    if n-1 = 0 then fib := 1
    else if n-2 = 0 then fib := 1
    else fib := fib(n-1) + fib(n-2)
  end fib;
```

The benchmark results are as follows:

	CPU	FPGA
Time	35.5 s	50 s
Clock	2.4 GHz	137 MHz
Cycles	85.2 B	6.85 B
Transistors	$\simeq$ 300 M	$\simeq$ 400 M
Utilisation	50%	2%
Tx (rel.)	5.62%	1,774.9%
Tx/trans (rel)	7.49%	1,331.1%

Note that the execution time on the FPGA is larger than on the CPU. This is to be expected, as the code is purely sequential and uses very little memory. This is precisely the code that CPUs are highly optimised to execute fast, and this is on top of the CPU working with a much faster clock.

However, one core of this dual-core CPU is fully occupied by this computation, leading to a 50% utilisation of resources. We could compute two instances of fib in parallel with no extra overhead. On the FPGA, the area occupied by the synthesised circuit is only 2%, which means we can run up to 50 instances of this circuit in parallel, with no overhead. Note that the utilisation bound (2%) is on total ALUTs rather than on memory (1%), which means that the overhead needed to handle recursion is manageable. Using spatial unfolding we can only run fib to a depth of recursion of about 5-6 (the expansion is exponential) whereas our temporal unfolding has a depth of 256 (and reduced use of resources).

A relative comparison of execution time versus utilisation gives the FPGA 1,774.9% (almost 18×) total throughput compared to the CPU (conversely, the CPU has 5.62% of the FPGA throughput).

Images of block diagram and resource utilisation density for the synthesised circuit are in Fig. 2. Note the row of RAM blocks, three of which are used to implement the stateful elements of recursion–they are the only memory overhead needed for implementing recursion.

It is fair to take into account the fact that this particular FPGA has a larger transistor count than the corresponding CPU. Normalising throughput by this factor still gives the FPGA over 13× total computational throughput per transistor.

6.2 Fibonacci, call-by-value

The CBN evaluation makes the purely functional Fibonacci function staggeringly inefficient. An improvement on the naive algorithm forces the evaluation of the argument inside the function:

```
integer procedure fib(n);
  integer n;
  begin
    integer n0, n1, n2;
    n0 := n;
    if n0-1 = 0 then fib := 1
    else if n0-2 = 0 then fib := 1
```

```
    else begin
      n1 := fib(n0-1);
      n2 := fib(n0-2);
      fib := n1 + n2 end
  end fib;
```

The results are now better in absolute terms both on the CPU and the FPGA. The maximum clock frequency for the CBV `fib` is smaller, but a similar relative throughput advantage for the FPGA version still occurs.

	CPU	FPGA
Time	2.8 s	4.0 s
Clock	2.4 GHz	119 MHz
Cycles	6.78 B	.48 B
Transistors	$\simeq$ 300 M	$\simeq$ 400 M
Utilisation	50%	2%
Tx (rel.)	5.7%	1,735.9%
Tx/trans (rel)	7.6%	1,301.9%

As a sanity check, we can compare this implementation with a call-by-value implementation as used by more wide-spread compilers; Ocaml v3.10 computes `fib(36)` on the same CPU in 0.6 seconds, substantially better than Algol60 and Marst. However, the overall throughput of the FPGA remains higher.

In Fig. 3 we can see run-time snapshots taken with the Signal-Tap tool of the two circuits, indicating current calculated value, current value of the internal recursion counter and next value being calculated. We can notice in the CBN version the recursion counter cycling all the way back to 0 each time an argument needs to be (re)evaluated, whereas in the CBV version the argument is picked up from the local variable.

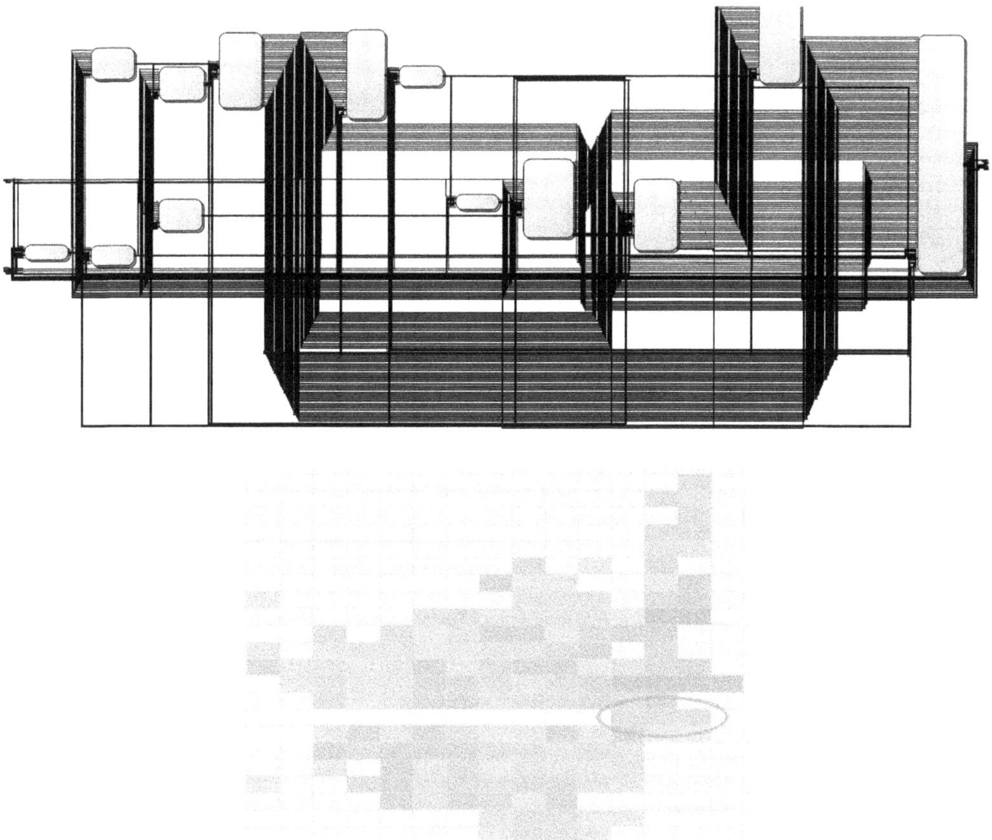

Figure 2. Synthesised FPGA layout for `fib`: block diagram and resource utilisation density (zoom-in)

6.3 Expressiveness

The fact that the recursion operator can only be applied to syntactically closed functions is not a major restriction in terms of expressiveness. Affine recursion has been studied in the context of closed recursion in the lambda calculus [AFFM07] and is in fact the style of recursion used in Goedel's System T [AFFM10], where it is called *iteration*. We prefer "affine recursion" as iteration may incorrectly suggest repeated serial application rather than true, nested, recursion.

As a test of the expressiveness of the compiler we programmed Escardo's implementation of the Bailey-Borwein-Plouffe spigot algorithm for the computation of the n-th digit of π [BBP97]. The implementation is written in Haskell and it uses higher-order functionals to give precise representations to real numbers as streams of digits [Esc09]. The program was successfully compiled to VHDL and synthesised on the same Altera-based FPGA-board. Note that our language does not offer direct support for lists and streams, which needed to be coded up in the standard way into the underlying lambda calculus.

This test was done only to evaluate the expressiveness of the compiler, as without direct semantic support for lists or streams the run-time performance cannot be realistically assessed. Even so, the fact that ALUT utilisation stood at only 12% and the BRAM utilisation at only 8% indicates that the overall footprint is small and the overhead imposed by recursion manageable.

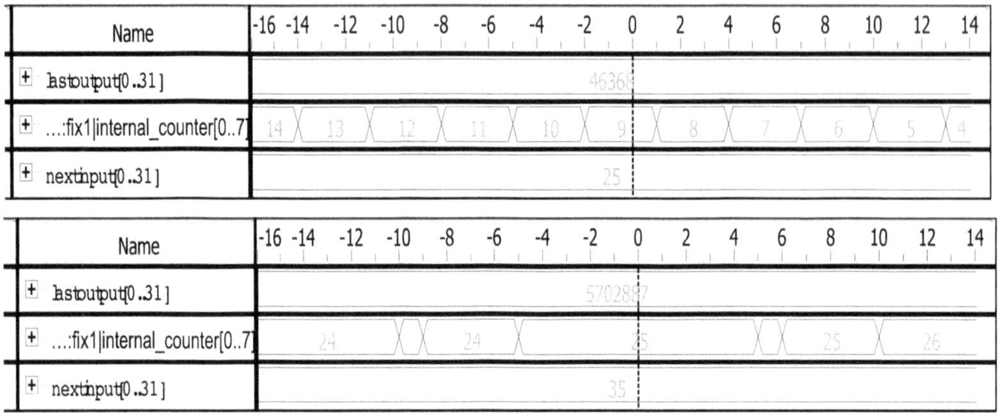

Figure 3. Run-time snapshots of CBN and CBV `fib`

7. Summary

We have shown a systematic approach for compiling programs using affine recursion into correct circuits implemented on FPGAs which operate between the 110 MHz to 140 MHz range (so the critical path is respectable) and these circuits can use far fewer cycles to compute a result than the corresponding software implementation. However, unlike the software version we can systematically explore space and time trade-offs by unrolling function calls through effectively inlining which in turn can increase throughput at the cost of area. Our initial preliminary results are encouraging and we are developing the system further by allowing the processing of off-chip dynamic data-structures and streams. By understanding how to effectively synthesize recursive descriptions we get one step closer to the ability to transform programs into circuits for implementations that have superior computational throughput or reduced energy consumption.

References

[AFFM07] Sandra Alves, Maribel Fernández, Mário Florido, and Ian Mackie. The power of closed reduction strategies. *Electr. Notes Theor. Comput. Sci.*, 174(10):57–74, 2007.

[AFFM10] Sandra Alves, Maribel Fernández, Mário Florido, and Ian Mackie. Gödel's system tau revisited. *Theor. Comput. Sci.*, 411(11-13):1484–1500, 2010.

[AJ92] Samson Abramsky and Radha Jagadeesan. New foundations for the Geometry of Interaction. In *IEEE Symposium on Logic in Computer Science (LICS)*, pages 211–222, 1992.

[Bat68] Kenneth E. Batcher. Sorting networks and their applications. In *AFIPS Spring Joint Computing Conference*, pages 307–314, 1968.

[BBP97] D. Bailey, P. Borwein, and S. Plouffe. On the rapid computation of various polylogarithmic constants. *Mathematics of Computation*, 66(218):903–914, 1997.

[BCSS98] Per Bjesse, Koen Claessen, Mary Sheeran, and Satnam Singh. Lava: Hardware design in Haskell. In *The International Conference on Functional Programming (ICFP)*, New York, NY, USA, 1998. ACM.

[BH98] P. Bellows and B. Hutchings. JHDL: an HDL for reconfigurable systems. In *IEEE Symposium on FPGAs for Custom Computing Machines*, Apr 1998.

[Esc09] Martin H. Escardo. Computing with real numbers represented as infinite sequences of digits in haskell. In *Computability and complexity analysis*, Ljubljana, Slovenia, 2009. (code available at the author's web page).

[FG06] George Ferizis and Hossam El Gindy. Mapping recursive functions to reconfigurable hardware. In *Field Programmable Logic and Applications, 2006. FPL '06. International Conference on*, pages 1–6, 2006.

[Ghi07] Dan R. Ghica. Geometry of Synthesis: a structured approach to VLSI design. In *ACM Symposium on Principles of Programming Languages (POPL)*, pages 363–375, 2007.

[Ghi09] Dan R. Ghica. Applications of game semantics: From software analysis to hardware synthesis. In *IEEE Symposium on Logic in Computer Science (LICS)*, pages 17–26, 2009.

[Ghi11] Dan R. Ghica. Functions interface models for hardware compilation. In *ACM/IEEE Ninth International Conference on Formal Methods and Models for Codesign (MEMOCODE)*, 2011. (forthcoming)

[GM00] Dan R. Ghica and Guy McCusker. Reasoning about Idealized Algol using regular languages. In *The International Colloquium on Automata, Languages and Programming (ICALP)*, pages 103–115, 2000.

[GM10] Dan R. Ghica and Mohamed N. Menaa. On the compositionality of round abstraction. In *The International Conference on Concurrency Theory (CONCUR)*, pages 417–431, 2010.

[GM11] Dan R. Ghica and Mohamed N. Menaa. Synchronous game semantics via round abstraction. In *The International Conference on Foundations of Software Science and Computation Structures (FoSSaCS)*, pages 350–364, 2011.

[GS10] Dan R. Ghica and Alex Smith. Geometry of Synthesis II: From games to delay-insensitive circuits. *Electr. Notes Theor. Comput. Sci.*, 265:301–324, 2010.

[GS11] Dan R. Ghica and Alex Smith. Geometry of Synthesis III: Resource management through type inference. In *ACM Symposium on Principles of Programming Languages (POPL)*, pages 345–356, 2011.

[HD08] Scott Hauck and André DeHon, editors. *Reconfigurable Computing*, chapter Specifying Circuit Layout in FPGAs. Systems on Silicon. Morgan Kaufmann Publishers, 2008.

[JSV96] André Joyal, Ross Street, and Dominic Verity. Traced monoidal categories. *Mathematical Proceedings of Cambridge Philosophical Society*, 119:447–468, 1996.

[KL80] G. M. Kelly and M. L. Laplaza. Coherence for compact closed categories. *Journal of Pure and Applied Algebra*, 19:193–213, 1980.

[Mac94] Ian Mackie. *The Geometry of Implementation*. PhD thesis, Imperial College, University of London, 1994.

[Mac95] Ian Mackie. The geometry of Interaction machine. In *ACM Symposium on Principles of Programming Languages (POPL)*, pages 198–208, 1995.

[McC02] Guy McCusker. A fully abstract relational model of Syntactic Control of Interference. In *The Conference on Computer Science Logic (CSL)*, pages 247–261, 2002.

[McC07] Guy McCusker. Categorical models of syntactic control of interference revisited, revisited. *LMS Journal of Computation and Mathematics*, 10:176–216, 2007.

[McC10] Guy McCusker. A graph model for imperative computation. *Logical Methods in Computer Science*, 6(1), 2010.

[MTH99] Tsutomu Maruyama, Masaaki Takagi, and Tsutomu Hoshino. Hardware implementation techniques for recursive calls and loops. In *The International Conference on Field Programmable Logic and Applications (FPL)*, pages 450–455, 1999.

[Nik04] Rishiyur Nikhil. Bluespec SystemVerilog: Efficient, correct RTL from high-level specifications. *Formal Methods and Models for Co-Design (MEMOCODE)*, 2004.

[OPTT99] Peter W. O'Hearn, John Power, Makoto Takeyama, and Robert D. Tennent. Syntactic control of interference revisited. *Theor. Comput. Sci.*, 228(1-2):211–252, 1999.

[OT81] Peter O'Hearn and Robert D. Tennent. *Algol-like languages*. Birkhauser, Boston, 1981.

[Red96] Uday S. Reddy. Global state considered unnecessary: An introduction to object-based semantics. *Lisp and Symbolic Computation*, 9(1):7–76, 1996.

[Rey78] John C. Reynolds. Syntactic control of interference. In *ACM Symposium on Principles of Programming Languages (POPL)*, pages 39–46, 1978.

[Rey81] John C. Reynolds. The essence of Algol. In *Proceedings of the 1981 International Symposium on Algorithmic Languages*, pages 345–372. North-Holland, 1981.

[Rey89] John C. Reynolds. Syntactic control of inference, part 2. In *The International Colloquium on Automata, Languages and Programming (ICALP)*, pages 704–722, 1989.

[Sel09] Peter Selinger. *New Structures for Physiscs*, chapter A survey of graphical languages for monoidal categories. Springer Lecture Notes in Physics, 2009.

[Skl04] Valery Sklyarov. FPGA-based implementation of recursive algorithms. *Microprocessors and Microsystems*, 28(5-6):197 – 211, 2004. Special Issue on FPGAs: Applications and Designs.

[TL07] D.B. Thomas and W. Luk. A domain specific language for reconfigurable path-based monte carlo simulations. In *International Conference on Field-Programmable Technology (ICFPT)*, pages 97 –104, 2007.

[Wal04] Matthew Wall. *Games for Syntactic Control of Interference*. PhD thesis, University of Sussex, 2004.

A Hierarchy of Mendler style Recursion Combinators *

Taming Inductive Datatypes with Negative Occurrences

Ki Yung Ahn Tim Sheard

Portland State University

{kya,sheard}@cs.pdx.edu

Abstract

The Mendler style catamorphism (which corresponds to weak induction) always terminates even for negative inductive datatypes. The Mendler style histomorphism (which corresponds to strong induction) is known to terminate for positive inductive datatypes. To our knowledge, the literature is silent on its termination properties for negative datatypes. In this paper, we prove that histomorphisms do not always termintate by showing a counter-example. We also enrich the Mendler collection of recursion combinators by defining a new form of Mendler style catamorphism (*msfcata*), which terminates for all inductive datatypes, that is more expressive than the original. We organize the collection of combinators by placing them into a hierarchy of ever increasing generality, and describing the termination properties of each point on the hierarchy. We also provide many examples (including a case study on a negative inductive datatype), which illustrate both the expressive power and beauty of the Mendler style. One lesson we learn from this work is that weak induction applies to negative inductive datatypes but strong induction is problematic. We provide a proof of weak induction by exhibiting an embedding of our new combinator into F_ω. We pose the open question: Is there a safe way to apply strong induction to negative inductive datatypes?

Categories and Subject Descriptors D.3.3 [*Programming Languages*]: Langauge Constructs and Features—abstract data types, polymorphism, control structure, recursion; F.3.3 [*Logics and Meanings of Programs*]: Study of Program Constructs—control primitives, functional constructs, program and recursion schemes, type structure; F.4.1 [*Mathematical Logic and Formal Languages*]: Mathematical Logic—lambda calculus and related systems

General Terms Languages

Keywords catamorphism, histomorphism, higher-order abstract syntax, parametric polymorphism, parametricity, recursion schemes, recursion combinators, termination, totality

1. Introduction

This paper explores a family of terminating recursion combinators over a wide class of inductive datatypes. The functional programming community has traditionally focused on families of combinators that work well in Hindley-Milner languages, characterized by folds and catamorphisms. This paper explores a more expressive family called Mendler style combinators. The Mendler style combinators were originally developed in the context of the Nuprl [8] type system. Nuprl made extensive use of dependent types. General type checking in Nuprl was done by interactive theorem proving — not by type inference. The Mendler style combinators are considerably more expressive than the conventional Squiggol [5] school.

Recently, Mendler style combinators have been studied in the context of modern functional languages with advanced type system features, including higher-rank polymorphism and generalized algebraic data types. This paper extends that analysis by

- Illustrating that the Mendler style approach applies to useful examples of negative datatypes, through the case study of the HOAS formatting function (§4).
- ★Extending the Mendler style catamorphism by using the inverse trick first described by Fegaras and Sheard [13], and later refined by Washburn and Weirich [37] (§4).
- Providing an intuitive explanation of why the Mendler style catamorphism ensures termination (§3.3) even for negative datatypes (§3.8). We illustrate a semi-formal proof of termination by encoding the extended catamorphism in the F_ω fragment in Haskell (Figure 6, §8)
- ★Providing an intuitive explanation of why the Mendler style histomorphism terminates for positive datatypes (§3.4), but may fail to terminate for negative datatypes (§3.8) by showing a counter-example to termination.
- Organizing a large class of Mendler style recursion combinators into an intuitive hierarchy, of increasing generality, that is expressive enough to cover regular dataypes (§3.1, §3.4), nested datatypes (§3.5), indexed datatypes (GADTs) (§3.6), mutually recursive datatypes (§3.7), and negative datatypes (§3.8, §4).
- Providing a detailed set of examples, all written in Haskell, in both the conventional and Mendler style, that illustrate most points in the hierarchy.

The ★-items are original contributions, and the others are collective observations of common patterns arising from the study of both the previously known combinators and our new combinators.

We demonstrate the Mendler style combinators in the Glasgow Haskell Compiler [31] (GHC) dialect of Haskell. However, this demonstration depends on a set of conventions. We assert that all our code fragments conform with our conventions. The conventions include: (1) all values of algebraic data types are inductive (finite), (2) certain conventions of data abstraction not enforced by Haskell, and (3) we can control or delineate other sources of nontermination.

The motivation for this investigation is the design of Trellys, a full-featured language with dependent types being developed by a cooperative project of Portland State University, the University of

* work supported by the National Science Foundation under grant 0910500.

ICFP '11, September 19–21, 2011, Tokyo, Japan

Iowa, and the University of Pennsylvania. A design goal of Trellys is to develop an inference mechanism which determines what terms of the language are safe to use as a logic, and what terms can only be used as programs. We call this analysis *logicality inference.* The intent is that logical values can be interpreted as proof objects by a Curry-Howard style interpretation, while programmatic values are allowed to express arbitrary computations (including non-termination). The usability of Trellys requires that it be as expressive as possible over natural forms of inductive and recursive argument. Hence our motivation to fully understand the Mendler style recursion combinators. It is our intention that the three conventions discussed in the previous paragraph will be enforced in the Trellys system, and our use of Haskell to illustrate the Mendler style, will soon be unnecessary.

The use of Mendler style combinators is characterized by splitting the definition of a recursive type into a generating functor (or a base datatype) and an explicit application of the appropriate datatype fixpoint operator. There exists an infinite series of datatype fixpoint operators, each of a different rank, in this paper we illustrate only the first two ranks. The rank of a datatype depends upon the kind of its *type indexes* (as opposed to its *type parameters*).[1]

2. Background - Termination and Negativity

Mendler [23] showed that diverging computations can be expressed using inductive datatypes with negative occurrences of the datatype being defined. No explicit recursion at the value level is required to elicit non-termination. We can illustrate this in Haskell as follows:

$\mathbf{data}\ T = C\ (T \to ())$	$w\ (C\ w)$
$p :: T \to (T \to ())$	$\rightsquigarrow (p\ (C\ w))\ (C\ w))$
$p\ (C\ f) = f$	$\rightsquigarrow w\ (C\ w)$
$w :: T \to ()$	$\rightsquigarrow (p\ (C\ w))\ (C\ w))$
$w\ x = (p\ x)\ x$	$\rightsquigarrow \cdots$

On the left is a data definition of the negative datatatpe T, and the non-recursive functions p and q. On the right is a diverging computation ($\rightsquigarrow$ denotes a reduction step).

Note, the term $w\ (C\ w) :: T$ diverges even though the functions p and w are non-recursive. The cause of this divergence can be attributed to the "hidden" self application in the term $w\ (C\ w) :: T$. The negative occurrence of T in the datatype definition of T is what enables this self application to be well typed.

For this reason, many systems (e.g., Hagino's CPL [14], and Coq [26]) supporting inductive datatypes require all datatypes to be positive (or covariant) in order to ensure normalization. Uustalu and Vene [33] call this style, limiting datatypes to positive occurrences, the *conventional* style, in contrast to what they name the Mendler style [24].

In the Mendler style, datatypes are not limited to induct over positive occurrences, yet functions expressible via catamorphism always terminate. This was first reported by Uustalu [32] and Matthes [19], but the search for exciting examples of negative datatypes was postponed until another time (considering it "may have a theoretical value only"[33]). Subsequent work [1, 2, 35, 36], that pioneered the Mendler style in practical functional programming, also failed to produce good examples that make use of negative datatypes in the Mendler style.

In the functional programming community, there are both well-known and useful examples of negative and mixed datatypes (e.g., delimited control[29][2]). One of the classic examples is Higher-Order Abstract Syntax (HOAS) [7, 27]. A non-standard definition of HOAS in Haskell is:[3]

$$\mathbf{data}\ \mathit{Exp} = \mathit{Lam}\ (\mathit{Exp} \to \mathit{Exp}) \mid \mathit{App}\ \mathit{Exp}\ \mathit{Exp} \mid \mathit{Var}\ \mathit{String}$$

We can define a function $\mathit{showExp} :: \mathit{Exp} \to \mathit{String}$ that formats an HOAS expression into a string. For example,

$$\mathit{showExp}\ (\mathit{Lam}\ (\lambda x \to x)) \rightsquigarrow \texttt{"(\textbackslash a->a)"}$$
$$\mathit{showExp}\ (\mathit{Lam}\ (\lambda x \to \mathit{App}\ x\ x)) \rightsquigarrow \texttt{"(\textbackslash a->(a a))"}$$

The function $\mathit{showExp}$ is total, provided the function values embedded in the Lam data constructor are total (which is one of the things the Trellys' logicality inference provides). This paper illustrates that this example (a negative datatype), and many others examples including non-regular datatypes and mutually recursive datatypes can all be easily written as Mendler style recursion, whose termination properties are known.

3. A Tour of the Mendler style Approach

In this section we give a tour of the Mendler style approach, to orient the reader, before diving into our case study on HOAS formatting in §4. First, we introduce both the catamorphism (§3.3) and histomorpism (§3.4) combinators of rank 0 for regular datatypes. Second, we provide intuition why Mendler style recursion combinators ensure termination for positive datatypes. Third, we move our focus from regular datatypes to more expressive datatypes which need rank 1 recursion combinators. These include nested datatypes (§3.5), indexed datatypes(GADTs) (§3.6), and mutually recursive datatypes (§3.7). Fourth, we give intuition why the Mendler style catamorphism ensures termination even for negative datatypes (§3.8). Finally, we present the case study focusing on HOAS in §4.

All of our results are summarized in Figures 2, 3, and 4. In Figure 2, we define the Mendler style datatype fixpoint operators (i.e. μ_0 and μ_1). These are datatype definitions in Haskell that take type constructors as arguments. They are used to tie the recursive knot through the generating functor (or base datatype) that they take as an argument.

In Figure 3, we provide the types of 8 Mendler style combinators distributed over the two ranks that we consider, along with the type of a conventional catamorphism for comparison. The combinators can be organized into a hierarchy of increasing generality, and juxtaposing the types of the combinators makes it clear where in the hierarchy each combinator appears, and how each is related to the others.

In Figure 4, we define the combinators themselves, again distributed over two ranks. The definition of the corresponding combinators in the two ranks are textually identical, although they must be given different types in each rank.

In Figures 7, 8, and 9, 10, and 11, we provide examples[4] selected for each of the combinators mcata_0, mhist_0, mcata_1, and mhist_1. We discuss the remaining combinators of the inverse augmented fixpoints in §4, where we culminate with the HOAS formatting example. We have structured each of the examples into two, side by side, parts. On the left, we provide a general recursive encoding, and on the right, a Mendler style encoding.

[1] In general, we define a fixpoint μ_κ for each kind κ. For example, μ_* is μ_0 and $\mu_{*\to *}$ is μ_1. There are multiple fixpoints for each rank higher than rank 0. For example, another rank 1 fixpoint with two indices can be defined as $\mathbf{data}\ \mu_{*\to *\to *}\ f\ i\ j = \mathsf{In}_{*\to *\to *}\ \{\mathsf{out}_{*\to *\to *} :: f\ (\mu_{*\to *\to *}\ f)\ i\ j\}$.

[2] A Haskell datatype definition for this can be found at
http://lists.seas.upenn.edu/pipermail/types-list/2004/000267.html

[3] The standard definition of HOAS, which omits the Var constructor, makes it more challenging to define $\mathit{showExp}$, as we shall see in §4.

[4] Some of the examples (Figures 7, 8, and 9) are adopted from [1, 2, 35, 36].

$$\textbf{newtype}\ \mu_0\ (f :: * \to *) = \mathsf{In}_0\ \{\mathsf{out}_0 :: f\ (\mu_0\ f)\ \}$$
$$\textbf{newtype}\ \mu_1\ (f :: (* \to *) \to (* \to *))\ i = \mathsf{In}_1\ \{\mathsf{out}_1 :: f\ (\mu_1\ f)\ i\}$$

$$\textbf{data}\ \breve{\mu}_0\ (f :: * \to *)\ a = \breve{\mathsf{In}}_0\ \{\breve{\mathsf{out}}_0 :: f\ (\breve{\mu}_0\ f\ a)\ \}\ \mid \mathsf{Inverse}_0\ a$$
$$\textbf{data}\ \breve{\mu}_1\ (f :: (* \to *) \to (* \to *))\ a\ i = \breve{\mathsf{In}}_1\ \{\breve{\mathsf{out}}_1 :: f\ (\breve{\mu}_1\ f\ a)\ i\}\ \mid \mathsf{Inverse}_1\ a$$

Figure 2. Standard (left) and inverse augmented (right) datatype fixpoints for rank 0 (first line) and rank 1 (second line)

		abstract inverse	abstract unroll	abstract recursive call	combining function	input value	answer
$cata$	$:: Functor\ f \Rightarrow ($				$(f\ a \to a)) \to$	$\mu_0\ f$	$\to a$
$mcata_0$	$:: (\forall r.$			$(r \to a) \to$	$(f\ r \to a)) \to$	$\mu_0\ f$	$\to a$
$mcata_1$	$:: (\forall r\ i.$			$(\forall i.r\ i \to a\ i) \to$	$(f\ r\ i \to a\ i)) \to$	$\mu_1\ f\ i$	$\to a\ i$
$mhist_0$	$:: (\forall r.$		$(r \to f\ r) \to$	$(r \to a) \to$	$(f\ r \to a)) \to$	$\mu_0\ f$	$\to a$
$mhist_1$	$:: (\forall r\ i.$		$(\forall i.\ r\ i \to f\ r\ i) \to$	$(\forall i.r\ i \to a\ i) \to$	$(f\ r\ i \to a\ i)) \to$	$\mu_1\ f\ i$	$\to a\ i$
$msfcata_0$	$:: (\forall r.$	$(a \to r\ a) \to$		$(r\ a \to a) \to$	$(f\ (r\ a) \to a)) \to$	$(\forall a.\breve{\mu}_0\ f\ a)$	$\to a$
$msfcata_1$	$:: (\forall r\ i.$	$(\forall i.a\ i \to r\ (a\ i)\ i) \to$		$(\forall i.r\ (a\ i)\ i \to a\ i) \to$	$(f\ (r\ (a\ i))\ i \to a\ i)) \to$	$(\forall a.\breve{\mu}_1\ f\ (a\ i)\ i)$	$\to a\ i$
$msfhist_0$	$:: (\forall r.$	$(a \to r\ a) \to$	$(\forall a.\ r\ a \to f\ (r\ a)) \to$	$(r\ a \to a) \to$	$(f\ (r\ a) \to a)) \to$	$(\forall a.\breve{\mu}_0\ f\ a)$	$\to a$
$msfhist_1$	$:: (\forall r\ i.$	$(\forall i.a\ i \to r\ (a\ i)\ i) \to$	$(\forall a\ i.r\ (a\ i)\ i \to f\ (r\ (a\ i))\ i) \to$	$(\forall i.r\ (a\ i)\ i \to a\ i) \to$	$(f\ (r\ (a\ i))\ i \to a\ i)) \to$	$(\forall a.\breve{\mu}_1\ f\ (a\ i)\ i)$	$\to a\ i$

Figure 3. Type signatures of recursive combinators. Note the heavy use of higher-rank types.

$$
\begin{array}{lll}
cata\quad s\ (\mathsf{In}_0\ x) & = s\ (fmap\ (cata\ s)\ x) & \\
mcata_0\ \varphi\ (\mathsf{In}_0\ x) & = \varphi & (mcata_0\ \varphi)\ x \\
mcata_1\ \varphi\ (\mathsf{In}_1\ x) & = \varphi & (mcata_1\ \varphi)\ x \\
mhist_0\ \varphi\ (\mathsf{In}_0\ x) & = \varphi\ \mathsf{out}_0 & (mhist_0\ \varphi)\ x \\
mhist_1\ \varphi\ (\mathsf{In}_1\ x) & = \varphi\ \mathsf{out}_1 & (mhist_1\ \varphi)\ x
\end{array}
$$

$$
\begin{array}{l}
msfcata_0\ \varphi\ r = msfcata\ \varphi\ r\ \textbf{where} \\
\quad msfcata\ \varphi\ (\breve{\mathsf{In}}_0\ x) \quad = \varphi\ \mathsf{Inverse}_0\ (msfcata\ \varphi)\ x \\
\quad msfcata\ \varphi\ (\mathsf{Inverse}_0\ z) \quad = z \\
msfcata_1\ \varphi\ r = msfcata\ \varphi\ r\ \textbf{where} \\
\quad msfcata :: (\forall r\ i.(\forall i.a\ i \to r\ (a\ i)\ i) \\
\qquad\qquad \to (\forall i.r\ (a\ i)\ i \to a\ i) \\
\qquad\qquad \to (f\ (r\ (a\ i))\ i \to a\ i)) \to \breve{\mu}_1\ f\ (a\ i)\ i \to a\ i \\
\quad msfcata\ \varphi\ (\breve{\mathsf{In}}_1\ x) \quad = \varphi\ \mathsf{Inverse}_1\ (msfcata\ \varphi)\ x \\
\quad msfcata\ \varphi\ (\mathsf{Inverse}_1\ z) \quad = z
\end{array}
$$

$$
\begin{array}{l}
msfhist_0\ \varphi\ r = msfhist\ \varphi\ r\ \textbf{where} \\
\quad msfhist :: (\forall r.(a \to r\ a) \\
\qquad\qquad \to (\forall a.r\ a \to f\ (r\ a)) \\
\qquad\qquad \to (r\ a \to a) \\
\qquad\qquad \to (f\ (r\ a) \to a) \qquad) \to \breve{\mu}_0\ f\ a \quad \to a \\
\quad msfhist\ \varphi\ (\breve{\mathsf{In}}_0\ x) \quad = \varphi\ \mathsf{Inverse}_0\ \breve{\mathsf{out}}_0\ (msfhist\ \varphi)\ x \\
\quad msfhist\ \varphi\ (\mathsf{Inverse}_0\ z) \quad = z \\
msfhist_1\ \varphi\ r = msfhist\ \varphi\ r\ \textbf{where} \\
\quad msfhist :: (\forall r\ i.(\forall i.a\ i \to r\ (a\ i)\ i) \\
\qquad\qquad \to (\forall a\ i.r\ (a\ i)\ i \to f\ (r\ (a\ i))\ i) \\
\qquad\qquad \to (\forall i.r\ (a\ i)\ i \to a\ i) \\
\qquad\qquad \to (f\ (r\ (a\ i))\ i \to a\ i) \qquad) \to \breve{\mu}_1\ f\ (a\ i)\ i \to a\ i \\
\quad msfhist\ \varphi\ (\breve{\mathsf{In}}_1\ x) \quad = \varphi\ \mathsf{Inverse}_1\ \breve{\mathsf{out}}_1\ (msfhist\ \varphi)\ x \\
\quad msfhist\ \varphi\ (\mathsf{Inverse}_1\ z) \quad = z
\end{array}
$$

Figure 4. Definitions of recursive combinators. Note identical textual definitions for the same operators at different ranks, but with types specialized for that rank.

$$
\begin{array}{l}
mcata_0\quad \varphi\ r = mhist_0\ (const\ \varphi)\ r \\
mcata_1\quad \varphi\ r = mhist_1\ (const\ \varphi)\ r \\
msfcata_0\ \varphi\ r = msfhist_0\ (\lambda inv\ \_ \to \varphi\ inv)\ r \\
msfcata_1\ \varphi\ r = msfhist_1\ (\lambda inv\ \_ \to \varphi\ inv)\ r
\end{array}
$$

Figure 5. Alternative definition of catamorphism via histomorphism.

$$
\begin{array}{l}
\textbf{type}\ \mu_0\ f = \forall a.(\forall r.(r \to a) \to f\ r \to a) \to a \\
mcata_0 :: (\forall r.(r \to a) \to f\ r \to a) \to \mu_0\ f \to a \\
mcata_0\ \varphi\ r = r\ \varphi \\
in_0 :: f\ (\mu_0\ f) \to \mu_0\ f \\
in_0\ r\ \varphi = \varphi\ (mcata_0\ \varphi)\ r
\end{array}
$$

Figure 6. F_ω encoding of μ_0 and $mcata_0$ in Haskell

3.1 Defining recursive regular datatypes

In the Mendler style approach, we define Mendler style inductive datatypes as fixpoints of non-recursive base datatypes. For example, the following are definitions of the natural number type in the general recursion style (left) and in the Mendler style (right).

	data $N\ r = Z \mid S\ r$
data Nat	**type** $Nat = \mu_0\ N$
$= Z$	$zero \quad = \mathsf{In}_0\ Z$
$\mid S\ Nat$	$succ\ n = \mathsf{In}_0\ (S\ n)$

Note, in Mendler style, we define Nat by applying the fixpoint μ_0 to the base N. The type argument r in the base N is intended to denote the points of recursion in the inductive type. Here, we have only one point of recursion at S, the successor data constructor. Then, we define the shorthand constructors $zero$ and $succ$ (on the right), which correspond to the data constructors Z and S of the natural number datatype in the general recursive encoding (on the left). We can express the number 2 as $S\ (S\ Z)$ in the general recursive encoding, and $succ\ (succ\ zero)$ or $\mathsf{In}_0\ (S\ (\mathsf{In}_0\ (S\ (\mathsf{In}_0\ Z))))$ in the Mendler style encoding.

We can also define parameterized datatypes, such as lists, in the Mendler style, using the same datatype fixpoint μ_0, provided that we consistently order the parameter arguments (p) to come before the type argument that denotes the recursion points (r) in the base datatype definition ($L\ p\ r$):

	data $L\ p\ r = N \mid C\ p\ r$
data $List\ p$	**type** $List\ p = \mu_0\ (L\ p)$
$= N$	$nil \quad\quad = \mathsf{In}_0\ N$
$\mid C\ p\ (List\ p)$	$cons\ x\ xs = \mathsf{In}_0\ (C\ x\ xs)$

Note, we define $List\ \ p$ as $\mu_0\ \ (L\ \ p)$, which is the fixpoint of the partial application of the base L to the parameter p. We can express the integer list with two elements 1 and 2 as $C\ 1\ (C\ 2\ N)$ in the general recursive encoding, and $cons\ \ 1\ \ (cons\ \ 2\ \ nil)$ or $\mathsf{In}_0\ (C\ 1\ (\mathsf{In}_0\ (C\ 2\ (\mathsf{In}_0\ N))))$ in the Mendler style encoding.

3.2 Conventional Catamorphism for regular datatypes

The conventional catamorphism[5] is defined on the very same fixpoint, μ_0, as is used in the Mendler style, provided that the base datatype f is a functor. This, more widely known approach [14], was developed independently, and at about the same time, as the Mendler style.

The additional requirement, that the base datatype (f) is a functor, shows up as a type class constraint ($Functor\ \ f$) in the type signature of the conventional catamorphism combinator $cata$:

$cata :: Functor\ f \Rightarrow (f\ a \to a) \to \mu_0\ f \to a$ (Figure 3).

This is necessary because $cata$ is defined in terms of $fmap$ (a method of the $Functor$ class):

$cata\ \varphi\ (\mathsf{In}_0\ x) = \varphi\ (fmap\ (cata\ \varphi)\ x)$ (Figure 4).

The combinator $cata$ takes a combining function $\varphi :: f\ \ a \to a$, which assumes the recursive subcomponents (e.g., tail of the list) have already been turned into a value of answer type (a) and combines the overall result.

A typical example of catamorphism is the list length function. We can define the list length function len_c in conventional style, which corresponds to the list length function len in the general recursion style in the left-hand side of Figure 7, as follows:

$$
\begin{array}{l}
len_c :: List\ p \to Int \\
len_c = cata\ \varphi\ \textbf{where} \\
\quad \varphi\ N \qquad\qquad = 0 \\
\quad \varphi\ (C\ x\ xslen) = 1 + xslen
\end{array}
$$

[5] In Haskell-ish words, $foldr$ on lists generalized to other dataypes

We need the functor instance for the base $L\ \ p$, which properly defines $fmap$, to complete the definition:

$$
\begin{array}{l}
\textbf{instance}\ Functor\ (L\ p)\ \textbf{where} \\
\quad fmap\ f\ N \qquad\quad = N \\
\quad fmap\ f\ (C\ x\ xs) = C\ x\ (f\ xs)
\end{array}
$$

The conventional catamorphism is widely known, especially on the list type, as $foldr$. The conventional catamorphism is more often used than the Mendler catamorphism, but it does not generalize easily to more exotic datatypes such as GADTs, or nested datatypes.

3.3 Mendler style Catamorphism for regular datatypes

The Mendler catamorphism $mcata_0$ lifts the restriction that the base type be a functor, but still maintains the strict termination behavior of $cata$. This restriction is lifted by using two devices.

- The combining function φ becomes a function of 2 arguments rather than 1. The first argument is a function that represents a recursive placeholder, and the second is the base structure that must be combined into an answer. The recursive placeholder allows the programmer to direct where recursive calls must be made. The Functor class requirement is lifted, because no call to $fmap$ is required in the definition of $mcata_0$:

  $$mcata_0\ \varphi\ (\mathsf{In}_0\ x) = \varphi\ (mcata_0\ \varphi)\ x$$

- The second device is the use of higher-rank polymorphism to insist that the recursive placeholder, with type $(r \to a)$, and the base structure, with type $(f\ \ r)$, work over an abstract type, denoted by (r).

  $$mcata_0 :: (\forall r.(r \to a) \to (f\ r \to a)) \to \mu_0\ f \to a$$

Under what conditions do $mcata_0$ calls always terminate? Although we defined μ_0 as a newtype and $mcata_0$ as a function in Haskell, you should consider them as an information hiding abstraction. The rules of the game (which will be enforced in Trellys) require programmers to construct values using the In_0 constructor (as in $zero$, $succ$, nil and $cons$), but forbid programmers from deconstructing those values by pattern matching against In_0 (or, by using the selector function out_0). These operations are hidden by the abstraction boundary (or in the case of Trellys' logicality inference, lead to classifying a term as programatic, rather than as logical). To remain in the logical (terminating) classification, whenever you need to decompose values of inductive datatypes you must do it via $mcata_0$ (or, any of the other terminating Mendler style combinators). To conform to these rules, all functions over positive inductive datatypes, except the trivial ones such as identity and constant functions (which don't inspect their structure), need to be implemented in terms of the combinators described in Figure 3. For negative inductive datatypes only the combinators in the catamorphism family ensure termination.

The intuitive reasoning behind the termination property of $mcata_0$ for all positive inductive datatypes is that (1) $mcata_0$ strips off one In_0 constructor each time it is called, and (2) $mcata_0$ only recurses on the direct subcomponents (e.g., tail of a list) of its argument (because the type of the recursive placeholder won't allow it to be applied to anything else). Once we observe these two properties, it is obvious that $mcata_0$ always terminates since those properties imply that every recursive call to $mcata_0$ decreases the number of In_0 constructors in its argument.[6]

The first property is easy to observe from the definition of $mcata_0$ in Figure 4, in particular, the pattern matching of the

[6] We assume that the values of inductive types are always finite. We can construct infinite values (or, co-inductive values) in Haskell exploiting lazyness, but we exclude such infinite values from our discussion in this work, and this property is a fundamental design decision in Trellys.

$$
\begin{array}{ll}
\textbf{data } List\ p & \textbf{data } L\ p\ r = N \mid C\ p\ r \\
\quad = N & \textbf{type } List\ p = \mu_0\ (L\ p) \\
\quad \mid\ C\ p\ (List\ p) & nil \quad = \mathsf{In}_0\ N \\
 & cons\ x\ xs = \mathsf{In}_0\ (C\ x\ xs) \\
 & len_m :: List\ p \to Int \\
len :: List\ p \to Int & len_m = mcata_0\ \varphi \textbf{ where} \\
len\ N \quad = 0 & \quad \varphi\ len\ N \quad = 0 \\
len\ (C\ x\ xs) = 1 + len\ xs & \quad \varphi\ len\ (C\ x\ xs) = 1 + len\ xs
\end{array}
$$

Figure 7. $mcata_0$ example: list length function

second argument with $(\mathsf{In}_0\ x)$. The second property is enforced by the parametricity in the type of the combining function φ of the $mcata_0$ combinator as shown in Figure 3,

In Figure 7, we redefine the length function (len_m on the right), this time, using a Mendler style catamorphism. In the definition of len_m, we name the first argument of φ, the recursive placeholder, to be len. We use this len exactly where we would recursively call the recursive function in the general recursion style (len on the left).

However, unlike the general recursion style, it is not possible to call $len :: r \to Int$ on anything other than the tail $xs :: r$. Using general recursion, we could easily err (by mistake or by design) causing length to diverge, if we wrote its second equation as follows: $len\ (C\ x\ xs) = 1 + len\ (C\ x\ xs)$.

We cannot encode such diverging recursion in Mendler style because $len :: r \to Int$ requires its argument to have the parametric type r, while $(C\ x\ xs) :: L\ p\ r$ has more specific type than r. The parametricity enforces weak structural induction.

The scheme of having the combining function φ abstract over the recursive placeholder len is a powerful one. We will reuse this strategy, generalizing φ to abstract over additional arguments, in order to generalize $mcata_0$ to become more expressive.

3.4 Mendler style Histomorphism for regular datatypes

Some computations are not easily expressible by a catamorphism, since a catamorphism only recurses on the direct subcomponents (e.g., tail of a list). Recursing on deeper subcomponents (e.g., tail of tail of a list) requires complex encodings in the conventional setting. Unfortunately, functional programmers often write simple recursive functions using nested pattern matching that recurse on deep subcomponents exposed by the nested patterns. A typical example is the Fibonacci function:

$$
\begin{array}{l}
fib\ Z \qquad\quad = 0 \\
fib\ (S\ Z) \qquad = 1 \\
fib\ (S\ (S\ m)) = fib\ (S\ m) + fib\ m
\end{array}
$$

Note, in the third equation fib recurses on both the predecessor $(S\ m)$, which is a direct subcomponent of the argument, and the predecessor of the predecessor m, which is a deeper subcomponent of the argument. The Histomorphism [34] captures such patterns of recursion often called a course-of-values recursion.

In the conventional style, histomorphisms are defined through co-algebraic construction of an intermediate stream data structure that pairs up the current argument and the results from the previous steps. There are two ways of implementing this. One is a memoizing bottom-up version, and the other is a non-memoizing version that repeats the computation of the previous steps. We are not going to show or discuss those implementations here, but the point we want to make is that both versions need to be implemented through co-algebraic construction [35, 36]. Course-of-values recursion expressed in terms of this co-algebraic style will look very different from its equivalent in general recursion style. One needs to extract both the original arguments and the deep result values from the stream explicitly calling on stream-head and stream-tail operations.

$$
\begin{array}{ll}
 & \textbf{data } N\ r = Z \mid S\ r \\
\textbf{data } Nat & \textbf{type } Nat = \mu_0\ N \\
\quad = Z & zero \quad = \mathsf{In}_0\ Z \\
\quad \mid\ S\ Nat & succ\ n = \mathsf{In}_0\ (S\ n) \\
 & fib_m = mhist_0\ \varphi \textbf{ where} \\
fib\ Z \quad = 0 & \quad \varphi\ \mathsf{out}\ fib\ Z \quad = 0 \\
fib\ (S\ n) = & \quad \varphi\ \mathsf{out}\ fib\ (S\ n) = \\
\quad \textbf{case } n \textbf{ of} & \qquad \textbf{case out } n \textbf{ of} \\
\qquad Z \quad \to 1 & \qquad\quad Z \quad \to 1 \\
\qquad S\ n' \to fib\ n + fib\ n' & \qquad\quad S\ n' \to fib\ n + fib\ n'
\end{array}
$$

Figure 8. $mhist_0$ example: Fibonacci function

However, in Mendler style, we do not need such co-algebraic construction at the user level[7].

In the Mendler style Histomorphism, we play the same trick we played in the Mendler style Catamorphism. We arrange for the combining function to take additional arguments (Figures 3 and 4).

- The combining function φ now becomes a function of 3 arguments. The first argument is a function that represents an abstract unrolling function that projects out the value embedded inside the data constructor In_0 by accessing the projection function out_0 given in the definition. As in $mcata_0$, the next argument represents a recursive placeholder, and the last argument represents the base structure that must be combined into an answer.

  $mhist_0\ \varphi\ (\mathsf{In}_0\ x) = \varphi\ \mathsf{out}_0\ (mhist_0\ \varphi)\ x$
- Again we use higher-rank polymorphism to insist that the abstract unrolling function, with type $(r \to f\ r)$, the recursive placeholder function, with type $(r \to a)$, and the base structure, with type $(f\ r)$, only work over an abstract type, denoted by (r).

  $mhist_0 :: (\forall r.(a \to f\ a) \to (r \to a) \to (f\ r \to a)) \to \cdots$

The Mendler style histomorphism is much handier when expressing course-of-values recursion than the conventional histomorphism [35]. For example, in Figure 8, the definition for the Fibonacci function in general recursion style (left) and the definition in Mendler style (right) look almost identical. Particularly, when we have unrolled the nested pattern matching in the general recursive definition into a case expression. The only difference between the two, is that in the Mendler style (left), we pattern match over $\mathsf{out}\ n$ in the case expression, in the Traditional-style (right) we pattern match over n.

Let us visually relate the definition of $mhist_0$ with the second equation of φ in the definition of the Fibonocci function as follows:

$$
\begin{array}{llll}
mhist_0\ \varphi\ (\mathsf{In}_0\ x) = & \varphi\ \mathsf{out}_0 & (mhist_0\ \varphi) & x \\
 & \vdots & \vdots & \vdots \\
 & \varphi\ \mathsf{out} & fib & (S\ n) = \\
 & \quad \textbf{case out } n \textbf{ of} & & \\
 & \qquad Z \quad \to 1 & & \\
 & \qquad S\ n' \to fib\ n + fib\ n' & &
\end{array}
$$

The abstract unrolling function out and the recursive placeholder fib stand for the actual arguments out_0 and $(mhist_0\ \varphi)$, but the higher-rank type of the combining function φ ensures that they are only used in a safe manner. The abstract unrolling function out enables us to discharge In_0 as many times as we want inside φ.

[7] The Mendler style histormophism combinators implemented here are the non-memoizing ones. Vene [36] suggests how to implement a memoizing Mendler style histomorphism, which uses co-algebraic construction.

From the programmers perspective, out_0 is a hidden primitive, hidden by the histomorphism abstraction. But, inside the definition of the combining function φ, the programmer can actually access the functionality of out_0 through the abstract unrolling function out. The higher-rank types limit the use of this abstract unrolling function out to values of type r.

In a positive inductive datatype, the only functions with domain r are the abstract unroller, and the recursive placeholder. The programmer can only *whittle down* the r values inside the base structure, of type $(f\ r)$, into smaller structures, of type $(f\ r)$. The programmer can then decompose these into even smaller r values by pattern matching against the data constructors of the base f. However, there is no way to combine any of these decomposed r values to build up larger r values. The only possible use of the decomposed r values is to call the recursive placeholder, with type $(r \to a)$.

For example, in Figure 8, we pattern match over $(\mathsf{out}\ n)$, discharging the hidden In_0 constructor of n. Note the types inside the $(S\ n')$ pattern matching branch: $n :: r$; $(\mathsf{out}\ n) :: (N\ r)$; and $n' :: r$. What can we possibly do with n and n', of type r? The only possible computation is to call $fib :: r \to Int$ on n and n', as we do in $fib\ n + fib\ n'$. It is a type error to call $fib :: r \to Int$ on either $(S\ n) :: N\ r$ or $(S\ n') :: N\ r$. This is why the termination property of $mhist_0$ continues to hold for positive datatypes.

For negative datatypes, however, we have additional functions with domain r. Inside the φ function passed to $mhist_0$, the embedded functions with negative occurrences, will have type r as their domain. These can be problematic. The counter-example to termination of $mhist_0$ is in Figure 13, which will discussed in more detail in §3.8.

3.5 Nested datatypes

The datatypes Nat and $List$, defined in §3.1, are regular datatypes. Non-recursive datatypes (e.g., $Bool$) and recursive (or inductive) datatypes without any type arguments (e.g., Nat) are always regular. Among the recursive datatypes with type arguments, those datatypes where all of the recursive occurrence on the right-hand side have exactly the same type argument as the left-hand side (in the same order) are considered regular. For example, the list datatype $\mathbf{data}\ List\ p = N \mid C\ p\ (List\ p)$ is regular since $(List\ p)$ appearing on right-hand side takes exactly the same argument p as the $(List\ p)$ in the left-hand side ($\mathbf{data}\ List\ p = \ldots$).

Note, every concrete *instantiation* of the list datatype has an equivalent non-parameterized datatype definition. For instance, $List\ Bool$ is equivalent to the following datatype:

$$\mathbf{data}\ List_{Bool} = N_{Bool} \mid C_{Bool}\ Bool\ List_{Bool}$$

This em instantiation property does *not* hold for nested datatypes.

Type arguments that never change in any recursive occurrences in a datatype definition are called *type parameters*. Type arguments that do change are called *type indices*. Datatypes with only type parameters are always regular. Nested datatypes [3] are non-regular datatypes where type arguments in some of the recursive occurrences in the recursive datatype equation differ from the left-hand side of the datatype equation.

Such types can be expressed in Haskell and ML without using GADT extensions. We introduce a well-known example of the bush datatype, and a function that sums up the elements of bush (Figure 9). Nested datatypes require us to move from rank 0 Mendler combinators to rank 1 Mendler combinators.

The bush datatype is defined as follows (also in Figure 9):

$$\mathbf{data}\ Bush\ i = N_B \mid C_B\ i\ (Bush\ (Bush\ i))$$

The type argument i for $Bush$ is a type index, since the type argument $(Bush\ i)$ occurring on the right-hand side is different from i appearing on the left-hand side. What is intriguing about $Bush$ is that the variation on the type index involves itself. Matthes [20] calls such datatypes, like $Bush$, *truly nested datatypes*. Here are some examples of bush values:

$$\begin{array}{lll} bs & = C_B\ 1\ bs' & :: Bush\ Int \\ bs' & = C_B\ (C_B\ 2\ N_B)\ bs'' & :: Bush\ (Bush\ Int) \\ bs'' & & :: Bush\ (Bush\ (Bush\ Int)) \\ bs'' & = C_B\ (C_B\ (C_B\ 3\ N_B)\ (C_B\ (C_B\ (C_B\ 4\ N_B)\ N_B)\ N_B))\ N_B & \end{array}$$

The tail of bs is bs', and the tail of bs' is bs''. We can observe that the shape of the elements becomes more deeply nested as we move towards latter elements.

We can define a function that sums up all the nested elements in a bush. Let us first take a look at the function $bsum$ in the general recursion style, on the left-hand side of Figure 9. This function takes 2 parameters: a bush to sum up and a function that turns elements into integers. The key part in the definition of $bsum$ is constructing the function $(\lambda ys \to bsum\ ys\ f) :: Bush\ i \to Int$. We must construct this function, on the fly, in order to make the recursive call of $bsum$ on its tail $xs :: Bush\ (Bush\ i)$. Without this function, the recursive call wouldn't know how to sum up bushed elements.

We can specialize $bsum$, for instance, for integer bushes as follows by supplying the identity function:

$$\begin{array}{l} sumB :: Bush\ Int \to Int \\ sumB\ xs = bsum\ xs\ id \end{array}$$

Using $sumB$, we can sum up bs defined above: $sumB\ bs \rightsquigarrow 10$.

Before discussing the Mendler style version, let us take a look at yet another general recursive version of the function $bsum'$, which explicitly wraps up the answer values of type $(i \to Int) \to Int$ inside the newtype $Ret\ i$. The relations between the plain vanilla version and the wrapped up version are simply:

$$\begin{array}{rl} bsum = & unRet \circ bsum' \\ Ret \circ bsum = & bsum' \end{array}$$

The wrapped up version $bsum'$ has the same structure as the Mendler style version $bsum_m$ found on the right-hand side of Figure 9. The wrapping of the answer type is for purely technical reasons: to avoid the need for higher-order unification. If we were to work with the unwrapped answer type in the Mendler style, the type system would need to unify $(a\ i)$ with $((i \to Int) \to Int)$, which is a higher-order unification, whereas unifying $(a\ i)$ with the wrapped answer type $(Ret\ i)$ is first-order. The type inference algorithm of Haskell (and most other languages) does not support higher-order unification.[8]

Finally, let us discuss the summation function for bushes using the Mendler style, found on the right-hand side in Figure 9. First, we give Mendler style datatype definitions for bushes. As usual, we define the datatype $Bush$ as a fixpoint of the base $BushF$. However, an important difference that readers should notice is the use of fixpoint μ_1 for rank 1 bases, instead of μ_0, for the rank 0 bases inducing regular datatypes.

That the type argument i in $Bush\ i$ is a type index that forces us to choose the rank 1 fixpoint (and its related recursion combinators). Note, in the definition of the base type $BushF$, we place the index i after the type argument r for the recursion points. This is the convention we use. We always write parameters (p), before the recursion point arugment (r), followed by indices (i). Figure 10, which we will shortly discuss in §3.6, contains an example where there are both type parameters and type indices in a datype $(Vec\ p\ i)$.

Getting back to the right-hand side of Figure 9, since we used μ_1 to define the inductive datatypes, we use $mcata_1$, the Mendler style catamorphism combinator for rank 1, to define the functions. The

[8] We may avoid higher-order unification, either by making the Mendler style combinators language constructs (rather than functions) so that the type system treats them with specialized typing rules; or by providing a version of the combinators with syntactic Kan-extension as in [2].

```
data Bush i = N_B | C_B i (Bush (Bush i))

bsum :: Bush i → (i → Int) → Int
bsum N_B         = (λf → 0)
bsum (C_B x xs) = (λf →
                    f x + bsum xs (λys → bsum ys f))
newtype Ret i = Ret {unRet :: (i → Int) → Int}
bsum' :: Bush i → Ret i
bsum' N_B         = Ret (λf → 0)
bsum' (C_B x xs) = Ret (λf →
                    f x + bsum'' xs (λys → bsum'' ys f))
      where bsum'' :: Bush i → (i → Int) → Int
            bsum'' = unRet ∘ bsum'
```

```
data BushF r i = N_B | C_B i (r (r i))
type Bush i = μ₁ BushF i
nil_B        = In₁ N_B
cons_B x xs = In₁ (C_B x xs)
bsum :: Bush i → (i → Int) → Int
bsum = unRet ∘ bsum_m
bsum_m :: Bush i → Ret i
bsum_m = mcata₁ φ where
  φ :: ∀r i'.(∀i.r i → Ret i) → BushF r i' → Ret i'
  φ bsum' N_B         = Ret (λf → 0)
  φ bsum' (C_B x xs) = Ret (λf →
                          f x + bsum'' xs (λys → bsum'' ys f))
        where  bsum'' :: r i → (i → Int) → Int
               bsum'' = unRet ∘ bsum'
```

Figure 9. Summing up a bush ($Bush$), a recursively nested datatype, expressed in terms of $mcata_1$.

beauty of the Mendler style approach is that the implementation of the recursion combinators for higher-ranks are *exactly the same* as their rank 0 counterparts. The definitions differ only in their type signatures. As you can see in Figures 3 and 4, $mcata_1$ has a richer type than $mcata_0$, but their implementations are *exactly the same*! This is not the case for the conventional approach. The definition of $cata$ won't generalize to nested datatypes in a trivial way. There has been several approaches [4, 15, 18] to extend folds or catamorphisms for nested datatypes in the conventional setting.

3.6 Indexed datatypes (GADTs)

A recent, popular extension to the GHC Haskell compiler is generalized algebraic datatypes (GADTs) [30]. In our nested examples, the variation of type indices always occurred in the arguments of the data constructors. GADTs are indexed datatypes, where the index may vary in the result types of the data constructors. Haskell's normal **data** declaration, which uses an "equation" syntax, makes the assumption that the result types of every constructor is the "same" type with no variation. GHC's GADT datatype extension is more expressive than the recursive **data** declaration. The GHC compiler extends the $datatype$ syntax, so that each datatype constructor is given its full type. The datatype definition for vectors (or size indexed lists) is a prime example:

```
data Vec p i where
  N_V :: Vec p Z
  C_V :: p → Vec p i → Vec p (S i)
```

Note, the indices[9] vary in the *result types* of the data constructors: Z in the type of N_V and $(S\ i)$ in the type of C_V.

Nested datatypes, which we discussed earlier, are a special case of indexed datatypes that happened to be expressible within the recursive type equation syntax of Haskell, because the indices only vary in the recursive arguments of the data constructors, but not in the result type. For a clearer comparison, we express the bush datatype in GADT syntax as follows: [10]

```
data Bush i where
  N_B :: Bush i
  C_B :: i → Bush (Bush i) → Bush i
```

Note, the type argument varies in second argument of C_B, which is $Bush\ (Bush\ i)$, but both the result type of N_P and C_P are $Bush\ i$.

[9] The Z and S used in Vec are type level representations of natural numbers, which are empty types that are not inhabited by any value. They are only intend to be used as indices.

[10] We can translate any recursive type equation into a definition using the GADT syntax since GADTs are indeed *generalized* algebraic datatypes.

In Figure 10, we define the vector datatype Vec as $\mu_1\ (V\ p)\ i$, in the Mendler style. That is, we apply μ_1 to the partial application of the base V to the parameter p, and then apply the resulting fixpoint to the index i. The base datatype $V\ p\ r\ i$ is a GADT with a parameter p and an index i. Recall that by convention we place the parameter p before the type argument r for recursion points, followed by the index i. We can express the $copy$ function that traverses a given vector and reconstructs that vector with the same elements, in Mendler style, using the rank 1 Mendler catamorphism combinator $mcata_1$. We can express the $switch2$ function that switches every two elements of the given vector, in Mendler style, using the rank 1 histomorphism combinator $mhist_1$. The definitions for $mcata_1$ and $mhist_1$ are exactly the same as the definitions for $mcata_0$ and $mhist_0$, except that $mcata_1$ and $mhist_1$ have richer type signatures (see Figures 3 and 4). Thus, defining functions using $mcata_1$ and $mhist_1$ is no more complicated than defining the functions for regluar datatypes using $mcata_0$ and $mhist_0$. The one proviso to this statement is that we need to give explicit type signatures for φ because GHC does not support type inference for higher rank types (i.e., types with inner $\forall$s that are not top-level). Again, in a language where the Mendler style combinators were language constructs rather than functions, we believe this annoying burden could be lifted.

3.7 Mutually recursive datatypes

We can express mutual recursion over mutually recursive datatypes in Mendler style using an indexed base dataype. The context extension function $extend$ and the expression evaluation function $eval$ in Figure 11 are mutually recursive functions over the mutually recursive datatypes of declaration Dec and expression Exp. The general recursive version on left-hand side of Figure 11 is a self-explanatory standard evaluator implementation for the expression.

To express this in Mender-style (right), we first define the common base $DecExpF$ which is indexed by D and E. Note, the data constructors of $DecExpF$ include both the data constructors of declarations (Def) and expressions (Var, Val, Add, and Let). The data constructor for declaration is indexed by D, and the other data constructors for expressions are indexed by E in their result types. Then, we can define Dec as $\mu_1\ DecExpF\ D$ and Exp as $\mu_1\ DecExpF\ E$. We wrap up the return types of the $eval$ and $extend$ functions with the data family Ret, for reasons similar to the return types of the summation functions in §3.5. We also define the projection functions $\pi_D :: Ret\ D \to (Env \to Env)$ and $\pi_E :: Ret\ E \to (Env \to Int)$ to open up the return type. Then, we can express the mutually recursive functions, both $eval$ and

```
data Z
data S i
data Vec p i where
  N_V :: Vec p Z
  C_V :: p → Vec p i → Vec p (S i)

copy :: Vec p i → Vec p i
copy N_V         = N_V
copy (C_V x xs) = C_V x (copy xs)

switch2 :: Vec p i → Vec p i
switch2 N_V          = N_V
switch2 (C_V x xs)  =
        case xs of
          N_V         → C_V x N_V
          C_V y ys → C_V y (C_V x (switch2 ys))
```

```
data V p r i where
  N_V :: V p r Z
  C_V :: p → r i → V p r (S i)
type Vec p i = μ1 (V p) i
nil_V        = In1 N_V
cons_V x xs = In1 (C_V x xs)
copy :: Vec p i → Vec p i
copy = mcata1 φ where
  φ :: (∀i.r i → Vec p i) → V p r i → Vec p i
  φ cp N_V         = nil_V
  φ cp (C_V x xs) = cons_V x (cp xs)
switch2 :: Vec p i → Vec p i
switch2 = mhist1 φ where
  φ :: (∀i.r i → V p r i) →
       (∀i.r i → Vec p i) → V p r i → Vec p i
  φ out sw2 N_V          = nil_V
  φ out sw2 (C_V x xs)  =
            case out xs of
              N_V         → cons_V x nil_V
              C_V y ys → cons_V y (cons_V x (sw2 ys))
```

Figure 10. Recursion (*copy*) and course-of-values recursion (*switch2*) over size indexed lists (*Vec*) expressed in terms of $mcata_1$ and $mhist_1$.

```
type Name = String
type Env = [(Name, Int)]

data Dec = Def Name Exp
data Exp = Var Name
         | Val Int
         | Add Exp Exp
         | Let Dec Exp

extend :: Dec → Env → Env
extend (Def x e) = λσ → (x, eval e σ) : σ
eval    :: Exp → Env → Int
eval (Var x)       = λσ → fromJust (lookup x σ)
eval (Val v)       = λσ → v
eval (Add e1 e2)  = λσ → eval e1 σ + eval e2 σ
```

```
data D
data E
data DecExpF (r :: * → *) (i :: *) where
  Def :: Name → r E → DecExpF r D
  Var :: Name        → DecExpF r E
  Val :: Int         → DecExpF r E
  Add :: r E → r E  → DecExpF r E
  Let :: r D → r E  → DecExpF r E
type Dec = μ1 DecExpF D
type Exp = μ1 DecExpF E
data family Ret i :: *
newtype instance Ret D = Ret_D (Env → Env)
newtype instance Ret E = Ret_E (Env → Int)
π_D    f = λx → case f x of Ret_D f_D → f_D
π_E    f = λx → case f x of Ret_E f_E → f_E
extev :: μ1 DecExpF i → Ret i
extev = mcata1 φ where
  φ :: (∀i.r i → Ret i) → DecExpF r i → Ret i
  φ f (Def x e)   = Ret_D $ λσ → (x, ev e σ) : σ
                 where ev = π_E f
  φ f (Var x)     = Ret_E $ λσ → fromJust (lookup x σ)
  φ f (Val v)     = Ret_E $ λσ → v
  φ f (Add e1 e2) = Ret_E $ λσ → ev e1 σ + ev e2 σ
                 where ev = π_E f
extend :: Dec → Env → Env
extend = π_D extev
eval    :: Exp → Env → Int
eval    = π_E extev
```

Figure 11. Mutual recursion (*extend* and *eval* over *Dec* and *Exp*) expressed in terms of $mcata_1$ over an indexed datatype *DecExpF* *extend*, combined in one function definition *extev* using $mcata_1$. You can observe that the definition of φ is very close to the definitions of the general recursive version of *extend* and *eval* on the left. The difference is that we project out *ev* from f, which is the handle for combined mutually recursive function, when we need to call the evaluation function for the recursion. Once we have defined the combined function *extev*, we can project out *extend* and *eval* using π_D and π_E.

3.8 Negative datatypes, a second look

Let us revisit the negative inductive datatype T (from §2) from which we constructed a diverging computation. We can define a Mendler style version of T, called T_m, as follows:

```
data TBase r = C_m (r → ())
type T_m = μ_0 TBase
```

If we can write two functions $p_m :: T_m \to (T_m \to ())$, and $w_m :: T_m \to ()$, corresponding to p and w from §2, we can reconstruct the same diverging computation. The function

```
w_m x = (p_m x) x
```

is easy. The function p_m is problematic. By the rules of the game, we cannot pattern match on In_0 (or use out_0) so we must resort to using one of the combinators, such as $mcata_0$. However, it is not possible to write p_m in terms of $mcata_0$. Here is an attempt (seemingly the only one possible) that fails:

```
p_m :: T_m → (T_m → ())
p_m = mcata_0 φ where
        φ :: (r → (T_m → ())) → TBase r → (T_m → ())
        φ _ (C_m f) = f
```

We write the explicit type signature for the combining function φ (even though the type can be inferred from the type of $mcata_0$), to make it clear why this attempt fails to type check. The combining function φ take two arguments. The recursive placeholder (for which we have used the pattern _, since we don't intend to call it) and the base structure $(Cm\ f)$, from which we can extract the function $f :: r \to ()$. Note that r is an abstract (universally quantified) type, and the result type of φ requires $f :: T_m \to ()$. The types r and T_m can never match, if r is to remain abstract. Thus, p_m fails to type check.

There is a function, with the right type, that you can define:

```
pconst :: T_m → (T_m → ())
pconst = mcata_0 φ where φ g (C f) = const ()
```

Not surprisingly, given the abstract pieces composed of the recursive placeholder $g :: r \to ()$, the base structure $(C\ f) :: TBase\ r$, and the function we can extract from the base structure $f :: r \to ()$, the only function that returns a unit value (modulo extensional equivalence) is, in fact, the constant function returning the unit value.

This illustrates the essence of how Mendler catamorphism guarantees normalization even in the presence of negative occurrences in the inductive type definition. By quantifying over the recursive type parameter of the base datatype (e.g. r in $TBase\ r$), it prevents an embedded function with a negative occurrence from flowing into any outside terms (especially terms embedding that function).

Given these restrictions, the astute reader may ask, are types with embedded function with negative occurrences good for anything at all? Can we ever call such functions? A simple example which uses an embedded function inside a negative inductive datatype is illustrated in Figure 13. The datatype *Foo* (defined as a fixpoint of *FooF*) is a list-like data structure with two data constructors *Noo* and *Coo*. The data constructor *Noo* is like the nil and *Coo* is like the cons. Interestingly, the element (with type $Foo \to Foo$) contained in *Coo* is a function that transforms a *Foo* value into another *Foo* value. The function *lenFoo*, defined with $mcata_0$, is a length like function, but it recurses on the transformed tail, $(f\ xs)$, instead of the original tail xs. The intuition behind the termination of $mcata_0$ for this negative datatype *Foo* is similar to the intuition for positive dataypes. The embedded function $f :: r \to r$ can only apply to the direct subcomponent of its parent, or to its sibling, xs and its transformed values (e.g. $f\ xs$, $f\ (f\ xs), \ldots$), but no larger values that contains f itself. We illustrate a general proof on termination of $mcata_0$ in Figure 6.

```
data FooF r = Noo | Coo (r → r) r
type Foo = μ_0 FooF
noo      = In_0 Noo
coo f xs = In_0 (Coo f xs)

lenFoo :: Foo → Int
lenFoo = mcata_0 φ where
  φ len Noo          = 0
  φ len (Coo f xs) = 1 + len (f xs)

loopFoo :: Foo → Int
loopFoo = mhist_0 φ where
  φ out len Noo          = 0
  φ out len (Coo f xs) = case out xs of
                             Noo      → 1 + len (f  xs)
                             Coo f' _ → 1 + len (f' xs)

foo :: Foo   -- loops for loopFoo
foo = coo_0 (coo_1 noo) where coo_0 = coo id
                              coo_1 = coo coo_0
```

Figure 13. An example of a total function *lenFoo* over a negative datatype *Foo* defined with $mcata_0$, and a counter-example *loopFoo* illustrating that $mhist_0$ can diverge for negative datatypes.

While all functions written in terms of $mcata_0$ are total, the same cannot be said of function written in terms of $mhist_0$. The function *loopFoo* defined with $mhist_0$ is a counter-example to totality, which shows that Mendler style histomorphisms do not always terminate. Try evaluating *loopFoo foo*. It will loop. This function *loopFoo* is similar to *lenFoo*, but has an additional twist. At the very end of the function definition, we recurse on the transformed tail $(f'\ xs)$, when we have more than two elements where the first and second elements are named f and f', respectively. Note, f' is an element embedded inside the tail xs. Thus, $(f'\ xs)$ is dangerous since it applies f' to a larger value xs, which contains f'. The abstract type of the unrolling function $(\mathsf{out} :: r \to f\ r)$, prevents the recursive placeholder from being applied to a larger value, but it does not preclude the risk of embedded functions, with negative domains, being applied to larger values which contain the embedded function itself.

4. Formatting Higher-Order Abstract Syntax

To lead up to the Mendler style solution to formatting HOAS, we first review some earlier work on turning expressions, expressed in Higher-Order Abstract Syntax (HOAS)[7, 27], into strings. This solution was suggested by Fegaras and Sheard [13]. They were studying yet another abstract recursion scheme described by Paterson [25] and Meijer and Hutton [22] that could only be used if the combining function had a true inverse. This seemed a bit limiting, so Fegaras and Sheard introduced the idea of a syntactic inverse. The syntactic inverse was realized by augmenting the μ_0 type with a second constructor. This augmented μ_0 had the same structure as $\check{\mu}_0$ in Figure 2, but with a different type.

The algorithm worked, but, the augmentation introduces junk. Washburn and Weirich [37] eliminated the junk by exploiting parametricity. It is a coincidence that Mendler style recursion combinators also use the same technique, parametricity, for a different pur-

```
data Exp_g = Lam_g (Exp_g → Exp_g) | App_g Exp_g Exp_g | Var_g String
showExp_g :: Exp_g → String
showExp_g e = show′ e vars where show′ (App_g x y) = λvs       → "(" ++ show′ x vs ++ " " ++ show′ y vs ++ ")"
                                 show′ (Lam_g z)   = λ(v : vs) → "(\\" ++ v ++ "->" ++ show′ (z (Var_g v)) vs ++ ")"
                                 show′ (Var_g v)   = λvs       → v

data ExpF r = Lam (r → r) | App r r
type Exp′ a = μ̆_0 ExpF a
type Exp = ∀a.Exp′ a
lam e   = In̆_0 (Lam e)
app f e = In̆_0 (App f e)
showExp :: Exp → String
showExp e = msfcata_0 φ e vars where
        φ :: (([String] → String) → r) → (r → ([String] → String)) → ExpF r → ([String] → String)
        φ inv show′ (App x y) = λvs       → "(" ++ show′ x vs ++ " " ++ show′ y vs ++ ")"
        φ inv show′ (Lam z)   = λ(v : vs) → "(\\" ++ v ++ "->" ++ show′ (z (inv (const v))) vs ++ ")"

vars = [[i] | i ← ['a'..'z']] ++ [i : show j | j ← [1..], i ← ['a'..'z']] :: [String]
```

Figure 14. $msfcata_0$ example: String formatting function for Higher-Order Abstract Syntax (HOAS)

pose, to guarantee termination. Fortunately, these two approaches work together without getting in each other's way.

4.1 A general recursive implementation for open HOAS

The recursive datatype Exp_g in Figure 14 is an open HOAS. By *open*, we express that Exp_g has a data constructor Var_g, which enables us to introduce free variables. The constructor Lam_g holds an embedded function of type $(Exp_g \to Exp_g)$. This is called a shallow embedding, since we use functions in the host language, Haskell, to represent lambda abstractions in the object language Exp_g. For example, using the Haskell lambda expressions, we can construct some Exp_g representing lambda expressions as follows:

$$
\begin{aligned}
k_g &= Lam_g\ (\lambda x \to Lam_g\ (\lambda y \to x)) \\
s_g &= Lam_g\ (\lambda x \to Lam_g\ (\lambda y \to Lam_g\ (\lambda z \to \\
&\qquad App_g\ (App_g\ x\ z)\ (App_g\ y\ z)))) \\
w_g &= Lam_g\ (\lambda x \to App_g\ x\ x)
\end{aligned}
$$

Since we can build any untyped lambda expressions with Exp_g, even the problematic self application expression w_g, it is not possible to write a terminating evaluation function for Exp_g. However, there are many functions that recurse over the structure of Exp_g, and when they terminate produce something useful. One of them is the string formatting function $showExp_g$ defined in Figure 14.

Given an expression (Exp_g) and a list of fresh variable names $([String])$, the function $show'$ (defined in the **where** clause of $showExp_g$) returns a string $(String)$ that represents the given expression. To format an application expression $(App_g\ x\ y)$, we simply recurse over each of the subexpressions x and y. To format a lambda expression, we take a fresh name v to represent the binder and we recurse over $(z\ (Var_g\ v))$, which is the application of the embedded function $(z :: Exp_g \to Exp_g)$ to a variable expression $(Var_g\ v :: Exp_g)$ constructed from the fresh name. Note, we had to create a new variable expression to format the function body since we cannot look inside the function values of Haskell. To format a variable expression $(Var_g\ v)$, we only need to return its name v. The local function $show'$ (and hence also $showExp_g$), are total as long as the function values embedded in the Lam_g constructors are total.

We can use $showExp_g$ to print out the terms as follows:

```
> putStrLn (showExp_g k_g)
(\a->(\b->a))
> putStrLn (showExp_g s_g)
(\a->(\b->(\c->((a c) (b c)))))
> putStrLn (showExp_g w_g)
(\a->(a a))
```

Note that $show'$ is not structurally inductive in the Lam_g case. The recursive argument $(z\ (Var_g\ v))$, in particular $Var_g\ v$, is not a subexpression of $(Lam_g\ z)$. Thus the recursive call to $show'$ may not terminate. This function terminated only because the embedded function z was well behaved, and the argument we passed to z, $(Var_g\ v)$, was well behaved. If we had applied z to the expression $(Lam_g\ (\lambda x \to x))$ in place of $Var_g\ v$, or z itself had been divergent, the recursive call would have diverged. If z is divergent, then obviously $show'\ (z\ x)$ diverges for all x. More interestingly, suppose z is not divergent (perhaps something as simple as the identity function) and $show'$ was written to recurse on $(Lam_g\ (\lambda x \to x))$, then what happens?

```
show′ (Lam_g z) (v : vs) = "(\\" ++ v ++ "->" ++
                            show′ (z (Lam_g (λx → x)) vs ++ ")"
```

The function is no longer total. To format $(z\ (Lam_g\ (\lambda x \to x)))$ in the recursive call, it loops back to the Lam_g case again, unless z is a function that ignores its argument. This will form an infinite recursion, since this altered $show'$ forms yet another new $Lam_g\ (\lambda x \to x)$ expression and keeps on recursing.

4.2 A Mendler style solution for closed HOAS

Our exploration of the code in Figure 14 illustrates three potential problems with the general recursive approach.

- The embedded functions may not terminate.
- In a recursive call, the arguments to an embedded function may introduce a constructor with another embedded function, leading to a non terminating cycle.
- We got lucky, in that the answer we required was a $String$, and we happened to have a constructor $Var_g :: String \to Exp_g$. In general we may not be so lucky.

In Figure 14, we defined Exp_g in anticipation of our need to write a function $showExp_g :: Exp_g \to String$, by including a constructor $Var_g :: String \to Exp_g$. Had we anticipated another function $f :: Exp_g \to Int$ we would have needed another constructor $C :: Int \to Exp_g$. Clearly we need a better solution. The solution is to generalize the kind of the datatype from $Exp_g :: *$ to $Exp :: * \rightarrow *$, and add a universal inverse.

$$
\begin{aligned}
&\mathbf{data}\ Exp\ a = App\ (Exp\ a)\ (Exp\ a) \\
&\qquad\qquad\quad \mid Lam\ (Exp\ a \rightarrow Exp\ a) \\
&\qquad\qquad\quad \mid Inv\ a \\
&countLam :: Exp\ Int \rightarrow Int \\
&countLam\ (Inv\ n) = n \\
&countLam\ (App\ x\ y) = countLam\ x + countLam\ y \\
&countLam\ (Lam\ f) = countLam\ (f\ (Inv\ 1))
\end{aligned}
$$

Generalizing from $countLam$ we can define a function from Exp to any type. How do we lift this kind of solution to the Mendler style? Fegaras and Sheard [13] proposed moving the general inverse from the Base type to the datatype fixpoint. Later this approach was refined by Washburn and Weirich [37] to remove the junk introduced by that augmentation (i.e. things like $App\ (Inv\ 1)\ (Inv\ 1)$).

We use the same inverse augmented datatype fixpoint appearing in Washburn and Weirich [37]. Here, we call it $\breve{\mu}_0$ (see Figure 2). The inverse augmented datatype fixpoint $\breve{\mu}_0$ is similar to the standard datatype fixpoint μ_0. The difference is that $\breve{\mu}_0$ has an additional type index a and an additional data constructor $\mathsf{Inverse}_0 :: a \rightarrow \breve{\mu}_0\ a\ i$, corresponding to the universal inverse. The data constructor $\breve{\mathsf{In}}_0$ and the projection function $\breve{\mathsf{out}}_0$ correspond to In_0 and out_0 of the normal fixpoint μ_0. As usual we restrict the use of $\breve{\mathsf{out}}_0$, or pattern matching against $\breve{\mathsf{In}}_0$.

We illustrate this in the second part of Figure 14. As usual, we define $Exp'\ a$ as a fixpoint of the base datatype $ExpF$ and define shorthand constructors lam and app. Using the shorthand constructor functions, we can define some lambda expressions:

$$
\begin{aligned}
k &= lam\ (\lambda x \rightarrow lam\ (\lambda y \rightarrow x)) \\
s &= lam\ (\lambda x \rightarrow lam\ (\lambda y \rightarrow lam\ (\lambda z \rightarrow \\
&\qquad app\ (app\ x\ z)\ (app\ y\ z)))) \\
w &= lam\ (\lambda x \rightarrow app\ x\ x)
\end{aligned}
$$

However, there is another way to construct Exp' values that is problematic. Using the constructor $\mathsf{Inverse}_0$, we can turn values of arbitrary type t into values of $Exp'\ t$. For example, $\mathsf{Inverse}_0\ True :: Exp'\ Bool$. This value is junk, since it does not cooresponnd to any lambda term. By design, we wish to hide $\mathsf{Inverse}_0$ behind an abstraction boundary. We should never allow the user to construct expressions such as $\mathsf{Inverse}_0\ True$, except for using them as placeholders for intermediate results during computation.

We can distinguish pure expressions that are inverse-free from expressions that contain inverse values by exploiting parametricity. The expressions that do not contain inverses have a fully polymorphic type. For instance, k, s and w are of type $(Exp'\ a)$. The expressions that contain $\mathsf{Inverse}_0$ have more specific type (e.g., $(\mathsf{Inverse}_0\ True) :: (Exp'\ Bool)$). Therefore, we define the type of Exp to be $\forall a. Exp'\ a$. Then, expressions of type Exp are guaranteed to be be inverse-free. Using parametricity to sort out junk introduced by the inverse is the key idea of Washburn and Weirich [37], and the inverse augmented fixpoint $\breve{\mu}_0$ is the key idea of Fegaras and Sheard [13]. The contribution we make in this work is putting together these ideas in Mender-style setting. By doing so, we are able define recursion combinators over types with negative occurrences, which have well understood termination properties enforced by parametricity. We define 4 such combinators: $msfcata_0$, $msfhist_0$, $msfcata_1$, and $msfhist_1$. The combinator $msfcata_0$ is the simplest, to define it we generalize over $mcata_0$ by using the same device we used earlier, we abstract the combining function over an additional argument, this time an abstract inverse.

- The combining function φ becomes a function of 3 arguments. An abstract inverse, an recursive placeholder, and a base structure.

$$
\begin{aligned}
&msfcata\ \varphi\ (\breve{\mathsf{In}}_0\ x) \quad\ \ = \varphi\ \mathsf{Inverse}_0\ (msfcata\ \varphi)\ x \\
&msfcata\ \varphi\ (\mathsf{Inverse}_0\ z) = z
\end{aligned}
$$

- For inverse values, return the value inside $\mathsf{Inverse}_0$ as it is.
- We use higher-rank polymorphism to insist that the abstract inverse function, with type $(a \rightarrow r\ a)$, the recursive placeholder function, with type $(r\ a \rightarrow a)$, and the base structure, with type $(f\ (r\ a))$, only work over an abstract type constructor, denoted by (r).

$$
\begin{aligned}
msfcata_0 :: (\forall r.(&a \rightarrow r\ a) \rightarrow \\
&(r\ a \rightarrow a) \rightarrow \\
&(f\ (r\ a) \quad \rightarrow a)) \rightarrow (\forall a. \breve{\mu}_0\ f\ a) \rightarrow a
\end{aligned}
$$

- Note, the abstract recursive type r is parameterized by the answer type a because the augmented datatype fixpoint $\breve{\mu}_0$ is parameterized by the answer type a.

  Also, note, the second argument of $msfcata_0$, the object being operated on, has the higher-rank type $(\forall a. \breve{\mu}_0\ f\ a)$, insisting the input value to be inverse-free by enforcing a to be abstract.

In Figure 14, using $msfcata_0$, it is easy to define $showExp$, the string formatting function for Exp, as in Figure 14. The App case is similar to the general recursive implementation. The body of φ is almost textually identical to the body of $show'$ in the general recursive solution, except we use the inverse expression $inv\ (const\ v)$ to create an abstract r value to pass to the embedded function z. Note, $const\ v$ plays exactly the same roll as $(Var_g\ v)$ in $show'$.

Does $msfcata_0$ really guarantee termination? To prove this we need to address the first two of the three potential problems described at the beginning of Section 4.2. The first problem (embedded functions may be partial) is addressed using logicality analysis. The second problem (cyclic use of constructors as arguments to embedded functions) is addressed by the same argument we used in Section 3.8. The abstract type of the inverse doesn't allow it to be applied to constructors, they're not abstract enough. Just as we couldn't define p_n (in Section 3.8) we can't apply z to things like $(Lam\ (\lambda x \rightarrow x))$. In §5 we provide an embedding of $msfcata$, along with several examples (including the HOAS formatting example), into the strongly normalizing language F_ω. This constitutes a proof that $msfcata$ terminates for all inductive datatypes, even those with negative occurrences.

4.3 A graph datatype with cycles and sharing

Another example of negative datatype is a graph with cycles and sharing. Due to the space limitation, we only give its implementation in Figure 15. For further details, see Fegaras and Sheard [13].

4.4 Additional generalization

The combinator $msfhist_0$ generalizes $mhist_0$ by adding an abstract inverse to a combinator that already has an abstract unroller. The combining function φ becomes a function of 4 arguments: an abstract inverse, an abstract unroll, a recursive placeholder, and a base structure.

The rank 1 combinators $msfcata_1$ and $msfhist_1$ generalize the rank 0 combinators $msfcata_0$ and $msfhist_0$ to combinators on types with an index. The pattern of generalization is quite evident in Figures 3, and 4, and the reader is encouraged to study those Figures for a complete understanding of the results of this paper.

We believe $msfcata_1$ would be useful for writing functions over negative datatypes with type indices. The combinator, $msfhist_1$, like its rank 0 counterpart $msfhist_0$, may not terminate given ill-behaved φ functions that extract embedded functions, and then apply them to parts of the tree which contain those functions. Yet, they are nevertheless useful functions.

```
data G p r = N p [r] | R (r → r) | S (r → r) r
type Graph p = ∀a.μ̆0 (G p) a
node v gs = In̆0 (N v gs)
rec f     = In̆0 (R f)
share f g = In̆0 (S f g)
flatG :: Graph a → [a]
flatG = msfcata0 φ where
  φ inv flat (N v gs)   = v : concatMap flat gs
  φ inv flat (R f)      = flat (f (inv []))
  φ inv flat (S f g)    = flat (f g)
sumG :: Graph Int → Int
sumG = msfcata0 φ where
  φ inv sumg (N n gs)  = n + sum (map sumg gs)
  φ inv sumg (R f)     = sumg (f (inv 0))
  φ inv sumg (S f g)   = sumg (f g)
g0 :: Graph Int  --
```

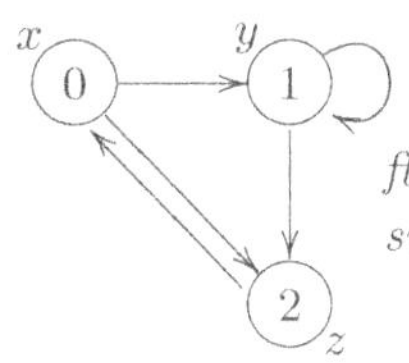


```
                  flatG ⇝ [0, 2, 1, 2]
                  sumG ⇝ 5

g0 = rec (λx →
        share  (λz → node 0 [z, rec (λy → node 1 [y, z])])
               (node 2 [x]))
```

Figure 15. A graph datatype with cycles and sharing [13]

```
type μ̆0 f r a = (r a) + (((r a → a) → f (r a) → a) → a)
newtype Id x = Id {unId :: x}
msfcata :: (∀r.(a → r a) → (r a → a) → f (r a) → a)
        → (∀a.μ̆0 f Id a) → a
msfcata φ x = case+ x unId (λf → f (φ Id))
lift :: ((Id a → a) → f (Id a) → a) → μ̆0 f Id a → Id a
lift h x = case+ x id (λx → Id (x h))

type a + b = ∀c.(a → c) → (b → c) → c
inL :: a → (a + b)
inL a = λf g → f a
inR :: b → (a + b)
inR b = λf g → g b
case+ :: (a + b) → (a → c) → (b → c) → c
case+ x f g = x f g
```

Figure 16. F_ω encoding of $\breve{\mu}_0$, $msfcata_0$, and the sum type (+).

5. F_ω encoding of $\breve{\mu}_0$ and $msfcata_0$

Figure 16 is the F_ω encoding of the inverse augmented datatype $\breve{\mu}_0$ and its catamorphism $msfcata_0$. We use the sum type to encode $\breve{\mu}_0$ since it consists of two constructors, one for the inverse and the other for the recursion. The newtype *Id* wraps answer values inside the inverse. The catamorphism combinator $msfcata_0$ unwraps the result ($unIn$) when x is an inverse. Otherwise, $msfcata_0$ runs the combining function φ over the recursive structure ($\lambda f \to f\ (\varphi\ Id)$). The utility function *lift* abstracts a common pattern, useful when we define the shorthand constructors (*lam* and *app*).

Figure 16 also contains the F_ω encoding of the sum type (+) and its constructors (or injection functions) in_L and in_R. The case expression $case_+$ for the sum type is just binary function application. In the F_ω encoding, they could be omitted (i.e., $case_+\ x\ f\ g$ simplifies to $x\ f\ g$). But, we choose to write in terms of $case_+$ to make the definitions easier to read.

```
data ExpF x = App x x | Lam (x → x)
type Exp' a = μ̆0 ExpF Id a
type Exp = ∀a.Exp' a
app :: Exp' a → Exp' a → Exp' a
app x y = inR (λh → h unId (App (lift h x) (lift h y)))
lam :: (Exp' a → Exp' a) → Exp' a
lam f = inR (λh → h unId (Lam (λx → lift h (f (inL x)))))
showExp :: Exp → String
showExp e = msfcata φ e vars where
  φ inv show' (App x y) = λvs       →
     "(" ++ show' x vs ++ " " ++ show' y vs ++ ")"
  φ inv show' (Lam z)   = λ(v : vs) →
     "(\\" ++ v ++ "->" ++ show' (z (inv (const v))) vs ++ ")"
```

Figure 17. HOAS string formatting example in F_ω.

In Figure 17, we define both an inductive datatype for HOAS (*Exp*), and the string formatting function (*showExp*), with these F_ω encodings, just as we did in §4.2. We can define simple expressions using the shorthand constructors and print out those expressions using *showExp*. For example,

```
> putStrLn (showExp (lam (λx → lam (λy → x))))
(\a->(\b->a))
```

6. Limitations

While the Mendler style is quite expressive, there are functions we have not been able to express easily. The first class are functions that transform their subcomponents before making a recursive call. For example: $length\ (x : xs) = 1 + length\ (reverse\ xs)$. It is also known that the parallel reduction is not expressible[12].

Neither *mcata* nor *cata* can express constant time predecessor function. Crary and Weirich [9] defined an interesting variation of a Mendler style recursion combinator (defined as a language construct), which allows constant time predecessor function for positive datatypes, but its termination properties for negative datatype has not been studied.

7. Related Work

Matthes [21] formalized a version of Mendler style calculi in Coq to prove properties on map fusion for nested datatypes. On the conventional side, Hinze [16] tries to unify various morphisms using the concept he calls *adjoint folds*. But, it remains to be seen whether more exotic species of combinators, such as histomorphisms, can be subsumed by this framework. Since most formal proof systems such as Coq do not support induction over negative datatypes, work on HOAS in such systems (e.g. [6]) are often based on Weak HOAS[11, 17] to avoid negative occurrences. Despeyroux et al. [12] introduced a primitive recursion for HOAS in a modal λ-calculus, and later tried to extended it to dependent types[10].

8. Conclusion and Future Work

We have described a hierarchy of Mendler style recursion combinators, gave examples of their use, and discussed their termination properties. We summarize our results in the table below. For each combinator we provide evidence of the termination behavior for that combinator over both positive and negative inductive types, plus pointers to examples that illustrate the use of that combinator.

	positive	negative	example
cata	proof [14]	undefined	*len* §3.2
$mcata_0$	proof Fig. 6	proof Fig. 6	*len* Fig. 7
$mhist_0$	proof [36]	no	*fib* Fig. 8
$msfcata_0$	proof §5	proof §5	*showExp* Fig. 14
$msfhist_0$	argument §3.4	no	*loopFoo* Fig. 13
$mcata_1$	proof [2]	proof [2]	*bsum* Fig. 9
			extev Fig. 11
$mhist_1$	?	no	*switch2* Fig. 10
$msfcata_1$	similar §5	similar §5	
$msfhist_1$	?	no	

The proof in Figure 6 for $mcata_0$ is a translation from Abel et al. [2], who also discuss the applicability of such proofs to arbitrary ranks. The proof is an embedding of μ_0 and $mcata_0$ into F_ω. It is a proof of termination provided that F_ω extended with non-recursive datatypes is normalizing. Section 5 is an extension of this proof to $msfcata_0$.

Figure 5 illustrates the well known fact that catamorphism is a special case of histomorphism. Although we do not have a formal argument, it seems quite evident that we can simulate all the standard combinators (e.g., $mcata_0$) via its inverse augmented counterparts (e.g., $msfcata_0$).

We pose the open question whether there is a safe way to apply strong induction (or histomorphism) to negative inductive datatypes. We only have preliminary thoughts that there may be a way of ramifying [28] the abstract type r in histomorphism combinators to prevent embedded functions from being applied to a larger term. We are also looking for interesting functional programming examples, which can show practical use of the histomorphism family of combinators for negative inductive datatypes.

Acknowledgments

This work was supported by the NSF grant 0910500. Thanks to Nathan Collins and Jim Hook for discussion and feedback.

References

[1] A. Abel, R. Matthes, and T. Uustalu. Generalized iteration and coiteration for higher-order nested datatypes. In *FoSSaCS*, volume 2620 of *LNCS*, pages 54–69. Springer, 2003.

[2] A. Abel, R. Matthes, and T. Uustalu. Iteration and coiteration schemes for higher-order and nested datatypes. *Theoretical Computer Science*, 333(1-2):3 – 66, 2005. ISSN 0304-3975.

[3] Bird and Meertens. Nested datatypes. In *MPC: 4th International Conference on Mathematics of Program Construction*. LNCS, Springer-Verlag, 1998.

[4] R. Bird and R. Paterson. Generalised folds for nested datatypes. *Formal Aspects of Computing*, 11:11–2, 1999.

[5] R. S. Bird and O. de Moor. *Algebra of Programming*. Prentice-Hall, 1997.

[6] A. Chlipala. Parametric higher-order abstract syntax for mechanized semantics. ICFP '08, pages 143–156. ACM, 2008.

[7] A. Church. A formulation of the simple theory of types. *Journal of Symbolic Logic*, 5(1):56–68, 1940.

[8] R. L. Constable, S. F. Allen, H. M. Bromley, W. R. Cleaveland, J. F. Cremer, R. W. Harper, D. J. Howe, T. B. Knoblock, N. P. Mendler, P. Panangaden, J. T. Sasaki, and S. F. Smith. *Implementing mathematics with the Nuprl proof development system*. Prentice-Hall, Inc., Upper Saddle River, NJ, USA, 1986. ISBN 0-13-451832-2.

[9] K. Crary and S. Weirich. Flexible type analysis. In *ICFP*, pages 233–248, 1999.

[10] J. Despeyroux and P. Leleu. Primitive recursion for higher-order abstract syntax with dependant types. In *Informal proceedings of the FLoC'99 IMLA*, June 1999.

[11] J. Despeyroux, A. P. Felty, and A. Hirschowitz. Higher-order abstract syntax in coq. In *Proceedings of the Second International Conference on Typed Lambda Calculi and Applications*, pages 124–138, London, UK, 1995. Springer-Verlag.

[12] J. Despeyroux, F. Pfenning, and C. Schürmann. Primitive recursion for higher-order abstract syntax. In P. de Groote, editor, *TLCA*, volume 1210 of *LNCS*, pages 147–163. Springer, 1997. ISBN 3-540-62688-3.

[13] L. Fegaras and T. Sheard. Revisiting catamorphisms over datatypes with embedded functions (or, programs from outer space). POPL '96, pages 284–294. ACM, 1996.

[14] T. Hagino. *A Categorical Programming Language*. PhD thesis, University of Edinburgh, 1987.

[15] R. Hinze. Efficient generalized folds. In J. Jeuring, editor, *Proc. of 2nd Workshop on Generic Programming*. July 2000.

[16] R. Hinze. Adjoint folds and unfolds. In C. Bolduc, J. Desharnais, and B. Ktari, editors, *Mathematics of Program Construction*, volume 6120 of *LNCS*, pages 195–228. Springer Berlin / Heidelberg, 2010.

[17] Honsell, Miculan, and Scagnetto. An axiomatic approach to metareasoning on nominal algebras in HOAS. In *ICALP: Annual International Colloquium on Automata, Languages and Programming*, 2001.

[18] C. E. Martin, J. Gibbons, and I. Bayley. Disciplined, efficient, generalised folds for nested datatypes. *Formal Aspects of Computing*, 16 (1):19–35, 2004.

[19] R. Matthes. *Extensions of System F by Iteration and Primitive Recursion on Monotone Inductive Types*. PhD thesis, Ludwig-Maximilians Universität, May 1998.

[20] R. Matthes. An induction principle for nested datatypes in intensional type theory. *Journal of Functional Programming*, 19(3-4):439–468, June 2009.

[21] R. Matthes. Map fusion for nested datatypes in intensional type theory. *Sci. Comput. Program.*, 76:204–224, March 2011.

[22] E. Meijer and G. Hutton. Bananas in space: extending fold and unfold to exponential types. FPCA '95, pages 324–333. ACM, 1995.

[23] N. P. Mendler. Recursive types and type constraints in second-order lambda calculus. In *LICS*, pages 30–36. IEEE Computer Society, 1987.

[24] N. P. Mendler. Inductive types and type constraints in the second-order lambda calculus. *Ann. Pure Appl. Logic*, 51(1-2):159–172, 1991.

[25] R. Paterson. Control structures from types. Unpublished draft, 1993.

[26] C. Paulin-Mohring. Inductive definitions in the system Coq - rules and properties. In M. Bezem and J. F. Groote, editors, *TLCA*, volume 664 of *LNCS*, pages 328–345. Springer, 1993.

[27] F. Pfenning and C. Elliot. Higher-order abstract syntax. PLDI '88, pages 199–208. ACM, 1988.

[28] B. Russell. Mathematical logic as based on the theory of types. *American Journal of Mathematics*, 30:222–262, 1908.

[29] C.-C. Shan. A static simulation of dynamic delimited control. *Higher Order Symbol. Comput.*, 20:371–401, December 2007.

[30] T. Sheard. Putting curry-howard to work. In *Proceedings of the 2005 ACM SIGPLAN workshop on Haskell*, pages 74–85. ACM, 2005.

[31] The GHC Team. *The Glorious Glasgow Haskell Compilation System User's Guide, Version 7.0.1*, 2010.

[32] T. Uustalu. *Natural Deduction for Intuitionistic Least and Greatest Fixedpoint Logics, with an Application to Program Construction*. PhD thesis, Dept. of Teleinformatics, Royal Inst. of Technology, Stockholm, May 1998.

[33] T. Uustalu and V. Vene. Mendler-style inductive types, categorically. *Nordic Journal of Computing*, 6(3):343–361, 1999.

[34] T. Uustalu and V. Vene. Primitive (co)recursion and course-of-value (co)iteration, categorically. *Informatica, Lith. Acad. Sci*, 10(1):5–26, 1999.

[35] T. Uustalu and V. Vene. Coding recursion à la Mendler (extended abstract). In J. Jeuring, editor, *Proc. of 2nd Workshop on Generic Programming*, pages 69–85. 2000.

[36] V. Vene. *Categorical Programming with Inductive and Coinductive Types*. PhD thesis, Dept. of Computer Science, Univ. of Tartu, 2000.

[37] G. Washburn and S. Weirich. Boxes go bananas: encoding higher-order abstract syntax with parametric polymorphism. ICFP '03, pages 249–262. ACM, 2003.

Typed Self-Interpretation by Pattern Matching

Barry Jay
University of Technology, Sydney
Barry.Jay@uts.edu.au

Jens Palsberg
University of California, Los Angeles
palsberg@ucla.edu

Abstract

Self-interpreters can be roughly divided into two sorts: self-recognisers that recover the input program from a canonical representation, and self-enactors that execute the input program. Major progress for statically-typed languages was achieved in 2009 by Rendel, Ostermann, and Hofer who presented the first typed self-recogniser that allows representations of different terms to have different types. A key feature of their type system is a type:type rule that renders the kind system of their language inconsistent.

In this paper we present the first statically-typed language that not only allows representations of different terms to have different types, and supports a self-recogniser, but also supports a self-enactor. Our language is a factorisation calculus in the style of Jay and Given-Wilson, a combinatory calculus with a factorisation operator that is powerful enough to support the pattern-matching functions necessary for a self-interpreter. This allows us to avoid a type:type rule. Indeed, the types of System F are sufficient. We have implemented our approach and our experiments support the theory.

Categories and Subject Descriptors D.3.4 [*Processors*]: Interpreters; D.2.4 [*Program Verification*]: Correctness proofs, formal methods; F.3.2 [*Semantics of Programming Languages*]: Operational semantics

General Terms Languages, Theory

Keywords self-interpretation, pattern matching

1. Introduction

An interpreter implements a programming language, and a *self-interpreter* is an interpreter written in the language that it implements. Self-interpreters are popular and available for Standard ML [34], Haskell [28], Scheme [1], JavaScript [12], Python [33], Ruby [41], λ-calculus [2, 4, 5, 21, 25, 26, 32, 35], and many other languages [23, 38, 42]. A self-interpreter enables programmers to easily modify, extend, and grow a language [31], do other forms of meta-programming [8], and even derive an algorithm for normalisation by evaluation [6].

These self-interpreters can be roughly divided into two sorts: *self-recognisers* that recover the input program from a canonical representation, and *self-enactors* that execute the input program. While we will review the rich literature on self-interpretation in Sections 2 and 9, two highlights are papers by Mogensen [25], and by Berarducci and Bohm [5], that each defined a single program representation for an untyped language that supports both a self-recogniser and a self-enactor, with proofs of correctness.

Now consider statically typed languages. Most previous work on self-interpreters for these give all program representations the same, universal type. The use of a universal type ignores the type of the input program and thereby misses an important opportunity for static type checking of self-interpreters. Major progress was achieved in 2009 when Rendel, Ostermann, and Hofer [31] presented the first self-recognizer for a statically-typed language in which representations of different terms can have different types.

The challenge Rendel, Ostermann, and Hofer left open the problem of typing a self-enactor. Additionally, their type system has a type:type rule that renders the kind system of their language inconsistent.

Our results In this paper we present the first statically-typed language in which representations of different terms can have different types and in which we can program and statically type both a self-recogniser and a self-enactor. Our language uses System F types and so has no rule asserting type:type. Our approach differs from previous work by adopting a pattern-matching perspective that we summarize next.

The representation of a term t is a data structure $'t$ so it is natural to consider an interpreter as a pattern-matching function in which each evaluation rule `left` $\to$ `right` of the source language can be represented by a case, with a pattern derived from `left` and a body derived from `right`.

So the fundamental question becomes how to represent pattern-matching. Berarducci and Bohm achieved this by considering how to solve equations inside lambda calculus but now there is a more direct and powerful method, in the *pattern calculus* of Jay and Kesner [16, 18, 19]. Although it may be possible to achieve our main goals in pure pattern calculus (or even static pattern calculus), this paper adopts a simpler and more direct approach.

Recent work on *factorisation calculus* by Jay and Given-Wilson [17] supports combinatory calculi that are more expressive than traditional combinatory calculi (based on S and K), in being able to analyse the internal structure of any normal form, e.g. to recover X from SKX. More generally, they can define pattern-matching functions that are powerful enough to interpret themselves. This compares well with previous approaches in which functions at one level are analysed by functions at the next higher level, as in the higher-order polymorphic λ-calculus F_ω and even F_ω^* which adds the rule type:type.

The pure factorisation calculus [17] is a combinator calculus with just two operators, S and F, where S is known from SK-combinators, and F is a factorization operator that is able to decompose *compounds* (e.g. closed normal forms) into their components. In this paper we add a constructor B to block evaluation,

ICFP'11, September 19–21, 2011, Tokyo, Japan.

and together S, F, and B are sufficient to represent programs in an untyped manner and to define an untyped self-recogniser and an untyped self-enactor. An additional benefit of this approach is that there is a term that decides equality of representations of combinators (closed terms). By comparison, such a term is not known to exist for higher-order abstract syntax of untyped λ-calculus when the meta-language is the untyped λ-calculus itself.

We meet the goals of static type checking by adding three more operators, the traditional operator K, a fixpoint operator Y and an operator E that tests for equality of operators. Although the types are relatively simple, being those of System F, they are used in two unusual ways. First, the F operator cannot be typed with Hindley-Milner types alone. Rather, it takes an argument of polymorphic type, since the types of components are not determined by the type of their compound. Second, the operator E doesn't have a principal type scheme, for reasons that can be traced back to the typing of pattern-matching functions in pattern calculus. This creates difficulties when interpreting E itself, which are overcome by replacing explicit references to E in patterns by binding symbols which are shown to match with E only.

We have implemented the entire approach and performed experiments that support our theory.

The rest of this paper. We will discuss the nature of self-interpretation and closely related work (Section 2), and we will define our language (Section 3), syntactic sugar (Section 4), self-recogniser (Section 5), self-enactor (Section 6), type system (Section 7), including proofs that our self-interpreters type check, and experimental results (Section 8). We also discuss additional related work (Section 9).

2. The Nature of Self-Interpretation

This section fixes the terminology for the various sorts of self-interpreters to be considered. Definitions have been chosen so that they apply as widely as possible, i.e. both to λ-calculi and other rewriting systems, and to programming languages with their evaluation strategies. Since the calculi emphasise static interpreters, while the programming language community emphasise dynamic ones, we propose new names for the various special cases.

Self-interpretation involves two steps. The first is a process of *quotation* that transforms the syntax of a term t into a value or normal form $'t$ (pronounced "quote t") ready for interpretation. The second is the application of a self-interpreter to $'t$ to produce something that has the same meaning as t. Researchers have identified two sorts of meaning here: a static approach that focuses on program structure, and a dynamic approach that focuses on program behaviour. Let us examine each of them in turn.

A *self-recogniser* is a self-interpreter `unquote` that can recognise a term from its quotation, by reversing the quotation process:

$$\textbf{Self-Recogniser:} \quad \texttt{unquote}('t) \approx t \qquad (1)$$

where $\approx$ denotes *behavioural equivalence*. For example, quotation may add tags that block evaluation, which are then removed by `unquote`. The first self-recogniser is due to Kleene [21] who introduced a notion of quotation and `unquote` for pure λ-calculus, and established (1) as a consequence of β-equality. Barendregt [2] cited Kleene's paper and used the term *self-interpreter* for any λ-term `unquote` that satisfies $\texttt{unquote}('t) =_\beta t$. Barendregt [2], Mogensen [25, 26], Berarducci and Böhm [5], and Bel [4] all presented λ-terms `unquote` that satisfy Equation (1). The name *self-recognisers* seems apt because the interpretation can recover, or recognise, (something equivalent to) the original term.

The process of quotation tends to cause code expansion, with $\texttt{unquote}('t)$ being a much larger program than t. This problem is mitigated if the self-recogniser is *strong* in the sense that:

$$\textbf{Strong Self-Recogniser:} \quad \texttt{unquote}('t) \longrightarrow^* t$$

where $\longrightarrow^*$ denotes reduction in a calculus, or a small-step operational semantics of a programing language. Among the examples above, those of Mogensen [25, 26] and Berarducci and Böhm [5] are strong.

A *self-enactor* is a self-interpreter `enact` that mimics evaluation:

$$\textbf{Self-Enactor:} \quad t \Rightarrow^* v \quad \text{implies} \quad \texttt{enact}('t) \approx {'v} . \qquad (2)$$

That is, if t evaluates to a *value* v then $\texttt{enact}('t)$ is behaviourally equivalent to $'v$. Note that this account requires knowledge of the values v and the evaluation process $\Rightarrow^*$. Also, a self-enactor cannot be a self-recogniser unless $'v \approx v$ which usually fails. That is, preservation of meaning by a self-enactor is different to that of a self-recogniser. That said, a self-enactor `enact` can be combined with a self-recogniser `unquote` to produce a self-interpreter that maps t to $\texttt{unquote}(\texttt{enact}('t))$.

The first use of self-enactors is due to Mogensen [25] who proved the existence of such a term in pure λ-calculus. He used the term *self-reducer* for any λ-term `enact` that satisfies Equation (2). Mogensen [25], Berarducci and Böhm [5] (who preferred the term *reductor*), and Song, Xu, and Qian [35] presented λ-terms `enact` that satisfy Equation (2). The name *self-enactor* seems apt because Equation (2) implies that `enact` must do work to turn a quotation into action. The technical details of Mogensen's paper [25] strongly suggest that a self-enactor is more complex than a self-recogniser. This makes sense since, unlike a self-recogniser, a self-enactor must do actual evaluation.

A *strong self-enactor* satisfies the following stronger requirement:

$$\textbf{Strong Self-Enactor:} \quad t \Rightarrow^* v \quad \text{implies} \quad \texttt{enact}('t) \Rightarrow^* {'v} .$$

Among the examples already mentioned, only that of Berarducci and Böhm is a strong self-enactor.

The self-interpreters for Standard ML [34], Haskell [28], Scheme [1], JavaScript [12], Python [40], and Ruby [41] all do evaluation. The documentations suggest that the programmers intended them to be self-enactors or, in some case, a self-enactor followed by an application of a self-recognizer to print a value rather than a representation of a value.

A desirable quality of program representation is that we can decide equality of program representations by a term `equal`, as in:

Equality of Representations:

$$\texttt{equal}('s, 't) \Rightarrow \begin{cases} '\texttt{true} & \text{if } 's = {'t} \\ '\texttt{false} & \text{otherwise.} \end{cases}$$

Some quotation mechanisms support that; some don't. Even the presence of `unquote` doesn't guarantee the existence of `equal`. For example, many of the above papers represent λ-terms by higher-order abstract syntax with a meta-language that itself is the untyped λ-calculus. For such representations, no term `equal` is known to exist. Binding operations complicate the issues because in λ-calculus, closed terms are built from open terms. Kleene [21] avoided the problems with open terms by representing programs with only closed terms that are built from combinators, that is, small, closed λ-terms. In general, combinatory calculi present an easier equality-checking problem.

3. Blocking Factorisation Calculus

3.1 Overview

Our language is a combinatory calculus called the *blocking factorisation calculus* which has all the properties above: decidable equality of quotations, a self-recogniser and a self-enactor. It is a *factorisation calculus* in the sense of Jay and Given-Wilson [17]. Factorisation calculi are more expressive than traditional SK-combinators [17], which may seem surprising since SK-calculus is *combinatorially complete* [20]. However, its factorisation operator F can decompose an identity function SKX to recover the value of the combinator X, something that cannot be done using S and K alone. Note that the corresponding logic would be unsound if F could decompose an arbitrary application, e.g. to recover X from KKX. To ensure soundness, the reduction rules for F require its first argument to be *factorable*, that is, a partial application of an operator. As a result, the factorisation calculus is confluent, which implies soundness of the corresponding logic. This expressive power supports analysis of normal forms such as quotations, including decidable equality of program representations. More generally, it supports *pattern matching* that is expressive enough to support self-interpreters.

3.2 Syntax

We assume a countable set of *variables* (meta-variables w, x, y, z). The *operators* (meta-variable O) of our language are given by:

$$\text{(Operator)} \quad O \quad ::= \quad Y \mid K \mid S \mid F \mid E \mid B\,.$$

Each operator has an *arity*, given by $1, 2, 3, 3, 4$ and ∞, respectively, that helps us define the intended semantics. S and K take their usual meanings from combinatory logic. Y is a fixed-point operator. In a pure setting it could be defined from S and K but this interpretation will not support the typing. F is the *factorisation* operator used to decompose compounds, as described later. Perhaps surprisingly, it cannot be defined in terms of S and K [17]. E is an equality operator that takes four arguments; two to compare, and two alternative results, chosen according to whether the compared arguments are the same operator or not. B is used to block evaluation.

The *terms* (meta-variables p, q, r, s, t, u) of our *term calculus* are given by:

$$\text{(Term)} \quad t \quad ::= \quad x \mid O \mid t\ t\,.$$

Terms are generated by the variables and operators and they are closed under application.

The *free variables* of a term are all the variables that occur in the term, since there are no binding operations. A term t *avoids* a variable x if x is not a free variable of t. *Term substitutions* σ are defined and applied in the usual manner. The substitution of the term u_i for the variable x_i for $1 \leq i \leq n$ in the term t may be denoted $[u_1/x_1, u_2/x_2, \ldots, u_n/x_n]$.

A *combinator* is a term built without any variables, the collection of which forms the corresponding *combinatory calculus* [15]. Conceptually, the combinatory calculus is more fundamental than the term calculus, but to define operations such as pattern-matching on combinators requires the larger, term calculus, so that our efforts will focus there.

A term is *factorable* if it is a partial application of an operator, as determined by its arity. That is, $O\ t_1\ \ldots\ t_k$ is a partial application of operator O if k is strictly less than the arity of O. In particular, all operators are factorable. A *compound* is a factorable application.

$$\frac{t \rightharpoonup t'}{t \longrightarrow t'} \qquad \frac{r \longrightarrow r'}{r\ u \longrightarrow r'\ u} \qquad \frac{u \longrightarrow u'}{r\ u \longrightarrow r\ u'}$$

Figure 1. The Reduction Relation

3.3 Reduction Semantics

The *reduction rules* are:

$$\begin{array}{rcll} Y\ t & \rightharpoonup & t\ (Y\ t) & \\ K\ s\ t & \rightharpoonup & s & \\ S\ s\ t\ u & \rightharpoonup & s\ u\ (t\ u) & \\ F\ O\ s\ t & \rightharpoonup & s & \text{if } O \text{ is an operator} \\ F\ (p\ q)\ s\ t & \rightharpoonup & t\ p\ q & \text{if } p\ q \text{ is a compound} \\ E\ O\ O\ s\ t & \rightharpoonup & s & \text{if } O \text{ is an operator} \\ E\ p\ q\ s\ t & \rightharpoonup & t & \text{otherwise, if } p \text{ and } q \text{ are factorable.} \end{array}$$

That is, Y is the *fixed-point* operator, K eliminates its second argument, and S duplicates its third argument, all as usual. The *factorisation* operator F branches according to the value of its first argument. If this is a compound then apply the third argument to the components, else return the second argument. The *equality* operator E decides equality of operators. If the first two arguments are the same operator then return the third argument, else if the first two arguments are both factorable (whether equal or not) then return the fourth argument. Note that there are no reduction rules for B, which may thus be thought of as a *constructor*.

The *reduction relation* $\longrightarrow$ is obtained by applying the reduction rules to arbitrary sub-terms, as described in Figure 1. As usual in rewriting, the transitive closure of a relation is denoted by $(-)^+$ as in $\longrightarrow^+$ and the reflexive, transitive closure by $(-)^*$ as in $\longrightarrow^*$. If $t \longrightarrow^* t'$ then t *reduces* to t'.

The basic properties of the calculus are easily established.

THEOREM 3.1. *Reduction is confluent.*

Proof. If $p\ q$ is a compound then, by inspecting the arities, it is clear that it is not an instance of any reduction rule. Hence, any reduction of $p\ q$ is a reduction of p or of q which implies that there are no critical pairs [37] involving $F\ (p\ q)\ s\ t$. Similarly, there are no other critical pairs. □

THEOREM 3.2. *Every combinator in normal form is factorable.*

Proof. The proof is by induction on the structure of the combinator. For example, if it is of the form $F\ p\ s\ t$ then induction implies p is a factorable form, so that a reduction rule applies. Similar remarks apply to combinators of the form $E\ p\ q\ s\ t$. The other cases are straightforward. □

This theorem provides a form of progress property, in that evaluation of the operators, especially F and E, cannot get blocked. Note, however, that if Ω does *not* have a normal form then $F\ \Omega\ K\ K$ cannot become an instance of a rule.

4. Syntactic Sugar

For the purpose of practical programming, particularly of our two self-interpreters, we use five forms of syntactic sugar:

- identity operator, written `I`,
- λ-abstraction, written $\lambda^* x.s$ and, in typewriter font, `x -> s`,
- let binding, written `let x = s in t`,
- let rec binding, written `let rec x = t` and
- extensions, written `p -> s | t`.

We de-sugar terms with such constructs before executing them. De-sugaring maps closed terms to closed terms. The type-writer font is used when the emphasis is on programming, rather than the calculus.

4.1 Identity, λ-abstraction, let, and let rec

We de-sugar I to the combinator SKK.

One of the oldest results on computability is that λ-abstraction can be defined by SK-terms (e.g. [15]). The definition of $\lambda^* x.t$ is as follows.

$$\begin{array}{rcll} \lambda^* x.x & = & I & \\ \lambda^* x.t & = & K\, t & \text{if } t \text{ avoids } x \\ \lambda^* x.t\, x & = & t & \text{if } t \text{ avoids } x \\ \lambda^* x.(r\, u) & = & S(\lambda^* x.r)\,(\lambda^* x.u) & \text{otherwise .} \end{array}$$

The use of η-contraction in the third line above is not theoretically necessary but makes a big difference in the size of the resulting term.

LEMMA 4.1. *For all terms s and u and variable x there is a reduction*

$$(\lambda^* x.s)\, u \longrightarrow^* [u/x]s\ .$$

Proof. The proof is by induction on the structure of the term s. If s is x then $(\lambda^* x.s)u = I\ u \longrightarrow^* u = [u/x]s$. If s avoids x then $(\lambda^* x.s)u = K\ s\ u \longrightarrow s = [u/x]s$. If s is of the form $t\ x$ where t avoids x then $(\lambda^* x.s)u = t\ u = [u/x]s$. Otherwise, if s is of the form $s_1 s_2$ then

$$\begin{array}{rcl} (\lambda^* x.s)u & = & S(\lambda^* x.s_1)(\lambda^* x.s_2)u \\ & \longrightarrow & (\lambda^* x.s_1)u((\lambda^* x.s_2)u) \\ & \longrightarrow^* & [u/x]s_1([u/x]s_2) \\ & = & [u/x]s \end{array}$$

by two applications of induction. □

We de-sugar the syntax `let x = u in t` to $(\lambda^* x.t)u$ and we de-sugar `let rec f = t` to $Y\ (\lambda^* f.t)$, as usual.

4.2 Extensions

A *pattern-matching function* of the form

$$\begin{array}{l} p_1 \rightarrow s_1 \\ \mid p_2 \rightarrow s_2 \\ \quad \ldots \\ \mid p_n \rightarrow s_n \\ \mid x \rightarrow s \end{array}$$

can be built as a sequence of *extensions* of the form `p -> s | t` by declaring the vertical bar to be right-associative, and replacing the final case by $\lambda^* x.s$. In such an extension, the first subterm `p` is a *pattern*, which is a term in normal form. While generalisations are possible, our notion of extension is sufficient for typed self-interpretation, and already generalises the usual approaches to pattern matching in functional programming. Traditionally, pattern matching is a technique for destructing values of a given algebraic data type, each pattern being headed by one of the type's constructors. In contrast, we allow patterns such as `(y x)` that is not headed by any constructor, but rather denotes an arbitrary compound data structure. Our notion of pattern matching is widely applicable; for example, it is easy to program an equality checker for normal forms.

We use the following recursive function to de-sugar extensions:

$$\begin{array}{rcl} x \rightarrow s \mid r & = & \lambda^* x.s \\ O \rightarrow s \mid r & = & \lambda^* x.E\ O\ x\ s\ (r\ x) = S(S(E\ O)(K\ s))r \\ p\, q \rightarrow s \mid r & = & \lambda^* x.F\ x\ (r\ x) \\ & & (\lambda^* y.(p \rightarrow (q \rightarrow s \mid r'\ y) \mid r')\ y) \\ & & (\text{where } r' = \lambda^* y.\lambda^* z.r\ (y\ z) = S(K\ r)) \end{array}$$

where x is chosen fresh. The first two rules are clear enough. The third defines matching against an applicative pattern $p\ q$ by matching the components of the argument against p and then against q. The complexity of the term is caused by the need to handle the various sorts of match failure.

The intended semantics is given by defining matching. A *match* is either a *successful match* given by `Some` σ where σ is a substitution, or a *match failure* `None`. The *disjoint union* $\uplus$ of successful matches is the successful match obtained from the disjoint union of their substitutions, if this exists. All other disjoint unions are `None`. The *matching* $\{u/p\}$ of a pattern p against a term u is defined by the rules

$$\begin{array}{rcll} \{u/x\} & = & \texttt{Some}\ [u/x] & \\ \{O/O\} & = & \texttt{Some}\ [\,] & \\ \{u_1\, u_2/p_1\, p_2\} & = & \{u_1/p_1\} \uplus \{u_2/p_2\} & \text{if } u_1\ u_2 \text{ is factorable} \\ \{u/p\} & = & \texttt{None} & \text{otherwise, if } u \text{ is factorable} \\ \{u/p\} & = & \text{undefined} & \text{otherwise} \end{array}$$

corresponding to those of static pattern calculus [16].

LEMMA 4.2. *Extensions satisfy the following derived reduction rules:*

$$\begin{array}{lcll} (p \rightarrow s \mid r)\ u & \longrightarrow^* & \sigma s & (\textit{if } \{u/p\} = \texttt{Some}\ \sigma) \\ (p \rightarrow s \mid r)\ u & \longrightarrow^* & r\ u & (\textit{if } \{u/p\} = \texttt{None}). \end{array}$$

Proof. The proof is a routine induction on the structure of the pattern, given Lemma 4.1. □

This style of pattern matching, also known as *path polymorphism* [16, 18, 19], cannot be expressed in pure λ-calculus or even in a combinator calculus with the operators Y, S, K, B. So, our calculus has the operator F and the novel operator E, and we make them play key roles when we de-sugar pattern matching.

For example, to unblock reduction we will use `unblock` defined by

```
B x -> x
| x -> x
```

which de-sugars to the combinator

$$\begin{array}{l} B\ x \rightarrow x \mid x \rightarrow x \\ = \lambda^* x.F\ x\ (I\ x)\ (\lambda^* y.(B \rightarrow (x \rightarrow x \mid r'\ y) \mid r')\ y) \\ = \lambda^* x.F\ x\ (I\ x)\ (\lambda^* y.(B \rightarrow I \mid r')\ y) \\ = \lambda^* x.F\ x\ (I\ x)\ (B \rightarrow I \mid r') \\ = \lambda^* x.F\ x\ (I\ x)\ (S(S(E\ B)(K\ I))r') \\ = S(S\ F\ I)(K(S(S(E\ B)(K\ I))(S(K\ I)))) \end{array}$$

where $r' = S(K\ I)$.

5. Self-Recognisers

5.1 Quotation

Quotation for both our self-interpreters is given by

$$\begin{array}{rcl} {}'x & = & x \\ {}'O & = & BO \\ {}'(s\,t) & = & {}'s\,{}'t \end{array}$$

Clearly, quoted terms are always normal forms, whose internal structure can be examined by factorising.

THEOREM 5.1. *There is a decidable equality of quotations of closed terms.*

Proof. The booleans are given by K (true) and $K\ I$ (false) as usual. The required equality term is

$$\frac{t \rightharpoonup t'}{t \Rightarrow t'} \qquad \frac{r \Rightarrow r'}{r\;u \Rightarrow r'\;u} \qquad \frac{p \Rightarrow p'}{F\;p \Rightarrow F\;p'}$$

$$\frac{p \Rightarrow p'}{E\;p \Rightarrow E\;p'} \qquad \frac{q \Rightarrow q'}{E\;p\;q \Rightarrow E\;p\;q'}$$

Figure 2. Call-by-Name Evaluation

```
let rec equal =
  x1 x2 -> (
    y1 y2 -> (equal x1 y1) (equal x2 y2) (K I)
  | y -> K I)
| x -> | y -> E x y K (K I)
```

It decides equality of arbitrary closed normal forms, be they quotations or not. If applied to two compounds then it checks equality of both components (by applying the boolean `(equal x1 y1)` to `(equal x2 y2)` and `(K I)` to represent the conditional for conjunction). Alternatively, if the first argument is an operator then E is applied. □

5.2 A Self-Recogniser

Define `unquote` by

```
let rec unquote =
  B x -> x
| y x -> (unquote y) (unquote x)
| x -> x
```

THEOREM 5.2. `unquote` *is a strong self-recogniser with respect to* $\longrightarrow^*$.

Proof. The proof is a straightforward induction on the structure of t. If t is a variable or operator then `unquote`$('t) \longrightarrow^* t$. If t is an application $t_1\;t_2$, then $'t$ is a compound $'t_1\;'t_2$ (since all quotations are headed by B). Hence `unquote`$('t) =$ `unquote`$('t_1\;'t_2) \longrightarrow^*\;'t_1\;'t_2$ by two applications of induction. □

6. Self-Enactors

6.1 Evaluation

We choose a call-by-name semantics, given by an *evaluation relation* $\Rightarrow$ as defined in Figure 2. There is not much scope for variation here; the operator F behaves like other branching constructs, such as conditionals, being eager in its first argument but deferring evaluation of the other two; and E evaluates its first two arguments to factorable forms, as required to support its reduction.

To define behavioural equivalence requires a notion of value and of context. Define a *value* to be a term that is irreducible with respect to $\Rightarrow$. A term t *has* a value if there is a value v such that $t \Rightarrow^* v$.

Usually, a context is described as a term with a hole in it but our terms contain free variables that cannot be bound, so a context $C[-]$ here must also allow a term substitution σ that is to be applied to the term that fills the hole.

Now, two terms t_1 and t_2 are *behaviourally equivalent* (written $t_1 \approx t_2$) if, for any context $C[-]$, the term $C[t_1]$ has a value if and only if $C[t_2]$ does. The following lemma will be our main tool in establishing behavioural equivalence.

LEMMA 6.1. *If* $t_1 \longrightarrow t_2$ *then* $t_1 \approx t_2$.

Proof. The proof is by case analysis on the reduction rules. □

Before giving the self-enactor for the blocking factorisation calculus that we will type, the approach can be illustrated by a pair of simpler examples.

6.2 A Self-Enactor for SK-calculus

Consider the interpretation of SK-calculus in the blocking factorisation calculus. There are two natural approaches to the representation of a rule `left` $\rightarrow$ `right` as a case, namely the *reduction approach* and the *meta-circular approach* (pace [32]). The reduction approach represents the rule by the case

$$|\;'\texttt{left} \rightarrow \texttt{enact}\;'\texttt{right}$$

where the left- and right-hand sides of the rule have been quoted. For the reduction rule for S, this yields

```
| B S x3 x2 x1 -> enact (x3 x1 (x2 x1))
```

The meta-circular approach replaces $'$`right` above by an application of the operator that is the subject of the rule. For S this yields

```
| B S x3 x2 x1 -> enact (S x3 x2 x1)
```

Although the meta-circular approach is sometimes more concise, and so will be preferred, it won't always be applicable.

The interpretation of SK-calculus is thus given by the combinator `enactSK` defined by

```
let rec enactSK =
  let enact1 =
    B K x2 x1 -> enactSK (K x2 x1)
  | B S x3 x2 x1 -> enactSK (S x3 x2 x1)
  | x1 -> x1
  in
    x2 x1 -> enact1 (enactSK x2 x1)
  | x1 -> x1
```

The function `enact1` tries to perform one step of the evaluation. It is a pattern-matching function with one case for each reduction rule of the calculus, which then performs a recursive call to `enactSK`. This stops if no reduction rule can be applied, as indicated by the default identity function. This handles partially applied operators. The pattern-matching function for `enactSK` itself has two cases: that for a compound enacts the left-hand component and then reduces the whole by `enact1`.

For example,

$$\begin{array}{ll} \texttt{enactSK '(K S K)} & \\ \quad = & \texttt{enactSK (B K (B S) (B K))} \\ \quad \longrightarrow^* & \texttt{enact1 (enactSK (B K (B S)) (B K))} \\ \quad \longrightarrow^* & \texttt{enact1 (B K (B S) (B K))} \\ \quad \longrightarrow^* & \texttt{enactSK (B S)} \\ \quad \longrightarrow^* & \texttt{B S} = \texttt{'S} \end{array}$$

Note that the evaluation is lazy. To make it eager the special case for `enactSK` must be changed to

```
x2 x1 -> enact1 (enactSK x2 (enactSK x1))
```

6.3 An Explicit Self-Enactor

Figure 3 displays a self-enactor for the blocking factorisation calculus that mentions `E` explicitly, but will resist typing later on. The case for `Y` uses the reduction approach, as the meta-circular approach as the term `Y x1` reduces to `x1 (Y x1)` instead of the intended `x1 (B Y x1)`. The operators `K` and `S` are handled using the meta-circular approach, as before. The rules for `F` and `E` are also meta-circular, which proves to be more concise than writing out all of the alternative elaborations of the rules. The role of `evalop` can

```
let rec enactexp =
  let unblock = B x -> x | x -> x in
  let evalop = x -> unblock (enactexp x) in
  let enact1 =
    B Y x1 -> enactexp (x1 (B Y x1))
  | B K x2 x1 -> enactexp (K x2 x1)
  | B S x3 x2 x1 -> enactexp (S x3 x2 x1)
  | B F x3 x2 x1 -> enactexp (F (evalop x3) x2 x1)
  | B E x4 x3 x2 x1 ->
      enactexp (E (evalop x4) (evalop x3) x2 x1)
  | x1 -> x1
  in
    x2 x1 -> enact1 (enactexp x2 x1)
  | x1 -> x1
```

Figure 3. A Self-Enactor that Handles E Explicitly

be illustrated by an example. Consider

$$
\begin{array}{ll}
 & \texttt{enactexp '(F K S K)} \\
= & \texttt{enactexp (B F (B K) (B S) (B K))} \\
\longrightarrow^* & \texttt{enact1 (B F (B K) (B S) (B K))} \\
\longrightarrow^* & \texttt{enactexp (F (evalop (B K)) (B S) (B K)}
\end{array}
$$

If `evalop (B K)` were replaced by `enact (B K)` then `F` would be applied to `B K` when it should be applied to `K`. So `evalop` is used to "unquote" operators while leaving everything else unchanged. Similar remarks apply to the interpretation of `E`. Note that there is no case for `B` in `enact1` as it has no reduction rules.

6.4 An Implicit Self-Enactor

The type machinery developed in Section 7 is not able to type patterns that contain `E`. Even though this has only arisen once, in the self-enactor in Figure 3, it creates a major technical challenge: we want the self-enactor to use a pattern-matching function with one case per construct in the language, but at the same time we aren't allowed to use E in a pattern! We overcome this difficulty by applying the dictum of *Sherlock Holmes*:

> *"Eliminate all other factors, and the one which remains must be the truth."* Sherlock Holmes [11].

That is, by first giving cases for all the other five operators (including a "dummy" case for B) we can infer the presence of E without naming it explicitly in a pattern. The resulting self-enactor in which `E` is handled implicitly is in Figure 4.

6.5 Correctness

LEMMA 6.2. *If v is a factorable form then* $\texttt{enact}('v) \longrightarrow^* {}'v$.

Proof. The proof is by a straightforward case analysis on the nature of factorable forms, since none of the special cases of `enact1` apply. □

LEMMA 6.3. *If $t_1 \longrightarrow t_2$ then* $\texttt{enact}('t_1)$ *and* $\texttt{enact}('t_2)$ *have a common reduct.*

Proof. The proof is by induction on the length of the reduction. If $t_1 \rightarrow t_2$ then routine case analysis shows that there is a reduction $\texttt{enact}\ 't_1 \longrightarrow^+ \texttt{enact}\ 't_2$. For example, if t_1 is $E\ O\ O\ s\ r$ and t_2 is s then $'t_1$ is the term $B\ E\ (B\ O)\ (B\ O)\ 's\ 'r$ and

$$
\begin{array}{llll}
\texttt{evalop}\ (B\ O) & \longrightarrow^* & \texttt{unblock}\ (\texttt{enact}\ (B\ O)) & \\
 & \longrightarrow^* & \texttt{unblock}\ (B\ O) & \text{(by Lemma 6.2)} \\
 & \longrightarrow^+ & O &
\end{array}
$$

and so $\texttt{enact}\ 't_1 \longrightarrow^* \texttt{enact}\ (E\ O\ O\ 's\ 'r) \longrightarrow \texttt{enact}\ 's$.

```
let rec enact =
  let unblock = B x -> x | x -> x in
  let evalop = x -> unblock (enact x) in
  let enact1 =
    B Y x1 -> enact (x1 (B Y x1))
  | B K x2 x1 -> enact (K x2 x1)
  | B S x3 x2 x1 -> enact (S x3 x2 x1)
  | B F x3 x2 x1 -> enact (F (evalop x3) x2 x1)
  | B B x4 x3 x2 x1 -> B B x4 x3 x2 x1
  | B x5 x4 x3 x2 x1 ->
      enact (x5 (evalop x4) (evalop x3) x2 x1)
  | x1 -> x1
  in
    x2 x1 -> enact1 (enact x2 x1)
  | x1 -> x1
```

Figure 4. A Self-Enactor that Handles E Implicitly

Again, if t_1 is $E\ O\ u\ s\ r$ where u is a factorable form other than O and t_2 is r then $'t_1$ is the term $B\ E\ (B\ O)\ 'u\ 's\ 'r$. If u is an operator O_1 (other than O) then $\texttt{evalop}\ (B\ O_1) \longrightarrow^* O_1$ as before, and so $B\ E\ (B\ O)\ 'u\ 's\ 'r \longrightarrow^* E\ O\ O_1\ 's\ 'r \longrightarrow {}'r$ as required. Similarly, if u is some compound then $\texttt{evalop}\ 'u$ reduces to a compound q and so $B\ E\ (B\ O)\ 'u\ 's\ 'r \longrightarrow^* E\ O\ q\ 's\ 'r \longrightarrow {}'r$ as required.

If t_1 is an application $r_1\ u_1$ and $r_1 \longrightarrow r_2$ then, by induction, $\texttt{enact}\ 'r_1$ and $\texttt{enact}\ 'r_2$ have a common reduct r_3. Hence $\texttt{enact}\ 't_1$ reduces to the term $\texttt{enact1}\ (\texttt{enact}\ 'r_1\ 'u_1)$ which has a common reduct with $\texttt{enact1}\ (\texttt{enact}\ 'r_2\ 'u_1)$ which is a reduct of $\texttt{enact}\ '(r_2\ u_1)$. A similar argument applies if $u_1 \longrightarrow u_2$.

If t_1 is some $F\ p\ s\ r$ and $p_1 \longrightarrow p_2$ then, by induction, $\texttt{enact}\ 'p_1$ and $\texttt{enact}\ 'p_2$ have a common reduct p_3. Thus $\texttt{enact}('t_1)$ and $\texttt{enact}('t_2)$ both reduce to

$$\texttt{enact}\ (F\ (\texttt{unblock}\ p_3)\ 's\ 'r)\ .$$

Similar arguments apply if t_1 is of the form $E\ p\ s\ r\ q$. □

LEMMA 6.4. *Let t be a term. If* $\texttt{enact}\ 't$ *reduces to a factorable form v then v is a quotation of some t_1 such that $t \longrightarrow^* t_1$.*

Proof. The proof is by induction upon the length of the reduction to v.

If t is an operator O then the only factorable form $\texttt{enact}\ 't$ can reduce to is $'O$ as required.

If t is an application $r\ u$ then any reduction of $\texttt{enact}\ 't$ produces the term $\texttt{enact1}\ (\texttt{enact}\ 'r\ 'u)$. Now if $\texttt{enact}\ 't$ is to produce a factorable form then $\texttt{enact}\ 'r$ must reduce to a factorable form which, by induction, is some $'v_1$ where v_1 is factorable. Now consider the cases of `enact1` in turn. If v_1 is Y then the whole reduces to $\texttt{enact}\ ('u\ (B\ Y\ 'u))$ which is $\texttt{enact}\ 't_1$ where $t_1 = u\ (Y\ u)$ arises from the reduction of t. Now apply induction to t_1.

Similar arguments apply if v_1 is of the form $K\ x_2$ or $S\ x_3\ x_2$.

Suppose that v_1 is of the form $F\ x_3\ x_2$. If the whole is to produce a factorable form then $\texttt{enact}\ 'x_3$ must produce a factorable form which, by induction, must be a quotation $'p_1$ where $x_3 \longrightarrow^* p_1$. If p_1 is an operator O then $\texttt{evalop}\ 'p_1$ reduces to O and the whole reduces to $\texttt{enact}\ 'x_2$ so induction applies as $F\ x_3\ x_2\ x_1 \longrightarrow x_2$. Alternatively, if p_1 is a compound $p_2\ p_3$ then the whole reduces to $\texttt{enact}\ ('u\ 'p_2\ 'p_3)$ to which induction can be applied.

Suppose that v_1 is of the form $B\ x_4\ x_3\ x_2$. Then the whole produces $'(v_1\ u)$ which is a quotation of a reduct of t.

Suppose that v_1 is of the form $x_5\ x_4\ x_3\ x_2$. Then it must be that x_5 is E. Now proceed as before.

Otherwise, $v_1\ u$ is a factorable form and the whole reduces to $'(v_1\ u)$ as required. □

THEOREM 6.5. *If t is a term such that* `enact` *$'t$ reduces to some factorable form n then t reduces to some factorable form v. Conversely, if t reduces to some factorable form v then* `enact` *$'t$ reduces to $'v$. Hence* `enact` *is a self-enactor for the blocking factorisation calculus.*

Proof. If `enact` $'t$ has a factorable form, then apply Lemma 6.4. Conversely, suppose that $t \longrightarrow^* v$ where v is factorable. By Lemma 6.3, `enact` $'t$ and `enact` $'v$ have a common reduct and Lemma 6.2 implies that the latter term evaluates to $'v$ which is normal, as required. □

7. Static Type System

7.1 Overview

We approach typing from a Curry-style perspective, in that the terms are fixed in advance, with types merely used to describe terms. This has several consequences, which will be noted when appropriate. Our type system uses the types of System F [13], given by

$$T ::= X \mid T \to T \mid \forall X.T$$

where $X, Y Z, \ldots$ are meta-variables for *type variables*, and U and T are meta-variables for *types*. These are much simpler than those of F^*_ω. The key enabler is the ability to factorise functions in situ, without rising a level in the type hierarchy.

Each operator O other than E has a *principal type* $\mathsf{Ty}[O]$ of the form

$$\begin{array}{lcl} Y & : & (X \to X) \to X \\ K & : & X \to Y \to X \\ S & : & (X \to Y \to Z) \to (X \to Y) \to X \to Z \\ F & : & X \to Y \to (\forall Z.(Z \to X) \to Z \to Y) \to Y \\ B & : & X \to X\,. \end{array}$$

For later convenience, these types are not quantified, but the type variables are typically assumed fresh.

The types for Y, S and K are all standard. Indeed, there is an embedding of Curry-style System F [3] into the blocking factorisation calculus. Hence, the undecidability of type inference for System F [39] carries over to here. However, we have designed and implemented a partial type inference algorithm that can type check our self-interpreters and also catch some mistakes in self-interpreters.

The operator B has type $X \to X$. A consequence of the type of B is that our notion of quotation is type-preserving: if a program has type T, then its representation has type T, too. This shows that different quotations may have different types. An alternative would be to follow Rendel, Ostermann, and Hofer and introduce a new type Expr T of program representations so that terms cannot be confused with their representations; we leave this for future work.

Following Jay and Given-Wilson [17], the type for F contains a quantified argument type

$$\forall Z.(Z \to X) \to Z \to Y\,.$$

The variable Z is used to represent the unknown type of the second component of a compound. This is unnecessary when every pattern is headed by a constructor that determines the types, but knowing that the pattern $x\ z$ has type X conveys no information about the type Z of z.

It is easy to specify a type scheme for E, namely

$$X \to X \to Y \to Y \to Y$$

but this is not sufficiently general to type the pattern-matching functions of interest, as each case may have a type that specialises the default type with respect to its pattern. For example, consider an extension of the form

$$O \to s \mid r$$

where $r : U \to T$ and $s : S$. Its de-sugared form is

$$\lambda^* x.E\ O\ x\ s\ (r\ x) = S(S(E\ O)(K\ s))r\,.$$

Now this should have type $U \to T$ so take $x : U$. Then E must have type

$$\mathsf{Ty}[O] \to U \to S \to T \to T\,.$$

Of course, this is type-safe if $S = T$ but, following the approach developed in pattern calculus [16], it is enough that any solution of $\mathsf{Ty}[O] = U$ also solves $S = T$.

Define $\{T_1 = T_2\}$ to be the *most general unifier* of T_1 and T_2. This is computed in the obvious manner, using α-conversion to align quantified type variables.

Returning to our example, $S = \{\mathsf{Ty}[O] = U\}T$ and so E must have the type

$$E : \mathsf{Ty}[O] \to U \to \{\mathsf{Ty}[O] = U\}T \to T \to T$$

for any operator O other than E. It is clear from this that E cannot have a principal type, and so is excluded from this analysis.

This is good enough for the Curry-style, but from the perspective of the Church-style, or types-as-propositions, this is all very ad hoc, and yet it is not clear how the situation might be better managed. The typing suggests that E be replaced by a family of operators E_O for each operator O. Yet each of these would in turn require an equality operator, even though they would not have principal types. We leave such considerations to future work.

There remains the challenge of typing patterns involving E itself. To date, we have not found a technique that works, and so will confine attention to the self-enactor in Figure 4 in which E does not appear explicitly.

A final issue concerns the typing of lambda-abstractions. When type-level operations are explicit in System F then the standard approach to instantiating a quantified type asserts that if $t : \forall X.T$ then $t : \{U/X\}T$ for any type U. However, given $f : S \to \forall X.T$ then the instantiation of X is achieved by first applying f to some fresh variable $x : S$ then instantiating at U and finally abstracting with respect to x to get $\lambda x.f\ x\ U : S \to \{U/X\}T$. In the Curry-style, this becomes $\lambda x.f\ x : S \to \{U/X\}T$. Mitchell [24], and later Remy [30], considered the consequences of adding η-contraction to System F. For us, the situation is not quite the same, as $\lambda^* x.f\ x$ is *defined* to be f. So we require a type-derivation rule of the form

$$\frac{t : S \to \forall X.T}{t : S \to \{U/X\}T}\,.$$

More generally, we need a subsumption rule with respect to a type instantiation relation $\prec$ which generalises the usual type manipulations.

7.2 Typing Rules

A *context* is given by a sequence Δ of type variables, so that the judgments take the form $\Delta \vdash T_1 \prec T_2$ which asserts that T_2 is an instance of T_1 in context Δ. For example, $\Delta \vdash T \prec \forall X.T$ whenever X is not free in Δ.

The rules for the *type instantiation order* $\prec$ are given in Figure 5, where $\mathsf{FV}(S)$ is the free type variables of S.

A *type context* Γ is a sequence of distinct, typed term variables $x_1 : T_1, \ldots, x_n : T_n$ as usual. The *free type variables* $\mathsf{FV}(\Gamma)$ of Γ is the union of the free type variables of each type T_i appearing within it. The type derivation rules are given in Figure 6.

$$\frac{}{\Delta \vdash \forall X.T \prec [U/X]T} \qquad \frac{}{\Delta \vdash T \prec \forall X.T}\ X \notin \Delta$$

$$\frac{\Delta, \mathsf{FV}(S) \vdash T_1 \prec T_2}{\Delta \vdash S \to T_1 \prec S \to T_2} \qquad \frac{\Delta \vdash S_2 \prec S_1}{\Delta \vdash S_1 \to T \prec S_2 \to T}$$

Figure 5. Type Instantiation

THEOREM 7.1. *If* $\Gamma \vdash t : T$ *and* $t \longrightarrow u$ *then* $\Gamma \vdash u : T$.

Proof. Consider the reduction $E\ O\ O\ s\ t \longrightarrow s$. Since U is a type for O and $v = \{U = \mathsf{Ty}[O]\}$ exists it follows that the domain of v can be limited to the free type variables of $\mathsf{Ty}[O]$ so that $t : \{\mathsf{Ty}[O] = U\}T = T$ as required. That the other reduction rules preserve typing is routine. □

7.3 Derived Typing Rules

LEMMA 7.2. *The following rule can be derived for abstractions*

$$\frac{\Gamma, x : U \vdash t : T}{\Gamma \vdash \lambda^* x.t : U \to T}\ .$$

Proof. The proof is by induction on the structure of the type derivation for t. If the last step in the derivation uses a type instantiation $\mathsf{FV}(\Gamma, x : U) \vdash T_1 \prec T$ then it follows that $\mathsf{FV}(\Gamma) \vdash U \to T_1 \prec U \to T$ so induction applies. The remaining possibilities follow the structure of t. If t is x then T is U and so $\lambda^* x.x = I : \forall X.X \to X \prec U \to U = U \to T$ as required. If x is not free in t then $\lambda^* x.t = K\ t$ and $\Gamma \vdash K\ t : U \to T$ as required. If t is of the form $r\ x$ where x is not free in r then $\lambda^* x.r\ x$ is r. Now the type derivation for t ends with some

$$\frac{\Gamma, x : U \vdash r : U_1 \to T \quad \Gamma, x : U \vdash x : U_1}{\Gamma, x : U \vdash r\ x : T}\ .$$

It follows that $\mathsf{FV}(\Gamma, x : U) \vdash U \prec U_1$ and so $\mathsf{FV}(\Gamma, x : U) \vdash U_1 \to T \prec U \to T$ by contravariance of the order with respect to argument types, which yields the desired typing for r. Otherwise, if t is an application $t_1\ t_2$ then there are types T_1 and T_2 such that $\Gamma \vdash t_1 : T_2 \to T$ and $\Gamma \vdash t_2 : T_2$. By two applications of induction, it follows that $\Gamma \vdash \lambda^* x.t_1 : U \to T_2 \to T$ and $\Gamma \vdash \lambda^* x.t_2 : U \to T_2$ whence $\lambda^* x.t = S(\lambda^* x.t_1)(\lambda^* x.t_2)$ has type $U \to T$ as required.

□

The intended typing rules for extensions depend upon patterns taking their most general types, as described by type judgments of the form $\Delta; B \vdash p : P$ where Δ is as before and B (big beta) is a type context in which each term takes a mono-type. The rules are presented in Figure 7. In the last rule it is implicit that the type variables in Δ_1, Δ_2 and X are distinct. Note that E does not have a principal type, and so cannot appear in patterns.

THEOREM 7.3. *The following rule can be derived for extensions*

$$\frac{\Gamma \vdash r : U \to T \quad \Delta; B \vdash p : P \quad v(\Gamma, B) \vdash s : vT \qquad \Delta \cap (\mathsf{FV}(\Gamma) \cup \mathsf{FV}(U \to T)) = \{\} \quad v = \{U = P\}}{\Gamma \vdash p \to s \mid r : U \to T}\ .$$

Proof. The proof is by induction upon the structure of p.

If p is a variable then apply Lemma 7.2.

If p is an operator O other than E then $p \to s \mid r = \lambda^* x.E\ O\ x\ s\ (r\ x) : U \to T$ as required.

If p is an application $p_1 p_2$ then $p \to s \mid r = \lambda^* x.F\ x\ (r\ x)$ $(\lambda^* y.(p_1 \to (p_2 \to s \mid r'\ y) \mid r')\ y)$ where $r' = S(K\ r)$. This has type $U \to T$ if there is derivation of

$$\Gamma, y : Z \to U \vdash (p_1 \to (p_2 \to s \mid r'\ y) \mid r')\ y : Z \to T$$

or, equivalently

$$\Gamma, y : Z \to U \vdash p_1 \to (p_2 \to s \mid r'\ y) \mid r' : (Z \to U) \to Z \to T\ .$$

Now the typing of the pattern $p_1\ p_2$ is of the form

$$\frac{\Delta_1; B_1 \vdash p_1 : P_1 \quad \Delta_2; B_2 \vdash p_2 : P_2}{\Delta_1, \Delta_2; v(B_1, B_2) \vdash p_1\ p_2 : vX}\ v = \{P_1 = P_2 \to X\}.$$

Hence, it is enough to prove that

$$v_1(\Gamma, y : Z \to U, B_1) \vdash p_2 \to s \mid r'\ y : v_1(Z \to T)$$

where $v_1 = \{P_1 = Z \to U\}$. Since $r'\ y$ has the desired type, this hold s if

$$v_2(v_1(\Gamma, B_1, B_2)) \vdash s : v_2(v_1 T)$$

where $v_2 = \{P_2 = v_1 Z\}$. Further, we have the premise

$$\{U = vX\}(v(\Gamma, B_1, B_2)) \vdash s : \{U = vX\}(v(T))\ .$$

Hence, it is enough to show that the restrictions of the compositions $v_2 \circ v_1$ and $\{U = vX\} \circ v$ to Γ, B_1, B_2 and T are the same.

Now the former is the most general solution of $P_1 = Z \to U$ and $Z = P_2$ or, equivalently, of $P_1 = P_2 \to U$ and $Z = P_2$. Similarly, the latter is the most general solution of $P_1 = P_2 \to X$ and $X = U$ or, equivalently, of $P_1 = P_2 \to U$ and $X = U$. As neither restriction involves X or Z it follows that both are simply $\{P_1 = P_2 \to U\}$. □

$$\frac{x : T \in \Gamma}{\Gamma \vdash x : T}$$

$$\frac{}{\Gamma \vdash O : \mathsf{Ty}[O]}$$

$$\frac{\mathsf{FV}(\mathsf{Ty}[O]) \cap \mathsf{FV}(U \to T) = \{\}}{\Gamma \vdash E : \mathsf{Ty}[O] \to U \to \{\mathsf{Ty}[O] = U\}T \to T \to T}$$

$$\frac{\Gamma \vdash t : U \to T \quad \Gamma \vdash u : U}{\Gamma \vdash t\ u : T}$$

$$\frac{\Gamma \vdash t : T_1 \quad \mathsf{FV}(\Gamma) \vdash T_1 \prec T_2}{\Gamma \vdash t : T_2}$$

Figure 6. Type Rules for Terms

COROLLARY 7.4. *The following rule can be derived for extensions*

$$\frac{\Gamma \vdash r : \forall X.X \to X \quad \Delta; B \vdash p : X \quad \Gamma, B \vdash s : X \qquad \mathsf{FV}(\Gamma) \cap \Delta = \{\}}{\Gamma \vdash p \to s \mid r : \forall X.X \to X}\ .$$

Proof. Instantiate the type of r to be $Y \to Y$ for some fresh variable Y and apply the theorem with $\{Y = X\}$ mapping Y to X. □

Note that although the corollary above will be sufficient to type our self-interpreters, it is not clear how to prove the corollary without first proving the more general theorem, since the typing of an extension with a compound pattern requires unification to handle the quantified type of the third argument of F.

7.4 Type Checking the Self-Interpreters

THEOREM 7.5. *We have* $\Gamma \vdash t : T$ *if and only if* $\Gamma \vdash {}'t : T$.

Proof. Each direction is straightforward by induction on t. □

THEOREM 7.6. *The function* `equal` *defined in Section 5 has typing*

$$\emptyset \vdash \mathtt{equal} : \forall X.\forall Y.X \to Y \to \mathtt{Bool}$$

$$\frac{}{X; x : X \vdash x : X} \qquad \frac{}{\mathsf{FV}(\mathsf{Ty}[O]) \vdash O : \mathsf{Ty}[O]}$$

$$\frac{\Delta_1; B_1 \vdash p_1 : P_1 \quad \Delta_2; B_2 \vdash p_2 : P_2}{\Delta_1, \Delta_2, X; \upsilon(B_1, B_2) \vdash p_1\, p_2 : \upsilon X}\ \upsilon = \{P_1 = P_2 \to X\}$$

Figure 7. Type Rules for Patterns

where Bool $= \forall Z.Z \to Z \to Z$.

Proof. This is a consequence of derived type inference rule for extensions. The calculations are relatively straightforward since the body of each case has the same type `Bool`. □

THEOREM 7.7. *The self-recogniser* `unquote` *defined in Section 5 has typing*

$$\emptyset \vdash \texttt{unquote} : \forall X.X \to X\ .$$

Proof. Apply Corollary 7.4. □

THEOREM 7.8. *The self-enactor defined in Figure 4 has type*

$$\emptyset \vdash \texttt{enact} : \forall X.X \to X\ .$$

Proof. The proof is by repeated applications of Corollary 7.4. □

Notice that we can easily type check self-applications of `unquote` and `enact`, such as `enact('enact)`.

7.5 Adequacy

A weakness of our approach is that the type system does not distinguish terms from their quotations. A more refined approach associates to each type T a new type form `Expr` T to type its quoted expressions. Then quotation is said to be *adequate* [31] if each closed normal form of type `Expr` T is the quotation of some term.

Future work may well adapt the self-interpreters given here to make them adequate. In the meantime, observe that there is not much scope for confusion, as there is a simple test for being a quotation, given by

```
let rec isquote =
  B (x y) -> false
| B x -> true
| x y -> isquote x && (isquote y)
| x -> false
```

where `&&` is conjunction. Similarly, given an interpretation of strings there is a pretty printer for quotations given by

```
let rec pretty_print  =
  B Y -> "Y"
| B K -> "K"
| B S -> "S"
| B F -> "F"
| B E -> "E"
| B B -> "B"
| x y -> pretty_print x ^ "(" ^ pretty_print y ^ ")"
| x -> "<not a quotation>"
```

8. Experimental Results

We have two implementations of both reduction and desugaring, one in bondi [7] and one in Scheme.

Type inference in the **bondi** interpreter confirms that all examples have the expected types. For example, `enact` in Figure 4 has the same type as the polymorphic identity function. The inference algorithm adapts the standard techniques by adding a rule for typing extensions. This is delicate as it is not obvious how any type substitutions required to infer a type for the body of the extension can be incorporated into the result without forcing the default to take the type of the special case. For our purposes, it is sufficient to merely check the type of the body, without propagating any changes.

In converting the (well-typed) extensions into combinators, it is worth adopting some optimisations when de-sugaring extensions with compound patterns.

A common situation concerns

$$p\, x \to s \mid r$$

which, when de-sugared, reduces to

$$S\ (S\ F\ r)(K(p \to \lambda^* x.s \mid (S(K\ r))).$$

Otherwise, when desugaring $p\, q \to s \mid r$ the default term r appears three times. When this is inefficient, the extension $p \to s \mid r$ will be interpreted by its β-expansion

$$(\lambda^* x.(p \to s \mid x))\ r$$

to avoid the copying.

After de-sugaring, `unquote` is:

```
Y(S(K(S(S(K S)(S F))(S(K K)(S(K(S(S(E B)(K(S K K)))))
(S(K S) K)))))(S(K(S(S F(S K K))))(S(K K)(S(S(K S)
(S(K(S(K S)))(S(K K))))K))))
```

which is built from 50 operators. The combinator for `enact` is shown in Figure 8; it uses 1185 operators. Both work fine in all our experiments, which have tested all of the cases in the extensions used in defining `enact`.

9. Related Work on Typed Self-Interpretation

A major source of difficulties for static type checking is that programs must be of function type, while their quotations must be data structures, amenable to analysis. The issues are well illustrated by Naylor's [28] self-interpreter for Haskell that has type:

$$\texttt{[(FunId, Exp)]} \to \texttt{Exp}\ .$$

The input is a list of function definitions that each pairs a function identifier with an expression, and the output is also an expression. The key thing to note is that the type `Exp` is a tagged union of integers, variables, abstractions, applications, etc:

```
data Exp =  App Exp Exp   |  Lambda VarId Exp
         |  Fun FunId     |  Var VarId
         |  Int Int       |  Lam (Exp -> Exp)
```

This type supports pattern-matching of the traditional kind (driven by the structure of an algebraic data type) but also brings some disadvantages too. Note that, although it is straightforward to decide equality of the five forms of expression that are used to represent input programs, the presence of arbitrary Haskell functions (tagged by the constructor `Lam`) within expressions will complicate any analysis of interpretations. More significant for the typing is that the resulting quotation process gives all program representations the same type `Exp`, which severely limits the usefulness of static type checking. The self-interpreter uses tagging and untagging operations at every step of computation, which amounts to little more than dynamic type checking.

Others have used tags in a similar manner, including Rossberg in his self-interpreter [34] for Standard ML, and Läufer and Odersky [22] in their self-interpreter for a typed version of the SK combinator calculus. Taha, Makholm, and Hughes [36], and also Danvy and López [10], showed how to eliminate superfluous tags.

```
Y(S(S(S(KS)(S(KK)(S(S(KS)(S(KK)(S(K(S(K(S(SF(SKK))))))(S(K(S(KK))(S(K(S(S(KS)(S(KK)(S(KS)K))))K)))))(S(S(KS)(S(KK)(S
(K(S(S(KS)(SF))))(S(K(S(KK))(S(S(KS)(S(KK)(S(K(S(S(KS)(SF))))(S(K(S(KK))(S(S(KS)(S(K(S(KS)))(S(S(KS)(S(K(S(KS)))(S(K
(S(K(S(KS)))))(S(K(S(K(S(K(S(EB))))))(S(K(S(K(S(KK)))))(S(S(KS)(S(KK)(S(KS)(S(KK)(S(KS)(S(K(S(EY)))(S(KK)(S(S(KS)K)(K
(S(SKK)(BY))))))))))(K(S(KS)K)))))))(K(S(KK)(S(KS)K))))))(K(K(SKK)))))))(K(S(KS)K))))))(S(S(KS)(S(KK)(S(K(S(S(KS)(
SF))))(S(K(S(KK)))(S(K(S(S(KS)(S(K(SF))(S(KS)K)))))(S(K(S(KK)))(S(S(KS)(S(KK)(S(K(S(S(KS)(SF))))(S(K(S(KK)))(S(S(KS)(S
(K(S(KS)))(S(S(KS)(S(K(S(KS)))(S(K(S(K(S(KS)))))(S(K(S(K(S(K(S(EB))))))(S(K(S(K(S(KK)))))(S(S(KS)(S(KK)(S(KS)(S(KK)(S
(KS)(S(K(S(EK)))(S(KK)(S(S(KS)(S(KK)(S(KS)K)))(KK)))))))))(K(S(KS)K)))))))(K(S(KK)(S(KS)K))))))(K(K(SKK)))))))(K(S(K
S)(S(KK)(S(KS)K))))))))))(S(S(KS)(S(KK)(S(K(S(S(KS)(SF))))(S(K(S(KK)))(S(K(S(S(KS)(S(K(SF))(S(KS)K)))))(S(K(S(KK)))(S
(K(S(S(KS)(S(K(SF))(S(KS)(S(KK)(S(KS)K)))))))(S(K(S(KK)))(S(S(KS)(S(KK)(S(K(S(S(KS)(SF))))(S(K(S(KK)))(S(S(KS)(S(K(S(K
S)))(S(S(KS)(S(K(S(KS)))(S(K(S(K(S(KS)))))(S(K(S(K(S(K(S(EB))))))(S(K(S(K(S(KK)))))(S(S(KS)(S(KK)(S(KS)(S(KK)(S(KS)(S
(K(S(ES)))(S(KK)(S(S(KS)(S(KK)(S(KS)(S(KK)(S(KS)K)))))(KS)))))))))(K(S(KS)K)))))))(K(S(KK)(S(KS)K))))))(K(K(SKK)))))
))(K(S(KS)(S(KK)(S(KS)(S(KK)(S(KS)K)))))))))))))(S(S(KS)(S(K(S(K(S(S(KS)(SF))))))(S(K(S(K(S(KK)))))(S(K(S(K(S(S(KS)(
S(K(SF))(S(KS)K)))))))(S(K(S(K(S(KK)))))(S(K(S(K(S(S(KS)(S(K(SF))(S(KS)(S(KK)(S(KS)K))))))))(S(K(S(K(S(KK)))))(S(S(KS
)(S(K(S(KS)))(S(K(S(KK)))(S(K(S(K(S(S(KS)(SF))))))(S(K(S(K(S(KK)))))(S(S(KS)(S(K(S(KS)))(S(K(S(K(S(KS)))))(S(S(KS)(S(K
(S(KS)))(S(K(S(K(S(KS)))))(S(K(S(K(S(K(S(KS)))))))(S(K(S(K(S(K(S(K(S(EB))))))))(S(K(S(K(S(K(S(KK)))))))(S(S(KS)(S(K(S
(KS)))(S(K(S(KK)))(S(K(S(KS)))(S(K(S(KK)))(S(K(S(KS)))(S(K(S(K(S(EF)))))(S(K(S(KK)))(S(S(KS)(S(KK)(S(KS)(S(KK)(S(KS)(S
(KK)(S(KS)K)))))))(K(S(KF)))))))))))(K(K(S(KS)K))))))))))(K(K(S(KK)(S(KS)K))))))))(K(K(K(SKK))))))))))(K(K(S(KS)(S(KK
)(S(KS)(S(KK)(S(KS)K))))))))))))))(S(K(S(K(S(S(KS)(SF))(S(KK)(S(S(KS)(S(K(SF))(S(KS)K)))(S(KK)(S(S(KS)(S(K(SF))(S(KS)
(S(KK)(S(KS)K)))))(S(KK)(S(S(KS)(S(K(SF))(S(KS)(S(KK)(S(KS)(S(KK)(S(KS)K)))))))(S(KK)(S(K(S(S(KS)(SF))(S(KK)(S(S(KS)(S
(S(KS)(S(K(S(KS)))(S(K(S(K(S(EB)))))(S(K(S(KK)))(S(K(S(K(S(S(EB)(K(BB)))))))(S(KS)K))))))(S(KK)(S(KS)K)))(K(SKK)))))
(S(KS)(S(KK)(S(KS)(S(KK)(S(KS)(S(KK)(S(KS)K)))))))))))))))))(S(K(S(K(S(SF(SKK))))))(S(K(S(KK)))(S(K(S(K(S(SF(S(K(SKK
))))))))(S(K(S(KK)))(S(K(S(K(S(SF(S(K(S(K(SKK)))))))))(S(K(S(KK)))(S(K(S(K(S(SF(S(K(S(K(S(K(SKK))))))))))))(S(K(S(KK)
))(S(K(S(K(S(SF(S(K(S(K(S(K(S(K(SKK))))))))))))))(S(K(S(KK)))(S(S(KS)(S(K(S(KS)))(S(K(S(K(S(EB)))))(S(K(S(KK)))(S(S(KS
)(S(KK)(S(KS)(S(KK)(S(KS)(S(KK)(S(KS)(S(KK)(S(KS)(S(KK)(S(KS)K))))))))))))(K(S(S(KS)(S(K(S(KS)))(S(K(S(K(S(KS)))))(S(K(
S(K(S(KK)))))(S(K(S(S(KS)K)))K)))))(S(KK)K))))))))(K(K(S(K(S(K(S(K(S(K(S(K(S(K(SKK))))))))))))))))))))))))))))))(S(K(S(S
(KS)K)))K))(K(S(SF(SKK))(K(S(S(EB)(K(SKK)))(S(K(SKK)))))))
```

Figure 8. `enact` de-sugared

In the examples above, tags arise as constructors of an algebraic data type of expressions. Certainly, our approach is not tagged in this sense. Rather, intensionality is built into the calculus in a fundamental way. Since equality is decidable for normal forms, including operators, there is no need for any additional tagging.

Before these efforts, Hagiya [14] presented a self-interpreter for a λ-calculus which implicitly defines a type system and does dynamic type checking.

While typing is unnecessary for self-interpretation in general, we are inspired by typability-preserving compilers [27] that compile a typed source program to a typed target program and enable implementers to catch compiler errors by type checking the target program.

An entirely different approach to typed interpretation is to use polymorphic types instead of a single universal type for all program representations. Significant progress in this direction was made by Pfenning and Lee [29] who studied the polymorphic λ-calculus and presented an interpreter for F_2 written in F_3 as well as an interpreter for F_ω written in F_ω^+, and by Carette, Kiselyov, and Shan [9] who wrote tagless interpreters in OCaml and Haskell for a simply-typed λ-calculus. They showed the viability of program representations with polymorphic types, without presenting self-interpreters.

The literature contains just one example (as far as we know) of a self-interpreter for a statically-typed language without a universal type. Rendel, Ostermann, and Hofer [31] presented a self-recogniser for F_ω^*, which is an extension of the higher-order polymorphic λ-calculus F_ω that has a type:type rule. The self-recogniser has type:

$$\forall X.(\mathsf{Expr}\ X) \to X$$

Their notion of quotation is *type-monomorphic* in that if $'s$ and $'t$ have the same type, then s and t have the same type too. Equivalently, terms of distinct types yield representations of distinct types. The use of type-monomorphic quotation is a radical departure from the use of a single universal type for all program representations, where all $'s$ and $'t$ have the same type, irrespectively of the types of s and t. They presented a self-recogniser (not strong), and left open the problems of writing an equality checker and a self-enactor. Their results inspired our work.

Rendel, Ostermann, and Hofer discuss the notion of typed self-representation, that is, "representing terms of a programming language in the language itself" [31, Section 2], and list five desirable properties. Let us evaluate how many of those properties our language, type system, and self-interpreters have. We list each property in *this font*, followed by our evaluation.

1. **Representation.** *There is a family of types* $(\mathsf{Expr}\ T)$ *such that* $'t$ *has type* $(\mathsf{Expr}\ T)$ *if and only if* t *has type* T. We use $(\mathsf{Expr}\ T) = T$ and the stated equivalence is our Theorem 7.5.
2. **Adequacy.** *Every term* s *of type* $(\mathsf{Expr}\ T)$ *corresponds to a term* t *of type* T, *which means that for every* s *as above there exists a* t *such that* $s = {'t}$. Our definition of quotation doesn't have this property; the reason is that we use $(\mathsf{Expr}\ T) = T$ so an unquoted term of type T also has type $(\mathsf{Expr}\ T)$.
3. **First class interpretations.** *It is possible to express operations on quoted terms so that they are well-typed for all terms of type* $(\mathsf{Expr}\ T)$, *without the need to refer to any specific such terms.* Our language doesn't have this property; rather, we use pattern matching pervasively.
4. **Self interpretation.** *There is a family of contexts* $\mathsf{eval}_T\langle\rangle$ *such that* $\mathsf{eval}_T\langle 't\rangle$ *is observationally equivalent to* t *if* t *has type* T. This property is essentially Equation (1) which is implied by our Theorem 5.2.
5. **Reflection.** $'t$ *exhibits the intensional structure of* t *in a useful way.* Our self-enactor is a good example of how we can make good use of the intensional structure of a quoted term.

In summary, our language, type system, and self-interpreters have three of those properties (1,4,5), while our language intentionally doesn't have property 3, and we leave property 2 for future work.

The approach of Rendel, Ostermann, and Hofer can be characterised as follows. A function at one level of the type hierarchy can be tagged to become a data structure at the next level. This requires a countable sequence of levels. By contrast, the ability to factorise means that functions (in normal form) *are already* data structures without any need to tag them or shift levels. Hence, the types of System F are good enough.

The other notable difference is that both applications of terms to types, and type abstractions, are explicit in their work but implicit here. This saves us from having to factorise type applications, but at the cost of type inference being undecidable.

10. Future Work

The use of factorisation to support self-interpreters raises many interesting questions about foundations and self-interpretation, as well as several practical questions.

When pattern-matching is driven by the definition of an algebraic data type then it is easy to decide whether a pattern-matching function covers all cases, but here "all cases" must include every factorable form of the calculus. Such analyses of coverage await development. In practice, such open-ended, or *extensible* functions prove quite useful. For example, a pretty-printer of type $\forall X.X \rightarrow$ `String` may have default behaviour that produces an exception, but as new types are declared, new cases are added for the new term forms.

It seems likely that the calculus without the fixpoint operator Y is strongly normalising, for reasons similar to those for *query calculus* [16] which extends System F with generic queries for searching and updating. A more interesting challenge is whether the results in this paper can be applied to a strongly normalising calculus. After all, if the basic calculus is strongly normalising, why shouldn't the interpretations be so too? To put it another way, can the Y operator be replaced by something that is strongly normalising?

By contrast, the denotational semantics of factorisation is quite undeveloped. For example, there is not yet an account of compounds and atoms in category theory.

Open questions within self-interpretation include the following. Is there a self-interpreter that is adequate, in the sense of Rendel, Ostermann, and Hofer? This seems plausible, at the price of making everything somewhat more obscure. Is there a self-interpreter for a language with decidable type-checking? This is a harder question, since it is not clear how to factorise the application of a term to a type.

Practical questions include the following. Does the calculus admit an efficient implementation? This seems plausible, since factorisation is a formalisation of the `car` and `cdr` of Lisp. Can these techniques be applied to λ-abstractions without first converting to combinators? How easy is it to adapt the given self-interpreters to explore alternative interpretations, e.g. to handle closures?

11. Conclusion

The blocking factorisation calculus is statically typed and supports a quotation mechanism that preserves types and supports both a typed self-recogniser and a typed self-enactor. Building on the ground-breaking work of Rendel, Ostermann, and Hofer, it brings the status of self-interpreters for typed calculi close to the standard set for pure λ-calculus by Mogensen and then Berarducci and Bohm. Future work may develop strong self-recognisers and self-enactors, and support types of the form `Exp` T for representations that are distinct from the type T of source programs.

The self-recogniser and self-enactors developed for the blocking factorisation calculus have a very natural development as pattern-matching functions. Each evaluation rule becomes a case of the one-step reducer `enact1` with the evaluation strategy captured by the nature of the recursion within which this is embedded. It will be easy enough to modify the strategy, or the reduction rules to suit evolving tastes. In a sense, all self-interpreters can be seen as encodings of such pattern-matching functions.

Further, we anticipate using this approach to model various program transformations, e.g. to produce code in continuation-passing style, and also evaluation strategies involving, say, closures. In general, this work opens up new possibilities for the interpretation of typed programming languages during compiler construction.

More generally, this work illustrates some of the expressive power that the pattern-matching approach brings to bear when one is able to analyse internal structure with the same facility used to apply functions.

Acknowledgments. The second author thanks Oleg Kiselyov, Torben Mogensen, Klaus Ostermann, Frank Pfenning, Andreas Rossberg, Jeff Siskind, Aaron Stump, Walid Taha, and Mitch Wand for discussions about the state of the art of self-interpretation. We thank Thomas Given-Wilson, Shu-yu Guo, Mohsen Lesani, Todd Millstein and Jose Vergara for helpful comments on a draft of the paper.

References

[1] Harold Abelson, Gerald Jay Sussman, and Julie Sussman. *Structure and Interpretation of Computer Programs.* MIT Press, 1985.

[2] Henk Barendregt. Self-interpretations in lambda calculus. *J. Funct. Program*, 1(2):229–233, 1991.

[3] HP Barendregt. *Handbook of Logic in Computer Science (vol. 2): Background: Computational Structures: Abramski,S (ed)*, chapter Lambda Calculi with Types. Oxford University Press, Inc., New York, NY, 1993.

[4] Michel Bel. A recursion theoretic self interpreter for the lambda-calculus. http://www.belxs.com/michel/#selfint.

[5] Alessandro Berarducci and Corrado Böhm. A self-interpreter of lambda calculus having a normal form. In *CSL*, pages 85–99, 1992.

[6] Mathieu Boespflug. From self-interpreters to normalization by evaluation. In Olivier Danvy, editor, *Proceedings of Workshop on Normalization by Evaluation*, 2009.

[7] bondi programming language. `www-staff.it.uts.edu.au/~cbj/bondi`.

[8] Reg Braithwaite. The significance of the meta-circular interpreter. http://weblog.raganwald.com/2006/11/significance-of-meta-circular_22.html, November 2006.

[9] Jacques Carette, Oleg Kiselyov, and Chung chieh Shan. Finally tagless, partially evaluated: Tagless staged interpreters for simpler typed languages. *Journal of Functional Programming*, 19(5):509–543, 2009.

[10] Olivier Danvy and Pablo E. Martínez López. Tagging, encoding, and Jones optimality. In *Proceedings of ESOP'03, European Symposium on Programming*, pages 335–347. Springer-Verlag (*LNCS*), 2003.

[11] Sir Arthur Conan Doyle. *The Sign of the Four.* Lippincott's Monthly Magazine, February 1890.

[12] Brendan Eich. Narcissus. `http://mxr.mozilla.org/mozilla/source/js/narcissus/jsexec.js`, 2010.

[13] J-Y. Girard, Y. Lafont, and P. Taylor. *Proofs and Types.* Tracts in Theoretical Computer Science. Cambridge University Press, 1989.

[14] Masami Hagiya. Meta-circular interpreter for a strongly typed language. *Journal of Symbolic Computation*, 8(6):651–680, 1989.

[15] R. Hindley and J.P. Seldin. *Introduction to Combinators and Lambda-calculus.* Cambridge University Press, 1986.

[16] Barry Jay. *Pattern Calculus: Computing with Functions and Structures.* Springer, 2009.

[17] Barry Jay and Thomas Given-Wilson. A combinatory account of internal structure. *Journal of Symbolic Logic*, 2011. To appear. `http://www-staff.it.uts.edu.au/~cbj/Publications/factorisation.pdf`.

[18] Barry Jay and Delia Kesner. First-class patterns. *Journal of Functional Programming*, 19(2):191–225, 2009.

[19] C.B. Jay. The pattern calculus. *ACM Transactions on Programming Languages and Systems (TOPLAS)*, 26(6):911–937, November 2004.

[20] S.C. Kleene. *Introduction to Methamathematics*. van Nostrand, 1952.

[21] Stephen C. Kleene. λ-definability and recursiveness. *Duke Math. J.*, pages 340–353, 1936.

[22] Konstantin Läufer and Martin Odersky. Self-interpretation and reflection in a statically typed language. In *Proceedings of OOPSLA Workshop on Reflection and Metalevel Architectures*. ACM, October 1993.

[23] Oleg Mazonka and Daniel B. Cristofani. A very short self-interpreter. http://arxiv.org/html/cs/0311032v1, November 2003.

[24] J.C. Mitchell. Polymorphic type inference and containment. *Information and Computation*, 1985.

[25] Torben Æ. Mogensen. Efficient self-interpretations in lambda calculus. *Journal of Functional Programming*, 2(3):345–363, 1992. See also DIKU Report D–128, Sep 2, 1994.

[26] Torben Æ. Mogensen. Linear-time self-interpretation of the pure lambda calculus. *Higher-Order and Symbolic Computation*, 13(3):217–237, 2000.

[27] Greg Morrisett, David Walker, Karl Crary, and Neal Glew. From System F to typed assembly language. In *Proceedings of POPL'98, 25th Annual SIGPLAN–SIGACT Symposium on Principles of Programming Languages*, pages 85–97, 1998.

[28] Matthew Naylor. Evaluating Haskell in Haskell. *The Monad.Reader*, 10:25–33, 2008.

[29] Frank Pfenning and Peter Lee. Metacircularity in the polymorphic λ-calculus. *Theoretical Computer Science*, 89(1):137–159, 1991.

[30] Didier Rémy. Simple, partial type-inference for System F based on type-containment. In *Proceedings of the tenth ACM SIGPLAN international conference on Functional programming*, ICFP '05, pages 130–143, New York, NY, USA, 2005. ACM.

[31] Tillmann Rendel, Klaus Ostermann, and Christian Hofer. Typed self-representation. In *Proceedings of PLDI'09, ACM SIGPLAN Conference on Programming Language Design and Implementation*, pages 293–303, June 2009.

[32] John C. Reynolds. Definitional interpreters for higher-order programming languages. In *Proceedings of 25th ACM National Conference*, pages 717–740. ACM Press, 1972. The paper later appeared in Higher-Order and Symbolic Computation, 11, 363–397 (1998).

[33] Armin Rigo and Samuele Pedroni. Pypy's approach to virtual machine construction. In *OOPSLA Companion*, pages 044–953, 2006.

[34] Andreas Rossberg. HaMLet. http://www.mpi-sws.org/ rossberg/hamlet, 2010.

[35] Fangmin Song, Yongsen Xu, and Yuechen Qian. The self-reduction in lambda calculus. *Theoretical Computer Science*, 235(1):171–181, March 2000.

[36] Walid Taha, Henning Makholm, and John Hughes. Tag elimination and Jones-optimality. In *Proceedings of PADO'01, Programs as Data Objects, Second Symposium*, pages 257–275, 2001.

[37] Terese. *Term Rewriting Systems*, volume 53 of *Tracts in Theoretical Computer Science*. Cambridge University Press, 2003.

[38] John Tromp. Binary lambda calculus and combinatory logic. In *Kolmogorov Complexity and Applications*, 2006. A Revised Version is available at http://homepages.cwi.nl/ tromp/cl/LC.pdf.

[39] J. B. Wells. Typability and type checking in the second-order λ-calculus are equivalent and undecidable. In *Proceedings of LICS'94, Ninth Annual IEEE Symposium on Logic in Computer Science*, 1994.

[40] Wikipedia. Pypy. http://en.wikipedia.org/wiki/PyPy, 2010.

[41] Wikipedia. Rubinius. http://en.wikipedia.org/wiki/Rubinius, 2010.

[42] Tetsuo Yokoyama and Robert Glück. A reversible programming language and its invertible self-interpreter. In *Proceedings of PEPM'07, ACM Symposium on Partial Evaluation and Semantics-Based Program Manipulation*, 2007.

Using Camlp4 for Presenting Dynamic Mathematics on the Web: DynaMoW, an OCaml Language Extension for the Run-Time Generation of Mathematical Contents and their Presentation on the Web

An experience report

Frédéric Chyzak *
INRIA (Rocquencourt, France)
frederic.chyzak@inria.fr

Alexis Darrasse *
LIP6 (Paris, France)
alexis.darrasse@lip6.fr

Abstract

We report on the design and implementation of a programming tool, DynaMoW, to control interactive and incremental mathematical calculations to be presented on the web. This tool is implemented as a language extension of OCaml using Camlp4. Fragments of mathematical code written for a computer-algebra system as well as fragments of mathematical web documents are embedded directly and naturally inside OCaml code. A DynaMoW-based application is made of independent web services, whose parameter types are checked by the OCaml extension. The approach is illustrated by two implementations of online mathematical encyclopedias on top of DynaMoW.

Categories and Subject Descriptors D.1.1 [*PROGRAMMING TECHNIQUES*]: Applicative (Functional) Programming; H.3.5 [*INFORMATION STORAGE AND RETRIEVAL*]: On-line Information Services; I.1.3 [*SYMBOLIC AND ALGEBRAIC MANIPULATION*]: Languages and Systems

General Terms Languages, Web Applications, Computer Algebra, Symbolic Computation

Keywords mathematical encyclopedias, quotations, antiquotations, metaprogramming, web services

1. Introduction

The communication of scientific knowledge is still commonly carried out via written media. Such documents are essentially fixed, even though they can now and then be brought up to date through successive editions. In contrast, the web has in recent times allowed a rapid and reactive diffusion of information, as well as an interactive access to electronic content. Encyclopedias and handbooks specialised in specific fields of mathematics are subject to this change from written media to web content, as their readers now prefer obtaining the mathematical formulas they need online, rather than from books on their shelves. Two ambitious realisations of this kind are the On-Line Encyclopedia of Integer Sequences[1], which is essentially a database with predefined mathematical queries, and the Digital Library of Mathematical Functions[2], which is a human-written mathematical text, specially typeset for the web. Both are successors of best-seller books [1, 5].

But other encyclopedias make essential use of symbolic calculations performed by computer-algebra systems, that is, calculations with terms representing exact algebraic quantities constructed over integers and symbols: polynomials, matrices, differential equations, etc. Two such projects are the Encyclopedia of Combinatorial Structures ("ECS") and the Encyclopedia of Special Functions ("ESF")[3]. There, the symbolic calculations were performed once and their results stored statically, before publishing the web sites. But, in the context of symbolically-generated mathematical knowledge, a natural desire is to perform symbolic computations at run-time. For instance, ECS identifies a combinatorial structure selected by the user through its first terms. The reply by the system consists in a collection of data statically attached to the sequence and merely retrieved from a database: name, combinatorial interpretation, references, etc. A natural wish of the user would be, via new requests, to obtain an arbitrary number of terms of the sequence, or to draw an instance of the structure randomly. This new, dynamic information would be calculated at the time of the request by a computer-algebra server. For its part, ESF provides, for a special function given by the user, a large number of formulas satisfied by the function, and several evaluation graphics. In this output, a series expansion of a certain order, for example, should be extendible at will, based on a user-supplied parameter. Similarly, graphics should be able

* Frédéric Chyzak was partially supported by the Microsoft Research – INRIA Joint Centre and most of the work was done when Alexis Darrasse was a postdoctoral fellow there.

ICFP'11, September 19–21, 2011, Tokyo, Japan.

[1] `http://oeis.org/`

[2] `http://dlmf.nist.gov/`

[3] The first author has maintained some part of ECS and has seen the development of ESF by close colleagues at INRIA.

to be recomputed and replotted interactively with respect to different ranges of the variable.

Part of our project consists in developing these encyclopedias towards more interactivity, and this triggered the development of the present work: a tool to help developing the above-mentioned encyclopedias. More than just assisting the typing and typesetting of mathematical formulas, a human-process that is prone to errors, what we needed was a programming environment for the dynamic (run-time) generation of (mathematical) symbolic content and its presentation online. We view this as *dynamic mathematics on the web*, whence the name of our library and system, DynaMoW[4]. Beside generated encyclopedias, we believe this tool can have applications to design environments whose users are no expert of computer algebra, but need some sort of symbolic calculations following a number of fixed scenarios. This would be the case, for instance, in education.

1.1 Desired Features

On the application level. Our main need was *interactivity*, requiring the ability for run-time symbolic (re)computations. This is well exemplified by our successor of ESF, the Dynamic Dictionary of Mathematical Functions (DDMF)[5] [3]. For example, its end users need to change parameters like: ranges of plots, orders of asymptotic expansions, precisions in numerical evaluations, etc. Likewise, interaction with ECS allows randomness in a page, to display random generated combinatorial structures. Thus, the system to be developed as a programming environment had to be able to simultaneously monitor calculations in a computer-algebra system and the generation of mathematical web documents.

System architecture: proper role of the computer-algebra system. ECS and ESF are based on the general-purpose computer-algebra system Maple[6] for their algebraic manipulations, but new encyclopedias could use other systems, including smaller ones specialised to various branches of mathematics. Besides, specific scientific communities with different habits could conceivably prefer another system, whence the need for possibly several cooperating computer-algebra systems in a future application.

For system tasks, both ECS and ESF have been excessively Maple-centric, with a minimal part of the software in Perl (the CGI). The choice of ESF to perform file manipulations and generation of XML documents inside Maple hinders the versatility towards various computer-algebra systems. Generating Maple and HTML by Perl (ECS) or just HTML by Maple (ESF) goes with heavy quotations of strings of the guest language in print formats, as computer-algebra system is typically not well suited for string manipulations. By not dissociating the application from this generation (ECS), any modification of the application requires changing the quotations again.

For both reasons, implementing the system in a computer-algebra system was not an option, and the main language naturally had to be a general-purpose language.

In addition, as we planned developing applications for end users with limited knowledge of computer-algebra, we could not expect any computer-algebra system to be installed on the user side. Thus, we confined ourselves to a client-server architecture, with no local computation.

Ease of programming and readability. The expected close interaction between symbolic calculations and the rest of the flow control suggested that computer-algebra code could not be kept separate from the rest of the source. In earlier projects, we had implemented as much as possible in the computer-algebra system, with induced heaviness. Here, we wanted several natures of programming languages to be mixed naturally in the same source files: a general-purpose language for the general control flow of the application; one or several computer-algebra languages; some string representation of literal fragments of web documents. Indeed, the ease to merge variables and HTML in PHP[7] has influenced our development.

Also, values have to migrate naturally between computer-algebra systems, control, and presentation, and, for readability, we wanted to be able to write a symbolic expression where it is used in the computer-algebra source code, rather than postponed (if using a notation of formats like with `printf`) or with an interruption in the syntax (if using a notation of concatenated strings). This all spoke in favour of a mechanism of *quotations and antiquotations*.

As to the general-purpose language, the wish for the comfort of a reasonably typed language immediately precluded a computer-algebra system as the main language. (One possible exception could have been Sage, which, however, was not so much developed at the time we started.)

1.2 Related Work

Ocsigen [2] is a complete system that provides facilities for programming the web in a type-safe environment. It is meant as a replacement for the pair Apache/PHP. It is written in OCaml and proposes an OCaml extension, Eliom, to develop OCaml applications. Our system DynaMoW works on the same level as Eliom and could be extended into a module for Ocsigen, so as to rely on it as a web server.

The free open-source mathematics software named Sage[8]. This project provides a unified interface to the major free computer-algebra systems in a minimal variant of the Python interpreter. Over the years, Sage has also become a computer-algebra system per se: besides libraries exposed from other systems, new code is being developed natively for Sage. It provides users with a textual read-eval-print loop, and thus is a system potentially used by DynaMoW[9]. Sage also exports a web-presented symbolic shell, which is thus mostly targeted at computer-algebra expert users. Sage embeds literally dozens of computer-algebra systems (whether big, general-purpose ones or smaller, dedicated ones). This makes it a large application (around half a gigabyte to download for the current release, 2.4 GB once uncompressed and installed). By contrast, DynaMoW is designed with web presentation as its main application and is very lightweight. Another difference is that Sage implements all mathematical notions as objects, and manipulates them mostly by interpreted Python libraries, with critical sections written in the related but different compiled language Cython[10], while DynaMoW is intended for compiled OCaml applications and does not require programmers to use any OCaml object facility.

[4] `http://ddmf.msr-inria.inria.fr/DynaMoW/`. Roughly 3800 lines of OCaml code in the current version, DynaMoW-1.0.0beta.

[5] `http://ddmf.msr-inria.inria.fr/`

[6] commercial product by Maplesoft, `http://www.maplesoft.com/`

[7] `http://www.php.net/`. PHP: Hypertext Preprocessor.

[8] `http://www.sagemath.org/`. Sage Mathematics Software.

[9] Indeed, we have a prototype plugin to glue to Sage.

[10] `http://www.cython.org/`. Cython: C-Extensions for Python.

2. Interfacing a Computer-Algebra System

2.1 Types for Values in a Mathematical Shell

Few developers use computer-algebra libraries, and all general-purpose computer-algebra systems behave as symbolic shells, that is, users interact with them through a textual read-eval-print loop. This makes a notion of a *symbolic session* central to the application. The OCaml level in DynaMoW thus makes successive interactions with the symbolic session, and needs to refer to values that persist in the symbolic memory inbetween.

To allow for several computer-algebra systems to be used in the same application, parametrised types have been used to represent symbolic values: the type for external symbolic values is 't DynaMoW.symb, with an abstract type parameter 't exported by the module implementing a computer-algebra system. This parameter can itself be parametrised, to express different datatypes in the same computer-algebra system. Thus, a symbolic value is typically of a type 'a MyCAS.t DynaMoW.symb: the first level of parametrisation protects against using a value from some computer-algebra system with another, while the second level can be used to protect against mixing types within the same system, provided the application properly defines and uses several types for 'a.

2.2 Computer-Algebra Programs as Quotations

In order to embed computer-algebra programs as directly as possible inside OCaml source, the technique of choice is *quotations*, which are available in OCaml by using Camlp4, in the notation <:id<...>>, where id stands for an identifier of the kind of quotation, and ... is the quoted text. We believe that quotations were introduced into the (O)Caml family by Mauny and de Rauglaudre [4].

The main kind of symbolic quotation is of the form <:symb<...>>, and quotes a literal fragment of symbolic code. The interpretation of such a quotation is, after evaluation of the code by a computer-algebra system, a reference to an externally-living symbolic value, represented by some type 'a DynaMoW.symb.

The previous quotation is meaningful for values that can have no OCaml counterpart, and thus have to remain external. Beside this, we made the informal assumption that a computer-algebra system has types that correspond to OCaml int, bool, and string, and designed additional quotations of the forms <:int<...>>, <:bool<...>>, and <:string<...>>, to denote computations whose results can be returned as native OCaml datatypes. As typical programming in a computer-algebra system uses a lot of side effects, we added a quotation <:unit<...>> that evaluates some code in the computer-algebra system, without actually returning any value to OCaml.

Symbolic calculations need to be parametrised by OCaml-generated values. *Antiquotations* are the dual of quotations to address this need, and we followed the Camlp4 notation: the syntax $(tau:expr) appearing in a quoted fragment stands for an escape, to be replaced before symbolic evaluation with a representation of the OCaml expression expr of type tau that can be parsed by the computer-algebra system. Thus,

```
let a = 3 in <:symb< f($(int:a)) >>
```

is intended to evaluate f(3) in the guest language, typically a function call.

Each antiquotation is intended to take the role of a syntactic entity in the guest language. For example,

```
let a = 3 in <:symb< f$(int:a) >>
```

expands as f (3) rather than f3. When Maple is the guest language, the former results in a function call, while the latter would be a Maple name[11]. We do not go beyond this in ensuring the validity of the generated fragment, and in particular we perform no parsing inside quotations.

The type of a <:symb<...>> quotation is 'a MyCAS.t DynaMoW.symb: if the application programmer wants to use different types of symbolic objects, it is his responsibility to confine the use of <:symb<...>> quotations to an unsafe section of the code, and to export safe functions, with more limited types for 'a, to be used in the rest of the application.

2.3 Computer-Algebra System Plugins

Computer-algebra systems can be used with DynaMoW through dedicated plugins, which are modules that abide by a fixed interface. Currently distributed plugins are a well tested Maple plugin, a simple OCaml plugin that serves as an example, as well as experimental Mathematica and Sage plugins. User-implemented plugins can also be developed.

A module is considered a plugin when it exports what enables DynaMoW to view the computer-algebra system as a shell, interacting with it through a read-eval-print loop:

- a type cas_code to store the symbolic commands after expansion of antiquotations inside <:symb<...>> quotations;
- "evaluators" that run a symbolic command and return either a reference to the symbolic result (evaluator_symbolic : cas_code -> 'a t DynaMoW.symb), or a LaTeX representation of the result (evaluator_latex: cas_code -> latex), or an OCaml value (evaluator_int: cas_code -> int for an integer value, and similarly for boolean, strings, etc.);
- a serialisation function, used internally for argument passing between services;
- a function to return a string containing a reference to a symbolic value living in the computer-algebra system, used internally to implement the $(symb:...) antiquotation;
- a start and a reset function, used automatically by DynaMoW to monitor a separate session for each service, so that users do not need to run/quit sessions explicitly;
- additional pretty-printing and related functions.

To simplify the creation of plugins, the provided functor DynaMoW_cas.Shell.Generic should be well adapted to generate plugins for most computer-algebra systems with a command-line interface. This functor takes as input a brief module that contains a string for each symbolic command needed by DynaMoW.

2.4 Interaction between Functional and Imperative Programming Styles

DDMF is the main application developed using DynaMoW. It consists of a mixture of functional code in OCaml and of imperative code in Maple. As of version 1.6, it is made of:

- 5 kloc of OCaml with Maple quotations,
- 8 kloc of generated OCaml with Maple quotations,

[11] For the sake of comparison, the quoted text in the preceding example really expands in the implementation as f((3)), which has the same interpretation as the announced f(3).

- 12 kloc of external Maple library (only a part is used).

At one end of the system, OCaml is used to organise the structure of the produced web documents, the interplay between the web services that produce them, and the interactivity with the user. At the other end, Maple libraries dedicated to the manipulation of the so-called "special functions" of mathematics are called by Maple quotations in the OCaml source. Additionally, one of our goals with DDMF was to keep traces of the underlying symbolic calculations, so as to be able to generate human-readable texts describing the ongoing calculations. Doing so was made possible by *instrumenting* some part of our existing Maple library, Algolib[12]. In quite a few cases, this instrumentation in fact required us to port some of the Maple code to OCaml. What we originally thought would be just syntactic transformation became in a few cases a more involved manual operation.

Maple originally had no kind of records or data structure with named fields. Although records have been introduced in the language (rather recently), efficiency issues remain and, more importantly, a huge amount of legacy code, including a large part of ours, does not use them. Instead, the traditional programming style in Maple bases on "lists", which are in fact immutable arrays of heterogeneous values. The same approach of dereferencing by the position applies to accessing the "fields" of most Maple data structures: terms in a polynomial, coefficients in a series, etc. Additionally, the design of a data structure in a Maple application makes very often the convention that a few of the first or last elements provide information on the rest, which is then a collection of values of the same type. Maple lists being immutable, they are copied when modified, which makes one avoid accumulating values in a list: this would cause a use of memory quadratic in the length of the final list and lead to a slowdown, owing to the interaction of the garbage collector. Instead, the typical idiom is to generate data into a mutable structure (a hash table), before flattening it into a list.

As OCaml lists behave differently, it made no sense to keep this heavier approach in the port, and we constructed OCaml lists directly, by mapping over an integer interval.

Finally, there remains needs for alternative iteration on an iterable Maple data structure and its OCaml counterpart. To this end, we provided two functions

```
symb_of_symb_list : 'a maple list -> 'a maple
symb_list_of_symb : 'a maple -> 'a maple list
```

(`'a maple` is a shorthand for `'a Maple.t DynaMoW.symb`).

The latter takes a Maple object assumed to be a Maple list and returns an OCaml list of Maple objects. The former performs the opposite operation: it inputs an OCaml list of Maple objects and returns a new Maple object, hiding (and forgetting) that it is a Maple list.

3. Interfacing the Mathematical Web

3.1 Services as Modules

A DynaMoW application is structured around special OCaml modules that we call *services*. Rather than OCaml functions, these are independent components, communicating over the network by serialization and deserialisation. Their general role is the computation of symbolic OCaml values enriched with some presentation format. To this end, a service returns a product of the form `doc * obj`, where type `doc` represents a document that can be serialised and served by a CGI and type `obj` is the type of returned values. Services can call one another, taking decisions based on the symbolic values (`obj` types) so as to recombine the document values (`doc` types).

Services share a lot of (parametrised) logistic code, still, they could not be generated by a mere functor application. Instead, a service is declared through a dedicated keyword `let_service` whose expansion by Camlp4 reveals a large boilerplate. The returned module just exports the input and output types of the service, together with the optional default values of its parameters and functions to call it. As an example, suppose we want a service named `LogInt` to calculate the integral of the nth power of the logarithm function. This can be declared as follows:

```
# let_service LogInt (n : int) : string * maple =
    let res = <:symb< int(log(x)^$(int:n), x) >> in
    (<:string< sprintf("%a", $(res)) >>, res)
```

Here the "document" returned by the service is a `string`, the result of letting Maple pretty print the algebraic quantity by `sprintf`; the next section will explain how more general web documents can be generated.

Often, the pair calculated by a service corresponds to the same symbolic value in two forms: the first intended for presentation to the end user, the second for further processing in OCaml. A more pragmatical view is that `obj` is only that part of the computed symbolic object that is really needed in further calculations. So, for some services and typically those that generate a whole web page rather than a section in a web page, `obj` is just OCaml's `unit`. (Compare files `Definition.ml` and `GeneralFormulaForTaylorBound.ml` in the DDMF source, available from the DDMF web site.)

When calling a service, the caller has access to either output via the functions `obj` and `descr`: Function `obj` immediately computes and returns the value in symbolic form:

```
# LogInt.obj (3, ()) ;;
- : LogInt.obj = << ln(x)^3*x-3*x*ln(x)^2+6*x*ln(x)-6*x >>
```

Function `descr` delays evaluation: it creates a descriptor that can later be used with function `DynaMoW_services.Services.call` to obtain the presentation as a string:

```
# let descr = LogInt.descr 3 None ;;
val descr : LogInt.doc_type DynaMoW_services.service_descr
  = <abstr>
# DynaMoW_services.Services.call descr ;;
- : DynaMoW_services.Services.service_type * string =
  ("Binary", "ln(x)^3*x-3*x*ln(x)^2+6*x*ln(x)-6*x")
```

Most computer-algebra systems leave a lot of side effects in a running session. To achieve some context independence of web services, we chose to make each symbolic session local to one service execution. This immobilises much resource, which made it not desirable to allow for recursive services. (And we have not felt the need for it in practice.) To forbid this, the two functions `obj` and `descr` are not exposed to the service definition.

3.2 Web Documents as Nested Quotations

Web documents are structured, tree-like documents that are usually stored in some XML string representation, often a combination of HTML, MathML, SVG, and similar XML dialects. Each variant language is specific to some kind of data to be displayed—MathML for mathematics, SVG for graphics—, but XML dialects all describe static trees. And all such languages share, by nature, a source of heaviness: the markups used to create a very regularly well-balanced

[12] http://algo.inria.fr/libraries/

language. This makes them better suited for automatic document generation than for human generation.

Concerning the generation of dynamic web documents, PHP was our first candidate. But we rejected this choice as it could not accommodate the symbolic code as easily as the document code, and also, we have to admit, for a matter of taste against the programming style. Another option to be considered was JavaScript, which embeds naturally in HTML. JavaScript allows to refer to the document, but in too low a level, and would also not have accommodated the symbolic code nicely.

Just as symbolic programs have been incorporated directly into OCaml code, we wanted to be able to write the pieces of text that make up a mathematical web document as quotations. Additionally, let us remark that some literal mathematics have to be part of the source code, typically to display equations of the form "$f(x)$ = computed value". This could be obtained in DynaMoW by an expression of the form `<:imath<f(x) = $(symb:v)>>`. For the literal part, `f(x) =` in the example, we had to choose a language that a human would easily type, and LaTeX looked like the only reasonable choice: MathML was ruled out by its verbosity. Thus, although we defined few quotation kinds for documents, an added complexity came from more levels of possible nesting, as a consequence of three input kinds that can contribute to texts in documents:

- literal strings, playing a role akin to the "character data" (CDATA) of XML, to write natural-language text;
- literal LaTeX code fragments, which appear as escapes from literal strings to denote a mathematical formula;
- symbolic code fragments, which appear as escapes from LaTeX code to denote a symbolic calculation whose result has to be displayed.

Literal strings with LaTeX escapes are introduced by either of the two quotations kinds `<:par<...>>` and `<:text<...>>`, which correspond respectively: *(i)* to full paragraphs possibly disrupted by displayed mathematical formulas; *(ii)* to linear text used for titles and the like, as well as to portions of sentences that have to receive a special rendering style. Literal LaTeX is introduced by either of the two quotations kinds `<:imath<...>>` and `<:dmath<...>>`, which stand respectively for an inline and for a displayed mathematical formula. Finally, the same notation `<:symb<...>>` as used directly in OCaml allows the inclusion of generated LaTeX, by introducing a symbolic evaluation whose output is converted to LaTeX by the symbolic plugin before presentation. (The plugin will typically use the computer-algebra system for this task if it exports a conversion facility.)

On the implementation side, nesting quotations no longer rely solely on the ability of Camlp4 to detect quoted strings by parsing OCaml. But, fortunately, the analysis of nested quotations does not require more than counting opening and closing parentheses, making the implementation very simple.

In addition to quotations, natural antiquotations allow insertion of simple datatypes in literal text and LaTeX, and content-manipulation functions can next be used to transform or combine the quotation-generated contents. Thus,

```
let l = [2; 3; 5; 7] in let n = List.length l in
List.fold_left
  (fun s a = s @:@ <:par<, $(int:a)>>)
  <:par<There are $(int:n) elements \
    in this list, viz.>> l
```

where (`@:@`) is a DynaMoW operator to merge the contents of two `<:par<...>>`, results in the display

There are 4 *elements in this list, viz.,* 2, 3, 5, 7

More functions combine paragraphs into lists, sections, etc.

These content quotations in DynaMoW have to be contrasted with the quotations proposed by another OCaml-based tool, OCamlDuce, a general XML transducer and validator: its quotations embed general XML strings, including XML markups (or, provided a DTD is given, this can be a string in some XML dialect). By contrast, the `<:par<...>>` and `<:text<...>>` quotations of DynaMoW allow no HTML markup. Indeed, the choice with DynaMoW is to generate a web document by calling constructors directly on subdocuments, much like using the module `XHTML.M` in Eliom, the OCaml language extension that comes with the web programming framework Ocsigen [2]. A difference is that DynaMoW proposes a restricted set of document constructs, rather than arbitrary HTML markups: the rationale here is to make it easier to achieve the uniformity of presentation over a whole generated web site.

3.3 Mathematical Presentation Online

Beside symbolic computations, *mathematical presentation* is another key component of DynaMoW. At the time of writing, no technical solution is as good as what we would want for our purpose, as the existing tools either provide with no completely nice rendering or are too slow for dynamic use, as they were implemented for static-only presentation.

The oldest method for presenting mathematical formulas is to embed Gif or PNG pictures. Fast conversion from LaTeX is nowadays possible on the server, and we use `latex` and `dvipng` for this task. However, this approach is subject to pixelisation when the user zooms in.

A more modern way is to let the client do the rendering. A nice tool for this is jsMath, implemented in JavaScript. Here, mathematical formulas are embedded directly into the web page, using dedicated markups. On the client, jsMath processes the LaTeX, typesetting it very much like LaTeX would, and using LaTeX mathematical fonts for the display. The rendering is very fine, but JavaScript can lead to unwanted latency and can be slow on some systems[13].

MathML is what is presented as the future, although, at the time of writing, it is reliably supported by Firefox only. The rendering is as fast as non-mathematical text, but it is a bit less nice than a typical LaTeX rendering, owing mostly to too rigid alignments. As LaTeX is the necessary format at an intermediate stage of our translation process, we had to use a converter from LaTeX to MathML. We could find no perfect tool for this:

- Distler's itex2MML (in C) is as fast as we need, but it understands a variant of TeX that we could not produce easily (spaces are needed to denote mathematical products) and cannot easily be extended to understand the AMS-TeX constructs we use;
- Miller's LaTeXML (in Perl) does an excellent job in producing very nice LaTeX, but it is meant to be used offline, and is too slow by a factor 100 to be used for run-time generation of MathML (the slowness is caused by the very general LaTeX parser).

The current version of DynaMoW uses a cocktail of solutions (MathML produced by LaTeXML, jsMath, and PNG produced by `dvipng`) so as to get reasonable results

[13] Internet Explorer, whether 8 or 9, on Windows 7. It is not clear whether this is due to IE itself or to the specific glue of jsMath.

on the main five browser families. At the same time, we continue evaluating MathJax, a new software under very active development, which should supersede our solutions above; MathJax has specific code for Internet Explorer, but still was too slow for our needs at the time of writing.

4. Security and Performance Issues

Security and robustness. Minimal measures prevent simple attacks on the server: parameter passing between services is secured by authentication to prevent injection of symbolic code; an instance of a computer-algebra system will be given limited time and memory resources to avoid denial of service.

Scalability and efficiency. A large effort, both in the design of DynaMoW and in the implementation of our applications, has been put to realise the *statelessness* of each service. This allows the replication of servers, and, as a bonus, independent page fragments are loaded asynchronously and can be calculated in parallel, with no need for any explicit syntax when programming: the right server configuration automates parallelism provided the programmer implements in a sufficiently modular way. This is well exemplified by the file `SpecialFunction.ml` in the DDMF source, which encodes the skeleton of each article in DDMF: each of the eight calls to `DC.inline_service` results in a different section in the web page, which is computed asynchronously.

With respect to our server architecture, DDMF and ECS use for now a simple model with one instance of a computer-algebra system per DynaMoW instance, setting up several DynaMoW instances behind a web server. In the future, we plan to have a single DynaMoW instance with potentially many instances of the same computer-algebra system and a cache for both documents and symbolic values (caching outputs from each service, keyed by the inputs). This will counterbalance the need for repeating some calculations in order to maximise independence of page fragments.

Still, computing a full fresh web page can require a dozen seconds of sequential calculations, primarily because of complex symbolic calculations. To mitigate this, we rely heavily on the web-server cache for better performance, which proves beneficial especially when the site is visited by web crawlers.

Text-based communication with the computer-algebra system is the main bottleneck. Using an API like OpenMaple will give better performance but is more system specific.

Client-side calculations One could think to take advantage of client-side resources for both scalability and efficiency. A typical general-purpose computer-algebra system is too large an application to be transmitted from server to client (not to mention license issues). A reimplementation in, say JavaScript, seems unfeasible, even for a limited set of functionality, and could prove to be too slow. Additionally, it would hardly be portable, as linking to C libraries would be necessary (at least for arbitrary-precision integers). A more appealing approach would be to run another instance of a DynaMoW plugin on the client side, with the computer-algebra system installed on the client.

5. Conclusions

Development and debugging process. The source of DDMF shows two extremes of coding styles: one with long symbolic quotations and no call to any external symbolic library, another with short quotations to a large external library. (Compare files `DiffeqToRecurrence.ml` and `TaylorExpansion.ml` in the DDMF source.) The first case is needed for an intrusive instrumentation of preexisting Maple libraries. With time, we want to show more certificates of the computed data on the web site, which will lead to more instrumented Maple code and increase the proportion of quotations. To modify code, we either modify the external Maple library or the OCaml code, or both. Introducing an adequate ocamltop that is able to call Maple and display (external) symbolic values made the debugging much easier.

Advantages of functional style. Using a language that favours functional style had two main advantages:

First, it made it very easy to deal with the content trees representing web documents. By making us have a recursive representation of the final document, we could now easily implement a translator to a different document format (say, PDF). By contrast, in an earlier implementation in imperative style, we just printed HTML along the execution of our symbolic calculations.

Second, and maybe more importantly, it incited and helped us to refactor the symbolic code in more independent functions. This made the interactivity of the site and the reactivity of the server easier to achieve, by enabling incremental and/or distributed calculations of independent parts.

Types in antiquotations. The main torment in the prototyping phase concentrated around the adequacy of Camlp4 to our project, to the point that it has not been clear immediately that DynaMoW should be an OCaml library. Indeed, for our first prototype (used before DDMF v1.5), we wrote an (OCaml) interpreter for a "BASIC with quotations and antiquotations". In the end, the main drawback with the final choice is that Camlp4 does not offer type analysis at preprocessing-time. This leads to too much type annotation. The following example makes this clear:

```
let a = 3 in <:symb< f($(int:a)) >>
```

If the preprocessing stage done by Camlp4 was aware of types, we could simplify `$(int:a)` to `$(a)`. Our source of DDMF proves that a typical application will have many such annotations. We could partially alleviate this by choosing default antiquotation types, but ironically enough, such annotations were not needed in our first "BASIC" prototype. It turns out that we chose Camlp4 as it provides syntax extensions and quotations in the same tool, but there clearly is room for a quotation/antiquotation extension tool that could infer type information and perform different calculations based on it.

Declarations of services: Functor application is not enough. The main reason why services require a language extension and cannot be obtained just by a functor application is the need for serialisation and deserialisation of the parameters exchanged between services via query strings in URLs. As the number and types of parameters vary, we could generate serialisation and deserialisation functions only on the meta-level, using Camlp4. For comparison sake, the Eliom module `Eliom_parameters` also provides a representation for the GET parameters of a service, and also requires a language extension. A difference is that services are not intended to be called from the OCaml code (with the exception, to some extent, of the use of the function `Eliom_services.preapply`). Service declarations and calls in DynaMoW resemble function calls, whereas declarations of service parameters in Eliom are done by providing the parameter names as strings together with a representation of their types to a service registering function (`Eliom_services.new_service`).

A nice side effect of the language extension for service declaration in DynaMoW is also to avoid repetitions in boilerplate (argument names, etc.).

Mathematical rendering. It seems our applications naturally generate web pages with larger formulas than what the online presentation tools are targeting. This made it difficult for us to find the right trade-off between a nice and a fast mathematical rendering (see section 3.3).

In particular, even jsMath and its successor MathJax provide too slow rendering on certain systems. But we had no time to test the version 1.1 of MathJax, which has been released very little time before the present submission, and promises "a number of performance improvements".

Interfacing with Ocsigen. We have not used Ocsigen in DynaMoW as it provides with more general XML than what we wanted to expose to our programmers (see end of §3.2)[14]. Thus, we still rely on an external general-purpose web server (Apache or lighttpd), with DynaMoW a FastCGI[15]. We want to explore the possibility of making DynaMoW a module for Ocsigen and expect added efficiency by doing so.

Expressivity of interactivity. Although the ability of Sage with respect to web display is merely to display classical symbolic sheets using HTML and JavaScript, in a way that is not intended for an all-user web site, Sage contains a few nice interaction functionalities. Particularly so is the `@interact` function, which from the user's point of view presents the input of a parameter in a range as a draggable slider. Besides being nice, this solves the question of soundness checking of the input data. In the same vein, the interaction with parameters limited to a (closed) enumeration type could be rendered better than by using textual fields. We plan to develop such aspects in the future.

(Symbolic) Code extraction. Early in the development of the project, we realised that instrumenting a symbolic library under continued development would lead to the need of double maintenance. Indeed, we need to keep a version of the library for computations off the web. We have prototyped the extraction of pure Maple libraries from our OCaml-with-Maple application just enough to realise that a complete code extraction would imply automatically undoing some of the paradigm-changing port described in section 2.4. This automation is not mature yet and will be the subject of future work.

Acknowledgments

The conception of DynaMoW has benefited greatly from discussions with James Leifer, Marc Mezzarobba, Nicolas Pouillard, and Didier Rémy. As DynaMoW was initially developed as the underlying engine of DDMF, it has also been influenced a lot by discussions with DDMF developers.

References

[1] M. Abramowitz and I. A. Stegun, editors. *Handbook of mathematical functions*. Dover, New York, 1992.

[2] V. Balat, J. Vouillon, and B. Yakobowski. Experience report: Ocsigen, a web programming framework. In A. Tolmach, editor, *ICFP'09*, pages 311–315, 2009.

[14] and for unclear license issues

[15] http://www.fastcgi.com/

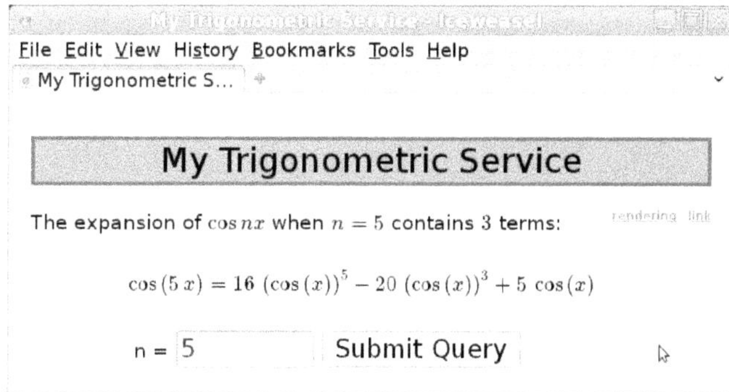

File `Trigo.ml`:

```
use_cas Maple
type_symb maple = unit Maple.t DynaMoW.symb

let_service Trigo (n : int = 2) :
  DynaMoW_services.Content.sec_entities * unit =
  let m_expr = << cos($(int:n) * x) >> in
  let s = Expand.obj (m_expr, ()) in
  let par_intro =
    <:par<The expansion of <:imath<\cos nx>>
      when <:imath<n = $(int:n)>>
      contains <:imath<$(int:s)>> terms:>>
  and par_math =
    DynaMoW_services.Content.inline_service
      (Expand.descr m_expr None) in
  let par =
    DynaMoW_services.Content.(@@@) par_intro par_math in
  (DynaMoW_services.Content.section
     <:text<My Trigonometric Service>> par,
   ())
```

File `Expand.ml`:

```
use_cas Maple
type_symb maple = unit Maple.t DynaMoW.symb

let_service Expand (expr : maple) :
  DynaMoW_services.Content.sec_entities * int =
  let s = << expand($(expr)) >> in
  (<:par<<:dmath<$(symb:expr) = $(symb:s)>>>>,
   <:int< nops($(s)) >>)
```

Table 1. Code for a simple service `Trigo` that calls a simple service `Expand` and, at the top, the resulting display. Proper configuration makes it available from the URL `http://.../example?service=Trigo&rendering=jsMath&n=5`. After entering the default web page (without final `&n=5`), which rendered the case $n = 2$, we changed the value to 5 in the form so as to get the display above.

[3] A. Benoit, F. Chyzak, A. Darrasse, S. Gerhold, M. Mezzarobba, and B. Salvy. The Dynamic Dictionary of Mathematical Functions (DDMF). In *The Third International Congress on Mathematical Software (ICMS 2010)*, volume 6327 of *Lecture Notes in Computer Science*, pages 35–41, 2010.

[4] M. Mauny and D. de Rauglaudre. A complete and realistic implementation of quotations for ML. In *Proc. of the Workshop on ML and its applications*, 1994.

[5] N. J. A. Sloane and S. Plouffe. *The Encyclopedia of Integer Sequences*. Academic Press, 1995.

Secure Distributed Programming with Value-Dependent Types

Nikhil Swamy[1] Juan Chen[1] Cédric Fournet[1] Pierre-Yves Strub[2] Karthikeyan Bhargavan[3] Jean Yang[4]

Microsoft Research[1] MSR-INRIA[2] INRIA[3] MIT[4]

Abstract

Distributed applications are difficult to program reliably and securely. Dependently typed functional languages promise to prevent broad classes of errors and vulnerabilities, and to enable program verification to proceed side-by-side with development. However, as recursion, effects, and rich libraries are added, using types to reason about programs, specifications, and proofs becomes challenging.

We present F*, a full-fledged design and implementation of a new dependently typed language for secure distributed programming. Unlike prior languages, F* provides arbitrary recursion while maintaining a logically consistent core; it enables modular reasoning about state and other effects using affine types; and it supports proofs of refinement properties using a mixture of cryptographic evidence and logical proof terms. The key mechanism is a new kind system that tracks several sub-languages within F* and controls their interaction. F* subsumes two previous languages, F7 and Fine. We prove type soundness (with proofs mechanized in Coq) and logical consistency for F*.

We have implemented a compiler that translates F* to .NET bytecode, based on a prototype for Fine. F* provides access to libraries for concurrency, networking, cryptography, and interoperability with C#, F#, and the other .NET languages. The compiler produces verifiable binaries with 60% code size overhead for proofs and types, as much as a 45x improvement over the Fine compiler, while still enabling efficient bytecode verification.

To date, we have programmed and verified more than 20,000 lines of F* including (1) new schemes for multi-party sessions; (2) a zero-knowledge privacy-preserving payment protocol; (3) a provenance-aware curated database; (4) a suite of 17 web-browser extensions verified for authorization properties; and (5) a cloud-hosted multi-tier web application with a verified reference monitor.

Categories and Subject Descriptors D.3.1 [*Formal Definitions and Theory*]: Syntax and Semantics

General Terms Security, Verification, Languages, Theory

Keywords Security type systems, refinement types

1. Introduction

Distributed applications are difficult to program reliably and securely. To address this problem, researchers have designed new languages with security verification in mind. Early work in this space developed *ad hoc* type systems targeting verification of specific security idioms, including systems for information flow controls, starting with Volpano et al. (1996); for proving authentication properties in cryptographic protocols (Gordon and Jeffrey 2003); and, more recently, for protocols that use zero-knowledge proofs (Backes et al. 2008). More general type systems for security verification have also been proposed, e.g., Fable (Swamy et al. 2008), F7 (Bengtson et al. 2008; Bhargavan et al. 2010), Aura (Jia and Zdancewic 2009; Jia et al. 2008; Vaughan et al. 2008), Fine (Chen et al. 2010; Swamy et al. 2010), and PCML5 (Avijit et al. 2010). All these languages use various forms of dependent types to reason about security, following a long tradition of dependent typing for general-purpose theorem proving and program verification, e.g., Coq (Bertot and Castéran 2004) and Agda (Norell 2007).

Although these languages are successful in many aspects, for large-scale distributed programming, we desire languages that (1) feature general programming constructs like effects and recursion, which, while invaluable for building real systems, make it hard to formally reason about programs, specifications, and proofs; (2) support various styles of proofs and evidence, ranging from cryptographic signatures to logical proof terms; (3) produce proofs that can be efficiently communicated between agents in the system.

This paper presents F*, a full-fledged design and implementation of a new dependently-typed programming language that addresses all these challenges. F* subsumes both F7 and Fine. Unlike prior languages, F* provides arbitrary recursion while maintaining a logically consistent core, resolving the tension between programmability and consistency by restricting the use of recursion in specifications and proofs; it enables modular reasoning about state and other effects and allows specifying refinement properties on affine values; it supports proofs of refinement properties using a mixture of cryptography and logical proof terms; and it allows selective erasure and reconstruction of proofs to reduce the overhead of communicating proofs.

By compiling to verifiable .NET bytecode, F* provides access to libraries for concurrency, networking, cryptography, and interoperability with C#, F#, and other .NET languages. We have formalized the metatheory of F*, and mechanized a significant part of the metatheory in Coq. We have developed a prototype compiler for F* (35,000 lines of F#), and used F* to program and verify more than 20,000 lines of code. We believe F* is the first language of its kind with such a scale of implementation and evaluation.

Next, we give an overview of F* and our main contributions.

A novel kind system. A central feature of F* is its kind system, which tracks several sub-languages—for terms, proofs, affine resources, and specifications. This kind system controls the interaction between those, while still providing a single unified language to specify, program, verify, and deploy secure distributed systems.

We use kinds $\star$ for program terms and P for proofs. Program terms that may be effectful and divergent reside in the universe of $\star$ types. Within $\star$, P identifies a universe of pure, total functions; P terms are used (mainly) in the construction of proof terms. Additionally, we use A, the kind of affine (used-at-most-once), stateful resources, to model and reason about effects in a modular style. Finally, the kind E is for types that may have no inhabitants at all. We

ICFP'11, September 19–21, 2011, Tokyo, Japan.

use E to control the selective erasure of proof terms, when these proofs are either impossible to construct in a distributed setting (e.g., due to cryptography or due to the design of legacy libraries); when the presence of a proof term would curtail expressiveness (e.g., when speaking of properties of affine values); or when proof terms would be too voluminous to construct. As such, E identifies a sub-language that plays a purely specificational role. To improve code reuse, we provide a sub-kinding relation, $P <: \star <: E$, with A unrelated to the others.

Two flavors of refinements. Refinement types are commonly used to specify program properties. In contrast with prior languages, F* features both *concrete* and *ghost* refinements; §2 illustrates the need for both for secure distributed programming. To reason about the security of distributed applications, with minimal trust between components, explicit proofs of security sometimes need to be communicated and checked at runtime.

Concrete refinements are pairs representing a value and a proof term serving as a logical evidence of the refinement property, similar to those in Coq and Fine. One novelty of F* is that it assigns a special kind P for proof terms, and restricts types and proof terms in the P universe to guarantee logical consistency.

Ghost refinements are used to state specifications for which proof terms are not maintained at run time. Ghost refinements have the form $\mathsf{x}{:}\mathsf{t}\{\phi\}$ where x is a value variable, t is a type, and ϕ is a logical formula, itself represented as a type that must have kind E and may depend on x and other in-scope variables. Ghost refinements are similar to those of F7; they are smoothly integrated in F* using the E kind. Ghost refinements provide the following benefits: (1) they enable precise symbolic models for many cryptographic patterns and primitives, and evidence for ghost refinement properties can be constructed and communicated using cryptographic constructions, such as digital signatures; (2) they benefit from a powerful subtyping relation: $\mathsf{x}{:}\mathsf{t}\{\phi\}$ is a subtype of t; this structural subtyping is convenient to write and verify higher-order programs; (3) they provide precise specification to legacy code without requiring any modifications; and (4) when used in conjunction with concrete refinements, they support *selective erasure* and *dynamic reconstruction* of evidence, enabling a variety of new applications and greatly reducing the performance penalty for runtime proofs.

Refinements on affine state. Prior work has shown the usefulness of affine types in reasoning about programs that use mutable state (Borgstrom et al. 2011; Lahiri et al. 2011). Relying on its kind system, F* freely allows the use of affine values within its specifications fragment, while still guaranteeing that affine values are used at most once elsewhere in the code. In §4, we exploit this feature extensively in implementing a new, flexible approach (Deniélou and Yoshida 2011) to enforce protocols on multi-party session types. Prior systems that integrate substructural and dependent types (e.g., Fine and Linear LF by Cervesato and Pfenning 2002) disallow refinements to speak directly about affine values, and have to rely instead on various encodings to work around this limitation, which is unsuitable for source programming.

Automation and logic parametricity. Proof automation is critical for developing large-scale programs. F* is carefully designed to be parametric in the logic used to describe programming properties and their proofs. §2.5 shows examples with a simple modal authorization logic and an *ad hoc* logic for database provenance. Logic parametricity enables working with custom authorization logics and, importantly, makes it easy to integrate F* with SMT solvers for logics extended with specific theories. Thus, program verification in F* benefits from significant automation—our implementation uses the Z3 SMT solver (de Moura and Bjørner 2008) and scales up to large programs and specifications. Languages like Aura, PCML5, Coq, and Agda commit to a specific logic, limiting their flexibility. This limitation is significant since diverse logics are used and even designed when reasoning about security policies and properties—see Chapin et al. (2008) for a recent survey.

Metatheory. We establish several properties of F*. First, we prove the soundness of F* in terms of progress and preservation. From this, we derive a safety property for ghost refinements called global deducibility. Next, we show that the P-fragment of F* is consistent by giving a typed embedding of this fragment into CiC and proving that the translation is a simulation. We also give a typed embedding of a core subset of RCF (the core calculus of F7) into F*. The subject reduction result (modulo the admission of a few standard lemma) has been mechanized in Coq—we plan to continue to develop our Coq formalization to include the other results.

Since our P-fragment is strongly normalizing, one might imagine extending F* to permit arbitrary P-terms to index types. However, term reduction in types, particularly with dynamic assumptions and affinity, poses a significant challenge for the metatheory. We remain with value dependency in F*, while acknowledging that it is less expressive than having expressions in types. However, value dependency is a practical design choice that has not hindered the construction and verification of the programs we have built.

Compiler implementation. We have implemented a compiler for F* based on our prior work on a compiler for Fine. The F* compiler accepts both Fine and F7 programs as input. To validate this feature, we typecheck and compile a large F7 library implementing symbolic cryptography (Bhargavan et al. 2010).

Our compiler translates F* to RDCIL, a dependently typed dialect of .NET bytecode. This translation is considerably more efficient than the one we used for Fine. Due to the use of ghost refinements and the availability of polymorphic kinds, bytecode emitted by the F* compiler is an order of magnitude (in some cases 45x) smaller than the bytecode emitted by the Fine compiler.

Experimental evaluation on a large suite of examples. We have implemented several libraries and applications in F*, verifying a large corpus of code for various properties. Prominent among our examples are (1) secure implementations of multi-party sessions protocols; (2) a prototype of a new zero-knowledge privacy scheme; (3) a provenance-aware curated database; (4) a suite of 17 web-browser extensions verified for authorization properties; and (5) an Azure-hosted multi-tier web application with a reference monitor verified for stateful authorization properties.

Due to space constraints, we leave the complete semantics of F*, manual proofs of the metatheory, and additional examples to a technical report, which, along with the compiler source code, the Coq development, and all our example programs, can be found at `http://research.microsoft.com/fstar`.

2. F* by example

This section introduces F* informally. The syntax of F* is based loosely on OCaml, F# and related languages in the ML family—notations specific to F* are primarily in support of its more expressive type and kind language. The dynamic semantics is also in the spirit of ML, in call by value, but the static semantics is significantly more complex. The examples in this section, together with those in §4, are intended to motivate and exercise its main features.

We organize our presentation around the new kind system of F*. We start with simple programs that use P-kind and F*'s sub-language of total functions to construct proof terms for concrete refinements. Next, we discuss E-kind and its use in two different scenarios with ghost refinements—first, when giving specifications to legacy libraries where the construction of explicit proof terms is impractical; and, second, when verifying implementations of cryptographic protocols, where the construction of proof terms is simply impossible. We then turn to A-kind, which, in conjunction with E-kind, can specify and verify properties of stateful computations. We conclude the section with an example that exploits the interaction between P-kind and E-kind, via the sub-kinding relation $P <: \star <: E$, to construct a model of a high-integrity database with precise data-provenance properties.

2.1 Concrete refinement types and total proof terms

Consider a partial specification for a very simple program, tail, that returns the tail of a list:

```
val tail: ∀α::⋆. l1:list α → {l2:list α | ∀x. Mem x l2 ⟹ Mem x l1}
```

This type is polymorphic, of the form ∀α::k. t where k is the kind of the abstracted type variable—kinds are ascribed to types using double colons. Here, α has kind $\star$, the kind given to types that admit arbitrary recursion and effects, i.e., the standard kind of fully-applied types in an ML-like system. Following ML, by default we omit explicit quantifiers for prenex-quantified type variables, and omit type applications when they can be determined by the context.

The rest of the type of tail shows a dependent function, of the form x:t → t' where the formal parameter x of type t is named, and is in scope in t'. When the function is not dependent, we simply write t → t'. The range type of tail shows our syntax for concrete refinements, {x:t | ϕ}, where ϕ is itself a type representing a logical formula, in which the name x is bound. Here, the formula states that the tail l2 contains at most the elements of l1.

Concrete refinements and constructive proofs. Also called subset types or Σ-types (Sozeau 2007), concrete refinements in F* are desugared into dependent pairs (as is usual in, say, Coq). The type below shows this desugaring, where the type x:t ∗ t' denotes a dependent pair, where x names the t-typed first component and is bound in t', the type of the second component.

```
val tail: l1:list α → (l2:list α ∗ (x:α → Mem x l2 → Mem x l1))
```

When desugaring formulas, quantifiers are desugared to dependent functions, and implications to non-dependent functions. The predicate Mem x l2 is itself a type, which we show below. As such, concrete refinements are represented as pairs of the underlying value, and a proof term witnessing the validity of the refinement formula.

A total sub-language for proof terms. We must be careful when representing quantifiers and implication with function arrows. For logical consistency, we require the function arrows that represent the type of proof terms to be total, whereas arrows used in the rest of the program (where we certainly want to use arbitrary recursion) can be partial. Thus, we need to ensure that potential divergence in the program never leaks into fragments of a program used for building proof terms. We achieve this by introducing a kind P, a subkind of $\star$, where types residing in P are guaranteed to be total.

Using P-kind, we define Mem, an inductive type that axiomatizes list membership in constructive style. Its kind is of the form α::k ⇒ k', where α binds a k-kinded formal type parameter in the kind k' of the constructed type. Type constructors can also be applied to values; such constructors have kinds of the form x:t ⇒ k where x names the formal argument, a value of type t, and is in scope in k. Below, the kind of Mem says that it is a dependent type constructor that constructs a type of kind P from a type α, a value x of type α, and a value l of type list α. (When x:α, we write Mem x l instead of Mem α x l.)

```
type Mem :: α::⋆ ⇒ α ⇒ list α ⇒ P =
  | Mem_hd : x:α → tl:list α → Mem x (Cons x tl)
  | Mem_tl : x:α → y:α → tl:list α → Mem y tl → Mem y (Cons x tl)
```

Inductive types defined in P-kind are required to be strictly positive, and we place other restrictions (§3.2) on the elimination rules for P-kinded types to ensure totality. A function type x:t → t' inherits the kind of its range type—it has P kind and is a total function when t'::P. Theorem 2 (Logical consistency of P) provides a well-typed embedding of terms residing in the P-fragment into CiC, ensuring that terms in the P-fragment are valid proof terms.

Non-constructive proofs, automation, and logic parametricity. Programming explicitly with proof terms for non-trivial program properties quickly becomes impractical. The F* implementation provides automation by calling Z3, an SMT solver, to try to decide refinement properties, and then constructing proof terms from the deduction traces reported by Z3. However, since Z3 (and many other automated provers) use classical logics, the proof terms produced in this manner are not constructive.

To support non-constructive proof terms (and more generally, to permit custom logics), F* allows to define custom proof kernels. A specific proof kernel (the type pf below), is defined in the standard library of F* and axiomatizes a classical logic, extended with axioms for commonly used data types such as list.

```
type pf :: P ⇒ P =
  | Exc_middle: pf (Or α (Not α))
  | Not_elim: pf (Not α) → pf α → pf β
  | Not_in_nil: x:α → pf (Not (Mem x Nil))
  | ... (∗ many constructors omitted ∗)
  | Unit_pf: α → pf α
  | Bind_pf: pf α → (α → pf β) → pf β
```

Each constructor in this kernel is an axiom in the logic, such as the excluded middle; introduction and elimination forms for the standard logical connectives (where Or, Not etc. are also type constructors); and axioms like Not_in_nil, which are necessary for reasoning in a non-constructive setting, where exhaustiveness arguments for inductive types are inapplicable. The pf kernel also includes constructors Unit_pf and Bind_pf that allow proofs to be composed monadically. This is particularly useful since F* is a call-by-value language—Bind_pf lets us compose proofs simply by constructor application, without triggering evaluation.

Using this approach, F* translates the type of tail to the type below. Relying on automated proof extraction from Z3, programmers write the code shown below, and the F* compiler inlines the proof term and compiles (while carrying proofs) to RDCIL (§5), our dependently typed .NET bytecode. Concrete refinements in this form are based on a similar construct in Fine. Through the use of P-kind (which Fine lacks), F* proof terms are logically consistent evidence of refinement properties.

```
val tail: l1:list α → (l2:list α ∗ pf (x:α → pf (Mem x l2) → pf (Mem x l1)))
let tail = function [] → [] | hd::tl → tl
```

2.2 Ghost refinements for lightweight specifications

Concrete refinements have a long tradition and a well-understood theory. However, as discussed below, we find them inappropriate for use in some scenarios. As an alternative, F* also provides ghost refinements, based on a construct of F7, and integrates them with the other features of the system, notably higher kinding, quantification over predicates, and refinements for substructural state.

We illustrate the use of ghost refinements for the problem of verifying clients of libraries, where the libraries are authored separately and are unmodifiable. In recent work, Guha et al. (2011) consider programming secure *web browser extensions* using F*. For this scenario, we use ghost refinement types to specify pre- and post-conditions on the interface provided by the browser, and use the specifications to verify access control properties of extensions. The listing below illustrates this approach on a tiny program—§5 reports new results for compiling a suite of 17 such extensions in a type-preserving style to .NET bytecode.

We aim to enforce a policy that untrusted extensions (line 10) only read data from the header of a web page and not the body.

This policy is specified using an assumption at line 8, which states, informally, that extensions hold the CanRead e privilege on DOM nodes e, for which the property EltTagName e "head" is derivable. Unlike the Mem predicate in §2.1 (which has P kind), EltTagName and CanRead construct erasable, or E-kinded, types. Erasable types are generally uninhabited and have no constructors. Instead, we use them for specifications, as in the types of innerText and tagName.

```
1  (* Fragment of DOM API *)
2  type elt
3  type EltTagName :: elt ⇒ string ⇒ E
4  type CanRead :: elt ⇒ E
5  val innerText: e:elt{CanRead e} → string
6  val tagName: e:elt → t:string{EltTagName e t}
7  (* Extension policy *)
8  assume ∀e. EltTagName e "head" ⟹ CanRead e
9  (* Extension code (untrusted) *)
10 let read e = if tagName e = "head" then innerText e else ""
```

The type of innerText has the form x:t{ϕ} → t', where the formula ϕ is a ghost refinement applied to the formal parameter x:t, and x is in scope in both ϕ and t'. The refinement CanRead e is a pre-condition indicating that clients must hold the CanRead e privilege before calling the function. Analogously, the post-condition of tagName relates the returned string t to the argument e, and clients may derive facts using this property and any other assumption (e.g., the policy assumption at line 8). For example, at the call to innerText in the **then**-branch at line 10, the F* checker (and Z3) uses the property that, for the value t returned by tagName e, we have EltTagName e t from the post-condition; t="head" from the equality test; and using the policy assumption, we can derive CanRead e, the pre-condition of innerText and authorize the call. Using this approach, once type checked, untrusted extension code need not be examined—only the policy (and the annotations on the DOM API) are trusted.

Two key properties of ghost refinements make them well-suited for use in our scenario. We discuss these below.

Ghost refinements and erasure. The type x:t{ϕ} is a subtype of t and the values of these two types have the same representation. This makes specifications using ghost refinements lightweight, since they do not require modifications to underlying code and data. For example, we did not need to modify or even wrap the DOM implementation in order to verify code in this style. Furthermore, the subtyping relation lifts naturally into the structure of function types, promoting reuse in higher order libraries.

Semantics of ghost refinement derivability. For every value v:t that inhabits x:t{ϕ} our type system ensures that the formula ϕ[v/x] is derivable. The definition of derivability is subtle and is made precise in §3. However, intuitively, derivability is a logical entailment relation defined relative to a context of dynamic assumptions $\mathscr{A}$. We think of $\mathscr{A}$ as a monotonically increasing *log* of events and formulas that are assumed during evaluation of the program. Formally, a call to tagName e reduces to t and has the *effect* of adding the formula EltTagName e t to the log. For values given ghost refinement types, there may be no concrete proof at run time to witness the derivability of the refinement formula. Indeed, when working with libraries like the DOM, explicit proof terms witnessing DOM invariants seem both infeasible and undesirable (as they may be very voluminous); ghost refinements fit the bill nicely.

Proof-irrelevance and P vs. E-kind. The distinction between P and E-kinds in F* may, at first, seem reminiscent of the distinction between Type and Prop in a system like Coq. The proof terms for concrete refinements in Coq are often from the Prop universe, indicating that they are computationally irrelevant (and so can be erased during code extraction). In contrast, concrete refinements in F* are accompanied by P-kinded proof terms, which are computationally *relevant*. We view proofs as useful runtime entities that carry important information. We choose to make proofs explicit and useful—§2.5 demonstrates a novel way of using concrete proof terms to construct precise provenance trails in a curated database. As such P-kind is closer to Coq's Type. Indeed, our embedding of F*'s P fragment in CiC translates P-kinded types to types that reside in Coq's Type universe.

E-kind in F* plays a role more similar to proof irrelevance in Coq. However, the semantics of E-kinded types and ghost refinements is considerably different. Not only are proofs for ghost refinements irrelevant, these proofs may not be constructible at all and E-kinded types may be uninhabited. Instead, the log-based semantics of ghost refinements makes trust assumptions in external code formal and explicit, and allows the definition of security properties for code that are robust even when code is composed with arbitrary attacker code. For example, Guha et al. (2011) used the log-based semantics to prove a robust safety property that ensures that verified extensions are authorization-safe even when composed with arbitrary untrusted JavaScript on a web page.

2.3 Ghost refinements and indexed types for cryptography

Refinement types (in the style of ghost refinements) have been used in F7 to verify implementations of cryptographic protocols. This section presents a small fragment of a library for public key cryptography implemented in a new style (see our website for a more complete library together with several client programs that use cryptography). This style is enabled by features of F* not available in F7, specifically, the integration of refinements with higher-kinded and indexed types. This example also illustrates the need for ghost refinements. As we will see, it is infeasible to construct concrete proof terms (whether constructive or not) to justify the soundness of cryptographic evidence.

The listing below shows the signature of a module Crypto that provides an interface to work with public key signatures. Informally, signatures provide a means for a party in a protocol to communicate a value and a property of its local environment to a remote party. For example, Alice can sign a message m and send it to Bob, and, if Bob trusts Alice, Bob can conclude that the message originated with Alice. Additionally, given a prior agreement on the usage of keys, Alice can convince Bob of some additional property Pred of the message m, e.g., that the message originated in Alice's file system. The property Pred need not be an intrinsic property of the contents of m—a constructive proof of Pred m in this setting may be nonsensical.

```
module Crypto
type dsig = bytes (* type of digital signatures *)
type prin (* name of a principal *)
type sk :: prin ⇒ α::⋆ ⇒ (α ⇒ E) ⇒ ⋆
val rsa_sign : ∀α::⋆, β::α⇒ E. p:prin → sk p α β → x:α {β x} → dsig
type pk :: prin ⇒ α::⋆ ⇒ (α ⇒ E) ⇒ ⋆
type Says :: prin ⇒ E ⇒ E
val rsa_verify : ∀α::⋆,β::α⇒ E.
  p:prin → pk p α β → x:α → dsig → r:bool{r=true ⟹ Says p (β x)}
```

Crypto provides a type dsig for digital signatures, here just an alias for bytes. It also exposes an abstract type prin for principal identifiers, and the type constructors sk and pk are for secret keys and public keys respectively.

A private key of type sk Alice α Pred belongs to the principal Alice:prin, who can use it to sign values m of type α that satisfy Pred m. The function rsa_sign allows clients to construct a dsig value by signing a message x:α, where the ghost refinement guarantees that the formula β x is derivable when rsa_sign is called. Public keys are complementary: rsa_verify verifies a signature using the public key pk p $\alpha\beta$ and, if it succeeds, the caller knows that Says p (β x) is derivable. The predicate Says p ϕ is the usual lifting of a proposition ϕ into a modality Says, similar to forms used in a variety of modal authorization logics (Chapin et al. 2008). Intuitively, Says p ϕ is weaker than ϕ, and the two coincide when principal p is trusted.

As in F7, an abstract implementation of the Crypto library can be verified against the specification shown above, and can be proved correct with respect to a Dolev-Yao adversary. However, in F7, types cannot be parametrized by predicates, so predicate parameters are instead simulated through a level of indirection. Instead of the F* type sk p α Pred, private keys in F7 are given a type of the form sk p α usage, and the predicate Pred is replaced by a global predicate SignSays, indexed by p and usage. Verification relies on a programming convention that each key usage must be unambiguously defined by recording an assumption of the form $\forall$p,usage,v, SignSays p usage v $\Longleftrightarrow$ Pred v. This convention is not enforced automatically in F7, and hence this style can lead to logical inconsistencies. In contrast, F* types are more concise, and require fewer dynamic assumptions and no programming discipline beyond typing.

2.4 Ghost refinements and affine-indexed types for state

F* is designed to enable reasoning about effectful programs, whether the effects be in the form of non-termination, state, or I/O. We have seen how *P*-kind serves to control non-termination and we consider I/O in §4. This section looks at how F* uses affine types, in combination with *E*-kinded types, to reason about state.

One innovation of F* is that it permits indexing types with affine values, allowing properties to be stated about affine values without having them be consumed immediately. We illustrate this feature by showing how to program with *linear maps*, a data type proposed by Lahiri et al. (2011) to verify heap-manipulating programs. For space reasons, we do not show a client program using linear maps—a complete example is available in the F* distribution.

Linear maps are a data structure that equips a Floyd-Hoare logic (using a *classical assertion logic*) with a form of local reasoning in the style of separation logic. Instead of modeling the heap of a program as a single monolithic map H:map $\alpha\beta$ from α-typed locations to β-typed values, the linear maps methodology advocates partitioning the heap H into several fragments $H_1, \ldots, H_n$ where the H_i have disjoint domains. Each H_i is a linear map of type lin $\alpha\beta$, and the disjoint domain condition ensures that modifications to H_i leave all the other H_j unmodified. This allows to formulate a kind of frame rule for programs that use linear maps. Since the assertion logic remains classical, linear map programs can be automatically verified using classical provers and SMT solvers.

```
type lin :: ⋆ ⇒ ⋆ ⇒ A
type Select :: α::⋆ ⇒ β::⋆ ⇒ lin αβ ⇒ α ⇒ β ⇒ E
type Update :: α::⋆ ⇒ β::⋆ ⇒ lin αβ ⇒ α ⇒ β ⇒ lin αβ ⇒ E
type InDomain :: α::⋆ ⇒ β::⋆ ⇒ α ⇒ lin αβ ⇒ E
```

The listing above defines an abstract type of linear maps and several predicates to model their properties. The kind of lin:: $\star \Rightarrow \star \Rightarrow A$ introduces the fourth base kind in F*: the kind *A* of affine types. To enforce the disjoint domains invariant on linear maps, Lahiri *et al.* require that linear maps be neither copied nor aliased. This corresponds directly to the use of affinity in F*: values of affine type can be used *at most once*.

The types Select and Update correspond to standard predicates implemented by SMT solvers like Z3: Select l x y states that the map l at the location x contains the value y; Update l x y m states that m is like the map l, except at the location x where it contains the value y. We omit the standard axiomatization of these predicates. Linear maps are partial maps and include a domain. The predicate InDomain x l has the obvious meaning.

Two operations to read and write locations in maps are shown below. (Other operations are omitted). The read function reads a location x out of a map m1 (when InDomain x m1), and returns the value y:β stored at x. Since m1 is affine, read threads m1 back to the caller as m2, where the refinement on m2 shows that it is unchanged. The write function is similar, and in both cases the Select and Update predicates specify the appropriate post-conditions.

```
val read: x:α → m1:lin αβ {InDomain x m1}
      → (y:β * (m2:lin αβ {m1=m2 && Select m1 x y}))

val write: x:α → y:β → m1:lin αβ {InDomain x m1}
      → (m2:lin αβ {Update m1 x y m2})
```

Predicates on affine values. While seemingly unremarkable, by refining affine values, the types shown above are a significant advance over prior languages that have included substructural and dependent types. For example, in systems like Fine and Linear LF (Cervesato and Pfenning 2002), types are required to be free of affine (or linear) indices, i.e., type constructors of kind t $\Rightarrow$ k, where t::*A* are forbidden. There are several reasons for this restriction in prior systems. Most prominently, expressing properties of affine values using concrete refinements requires constructing proof terms where, simply by using an affine resource in a proof term, the resource is consumed. While there are ways to work around this restriction (Borgstrom et al. 2011), they involve relatively complex whole-program transformations.

A key innovation of F* is to use the *E*-kind to allow stating properties on affine values directly. Specifically, since *E*-kinded predicates have no runtime significance, indexing these predicates with affine values does not consume them—in F*, kinds of the form t $\Rightarrow$ *E* are permitted, even when t::*A*. In our example, we use affine indexes on *E*-kinded types to state pre- and post-conditions using ghost refinements. However, when modeling linear maps programs, the dynamic log of assumptions (unlike when modeling DOM programs and cryptography) is constant, so F*'s metatheory guarantees that refinement formulas in pre- and post-conditions are derivable from the axiomatization of linear maps alone.

We defer further discussion of affine indexed types until §4, where we use affine indexes with higher-rank *E*-kinded types to model concurrent, message passing programs.

2.5 Selective erasure using concrete and ghost refinements

The preceding discussion of ghost refinements may lead the reader to believe that they are always to be preferred to refinements with concrete proof terms. This section illustrates that concrete proof terms are useful too, particularly when one is allowed to compute over these terms, to store them, and to communicate them over the network. The example discussed here is an excerpt from a larger program that models a database of scientific experiments, where each record contains a proof term indicating the *provenance* of the experiment and its "validity", according to some custom notion of validity. The full example brings together several elements, including the use of cryptography with a simple modal logic to authenticate experimental observations. For brevity, we focus just on one aspect: selective erasure and reconstruction of proofs, which may be implemented for both efficiency and confidentiality reasons.

Each experiment record in our database is given the type exp b (for some boolean parameter b, explained shortly). The record contains an optional primary key field xid; a field r:expsetup that defines what ingredients were used in the experiment; and, importantly, a proof term of type proof b (Valid r), where the proof term contains evidence recording the relationship of this experiment to other experiments in the database, i.e., the proof term reflects the provenance of the experiment.

```
type expsetup = list {reagent:string; quantity:int}
type Valid :: expsetup ⇒ E
type exp (b:bool) = (xid:option int * r:expsetup * proof b (Valid r))
```

The type proof b t represents a value from a proof kernel defining a custom logic tailored to this specific application—another example of F*'s logic parametricity. We show a selection of the constructors from this kernel below.

```
let full, partial = true, false
type proof :: bool ⇒ E ⇒ P=
| AndIntro: ... | AndElim1 : ... | ...
| ChemicalVolcano: proof full (Valid[{reagent="(NH4)2Cr2O7"; ...}])
| Combine: r1:expsetup → r2:expsetup → r3:expsetup → b:bool
        → proof b (And (Union r1 r2 r3) (And (Valid r1) (Valid r2)))
        → proof b (Valid r3)
| Prune: r:expsetup{Valid r} → xid:int → proof partial (Valid r)
```

The interplay between ghost and concrete proof terms is central in this example—it enables proof terms to be *selectively erased* and later *reconstructed*. This allows us to maintain compact, yet detailed and reliable provenance trails. The type proof full (Valid r) represents a fully explicated proof of Valid r, with no selective erasure applied. In contrast, values of type proof partial (Valid r) may have been partially erased—these values are not guaranteed to carry a complete provenance for the experiment setup r.

The constructors in the kernel include axioms for basic connectives and axioms like ChemicalVolcano which state validity of some well-known experiments. Axioms like Combine allow new valid experiments to be constructed from other valid ones. The most interesting constructor is Prune, which allows a ghost refinement of the validity of an experiment (r:expsetup{Valid r}) to be traded for a concrete proof term for the validity. To allow proofs to be reconstructed, Prune takes an extra argument, xid:int, the primary key of a record in the database that holds the complete provenance for r.

Now we can give a typed interface to our database (below). The database db is simply a list of experiments with full proofs. It supports operations to insert new experiments (returning an auto-generated private key); to lookup using the primary keys; and to look up just the provenance trail of a particular experiment setup, using a primary key for the experiment.

```
type db = list (exp full)
val insert: exp full → int
val lookup: xid → option (exp full)
val lookupProof: r:expsetup → xid:int → option (proof full (Valid r))
```

We implement a client-facing interface to the database that wraps the basic lookup and insert operations. On outbound request, we lookup an experiment by its primary key. But, rather than communicate a (potentially large) proof term with explicit provenance to the requestor, we erase the proof (using Prune) and send only a partial proof to the caller, recording the primary key xid in the proof term for later reconstruction. In our full implementation, rather than simply sending a Prune node, we send an authenticated proof term, signed under a key for the database, so that the requestor can conclude that the returned experiment is indeed valid.

```
(* Erasing outbound proofs *)
assume ∀(b:bool) (r:expsetup) (pf:proof b (Valid r)). b=full ⟹ Valid r
let readExp xid : option (exp partial) =
  match lookup xid with
    | Some (xid, r, pf) → Some (xid, r, Prune r xid)
    | None → None
```

To use the Prune constructor, we have to prove that r has the type r:expsetup{Valid r}. Although pf is full proof of Valid r, we cannot use pf directly to derive ghost refinement formulas. To connect concrete and ghost refinements, we introduce the assumption above. Given the soundness of the proof kernel, this assumption is admissible, and the type of Prune ensures that the database program never introduces partial proofs for experiments that do not have a valid provenance trail. Despite the fact that the Valid r type has no inhabitants, the introduction of this assumption does not lead to logical inconsistency. Formally, assumptions are simply recorded as effects in the log, and do not produce values that can be destructed, say, via pattern matching.

Finally, on requests to insert new records in the database, we can reconstruct proofs. The function expand below traverses the structure of a proof tree, and expands Prune nodes by looking them up in the database. The database maintains an invariant that each record in the database has a full proof and thus a fully explicated provenance trail, ensured via type soundness.

```
(* Reconstructing proof terms on inbound requests *)
let rec expand (c:bool) (pf:proof c α) : option (proof full α) =
  if c=full then Some pf
  else match pf with
    | Prune r xid → lookupProof r xid
    | AndElim1 c1 pf → (match expand c1 pf with
                         | Some pf' → Some (AndElim1 full pf')
                         | _ → None)
    | ...
(* Inserting a new record in the DB *)
let insertExp (r:expsetup) (c:bool) (pf: proof c (Valid r)) =
  match (expand c pf) with
    | Some pf' → Some (insert (None, r, pf'))
    | _ → None
```

The function expand is, in effect, a partial, effectful proof-search procedure. Despite the use of non-termination and effects, the type system guarantees that if this function terminates and returns Some pf, then pf is indeed a valid full proof in the P-fragment, F*'s logically consistent fragment of total functions.

3. Formalizing F*

This section presents the syntax and the semantics of F*. We focus on five main themes: (1) the stratification into expressions, types and kinds with the ability to describe functional dependences at each level; (2) the use of kinds to isolate sub-languages for proofs, specifications, and affinity; (3) relating logical effects described using ghost refinements to propositions witnessed by proof terms; (4) logic parametricity, allowing us to plug-in proof kernels and automated decision procedures for the logics they define; and (5) the consistency of a core universe of propositions, via strong normalization, and the ability to program over its values, to support applications with mobile proofs and selective erasure.

3.1 Syntax

The syntax of F* is shown below. Values include variables, lambda abstractions over values and types, and fully applied n-ary data constructors. The value v^ℓ is a technical device used to prove the soundness of affine typing—ℓ is an identifier drawn from a class of names distinct from term and type names. We use the notation $\overline{a}$ to stand for a finite sequence of elements $a_1, \ldots, a_n$, for arbitrary n; $(\overline{a})_k$ is a sequence $a_1, \ldots, a_{k-1}$. We adopt a (partially) let-normalized view of the expression language e, in particular requiring function arguments to always be values—this is convenient when using value-dependent types, since it ensures that expressions never escape into the level of types. The only other non-standard expression form is **assume** ϕ, which has the effect of adding a formula to the log and is explained in §3.3.

Types are ranged over by meta-variables t and ϕ—we use ϕ for types that stand for logical formulas. Types include variables α, constants T, dependent functions ranging over values whose domain may be values ($x{:}t \rightarrow t'$) or types ($\forall\alpha{::}\kappa.t$, written `'a::k -> t` in the concrete syntax), types applied to values ($t\ v$) and to types ($t\ t'$), type-level functions from values to types ($\lambda x{:}t.t'$, concretely written `fun (x:t) -> t'`), ghost refinements $x{:}t\{\phi\}$, and finally coercions to affine types $¡t$. This modal operator serves to qualify the type of a closure that captures an affine assumption; we include $¡t$ in the formalism to avoid duplicating

Syntax: expressions, types, kinds, signatures, environments

v	$::=$	$x \mid \lambda x{:}t.e \mid \Lambda\alpha{::}\kappa.e \mid D\,\bar{t}\,\bar{v} \mid v^{\ell}$	values
e	$::=$	$v \mid e\,v \mid e\,t \mid$ **assume** $\phi \mid$ **let** $x = e$ **in** e'	terms
	$\mid$	**match** x **with** $D\,\bar{\alpha}\,\bar{x} \rightarrow e$ **else** e'	
ϕ, t	$::=$	$\alpha \mid T \mid x{:}t \rightarrow t' \mid \forall\alpha{::}\kappa.t \mid t\,v \mid t\,t'$	types
	$\mid$	$\lambda x{:}t.t' \mid x{:}t\{\phi\} \mid ¡t$	
c	$::=$	$\star \mid P \mid A$	concrete kinds
b	$::=$	$c \mid E$	base kinds
κ	$::=$	$b \mid x{:}t \Rightarrow \kappa \mid \alpha{::}\kappa \Rightarrow \kappa'$	kinds
S	$::=$	$\cdot \mid T{::}\kappa\{\overline{D{:}t}\} \mid S, S'$	signature
Γ	$::=$	$\cdot \mid x{:}t \mid \alpha{::}\kappa \mid v_1 = v_2 \mid t_1 = t_2 \mid \Gamma, \Gamma'$	type env.
$\mathscr{A}$	$::=$	$\cdot \mid \phi \mid \ell \mid \hat{\ell} \mid \mathscr{A}, \mathscr{A}'$	dynamic log

the rules for function arrows, but concretely we write affine functions as `x:t >> t'` and `'a::k >> t` instead of $¡(x{:}t \rightarrow t')$ and $¡(\forall\alpha{::}\kappa.t)$.

Kinds κ include the four base kinds $\star$, P, A, and E—we distinguish the first three of these as *concrete kinds*, since they classify inhabitable types. As at the type level, we have kinds for dependent function spaces whose range are types and whose domain may be either values ($x{:}t \Rightarrow \kappa$) or types ($\alpha{::}\kappa \Rightarrow \kappa'$). Stratifying the language into terms, types, and kinds allows us to place key restrictions (discussed below) that facilitate automated verification, and to compile efficiently to .NET. However, stratification does come at a cost—several pieces of technical machinery are replicated across the levels.

Signatures S are finite lists of inductively defined types. Each inductive definition $T{::}\kappa\{\overline{D{:}t}\}$ introduces a type constructor T of kind κ and all its constructors $D_1{:}t_1, \ldots, D_n{:}t_n$. For simplicity, we do not include mutually inductive types, although these are supported by our implementation and their addition to the formalism poses no significant difficulties. We do not need a fixpoint form in the expression language since inductive types allow us to encode recursive functions. To show that terms given P-kinded types are strongly normalizing, a well-formedness condition on signatures imposes a positivity constraint on inductive definitions for P-kinded types. An additional constraint on signatures is that they must contain a declaration unit$::\star\{()$:unit$\}$ for the unit type and its one value (). Finally, typing environments Γ track in-scope value variables (x with type t), type variables (α with kind κ), and equivalences between values ($v_1 = v_2$) and types ($t_1 = t_2$) introduced when checking **match** expressions. We discuss the log $\mathscr{A}$ in conjunction with the dynamic semantics in §3.3. Briefly, $\mathscr{A}$ maintains a set of facts introduced by the dynamic assumption of ghost refinements, and also a set of names ℓ used to track affine values.

3.2 The F* type system

Figure 1 shows key rules from each judgment in the type system.

Well-formedness of kinds. The judgment $S;\Gamma \vdash \kappa$ ok(b) states that κ is well-formed and produces types of base kind b (when $\kappa = b$) or type constructors for b-kinded types. The rule (OK-TK) shows a key enhancement of F* over prior languages, e.g., Fine or Linear LF. Types can be constructed from affine values ($b_1 = A$), so long as the type constructed is purely specificational ($b_2 = E$). As illustrated in §2.4 and §4, this improves the expressiveness of affine typing significantly, enabling refinements on affine state. (OK-KK) is also an enhancement over Fine to allow dependences and to ensure that types parameterized by affine types are themselves affine. Although our formalism allows higher-kinds like $(\star \Rightarrow \star) \Rightarrow \star$, such kinds cannot be compiled to the type system of the .NET bytecode language and are currently rejected by our compiler. However, retargeting F* to a platform with a more flexible typing discipline would lift this restriction.

Kinding for value-indexed and affine types. The judgment $S;\Gamma \vdash t :: \kappa$ states that type t has kind κ. The rules shown here reveal a few subtle aspects of the type system, starting with affine typing and affine-value indexing. The rule (K-A) shows how the modal operator coerces the kind of a type. (K-Tv) allows a type function t to be applied to a value v; these type functions are introduced either using (K-Fun) or as type constructors T in the signature. Next, recall that we wish to allow affine values to be freely used at the type level, since specifications should not consume affine resources. For this reason, unlike prior languages, the values passed to type functions may use affine assumptions in the context Γ—the restrictions imposed by (OK-TK) ensure that such uses of affine assumptions at the type level cannot influence term-level reduction. The second premise of (K-Tv) uses the expression typing judgment, discussed shortly. This judgment has two modes ($m ::= \cdot \mid \varepsilon$) indicated on the turnstile. When the mode is ε (indicating that the term being typed occurs at the type-level, effectively as an index of an E-kinded type), affine assumptions in the context can be freely duplicated without resulting in their consumption. We discuss how this works shortly, in the context of the (T-X) rule.

Ghost refinements, total functions, and sub-kinding. (K-ϕ) requires that formulas in ghost refinements be erasable (E-kinded). Formulas in ghost refinements are erased at runtime and refinements apply only to types given concrete kinds c (the first premise of (K-ϕ)), i.e., inhabitable types. (K-Arr) handles dependent function arrows, which (as seen in §2.1) can be used to represent both quantified formulas in the logic as well as term-level function abstractions. A function arrow is P-kinded if its range type is P-kinded. Finally, (K-Sub) uses a sub-kinding judgment in its premise. Sub-kinding in F* is defined by the judgment $S;\Gamma \vdash \kappa_1 <: \kappa_2$. Sub-kinding is based on the relation $P <: \star <: E$, among base kinds, with $A <: A$ only. These base relations are lifted into the structure of arrow kinds, with co- and contravariance as usual. (K-Sub) includes premises to ensure that sub-kinding preserves well-formedness of kinds. We conjecture that these premises can be eliminated in favor of lemmas establishing that sub-kinding never introduces ill-formed kinds. We have yet to prove it, so we include these premises to facilitate our formal proof of well-formedness of kinds produced by derivations.

Expression typing. The judgment $S;\Gamma;X \vdash^m e : t$ states that expression e has type t, under signature S, environment Γ, and an affine environment $X ::= \cdot \mid \ell \mid x \mid X, X'$, where X, X' denotes disjoint union of sets of names. A well-formedness condition on contexts requires all variables $x \in X$ to also be bound in Γ. The context X represents a set of available affine assumptions, and usual context splitting rules apply to X when typing the sub-terms of an expression. (As in Fine, we choose not to split Γ itself, since this complicates well-formedness of contexts in the presence of dependent types.) Finally, as mentioned above, expression typing comes in two modes, indicated on the turnstile.

Affine typing in two modes. (T-XA) is typical of affine typing systems. To use an affine assumption x, we require x to be present in the affine environment X. In addition, (T-X) provides two exceptions to (T-XA): first, as is standard, we can use non-affine assumptions without requiring them to be present in X. Second, when the mode is ε, we are typing a term at the level of types; since this does not consume the affine resource, we are free to use it even when X is empty. (T-WknX) provides weakening for the affine context. Finally, (T-Abs) is a standard rule with one subtlety that the introduced function type is tagged with the affine modality (using $Q(X, x{:}t \rightarrow t')$) if the function closure captures an affine assumption. ((T-ℓ) is also related to affine typing, but, values v^{ℓ} are used solely to state our type soundness result—we discuss this rule in conjunction with the dynamic semantics.)

Ghost refinements and subtyping. The rules (T-As), (T-V), and the subtyping judgments introduce ghost refinement types. (T-As) in-

$$\boxed{S;\Gamma \vdash \kappa\ \text{ok}(b)} \quad \text{OK-b}\ \frac{}{S;\Gamma \vdash b\ \text{ok}(b)} \quad \text{OK-TK}\ \frac{b_2 = E \text{ if } b_1 = A \quad S;\Gamma \vdash t{::}b_1 \quad S;\Gamma,x{:}t \vdash \kappa\ \text{ok}(b_2)}{S;\Gamma \vdash x{:}t \Rightarrow \kappa\ \text{ok}(b_2)} \quad \text{OK-KK}\ \frac{b_2 \in \{A,E\} \text{ if } b_1 = A \quad S;\Gamma \vdash \kappa_1\ \text{ok}(b_1) \quad S;\Gamma,\alpha{::}\kappa_1 \vdash \kappa_2\ \text{ok}(b_2)}{S;\Gamma \vdash \alpha{::}\kappa_1 \Rightarrow \kappa_2\ \text{ok}(b_2)}$$

$$\boxed{S;\Gamma \vdash t :: \kappa} \quad \text{K-A}\ \frac{S;\Gamma \vdash t :: \star}{S;\Gamma \vdash \text{¡}t :: A} \quad \text{K-Tv}\ \frac{S;\Gamma \vdash t :: (x{:}t' \Rightarrow \kappa) \quad S;\Gamma;. \vdash^{\varepsilon} v : t'}{S;\Gamma \vdash t\ v :: \kappa[v/x]} \quad \text{K-Fun}\ \frac{S;\Gamma \vdash t :: b \quad S;\Gamma,x{:}t \vdash t' :: \kappa}{S;\Gamma \vdash \lambda x{:}t.t' :: x{:}t \Rightarrow \kappa}$$

$$\text{K-}\phi\ \frac{S;\Gamma \vdash t :: c \quad S;\Gamma,x{:}t \vdash \phi :: E}{S;\Gamma \vdash x{:}t\{\phi\} :: c} \quad \text{K-Arr}\ \frac{S;\Gamma \vdash t :: c \quad S;\Gamma,x{:}t \vdash t' :: c' \quad b = P \text{ if } c' = P \text{ and } \star \text{ o.w.}}{S;\Gamma \vdash x{:}t \rightarrow t' :: b} \quad \text{K-Sub}\ \frac{S;\Gamma \vdash t :: \kappa \quad S;\Gamma \vdash \kappa <: \kappa' \quad S;\Gamma \vdash \kappa\ \text{ok}(b) \quad S;\Gamma \vdash \kappa'\ \text{ok}(b)}{S;\Gamma \vdash t :: \kappa'}$$

$$\boxed{S;\Gamma \vdash \kappa_1 <: \kappa_2} \quad \text{SK-Refl}\ \frac{S;\Gamma \vdash \kappa \equiv \kappa'}{S;\Gamma \vdash \kappa <: \kappa'} \quad \text{SK-PStar}\ \frac{}{S;\Gamma \vdash P <: \star} \quad \text{SK-StarE}\ \frac{}{S;\Gamma \vdash \star <: \text{E}}$$

$$\text{SK-Prod}\ \frac{S;\Gamma \vdash t' <: t \quad S;\Gamma,x{:}t' \vdash \kappa <: \kappa'}{S;\Gamma \vdash (x{:}t \Rightarrow \kappa) <: (x{:}t' \Rightarrow \kappa')} \quad \text{SK-ProdK}\ \frac{S;\Gamma \vdash \kappa_1' <: \kappa_1 \quad S;\Gamma,\alpha{::}\kappa_1' \vdash \kappa_2 <: \kappa_2'}{S;\Gamma \vdash (\alpha{::}\kappa_1 \Rightarrow \kappa_2) <: (\alpha{::}\kappa_1' \Rightarrow \kappa_2')} \quad \text{SK-Trans}\ \frac{S;\Gamma \vdash \kappa <: \kappa_1 \quad S;\Gamma \vdash \kappa_1 <: \kappa'}{S;\Gamma \vdash \kappa <: \kappa'}$$

$$\boxed{S;\Gamma \vdash \kappa \equiv \kappa'} \quad \text{KE-Refl}\ \frac{}{S;\Gamma \vdash \kappa \equiv \kappa} \quad \text{KE-Prod}\ \frac{S;\Gamma \vdash t \equiv t' \quad S;\Gamma,x{:}t \vdash \kappa \equiv \kappa'}{S;\Gamma \vdash x{:}t \Rightarrow \kappa \equiv x{:}t' \Rightarrow \kappa'} \quad \text{KE-ProdK}\ \frac{S;\Gamma \vdash \kappa_1 \equiv \kappa_1' \quad S;\Gamma,\alpha{::}\kappa_1 \vdash \kappa_2 \equiv \kappa_2'}{S;\Gamma \vdash \alpha{::}\kappa_1 \Rightarrow \kappa_2 \equiv \alpha{::}\kappa_1' \Rightarrow \kappa_2'}$$

$$\boxed{S;\Gamma;X \vdash^m e : t} \quad \text{T-XA}\ \frac{S;\Gamma \vdash \Gamma(x) :: A}{S;\Gamma;x \vdash x : \Gamma(x)} \quad \text{T-X}\ \frac{S;\Gamma \vdash \Gamma(x){::}b \quad m = \varepsilon \text{ if } b = A}{S;\Gamma;. \vdash^m x : \Gamma(x)} \quad \text{T-WknX}\ \frac{S;\Gamma;X \vdash^m e : t}{S;\Gamma;X,X' \vdash^m e : t} \quad \text{T-Abs}\ \frac{S;\Gamma \vdash t{::}c \quad S;\Gamma,x{:}t;X,x \vdash^m e : t'}{S;\Gamma;X \vdash^m \lambda x{:}t.e : Q(X,x{:}t \rightarrow t')}$$

$$\text{T-As}\ \frac{S;\Gamma \vdash \phi :: E \quad t = x{:}\text{unit}\{\phi\}}{S;\Gamma;\cdot \vdash^m \textbf{assume}\ \phi : t} \quad \text{T-V}\ \frac{S;\Gamma;X \vdash^m v : t \quad S;\Gamma \vdash t :: c \quad S;\Gamma,x{:}t,x = v \models \phi \quad S;\Gamma,x{:}t \vdash \phi :: E}{S;\Gamma;X \vdash^m v : x{:}t\{\phi\}} \quad \text{T-Let}\ \frac{S;\Gamma;X_1 \vdash^m e_1 : t_1 \quad S;\Gamma,x{:}t_1;X_2,x \vdash^m e_2 : t_2 \quad \forall i.S;\Gamma \vdash t_i :: \kappa_i \quad \kappa_2 = P \Rightarrow \kappa_1 = P}{S;\Gamma;X_1,X_2 \vdash^m \textbf{let}\ x = e_1\ \textbf{in}\ e_2 : t_2}$$

$$\text{T-Match}\ \frac{\begin{array}{c} S;\Gamma;X_1 \vdash^m v : t_v \quad S;\Gamma \vdash t_v :: \kappa_v \quad \Gamma' = \Gamma,\overline{\alpha{::}\kappa},\overline{x{:}t} \quad \vdash S;\Gamma'\text{wf} \quad S;\Gamma';\bar{x} \vdash^m D\ \bar{\alpha}\ \bar{x} : t_p \quad FV(t_v,t_p) = \bar{\beta},\bar{y} \\ t_v\theta = t_p\theta \quad \theta = [\bar{t}/\bar{\beta},\bar{v}/\bar{y}] \quad S;\Gamma',\overline{\beta = t},\overline{y = v},v = D\ \bar{\alpha}\ \bar{x};X_2,\bar{x} \vdash^m e_1 : t \quad S;\Gamma;X_2 \vdash^m e_2 : t \quad S;\Gamma \vdash t :: \kappa_b \quad \kappa_b = P \Rightarrow \kappa_v = P \end{array}}{S;\Gamma;X_1,X_2 \vdash^m \textbf{match}\ v\ \textbf{with}\ D\ \bar{\alpha}\ \bar{x} \rightarrow e_1\ \textbf{else}\ e_2 : t}$$

$$\text{T-}\ell\ \frac{m \neq \varepsilon \Rightarrow X' = \ell \quad S;\Gamma;X \vdash^m v : t}{S;\Gamma;X,X' \vdash^m v^{\ell} : t} \quad \text{T-Sub}\ \frac{S;\Gamma;X \vdash e : t' \quad S;\Gamma \vdash t' <: t \quad S;\Gamma \vdash t' :: c \quad S;\Gamma \vdash t :: c}{S;\Gamma;X \vdash e : t} \quad \text{where} \quad \begin{array}{rcl} Q(\cdot,t) & = & t \\ Q(X,t) & = & \text{¡}t \end{array}$$

$$\boxed{S;\Gamma \vdash t <: t'} \quad \text{S-Refl}\ \frac{S;\Gamma \vdash t \equiv t'}{S;\Gamma \vdash t <: t'} \quad \text{S-}\phi\text{I}\ \frac{S;\Gamma \vdash t <: t' \quad S;\Gamma,x{:}t \models \phi'}{S;\Gamma \vdash t <: x{:}t'\{\phi'\}} \quad \text{S-}\phi\text{E}\ \frac{}{S;\Gamma \vdash x{:}t\{\phi\} <: t} \quad \text{S-Arr}\ \frac{S;\Gamma \vdash t_1' <: t_1 \quad S;\Gamma,x{:}t_1' \vdash t_2 <: t_2'}{S;\Gamma \vdash x{:}t_1 \rightarrow t_2 <: x{:}t_1' \rightarrow t_2'}$$

$$\boxed{\begin{array}{c} S;\Gamma \vdash t \equiv t' \\ S;\Gamma \vdash v \equiv v' \end{array}} \quad \text{EQ-T}\ \frac{t_1 = t_2 \in \Gamma}{S;\Gamma \vdash t_1 \equiv t_2} \quad \text{EQ-V}\ \frac{v_1 = v_2 \in \Gamma}{S;\Gamma \vdash v_1 \equiv v_2} \quad \text{EQ-}\beta\ \frac{}{S;\Gamma \vdash (\lambda x{:}t.t')v \equiv t'[v/x]} \quad \text{EQ-VApp1}\ \frac{S;\Gamma \vdash v \equiv v'}{S;\Gamma \vdash t\ v \equiv t\ v'}$$

$$\boxed{\vdash S\ \text{ok}} \quad \text{WFS-D}\ \frac{\begin{array}{c} S;\cdot \vdash \kappa\ \text{ok}(c) \quad \forall i.S,T{::}\kappa\{\};(\overline{\alpha{::}\kappa})_i \vdash \kappa_i\ \text{ok}(b_i) \quad \forall j.S,T{::}\kappa\{\};\overline{\alpha{:}\kappa},(\overline{x{:}t})_j \vdash t_j :: c_j \\ S,T{::}\kappa\{\};\overline{\alpha{:}\kappa},\overline{x{:}t} \vdash T\ \vec{t}'\ \vec{v}' :: c \quad \forall j.apos(c,T,t_j{::}c_j) \end{array}}{S \vdash T{::}\kappa\{D{:}\forall\overline{\alpha{::}\kappa}.\overline{x{:}t} \rightarrow T\ \vec{t}'\ \vec{v}'\}\ \text{ok}} \qquad \frac{(c' = A \Rightarrow c = A) \quad c = P \Rightarrow \forall 1 \leq i < n.T \notin FTC(t_i)}{apos(c,T,((x:t_1 \rightarrow \ldots \rightarrow t_n){::}c'))}$$

Figure 1. Selected static semantics of F*

troduces a unit refined with the assumed formula ϕ—no logical evidence is produced for ϕ. To justify this rule, the dynamic semantics of this expression adds a formula to the dynamic log $\mathscr{A}$. (T-V) allows value v to be refined with the formula ϕ when ϕ is derivable: $S;\Gamma' \models \phi$. The context Γ' includes bindings $x{:}t, x = v$ which allow the derivability relation to use information about v; however, for kind-correctness, we require the kinding of the introduced formula to not rely on the introduced equality. Ghost refinements have no impact on the representation of values, so they admit structural subtyping. The subtyping rules include (S-ϕI), like (T-V), an introduction form for ghost refinements and (S-ϕE), an elimination form. (S-Arr) lifts the relation into the structure of function types—omitted rules do the same for other constructions. In contrast, concrete refinements (i.e., the dependent pairs of Coq, Fine etc.) do not enjoy this structural subtyping relation. Instead, via a systematic translation to insert coercions (called *derefinement*) inherited from Fine, F* provides programmers with a weaker, non-structural subtyping relation on concrete refinements. Subtyping also includes type conversion, an equivalence relation according to the judgment $S;\Gamma \vdash t_1 \equiv t_2$. This relation, discussed briefly in conjunction with (T-Match), converts types using equations that appear in the context, and is available everywhere within the structure of types.

Logic parametricity is embodied by (T-V) and (S-ϕI): various definitions of the derivability relation ($S;\Gamma \models \phi$) can be "plugged in" to the type system, as long as the relation meets a few important admissibility constraints. Admissible relations must at least be the identity on refined assumptions ($S;x : (x{:}t\{\phi\}) \models \phi$); be closed under substitution of free variables in Γ; be allowed to use structural rules such as weakening, duplication and permutation; and be insensitive to the presence of derivable equality assumptions in the context ($S;\Gamma, v = v \models \phi \iff S;\Gamma \models \phi$). Pragmatically, we often plug in a decision procedure for first order logic with additional theories, as implemented by the Z3 theorem prover—the ability to use structural rules (e.g., weakening) in the logic, enabled by our restrictions on the use of affine indices in types, makes it easy to support automation. Formally, we also exploit logic parametricity to provide an embedding of F7's formal core, RCF, into F*, plugging into (T-V) RCF's entailment relation (which, unlike F*, includes the basic first-order connectives and equality, each satisfying their usual introduction and elimination forms).

Consistency of the P-universe requires placing restrictions in various parts of the type system. For an expression e to reside in P, e must be free of non-P expressions, since those may diverge—the last premise of (T-Let) enforces this property. We disallow discriminating on values that reside in $\star$ or A when constructing propositions in the branches of a **match**—the last premise of (T-Match) shows this. We also have constraints on the well-formedness of inductive type T (recall that we use $\overline{(\alpha{::}\kappa)}_i$ to mean $\alpha_1{::}\kappa_1,\ldots,\alpha_{i-1}{::}\kappa_{i-1}$). In (WFS-D), the first premise ensures that the kind κ of T is well-formed; the second and third premises ensure that the arguments of D are well-formed; the fourth premise ensures that the constructed type matches the kind expected for T; and the final premise imposes two key restrictions: (1) constructors with affine arguments must construct affine results—this is unrelated to totality of P-functions; (2) a positivity constraint on inductive P-kinded types. We use a relatively simple version of positivity, excluding the constructed type T in negative position in any argument of D.

These constraints are similar to those imposed by Aura on its Prop universe—to our knowledge, Aura is the only other language that embeds a strongly normalizing core within a language with arbitrary recursion. However, there are several important differences. First, Aura (like Coq) insists on Prop terms being computationally irrelevant, so its match rule forbids cross-universe elimination—Prop terms cannot be eliminated to construct values in Type. We explicitly wish to program over proofs, so F* permits P-to-$\star$ elimination. Next, Aura does not allow the branches of a match expression to use equality assumptions between the pattern and the scrutinized term. This makes it impossible to program on proof terms, as shown in §2.5, which make essential use of GADT-style programming patterns. In contrast, (T-Match) checks the **then**-branch e_1 in a context that includes equality assumptions induced by unifying the type of the pattern with the type of the scrutinee (the first three premises on the second line). These equality assumptions are used in $S;\Gamma \vdash t \equiv t'$ to allow typing derivations to freely refine both type and value indices within types. This feature complicates the consistency proof of F*'s P-fragment. We discuss this aspect when presenting the metatheory of F*.

3.3 Dynamic semantics: logical effects and affine names

The dynamic semantics of F* is a small-step reduction relation for a call-by-value language. It has the form $(\mathscr{A};e) \rightarrow_S (\mathscr{A};e')$ where the signature S is unvarying. The interesting part of this relation is the log $\mathscr{A}$, a non-decreasing set of logical facts ϕ and names ℓ for affine values. As mentioned in §2.2, the set of facts in $\mathscr{A}$ is used in the definition of ghost refinement derivability. Facts are added to the log using the **assume** ϕ form, which reduces as below.

$$\text{E-Log}\ \frac{}{(\mathscr{A};\textbf{assume}\ \phi) \rightarrow_S (\mathscr{A},\phi;())}$$

Foreshadowing our safety condition for ghost refinements (Corollary 1), we show that, when a well-typed program $e : x{:}t\{\phi\}$ reduces to a value, that is $(\cdot;e) \rightarrow_S^* (\mathscr{A};v)$, its refinement formula ϕ is derivable from the signature and all the accumulated logical effects: $S;\mathsf{Facts}(\mathscr{A}) \models \phi[v/x]$. This is in contrast to our soundness result for proof terms, expressions that reside in the P-fragment, for which we obtain a more traditional logical consistency property. In a distributed program, the log is an idealized global view of the logical state of all participants. Ghost refinements accompanied by cryptographic evidence (in the form of digital signatures) enable speaking about this distributed state.

The log also tracks affine values. We aim to show that well-typed programs destruct affine values at most once. For this purpose, we instrument the dynamic semantics to tag an affine value v with a fresh name when it is introduced, recording the name in the log (E-Newℓ). Names held in the log come in two variants: names ℓ are "live", while names $\hat{\ell}$ are "dead". When v appears in a destruct position (the context E in (E-Killℓ), which includes the function position of a β redex, and the scrutinee position of a match), we require the name ℓ to be "live" in the log for reduction to not get stuck, kill the name in $\mathscr{A}$, and then proceed. This instrumentation serves as our specification of the use-at-most-once property.

$$\text{E-New}\ell\ \frac{S;\mathsf{Facts}(\mathscr{A}) \vdash t :: A \qquad \text{fresh } \ell \\ S;\mathsf{Facts}(\mathscr{A});\mathsf{LiveNames}(\mathscr{A}) \vdash v : t}{(\mathscr{A};v) \rightarrow_S (\mathscr{A},\ell;v^\ell)}$$

$$\text{E-Kill}\ell\ \frac{}{(\mathscr{A}_1,\ell,\mathscr{A}_2;E[v^\ell]) \rightarrow_s (\mathscr{A}_1,\hat{\ell},\mathscr{A}_2;E[v])}$$

3.4 Metatheory of F*

Our first theorem is a type soundness result, stated in terms of standard progress and preservation lemmas. In addition to well-typed programs not getting stuck, this result ensures that affinely typed values are destructed at most once, and can thus be soundly implemented using destructive reads and mutation. (The theorem relies on an auxiliary judgment $S \vdash \mathscr{A} \Longrightarrow \Gamma;X$ which obtains a context $\Gamma;X$ from the dynamic log, where Γ includes the logical assumptions accumulated in $\mathscr{A}$, and live names in $\mathscr{A}$ recorded in X.)

THEOREM 1 (Type soundness). *For all S, $\mathscr{A}$, Γ, X, X', e, and t such that*

(1) $S \vdash \mathscr{A} \Longrightarrow \Gamma;X$,
(2) $\vdash S;\Gamma;X$ *wf, and*
(3) $S;\Gamma;X' \vdash e : t$ *where* $X' \subseteq X$,

either e is a value, or there exist $\mathscr{A}'$, e', Γ', and X'' such that

(1) $S \vdash \mathscr{A}' \Longrightarrow \Gamma';X''$,
(2) $X'' = (X' \setminus \mathsf{DeadNames}(\mathscr{A}')) \cup \mathsf{LiveNames}(\mathscr{A}' \setminus \mathscr{A})$,
(3) $\exists\Gamma''.\Gamma' = \Gamma,\Gamma''$, *and*
(4) $S;\Gamma';X'' \vdash e' : t$.

From type soundness, we obtain our main safety property for ghost refinements: their formulas are derivable from the logical effects accumulated in the log.

COROLLARY 1 (Safety for ghost refinements). *For all S, $\mathscr{A}$, Γ, e, ϕ, t, $\mathscr{A}'$, Γ', and v such that $\vdash S$ ok, $S \vdash \mathscr{A} \Longrightarrow \Gamma;X$, $S;\Gamma;X \vdash e : x{:}t\{\phi\}$, and $(\mathscr{A};e) \rightarrow_S^* (\mathscr{A}';v)$, there exists Γ' such that $S \vdash \mathscr{A}' \Longrightarrow \Gamma';\_$ and $S;\Gamma' \models \phi[v/x]$.*

Theorem 2 (Logical consistency of P) shows logical consistency of the P-fragment, by translating P-terms into CiC (The Coq Development Team 2010), which is widely believed to be strongly normalizing. Intuitively, the theorem states that the translation of F*'s P-fragment into CiC is a (weak) simulation, with regard to F* and CiC's reduction relations. Since in CiC, all reduction sequences are presumed to be finite, this guarantees the absence of infinite reduction sequences for F*'s P-terms. A direct proof of strong normalization of F*'s P-fragment is likely to be challenging since it involves inductive types like CiC. Our proof strategy borrows ideas from a proof of a related property in Aura. However, unlike Aura, F* supports implicit type conversions using equalities introduced by pattern matching—we find this essential for programming over proof terms. We translate this to CiC through the use of explicit, equality-witnessing conversions in CiC.

In the statement of the theorem below, $(S;\Gamma;\cdot \vdash_p e : t \hookrightarrow \tau)$ is the translation that marks non-P-lambdas in F* term e and translates them to a CiC term τ. $(\rightsquigarrow)$ is the reduction of P-terms; and $(\longrightarrow_{\beta,\iota,\delta})$ is term conversion in CiC.

THEOREM 2 (Logical consistency of P). *For all S, Γ, p, e, e', t, τ such that $\vdash S;\Gamma\ ok_E$ and $S;\Gamma \vdash t :: P$, if $S;\Gamma;\cdot \vdash_p e : t \hookrightarrow \tau$ and $e \rightsquigarrow e'$, then there exists τ' such that $\tau \longrightarrow^*_{\beta,\iota,\delta} \tau'$ and $S;\Gamma;\cdot \vdash_p e' : t \hookrightarrow \tau'$.*

Theorem 3 (Well-typed translation of RCF) is an embedding into F* of a core fragment of RCF without Public/Tainted kinds, without concurrency, and with restrictions on the use of RCF's isorecursive types. In the statement below, A is an RCF configuration; E is an RCF context; and $A \rightarrow A'$ is a single step of reduction in RCF. The notation $[\![\cdot]\!]$ means translation. The judgment $E \vdash \diamond$ means that E is well-formed. The translation is over the structure of RCF typing derivations. The theorem states, roughly, that well-typed RCF terms translate to well-typed F* terms, and that the translation is a simulation, i.e., reduction steps in RCF correspond to reductions in F*.

THEOREM 3 (Well-typed translation of RCF). *Given $E \vdash [\![A]\!] = (\mathscr{A};e)$, $\vdash [\![E]\!] = S;\Gamma$, and $E \vdash \diamond$, we have $S;\Gamma;. \vdash e : t$ where $E \vdash [\![T]\!] = t$. Additionally $A \rightarrow A'$ if and only if $(\mathscr{A};e) \rightarrow_S (\mathscr{A}';e')$ and $E \vdash [\![A']\!] = (\mathscr{A}';e')$.*

3.5 Coq formalization

The proofs of the metatheory of F* were initially done by hand. As we reached completion of the hand proofs, we started a formalization of the meta-theory of F* in the Coq proof assistant, using the SSREFLECT extension (Gonthier et al. 2011). At the time of writing, we had formalized the whole calculus definition, along with a major part of its metatheory, including all the key technical lemmas up to substitutivity, and a partial proof of the type soundness result. We found a few oversights in our pencil and paper proofs, which we have since corrected. We expect to have a fully mechanized type soundness proof in the near future. A more challenging, next step is a formalization of the embedding of the propositional part of F* to CiC. We plan to use the Barras's formalization of CiC[1] as a basis.

Our formalization in Coq is noteworthy in several ways. First, this is the first time the SSREFLECT package has been used to carry out a large development in programming language metatheory. We started out attempting to use the Coq code generator Ott (Sewell et al. 2010) to help reduce the gap between the formal and informal descriptions of our type system. Although this did help in the maintenance of the two versions of the type system, we found that with the many different kinds of variables in F*, the code produced by Ott resulted in a very large, incomplete set of lemmas.

Following this experience, we have developed a new framework for metatheory using SSREFLECT, and use it on F*—a particularly challenging test case, since it involves many kinds of names and binders, with subtle differences across the levels of terms, types and kinds. Furthermore, most central judgments in the type system are mutually recursive. Despite these complications, we are happy to note that our framework has allowed us to develop short, largely automated proofs. Our experience is encouraging initial progress towards an eventual goal: a general framework, based on the reflection pattern and the theory of the pure lambda calculus, dedicated to the study of type systems. We think that the development of the F* formal meta-theory will serve as a basis of such a framework.

4. Secure multi-party sessions in F*

This section shows how to use the libraries and programming idioms in §2 to write and verify realistic distributed security applications. The combination of cryptographic evidence, ghost refinements, and affine types proves crucial for this case study and enables more precise specifications and stronger proofs than earlier results obtained using F7 (Bhargavan et al. 2009).

4.1 Multi-party sessions

Multi-party sessions (Bhargavan et al. 2009; Deniélou and Yoshida 2011; Honda et al. 2008) offer a powerful method to structure and build distributed message-based applications when their message flow is fixed beforehand. Consider a 3-party session between a customer (c), a website (w), and a credit-card verifier (v), with the message flow below:

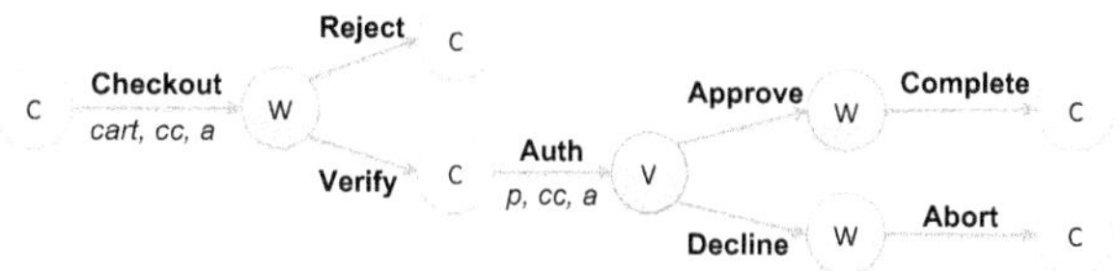

The customer initiates a Checkout session for buying some items (*cart*), billed to her credit card *cc* for the total amount a. The web site then either rejects the transaction outright, or asks for credit card verification. The customer is redirected to a verification server and provides a password (p) to authorize payment of a on her credit card *cc*. The verifier then either confirms or declines payment to the web site, who completes or aborts the session accordingly.

Such a session specifies a contract between component programs in a distributed application. Every program promises to play one role of the session, and in return, it expects the others to correctly play their roles. For instance, w promises not to charge more than a, and not to abort the transaction if the payment is approved: c can rest assured that if she receives an Abort message, her credit card has not been charged.

A variety of type systems have been proposed to verify that a program complies with a session role, and each type system is tailored to a specific set of session primitives and programming language features. Instead, we encode multi-party sessions as F* types. By standard F* typing, we can verify that a program correctly plays a session role. Even if some programs deviate from their role at run-time (because they have been taken over by an attacker, for example), we show how the rest of the application can protect itself by using a custom cryptographic protocol.

4.2 A session API in F*

We define a generic session API for distributed applications to enforce a multi-party session discipline. We start with a simplified version of our API, then build up to showing our model of more complex features.

To begin with, we ignore the values (*cart*, *cc*, a, p) passed in the session and aim to control the sequence of messages a session participant can send and receive. Using affine types, we can define a type for a *role process*, **type** role0::$E \Rightarrow A$, where the parameter of the role is a type describing an automaton. The types used to define these automata are purely specificational—they are given E-kind. A value of a role process type is a handle that gives a program the capability to enact the automaton. We show two simple automata types provided by our API, and a function that consumes and returns a role handle.

```
type Send0 :: 'm::★ ⇒ 'k::('m ⇒ E) ⇒ E
type Done :: E
val send: m:'m → role0 (Send0 m 'k) → role0 ('k m)
```

The Send0 automaton is indexed by two types—the first, a type 'm of the message to be sent by the process; the second, a type 'k representing a *continuation process*, where the process is dependent on the value of type 'm sent in the first state. Done represents a finished automaton. Using these automata, we can define the

[1] http://www.lix.polytechnique.fr/~barras/proofs/sets/

following role process type that represents a program that first sends an integer x, then an integer y greater than x, and then concludes. (In concrete syntax, we write **fun** (x:t) ⇒ t' for a type-level function $\lambda x{:}t.t'$; **fun** _ ⇒ t' ignores its type argument.)

```
role0 (Send0 int (fun (x:int) ⇒ Send0 (y:int{y > x}) (fun _ ⇒ Done)))
```

Our full API generalizes the automata types above with the notion of a global distributed store for session values; each participant maintains a local view of the store and we ensure, by typing, that these views are consistent. We show below the extended analogs of role0, Send0, and also automata types for receiving a message and for choice-points in the session graph. The type of a role process (role) is parametrized by a store value (of type 'st); automata types (Send, Recv) are indexed by binary predicates δ on 'st values that define the allowed changes to the store during the next step. The function send allows a client to send a message m and update the store from s0 to s1 given that the current role process is a Send and that the stores satisfy the predicate δ attached to Send—client programs calling send have to prove δ s0 s1 for some specific instantiation of δ, and our type checker uses Z3 to assist with the proof of such ghost refinement properties.

```
type role:: 'st::⋆ ⇒ E ⇒ 'st ⇒ A
type Send:: 'm::⋆⇒ 'st::⋆⇒ 'm⇒ ('st⇒ 'st⇒ E )⇒ 'k::('m⇒ E )⇒ E
type Recv:: 'm::⋆⇒ 'st::⋆⇒ 'm⇒ ('st⇒ 'st⇒ E )⇒ 'k::('m⇒ E )⇒ E
type Choice:: 'l::E ⇒ 'r::E ⇒ E
val send: m:'m → s0:'st → s1:'st{δ s0 s1}
        → role (Send 'm 'st m δ 'k) s0 → role ('k m) s1
```

The code below shows how we can use this session API to model the website role (w) in the example session of §4.1. The type msg defines the set of messages and the type store is the type of the distributed store (including, for this example, the names of each participant in the session, their view of the contents of the shopping cart, etc.) The process automaton involves an alternation of message send and receive, and this type uses two store update predicates (of kind store ⇒ store ⇒ E): Update_id_c_v_cart_cc_a allows initial assignments from the customer to id, c, v, cart, cc, and a; then Unchanged disallows any changes.

```
type msg = Checkout | Reject | Verify | Auth | Approve | (...)
type store = {id:nat; c:prin; w:prin; v:prin; cart:string; (...) }
type proc_w =
  Recv Checkout Update_id_c_v_cart_cc_a (fun _ ⇒ Choice
    (Send Reject Unchanged (fun _ ⇒ Done)
    (Send Verify Unchanged (fun _ ⇒ Choice
      (Recv Approve Unchanged (fun _ ⇒
           Send Complete Unchanged (fun _ ⇒ Done)))
      (Recv Decline Unchanged (fun _ ⇒
           Send Abort Unchanged (fun _ ⇒ Done)))))
```

Type soundness ensures that a well-typed program is guaranteed to comply with its declared role process. For example, a program that joins a session in role w obtains a role handle of type role proc_w init_store_w. It may then call the receive function (the counterpart of send, not shown here) to receive a Checkout message but cannot call send; subsequently, it may call send with either a Reject or a Verify message, but not both.

In earlier work, Bhargavan et al. (2009) showed how to encode multi-party sessions as refinement types in F7. However, since the F7 type system does not support generic predicate-indexed types, such as Send above, they encode the session using large session-specific logical formulas rather than types. Our use of F⋆ higher-order kinds here yields session specifications that are, in general, one-third the size of the corresponding F7 specifications. Moreover, F7 lacks affine types, and they have to prove by hand, with the help of an awkward continuation-passing style encoding, that their applications use role handles linearly.

4.3 Custom cryptographic protocols for session consistency

Distributed applications typically run in an untrusted environment, where the network and one or more of the session participants may be under the control of malicious adversaries. In this scenario, cryptographic mechanisms, such as digital signatures, can be used ensure that all honest session participants have consistent states. For example, when the client c receives an Abort message from the website w, it may demand that this message include a valid signature proving that card verifier v Declined, to prevent a malicious w from double-crossing c.

Bhargavan et al. (2009) show how to systematically use cryptographic evidence as proof of session compliance. They compile multi-party sessions to efficient custom cryptographic protocols that exchange and check a minimal number of digital signatures to ensure global session consistency. Their compiled protocols use session types and cryptography in the style of F7: without higher-order kinds, affinity, or predicate-indexed types.

We implement secure multi-party sessions in F⋆ using protocol libraries adapted from those of Bhargavan et al., but instead using the crypto library of §2.3 and the sessions API shown above. In our example session, the Abort message from w to c carries two digital signatures, one from w and one from v, each signature authenticating the last message sent by the corresponding principal and the values in its store at that time. On receiving the Abort message, c verifies these signatures and checks that they conform to the session type: in particular, that the signature from v says that v sent a Decline message and not an Approve. The resulting type for the recv_Abort function (a specialization of the generic receive function in our API) is as follows:

```
type Aborted:: w:prin ⇒ st_w:store ⇒ E
type Declined:: v:prin ⇒ st_v:store ⇒ E
val recv_Abort:
  st_c:store → role (RecvCompleteOrAbort) st_c →
  (st_c':store ∗ role Done st_c'){
    Unchanged st_c st_c' ∧
    Says st_c.w (∃ st_w. Aborted st_c.w st_w ∧ Unchanged st_w st_c') ∧
    Says st_c.v (∃ st_v. Declined st_c.v st_v ∧ Unchanged st_v st_c')}
```

The function takes the current store st_c at c and a role handle for c that must be in the state after c has sent Auth. The function returns an (unchanged) store st_c' and a new (completed) role handle. The E-kinded predicates Aborted and Declined represent the session states at the other roles. For example, Declined p st means that the principal p, playing role v previously sent a Decline when it had a store st. Hence, the post-condition says that the principals st_c.w and st_c.v (playing w, v) claim to be in the states Aborted st_c.w st_w and Declined st_c.v st_v where the stores st_w and st_v are the same as c's store st_c'. So if v is honest, then even if w is malicious, it cannot cause c to accept an Abort unless v sent a Decline. Note that the post-condition is a ghost refinement that is proved here using a combination of cryptographic evidence and F⋆ typechecking.

4.4 Encoding advanced session constructs in F⋆

The four automata types shown above are adequate to represent a wide variety of static sessions that do not use delegation or parallelism. Adding constructors for recursive sessions is straightforward. We now show how to extend our API to capture a limited form of parallelism, inspired by the dynamic multi-role session types of Deniélou and Yoshida (2011).

Distributed applications often run several instances of the same role in parallel, for scalability. For example, a web site may run several copies of a web server all connected to the same backend database. Or, a client may fork several processes that may communicate with a server in parallel, in an arbitrary order. To verify such applications we extend our sessions API with three new automata types: Fork, Join, and Await.

The Fork automaton (given below) enables a role to fork multiple instances of a child role, transfer control to them, and then wait for them to complete. These child role processes may either execute sequentially (in any order), or in parallel. Each child process is given a unique principal name which it can use when communicating with its parent or with other roles. The Join automaton enables the child role to transfer control back to the parent; and Await represents a parent role process waiting for its children to complete.

We illustrate Fork and its use in an application below, where we elide the store for simplicity (and so use role0 instead of role).

```
type Fork :: ps:list prin ⇒ 'ParentProc::E
        ⇒ 'ChildProc::(role0 (Await ps 'ParentProc) ⇒ prin ⇒ E)
        ⇒ E
let go ps : role0 Done =
  let client = startClient ps in
  let client, children = fork ps client in
  let children =
    map (fun (q, child) →
            let child = send0 Request child in
            let Response, child = receive0 child in
              (q, child)) children in
    join ps client children
```

The function go forks a number of children (indexed by a given list of principals ps). Each child sends a Request message, then receives a Response message and then joins its parent (p). Here, the variable client is a role handle that has an automaton type of the form Fork ps Done ChildRole, where the automaton ChildRole sends a Request, receives a Response and then Joins its parent. Since role handles have an affine type, the code here passes client in and out of every session operation. The variable children is given an affine list type, which guarantees that the different child processes cannot interfere with each other; in other words each Response can be accurately correlated with its corresponding Request.

5. Implementation and Measurement

This section describes the implementation of our prototype F* compiler and its performance measured on a variety of programs (about 20,000 lines of code in total), including cloud applications, cryptographic protocols, and secure browser extensions.

Compilation. The F* compiler consists of about 35,000 lines of F# code and is still under active development. It is based on the type-preserving compiler for Fine (Chen et al. 2010). It takes as input an F* program and typechecks the program by asking logical queries of Z3. The compiler also accepts Fine and F7 programs and translates them into F*. Source programs are then compiled to RDCIL, a small extension of a functional core of the .NET bytecode language CIL. Like DCIL, the target language of Fine, RDCIL extends CIL with type-level functions and value parameters (in addition to type parameters) in class declarations, to model value-dependent types in the source language. Unlike DCIL, RDCIL also supports ghost refinements. RDCIL encodes these additional type constructs as custom attributes, so RDCIL binaries can run on stock .NET virtual machines, access libraries of other .NET languages (e.g., C# and F#), and be called from those languages. RDCIL is fully typed and can be verified (with the help of Z3) for security, the same way F* is verified.

Checking two forms of refinements in RDCIL. Ghost refinement is a new feature of F* and RDCIL, not supported by Fine or DCIL. Ghost refinements in F* are translated to ghost refinements in RDCIL, and the typechecker for RDCIL verifies them using Z3.

Concrete refinements are handled similarly in F* and Fine. During source typechecking, the F* compiler extracts proofs of concrete refinements from the SMT solver and injects them as terms in the generated RDCIL. Hence, concrete refinements in the source program are translated to a pair of a value and an explicit proof in RDCIL, which can be verified by the RDCIL type checker.

Reducing the size of generated bytecode. Explicit proofs can be costly though. Carrying proofs increases the code size by 50x for a Fine benchmark. The F* compiler addresses this difficulty by relying on the RDCIL typechecker to reconstruct proofs by refinement type checking, rather than just depend on explicit proofs. As a result, RDCIL programs contain far fewer proofs compared to DCIL, and the overhead of proofs and types is only 60% for our benchmarks. The F* compiler also reduces the size of generated bytecode (ignoring proofs and custom attributes for types), because higher-order dependent kinds allow more concise translation of polymorphic types and higher-order code, which are prevalent in F* programs. Combining the two factors, the F* compiler produces binaries an order of magnitude smaller than those produced by Fine, as much as a 45x improvement.

5.1 Benchmarks and Measurements

Code size. We compile the Fine benchmarks in (Chen et al. 2010) with the F* compiler, treating all refinement types as ghost refinements. This way, no proofs are extracted. The table below shows the names of the benchmarks (column Bench.), the F* code size (in bytes) with and without custom attributes for the additional types (A+ and A- respectively), and Fine size (in bytes) with and without proofs reported in (Chen et al. 2010) (Pf+ and Pf- respectively). The Fine numbers reflect only proof overhead, not attributes.

	F* size		Fine size		A+/	A-/	A+/	A-/
Bench.	A+	A-	Pf+	Pf-	Pf+	Pf+	A-	Pf-
Authac	15k	12k	30k	20k	0.50	0.4	1.3	0.6
Iflow	27k	18k	840k	30k	0.03	0.02	1.5	0.6
Automaton	28k	15k	40k	20k	0.70	0.38	1.9	0.8
HealthWeb	76k	48k	2.1M	80k	0.04	0.02	1.6	0.6
Lookout	147k	81k	1.8M	120k	0.08	0.05	1.8	0.7
ConfRM	72k	51k	3.3M	110k	0.02	0.02	1.4	0.5
Total	365k	225k	8.1M	380k	0.05	0.03	1.6	0.6
ProofLib	7M	5M	51M	51M	0.14	0.1	1.4	0.1

Because of no proofs, the code size overhead is simply the custom attributes for encoding more expressive types than the CIL types. Column "A+/A-" shows that RDCIL code with those custom attributes is about 1.3x-1.9x of the code without the custom attributes, with an average 60% overhead for the custom attributes. Our current implementation simply uses compressed strings of pretty-printing types as custom attributes. A smarter encoding may further reduce the size overhead.

The RDCIL code is about an order of magnitude smaller than the DCIL code for the Fine benchmarks. Column "A+/Pf+" shows that the RDCIL code (with custom attributes) is about 3%-70% of the DCIL code (with proofs), with an average of 5%—a 20x improvement. Column "A-/Pf+" shows that the RDCIL code (without custom attributes) is about 2%-38% of the DCIL code (with proofs), with an average of 3%—indicating a 30x improvement in this configuration, although the accurate breakdown is hard to obtain because Fine numbers do not include custom attributes. Benchmarks with less proofs, e.g., Authac and Automaton, show less reduction. Column "A-/Pf-" shows that the pure code size of RDCIL is about 10% to 80% of that of DCIL, with an average of 60%—a 40% reduction because of a more expressive type language. Prooflib is purely refinement-free code. The 10x reduction in code size is entirely due to dependent higher kinds.

Compilation and typechecking times. The table below shows the time taken to typecheck and compile the Fine benchmarks as well as several new F* programs we develop ourselves. For each program, it shows number of lines of source code (LOC), source parsing and checking time (SC, in seconds), compilation of F* to RDCIL time (Trans), target checking time (TC), and the number of queries made to Z3 by the source checker (SQ) and target checker

(TQ). All measurements were performed on a 2.67 GHz two-core Intel Core i7 CPU running Windows 7.

Bench.	LOC	SC	Trans	TC	SQ	TQ
Authac	37	0.2	0.1	0.2	1	1
Iflow	119	0.8	0.4	0.5	25	18
Automaton	117	0.3	0.2	0.3	5	4
HealthWeb	330	2.3	1.9	1.1	33	10
Lookout	502	2.4	2.4	1.9	29	33
ConfRM	704	2.7	2.5	1.8	63	21
Prooflib	10694	20.8	258.3	14.7	0	0
HealthwebEnh	766	8.0	8.5	5.8	156	83
HigherOrderIter	150	1.0	3.5	1.6	13	13
HigherOrderFoldr	108	2.3	5.8	0.9	10	6
Permission	251	4.1	4.3	5.5	29	29
Iflow_state	204	0.8	0.6	0.8	7	14
Provenance	221	1.6	1.5	0.8	22	17
Browser exts	785	3.1	3.3	3.8	89	55
DynSessions	211	0.7	0.5	0.2	0	0

HealthwebEnh is a cloud application managing an electronic medical record database, interacting with code written in ASP.NET, C#, and F#. It is about twice as big as the Fine HealthWeb benchmark, and is deployable on Microsoft Windows Azure. HigherOrderIter and HigherOrderFoldr implement higher-order library functions that iterate over lists. Permission implements a stateful API of collections and iterators that guarantee that the collection underlying an iterator is never modified while an iteration is in progress. Iflow_state provides an information-flow tracking library for stateful programs. Provenance is a larger version of the curated database in §2.5. Browser exts is a suite of 17 browser extensions, verified for authorization and information flow properties. DynSessions is the example of §4, including fork/join parallelism.

Fine and F* source typechecking times are roughly equivalent. F* translation is faster than Fine because there are fewer proofs to translate. Conversely, typechecking RDCIL code with refinement types is slower than checking DCIL proofs, but in view of the many advantages of F*, such as smaller bytecode and more expressive types, we find this tradeoff worthwhile.

Verifying cryptographic applications. Finally, we report source code verification results for several cryptographic protocol examples, many of which were previously developed for F7, and are now verified by F*.

Example	LOC	SC	SQ
CryptoLib	1530	50.5	426
KeyManager	608	55.6	287
AuthRPC	232	67.9	335
SessionLib	32	0.4	0
Commit	126	1.5	28
Forward	131	1.3	22
Metering	111	0.6	3

CryptoLib is a large F7 library implementing symbolic cryptography, which is used in all subsequent applications. KeyManager is a key management application. AuthRPC implements an authenticated RPC protocol. SessionLib is the generic API for multiparty sessions (§4), used to securely implement a two-party session Commit and a three-party session Forward. Metering is a privacy-friendly zero-knowledge cryptographic protocol for smart metering (Rial and Danezis 2010).

6. Related work

We have compared F* to Fine, F7, Aura, Coq, Agda, and discussed other related work in detail throughout this paper. Here, we briefly cover a few more topics. Guts et al. (2009) show how to build cryptographic audit trails that can be verified by independent third parties; Vaughan et al. (2008) argue that logs of logical evidence could also build audit trails. Neither consider the combination of mobile logical and cryptographic proofs, augmented with selective erasure and reconstruction. Related work on session types focuses on enforcing session compliance in the absence of malicious adversaries. Honda et al. (2008) develop special-purpose type systems for multi-party asynchronous sessions. They do not consider security or source code verification. Kiselyov et al. (2010) add type functions to Haskell and show how these can be used to program simple two-party sessions.

References

K. Avijit, A. Datta, and R. Harper. Distributed programming with distributed authorization. In *TLDI*, 2010.

M. Backes, C. Hritcu, and M. Maffei. Type-checking zero-knowledge. In *CCS*, 2008.

J. Bengtson, K. Bhargavan, C. Fournet, A. D. Gordon, and S. Maffeis. Refinement types for secure implementations. In *CSF*, 2008.

Y. Bertot and P. Castéran. *Coq'Art: Interactive Theorem Proving and Program Development*. Springer Verlag, 2004.

K. Bhargavan, R. Corin, P.-M. Déniélou, C. Fournet, and J. Leifer. Cryptographic protocol synthesis and verification for multiparty sessions. In *CSF*, 2009.

K. Bhargavan, C. Fournet, and A. D. Gordon. Modular verification of security protocol code by typing. In *POPL*, 2010.

J. Borgstrom, J. Chen, and N. Swamy. Verifying stateful programs with substructural state and hoare types. In *PLPV '11*, Jan. 2011.

I. Cervesato and F. Pfenning. A linear logical framework. *Inf. Comput.*, 179 (1), 2002.

P. C. Chapin, C. Skalka, and X. S. Wang. Authorization in trust management: Features and foundations. *ACM Comput. Surv.*, 40, 2008.

J. Chen, R. Chugh, and N. Swamy. Type-preserving compilation of end-to-end verification of security enforcement. In *PLDI '10*. ACM, 2010.

L. de Moura and N. Bjørner. Z3: An efficient SMT solver. In *TACAS*, 2008.

P.-M. Deniélou and N. Yoshida. Dynamic multirole session types. In *POPL*, 2011.

G. Gonthier, A. Mahboubi, and E. Tassi. Research Report RR-6455, 2011.

A. D. Gordon and A. Jeffrey. Authenticity by typing for security protocols. *Journal of Computer Security*, 11(4):451–520, 2003.

A. Guha, M. Fredrikson, B. Livshits, and N. Swamy. Verified security for browser extensions. In *IEEE Symposium on Security and Privacy (Oakland)*, 2011.

N. Guts, C. Fournet, and F. Z. Nardelli. Reliable evidence: Auditability by typing. In *ESORICS*, 2009.

K. Honda, N. Yoshida, and M. Carbone. Multiparty asynchronous session types. In *POPL*, 2008.

L. Jia and S. Zdancewic. Encoding information flow in aura. In *PLAS*, 2009.

L. Jia, J. Vaughan, K. Mazurak, J. Zhao, L. Zarko, J. Schorr, and S. Zdancewic. Aura: A programming language for authorization and audit. In *ICFP*, 2008.

O. Kiselyov, S. P. Jones, and C. chieh Shan. Fun with type functions, 2010. Unpub.

S. K. Lahiri, S. Qadeer, and D. Walker. Linear maps. PLPV '11. ACM, 2011.

U. Norell. *Towards a practical programming language based on dependent type theory*. PhD thesis, Chalmers Institute of Technology, 2007.

A. Rial and G. Danezis. Privacy-friendly smart metering. Technical report, Microsoft Research, nov 2010.

P. Sewell, F. Z. Nardelli, S. Owens, G. Peskine, T. Ridge, S. Sarkar, and R. Strnisa. Ott: Effective tool support for the working semanticist. *JFP*, 20(1), 2010.

M. Sozeau. Subset coercions in coq. In *TYPES*, 2007.

N. Swamy, B. J. Corcoran, and M. Hicks. Fable: A language for enforcing user-defined security policies. In *S&P*, 2008.

N. Swamy, J. Chen, and R. Chugh. Enforcing stateful authorization and information flow policies in Fine. In *ESOP*, 2010.

The Coq Development Team. Chapter 4: Calculus of Inductive Constructions. Technical report, 2010. URL `http://coq.inria.fr`.

J. A. Vaughan, L. Jia, K. Mazurak, and S. Zdancewic. Evidence-based audit. In *CSF*, 2008.

D. Volpano, G. Smith, and C. Irvine. A sound type system for secure flow analysis. *Journal of Computer Security*, 4(3):167–187, 1996.

Frenetic: A Network Programming Language

Nate Foster
Cornell University

Rob Harrison
Princeton University

Michael J. Freedman
Princeton University

Christopher Monsanto
Princeton University

Jennifer Rexford
Princeton University

Alec Story
Cornell University

David Walker
Princeton University

Abstract

Modern networks provide a variety of interrelated services including routing, traffic monitoring, load balancing, and access control. Unfortunately, the languages used to program today's networks lack modern features—they are usually defined at the low level of abstraction supplied by the underlying hardware and they fail to provide even rudimentary support for modular programming. As a result, network programs tend to be complicated, error-prone, and difficult to maintain.

This paper presents Frenetic, a high-level language for programming distributed collections of network switches. Frenetic provides a declarative query language for classifying and aggregating network traffic as well as a functional reactive combinator library for describing high-level packet-forwarding policies. Unlike prior work in this domain, these constructs are—by design—fully compositional, which facilitates modular reasoning and enables code reuse. This important property is enabled by Frenetic's novel run-time system which manages all of the details related to installing, uninstalling, and querying low-level packet-processing rules on physical switches.

Overall, this paper makes three main contributions: (1) We analyze the state-of-the art in languages for programming networks and identify the key limitations; (2) We present a language design that addresses these limitations, using a series of examples to motivate and validate our choices; (3) We describe an implementation of the language and evaluate its performance on several benchmarks.

Categories and Subject Descriptors D.3.2 [*Programming Languages*]: Language Classifications—Specialized application languages

General Terms Languages, Design

Keywords Network programming languages, domain-specific languages, functional reactive programming, OpenFlow

1. Introduction

Today's networks consist of hardware and software components that are closed and proprietary. The difficulty of changing these components has had a chilling effect on innovation, and forced network administrators to express policies through complicated and frustratingly brittle interfaces. As discussed in recent a *New York Times* article [30], the rise of data centers and cloud computing have brought these problems into sharp relief and led a number of networks researchers to reconsider the fundamental assumptions that underpin today's network architectures.

In particular, significant momentum has gathered behind OpenFlow, a new platform that opens up the software that controls the network while also allowing packets to be processed using fast, commodity switching hardware [31]. OpenFlow defines a standard interface for installing flexible packet-forwarding rules on physical network switches using a programmable *controller* that runs separately on a stock machine. The most well-known controller platform is NOX [20], though there are several others [1, 8, 25, 39]. OpenFlow is supported by a number of commercial Ethernet switch vendors, and has been deployed in several campus and backbone networks. Using OpenFlow, researchers have already created a variety of controller applications that introduce new network functionality, like flexible access control [9, 33], Web server load balancing [21, 40], energy-efficient networking [22], and seamless virtual-machine migration [18].

Unfortunately, while OpenFlow and NOX now make it *possible* to implement exciting new network services, they do not make it *easy*. OpenFlow programmers must constantly grapple with several difficult challenges.

First, networks often perform multiple tasks, like routing, access control, and traffic monitoring. Unfortunately, decoupling these tasks from each other and implementing them independently in separate modules is effectively impossible, since packet-handling rules (un)installed by one module often interfere with overlapping rules (un)installed by other modules.

Second, the OpenFlow/NOX interface is defined at a very low level of abstraction. For example, the OpenFlow rule algebra directly reflects the capabilities of the switch hardware (*e.g.*, bit patterns and integer priorities). Simple high-level concepts such as set difference require multiple rules and priorities to implement correctly and more powerful "wildcard" rules are a limited hardware resource that programmers must manage by hand.

Third, controller programs only receive events for packets the switches do not know how to handle. Code that installs a forwarding rule might prevent another, different event-driven call-back from being triggered. As a result, writing programs for OpenFlow/NOX quickly becomes a difficult exercise in *two-tiered* programming—programmers must simultaneously reason about the packets that will processed on switches and those that will be processed on the controller.

Fourth, because a network of switches is a distributed system, it is susceptible to various kinds of race conditions. For example, a common NOX programming idiom is to handle the first packet of each network flow on the controller and install switch-level rules to handle the remaining packets. However, such programs can be susceptible to errors if the second, third, or fourth packets in a

ICFP'11, September 19–21, 2011, Tokyo, Japan.

flow arrive before the appropriate switch-level rule is computed and installed on the switches in the network.

To address these challenges, we present Frenetic, a new programming language for networks. Frenetic is organized around two levels of abstraction: (1) a set of source-level operators for constructing and manipulating streams of network traffic, and (2) a run-time system that handles all of the details of installing and uninstalling low-level rules on switches. The source-level operators draw on previous work on declarative database query languages and functional reactive programming (FRP) and are carefully constructed to support the following key principles:

Declarative Design. Where possible, we consider *what the programmer* might want, rather than *how the hardware* implements it. Hence, in many cases, we provide intuitive, high-level primitives, even though they are not directly supported by the hardware.

Modular Design. We have designed Frenetic's primitives to have *limited network-wide effects* and semantics that can be stated *independently of the context in which they are used*. This facilitates building modular programs with reuseable parts.

Single-tier Programming. Frenetic programmers do not have to worry that installing packet-handling rules may prevent the controller from analyzing other traffic. On the contrary, Frenetic supports a *see-every-packet abstraction* which guarantees that every packet is available for analysis, thereby side-stepping the many complexities of today's two-tiered programming model.

Race-free Semantics. Because Frenetic queries supply the run-time system with information about *what programmers want*, the run-time can suppress superfluous packets that arrive at the controller due to network race conditions. Automatic race detection and packet suppression simplifies the programming model.

Cost Control. In general, a danger of adopting high-level, declarative features is that it may difficult for users to understand or control the computational costs of the abstractions they use. To avoid this pitfall, Frenetic gives programmers guidance concerning the costs of programming constructs. In particular, the query language is carefully defined so that the core query logic can be executed on network switches, thereby keeping most packets in the fast path.

The above principles make Frenetic programs robust, compact, easy to write, easy to understand and easy to modify. Hence, to summarize, this paper makes the following contributions:

- Analysis of OpenFlow/NOX difficulties (Section 3): Using our combined expertise in programming languages and networks, we identify weaknesses of the current model that modern programming language principles can overcome.
- Frenetic language design (Section 4): Applying ideas from the disparate fields of database query languages and functional reactive programming, we present and analyze our design choices for Frenetic, a language for programming OpenFlow networks.
- Frenetic implementation (Section 5): We describe Frenetic's implementation architecture, paying particular attention to the run-time system—the enabling technology that allows us to raise the level of abstraction without sacrificing performance.
- Evaluation (Section 6): We discuss several applications implemented in Frenetic and NOX and compare them on several metrics: lines of code, controller load, and total traffic. The results demonstrate that Frenetic programs are more concise than their NOX counterparts and yet achieve comparable performance.

2. Background on OpenFlow and NOX

This section presents the main features of OpenFlow and NOX. To keep the presentation simple, we have elided a few details that are not important for understanding Frenetic. Readers interested in a complete description may consult the OpenFlow specification [3].

Integers	n
Rules	$r ::= \langle pat, pri, t, [a_1, \ldots, a_n] \rangle$
Patterns	$pat ::= \{h_1 : n_1, \ldots, h_k : n_k\}$
Priorities	$pri ::= n$
Timeouts	$t ::= n$ | `None`
Actions	$a ::=$ `output`(op) | `modify`(h, n)
Headers	$h ::=$ `in_port` | `vlan` | `dl_src` | `dl_dst` | `dl_type` | `nw_src` | `nw_dst` | `nw_proto` | `tp_src` | `tp_dst`
Ports	$op ::= n$ | `flood` | `controller`

Figure 1. OpenFlow Syntax. Prefixes `dl`, `nw`, and `tp` denote data link (MAC), network (IP), and transport (TCP/UDP), respectively.

Overview. In an OpenFlow network, a centralized *controller* manages a distributed collection of *switches*. While packets flowing through the network may be processed by the centralized controller, doing so is orders of magnitude slower than processing those packets on the switches. Hence, one of the primary functions of the controller is to configure the switches so that they process the vast majority of packets and only a few packets from new or unexpected flows need to be handled on the controller.

Configuring a switch primarily involves installing entries in its *flow table*: a set of *rules* that specify how packets should be processed. A rule consists of a *pattern* that identifies a set of packets, an integer *priority* that disambiguates rules with overlapping patterns, an optional integer *timeout* that indicates the number of seconds until the rule expires, and a list of *actions* that specifies how packets should be processed. For each rule in its flow table, the switch maintains a set of *counters* that keep track of basic statistics concerning the number and total size of packets processed.

Rules are defined formally by the grammar in Figure 1. A pattern is a list of pairs of header fields and integer values, which are interpreted as equality constraints. For instance, the pattern {`nw_src` : `10.0.0.1`, `tp_dst` : `80`} matches packets from source IP address `10.0.0.1` going to destination port `80`. We use standard notation for values in common header fields—*e.g.*, writing "`10.0.0.1`" instead of "`167772161`." Any header fields not appearing in a pattern are unconstrained. We call rules with unconstrained fields *wildcard rules*.

OpenFlow Switches. When a packet arrives at a switch, the switch processes it in three steps:

1. It selects a rule from its flow table whose pattern matches the packet. If there are no matching rules, the switch sends the packet to the controller for processing. Otherwise, if there are multiple matching rules, it picks the *exact-match* rule (*i.e.*, the rule whose pattern matches every header field in the packet) if one exists, or a wildcard rule with highest priority if not.
2. It updates the byte and packet counters associated with the rule.
3. It applies the actions listed in the rule to the packet in order, or drops the packet if the list is empty.

The action `output`(op) instructs the switch to forward the packet out on port op, which can either be a physical switch port n or one of the virtual ports `flood` or `controller`, where `flood` forwards it out on all physical ports (except the ingress port) and `controller` sends it to the controller. The action `modify`(h, n) instructs the switch to rewrite the header field h to n. The list of actions may contain both output and modify actions—*e.g.*, [`modify`(`nw_src`, `10.0.0.1`), `output`(2), `output`(`controller`)]

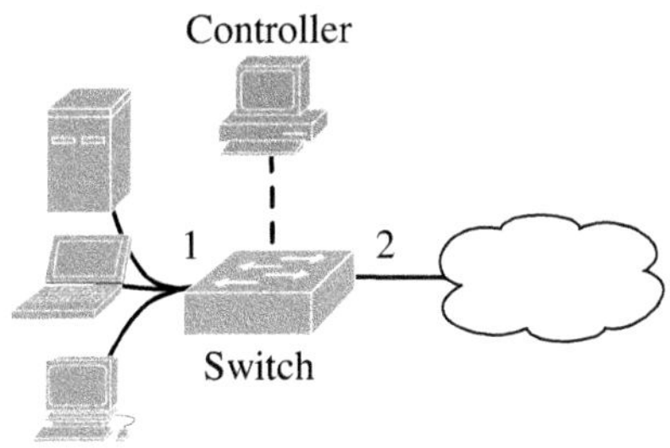

Figure 2. Simple Topology.

rewrites the source IP address of the packet to 10.0.0.1 and then outputs it on switch port 2 and sends it to the controller.

NOX Controller. The controller manages the set of rules installed on the switches in the network by reacting to network events. Most controllers are currently based on NOX, which is a simple operating system for networks that provides primitives for managing events as well as functions for communicating with switches [20]. NOX defines a number of events:

- *packet_in(switch, port, packet)*, triggered when *switch* forwards a *packet* received on physical *port* to the controller;
- *stats_in(switch, xid, pattern, packets, bytes)*, triggered when *switch* returns the *packets* and *bytes* counters in response to a request for statistics about rules contained in *pattern*. The *xid* parameter represents an identifier for the request.
- *flow_removed(switch, pattern, packets, bytes)*, triggered when a rule with *pattern* exceeds its timeout and is removed from *switch*'s flow table. The *packets* and *bytes* parameters contain the values of the counters for the evicted rule.
- *switch_join(switch)*, triggered when *switch* joins the network.
- *switch_exit(switch)*, triggered when *switch* exits the network.
- *port_change(switch, port, up)*, triggered when the link attached to a given physical *port* on *switch* goes up or down. The *up* parameter represents the new status of the link.

NOX also provides functions for sending messages to switches:

- *install(switch, pattern, priority, timeout, actions)*, installs a rule with the given *pattern*, *priority*, *timeout*, and *actions* in the flow table of *switch*.
- *uninstall(switch, pattern)*, removes all rules contained in *pattern* from the flow table of *switch*.
- *send(switch, packet, action)*, sends the given *packet* to *switch* and applies *action* to it there.
- *query_stats(switch, pattern)*, issues a request for statistics from all rules contained in *pattern* on *switch* and returns a request identifier *xid* that can be used to match up the asynchronous response from the switch.

The program running on the controller defines a handler for each of the events built into NOX, but may otherwise be structured as an arbitrary program.

Example. To illustrate the use of OpenFlow, consider a controller program written in Python that implements a simple repeater hub. Suppose that the network has a single switch connected to a pool of internal hosts on port 1 and a wide-area network on port 2, as shown in Figure 2. The `switch_join` handler below invokes the `repeater` when the switch joins the network. The `repeater` function installs rules on switch `s` that instruct the switch to forward packets from port 1 to port 2 and vice versa.

```
def switch_join(switch):
  repeater(switch)
def repeater(switch):
  pat1 = {in_port:1}
  pat2 = {in_port:2}
  install(switch,pat1,DEFAULT,None,[output(2)])
  install(switch,pat2,DEFAULT,None,[output(1)])
```

Note that both calls to `install` use the `DEFAULT` priority level and use `None` as the timeout, indicating that the rules are permanent.

3. Analysis of OpenFlow/NOX Difficulties

OpenFlow provides a standard interface for manipulating the rules installed on switches, which goes a long way toward making networks programmable. However, the programming model currently provided by NOX has several deficiencies that make it difficult to use in practice. This section presents four of the most substantial difficulties that arise when writing programs for OpenFlow/NOX. For concreteness, we focus on the NOX controller but other controllers for OpenFlow such as Onix [25], Beacon [1], and Nettle [39] suffer from similar issues.

3.1 Interactions Between Concurrent Modules

The first issue is that NOX programs do not compose. Suppose that we want to extend the repeater hub to monitor the total number of bytes of incoming web traffic. Rather than counting the web traffic at the controller, a monitoring application could install rules for web traffic, and periodically poll the byte and packet counters associated with those rules to collect the necessary statistics:

```
def monitor(switch):
  pat = {in_port:2,tp_src:80}
  install(switch,pat,DEFAULT,None,[])
  query_stats(switch,pat)
def stats_in(switch,xid,pattern,packets,bytes):
  print bytes
  sleep(30)
  query_stats(switch,pattern)
```

The `monitor` function installs a rule that matches all incoming packets with TCP source port 80 and issues a query for the counters associated with that rule. The `stats_in` handler receives the response from the switch, prints the byte count to the console, sleeps for 30 seconds, and then issues the next query.

Ideally, we would be able to compose this program with the repeater program to obtain a program that forwards packets and monitors traffic:

```
def repeater_monitor_wrong(switch):
  repeater(switch)
  monitor(switch)
```

Unfortunately, naively composing the two programs in this way will *not* work due to interactions between the rules installed by each program. In particular, because the programs install overlapping rules on the switch, when a packet arrives from port 80 on the source host, the switch is free to process the packet using either rule. But using the `repeater` rule will not update the counters needed for monitoring, while using the `monitor` rule will break the repeater program because its list of actions is empty (*i.e.*, packets will be dropped).

To obtain the desired behavior, we have to manually combine the forwarding logic from the first program with the monitoring policy from the second:

```
def repeater_monitor(switch):
  pat1 = {in_port:1}
  pat2 = {in_port:2}
  pat2web = {in_port:2,tp_src:80}
  install(switch,pat1,[output(2)],DEFAULT)
  install(switch,pat2web,[output(1)],HIGH)
  install(switch,pat2,[output(1)],DEFAULT)
  query_stats(switch,pat2web)
```

Performing this combination is non-trivial: the `pat2web` rule needs to include the `output(1)` action from the `repeater` program, and must be installed with `HIGH` priority to resolve the overlap with the `pat2` rule. In general, composing NOX programs requires careful, manual effort on the part of the programmer to preserve the semantics of the original programs. This makes it nearly impossible to factor out common pieces of functionality into reusable libraries and also prevents compositional reasoning about programs.

3.2 Low-Level Programming Interface

Another difficulty stems from the low-level nature of the programming interface, which is derived from the features of the switch hardware rather than being designed for ease of use. This makes programs unnecessarily complicated, as they must describe low-level details that do not affect the overall behavior of the program. For example, suppose that we want to extend the repeater and monitoring program to monitor all incoming web traffic *except* traffic destined for an internal server (connected to port 1) at address `10.0.0.9`. To do this, we need to express a logical "difference" of patterns, but OpenFlow patterns can only directly express positive constraints. Thus, to simulate the difference between two patterns, we have to install *two* overlapping rules on the switch, using priorities to disambiguate between them.

```
def repeater_monitor_noserver(switch):
  pat1 = {in_port:1}
  pat2 = {in_port:2}
  pat2web = {in_port:2,tp_src:80}
  pat2srv = {in_port:2,nw_dst:10.0.0.9,tp_src:80}
  install(switch,pat1,DEFAULT,None,[output(2)])
  install(switch,pat2srv,HIGH,None,[output(1)])
  install(switch,pat2web,MEDIUM,None,[output(1)])
  install(switch,pat2,DEFAULT,None,[output(1)])
  query_stats(switch,pat2web)
```

This program uses a separate rule to process web traffic going to the internal server—`pat2srv` matches incoming web packets going to the internal server, while `pat2web` matches all other incoming web packets. It also installs `pat2srv` at `HIGH` priority to ensure that the `pat2web` rule only processes (and counts!) packets going to hosts other than the internal server.

Describing packets using the low-level patterns supported by OpenFlow switches is cumbersome and error-prone. It forces programmers to use multiple rules and priorities to encode patterns that could be easily expressed using natural operations such as negation, difference, and union. It adds unnecessary clutter to programs and further complicates reasoning about their behavior.

3.3 Two-Tiered System Architecture

A third challenge stems from the two-tiered architecture used in NOX, where a controller program manages the network by installing and uninstalling switch-level rules. This indirection forces the programmer to specify the communication patterns between the controller and switch and deal with tricky concurrency issues such as coordinating asynchronous events. Consider extending the original repeater program to monitor the total amount of incoming traffic by destination host. Unlike the previous examples, we cannot install all of the rules we need in advance because, in general, we will not know the address of each host *a priori*. Instead, the controller must dynamically install rules for the packets seen at run time.

```
def repeater_monitor_hosts(switch):
  pat = {in_port:1}
  install(switch,pat,DEFAULT,None,[output(2)])
def packet_in(switch,inport,packet):
  if inport == 2:
    mac = dstmac(packet)
    pat = {in_port:2,dl_dst:mac}
    install(switch,pat,DEFAULT,None,[output(1)])
    query_stats(switch,pat)
```

The `repeater_monitor_hosts` function installs a single rule that handles all outgoing traffic. Initially, the flow table on the switch does not contain any entries for incoming traffic, so the switch sends all packets that arrive at port 2 to the controller. This causes the `packet_in` handler to be invoked; it processes each packet by installing a rule that handles future packets. Note that the controller only sees one incoming packet per host—the rule processes future traffic to that host directly on the switch.

As this example shows, NOX programs are actually implemented using *two* programs—one on the controller and another on the switch. While this design is essential for efficiency, the two-tiered architecture makes applications difficult to read and reason about, because the behavior of each program depends on the other—*e.g.*, installing/uninstalling rules on the switch changes which packets are sent up to the controller. In addition, the controller program must specify the communication patterns between the two programs and deal with subtle concurrency issues—*e.g.*, if we were to extend the example to monitor both incoming and outgoing traffic, the controller would have to issue multiple queries for the statistics for each host and synchronize the resulting callbacks.

Although NOX makes it possible to manage networks using arbitrary general-purpose programs, its two-tiered architecture forces programmers to specify the asynchronous and event-driven interaction between the programs running on the controller and the switches in the network. In our experience, these details are a significant distraction and a frequent source of bugs.

3.4 Network Race Conditions

One of the corollaries of NOX's explicit two-tier programming model is that programs are susceptible to subtle network race conditions. For example, a common NOX programming idiom is to analyze the first packet of every flow and calculate an action to apply to all future packets in the same network flow. In fact, this is how the `repeater_monitor_hosts` example described in the previous subsection worked. Unfortunately, our statement that the `packet_in` handler "processes each packet by installing a rule that handles *all future packets* to the same host" was a simplification. The installed rule usually handles all future packets—but not always! If a new packet in the same flow arrives before the switch has been able to install the new rule, that new packet will also be sent up to the controller. Consequently, if the controller routines are not carefully crafted to be idempotent when receiving multiple unexpected packets in the same flow, they will fail.

4. Frenetic Language Design

Frenetic is a new, domain-specific language for programming OpenFlow networks. It is embedded in Python and comprises two integrated sublanguages: (1) a limited, but high-level and declarative *network query language*, and (2) a general-purpose, functional and reactive *network policy management library*. The language offers a number of features that make programming more convenient

Queries	$q ::=$	`Select`(a) `*`
		`Where`(fp) `*`
		`GroupBy`([$qh_1, \ldots, qh_n$]) `*`
		`SplitWhen`([$qh_1, \ldots, qh_n$]) `*`
		`Every`(n) `*`
		`Limit`(n)
Aggregates	$a ::=$	`packets` | `sizes` | `counts`
Headers	$qh ::=$	`inport` | `srcmac` | `dstmac` | `ethtype` |
		`vlan` | `srcip` | `dstip` | `protocol` |
		`srcport` | `dstport` | `switch`
Patterns	$fp ::=$	`true_fp`() | qh`_fp`(n) |
		`and_fp`([$fp_1, \ldots, fp_n$]) |
		`or_fp`([$fp_1, \ldots, fp_n$]) |
		`diff_fp`(fp_1, fp_2) | `not_fp`(fp)

Figure 3. Frenetic query syntax

including a single-tier, "see-every-packet" abstraction; strong compositionality properties; a clear cost model; and a simple, race-free semantics. In the following subsections, we present the main features of the language and explain its semantic properties in detail.

4.1 The Network Query Language

The network query sublanguage allows Frenetic programs to *read* the state of network. To implement these reads efficiently, the Frenetic run-time system changes the state of the network by installing a variety of low-level rules on switches. However, from the high-level, abstract viewpoint of the Frenetic programmer, these reads and their implementation have no observable effect on network state. As a result, queries compose perfectly—both with each other and with the operations in the policy management library.

The key challenge in the design of Frenetic's query sublanguage involves finding a balance between expressiveness, simplicity, and control over cost. For example, the cost of evaluating a query can be defined as the number of packets that must be diverted from the fast path in the network and processed on the controller. Managing this cost is important because the latency of processing a diverted packet is orders of magnitude worse than processing it in hardware. Moreover, if many packets are diverted, the link between the switches and controller can become a bottleneck. Consequently, we deliberately limit the expressiveness of Frenetic query language to ensure that it has a simple, easy-to-understand cost model programmers can depend on.

Basic Concepts. Frenetic queries include constructs for *filtering* the set of all packets in the network using high-level patterns, subdividing this set by *grouping* on the basis of one or more header fields, further *splitting* these sets by arrival time or whenever a header field changes value, *limiting* the number of values returned, and *aggregating* by number or size of packets. The result produced by a query is an *event stream*—a data structure that represents an infinite, discrete, time-indexed stream of *values*. Though Frenetic is embedded in Python, an untyped language, it is useful to understand the types of events and event-driven programs.[1] The type α E denotes events carrying values of type α. For example, packet E is an event of packets and (switch $\times$ int) E is an event of pairs of switch identifiers and integers.

The syntax of Frenetic queries is given in Figure 3. Each top-level clause is optional, except for the `Select`, which identifies the type of event returned by the query—an event carrying packets, byte counts, or packet counts. In Python code, we use the infix operator `*` to combine clauses. We briefly explain the main syntactic elements below and follow up with illustrative examples.

[1] Though it is not central to this paper, we have implemented a dynamic typechecker for Frenetic that checks the types of operators dynamically.

A `Select`(a) clause aggregates the results returned by the rest of the query using method a, where a may be one of `packets` (return the packets themselves), `counts` (return the number of packets) or `bytes` (return the sum of the sizes of the packets).

A `Where`(fp) clause filters the results, retaining only those packets satisfying the *filter pattern* fp. Simple query patterns define sets of packets on the basis of packet header fields such as switch (`switch`), port (`inport`), source MAC address (`srcmac`), destination IP address (`destip`) and others. More complicated filter patterns can be constructed using natural set-theoretic operations such as intersection (`and_fp`), union (`or_fp`), difference (`diff_fp`), and complement (`not_fp`). These high-level patterns are compiled to OpenFlow-representable patterns by Frenetic.

A `GroupBy([`$qh_1, \ldots, qh_n$`])` clause subdivides the set of queried packets into subsets based on header fields qh_1 through qh_n. For example, grouping by `srcip` and `srcport` results in one subset for all packets with source IP 10.0.0.1 and TCP source port 80, a second subset for all packets with source IP 10.0.0.2 and TCP source port 80, a third subset for all packets with source IP 10.0.0.1 and source port 21, *etc.*

A `SplitWhen([`$qh_1, \ldots, qh_n$`])` clause, like a `GroupBy`, subdivides the set of selected packets into subsets. However, whereas `GroupBy` produces *one* subset for *all* packets with particular values for the given header fields, `SplitWhen` does not—it generates a new subset each time the value of one of the given fields *changes*. For example, suppose a query splits on source IP address, and packets with source IPs 10.0.0.1, 10.0.0.2 and 10.0.0.1 arrive in sequence. In this case, `SplitWhen` generates three subsets (the first and third packets are put in separate sets, because their IP addresses differ from the address of the preceding packet). If the arrival order was different, perhaps 10.0.0.1, 10.0.0.1, 10.0.0.2, then only two subsets would be generated.

An `Every`(n) clause partitions packets by time, grouping packets that arrive within the same n-second window together.

Finally, a `Limit`(n) clause limits the number of packets in each subset to n. The most common limit is 1.

Example Query. To get a taste of the Frenetic query language, consider the following web monitoring query, designed for the single-switch repeater network presented in the previous section.

```
def web_query():
  return \
    (Select(sizes) *
     Where(inport_fp(2) & srcport_fp(80))) *
     Every(30))
```

The infix operator `&` used in this query desugars into `and_fp`. When registered with the run-time system, it selects all packets arriving on physical port 2 and from TCP source port 80. It sums the sizes of all such packets every 30 seconds and returns an event stream carrying integers as a result.

The results of such queries may be used in a variety of ways in Frenetic programs—for traffic analysis, for security monitoring and for decisions about the forwarding policy. For now, all we will do is pipe the results to a printer:

```
def web_stats():
  web_query() >> Print()
```

Query Composition. To illustrate the modularity properties of Frenetic programs, let us carry the example a step further and extend it to monitor incoming traffic by host. As shown in Section 3.1, implementing this program in NOX is difficult—we cannot run the two smaller programs side-by-side because the rules for monitoring web traffic overlap with the rules for monitoring traffic by host.

Extending the Frenetic program, however, is simple. The following query summarizes the total volume of traffic arriving on physical port 2, grouped by destination host, every 60 seconds.

```
def host_query():
  return (Select(sizes) *
          Where(inport_fp(2)) *
          GroupBy([dstmac]) *
          Every(60))
```

This query may be composed with the web query using the Merge operator, a generic combinator that transforms a pair of events into an event of pairs of optional values.

```
def all_stats():
  Merge(host_query(),web_query()) >> Print()
```

The programmer who writes this program needs not know the details of the individual query routines, as neither query can interfere with the results produced by the other. Why is that? Unlike NOX, Frenetic supports the abstraction that queries merely read network state and do not modify it (even though the underlying run-time system will, in fact, modify the state of the network by installing rules on switches). Moreover, by design, Frenetic supports a programming model in which every query can "see every packet" in the network. Thus, installing one query in the run-time does not silently inhibit any other queries from seeing certain packets. Note that the host query and the web queries operate at different frequencies—60 seconds vs. 30 seconds. Implementing this functionality in Frenetic is as easy as declaring the desired intervals. Implementing it in NOX, on the other hand, would be difficult, as the programmer would have to code tedious bookkeeping routines in event handlers to keep track of which statistics to collect at which times. Frenetic's run-time system does this bookkeeping automatically. Hence, our design has changed query composition from a challenging, error-prone enterprise to a completely trivial one.

Race-Free Semantics. One of the most basic network programs is a *learning switch*, which discovers the identity of the hosts connected to each of its ports by recording the source MAC addresses contained in incoming packets. The following query could be used to implement the core functionality of a simple learning switch:

```
def learning_query():
  return (Select(packets) *
          Where(true_fp()) *
          GroupBy([srcmac]) *
          SplitWhen([inport]) *
          Limit(1))
def connection_printer():
  learning_query() >> Print()
```

When `learning_query` is executed, it generates an event that includes one packet for each distinct source MAC, unless the port associated with that source MAC changes (which might happen if a host, such as a laptop, were to move). This program is unremarkable except that it prints each new connection that it discovers exactly once because the query is limited to return *one* packet. Achieving the same effect in NOX is surprisingly tricky because of network race conditions. In the time it takes for a NOX program to generate and install a rule to suppress packets 2, 3, 4 with the same source MAC, those packets might already have arrived at the switch, be en route to the controller and be about to be processed by the handler. Consequently, the NOX programmer will have to remember to implement complex, error-prone bookkeeping if she wants to get it right. Such races affect the implementation of the Frenetic run-time system as well, but they are handled invisibly (and once-and-for-all) at that level, and are not exposed to the programmer. Unfortunately, the NOX implementation cannot mimic Frenetic as it does not have access to the high-level, semantic information expressed in the queries that allows Frenetic to squash superfluous packets.

The Query Cost Model. In order for programmers to use Frenetic effectively, they must have an understanding of the cost of applying the basic operations in the language. In particular, it is important that they have an understanding of the number of packets that must be diverted from the fast path in the network and sent to the controller due to a query.

The cost of executing a Frenetic query can be understood in terms of *microflows—i.e.*, sets of related packets that have identical header fields and arrive at the same switch. To illustrate recall the simple web query defined earlier:

```
def web_query():
  return \
    (Select(sizes) *
     Where(inport_fp(2) & srcport_fp(80))) *
     Every(30))
```

An example of a microflow pertinent to this query is the one represented by a tuple that contains `in_port 2`, `srcport 80`, `vlan 0`, `dl_src 0`, and so on, with a specific value for each header field. Another microflow pertinent to the query is the one with `in_port 2`, `srcport 80`, `vlan 1`, `dl_src 0`, and so on. Note the difference between the two flows is only in the value of the `vlan` field. Clearly, the total number of microflows is enormous, but a single microflow may contain arbitrarily many packets so there are dramatically fewer *inhabited microflows—i.e.*, flows for which the network actually witnesses a packet.

A *statistics query*, such as the web query above, measures the `counts` or `sizes` of a particular stream of packets. Such a query diverts one packet per inhabited microflow to the controller. After that single packet has been diverted, the run-time system installs a rule on the switch for processing subsequent packets in that microflow.[2] Every 30 seconds, the system gathers statistics for the query, not by diverting additional packets, but by querying the counters maintained by the switches.

There are two additional considerations in this cost analysis for statistics queries. First, if multiple statistics queries are interested in information about the same microflow, then the costs are shared—no matter how many statistics queries are interested in a microflow at most one packet will diverted to the controller. Second, if the underlying forwarding policy changes then the installed microflow rules must be uninstalled as the actions associated with the rules may be wrong. The reason is that the rules used to collect statistics on the switch are also used to perform forwarding and may, for example, be forwarding the given microflow out on one port in the old policy and a different port in the new policy. Thus, when the policy changes, additional packets may be diverted from the fast path as the network adapts to the change.

The above analysis applies specifically to statistics queries, as statistics can be tabulated on switches and collected later by the controller. Packet queries are different because every packet that appears in the result of a packet query must go to the controller. Hence packet queries without a `Limit` clause are inherently expensive—in effect, the switch hardware cannot be used at all because every packet in each pertinent microflow must be diverted to the controller. With a `Limit` clause, the costs are reduced. For example, with a `Limit(1)`, as in the query used in the learning

[2] Of course, due to network race conditions and the non-zero latency of switch-controller communication, it may be the case that prior to installing the new rule, a few additional packets in the same microflow hit the switch and are diverted to the controller. Hence, to be perfectly accurate, one packet "modulo network race conditions" is diverted from the fast path.

switch, the cost of a packet query is similar to the cost of an analogous statistics query.

Deep Packet Inspection. To implement deep packet inspection in Frenetic, one only needs to write a query that returns the packets to inspect—*e.g.*, the following query returns all web traffic:

```
def web_packets_query():
  return (Select(packets) *
          Where(srcport_fp(80)))
def dpi():
  web_packets_query() >> analyze_packet()
```

Of course, as just explained, unrestricted packet queries such as this one do not make effective use of switch hardware and divert many packets to the controller. However, this is not a limitation of the Frenetic design, it is a limitation of the popular OpenFlow platform on which Frenetic sits. In the future, OpenFlow switches may well be extended to allow efficient querying of additional bits of every packet in hardware. When such extensions are available, we anticipate it will be straightforward to extend the Frenetic query language to support deep packet inspection efficiently. For now, to maintain a clear cost model for Frenetic queries—*i.e.*, one where cost depends on the number of microflows, not the number of packets in a microflow (except for packets returned by the query)—we do not support deep packet inspection in queries themselves.

Summary. The Frenetic query language supports a collection of orthogonal, high-level query operators. The Frenetic run-time system supports the abstraction that these operators read, but do not modify network state. The key consequence of this abstraction is that queries compose seamlessly with one another. The Frenetic run-time system also suppresses superfluous packets that occur due to race conditions in the underlying network, giving queries a simple race-free semantics. Finally, Frenetic queries have a simple, clear cost model that depends primarily on the number of inhabited microflows, not the number of packets within a microflow.

4.2 The Network Policy Management Library

Frenetic programmers manage the policy that governs the forwarding of packets through the network using a combinator library for functional, reactive programming (FRP). The library design is inspired by Yampa [12] (a language for programming robots) and its implementation is based on the strategy used in FlapJax [32] (a library for web programming). However, there is still significant novelty in applying these old ideas to a new domain. In addition, Frenetic's query language, its representation of network state in the run-time system, and its library of FRP combinators, are all carefully designed to work well together.

Basic Concepts. One of the basic operations performed by a Frenetic program is to construct packet-forwarding *rules* for installation on switches. These rules are created using the `Rule` constructor, which takes a *pattern* and a list of *actions* as arguments. Patterns are similar to the filter patterns used in the query language—the only difference is that rule patterns do not mention switches. Actions include *forwarding* through a particular port p (`forward(`p`)`), flooding through all ports (`flood()`), sending the packet to the controller (`controller()`), and modifying header field f to a new value v (`modify(`f`,`v`)`). There is no explicit drop action. The empty list is interpreted as a directive to drop packets.

To associate rules with switches, Frenetic programs must create *network policies*. We represent policies in Python as dictionaries mapping switches to lists of rules.

Frenetic programs control the installation of policies in a network *over time* by generating *policy events*. Policy events are infinite, time-indexed streams of values, just like the events generated from queries that we saw in the previous subsection. In addition to policy events and query-generated events, Frenetic also contains the primitive events `Seconds`, which contains the number of seconds since the epoch, `SwitchJoin` and `SwitchExit`, which contains the identifiers of switches joining or leaving the network, and `PortChange`, which contains triples comprising a switch, a port number, and a boolean value. In this last event, the boolean value indicates whether the given port on the switch is enabled.

Frenetic also contains *Listeners*, which represent event consumers. One example of a listener is the primitive `Print` listener, which consumes string events by printing them to the console. Another example is the `Send` listener, which consumes events carrying a switch, packet, and action list by sending each packet to the switch and applying the actions to it there. The `Register` lis-

Events

`Seconds` $\in$ int E
`SwitchJoin` $\in$ switch E
`SwitchExit` $\in$ switch E
`PortChange` $\in$ (switch $\times$ int $\times$ bool) E
`Once` $\in \alpha \to \alpha$ E

Basic Event Functions

`>>` $\in \alpha$ E $\to \alpha\ \beta$ EF $\to \beta$ E
`Lift` $\in (a \to \beta) \to \alpha\ \beta$ EF
`>>` $\in \alpha\ \beta$ EF $\to \beta\ \gamma$ EF $\to \alpha\ \gamma$ EF
`ApplyFst` $\in \alpha\ \beta$ EF $\to (\alpha \times \gamma)\ (\beta \times \gamma)$ EF
`ApplySnd` $\in \alpha\ \beta$ EF $\to (\gamma \times \alpha)\ (\gamma \times \beta)$ EF
`Merge` $\in (\alpha$ E $\times\ \beta$ E$) \to (\alpha$ option $\times\ \beta$ option$)$ E
`BlendLeft` $\in \alpha \times \alpha$ E $\times\ \beta$ E $\to (\alpha \times \beta)$ E
`BlendRight` $\in \beta \times \alpha$ E $\times\ \beta$ E $\to (\alpha \times \beta)$ E
`Accum` $\in (\gamma \times (\alpha \times \gamma \to \gamma) \to \alpha\ \gamma$ EF
`Filter` $\in (\alpha \to$ bool$) \to \alpha\ \alpha$ EF

Listeners

`>>` $\in \alpha$ E $\to \alpha$ L $\to$ unit
`Print` $\in \alpha$ L
`Register` $\in$ policy L
`Send` $\in$ (switch $\times$ packet $\times$ action) L

Rules and Policies

`Rule` $\in$ pattern $\times$ action list $\to$ rule
`MakeForwardRules` $\in$ (switch $\times$ port $\times$ packet) policy EF
`AddRules` $\in$ policy policy EF

Figure 4. Selected Frenetic Operators.

```
# query returning one packet per source IP
def src_ips() =
  return (Select(packets) *
          Where(inport_fp(1)) *
          GroupBy([srcip]) *
          Limit(1))

# helper to add switch to a port-packet pair
def add_switch(port,packet):
  return (switch(header(packet)),port,packet)

# parameterized load balancer
def balance(balancer):
  return \
    (src_ips()           >> # (IP*packet) E
     ApplyFst(balancer)  >> # (port*packet) E
     Lift(add_switch)    >> # (switch*port*packet) E
     MakeForwardRules()  >> # policy E
     AddRules())            # policy E
```

Figure 5. A Parameterized Load Balancer

tener applies a network policy to a network. The type of listeners of events α E is written α L.

Frenetic programs analyze or transform events using *event functions*. The type of event functions from α E to β E is written α β EF. Many such event functions are based on standard operators found in previous work on FRP. For example, Merge, which we saw in previous sections, transforms a pair of events into an event of pairs of options. Lift(f) transforms an ordinary function f of type $(\alpha \rightarrow \beta)$ into an event function of type α β EF that applies f to each value in its input event. Frenetic also supplies a derived library of event functions useful specifically in a networking context. For example, MakeForwardRules converts an event of triples containing a switch, port number, and packet into a forwarding policy that forwards packets with the same header out the given port. AddRules folds over the values in its incoming policy event by repeatedly merging the policies it receives and returning, at each time step, the total accumulated policy so far.

In the following paragraphs, we will further explain these concepts using examples. For reference, Figure 4 lists a selected set of the most important Frenetic operators and their types. Note that the composition operator >> is overloaded and can be used to compose events with event functions, event functions with other event functions, and events with listeners.

A First Example. The simplest forwarding program just installs static packet-forwarding rules. The Frenetic program below mimics the NOX repeater hub presented in Section 3:

```
rules = [Rule(inport_fp(1),[forward(2)]),
         Rule(inport_fp(2),[forward(1)])]
def repeater():
  (SwitchJoin() >>
   Lift(lambda switch:{switch:rules}) >>
   Register())
```

The network policy in this program contains two rules. The first matches all packets arriving at port 1 and forwards them out port 2. Conversely, the second matches packets arriving on port 2 and forwards them out port 1. The repeater function passes the SwitchJoin event stream to a lifted function that builds an event carrying dictionaries with switches as keys and the list of rules as the corresponding value. It then pipes this policy to the Register listener, which installs it in the run-time system.

One of the first things to notice about this example is that it composes effortlessly with the network monitoring programs developed in the previous subsection:

```
def repeater_web_monitor():
  repeater()
  all_stats()
```

Unlike the NOX code we saw before, in Frenetic there is no need to rewrite and interleave overlapping monitoring code and forwarding policy code. Because Frenetic presents the abstraction that queries read, but do not modify the network, these reads do not interfere with the forwarding policy. Conversely, because queries "see every packet", forwarding does not interfere with the *semantics* of a query (though, of course, sending packets along a monitored link does affect the *results* of a query). Under the hood, the Frenetic run-time system manages the interactions between the OpenFlow rules generated by queries implementation and the rules generated by the network policy.

A Simple Load Balancer. A load balancer is a switch that receives traffic on its incoming ports and multiplexes that traffic out its outgoing ports. Our load balancer will multiplex traffic based on source IPs: traffic from the same source IP will be forwarded through the same output port; traffic from different source IPs may be forwarded through different output ports.

```
# Filter away rules involving
# elements of ip_list from policy
def filter_ips(ip_list,policy):
  secure_policy = policy
  for ip in ip_list:
    secure_policy = delete_ip(ip,secure_policy)
  return secure_policy

# Filter away rules involving
# elements of bad_ips() from policyE
def secure(policyE):
  return (BlendLeft({},bad_ips(),policyE) >>
          Lift(filter_ips))

# Apply the load balancer followed
# by the security filter
def secure_balance():
  (secure(balance(weighted_balancer())) >>
   Register())
```

Figure 6. Securing the weighted balancer. The bad_ips event and delete_ip function are elided.

Figure 5 presents the code for the core load balancing algorithm. The code uses a query (defined by src_ips) to generate an event with one value for each new source IP in a packet arriving on port 1. The main routine, balance, takes an argument balancer, which is an event function that transforms IP addresses into ports (we assume traffic will be multiplexed through ports 2 through OUTPORTS). The balance function itself runs the src_ips query to generate an event for each new IP address seen, runs the balancer to determine the appropriate port through which to forward those packets, and uses library functions to construct the network policy as the result.

The balancer can be instantiated in many different ways. For example, the programmer might assume a uniform distribution of traffic across IP addresses and hash each source IP to a port,

```
def hash_balancer():
  return Lift(lambda ip,port:hash_ip_to_port(ip))
```

or they might implement round-robin load balancing:

```
def rr_balancer():
  next = lambda ip,port:(port%(OUTPORTS-1))+2
  return (Accum(1,next))
```

Yet another possibility is to monitor the load on the switch and implement the load balancer using dynamic traffic levels. The ip_monitor program below queries the packet counts by IP address every INTERVAL seconds. Then weighted_balancer pipes the result of the query into an event function weighted_choice (whose definition is elided), that selects the next port to forward through based on current traffic levels.

```
def ip_monitor():
  return (Select(counts) *
          Where(inport_fp(1)) *
          GroupBy([srcip]) *
          Every(INTERVAL))

def weighted_balancer():
  return (ip_monitor() >>
          weighted_choice())
```

Any of the above balancing functions can be used in conjunction with the generic balancer as follows.

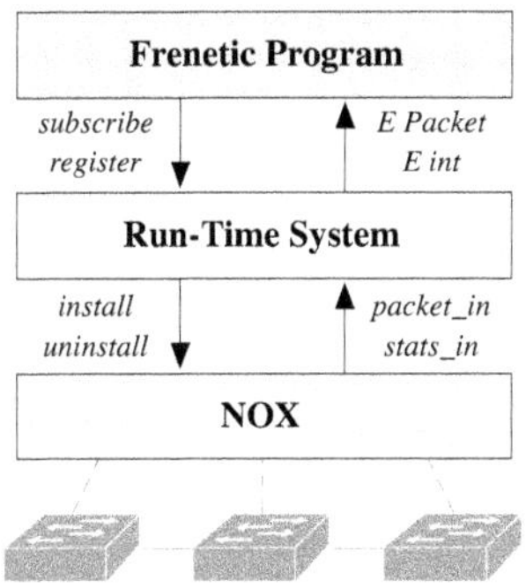

Figure 7. Frenetic architecture.

```
def balance_switch():
  balance(weighted_balancer()) >>
  Register()
```

Interestingly, while creating this parameterized load balancer with Frenetic is a relatively straight-forward exercise in functional programming, simulating it in NOX is substantially more difficult. The crux of the problem is that the parameterized balancing algorithm (the function `balance`) cannot be defined in NOX without risking interference from the monitoring rules needed by components such as `weighted_balance`. The simplest NOX solution is likely to make multiple copies of the code—one for each separate balancing function—and handle interfering rules manually. Frenetic's run-time system handles all such interference automatically.

Composing Forwarding Decisions. The previous examples illustrate composition of queries with each other and with a single policy module. It is also possible to compose a routine that computes a forwarding policy with separate routines that transform or alter the policy. A typical example is a security module that prevents known bad source IPs from sending traffic, as shown in Figure 6. Frenetic's functional style makes such examples easy to code. It is typically much more difficult to compose the forwarding policies computed by different NOX modules, unless those modules act on completely disjoint sets of packets.

Summary. Most network programs involve a combination of monitoring and forwarding. Because queries can always "see every network packet" independently of the forwarding policies expressed by other modules, monitoring and policy components compose seamlessly in Frenetic. Moreover, because of Frenetic's functional style, post-facto application of policy modifiers, such as our security module, is trivial. Overall, it is far easier to write simple, modular, reuseable programs in Frenetic than it is in NOX.

5. Frenetic Implementation

Frenetic provides high-level abstractions that free programmers from having to reason about a host of low-level details involving the underlying switch hardware. However, the need to deal with these low-level details does not just disappear because programs operate at a higher level. The rubber meets the road in the implementation, which is described in this section.

We have implemented a complete working prototype of Frenetic as an embedded combinator library in Python. Figure 2 depicts its architecture, which is organized around three main pieces: the language itself, the run-time system, and NOX. The use of NOX is convenient but not essential—we could also use any other controller as a back-end.

```
function packet_in(packet, inport)
  isSubscribed := false
  actions := []
  for (query, event, counters, requests) ∈ subscribers do
    if query.matches(packet.header) then
      event.push(packet)
      isSubscribed := true
  for rule ∈ rules do
    if (rule.pattern).matches(packet.header) then
      actions.append(rule.actions)
  if isSubscribed then
    send_packet(packet, actions)
  else
    install(packet.header, DEFAULT, None, actions)
    flows.add(packet.header)

function stats_in(xid, packets, bytes)
  for (query, event, counters, requests) ∈ subscribers do
    if requests.contains(xid) then
      counters.add(packets, bytes)
      requests.remove(xid)
      if requests.is_empty() then
        event.push(counters)

function stats_loop()
  while true do
    query := next_stats()
    counters.reset()
    for pattern ∈ flows do
      if query.matches(pattern) then
        xid := stats_request(pattern)
        requests.add(xid)
    sleep(next_stats_window())
```

Figure 8. Frenetic run-time system handlers

The central piece of the implementation is the run-time system, which sits between the high-level program and NOX. It manages all of the bookkeeping related to installing and uninstalling rules on switches and also generates the necessary communication patterns between switches and the controller. To do all of this, the run-time maintains several global data structures:

- *policy*, a dictionary from switches to sets of high-level rules that describes the current packet-forwarding policy,
- *flows*, a set of low-level rules currently installed on the switches in the network, and
- *subscribers*, a set of tuples containing a defining query, an event for that subscriber, byte and packet counts, and a list of outstanding statistics requests.

To translate the high-level forwarding policy registered in the run-time into switch-level rules, the run-time uses a simple strategy that *reacts* to flows of network traffic as they occur. At the start of the execution of a program, the flow table of each switch in the network is empty, so every packet is sent to the controller and passed to the `packet_in` handler. When it receives a packet, this function first iterates through the set of subscribers and propagates the packet to each subscriber whose defining query includes the packet in its result. Next, it traverses the policy and collects up the list of actions specified in all rules. Finally, it processes the packet in one of two ways: If there are no subscribers for the packet, then it installs a switch-level rule that processes future packets with the same header fields without involving the controller. Or, if there are subscribers for the packet, then the run-time sends the packet back

		Connectivity			Heavy Hitters			Web Stats		
		HUB	*LSW*	*LFLSW*	*HUB*	*LSW*	*LFLSW*	*HUB*	*LSW*	*LFLSW*
NOX	Lines of Code	20	55	75	110	198		104	135	
	Controller Traffic (kB)	12.8	13.5	31.3	9.3	10.3	⋆	4.5	4811	⋆
	Aggregate Traffic (kB)	69.2	42.3	64.1	57.2	36.1		14.1	9.0	
Frenetic	Lines of Code	6	30	58	29	53	81	13	37	65
	Controller Traffic (kB)	9.1	12.0	12.4	11.1	10.6	10.9	4.5	5.1	5.8
	Aggregate Traffic (kB)	65.6	41.0	41.5	55.0	36.4	36.9	13.6	9.20	9.9

Table 1. Experimental results.

to the switch and applies the actions there, but does not install a rule, as doing so would prevent future packets from being sent to the controller (and, by extension, the subscribers that need to be supplied with those packets). In effect, this strategy dynamically unfolds the forwarding policy expressed in the high-level rules into switch-level rules, moving processing off the controller and onto switches in a way that does not interfere with any subscriber.

The run-time uses a slightly different strategy to implement aggregate statistics subscribers, making use of the byte and packet counters maintained by the switches. The run-time system executes a loop that waits until the window for a statistics subscriber expires. At that point, it traverses the *flows* set and issues a request for the byte and packet counters from each switch-level rule whose pattern matches the query, adding the request identifier to the set of outstanding requests maintained for this subscriber in *subscribers*. The `stats_in` handler receives the asynchronous replies to these requests, adds the byte and packet counters to the counters maintained for the subscriber in *subscribers*, and removes the request id from the set of outstanding requests. When the set of outstanding requests becomes empty, it pushes the counters, which now contain the correct statistics, onto the subscriber's event stream.

Figure 8 gives pseudo-code for the NOX handlers used in the Frenetic run-time system. These algorithms describe the basic behavior of the run-time, but elide some additional complications and details[3] that the actual implementation has to deal with such as spurious packets that get sent to the controller due to race conditions between the receipt of a message to install a rule and the arrival of the packet at the switch.

The other piece of the Frenetic implementation is the library of FRP operators themselves. This library defines representations for events, event functions, and listeners, as well as each of the primitives in Frenetic. Unlike classic FRP implementations, which support continuous streams called *behaviors* as well as discrete streams called *events*, Frenetic focuses almost exclusively on discrete streams. This means that the pull-based strategy used in most previous FRP implementations, which is optimized for behaviors, is not a good fit for Frenetic. Accordingly, our FRP library uses a push-based strategy to propagate values from inputs to outputs.

The run-time system's use of exact-match rules follows the approach used in Ethane [9] and many OpenFlow-based applications [18, 21], and is well-suited for dynamic settings. Moreover, exact-match rules use the plentiful conventional memory (*e.g.*, SRAM) many switches provide, as opposed to the small, expensive, power-hungry Ternary Content Addressable Memories (TCAMs) needed to support wildcards. Still, wildcard rules are more concise and well-suited for static settings. We plan to develop a proactive, priority-based wildcard approach as part of Frenetic's run-time in the near future. Longer term, we plan to extend the run-time to *adaptively* select between exact-match and wildcard rules, depending on the capabilities of the switches in the network.

[3] For example, when the forwarding policy changes, some of the rules installed on switches may be stale and must be uninstalled. But when the run-time uninstalls a rule on a switch, the byte and packet counters associated with the switch-level rule must not be lost. Thus, the Frenetic run-time defines a `flow_removed` handler that receives the counters for uninstalled rules and adds them to the counters maintained on the controller.

6. Evaluation

To evaluate our design for Frenetic, we implemented several simple applications in Frenetic and compared them against equivalent NOX programs on three metrics: lines of code, traffic to controller, and total traffic. The *lines of code* metric gives a measure of the complexity of each program, as well as the savings from code reuse when modules are composed. The *controller traffic* measures the total amount of communication between the switch and controller, which quantifies the overhead of managing switch-level rules using a run-time system. Finally, the *aggregate traffic* metric measures the total amount of traffic on every link in the network.

Setup and Methodology. We ran our experiments using the Mininet virtualization environment [26] on a Linux host with a 2.4GHz Intel Core2 Duo processor and 4GB of RAM. Mininet does not provide performance fidelity but does give accurate traffic measurements. For the lines of code metric, we counted up to 80 characters of properly-indented Python excluding whitespace. We used Wireshark to tally controller and total traffic.

Microbenchmarks. We compared the performance of Frenetic against NOX using the following microbenchmarks:

- **All-Pairs Connectivity:** each host sends and receives ICMP (ping) packets to/from all other hosts. This benchmark tests whether the forwarding policy establishes basic connectivity.
- **Web Statistics:** each host generates a single request to a web server and the controller monitors the aggregate HTTP traffic every five seconds. This tests the performance of simple monitoring—a common network administration task.
- **Heavy Hitters:** each host sends and receives ICMP packets to/from a variety of other hosts in the network. The controller collects per-host statistics and reports the top-k traffic sources. This illustrates a more sophisticated monitoring application.

Note that none of these microbenchmarks specify the underlying policy used to forward packets in the network. We ran each microbenchmark using several different policies:

- **Hub:** The hub (HUB) policy floods packets received on one port out on all other ports, except the port the packet arrived on.
- **Learning Switch:** The learning switch (LSW) policy dynamically learns the association between hosts and ports as it sees traffic. It floods packets to unknown destinations but outputs packets to known hosts on the port the host is connected to.

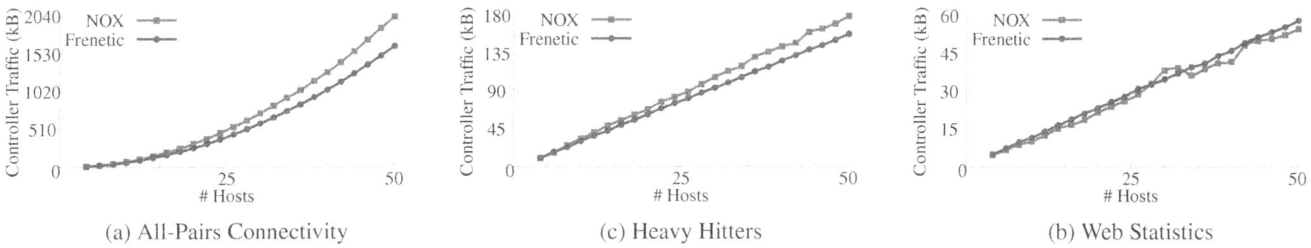

Figure 9. Scalability experimental results.

		Connectivity	Multi-get
NOX	Controller Traffic (kB)	5.9	3.2
	Aggregate Traffic (kB)	34.8	30.1
Frenetic	Controller Traffic (kB)	12.0	11.8
	Aggregate Traffic (kB)	41.0	38.9

Table 2. Wildcard experimental results.

- **Loop-Free Learning Switch:** The loop-free learning switch (LFLSW) learns the host-port mapping and the network topology using custom protocols of our own design. From these two pieces of information, it calculates a spanning tree and uses this to avoid forwarding loops when flooding packets.

Results. The results of our experiments are given in Table 1. They demonstrate a few key points. First, on these benchmarks, Frenetic performs comparably with hand-written NOX programs despite being implemented using a run-time system. Second, Frenetic provides substantial code savings to the network programmer. In particular, Frenetic's compositional semantics allowed us to easily compose the monitoring modules with each of the forwarding policies—the size of each composition is exactly the sum of the sizes of the inputs (the monitoring queries for Web Stats and Heavy Hitters are 23 and 7 lines, respectively)—unlike the NOX programs, which had to be manually refactored to correctly implement each version of the microbenchmark.[4] Finally, the aggregate traffic statistics for LFLSW on the connectivity experiment demonstrate that by using Frenetic, programmers can write sophisticated network programs that actually consume *less* network capacity than hand-written NOX programs. The reason for this difference is that the Frenetic LFLSW dynamically reacts to network events while the NOX version uses periodic polling to discover the network topology, which produces more total traffic on the network.

These microbenchmarks demonstrate that Frenetic's run-time system achieves adequate performance in some common scenarios. But they are far from comprehensive. There are certainly many situations where Frenetic's run-time system does not perform as well as hand-written NOX programs—*e.g.*, when the optimal implementation of the forwarding policy uses wildcard rules. To demonstrate such a situation, we implemented a "wildcard learning switch" which is similar to the standard MAC learning switch distributed with NOX but installs wildcard rules instead of microflow rules. More specifically, the controller installs flow table entries that constrain only the learned source and destination MAC addresses, but leave all other header fields as wildcards. In situations where two hosts communicate across multiple distinct microflows sharing a common source and destination MAC address, the wildcard learning switch will perform better, according to these metrics. Table 2, compares the wildcard learning switch to the Frenetic run-time system on the connectivity benchmark and another benchmark called multi-get, which generates multiple concurrent HTTP requests to different TCP ports—*i.e.*, two hosts with the same source and destination MACs communicate using multiple distinct microflows. As the results show, the NOX application which uses wildcards significantly outperforms the reactive, microflow based approach used in Frenetic. We are currently working to extend the run-time system to support wildcard rules.

Scalability Experiments. For each microbenchmark, we also conducted a scalability experiment to evaluate whether Frenetic programs would continue performing comparably to NOX programs as the number of hosts in the network grows. In each experiment, we used a single switch running the learning switch forwarding policy, but scaled the number of hosts up from 1 to 50. The results in Figure 9 confirm that Frenetic performance *scales* comparably—and in many cases better than—NOX. We hypothesize a simple reason for this difference: a common NOX idiom, which we used in our implementations of the NOX benchmarks, is to install rules with timeouts. This ensures that rules "self-destruct" without the programmer having to perform extra bookkeeping to remember all of the installed rules. However, such timeouts result in additional packets being sent to the controller, both in *flow_removed* messages and for subsequent flow setups. In contrast, Frenetic's run-time system reacts to changes in the forwarding policy and manages the set of installed rules automatically, obviating the need for timeouts.

Further Experience. In addition to the quantitative benchmarks discussed so far, we have implemented a collection of network utilities in Frenetic to validate our language design. This list of programs ranges from essential network functions to novel applications that implement new functionality. Frenetic's modular design makes it easy to build new tools out of simpler, reuseable parts. Code for these examples is hosted on the Frenetic web site [2].

- **Discovery.** Discovers the network topology.
- **Spanning Tree.** Computes a spanning tree from the topology.
- **All-Pairs Shortest-Path Routing.** Uses the topology to compute a forwarding policy based on shortest paths.
- **Load Balancer.** Connects incoming traffic to one of several replica servers. Can be instantiated with many heuristics to balance incoming traffic across back-end servers.
- **Fault-tolerant Routing.** Connects incoming traffic to one of several replica switches, organized into several layers. When a switch goes down, traffic is routed through the other switches in the same layer.

[4] In fact, refactoring the benchmarks to use the loop-free learning switch was sufficiently difficult that we did not complete it, despite the fact that NOX provides a topology module and we had already implemented hub and learning switch versions of the benchmarks.

- **Address Resolution Protocol (ARP) Server.** Implements ARP *in the network*, by maintaining a global view of the IP-MAC address mapping.
- **Dynamic Host Configuration (DHCP) Server.** Implements DHCP to bootstrap network hosts with logical (IP) addressing information.
- **Memcached Query Router.** Connects clients to virtual servers implementing a key-value store. The switch translates between the virtual addresses assigned to servers and the servers' physical addresses. When servers fail, it reassigns its virtual addresses to another server; when new servers becomes available, virtual addresses from other servers are remapped to it.
- **Scan-Free Learning Switch.** Generalized learning switch. Detects and blocks malicious hosts that scan the network.
- **DDoS Defense.** Detects anomalies in the amount of traffic sent over the network and drops packets from the offending hosts.

7. Related Work

This paper extends preliminary work by some of the authors, which was presented at a workshop on programmable network devices [19]. The earlier paper did not describe a run-time system, query language, or any significant applications, and did not provide an evaluation of the language's design or its implementation.

The OpenFlow platform provides a uniform interface for programming physical network switches [3, 30, 31]. Many other platforms for programming network devices have also been proposed. The Click modular router [24] shares the general goal of making network devices programmable and, like Frenetic, emphasizes modularity as an organizing design principle. But Click exclusively targets software switches (implemented as a Linux kernel module) while Frenetic can be used with physical switches (implemented using special-purpose hardware). RouteBricks [15] attempts to obtain better performance from software switches implemented using stock machines. Bro [35] and Snortran [16] allow programmers to express rich packet-filtering and monitoring policies for securing networks and detecting intrusions while Shangri-La [10] and FPL-3E [14] compile high-level packet-processing programs down to special packet-processing hardware and FPGAs. The key difference between Frenetic and all of these systems is that they are limited to a single device. Thus, they do not address the issue of how to program a collection of interconnected switches.

The Frenetic implementation uses the NOX controller [20], which provides convenient C++ and Python APIs for handling raw events and communicating with switches. Several other OpenFlow controllers have also been proposed. Beacon [1] is similar to NOX but provides a Java API. Maestro [8] provides a modular mechanism for managing network state using programmer-defined views. It is also multi-threaded, which increases throughout dramatically. Onix [25] provides abstractions for partitioning and distributing network state onto multiple distributed controllers, which addresses the scalability and fault-tolerance issues that arise when using a centralized controller. SNAC [4] provides high-level patterns (similar to Frenetic's filter patterns) for specifying access control policies as well as a graphical monitoring tool but is not a general programming environment. The Flow Management Language [23] also provides a high-level pattern language for specifying security policies in OpenFlow networks [23].

Frenetic's event functions are modeled after functional reactive languages such as Yampa and others [17, 32, 34, 36], and many of our primitives are borrowed directly from these languages. Frenetic's push-based implementation of the functional reactive combinators is based on FrTime [11] and is also similar to adaptive functional programming [5]. The Flask [29] language applies functional reactive programming to sensor networks in a staged language. The key differences between Frenetic and all of these languages are in the application domain (networking as opposed to animation, robotics, and others) and in the design of our query language and run-time system, which uses the capabilities of switches to avoid sending packets to the controller.

At a high level, Frenetic is also similar to streaming languages such as StreamIt [38], CQL [6], Esterel [7], Brooklet [37], etc. The FRP operators used in Frenetic are more to our taste, but one could easily build a system that retained the main elements of our design (e.g., the query language and the run-time system) but used different constructs for processing streams of network events.

The Nettle [39] language also uses FRP combinators to program OpenFlow switches. A Nettle program takes a stream of raw OpenFlow events as input (e.g., *switch_join*, *port_change*, *packet_in*, etc.) and produces a stream of raw OpenFlow messages as output (e.g., *install*, *uninstall*, *query_stats*, etc.). Although Nettle and Frenetic appear superficially similar—both use FRP for OpenFlow networks—a closer inspection reveals substantial differences. The most important difference is that Nettle operates at a lower level of abstraction than Frenetic: it is an effective *substitute* for NOX while Frenetic *sits on top of* NOX (and, in the future, could potentially sit on top of Nettle). Nettle does not offer any analog of Frenetic's query language or its run-time system and so Nettle programs work in terms of low-level OpenFlow concepts such as switch-level rules, priorities, and timeouts. As such it suffers from all of the limitations of NOX discussed in Section 3—e.g., Nettle programs cannot be easily composed and are susceptible to network race conditions.

NDLog, an extension of Datalog developed by Loo, Hellerstein, et al. has been used to specify and implement routing protocols, overlay networks, and services such as distributed hash tables [27, 28]. Both Frenetic and NDLog use high-level languages to program networks, but there are some important differences. One is NDLog's focus on routing protocols and overlay networks, whereas Frenetic programs can be used to implement finer-grained packet-processing including rewriting header fields. Another difference is that NDLog programs are written in an explicitly distributed style while Frenetic offers the programmer the abstraction of a centralized view of the network. This dramatically changes the way that programs must be written: an NDLog programmer crafts a single query that is evaluated on every router in the network while a Frenetic programmer writes a program from the omniscient perspective of the controller and run-time system distributes low-level rules to the switches in the network. Finally, deploying NDLog in a production network would require deep changes to the way that switches are built, as it requires each switch to run a custom Datalog engine. Frenetic targets OpenFlow, which is already supported by several vendors, and so can be deployed immediately.

One of the main challenges in the implementation of Frenetic is splitting work between the (powerful but slow) controller and the (fast but limited) switches. Gigascope [13], a stream database for monitoring networks, addresses the same problem but, unlike Frenetic, only supports querying traffic and cannot be used to control the processing of packets in the network.

8. Conclusions and Future Work

This paper describes the design and implementation of Frenetic, a new language for programming OpenFlow networks. Frenetic addresses some serious problems with the OpenFlow/NOX programming model by introducing a collection of high-level and compositional operators for querying and transforming streams of network traffic. A run-time system handles all of the details related to installing and uninstalling low-level rules. An experimental evaluation demonstrates that the performance of Frenetic's run-time system is competitive with hand-written OpenFlow/NOX programs.

We are currently working to extend Frenetic in several directions. One thread of work is developing security applications for performing authentication and access control, and for ensuring isolation between logical networks that share a common physical infrastructure. We are also designing a new run-time system that generates rules from the registered subscribers and forwarding rules eagerly. We plan to compare the tradeoffs between different rule-generation strategies empirically.

Acknowledgments. We wish to thank Matthew Meola, Mark Reitblatt, and Minlan Yu for many helpful discussions, and the anonymous ICFP reviews for their insightful comments. Our work is supported in part by ONR grants N00014-09-1-0770 *Networks Opposing Botnets* and N00014-09-1-0652 *Fabric: A Higher-Level Abstraction for Building Secure Distributed Applications*. Any opinions, findings, and recommendations are those of the authors and do not necessarily reflect the views of the ONR.

References

[1] Beacon: A java-based OpenFlow control platform. See `http://www.beaconcontroller.net`, Nov 2010.

[2] The Frenetic language. See `http://www.frenetic-lang.org/`, Nov 2010.

[3] OpenFlow. See `http://www.openflowswitch.org`, Nov 2010.

[4] SNAC. See `http://snacsource.org/`, 2010.

[5] Umut A. Acar, Guy E. Blelloch, and Robert Harper. Adaptive functional programming. *TOPLAS*, 28:990–1034, November 2006.

[6] Arvind Arasu, Shivanth Babu, and Jennifer Widom. The CQL continuous query language: Semantic foundations and query execution. *The VLDB Journal*, 15:121–142, Jun 2006.

[7] Gérard Berry and Georges Gonthier. The Esterel synchronous programming language: Design, semantics, implementation. *Science of Computer Programming*, (2):87–152, 1992.

[8] Zheng Cai, Alan L. Cox, and T. S. Eugene Ng. Maestro: A system for scalable OpenFlow control. Technical Report TR10-08, Rice University, Dec 2010.

[9] Martin Casado, Michael J. Freedman, Justin Pettit, Jianying Luo, Natasha Gude, Nick McKeown, and Scott Shenker. Rethinking enterprise network control. *Trans. on Networking.*, 17(4), Aug 2009.

[10] Michael K. Chen, Xiao Feng Li, Ruiqi Lian, Jason H. Lin, Lixia Liu, Tao Liu, and Roy Ju. Shangri-la: Achieving high performance from compiled network applications while enabling ease of programming. In *PLDI*, pages 224–236, Jun 2005.

[11] Gregory H. Cooper and Shriram Krishnamurthi. Embedding dynamic dataflow in a call-by-value language. In *ESOP*, pages 294–308, 2006.

[12] Antony Courtney, Henrik Nilsson, and John Peterson. The Yampa arcade. In *Haskell Workshop*, pages 7–18, Aug 2003.

[13] Chuck Cranor, Theodore Johnson, Oliver Spataschek, and Vladislav Shkapenyuk. Gigascope: A stream database for network applications. In *SIGMOD*, pages 647–651, 2003.

[14] Mihai Lucian Cristea, Claudiu Zissulescu, Ed Deprettere, and Herbert Bos. FPL-3E: Towards language support for reconfigurable packet processing. In *SAMOS*, pages 201–212. Jul 2005.

[15] Mihai Dobrescu, Norbert Egi, Katerina Argyraki, Byung-Gon Chun, Kevin Fall, Gianluca Iannaccone, Allan Knies, Maziar Manesh, and Sylvia Ratnasamy. RouteBricks: Exploiting parallelism to scale software routers. In *SOSP*, Oct 2009.

[16] Sergei Egorov and Gene Savchuk. *SNORTRAN: An Optimizing Compiler for Snort Rules*. Fidelis Security Systems, 2002.

[17] Conal Elliott and Paul Hudak. Functional reactive animation. In *ICFP*, pages 163–173, Jun 1997.

[18] David Erickson et al. A demonstration of virtual machine mobility in an OpenFlow network, Aug 2008. Demo at *ACM SIGCOMM*.

[19] Nate Foster, Rob Harrison, Matthew L. Meola, Michael J. Freedman, Jennifer Rexford, and David Walker. Frenetic: A high-level langauge for OpenFlow networks. In *PRESTO*, Nov 2010.

[20] Natasha Gude, Teemu Koponen, Justin Pettit, Ben Pfaff, Martín Casado, Nick McKeown, and Scott Shenker. NOX: Towards an operating system for networks. *SIGCOMM CCR*, 38(3), 2008.

[21] Nikhil Handigol, Srinivasan Seetharaman, Mario Flajslik, Nick McKeown, and Ramesh Johari. Plug-n-Serve: Load-balancing web traffic using OpenFlow, Aug 2009. Demo at *ACM SIGCOMM*.

[22] Brandon Heller, Srini Seetharaman, Priya Mahadevan, Yiannis Yiakoumis, Puneet Sharma, Sujata Banerjee, and Nick McKeown. ElasticTree: Saving energy in data center networks. In *NSDI*, Apr 2010.

[23] Timothy L. Hinrichs, Natasha S. Gude, Martin Casado, John C. Mitchell, and Scott Shenker. Practical declarative network management. In *WREN*, pages 1–10, 2009.

[24] Eddie Kohler, Robert Morris, Benjie Chen, John Jannotti, and M. Frans Kaashoek. The Click modular router. *ACM Transactions on Computer Systems*, 18(3):263–297, Aug 2000.

[25] Teemu Koponen, Martin Casado, Natasha Gude, Jeremy Stribling, Leon Poutievski, Min Zhu, Rajiv Ramanathan, Yuichiro Iwata, Hiroaki Inoue, Takayuki Hama, and Scott Shenker. Onix: A distributed control platform for large-scale production networks. In *OSDI*, Oct 2010.

[26] Bob Lantz, Brandon Heller, and Nick McKeown. A network in a laptop: Rapid prototyping for software-defined networks. In *HotNets*, pages 1–6, 2010.

[27] Boon Thau Loo, Tyson Condie, Joseph M. Hellerstein, Petros Maniatis, Timothy Roscoe, and Ion Stoica. Implementing declarative overlays. *SIGOPS*, 39(5):75–90, 2005.

[28] Boon Thau Loo, Joseph M. Hellerstein, Ion Stoica, and Raghu Ramakrishnan. Declarative routing: Extensible routing with declarative queries. In *SIGCOMM*, pages 289–300, 2005.

[29] Geoffrey Mainland, Greg Morrisett, and Matt Welsh. Flask: Staged functional programming for sensor networks. In *ICFP*, pages 335–346, 2008.

[30] John Markoff. Open networking foundation pursues new standards. *The New York Times*, Mar 2011. See `http://nyti.ms/eK3CCK`.

[31] Nick McKeown, Tom Anderson, Hari Balakrishnan, Guru Parulkar, Larry Peterson, Jennifer Rexford, Scott Shenker, and Jonathan Turner. Openflow: Enabling innovation in campus networks. *SIGCOMM CCR*, 38(2):69–74, 2008.

[32] Leo A. Meyerovich, Arjun Guha, Jacob Baskin, Gregory H. Cooper, Michael Greenberg, Aleks Bromfield, and Shriram Krishnamurthi. Flapjax: A programming language for Ajax applications. In *OOPSLA*, pages 1–20, 2009.

[33] Ankur Nayak, Alex Reimers, Nick Feamster, and Russ Clark. Resonance: Dynamic access control in enterprise networks. In *WREN*, Aug 2009.

[34] Henrik Nilsson, Antony Courtney, and John Peterson. Functional reactive programming, continued. In *Haskell Workshop*, pages 51–64, Oct 2002.

[35] Vern Paxson. Bro: A system for detecting network intruders in real-time. *Computer Networks*, 31(23–24):2435–2463, Dec 1999.

[36] John Peterson, Paul Hudak, and Conal Elliott. Lambda in motion: Controlling robots with Haskell. In *PADL*, Jan 1999.

[37] Robert Soulé, Martin Hirzel, Robert Grimm, Buğra Gedik, Henrique Andrade, Vibhore Kumar, and Kun-Lung Wu. A universal calculus for stream processing languages. In *ESOP*, pages 507–528, 2010.

[38] William Thies, Michal Karczmarek, and Saman Amarasinghe. Streamit: A language for streaming applications. In *International Conference on Compiler Construction*, pages 179–196, Apr 2002.

[39] Andreas Voellmy and Paul Hudak. Nettle: Functional reactive programming of OpenFlow networks. In *PADL*, Jan 2011.

[40] Richard Wang, Dana Butnariu, and Jennifer Rexford. OpenFlow-based server load balancing gone wild. In *Hot-ICE*, Mar 2011.

Forest: A Language and Toolkit for Programming with Filestores

Kathleen Fisher
Tufts University

Nate Foster
Cornell University

David Walker
Princeton University

Kenny Q. Zhu
Shanghai Jiao Tong University

Abstract

A *filestore* is a structured collection of data files housed in a conventional hierarchical file system. Many applications use filestores as a poor-man's database, and the correct execution of these applications requires that the collection of files, directories, and symbolic links stored on disk satisfy a variety of precise invariants. Moreover, all of these structures must have acceptable ownership, permission, and timestamp attributes. Unfortunately, current programming languages do not provide support for documenting assumptions about filestores, detecting errors in them, or safely loading from and storing to them.

This paper describes the design, implementation, and semantics of Forest, a new domain-specific language for describing filestores. The language uses a type-based metaphor to specify the expected structure, attributes, and invariants of filestores. Forest generates loading and storing functions that make it easy to connect data on disk to an isomorphic representation in memory that can be manipulated as if it were any other data structure. Forest also generates metadata that describes the degree to which the structures on the disk conform to the specification, making error detection easy. In a nutshell, Forest extends the rigorous discipline of typed programming languages to the untyped world of file systems.

We have implemented Forest as an embedded domain-specific language in Haskell. In addition to generating infrastructure for reading, writing and checking file systems, our implementation generates type class instances that make it easy to build generic tools that operate over arbitrary filestores. We illustrate the utility of this infrastructure by building a file system visualizer, a file access checker, a generic query interface, description-directed variants of several standard UNIX shell tools and (circularly) a simple Forest description inference engine. Finally, we formalize a core fragment of Forest in a semantics inspired by classical tree logics and prove round-tripping laws showing that the loading and storing functions behave sensibly.

Categories and Subject Descriptors D.3.2 [*Programming Languages*]: Language Classifications—Specialized application languages

General Terms Languages, Design, Theory

Keywords Data description languages, file systems, filestores, domain-specific languages, ad hoc data, Haskell, bidirectional transformations, generic programming

ICFP'11, September 19–21, 2011, Tokyo, Japan.

1. Introduction

Databases are an effective, time-tested technology for storing structured and semi-structured data. Nevertheless, many computer users eschew the benefits of structured databases and store important semi-structured information in collections of files and directories in a conventional file system instead. For example, the Princeton Computer Science Department stores records of undergraduate student grades in a structured set of directories and uses scripts to compute averages and study grading trends. Similarly, Michael Freedman collects sets of log files from CoralCDN, a distributed content distribution network [11, 12]. The logs are organized in hierarchical directory structures based on machine name, time and date. Freedman mines the logs for information on system security and performance. At Harvard, physics professor Vinothan Manoharan stores his experimental data in sets of files and extracts information using python scripts. At AT&T, vast structured repositories contain network monitoring information, phone call records, and billing data. Many software code bases, including Haskell and its associated Cabal libraries, require that specific files exist in particular formats at precise locations described in other files. Similarly, version control systems like `cvs` utilize the file system to store revision information. Web sites require various types of files to exist in particular directories according to content type, and security considerations often require particular permissions on these files. Many other examples exist across the computational sciences and social sciences, in computer systems research, in computer systems administration and in industry.

Users choose to implement ad hoc databases in this manner for a number of reasons. A key factor is that using databases often requires paying substantial up-front costs such as: (1) finding and evaluating the appropriate database software (and possibly paying for it); (2) learning how to load data into the database; (3) writing programs to transform the raw data for loading into the database; (4) learning how to access the data once it is in the database; and (5) interfacing the database with a conventional programming language to support applications that use the data. Finally, it may be the case that the database optimizes for a pattern of use not suited to the actual application, which makes the overhead of the database system even less desirable.

Rather than paying these costs, programmers often store data in the file system, using a combination of directory structure, file names, file contents, and symbolic links to organize the data. We call such a data representation a *filestore*. The "query language" for a filestore is often a shell script or conventional programming language.

Unfortunately, despite their initial convenience, using filestores can have a number of negative consequences. First, there is generally no documentation, which means it can be hard to understand the data and its organization. New users struggle to learn the structure, and if the system administrator leaves, knowledge of the data organization may be lost. Second, the structure of the filestore tends to evolve: new elements are added and old formats are changed, sometimes accidentally. Such evolution can cause hacked-up data processing tools to break or return erroneous results; it also further complicates understanding the data. Third, there is often no systematic means for detecting errors even though data errors can be immensely important. For example, for filestores containing monitoring information, errors can signal that some portion of the monitored system is broken. Fourth, analyses tend to be built from scratch. There is no auxiliary query or tool support and no help with debugging. Tools tend to be "one-off" efforts that are not reuseable. Fifth, dealing with large data sets, which are common in this setting, imposes extra difficulties. For example, standard shell tools such as `ls` fail when more than 256 files appear on the command line. Hence, programmers must break up their data and process it in smaller sets, a tedious task.

We propose a better way: A type-based specification language, programming environment and toolkit for describing and managing filestores. This language, called Forest, is implemented as an embedded domain-specific language in Haskell. Forest allows programmers to describe the expected shape of a filestore and to materialize it as typed, format-specific Haskell data structures. Conversely, given data structures with the appropriate type, Forest makes it straightforward to dematerialize these structures and write them out to disk.

The first benefit of the Forest system is that Forest descriptions provide *executable documentation* that can be used to check whether a given filestore conforms to its specification. For example, Unix file systems should be laid out according to the informal standard set forth by the Filesystem Hierarchy Standard Group [3], which requires, among other things, that certain directories *only* contain certain files, presumably for security reasons. Forest provides a language for expressing standards precisely and for checking that given file systems conform to them. As another example, the Pads website [25] contains a complex set of scripts and data files to implement an online demo. Unless all of the required data files, directories, and symbolic links are configured correctly, the web demo fails with an inscrutable error message. Forest allows the Pads webmaster to precisely document all of these requirements and to detect specification violations, making it easy to find and repair errors. And, of course, if the current webmaster were to leave her post, her successor could use the Forest description to help understand the system.

As well as serving as executable documentation, Forest provides substantial additional support for programmers. The goal is for programmers to obtain a whole range benefits by writing one simple, compact file system specification. The automatically generated auxiliary support includes: (1) a set of type declarations to represent the filestore in memory; (2) a set of type declarations that capture errors and file system attributes for the filestore; (3) a loading function to populate these in-memory structures; (4) a storing function to push possibly updated structures back out to disk; (5) type class instance declarations that make it possible for programmers to query, analyze, and transform filestore data using generic functions; and (6) a set of useful generic functions/scripts that operate over instances of these type classes.

The main contribution of this work is conceptual: We propose the idea of extending a modern programming language with tightly integrated linguistic features for describing and manipulating filestores. To demonstrate the potential of this idea, the following sections flesh out our proposal in greater depth:

- Section 2 begins with two concrete motivating examples, drawn from the authors' day-to-day experience managing computer systems. While there are just two central examples in this paper, the Forest web site [9] contains a number of further examples and case studies.
- Section 3 describes a concrete language design. The design is characterized by a simple, intuitive and compositional syntax that is tightly integrated with Haskell, our host language. The design is also tightly integrated with Pads/Haskell, a domain-specific language for describing individual files (as opposed to entire filestores), inspired by past work on related data description languages [5, 6, 7, 22]. This tight integration was a crucial design goal as it allows programmers to transition seamlessly between ordinary Haskell data structures, file internals and file collections, all in a uniform syntax.
- Section 4 explains how to write Haskell programs that operate over filestores described in Forest. The goal of this section is to provide a sense of how easy it is to write simple filestore scripts or queries.
- Section 5 shows that it is possible to use Forest to make the management of filestores even easier by developing generic tools capable of operating over any filestore. We have developed several such tools including a generic query interface, a file system visualization tool, an access-control permission checker, and a series of UNIX-like scripting tools. We have also built a simple description-inference tool to help users write a new description for an existing file system. These tools are interesting in their own right and also as case studies of putting generic programming techniques into practice. In addition, they provide evidence that our design is effectively integrated into the Haskell ecosystem.
- Section 6 explains our implementation, which is complete and may be downloaded at the Forest web site [9]. In addition to delivering a useful tool, our engineering work has the auxiliary benefit of serving as a case study in domain-specific language implementation. In fact, it has already had significant impact as such: the Haskell team modified and extended Haskell's quasiquoting mechanism in response to our needs.
- Section 7 describes the formal semantics for core Forest and states theorems demonstrating that the mappings between the filestore and in-memory structures behave correctly. These theorems are inspired by the "round-tripping" laws for well-behaved lenses [10], but are significantly more complicated as the load and store functions have to deal with inconsistencies stemming from dependencies, duplication, and invalid data.
- Section 8 contains a discussion of related work. There has been much past work on domain-specific languages for describing, parsing and printing individual data files. Examples include Lex, Yacc, Antlr [26], Parsec [19] and Pads [7], to name just a few. However, Forest differs substantially from any of these systems because it focuses on technology for describing *entire filestores*. A key difference is that simple filestores are *trees* and complex ones with symbolic links are *graphs*, whereas files are *sequences* (of characters or tokens). Consequently, the language design, formal systems, semantic issues, and underlying implementation technology are all entirely different.

2. Example Filestores

In this section, we present two example filestores. We use these examples to motivate and explain the design of Forest.

The first filestore contains information about students in Princeton's undergraduate computer science program. The faculty use the information to decide on undergraduate awards and to track grading trends. Its format has changed over time—something that is typical for ad hoc filestores. Naturally, any description needs to cope with the variations introduced as formats evolve.

Figure 1 shows a snippet of the (anonymized) student filestore designed to illustrate its structure. At the top level, there are

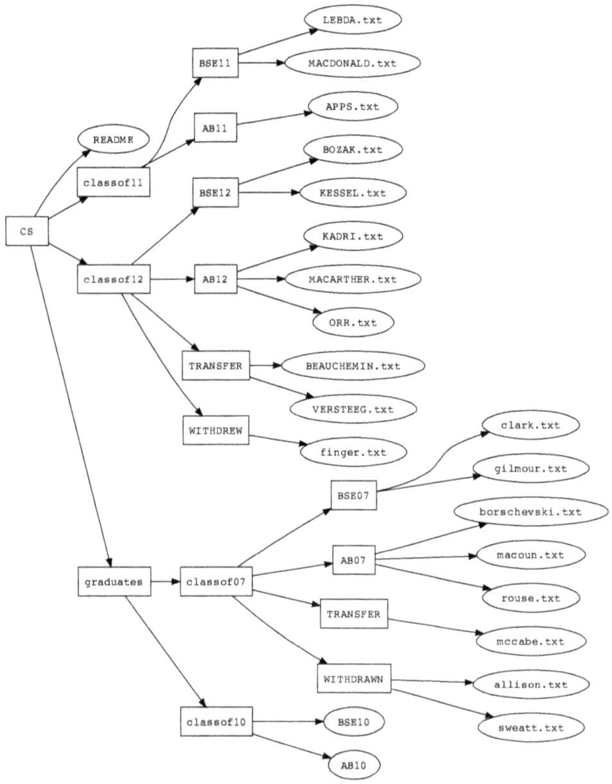

Figure 1. Anonymized snippet of Princeton computer science undergraduate data. A shaded node denotes denotes an error; in this case, missing files.

three directories: `classof11` (seniors), `classof12` (juniors) and `graduates` (students who have graduated). There is also a `README` file containing a collection of notes. Inside `graduates`, there is set of directories named `classofYY` where `YY` dates back to 92. Inside each `classofYY` directory, there are at least the two degree subdirectories `ABYY` and `BSEYY` as the computer science department gives out both Arts and Science (AB) and Engineering (BSE) degrees. Optionally, there are also subdirectories for students who withdrew from Princeton or transferred to another program. Within any degree subdirectory, there is one text file per student that records the courses taken and the corresponding grades. Each degree directory may also contain a template file named `sss.txt` or `sxx.txt` for creating new students.

The second filestore contains log files for CoralCDN [11, 12]. To monitor the performance and security of the system, the hosts participating in CoralCDN periodically send usage statistics back to a central server. These statistics are collected in a filestore similar to the one depicted in Figure 2. The filestore has a top-level directory named `dat`, which contains a set of subdirectories, one for each host. Each of those directories contain another set of directories, labeled by date and time. Finally, each of the date/time directories contain one or more compressed log files. For the purposes of this example, we will focus on the `coralwebsrv.log.gz` log file, which contains detailed information about the web requests made on the host during the preceding time period. In addition to exploring this primary filestore, we also explore a secondary, derived filestore. This secondary store, named `stats`, contains files that store statistics generated by Forest/Haskell scripts that analyze and summarize the raw CoralCDN server data. These system-wide summaries are representative of the statistics reported by Freedman in his CoralCDN report [11].

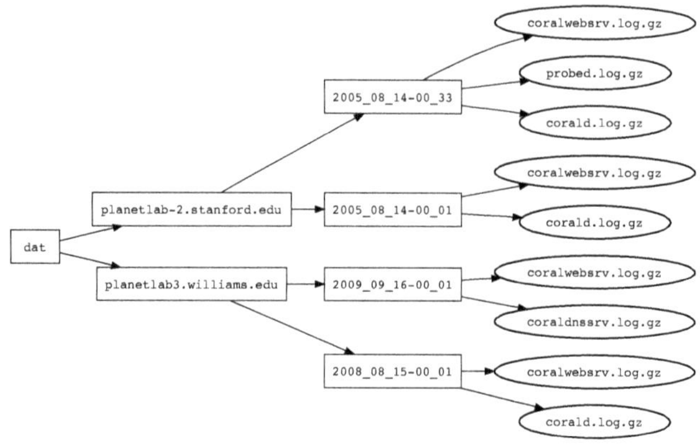

Figure 2. Coral system log data.

3. Forest Design

Data stored in filestores shares many characteristics of data stored in ordinary, in-memory data structures. Consequently, Forest uses the same sort of language to describe filestores as one uses to describe ordinary data structures — the language of types. Simple base types describe individual file system objects[1] and more complex types describe organized collections of file system objects. This idea forms the basis for our design.

Embedding Forest in Haskell. In order to write lightweight scripts, programmers must be able to manipulate and transform file system objects side-by-side with ordinary data structures. Consequently, a language like Forest must be embedded within a more general host programming language. We chose Haskell as the host language primarily because of its rich support for type-directed programming, which facilitates the construction of generic tools that can operate over any Forest description. As a bonus, Haskell's quasiquoting mechanism [21] proved a useful way to implement Forest. It enabled tight integration of the two languages while admitting fine-grained control over Forest syntax.

To introduce new Forest declarations within a Haskell program, the programmer simply opens the Forest sublanguage using quasiquoting notation:

```
[forest| ... forest declarations ... |]
```

When processing such a quasiquote, the Haskell compiler invokes the Forest compiler, which converts the given Forest declarations into a sequence of plain Haskell declarations that collectively implement the Forest declarations.

Forest Structure and Interpretations. Once within the Forest sublanguage, the programmer writes declarations that resemble extended Haskell type declarations. Each such type declaration has three primary semantic interpretations:

1. An interpretation as an *expected on-disk shape* of a file system fragment.
2. An interpretation as an ordinary Haskell type for the in-memory *representation* that will be constructed when the file system fragment is loaded into a Haskell program.
3. An interpretation as an ordinary Haskell type for the in-memory *metadata* that will be generated when the file system fragment is loaded.

All three interpretations are used by the tool that loads data from the filestore into memory as specified by a Forest description. When

[1] We use the term *file system object* or more simply *object* to denote either a file, a directory, or a symbolic link.

supplied with a *current path*, the loader uses the first interpretation to validate that the filestore rooted at that path has the correct shape. If the expected shape is complicated, possibly involving several nested subshapes (and hence traversal through several subdirectories), the semantics of Forest dictates how the loader should adjust the current path as it goes. When validation (also called *matching*) succeeds, we say the filestore fragment *matches* the description. The second interpretation is used when the loader lazily pulls the on-disk data into memory. The in-memory data structure is guaranteed to have the Haskell type given by the second interpretation. The third interpretation provides a type for the metadata structure generated by the loader. Such metadata includes error information (missing file, insufficient permissions, *etc.*) as well as file system attributes (owner, size, *etc.*).

The effectiveness of the Forest language comes in part from the fact that these three interpretations all arise from a single compact description. Moreover, to aid the programmer in navigating between interpretations, we align the syntax of Forest with the syntax of Haskell where possible. For example, if the Haskell types for the in-memory representation and metadata are record types, then the Forest syntax is designed to look similar to a Haskell record type. Likewise, if the Haskell types for the in-memory representation and metadata are Maybe types then the Forest syntax is designed to look similar to a Haskell Maybe type. Many of these high-level design considerations were adopted from earlier work on Pads [5, 7, 22], although the semantics of Forest (which operates over graph-based filestores) is substantially different from the semantics of Pads (which operates over sequence-based strings).

Errors. As with Pads [5, 7, 22], we do not assume that a given filestore conforms perfectly to its associated Forest description. Instead, when loading data, we check that a filestore conforms and mark discrepencies in the metadata. This design allows users to respond in application-specific ways to errors. It also allows Forest to check the arbitrarily complex conditions that may be specified by Forest's dependent types.[2] Because Forest loads data lazily, this choice means errors will not be detected unless the user program needs to touch the portion of the filestore with the error. The user can force a complete conformance check by accessing the top-level error count. It is possible for the filestore to change during or after this check. For the filestores we have seen in practice, there are extra-linguistic procedures in place to prevent such concurrent modifications; we leave to future work the possibility of using operating system support to monitor and/or prevent such changes automatically.

Onward. In the remainder of this section, we discuss the specific type constructors that constitute the Forest language and illustrate their use in our running examples.

3.1 Base Types: Files

Forest provides a small collection of base types for describing individual files: `TextFile` for ASCII files, `BinaryFile` for binary files, and `AnyFile` for arbitrary files. As with all Forest types, each of these types specifies a representation type, a metadata type, and loading and storing functions. For all three file types, the representation type is a `ByteString`. Similarly all three share a metadata type, which pairs file-system metadata with metadata describing properties of the file contents. The file-system metadata has type `Forest_md`, shown in Figure 3. This structure stores two kinds of information:

```
data Forest_md = Forest_md
   { numErrors :: Int
   , errorMsg  :: Maybe ErrMsg
   , fileInfo  :: FileInfo }

data FileInfo = FileInfo
   { fullpath     :: FilePath
   , owner        :: String
   , group        :: String
   , size         :: COff
   , access_time  :: EpochTime
   , mod_time     :: EpochTime
   , read_time    :: EpochTime
   , mode         :: FileMode
   , isSymLink    :: Bool
   , kind         :: FileType }
```

Figure 3. Forest metadata types.

1. the number and kind of any errors that occurred during loading
2. the attributes associated with the file (`fileInfo`)

File-content metadata describes errors within the file. For these three file types, there is no meaningful content metadata and so this type is the unit type. Leveraging Haskell's laziness, the loading functions create the in-memory representations and set the metadata on demand. The storing functions, which are described in more detail in Section 4, do the inverse.

Although useful, these three base types are not sufficient for describing the wide range of files used in practice, including XML documents, Makefiles, source files in various languages, shell scripts, *etc.* The appropriate representation and content metadata types for each such file varies. To support such files, Forest provides a plug-in architecture, allowing third-party users to define new file types by specifying a representation type, a metadata type, and corresponding loading and storing functions.

A common class of files are *ad hoc data files* containing semi-structured information, an example of which is the Princeton student record file format. In such cases, Forest can leverage the Pads/Haskell [8] data description language to define format-specific in-memory representations, content metadata, and loading and storing functions. Pads/Haskell is a recently developed version of Pads [5, 7, 22]. Like Forest, Pads/Haskell is embedded in Haskell using quasiquotation. For example, the following code snippet begins the Pads specification of the Princeton student record format:

```
[pads| data Student(name::String) = Student
         { person  :: Line (Person name)
         , Header
         , courses :: [Line Course]
         , Trailer
         }
       ...  |]
```

This description is parameterized by the name of the student whose data is in the file; the complete description appears in the companion technical report [4]. From this specification, the Pads compiler generates an in-memory representation type `Student`, a content metadata type `Student_md`, and parsing and printing functions.

Forest provides the `File` type constructor to lift Pads types to Forest file types. For example, the declaration

```
[forest| type SFile(n::String) = File(Student n) |]
```

introduces a new file type named `SFile` whose format is given by the Pads type `Student`. As with the Pads type, `SFile` is parameterized by the name of the student.

[2] Validation that a filestore obeys a Forest specification is akin to type checking. However, it is akin to type checking closed, zero-order values (trees and graphs) as opposed to type checking parameterized, higher-order values (functions). Consequently, even though Forest has dependent types, type checking is not algorithmically challenging. For example, Forest does not have to decide equivalence of expressions with free variables as one must do when type checking a dependent lambda calculus.

Using Pads/Haskell descriptions in Forest not only helps specify the structure of ad hoc data files, but it also generates a structured in-memory representation of the data, allowing Haskell programmers to traverse, query and otherwise manipulate such data. We designed Pads/Haskell and Forest to work seamlessly together. From the perspective of the Haskell programmer traversing a resulting in-memory data structure, there is effectively no difference between iterating over files in a directory or structured sequences of lines or tokens within a file.

While Pads/Haskell is independently interesting, this paper focuses on Forest. Henceforth, any unadorned declarations occur within the Forest scope `[forest| ... |]` unless otherwise noted. Any declarations prefixed by > are ordinary Haskell declarations.

3.2 Base Type: Symbolic Links

When symbolic links occur in a described filestore, Forest follows the symbolic link to its target, mimicking standard shell behavior. However, Forest allows programmers to specify explicitly that a particular file is a symbolic link using the base type `SymLink`. The in-memory representation for an explicit symbolic link is the path that is the target of the link. It is possible to use constraints (Section 3.6) to specify desired properties of the link target, such as requiring it to be to a specific file.

In Forest, any file system object may be described in multiple ways. Hence, in the case of a symbolic link, it is possible to use one declaration to specify that the object is a symbolic link and a second to specify the type of the link target. We will see an example of such a specification in Section 3.4

3.3 Maybe: Optional File System Objects

Sometimes, a given file (or directory or symbolic link) may or may not be present in the file system, and either case is valid. To handle this situation, we leverage the idea of an option type by providing a Forest-level `Maybe` type constructor that maps the optional file system object to a `Maybe` type in Haskell. In particular, if `T` is a Forest type, then `Maybe T` is the Forest type denoting an optional `T`. The type `Maybe T` succeeds and returns representation `None` when the current path does not exist in the file system. `Maybe T` also succeeds and returns `Just v` for some `v` of type `T` when the current path exists and matches `T`. `Maybe T` registers an error in the metadata when the current path exists but the corresponding object does not match `T`.

3.4 Records: Directories

Forest directories are record-like datatype constructors that allow users to specify directory structures. For example, to specify the root directory of the student repository in Figure 1, we might use the following declaration. This declaration assumes that we have already defined `Class y`, a parameterized description that specifies the structure of a directory holding data for the class of year `y`, and `Grads`, a description that specifies the structure of the directory holding all graduated classes.

```
type PrincetonCS_1 = Directory
  { notes   is "README"      :: TextFile
  , seniors is "classof11"   :: Class 11
  , juniors is "classof12"   :: Class 12
  , grads   is "graduates"   :: Grads }
```

Each field of the record describes a single file system object. It has three components: (1) an internal name (*e.g.*, `notes` or `seniors`) that must be a valid Haskell record label, (2) an external name specified as a value of type `String` (*e.g.*, `"README"` or `"classof11"`) that gives the name of the object on disk, and (3) a Forest description of the object (*e.g.*, `TextFile` or `Class 11`).

When the external name is itself a valid Haskell label, users may omit it, in which case Forest uses the label as the on-disk name:

```
type PrincetonCS_2 = Directory
  { notes is "README" :: TextFile
  , classof11 :: Class 11
  , classof12 :: Class 12
  , graduates :: Grads }
```

We could not abbreviate the `notes` field because labels must start with a lowercase letter in Haskell.

Matching. For a file system object to match a directory description, the object must be a directory and each field of the record must match. A field `f` matches when the object whose path is the concatenation of the current path and the external name of `f` matches the type of `f`.

It is possible for the same file system object to match multiple fields in a directory description at the same time. For example, if `"README"` were actually a symbolic link, it is possible to document that fact by mentioning it twice in the directory description, once as a text file and once as a symbolic link:

```
type PrincetonCS_3 = Directory
  { link  is "README" :: SymLink
  , notes is "README" :: TextFile
  , ... }
```

It is also possible for a directory to contain objects that are unmatched by a description. We allow extra items because it is common for directories to contain objects that users do not care about. For example, a directory structure may contain extra files or directories related to a version control system, and a description writer may not want to clutter the Forest specification with that information. We will see shortly that it is possible to specify the absence of file system objects using constraints.

As suggested by the syntax, the in-memory representation of a directory is a Haskell record with the corresponding labels. The type of each field is the representation type of the Forest type for the field. The metadata has a similar structure. The metadata for each field has two components: file-system attribute information of type `Forest_md` and field-specific metadata whose type is derived from the Forest type for the field. In addition, the directory metadata contains an additional value of type `Forest_md` that summarizes the errors occurring in directory components and stores the `FileInfo` structure for the directory itself. When loading a directory, Forest constructs the appropriate in-memory representation for each field that matches and puts the corresponding metadata in the metadata structure. For fields that do not match, Forest constructs default values and marks the metadata with suitable error information.

Computed Paths The above descriptions are a good start for our application, but they are not ideal. Every year, the directory for graduating seniors (*i.e.*, `classof11`) is moved into the graduates directory, the juniors are promoted to seniors and a new junior class is created. As it stands, we would have to edit the description every year. An alternative is to parameterize the description with the current year and to *construct* the appropriate file names using Haskell functions:

```
> toStrN i n = (replicate(n - length(show i)) '0')
>               ++ (show i)
> mkClass y = "classof" ++ (toStrN y 2)
```

```
type PrincetonCS (y::Integer) = Directory
  { notes   is "README" :: TextFile
  , seniors is <|mkClass y     |> :: Class y
  , juniors is <|mkclass (y+1)|> :: Class <|y+1|>
  , graduates :: Grads }
```

The bracket syntax `<| ... |>` provides an escape so that we may use Haskell within Forest code to specify arbitrary computations. When an expression is a constant or variable, it may be supplied directly. When an argument is more complex, however, it must be written in brackets to escape to Haskell. This example also illustrates abstraction: any Forest declaration may be parameterized by specifying a legal Haskell pattern and its type. The types of the fields for `seniors` and `juniors` illustrate the use of parameterized descriptions.

Approximate Paths As filestores evolve, naming conventions may change. Additionally, directory structures with multiple instances may have minor variations in the names of individual files across instances. For example, in each Princeton class directory, there may (or may not) be some number of students that have withdrawn from the program, transferred to a different program, or gone on leave. Over the years, slightly different directory names have been used to represent these situations.

To accommodate this variation, Forest includes the matching construct to approximate file names. We can use this mechanism to describe the class directory:

```
> transRE = RE "TRANSFER|Transfer"
> leaveRE = RE "LEAVE|Leave"
> wdRE    = RE "WITHDRAWN|WITHDRAWAL|Withdrawn"

type Class (y::Integer) = Directory
  { bse is <|"BSE" ++ (toString y)|> :: Major
  , ab  is <|"AB"  ++ (toString y)|> :: Major
  , trans matches transRE :: Maybe Major
  , withd matches wdRE    :: Maybe Major
  , leave matches leaveRE :: Maybe Major }
```

A field with the form `<label> matches <regexp> :: T` finds the set of paths in the files system that match `currentPath/<regexp>`. If there are zero or one such files, the `matches` form acts just as the `is` form. If more than one file matches, one of the matches is selected non-deterministically, a multiple match error is registered in the metadata, and matching continues as it would with the `is` form. In addition to regular expressions, the matching construct also allows *glob patterns*, (*i.e.*, patterns such as `*.txt`), to specify the names of files on disk. An example appears in the next subsection.

3.5 Lists

Just as Haskell has both records and lists, so too does Forest. Records allow programmers to specify a fixed number of file system objects, each with its own type. Lists, on the other hand, allow programmers to specify an arbitrary number of file system objects, each with the same type. As an example, we can use a list to specify the `Grads` directory from Figure 1. We borrow Haskell's notation for list comprehensions to specify the names of the file system objects:

```
> getYear s =
>   toInteger $ reverse $ take 2 $ reverse s
> cRE = RE "classof[0-9][0-9]"

type Grads =
  [c :: Class <|getYear c|> | c <- matches cRE]
```

In this specification, `Grads` is a directory fragment containing a number of `Class` subdirectories with names `c` that match the regular expression `cRE`. The Haskell function `getYear` extracts the last two digits from the name of the directory, converts the string digits to an integer year, and passes the year to the underlying `Class` specification. More generally, Forest lists have the form `[path :: T | id <- gen, pred]` where `id` is bound in turn to each of the file names generated by `gen`, which may be a `matches` clause (used to match against the files at the current path as in the previous section) or a list computed in Haskell. These generated `id`s are filtered by the optional predicate `pred`. For each such legal `id`, there is a corresponding expression `path`, which Forest interprets as extending the current path. The object at each such path should have the Forest type `T`. The identifier `id` is in scope in `pred`, `path`, and `T`.

The in-memory representation of a Forest list is a Haskell list containing pairs of the name of a matching object and its representation. The metadata is a list of the metadata of the matching objects paired with a summary metadata structure of type `Forest_md`.

Representation Transformations. Although the list representation for comprehensions is useful, it can be desirable to use a more sophisticated data structure to represent such collections. To support this usage, Forest allows programmers to prefix a list comprehension with any type constructor that belongs to a Forest-defined container type class. This type class contains functions that specify how to convert between the list representation and the desired container representation. We have provided such instance declarations for Haskell's `Map` and `Set` type constructors.

As an example, consider the specification of the `Major` directory. Each such directory contains a list of student files and an additional template file named either `sss.txt` or `sxx.txt`. The declaration below specifies the collection of student files by matching with a glob pattern and filtering to exclude template files. It uses the `Map` type constructor to specify that the data and metadata should be collected in a `Map` rather than a list.

```
> template s = s `elem` ["sss.txt", "sxx.txt"]
> txt = GL "*.txt"

type Major = Map
   [ s :: File (Student <|dropExtension s|>)
   | s <- matches txt, <|not (template s)|>]
```

3.6 Dependent Types: Attributes and Constraints

Every file system object has a number of *attributes* associated with it, such as its owner, group, permissions, and size. In general, if a Forest identifier `id` refers to a path, then the identifier `id_att` refers to the corresponding attributes. This attribute identifier has type `Forest_md`, shown in Figure 3. Forest defines helper functions to access these attributes, some of which are listed in Figure 4.

Constrained types are a simple form of dependent types that allow users to specify required attributes. For example, the type `PrivateFile` specifies a text file accessible only by its owner.

```
type PrivateFile = TextFile
      where <|get_modes this_att == "-rw-------"|>
```

The keyword **where** introduces a constraint on the underlying type. The load function for the type `PrivateFile` checks this constraint during loading. If the constraint is false, it records that fact in the metadata. Within constraints, the special identifier `this` refers to the representation of the underlying object, `this_att` refers to its attributes and `this_md` to its complete metadata.

Using attributes, we can write a *universal directory description*, which is sufficiently general to describe any directory:

```
type Universal = Directory
  { asc is [ f :: TextFile
           | f <- matches <| GL "*" |>,
           <| get_kind f_att == AsciiK |> ]
  , bin is [ b :: BinaryFile
           | b <- matches <| GL "*" |>,
           <| get_kind b_att == BinaryK |> ]
  , dir is [ d :: Universal
           | d <- matches <| GL "*" |>,
           <| get_kind d_att == DirectoryK |> ]
  , sym is [ s :: SymLink
           | s <- matches <| GL "*" |>,
           <| isJust (get_symLink s_att) |> ] }
```

function name	information
get_group	object group
get_kind	the sort of file or directory
get_modes	permission string
get_owner	object owner
get_size	object size

Figure 4. Selected file attribute functions.

When a directory is loaded using the Universal description, all the ASCII files will end up the in asc field, all the binary files in bin, all the directories in dir, and all the symbolic links in sym. Note that the description uses recursion to describe nested directories. In the case that a symbolic link creates a cycle in the file system by pointing to a parent directory, the Haskell in-memory representation is a (lazy) infinite data structure. We view the fact that it is possible to write such a universal description in Forest as evidence that the language is appropriately expressive. This description also serves as an example of how to describe a filestore by its *structure* rather than its *names*.

We can also use constraints to specify that certain files *do not* appear in certain places. As an example, we might want to require that no binaries appear in a directory given to an untrusted user as scratch space. The description below flags an error during loading if a binary file exists in the directory.

```
type NoBin =
 [ b :: BinaryFile | b <- matches <| GL "*" |>,
                  <| get_kind b_att == BinaryK |> ]
  where <|length this == 0|>
```

3.7 Specialized Constructors: Gzip and Tar

Some files need to be processed before they can be used. A typical example is a compressed file such as the gzipped log files in CoralCDN. Forest provides processing-specific type constructors to describe such files. For example, if CoralLog is a Pads/Haskell description of a CoralCDN log file then

```
type Info = Gzip (File CoralLog)
```

describes a gzipped log file. Likewise, suppose logs.tar.gz is a gzipped tar file and that the type ManyLogs describes the directory of log files that logs.tar expands to when untarred. Such a situation can be described using a combination of the Tar and Gzip type constructors:

```
type MoreInfo = Gzip (Tar ManyLogs)
```

3.8 Putting it all together

The preceding subsections give an overview of Forest's design. Figures 5 and 6 give the specifications for the two running examples, minus the associated Pads/Haskell and Haskell declarations. The complete descriptions of these filestores and additional descriptions are available in a technical report [4], including descriptions of the Pads website, a Gene Ontology filestore, and CVS repositories.

4. Programming with Forest

Many Forest programs work in two phases. In the first phase they use Forest to load relevant portions of the file system into memory, and in the second phase they use an ordinary Haskell function to traverse the in-memory representation of the data (or its associated metadata) and compute the desired result. Some Forest programs add a third phase in which they store updated structures back to the filestore.

```
[forest|
 data PrincetonCS (y::Integer) = Directory
   { notes    is "README" :: TextFile
   , seniors is <|mkClass y     |> :: Class y
   , juniors is <|mkclass (y+1)|> :: Class <|y+1|>
   , graduates :: Grads }

 data Class (y::Integer) = Directory
   { bse is <|"BSE" ++ (toString y)|> :: Major
   , ab  is <|"AB"  ++ (toString y)|> :: Major
   , trans matches transRE :: Maybe Major
   , withd matches wdRE    :: Maybe Major
   , leave matches leaveRE :: Maybe Major }

 type Grads =
   [c :: Class <|getYear c|> | c <- matches cRE]

 type Major = Map
    [ s :: File (Student <|dropExtension s|>)
    | s <- matches txt, <|not (template s)|>] |]
```

Figure 5. Forest description of Princeton filestore.

```
[forest|
 type Stats = Directory
   { last :: File Last, topk :: File Topk }
 type Dat    = [ s :: Site | s <- matches site ]
 type Site   = [ d :: Log  | d <- matches time ]
 data Log = Directory
   { log is coralwebsrv :: Gzip (File CoralLog) } |]
```

Figure 6. Forest description of CoralCDN filestore.

Representation Types:

```
newtype Stats = Stats {last :: Last, topk :: Topk}
newtype Dat   = Dat   [(String, Site)]
newtype Site  = Site  [(String, Log)]
data    Log   = Log   {log :: CoralLog}
```

Metadata Types:

```
type Stats_md = (Forest_md, Stats_inner_md)
data Stats_inner_md = Stats_inner_md
    {last_md :: (Forest_md, Last_md),
     topk_md :: (Forest_md, Topk_md)}
type Dat_md    = (Forest_md, [(String, Site_md)])
type Site_md   = (Forest_md, [(String, Log_md)])
type Log_md    = (Forest_md, Log_inner_md)
data Log_inner_md = Log_inner_md
    {log_md :: (Forest_md, CoralLog_md)}
```

Load Functions:

```
stats_load :: FilePath -> IO (Stats, Stats_md)
dat_load   :: FilePath -> IO (Dat, Dat_md)
site_load  :: FilePath -> IO (Site, Site_md)
log_load   :: FilePath -> IO (Log, Log_md)
```

Store Functions:

```
stats_manifest :: (Stats, Stats_md) -> IO Manifest
dat_manifest   :: (Dat, Dat_md)     -> IO Manifest
site_manifest  :: (Site, Site_md)   -> IO Manifest
log_manifest   :: (Log, Log_md)     -> IO Manifest
storeAt        :: FilePath -> Manifest -> IO ()
store          ::             Manifest -> IO ()
```

Figure 7. Artifacts generated from the CoralCND description.

To facilitate this style of programming, the Forest compiler generates several Haskell types and functions from every Forest declaration. Collectively, these types and functions define an instance of the `Forest` type class:

```
class (Data rep, ForestMD md)
    => Forest rep md | rep -> md  where
  load     :: FilePath -> IO(rep, md)
  manifest :: (rep,md) -> IO Manifest
  ...
```

In this type class, the type `rep` is the generated in-memory representation type of the corresponding on-disk data. The type `md` is the generated type for the associated metadata. The `ForestMD` type class provides operations for manipulating Forest metadata; all generated metadata types belong to this type class.

The generated load function lazily traverses the file system and reads the files, directories, and symbolic links mentioned in the description into a pair of the in-memory representation and its metadata. To reverse the process of reading data in to memory, Forest also generates a *manifest function*, which reads an in-memory data structure, writes its contents out to disk in a temporary space, and prepares a *manifest log*. The manifest log records inconsistencies detected during this process as well as the sequence of operations necessary to move data from the temporary space to its final resting point. Inconsistences can arise when a programmer creates an erroneous in-memory representation of a filestore. The dependencies that may be present in Forest descriptions mean that not all such inconsistencies can be detected statically by the Haskell type system. After creating a manifest, a programmer may analyze it and decide whether to execute the generic `store` or `storeAt` functions, which move a manifest (inconsistencies and all) to its rightful position on disk. Details concerning the semantics of storing, especially where it concerns inconsistencies, are explained in further depth in Section 7.

As an example, consider the CoralCDN logs described in Figure 6. The corresponding load and store functions, the representation types, and the metadata types appear in Figure 7.[3] Note that the structure of each of these artifacts mirrors the structure of the Forest description that generated them. This close correspondence makes it easy for programmers to write programs using these Forest-generated artifacts.

For instance, consider the `Dat` description in Figure 6. The `dat_load` function takes a path as an argument and produces the representation and metadata obtained by loading each of the site directories contained in the directory at that path:

```
(rep,md) <- dat_load "/var/log/coral/dat"
```

Because `Dat` is a Forest list, the `rep` is a Haskell list. More specifically, `rep` has the form

```
Coral [("planetab2.eecs.wsu.edu", Site [...]),
       ("planetlab3.williams.edu",Site [...]),...]
```

where the list contains pairs of names of subdirectories and representations for the data loaded from those directories. The metadata is a pair consisting of a generic header of type `Forest_md` and a list of pairs of names of subdirectories and their associated metadata. The header collects information about errors encountered during loading and it stores the file system attributes of each file, directory, or symbolic link loaded from the file system. The following is the pretty-printed version of such a structure:

```
Forest_md
  { numErrors = 0,
    errorMsg = Nothing,
    fileInfo = FileInfo
      { fullpath = /var/log/coral/dat,
        owner = alice, group = staff, size = 102,
        access_time = Fri Nov 19 01:47:09 2010,
        mod_time = Thu Nov 18 20:42:37 2010,
        read_time = Fri Nov 19 01:47:28 2010,
        mode = drwxr-xr-x, isSymLink = False,
        kind = Directory } },
[("planetlab2.eecs.wsu.edu", Forest_md {...}),
 ("planetlab3.williams.edu", Forest_md {...}), ...]
```

Using these functions and types, it is easy to formulate many useful queries as simple Haskell programs. For instance, to count the number of sites we can simply compute the length of the nested list in `rep`:

```
num_sites = case rep of Dat l -> List.length l
```

More interestingly, since the internals of the web log are specified using Pads/Haskell (see the technical report [4] for details), it is straightforward to dig in to the file data and combine it with file metadata or attributes in queries. For example, to calculate the time when statistics were last reported for each site, we can zip the lists in `rep` and `md` together and project out the site name and the `mod_time` field from each element in the resulting list of pairs:

```
get_site = fst
get_mod (_,(f,_)) = mod_time . fileInfo $ f
sites_mod () =
  case (rep,md) of (Dat rs, (_,ms)) ->
    map (get_site *** get_mod) (zip rs ms)
```

As this example shows, Forest blurs the distinction between data represented on disk and in memory. After writing a suitable Forest description, programmers can write programs that work on file system data as if it were in memory. Moreover, because Forest uses Haskell's lazy I/O operations, many simple programs do not require constructing an explicit representation of the entire directory being loaded in memory—a good thing as the directory of CoralCDN logs contains approximately 1GB of data! Instead, the load functions only read the portions of the file system that are needed to compute the result—in this case, only the site directories and not the gzipped log files contained within them.

As a final analysis example, consider a program that computes the top-k requested URLs from all CoralCDN nodes by size. The CoralCDN administrators compute this statistic periodically to help monitor and tune the performance of the system [11]. We define the analogous function in Haskell using helper functions such as `get_sites` to project out components of `rep`:

```
topk k =
  take k $ sortBy descBytes $ toList $
  fromListWith (+)
    [ (get_url e, get_total e)
    | (site,sdir) <- get_sites rep,
      (datetime,ldir) <- get_dates sdir,
      e <- get_entries ldir,
      is_incoming e ]
```

Reading this program inside-out, we see that it first uses a list comprehension to iterate through `rep`, collecting the individual log entries corresponding to incoming requests using the `is_incoming` predicate. It then projects out the URL requested and the total size of the request. It then sums the sizes of all requests for the same URL using the `fromListWith` function from the `Data.Map` module. Next, it sorts the entries in descending order. Finally, it returns the first k entries of the list as the final result.

Having implemented these analyses, a programmer may wish to store their results. She may do so via the following code, which

[3] In the following examples, for the sake of clarity, we use type-specific names such as `dat_load` and `dat_manifest`, rather than the overloaded names `load` and `manifest`.

uses `stats_manifest` to generate a manifest and `store` to copy it over to the `stats` directory. In addition, the code uses `stats_defaultMd`, a function that constructs default metadata for stats structures (a useful function in situations that require storing newly constructed data).

```
let result = Stats { last = sites_mod ()
                   , topk = topk 10 }
manifest <- stats_manifest
  ( result
  , stats_defaultMd result "/var/log/coral/stats" )
store manifest
```

Overall, the main thing to take away from this section is how Forest and its tight integration with Haskell facilitates exploratory data analysis, enabling remarkably terse queries over the combination of file contents, file attributes and directory structures.

5. Generic Tools

Third-party developers can use generic programming [18] to generate tools that will work for any filestore that has a Forest description. An advantage of these tools compared to tools that work directly on the untyped file system is that they are specific to the fragment of the file system relevant to the filestore. This fragment can be difficult to specify when using conventional tools since it can rely on the contents of configuration files, file naming conventions, file system attributes, *etc.* It is precisely these relationships that Forest descriptions capture concisely; tools written to use Forest specifications can leverage that information.

As a proof of concept, we have written a number of such tools, which we describe in this section.

5.1 Generic Querying

One simple application of generic programming is querying metadata to find files with a particular collection of attributes. The `findFiles` function

```
findFiles :: (ForestMD md) =>
     md -> (FileInfo -> Bool) -> [FilePath]
```

takes as input any Forest metadata value (*i.e.*, any value of type `md` where `md` belongs to the Forest metadata class `ForestMD`) and a predicate on `FileInfo` structures, and returns the list of all `FilePaths` anywhere in the input metadata whose associated `FileInfo` satisfies the predicate. For example, if `cs_md` is the metadata associated with the Princeton computer science department filestore, then the code

```
dirs  = findFiles cs_md (\(r::FileInfo) ->
                          (kind r) == DirectoryK)
other = findFiles cs_md (\(r::FileInfo) ->
                          (owner r) /= "bwk")
```

binds `dirs` to the list of all directories in the data set and `other` to all the directories and files not owned by user `"bwk"`.

To implement the `findFiles` function, we use the generic Haskell function `listify`:

```
findFiles md pred = map fullpath (listify pred md)
```

The return type of the polymorphic `listify` function is instantiated to match the argument type of its predicate argument. We map the `fullpath` function over the resulting list of `FileInfo` structures to return only the `FilePaths`.

5.2 File System Visualization

`ForestGraph` generates a graphical representation of any directory structure that matches a Forest specification. We generated the graphs in Figures 1 and 2 using this tool. In the default configuration, `ForestGraph` uses boxes to denote directories and ovals to denote files. Borders of varying thickness distinguish between ASCII and binary files. Dashed node boundaries indicate symbolic links and shaded nodes flag errors.

The core functionality of `ForestGraph` lies in the Haskell function `mdToPDF`:

```
mdToPDF :: ForestMD md =>
     md -> FilePath -> IO (Maybe String)
```

The function takes as input any metadata value and a filepath that specifies where to put the generated PDF file. It optionally returns a string (`Maybe String`); if the option is present, the string contains an error message. The `IO` type constructor indicates that there can be side effects during the execution of the function. A use of this function to generate the graph for the Princeton computer science department filestore looks like:

```
do { (cs_rep,cs_md) <- CS_load  "facadm"
   ; mdToPDF cs_md "Output/CS.pdf"        }
```

Note that this code needs only the metadata to generate the graph; laziness means Forest will not load the representation in this case.

The related function `mdToPDFWithParams` takes an additional argument that allows the user to specify how to draw the nodes and edges in the output graph. Among other things, this parameter specifies how to map a value of type `Forest_md` into GRAPHVIZ [13, 14] attributes. By appropriately setting the parameter, a user can customize the formatting of each node according to its owner, group, or permissions, *etc.*, as well as specify global properties of the graph such as its orientation and size. `ForestGraph` uses the Haskell binding of the GRAPHVIZ library to lay out and render the graphs, so all customizations provided by GRAPHVIZ are available.

The `listify` function is at the heart of the implementation of this tool; we use it to convert the input metadata to the list of `FileInfos` in the metadata. We then convert this list into a graph data structure suitable for use with the GRAPHVIZ library.

5.3 Permission Checker

The permission tool is designed to check the permissions on the files and directories in a Forest description on a multi-user machine. In particular, it enables one user to determine which files a second user can read, write, or execute. If the second user cannot access a file in a particular way, the tool also reports the names of the files and directories whose permissions have to change to allow the access. The tool is useful when trying to share files with a colleague. It helps the first user ensure that all the necessary permissions have been set properly to allow the second user access. The key to the implementation of this tool is again applying the `listify` function to the metadata for the Forest description.

5.4 Shell Tools

We have implemented analogs of many shell tools that work over a file system fragment defined by a Forest description:

```
ls   :: (ForestMD md) => md -> String -> IO String
grep :: (ForestMD md) => md -> String -> IO String
tar  :: (ForestMD md) => md -> FilePath -> IO ()
cp   :: (ForestMD md) => md -> FilePath -> IO ()
```

All of these functions work by extracting the relevant file names from the argument metadata structure using `listify` and then calling out to a shell tool to do the work. For `ls`, the second argument gives the command-line arguments to pass to the shell version of `ls`, and the result is the resulting output. The implementation uses `xarg` to lift the restriction on the number of files that can be passed to `ls`. For `grep`, the second argument is the search string and result is the output of the shell version of `grep`. For `tar`, the second argument specifies the location for the resulting tarball. The implementation uses a file manifest to allow `tar` to work regardless of the number of files involved. The `cp` tool uses the `tar` tool to move the files mentioned in the metadata to the location specified by the second argument *while retaining the same directory structure*. The module that implements these tools is approximately 80 lines of Haskell code.

5.5 Description Inference Tool

This tool allows the user to generate a Forest description from the contents of the file system. The function

```
getDesc :: FilePath -> IO String
```

takes as an argument the path to the root of the directory structure to infer. It returns a string containing the generated representation. For example, below we show a fragment of the results when `getDesc` is invoked on the `classof11` directory:

```
data classof11 = Directory {
    aB11 is "AB11" :: aB11,
    bSE11 is "BSE11" :: bSE11,
    tRANSFER is "TRANSFER" :: tRANSFER,
    wITHDREW is "WITHDREW" :: wITHDREW }
data tRANSFER = Directory {
    bEAUCHEMINtxt is "BEAUCHEMIN.txt" :: File Text,
    vERSTEEGtxt is "VERSTEEG.txt" :: File Text }
...
```

The description is not perfect: the label names are generated from the file name, for example. Nevertheless, the tool improves programmer productivity as it is easier for a programmer to edit a generated description than to start from scratch. Our first tool in this vein is simple; a more sophisticated variant would collapse records of files into lists when a width limit was exceeded or other criteria were met. Another variant might collapse deeply nested directories into a universal directory description when a depth limit was exceeded. The `getDesc` function works by using the universal description to load the contents of the file system starting from the supplied path. It then walks over the resulting metadata to generate a Forest parse tree, which it then pretty prints.

6. Implementation

The current implementation of Forest is available from the project web site: `forestproj.org`.

Haskell provides powerful language features and libraries that greatly facilitated implementation of Forest. The most obvious of these features is the quasiquotation mechanism [21] that we used to embed Forest into Haskell. This mechanism provided the benefits of being an embedded domain-specific language without having to sacrifice the flexibility of defining our own syntax. To use quasiquoting, we defined a Haskell value `forest` of type `QuasiQuoter` which specifies how to convert an input string representing a sequence of Forest declarations into the Template Haskell [27] data structures that represent the syntax of the corresponding collection of Haskell declarations. The Haskell compiler calls the `forest` "compilation" function during the compilation of any Haskell source file containing a Forest quasiquotation. The quasiquoted syntax `[forest| <input> |]` is legal anywhere the identifier `forest` is in scope. When the Haskell compiler processes this declaration, it first passes `<input>` as a string to the `forest` quasiquoter, and then it compiles the resulting Template Haskell data structures as if the corresponding Haskell code had appeared in the input at the location of the quasiquote. Early versions of quasiquoting supported quoting only expression and pattern forms. Simon Peyton Jones extended the mechanism to permit declaration and type quasiquoting partly to enable the Forest implementation. We used this same approach to implement Pads/Haskell, which we built concomitantly.

Note that in implementing Forest, we had to use Template Haskell rather than any of the other libraries that support generic programming, both because that is what the quasiquote library expects and because we need to generate type and datatype declarations (and to do so at compile time). Other available generic libraries do not support the latter functionality.

Parsing. We used the parsec 3.1.0 parser combinator library [19] to implement the Forest parser. One key element of the Forest design is to allow arbitrary Haskell expressions in various places inside Forest descriptions. We did not want to reimplement the grammar for Haskell expressions, which is quite complicated. Instead, we structured the Forest grammar so we could always determine the extent of any embedded Haskell code. We then used the Haskell Source Extension package [15] to parse these fragments. The data structure that this library returns is unfortunately not the data structure that Template Haskell requires, so we used yet another library, the Haskell Source Meta package [16], that does this translation.

Type checking. We would like to give users high-quality error messages if there are type errors in their Forest declarations. At the moment, typechecking occurs, but only after the Forest declarations have been expanded to the corresponding Haskell code. Although these error messages can be quite informative, it is sub-optimal to report errors in terms of generated code. Type checking the Forest source is complicated by the embedded fragments of Haskell. As with the syntax, we do not want to reimplement the Haskell typechecker! There is an active proposal [29] to extend the Template Haskell infrastructure with functions that would enable us to ask the native Haskell typechecker for the types of embedded expressions and to extend the current type environment with type bindings for new identifiers. With this combination of features, we would be able to type check Forest sources directly.

Runtime. Although Forest facilitates treating the file system as a persistent store, it does not provide the ACID guarantees familiar from databases. None of the filestores we have encountered in practice are implemented in a system that provides such support; users instead have extra-linguistic mechanisms to make sure they do not corrupt their data with ill-timed concurrent reads and writes. That said, the Forest language does not preclude an implementation from providing such guarantees. We consider this issue very interesting future work.

Forest uses Haskell's `unsafeInterleaveIO` to load each portion of a filestore only when needed by an application program. We have not systematically measured the performance overhead of using Forest. However, we have used our mostly-unoptimized implementation to manipulate filestores on the order of many gigabytes and found the performance acceptable for many applications.

The running time of storing operations is proportional to the "footprint" of the described filestore. However, the Forest compiler generates `load` and `manifest` functions for each named type in a description. Thus, updates may be made at any granularity for which there is a named type, which is typically at the level of individual files. We plan to investigate better support for incremental updates in future work.

7. Core Calculus

This section presents a core calculus for Forest, which formalizes the essential features of the language in a simple setting. The calculus is based on classical (*i.e.*, not separating, substructural, or ambient) unordered tree logics, but has a number of features tailored to file systems. We used it to study various features of Forest as we were developing it, and to prove key theorems like the round-tripping properties described at the end of the section.

Basic definitions

$$\begin{aligned}
\textit{Integers}\ n &\in \mathbb{Z}\\
\textit{Strings}\ u &\in \Sigma^*\\
\textit{Values}\ v &::= n \mid u \mid r \mid \mathit{True} \mid \mathit{False} \mid () \mid (v_1, v_2)\\
&\quad \mid \mathit{Just}\ v \mid \mathit{Nothing} \mid [v_1, .., v_n]\\
\textit{Types}\ \tau &::= \mathit{String} \mid \mathit{Int} \mid \mathit{Path} \mid \mathit{Bool} \mid () \mid (\tau_1, \tau_2)\\
&\quad \mid \mathit{Maybe}\ \tau \mid [\tau]\\
\textit{Environments}\ \mathcal{E} &::= \emptyset \mid \mathcal{E}, x \mapsto v\\
\textit{Expressions}\ e &::= x \mid \lambda x.\, e \mid e_1\, e_2 \mid \ldots
\end{aligned}$$

Forest definitions

$$\begin{aligned}
\textit{Paths}\ r &::= \cdot \mid r\,/\,u\\
\textit{Attributes}\ a &::= v\\
\textit{Contents}\ T &::= \mathsf{File}\ u \mid \mathsf{Link}\ r \mid \mathsf{Dir}\ \{u_1, .., u_n\}\\
\textit{File systems}\ F &::= \{\!|\, r_1 \mapsto (a_1, T_1), .., r_n \mapsto (a_k, T_n) \,|\!\}\\
\textit{Specifications}\ s &::= k_{\tau_1}^{\tau_2} \mid e{::}s \mid \langle x{:}s_1, s_2\rangle \mid [s \mid x \in e] \mid \mathsf{P}(e) \mid s?
\end{aligned}$$

Figure 8. Forest calculus syntax.

7.1 Data Model

Forest calculus specifications manipulate instances of a simple file system model, which is given in Figure 8. A path r is a sequence of strings u,[4] and a file system F is a finite map from paths to pairs (a, T) of attributes a and file system contents T. We do not specify the syntax of attributes precisely, but expect that they will contain the usual fields including owner, group, permissions, modification date and time, *etc.* A special attribute a_{default} contains default values for all fields. The contents T of a node in the file system is either a file $\mathsf{File}\ u$, where u is the string contents of the file; a symbolic link $\mathsf{Link}\ r$, where r is the path pointed to by the link; or a directory $\mathsf{Dir}\ \{u_1, .., u_n\}$, where u_1 to u_n are the names of the elements of the file system located below the node. We write $\mathsf{dom}(F)$ for the set of paths F is defined on, $F(r)$ for the contents at r, $F(r) = \bot$ when r is not in $\mathsf{dom}(F)$, and $F[r := (a, T)]$ or $F[r := \bot]$ for the file systems obtained from F by overwriting the mapping for r to (a, T) or deleting the mapping for r respectively.

A file system F is *well-formed* if it encodes a tree with directories at the internal nodes and files and symbolic links at the leaves. More formally, F is well-formed if the following conditions hold:

- $\mathsf{dom}(F)$ is prefix-closed,
- $F(r) = (a, \mathsf{Dir}\ \{u_1, .., u_n\})$ implies $r\,/\,u_i \in \mathsf{dom}(F)$ for all i from 1 to n, and
- $F(r) = (a, \mathsf{File}\ u)$ or $F(r) = (a, \mathsf{Link}\ r')$ implies $r\,/\,u' \notin \mathsf{dom}(F)$ for all u'.

Note that although these conditions imply that the structure of a well-formed file system F must be tree-shaped, cycles can be expressed using symbolic links that point "up" in the file system.

7.2 Specifications

The syntax of specifications s is given in Figure 8. The calculus models the most important features of the full Forest language in the simplest possible way, using orthogonal, independent constructs. The set of specifications is parameterized over a collection of constants $k_{\tau_1}^{\tau_2}$, where τ_1 is the type of the generated representation and τ_2 is the type of the generated metadata. We omit the type annotations in examples. For the purpose of illustration, we will assume that constants for describing files File, directories Dir, and symbolic links Link all exist, as well as constants $\mathsf{Adhoc}(p)$ parameterized on Pads/Haskell descriptions p for describing the contents of files in more detail. Path specifications $e{::}s$ are parameterized on an expression e, which must evaluate to a string (to be appended to the current path), and a specification s that describes the fragment of the file system at the extended path. We leave the syntax of expressions e abstract but assume that it contains the features of a simple functional language (of course, in the full Forest language, expressions can be arbitrary fragments of Haskell code). We assume a semantic function $[\![e]\!]_\tau^{\mathcal{E}}$ that evaluates e in environment $\mathcal{E}$, yielding a value v of type τ. Dependent pairs are written $\langle x{:}s_1, s_2\rangle$ where s_1 and s_2 are specifications that describe possibly overlapping fragments of the file system. When a dependent pair is evaluated, the variables x and x_{md} are bound to the value and metadata computed for s_1 and may be used in s_2. Comprehensions are written $[s \mid x \in e]$, where e is an expression that evaluates to a set of values, and s is a specification that describes a fragment of the file system for each value of x. Predicates $\mathsf{P}(e)$ succeed when the expression e evaluates to *True* and fail when it evaluates to *False* under the current environment. Finally, the specification $s?$ describes either a filesystem that is undefined at the current path, or a file system containing the current path and satisfying s.

To develop some intuitions about these constructs, let us encode a few of the more complicated features of the full Forest language in the calculus. In the full language, records and paths are specified using a single construct:

```
Directory
  { c is "c.txt" :: C,
    d is "d.txt" :: D c,
    e is "e.bin" :: E d }
```

The calculus, however, only has dependent pairs, not full-blown records, and has a separate construct for describing paths. Thus, to encode the specification above, we use the following specification:

$$\langle c : (\texttt{"c.txt"}{::}C)\ , \langle d : (\texttt{"d.txt"}{::}D\ c)\ , \texttt{"e.bin"}{::}E\ d\rangle\rangle$$

Similarly, a comprehension written as

```
[c :: C | c <- matches <| GL "*" |> ]
```

in the full language is encoded in the calculus as

$$\langle d{:}\mathsf{Dir}\ , [\ c{::}C \mid c \in d\ ]\rangle$$

The value returned by the Dir constant is the set of names of the immediate children of the directory. Finally, in the full language, constraints are written as

```
s where e
```

but are encoded in the calculus as a dependent pair and predicate:

$$\langle \mathit{this}{:}s, \mathsf{P}(e)\rangle$$

When evaluated, the predicate encodes the success or failure of the constraint expressed by e in the metadata for the second component of the pair.

7.3 Semantics

The semantics of the Forest calculus is organized into four separate definitions, one for each of the major artifacts generated by the compiler. These artifacts include a type for the representations, a type for metadata, a function *load* for loading data from the file system, and a function *store* for storing it back. They are carefully designed to fit together in a particular way—*e.g.*, the *load* and *store* functions manipulate representations and metadata of

[4] For simplicity, we do not model special path elements such as ".." and ".". It would be easy to add these at the cost of complicating the semantics.

the appropriate type and are guaranteed (under certain precisely identified circumstances) to preserve data on round trips.

Types. The definitions of the types for the representations ($\mathcal{R}[\![s]\!]$) and metadata ($\mathcal{M}[\![s]\!]$) generated for each specification s appear in Figure 10. The representation type for constants $k_{\tau_1}^{\tau_2}$ is simply read off from τ_1. For other specifications, representation types are built out of the types for sub-specifications in the obvious way—*e.g.*, for pairs $\langle x{:}s_1, s_2\rangle$, the type is a product $(\mathcal{R}[\![s_1]\!], \mathcal{R}[\![s_2]\!])$. The types for metadata are more interesting. In the Forest calculus we represent metadata using structured datatypes containing a boolean value at each level of structure. Intuitively, this value indicates whether there were any errors during loading. The Md constructor provides a uniform representation for these structures,

$$\begin{array}{lcl} MdHeader & = & Bool \\ Md\ \tau & = & (MdHeader, \tau), \end{array}$$

and the function $valid(d)$ extracts the boolean value, returning $True$ if there are no errors in the structure, and $False$ otherwise. Each of the the $load$ functions generated from specifications maintain the invariant that the the boolean value at each level of structure is $True$ if and only if all of the nested values are also $True$. Thus, one can test for errors during loading simply by examining the top-level boolean value. Note that it would be simple to augment this structure with additional information, such as the number of errors, an optional error message, or file system attributes, as in Figure 3; one would simply have to change the $MdHeader$ type and the $valid(d)$ function.

Load Functions. The most common use of Forest is as a tool for loading data from the file system into an in-memory representation. The functions defined by the inference rules in Figure 10 (a) implement this task. Formally, the judgment $\mathcal{E}; r; s \vdash \mathsf{load}\ F \ \triangleright\ (v, d)$ holds if loading the specification s from the file system F at path r in environment $\mathcal{E}$ yields a pair (v, d) of representation and metadata. This judgment may be seen as describing a total function from $\mathcal{E}$, r, s and F to (v, d). The fact that the load function is total is useful—it allows the programmer to explore fragments of the file system that do not match s exactly. When F does not match s, the function puts default values in the representation v and records an error in the metadata d.

Let us examine the inference rules that define the load functions in detail. We assume that each constant $k_{\tau_1}^{\tau_2}$ has an associated $load_k$ function. For example, the $load$ function for the File construct, which describes any file (but not symbolic links or directories), takes an environment $\mathcal{E}$, a file system F, and a path r as arguments, and either returns the contents and attributes of the file at path r, or "" and default attributes if $F(r)$ is undefined or not a file.

$$load_{\mathsf{File}}\ (\mathcal{E}, F, r) = \begin{cases} (u, (True, a)), \mathrm{if} F(r) = (a, \mathsf{File}\ u) \\ (``\,", (False, a_{\mathsf{default}})), \mathrm{otherwise} \end{cases}$$

The $load$ function for symbolic links is similar:

$$load_{\mathsf{Link}}\ (\mathcal{E}, F, r) = \begin{cases} (r', (True, a)), \mathrm{if} F(r) = (a, \mathsf{Link}\ r') \\ (\cdot, (False, a_{\mathsf{default}})), \mathrm{otherwise} \end{cases}$$

Note that this function only returns the path r' contained in the link and not the directory or file pointed to by it. To access the contents of the file system at r', the programmer could bind the path value returned by Link to a variable, and use the path construct to navigate to that path, as in the following specification:

$$\langle x : \mathsf{Link}\ , (x{::}\mathsf{File})\ \rangle$$

Alternatively, one could design another constant for symbolic links that implements a "deep" lookup in the file system.

The load function for path specifications $e{::}s$ evaluates the expression r/e to a path r', and invokes the load function for s from r'. The load function for dependent pairs $\langle x{:}s_1, s_2\rangle$ first invokes the load function for s_1, yielding a representation v_1 and metadata d_1, and then invokes the load function for s_2 in an extended environment where x is bound to v_1 and x_{md} to d_1, yielding v_2 and d_2. It returns (v_1, v_2) and $(valid(d_1) \wedge valid(d_2), (d_1, d_2))$ as the result. The load function for comprehensions $[s \mid x \in e]$ is similar. It evaluates the expression e to a list $[w_1, .., w_n]$, invokes the load function for s n times, in a series of environments with x bound to each w_i, and collects up the results into lists of representations $[v_1, .., v_n]$ and metadata $[d_1, .., d_n]$.

The load function for predicates $\mathsf{P}(e)$ tests whether the expression e is holds in the environment $\mathcal{E}$. It returns $()$ as the representation and $(b, ())$ as the metadata, where b is $[\![e]\!]_{bool}^{\mathcal{E}}$. The final load function, for options, $s?$ is defined using two inference rules. The first handles the case where the current path r exists in the file system. It uses s's load function to obtain a representation and metadata and injects both into the $Maybe$ type using the Just constructor. The second handles the case where r does not exist in the file system. It returns $Nothing$ for both the representation and metadata.

Store Functions. Just as they can be used for loading from the file system, Forest specifications can also be used to store data back to the file system. The inference rules in Figure 10 (b) define the judgment $\mathcal{E}; r; s \vdash \mathsf{store}\ (F, v, d)\ \triangleright\ (F', \phi')$, which holds if storing (v, d) into F at r using specification s with respect to $\mathcal{E}$ yields a modified file system F' and a *validator* ϕ'. This last element, the validator, is a predicate on file systems that tests for inconsistencies during storing — it will be described in greater detail momentarily. As with load functions, the store judgment may be read as a total function; it maps $\mathcal{E}$, r, s, F, and (v, d) to (F', ϕ').

Intuitively, it should be obvious that there are numerous ways that storing data back to the file system could go wrong. For example, the representation v and metadata d might not be consistent with the existing information on the file system, or with each other. Even worse, storing v and d back to F could involve overwriting the same file (or link, or directory) with multiple pieces of data—a conflict. Thus, to reliably use store functions to manipulate the file system, we need a way way to track the intricate constraints on the data in the representation, metadata, and file system implied by the specification.

The validator ϕ' produced by the store function does exactly this—it keeps track of the conditions needed to ensure that storing the representation and metadata back to F will accurately reflect all of the information they contain. As a simple example that shows why validators are necessary, consider a specification s defined as $\langle x{:}\mathsf{File}, \mathsf{File}\rangle$ and suppose that we invoke s's load function with $\mathcal{E}$, F, and r where $F(r)$ is $(a, \mathsf{File}\ u)$. According to the semantics of the load functions described above, the representation v will be a pair (u, u) containing two copies of the file contents at r and the metadata d will also be a pair $((True, a), (True, a))$ containing two copies of the attributes associated to that file. Now suppose that we change the representation to (u, u'), where $u \neq u'$, and store the result back to the file system. Because this new representation does not satisfy the dependency between the two components of the pair implied by s, the store function cannot produce a new file system containing the information in both u and u'. It must store one of the strings and discard the other. The validator ϕ' detects this inconsistency. In this case, the validator will be equivalent to the following predicate on file systems:

$$\lambda F'.\ (F'(r) = (a, \mathsf{File}\ u)) \wedge (F'(r) = (a, \mathsf{File}\ u'),$$

which is clearly not satisfiable unless $u = u'$.

The store functions also use validators to detect internal inconsistencies between the representation and metadata. For example, consider the specification s defined as $s_1?$, and suppose that invoking s's load function with $\mathcal{E}$, F, r where $F(r)$ is undefined. The representation and metadata will be *Nothing* and (*True*, *Nothing*) respectively. Now suppose that we change the representation to *Just* u', and invoke s's store function. Even though the pair (*Just* u', (*True*, *Nothing*)) would never be produced by s's load function, the store function must still do something reasonable with it. A reasonable choice—the one used in our semantics—is to update the file system contents by passing (File u', a_{default}) to s's store function, but produce a validator $\phi' = \lambda F'.\ \mathit{False}$ that records the inconsistency between the representation and metadata. This informs the programmer that if they invoke the load function on the new file system, the representation and metadata may not be preserved—*e.g.*, loading using s_1 could result in an error.

Now let us examine the inference rules in detail. We assume that each constant defines a $store_k$ function. The $store$ function for File is defined as follows:

$$store_{\text{File}}\ (\mathcal{E}, F, r, v, d) =$$
$$\begin{cases} (F[r := (a, \text{File } v)], \\ \lambda F'.\ (F'(r) = (a, \text{File } v))) & \text{if } d = (\mathit{True}, a) \\ (F[r := \bot], \\ \lambda F'.\ (v = \text{``''} \wedge a = a_{\text{default}} \wedge F'(r) \neq (\_, \text{File } \_))) & \text{if } d = (\mathit{False}, a) \wedge F(r) = (\_, \text{File } \_) \\ (F, \\ \lambda F'.\ (v = \text{``''} \wedge a = a_{\text{default}} \wedge F'(r) \neq (\_, \text{File } \_))) & \text{if } d = (\mathit{False}, a) \wedge F(r) \neq (\_, \text{File } \_) \end{cases}$$

It overwrites the contents of the file system F at path r with $(a, \text{File } v)$ if d is valid, deletes the contents of F at r if d is not valid but $F(r)$ contains a file, and returns F unchanged otherwise. The validator ϕ' also has three cases: in the first, it tests whether $F'(r)$ is $(a, \text{File } v)$; in the second and third cases it tests whether $F'(r)$ is not a file and (v, a) is the default (“”, a_{default}) generated by the *load* function. These constraints are necessary to prove the round-tripping properties described at the end of this section.

The rule for path specifications $e{::}s$ simply passes off control to the store function for s after replacing the current path r with $[\![r\,/\,e]\!]^{\mathcal{E}}_{path}$. The rule for dependent pairs $\langle x{:}s_1, s_2\rangle$ is more interesting. Given a pair (v_1, v_2) as the representation and $(b, (d_1, d_2))$ as the metadata, it invokes the store function for s_1 on (v_1, d_1), yielding an updated file system F'_1 and validator ϕ'_1, and then invokes the store function for s_2 on (v_2, d_2) in an extended environment where x is bound to v_1 and x_{md} is bound to d_1, yielding another updated file system F'_2 and validator ϕ'_2. It combines the updated file systems using the right-biased file system concatenation operator defined as follows:

$$(F_1{+}{+}F_2)(r) =$$
$$\begin{cases} (a_2, \text{Dir } (U_1 \cup U_2)) & \text{if } F_1(r) = (a_1, \text{Dir } U_1) \wedge \\ & \quad F_2(r) = (a_2, \text{Dir } U_2) \\ F_1(r) & \text{if } F_2(r) = \bot \\ F_2(r) & \text{otherwise} \end{cases}$$

Finally, it conjoins the two validators ϕ'_1 and ϕ'_2. The result is a file system that contains the consistent changes made to the file system by the store functions for s_1 and s_2 as well as a validator that checks for the consistency of all the changes. The store function for comprehensions is similar.

The store function for predicates $\mathsf{P}(e)$ returns the input file system F unchanged and a validator ϕ' that checks whether e evaluates to b, the boolean value stored in the metadata. The store function for options $s_1?$ is defined by three inference rules. The first handles the case where the representation is *Just* v_1 and the metadata is *Just* d_1 by simply unpacking the encapsulated values and invoking s_1's store function. The second handles the case where the representation is *Nothing*. It deletes the file and returns a validator that checks whether the metadata d is also *Nothing* and the file system is undefined on the path r. The third rule handles the case where the representation is *Just* v_1 and the metadata is *Nothing*. It invokes s_1's store function on v_1 and default metadata and returns a validator that always evaluates to *False*, reflecting the inconsistency in the representation and metadata.

s	$\mathcal{R}[\![s]\!]$	$\mathcal{M}[\![s]\!]$
$k^{\tau_2}_{\tau_1}$	τ_1	$Md\ \tau_2$
$e{::}s$	$\mathcal{R}[\![s]\!]$	$\mathcal{M}[\![s]\!]$
$\langle x{:}s_1, s_2\rangle$	$(\mathcal{R}[\![s_1]\!], \mathcal{R}[\![s_2]\!])$	$Md\ (\mathcal{M}[\![s_1]\!], \mathcal{M}[\![s_2]\!])$
$[s \mid x \in e]$	$[\mathcal{R}[\![s]\!]]$	$Md\ [\mathcal{M}[\![s]\!]]$
$\mathsf{P}(e)$	$()$	$Md\ ()$
$s?$	$Maybe\ \mathcal{R}[\![s]\!]$	$Md\ (Maybe\ \mathcal{M}[\![s]\!])$

Figure 9. Forest calculus representation and metadata types.

7.4 Formal Properties

The semantics of Forest calculus specifications is carefully designed to ensure some essential correctness properties. The first is a basic type safety property, which states that the load function for specifications s generates representations and metadata belonging to $\mathcal{R}[\![s]\!]$ and $\mathcal{M}[\![s]\!]$ respectively.

Proposition 1 (Load Type Safety)
If $\mathcal{E}; r; s \vdash \text{load } F\ \rhd\ (v, d)$ *and* $\mathcal{R}[\![s]\!] = \tau_{\mathcal{R}}$ *and* $\mathcal{M}[\![s]\!] = \tau_{\mathcal{M}}$ *then* $\vdash v : \tau_{\mathcal{R}}$ *and* $\vdash d : \tau_{\mathcal{M}}$.

This property demonstrates that our type definitions are properly aligned with the semantics of loading.

To ensure that the semantics of loading is aligned with the semantics of storing, we also prove the following pair of round-tripping properties.

Theorem 2 (LoadStore)
Let $\mathcal{E}$ *be an environment,* F *a file system,* r *a path,* s *a specification,* v *a representation, and* d *metadata. If*

$$\mathcal{E}; r; s \vdash \text{load } F\ \rhd\ (v, d)$$
$$\mathcal{E}; r; s \vdash \text{store } (F, v, d)\ \rhd\ (F', \phi)$$

then $F = F'$ *and* $\phi'(F')$.

Theorem 3 (StoreLoad)
Let $\mathcal{E}$ *be an environment,* F *and* F' *file systems,* r *a path,* s *a specification,* v *a representation,* d *and* d' *metadata, and* ϕ' *a validator. If*

$$\mathcal{E}; r; s \vdash \text{store } (F, v, d)\ \rhd\ (F', \phi') \qquad \phi'(F')$$
$$\mathcal{E}; r; s \vdash \text{load } F'\ \rhd\ (v', d')$$

then $(v', d') = (v, d)$.

The first theorem states that loading from a file system F and immediately storing the resulting representation and metadata yields the original file system and, moreover, that this file system will satisfy the validator produced by the store function. This guarantees that the store function will not disturb information in the file system if possible, such as the information outside of the fragment of the

$$\boxed{\mathcal{E}; r; s \vdash \text{load } F \rhd (v, d)}$$

$$\frac{}{\mathcal{E}; r; k_{\tau_1}^{\tau_2} \vdash \text{load } F \rhd (\mathit{load}_k(\mathcal{E}, F, r))}$$

$$\frac{\mathcal{E}; [\![r\,/\,e]\!]^{\mathcal{E}}_{Path}; s \vdash \text{load } F \rhd (v, d)}{\mathcal{E}; r; e{::}s \vdash \text{load } F \rhd (v, d)}$$

$$\frac{\begin{array}{c}\mathcal{E}; r; s_1 \vdash \text{load } F \rhd (v_1, d_1) \\ (\mathcal{E}, x \mapsto v_1, x_{md} \mapsto d_1); r; s_2 \vdash \text{load } F \rhd (v_2, d_2) \\ b = \mathit{valid}(d_1) \wedge \mathit{valid}(d_2)\end{array}}{\mathcal{E}; r; \langle x{:}s_1, s_2 \rangle \vdash \text{load } F \rhd ((v_1, v_2), (b, (d_1, d_2)))}$$

$$\frac{\begin{array}{c}[\![e]\!]^{\mathcal{E}}_{[\tau]} = [w_1, .., w_k] \\ \forall i \in \{1, ..., k\}.\ (\mathcal{E}, x \mapsto w_i); r; s \vdash \text{load } F \rhd (v_i, d_i) \\ b = \bigwedge_i^k \mathit{valid}(d_i) \quad vs = [v_1, .., v_k] \quad ds = [d_1, .., d_k]\end{array}}{\mathcal{E}; r; [s \mid x \in e] \vdash \text{load } F \rhd (vs, (b, ds))}$$

$$\frac{b = [\![e]\!]^{\mathcal{E}}_{Bool}}{\mathcal{E}; r; \mathsf{P}(e) \vdash \text{load } F \rhd ((), (b, ()))}$$

$$\frac{r \notin \mathsf{dom}(F)}{\mathcal{E}; r; s_1? \vdash \text{load } F \rhd (\mathit{Nothing}, (\mathit{True}, \mathit{Nothing}))}$$

$$\frac{r \in \mathsf{dom}(F) \quad \mathcal{E}; r; s_1 \vdash \text{load } F \rhd (v_1, d_1)}{\mathcal{E}; r; s_1? \vdash \text{load } F \rhd (\mathit{Just}\ v_1, (\mathit{valid}(d_1), \mathit{Just}\ d_1))}$$

(a)

$$\boxed{\mathcal{E}; r; s \vdash \text{store } (F, v, d) \rhd (F', \phi')}$$

$$\frac{}{\mathcal{E}; r; k_{\tau_1}^{\tau_2} \vdash \text{store } (F, v, d) \rhd (\mathit{store}_k(\mathcal{E}, F, r, v, d))}$$

$$\frac{\mathcal{E}; [\![r\,/\,e]\!]^{\mathcal{E}}_{Path}; s \vdash \text{store } (F, v, d) \rhd (F', \phi')}{\mathcal{E}; r; e{::}s \vdash \text{store } (F, v, d) \rhd (F', \phi')}$$

$$\frac{\begin{array}{c}\mathcal{E}; r; s_1 \vdash \text{store } (F, v_1, d_1) \rhd (F'_1, \phi'_1) \\ (\mathcal{E}, x \mapsto v_1, x_{md} \mapsto d_1); r; s_2 \vdash \text{store } (F, v_2, d_2) \rhd (F'_2, \phi'_2) \\ \phi' = \lambda F'.\ (b = \mathit{valid}(d_1) \wedge \mathit{valid}(d_2)) \wedge \phi'_1(F') \wedge \phi'_2(F')\end{array}}{\mathcal{E}; r; \langle x{:}s_1, s_2 \rangle \vdash \text{store } (F, (v_1, v_2), (b, (d_1, d_2))) \rhd (F'_1{+}{+}F'_2, \phi')}$$

$$\frac{\begin{array}{c}vs = [v_1, .., v_j] \quad ds = [d_1, .., d_l] \\ [\![e]\!]^{\mathcal{E}}_{[\tau]} = [w_1, .., w_m] \quad k = \min(j, l, m) \\ \forall i \in \{1, ..., k\}.\ (\mathcal{E}, x \mapsto w_i); r; s \vdash \text{store } (F, v_i, d_i) \rhd (F'_i, \phi'_i) \\ \phi' = \lambda F'.\ (j = l = m) \wedge (b = \bigwedge_i^k \mathit{valid}(d_i)) \wedge (\bigwedge_i^k \phi'_i(F'))\end{array}}{\mathcal{E}; r; [s \mid x \in e] \vdash \text{store } (F, vs, (b, ds)) \rhd (F'_1{+}{+}..{+}{+}F'_k, \phi')}$$

$$\frac{\phi' = \lambda F'.\ (b = [\![e]\!]^{\mathcal{E}}_{Bool})}{\mathcal{E}; r; \mathsf{P}(e) \vdash \text{store } (F, (), (b, ())) \rhd (F, \phi')}$$

$$\frac{\begin{array}{c}\mathcal{E}; r; s_1 \vdash \text{store } (F, v_1, d_1) \rhd (F', \phi'_1) \\ \phi' = \lambda F'.\ (b = \mathit{valid}(d_1)) \wedge (r \in \mathsf{dom}(F')) \wedge \phi'_1(F')\end{array}}{\mathcal{E}; r; s_1? \vdash \text{store } (F, \mathit{Just}\ v_1, (b, \mathit{Just}\ d_1)) \rhd (F', \phi')}$$

$$\frac{\phi' = \lambda F'.\ (d = \mathit{Nothing}) \wedge b \wedge r \notin \mathsf{dom}(F')}{\mathcal{E}; r; s_1? \vdash \text{store } (F, \mathit{Nothing}, (b, d)) \rhd (F[r := \bot], \phi')}$$

$$\frac{\begin{array}{c}\mathcal{E}; r; s_1 \vdash \text{store } (F, v_1, d^{s_1}_{\mathsf{default}}) \rhd (F', \phi'_1) \\ \phi' = \lambda F'.\ \mathit{False}\end{array}}{\mathcal{E}; r; s_1? \vdash \text{store } (F, \mathit{Just}\ v_1, (b, \mathit{Nothing})) \rhd (F', \phi')}$$

(b)

Figure 10. Forest calculus semantics for (a) loading and (b) storing.

file system described by the specification. It also establishes that the validator is not the trivial predicate on file systems that always returns false.

The second theorem states that storing an arbitrary representation and then loading the resulting file system yields the same representation and metadata, provided the stored file system satisfies the validator. This theorem ensures that the store function reflects all of the information contained in the representation in the updated file system.

These properties are based on the general correctness conditions that have been proposed for bidirectional transformations in the context of lenses [10], but are generalized here to accommodate the inconsistencies that can arise when working with imperfect, ad hoc data. The proofs of these theorems can be found in the accompanying technical report.

8. Related Work

The work in this paper builds upon ideas developed in the Pads project [5, 7]. Pads uses extended type declarations to describe the grammar of a document and simultaneously to generate types for parsed data and a suite of data-processing tools. The obvious difference between Pads (and other parser generators) and Forest is that Pads generates infrastructure for processing strings (the insides of a single file) whereas Forest generates infrastructure for processing entire filestores. In addition, Forest (and Pads/Haskell) is architecturally superior to previous versions of Pads in the tight integration with its host language and in its support for third-party generic programming and tool construction.

More generally, Forest shares high-level goals with other systems that seek to make data-oriented programming simpler and more productive. For example, Microsoft's LINQ [20] extends the .NET languages to enable querying any data source that supports the `IEnumerable` interface using a simple, convenient syntax. LINQ differs from Forest in that it does not provide support for declaratively specifying the structure of, and then ingesting, filestores. As a second example, *Type Providers* [28], an experimental feature of F#, help programmers materialize standard data sources equipped with predefined schemas (such as XML documents or databases) in memory in an F# program. Type Providers do not themselves provide a new means for describing data sources (as Forest does).

Several XML-based languages for specifying file formats, file organization and file locations have been proposed. One example of such a language is XFiles [1]. XFiles uses RDF specifications to describe the location, permissions, ownership, and other attributes of files, as well as the name of an application capable of parsing specific files. The key difference between XFiles and Forest is that Forest is tightly integrated into a general-purpose, conventional programming language. Forest declarations generate types, functions and data structures that materialize the data within a surrounding Haskell program while XFiles does not interoperate directly with a conventional programming language.

A recent MSc thesis by Ntzik proposes using an extension of context logic [2] to reason about the effects of updates made to file systems using standard POSIX commands [24]. The core goal of Ntzik's work is to create a new kind of Hoare Logic, and consequently, it is quite different from Forest.

The round-tripping properties that core Forest programs obey are based on laws that have been proposed in the context of well-behaved bidirectional transformations, often called lenses [10]. As far as we are aware, lenses for file systems have not been developed but some of the same fundamental issues that arise in core Forest have been studied by Hu and his colleagues, including languages that handle data with internal dependencies [23] and ones that handle graph structures [17].

9. Conclusions

In this paper, we propose the idea of extending a modern, high-level programming language with tightly integrated features for processing coherent file system fragments, which we call filestores. To demonstrate the potential of this idea, we designed Forest, a domain-specific language embedded in Haskell for describing and managing filestores.

The Forest design has been informed by both theoretical analysis and practical experience. On the theoretical side, we developed a formal calculus that models the core Forest functionality and we proved that our calculus obeys round-tripping laws derived from previous work on bi-directional programming paradigms. On the practical side, we illustrated the utility of our design by describing several example filestores, and showing how to use these descriptions to build simple Haskell scripts that query, analyze, and transform the example data in useful ways. We also provided evidence that Forest has effective support for building generic, description-directed tools by implementing a number of such tools ourselves, including a filestore visualizer, a generic query interface, an access control checker, and (circularly) a simple description inference engine. An ancillary benefit of this engineering work is that it serves as an extensive case study in domain-specific language design, and, as such, inspired changes in the design of Template Haskell.

For further information about Forest, we direct readers to the Forest web site [9], where they may find our open source implementation and a number of additional examples.

Acknowledgments

We wish to thank Simon Peyton Jones for extending Haskell's quasiquoting mechanism to support the Forest design and for assisting us in its use, John Launchbury for helping us design and implement Pads/Haskell, and the anonymous ICFP reviewers for many insightful comments and suggestions.

This work was supported in part by the NSF under grant CCF-1016937, the ONR under grant N00014-09-1-0652, and the NSFC under grant 6103302. Any opinions, findings, and recommendations expressed in this material are those of the authors and do not necessarily reflect the views of these agencies.

References

[1] S.-C. Buraga. An XML-based semantic description of distributed file systems. In *RoEduNet*, pages 41–48, 2003.

[2] C. Calcagno, P. Gardner, and U. Zarfaty. Context logic and tree update. In *POPL*, pages 271–282, 2005.

[3] Filesystem Hierarchy Standard Group. Filesystem hierarchy standard. `http://www.pathname.com/fhs/`, 2004.

[4] K. Fisher, N. Foster, D. Walker, and K. Q. Zhu. Forest 1.0: A Language and Toolkit for Programming with Filestores. Technical Report TR-904-11, Princeton University, June 2011.

[5] K. Fisher and R. Gruber. PADS: A domain specific language for processing ad hoc data. In *PLDI*, pages 295–304, June 2005.

[6] K. Fisher, Y. Mandelbaum, and D. Walker. The next 700 data description languages. In *POPL*, Jan. 2006.

[7] K. Fisher, Y. Mandelbaum, and D. Walker. The next 700 data description languages. *JACM*, 57:10:1–10:51, February 2010.

[8] K. Fisher and D. Walker. The PADS project: An overview. In *Proceedings of the 14th International Conference on Database Theory*, ICDT '11, pages 11–17, New York, NY, USA, 2011. ACM.

[9] Forest: A language and toolkit for programming with file system fragments. `http://forestproj.org`, 2010.

[10] J. N. Foster, M. B. Greenwald, J. T. Moore, B. C. Pierce, and A. Schmitt. Combinators for bidirectional tree transformations: A linguistic approach to the view update problem. *TOPLAS*, 29(3), May 2007.

[11] M. J. Freedman. Experiences with CoralCDN: A five-year operational view. In *NSDI*, pages 7–7, 2010.

[12] M. J. Freedman, E. Freudenthal, and D. Mazieres. Democratizing content publication with Coral. In *NSDI*, pages 18–18, 2004. See also `http://www.coralcdn.org/`.

[13] E. R. Gansner and S. C. North. An open graph visualization system and its applications to software engineering. *Softw. Pract. Exper.*, 30:1203–1233, September 2000.

[14] Haskell Graphviz Package. `http://hackage.haskell.org/package/graphviz`.

[15] Haskell Source Extensions Package. `http://hackage.haskell.org/package/haskell-src-exts`.

[16] Haskell Source Meta Package. `http://hackage.haskell.org/package/haskell-src-meta`.

[17] S. Hidaka, Z. Hu, K. Inaba, H. Kato, K. Matsuda, and K. Nakano. Bidirectionalizing graph transformations. In *ICFP*, pages 205–216, 2010.

[18] R. Lämmel and S. P. Jones. Scrap your boilerplate: A practical design pattern for generic programming. In *TLDI*, pages 26–37, 2003.

[19] D. Leijen and E. Meijer. Parsec: Direct style monadic parser combinators for the real world. Technical Report UU-CS-2001-27, Department of Computer Science, Universiteit Utrecht, 2001.

[20] LINQ: .NET language-integrated query. `http://msdn.microsoft.com/library/bb308959.aspx`, Feb. 2007.

[21] G. Mainland. Why it's nice to be quoted: Quasiquoting for Haskell. In *Haskell Workshop*, pages 73–82, 2007.

[22] Y. Mandelbaum, K. Fisher, D. Walker, M. Fernández, and A. Gleyzer. PADS/ML: A functional data description language. In *POPL*, Jan. 2007.

[23] S.-C. Mu, Z. Hu, and M. Takeichi. An algebraic approach to bi-directional updating. In *APLAS*, pages 2–20, Nov. 2004.

[24] G. Ntzik. Local reasoning for filesystems. Master's thesis, Imperial College, Sept. 2010.

[25] PADS project. `http://www.padsproj.org/`, 2007.

[26] T. J. Parr and R. W. Quong. ANTLR: A predicated-$LL(k)$ parser generator. *Softw. Pract. Exper.*, 25(7):789–810, July 1995.

[27] T. Sheard and S. P. Jones. Template meta-programming for Haskell. In *Haskell Workshop*, pages 1–16, 2002.

[28] D. Syme. Looking Ahead with F#: Taming the Data Deluge. Presentation at the Workshop on F# in Education, Nov. 2010.

[29] Template Haskell Extension Proposal. `hackage.haskell.org/trac/ghc/blog/Template%20Haskell%20Proposal`.

Making Standard ML a Practical Database Programming Language *

Atsushi Ohori   Katsuhiro Ueno

Research Institute of Electrical Communication
Tohoku University
{ohori, katsu}@riec.tohoku.ac.jp

Abstract

Integrating a database query language into a programming language is becoming increasingly important in recently emerging high-level cloud computing and other applications, where efficient and sophisticated data manipulation is required during computation. This paper reports on seamless integration of SQL into SML# – an extension of Standard ML. In the integrated language, the type system always infers a principal type for any type consistent SQL expression. This makes SQL queries first-class citizens, which can be freely combined with any other language constructs definable in Standard ML. For a program involving SQL queries, the compiler separates SQL queries and delegates their evaluation to a database server, e.g. PostgreSQL or MySQL in the currently implemented version.

The type system of our language is largely based on Machiavelli, which demonstrates that ML with record polymorphism can represent type structure of SQL. In order to develop a practical language, however, a number of technical challenges have to be overcome, including static enforcement of server connection consistency, proper treatment of overloaded SQL primitives, query compilation, and runtime connection management. This paper describes the necessary extensions to the type system and compilation, and reports on the details of its implementation.

Categories and Subject Descriptors H.2.3 [*Database Management*]: Languages—Database (persistent) programming languages

General Terms Design, Languages

Keywords SQL, Polymorphism, Type System, Interoperability, SML#

1. Introduction

Smooth integration of a database query language into a programming language is essential for any high-level applications that require efficient processing of large amount of data. The need of this integration will become particularly important in recently emerging high-level cloud computing, where sophisticated data manipulation beyond simple data aggregation will be required. Query language integration will also make currently wide-spread Web programming through various meta-level "framework" such as Ruby on Rails much more reliable.

The need of proper integration of a database query language and a programming language has been recognized and investigated in database programming community for more than two decades. See [4] for an early survey in this area. Since then a number of query language bindings and embeddings in general purpose programming languages have been proposed and implemented. Examples include SQLJ [13] and more recent LINQ [23] and Ferry [16] middle-ware. Compared with SQL command string interface to database servers, these database binding frameworks certainly increase flexibility and ease of use in accessing databases from programming languages. However, they still do not achieve seamless integration of a database query language into a host language type system. Existing database bindings either restrict full functionality and generality provided by their target database servers, or they do not treat database queries as first-class citizens in the type systems of the host programming languages.

There have also been a number of proposals for high-level database programming languages that integrate declarative queries in their type systems. Some notable examples include GemStone (OPAL) [11], Machiavelli [30], O_2 [19], and Fibonacci [2] to name a few. While these approaches provide uniform integration of database queries in a programming language, it remains to be seen whether or not some of these approaches would become a practical alternative to SQL. Based on long and intensive research and development of the relational data model [8], relational database systems have realized highly optimized data manipulation for large amount of data with various practical supports such as transaction management and network access. All of these features are made available through SQL, which is the well established and standardized query language for relational database systems. Perhaps due to this reason, most of applications that require both efficient database manipulation and programming still use general purpose programming languages such as C or Java with SQL command string interface to a relational database server.

This situation indicates that an "impedance mismatch" [22] between a database system and a programming language still exists *in practice*.

To eliminate this mismatch, we must develop a high-level programming language that seamlessly integrates SQL in such a way that SQL queries are first-class citizens in the language type system and that they are evaluated by a practical database server. This paper reports on one such integration, where SQL is seamlessly integrated in SML# [32], an extension of Standard ML [24]. In our

* The authors were partially supported by the Japan Society for the Promotion of Science Grant-in-Aid for Basic Research (C) grant no. 22500023.

ICFP'11, September 19–21, 2011, Tokyo, Japan.

development, we adopt polymorphic typing of Machiavelli [30], where the authors suggested that the programming language ML can be extended with an SQL-style declarative query language. The language proposed in [30] is, however, conceptual one focusing only on typing issues; no implementation strategy is considered or developed. As outlined in the next section, a number of technical challenges have to be overcome before a practical language can become a reality. In the present paper, we have solved those problems and have developed a compiler for SML# extended with SQL. In this extended language, SQL queries are first-class expressions directly definable in the language type system, and are evaluated by an external database server. Thanks to this feature, Standard ML programmers can readily enjoy efficient and practical database programming in their Standard ML code.

In addition to solving technical problems in language design and typing, we have also developed an implementation technique for connecting static semantics of SQL in the host language type system, and its dynamic semantics realized by an external database server. This should be useful for extending a typed higher-order language with various domain specific languages, not restricted to SQL.

All the results reported in this paper has been implemented in our SML# compiler. Most of them have already been made available in SML# version 0.60 or later releases [32].

1.1 Related works

Before presenting our technical development, we compare our approach with some more related works.

The conventional and still widely used approach to database programming is to construct SQL command strings directly and send them to a database server using low-level database server interfaces such as SQL/CLI and JDBC. Embedded SQL such as ECPG of PostgreSQL and SQLJ [13] supports a form of macro SQL statements that are expanded by a preprocessor to those low-level database library calls. Both of them are unsatisfactory in many ways; type-checking is far from adequate, and the interaction with the host language construct is rather limited. In order to improve type safety and host language interface of preprocessor-based approach, several domain specific embedded languages [18] have been proposed and implemented. HaskellDB [20] implements a set of monadic term constructors corresponding to relational operators. ARARAT [14] provides C++ template for composing SQL queries. Ur/Web [7] provides a meta-programming framework for the programmer to generate type-consistent SQL queries through type computation. LINQ [23] and Ferry [16] attempt to provide a language independent layer for querying various data structures including relational database. DHS [15] implements a combinator library for generic manipulation of collection types that are to be compiled to Ferry. While these approaches provide high-level database access, they do not fully achieve seamless integration of SQL into a general purpose programming language to the extent we wish to achieve.

We note that SQL is an algebraic language based on the relational algebra. In this language, relation-valued expressions including SELECT expressions can be used to construct another query expression. This properly makes SQL an elegant and powerful data algebra for relations. Seamlessly integrating SQL in a programming language must at least mean that relations are first-class citizens and their operations are freely combined with other language constructs in the host programming language. This is a common-sense knowledge in functional programming. For example, consider the case of integrating an algebra of *lists* in ML. Everyone unanimously expects that lists are first-class citizens and associated operators to construct and manipulate lists can be freely combined with any other language constructs. SQL should be given the same status, without scarifying its features specified in the standardized language definition and its efficiency realized by a matured external database server. Unfortunately, however, there does not seem to exist any implemented general purpose programming language that achieves this status for SQL. This is the property we attempt to achieve in SML#.

Since relations are well-defined mathematical objects, it should be possible to extend a type theory of programming languages with data algebra on relations. Based on this general observation, several database programming languages have been proposed, including GemStone [11], Machiavelli [30], Napier88 [26], Iris [3], Fibonacci [2], and Kleisli [34]. All of those languages, by their construction, seamlessly integrate advanced database queries in their type systems and evaluation models. See [33] for various typing issues in database queries, and [21] for a survey on various approaches to database and language integration. However, it is non-trivial to make those languages practical database programming languages that can handle hundreds of millions of tuples efficiently. Compared with the high maturity of optimization and implementation techniques of relational database systems, optimization and implementation techniques for advanced data models realized in those new database programming languages do not seem to have been well developed.

The goal of the present paper is to make the SQL itself seamlessly available in a practical general purpose programming language. For this purpose, we must first extend the type system of the host programming language so that SQL statements can be representable as typed expressions. An extension of ML type inference for generalized relational algebra presented in [29] is perhaps the first such example. This type system and its refinement [28] were the basis of the type system of Machiavelli [6, 30]. We design our type system largely based on this approach. However, in this paper, instead of uniformly integrating generalized relational algebra in its type system and evaluation model, we develop a type system that precisely represents polymorphic typing of the SQL language itself as defined in its language standard, and develop a compilation method to delegate their evaluation to an external database server. This requires careful design and development beyond the language design reported in [6, 30].

Another approach to integrate database queries and programming constructs is to compile high-level expressions into SQL [9]. Links [10] takes this approach in designing a Web programming system. The type system sketched in [10] appears to be based on the observation similar to [6, 30] – it uses sorted row variables [31] instead of kinded typing [28, 29], but these two formalisms on record polymorphism are equivalent for typing query expressions. Links compiles relation-valued expressions, possibly involving function applications and other language constructs, into SQL. The resulting system achieves integration of database queries and programming language constructs, but this is only to the extent that the language constructs can be compiled to SQL commands. While this compile-to-SQL approach would be useful for some target areas such as Web programming, it is not obvious that this approach scales up to large and complex application development that requires a general purpose programming language and the full functionality of SQL.

We note that any practical general purpose programming language involves a number of advanced features to form a complex system whose semantics can (at least under the current state-of-the-art) only be realized by a sophisticated compiler. This is true for Standard ML. SML# compiler, for example, contains more than 0.3 million lines of code. The SQL language itself also contains various features such as grouping and duplicate controls in SELECT lists, and transaction management in data manipulation. All these features are indispensable for serious application development. Our major technical contribution is to design a type system that can precisely represent the SQL language in Standard ML, to develop a compilation method that seamlessly combines the dynamic semantics of Standard ML expressions realized by a Standard ML compiler and the semantics of SQL queries realized by an external database server, and to implement it in the SML# compiler that compiles the full set of Standard ML.

1.2 Paper organization

The rest of this paper is organized as follows. Section 2 discusses the problems to be overcome and outlines our strategy. Section 3 describes the language and its type system. Section 4 describes the details of its implementation. Section 5 concludes the paper with suggestions for further investigations.

2. Problems and our strategy

We have chosen Standard ML as the base language for our database extension. This is not accidental. In this section, we review the requirements and problems in achieving our goal of seamless integration, and outline our development.

2.1 Expressions and typing of SQL

We begin by reviewing the basic properties of SQL in the perspective of programming languages.

SQL can be characterized as a *impure functional language*. Its main components, i.,e. SELECT statements, are relation-valued expressions that can be freely composed as far as each sub-phrase is type consistent. For example, a query such as

```
SELECT name, age
FROM people                (Q)
WHERE age >= 25
```

is an expression denoting a set of tuples of `name` and `age` and can be used as a source relation in any other queries. SQL programming consists of composing those relation-valued expressions. In addition to those functional expressions, SQL also contains imperative features such as those for updating the database state and transaction management, which assumes sequential evaluation. To represent those expressions, eager functional programming is the most appropriate framework. Moreover, since SQL programming involves manipulation of record structures across multiple tables, it is essential to enforce type discipline that statically checks complex queries before sending them to a remote database server. As observed in [30], SQL expressions are inherently polymorphic in the structures they manipulates. For example, the above very simple query is polymorphic in several ways: this query can be issued against any database that contains at least a `people` table having at least `name` field of any type and `age` field of numerical type. This indicate that a language containing SQL should have a polymorphic type system preferably with type inference.

Base on these observations, a basic strategy of extending ML to represent SQL-style database queries was proposed in [29, 30]. In their approach, a query expression is considered as a *polymorphic function* acting on an appropriate structure composed of labeled record and set data types. For example, the query Q above would be given a polymorphic type of the following form (in the notations we use in this paper):

```
Q : ['a,'b#{name:'a, age:int},'c#{people:'b}.
      'c db -> 'b relation]
```

This is the type `'c db -> 'b relation` in prenex form where the set of bound type variables are explicitly listed in its prefix `'a,'b#{name:'a, age:int},'c#{people:'b}`. Notation `'b#{name:'a, age:int}` represents a type variable `'b` with a *kind* constraint `#{name:'a, age:int}` indicating the fact that any instance of `'b` must be a labeled record (tuple) type that contains at least `name:'a` and `age:int` fields. By this polymorphic typing with record kind constraints, their approach represents the precise polymorphic nature of Q, i.e. it is a query that can be evaluated against any database that contains at least a `people` table each of whose tuples contains at least integer-valued `age` column and `name` column of any type.

We roughly follow this approach. Among the ML family of languages, we consider Standard ML the most appropriate one for the following reasons.

Its eager functional semantics with imperative features make an ideal framework for integrating relation-valued query expressions with imperative features such as transactions.

Its type system and operational semantics has been rigorously specified and their details are well documented [24].

The type theory and implementation method for extending Standard ML with record polymorphism has been well established [28, 31].

We base our development on SML#, which is an extension of Standard ML with record polymorphism [28] and interoperability with C language. These two features provide sufficient basis for seamless extension of Standard ML with SQL.

2.2 The remaining problems

The solutions so far proposed in the literature are, however, only partial for extending Standard ML with SQL. There are a number of problems that have to be worked out before realizing a practical language that achieves truly seamless integration of SQL. Among them, the following are major technical challenges.

1. *Extensions of the type system.* Record polymorphism is useful in achieving the integration but adding this alone to Standard ML type system does not yield a type system for SQL. We need to construct typing mechanisms for the following.
   (a) *Server typing and type checking.* We need to develop a typing mechanism to declare a database schema on a database server, and to type check its correctness against actual contents of the server.
   (b) *Server connection typing and its consistency enforcement.* Since an SQL command needs to be sent to a database server, all the query components consisting of the command must only reference to a unique server connection. With higher-order functions, enforcing this requirement turns out to be a subtle typing problem.
   (c) *A proper treatment of null values.* Since a column may contain null values, we cannot simply infer a typing of the form `'a::{age:int}` for expression `age >= 25`.
   (d) *Overloaded operator and constants.* Literals such as 25 above play double roles; one for a constant of the host language, and one that denotes the same constant in a remote database server. These two have different representations. Even worse, 25 in an SQL query represents not only an integer but also a floating-point number. In addition, operator such as > for comparison is overloaded with several atomic types. In Standard ML definition, overloading is resolved statically. If we simply adopt the same strategy, then the flexibility of SQL expressions would be severely limited. Again, developing a precise typing mechanism to treat these overloading requires delicate development.
2. *Compilation and evaluation.* Expressions in a functional language is compiled to a code and executed with a runtime system with a specialized memory management. It is relatively

straightforward to add compilation rules for their own query constructs and execute them in their own runtime system. For this purpose, it is sufficient to define a data structure for tuples and relations and evaluation strategy for each primitive operations in the relational algebra. Newly designed database programming languages usually adopt this strategy. Our purpose is different. Instead of developing a query execution engine inside of the language runtime system, we need to call an existing SQL database server. For this purpose, we need to develop both a compilation method and a runtime mechanism for delegating evaluation of SQL query expressions to a remote database server. Since Standard ML is a higher-order functional language, seamless integration of SQL implies that SQL queries are intermixed with function definitions and function applications. This requires us to carefully design the compilation algorithm so that it separates SQL query expressions appearing in a given expression.

2.3 Summary of our development

We have worked out these problems, have developed compilation algorithms and have implemented a new generation of Standard ML that seamlessly integrates SQL by extending our SML# compiler. The extension to Standard ML syntax is carefully designed so that it maintains backward compatibility with the Definition of Standard ML. In our development, we have used PostgreSQL and MySQL for our target database servers, considering their wide availability; other DBMS should equally be possible, as described later in section 4.6.

In SML# with our extension, the query Q is written as follows.

```
val Q =
  _sql db => select #person.name as name,
                    #person.age as age
             from #db.people as person
             where SQL.>= (#person.age, 25)
```

where `SQL.>=` is the greater-or-equal comparison for SQL values. One can see that the above expression is a direct representation of (a verbose version of) the query Q. Similar expressions may be possible in some programming languages with embedded SQL commands, which are translated to a sequence of primitive statements. Different from those syntactic shorthands, this is an expression in the language. The extended SML# compiler type checks this and infers the following polymorphic type.

```
val Q = fn
: ['a#{people: 'b},
   'b#{age: int, name: 'd},
   'c,
   'd::{int, word, char, string, real, 'e option},
   'e::{int, word, char, bool, string, real}.
   ('a, 'c) SQL.db
     -> {age:int, name:'d} SQL.query]
```

This type indicates that Q is a function that takes a database of type `('a, 'c) SQL.db` whose contents is of type `'a#{people:'b}`, and returns a query of type `{age:int,name:'d}`. The extra parameter `'c` to a database type `'a#{people:'b}` is there to ensure the consistent usage of connection and will be explained later. `'d::{ }` constrains that `'d` can be instantiated only with a type shared among ML and SQL. It should be intuitively clear that the inferred type represents the precise polymorphic nature of the query Q, and indeed it is a principal type for Q.

In an ML-style type system, the fact that a principal type is inferred for this expression immediately means that this expression can be freely combined with any other language constructs as far as its usage is type consistent. Figure 1 shows example programs to define a database server, to connect it, to insert tuples, to execute query Q, and to fetch the results as a list of SML# records. It shows an actual interactive session in SML#. The lines starting with prompt "`#`" and ending with delimiter "`;`" are user input, which are followed by a system response.

3. SML# extended with SQL

This section presents the language we develop. We first introduce SML#, and develop necessary extensions in syntax, typing mechanisms, and operational semantics. We then show a programming example demonstrating the benefit of seamless integration of SQL into SML#.

3.1 SML#: Standard ML with record polymorphism and interoperability with C

SML# embodies record polymorphism and infers a polymorphic type for record operations as seen in the following example:

```
# fun getName x = #Name x;
val getName = fn : ['a#{Name:'b}, 'b. 'a -> 'b]
```

where `#`l selects the l field from a record. `getName` takes a record and returns its `Name` field. This record polymorphism provides a basis to extend Standard ML with SQL expressions.

In addition, SML# supports interoperability with the C language through its *natural data representation* [27]. Under this scheme, internal data representations in SML# and C have the following correspondence: atomic types including `int` and `real` are the same as `int` and `double` in C; τ `array` has the same representation as a pointer to an array of τ in C; and a labeled record type $\{l_1:\tau_1, \ldots, l_n:\tau_n\}$ has the same representation as a pointer to a structure in C that contains the elements of types $\{\tau_1, \ldots, \tau_n\}$ in the lexicographical order of their labels $\{l_1, \ldots, l_n\}$. Based on these properties, SML# allows the programmer to declare an external library function defined in C and use it as an ordinary ML function. The following example code imports C library function `sin`:

```
# val sin =
      dlsym (dlopen "/usr/lib/libm.so", "sin")
      : _import real -> real;
val sin = fn : real -> real;
# sin 1.0;
val it = 0.841470984807 : real
```

where `dlopen` and `dlsym` are built-in library functions that open and find a pointer to the named dynamically linked library function. After this declaration, `sin` is used as an ordinary ML expression of type `real -> real`, but application of `sin` directly calls the C library function without any data conversion. In our development, we use this feature to bind database server library functions provided for C.

The syntax of SML# is that of Standard ML. For the explanation purpose in this paper we consider the following subset of its core language.

$$e \ ::= \ x \mid \texttt{fn}\ x\ \texttt{=>}\ e \mid e\ e \mid \{l_1\texttt{=}e_1, \ldots, l_n\texttt{=}e_n\} \mid \texttt{\#}l\ e$$

x ranges over the set of variables. `fn` x `=>` e defines a (first-class) function. $\{l_1=e_1, \ldots, l_n=e_n\}$ constructs a labeled record. Other features are mostly orthogonal to our SQL extension and can be used without any problem. In examples, we also use the following syntax.

`val` x `=` e binds a variable x to an expression e.

`SQL.`x is a variable x defined in the module named `SQL`. In our implementation, which we shall describe in Section 4, most

```
# val server =
      _sqlserver "host=127.0.0.1 dbname=test"
      : {people: {name: string, age: int}};
val server = "host=127.0.0.1 dbname=test"
  : {people: {age: int, name: string}} SQL.server

# val db = SQL.connect server;
val db = <conn>
  : {people: {age: int, name: string}} SQL.conn

# val q =
      _sql db =>
          insert into #db.people (name, age)
          values ("Alice", 24);
val q = fn
  : ['a#{people: {age: int, name: string}},
     'b.
     ('a, 'b) SQL.db -> SQL.command]

# val r = _sqlexec q db;
val r = () : unit

# val q =
      _sql db =>
          insert into #db.people (name, age)
          values ("Bob", 25);
val q = fn
  : ['a#{people: {age: int, name: string}},
     'b.
    ('a, 'b) SQL.db -> SQL.command]

# val r = _sqlexec q db;
val r = () : unit

# val Q =
      _sql db =>
          select #person.name as name,
                 #person.age as age
          from #db.people as person
          where SQL.>= (#person.age, 25);
val Q = fn
  : ['a#{people:'b},
     'b#{age:int, name:'d},
     'c,
     'd::{int, word, char, string, real, 'e option},
     'e::{int, word, char, bool, string, real}.
     ('a, 'c) SQL.db
     -> {age: int, name: 'd} SQL.query]

# val r = _sqleval Q db;
val r = <rel> : {age: int, name: string} SQL.rel

# val x = SQL.fetchAll r;
val x = [{age = 25, name = "Bob"}]
  : {age: int, name: string} list
```

Figure 1. Example Program in SML#

resources (functions and types) for the SQL extension are organized into the `SQL` module, and they are referenced through this notation.

Its type system is that of Standard ML extended with record kinds on type variables. We let C range over type constructors such as `list` or `array`. Sometimes we use `option` type constructor to represent values possibly containing null. We use the following syntax for types.

The set of monomorphic types (ranged over by τ) is given by the following syntax

$$\tau ::= b \mid \tau \texttt{ -> } \tau' \mid \{l_1 : \tau_1, \ldots, l_n : \tau_n\} \mid \tau\ C$$

where b ranges over atomic base types such as `int`; τ `->` τ' is a function type; $\{l_1 : \tau_1, \ldots, l_n : \tau_n\}$ is a labeled record type; and $\tau\ C$ is a constructor type such as `int list`.

`'a`, `'b`, ... are type variables (ranged over by t).

$[t_1\#k_1, \ldots, t_n\#k_n.\tau]$ is a polymorphic type of τ with bound type variables $t_1, \ldots, t_n$. Each t_i is constrained with a kind k_i. A kind k is either empty indicating no constraint or a record kind $\{l_1 : \tau_1, \ldots, l_n : \tau_n\}$ denoting all possible records that contain at least the specified fields.

3.2 Syntax extension for SQL

To represent SQL, we need to introduce the following.

A server definition on which SQL is run.

SQL "commands". Among them a `SELECT` command is an algebraic (functional) expression that returns a relation. The others are those that change the server state.

Our aim is to represent SQL queries as directly as possible, and allow them as first-class citizens in the language. The important step to achieve this goal is to identify all the syntactic elements that are implicit in a `SELECT` command and introducing them as expressions in SML#. Introduction of a server definition and other SQL commands are relatively straightforward.

To identify those implicit syntactic shorthands, let us examine the following simple `SELECT` command.

```
SELECT name FROM people WHERE age >= 25
```

This implicitly assumes the following.

1. Field names `name` and `age` in `SELECT` and `WHERE` clauses denote the results of the corresponding field selections from a tuple in the table given in `FROM` clause.
2. `SELECT` phrase creates a tuple whose labels are inherited from the field names.
3. This query is executed against a given database connection. This implies that the table name `people` in `FROM` clause represents the selection of the `people` table from a database consisting of a named collection of tables.

The first two points are made explicit by the following more verbose version of the same SQL command

```
SELECT person.name AS name, person.age AS age
FROM people AS person
WHERE (person.age >= 25)
```

where a variable `person` is bound to a representative tuple, from which the mentioned fields are extracted. To represent the third point, we represent a query expression as a function that explicitly takes a database connection `db` as a parameter and selects the referenced table `people` from `db`. This analysis yield the example expression we gave in Section 2.

```
e   ::=  ...                              (SML# expressions)
      |  _sqlserver [string] : τ          (server definition)
      |  _sql x => sql                    (SQL expressions)
      |  _sqleval e                       (query evaluation)
      |  _sqlexec e                       (command execution)
      |  #x.l                             (selection)

sql  ::=  select | insert | update | begin | commit | rollback

select  ::=  select e [ as l ] ... e [ as l ]
             [ from e as x ... e as x ]
             [ where e ]
               (other clauses)
insert  ::=  insert into #x.l (l, ..., l)
             values ( {e|default}, ..., {e|default})
update  ::=  update #x.l [ as x ]
             set (l, ..., l) = (e, ..., e)
             [ from e as x ... e as x ]
             [ where e ]
delete  ::=  delete from #x.l [ as x ]
             [ where e ]
```

Figure 2. The syntax of SQL extension in SML#

We also need to introduce syntax for executing an SQL query command against a database connection. There should be two forms, one for SELECT, which returns a relation, and the other for all the other commands which do not return any value.

Based on these analyses, we define the syntax extension to SML# as shown in Figure 2. In this definition, note that e ranges over any expressions including those of SML#. Those who are familiar with SQL should immediately recognize that these extensions are direct representation of (a subset of) SQL. SQL contains more features, which can be added without any problem, as we discuss later.

3.3 Typing extension for SQL

We should emphasize that these SQL expressions are not macro but they are all legal expressions that can be freely combined with other SML# expressions. Moreover, each sub-expression e appearing in those SQL syntax can be any expression definable in SML#. Of course not all syntactically well-formed expressions are legal; the set of expressions that have well-defined meaning are those that have a *type* inferred by the type system.

Our goal is to extend the type system of SML# so that it always infers a most general type for any legal SQL expression. Since the type system guarantees that any typable expression can be freely combined as far as its type is consistent, this achieves our goal of seamless integration of SQL into Standard ML.

The type system is defined through a set of typing rules to derive typing judgments in the style of [24]. We have worked out the details of the typing rules for the above SQL extension. In this section, rather than giving a formal typing derivation system, we present the type system by explaining the meanings of new type constructors and the behavior of the associated typing rules.

3.3.1 The set of new type constructors

The set of types of SML# is extended with the following new type constructors for the SQL extension.

```
τ  :=     | τ server | τ conn | τ query | command | τ rel
     |  (τ, τ') db | (τ, τ') table | (τ, τ') row
     |  (τ, τ') value
```

Intuitive meanings of these types are the following; their precise meaning will become clear when we explain typing properties of associated operations. τ `server` denotes a server of a database of type τ by which SQL expressions are evaluated. In what follows, we call such a server as an SQL server. τ `conn` represents an established connection to an SQL server of type τ `server`. τ `query` represents an SQL `SELECT` command that return a relation of type τ. `command` is the type of the other SQL commands such as `insert` and `rollback`, which cause some side effects to the SQL server state. τ `rel` represents a relation containing tuples of type τ returned from an SQL server as a result of query evaluation. The other four types (τ_1, τ_2) `db`, (τ_1, τ_2) `table`, (τ_1, τ_2) `row`, and (τ_1, τ_2) `value` are used to type expressions inside of SQL queries and commands. They respectively denote an active database connection of type τ_1, a table of type τ_1 in an active database connection, a tuple of type τ_1 in an active database connection, and an atomic value of type τ_1 in an active database connection. τ_1 of type `value` is either an atomic base type b for values without null or b `option` for values possibly containing null. The extra second type parameter τ_2 in these types is introduced to ensure the consistency of database connections in SQL queries we shall explain below.

Using these types, we represent legal SQL expressions through SQL constructs. In the following, we introduce SQL constructs and explain their typing relations.

3.3.2 SQL servers

A server expression `_sqlserver` [*string*] : τ declares that there is an SQL server of type τ at the location specified by *string*. This *string* may also contain some extra information to establish a connection to the server. In our current version, the location specification *string* is designed so that it is expressive enough for PostgreSQL or MySQL servers. τ specifies the set of tables in the database as a form of record type. This expression is always well typed with type τ `server`. Note that giving a type to servers makes them first-class values. This feature gives flexibility to database programming. For example, a function can take list of servers with additional information such as their capacities and can dynamically choose appropriate one at runtime.

A runtime value of a server expression is a server object consisting of the server information including its location and a runtime representation of its type τ. The only operation on a server object is the primitive function

```
SQL.connect : ['a. 'a server -> 'a conn].
```

This primitive attempts to connect the SML# runtime system to the SQL server using the location information stored in the server object of type τ `server`. If the attempt succeeds, then it dynamically checks that the connected server has indeed the type τ stored in the server object. This typechecking is done by retrieving database schema information from the remote SQL server. If the typecheck succeeds, then the primitive succeeds and returns a connection object of type τ `conn`, which can be used to issue SQL commands. If either the connection attempt or the typecheck fails then this primitive raises a runtime exception.

3.3.3 Consistency of database connection

A distinguishing features of our language is that all the components of SQL are given types so that they are treated as first class values. This achieves powerful SQL programming using higher-order functions. As we noted above, in our system, database servers and the corresponding database connections are all first-class values. As a consequence, one can write a program that manipulates multiple database connections to different database servers. This flexibility raises one subtle issue in ensuring well-definedness of SQL query execution. A straightforward combination of higher-order functions and first-class database connections would inadvertently admit an SQL query that involves multiple database connections. However, an SQL query needs to be evaluated by a single SQL server through a single database connection. To see the problem, consider the following example.

```
fun f db1 =
    _sql db2 => select #r1.c1, #r2.c2
                from #db1.t1 as r1, #db2.t2 as r2
```

The function `f` generates an SQL SELECT command for a database connection `db2`, but it uses another database connection `db1` received as a parameter. This function definition is valid only when `db1` and `db2` denote the identical connection. The following example is an invalid use of `f`.

```
val conn1 = SQL.connect (_selserver "DB1");
val conn2 = SQL.connect (_selserver "DB2");
_sqleval
  (_sql db =>
       select    from
       where    (_sqleval f db conn1)    )
  conn2
```

This results in sending to an SQL server "DB1" a query that involves a reference to another database server "DB2". A sound integration of SQL into SML# type system requires that the extended type system should statically detect this form of inconsistency due to multiple database connections in one SQL query.

We solve this problem using existential types proposed in [25]. The idea is to consider a database connection of type τ_1 `conn` as an abstract package of type

$$\tau_1\ \texttt{conn} = \exists\tau_2.(\tau_1, \tau_2)\ \texttt{db}$$

where τ_2 is an abstract witness representing a unique connection established for a particular connection to a database. Since existential types are second-order types, general introduction of this mechanism is beyond the power of ML typing on which SML# is based. So we introduce this mechanism only for the expressions `_sqleval` and `_sqlexec` that use a database connection. These expressions temporally opens the package by generating a unique τ_2 and converting a database connection type τ_1 `conn` into a database type (τ_1, τ_2) `db`. All the database components (tables and values) that forms an argument to the same `_sqleval` or `_sqlexec` are typed with the same unique witness type τ_2. This ensures the consistent use of connection without introducing ad-hoc restriction on the usage of first-class SQL constructs. The second type parameter τ_2 in (τ_1, τ_2) `db`, (τ_1, τ_2) `table`, (τ_1, τ_2) `row`, and (τ_1, τ_2) `value` are introduced for this purpose. The precise typing rule is rather involved, but it is a standard application of existential types. As we shall describe below, our implementation achieves an efficient and simple type inference method specialized for `_sqleval` and `_sqlexec`.

3.3.4 Component selection expression

The `select` expressions and other SQL commands contains component selection expressions of the form $\#x.l$, which denotes the l component of the value denoted by x. The value may be a database or a tuple, both of which have a labeled record structure. Correctly inferring the most general type of this construct is a key to achieving seamless integration of SQL into SML#.

For this expression, the type inference system performs the following.

Infer a type of x. The result should be either a database type (τ_1, τ_2) `db` or a tuple type (τ_1, τ_2) `row`. In these types, τ_1 is a record type representing their structure, and τ_2 represents a unique database connection.

It unifies τ_1 with a fresh type variable with a record kind `'a#`$\{l$`:'b`$\}$.

If unification succeed, then the type inference system computes an instance of the component type `'b`. Let the result be τ_3. The type inference system returns (`'b`, τ_3) `table` if $\#x.l$ appears in a context that requires a table, otherwise it returns (`'b`, τ_3) `value`.

3.3.5 SQL SELECT command

With these extensions, SQL `SELECT` command can be typed. Its syntax in our extension has the following form.

`_sql db => select` e_1 `as` l_1 ... e_n `as` l_n
`from` e^1 `as` x^1 ... e^k `as` x^k
`where` e_w

For this expression, the typechecker performs the following.

Infer a type τ for e_w and unify τ with (`bool`, τ_0) `value`.

For each e^i, infer types τ^i and unify τ^i with $(\tau^{i\prime}, \tau_0)$ `table`, and add the bindings $\{x^i : (\tau^{i\prime}, \tau_0)\ \texttt{row}\}$ to the typing environment.

Under the extended typing environment, infer types $\tau_1, \ldots, \tau_n$ for $e_1, \ldots, e_n$.

If all the inference steps succeed, then it returns the type $\{l_1 : \tau_1, \ldots, l_n : \tau_n\}$ `query` as a result.

3.3.6 Sub queries

SQL allows arbitrary nesting of SELECT commands by treating the result of a SELECT command as a table. This is simply done by the introduction of the following typed primitive.

```
SQL.subquery : ['a, 'b.
                 (('a, 'b) db -> 'a query)
                  -> ('a, 'b) db -> ('a, 'b) table
```

The first parameter is a `select` expression, and the second parameter is the current database connection. This converts the `select` expression to a virtual table on that connection.

3.3.7 Overloaded operators

In addition to the mechanism above, one more extension is required to infer a desired polymorphic type for SQL expressions. To explain this, we note that an SQL expression is not only polymorphic in the database structures it manipulates but it also implicitly uses overloaded operators such as comparison >. Since conventional SQL commands are executed under a fixed monomorphic database, all the overloading are resolved by the server without any problems. However, if we treat a query as a first-class value, then we need to represent the overloaded operators as first-class values as well. To see the need, consider the following query.

```
fun f x =
    _sql db => select #person.name as name
               from #db.people as person
               where SQL.> (#person.age, x)
```

There are multiple possible types for `age` and accordingly there are possible multiple instances of `SQL.>`. Since SML# is a typed language, we must infer a polymorphic type of this function. Instead of introducing a general mechanism for overloading such as type classes [17], which would significantly complicate the underlying type system of Standard ML, our solution is to introduce a new kinded type variable of the form `'a::`$\{\tau_1, \ldots, \tau_n\}$ representing the fact that type variable 'a is an overloaded type whose instance is restricted to one of its list $\tau_1, \ldots, \tau_n$. The type of the parameter x in the above function is type variable 'a with the following kinding:

```
'a::{int, word, char, string, real, 'b option},
'b::{int, word, char, bool, string, real}
```

The listed types are atomic types shared among ML and SQL. Since the age column in the actual database may contain null, the set of instances must contain int option as well as int etc. Thus, the set of all possible instances of 'a is {int, word, char, string, real, int option, word option, char option, bool option, string option, real option} which is the standard set of types allowed for the age field in an SQL database. The same restriction applies to the result value of a column selection expression such as #person.name.

Combining all the typing mechanisms, our type system always infers a principal type for any type-correct SQL expression. For the above f, for example, the following type is inferred.

```
val it = fn
 : ['a::{int, word, char, string, real, 'b option},
    'b::{int, word, char, bool, string, real},
    'c.
    ('a, 'c) SQL.value
    -> ['d#{people: 'e},
        'e#{age: 'a, name: 'f},
        'f::{int, word, char, string, real,
             'g option},
        'g::{int, word, char, bool, string, real}.
        ('d, 'c) SQL.db -> {name:'f} SQL.query]]
```

Although the inferred type is notationally involved, it is not hard to see that this is exactly the constraint imposed by the above SQL query. It is this precise typing that achieves seamless integration of SQL into a typed polymorphic high-order functional language.

3.4 The operational semantics

Once we have worked out the typing structures of all the components of SQL, the next step is to develop an evaluation model for the SQL extension and to combine it in the compilation steps in SML#. An expression in a functional language is compiled to a code that generates a value denoted by the expression. In order to seamlessly integrate SQL in this general model, we adopt the following strategy. For various SQL components that appear inside of SQL expressions, we define their values to be the syntax tree representing the component whose leaves may contain atomic SML# values, and represent the runtime value of each primitive functions operating on SQL components as a function that combines abstract syntax trees. SQL construct _sql x => sql is compiled to a code that takes a database connection and returns an abstract syntax tree representing the corresponding SQL command to be sent to the server through the connection. _sqleval and _sqlexec are implemented as functions that take an abstract syntax tree, generate an SQL string from the tree, and sends it to the server. In actual implementation, we do not explicitly generate an abstract syntax tree but generate its string representation on the fly.

In the case of _sqleval, it must perform additional task of converting the returned result to the SML# runtime values. We solve this problem by associating _sqleval with a function that generates SML# values from the server's result. The runtime representation of τ rel is a value containing such a function. SQL.fetchAll : τ rel -> τ list converts a query result to an SML# list of records by invoking the conversion function.

3.5 Other SQL features and examples

The syntax of SQL contains additional components other than those defined in the syntax extension in section 3.2. For example, SELECT command has many clauses other than FROM and WHERE such as ORDER BY. Some of those additional components require extension to the syntax, and others are realized by adding primitive functions. In this section, we take ORDER BY clause of SELECT command as an example for the former, and logical operators including EXISTS predicate for the latter. Other components can be introduced similarly to one of these two.

The ORDER BY clause of SQL sorts tuples in the query result according to columns in the select list as well as those of the tables appearing in FROM clause. Original ORDER BY clause refers the select list in anonymous way. To realize this behavior in our syntax, we need to explicitly introduce a variable which is bound to a result tuple. We use into keyword for this binding. The syntax of select command is refined as follows.

$select$ ::= select e [as l] ... e [as l] into x

order by e [{asc|desc}] e [{asc|desc}]

The type of x following into is (τ_1, τ_2) row where τ_1 is a record type representing the type of the result tuple. This x can be seen from sub-expressions in the order by clause and is used to refer to the select list.

Some of primitive operations in SQL expressions can be represented as typed primitive functions. The following typed primitives represent SQL logical operators.

```
SQL.andAlso :
    ['a. (bool,'a) value * (bool,'a) value
       -> (bool, 'a) value]
SQL.orElse  :
    ['a. (bool,'a) value * (bool,'a) value
       -> (bool,'a) value]
```

EXISTS subquery expression can be introduced by the following typed primitive, similar to SQL.subquery.

```
SQL.exists :
    ['a, 'b. (('a, 'b) db -> 'a query)
             -> ('a, 'b) db -> (bool, 'b) value]
```

Using those features, the programmer can enjoy database programming with full spectrum of SQL directly in Standard ML. Figure 3 shows an example that retrieves employee information from an employment database and constructs a nested list of employees for each department. employees is a polymorphic query that receives a condition for where clause and returns a list of pairs of an employee's name and his/her salary in descending order of salary. employees' is another polymorphic query obtained from employees by applying it to a partial condition. depts holds the list of pairs of a department name and its ID. The map function in the definition of forEachDept performs iteration over the department list and constructs and emits a query for each department. l1 and l2 hold resulting employee lists under different conditions.

4. Implementation

We have implemented the presented extension in SML# compiler. Through our effort of modular and systematic extension of a complex system of SML# compiler, we have developed an implementation technique for connecting static semantics of SQL in the host language, SML#, and its dynamic semantics realized by an external SQL server. This technique should be useful for extending a compiler with a domain specific language. In the next subsection, we discuss the problem in extending an existing compiler and describe

```
val db = _sqlserver "dbname=employment"
         : {employee: {name:string, age:int,
                       salary:int, deptId:int},
            department: {id:int, name:string}}

val conn = SQL.connect db

fun employees condFn =
    _sql db => select #r.name, #r.salary
               from #db.employee as r
               where condFn r
               order by #r.salary desc

fun employees' condFn deptId =
    employees
      (fn r => SQL.andAlso
                 (SQL.== (#r.deptId, deptId),
                  condFn r))

val depts =
    SQL.fetchAll
      (_sqleval
         (_sql db =>
            select #r.name as deptName,
                   #r.id as deptId
            from #db.department as r
            order by #r.name)
         conn)

fun forEachDept queryFn =
    map (fn {deptId, deptName} =>
            {deptName = deptName,
             employees =
               SQL.fetchAll (queryFn deptId) conn})
        depts;

val q1 = employees' (fn r => SQL.> (#r.salary, 5000))
val l1 = forEachDept (fn i => _sqleval (q1 i));

val q2 = employees' (fn r => SQL.> (#r.age, 50))
val l2 = forEachDept (fn i => _sqleval (q2 i));
```

Figure 3. example of combination of ML and SQL

the implementation technique we have developed. We then reports the details of the implementation in the subsequent subsections.

4.1 Implementation strategy

A natural way of extending a compiler with SQL would be to add its syntax and the corresponding intermediate representations, and then to add to each compilation phase the cases that process the new components in such a way that the added SQL components achieve the intended typing and runtime behavior. This approach requires detailed analysis on interaction between the existing system and new components, and is difficult for a large and complex language such as a compiler of Standard ML including SML# compiler, which contains more than 300K line of code organized in more than 20 compilation phases. This natural strategy would also be problematic in extensibility and maintenance, since the added extensions will become tightly built-in the core of the compiler. In order to extend the SML# compiler efficiently and reliably, we should localize the extensions and minimize the modifications of the core of the compiler. Our basic strategy for achieving this goal is to use the compiler's functions as far as possible.

Extending a typed language with some new constructs requires to implement their *static semantics*, which infers types and properly propagates them to the rest of the language, and their *dynamic semantics*, which realizes the desired runtime effect. In our implementation, we have successfully organized the SQL extension in such a way that both static and dynamic evaluation are realized systematically using the existing functionality of the SML# compiler. This is based on our following observations.

Components of SQL expressions including "databases", "tables", and "rows" are all labeled record structures combined with a type constructor for collections (relations). These components can be represented in the type system of SML#, which supports record polymorphism. We can then directly implement any SQL expression as a source program in SML#. This would yield a *toy implementation* of SQL in SML#. Of course, such a toy implementation is not what we really want. Our goal is to seamlessly extend SML# with SQL in such a way that the SQL part is evaluated by an efficient practical database server. However, as far as typing is concerned, such a toy implementation is good enough; for each SQL expression, we can generate a toy program whose type is the same as that of the SQL expression. This means that we can obtain the desired static semantics of an SQL expression by constructing an appropriate toy source program that corresponds to the SQL expression. Moreover, types are only used for static enforcement of legal combination of SQL expressions with other language constructs, and are not needed at runtime. A dynamic semantics of an SQL expression is realized by generating an SQL command string and sending them to an SQL server without using type information. This process is also easily represented by an SML# program. The desired SQL extension can then be realized by connecting the static semantics realized by a toy implementation and the dynamic semantics realized by a database server.

The above observation leads us to the following implementation strategy. The compiler first translates an SQL expression to a source program that computes a pair of a toy implementation and a target SQL command string. Each primitive operation of SQL is translated to a source program that simultaneously composes both the toy implementation and the target SQL command string. It is not hard to define a data type for the source program so that the type of the toy implementation becomes the type of the entire result. The value of the translated program is a pair of the toy implementation and the target SQL command string. So the remaining thing for the compiler to achieve the desired dynamic semantics is to compile `_sqleval` and `_sqlexec` to a source program that takes the source program generated from an SQL expression, runs the program to obtain a pair, throws away the first component, and sends SQL command string stored in the second component to the database server.

The first major phase of the SML# compiler is *elaboration*, which translates a given abstract syntax to a basic source program, called a *core ML program*, by expanding derived forms (sugared syntax). Since most of the above process are definable in the core ML language, the major part of SQL compilation can be implemented by extending the elaboration phase of the SML# compiler so that it translates SQL expressions to appropriate core ML programs described above.

In order to carry out the implementation based on this strategy, we have to develop the following components and integrate them in the SML# compiler.

1. *Extension to the SML# type system.* Although most of SQL type structures can be representable in the core ML language of SML#, a complete representation of actual SQL expressions requires some extensions to its type system. The major one is the introduction of existential types we explained in Section 3 to ensure that all the components in one SQL expression refer

to the same database connection. Introduction of this feature requires to extend the typed intermediate language of the SML# compiler and its type inference system.

2. *SQL type definitions.* Under our strategy, the compiler generates a core ML program that achieves the static semantics of the original SQL program. Those generated programs need to reference types of SQL component such as "tables" and "rows". This means that these types should be predefined and loaded before the compilation.
3. *Core ML program generation.* After the preparation of the above two steps, the compiler generates a core ML program from a given SQL expression.
4. *Connection management.* In addition to compile SQL expressions, the compiler and runtime system must also manage server connection. An important additional role beside making server connection is to dynamically check type conformance of the sever database against the declared server type. Since types are static entities that only exists during compilation, a special compiler support is necessary for this purpose.
5. *SQL server binding.* To communicate with an SQL server process, we need primitive functions to access an SQL server. Modern SQL servers usually provide such features as their own low-level APIs. To make our implementation independent of particular SQL server as much as possible, we introduce a *server binding* module to abstract the low-level communication.

The following five subsections explain these major components.

4.2 Extension to the SML# type system

New typing mechanisms necessary for SQL expressions include overloading and existential types.

4.2.1 Overloading compilation for SQL primitives

As we have explained in 3.3.7, we need to represent constant literals and primitives in SQL expressions. For this purpose, we have introduced a simple first-class overloading mechanism based on polymorphic record compilation. Compared with type classes in Haskell [17], the modification to SML# type system is simple, and it can be implemented by small modification to the existing mechanism for record compilation. Here, we outline the necessary extension to SML# type system and the implementation. For the sake of explanation, we consider an overloaded primitive O whose instances is represented by a polymorphic type of the form

$$O : \forall t :: \{b_1, \ldots, b_n\}.\tau$$

where $\{b_1, \ldots, b_n\}$ is a set of base types. For this simplified setting, each of instance functions of O is identified by a base type b listed in the kind, which we write O_b.

To deal with overloading specified in the definition of Standard ML, the original SML# type system already contains overloaded kind of free type variables of the form $t :: \{b_1, \ldots, b_n\}$, where $b_1, \ldots, b_n$ are distinct base types. If these type variables remain free at the top-level, they are not generalized but are instantiated with the first component b_1 of the list of types $\{b_1, \ldots, b_n\}$. To extend the type inference system with first-class overloading, we have only to allow these type variables with overloaded kind to be generalized. The kinded type system of SML# correctly propagates and resolves overloaded instance types.

The above modified type inference system of course does not reflect the dynamic semantics of overloaded primitive O. The compiler needs to resolve overloading by selecting appropriate instance O_b according to an instance b of t. For this purpose, we apply the idea of polymorphic record compilation and compile a term with of overloaded primitive O to a higher-order function that takes an appropriate overloaded instance as an extra parameter. For this purpose, in the target language, an overload kind is extended to be a pair $(\{O_1, \ldots, O_m\}, \{b_1, \ldots, b_n\})$ by including the set $\{O_1, \ldots, O_m\}$ of overloaded primitives involved. When type variables with overloaded kinds are unified, the type system takes the intersection of instance sets and the union of the primitive sets. When polymorphic generalization is performed on those overloaded variables, extra bound variable for each O_i is introduced, and when polymorphic instantiation is performed, the actual instance primitive is passed as an additional parameter. With this preparation, the compilation process is essentially the same as that of polymorphic record compilation. For example, a function

```
val f = fn x => +(x,*(x,x))
        : ['a::{int, real}. 'a -> 'a]
```

is compiled to the following term:

```
val f = fn I+ => fn I  => fn x => I+(x,I (x,x))
        : ['a::({+,*},{int, real}).
           Inst(+,'a) -> Inst(*,'a) -> 'a -> 'a]
```

where $Inst($`+, 'a`$)$ is the singleton type that denotes the primitive `+` for the type `'a`.

In our actual extension, we allow each overloaded instance type b_i to take another overloaded type variable as its type parameter to represent *nested* overloaded instances. By allowing the nesting, we can define overloaded primitives not only over base types but also over constructed types. This is needed to represent the set of types shared among ML and SQL as described in section 3.3.7. For example, in our SQL extension, the type of `SQL.>`, which is a comparison primitive for SQL queries, is declared as follows:

```
['a,
 'b::{int, word, char, bool, string, real},
 'c::{int, word, char, string, real, 'b option}.
 ('c, 'a) SQL.value * ('c, 'a) SQL.value
   -> (bool option, 'a) SQL.value ]
```

Overloaded type variable `'c` in this example refers to another overloaded type variable 'b to form a nested instance set, which represents the set of types for which comparison operation is defined in SQL. The necessary extension to the SML# compiler is small and modular.

4.2.2 Existential types for database connections

In order for an SQL expression `_sql db =>` *sql* to have well-defined meaning, any component in *sql* must reference to the same server connection. As we have pointed out, one way to ensure this restriction is to consider the database connection `db` as an abstract package having an existential type $\exists t.\sigma$ providing the capability of accessing its component tables and columns therein. The resulting type system yields sound typing for SQL expressions, successfully excluding anomalous terms such as the example shown in Section 3.3.3. However, introduction of existential types in their general form makes the type inference system of ML incomplete. Our solution is to restrict existential types to the combination of `_sql db =>` *sql* and `_sqleval` (or `_sqlexec`.) Here we only explain the case for `_sqleval`. The case for `_sqlexec` is the same. The basic role of the construct `_sqleval (_sql db =>` *sql*`) conn` is to bind `db` to a connection denoted by `conn`. In addition, the type system generates a unique witness type and propagated through all the `db` component in *sql*. To represent this effect, the type system treats this application specially. When typechecking the above application, the type system generates a new type `'a dbi`, unifies the type of `db`, infers the application, and finally checks that the newly generated type variable `'a` does not occur in both the type environment and the type judgment. This final check ensures that all the elements in *sql* reference to the same server connection denoted by conn.

4.3 SQL type definitions

Our strategy is to translate SQL expressions to core ML programs of SML#. This requires that all the types of SQL component such as "database" and "tables" used in the generated programs should have been defined. For this purpose, we extend the set of built-in types of SML# with the following types.

```
datatype ('a, 'b) db =
         DB of 'a * 'b dbi
datatype ('a, 'b) table =
         TABLE of 'a * string * 'b dbi
datatype ('a, 'b) row =
         ROW of 'a * string * 'b dbi
datatype ('a, 'b) value =
         VALUE of 'a * string * 'b dbi
```

The first type argument 'a of db, table, row, and value is the type of the toy program. The second type parameter 'b is used to propagate a unique connection type explained above. The string component in the implementations of table, row, and value holds the (partially constructed) target SQL command string.

4.4 Core ML program generation

Using these types and their data constructors, the compiler generates core ML programs of SML# from SQL expressions. This is done by adding a case for each of SQL expression syntax to the SML# elaboration phase, which recursively traverse a given source program. Each case is largely mechanical with a special care of ensuring that a unique connection type should be properly propagated. As a simple example, component selection, #*x*.*l*, in a source program is translated to the following core ML program.

```
case x of DB (y, {l=z,...}) => TABLE ("l", y, z)
```

In this program, "*l*" is a string literal to appear in the SQL command string being generated, the part {*l*=*z*,...} => *z* is the toy implementation that generates polymorphic typing of this selection, and *y* => *y* is for propagating a unique connection type. Each SQL operation is translated to a program that composes the toy parts, concatenates the SQL command strings, and propagates the unique connection type.

Since some of SQL components only concatenate the SQL command strings, connection types need to be propagated through SQL command string concatenation. For this purpose, we introduce a special string concatenation function concatQuery of type (string * 'a dbi) list -> string, and passes component strings together with connection witnesses to this function. This function concatenates a list of string with the typing effect of unifying all their connection types to the same type. This achieves the desired typing effect.

There is one more subtlety that should be take care of in achieving seamless integration of SQL into SML#. We have so far identified SQL rows (tuples) with Standard ML labeled records. This identification works fine for component selection and its typing. However, internal representations of SQL rows returned from an SQL server are different from those of ML record representation. This implies that a row fetched from the result of an SQL expression returned from a server should be converted to the internal representation of Standard ML. Under our strategy, this requires to generate a core ML program that performs such conversion. Moreover, we need to generate such a conversion function for each SQL query using its type information. This is best done at the time of translating a query expression, when all the necessary type information is available. Our source level translator generates a core ML program that performs this conversion just after an entire query is constructed. The result of our translation of an SQL query is then a core ML program having the following type.

```
datatype 'a query =
         QUERY of string * 'a * (result -> 'a)
```

The first component is an SQL command string to be sent to a server, the second component is a toy implementation, and the third component is the conversion function.

Figure 4 shows an example of translating a query expression into a core ML program.

Source program:

```
_sql db =>
  select #person.name as name
  from #db.people as person
```

Translated core ML terms:

```
fn db as DB (dbi, _) =>
   let
     val (tabname, person) =
         case (case db of
                     DB (i, {people = w, ...}) =>
                     TABLE (("people", i), w)) of
           TABLE (t as (_, i), w) =>
           (t, ROW (("person", i), w))
     val VALUE (nameExp, nameW) =
         case person of
           ROW (n, {name = w, ...}) =>
           VALUE (concatDot (n, "name"), w)
     val witness = {name = nameW}
   in
     QUERY
       (concatQuery [("SELECT ", DBI),
                     nameExp,
                     (" AS name FROM ", DBI),
                     tabname,
                     (" AS person", DBI)],
          witness,
          fn RESULT result =>
             {name = fromSQL
                     (0, result, #name witness)})
   end
```

Figure 4. example of query translation

4.5 Connection management

The remaining component of our extension is connection management. This is responsible for defining a server, establishing a connection, and sending a query over connection. Among them, the third one is a simple source level library function that calls one of C API provided by the database server through SML# C function interface described earlier. Server definition and connection establishment need to perform runtime typechecking to ensure the type safety of SQL expressions.

We have developed a typing machinery to infer a most general type for any legal SQL query expression. This inferred type should be checked against the type of a database stored in a database server to be connected. Since a database server is external to SML# programs, we model a database server as an object of type dynamic as proposed in [1]. In this formalism, an expression having a type dynamic is used with an explicit type annotation. Its runtime representation is a pair of its value and its runtime type information. This runtime type information is checked against the explicit type annotation only once when this object is loaded (linked) in a program.

In our language, this model is implemented by checking that the internal type of the connected database server is the same as the static type specified in `_sqlserver` expression when a database server is connected by `SQL.connect` primitive. This is done as follows. `_sqlserver` expression is translated to a core ML code that generates a string representation of the annotated type τ together with the location information of the server. `SQL.connect` primitive is implemented as a core ML function. This function takes a server object of type τ `server` containing a server location and type information, opens a connection using the server location information, and issues a query to the database to obtain its scheme information, and then it checks that the connected database has the type τ using its string representation and the obtained scheme information. If the type check succeeds then `SQL.connect` succeeds and yields a value of type τ `conn`, otherwise it raises runtime exception. After this connection, a database is safely used with typed first-class SQL query expressions.

4.6 SQL server bindings

Since the SQL syntax of our language is (a subset of) the standardized SQL language, our language should be independent of any particular SQL server implementation. However, C APIs needed to implement the connection management are varied with SQL servers. For our system to work with any server that conform to the SQL standard, we introduce a server binding module and its interface which absorbs the difference of low-level C APIs. Any user-level primitive features of SQL extentions, such as `SQL.fetchAll` and `SQL.connect` functions, are implemented by using this binding module.

The server binding interface requires the binding module implementator to provide the following functions.

1. Low-level connection management functions through abstract connection handles, and string-based query execution functions.
2. A function to obtain schema information for runtime typechecking.
3. A mapping of type names from database types to ML types, and the corresponding set of conversion functions from query results to ML values.

With the functionality provided by any modern SQL database systems, it is routine to implement these functions by writing a small amount of code. On the requirement 1, database systems usually offer such a string-based low-level query interface, as discussed in section 1.1. The requirement 2 can be easily realized by a series of SQL queries issued through the low-level query interface since database systems usually implement system catalogs as tables which is accessible to an ordinary SELECT command. The requirement 3 can be implemented by composing low-level methods to retrieve tuples and fields from the query result and representation conversion functions. This is also streightforward except that a little care is needed to define the type name mapping.

We have implemented binding modules for PostgreSQL and MySQL. Any other database systems can be supported just by writing a binding module for the database.

5. Conclusions and Future Works

We have presented a new generation of Standard ML that seamlessly integrates SQL. In this language, a legal SQL expression is a polymorphically typed first-class citizen that are freely combined with any features of Standard ML, including high-order functions, data type definition, and its module system. The distinguishing feature of our language is that those SQL expressions are not evaluated in the ML language runtime, but they are sent to a real database server. This makes efficient practical database programming directly available in a high-level and reliable functional programming language.

We have solved a number of typing and implementation issues and have implemented the language. The implementation is done by extending the compiler of SML#, which is an extension of Standard ML with record polymorphism. Since the only crucial technical typing device we have used is record polymorphism presented in [28], we also expect that our method can be transferred to any other ML-style language as far as its type system contains a typing mechanism that is at least as powerful as record polymorphism such as OCaml objects based on Remy's record polymorphism [31] or Haskell type classes [17].

This is a step toward making practical database programming seamlessly available in a typed high-level programming language. A number of interesting future issues remain to be investigated. We briefly mention some of them below.

As mentioned in Section 1.1, there are several proposals for high-level query languages for advanced applications. One way of making these approaches practical and scalable would be to implement those advanced data models on top of SQL running on an efficient database server. The idea would be to make SQL relations as basic data structures to implement those high-level data model primitives. Since in our language various components in SQL databases are first-class values that are freely and directly manipulated by programs, our language should serve as an ideal basis for those applications.

Web programming framework is also a promising application area of our language. Interoperation between languages and databases are crucial in Web programming, and most of practical Web application framework such as Ruby on Rails provides various database access supports. Seamless integration of SQL with higher-order functional language would open up high-level Web application framework supporting various features such as "mashup" of variety of data sources and services.

Another interesting future work is to design a large scale distributed data manipulation system based on our language. Such a system would provide high-level and powerful alternative to mapreduce model [12]. As observed in [5], many future cloud applications would be benefited from database capability such as the ability to join various data sources.

References

[1] M. Abadi, L. Cardelli, B. Pierce, and G. Plotkin. Dynamic typing in a statically-typed language. *ACM Trans. Program. Lang. Syst.*, 13(2):207–268, 1991.

[2] A. Albano, G. Ghelli, and R. Orsini. Fibonacci: a programming language for object databases. *The VLDB Journal*, 4(3):403–444, 1995.

[3] J. Annevelink. Database programming languages: a functional approach. In *Proceedings of the ACM SIGMOD International Conference on Management of Data*, pages 318–327, 1991.

[4] M.P. Atkinson and O.P. Buneman. Types and persistence in database programming languages. *ACM Computing Surveys*, 1987.

[5] S. Blanas, J. M. Patel, V. Ercegovac, J. Rao, E. J. Shekita, and Y. Tian. A comparison of join algorithms for log processing in mapreduce. In *Proceedings of the ACM SIGMOD International Conference on Management of Data*, pages 975–986, 2010. ACM.

[6] P. Buneman, S. Naqvi, V. Tannen, and L. Wong. Principles of programming with complex objects and collection types. *Theor. Comput. Sci.*, 149(1):3–48, 1995.

[7] A. Chlipala. Ur: statically-typed metaprogramming with type-level record computation. In *Proceedings of the ACM SIGPLAN Conference*

on Programming Language Design and Implementation, pages 122–133, 2010.

[8] E. F. Codd. A relational model for large shared databank. *Communications of the ACM*, 13(6):377–387, 1970.

[9] E. Cooper. The script-writer's dream: How to write great SQL in your own language, and be sure it will succeed. In *Proceedings of the International Symposium on Database Programming Languages*, pages 36–51, Springer-Verlag, 2009.

[10] E. Cooper, S. Lindley, P. Wadler, and J. Yallop. Links: web programming without tiers. In *Proceedings of the International Conference on Formal Methods for Components and Objects*, pages 266–296, Springer-Verlag, 2007.

[11] G. Copeland and D. Maier. Making smalltalk a database system. In *Proceedings of the ACM SIGMOD International Conference on Management of Data*, pages 316–325, 1984.

[12] J. Dean and S. Ghemawat. Mapreduce: simplified data processing on large clusters. *Commun. ACM*, 51(1):107–113, 2008.

[13] A. Eisenberg and J. Melton. SQLJ part 0, now known as SQL/OLB (object-language bindings). *SIGMOD Rec.*, 27(4):94–100, 1998.

[14] J. Gil and K. Lenz. Simple and safe SQL queries with C++ templates. *Science of Computer Programming*, 75(7):573–595, 2010.

[15] G. Giorgidze, T. Grust, T. Schreiber, and J. Weijers. Haskell boards the Ferry: Database-supported program execution for Haskell. In *Proceedings of the 22nd international symposium on Implementation and Application of Functional Languages*, to appear.

[16] T. Grust, M. Mayr, J. Rittinger, and T. Schreiber. FERRY: database-supported program execution. In *Proceedings of the SIGMOD International Conference on Management of Data*, pages 1063–1066, 2009.

[17] C. V. Hall, K. Hammond, S. L. Peyton Jones, and P. L. Wadler. Type classes in haskell. *ACM Trans. Program. Lang. Syst.*, 18(2):109–138, 1996.

[18] P. Hudak. Building domain-specific embedded languages. *ACM Comput. Surv.*, page 196, 1996.

[19] C. Lécluse and P. Richard. The O_2 database programming language. In *Proceedings of the International Conference on Very Large Data Bases*, pages 423–432, Morgan Kaufmann Publishers Inc, 1989.

[20] D. Leijen and E. Meijer. Domain specific embedded compilers. In *Proceedings of the 2nd USENIX Conference on Domain Specific Languages*, pages 109–122, 1999.

[21] Y. Leontiev, M. T. Özsu, and D. Szafron. On type systems for object-oriented database programming languages. *ACM Comput. Surv.*, 34(4):409–449, 2002.

[22] D. Maier. Why database languages are a bad idea. In F. Bancilhon and P. Buneman, editors, *Proceedings of the International Workshop on Database Programming Languages*, Addison-Wesley, 1989.

[23] E. Meijer, B. Beckman, and G. Bierman. LINQ: Reconciling object, relations and XML in the .NET framework. In *Proceedings of the ACM SIGMOD International Conference on Management of Data*, pages 706–706, 2006.

[24] R. Milner, M. Tofte, R. Harper, and D. MacQueen. *The Definition of Standard ML*. The MIT Press, revised edition, 1997.

[25] J.C. Mitchell and G.D. Plotkin. Abstract types have existential type. *ACM Trans. Program. Lang. Syst.*, 10(3):470–502, 1988.

[26] R. Morrison, F. Brown, R. Connor, Q. Cutts, A. Dearle, G. Kirby, and D. Munro. Napier88 reference manual. Technical report, University of St. Andrews, 1996.

[27] H-D. Nguyen and A. Ohori. Compiling ml polymporphism with explicit layout bitmap. In *Proceedings of the ACM Conference on Principles and Practice of Declarative Programming*, pages 237–248, 2006.

[28] A. Ohori. A polymorphic record calculus and its compilation. *ACM Trans. Program. Lang. Syst.*, 17(6):844–895, 1995. A preliminary summary appeared at ACM POPL, 1992 under the title "A compilation method for ML-style polymorphic record calculi".

[29] A. Ohori and P. Buneman. Type inference in a database programming language. In *Proceedings of the ACM Conference on LISP and Functional Programming*, pages 174–183, 1988.

[30] A. Ohori, P. Buneman, and V. Breazu-Tannen. Database programming in Machiavelli – a polymorphic language with static type inference. In *Proceedings of the ACM SIGMOD International Conference on Management of Data*, pages 46–57, 1989.

[31] D. Remy. Typechecking records and variants in a natural extension of ML. In *Proceedings of the ACM Symposium on Principles of Programming Languages*, pages 242–249, 1989.

[32] SML#. http://www.riec.tohoku.ac.jp/smlsharp/.

[33] J. Bussche, D. Van Gucht, and S. Vansummeren. A crash course on database queries. In *Proceedings of the ACM SIGMOD-SIGACT-SIGART Symposium on Principles of Database Systems*, pages 143–154, 2007.

[34] Limsoon Wong. Kleisli, a functional query system. *J. Funct. Program.*, 10(1):19–56, 2000.

Nameless, Painless

Nicolas Pouillard
INRIA
Nicolas.Pouillard@inria.fr

Abstract

De Bruijn indices are a well known technique for programming with names and binders. They provide a representation that is both simple and canonical.

However, programming errors tend to be really easy to make. We propose a safer programming interface implemented as a library. Whereas indexing the types of names and terms by a numerical bound is a famous technique, we index them by worlds, a different notion of index that is both finer and more abstract. While being more finely typed, our approach incurs no loss of expressiveness or efficiency.

Via parametricity we obtain properties about functions polymorphic on worlds. For instance, well-typed world-polymorphic functions over open λ-terms commute with any renaming of the free variables.

Our whole development is conducted within Agda, from the code of the library, to its soundness proof and the properties of external functions. The soundness of our library is demonstrated via the construction of a logical relations argument.

Categories and Subject Descriptors D.3.3 [*Programming Languages*]: Language Constructs and Features—Data types and structures; Polymorphism

General Terms Design, Languages, Theory

Keywords names, binders, meta-programming, name abstraction, de Bruijn indices

1. Introduction

It is quite common in the programming realm to deal with the mundane business of data structures with names and binders. Compilers, code generators, static analysers, theorem provers, and type-checkers have this in common. They manipulate programs, formulae, proofs, and types. When seen as pieces of data, there is a common difficulty: the representation of variables (names and binders).

One traditional approach is to represent all the occurrences of a bound variable identically by using character strings or integers. While being the most obvious representation it is known to cause a lot of trouble when dealing with operations like substitution. In particular we name it the capture-avoiding substitution because it has to rename some variables to avoid accidental changes called captures.

ICFP'11, September 19–21, 2011, Tokyo, Japan.

In this article we focus on a different kind of representation, namely de Bruijn indices [6]. This representation is said to be nameless because variables are no longer identified by a name but a notion of "distance" to the binding point. De Bruijn indices are the most famous nameless representation and in the following we will use the term "nameless" as a synonym for "de Bruijn indices".

The nameless approach solves part of the problem by providing a canonical representation. More precisely binding occurrences are no longer named (we now use λ`.` instead of λ`x.`). Then bound variables are represented by the "distance" to the binding λ. This distance is the number of λs to cross in order to reach the binding λ.

A major issue with this nameless representation is its arithmetic flavor. Indeed properties about names and binders are turned into arithmetic formulae. The result can be harder to understand, and worse, easier to get wrong. To remedy this, several techniques have been proposed to give finer grained types to these representations [1, 2, 5, 7]. We continue further in this direction by providing a safer system to program with a nameless representation.

1.1 Contributions

In a previous paper [10] we developed an abstract interface to program with names and binders. The interface can be both implemented in a named or a nameless style. Here by focusing on a nameless representation we greatly simplify the programming interface needed to achieve our safety goals. This is at the expense of some loss of abstraction. However while the goals are less ambitious, the results are significantly more applicable since simpler and closer to a concrete representation.

Our previous nameless implementation was relying on the `Fin` approach (described in section 1.4.3). The notion of worlds presented here (in section 2.3) is significantly more precise than `Fin`. However the worlds were already abstract to the programmer and they still are. Indeed abstraction is necessary to retain the parametricity properties we want from world-polymorphic functions.

While a fair amount of proofs were already mechanized in [10], the logical relation argument was still largely on paper. Here we not only finished these mechanized proofs but have every part well connected in one single setup. The code and proofs are accessible online at [9] and we encourage the reader to have a look for reference on technical details and applications.

1.2 Outline of the paper

This paper is organized as follows. In the remainder of this section we present several nameless techniques to represent data structures with bindings. In section 2 we detail our approach to the problem. In section 3 we give some examples and advanced operations. In section 4 we develop a logical relation construction which ensures the soundness properties we want, and we show how to exploit these properties on concrete examples. All the construction is built in the AGDA language, our system is an AGDA library and its soundness proof is done in AGDA as well.

1.3 A brief introduction to AGDA notation

Throughout the paper, our definitions are presented in the syntax of AGDA. In AGDA, `Set` (or $\texttt{Set}_0$) is the type of small types like `Bool`, `Maybe (List Bool)`, or ℕ. $\texttt{Set}_1$ is the type of `Set`, `Set → Bool`, or `ℕ → Set`. The function space is written `A → B`, while the dependent function space is written `(x : A) → B` or `∀ (x : A) → B`. An implicit parameter, introduced via `∀{x : A} → B`, can be omitted at a call site if its value can be inferred from the context. There are shortcuts for introducing multiple arguments at once or for omitting a type annotation, as in `∀{A} {i j : A} x → e`. There is no specific sort for propositions in AGDA, everything is in `Set ℓ` for some ℓ. The unit type is a record type with no fields named ⊤, it also represents the `True` proposition. The empty type is an (inductive) data type with no constructors named ⊥, it also represents the `False` proposition. The negation `¬ A` is defined as `A → ⊥`.

The same name can be used for different data constructors. AGDA makes use of type annotations to resolve ambiguities.

As in Haskell, a definition consists of a type signature and a sequence of defining equations, which may involve pattern-matching. The `with` construct extends a pattern-matching-based definition with new columns. An ellipsis `...` is used to elide a redundant equation prefix.

AGDA is strict about whitespace: `x≤y` is an identifier, whereas `x ≤ y` is an application. This allows naming a variable after its type (deprived of any whitespace). We use mixfix declarations, such as `_⊕_`. We use some definitions from AGDA's standard library: natural numbers, booleans, lists, and applicative functors (`pure`, `_⊛_`).

For the sake of conciseness, the code fragments presented in the paper are sometimes not perfectly self-contained. However, a complete AGDA development is available online [9].

1.4 Related work: nameless representations

Various techniques have been discovered to build a nameless representation. We have chosen a few of them which gradually setup the stage.

1.4.1 `bare`: The original approach

We call this one `bare`, because it solely relies on natural numbers. To make things more concrete here is an example of its use when defining the untyped λ-calculus with local bindings (`let`). Our naming convention is as follows: we call `Tm` the type of λ-terms, `V` is the data constructor for variables, `_·_` is for the application, `ƛ` is for the λ-abstraction, and finally `Let` is for local bindings.

```
data Tm : Set where
  V    : (x    : ℕ)  → Tm
  _·_  : (t u  : Tm) → Tm
  ƛ    : (t    : Tm) → Tm
  Let  : (t u  : Tm) → Tm
```

From the point of view of the binding structure, it is striking that no difference appears between the constructors of the data type. It is completely up to the programmer to manage the scoping difference introduced by `ƛ` and `Let`. This is even more worrying in the `Let` case since we have no clue of difference between the arguments.

Here is an example using this representation to build the λ-term for `λf.λx.f x`.

```
appTm : Tm
appTm = ƛ (ƛ (V 1 · V 0))
```

The main advantages of this approach are its simplicity and its expressiveness. The expressiveness is almost maximal since no restriction is put on the usage of variables. Actually expressiveness is really maximal only in partial languages where all types are inhabited by a looping term. Indeed the absence of restrictions on data can be constraining when receiving data as argument. In a total language all cases have to be covered, even those we consider as impossible. For instance a function accepting only closed terms will have to provide a return value for the variable case anyway. Sometimes the return type is so constrained that the type is actually empty in this case, and so no dummy value can be returned. However, even in a partial language the expressiveness is maximal if we are willing to live in an error monad.

1.4.2 `Maybe`: The nested data type approach

The nested data type approach [2, 3, 5] is a first step towards better properties about the binding structure of terms. Let us start with the definition of `Tm` with this approach:

```
data Tm (A : Set) : Set where
  V    : (x : A)                          → Tm A
  _·_  : (t u : Tm A)                     → Tm A
  ƛ    : (t : Tm (Maybe A))               → Tm A
  Let  : (t : Tm A) (u : Tm (Maybe A))   → Tm A
```

There are three points to look at. The `Tm` type is parameterized by another type called `A`, so we can look at it as a kind of container. Note also that the variable case `V` does not hold a ℕ but an `A`. Last but not least the `ƛ` case holds a term whose parameter is not simply an `A` but a `Maybe A`.

This last point makes the `Tm` type a nested data type, also called a non-regular type. This has the consequence of requiring polymorphic recursion to write recursive functions on such a type.

To understand why this is an adequate representation of λ-terms one has to look a bit more at the meaning of `Maybe`. If types are seen as sets, then `Maybe` takes a set and returns a set with one extra element. So each time we cross a `ƛ`, there is one extra element in the set of allowed variables, exactly capturing the fact we are introducing a variable.

To see the difference with the previous approach, here is the `appTm` λ-term again:

```
appTm : Tm ⊥
appTm = ƛ (ƛ (V (just nothing) · V nothing))
```

Note the use of the empty type ⊥ to state the closedness of the `appTm` term. Stating this kind of properties was impossible to do with the previous approach, without resorting to logical properties on the side.

1.4.3 The `Fin` approach

Another approach already described and used in [1, 7] is to index everything (terms for example) by a bound. This bound is the maximum number of distinct free variables allowed in the value. This rule is enforced in two parts: variables have to be strictly lower than their bound, and the bound is incremented by one when crossing a name abstraction (a λ-abstraction for instance, called `ƛ` here).

The `Fin n` type is used for variables and represents natural numbers strictly lower than `n`. The name `Fin n` comes from the fact that it defines finite sets of size `n`. We call this approach `Fin` for its use of this type. The definition found in AGDA standard library is the following:

```
data Fin : ℕ → Set where
  zero : {n : ℕ} → Fin (suc n)
  suc  : {n : ℕ} (i : Fin n) → Fin (suc n)
```

Given this Fin type, one can define the Tm data type using this approach:

```
data Tm n : Set where
  V    : (x : Fin n)                    → Tm n
  _·_  : (t u : Tm n)                   → Tm n
  ƛ    : (t : Tm (suc n))               → Tm n
  Let  : (t : Tm n) (u : Tm (suc n))    → Tm n
```

As the previous approach, this representation helps enforcing some wellformedness properties, for instance Tm 0 is the type of closed λ-terms.

Here is the appTm λ-term in this approach:

```
appTm : Tm 0
appTm = ƛ (ƛ (V (suc zero) · V zero))
```

We can easily draw a link with the Maybe approach. Indeed, the Fin (suc n) type has exactly one more element than the Fin n type. Although they are not equivalent for at least two reasons. The Maybe approach can accept any type to represent variables. This makes the structure more like a container and this can be particularly helpful to define the substitution as the composition of mapTm : ∀{A B} → (A → B) → Tm A → Tm B and joinTm : ∀{A} → Tm (Tm A) → Tm A as in [2, 5]. The Fin approach has advantages as well, the representation is concrete and simpler since closer to the bare approach. However this apparent simplicity comes at a cost, we will see that its concrete representation is one root of the problem.

2. NaPa, a safer nameless representation

2.1 Motivation

While these nameless approaches easily guarantee wellformedness of terms, nothing is said about functions manipulating terms. How are the inputs of a function related to its output? What should a function be able to do given unknown free variables? We claim that free variables should be kept abstract. More precisely a function f operating on terms should commute with a renaming Φ of free variables, namely $f \circ \Phi = \Phi \circ f$. By renaming we mean a permutation of the free variables (more precisely an injective function). In fact this is a bit more flexible, depending on the type of the function f this property will be enforced or not, as we will see in section 4.5.

The goal is to catch some programming errors by having finer types for the manipulated values and for the functions manipulating values. We will show later that this is not a restriction by itself since the types do not force the programmer to be precise everywhere.

One common kind of programming error with these nameless representations is to forget to shift the free variables here and there. While these errors are already caught by the Maybe and the Fin approaches, in these approaches the programmer is provided with means to workaround the type error. In complex situations making the distinction between a valid coercion and a wrong one can be challenging. With finer types, the mistakes will result in more informative type errors.

2.2 A data definition kit

The three previous approaches are closely related. Just a few details change each time. We can capture all of them with a single abstraction: a triple (World, Name, _↑1) where World is the index of types like Tm, Name is the type for names (indexed by worlds) as used in the V constructor, and finally _↑1 is an operation to shift a world by one as used in the ƛ constructor.

In Agda, this triple can be defined with a record type named DataKit. This type is made universe polymorphic to accept the nested data types approach.

```
record DataKit {ℓ} : Set (suc ℓ) where
  constructor ⟨_,_,_⟩
  field
    World : Set ℓ
    Name  : World → Set
    _↑1   : World → World
```

The three previous approaches are summed up in figure 1 by defining their DataKit. Note that for the bare approach the index type is the unit type. In the Maybe approach the index type is Set and the type for names is directly the index so we use the identity function.

```
bareKit   : DataKit
bareKit   = ⟨ ⊤ , λ _ → ℕ , id ⟩

maybeKit  : DataKit
maybeKit  = ⟨ Set , id , Maybe ⟩

finKit    : DataKit
finKit    = ⟨ ℕ , Fin , suc ⟩
```

Figure 1. DataKits for the three previous approaches

We can now give a single definition of Tm generalizing the three previous ones. To this end, we simply take a DataKit as argument and use it to define the type Tm.

```
module DataTm {ℓ} (kit : DataKit {ℓ}) where
  open DataKit kit
  data Tm α : Set ℓ where
    V    : (x : Name α)                  → Tm α
    _·_  : (t u : Tm α)                  → Tm α
    ƛ    : (t : Tm (α ↑1))               → Tm α
    Let  : (t : Tm α) (u : Tm (α ↑1))    → Tm α
```

We claim that nothing more is required from the kit. As complex binding structures can be defined in the original nameless representation (bare), they can also be defined using this kit. In particular having an empty world or making an induction over a world is not necessary.

Translation between data types using different kits can be done modularly as we do in the Agda development. In any direction (any pair of kits k_1 k_2) one can define a function of type ∀ {α_1 α_2} → (Name k_1 α_1 → Name k_2 α_2) → Tm k_1 α_1 → Tm k_2 α_2. This function takes a mapping for free variables and lifts this mapping to terms.

Whereas using these translations is fine in many cases, when going from bare to a more precise representation, an issue arises. Since Agda is a total language, the initial mapping must be a total function. The bare approach ensuring nothing about free variables, one cannot supply the initial mapping to go to a closed term. One has to keep at least one free variable and then dynamically check for occurrences of the free variable in a second transformation.

We will now build on this DataKit abstraction to introduce our own solution.

```
World    : Set
∅        : World
_+1      : World → World
_↑1      : World → World
Name     : World → Set
_⊆_      : World → World → Set

napaKit : DataKit
napaKit = ⟨ World , Name , _↑1 ⟩
```

Figure 2. Core types of NAPA

```
zeroᴺ     : ∀ {α}       → Name (α ↑1)
addᴺ      : ∀ {α} k     → Name α
                        → Name (α +ᵂ k)
subtractᴺ : ∀ {α} k     → Name (α +ᵂ k)
                        → Name α
cmpᴺ      : ∀ {α} ℓ     → Name (α ↑ ℓ)
                        → Name (∅ ↑ ℓ)
                        ⊎ Name (α +ᵂ ℓ)
_==ᴺ_     : ∀ {α} (x y : Name α) → Bool
coerceᴺ   : ∀ {α β}     → α ⊆ β
                        → Name α → Name β
¬Name∅    : ¬(Name ∅)

syntax addᴺ      k x = x +ᴺ k
syntax subtractᴺ k x = x -ᴺ k
syntax cmpᴺ      ℓ x = x <ᴺ ℓ
```

Figure 3. Core operations on names

2.3 NAPA types

We call our approach NAPA as in **Na**meless, **Pa**inless. At the level of types, NAPA exposes the interface shown in figure 2. This is a superset of the `DataKit`, featuring an empty world, a `_+1` operation on worlds described later on, and a notion of world inclusion.

If we look closely at the notion of worlds in the `Fin` approach, we see that it gives us too much information. Indeed a function could look at the given world (by pattern-matching or induction) and behave differently for some values of the world.

On the other hand, `Fin` worlds are too coarse: a single number ℓ is used to represent a set, namely the complete interval $[0..\ell\text{-}1]$.

In NAPA, a world denotes a subset of $\mathbb{N}$ but is kept abstract (no pattern-matching nor induction). Only the empty world $\emptyset$ and two operations are given, namely `_+1` and `_↑1`. Semantically α +1 is defined by $\{x + 1 \mid x \in \alpha\}$ and $\alpha \uparrow 1$ by $\{0\} \cup (\alpha + 1)$.

Internally we represent worlds by lists of Boolean values. Having `true` at the nth position of the list means that n is in the world. Here are the AGDA definitions:

```
World : Set
World = List Bool

∅ : World
∅ = []

_+1 : World → World
α +1 = false :: α

_↑1 : World → World
α ↑1 = true :: α
```

These one step definitions `_+1` and `_↑1` are extended to any number to produce `_+ᵂ_` and `_↑_` of type `World → ℕ → World`.

To the best of our knowledge, making the distinction between two forms of shifting operations for worlds has never been investigated in the context of representing names and binders.

In NAPA the type for names is a refinement of $\mathbb{N}$, kept abstract by not exporting its definition. From a set point of view, inhabitants of `Name` α are members of α. However we want worlds to form static information only and to be able to erase them before running the programs. To do so we will use a pair of a natural number and a proof it belongs to its world. Here is the membership predicate and the record definition for names:

```
_∈_ : ℕ → World → Set
_      ∈ []              = ⊥
zero   ∈ (false :: _)    = ⊥
zero   ∈ (true  :: _)    = ⊤
suc n  ∈ (_     :: xs)   = n ∈ xs

record Name α : Set where
  constructor _,_
  field
    name    : ℕ
    name∈α  : name ∈ α
```

Thanks to our definition of world membership which is canonical, equality of the `name` field implies equality on whole `Name` values. This means we get provable proof-irrelevance for the `Name` type without requiring an additional axiom.

2.4 Operations on names

The core operations on names are given in figure 3. The simplest name is `zeroᴺ`, it represents 0 and lives in any world shifted by one. One can add any constant to a name in any world with `addᴺ`, the resulting world clearly shows that this function (if parametric in α) does exactly its job. One can do the opposite operation with `subtractᴺ`. Thanks to its precise type this function is total and the inverse of `addᴺ`. Figure 4 depict the core operations we have on names. Starting from the bottom, worlds of the form $\emptyset \uparrow$ `k` are names which are definitely bound. There value is completely known as stated by arrows with the `Fin k` type. Above we have names that may be bound or free (`Name` $(\alpha \uparrow$ `k`$)$), a dynamic test (`cmpᴺ`) can tell whether it is bound or not. Above we have names that are known to be greater than `k` (`Name` $(\alpha$ `+ᵂ k`$)$), apart from that they are free names. Above we have free names (`Name` α). On the top we have impossible names since they are said to belong to an empty world. From them we can derive everything.

Given any world α, a name in the world $\alpha \uparrow \ell$ is either strictly lower than ℓ (and so also lives in $\emptyset \uparrow \ell$), or greater or equal to ℓ (thus also lives in α `+ᵂ` ℓ). This is exactly what the `cmpᴺ` function is about. Given a name, it returns a disjoint sum of names which can be read in two parts. It first gives which side of the disjoint sum it stands, and second it gives a refined version of the input name.

The `coerceᴺ` function will be described in length in the next sub-section. The only way left to extract information from a name in an arbitrary world is to compare it with another name for equality

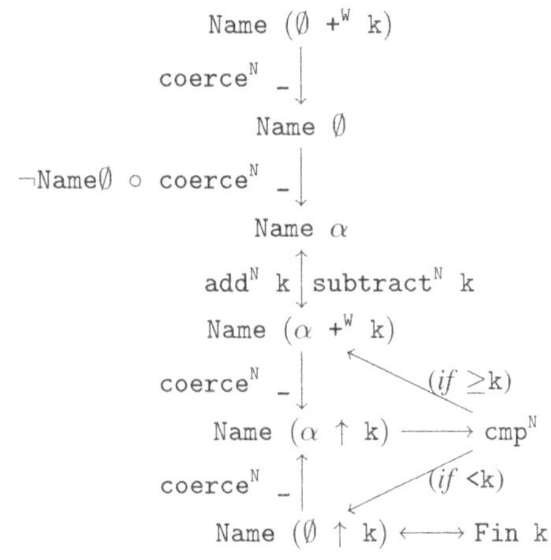

Figure 4. Operations on names

with `_==N_`. Finally ¬Name∅ asserts that no name lives in the empty world. In a total language this is of great use to tackle impossible cases.

These primitives are enough to show an isomorphism between `Fin n` and `Name (∅ ↑ n)`. From this, every program involving `Fin` can be translated into our system. This means that our system does not restrict the programmer more than the `Fin` approach. However as soon as one uses finer types than `Name (∅ ↑ n)`, then fewer "wrong programs" type-check and more properties hold as we will see later.

2.5 A type for world inclusion witnesses

Having finer types also implies being able to give more types to the same value. Then cheaply moving from different types is a must. We call a function which has an output type different from the input type and behaves as the identity a coercion. To capture a great deal of coercions from a world α to a world β we focus on the case where α is included in β. In NAPA a type `_⊆_` is introduced to witness the inclusion between two worlds. Then the `coerce`N function turns a $\alpha \subseteq \beta$ into an identity function of type `Name α → Name β`. Here is the `coerce`N function and its alias `_⟨-because_-⟩` which is useful to keep the code separated from the typing/proof, in particular what is between the angle brackets can be safely skipped.

```
coerceN : ∀ {α β} → α ⊆ β → Name α → Name β
coerceN α⊆β (x , x∈α) = (x , ⊆-sound α⊆β x x∈α)

infix 0 _⟨-because_-⟩
_⟨-because_-⟩ : ∀{α β}→ Name α → α ⊆ β → Name β
_⟨-because_-⟩ n pf = coerceN pf n
```

The inclusion relation also expresses the emptiness of a world α by using $\alpha \subseteq \emptyset$. We use this definition of emptiness as opposed to an equality with the empty world for two reasons. First $\emptyset$ is not the only empty world ($\emptyset$ `+1` is empty as well). Second having world equalities would require new definitions and would be heavy in comparison to the use of inclusions. Combining `coerce`N and ¬Name∅ turns any contradiction on names into an inclusion problem, reusing any automation done on this side.

```
¬Name : ∀ {α} → α ⊆ ∅ → ¬(Name α)
¬Name α⊆∅ = ¬Name∅ ∘ coerceN α⊆∅
```

```
⊆-refl    : ∀{α}→ α ⊆ α
⊆-trans   : ∀{α β γ}→ α ⊆ β → β ⊆ γ → α ⊆ γ
⊆-∅       : ∀{α}→ ∅ ⊆ α
⊆-∅+1     : ∅ +1 ⊆ ∅
⊆-↑1-↑1   : ∀{α β}→ α ⊆ β ↔ α ↑1 ⊆ β ↑1
⊆-+1-+1   : ∀{α β}→ α ⊆ β ↔ α +1 ⊆ β +1
⊆-+1-↑1   : ∀{α}→ α +1 ⊆ α ↑1
```

Figure 5. Rules for world inclusion

We expose the inclusion relation with a set of rules given in figure 5. This states that the inclusion relation is reflexive, transitive, and has the empty world as lowest element. The `⊆-∅+1` rule states that ∅ `+1` is empty. The inclusion is preserved both ways by the contexts `_↑1` and `_+1`. Finally `_+1` can be weakened in `_↑1`. This accounts for the fact that α `↑1` means `{0}` ∪ (α `+1`) and so is a superset of α `+1`. This set of rules has been shown sound according to a semantic definition of inclusion, namely ∀ `x` → `x` ∈ α → `x` ∈ β. On top of these base rules, we derived others that we omit to define here but some are used in the code.

Sometimes one has to build complex inclusion witnesses. While inference would be of great effect here, we propose a modest syntactic tool to build them, namely the `⊆-Reasoning` module. It gives access to the transitivity `⊆-trans` in a style which focuses more on the intermediate states of the reasoning rather than the steps. The syntax is a list of worlds interleaved by inclusion witnesses, with two ■ around the last world. There is one example of its use in the following section. The code for `⊆-Reasoning` is given below for reference and can be safely skipped.

```
module ⊆-Reasoning where
  infix  2 finally
  infixr 2 _⊆⟨_⟩_

  _⊆⟨_⟩_ : ∀ x {y z} → x ⊆ y → y ⊆ z → x ⊆ z
  _ ⊆⟨ x⊆y ⟩ y⊆z = ⊆-trans x⊆y y⊆z

  finally : ∀ x y → x ⊆ y → x ⊆ y
  finally _ _ x⊆y = x⊆y

  syntax finally x y x⊆y = x ⊆⟨ x⊆y ⟩■ y ■
```

2.6 Singleton worlds!

We said that our worlds denote finite subsets of $\mathbb{N}$ and are more precise than in the `Fin` approach. Actually they can be as precise as we wish, since any subset of $\mathbb{N}$ can be described by our operations on worlds (∅, `_+1`, and `_↑1`). In particular they can be singleton worlds. From singleton worlds we build singleton types for names:

```
World^s : ℕ → World
World^s n = ∅ ↑1 +^W n

Name^s : ℕ → Set
Name^s = Name ∘ World^s

_^s : ∀ n → Name^s n
_^s n = zero^N +^N n
```

Singleton worlds not only exist, they are also preserved by our two updating operations, namely add^{N} and subtract^{N}.

```
add^s : ∀ {n} k → Name^s n → Name^s (k +ℕ n)
add^s {n} k x = add^N k x
  ⟨-because ⊆-assoc-+ ⊆-refl n k -⟩

subtract^s : ∀ {n} k → Name^s (k +ℕ n) → Name^s n
subtract^s {n} k x = subtract^N k x
  ⟨-because ⊆-assoc-+′ ⊆-refl n k -⟩
```

3. Using NAPA: examples and advanced operations

3.1 Some convenience functions

Here are a few functions built on top of the interface (without using the concrete representation of names). suc^{N} is add^{N} 1 and suc^{N}↑ is a variant that includes a coercion from α +1 to α ↑1. The function _^{N} turns a number n into a name that inhabits any world with at least n+1 consecutive binders.

```
suc^N : ∀ {α} → Name α → Name (α +1)
suc^N = add^N 1

suc^N↑ : ∀ {α} → Name α → Name (α ↑1)
suc^N↑ = coerce^N ⊆-+1↑1 ∘ suc^N

_^N : ∀ {α} n → Name (α ↑ suc n)
_^N {α} n = zero^N +^N n
  ⟨-because α ↑1 +^W n ⊆⟨ ⊆-+-↑ n ⟩
            α ↑1 ↑  n ⊆⟨ ⊆-exch-↑-↑ 1 n ⟩∎
            α ↑ suc n ∎ -⟩
  where open ⊆-Reasoning
```

We call ℓ-bound, a name bound somewhere in the scope of ℓ binders. We call ℓ-free, a name free for all ℓ binders. In other words, a de Bruijn index is ℓ-bound if it is strictly less than ℓ; it is ℓ-free otherwise.

The exportName function tells whether a given name is ℓ-bound or ℓ-free. In case the name is free, an exported version of it is returned. This function forms the base case of exporting functions like exportTm explained later on.

```
-- Partial functions from A to B
A →? B = A → Maybe B

exportName : ∀ {α} ℓ →  Name (α ↑ ℓ)
                     →? Name α
exportName ℓ x
  with x <^N ℓ
...  | inj₁ _  = nothing
...  | inj₂ x′ = just (x′ -^N ℓ)
```

The function shiftName ℓ k pf shifts its argument by k if this name is ℓ-free, otherwise it leaves the ℓ-bound name untouched. This function makes use of cmp^{N} and coerces the outputs to the required type. It also perform a coercion on the fly, giving extra flexibility for free.

```
shiftName : ∀ {α} ℓ k → (α +^W k) ⊆ β
                      → Name (α ↑ ℓ)
                      → Name (β ↑ ℓ)
shiftName ℓ k pf x
 with x <^N ℓ
... | inj₁ x′ = x′
              ⟨-because pf₁ -⟩
... | inj₂ x′ = x′ +^N k
              ⟨-because pf₂ -⟩
  where
  pf₁ = ⊆-cong-↑ ⊆-∅ ℓ
  pf₂ = ⊆-trans (⊆-exch-+-+ ⊆-refl ℓ k)
                (⊆-ctx-+↑ pf ℓ)
```

The protect↑ function shifts a name transformer. Let f be a function from names to names. The function protect↑ ℓ f is a version of f that is applicable under ℓ binders. Let x be a name under ℓ binders. When x is ℓ-bound, it is left untouched by protect↑. When x is ℓ-free, we can subtract ℓ to x, give it to f, and then add ℓ to get the result. By combining protect↑ and add^{N} one obtain an alternative implementation of shiftName called shiftName′. However shiftName is more efficient since it avoids to subtracting ℓ to add it back after adding k.

```
protect↑ : ∀ {α β} ℓ
           → (Name α → Name β)
           → (Name (α ↑ ℓ) → Name (β ↑ ℓ))
protect↑ ℓ f x
 with x <^N ℓ
... | inj₁ x′ = x′
              ⟨-because ⊆-cong-↑ ⊆-∅ ℓ -⟩
... | inj₂ x′ = f (x′ -^N ℓ) +^N ℓ
              ⟨-because ⊆-+-↑ ℓ -⟩

shiftName′ : ∀ {α β} ℓ k → (α +^W k) ⊆ β
             → Name (α ↑ ℓ) → Name (β ↑ ℓ)
shiftName′ ℓ k pf = protect↑ (coerce^N pf ∘ add^N k) ℓ
```

3.2 Building terms

Building terms in NAPA is as easy as building them in the other nameless approaches we have seen. The structure is exactly the same, and the variables are made of numbers (of type ℕ) using _^{N}. Below we define the representation of the identity function as idTm, the application operator as appTm and finally the composition function as compTm:

```
idTm : ∀ {α} → Tm α
idTm = ƛ(V (0 ^N))

appTm : ∀ {α} → Tm α
appTm = ƛ(ƛ(V (1 ^N) · V (0 ^N)))

compTm : ∀ {α} → Tm α
compTm = ƛ(ƛ(ƛ(V (2 ^N)) · (V (1 ^N) · V (0 ^N)))))
```

3.3 Computing free variables

Our first example of functions over terms simply computes the list of free variables in the input term. The `fv` function below, while straightforward, has the subtle cases of binding constructs (`ƛ` and `Let`). In these cases we have to remove the bound variable from the list of free variables given by the recursive call. In this nameless representation this amounts to removing occurrences of 0 and subtract 1 to other name occurrences. This is done by the function `rm₀| which calls {agda|exportName 1` on each element of the list and merges the results. Note that forgetting to remove the bound variable will result in a type error. In the same vein the typing of `fv` ensures that all returned variables do appear free in the given term.

```
rm₀ : ∀ {α} → List (Name (α ↑1))
           → List (Name α)
rm₀ [] = []
rm₀ (x :: xs) with exportName 1 x
...                | just x'  = x' :: rm₀ xs
...                | nothing  = rm₀ xs

fv : ∀ {α} → Tm α → List (Name α)
fv (V x)          = [ x ]
fv (fct · arg)    = fv fct ++ fv arg
fv (ƛ t)          = rm₀ (fv t)
fv (Let t u)      = fv t ++ rm₀ (fv u)
```

3.4 Generic traversal

In order to build multiple traversal functions at once, we first define a generic function based on ideas from [8]. It is essentially a map/subst function where the free variables are transformed by a user-supplied function. Moreover a class of effects (an applicative functor) is allowed during the traversal. An applicative functor is halfway between a functor and a monad. Like a monad, an applicative functor has a unit called `pure`. It allows to embed any pure value as a potentially effectful one. The second operation called `_⊛_` is an effectful application, taking both an effectful function and argument and resulting in an effectful result.

```
module TraverseTm
          {E}    (E-app  : Applicative E)
          {α β} (trName : ∀ ℓ → Name (α ↑ ℓ)
                                  → E (Tm (β ↑ ℓ)))
  where
  open Applicative E-app

  tr : ∀ ℓ → Tm (α ↑ ℓ) → E (Tm (β ↑ ℓ))
  tr ℓ (V x)       = trName ℓ x
  tr ℓ (t · u)     = pure _·_ ⊛ tr ℓ t ⊛ tr ℓ u
  tr ℓ (ƛ t)       = pure ƛ   ⊛ tr (suc ℓ) t
  tr ℓ (Let t u) = pure Let ⊛ tr ℓ t
                             ⊛ tr (suc ℓ) u

  trTm : Tm α → E (Tm β)
  trTm = tr 0
```

To put this traversal at work we successively instantiate some of its arguments. For instance you may have noticed the special case we made for variables. Mapping names to terms will bring us capture avoiding substitution almost for free. However, in the mean time we build `trTm′` which maps names to names. It does so by applying `pure V` to the name to name function:

```
open TraverseTm

trTm′ :
  ∀ {E} (E-app : Applicative E) {α β}
    (trName : ∀ ℓ → Name (α ↑ ℓ)
                    → E (Name (β ↑ ℓ)))
  → Tm α → E (Tm β)
trTm′ E-app trName
  = trTm E-app (λ ℓ x → pure V ⊛ trName ℓ x)
    where open Applicative E-app
```

Renaming functions In many functions over terms the handling of variables shares a common part. Given a variable under ℓ binders, we test if the variable is ℓ-bound. If so we leave it untouched, otherwise we subtract ℓ and go on a specific processing after which we add ℓ again to the free variables of the result. The traversal function is augmented by this processing of bound variables to build `renameTmA`. Then by picking either the identity functor (`id-app`), or the `Maybe` one we build two functions (a total and a partial one) to perform renamings, namely `renameTm` and `renameTm?`:

```
renameTmA : ∀ {E} (E-app : Applicative E)
              {α β} (θ : Name α → E (Name β))
           → Tm α → E (Tm β)
renameTmA E-app θ
  = trTm′ E-app (protect↑A E-app θ)
```

```
renameTm : ∀ {α β} → (Name α → Name β)
                   → Tm α → Tm β
renameTm θ = trTm′ id-app (protect↑ θ)
-- or
-- renameTm = renameTmA id-app
```

```
renameTm? : ∀ {α β} → (Name α →? Name β)
                    → Tm α →? Tm β
renameTm? = renameTmA Maybe.applicative
```

Lifting name functions Any operation on names can now be lifted to terms:

```
addTm : ∀ {α} k → Tm α → Tm (α +ᵂ k)
addTm = renameTm ∘ addᴺ

subtractTm : ∀ {α} k → Tm (α +ᵂ k) → Tm α
subtractTm = renameTm ∘ subtractᴺ

exportTm? : ∀ {α} ℓ → Tm (α ↑ ℓ) →? Tm α
exportTm? = renameTm? ∘ exportName
```

While `coerceᴺ` can be lifted to terms in the same way, using `trTm′` directly enables to by-pass the `protect↑` dynamic tests and directly "protect" the inclusion witness with an appropriate inclusion rule.

```
coerceTm : ∀ {α β} → α ⊆ β → Tm α → Tm β
coerceTm pf = trTm′ id-app (coerceᴺ ∘ ⊆-cong-↑ pf)
-- or less efficiently:
-- coerceTm = renameTm ∘ coerceᴺ
```

Lifting add^N to terms can be done more efficiently (than using protect↑) as well. Here the dynamic test performed by protect↑ is necessary. However when the name is ℓ-free we subtract ℓ to add it back after adding k. The function shiftName avoids this extra computation, hence the following shiftTm:

```
shiftTm : ∀ {α β} k → (α +ᵂ k)⊆ β → Tm α → Tm β
shiftTm k p = trTm′ id-app (λ ℓ → shiftName ℓ k p)
-- or less efficiently:
-- shiftTm k pf = renameTm (coerceᴺ pf ∘ addᴺ k)
```

A special case of renameTm? is the so-called closeTm?. This function takes a term in any world and checks if the term is closed. If so, the same term is returned in the empty world. Otherwise the function fails by returning nothing:

```
closeTm? : ∀ {α} → Tm α →? Tm ∅
closeTm? = renameTm? (const nothing)
```

Capture avoiding substitution To implement capture avoiding substitution for the Tm type we solely need a specific trName function for trTm. Here substitutions are represented as functions from names to terms. The function substVarTm handles the case for variables. This function is very close to protect↑ but extended to functions returning terms.

```
substVarTm : ∀{α β} → (Name α → Tm β) →
             ∀ ℓ → Name (α ↑ ℓ) → Tm (β ↑ ℓ)
substVarTm f ℓ x
 with x <ᴺ ℓ
... | inj₁ x′ = V (x′
                ⟨-because ⊆-cong-↑ ⊆-∅ ℓ -⟩)
... | inj₂ x′ = shiftTm ℓ (⊆-+-↑ ℓ) (f (x′ -ᴺ ℓ))
```

The main function substTm instantiates trTm with the identity applicative functor and substVarTm:

```
substTm : ∀ {α β} → (Name α → Tm β)
                  → Tm α → Tm β
substTm = trTm id-app ∘ substVarTm
```

As an illustration, the function β-red takes the body of a λ-abstraction and calls substTm with the substitution that replaces 0 with a received replacement term:

```
β-red : ∀ {α} → Tm (α ↑1) → Tm α → Tm α
β-red {α} f a = substTm (ϕ ∘ exportName 1) f
  where ϕ : Maybe (Name α) → Tm α
        ϕ (just x) = V x
        ϕ nothing  = a
```

3.5 Deciding term α-equivalence

Our next example focuses on comparison of terms. We first define αEq, where αEq F is the type of functions comparing F structures.

```
αEq : (F : World → Set) (α β : World) → Set
αEq F α β = F α → F β → Bool
```

We show that all the subtle work is done at the level of names in a separate and reusable function called αeqName. This function takes a function that compares two free names and builds one that compares two names under ℓ bindings. It does so by comparing both of them to ℓ. If they are both bound they can be safely compared using $\_==^N\_$ since they now are of the same type. If they are both free, they can be compared using the function received as argument. Otherwise they are different.

```
αeqName : ∀ {α β} ℓ → αEq Name α β
                    → αEq Name (α ↑ ℓ) (β ↑ ℓ)
αeqName ℓ Γ x y with x <ᴺ ℓ | y <ᴺ ℓ
... | inj₁ x′ | inj₁ y′  = x′ ==ᴺ y′
... | inj₂ x′ | inj₂ y′  = Γ (x′ -ᴺ ℓ) (y′ -ᴺ ℓ)
... | _       | _        = false
```

The αeqTm function structurally compares two terms in a simple way, only keeping track of the number of traversed binders and calling αeqName at variables.

```
αeqTm : ∀ {α β} → αEq Name α β → αEq Tm α β
αeqTm {α} {β} Γ = go 0 where
  go : ∀ ℓ → αEq Tm (α ↑ ℓ) (β ↑ ℓ)
  go ℓ (V x)       (V y)       = αeqName ℓ Γ x y
  go ℓ (t · u)     (v · w)     = go ℓ t v ∧ go ℓ u w
  go ℓ (ƛ t)       (ƛ u)       = go (suc ℓ) t u
  go ℓ (Let t u)   (Let v w)   = go ℓ t v
                               ∧ go (suc ℓ) u w
  go _ _ _                     = false
```

4. Soundness using logical relations

Since our library is written in a type-safe language, one may wonder what soundness properties are to be proved. Moreover our names are indexed by worlds and hold membership proofs. The functions over names are given precise types and have been shown to be type-safe. However we still wish to show that our library respects a model of good behavior with respect to names and binders. Our model is based on logical relations indexed/directed by types. This technique [4] is independent of this work and enables to define a notion of program equivalence. We use this technique to capture good behavior of functions involving names and binders. Using this technique, the set of specific definitions is kept to a minimum of one per introduced type (World, Name, and $\_\subseteq\_$). One proof per value introduced has to be done, which keeps the development modular and forward-compatible to the addition of more features.

This section is organized as follows. First we recall the basics of logical relations. Then we give a toy example to practice a bit. Then relations for worlds, names, and world inclusions are given. Finally we make use of the construction to obtain free theorems [12] about world-polymorphic functions over the Tm type.

4.1 Recap of the framework

A relation is said to be type-directed when it is recursively defined on the structure of types. Let $\mathcal{R}$ be such a type-directed relation, and let τ be a type. Then, $\mathcal{R}\tau$ is a relation on values of type τ, namely $\mathcal{R}\tau : \tau \to \tau \to$ Set. Recall that Set is also the type of propositions in AGDA.

A type-directed relation is called "logical" when the case for functions is defined extensionally. Here extensionally means that two functions are related when they produce related results out of related arguments. Let A_r be a relation for the arguments and B_r a relation for results. Two functions f_1 and f_2 are related if and only if for every pair of arguments (x_1, x_2) related by A_r, the results $f_1\ x_1$ and $f_2\ x_2$ are related by B_r. This definition can be given in AGDA as well:

```
RelatedFunctions Aᵣ Bᵣ f₁ f₂ =
          ∀ {x₁ x₂} → Aᵣ x₁ x₂
                    → Bᵣ (f₁ x₁) (f₂ x₂)
```

We say that a program or a value fits a logical relation when it is related to itself by the relation indexed by its type. We say that a logical relation is universal if every well-typed program fits the logical relation. This notion of universality was originally coined by John Reynolds as the "Abstraction Theorem" [11]. We call the "AGDA logical relation" the one defined by Bernardy et al. [4] for a $\mathcal{PTS}$ (pure type system) and naturally extended as they suggest to other features of AGDA. While no complete mechanized proof has been done for this we will consider the AGDA logical relation as universal.

To simplify matters, the definitions shown here are not universe polymorphic. You can find universe-polymorphic definitions in our complete AGDA development [9].

To formally define a logical relation indexed by types, a common technique is to first inductively define the structure of types. This is known as a "universe of codes" U. Then one defines a function called El from codes to types. Finally one defines by induction a function called ⟦_⟧ from codes to relations on elements of type described by the given code. In AGDA the ⟦_⟧ function has the following type: (τ : U) → El τ → El τ → Set. Because, when types contain variables, a good deal of complexity is added to this scheme, we opt for a lighter scheme. We do not define U, El, and ⟦_⟧.

Instead, for each type constructor κ, we define a relation ⟦κ⟧ For the function type constructor the RelatedFunctions definition above is a good start. Actually this is a fine definition for non-dependent functions. The dependent version of RelatedFunctions, called ⟦Π⟧ here, passes the relation argument A_r x_1 x_2 called x_r to the relation for results B_r. In short the relation for results now depends on the relation for arguments. Here is the definition in AGDA:

```
⟦Π⟧ Aᵣ Bᵣ f₁ f₂ = ∀ {x₁ x₂} (xᵣ : Aᵣ x₁ x₂)
                     → Bᵣ xᵣ (f₁ x₁) (f₂ x₂)
```

Note that this definition generalizes the case of non-dependent functions and universal quantifications as well. For non-dependent functions we simply provide a relation for results which ignores its first argument (equivalent to RelatedFunctions and noted _⟦→⟧_ from now on). For universal quantifications, since the arguments are types, all we need is a relation for types (members of $\mathtt{Set}_0$) themselves. Following our convention we call this relation ⟦$\mathtt{Set}_0$⟧, its definition is the set of relations between its arguments:

```
⟦Set₀⟧ : Set₀ → Set₀ → Set₁
⟦Set₀⟧ A₁ A₂ = A₁ → A₂ → Set₀
```

For reference, full definitions for core type theory are given in figure 6. We now have all the building blocks of the meta-function ⟦_⟧ and we will not materialize it more here. We will apply the ⟦_⟧ function manually. To this end it suffices to replace each constructor κ by ⟦κ⟧, each non dependent arrow by ⟦→⟧, each dependent arrow (x : A) → B by ⟨ x_r : ⟦ A ⟧ ⟩⟦→⟧ ⟦ B ⟧. By convention we subscript the variables by r. Applications are translated to applications. Because of dependent types, this translation has to be extended to all terms but we will not do it here. Finally here are a few examples of the manual use of the ⟦_⟧ function:

```
⟦ ℕ → ℕ → Bool ⟧ =
⟦ℕ⟧ ⟦→⟧ ⟦ℕ⟧ ⟦→⟧ ⟦Bool⟧ =
λ f₁ f₂ →
  ∀ {x₁ x₂} (xᵣ : ⟦ℕ⟧ x₁ x₂)
    {y₁ y₂} (yᵣ : ⟦ℕ⟧ y₁ y₂)
  → ⟦Bool⟧ (f₁ x₁ y₁) (f₂ x₂ y₂)
```

```
data ⟦⊥⟧ : ⟦Set₀⟧ ⊥ ⊥ -- no constructors

data ⟦Bool⟧ : ⟦Set₀⟧ Bool Bool where
  ⟦true⟧  : ⟦Bool⟧ true  true
  ⟦false⟧ : ⟦Bool⟧ false false

data ⟦ℕ⟧ : ⟦Set₀⟧ ℕ ℕ where
  ⟦zero⟧ : ⟦ℕ⟧                  zero zero
  ⟦suc⟧  : (⟦ℕ⟧ ⟦→⟧ ⟦ℕ⟧) suc  suc

data _⟦⊎⟧_ {A₁ A₂ B₁ B₂} (Aᵣ : ⟦Set₀⟧ A₁ A₂)
                        (Bᵣ : ⟦Set₀⟧ B₁ B₂) :
           A₁ ⊎ B₁ → A₂ ⊎ B₂ → Set₀ where
  ⟦inj₁⟧ : (Aᵣ → Aᵣ ⟦⊎⟧ Bᵣ) inj₁ inj₁
  ⟦inj₂⟧ : (Bᵣ → Aᵣ ⟦⊎⟧ Bᵣ) inj₂ inj₂
```

Figure 7. Logical relations for data types

```
⟦ (A : Set₀) → A → A ⟧ =
⟦Π⟧ ⟦Set₀⟧ (λ Aᵣ → Aᵣ ⟦→⟧ Aᵣ) =
λ f₁ f₂ →
  ∀ {A₁ A₂} (Aᵣ : A₁ → A₂ → Set₀)
    {x₁ x₂} (xᵣ : Aᵣ x₁ x₂)
  → Aᵣ (f₁ A₁ x₁) (f₂ A₂ x₂)
```

```
-- Using the notation instead of ⟦Π⟧:
⟦ (A : Set₀) → List A ⟧ =
⟨ Aᵣ : ⟦Set₀⟧ ⟩⟦→⟧ ⟦List⟧ Aᵣ =
λ l₁ l₂ →
  ∀ {A₁ A₂} (Aᵣ : A₁ → A₂ → Set₀)
  → ⟦List⟧ Aᵣ (l₁ A₁) (l₂ A₂)
```

We now have the definition of the AGDA logical relation for the core type theory part. It extends nicely to inductive data types and records. The process is as follows: for each constructor κ of type τ, declare a new constructor ⟦κ⟧ whose type is ⟦ τ ⟧ κ κ. This process applies to type constructors and data constructors of data types, and type constructors and fields of record types. For reference, the logical relations for data types we use in this development are in figure 7.

4.2 An example: booleans represented by numbers

We wish to explain how logical relations can help build a safe interface to an abstract type. To do so we introduce a tiny example about booleans represented using natural numbers. We want 0 to represent false and any other number to represent true. Therefore the boolean disjunction can be implemented using addition. We show that logical relations help build a model, ensure that a given implementation respects this model, and finally show that a client that uses only the interface will also respect the model.

Note however that this is a toy example in several ways. There are no polymorphic functions in the interface, so no interesting free theorems are to be expected. While we could prove the safety by defining a representation predicate in unary style, the logical relations approach is different. It relies on comparing concrete data as opposed to mapping to abstract data. The unary construction would allow for a simpler construction, however this oversimplifies the problem here and would be no longer useful for proving NAPA.

Our tiny implementation of booleans using natural numbers is given below. It contains a type B that we want to keep abstract. It contains obvious definitions for true, false, and the disjunction

```
⟦Set₀⟧ : ∀ (A₁ A₂ : Set₀) → Set₁
⟦Set₀⟧ A₁ A₂ = A₁ → A₂ → Set₀

⟦Set₁⟧ : ∀ (A₁ A₂ : Set₁) → Set₂
⟦Set₁⟧ A₁ A₂ = A₁ → A₂ → Set₁

_⟦→⟧_ : ∀ {A₁ A₂ B₁ B₂} → ⟦Set₀⟧ A₁ A₂ → ⟦Set₀⟧ B₁ B₂ → ⟦Set₀⟧ (A₁ → B₁) (A₂ → B₂)
Aᵣ ⟦→⟧ Bᵣ = λ f₁ f₂ → ∀ {x₁ x₂} → Aᵣ x₁ x₂ → Bᵣ (f₁ x₁) (f₂ x₂)

infixr 0 _⟦→⟧_

⟦Π⟧ : ∀ {A₁ A₂} (Aᵣ : ⟦Set₀⟧ A₁ A₂)
        {B₁ B₂} (Bᵣ : (Aᵣ ⟦→⟧ ⟦Set₀⟧) B₁ B₂)
      → ((x : A₁) → B₁ x) → ((x : A₂) → B₂ x) → Set₁
⟦Π⟧ Aᵣ Bᵣ = λ f₁ f₂ → ∀ {x₁ x₂} (xᵣ : Aᵣ x₁ x₂) → Bᵣ xᵣ (f₁ x₁) (f₂ x₂)

syntax ⟦Π⟧ Aᵣ (λ xᵣ → f) = ⟨ xᵣ : Aᵣ ⟩⟦→⟧ f

⟦∀⟧ : ∀ {A₁ A₂} (Aᵣ : ⟦Set₀⟧ A₁ A₂)
        {B₁ B₂} (Bᵣ : (⟦Set₀⟧ ⟦→⟧ ⟦Set₀⟧) B₁ B₂)
      → ⟦Set₁⟧ ({x : A₁} → B₁ x) ({x : A₂} → B₂ x)
⟦∀⟧ Aᵣ Bᵣ = λ f₁ f₂ → ∀ {x₁ x₂} (xᵣ : Aᵣ x₁ x₂) → Bᵣ xᵣ (f₁ {x₁}) (f₂ {x₂})

syntax ⟦∀⟧ Aᵣ (λ xᵣ → f) = ∀⟨ xᵣ : Aᵣ ⟩⟦→⟧ f
```

Figure 6. Logical relations for core types

_∨_. It intentionally has a dubious function is42? which breaks our still informal expectations from such a module.

```
B : Set
B = ℕ

false : B
false = 0

true : B
true = 1


_∨_ : B → B → B
m ∨ n = m + n


is42? : B → B
is42? 42 = true
is42? _  = false
```

The next step is to define our expectations. To do so, we give a binary relation which tells when two B values have the same meaning. We do so with an (inductive) data type named ⟦B⟧ which states that 0 is related only with itself, and that any two non zero numbers are related:

```
data ⟦B⟧ : B → B → Set where
  ⟦false⟧ : ⟦B⟧ 0 0
  ⟦true⟧  : ∀ {m n} → ⟦B⟧ (suc m) (suc n)
```

When plugged into the machinery of logical relations this single definition suffices to define a complete model of well-typed programs. However, the plumbing requires some care. While the AGDA logical relation is universal, we have no such guarantee about the AGDA logical relation where the relation for B is no longer ⟦ℕ⟧ but ⟦B⟧. Fortunately changing the relation at a given type (B here) can be done safely. All we have to do is to consider programs abstracted away from B and its operations: true, false and _∨_. This can be done either through a mechanism for abstract types, or by requiring the client to be a function taking the implementation for B and its operations as argument.

However to use ⟦B⟧ as the relation for B, we have to show that the definitions which make use of the representation of B actually fit the relation. Since ⟦true⟧ and ⟦false⟧ are obvious witnesses for true and false, only _∨_ and is42? are left to be proved. Each time the goal to prove is mechanical: wrap the type with ⟦·⟧ on each constructor and put the name of the function twice to state we want it to be related to itself. Here is the definition for _⟦∨⟧_:

```
_⟦∨⟧_ : (⟦B⟧ ⟦→⟧ ⟦B⟧ ⟦→⟧ ⟦B⟧) _∨_ _∨_
```

The type of _⟦∨⟧_ means that given inputs related in the model, the results are related in the model as well. Once unfolded the type looks like:

```
_⟦∨⟧_ : ∀ {x₁ x₂} (xᵣ : ⟦B⟧ x₁ x₂)
          {y₁ y₂} (yᵣ : ⟦B⟧ y₁ y₂)
        → ⟦B⟧ (x₁ ∨ y₁) (x₂ ∨ y₂)
```

The fact that input arguments come as implicit arguments will greatly shorten definitions. Now, thanks to the inductive definition of _+_, simply pattern-matching on the first relation suffices to reduce the goal, and allows this nice looking definition where we see the usual lazy definition of the left biased disjunction:

```
⟦false⟧ ⟦∨⟧ x = x
⟦true⟧  ⟦∨⟧ _ = ⟦true⟧
```

Let us now consider a proof for the is42? function. Fortunately there is no such proof since this function gladly breaks the intended abstraction. Instead we simply prove its negation by exhibiting that given two related inputs (42 and 27) we get non related outputs (is42? 42 = 1 and is42? 27 = 0).

```
¬⟦is42?⟧ : ¬((⟦B⟧ ⟦→⟧ ⟦B⟧) is42? is42?)
¬⟦is42?⟧ ⟦is42?⟧ with ⟦is42?⟧ {42} {27} ⟦true⟧
...                  | () -- absurd
```

Note that is42? is rejected by our model with no considerations about the other exported functions. Indeed with another implementation of _∨_ there would be no way to produce 42 and so no way to expose the wrong behavior of is42? using the interface. Using a model provides a better forward compatibility and enables proofs to be done in a modular way.

4.3 Relations for NAPA

For NAPA, we apply the same process as with booleans. We define our expectations, by defining relations for introduced types (worlds, names, and inclusions). Finally we prove that each value/function exported fits the relation.

4.3.1 Relations for NAPA types

Valid names are those which belong to their worlds, names with the same meaning are those related by the relation between their worlds. What matters is not just the fact that two worlds are related, but "how" they are related. Indeed this will dictate when two names are related. We need to define a set of valid relations between worlds. The more relations are accepted, the more power it gives to the free theorems of world-polymorphic functions. However we want the equality test on names to be accepted. Thus we at least need the relation to preserve name equalities across the relation in both directions. We require these relations to be functional and injective:

```
FunctionalAndInjective 𝓡 =
  ∀ x₁ y₁ x₂ y₂ → 𝓡 x₁ x₂ → 𝓡 y₁ y₂
    → x₁ ≡ y₁ ↔ x₂ ≡ y₂
```

The relation ⟦World⟧ between two worlds α_1 and α_2 is the set of functional and injective relations between Name α_1 and Name α_2. Then, two names x (in α_1) and y (in α_2) are related by ⟦Name⟧ α_r if and only if they are related by the α_r relation.

For the _⟦⊆⟧_ relation, we exploit the fact there is only one way to use an inclusion witness, namely coerce^N. Thus, for the purpose of building the model, we identify inclusions with their use in coerce^N. Put differently, whatever the representation for inclusions is, the model takes them as functions from names to names. Yet another way to look at it is from the perspective of relation inclusions. A relation $\mathcal{R}_1$ is included in a relation $\mathcal{R}_2$ if and only if all pairs related by $\mathcal{R}_1$ are related by $\mathcal{R}_2$ as well. The coerce^N function behaving like the identity function all these definitions coincide. For instance if we expand the definitions for ⟦Name⟧ and ⟦→⟧, we get the definition for relation inclusion modulo the coercions:

```
_⟦⊆⟧_ αᵣ βᵣ p₁ p₂
  = ∀ {x₁ x₂} → (x₁ , x₂) ∈ αᵣ
      → (coerceᴺ p₁ x₁ , coerceᴺ p₂ x₂) ∈ βᵣ
```

We now have to define operations on worlds that fit the logical relation. The case for ⟦∅⟧ is trivial. Then α_r ⟦+1⟧ is defined by $\{ (x{+}1, y{+}1) \mid (x, y) \in \alpha_r \}$ and α_r ⟦↑1⟧ is defined by $\{(0,0)\} \cup \alpha_r$ ⟦+1⟧ . We shown that both operations preserve functionality and injectiveness. Here are the signatures that these operations fit the relation:

```
record ⟦World⟧ α₁ α₂ : Set where
  constructor _,_
  field
    𝓡 : Name α₁ → Name α₂ → Set
    𝓡-fun-inj : FunctionalAndInjective 𝓡

⟦Name⟧ : (⟦World⟧ ⟦→⟧ ⟦Set₀⟧) Name Name
⟦Name⟧ (𝓡 , _) x₁ x₂ = 𝓡 x₁ x₂

_⟦⊆⟧_ : (⟦World⟧ ⟦→⟧ ⟦World⟧ ⟦→⟧ ⟦Set₀⟧)
          _⊆_ _⊆_
_⟦⊆⟧_ αᵣ βᵣ α₁⊆β₁ α₂⊆β₂
  = (⟦Name⟧ αᵣ ⟦→⟧ ⟦Name⟧ βᵣ) (coerceᴺ α₁⊆β₁)
                               (coerceᴺ α₂⊆β₂)
```

Figure 8. Relations for NAPA types

```
⟦∅⟧      : ⟦World⟧ ∅ ∅
_⟦+1⟧    : (⟦World⟧ ⟦→⟧ ⟦World⟧) _+1 _+1
_⟦↑1⟧    : (⟦World⟧ ⟦→⟧ ⟦World⟧) _↑1 _↑1
```

4.3.2 NAPA values fit the relation

We now give a short overview of the proofs needed to show that our functions fit the relation. Thanks to the definition of _⟦↑1⟧, zero^N fits the relation by definition. Thanks to the definition of _⟦+1⟧, add^N 1 and subtract^N 1 fit the relation as well. These two are later extended to add^N k and subtract^N k by an induction on k. Since ⟦¬Name∅⟧ receives names in the empty world, it trivially holds. Here is for instance the type signature for ⟦add^N⟧:

```
⟦addᴺ⟧ : (∀⟨ αᵣ : ⟦World⟧    ⟩⟦→⟧
          ⟨ kᵣ : ⟦ℕ⟧         ⟩⟦→⟧
          ⟦Name⟧ αᵣ ⟦→⟧
          ⟦Name⟧ (αᵣ ⟦+ᵂ⟧ kᵣ)) addᴺ addᴺ
```

For _⟦==^{N}⟧_, once unfolded, the statement tells that the equality test commutes with a renaming. This means that the result of the equality test does not change when its inputs are consistently renamed. The proof for _⟦==^{N}⟧_ is done in two parts. First, we have to relate the Boolean-valued function _==^{N}_ to the fact it decides equality on names. Second, we make use of the two properties (functionality and injectiveness) of the relation between the two worlds.

The definition of cmp^N is not a simple induction on its first argument. It calls _<=_ (which does an induction) and returns a Boolean value. Based on this Boolean value, the function cmp^N returns either inj₁ or inj₂ (the constructors of _⊎_) with the same name (with a different proof). To prove _⟦cmp^N⟧_ we show the equivalence with a simpler inductive function and show that this simpler function is in the relation. Thanks to the extensionality of the logical relation, no additional axiom is required to show that cmp^N fits the relation.

Thanks to the definition of _⟦⊆⟧_, the proof that coerce^N fits the relation is a simple application of the hypotheses. Then the real job is to show that all the inclusion rules fit the relation. This means that they all behave as the identity function. All eleven rules stated in figure 5 have been shown to fit the relation.

4.4 On the strength of free theorems

Every well-typed function comes with a free theorem [12]. However depending on the type of the function the strength of the theorem varies a lot. For instance at type `Int` $\rightarrow$ `Bool` it says no more than the function is deterministic. At type $\forall$`{A : Set}` $\rightarrow$ `A` $\rightarrow$ `A` it says that the function behaves like the identity function, which is much stronger. We now give a few elements of what can affect the strength of free theorems in our context. We will continue to use our `Tm` type to represent some data structures with names and binders but it could be any other.

Various term types The weakest type we can give to a value with names and binders is `Tm` $(\emptyset \uparrow \ell)$ for a given ℓ. Such a term can have a statically unknown number of distinct free variables, but we know that these variables are comprised in the interval $[0 .. \ell\text{-}1]$. The free theorem of $\forall\{\ell\} \rightarrow$ `Tm` $(\emptyset \uparrow \ell) \rightarrow$ `Tm` $(\emptyset \uparrow \ell)$ says no more than "the function is deterministic". We also know because of typing that the resulting term cannot have ℓ-free occurrences.

A stronger type is to use any world instead of the empty world, but still have a known amount of bindings. A function of type $\forall\{\alpha\ \ell\} \rightarrow$ `Tm` $(\alpha \uparrow \ell) \rightarrow$ `Tm` $(\alpha \uparrow \ell)$ has a stronger free theorem. It says that the function commutes with a renaming of the variables in the world α (section 4.5). This is a common type to deal with open terms under a partial environment: $\forall\{\alpha\ \ell\} \rightarrow$ `Vec Info` $\ell \rightarrow$ `Tm` $(\alpha \uparrow \ell) \rightarrow$ `Tm` $(\alpha \uparrow \ell)$.

The strongest type for terms is to make no assumptions on their free variables. This can be done by quantifying by an arbitrary world. The free theorem associated with the type $\forall\ \{\alpha\} \rightarrow$ `Tm` $\alpha \rightarrow$ `Tm` α says that the function commutes with renamings of the free variables. This particular type is studied in detail in the section 4.5.

Extra arguments Note that adding extra arguments to a function can drastically affect the strength of its free theorem. An extreme example is the type $\forall\{\alpha\} \rightarrow (\alpha \equiv \emptyset) \rightarrow$ `Tm` $\alpha \rightarrow$ `Tm` α, which is ruined by its $\alpha \equiv \emptyset$ argument. While the above example is extreme, this is an important point to watch out for when adding extra arguments to a function. Another example is the type $\forall\{\alpha\ \beta\} \rightarrow$ `Tm` $\alpha \rightarrow$ `Tm` $\beta \rightarrow$ `Tm` β versus $\forall\{\alpha\ \beta\} \rightarrow$ (`Name` $\alpha \rightarrow$ `Name` $\beta \rightarrow$ `Bool`) $\rightarrow$ `Tm` $\alpha \rightarrow$ `Tm` $\beta \rightarrow$ `Tm` β, the first one cannot compare the free variables of the two given terms while the second can apply a user-supplied function to do so.

Shifting versus adding Last but not least using $+^{W}$ instead of $\uparrow$ significantly improves the strength of the associated free theorem. Consider the function:

```
protectedAdd : ∀ {α} ℓ k → Name (α ↑ ℓ)
                         → Name (α +ᵂ k ↑ ℓ)
protectedAdd ℓ k = protect↑ ℓ (addᴺ k)
```

Consider now a weaker type, namely:

```
protectedAdd↑ : ∀ {α} ℓ k → Name (α ↑ ℓ)
                          → Name (α ↑ k ↑ ℓ)
protectedAdd↑ ℓ k = protect↑ ℓ (addᴺ↑ k)
```

We simply replaced the occurrence of $+^{W}$ by $\uparrow$. The consequences of this change are disastrous: this type allows more behaviors for its functions. Indeed the add^{N} `k` function can be given the latter type (but not the former) when using the appropriate inclusion witness to exploit the commutativity of $\uparrow$:

```
unprotectedAdd : ∀ {α} ℓ k → Name (α ↑ ℓ)
                           → Name (α ↑ k ↑ ℓ)
unprotectedAdd ℓ k
  = coerceᴺ (⊆-exch-↑-↑′ ℓ k) ∘ addᴺ↑ k
```

In our previous work [10] we had only the $\uparrow$ operation. Our function `shiftName` (`protectedAdd` in this example) was defined with the `unprotectedAdd` behavior. It took us a long time to discover this mistake, since we thought that our logical relation argument was enough. In summary we want to emphasis that all the logical relations proofs have to be taken with great care. A weaker function type than expected can ruin the intended informal properties.

4.5 Using logical relations and parametricity

To formally show that a world-polymorphic function `f` of type $\forall\ \{\alpha\} \rightarrow$ `Tm` $\alpha \rightarrow$ `Tm` α commutes with a renaming of the free variables, we proceed as follows. First we recall the natural definition of logical relation on the type `Tm`. Second we present the type `Ren` of renamings as injective functions. Third renaming is shown equivalent to being related at the type `Tm`. Finally we prove our commutation lemma by using the free-theorem associated to the function `f`.

The logical relation for the type `Tm` is mechanical. It states that two terms are related if they have the same structure and related free variables:

```
data ⟦Tm⟧ {α₁ α₂} (αᵣ : ⟦World⟧ α₁ α₂) :
          Tm α₁ → Tm α₂ → Set where
  ⟦V⟧     : ∀ {x₁ x₂} (xᵣ : ⟦Name⟧ αᵣ x₁ x₂)
          → ⟦Tm⟧ αᵣ (V x₁) (V x₂)
  _⟦·⟧_   : ∀ {t₁ t₂ u₁ u₂}
            (tᵣ : ⟦Tm⟧ αᵣ t₁ t₂)
            (uᵣ : ⟦Tm⟧ αᵣ u₁ u₂)
          → ⟦Tm⟧ αᵣ (t₁ · u₁) (t₂ · u₂)
  ⟦ƛ⟧     : ∀ {t₁ t₂} (tᵣ : ⟦Tm⟧ (αᵣ ⟦↑1⟧) t₁ t₂)
          → ⟦Tm⟧ αᵣ (ƛ t₁) (ƛ t₂)
  ⟦Let⟧   : ∀ {t₁ t₂ u₁ u₂}
            (tᵣ : ⟦Tm⟧ αᵣ t₁ t₂)
            (uᵣ : ⟦Tm⟧ (αᵣ ⟦↑1⟧) u₁ u₂)
          → ⟦Tm⟧ αᵣ (Let t₁ u₁) (Let t₂ u₂)
```

Then we need a notion of renaming. We choose to use injective functions over names. The type for a renaming is `Ren`, and the functions $\langle\_\rangle$ and $\langle\langle\_\rangle\rangle$ respectively convert a renaming to a function over names, and to a relation over worlds:

```
Ren : (α β : World) → Set

⟨_⟩ : ∀ {α β} → Ren α β → Tm α → Tm β

⟪_⟫ : ∀ {α β} → Ren α β → ⟦World⟧ α β
```

We now observe that given a renaming Φ, it is equivalent for two terms t_1 and t_2 to be related by ⟦Tm⟧ ⟪ Φ ⟫ and for t_2 to be equal to t_1 renamed with Φ.

```
⟦Tm⟧⇔rename :
  ∀ {α β} (Φ : Ren α β) {t₁ t₂}
  → ⟦Tm⟧ ⟪ Φ ⟫ t₁ t₂ ⇔ (⟨ Φ ⟩ t₁) ≡ t₂
```

Finally given a function `f` and a proof $\texttt{f}_r$ that `f` is in the logical relation, we can show that any renaming Φ commutes with the function `f`. To prove so we apply our ⟦Tm⟧⇔`rename` lemma in both directions and use $\texttt{f}_r$ with the renaming Φ lifted as a ⟦`World`⟧.

```
ren-comm :
  (f : ∀ {α} → Tm α → Tm α)
  (fᵣ:(∀⟨ αᵣ : ⟦World⟧ ⟩⟦→⟧ ⟦Tm⟧ αᵣ ⟦→⟧ ⟦Tm⟧ αᵣ)f f)
  → ∀ {α β} (Φ : Ren α β)
  → ⟨ Φ ⟩ ∘ f ≗ f ∘ ⟨ Φ ⟩
ren-comm f fᵣ Φ t
    = ⟦Tm⟧⇒rename Φ
          (fᵣ ⟪ Φ ⟫ (rename⇒⟦Tm⟧ Φ ≡.refl))
```

5. Conclusion and future work

We have shown a new approach for a safer nameless programming interface. Our work relies on a different notion of worlds both finer and more abstract. The type of names while being represented as a natural number is kept abstract as well. Only a few functions are required from the interface to get complete expressiveness. Indeed while our worlds are more precise, nothing forces the programmer to be precise with them. Thus there is no loss of expressiveness compared to the `Fin` approach. Through concrete examples we have shown how we can program in this system using classical examples like capture avoiding substitution. However the most challenging result comes from the solid mechanized development we have made in AGDA. This development not only demonstrates the soundness of our approach but allows to derive properties of functions using the system. This way we have shown that world-polymorphic functions over terms commute with renamings of free variables. These soundness results are shown in a modular way and reuse the solid foundations of logical relations.

As future work we would like to explore more properties of this system. We have also seen that a major convenience problem in our system was to build world inclusion witnesses. We would like to address this problem through a witness inference system built within AGDA, using the recent reflection mechanism. Another time-consuming task was to apply the AGDA logical relations to types and operations, so we would like to explore the integration of inspection primitives and meta-programming facilities for AGDA, namely TEMPLATE AGDA. Finally we would like to investigate how this system could scale to representations of well-typed terms.

Acknowledgements Thanks to François Pottier, Jean-Philippe Bernardy, Alexandre Pilkiewicz, and the anonymous reviewers for providing us with very valuable feedback.

References

[1] Thorsten Altenkirch. A formalization of the strong normalization proof for System F in LEGO. In J.F. Groote M. Bezem, editor, *Typed Lambda Calculi and Applications*, LNCS 664, pages 13 – 28, 1993.

[2] Thorsten Altenkirch and Bernhard Reus. Monadic presentations of lambda terms using generalized inductive types. In *Computer Science Logic*, volume 1683 of *Lecture Notes in Computer Science*, pages 453–468. Springer, 1999.

[3] Françoise Bellegarde and James Hook. Substitution: A formal methods case study using monads and transformations. *Sci. Comput. Program.*, 23(2-3):287–311, 1994.

[4] Jean-Philippe Bernardy, Patrik Jansson, and Ross Paterson. Parametricity and dependent types. In *Proceedings of the 15th ACM SIGPLAN international conference on Functional programming*, ICFP '10, pages 345–356, New York, NY, USA, 2010. ACM.

[5] Richard Bird and Ross Paterson. de Bruijn notation as a nested datatype. *Journal of Functional Programming*, 9(1):77–91, January 1999.

[6] Nicolaas G. de Bruijn. Lambda-calculus notation with nameless dummies: a tool for automatic formula manipulation with application to the Church-Rosser theorem. *Indag. Math.*, 34(5):381–392, 1972.

[7] Conor McBride and James McKinna. The view from the left. *J. Funct. Program.*, 14:69–111, January 2004.

[8] Conor McBride and Ross Paterson. Applicative programming with effects. *Journal of Functional Programming*, 18(1):1–13, 2008.

[9] Nicolas Pouillard. Nameless, painless (Agda code), 2011. `http://tiny.nicolaspouillard.fr/NaPa.agda`.

[10] Nicolas Pouillard and François Pottier. A fresh look at programming with names and binders. In *Proceedings of the 15th ACM SIGPLAN international conference on Functional programming*, ICFP '10, pages 217–228, New York, NY, USA, September 2010. ACM.

[11] John C. Reynolds. Types, abstraction and parametric polymorphism. In *Information Processing 83*, pages 513–523. Elsevier Science, 1983.

[12] Philip Wadler. Theorems for free! In *Conference on Functional Programming Languages and Computer Architecture (FPCA)*, pages 347–359, September 1989.

Binders Unbound

Stephanie Weirich   Brent A. Yorgey
University of Pennsylvania
{sweirich,byorgey}@cis.upenn.edu

Tim Sheard
Portland State University
sheard@cs.pdx.edu

Abstract

Implementors of compilers, program refactorers, theorem provers, proof checkers, and other systems that manipulate syntax know that dealing with name binding is difficult to do well. Operations such as α-equivalence and capture-avoiding substitution seem simple, yet subtle bugs often go undetected. Furthermore, their implementations are tedious, requiring "boilerplate" code that must be updated whenever the object language definition changes.

Many researchers have therefore sought to specify binding syntax declaratively, so that tools can correctly handle the details behind the scenes. This idea has been the inspiration for many new systems (such as Beluga, Delphin, FreshML, FreshOCaml, Cαml, FreshLib, and Ott) but there is still room for improvement in expressivity, simplicity and convenience.

In this paper, we present a new domain-specific language, UNBOUND, for specifying binding structure. Our language is particularly expressive—it supports multiple atom types, pattern binders, type annotations, recursive binders, and nested binding (necessary for telescopes, a feature found in dependently-typed languages). However, our specification language is also simple, consisting of just five basic combinators. We provide a formal semantics for this language derived from a locally nameless representation and prove that it satisfies a number of desirable properties.

We also present an implementation of our binding specification language as a GHC Haskell library implementing an embedded domain specific language (EDSL). By using Haskell type constructors to represent binding combinators, we implement the EDSL succinctly using datatype-generic programming. Our implementation supports a number of features necessary for practical programming, including flexibility in the treatment of user-defined types, best-effort name preservation (for error messages), and integration with Haskell's monad transformer library.

Categories and Subject Descriptors D.2.3 [*Coding Tools and Techniques*]; D.1.1 [*Applicative (Functional) Programming*]; E.1 [*Data Structures*]

General Terms Algorithms, Languages.

Keywords generic programming, Haskell, name binding, patterns

1. Introduction

Name binding is one of the most annoying parts of language implementations. Although functional programming languages such as Haskell and ML excel at the implementation of type checkers, compilers, and interpreters, there is an impedance mismatch between the free structure provided by algebraic datatypes and the syntax identified up to α-equivalence that we actually want to model. Although there are many techniques for implementing name binding, they require subtle invariants that pervade the system. Implementation flaws cause bugs that are difficult to track down. Furthermore, the implementations themselves are tedious, requiring boilerplate that must be maintained as the implemented language evolves. While such boilerplate is straightforward, it causes friction for developers who just want to get the job done.

And all this work is for something so "obvious" that it is often elided from language definitions!

There has been much research towards solving this problem. Recently introduced languages and tools provide primitive support for variable-binding, based on first-order [6, 21, 30, 31] and higher-order representations [18, 20]. These tools handle the details behind the scenes, relieving programmers of the tedium and subtle bugs described above. However, these tools must also satisfy the practical needs of programmers, and here they fall short:

Expressiveness: These tools provide *binding specification languages* that specify what variables are bound where. As unary lexical scoping (binding a single variable in a single location) is not sufficient for many applications, many of these tools support a language for patterns in binding specifications. Despite this flexibility, it is still not enough—there are patterns that we would like to use that cannot be defined by existing specification languages.

Availability: Programmers want to write code in their language, and they want to do it directly. Tools that are wrappers for existing languages are preferred to completely new systems, but such tools still require update with each new version of the language. Libraries are more stable and have the added benefit of simple distribution, some degree of portability and familiar syntax.

Choice of implementations: These tools each provide only *one* implementation for any given binding specification. However, name binding involves a number of different operations and some implementations may favor one over the other. Programmers should be able to swap out implementations (or write their own) if they find one that works better with their application.

In this paper, we present a new domain-specific language, UNBOUND, for specifying binding structure that addresses these issues. Concretely, our contributions are as follows:

- We describe a small, compositional set of abstract combinators which form the entire basis for UNBOUND. This interface succinctly characterizes our specification language.
- We show, via examples (§ 2, § 3), that UNBOUND is nonetheless expressive. In particular, it supports multiple atom types,

pattern binders, type annotations, recursive binders, and nested binders. The last are necessary to model *telescopes* and are not supported by any existing specification language.

- We give a formal semantics for our specification language (§ 4) based on a locally nameless representation and prove its correctness (§ 5). Our choice of representation leads to a simple semantics and straightforward metatheory. Alternative meanings are also possible; the simplicity of ours makes it a good reference for more sophisticated implementations.
- We have implemented our framework as a Haskell library (§ 6), using Haskell's generic programming support to automatically derive standard operations. Our library is available for download from Hackage,[1] along with extensive documentation and examples. (Note GHC 7 is required.)

Although UNBOUND is designed for object language *implementation*, this specification language and semantics are also appropriate for formal object language *reasoning*. That application is beyond the scope of this paper; we discuss the connections to mechanized metatheory in § 8 and § 9.

2. The UNBOUND Specification Language

We begin with a simple UNBOUND specification.[2] Functional programmers are accustomed to using algebraic datatypes to specify the abstract syntax of a programming language. UNBOUND introduces type combinators that encode binding structure into the algebraic datatype itself. For example, to represent the untyped lambda calculus, we use the E datatype below:

```
type N = Name E
data E = Var N
       | Lam (Bind N E)
       | App E E
```

The abstract type Name (provided by UNBOUND) represents variables, and is indexed by the type of values which can be substituted for them (here, E). For convenience, we define N as a synonym for Name E. Lambda abstractions are represented using the type Bind N E, indicating a name paired with an expression in which the name is bound. Application does not involve binding, so it is simply a pair of E values as expected.

UNBOUND uses this datatype definition to derive standard operations for working with syntax, such as α-equivalence, free variable calculation, and capture-avoiding substitution. For example, suppose we want to implement parallel reduction for untyped lambda calculus terms. This operation looks throughout a term for β- and η-reductions, even under lambda abstractions, transforming it into a simpler form. An implementation is shown in Figure 1. The signatures for the UNBOUND-derived operations that this code relies on are at the top of the figure. All of these functions are automatically derived by UNBOUND.

The function *red* has three cases. (Note that the *Fresh* constraint on m also implies a *Monad* constraint, enabling the use of **do**-notation.) The *Var* case is trivial. The *Lam* case must handle the possibility of η-reduction, so we must break the lambda into its two constituent parts—its bound variable, and its body. Note that the type Bind N E type is abstract, so we cannot use pattern matching to extract its components. Instead, the monadic *unbind* operation decomposes the binding, ensuring that the name x does not conflict with other names currently in scope.

[1] `http://hackage.haskell.org/package/unbound/`

[2] While our examples are presented in Haskell, using our Haskell library, the examples themselves are language neutral.

UNBOUND operations used in this example:

```
bind   :: N → E → (Bind N E)
unbind :: Fresh m ⇒ (Bind N E) → m (N, E)
fv     :: E → Set N
subst  :: N → E → E
```

Parallel reduction:

```
red :: Fresh m ⇒ E → m E
red (Var x) = return (Var x)
red (Lam b) = do
  (x, e) ← unbind b
  e'     ← red e
  case e' of      -- η-reduction: (λ x.e x) = e
    App e'' (Var y) | x ≡ y ∧ ¬ (x ∈ fv e'') → return e''
    _ → return (Lam (bind x e'))
red (App e1 e2) = do
  e1' ← red e1
  e2' ← red e2
  case e1' of     -- β-reduction: (λ x.e) t = e[t/x]
    Lam b → do
      (x, e') ← unbind b
      return (subst x e2' e')
    _      → return (App e1' e2')
```

Figure 1. Parallel reduction for E

$T \in \mathbb{T}$	
Name T	Names for Ts
R	Regular datatype containing only terms
Bind P T	Bind pattern P in body T
$P \in \mathbb{P}$	
Name T	Single binding name
R_P	Regular datatype containing only patterns
Embed T	Embedded term (§ 3.1)
Rebind P P	Nested binding pattern (§ 3.2)
Rec P	Recursive binding pattern (§ 3.3)

Figure 2. UNBOUND type combinators

Once the body of the lambda expression has been reduced, the code checks to see if it can do an η-reduction. This is possible when the body is exactly the application of some other term e'' to the variable x, where x does not appear free in e''. If an η-reduction is not possible, the binding is reformed using the *bind* constructor for the Bind N E type. A similar unbinding occurs in the application case, when a β-reduction has been detected, followed by an invocation of a capture-avoiding substitution operation also provided by UNBOUND.

At this point, one may ask: *Where do these operations come from? What do they mean? How do we know that the code given for red correctly implements parallel reduction for the lambda calculus?* The first question we answer in § 6 where we discuss the Haskell implementation of UNBOUND. The other questions motivate our semantics (§ 4) and the theorems we choose to prove about it (§ 5).

3. Beyond single binding

A key feature of UNBOUND is that programmers are not limited to binding a single variable at a time. Instead, the *bind* constructor takes a pattern containing variables and abstracts over all of them. A large class of types may be used as patterns. As a simple example, lists of names are patterns. If we wanted to allow the syntax $\lambda x\ \ y\ \ z \ \rightarrow\ \dots$ as a convenient shorthand for $\lambda x \rightarrow \lambda y \rightarrow \lambda z \rightarrow \dots$, where x, y, and z are distinct names,[3] we could change our definition of E to the following:

$$\begin{aligned}\textbf{data}\ E = &\ \mathit{Var}\ N\\ |&\ \mathit{Lam}\ (\mathsf{Bind}\ [N]\ E)\\ |&\ \mathit{App}\ E\ E\end{aligned}$$

In general, UNBOUND uses two sorts of types: those that may be used as *patterns*, where names are binding occurrences, and those that are *terms*, where names are references to binding sites. Figure 2 summarizes these two classes, written $\mathbb{P}$ and $\mathbb{T}$ respectively. The Bind type combinator takes a pattern type as its first argument and a term type as its second argument and returns a term type. Other term types include Name (representing free variables) and *regular* datatypes—those built using unit, base types, sums, products, and least fixpoint—that contain only term types. By convention, we use the metavariable P for pattern types and T for term types.

The expressiveness of UNBOUND is determined by $\mathbb{P}$, the collection of types that can be used as patterns. These types include Names, of course, as well as regular datatypes that contain only other pattern types. This mean that some types, such as *Int* and *String*, can be used as both terms and patterns. We describe the three remaining UNBOUND pattern combinators (Embed, Rebind and Rec) in more detail in the next subsections.

As a more sophisticated example of pattern binding, consider adding pattern matching to the E language with a case statement. Each branch is encoded as Bind $\ Pat\ \ E$, where Pat is a new datatype representing object-language patterns. Every name occurring in a Pat will be bound in the respective body.

$$\begin{aligned}&\textbf{data}\ \mathit{Pat} = \mathit{PVar}\ N \mid \mathit{PCon}\ \mathit{String}\ [\mathit{Pat}]\\ &\textbf{data}\ E\ \ = \dots\\ &\qquad \mid \mathit{Con}\ \mathit{String}\ [E] \qquad \text{-- data constructors}\\ &\qquad \mid \mathit{Case}\ E\ [\mathsf{Bind}\ \mathit{Pat}\ E] \quad \text{-- pattern matching}\end{aligned}$$

It is not hard to check that Pat is a valid pattern type (since it contains only Names and *String*s), justifying its use as the first argument to Bind.

3.1 Embedding terms in patterns

In many situations it is convenient to be able to embed terms within patterns. Such embedded terms do not bind variables along with the rest of the pattern. For example, suppose we wanted to extend our E language with simple let-binding, let $x{=}e_1$ in e_2. Here x is bound in e_2 but not in e_1.

A semantically correct encoding puts the e_1 in the abstract syntax before binding x in e_2, "lifting" e_1 outside the binding so it does not participate.

$$\begin{aligned}&\textbf{type}\ E_1 = E\\ &\textbf{type}\ E_2 = E\\ &\textbf{data}\ E = \dots\\ &\qquad \mid \mathit{Let}\ E_1\ (\mathsf{Bind}\ N\ E_2)\end{aligned}$$

(We use the type synonyms E_1 and E_2 to indicate which sub-terms of Let correspond to e_1 and e_2.) However, this encoding forces us to write the terms in an unnatural order; moreover, it fails to express the relationship between the name being let-bound and its definition. We can craft a more satisfying solution using the embedding combinator Embed provided by UNBOUND.

[3] Although UNBOUND supports shadowing, a single pattern must be linear (*i.e.* not contain repeated variables).

$$\begin{aligned}&\textbf{data}\ E = \dots\\ &\qquad \mid \mathit{Let}\ (\mathsf{Bind}\ (N, \mathsf{Embed}\ E_1)\ E_2)\end{aligned}$$

Embed may only occur within pattern types, where it serves as an "escape hatch" for embedding terms which do not bind any names. Note that a term type within an Embed may itself contain pattern types (inside the left-hand side of Bind) which may contain Embedded term types, and so on.

This formulation with Embed also enables us to extend our let expressions to multiple bindings, by using a pattern list:

$$\begin{aligned}&\textbf{data}\ E = \dots\\ &\qquad \mid \mathit{Let}\ (\mathsf{Bind}\ [(N, \mathsf{Embed}\ E)]\ E)\end{aligned}$$

Without Embed, we could encode this binding specification by "unzipping" the list of name-definition pairs and lifting the definitions outside of the Bind:

$$\begin{aligned}&\textbf{data}\ E = \dots\\ &\qquad \mid \mathit{Let}\ [E]\ (\mathsf{Bind}\ [N]\ E)\end{aligned}$$

But this example is even worse than the corresponding encoding of let with a single binding. Not only does it force us to use an unnatural order and fail to encode the relationship between names and their respective definitions, it also admits "junk" terms with lists of different lengths. Embed enables an encoding where names and their definitions are paired, as they should be.

3.2 Nested binding

Consider now a let* construct, let* $x_1{=}e_1, \dots, x_n{=}e_n$ in e, where each x_i is bound in e and *also* in all the e_j with $j > i$. One way to encode this pattern is by iterating the encoding for single let bindings discussed above:

$$\begin{aligned}&\textbf{data}\ \mathit{LetList} = \mathit{Body}\ \ \ \ E\\ &\qquad\qquad \mid \mathit{Binding}\ (\mathsf{Bind}\ (N, \mathsf{Embed}\ E)\ \mathit{LetList})\\ &\textbf{data}\ E\qquad = \dots\\ &\qquad\qquad \mid \mathit{LetStar}\ \mathit{LetList}\end{aligned}$$

This succeeds in capturing the binding structure of let*, and may be sufficient for some purposes. However, it does have one major drawback: in order to extract the body of the let* expression, we must first recurse through all the bindings. It is more convenient to encode a let* expression by *pairing* a list of bindings and a body, so the body can be accessed without first processing the bindings. As a first try, we could write

$$\begin{aligned}&\textbf{data}\ E = \dots\\ &\qquad \mid \mathit{LetStar}\ (\mathsf{Bind}\ [(N, \mathsf{Embed}\ E)]\ E)\end{aligned}$$

but this is just the multiple binding example from the previous subsection. With this specification, the x_i are bound *only* in the body of the let*, not in the definitions of subsequent variables. We evidently want a way to *nest* additional binding structure within the pattern of the outermost Bind.

UNBOUND provides a novel *rebinding* pattern combinator for precisely this purpose. Rebind $P_1\ \ P_2$ acts like the pattern type (P_1, P_2), except that P_1 also scopes over P_2, so the binders in P_1 may be referred to by terms embedded within P_2. (The fact that P_1 scopes over P_2 in this way has no effect on the *pattern* portion of P_2.) For example, consider the specification

$$\begin{aligned}&\textbf{type}\ N_1 = \mathsf{Name}\ E\\ &\textbf{type}\ N_2 = \mathsf{Name}\ E\\ &\mathsf{Bind}\ (\mathsf{Rebind}\ N_1\ (N_2, \mathsf{Embed}\ E_1))\ E_2\end{aligned}$$

Here N_1 and N_2 are bound in E_2, and additionally N_1 is also bound within E_1.

Using rebinding, we can faithfully encode the binding structure of let* as follows:

$$\begin{aligned}\textbf{data}\ Lets &= Nil\\ &\mid Cons\ (\mathsf{Rebind}\ (N, \mathsf{Embed}\ E)\ Lets)\\ \textbf{data}\ E &= \ldots\\ &\mid LetStar\ (\mathsf{Bind}\ Lets\ E)\end{aligned}$$

All the names within the sequence of definitions are bound in the body of the let*-expression (Bind $Lets$ E); additionally, each name (paired with its definition as an embedded term) is bound within any $Embeds$ occurring in the remainder of the sequence—that is, within the definitions of subsequent names.

Telescopes A particularly important example of a binding pattern that requires Rebind is a *telescope*. Telescopes were invented by de Bruijn [9] to model dependently-type systems. They are used frequently in specifications of dependently-typed languages, including Epigram [15] and Agda [17].

A telescope, Δ, is a sequence of variables paired with their types:

$$x_1 : A_1, \ldots, x_n : A_n.$$

However, each variable scopes over the types that occur later in the telescope. For example, here x_1 may occur in A_2, A_3, and so on. The name *telescope* comes from the optical device, which is built as as a sequence of segments that slide into one another.

Telescopes are used for "aggregate binding". For example, consider the following (very simple) fragment of a dependently-typed language. In this language, functions can take multiple parameters and be applied to multiple arguments. However, because of dependent types, the type of each parameter is allowed to mention earlier parameters.

$$A, B, M, N ::= x \mid \Pi\Delta.B \mid \lambda\Delta.M \mid M\ (N_1 \ldots N_n)$$

Telescopes gather together all of the parameters of the function in both its definition ($\lambda\Delta.M$) and its type ($\Pi\Delta.B$). Because telescopes are essentially typing contexts, the typing rule for abstractions merely appends the telescope to the current typing context:

$$\frac{\Gamma, \Delta \vdash M : B}{\Gamma \vdash \lambda\Delta.M : \Pi\,\Delta.B}$$

Type checking the multi-applications requires an auxiliary judgment that determines if the vector of arguments "fits into" the telescope.

$$\frac{}{\Gamma \vdash : .} \qquad \frac{\Gamma \vdash N_1 : A \quad \Gamma \vdash N_2 \mathinner{..} N_n : \Delta[x \mapsto N_1]}{\Gamma \vdash N_1\ N_2 \mathinner{..} N_n : (x : A, \Delta)}$$

This judgment verifies that all of the arguments have the right types. Computing the result type of the application requires substituting all of the arguments for each binding variable in the telescope.

$$\frac{\begin{array}{l}\Gamma \vdash M : \Pi\,\Delta.A \quad \Gamma \vdash N_1 \mathinner{..} N_n : \Delta\\ dom\,(\Delta) = x_1 \mathinner{..} x_n\end{array}}{\Gamma \vdash M(N_1 \mathinner{..} N_n) : B[x_1 \mathinner{..} x_n \mapsto N_1 \mathinner{..} N_n]}$$

This fragment demonstrates the important features of telescopes. Sometimes they are used as binding patterns and sometimes they are used as the types of vectors, independent of binding. Implementing this language using traditional unary binding would be tiresome because one would have to traverse the entire telescope to see the body of the function or the body of the dependent type. That is not so much of an issue in this simple example, but the semantics of features like inductive families (with eliminators based on induction principles or dependent pattern matching) is greatly simplified by the aggregate binding that telescopes provide.

In UNBOUND, we can represent the language fragment above using Rebind:

$$\begin{aligned}\textbf{data}\ E &= Var\ N\\ &\mid Pi\ (\mathsf{Bind}\ Tele\ E)\\ &\mid Lam\ (\mathsf{Bind}\ Tele\ E)\\ &\mid App\ E\ [E]\\ \textbf{data}\ Tele &= Empty \mid \mathsf{Rebind}\ (N, \mathsf{Embed}\ E)\ Tele\end{aligned}$$

Furthermore, UNBOUND automatically provides all of the machinery necessary for working with telescopes, including calculation of their binding variables, multiple substitution in terms, and substitution through the telescopes.

3.3 Recursive binding

Our E language is looking nice, but what if we want to add some recursion? We can try to encode a letrec construct,

$$\mathsf{letrec}\ x_1{=}e_1, \ldots, x_n{=}e_n\ \mathsf{in}\ e,$$

where this time, the x_i are bound in e as well as *all* the e_i. This is straightforward if we are willing to lift all the x_i out to the front:

$$\begin{aligned}\textbf{data}\ E &= \ldots\\ &\mid Letrec\ (\mathsf{Bind}\ [N]\ ([E], E))\end{aligned}$$

However, the problems with this sort of encoding have already been discussed. We would like to encode letrec in such a way that names and definitions are paired.

Rebind doesn't help, because it forces us to separate binders from the terms over which they scope, just like Bind. We need a way to freely mix patterns and terms bound by the patterns in the same data structure. UNBOUND provides the Rec combinator for this purpose. In Rec P, names in the pattern P scope recursively over any terms embedded in P itself. However, Rec P itself is also a pattern, so names in P also scope externally over any term that binds Rec P. Intuitively, Rec is just a "recursive" version of Rebind.

An appropriate encoding of letrec is therefore:

$$\begin{aligned}\textbf{data}\ E &= \ldots\\ &\mid Letrec\ (\mathsf{Bind}\ (\mathsf{Rec}\ [(N, \mathsf{Embed}\ E)])\ E)\end{aligned}$$

Here the pattern $[(N, \mathsf{Embed}\ E)]$ scopes over itself—hence all the names are bound in all the definitions—as well as over the body of the letrec.

4. Semantics

In the previous section, we gave a number of examples of specifying different sorts of binding patterns found in programming languages. However, we have been fairly vague about what those specifications actually mean. In this section, we fill in the details by giving it a semantics.

Our semantics comes in two parts. We first define the *representation* of syntax with binders, and specify smart constructors and destructors that work with this representation. Second, we define the *action* of UNBOUND operations (α-equivalence, free variable calculation and substitution) in terms of this representation. Once we have formally defined this semantics, we prove that it satisfies the properties we expect (§ 5) and discuss the correspondence between it and our concrete Haskell implementation (§ 6).

4.1 Representation

For simplicity, we use a *locally nameless* representation of terms with binding structure. This representation provides a straightforward semantics for UNBOUND, one that is both simple to implement and simple to reason about. Using a locally nameless representation is an old idea—we give more details about its history later § 8.

A locally nameless representation of terms with binding structure separates bound variables, represented by de Bruijn indices, from free variables, represented by *atoms*. (Atoms are often taken to be strings, but any countably infinite set with decidable equality

$$\mathbb{A} ::= \{\mathsf{x}, \mathsf{y}, \mathsf{z}, \ldots\}$$
$$b ::= j@k$$
$$t ::= \mathsf{x} \mid b \mid \mathsf{K}\ t_1 \ldots t_n \mid \mathsf{Bind}\ p\ t$$
$$p ::= -_{\mathsf{x}} \mid \mathsf{K}\ p_1 \ldots p_n \mid \mathsf{Rebind}\ p\ p \mid \mathsf{Embed}\ t \mid \mathsf{Rec}\ p$$

Figure 3. Syntax of atoms, indices, terms, and patterns

will do.) This representation has the advantage that α-equivalence is simply structural equality. Distinguishing bound variables from free variables in this way also means that we do not need to keep track of the current *scope* of a free variable and shift it as we move from one scope to another, as we would with a purely de Bruijn-indexed representation.

The locally nameless syntax we use to represent terms with binding structure is shown in Figure 3. As in Figure 2, we separate terms from patterns. Terms t have term types T, whereas patterns have pattern types P.

Names that appear in terms can either be free names, x, or bound names, b. Free names are drawn from the set $\mathbb{A}$ of atoms. (In the interest of simplicity, the semantics we describe here only includes a single sort for atoms; extending to multiple atom sorts is straightforward.) Terms also include applications of constructor constants K to zero or more subterms. Note that constructor application covers all terms with some regular type R; in the semantics they are all handled in precisely the same way. Indeed, thanks to generic programming, this is actually a faithful reflection of our Haskell implementation, which handles all data constructors other than the special UNBOUND combinators uniformly.

Like terms, patterns can be formed by the application of constructors to subpatterns. Names inside patterns are *binders*, written $-_{\mathsf{x}}$, which represent binding occurrences of names. We denote binders with special syntax to emphasize that we should think of them as placeholders with an associated name.

The astute reader may note that we are punning a bit with our syntax: in earlier examples, Bind and friends showed up as *types*, whereas here they are playing the role of *data*. The resolution of the apparent inconsistency is that Bind, Embed, Rebind, and Rec are all *singleton types* with eponymous constructors.

For example, we can define an operation that lists all of the atoms that a pattern will bind as shown below.

$$
\begin{array}{ll}
binders :: P \to [\mathbb{A}] & \\
binders\ -_{\mathsf{x}} & = [x] \\
binders\ (\mathsf{K}\ p_1 \ldots p_n) & = binders\ p_1 +\!\!+ \ldots +\!\!+ binders\ p_n \\
binders\ (\mathsf{Rebind}\ p_1\ p_2) & = binders\ p_1 +\!\!+ binders\ p_2 \\
binders\ (\mathsf{Embed}\ t) & = \varnothing \\
binders\ (\mathsf{Rec}\ p) & = binders\ p
\end{array}
$$

Note that even though we are using Haskell-like syntax, this definition is type-directed. It works for any pattern of any pattern type; the type of $binders$, $P \to [\mathbb{A}]$, is an abbreviation for $\forall\ P : \mathbb{P}, P \to [\mathbb{A}]$. In our Haskell implementation, to be discussed in more detail in § 6, each clause of a definition such as this one corresponds to a method definition in a type class instance.

4.2 Names, indices and patterns

Bound names b consist of two natural number indices, $j@k$. The first index j references a pattern, counting outwards from zero; the second index k is an offset. It references a particular binder within the given pattern, counting from left to right, also starting from zero. For example, in

$$\mathsf{Bind}\ (-_{\mathsf{x}}, -_{\mathsf{y}}, -_{\mathsf{z}})\ (\mathsf{Bind}\ -_{\mathsf{q}}\ 1@2)$$

the bound variable $1@2$ refers to $-_{\mathsf{z}}$, the index-2 binder within the index-1 enclosing pattern.

Therefore, an important part of this representation is the connection between patterns and offsets. We make this connection precise with the operations *nth* and *find* (although we omit their definitions in the interest of space):

$$
\begin{array}{l}
nth :: P \to \mathbb{N} \to \mathsf{Maybe}\ \mathbb{A} \\
find :: P \to \mathbb{A} \to \mathsf{Maybe}\ \mathbb{N}
\end{array}
$$

nth takes a pattern and a natural number n and finds the *nth* name bound in that pattern, failing if there are not enough binders. *find* takes a pattern and a name and finds the first index of that name in the pattern, failing if the name does not occur.

4.3 Close and open

The two most important operations for the locally nameless representation are *close* and *open*. The former is used for binding terms: it converts atoms (*i.e.* free names) to indices (*i.e.* bound names). The latter does the reverse, replacing indices that resolve to a particular binding location by free names.

We call the first operation *close*, as we are closing the term with respect to the free names listed in a pattern. Likewise, we call the inverse operation *open*, as we may use it to open up a binder in order to recurse through its subcomponents. These two operations are standard components for working with a locally nameless representation [2, 11]. Here we modify them to close and open terms with respect to a *pattern* instead of a single variable, and also to close and open the terms embedded inside patterns.

The *close* operation is defined in Figure 4. It takes as input a natural number *level*, a pattern, and a term, and returns a new term where free variables matching binders in the pattern have been replaced by bound variables at the given level. In the free variable case, it uses *find* to look for a matching binder and generate the appropriate index if one is found. We also define a version of *close* for patterns, $close_{\mathsf{P}}$, whose job is to recurse through patterns looking for Embedded terms to which *close* can be applied. When recursing under a binder (Bind, Rebind, or Rec), both *close* and $close_{\mathsf{P}}$ increment the current level.

The *open* operation is also defined in Figure 4. It takes a natural number level, a pattern, and a term, and "opens" the term by interpreting bound variables at the given level as references into the pattern, replacing them by the free variable attached to the referenced binder.[4] Similarly to *close*, *open* is mutually defined with a pattern version $open_{\mathsf{P}}$. In the case where a bound variable is found which matches the current level, *open* uses *nth* to index into the pattern and pick out the free variable associated with the referenced binder.

We use $close\ p\ t$ and $open\ p\ t$ as convenient synonyms for $close\ 0\ p\ t$ and $open\ 0\ p\ t$, respectively.

4.4 Constructing terms and patterns

Figure 5 lists the smart constructors and destructors that are part of the interface to the type combinators exported by UNBOUND. In

[4] In the locally nameless literature, *open* is sometimes defined as *bound-variable substitution* and generalized to replace bound variables with terms instead of with free variables. Such definitions save effort, since the next step after opening is often to substitute for the new free variable. In that case, the definition of *open* is a little more complex than what is presented here in order to deal with substituting terms with dangling bound variable references. We prefer our reference semantics to be as simple as possible so we avoid such complications.

$$
\begin{array}{ll}
\mathit{close} :: \mathbb{N} \to P \to T \to T & \\
\mathit{close}\ l\ p\ b & = b \\
\mathit{close}\ l\ p\ \mathsf{x} & = \textbf{case}\ \mathit{find}\ p\ \mathsf{x}\ \textbf{of} \\
& \quad \mathsf{Just}\ i \quad \to l@i \\
& \quad \mathsf{Nothing} \to \mathsf{x} \\
\mathit{close}\ l\ p\ (\mathsf{K}\ t_1 \ldots t_n) & = \mathsf{K}\ (\mathit{close}\ l\ p\ t_1) \ldots \\
& \quad (\mathit{close}\ l\ p\ t_n) \\
\mathit{close}\ l\ p\ (\mathsf{Bind}\ p'\ t) & = \mathsf{Bind}\ (\mathit{close}_{\mathsf{P}}\ l\ p\ p') \\
& \qquad (\mathit{close}\ (l+1)\ p\ t)
\end{array}
$$

$$
\begin{array}{ll}
\mathit{close}_{\mathsf{P}} :: \mathbb{N} \to P \to P \to P & \\
\mathit{close}_{\mathsf{P}}\ l\ p\ \_{\mathsf{x}} & = \_{\mathsf{x}} \\
\mathit{close}_{\mathsf{P}}\ l\ p\ (\mathsf{K}\ p_1 \ldots p_n) & = \mathsf{K}\ (\mathit{close}_{\mathsf{P}}\ l\ p\ p_1) \ldots \\
& \quad (\mathit{close}_{\mathsf{P}}\ l\ p\ p_n) \\
\mathit{close}_{\mathsf{P}}\ l\ p\ (\mathsf{Rebind}\ p_1\ p_2) & = \mathsf{Rebind}\ (\mathit{close}_{\mathsf{P}}\ l\ p\ p_1) \\
& \qquad (\mathit{close}_{\mathsf{P}}\ (l+1)\ p\ p_2) \\
\mathit{close}_{\mathsf{P}}\ l\ p\ (\mathsf{Embed}\ t) & = \mathsf{Embed}\ (\mathit{close}\ l\ p\ t) \\
\mathit{close}_{\mathsf{P}}\ l\ p\ (\mathsf{Rec}\ p') & = \mathsf{Rec}\ (\mathit{close}_{\mathsf{P}}\ (l+1)\ p\ p')
\end{array}
$$

$$
\begin{array}{ll}
\mathit{open} :: \mathbb{N} \to P \to T \to T & \\
\mathit{open}\ l\ p\ (j@k) \mid j \equiv l & = \textbf{case}\ \mathit{nth}\ p\ k\ \textbf{of} \\
& \quad \mathsf{Just}\ \mathsf{x} \quad \to \mathsf{x} \\
& \quad \mathsf{Nothing} \to j@k \\
\mathit{open}\ l\ p\ \mathsf{x} & = \mathsf{x} \\
\mathit{open}\ l\ p\ (\mathsf{K}\ t_1 \ldots t_n) & = \mathsf{K}\ (\mathit{open}\ l\ p\ t_1) \ldots \\
& \quad (\mathit{open}\ l\ p\ t_n) \\
\mathit{open}\ l\ p\ (\mathsf{Bind}\ p'\ t) & = \mathsf{Bind}\ (\mathit{open}_{\mathsf{P}}\ l\ p\ p') \\
& \qquad (\mathit{open}\ (l+1)\ p\ t)
\end{array}
$$

$$
\begin{array}{ll}
\mathit{open}_{\mathsf{P}} :: \mathbb{N} \to P \to P \to P & \\
\mathit{open}_{\mathsf{P}}\ l\ p\ (\mathsf{K}\ p_1 \ldots p_n) & = \mathsf{K}\ (\mathit{open}_{\mathsf{P}}\ l\ p\ p_1) \ldots \\
& \quad (\mathit{open}_{\mathsf{P}}\ l\ p\ p_n) \\
\mathit{open}_{\mathsf{P}}\ l\ p\ \_{\mathsf{x}} & = \_{\mathsf{x}} \\
\mathit{open}_{\mathsf{P}}\ l\ p\ (\mathsf{Rebind}\ p_1\ p_2) & = \mathsf{Rebind}\ (\mathit{open}_{\mathsf{P}}\ l\ p\ p_1) \\
& \qquad (\mathit{open}_{\mathsf{P}}\ (l+1)\ p\ p_2) \\
\mathit{open}_{\mathsf{P}}\ l\ p\ (\mathsf{Embed}\ t) & = \mathsf{Embed}\ (\mathit{open}\ l\ p\ t) \\
\mathit{open}_{\mathsf{P}}\ l\ p\ (\mathsf{Rec}\ p') & = \mathsf{Rec}\ (\mathit{open}_{\mathsf{P}}\ (l+1)\ p\ p')
\end{array}
$$

Figure 4. *close* and *open*

the next two subsections, we discuss the implementations of these operations.

We use *close* to define the constructors for binding abstractions. Closing a term with respect to the pattern binds the pattern variables in the term.

$$\mathit{bind}\ p\ t = \mathsf{Bind}\ p\ (\mathit{close}\ p\ t)$$

Effectively, this replaces all free occurrences of variables that appear in the pattern with indices. For example, binding a pair of variables in a term that references both variables will produce indices that refer to the same pattern, but at different offsets. In contrast, nesting the binders produces indices that refer to the different binding locations, but each one at the same offset (the zeroth variable in the pattern).

$$
\begin{array}{ll}
\mathit{bind}\ (\_{\mathsf{x}}, \_{\mathsf{y}})\ (x, y) & = \mathsf{Bind}\ (\_{\mathsf{x}}, \_{\mathsf{y}})\ (0@0, 0@1) \\
\mathit{bind}\ \_{\mathsf{x}}\ (\mathit{bind}\ \_{\mathsf{y}}\ (x, y)) & = \mathsf{Bind}\ \_{\mathsf{x}}\ (\mathsf{Bind}\ \_{\mathsf{y}} \\
& \qquad (1@0, 0@0))
\end{array}
$$

Likewise, for pattern combinators that introduce internal binding, we also use *close* to replace occurrences of the bound variable with indices. Note that in the case of recursive binding, we close the pattern with respect to itself.

$$
\begin{array}{ll}
\mathit{string2Name} & :: \mathit{String} \to \mathsf{Name}\ T \\
\mathit{name2String} & :: \mathsf{Name}\ T \to \mathit{String} \\
\\
\mathit{bind} & :: P \to T \to \mathsf{Bind}\ P\ T \\
\mathit{unbind} & :: \mathit{Fresh}\ m \Rightarrow \mathsf{Bind}\ P\ T \to m\ (P, T) \\
\\
\mathit{rebind} & :: P_1 \to P_2 \to \mathsf{Rebind}\ P_1\ P_2 \\
\mathit{unrebind} & :: \mathsf{Rebind}\ P_1\ P_2 \to (P_1, P_2) \\
\\
\mathit{rec} & :: P \to \mathsf{Rec}\ P \\
\mathit{unrec} & :: \mathsf{Rec}\ P \to P \\
\\
\mathit{embed} & :: T \to \mathsf{Embed}\ T \\
\mathit{unembed} & :: \mathsf{Embed}\ T \to T
\end{array}
$$

Figure 5. Constructors and destructors

$$
\begin{array}{ll}
\mathit{rebind}\ p_1\ p_2 & = \mathsf{Rebind}\ p_1\ (\mathit{close}_{\mathsf{P}}\ p_1\ p_2) \\
\mathit{rec} \qquad p & = \mathsf{Rec}\ (\mathit{close}_{\mathsf{P}}\ p\ p)
\end{array}
$$

Finally, *embed* does not need to do any closing, and merely applies the Embed constructor to the given term. Likewise, *unembed* merely returns the nested term.

$$
\begin{array}{ll}
\mathit{embed} \qquad t & = \mathsf{Embed}\ t \\
\mathit{unembed}\ (\mathsf{Embed}\ t) & = t
\end{array}
$$

4.5 Freshening and unbinding

Unbinding is not quite as straightforward as binding. Given a term Bind p t, it is only safe to call *open* p t if none of the binding variables of p clash with existing free variables in t. Therefore, before opening, we must first *freshen* p by assigning suitably fresh names to its binders. At this point, we leave the precise meaning of "suitably fresh" open to interpretation; some concrete alternatives are discussed in § 6.4. We omit the formal definition of freshening since it is straightforward: it simply walks over a pattern, assigning a suitably fresh name to each binder encountered, and stopping at occurrences of Embed, since these are not part of the pattern. In our implementation, freshening also returns a permutation which describes how the variables were renamed, but we omit that here.

We can now define *unbind* as the operation that freshens the binding variables in the pattern and then opens the body of the binder with the new pattern.

$$
\begin{array}{l}
\mathit{unbind}\ (\mathsf{Bind}\ p\ t) = \textbf{do} \\
\quad p' \leftarrow \mathsf{freshen}\ p \\
\quad \mathit{return}\ (p', \mathit{open}\ p'\ t)
\end{array}
$$

In contrast, the destructors for Rebind and Rec *do not* freshen before opening the rest of the pattern. Instead, they use the preexisting names:

$$
\begin{array}{lll}
\mathit{unrebind} & (\mathsf{Rebind}\ p_1\ p_2) & = (p_1, \mathit{open}_{\mathsf{P}}\ p_1\ p_2) \\
\mathit{unrec} & (\mathsf{Rec}\ p) & = \mathit{open}_{\mathsf{P}}\ p\ p
\end{array}
$$

One might wonder: why the difference?

When opening a Bind, we must generate fresh names for its binders. However, by the time we come to opening a *nested* binding, fresh names will have already been chosen for its binders when the enclosing Bind was opened. Hence there is no need to choose new names. In fact, we *must not* choose fresh names, since there may exist corresponding free variables over which we have no control. For example, consider the term Bind (Rebind p_1 p_2) t, in which t may contain references to binders in p_1. If we use *unbind* to take it apart into Rebind p_1' p_2' and t', there will now be free variables in t' which match the names on binders in p_1'. Freshening p_1' again when opening the Rebind would destroy this connection, and in particular would mean that we could not reassemble the original term using *rebind* and *bind*. This is also why we must have Bind and Rebind as distinct combinators: if we used Bind everywhere, *unbind* would have no way of knowing whether it was opening a top-level Bind (which must first be freshened) or a nested one (which must not be).

4.6 Free variables, α-equivalence and substitution

Now we come to the real payoff of our representation, as we specify the basic UNBOUND operations of α-equivalence, free variable calculation, and capture-avoiding substitution, all shown in Figure 6. Their specifications are entirely straightforward—and, as described in the next section, reasoning about them is not much harder!

The α-equivalence relation on terms is defined mutually with a notion of equivalence for patterns which ignores binders and checks that embedded terms are α-equivalent. This α-equivalence relation is *essentially* structural equality—the only reason it is not precisely structural equality is that name annotations on binders are ignored in PEQ_BINDER.

Computing free variables is equally straightforward. Since free and bound variables are distinguished syntactically, we need only recurse through terms and patterns collecting all the free variables we find.

Finally, we define substitution into terms and patterns. If we see the free variable we are substituting for, we replace it with the term being substituted; otherwise we simply recurse. We need do nothing special when recursing through binders: since free and bound variables are distinguished syntactically, we are in no danger of mistaking a bound variable for a free variable we should substitute for, or of accidentally capturing any free variables in the substituted term.

5. Metatheory

We've now defined a simple semantics for our pattern specification language in terms of a locally nameless representation. But how can we know whether this semantics is at all meaningful? Well, we prove stuff, of course!

In the previous section, we noted how straightforward the definitions of various operations were. Likewise, most of the proofs regarding these operations are also straightforward (but full of fiddly details). We therefore omit most of the proofs and give only brief sketches of a few. The fact that the proofs are straightforward is a testament to the elegance of the locally nameless representation.

There is already a lot of work to draw on from the metatheory of locally nameless representations in the single binder case [1, 2]; much of the metatheory here can be seen as an extension of that prior work.

5.1 Local closure

One important property of the locally nameless representation is that only some terms are good representations. In particular, there is some "junk" in our representation, and we would like to know that we (and users of our library) never need to deal with it. The *local closure* relation in Figure 7 is an invariant for our representation which excludes terms with "dangling" bound variables. For example, the term 0@0, a bound variable with no surrounding binder, is not locally closed.[5]

By making the type combinators of our library abstract, we can demonstrate a central property of our interface: *users of the library can only construct locally closed patterns and terms.*

[5] This relation is an extension of McKinna and Pollack's VClosed relation [16].

$$
\begin{array}{llll}
\multicolumn{4}{l}{\approx :: T \to T \to \mathit{Bool}} \\
\mathsf{x} & \approx \mathsf{y} & = \mathsf{x} \equiv \mathsf{y} & \\
b_1 & \approx b_2 & = b_1 \equiv b_2 & \\
(\mathsf{K}\ s_1 \ldots s_n) & \approx (\mathsf{K}\ t_1 \ldots t_n) & = s_1 \approx t_1 \wedge \ldots \wedge s_n \approx t_n & \\
(\mathsf{Bind}\ p_1\ t_1) & \approx (\mathsf{Bind}\ p_2\ t_2) & = p_1 \approx_{\mathsf{P}} p_2 \wedge t_1 \approx t_2 &
\end{array}
$$

$$
\begin{array}{lll}
\multicolumn{3}{l}{\approx_{\mathsf{P}} :: P \to P \to \mathit{Bool}} \\
-_{\mathsf{x}} & \approx_{\mathsf{P}} -_{\mathsf{y}} & = \mathsf{True} \\
(\mathsf{K}\ p_1 \ldots p_n) & \approx_{\mathsf{P}} (\mathsf{K}\ q_1 \ldots q_n) & = p_1 \approx_{\mathsf{P}} q_1 \wedge \ldots \\
 & & \quad \wedge\ p_n \approx_{\mathsf{P}} q_n \\
(\mathsf{Rebind}\ p_1\ p_2) & \approx_{\mathsf{P}} (\mathsf{Rebind}\ q_1\ q_2) & = p_1 \approx_{\mathsf{P}} q_1 \wedge p_2 \approx_{\mathsf{P}} q_2 \\
(\mathsf{Embed}\ t_1) & \approx_{\mathsf{P}} (\mathsf{Embed}\ t_2) & = t_1 \approx t_2 \\
(\mathsf{Rec}\ p_1) & \approx_{\mathsf{P}} (\mathsf{Rec}\ p_2) & = p_1 \approx_{\mathsf{P}} p_2
\end{array}
$$

$$
\begin{array}{ll}
\multicolumn{2}{l}{\mathit{fv} :: T \to \mathit{Set}\ \mathbb{A}} \\
\mathit{fv}\ \mathsf{x} & = \{\mathsf{x}\} \\
\mathit{fv}\ b & = \varnothing \\
\mathit{fv}\ (\mathsf{K}\ t_1 \ldots t_n) & = \mathit{fv}\ t_1 \cup \cdots \cup \mathit{fv}\ t_n \\
\mathit{fv}\ (\mathsf{Bind}\ p\ t) & = \mathit{fv}_{\mathsf{P}}\ p \cup \mathit{fv}\ t
\end{array}
$$

$$
\begin{array}{ll}
\multicolumn{2}{l}{\mathit{fv}_{\mathsf{P}} :: P \to \mathit{Set}\ \mathbb{A}} \\
\mathit{fv}_{\mathsf{P}}\ -_{\mathsf{x}} & = \varnothing \\
\mathit{fv}_{\mathsf{P}}\ (\mathsf{K}\ p_1 \ldots p_n) & = \mathit{fv}_{\mathsf{P}}\ p_1 \cup \cdots \cup \mathit{fv}_{\mathsf{P}}\ p_n \\
\mathit{fv}_{\mathsf{P}}\ (\mathsf{Rebind}\ p_1\ p_2) & = \mathit{fv}_{\mathsf{P}}\ p_1 \cup \mathit{fv}_{\mathsf{P}}\ p_2 \\
\mathit{fv}_{\mathsf{P}}\ (\mathsf{Embed}\ t) & = \mathit{fv}\ t \\
\mathit{fv}_{\mathsf{P}}\ (\mathsf{Rec}\ p) & = \mathit{fv}_{\mathsf{P}}\ p
\end{array}
$$

$$
\begin{array}{ll}
\multicolumn{2}{l}{\mathit{subst} :: \mathbb{A} \to T \to T \to T} \\
\mathit{subst}\ \mathsf{x}\ s\ \mathsf{y} \mid \mathsf{x} \equiv \mathsf{y} & = s \\
\qquad\qquad\ \ \mid \mathit{otherwise} & = \mathsf{y} \\
\mathit{subst}\ \mathsf{x}\ s\ b & = b \\
\mathit{subst}\ \mathsf{x}\ s\ (\mathsf{K}\ t_1 \ldots t_n) & = \mathsf{K}\ (\mathit{subst}\ \mathsf{x}\ s\ t_1) \ldots (\mathit{subst}\ \mathsf{x}\ s\ t_n) \\
\mathit{subst}\ \mathsf{x}\ s\ (\mathsf{Bind}\ p\ t) & = \mathsf{Bind}\ (\mathit{subst}_{\mathsf{P}}\ \mathsf{x}\ s\ p)\ (\mathit{subst}\ \mathsf{x}\ s\ t)
\end{array}
$$

$$
\begin{array}{ll}
\multicolumn{2}{l}{\mathit{subst}_{\mathsf{P}} :: \mathbb{A} \to T \to P \to P} \\
\mathit{subst}_{\mathsf{P}}\ \mathsf{x}\ s\ -_{\mathsf{y}} & = -_{\mathsf{y}} \\
\mathit{subst}_{\mathsf{P}}\ \mathsf{x}\ s\ (\mathsf{K}\ p_1 \ldots p_n) & = \mathsf{K}\ (\mathit{subst}_{\mathsf{P}}\ \mathsf{x}\ s\ p_1) \ldots \\
 & \qquad (\mathit{subst}_{\mathsf{P}}\ \mathsf{x}\ s\ p_n) \\
\mathit{subst}_{\mathsf{P}}\ \mathsf{x}\ s\ (\mathsf{Rebind}\ p_1\ p_2) & = \mathsf{Rebind}\ (\mathit{subst}_{\mathsf{P}}\ \mathsf{x}\ s\ p_1) \\
 & \qquad (\mathit{subst}_{\mathsf{P}}\ \mathsf{x}\ s\ p_2) \\
\mathit{subst}_{\mathsf{P}}\ \mathsf{x}\ s\ (\mathsf{Embed}\ t) & = \mathsf{Embed}\ (\mathit{subst}\ \mathsf{x}\ s\ t) \\
\mathit{subst}_{\mathsf{P}}\ \mathsf{x}\ s\ (\mathsf{Rec}\ p) & = \mathsf{Rec}\ (\mathit{subst}_{\mathsf{P}}\ \mathsf{x}\ s\ p)
\end{array}
$$

Figure 6. α-equivalence, free variables, and substitution

Theorem 1 (Constructors and destructors preserve local closure). *All exported term and pattern constructors and destructors preserve local closure.*

Proof. Requires considering the action of each constructor and destructor individually, appealing to a number of properties about the interaction of local closure, open and close. □

Theorem 2 (Substitution preserves local closure).

- *If LC t and LC t′ then LC* $\mathit{subst}\ \mathsf{x}\ t\ t'$.
- *If LC t and LC p then LC* $\mathit{subst}_{\mathsf{P}}\ \mathsf{x}\ t\ p$.

Proof. Straightforward induction using a generalized version of local closure. □

$\boxed{\mathsf{LC}\ t}$ t is locally closed

$$\frac{}{\mathsf{LC}\ \mathsf{x}}\ \textsc{LC\_Free}$$

$$\frac{\mathsf{LC}\ t_1\ ..\ \mathsf{LC}\ t_n}{\mathsf{LC}\ \mathsf{K}\ t_1\ ..\ t_n}\ \textsc{LC\_Con}$$

$$\frac{\mathsf{LC}\ p\quad \mathsf{LC}\ (open\ p\ t)}{\mathsf{LC}\ \mathsf{Bind}\ p\ t}\ \textsc{LC\_Bind}$$

$\boxed{\mathsf{LC}\ p}$ p is locally closed

$$\frac{}{\mathsf{LC}\ -_{\mathsf{x}}}\ \textsc{LCP\_Binder}$$

$$\frac{\mathsf{LC}\ p_1\ ..\ \mathsf{LC}\ p_n}{\mathsf{LC}\ \mathsf{K}\ p_1\ ..\ p_n}\ \textsc{LCP\_Con}$$

$$\frac{\mathsf{LC}\ p_1\quad \mathsf{LC}\ (open_{\mathsf{P}}\ p_1\ p_2)}{\mathsf{LC}\ \mathsf{Rebind}\ p_1\ p_2}\ \textsc{LCP\_Rebind}$$

$$\frac{\mathsf{LC}\ t}{\mathsf{LC}\ \mathsf{Embed}\ t}\ \textsc{LCP\_Embed}$$

$$\frac{\mathsf{LC}\ (open_{\mathsf{P}}\ p\ p)}{\mathsf{LC}\ \mathsf{Rec}\ p}\ \textsc{LCP\_Rec}$$

Figure 7. Local closure of terms and patterns

Lemma 3 (Freshening preserves local closure)**.** *If* LC p *and* freshen $p \to p'$, *then* LC p'.

Proof. Easy induction; freshening only changes names on binders, which the LC relation ignores. □

Next, we show that α-equivalence is an equivalence relation that is respected by the operations of our library.

Theorem 4. $- \approx -$ *is an equivalence.*

Proof. Reflexivity, symmetry, and transitivity can each be established by straightforward induction. □

Theorem 5 (fv respects α-equivalence)**.** *If* $t_1 \approx t_2$, *then* $fv\ t_1 = fv\ t_2$.

Proof. Straightforward induction on $fv\ \ t_1$ along with a similar proof for fv_{P}. □

Theorem 6 (Substitution respects α-equivalence)**.** *If* $t_1 \approx t_2$ *and* $s_1 \approx s_2$, *then* $[x \mapsto s_1]t_1 \approx [x \mapsto s_2]t_2$.

Proof. Straightforward induction on the derivation of $t_1 \approx t_2$, along with a similar proof for pattern substitution. □

We next specify how the operations of α-equivalence, free variable calculation, and substitution interact with Bind. The proofs of these remaining theorems rely on properties about the interactions between *close* and each of the operations.

The first theorem states the interaction between binding and α-equivalence. It states that two bindings are α-equivalent when we can freshen two patterns to the same new result, and then show that their bodies are α-equivalent under a consistent renaming. Below, π_1 and π_2 are the permutations returned by freshen and $\pi_1 \cdot t_1$ is the application of a permutation to a term.

```
type N = Name E
data E = Var N
       | App E E
       | Lam (Bind N E)
  deriving Show
$(derive [''E])
instance Alpha E
instance Subst E E where
  isvar (Var n) = Just (SubstName n)
  isvar _       = Nothing
```

Figure 8. Representing the untyped lambda calculus

Theorem 7. *If* freshen $p_1 \to p, \pi_1$ *and* freshen $p_2 \to p, \pi_2$ *and* $\pi_1 \cdot t_1 \approx \pi_2 \cdot t_2$ *then* $bind\ p_1\ t_1 \approx bind\ p_2\ t_2$.

The second theorem specifies the behavior of fv for binders.

Theorem 8. $fv\ (bind\ p\ t) = fv_{\mathsf{P}}\ p \cup (fv\ t - binders\ p)$.

Finally, we specify the conditions when substitutions are permitted to commute through bindings.

Theorem 9. *If* $\{x\} \cup fv\ t$ *is disjoint from* $binders\ p$, *then* $subst\ x\ t\ (bind\ p\ t') = bind\ (subst_{\mathsf{P}}\ x\ t\ p)\ (subst\ x\ t\ t')$.

6. Implementation

The UNBOUND specification language is implemented as an embedded domain specific language (EDSL) in GHC Haskell, including all of the functionality described above and more. Terms and patterns are normal Haskell datatypes, and combinators such as Name, Bind and Rebind are abstract types provided by our library. The implementation of UNBOUND closely follows the semantics that we presented in the previous section, with UNBOUND operations such as fv, $subst$ and $\cdot \approx \cdot$ provided for user-defined datatypes via generic programming.

Below, we give an overview of our library, first by giving a short example of how it may be used in a Haskell program, and then discussing the implementation details. Figure 9 summarizes the important UNBOUND operations that we discuss in this section.

Figure 8 shows a definition of the untyped lambda calculus using UNBOUND. The first part of the figure is the same as in § 2. The rest of the figure includes the small amount of "boilerplate" necessary to use UNBOUND with the type E.

We implement UNBOUND using the REPLIB generic programming library [35]. REPLIB works by producing generic representation instances for each type. Roughly, a representation instance records the *structure* of a datatype by analyzing its **data** declaration. In this case, the call $(*derive* [''$E$]) uses Template Haskell [29] to generate the generic representation for E. This structure information is used to automatically generate particular functions over E on demand.

The following line in the figure declares E to be an instance of the *Alpha* type class, which governs α-equality, free variable and freshening operations. Happily, default implementations for the methods of *Alpha* are defined generically. Guided by the occurrences of Bind and Name in the definition of E, the default definitions of these methods behave exactly like their specifications in the semantics section.

Capture-avoiding substitution is governed by the *Subst* class, and requires a tiny bit of work on our part: we must indicate where variables are located in datatypes. Beyond that, the generic default implementation suffices. In general, the type of *subst* declares that values of type b may be substituted for free variables occurring in

$\cdot \approx \cdot$	$:: Alpha\ a \Rightarrow a \rightarrow a \rightarrow Bool$	-- alpha equivalence
$acompare$	$:: Alpha\ a \Rightarrow a \rightarrow a \rightarrow Ordering$	-- alpha-respecting comparison
fv	$:: (Alpha\ a, Rep\ b, Collection\ c) \Rightarrow a \rightarrow c\ (\mathsf{Name}\ b)$	-- free names (single sort)
$fvAny$	$:: (Alpha\ a, Collection\ c) \Rightarrow a \rightarrow c\ AnyName$	-- free names (all)
fv_{P}	$:: (Alpha\ a, Rep\ b, Collection\ c) \Rightarrow a \rightarrow c\ (\mathsf{Name}\ b)$	-- free names in annotations (single)
$fv_{\mathsf{P}}Any$	$:: (Alpha\ a, Collection\ c) \Rightarrow a \rightarrow c\ AnyName$	-- free names in annotations (all)
$binders$	$:: (Alpha\ a, Rep\ b, Collection\ c) \Rightarrow a \rightarrow c\ (\mathsf{Name}\ b)$	-- binding names (single sort)
$bindersAny$	$:: (Alpha\ a, Collection\ c) \Rightarrow a \rightarrow c\ AnyName$	-- binding names (all)
$freshen$	$:: (Alpha\ a, Fresh\ m) \Rightarrow a \rightarrow m\ (a, Perm\ AnyName)$	-- rename with fresh variables (returns a permutation)
$swaps$	$:: Alpha\ a \Rightarrow Perm\ AnyName \rightarrow a \rightarrow a$	-- permute variables
$subst$	$:: Subst\ b\ a \Rightarrow \mathsf{Name}\ b \rightarrow b \rightarrow a \rightarrow a$	-- single substitution
$substs$	$:: Subst\ b\ a \Rightarrow [(\mathsf{Name}\ b, b)] \rightarrow a \rightarrow a$	-- simultaneous substitution

Figure 9. Overview of selected UNBOUND operations

values of type a, so the $Subst\ E\ E$ instance shown declares that E values may be substituted for Vars in other E values.

By making $Subst$ a multiparameter type class we have flexibility and safety. Imagine a different declaration of the type E which contains both variables abstracting E, and type variables abstracting Typ. An instance $Subst\ E\ E$ declares that E variables can be replaced with Es, and another instance $Subst\ Typ\ E$ would declare that Typ variables can be replaced with Typs inside Es. In the latter case, we would use the default definition of $isvar$ as there is no way to replace Typ variables with Typs an get an E. In fact, the type indices of Name and $SubstName$ would not allow us to give a definition of $isvar$ that would confuse Typ and E variables.

The operations fv, $bind$, $unbind$ and $subst$ are implemented in terms of the $Alpha$ and $Subst$ type classes. Therefore, Figure 8 provides all the necessary definitions for the parallel reduction example in Figure 1 (which is valid Haskell code).

6.1 Multi-sorted names and $AnyName$

Instead of a single homogeneous set of atomic names, UNBOUND has multisorted names. Consider the type declarations in Figure 9. Names are indexed by a type, and the type of $subst$ ensures that only things of type t may be substituted for t-indexed names. The fv, fv_{P}, and $binders$ functions are also polymorphic in their result type, ignoring names whose type index does not match the requested result type. In this way, one may calculate, say, just the free term variables or just the free type variables from an expression. These functions are overloaded, so type inference determines precisely what sort of names will be calculated, and what sort of data structure (list, set, etc.) will be used to collect them.

However, sometimes we would like to know all free names, no matter what their sort. Therefore, UNBOUND also provides the type $AnyName$, which existentially hides the type index on a name, and the functions $fvAny$ and $bindersAny$ which return *all* appropriate names wrapped in $AnyName$ constructors.

6.2 The $Alpha$ type class

One way in which our implementation differs from our semantics is that while the semantics statically differentiates between *terms* and *patterns*, the implementation does not. Due to limitations of REPLIB, instead of having two type classes $Term\ a$ and $Pattern\ a$ we must have a single type class $Alpha\ a$ which serves both purposes. This conflation means that our implementation cannot statically prevent meaningless types which use a pattern as a term (*e.g.* Embed (Embed N)) or a term as a pattern (*e.g.* Bind (Bind N E) E).[6]

However, this conflation does have an advantage. Many of the methods of the $Alpha$ class are parameterized by a *mode* which determines whether the type is being used as a term or a pattern. For example, the α-equivalence method, called aeq', is declared as:

$$aeq' :: AlphaCtx \rightarrow a \rightarrow a \rightarrow Bool$$
$$aeq' = aeqR1\ rep1$$

The first argument, of type $AlphaCtx$, specifies whether alpha-equivalence should operate in term or pattern mode, generalizing the $\approx$ and $\approx_{\mathsf{P}}$ functions shown in Figure 6. The second line of the declaration is the default definition, which calls the datatype-generic function $aeqR1$ (not shown) with the type representation $rep1$ (derived with Template Haskell). Instances of $Alpha$ can override this generic implementation. For example, in the Name instance, the mode determines whether the names should be compared or always considered equivalent.

```
instance Alpha Name where
  ...
  aeq' c x y | mode c ≡ Term = x ≡ y
  aeq' c _ _ | mode c ≡ Pat  = True
```

Many types (such as products and sums) are parametric in the mode and use the same behavior in both cases.

Overall, the $Alpha$ type class includes mode-generalized versions of the operations shown in Figure 9, the predicates for distinguishing between terms and patterns, and the necessary machinery for the locally nameless representation ($open$, $close$, $find$ and nth).

6.3 Specific instances for $Alpha$

Default implementations for all $Alpha$ methods are defined via generic programming, but they may be overridden for greater control or customization. This capability is necessary in practical uses of UNBOUND for specific types.[7]

For example, suppose we would like to tag variables with source position information in our abstract syntax:

[6] We do, however, provide dynamic checks $isPat$ and $isTerm$ that can be used to ensure the invariants are maintained.

[7] This capability for overriding generic functions is inspired by the SYB3 library [14].

```
class Monad m ⇒ Fresh m where
  fresh :: Name a → m (Name a)

class Monad m ⇒ LFresh m where
  lfresh :: Rep a ⇒ Name a → m (Name a)
  avoid :: [AnyName] → m a → m a
```

Figure 10. The *Fresh* and *LFresh* type classes

```
data E = ...
       | Var SourcePos N
```

To make E an instance of *Alpha*, we need *SourcePos* to also be an instance of *Alpha*, because it appears inside the E type. If we would like α-equivalence to ignore source positions, we can simply override the default definition of α-equivalence for *SourcePos*. By identifying all source positions as equivalent, we ensure that expressions appearing in different positions can still be determined to be α-equivalent.

```
instance Alpha SourcePos where
  aeq' _ _ _ = True
```

6.4 Freshness monads

Since the freshen operation relies on the generation of fresh names, operations which make use of it (such as *unbind*) must execute within a monad. The *Fresh* type class, shown in Figure 10, governs those monads which can be used for this purpose, and is used to avoid tying users down to one particular concrete monad.

The *Fresh* class is quite simple: it requires only a single operation *fresh*, which takes a name as input and generates a new name (based on the given name) which is guaranteed to be "globally fresh" in some appropriate sense. For example, a simple concrete implementation might keep track of a global counter which is incremented every time *fresh* is called, appending the new counter value to the given base variable name.

However, this is unsatisfactory in many instances. For example, consider the simple pretty-printer for the untyped lambda calculus shown in Figure 11. If we pass it the term $\lambda -_x \lambda -_y \lambda -_z$ 2@0 (1@0 0@0), it produces `\x. \y1. \z2 -> x (y1 z2)`. We can see perfectly well that the numeric suffixes on y and z are unnecessary, since the existing names do not clash, but the *fresh* operation does not have enough information to make this assessment.

For this reason, we also provide the more sophisticated *LFresh* type class for monads which can generate *locally fresh* names. *lfresh* works much like *fresh*, but it has more to go on: *avoid ns m* allows us to specify that the names *ns* should be avoided by calls to *lfresh* in the subcomputation *m*. Unlike *fresh*, *lfresh* is not guaranteed to pick *globally* fresh names; it only guarantees not to pick names proscribed by an enclosing call to *avoid*. The intention is that it will return its argument unchanged when that name is not specifically to be avoided.

Using *LFresh*, we can rewrite the pretty-printer so that names are chosen fresh with respect to exactly those names currently in scope. To accomplish this we need only use *LFresh* instead of *Fresh* and *lunbind* instead of *unbind*; *lunbind* generates names for the binder using *lfresh*, then hands the body to a continuation wrapped in a call to *avoid*.

UNBOUND provides several concrete implementations for *Fresh* and *LFresh*, including transformer versions for adding fresh name generation capabilities to existing monads, and instances allowing their use with all the standard monad transformers in the `transformers` package.[8]

```
type N = Name E
data E = Var N
       | Lam (Bind N E)
       | App E E

ppr :: Fresh m ⇒ E → m String
ppr = ppr' 0
  where ppr' _ (Var x) = return (show x)
        ppr' p (Lam b) = do
          (x, e) ← unbind b
          e'     ← ppr' 0 e
          return $ parens (p > 0)
            ("\\" ++ show x ++ ". " ++ e')
        ppr' p (App e1 e2) = do
          e1' ← ppr' 1 e1
          e2' ← ppr' 2 e2
          return $ parens (p > 1) (e1' ++ " " ++ e2')
        parens True x = "(" ++ x ++ ")"
        parens _ x = x
```

Figure 11. A pretty-printer for the untyped lambda calculus

6.5 Simultaneous unbinding

Up to now, we have seen only examples of opening a single abstraction with *arbitrary* fresh names. However, some situations require simultaneously opening two or more abstractions with the *same* fresh names. For example, in order to check the convertibility of two LF Π-types, we must open them with the same fresh name and recursively check the convertibility of the bodies.

In order to simultaneously open two abstractions Bind p_1 t_1 and Bind p_2 t_2, we require only that p_1 and p_2 have the same number of binders. Requiring a stronger match between p_1 and p_2 would be unnecessarily limiting. For example, continuing our LF checking example, p_1 and p_2 might contain type annotations which are convertible but not α-equivalent.

Therefore, UNBOUND provides a function $unbind_2$ that simultaneously opens two related bindings.

```
unbind2 :: (Fresh m, Alpha p1, Alpha p2,
                    Alpha t1, Alpha t2) ⇒
           Bind p1 t1 → Bind p2 t2 →
           m (Maybe (p1, t1, p2, t2))
unbind2 (B p1 t1) (B p2 t2) = do
  case mkPerm (bindersAny p1) (bindersAny p2) of
    Just π → do
      (p1', π') ← freshen p1
      return (Just (p1', open p1' t1,
                    swaps (π' ∘ π) p2, open p1' t2))
    Nothing → return Nothing
```

This function works by first matching the binding variables of the two patterns together to create a permutation π. This operation will fail if the patterns bind different numbers of variables. Next, it freshens the first pattern p_1 and uses the result to open t_1 and t_2. Finally, it must compose the permutation from freshening p_1 with that from the match, and use the new permutation to rename the second pattern.

[8] `http://hackage.haskell.org/package/transformers`

7. Discussion

7.1 Nominal semantics

We have presented a semantics for the UNBOUND specification language in terms of a locally nameless representation, but this is not our only possible choice. UNBOUND could also be specified via an equivalent *nominal* semantics [19], and we are working in parallel on a nominal-style Haskell implementation. Such an alternative semantics would provide differences in running time/space, but otherwise would behave identically to the locally nameless version. In future work, we plan to formalize the precise connection between the two formulations and prove their equivalence with respect to the abstract interface provided by the library.

Although a nominal semantics might appear more natural to think about, in our experience the locally nameless semantics is far easier to understand when it comes to generalized binding patterns, especially with nesting. Therefore, an important contribution of this work is the identification of a *simple* semantics for pattern binding.

7.2 $C\alpha$ml-style specifications

François Pottier's $C\alpha$ml system [21] features a single-argument *abstraction* constructor, inside which patterns and terms (both bound and unbound) can be mixed. Directly inside an abstraction is a pattern, with terms embedded via outer (indicating a term outside the scope of the pattern) or inner (indicating that the pattern binds names in the term). $C\alpha$ml's abstraction constructor $\langle p \rangle$ is easily definable with UNBOUND as Bind (Rec p) (). Within that pattern, occurrences of Embed are analogous to occurrences of inner in $C\alpha$ml. To account for $C\alpha$ml's outer scope specification, we generalize the Embed combinator by adding a natural number subscript. When encountering Embed_n while doing an *open* or *close* operation, we *decrement* the level by n. Hence, Embed_0 corresponds to the original Embed, and Embed_1 corresponds to $C\alpha$ml's outer construct, since it shifts the scope of an embedded term out to the next enclosing level.

In UNBOUND we implement indexed embedding by adding a new type combinator Shift P. This type increments the index of its argument, so Shift (Embed T) corresponds to Embed_1 T, and Shift (Shift (Embed T)) is Embed_2 T. Operationally, all Shift does is decrement the binding level when the pattern is opened or closed so that variables will resolve to an outer scope.

7.3 UNBOUND in practice

We have been using UNBOUND in the TRELLYS project, in the context of type checking and evaluation of an experimental dependently-typed language. In this context, UNBOUND support for telescopes is essential. Our experience with TRELLYS has allowed us to find and correct a few bugs in our implementation of UNBOUND, but for the most part the use of UNBOUND has been unremarkable, in the sense that it seems to "just work". The only drawback to using UNBOUND is the lack of pattern matching for the abstract type Bind.

TRELLYS is an ideal client for UNBOUND, in that it is a prototype language with a greater emphasis on semantics than performance. Because UNBOUND is implemented using generic programming, it will be slower than a hand-coded implementation [25]. If necessary, we could easily replace the generic definitions with hand-coded operations by overriding the *Alpha* type class instances.

The locally nameless representation does have some performance concerns with respect to its use of *open* and *close*. While the standard operations *fv*, *subst*, and $\cdot \approx \cdot$ are linear in the size of terms, operations that are defined in the freshness monad must open and close the terms for each binding level, which could be expensive. Although we have not had any difficulties of this sort in TRELLYS (our experiments are still small) it is possible that with larger programs and deeper binding depths, these operations could dominate. To mitigate this difficulty, UNBOUND supports an "experts-only" interface, where critical operations can be written directly over the terms (in a manner similar to our implementations of *fv*, *subst* and $\cdot \approx \cdot$).

We have not explored the interaction of UNBOUND with standard optimizations [28]. For example, by caching free names, an implementation of substitution could stop early if the name being substituted for is not cached. If we remove names from bound patterns (which are preserved only for error messages) the locally nameless representation interacts nicely with hash-consing, as all α-equivalent terms have the same representation.

We are also working on bringing our nominal implementation of UNBOUND up to date with our reference locally nameless implementation. Both implementations provide the same interface to clients. When using the *LFresh* monad, the nominal implementation could avoid freshening when unbinding patterns if the patterns were already "sufficiently" fresh. However, there are trade-offs involved; for example, α-equivalence can be more expensive with the nominal version.

One important contribution of UNBOUND is that it provides an abstract interface to name binding. Clients can write their code against this interface, and, depending on their particular application, choose the most appropriate implementation. Importantly, our locally nameless implementation provides a simple reference semantics for this interface, and alternative implementations may use this semantics to prove their correctness.

8. Related Work

Locally nameless representation The locally nameless representation dates back to the introduction of de Bruijn indices, and is mentioned in the conclusion of de Bruijn's paper [8]. The key idea is even older. It rests on the separation of names into two distinct classes: variables (for locally bound variables) and parameters (for free, or globally bound variables) and goes back to Kleene [13], Prawitz [24] and Gentzen [10]. The full history of the locally nameless representation is outside the scope of this paper, but we refer to Aydemir et al [2] and Charguéraud [4] which discusses it in detail. Instead, we focus on the interaction between this representation, generic programming and binding specifications.

Charguéraud's paper [4] also gives several examples of locally-nameless representations of languages with specific binding forms, including binding a list of variables, pattern matching (with embedded terms), and recursive bindings. However, he does not consider a compositional framework for describing generalized binding.

Zappa Nardelli's locally nameless backend [36] for the OTT tool [27] automatically generates definitions for the Coq proof assistent given a specification of a language (with single binding only). These definitions include a locally nameless representation of the syntax, *open* and *close* operations, α-equivalence, substitution, and free variable calculation. The LNgen tool of Aydemir and Weirich [1] augments this output with generic proofs about this representation, including many of the properties of § 5.

Tools for general bindings Cirstea *et al.* [7] define the *ρ-calculus*, a λ-calculus-like system for expressing rewriting strategies, which features generic binders represented by any term.

Herman and Wand define a specification language for binding structure in the service of α-converting Scheme programs containing macros [12]. Although it only allows single variables as binding patterns, it is flexible about the subterms in which each variable should be bound.

The OTT tool provides an expressive specification language for generalized binding in programming languages. In conjunction with a specification of the abstract syntax, OTT allows the definition of *bindspecs*: functions that arbitrarily select the binding variables that appear in terms and bind them elsewhere in the abstract syntax. They give a semantics of this specification language using a representation with concrete variable names [26] and show that under appropriate conditions, their concrete substitution functions respect α-equivalence and coincide with capture-avoiding substitution.

Inspired by the OTT specification language, Urban and Kaliszyk recently extended the Nominal Isabelle proof assistant with support for general bindings [34]. Their system works by using the OTT binding specifications (with some restrictions) to define α-equivalence classes of syntax with binders which they use to model nominal-logic specifications. While a direct comparison is difficult, their restrictions prevent variables from being bound by two different bindspecs, which seems necessary for telescopes. On the other hand, they also add two forms of *set* bindings to their specifications, allowing binders to be equivalent up to permutation and weakening of their patterns.

As discussed in § 7.2, there is a close connection between UNBOUND and Francois Pottier's Cαml system [21], based on a nominal semantics for binding. One major difference is that Cαml explicitly does not include support for nested binders. Another difference is that Cαml is an external tool that performs a preprocessing step, whereas UNBOUND is a library. However, this is not a fundamental difference; Cαml could be made into a library as well if OCaml had better support for generic programming (likewise, UNBOUND could be ported to languages without support for generic programming by making it into an external tool).

Cheney's FreshLib [6] is a Haskell library which served as an inspiration for UNBOUND. Like UNBOUND, it uses generic programming to automatically define α-equivalence and substitution functions (although FreshLib is based on a nominal semantics for name binding, so the generic operations that establish its semantics are different). FreshLib also supports some forms of generalized binding, but does not give a generic treatment of patterns.

Other tools based on nominal logic include FreshML [31] and FreshOCaml [30]. However, they support limited forms of binding patterns which do not include embeddings, recursive or nested bindings. Likewise, the Haskell Nominal Toolkit [3] is a library that supports single binding for a fixed term structure.

9. Future work

Although we believe UNBOUND is useful in its current state, there are several directions in which we would like to extend it.

Other forms of "exotic" binding Cheney [5] gives a catalogue of "exotic" binding, renaming, and structural congruence situations. Although UNBOUND can express many of these examples, we hope to extend UNBOUND with better support for "global" binding, such as that used for objects and modules. Furthermore, we would also like to add support for set binding similar to Nominal Isabelle [34]. However, implementing $unbind_2$ in the presence of such bindings is a nontrivial task.

Better static distinction between names and patterns As discussed in § 6.2, an infelicity of our current design is the ability to get terms and patterns mixed up. UNBOUND inherits this limitation from REPLIB; it is possible that an alternative framework for generic programming would perform better in this respect.

Scoping UNBOUND does not keep track of the scope of names once they have been unbound. While this laxity leads to a familiar and flexible interface, it does not rule out bugs that could occur from names escaping their scope. Pottier *et al.* have made progress in this respect [22, 23], and we would like to explore a variant interface for UNBOUND that provides this tighter control.

Mechanized metatheory The UNBOUND specification language seems ideal for incorporation into tools like Ott, LNgen and Nominal Isabelle that assist in the formalization of programming language metatheory. Indeed, locally nameless representations have already proved useful for that sort of reasoning.

However, in the context of formal reasoning, we must be more careful about scoping. Allowing bound names to escape their scope can lead to unsoundness (see Urban [32]). Such functions violate the "Freshness Condition for Binders", a side condition required for all function definitions in Nominal Isabelle [33]. Adapting UNBOUND to mechanized reasoning would require a similar side condition for function definitions.

10. Conclusion

UNBOUND is an expressive specification language for generalized binding structures, defined with a simple compositional semantics, proven correct, and immediately available to the GHC user community. Because it supports the rapid development of typecheckers, compilers, and interpreters, it is a valuable tool for exploration in programming language design. Furthermore, we hope that the design of UNBOUND itself will be a model for future work on library support for expressive binding structure.

Acknowledgments

Chris Casinghino, Vilhelm Sjöberg and the rest of the TRELLYS team provided valuable feedback on this work. Thanks are also due to the Penn PLClub for feedback on an early draft of this paper. Finally, we thank the anonymous referees for their many helpful corrections, comments, and suggestions. This material is based upon work supported by the National Science Foundation under grant 0910500.

References

[1] B. Aydemir and S. Weirich. LNgen: Tool support for locally nameless representations. Technical Report MS-CIS-10-24, Computer and Information Science, University of Pennsylvania, June 2010.

[2] B. Aydemir, A. Charguéraud, B. C. Pierce, R. Pollack, and S. Weirich. Engineering formal metatheory. In *ACM SIGPLAN-SIGACT Symposium on Principles of Programming Languages (POPL)*, pages 3–15, Jan. 2008.

[3] C. Calvès. A Haskell nominal toolkit. `http://www.inf.kcl.ac.uk/pg/calves/hnt/`, Jan. 2009.

[4] A. Charguéraud. The locally nameless representation. *Journal of Automated Reasoning, Special Issue on the POPLmark Challenge*, 2011. To appear.

[5] J. Cheney. Toward a general theory of names: binding and scope. In *Proceedings of the 3rd ACM SIGPLAN workshop on Mechanized reasoning about languages with variable binding*, MERLIN '05, pages 33–40, New York, NY, USA, 2005. ACM.

[6] J. Cheney. Scrap your nameplate: (functional pearl). In *Proceedings of the tenth ACM SIGPLAN international conference on Functional programming*, ICFP '05, pages 180–191, New York, NY, USA, 2005. ACM. ISBN 1-59593-064-7.

[7] H. Cirstea, C. Kirchner, L. Liquori, and B. Wack. Rewrite strategies in the rewriting calculus. In B. Gramlich and S. Lucas, editors, *Proceedings of the Third International Workshop on Reduction Strategies in Rewriting and Programming* , Valencia, Spain, June 2003. Electronic Notes in Theoretical Computer Science.

[8] N. G. de Bruijn. Lambda calculus notation with nameless dummies, a tool for automatic formula manipulation, with application to the Church-Rosser theorem. *Indagationes Mathematicae*, 34(5):381–392, 1972.

[9] N. G. de Bruijn. Telescopic mappings in typed lambda calculus. *Information and Computation*, 91(2):189 – 204, 1991.

[10] G. Gentzen. *The Collected Papers of Gerhard Gentzen*. North-Holland, 1969. Edited by Mandred Szabo.

[11] A. D. Gordon. A mechanisation of name-carrying syntax up to alpha-conversion. In J. Joyce and C. Seger, editors, *Higher-order Logic Theorem Proving And Its Applications, Proceedings, 1993*, volume 780 of *Lecture Notes in Computer Science*, pages 414–426. Springer, 1994.

[12] D. Herman and M. Wand. A theory of hygienic macros. In *ESOP '08: Proceedings of the Seventeenth European Symposium On Programming*, Mar. 2008.

[13] S. Kleene. *Introduction to Metamathematics*. ban Nostrand Rheinhold, Princeton, USA, 1952.

[14] R. Lämmel and S. Peyton Jones. Scrap your boilerplate with class: extensible generic functions. In *Proceedings of the ACM SIGPLAN International Conference on Functional Programming (ICFP 2005)*, pages 204–215. ACM Press, Sept. 2005.

[15] C. McBride. *Dependently Typed Functional Programs and their Proofs*. PhD thesis, University of Edinburgh, 1999. Available from `http://www.lfcs.informatics.ed.ac.uk/reports/00/ECS-LFCS-00-419/`.

[16] J. McKinna and R. Pollack. Some lambda calculus and type theory formalized. *Journal of Automated Reasoning*, 23(3–4):373–409, 1999.

[17] U. Norell. *Towards a practical programming language based on dependent type theory*. PhD thesis, Department of Computer Science and Engineering, Chalmers University of Technology, SE-412 96 Göteborg, Sweden, September 2007.

[18] B. Pientka and J. Dunfield. Beluga: A framework for programming and reasoning with deductive systems (system description). In J. Giesl and R. Hähnle, editors, *IJCAR*, volume 6173 of *Lecture Notes in Computer Science*, pages 15–21. Springer, 2010.

[19] A. M. Pitts. Nominal logic, a first order theory of names and binding. *Information and Computation*, 186:165–193, 2003.

[20] A. Poswolsky and C. Schürmann. System description: Delphin – a functional programming language for deductive systems. *Electron. Notes Theor. Comput. Sci.*, 228:113–120, January 2009.

[21] F. Pottier. An overview of Cαml. In *ACM Workshop on ML*, pages 27–52, Mar. 2006.

[22] F. Pottier. Static name control for FreshML. In *In IEEE Symposium on Logic in Computer Science*, pages 356–365, 2007.

[23] N. Pouillard and F. Pottier. A fresh look at programming with names and binders. In *Proceedings of the 15th ACM SIGPLAN international conference on Functional programming*, ICFP '10, pages 217–228, New York, NY, USA, 2010. ACM. ISBN 978-1-60558-794-3.

[24] D. Prawitz. *Natural Deduction: Proof Theoretical Study*. Almquist and Wiksell, Stockholm, 1965.

[25] A. Rodriguez, J. Jeuring, P. Jansson, A. Gerdes, O. Kiselyov, and B. C. d. S. Oliveira. Comparing libraries for generic programming in Haskell. *SIGPLAN Not.*, 44:111–122, September 2008.

[26] S. Sarkar, P. Sewell, and F. Zappa Nardelli. Binding and substitution. `www.cl.cam.ac.uk/~pes20/ott/bind-doc.pdf`, Oct. 2007.

[27] P. Sewell, F. Z. Nardelli, S. Owens, G. Peskine, T. Ridge, S. Sarkar, and R. Strniša. Ott: Effective tool support for the working semanticist. *Journal of Functional Programming*, 20(1):71–122, 2010.

[28] Z. Shao. Implementing typed intermediate language. In *Proc. 1998 ACM SIGPLAN International Conference on Functional Programming (ICFP'98)*, pages 313–323, Baltimore, Maryland, September 1998.

[29] T. Sheard and S. P. Jones. Template meta-programming for Haskell. *SIGPLAN Not.*, 37:60–75, December 2002.

[30] M. Shinwell and A. Pitts. *Fresh Objective Caml User Manual*. Cambridge University Computer Laboratory, Feb. 2005.

[31] M. R. Shinwell, A. M. Pitts, and M. J. Gabbay. FreshML: Programming with binders made simple. In *Eighth ACM SIGPLAN International Conference on Functional Programming (ICFP 2003), Uppsala, Sweden*, pages 263–274. ACM Press, Aug. 2003.

[32] C. Urban. How to prove false using the variable convention. Appears as a poster at TTVSI, 1 page, mar 2008.

[33] C. Urban. Nominal techniques in Isabelle/HOL. *Journal of Automated Reasoning*, 40:327–356, 2008. ISSN 0168-7433. URL `http://dx.doi.org/10.1007/s10817-008-9097-2`.

[34] C. Urban and C. Kaliszyk. General bindings and alpha-equivalence in Nominal Isabelle. In G. Barthe, editor, *Programming Languages and Systems*, volume 6602 of *Lecture Notes in Computer Science*, pages 480–500. Springer Berlin / Heidelberg, 2011. URL `http://dx.doi.org/10.1007/978-3-642-19718-5_25`.

[35] S. Weirich. RepLib: A library for derivable type classes. In *Haskell Workshop*, pages 1–12, Portland, OR, USA, Sept. 2006.

[36] F. Zappa Nardelli. A locally-nameless backend for Ott. `moscova.inria.fr/~zappa/projects/ln_ott/`, 2009.

Recursion principles for syntax with bindings and substitution

Andrei Popescu
Technical University Munich
University of Illinois at Urbana-Champaign
Institute of Mathematics Simion Stoilow of the Romanian Academy
uuomul@yahoo.com

Elsa L. Gunter
University of Illinois at Urbana-Champaign
egunter@uiuc.edu

Abstract

We characterize the data type of terms with bindings, freshness and substitution, as an initial model in a suitable Horn theory. This characterization yields a convenient recursive definition principle, which we have formalized in Isabelle/HOL and employed in a series of case studies taken from the λ-calculus literature.

Categories and Subject Descriptors F.3.1 [*Specifying and Verifying and Reasoning about Programs*]: Mechanical verification

General Terms Languages, Verification

Keywords Syntax with bindings, Recursion, Lambda calculus, Substitution

1. Introduction

Bindings and substitution, i.e., the notions of *binding a variable in a term* and *substituting a term or value for a variable in a term*, respectively, are pervasive in logic and programming languages. Formal/rigorous reasoning about syntax with bindings is notoriously hard, as observed by many authors (e.g., [8, 11, 14, 19, 22, 28, 32, 39, 45]). In particular, basic lemmas about *composing and commuting substitutions* turn out, in practice, to be problematic.

In this paper, we introduce a recursor for terms with bindings with *built-in substitution*, which ensures, in exchange for checking a few conditions on the target domain, both the correctness of the definition and compositionality w.r.t. freshness and substitution. Our contribution is formalized in the Isabelle theorem prover [26], and is in general guided by formalization goals.

Apart from this introduction and Section 8 which draws conclusions and discusses related work, this paper has two main parts. The first part, consisting of Sections 2, 3, 4, and 5, motivates, presents and illustrates our mathematical contribution. In Section 2, we discuss two standard situations occurring in formal reasoning: defining a semantic domain interpretation map and a Higher-Order Abstract Syntax (HOAS) representation map. In order to go through, these definitions traditionally require a tedious treatment of bindings and α-equivalence. Moreover, later development usually requires that the involved interpretation/representation maps be shown to *preserve freshness* and be *compositional w.r.t. to substitution*. These "basic", "low-level" facts require serious effort from the developer, which contrasts with their highly intuitive character; and this discrepancy is of course even more dramatic if one is interested in a formal development (in a theorem prover). All the above motivate our approach, described in Section 3. The main idea is to integrate freshness and substitution in the definition (of the desired map from terms to another set), resolving "at definition time", both the issue of well-definedness (i.e., compatibility with α-equivalence) and that of substitution compositionality. Mathematically, this is based on a characterization of the term model as initial in a suitable Horn theory in the first-order language of the term-constructor, freshness and substitution operators. We show how our approach handles the aforementioned two situations – e.g., for HOAS, both the definition of the map and its so-called *adequacy* are established during the definition. Our thesis is that many situations from formal reasoning about syntax with bindings fall under the scope of this substitution-based definition principle. In Section 4, we bring evidence for this thesis by means of other examples taken from the λ-calculus literature. We also discuss cases where our principle does not apply. Finally, in Section 5, we explore the notion of inferring more facts about the maps defined by our methodology. It turns out that this is indeed possible (and, as witnessed by examples, useful). In particular, we obtain an internal characterization of the term model, expressed solely in terms of the basic operators: syntactic constructs, freshness and substitution.

The second part, consisting of Sections 6 and 7, deals with formalization aspects. Indeed, the main goal of our theoretical contribution is facilitating rigorous, and indeed *formal*, definitions of substitution-compositional maps on terms with bindings. Therefore, formalizing our results and applying them in actual formal developments is an important test for their relevance. In Section 6, we discuss the formal resolution in Isabelle/HOL [26] of one of our motivating problems, namely, adequate HOAS representation. In Section 7, we employ our characterization from Section 5 to relate by isomorphisms our formalization with other Isabelle formalizations of λ-calculus terms: Nominal [42], Hybrid [8] and *locally named* [38]. Indeed, our characterizations of terms as an abstract data type (ADT) is up to isomorphism – any model satisfying our properties yields an isomorphism to our own model (and to any correct model). We propose this methodology (of establishing such ADT isomorphisms) as a basis for certifying formalizations and transporting results across different formalizations.

The appendix contains more details on the Isabelle formalization of this paper's results and examples (made available at [4] for the interested reader). An extended version of the material presented in this paper, including technical details and explanations, can be found in [36] (as the largely self-contained chapter 2 from there).

Conventions and notations. We employ the standard symbols for functional and logical connectives and quantifiers (λ for functional

ICFP'11, September 19–21, 2011, Tokyo, Japan.

abstraction, $\wedge$ for conjunction, $\Longrightarrow$ for implication, $\forall$ for the universal quantifier), only in the meta-language of this paper, and *not* in the various formal languages that we discuss.

We fix a countable set **var** of variables, ranged over by x, y, z, and consider the set **term**, of terms, ranged over by X, Y, Z, to be generated by the following grammar:

$$X \ ::= \ \mathsf{Var}\, x \mid \mathsf{App}\, X\, Y \mid \mathsf{Lm}\, x\, X$$

where, within $\mathsf{Lm}\, x\, X$, any occurrence of x in X is assumed bound. Thus, we use lower cases for variables and upper cases for terms. $\mathsf{Var}\, x$ is the variable x regarded as a term, $\mathsf{App}\, X\, Y$ is an application, "X applied to Y", and $\mathsf{Lm}\, x\, X$ is a λ-abstraction, of x in X. We usually omit spelling the variable-injection operator Var, writing x instead of $\mathsf{Var}\, x$. Terms are identified modulo the notion of α-equivalence standardly induced by the above bindings. The freshness and substitution operators,

- fresh : **var** $\rightarrow$ **term** $\rightarrow$ **bool** and
- $\_[\_/\_]$: **term** $\rightarrow$ **term** $\rightarrow$ **var** $\rightarrow$ **term**,

are the standard ones, namely: $\mathsf{fresh}\, x\, X$ holds iff the variable x is fresh for (i.e., does not appear free in) the term X; $X[Y/y]$ is the term obtained from X by substituting, in a capture-free manner, all occurrences of y with Y.

We refer to the above type, **term** with the syntactic constructors (C), freshness (F) and substitution (S), as $\mathbf{term}_{C,F,S}$. Besides syntactic constructs and substitution, we occasionally consider the swapping operator, $\_[\_\wedge\_]$: **term** $\rightarrow$ **var** $\rightarrow$ **var** $\rightarrow$ **term**, where $X[x \wedge y]$ is obtained from X by swapping (interchanging) all occurrences of x and y.

2. Two problems of rigorous/formal reasoning

We next recall two typical situations arising in formal reasoning on syntax with bindings – semantic domain interpretation and Higher Order Abstract Syntax (HOAS) representation – as motivation for the desire to have convenient (conceptual and formal) tools for recursive definitions sensible to the mechanisms of binding *and substitution*.

2.1 Problem I – Interpretation of syntax in semantic domains

Suppose we want to interpret terms in a semantic domain D (ranged over by d) endowed with operators $\mathsf{APP} : D \rightarrow D \rightarrow D$ and $\mathsf{LM} : (D \rightarrow D) \rightarrow D$, by matching the syntactic App and Lm with the semantic APP and LM, mapping syntactic binders to functional binders. For this, we need the collection of valuations (of variables into the domain), $\mathbf{val} = (\mathbf{var} \rightarrow D)$, ranged over by ρ. Then, the definition of the interpretation, $[\_] : \mathbf{term} \rightarrow \mathbf{val} \rightarrow D$, needs to proceed recursively on the structure of terms:

(1) $[x]\ \rho = \rho\ x$, **(2)** $[\mathsf{App}\ X\ Y]\ \rho = \mathsf{APP}\ ([X]\ \rho)\ ([Y]\ \rho)$,
(3) $[\mathsf{Lm}\ x\ X]\ \rho = \mathsf{LM}\ (\lambda d : D.\ [X]\ (\rho[x \leftarrow d]))$,

where $\rho[x \leftarrow d]$ is the valuation ρ updated at x with d. Moreover, we usually wish to prove the following:

- Obliviousness of the interpretation to the variables fresh for the represented term: **(4)** $\mathsf{fresh}\ x\ X\ \wedge\ \rho =_x \rho' \Longrightarrow [X]\ \rho = [X]\ \rho'$, where $\rho =_x \rho'$, read "ρ equals ρ' everywhere but in x", is defined to be $\forall y \neq x.\ \rho\ y = \rho'\ y$.
- Compositionality of substitution w.r.t. environment update, a.k.a. the *substitution lemma*: **(5)** $[Y[X/x]]\ \rho = [Y]\ (\rho[x \leftarrow [X]\ \rho])$.

Parenthesis. The above recursive definition and facts to be proved follow a canonical pattern of interpreting syntax in denotational semantics and formal logic. To give another well-known example, the semantics of FOL formulas φ is typically given as a relation $M \models_\rho \varphi$, read "M satisfies φ for the valuation ρ : **var** $\rightarrow M$"; and the clause for the universal quantifier, which we denote by All, is the following: $M \models_\rho \mathsf{All}\ x\ \varphi$ iff $\forall m \in M.\ M \models_{\rho[x \leftarrow m]} \varphi$. Despite the different notation, this clause is of the same nature as that for Lm, in that the syntactic variable binding is captured in both cases by a semantic abstraction (functional in one case, universal in the other) in conjunction with environment update. Moreover, here (in FOL) we also wish to prove that the interpretation does not depend on the fresh variables and that the substitution lemma holds. In fact, most of the basic properties of FOL, including those necessary for the proof of the completeness theorem, rely on these two. The solution discussed below also applies to this FOL example and to many others in the same category. **End of parenthesis.**

The problem with the above definition of $[\_]$ is that, at the Lm-clause, we have to show the choice of the representatives x and X in $\mathsf{Lm}\, x\, X$ immaterial. In other words, this clause proceeds as if Lm were a *free* construct on terms, while it is not (since there exist x, X, x', X' such that $(x, X) \neq (x', X')$ and $\mathsf{Lm}\, x\, X = \mathsf{Lm}\, x'\, X'$). Here is another way to express the problem. Let us call "quasi-terms" the absolutely free data type generated by the constructors Var, App and Lm, without factoring to α-equivalence. What we called "terms" are thus quasi-terms factored by α, i.e., α-classes of quasi-terms. Now, the above is a valid definition if regarded on quasi-terms; however, to lift this to an operator on terms, we need to prove that it preserves α-equivalence. This problem is typically by-passed in informal texts, relying on "folklore", but needs to be faced and solved within a formalization. This folklore problem is more challenging than it may look at first. We urge the reader to try to solve it before reading our solution. (A proof of compatibility with α does not go through by induction directly; other auxiliary facts need to be discovered and proved in parallel; and care is required for the choice of these facts.)

2.2 Problem II – Compositional HOAS representation

HOAS [22, 31] prescribes the representation of formal systems of interest, referred to as the *object systems*, into a fixed, but customizable *logical framework*, a.k.a. the *meta system*, by capturing object-level features such as binding mechanisms directly as corresponding meta-level features. While logical frameworks in current use are typically more complex (LF [22], intuitionistic HOL [30], etc.), here we restrict ourselves to the λ-calculus augmented with constants as the logical framework (as in [7, 8, 25]). But our discussion also applies to the above more complex frameworks.

To augment the λ-calculus with constants, we fix **const**, ranged over by c, a set of *constants*. We extend the syntax of λ-calculus with these constants as usual, so that the new terms, which we call **const**-terms and whose set we denote by **term**(**const**), are now: either (injections of) variables x, or applications $\mathsf{App}\, X\, Y$, or λ-abstractions $\mathsf{Lm}\, x\, X$ (as before), or injections of constants, $\mathsf{Ct}\, c$. Constants do not participate in bindings and are unaffected by substitution. Just like for variables, we usually omit the constant-injection Ct, writing c instead of $\mathsf{Ct}\, c$.

We take **term**(**const**) as our logical framework. (A complete logical framework, of course, also has judgment mechanisms, typically given by a type system in combination with a reduction relation; for instance, in our case, reduction may be β or $\beta\eta$-reduction. Here, we ignore the largely orthogonal judgment aspect of HOAS and consider the syntax representation aspect only.) Say our object system is the λ-calculus itself (without constants). Its natural HOAS representation into **term**(**const**) proceeds as follows:

- Instantiate **const** to a two-element set, $\{\mathsf{APP}, \mathsf{LM}\}$, to match the two syntactic constructors App and Lm. (Note that one does not represent object-level variables and their injection into terms explicitly, as they will be captured directly by the meta-level items.)
- Define the representation map rep : **term** $\rightarrow$ **term**($\{\mathsf{APP}, \mathsf{LM}\}$) recursively on the structure of terms: **(1)** $\mathsf{rep}\ x = x$;
(2) $\mathsf{rep}(\mathsf{App}\ X\ Y) = \mathsf{App}\ (\mathsf{App}\ \mathsf{APP}\ (\mathsf{rep}\ X))\ (\mathsf{rep}\ Y)$;
(3) $\mathsf{rep}(\mathsf{Lm}\ x\ X) = \mathsf{App}\ \mathsf{LM}\ (\mathsf{Lm}\ x\ (\mathsf{rep}\ X))$.

Much of what makes HOAS encodings so convenient is *substitution compositionality*: **(4)** $\mathsf{rep}(Y[X/x]) = (\mathsf{rep}\ Y)[(\mathsf{rep}\ X)/x]$, and indeed this is the main fact that is typically proved informally, by "pen-and-paper", about a HOAS representation. Preservation of freshness is another fact that turns out to be useful (see, e.g., [21], page 657), even though this is seldom acknowledged explicitly: **(5)** $\mathsf{fresh}\ x\ X \Longrightarrow \mathsf{fresh}\ x\ (\mathsf{rep}\ X)$. As before, the problem with the definition of rep and with the (customary) informal proof of compositionality is the non-rigorous treatment of the Lm-case.

3. Horn-based recursion with built-in substitution

In this section, we show that we can regard $\mathbf{term}_{C,F,S}$ as an "ordinary" data type, of the same kind with, say, finite sets or bags; namely, we can regard it as the initial model of a suitable Horn theory. But in order to explain the intuition behind this view, we first recall how "ordinary" data type recursion is standardly obtained and how the initial model of a Horn theory is constructed.

3.1 Ordinary data types

To define a function H (primitively) recursively from an inductive data type, say, $I\!N$, to another set A, $H : I\!N \to A$, one needs to express the behavior of H w.r.t. the number constructors, 0 and Suc, i.e., write equations of the forms **(1)** $H\,0 = 0_A$ and **(2)** $H\,(\mathsf{Suc}\ n) = \mathsf{Suc}_A\ (H\ n)$, where $0_A \in A$ and $\mathsf{Suc}_A : A \to A$. In other words, one needs to endow A with "number-like" operations, 0_A and Suc_A, i.e., organize A as a *model* for the signature having a constant symbol, 0, and a unary operation symbol, Suc.

The above simple recipe is valid for defining functions from an *absolutely free* data type such as $I\!N$. When the constructors are not free, simply defining on the target domain operations matching these constructors may not suffice for properly defining a function. For example, consider the data type $\mathbf{P}_f(U)$ of finite sets with elements in a fixed universe U (ranged over by u), with the singleton and the union constructors. To define a function H from $\mathbf{P}_f(U)$ to a set A, it does not suffice to endow A with operations $\{\_\}^A : U \to A$ and $\cup^A : A \to A \to A$, and state **(3)** $H\,\{x\} = \{x\}^A$ and **(4)** $H\,(S \cup T) = (H\ S) \cup^A (H\ T)$. Indeed, an H satisfying (3) and (4) may not exist. However, we know that $\mathbf{P}_f(U)$ is a data type *specifiable by equations*: if we start with formal expressions E given by the grammar $E ::= \{u\} \mid E_1 \cup E_2$ (where $\{\_\}$ and $\cup$ do not have any set-theoretic meaning, but are just free constructors) and then factor these expressions by all equalities deducible from associativity, commutativity and idempotence (ACI), we obtain a data type isomorphic to $\mathbf{P}_f(U)$. A useful consequence of this is that the clauses (3) and (4) do yield a valid definition of a function H provided the ACI properties hold for $\{\_\}^A$. (In other words, $\mathbf{P}_f(U)$ is the *initial ACI model.*) In this sense, $\mathbf{P}_f(U)$ is an "ordinary" data type, i.e., one freely generated by some constructors modulo some equations.

3.2 Terms as an ordinary data type

So is $\mathbf{term}_{C,F,S}$ also "ordinary"? To answer this question, we first remark that, due to the freshness operator, which is better regarded as a relation, we need to slightly relax our notion of "ordinary" data type, accepting not only operations, but also relations, and not only equations, but more generally *Horn clauses* – fortunately, this relaxation is unproblematic (w.r.t. our goal of obtaining a recursion principle), since Horn theories also admit initial models.

Next, we recall the way in which the initial model of a given Horn theory $\mathcal{H}$ is constructed: start, as before, with formal expressions built using the involved operation symbols, and then proceed to define the equality relation (by which one will need to factor to obtain the end-product type) as well as the other relations (corresponding to the relation symbols) *minimally*, as containing just what can be inferred from $\mathcal{H}$; therefore, the construction of the initial Horn model proceeds as if defining equality and all the relations *mutually recursively*. By contrast, term equality, i.e., α-equivalence, and substitution (main components of $\mathbf{term}_{C,F,S}$) are traditionally defined in a rather cumbersome manner: first substitution is defined on quasi-terms (i.e., "raw" terms, not yet factored to α) via an auxiliary "pick fresh" operator, then α is defined using substitution (or sometimes swapping) on quasi-terms, and finally substitution is shown to not depend on the choice made by "pick fresh" and to be compatible with α. Such traditional definitions are hardly exciting as a basis for a useful Horn specification (hence a useful recursion principle), due to the "immaterial" presence of "pick fresh".

Therefore, our original question becomes: can we have simple (yet complete) mutually recursive definitions of α-equivalence, freshness and substitution? It turns out the answer is positive,[1] if we renounce the ambition of having substitution *fully specified on quasi-terms*. Namely, in the Lm-case, when variable capture occurs, instead of eagerly "picking fresh" in order for substitution to go under Lm, as in $(\mathsf{Lm}\ x\ X)[Z/z] = \mathsf{Lm}\ x'\ (X[x'/x][Z/z])$ where $x' = \mathsf{pickFresh}\ \{z, Z\}$ (as is customarily done), we choose to lazily "define" substitution only when interaction with Lm is smooth, namely, $x \neq z \ \wedge\ \mathsf{fresh}\ x\ Z \Longrightarrow (\mathsf{Lm}\ x\ X)[Z/z] = \mathsf{Lm}\ x\ (X[Z/z])$; for the rest of the cases, an α-renaming clause, $x \neq y \wedge \mathsf{fresh}\, y\, X \Longrightarrow \mathsf{Lm}\, y\, (X[y/x]) = \mathsf{Lm}\, x\, X$, will eventually "make way" for substitution under Lm. (The latter two clauses are reflected in the definition of FSb-models below, as S4 and A.)

These observations lead to a simple Horn characterization of $\mathbf{term}_{C,F,S}$ and to a corresponding recursion principle; the latter states that, given a model of this Horn theory, there exists a (unique) constructor-, freshness- and substitution- compositional map from the term model to it. We think of such models as containing "generalized" terms, i.e., items with term-like operations on them (which we later refer to as "generalized" constructor, freshness and substitution operators) satisfying term-like properties (Horn clauses) – hence the prefix "g" in the notations below.

A *fresh-substitution-model* (*FSb-model*) consists of a set A (ranged over by gX, gY, gZ) together with operations and relation $\mathsf{gVar} : \mathbf{var} \to A$, $\mathsf{gApp} : A \to A \to A$, $\mathsf{gLm} : \mathbf{var} \to A \to A$, $\_[\_/\_]^g : A \to A \to \mathbf{var} \to A$, $\mathsf{gFresh} : \mathbf{var} \to A \to \mathbf{bool}$, satisfying the following properties:

F1: $x \neq z \Longrightarrow \mathsf{gFresh}\ z\ (\mathsf{gVar}\ x)$,
F2: $\mathsf{gFresh}\ z\ gX \ \wedge\ \mathsf{gFresh}\ z\ gY \Longrightarrow \mathsf{gFresh}\ z\ (\mathsf{gApp}\ gX\ gY)$,
F3: $\mathsf{gFresh}\ z\ (\mathsf{gLm}\ z\ gX)$,
F4: $\mathsf{gFresh}\ z\ gX \Longrightarrow \mathsf{gFresh}\ z\ (\mathsf{gLm}\ x\ gX)$,
S1: $(\mathsf{gVar}\ z)[gZ/z]^g = gZ$,
S2: $x \neq z \Longrightarrow (\mathsf{gVar}\ x)[gZ/z]^g = \mathsf{gVar}\ x$,
S3: $(\mathsf{gApp}\ gX\ gY)[gZ/z]^g = \mathsf{gApp}\ (gX[gZ/z]^g)\ (gY[gZ/z]^g)$,
S4: $x \neq z \wedge \mathsf{gFresh}\ x\ gZ \Longrightarrow (\mathsf{gLm}\ x\ gX)[gZ/z]^g = \mathsf{gLm}\ x\ (gX[gZ/z]^g)$,
A: $x \neq y \wedge \mathsf{gFresh}\ y\ gX \Longrightarrow \mathsf{gLm}\ y\ (gX[(\mathsf{gVar}\ y)/x]^g) = \mathsf{gLm}\ x\ gX$.

Note that, indeed, the above properties, F1-F4, S1-S4 and A, form an (infinitary) Horn theory $\mathcal{H}$ over the first-order language having:
- a binary operation symbol for application;
- for each variable x:
— a constant symbol for the x-injection as a term,
— a unary operation symbol for λx-abstraction,
— a binary operation symbol for substitution for x,
— a binary relation symbol for freshness of x.

(Note that negative conditions such as $x \neq z$ are *not* part of the $\mathcal{H}$ clauses, but are meta-level conditions – thus, e.g., F1 represents an infinite collection of Horn clauses, one for each pair of variables (x, z) with $x \neq z$.)

[1] Interestingly, the answer becomes negative if we remove any of the three – this is further evidence for the suitability of taking freshness and substitution as "built-ins" in the syntax.

Terms form of course a model of $\mathcal{H}$, since the latter consists of well-known properties of terms;[2] and the next theorem says this model is *initial* in $\mathcal{H}$:

THEOREM 1. *Let A be an FSb-model. Then there exists a unique map H :* **term** $\rightarrow A$ *commuting with the constructors, i.e.:*
(a) $H\ x = \mathsf{gVar}\ x$, **(b)** $H\ (\mathsf{App}\ X\ Y) = \mathsf{gApp}\ (H\ X)\ (H\ Y)$,
(c) $H\ (\mathsf{Lm}\ x\ X) = \mathsf{gLm}\ x\ (H\ X)$.
Additionally, H commutes with substitution and preserves freshness, i.e.: **(d)** $H\ (Y[X/x]) = (H\ Y)[(H\ X)/x]^g$,
(e) $\mathsf{fresh}\ x\ X \Longrightarrow \mathsf{gFresh}\ x\ (H\ X)$.

Proof sketch. **Existence:** First, note that, if H : **term** $\rightarrow A$ is an $(\mathsf{Var}, \mathsf{App}, \mathsf{Lm})$-morphism, i.e., if it commutes with the indicated three operators, then it also commutes with substitution and preserves freshness. This can be proved by induction on terms, using F1-F4, S1-S4, and the fact that **term** itself satisfies the corresponding clauses. This fact allows us to focus on the simpler task of finding a $(\mathsf{Var}, \mathsf{App}, \mathsf{Lm})$-morphism between **term** and A.

Next, recall that **term** consists of "terms up to α" i.e., of α-equivalence classes. We call *quasi-terms* the items not yet factored by α and let qVar, qApp, qLm, qFresh and $\_[\_ \wedge \_]^q$ be the corresponding operarors (variable injection, application, abstraction, and swapping) on quasi-terms. Let F : **qTerm** $\rightarrow A$ be the unique $(\mathsf{Var}, \mathsf{App}, \mathsf{Lm})$-morphism given by the absolute initiality of **qTerm**. I.e., F is defined by standard recursion:
- $F(\mathsf{qVar}\ x) = \mathsf{gVar}\ x$;
- $F(\mathsf{qApp}\ P\ Q) = \mathsf{gApp}\ (F\ P)\ (F\ Q)$;
- $F(\mathsf{qLm}\ x\ P) = \mathsf{gLm}\ x\ (F\ P)$.

Using F1-F4, one can show by induction on quasi-terms that F preserves freshness, namely:
(1) $\mathsf{qFresh}\ x\ P \Longrightarrow \mathsf{gFresh}\ x\ (F\ P)$.

Next, using (1), S1-S4, F1-F4 and A, one can show by induction on quasi-terms that, under an appropriate freshness assumption, F commutes with swapping versus substitution, namely:
(2) $\mathsf{qFresh}\ y_1\ P \Longrightarrow F\ (P[y_1 \wedge y]^q) = (F\ P)[(\mathsf{gVar}\ y_1)/y]^g$.
(Above, considering swapping on the left-hand side of the equality is much more convenient than considering variable-for-variable substitution, as the latter is not well-behaved on quasi-terms.)

Next, using (1), (2), S1-S4, F1-F4 and A, one can show by induction on quasi-terms that F respects α-equivalence, i.e.,
(3) $P \simeq_\alpha Q$ implies $F\ P = F\ Q$.

Finally, (3), together with the definitional clauses of F and the fact that α is a congruence on quasi-terms imply standardly (by the universal property of quotient FOL models) the existence of a $(\mathsf{Var}, \mathsf{App}, \mathsf{Lm})$-morphism H : **term** $\rightarrow A$, as desired.
Uniqueness: By an easy induction on terms. □

We call a map H as in Thm. 1 an *FSb-morphism*. Thus, Thm. 1 provides the following recursion principle: if one defines an FSb-model on the desired target domain (and thus discharges the resulted proof obligations, namely, F1-F4, S-S4 and A), then one obtains a compositional map between terms and the target domain, i.e., an FSb-morphism. Note that the particular "implementation" of this FSb-morphism is completely irrelevant (and is "hidden" in the proof of Thm. 1), since its abstract properties (a)-(c) characterize it uniquely, and, together with (d) and (e), form a convenient basis for working with it. We are now ready to present the promised solutions to the problems from Section 2.

3.3 Solution to Problem I

We let A, the set of *semantic values*, ranged over by s, t, be **val** $\rightarrow D$. We organize A as an FSb-model. The desired recursive equations from Section 2 leave us no choice about the generalized constructor operators on A:
- $\mathsf{gVar}\ x = \lambda\rho.\ \rho\ x$;
- $\mathsf{gApp}\ s\ t = \lambda\rho.\ \mathsf{APP}\ (s\ \rho)\ (t\ \rho)$;
- $\mathsf{gLm}\ x\ s = \lambda\rho.\ \mathsf{LM}\ (\lambda d.\ s\ (\rho[x \leftarrow d]))$.

Moreover, the desired freshness obliviousness property imposes that generalized freshness on A be at least as strong as the following relation, and we choose to define it as precisely this relation: $\mathsf{gFresh}\ x\ s = (\forall \rho, \rho'.\ \rho =_x \rho' \Longrightarrow s\ \rho = s\ \rho')$.

Finally, the desired substitution compositionality leaves us no choice about the definition of generalized substitution on A: $s[t/x]^g = \lambda\rho.\ s\ (\rho[x \leftarrow t\ \rho])$.

Thus, saying that the clauses and desired facts listed in Section 2 hold is the same as saying that the map $[\_]$ is an FSb-morphism. For instance, substitution compositionality, i.e.,
$\forall x\ Y\ X\ \rho.\ [Y[X/x]]\ \rho = [Y]\ (\rho[x \leftarrow [X]\ \rho])$
means $\forall x\ Y\ X.\ [Y[X/x]] = \lambda\ \rho.\ [Y]\ (\rho[x \leftarrow [X]\ \rho])$,
which means $\forall x\ Y\ X.\ [Y[X/x]] = [Y]\ [[X]/x]^g$,
which means: $[\_]$ commutes with substitution.

According to Thm. 1, what remains to do in order to have Problem I resolved is checking that A with the above structure is indeed an FSb-model, i.e., satisfies the clauses F1-F4, S1-S4 and A. It turns out that here, *as well as in most of the examples we consider later*, checking these facts is trivial (and usually automatically discharged in Isabelle – see Section 6). For instance, the most complex of them, A, here requires that $\forall\ \rho_1\ \rho_2.\ \rho_1 =_y \rho_2 \Longrightarrow s\ \rho_1 = s\ \rho_2$ implies $s(\rho[y \leftarrow d][x \leftarrow d]) = s(\rho[x \leftarrow d])$, which can be discharged immediately.

3.4 Solution to Problem II

We take A to be **term**$(\{\mathsf{APP}, \mathsf{LM}\})$ (the set of λ-terms with two constants). We organize A as an FSb-model.

Again, the generalized constructor operators, the weakest notion of freshness, and the generalized substitution on A are all predetermined by the desired recursive equations:
(1) $\mathsf{gVar}\ x = x$; **(2)** $\mathsf{gApp}\ X\ Y = \mathsf{App}\ (\mathsf{App}\ \mathsf{APP}\ X)\ Y$;
(3) $\mathsf{gLm}\ x\ X = \mathsf{App}\ \mathsf{LM}\ (\mathsf{Lm}\ x\ X)$; **(4)** $\_[\_/\_]^g = \_[\_/\_]$;
(5) $\mathsf{gFresh} = \mathsf{fresh}$.

Notice that gApp and gLm are different from App and Lm, while, to the contrary, gFresh and $\_[\_/\_]^g$ are just regular freshness and substitution – indeed, a main point of HOAS is the reuse of substitution. Again, it is immediate to check that A is an FSb-model, yielding, by Thm. 1, the existence of a map rep : **term** $\rightarrow$ **term**$(\{\mathsf{APP}, \mathsf{LM}\})$ satisfying the desired recursive equations and in addition preserving freshness and substitution.

3.5 Bottom line to our solutions

There are two advantages in employing the described recursors instead of directly attempting a representative-independent definition (perhaps proved to be so, dynamically, at definition-time): **(I)** clear a priori picture of what needs to be proved; **(II)** extra built-in compositionality results.

4. More examples

Our Horn-based principle is surprisingly general. We could not find in the literature any example of a syntactic map supposed to feature compositionality (of some kind) w.r.t. substitution and not falling in the scope of this principle. In this section we give more examples.

As seen in the solutions for Problems I and II, listing all the desired clauses – those for the term constructors, the *weakest* one for freshness, and the one for substitution – determines a model. Therefore, when discussing the next examples, we only spell out the clauses, leaving implicit the construction of the corresponding model.

[2] Note also that clauses S1-S4 coincide with the usual Nominal Logic definition of substitution, which also exploits the aforementioned idea of "lazy" clauses, however *not* with the purpose of obtaining a substitution-compositional recursor as we do here – see also Section 8.

4.1 The number of free occurrences of a variable in a term

Given a variable z, the intended definitional clauses of the map $\mathsf{no}^z : \mathbf{term} \to I\!N$, taking any term X to the number of free occurrences of z in X, are the following:

- $\mathsf{no}^z\ x = \mathsf{if}\ x = z\ \mathsf{then}\ 1\ \mathsf{else}\ 0$;
- $\mathsf{no}^z(\mathsf{App}\ X\ Y) = (\mathsf{no}^z\ X) + (\mathsf{no}^z\ Y)$;
- $\mathsf{no}^z(\mathsf{Lm}\ x\ X) = \mathsf{if}\ x = z\ \mathsf{then}\ 0\ \mathsf{else}\ \mathsf{no}^z\ X$.

To make them into a rigorous definition, we need to ask: what is the desired/necessary relationship between no^z and freshness on one hand and no^z and substitution on the other. (In fact, an employment of this map in larger developments would typically need to ask these questions anyway.)

The answer to the the first question is the simpler one:
- $\mathsf{fresh}\ z\ X \Longrightarrow \mathsf{no}^z\ X = 0$.

To the substitution question however, we cannot answer for a fixed z, but need to consider all no^z's at the same time, obtaining:

- $\mathsf{no}^z(X[Y/y]) = \begin{cases} (\mathsf{no}^y\ X) * (\mathsf{no}^z\ Y), & \text{if } y = z \\ (\mathsf{no}^z\ X) + (\mathsf{no}^y\ X) * (\mathsf{no}^z\ Y), & \text{otherwise} \end{cases}$

This of course suggests considering the simultaneous version of the map, $\mathsf{no} : \mathbf{term} \to (\mathbf{var} \to I\!N)$, where $\mathsf{no}\ X\ z$ now denotes what used to be $\mathsf{no}^z\ X$. We obtain:

- $\mathsf{no}\ x\ z = \mathsf{if}\ x = z\ \mathsf{then}\ 1\ \mathsf{else}\ 0$;
- $\mathsf{no}\ (\mathsf{App}\ X\ Y)\ z = (\mathsf{no}\ X\ z) + (\mathsf{no}\ Y\ z)$;
- $\mathsf{no}\ (\mathsf{Lm}\ x\ X)\ z = \mathsf{if}\ x = z\ \mathsf{then}\ 0\ \mathsf{else}\ \mathsf{no}\ X\ z$.
- $\mathsf{fresh}\ z\ X \Longrightarrow \mathsf{no}\ X\ z = 0$;
- $\mathsf{no}\ (X[Y/y])\ z = \begin{cases} (\mathsf{no}\ X\ y) * (\mathsf{no}\ Y\ z), & \text{if } y = z \\ (\mathsf{no}\ X\ z) + (\mathsf{no}\ X\ y) * (\mathsf{no}\ Y\ z), & \text{otherwise,} \end{cases}$

which do work as a definition of no by our method, in that our method yields the existence of a (unique) function no such that the above 5 facts hold. (Discharging the resulted proof goals is trivial arithmetic.)

4.2 CPS transformation

Consider the task of defining the call-by-value to call-by-name continuation passing-style (CPS) transformation discussed in [34] in the context of λ-calculus. The transformation goes recursively by the following clauses on the syntax of terms:

- $\mathsf{cps}\ x = \mathsf{Lm}\ k\ (\mathsf{App}\ k\ x)$, for some $k \neq x$;
- $\mathsf{cps}(\mathsf{Lm}\ x\ X) = \mathsf{Lm}\ k\ (\mathsf{App}\ k\ (\mathsf{Lm}\ x\ (\mathsf{cps}\ X)))$, for fresh $k \in \mathbf{var}$;
- $\mathsf{cps}\ (\mathsf{App}\ X\ Y) =$
$\mathsf{Lm}\ k\ (\mathsf{App}\ (\mathsf{cps}\ X)$
$\quad (\mathsf{Lm}\ x\ (\mathsf{App}\ (\mathsf{cps}\ Y)$
$\quad\quad (\mathsf{Lm}\ y\ (\mathsf{App}\ (\mathsf{App}\ x\ y)\ k)))))$,

for fresh distinct variables k, x, y.

(Above, the most specific clause is the one for App, which follows the usual sequential interpretation of CPS. Namely, let X' and Y' be $\mathsf{cps}\ X$ and $\mathsf{cps}\ Y$, i.e., the CPS-transformed versions of X and Y. Then, given any continuation k, $\mathsf{cps}\ (\mathsf{App}\ X\ Y)$ is evaluated as follows:

- X' is evaluated and the result is passed, as x, to the continuation starting with "$\mathsf{Lm}\ x$",
- which in turn evaluates Y' and passes the result, as y, to the continuation starting with "$\mathsf{Lm}\ y$",
- which in turn evaluates $\mathsf{App}\ x\ y$ and finally passes the result to the original continuation, k.

Consequently, call-by-value behavior is achieved with call-by-name mechanisms.)

As before, the problem is making the above definition rigorous. Now, trying to approach this directly using our Horn machinery for the **term** syntax does not work for the following reason: the desired transformation does not commute with arbitrary substitution, but only with substitution of *values* for variables, where a value is a term which is either a variable or a Lm-abstraction. I.e., as shown in [34] (Lemma 1 on page 149), $\mathsf{cps}\ (X[Yvl/y]) = (\mathsf{cps}\ X)\ [(\mathsf{cps}\ Yvl)/y]$ does hold for all values Yvl, but not for arbitrary terms. Interestingly, the solution lays here in recognizing the proper granularity of the syntax suggested above. Indeed, the aforementioned restricted substitution compositionality, *as well as all the rest of the call-by-value theory developed in [34]*, requires that, under call-by-value, the syntactic categories emphasize value terms. Namely, we are better off if we work with the following variation of **term**, split in two syntactic categories: $\mathbf{term}_{fl}$, of *full terms*, ranged over by X, Y, and $\mathbf{term}_{vl}$, of *value terms*, (or, simply, *values*), ranged over by Xvl, Yvl, defined mutually recursively by:

$X ::= \mathsf{InVl}\ Xvl \mid \mathsf{App}\ X\ Y \qquad Xvl ::= x \mid \mathsf{Lm}\ x\ X$

Thus, $(\mathbf{term}_{fl}, \mathbf{term}_{vl})$ is **term** with values singled out as a separate category (InVl being the injection of values into full terms). Here, only substitution of values for variables makes sense, "institutionalizing" the following semantic remark from [34] on page 135: "free variables should be thought of as ranging over values and not arbitrary terms". In this two-sorted context, the corresponding version of our recursion principle does the job of defining the mutually recursive maps $\mathsf{cps} : \mathbf{term}_{fl} \to \mathbf{term}$ and $\mathsf{cps}_{vl} : \mathbf{term}_{vl} \to \mathbf{term}$, together with the (proved) statements of their freshness and substitution preservation, by the clauses:

(1) $\mathsf{cps}_{vl}\ x = x$; **(2)** $\mathsf{cps}_{vl}\ (\mathsf{Lm}\ x\ X) = \mathsf{Lm}\ x\ (\mathsf{cps}\ X)$;
(3) $\mathsf{cps}(\mathsf{InVl}\ Xvl) = \mathsf{Lm}\ k\ (\mathsf{App}\ k\ (\mathsf{cps}_{vl}\ Xvl))$, for a fresh $k \in \mathbf{var}$;
(4) $\mathsf{cps}(\mathsf{App}\ X\ Y) = \langle\text{same as before}\rangle$
(5) $\mathsf{fresh}\ y\ X \Longrightarrow \mathsf{fresh}\ y\ (\mathsf{cps}\ X)$;
(6) $\mathsf{fresh}\ y\ Xvl \Longrightarrow \mathsf{fresh}\ y\ (\mathsf{cps}_{vl}\ Xvl)$;
(7) $\mathsf{cps}_{vl}\ (Xvl\ [Yvl/y]) = (\mathsf{cps}_{vl}\ Xvl)\ [(\mathsf{cps}_{vl}\ Yvl)/y]$;
(8) $\mathsf{cps}\ (X[Yvl/y]) = (\mathsf{cps}\ X)\ [(\mathsf{cps}\ Yvl)/y]$.

Note that the originally intended behavior for variables and Lm-abstractions now follows by inlining cps_{vl}, for InVl-wrapped values: **(a)** $\mathsf{cps}\ (\mathsf{InVl}\ x) = \mathsf{Lm}\ k\ (\mathsf{App}\ k\ x)$; **(b)** $\mathsf{cps}\ (\mathsf{InVl}\ (\mathsf{Lm}\ x\ X)) = \mathsf{Lm}\ k\ (\mathsf{App}\ k\ (\mathsf{Lm}\ x\ (\mathsf{cps}\ X)))$.

Checking the clauses necessary for the definition to work (i.e., the clauses defining FSb-models for the considered two-sorted syntax $(\mathbf{term}_{fl}, \mathbf{term}_{vl})$) is again routine, provided several basic properties of freshness and substitution are available. There is of course the question whether it is worth "storing" call-by-value λ-calculus in a different data type from standard λ-calculus, or should one rather define values inside standard λ-calculus and work with these. This is an engineering, not a mathematical question. But if one opts for a different data type, then the isomorphism between $\mathbf{term}_{fl}$ and **term** is yet another (trivial) application of our recursion principle.

4.3 Other examples

These include the classic de Bruijn interpretation map from [12], the CPS transformation in the opposite direction (from call-by-name to call-by-value) from [34] and the translation of the LF syntax into untyped λ-calculus (meant to be subsequently Curry-style typed) employed in the proof of strong normalization for the LF reduction [22]. The reader is invited to try our method on his/her own examples pertaining to syntax with bindings – again, we believe it is very likely to work provided a substitution lemma of some kind is in sight.

4.4 Non-examples

Of course, not everything one wants to define is compositional w.r.t. substitution. Such cases fall out of the scope of our definitional principle. These include, e.g., the depth operator – an immediate symptom showing why our principle cannot handle this example is the fact that we cannot compute the depth of $X[Y/y]$ based on the depths of X and Y; in other words, we cannot answer the substitution question. So this example is problematic because it is, in some sense, syntactically under-specified, as it "ignores" substitution. An example problematic because of a somewhat opposite reason is the so-called *complete development*, $\mathsf{cdev} : \mathbf{term} \to \mathbf{term}$, introduced in [41] as a means to simplify the proof of the Church-Rosser the-

orem (and of other results):
(1) cdev $x = x$; **(2)** cdev $(\mathsf{Lm}\ x\ X) = \mathsf{Lm}\ x\ (\mathsf{cdev}\ X)$;
(3) cdev $(\mathsf{App}\ X\ Y) = \mathsf{App}\ (\mathsf{cdev}\ X)\ (\mathsf{cdev}\ Y)$, if $\mathsf{App}\ X\ Y$ is not a β-redex (i.e., if X does not have the form $\mathsf{Lm}\ y\ Z$);
(3') cdev $(\mathsf{App}\ (\mathsf{Lm}\ y\ X)\ Y) = (\mathsf{cdev}\ X)[(\mathsf{cdev}\ Y)/y]$.

cdev reduces all the (arbitrarily-nested) β-redexes in a term. It does not commute with substitution, mainly because it is not a "purely syntactic" map, but includes some "operational semantics". Note however that, even if the codomain consists of terms, our method does not require that substitution on the domain of terms be mapped to *standard* substitution on the codomain, but to any well-behaved notion of "generalized substitution". We therefore could define a non-standard substitution (on standard terms) that will eventually yield preservation of substitution, but this would be unnecessarily complicated *and artificial*. Our principle is not intended to have its users work hard to have their definitions go through; rather, it is aimed at situations where the issues of preservation of freshness and substitution appear naturally as further desired properties. In our formalization, we have incorporated a work-around that handles the cdev operator by a variation of our approach that renounces the substitution compositionality goal, replacing it with the less ambitious one of swapping compositionality (see Appendix A).

5. Pushing the Horn approach even further

Besides having the "up to α" definitions go through, our Horn approach infers some extra information about the defined maps: compositionality w.r.t. freshness and substitution. Can we infer even more? The answer is: yes, if we prove more facts about the constructed model. Next we state criteria for three commonly encountered properties: freshness reflection, injectiveness, surjectiveness.

An FSb-model is said to be:
- *fresh-reversing*, if the following facts (converse to F1-F4 from Section 3), hold for it: **(a)** $\mathsf{gFresh}\ z\ (\mathsf{gVar}\ x) \Longrightarrow x \neq z$, **(b)** $\mathsf{gFresh}\ z\ (\mathsf{gApp}\ gX\ gY) \Longrightarrow (\mathsf{gFresh}\ z\ gX \wedge \mathsf{gFresh}\ z\ gY)$, **(c)** $\mathsf{gFresh}\ z\ (\mathsf{gLm}\ x\ gX) \Longrightarrow (z = x \vee \mathsf{gFresh}\ z\ gX)$;
- *constructor-injective*, if its constructor operators are mutually injective, i.e.: **(a)** $\mathsf{gVar}\ x$, $\mathsf{gApp}\ X\ Y$ and $\mathsf{gLm}\ z\ Z$ are mutually distinct; **(b)** gVar, gApp (regarded as an uncurried binary operation) and $\mathsf{gLm}\ x$ are injective;
- *inductive*, if the following induction principle is true: for all predicates φ, $\forall gX.\ \varphi\ gX$ holds provided the following hold: **(a)** $\forall x.\ \varphi\ (\mathsf{gVar}\ x)$, **(b)** $\forall gX\ gY.\ \varphi\ gX \wedge \varphi\ gY \Longrightarrow \varphi\ (\mathsf{gApp}\ gX\ gY)$, **(c)** $\forall x\ gX.\ \varphi\ gX \Longrightarrow \varphi\ (\mathsf{gLm}\ x\ gX)$.

The next theorem follows easily by structural induction on terms:

THEOREM 2. *Let A be an FSb-model and let H be the map from Thm. 1. Then, if A is fresh-reversing (construct-injective, inductive), then H is, respectively, fresh-reflecting (injective, surjective), where "fresh-reflecting" means:* $\mathsf{fresh}\ x\ (H\ X) \Longrightarrow \mathsf{fresh}\ x\ X$.

The above result integrates even more facts as "built-ins" of the recursive definition. E.g.: the HOAS operator from Section 2 is freshness-reflective and injective; the "number of free occurrences" operator from Section 4.1 is freshness-reflecting; the CPS operator from Section 4.2 is freshness-reflective and injective. Putting together these 3 criteria, we obtain the following characterization:

THEOREM 3. *If an FSb-model A is fresh-reversing, constructor-injective and inductive, then the map H from Thm. 1 is an isomorphism of FSb-models (where "isomorphism of FSb-models" is the usual notion from first-order model theory, namely: "bijection preserving the constructors and substitution and preserving and reflecting freshness").*

This characterization of the term model is *internal*, in that it does not rely on things from "outside" the model itself (such as morphisms and other models), as does the characterization as initial Horn model. Although such an internal characterization is not the first one from the literature (see, e.g., [19], [28]), it appears to be the first expressed in terms of essential ingredients only – syntactic constructors, freshness and substitution – and also the first to be formalized and put to use (see Section 7).

6. Isabelle formalization

Above, we have presented our results for the syntax of λ-calculus terms. However, one can see that similar results hold for any other (possibly multiple-sorted) syntax with bindings, such as, e.g., that of LF [22]. For the sake of generality and reusability, we chose to formalize these results parameterizing by an *arbitrary binding signature*, within a theory of syntax consisting of:
- a wide collection of basic facts on freshness, substitution and swapping;
- customized induction principles, including fresh induction in the style of [32, 45];
- customized recursion principles (the topic of this paper).

Moreover, we have formalized all the examples discussed in this paper, in their particular syntaxes instantiated from the aforementioned general theory. We have also employed these examples in larger development, notably the formalization of a large part of Plotkin's classic paper [34].

A detailed presentation of our formal development, available at [4], falls outside the scope of this paper (but the appendix offers a few details for the interested reader). Here, we illustrate our approach by presenting the Isabelle formalization of Problem II from Sections 2.2 and 3.4 (contained in theory HOAS from [4]).

In order to relate the formal scripts described below to the mathematical notations from Sections 2.1 and 3.4, we note the following:
-(1) Unlike in the paper, in the formalization we distinguish terms from *abstractions*, an abstraction being essentially a pair (variable,term) up to α. We write Abs for the abstraction constructor (taking a variable and a term and returning an abstraction). In this setting, a binding operator such as λ no longer takes a variable and a term, but takes an abstraction (and returns a term); we write Lam for this operator. (Thus, our operator Lm from the paper can be obtained as $\mathsf{Lm}\,x\,X = \mathsf{Lam}\,(\mathsf{Abs}\ x\ X)$; the latter is actually defined as an abbreviation in our scripts.) This setting is reflected in the notion of an FSb-model too, where we have both "generalized terms" and "generalized abstractions" (and corresponding "generalized operators").
-(2) In the formalization we use a more general notion of FSb-model than in the paper, supporting not merely iteration, but full (primitive) recursion. This is reflected in the presence of extra arguments for the model operations, which take not only "generalized terms" (corresponding to the recursively computed result), but also genuine syntactic terms (corresponding to the original input at recursion time).
-(3) In the formalization, the problem setting is itself slightly more general than that in the paper. Namely, let us write **term**(**const**) for the syntax of the λ-calculus over a set of constants **const**. Then the object syntax is **term**(**const**), and the meta syntax is **term**(**metaConst**), where the set **metaConst**, of *meta-constants*, consists of copies $\mathsf{Const}\,c$ of elements $c \in$ **const** and of the new constants APP and LM.

We use the prefixes "Obj" and "Meta" for operators pertaining to the object syntax and to the meta syntax, respectively. Moreover, we write $\_[\_/_o\ \_]$ and $\_[\_/_m\ \_]$ for the object level and meta level substitutions, respectively. The Isabelle definition of the desired FSb-model, called rep_MOD, is the following:

```
definition rep_MOD :: ('const, 'const metaConst term,
'const metaConst abs)model
where rep_MOD ==
  gVar_vlm = Meta_Var,
  gAbs_lm_lm = λ y X mX. Meta_Abs y mX,
  gCt = λ c. Meta.Ct (Const c),
  gApp = λ X mX Y mY.
         Meta.App (Meta.App (Meta.Ct APP) mX) mY,
  gLam = λ A mA. Meta.App (Meta.Ct LM) (Meta.Lam mA),
  gFresh_vlm_lm = λ y X mX. Meta_fresh y mX,
  gFresh_vlm_lm_lm = λ y A mA. Meta_freshAbs y mA,
  gSubst_vlm_lm = λ Y mY y X mX. mX [mY /m y],
  gSubst_vlm_lm_lm = λ Y mY y A mA. mA [mY /m y]
```

Above, the type of rep_MOD (on the first 2 lines) is the record type of "(FSb-)models for the **term**(**const**) syntax", hence the first parameter **const**; the other two parameters from this type represent the carriers of the model, which are the meta-terms and meta-abstractions. Then there are defined the record components, i.e., the "generalized operators" on the model – X, Y and A range over object terms and abstractions, and mX, mY and mA over meta terms and abstractions. The "lm" and "vlm" suffixes from the operators' names are a reminiscence of our many-sorted setting: they refer to the only variable sort (vlm) and term sort (lm) for the syntax **term**(**const**).

Modulo these explanations, the reader should now recognize the definition from our resolution of Problem II in Section 3.4. E.g., the above definition of gAbs_lm_lm corresponds to the HOAS-specific recursive clause repAbs (Obj.Abs x X) $=$ Meta.Abs x (rep X), where rep denotes, as in Sections 2.1 and 3.4, the representation map on terms, and repAbs is its abstraction counterpart.

For each of the Isabelle lemmas listed below, after the keyword "lemma" comes the name of the lemma, followed by a colon, followed by the stated fact in double quotes. We omit their formal proofs. (Each of the proofs has at most 2 lines and proceeds by merely unfolding definitions and calling the automatic simplifier tool.)

Once the model has been defined, we need to check that it is indeed a "well-structured" FSb-model (expressed as the Isabelle predicate wlsFSb), i.e., that it satisfies the involved clauses for freshness and substitution (F1-F4, S1-S4 and A) – in this case, these goals are discharged automatically:

```
lemma wlsFSb_rep_MOD: "wlsFSb rep_MOD"
```

This is all we needed to check to have our recursive definition go through. However, we wish to infer some further facts for our morphism, in this case freshness reflection and injectiveness. For these, the first 2 points of Thm. 2 tell us that it suffices that the reversed fresh clauses hold (expressed by the Isabelle predicate gFresh_cls_rev) and that the generalized constructors be injective (expressed by the Isabelle predicate gCons_inj). The latter facts can again be proved automatically:

```
lemma gFresh_cls_rev_rep_MOD:"gFresh_cls_rev rep_MOD"

lemma gCons_inj_rep_MOD: "gCons_inj rep_MOD"
```

This concludes the creative part of the HOAS development. The rest is "bureaucracy", and goes the same way for all recursive definitions, as it relies on our general theory.

Parenthesis: Our Isabelle formalization of the recursion theorem Thm. 1 takes advantage of the Hilbert choice operator, building the constant rec_lm out of the "exists unique" statement from Thm. 1 (and the corresponding constant rec_lm_lm for abstractions) – i.e., given any FSb-model M, rec_lm M and rec_lm_lm M correspond to the function H from Thm. 1. Then theorem "wlsFSb rec term_FSb_morph", which is the Isabelle version of Thm. 1, says that, if M is an FSb-model, then rec_lm M and rec_lm_lm M form an FSb-morphism from terms to M. (All these are presented and illustrated in detail in the commented theory L from [4].)

Back to the HOAS development, we let rep and repAbs denote the recursive functions associated to the particular model rep_MOD, thus mapping object terms and abstractions to meta terms and abstractions:

```
definitions rep where "rep X ≡ rec_lm rep_MOD X"
and repAbs where "repAbs A ≡ rec_lm_lm rep_MOD A"
```

We now apply the aforementioned recursion theorem, "wlsFSb rec term_FSb_morph", obtaining that (rep, repAbs) is an FSb-morphism:

```
lemma term_FSb_morph_rep:
"term_FSb_morph rep repAbs rep_MOD"
```

Unfolding definitions, we see the morphism property in familiar format (similar to the one from Section 2.2):

```
lemma rep_simps:
"rep (Obj_Var x) = Meta_Var x"
"rep (Obj.Ct c) = Meta.Ct (Const c)"
"rep (Obj.App X Y) =
 Meta.App (Meta.App (Meta.Ct APP) (rep X)) (rep Y)"
"rep (Obj_Lm y X) =
 Meta.App (Meta.Ct LM) (Meta_Lm y (rep X))"

lemma rep_subst:
"rep (X [Y /o y]) = (rep X) [(rep Y) /m y]"

lemma rep_preserves_fresh:
"Obj_fresh y X  ==>  Meta_fresh y (rep X)"
```

Thus, Lemmas rep_simps, rep_subst and rep_preserves_fresh correspond to clauses (1)-(3), (4), and (5), respectively, from Section 2.2.

Additionally, we use (the Isabelle formalization of) the first 2 points of Thm. 2, to infer that this morphism is additionally freshness reflecting and injective:

```
lemma refl_freshAll_rep:
"refl_freshAll rep repAbs rep_MOD"

lemma is_injAll_rep:
"is_injAll rep repAbs"
```

And again, by unfolding definitions, we obtain more readable versions of these results:

```
lemma rep_reflects_fresh:
"Meta_fresh y (rep X) ==> Obj_fresh y X"

lemma rep_inj:
"(rep X = rep Y) = (X = Y)"
```

This concludes the definition of the HOAS representation map *and the proof of its syntactic adequacy*. Notice the high degree of automation of the development, as the proof goals generated by the FSb-model requirement are automatically discharged – this is the case for most applications of Thm. 1 and Thm. 2 throughout our formal development.

7. Certifying and relating formalizations of terms

The literature on λ-calculus theory and theorem proving abounds in approaches to representing syntax with bindings, such as α-classes, de Bruijn levels [13], de Bruijn indexes [13], locally nameless [8, 9, 18, 19], locally named [35, 38], proper weak-HOAS functions [14, 20], partial functions [42] (to list only a few; see [29] for an overview of several of these and others).

These representations have various merits: of being more efficient, more insightful w.r.t. definition and proof principles, etc.

However, all these approaches are aimed at capturing *the same Platonic notion of syntax*. So what makes them correct? Typically, work proposing such a new implementation/representation justifies its correctness by showing it isomorphic to a more standard representation, or to one that has been used many times and has a high degree of trustability. E.g., in [42], the new partial-function based representation of λ-terms from the Nominal package is proved isomorphic to the α-class-based one; in [35], the *locally named* representation is proved isomorphic to the nominal representation.

Our Thm. 3 provides a common formal basis for establishing such isomorphisms, and, in general, for proving a novel representation to be correct, namely, by *showing that it forms a fresh-reversing, constructor-injective and inductive FSb-model* (as the latter notion is unique up to fresh [preserving and reflecting] and substitution preserving isomorphism). Following this methodology, we have established in Isabelle formal isomorphisms between our representation and each of the following:
-(1) the Nominal representation [42];
-(2) the locally nameless representation underlying the Hybrid system [8, 15, 24, 25];
-(3) the *locally named* representation [35, 38].

(1) The connection with Nominal is formalized in the theory C_Nominal from [4]. We connect the λ-terms from the theory Lam_funs (located in the Nominal directory in the Isabelle distribution) with our *pure* λ-terms. The latter are λ-terms without constants, defined in our theory Pure. (We use pure terms here, since the terms in the aforementioned Nominal theory happen to not include constants.) First, we establish a bijection toNA, read "to Nominal atom" between our variables and the Nominal atoms, called "names" here – this is immediate, since both collections are countable. Then we proceed to organize the Nominal terms as an FSb-model with the required additional properties, yielding an isomorphism toN, read "to Nominal", between our pure terms and their terms. Checking the facts necessary for obtaining this isomorphism was immediate, given that Lam_funs and the underlying Nominal package provide a rich pool of basic facts. To give an example of the potential usefulness of the above isomorphism, for both parties:
- our rich theory of substitution is now available for this Nominal theory;[3]
- advanced Nominal techniques pertaining to rule induction are now available in our λ-calculus theory.

(2) For the connection with the Hybrid terms, we imported the theory Expr from the Hybrid scripts (http://hybrid.dsi.unimi.it). On top of Expr, Hybrid has several other HOAS layers – however, we were only interested in this very basic implementation layer. The connection, developed in our theory C_Hybrid (from [4]), took a little more work, given that the Hybrid representation is HOAS-oriented, hence it lacks a first-order binding operator, which we had to add ourselves. Then the Hybrid terms were organized as an FSb-model, yielding an isomorphism between our terms with constants and their terms with constants.

(3) The locally named representation from [35] is based on a distinction between parameters (or global variables), and (local) variables, only the latter being allowed (and required) to be bound. As mentioned, this representation has already been proved isomorphic to the Nominal one discussed above, by defining a relation and showing it to be total and deterministic, yielding a function – note that a main motivation of our approach is to avoid the roundabout route of defining a function first as a relation. The connection is developed in our theory C_Sato_Pollack from [4] (named after the two authors of the approach), importing a couple of theories from the scripts associated to the paper [35], available from the first author's home page: http://homepages.inf.ed.ac.uk/rpollack. Similarly to before, we define a bijection toP between our variables and their parameters, and then organize their terms as an FSb-model, yielding an isomorphism between our pure terms and their terms.

[3] Substitution is of course definable with the Nominal package, but its many relevant properties of interaction with the other operators, including, e.g., the very recursion principles proposed in this paper, do not come with this definition, but would need to be established individually.

8. Conclusions and related work

Next we discuss other approaches to the main contribution of this paper – convenient recursion principles for terms with bindings. (See Section 2.10 in [36] for much more details.)

Nominal Logic is originally a non-standard logic, parameterized by various categories of *atoms* (a.k.a. names, or variables); there are built-in notions of swapping (primitive) and freshness of an atom for an object (derived) and an underlying assumption of *finite support*, essentially saying that, for each object, all but a finite number of atoms are fresh for it; all the expressible predicates have a property called *equivariance* (invariance under swapping). This non-standard logic is discussed, e.g., in [17]. However, the nominal approach can also be developed in a standard logic such as classic HOL, as shown by the Isabelle/HOL Nominal Package [42, 43, 45].

The Nominal recursor [33, 42] on terms with bindings employs the syntactic constructors Var, App and Lm, as well as a notion of permutation swapping. All the operators involved in the recursive clauses in a presumptive definition with target domain A (assumed to have a permutation swapping operator on it), in our notation gVar : **var** $\rightarrow A$, gApp : **term** $\rightarrow A \rightarrow$ **term** $\rightarrow A \rightarrow A$ and gLm : **var** $\rightarrow$ **term** $\rightarrow A \rightarrow A$, are required to have *finite support*. Moreover, a technical condition, *Freshness Condition for Binders* (FCB) (a form of freshness preservation for gLm), is required to hold. Under the above conditions, one obtains an operator H : **term** $\rightarrow A$ which is "almost a morphism" w.r.t. the syntactic constructors, in that it commutes with Var and App in the usual sense and commutes with Lm for fresh names only, namely: H (Lm x X) = gLm x X (H X) provided gFresh x gVar, gFresh x gApp and gFresh x gLm hold.

Compared to our main substitution-based recursion combinator (henceforth abbreviated SRC), the above Nominal recursion combinator (henceforth abbreviated NRC) has the advantage of uniformity and economy of structure (only swapping is primitive, and everything is based on it). Moreover, the consideration of the aforementioned "almost morphisms" as targets of definitions, w.r.t. which freshness for parameters may be assumed, provides extra generality to the NRC. On the other hand, the conditions that SRC requires to be checked by the user are simpler than those required by NRC, the latter involving a certain quantifier complexity, notably when considering the support of functions (although, like ours, often these conditions can be checked automatically, as shown by the various examples considered by work using the Nominal Package). Moreover, there is some benefit in staying first-order as in our Horn approach, and not getting into the second-order issue of finiteness of support. E.g., as soon as one deals with more semantic situations, such as our semantic-domain interpretation in Section 2, the finite support conditions are no longer satisfied, but a complex combination of induction and recursion is needed to have a Nominal definition eventually go through, as shown in [33] (on page 492) for this very example. Another difference between NRC and SRC is of course the presence in SRC of built-in compositionality, which relates to the user as both an obligation and a reward.

Michael Norrish's work. [27] introduces a recursor for λ-calculus involving swapping and the free-variable operator FV, and also considers parameters à la Nominal. If we ignore the largely orthogonal extra generality of [27] w.r.t. parameters, and replace the use of FV : **term** $\rightarrow$ $\mathbf{P}_f$(**var**) with the (complementary) use of fresh : **var** $\rightarrow$ **term** $\rightarrow$ **bool**, we find that [27] did in fact propose a Horn-like recursive principle for syntax with bindings. Interestingly, [27] also contemplates considering substitution, but renounces in favor of swapping because "permutations move around terms much more readily than substitution" ([27], page 248). However, as we show in this paper, the (indeed harder) task of having substitution "move around terms" results in a recursion principle which is *not* harder to apply (from the user's perspective), while bringing the convenience of substitution compositionality.

Non-standard-model approaches to syntax, based on functor categories [7, 16, 23]. These approaches add more structure to terms, regarding them as *terms in contexts* – this is inspired by the method of *de Bruijn levels* [13], and consists conceptually in "turning the free-variable function FV : **term** $\rightarrow$ **P**(**var**) into extra structure on terms" ([16], page 3). Here, there is no single set of terms, but rather terms form a family of sets indexed by the "contexts", with additional categorical structure (i.e., as presheaves). The flexibility of moving between different contexts allows one to overcome the typical problems with recursive definitions on syntax. Compared to the more elementary settings discussed previously (which include our own), the non-standard model approach has the advantage of "syntactic purity" (as only the term constructors are involved) and mathematical elegance, but does have a couple of disadvantages too. Thus, it is harder to formalize in a standard theorem prover, due to the fancy category theory involved (although this is more of a (solvable) problem for the implementor, not for the user). More importantly, it seems rather tedious to employ in order to define concrete operators. Indeed, the target domain would have to be organized each time as an algebra for a suitable functor on presheaves, which means that a lot of structure and verifications would need to be provided and performed by the user. On the other hand, a category theorist may argue that all this effort would not go in vain, as the extra structure will be helpful later in proofs – and this is much like our argument in favor of built-in substitution made in this paper. Concerning the latter, both [23] and [16] show how to define substitution using their iterator. Moreover, [16] goes further and integrates substitution in the algebraic structure, inferring a version of recursion with a built-in substitution lemma, which is essentially what we do in this paper in a more standard setting.

Formalizations and case studies. Norrish has formalized his swapping-based recursion principle for the syntax of untyped λ-calculus and has included it in the distribution of the HOL4 system [6].

The Nominal package [46] has been used in several formal developments, including proofs of Church-Rosser and Standardization for λ-calculus – the latter classic result, presented, e.g., in Barendregt, is different than the call-by-name and call-by-value standardization theorems from [34] that we have formalized, in that the latter deals with more programming-oriented strategies, not allowing rewrites under λ-abstractions. Recent work at the Nominal Package [44] allows syntax with multiple (concurrent) binders, while our notion of binding signature allows only one binder at a time.

HOAS versus FOAS. In this paper, we took a *first-order abstract syntax (FOAS)* view of syntax with bindings, where variables are bound in terms by first-order operators such as Lm. By contrast, HOAS [22, 31] employs higher-order types for the binding operators. HOAS-based theorem proving and programming is currently a topic of intensive research, e.g., [1–3, 10]. HOAS recursion principles can be found, e.g., in [14, 19, 37, 40]. (See Section 3.7 in [36] for details.)

While HOAS is often more elegant than FOAS, it is not always an alternative to FOAS. For instance, the very foundations of HOAS, consisting of the definition of the meta and object logics and the associated adequacy proof, rely on (some form of) FOAS. In spite of the extensive and growing interest in HOAS and its meta-theory, our *formal* HOAS adequacy proof discussed in Section 6 seems to be the first reported in the literature. Even though it is performed for a fairly simple (albeit standard) logical framework, λ-calculus with constants, the actual proof technique works for more complex frameworks such as LF too. An important part of the meta-theory of LF has been formalized using the Nominal package, but we are not aware of actual representations and adequacy proofs performed in this setting.

Acknowledgments. We are indebted to the referees for helpful comments and suggestions. This work was supported in part by the National Science Foundation (NSF) Award number 0917218. The content is solely the responsibility of the authors and does not necessarily represent the official views of the NSF.

References

[1] Bedwyr. `http://slimmer.gforge.inria.fr/bedwyr`.

[2] Beluga. `http://www.cs.mcgill.ca/~complogic/beluga`.

[3] Delphin. `http://cs-www.cs.yale.edu/homes/carsten/delphin`.

[4] `http://www4.in.tum.de/~popescua/Scripts.zip`.

[5] The Twelf Project, 2009. `http://twelf.plparty.org`.

[6] The HOL4 Theorem prover, 2010. http://hol.sourceforge.net/.

[7] S. J. Ambler, Roy L. Crole, and Alberto Momigliano. A definitional approach to primitive recursion over Higher Order Abstract Syntax. In *MERLIN*, 2003.

[8] Simon Ambler, Roy L. Crole, and Alberto Momigliano. Combining Higher Order Abstract Syntax with tactical theorem proving and (co)induction. In *TPHOLs*, pages 13–30, 2002.

[9] Brian E. Aydemir, Arthur Charguéraud, Benjamin C. Pierce, Randy Pollack, and Stephanie Weirich. Engineering formal metatheory. In *POPL*, pages 3–15, 2008.

[10] Jacques Carette, Oleg Kiselyov, and Chung chieh Shan. Finally tagless, partially evaluated. In *APLAS*, pages 222–238, 2007.

[11] Adam J. Chlipala. Parametric higher-order abstract syntax for mechanized semantics. In *ICFP*, pages 143–156, 2008.

[12] Pierre-Louis Curien. Categorical combinators. *Information and Control*, 69(1-3):188–254, 1986.

[13] N. de Bruijn. λ-calculus notation with nameless dummies, a tool for automatic formula manipulation, with application to the Church-Rosser theorem. *Indag. Math*, 34(5):381–392, 1972.

[14] Joëlle Despeyroux, Amy P. Felty, and André Hirschowitz. Higher-order abstract syntax in Coq. In *TLCA*, pages 124–138, 1995.

[15] Amy P. Felty and Alberto Momigliano. Hybrid: A definitional two-level approach to reasoning with Higher-Order Abstract Syntax. *CoRR*, abs/0811.4367, 2008.

[16] Marcelo Fiore, Gordon Plotkin, and Daniele Turi. Abstract syntax and variable binding (extended abstract). In *LICS*, pages 193–202, 1999.

[17] M. J. Gabbay. A theory of inductive definitions with α-equivalence. Ph.D. thesis, University of Cambridge, 2001.

[18] Andrew D. Gordon. A mechanisation of name-carrying syntax up to alpha-conversion. In *HUG*, pages 413–425, 1994. ISBN 3-540-57826-9.

[19] Andrew D. Gordon and Thomas F. Melham. Five axioms of alpha-conversion. In *TPHOLs*, pages 173–190, 1996.

[20] Elsa L. Gunter, Christopher J. Osborn, and Andrei Popescu. Theory support for weak Higher Order Abstract Syntax in Isabelle/HOL. In *LFMTP*, pages 12–20, 2009.

[21] Robert Harper and Daniel R. Licata. Mechanizing metatheory in a logical framework. *J. Funct. Program.*, 17(4-5):613–673, 2007.

[22] Robert Harper, Furio Honsell, and Gordon Plotkin. A framework for defining logics. In *LICS*, pages 194–204. IEEE, Computer Society Press, 1987.

[23] Martin Hofmann. Semantical analysis of higher-order abstract syntax. In *LICS*, page 204, 1999.

[24] Alberto Momigliano and Simon Ambler. Multi-level meta-reasoning with higher-order abstract syntax. In *FoSSaCS*, pages 375–391, 2003.

[25] Alberto Momigliano, Alan J. Martin, and Amy P. Felty. Two-level Hybrid: A system for reasoning using Higher-Order Abstract Syntax. *Electron. Notes Theor. Comput. Sci.*, 196:85–93, 2008.

[26] Tobias Nipkow, Lawrence C. Paulson, and Markus Wenzel. *Isabelle/HOL: A Proof Assistant for Higher-order Logic*. Springer, 2002.

[27] Michael Norrish. Recursive function definition for types with binders. In *TPHOLs*, pages 241–256, 2004.

[28] Michael Norrish. Mechanising lambda-calculus using a classical first order theory of terms with permutations. *Higher-Order and Symbolic Computation*, 19(2-3):169–195, 2006.

[29] Michael Norrish and René Vestergaard. Proof pearl: De Bruijn terms really do work. In *TPHOLs*, pages 207–222, 2007.

[30] L. C. Paulson. The foundation of a generic theorem prover. *J. Autom. Reason.*, 5(3), 1989.

[31] F. Pfenning and C. Elliot. Higher-order abstract syntax. In *PLDI*, pages 199–208, 1988.

[32] Andrew M. Pitts. Nominal logic: A first order theory of names and binding. In *TACS*, pages 219–242, 2001.

[33] Andrew M. Pitts. Alpha-structural recursion and induction. *J. ACM*, 53(3), 2006.

[34] Gordon D. Plotkin. Call-by-name, call-by-value and the lambda-calculus. *Theor. Comput. Sci.*, 1(2):125–159, 1975.

[35] Robert Pollack and Masahiko Sato. A canonical locally named representation of binding. To appear in Journal of Automated Reasoning.

[36] Andrei Popescu. Contributions to the theory of syntax with bindings and to process algebra. Ph.D. Thesis, Univ. of Illinois, 2010. Available at `http://hdl.handle.net/2142/18477`.

[37] Andrei Popescu, Elsa L. Gunter, and Christopher J. Osborn. Strong normalization of System F by HOAS on top of FOAS. In *LICS*, pages 31–40, 2010.

[38] Masahiko Sato and Robert Pollack. External and internal syntax of the lambda-calculus. *Journal of Symbolic Computation*, 45:598–616, 2010.

[39] Carsten Schurmann and Frank Pfenning. Automated theorem proving in a simple meta-logic for LF. In *CADE*, pages 286–300, 1998.

[40] Carsten Schurmann, Joelle Despeyroux, and Frank Pfenning. Primitive recursion for higher-order abstract syntax. *Theor. Comput. Sci.*, 266(1-2):1–57, 2001.

[41] Masako Takahashi. Parallel reductions in lambda-calculus. *Inf. Comput.*, 118(1):120–127, 1995.

[42] Christian Urban. Nominal techniques in Isabelle/HOL. *J. Autom. Reason.*, 40(4):327–356, 2008.

[43] Christian Urban and Stefan Berghofer. A recursion combinator for nominal datatypes implemented in Isabelle/HOL. In *IJCAR*, pages 498–512, 2006.

[44] Christian Urban and Cezary Kaliszyk. General bindings and alpha-equivalence in Nominal Isabelle. In *ESOP*, pages 480–500, 2011.

[45] Christian Urban and Christine Tasson. Nominal techniques in Isabelle/HOL. In *CADE*, pages 38–53, 2005.

[46] Christian Urban, James Cheney, and Stefan Berghofer. Mechanizing the metatheory of LF. In *LICS*, pages 45–56, 2008.

[47] Makarius Wenzel, Lawrence C. Paulson, and Tobias Nipkow. The isabelle framework. In *TPHOLs*, pages 33–38, 2008.

APPENDIX

In this appendix, we give more details on the Isabelle formalization of our results and examples from this paper.

The Isabelle scripts presented in pdf, html and native (runnable) Isabelle format can be found at [4]. These scripts are well documented by text inserted at the beginning of each theory/section and often at the beginning of subsections too. Next we give a brief outline of the part of this formalization which is relevant to the topic of this paper – much more details are given in Section 2.9 from [36].

A. Formalization of a general theory of syntax

As mentioned, we have formalized our recursion principles not only for the particular syntax of λ-calculus, but for an arbitrary syntax with bindings. In other words, we work with terms (modulo α) over a fixed, but arbitrary binding signature.

Our notion of binding signature is similar to, e.g., that of [16] – it is essentially an algebraic signature, where the operation symbols have associated *sorts* and *arities*, just that arities consider not only free, but also *bound* arguments. In our formalization, we also distinguish between *terms* and *abstractions*, the latter being pairs variable-term, up to α. Thus, a binding operator such as Lm takes an abstraction as argument, while a non-binding operator such as App takes terms as arguments.

More precisely, we fix an infinite set of variables, **var**, ranged over by x, y, z. Given any two sets I and A, we let $\mathbf{Input}(I, A)$ be the set of partial functions from I to A, which we call *I-indexed A-inputs*; elements of $\mathbf{Input}(I, \mathbf{term})$ (for some sufficiently large set I) will be used as inputs (i.e., families of arguments) to the operations of the binding signature. Given $f \in \mathbf{Input}(I, A)$ and $g \in \mathbf{Input}(I, B)$, we write $\mathsf{sameDom}\ f\ g$, read "f and g have the same domain", for $\forall\, i \in I.\ (f\ i \text{ defined }) \iff (g\ i \text{ defined })$.

A *binding signature* Σ is then a tuple
(**index**, **bindex**, **varSort**, **sort**, **opSym**, asSort, arOf, barOf), where:
- **index**, ranged over by i, j, is the set of *indexes* (meant to be used for building families of free arguments for the operators);
- **bindex**, also ranged over by i, j, is the set of *binding indexes* (*bindexes* for short) (meant to be used for building families of bound arguments for the operators);
- **varSort**, ranged over by xs, is the set of *variable sorts* (*varsorts* for short) (representing the various syntactic categories of variables);
- **sort**, ranged over by s, is the set of *sorts* (representing the various syntactic categories of terms);
- **opSym**, ranged over by δ, is the set of *operation symbols*;
- $\mathsf{asSort} : \mathbf{varSort} \to \mathbf{sort}$ is an injective map (this is the inclusion/injection of varsorts as (term) sorts – thus, for each sort of variables, we have precisely one sort of terms that can substitute them);
- $\mathsf{stOf} : \mathbf{opSym} \to \mathbf{sort}$, read "the (result) sort of";
- $\mathsf{arOf} : \mathbf{opSym} \to \mathbf{Input}(\mathbf{index}, \mathbf{sort})$, read "the (free) arity of";
- $\mathsf{barOf} : \mathbf{opSym} \to \mathbf{Input}(\mathbf{bindex}, \mathbf{varSort} \times \mathbf{sort})$, read "the bound arity of" ("barity of", for short).

We work with a fixed (but arbitrary) binding signature in an Isabelle locale, for which we first define many-sorted quasi-terms and quasi-abstractions (not yet factored to α), and then terms and abstractions as α-classes of quasi-terms and quasi-abstractions. Thus, we have:
- for each sort s, a collection $\mathbf{term}(\Sigma)_s$ of s-terms;
- for each varsort xs and sort s, a collection $\mathbf{abs}(\Sigma)_{(xs,s)}$ of (xs, s)-abstractions, binding xs variables in s-terms.

For instance, the binding signature Σ of the untyped λ-calculus is obtained as follows:
- since we have only one syntactic category of variables and one of

terms,
— **varSort** is a singleton set, say $\{\text{vlm}\}$;
— **sort** is a singleton set, say $\{\text{lm}\}$;
— asSort : **varSort** $\rightarrow$ **sort** maps vlm to lm;
- **opSym** is taken to contain symbols for application and λ-abstraction, namely, **opSym** $= \{\text{app}, \text{lam}\}$;
- **index** is taken to contain slots for each sort in the arity of each operation symbol, here **index** $= \{\text{lapp}_1, \text{lapp}_2\}$;
- **bindex** is taken to contain slots for each pair varsort-sort in the barity of each operation symbol, here **bindex** $= \{\text{llam}\}$;
- stOf : **opSym** $\rightarrow$ **sort** is defined by:
— stOf app $=$ lm;
— stOf lam $=$ lm;
- arOf : **opSym** $\rightarrow$ **Input**(**index**, **sort**) is defined by:
— arOf app $i =$ lm;
— arOf lam $i =$ undefined;
- barOf : **opSym** $\rightarrow$ **Input**(**bindex**, **varSort** $\times$ **sort**) is defined by:
— barOf app $i =$ undefined;
— barOf lam $i =$ lm.

Now, $\mathbf{term}(\Sigma)_{\text{lm}}$ and $\mathbf{abs}(\Sigma)_{(\text{vlm},\text{lm})}$ are precisely the terms and abstractions for the untyped λ-calculus (with Op app being precisely App, etc.)

(See Section 2.9.1 from [36] for much more details.)

Recursion principles. The theories Iteration and Recursion (from [4]) formalize the arbitrary-syntax generalization of the results pertaining to Horn-based recursion from Sections 3 and 5, as well as a couple of variations of these results employing swapping instead of substitution. (NB: What we called "recursion" in Section 3 is in fact *iteration*, i.e., a restricted form of (primitive) recursion, where in the defining equations one is able to use the recursively computed result, but *not* the recursive argument itself – see Sections 1.4.2 in [36] for details. We also formalized the general version.)

Next we discuss theory Recursion. Just like in Section 3, we use the prefix "g" for "generalized" items (here, not only "generalized" terms, but, as discussed in Section 6, also "generalized" abstractions). We have 4 kinds of models: FSb-models (formalizing the concept described in Section 3), and FSw-models, FSbSw-models and FSwSb-models, formalizing the aforementioned swapping-based variations.

For economy reasons, all these kinds of models share a common Isabelle record type, featuring operators for the syntactic constructors, freshness, swapping and substitution – such a record is called a "raw" model. The involved clauses, such as F1-F4, S1-S4 and A for FSb-models, stated as predicates on raw models, make such a raw model a specific model of one of the 4 kinds; if a certain feature is not needed for a certain kind of model (such as swapping for FSb-models), the corresponding operator is left undefined.

Then the four types of models are introduced by the predicates wlsFSb, wlsFSw, wlsFSbSw, wlsFSbSw, read "well-structured FSb-model" etc., which are conjunctions of the necessary clauses.

We only discuss here FSb-models. Given a raw model MOD, wlsFSb MOD is defined to be essentially a conjunction of 3 predicates:
- gFreshCls MOD, stating "the fresh clauses" (F1-F4 from Section 3);
- gSubstCls MOD, stating "the substitution clauses" (S1-S4 from Section 3);
- gAbsRen MOD, stating "the abstraction-renaming clause" (A from Section 3).

The expected notions of morphism from the term model to another FSb-model (generalizing the notion of FSb-morphism from Section 3) is given by the predicate termFSbMorph, stating preservation of freshness and substitution.

Given a FSb-model MOD as above, the associated recursive morphism from the term model comes as two maps rec MOD : **term** $\rightarrow$ **gTerm** and recAbs MOD : **abs** $\rightarrow$ gAbs. The recursion theorem (Thm. 1) is stated, split in two: **(a)** existence, as theorem wlsFSb_recAll_termFSbMorph (note that H from Thm. 1 is written in the scripts as rec MOD and recAbs MOD); **(b)** uniqueness, as theorem wlsFSb_recAll_unique_presCons (saying that (rec MOD, recAbs MOD) is the only pair of constructor-preserving maps from terms and abstractions to the target model).

The 3 criteria for extra morphism properties from Section 5, namely, Thm. 2, have also been formalized, as theorems wlsFSb_recAll_reflFreshAll, wlsFSb_recAll_isInjAll and wlsFSb_recAll_isSurjAll.

B. Formalized examples and larger developments

All the examples listed explicitly in this paper have been formalized. Our first example, namely, semantic interpretation (Problem I) has been included as a "built-in" in the general theory. The rest of the examples are formalized in roughly the same syntax in which they were presented in this paper (usually in a slightly more general format, allowing an unspecified number of constants too besides variables, application and λ-abstraction). Many of the examples appear in the formal scripts as parts of larger developments, the largest one being a formalization of a significant part of Plotkin's classic paper [34]. In all such cases, we claim that the overall development benefits highly from the possibility to *define the map with the desired properties and move on*, provided by our recursion principles, as opposed to trying to make the definition work by ad hoc bases.[4]

Semantic-domain interpretation. Due to its importance and generality, the semantic interpretation example (or, rather, class of examples) discussed as motivational Problem I has also been included in the general development (for an arbitrary syntax) – this is the topic of theory Semantic_Domains. A "well-structured" semantic domain (predicate wlsSEM) consists essentially of a type **sTerm**, of semantic values (called "semantic terms" in the scripts' comments), and of an interpretation of the operation symbols from a signature, where abstractions are treated as functions (thus the operations have second-order arguments to match bindings in the syntax, as for LM versus Lm at Problem I). A compositional interpretation map (predicate compInt) is a map, via valuations, of syntax to the semantic domain which is compositional with the syntactic constructors and with substitution and oblivious to freshness, as is $[\_]$ in Problem I. The main theorem, semIntAll_compInt, states that, for any given semantic domain SEM, the pair (semInt SEM, semIntAbs SEM) is indeed such a compositional interpretation map.

Instances of the general theory for particular syntaxes. So far, we have considered the following two instances:
(I) The syntax of the untyped λ-calculus with constants, with terms $X, Y, Z \in$ **term** and abstractions $A, B \in$ **abs**:
$X \ ::= \ \text{Var}\, x \mid \text{Ct}\, c \mid \text{App}\, X\, Y \mid \text{Lam}\, A \qquad A \ ::= \ \text{Abs}\, x\, X$
(II) The two-sorted value-based variation of the above (as at the CPS example in Section 4), with full terms $X, Y, Z \in \mathbf{term}_{fl}$, value terms $Xvl, Yvl, Zvl \in \mathbf{term}_{vl}$ and abstractions (of value variables in full terms) $A, B \in \mathbf{abs}_{(vl,fl)}$: $\;X \ ::= \ \text{InVl}\, Xvl \mid \text{App}\, X\, Y$
$Xvl \ ::= \ \text{Var}\, x \mid \text{Ct}\, c \mid \text{Lam}\, A \qquad A \ ::= \ \text{Abs}\, x\, X$
where InVl is the injection of value terms into full terms. For both syntaxes, we recover the notation from this paper's previous sections by letting $\text{Lm}\, x\, X$ be an abbreviation for $\text{Lam}\, (\text{Abs}\, x\, X)$.

Theories L1 and L are performing the instantiation of the general theory to the above syntax (I) (and LV1 and LV do the same for (II)). The instantiation process is performed in a completely uniform manner and will eventually be automated, but currently it is done by hand. Theories L1 and L most of the facts one needs to

[4] But see Section 8 from the main paper for a discussion of other means for handling such definitions uniformly.

know about the λ-calculus instance of the theory, including: **(1)** basic facts about freshness, substitution and swapping; **(2)** induction principles; **(3)** the Horn-based recursion principles. All these facts, especially those pertaining to (3) (present in L1), are documented and illustrated by comments inserted in between the formal scripts.

The theory of call-by-name λ-calculus. This is the content of theories CBN, CBN_CR and CBN_Std, following Section 5 of [34]. In theory CBN, we introduce all the necessary relations pertaining to $\beta\delta$-reduction (where δ refers to the presence of the so-called δ rules for reducing constants application.) – one-step left reduction, one-step reduction, parallel reduction, their reflexive-transitive closures, the associated CBN equational theory, etc. – as inductive definitions, and then prove several basic facts about them, such as fresh induction and inversion rules. The number-of-free-occurrences operator no : **term** $\rightarrow$ **var** $\rightarrow I\!N$ discussed in Section 4 plays an important role in the development, where a measure based on it needs to be assigned to parallel reduction (this measure roughly indicates the number of redexes available in parallel in one step). In CBN_CR, we prove the call-by-name Church-Rosser theorem (a prerequisite for [34]). In CBN_Std, we prove the call-by-name standardization theorem, (stated as Thm. 1 on page 146 in [34]) and its corollaries.

HOAS representation of λ-calculus into itself. This is the content of the theory HOAS. The first part of this theory deals with the representation of syntax, and has been described in Section 6 of the main paper.

As operational semantics for the object system we have chosen the call-by-name big-step reduction (as defined, e.g., in [34] on page 145, using the function Eval_N) – this is defined in our theory CBN as the relation Bredn : **Obj.term** $\rightarrow$ **Obj.term** $\rightarrow$ **bool**, with concrete syntax $==>_n$, where the index n is not a number, but a reminder of the "by name" style of reduction. (The choice was not important, we could have chosen any other reduction relation.) This relation is represented in the usual HOAS, LF-style fashion. The difference from LF though is that the simple logical framework considered here, **term(metaConst)**, does not have judgement mechanisms of its own, and therefore we use the inductive mechanism of Isabelle, which is here the "meta-meta level". Thus, we represent Bredn by an inductively defined relation MetaBredn : **Meta.term** $\rightarrow$ **Meta.term** $\rightarrow$ **bool**, with concrete syntax $==>_{nM}$, where the index "nM" stands for "by name, Meta". E.g., the β-clause in the definition of Bredn, namely,

$$\frac{X ==>_n \text{Obj.Lm}\ y\ Z' \qquad Z'[Y/y] ==>_n U''}{\text{Obj.App}\ X\ Y ==>_n U''}$$

is captured by the clause

$$\frac{mX ==>_{nM} \text{Meta.App LM}\ mV' \qquad \text{Meta.nf}\ (\text{Meta.App}\ mV'\ mY) ==>_{nM} mU''}{\text{Meta.App}\ (\text{Meta.App APP}\ mX)\ mY ==>_{nM} mU''}$$

where, as usual, we omitted spelling the meta-constant injection operator, Meta.Ct, and where Meta.nf : **Meta.term** $\rightarrow$ **Meta.term** associates to each meta-level term its $\beta\delta$-normal form if such a normal form exists and is undefined otherwise.

Notice that the meta-level rule does not involve any bindings – this was the whole purpose, to capture the involved bindings implicitly, by the meta-level mechanisms. The object-level action of substituting in Z' a previously bound variable (as $Z'[Y/y]$) is matched by meta-level application Meta.App mV' mY in conjunction with normalization – since in this correspondence Meta.App LM mV' will be the representation of Obj.Lm y Z', mV' will itself be a (meta-level) Lm-abstraction; the purpose of normalizing Meta.App mV' mY is therefore taking care of the resulting meta-level β-redex.

For this sample representation, we have chosen to normalize "on the fly", since this matches most faithfully the practice of logical frameworks. (For instance, in (generic) Isabelle [47], $(\lambda\ x.\ X)\ Y$ is a volatile entity, being instantaneously replaced by $X[Y/y]$, the latter being what the user sees.) Another approach would be not normalizing (i.e., not including Meta.nf in the above rule), but then stating the adequacy referring to normal forms – the latter is more common in the LF literature on adequacy [5, 22]. Yet another, newer approach, surveyed in [21], is to normalize at substitution time, via a notion of *hereditary substitution*. These approaches are equivalent, and they reflect the semantic intuition that the β (or $\beta\delta$, $\beta\eta$, etc.) equational theory is acting as the meta-level equality.

The semantic adequacy of the representation is stated as two theorems:

- rep_preserves_Bredn: If $X ==>_n X'$, then rep $X ==>_{nM}$ rep X'.
- rep_reflects_Bredn: If rep $X ==>_n mX'$, then there exists X' such that $X ==>_n X'$ and rep $X' = mX'$.

In particular, these theorems imply:

- corollary rep_Bredn_iff: rep $X ==>_{nM}$ rep X' holds iff $X ==>_n X'$ holds.

CPS transformation of call-by-value to call-by-name. This is the content of the theory CPS. It includes formalization of the discussion from Section 4.2. CPS imports the theory Embed, where the two-sorted value-based syntax is embedded in the (single-sorted) standard syntax. We defined two combinators, combIC : **term** $\rightarrow$ **term**, read "the identity-continuation combinator", and combAC : **term** $\rightarrow$ **term** $\rightarrow$ **term**, read "the application-continuation combinator", corresponding to the right-hand sides of clauses (3) and (4) from Section 4.2, by making choices of fresh variables (via the Isabelle Hilbert choice) and then showing that these choices are irrelevant. Thus, the aforementioned clauses appear in the scripts (in lemma cps_simps) as cps (InVl Xvl) = combIC (cps_{vl} Xvl)) and cps (App X Y) = combAC (cps X) (cps Y). The "built-in" freshness reflection and injectiveness of the morphism are also formalized, as lemmas cps_reflects_fresh and cps_inj.

A more technically involved example – connection with the de Bruijn representation. This example has not been described in the main body of the paper, so we enter more details here.

We use the following references:

-[a] P.-L. Curien, Categorical combinators. Information and Control, 69(1-3):188–254, 1986.

-[b] H. Ohtsuka. A proof of the substitution lemma in de Bruijn's notation. Inf. Process. Lett., 46(2):63–66, 1993.

De Bruijn indexes are a standard way to represent λ-calculus for efficient manipulation / implementation purposes. The set **dB**, of *de Bruijn terms*, ranged over by K, L, M, is defined by the following grammar, where n ranges over $I\!N$:

$$K \ ::= \ \text{VAR}\ n \mid \text{APP}\ K\ L \mid \text{LM}\ K$$

There are no variable bindings involved – rather, the index n of a de Bruijn variable VAR n indicates the "distance" between the given occurrence and its LM-binder (if any), i.e., the number of LM-operators interposed between that occurrence and its binder. Thus, e.g., the λ-term Lm x (Lm y (App y x)) corresponds to the de Bruijn term LM (LM (APP (VAR 0) (VAR 1))).

As it stands, this correspondence is not perfect, since, on one hand, there are λ-terms with free variables, and, on the other, there are de Bruijn terms with dangling indexes, i.e., indexes that fail to point to a valid binder (e.g., VAR 0, or LM (VAR 1)). A more serious discrepancy is that the processes of binding variables in terms are different: using Lm, one can choose any variable x to be bound, while using LM one binds the "default" de Bruijn variables waiting to be bound, namely, those with dangling level 0.

A closer mathematical connection, allowing one to actually relate de Bruijn versions of standard results with the "official" λ-versions (as is done, e.g., in [b]) can be achieved via parameterizing by variable orderings, as discussed in [a].

We model such orderings as injective valuations of variables into numbers, i.e., injective elements of **val** $=$ (**var** $\to \mathbb{N}$). Let **sem**, the set of semantic values, ranged over by s, be $\{\rho \in$ **val**. $\mathsf{inj}\ \rho\} \to$ **dB**, where inj : **val** $\to$ **bool** is the predicate stating that a valuation is injective. Then λ-terms are interpreted as de Bruijn terms by a map toDB : **term** $\to$ **sem**, read "to de Bruijn" as follows.

The clauses for variables and application are the obvious ones:
- (1) $\mathsf{toDB}\ x = \lambda\rho.\ \mathsf{VAR}(\rho\ x)$;
- (2) $\mathsf{toDB}\ X\ Y = \lambda\rho.\ \mathsf{APP}\ (\mathsf{toDB}\ X\ \rho)\ (\mathsf{toDB}\ Y\ \rho)$.

To interpret λ-abstraction, we first define mkFst : **var** $\to$ **val** $\to$ **val**, read "make first":
- $\mathsf{mkFst}\ x\ \rho = \lambda\ y.$ if $y = x$ then 0 else $(\rho\ y + 1)$.

(Thus, x is "made first" by assigning it the first position, 0, in ρ, and by making room for it through shifting the values of all the other variables.) Now, we set
- (3) $\mathsf{toDB}\ (\mathsf{Lm}\ x\ X) = \lambda\rho.\ \mathsf{LM}(\mathsf{toDB}\ X\ (\mathsf{mkFst}\ x\ \rho))$.

(Thus, in order to map $(\mathsf{Lm}\ x)$-abstractions to LM-abstractions, x is initially "made first", i.e., mapped to 0, the only value which LM "knows" how to bind.)

The above clauses are essentially Definition 2.3 on page 192 in [a] (under a slightly different notation). There are some similarities between these clauses and those from Problem I, but there are also some major differences, notably the interpretation of λ-abstractions and the restricted space of valuations here, which prevent us from reducing one problem to the other.

As usual, to make the definition rigorous, we ask the freshness and substitution questions.

What can we infer about x versus $\mathsf{toDB}\ X$ if we know that x is fresh for X? The answer to this is similar to that from Problem I: we can infer obliviousness to x of the interpretation:
- (4) $\mathsf{fresh}\ x\ X \Longrightarrow (\forall \rho\ \rho'.\ \rho =_x \rho' \Longrightarrow \mathsf{toDB}\ X\ \rho = \mathsf{toDB}\ X\ \rho')$.

As for the substitution question, the answer is given by a lemma stated in loc. cit.:
- (5) $\mathsf{toDB}\ (X[Y/y]) = \lambda\rho.\ (\mathsf{toDB}\ X)\ (\mathsf{mkFst}\ y\ \rho)\ [(\mathsf{toDB}\ Y\ \rho)/0]^b$;

where $\_[\_/\_]^b$: **dB** $\to$ **dB** $\to \mathbb{N} \to$ **dB** is de Bruijn substitution (i.e, plain FO-substitution):
— $(\mathsf{VAR}\ n)[M/m]^b =$ if $n = m$ then M else $\mathsf{VAR}\ n$,
— $(\mathsf{APP}\ K\ L)[M/m]^b = \mathsf{APP}\ (K[M/m]^b)\ (L[M/m]^b)$,
— $(\mathsf{LM}\ K)[M/m]^b = \mathsf{LM}\ (K[M/m]^b)$.

(Thus, the toDB treatment of substitution is similar to that of λ-abstraction: x is 0-indexed and then 0 is de Bruijn-substituted.)

Again, to have clauses (1)-(3) rigorously justified and clauses (4), (5) proved, one needs to check that the resulted model is an FSb-model. Unlike in the previous examples, here there are some complications, in that some of the FSb-model clauses simply do not hold on the whole space **sem**.

Fortunately however, a technical closure condition fixes this problem. Namely, if we take
sem$' = \{s \in$ **sem**. $\forall\sigma : \mathbb{N} \to \mathbb{N},\ \rho \in$ **val**. $\mathsf{inj}\ \sigma \wedge \mathsf{inj}\ \rho \Longrightarrow s\ (\sigma \circ \rho) = G\ \sigma\ (\mathsf{toDB}\ X\ \rho)\}$,
where $G : (\mathbb{N} \to \mathbb{N}) \to$ **dB** $\to$ **dB** is a map whose definition we give below, then **sem**$'$, with the FSb-structure given by clauses (1)-(5), indeed turns out to be an FSb-model – checking this is relatively easy, but does rely on some de Bruijn arithmetic.

The definition of G (having little importance beyond its technical role in the invariant that helps defining toDB), goes as follows:
- $G\ \sigma\ K = \mathsf{vmapDB}\ (\mathsf{cut}\ \sigma)\ 0\ K$, where
- $\mathsf{vmapDB} : (\mathbb{N} \to \mathbb{N} \to \mathbb{N}) \to \mathbb{N} \to$ **dB** $\to$ **dB**, read "variable map", is the natural de Bruijn analogue of, say, list map (also taking into account, like any "natural" de Bruijn function, the LM-depth, recursively):
— $\mathsf{vmapDB}\ \sigma\ n\ (\mathsf{VAR}\ i) = \mathsf{VAR}\ (\sigma\ n\ i)$,
— $\mathsf{vmapDB}\ \sigma\ n\ (\mathsf{APP}\ K\ L) = \mathsf{APP}\ (\mathsf{vmapDB}\ \sigma\ K)\ (\mathsf{vmapDB}\ \sigma\ L)$;
— $\mathsf{vmapDB}\ \sigma\ (\mathsf{LM}\ K) = \mathsf{LM}\ (\mathsf{vmapDB}\ \sigma\ (n+1)\ K)$;
- and $\mathsf{cut} : (\mathbb{N} \to \mathbb{N}) \to \mathbb{N} \to (\mathbb{N} \to \mathbb{N})$ is defined by
$\mathsf{cut}\ \sigma\ n\ i =$ if $i < n$ then i else $\sigma\ (i - n) + n$.

We conjecture that the difficulty we encountered with constructing an FSb-model for this example would be matched by a corresponding difficulty in making the definitions go through in an ad-hoc approach, where one would eventually have to discover a similar invariant (again, compared to our approach, with the disadvantage of having to do this discovery by repeated trial and error in the middle of inductive proofs, not knowing in advance what properties need to hold). Unfortunately, we have no way of testing this conjecture, as ours seems to be the first rigorous (let alone formal) treatment of this construction from the literature. In [a], one employs quasi-terms rather than terms, and α-equivalence is not even defined until after defining the above de Bruijn interpretation, and then its definition is non-standard: α-equivalence is taken to be the very kernel of this interpretation. Moreover, the substitution lemma is stated in [a] without a proof.

This example has been formalized as the theory C_deBruijn from [4]. The scripts follow quite closely the notations we used above. We import theory Lambda, the existing formalization of the de Bruijn representation from the Isabelle library. Then we develop some de Bruijn arithmetics facts, after which we proceed with the interpretation map toDB by means of the model toDB_MOD. (This naming convention, having the name of the model be the name of the desired map followed by "_MOD" is observed in all our formalized examples.) This time, since there are some nontrivial computations involved in the verification of the clauses, we prefer to first define the model components separately (operators ggWls, ggVar etc. in the scripts). Lemmas toDB_simps, toDB_preserves_fresh and toDB_subst are the end-products of the definition, i.e. correspond to clauses (1)-(5). (For these end-products, we also observe the same naming pattern, as seen here and in the HOAS case, for all our examples.)

Proving the Unique Fixed-Point Principle Correct

An Adventure with Category Theory

Ralf Hinze Daniel W. H. James

Department of Computer Science, University of Oxford, Wolfson Building, Parks Road, Oxford, OX1 3QD, England

{ralf.hinze, daniel.james}@cs.ox.ac.uk

Abstract

Say you want to prove something about an infinite data-structure, such as a stream or an infinite tree, but you would rather not subject yourself to coinduction. The unique fixed-point principle is an easy-to-use, calculational alternative. The proof technique rests on the fact that certain recursion equations have unique solutions; if two elements of a coinductive type satisfy the same equation of this kind, then they are equal. In this paper we precisely characterize the conditions that guarantee a unique solution. Significantly, we do so not with a syntactic criterion, but with a semantic one that stems from the categorical notion of naturality. Our development is based on distributive laws and bialgebras, and draws heavily on Turi and Plotkin's pioneering work on mathematical operational semantics. Along the way, we break down the design space in two dimensions, leading to a total of nine points. Each gives rise to varying degrees of expressiveness, and we will discuss three in depth. Furthermore, our development is generic in the syntax of equations and in the behaviour they encode—we are not caged in the world of streams.

Categories and Subject Descriptors D.2.4 [*Software/ Program Verification*]: correctness proofs, formal methods; F.3.1 [*Logics and Meanings of Programs*]: Specifying and Verifying and Reasoning about Programs—specification techniques

General Terms Languages, Theory, Verification

Keywords unique fixed-points, bialgebras, distributive laws

1. Introduction

"Whence cometh this?" Our aim is to provide an elegant proof of correctness for an elegant proof principle. Elegance comes, in large part, through simplicity, and specifically we value the simplicity afforded by the notion of naturality and initial/final algebra/coalgebra semantics. The key component for correctness of the unique fixed-point principle is a sound characterization of what gives a recursion equation a unique solution.

"Why does uniqueness matter?" Uniqueness has two complementary perspectives: programs and proofs. When read as a program, the unique solution implies that it is well-defined. When the unicity is utilized in a proof, we are able to show that two given solutions are equal—the unique fixed-point principle (UFP).

ICFP'11, September 19–21, 2011, Tokyo, Japan.

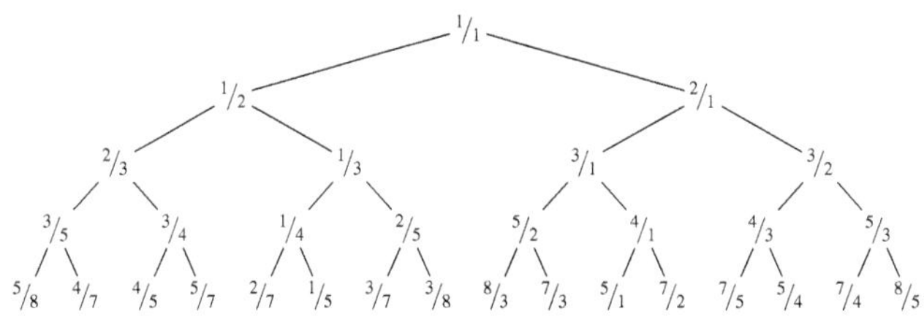

Figure 1. The Bird tree

"Why not a syntactic criterion?" In prior work [10] a simple syntactic criterion, specific to stream equations, was proffered, but this is unsatisfactory. A criterion must exclude all bad things and accept as many good things as possible. As criteria are complicated to accept more good things, so is the understanding and trust. Their syntactic nature makes them intrinsically fragile. Just as it is often easy to satisfy a criterion by a program transformation, it is just as easy to lose the satisfaction.

"Category complex" Our theoretical underpinnings, distributive laws and bialgebras, draw on Turi and Plotkin's mathematical operational semantics [21], and just as in theirs, the following pages contain plenty of category theory. However, our concern throughout is making the theory accessible. We do so by grounding it in an application, and targeting the categorical parlance to readers who are familiar with the Algebra of Programming [5]. This is the holy trinity of categories, functors and natural transformations, along with algebras and coalgebras, which we will summarize. For the categorically enlightened, we will note the more direct reasoning.

"Interpretation of categorical structures" We will introduce a selection of categorical structures and discuss their interpretation in this domain. It is well known that free monads can been seen as terms with variables and cofree comonads as labelled trees, but we will see how these and two other structures influence the expressivity of recursion equations, by the 'language features' they induce. These features are positioned in two dimensions. We will focus on just one, and we give a fuller account in the extended paper [11]. As a small exception, we will consider what Niqui and Rutten [16] calls *sampling* functions, and what we would more loosely describe as stream operators that consume more than they produce.

"Beauty and Elegance" We hope to showcase the beauty of the unique fixed-point principle. Its elegance is due, in no small part, to its calculational style, a style that proofs will follow throughout.

2. The Unique Fixed-Point Principle

2.1 Infinite Trees

In Figure 1 we can see the first five levels of the *Bird Tree* [9], an infinite tree in which you can find every positive rational number exactly once. It has several remarkable properties that come from its nature as a *fractal* object—its subtrees are similar to the whole tree. The tree can be transformed into its left subtree by incrementing and then taking the reciprocal of every element; the right subtree is obtained by swapping these operations. This description can be nicely captured by a *corecursive* definition (we will use Haskell as a meta-language for the category of sets and total functions):

$$\mathit{bird} = \mathit{Node}\ 1\ (1\ /\ (\mathit{bird} + 1))\ ((1\ /\ \mathit{bird}) + 1)\ .$$

The picture suggests that taking the reciprocal of each element is the same as mirroring the tree, $\mathit{mirror\,bird} = 1\ /\ \mathit{bird}$, and this is indeed the case. We shall see that we can prove this effortlessly using the unique fixed-point principle.

Before we get to the proof, we must introduce some definitions.

```
data Tree x = Node {root :: x, left :: Tree x, right :: Tree x}
```

The type Tree x is a so-called *coinductive datatype*. Its definition is similar to the textbook definition of binary trees, except that there are no leaves, so we cannot build a finite tree. And without leaves, *mirror* is a one-liner:

```
mirror (Node x l r) = Node x (mirror r) (mirror l) .
```

The definition of *bird* uses $+$ and $/$ lifted to trees. We obtain these liftings for free as Tree is a so-called *idiom* [14]:

```
class Idiom f where
  pure :: x → f x
  (⋄)  :: f (x → y) → (f x → f y)
instance Idiom Tree where
  pure x = t where t = Node x t t
  t ⋄ u  = Node (root t $ root u)
                (left t ⋄ left u) (right t ⋄ right u) .
```

The call *pure* x constructs an infinite tree of xs; idiomatic application $\diamond$ takes a tree of functions and a tree of arguments to a tree of results. Using *pure* and $\diamond$, we can lift arithmetic operations *generically* to idioms.

```
instance (Idiom f, Num x) ⇒ Num (f x) where
  fromInteger n = pure (fromInteger n)
  negate u      = pure negate ⋄ u
  u + v         = pure (+) ⋄ u ⋄ v   ...
```

Since the operations are defined pointwise, the familiar arithmetic laws also hold for trees. Mirroring a tree preserves the idiomatic structure, the function *mirror* is an *idiom homomorphism*: $\mathit{mirror}\,(\mathit{pure}\,x) = \mathit{pure}\,x$ and $\mathit{mirror}\,(x \diamond y) = \mathit{mirror}\,x \diamond \mathit{mirror}\,y$. This implies, for instance, that $\mathit{mirror}\,(u+v) = \mathit{mirror}\,u + \mathit{mirror}\,v$.

Let us return to the promised proof and the unique fixed-point principle. Consider the recursion equation $x = \mathit{Node}\ y\ l\ r$, where l and r possibly contain the variable x, but *not* the expressions $\mathit{root}\,x$, $\mathit{left}\,x$ or $\mathit{right}\,x$. Equations in this syntactic form possess a *unique solution*. Uniqueness can be exploited to prove that two infinite trees are equal: if they satisfy the same equation, then they are.

$$
\begin{aligned}
& \mathit{mirror\ bird} \\
= {} & \quad \{\ \text{definitions of } \mathit{mirror} \text{ and } \mathit{bird}\ \} \\
& \mathit{Node}\ 1\ (\mathit{mirror}\ ((1\ /\ \mathit{bird}) + 1))\ (\mathit{mirror}\ (1\ /\ (\mathit{bird} + 1))) \\
= {} & \quad \{\ \mathit{mirror} \text{ is an idiom homomorphism}\ \} \\
& \mathit{Node}\ 1\ ((1\ /\ \mathit{mirror\ bird}) + 1)\ (1\ /\ (\mathit{mirror\ bird} + 1)) \\
\propto {} & \quad \{\ x = \mathit{Node}\ 1\ ((1\ /\ x) + 1)\ (1\ /\ (x + 1)) \text{ has a unique sol.}\ \} \\
& \mathit{Node}\ 1\ ((1\ /\ (1\ /\ \mathit{bird})) + 1)\ (1\ /\ ((1\ /\ \mathit{bird}) + 1)) \\
= {} & \quad \{\ \text{arithmetic}\ \} \\
& 1\ /\ \mathit{Node}\ 1\ (1\ /\ (\mathit{bird} + 1))\ ((1\ /\ \mathit{bird}) + 1) \\
= {} & \quad \{\ \text{definition of } \mathit{bird}\ \} \\
& 1\ /\ \mathit{bird}
\end{aligned}
$$

The link $\propto$ indicates that the proof rests on the *unique fixed-point principle*; the recursion equation is given within the curly braces. The upper part shows that *mirror bird* satisfies the equation $x = \mathit{Node}\ 1\ ((1\ /\ x) + 1)\ (1\ /\ (x + 1))$; the lower part establishes that $1\ /\ \mathit{bird}$ satisfies the same equation. The symbol $\propto$ links the two parts, effectively proving the equality of both expressions.

We mentioned that the Bird Tree contains every positive rational exactly once. A proof that exclusively builds on the unique fixed-point principle can be found in Hinze [9].

2.2 Streams

Let us consider a second coinductive type, one that will accompany us for the rest of the paper: the type of streams, infinite sequences of elements.

```
data Stream x = Cons {head :: x, tail :: Stream x}
(≺)   :: x → Stream x → Stream x
x ≺ s = Cons x s
```

Like the type of infinite trees, Stream is an idiom.

```
instance Idiom Stream where
  pure x = s where s = x ≺ s
  s ⋄ t  = (head s $ head t) ≺ (tail s ⋄ tail t)
```

Using this vocabulary, we can define, for instance, the stream of Fibonacci numbers.

$$
\begin{aligned}
\mathit{fib} &= 0 \prec \mathit{fib}' \\
\mathit{fib}' &= 1 \prec \mathit{fib} + \mathit{fib}'
\end{aligned}
$$

The Fibonacci numbers satisfy a myriad of properties. For example, if we form the stream of their partial sums and increment the result, we obtain fib'. Again, we shall see that the UFP allows for a concise proof. But first, we have to capture summation as a stream operator.

$$\Sigma\, s = 0 \prec s + \Sigma\, s$$

Turning to the proof of $\Sigma\,\mathit{fib} + 1 = \mathit{fib}'$, we can either show that $\Sigma\,\mathit{fib} + 1$ satisfies the defining equation of fib', or that $\mathit{fib}' - 1$ satisfies the recursion equation of $\Sigma\,\mathit{fib}$. Both approaches work, the calculations are left as really (!) easy exercises to the reader.

A related property is the following: if we sum the Fibonacci numbers at odd positions, we obtain the Fibonacci numbers at even positions. The so-called *sampling functions* [16] *even* and *odd* enjoy simple corecursive definitions.

$$
\begin{aligned}
\mathit{even}\ s &= \mathit{head}\ s \prec \mathit{odd}\ \ (\mathit{tail}\ s) \\
\mathit{odd}\ \ s &= \qquad\qquad\quad \mathit{even}\ (\mathit{tail}\ s)
\end{aligned}
$$

Turning to the proof of $\Sigma\,(\mathit{odd\,fib}) = \mathit{even\,fib}$, we reason:

$$
\begin{aligned}
& \Sigma\,(\mathit{odd\,fib}) \\
= {} & \quad \{\ \text{definition of } \Sigma\ \} \\
& 0 \prec \mathit{odd\,fib} + \Sigma\,(\mathit{odd\,fib}) \\
= {} & \quad \{\ \text{definition of } \mathit{odd}\ \} \\
& 0 \prec \mathit{even\,fib}' + \Sigma\,(\mathit{odd\,fib}) \\
\propto {} & \quad \{\ x = 0 \prec \mathit{even\,fib}' + x\ \} \\
& 0 \prec \mathit{even\,fib}' + \mathit{even\,fib} \\
= {} & \quad \{\ \mathit{even} \text{ is an idiom homomorphism and arithmetic}\ \} \\
& 0 \prec \mathit{even}\ (\mathit{fib} + \mathit{fib}') \\
= {} & \quad \{\ \text{definitions of } \mathit{fib}' \text{ and } \mathit{odd}\ \} \\
& 0 \prec \mathit{odd\,fib}' \\
= {} & \quad \{\ \text{definitions of } \mathit{fib} \text{ and } \mathit{even}\ \} \\
& \mathit{even\,fib}\ .
\end{aligned}
$$

This completes our short survey. The UFP is not only easy-to-use, but also surprisingly powerful: in prior work [10] we have shown how to redevelop the theory of recurrences, finite calculus and generating functions using streams and stream operators, building solely on the cornerstone of unique solutions.

What remains to be done? We have been somewhat vague about the syntactic conditions that guarantee uniqueness. We shall see that systems of recursion equations can be classified along two dimensions, leading to a total of nine different points of interest. The system for *fib* falls into one ("consume one element, produce one"), the system for *even* into another ("consume many, but don't nest calls"). When defining streams we cannot mix styles. For instance, the equation $x = 0 \prec even\, x$ has infinitely many solutions. We shall see that we can capture the conditions that guarantee unicity semantically, using the categorical concept of naturality.

Furthermore, we abstract away from the type of infinite trees and streams. The development is generic both in the syntax and in the behaviour—which operations are defined and over which coinductive type. An appropriate setting is provided by the categorical notion of algebras and coalgebras which we introduce next. The resulting proofs are not only more general, they are also shorter than specific instances that have appeared in the literature [17, 19].

3. Initial Algebras and Final Coalgebras

We hope the reader has encountered the material of this section before, but we will reiterate it here as it serves as a simple demonstration of the power of *duality*. We will invoke the power to construct 'the opposite thing' time and time again.

Let $\mathsf{F} : \mathscr{C} \to \mathscr{C}$ be an endofunctor. An F-algebra is a pair $\langle A, a\rangle$ consisting of an object $A : \mathscr{C}$ and an arrow $a : \mathsf{F}\,A \to A : \mathscr{C}$. We say that A is the carrier and a is the action of the algebra; however, we often refer to the algebra simply by a as it determines the carrier. An F-homomorphism between algebras $\langle A, a\rangle$ and $\langle \mathsf{B}, b\rangle$ is an arrow $h : A \to \mathsf{B} : \mathscr{C}$ such that $h \cdot a = b \cdot \mathsf{F}\,h$.

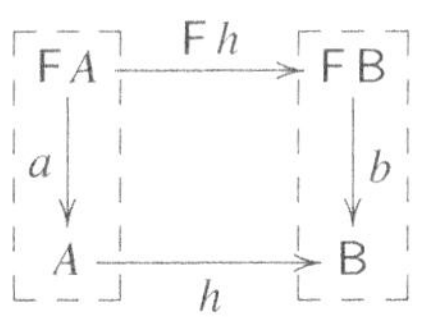

A characteristic of functors is that they preserve identity and composition; this entails that F-homomorphisms compose and have an identity. Consequently, F-algebras and F-homomorphisms form a category, called $\mathsf{F}\text{-}\mathbf{Alg}(\mathscr{C})$. If this category has an initial object, it is called the *initial* F*-algebra* $\langle \mu\mathsf{F}, in\rangle$. Initiality implies that it has a unique F-homomorphism to any F-algebra $\langle A, a\rangle$, which is written $(\!|a|\!)$ and called *fold*. It satisfies the *uniqueness property*

$$h = (\!|a|\!) \iff h \cdot in = a \cdot \mathsf{F}\,h \ . \tag{3.1}$$

We will now seize the opportunity to dualize these constructions to the opposite things: F*-coalgebras* and *unfolds*. An F-coalgebra is a pair $\langle C, c\rangle$ of an object $C : \mathscr{C}$ and an arrow $c : C \to \mathsf{F}\,C : \mathscr{C}$. An F-homomorphism between coalgebras $\langle C, c\rangle$ and $\langle D, d\rangle$ is an arrow $h : C \to D : \mathscr{C}$ such that $\mathsf{F}\,h \cdot c = d \cdot h$. In the same way, we can form a category $\mathsf{F}\text{-}\mathbf{Coalg}(\mathscr{C})$. If this category has a final object, it is called the *final* F*-coalgebra* $\langle \nu\mathsf{F}, out\rangle$. Being the final object, it has a unique F-homomorphism to it from any F-coalgebra $\langle C, c\rangle$, which is written $[\!(c)\!]$ and called *unfold*. It satisfies the following *uniqueness property*.

$$h = [\!(c)\!] \iff \mathsf{F}\,h \cdot c = out \cdot h \tag{3.2}$$

In case you were wondering, *final algebras* and *initial coalgebras* are unexciting, although we will find a use for them. The final algebra is $\langle 1, !_{\mathsf{F}\,1}\rangle$, and the initial coalgebra is $\langle 0, ¡_{\mathsf{F}\,0}\rangle$.

Let $\mathsf{F}, \mathsf{G} : \mathscr{C} \to \mathscr{C}$ be endofunctors, and $\alpha : \mathsf{F} \dot{\leftarrow} \mathsf{G}$ a natural transformation. We can turn α into a functor $\alpha\text{-}\mathbf{Alg} : \mathsf{F}\text{-}\mathbf{Alg} \to \mathsf{G}\text{-}\mathbf{Alg}$ between the categories of F- and G-algebras. (We use $\dot{\leftarrow}$ to highlight the contravariance between α and $\alpha\text{-}\mathbf{Alg}$.)

$$\alpha\text{-}\mathbf{Alg}\,\langle X, a : \mathsf{F}\,X \to X\rangle = \langle X, a \cdot \alpha\,X : \mathsf{G}\,X \to X\rangle \qquad \alpha\text{-}\mathbf{Alg}\,h = h$$

That $\alpha\text{-}\mathbf{Alg}$ is a functor follows from a more general construction given in Appendix B. We will see various instantiations of $\alpha\text{-}\mathbf{Alg}$ later on, where its functor properties will come in handy.

4. Meet Iniga and Finn

Once upon a time a teacher had a pair of bright and capable students, who, for better or worse, were hooked on category theory. The first, Iniga, was a go-getting student with plenty of initiative. Interestingly, this was in stark contrast to Finn, a reserved character who perceived the world with a sense of finality.

The teacher posed them the problem of demonstrating that a system of stream equations has a unique solution. Owing to their polar opposite outlooks, Iniga and Finn took divergent approaches to tackling the problem, but as we will discover, their approaches turned out to be two sides of the same coin.

The teacher started with a minimalistic example, asking them to consider the following stream equations.

$$\begin{aligned} &one &&= 1 \prec one \\ &plus\ (Cons\ m\ s, Cons\ n\ t) &&= (m + n) \prec plus\ (s, t) \end{aligned}$$

Streams of natural numbers are the resultant behaviour of these equations, so the teacher provided the functor $\mathsf{B}\,X = \mathbb{N} \times X$ as the *behaviour functor*. We can give this a Haskell rendering:

$$\mathbf{data}\ \mathsf{B}\ x = Cons\ (\mathbb{N}, x) \ .$$

For simplicity, the teacher fixed the element type of streams. An element of $\nu\mathsf{B}$, the carrier of the final coalgebra of the behaviour functor, is a stream of natural numbers: $\nu\mathsf{B} \cong \mathsf{Stream}\ \mathbb{N}$.

The stream constant *one* and the stream operator *plus* in the example stream equations are also modelled categorically with the functor $\mathsf{S}\,X = 1 + X \times X$ as the *syntax functor*.

$$\mathbf{data}\ \mathsf{S}\ x = One \mid Plus\ (x, x)$$

An element of $\mu\mathsf{S}$, the initial algebra carrier of the syntax functor, is a finite, closed term, built from the syntax constructors of S.

Iniga (taking the initiative): Ok, given these definitions we can model the stream equations by a simple function.

$$\begin{aligned} &\lambda\ (One) &&= Cons\ (1, One) \\ &\lambda\ (Plus\ (Cons\ (m, s), Cons\ (n, t))) &&= Cons\ (m + n, Plus\ (s, t)) \end{aligned}$$

Teacher: Observe that λ is really a natural transformation of type $\mathsf{S}{\circ}\mathsf{B} \dot{\to} \mathsf{B}{\circ}\mathsf{S}$. This is crucial: the syntactic requirements on stream equations to ensure uniqueness of solutions are captured by the naturality requirement on λ. Its type can be seen as a promise that only the head of the incoming stream will be inspected and that an element of the outgoing stream will be constructed. Can you see how the slogan "consume one, produce one" translates?

Iniga: Yes! An interpretation of the syntax is then given by an S-algebra $a : \mathsf{S}\,(\nu\mathsf{B}) \to \nu\mathsf{B}$ whose carrier is the final B-coalgebra $\langle \nu\mathsf{B}, out\rangle$. The algebra a takes a level of syntax over a stream and turns it into a stream.

Teacher: How do we model that a respects the stream equations captured by λ? Your algebra a has to satisfy the following law:

$$out \cdot a = \mathsf{B}\,a \cdot \lambda\,(\nu\mathsf{B}) \cdot \mathsf{S}\,out \ : \ \mathsf{S}\,(\nu\mathsf{B}) \to \mathsf{B}\,(\nu\mathsf{B}) \ . \tag{4.1}$$

The law states that unrolling the result of a is the same as unrolling the arguments of the syntax, $\mathsf{S}\,out$, applying the stream equations $\lambda\,(\nu\mathsf{B})$, and then interpreting the tail, $\mathsf{B}\,a$.

Iniga: Great, for our example I will rearrange the law to observe the Haskell convention of definition by pattern matching,

$a \cdot \mathsf{S}\, out^\circ = out^\circ \cdot \mathsf{B}\, a \cdot \lambda\,(\nu\mathsf{B})$. If I instantiate this law to our running example, I obtain a definition of the algebra a:

$$\begin{aligned}&a\ One\\&\quad = Out^\circ\ (Cons\ (1, a\ One))\\&a\ (Plus\ (Out^\circ\ (Cons\ (m,s)), Out^\circ\ (Cons\ (n,t))))\\&\quad = Out^\circ\ (Cons\ (m+n, a\ (Plus\ (s,t))))\ .\end{aligned}$$

With a, I can now define the semantic counterparts of *One* and *Plus*, the stream constant $\underline{one}$ and the stream operator $\underline{plus}$, underlined to emphasize that they are semantic entities:

$$\begin{aligned}\underline{one}\quad &= a\ One\\ \underline{plus}\ (s,t) &= a\ (Plus\ (s,t))\ .\end{aligned}$$

Teacher (interrupting): You are actually building upon the isomorphism $\mathsf{S}\,X \to X \cong (1 \to X) \times (X \times X \to X)$ here: the pair of functions, $\underline{one}$ and $\underline{plus}$, is just another way of writing the algebra a.

Iniga: Using $a \prec s$ as a shorthand for $Out^\circ\ (Cons\ (a,s))$, the definition of a is the same as,

$$\begin{aligned}&\underline{one} &&= 1 \prec \underline{one}\\&\underline{plus}\ (Cons\ m\ s, Cons\ n\ t) &&= m+n \prec \underline{plus}\ (s,t)\ ,\end{aligned}$$

that is $\underline{one}$ and $\underline{plus}$ satisfy the original stream equations. Again, the notation makes clear that we have to read the stream operators semantically—$\underline{one}$ and $\underline{plus}$ are the entities defined by the system.

Teacher: We can wrap this up by showing that the law (4.1) *uniquely* determines a:

$$\begin{aligned}&out \cdot a = \mathsf{B}\, a \cdot \lambda\,(\nu\mathsf{B}) \cdot \mathsf{S}\, out\\ \iff\ &\{\ \text{uniqueness of unfold (3.2)}\ \}\\ &a = [\!(\lambda\,(\nu\mathsf{B}) \cdot \mathsf{S}\, out)\!]\end{aligned}$$

So $[\!(\lambda\,(\nu\mathsf{B}) \cdot \mathsf{S}\, out)\!]$ is the unique solution of the stream equations. Furthermore, the fold $(\!|a|\!) : \mu\mathsf{S} \to \nu\mathsf{B}$ takes syntax to behaviour by evaluating a term. Finn, what are your thoughts?

Finn: To start with, I would write the stream equations differently. I find them too Haskell-like, and I prefer what Jan Rutten calls "behavioural differential equations" [17].

$$\begin{aligned}&head\ one = 1\\&tail\quad one = one\\&head\ (plus\ (s,t)) = head\ s + head\ t\\&tail\quad (plus\ (s,t)) = plus\ (tail\ s, tail\ t)\end{aligned}$$

A semantics is given by a B-coalgebra $c : \mu\mathsf{S} \to \mathsf{B}\,(\mu\mathsf{S})$ whose carrier is the initial S-algebra $\langle \mu\mathsf{S}, in\rangle$. The coalgebra c takes a term and produces the first number of the defined stream, and a term to generate the rest of the stream.

Teacher: Just as for Iniga, your coalgebra c has to satisfy the following law:

$$c \cdot in = \mathsf{B}\, in \cdot \lambda\,(\mu\mathsf{S}) \cdot \mathsf{S}\, c\ :\ \mathsf{S}\,(\mu\mathsf{S}) \to \mathsf{B}\,(\mu\mathsf{S})\ . \tag{4.2}$$

The law states that building a term and applying c is the same as giving a semantics to the subterms, $\mathsf{S}\,c$, applying the stream equations $\lambda\,(\mu\mathsf{S})$, and building a term in the tail of a stream, $\mathsf{B}\, in$.

Finn: I will follow Iniga's lead and specialize the law to our example, obtaining a definition of c:

$$\begin{aligned}&c\ (In\ One)\\&\quad = Cons\ (1, In\ One)\\&c\ (In\ (Plus\ (s,t)))\\&\quad = Cons\ (head\ (c\ s) + head\ (c\ t),\\&\qquad\qquad In\ (Plus\ (tail\ (c\ s), tail\ (c\ t))))\ ,\end{aligned}$$

where $head\,(Cons\,(a,s)) = a$ and $tail\,(Cons\,(a,s)) = s$. Given a *stream program*, my c gives the head of the stream and a stream program for the tail of the stream. I can now define the semantic counterparts of *head* and *tail*:

$$\begin{aligned}\underline{head}\ s &= head\ (c\ s)\\ \underline{tail}\quad s &= tail\quad (c\ s)\ .\end{aligned}$$

Teacher: You are building upon the isomorphism $X \to \mathsf{B}\,X \cong (X{\to}\mathbb{N}) \times (X{\to}X)$ here: $\underline{head}$ and $\underline{tail}$ is just another way of writing c.

Finn: Using *one* as a shorthand for *In One* and $plus\,(s,t)$ for $In\,(Plus\,(s,t))$, the definition of c is the same as,

$$\begin{aligned}&\underline{head}\ one = 1\\&\underline{tail}\quad one = one\\&\underline{head}\ (plus\ (s,t)) = \underline{head}\ s + \underline{head}\ t\\&\underline{tail}\quad (plus\ (s,t)) = plus\ (\underline{tail}\ s, \underline{tail}\ t)\ ,\end{aligned}$$

that is, $\underline{head}$ and $\underline{tail}$ satisfy the original stream equations. The notation emphasizes that we have to read the stream selectors semantically—$\underline{head}$ and $\underline{tail}$ are the entities defined by the system.

Teacher: Again, we can show that the law (4.2) determines c:

$$\begin{aligned}&c \cdot in = \mathsf{B}\, in \cdot \lambda\,(\mu\mathsf{S}) \cdot \mathsf{S}\, c\\ \iff\ &\{\ \text{uniqueness of fold (3.1)}\ \}\\ &c = (\!|\mathsf{B}\, in \cdot \lambda\,(\mu\mathsf{S})|\!)\end{aligned}$$

So $(\!|\mathsf{B}\, in \cdot \lambda\,(\mu\mathsf{S})|\!)$ is the *unique* solution of your stream equations. And the unfold $[\!(c)\!] : \mu\mathsf{S} \to \nu\mathsf{B}$ takes syntax to behaviour by unrolling a complete stream.

Iniga and Finn, you should reconcile your two viewpoints. Your semantic functions are of type $\mu\mathsf{S} \to \nu\mathsf{B}$, so is the fold of Iniga's algebra the same as the unfold of Finn's coalgebra: $(\!|a|\!) = [\!(c)\!]$? Did you notice that we made use of the naturality of λ: Iniga used λ at type $\nu\mathsf{B}$, while Finn required the $\mu\mathsf{S}$ instance? For now, we have only discussed a minimalistic example, and we are not immediately able to model stream equations such as the ones that define the Fibonacci stream: there is more to this story.

Epilogue

Now that we have met Iniga and Finn and got a taste for the problem that their teacher posed to them, we will move on to introduce the infrastructure that is needed for the reconciliation.

5. Bialgebras

Let $\mathsf{S}, \mathsf{B} : \mathscr{C} \to \mathscr{C}$ be functors. A bialgebra is a triple $\langle X, a, c\rangle$ consisting of an object $X : \mathscr{C}$, an arrow $a : \mathsf{S}\,X \to X : \mathscr{C}$, and an arrow $c : X \to \mathsf{B}\,X : \mathscr{C}$. It is an S-algebra and a B-coalgebra with a common carrier. Let $\langle X, a, c\rangle$ and $\langle Y, b, d\rangle$ be bialgebras and $h : X \to Y : \mathscr{C}$ an arrow. Then h is a bialgebra homomorphism if it is both an S-algebra homomorphism and a B-coalgebra homomorphism.

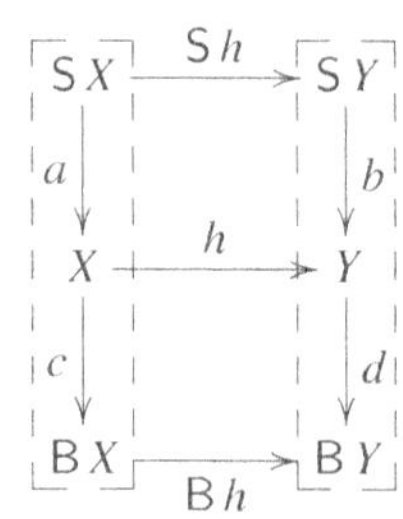

Identity is a bialgebra homomorphism and homomorphisms compose. Consequently, bialgebras and their homomorphisms form a category, called $\mathbf{Bialg}(\mathscr{C})$.

We are concerned with λ-bialgebras, which are bialgebras equipped with a so-called *distributive law* $\lambda : \mathsf{S}{\circ}\mathsf{B} \dot{\to} \mathsf{B}{\circ}\mathsf{S}$. This extra structure imposes a coherence condition on bialgebras.

$$c \cdot a = \mathsf{B}\, a \cdot \lambda\, X \cdot \mathsf{S}\, c \tag{5.1}$$

The condition is also called the *pentagonal law*.

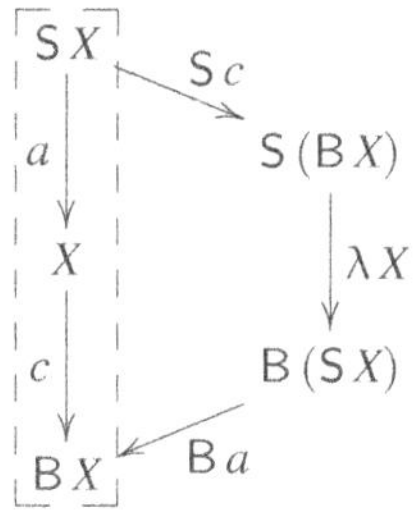

(5.2)

The category of bialgebras that satisfy the pentagonal law (5.2) is denoted λ-$\mathbf{Bialg}(\mathscr{C})$. It is a full subcategory of $\mathbf{Bialg}(\mathscr{C})$.

6. Iniga and Finn with Bialgebraic-tinted Glasses

We will now use λ-bialgebras to explicate Iniga and Finn's conversation with their teacher, and begin to reconcile their solutions.

Let $\mathsf{S}, \mathsf{B} : \mathscr{C} \to \mathscr{C}$ be functors, and $\lambda : \mathsf{S} \circ \mathsf{B} \dot{\to} \mathsf{B} \circ \mathsf{S}$ be a natural transformation. We will read these to imply syntax and behaviour functors, and a distributive law modelling a set of equations. Using λ-bialgebras, we will characterize the semantic function from syntax to behaviour—the arrow from the least fixed-point of S to the greatest fixed-point of B.

The algebra $\langle \mu\mathsf{F}, in \rangle$ is the initial object in F-$\mathbf{Alg}$. We will now show that from this we can form the initial object in λ-$\mathbf{Bialg}$. If the carrier has been fixed as $\mu\mathsf{S}$, then the coalgebra will have type $\mu\mathsf{S} \to \mathsf{B}\,(\mu\mathsf{S})$. This is exactly Finn's coalgebra, and his teacher has derived it: $(\!|\mathsf{B}\, in \cdot \lambda\,(\mu\mathsf{S})|\!)$. As one might guess, the laws the teacher provided came from λ-bialgebras. Let us take a step back to re-examine λ and the pentagonal law.

6.1 Lifting Endofunctors to Algebras

The pentagonal law confers a useful property both on the algebra and the coalgebra component of a λ-bialgebra. Let us illustrate this first for the coalgebra component by redrawing diagram (5.2).

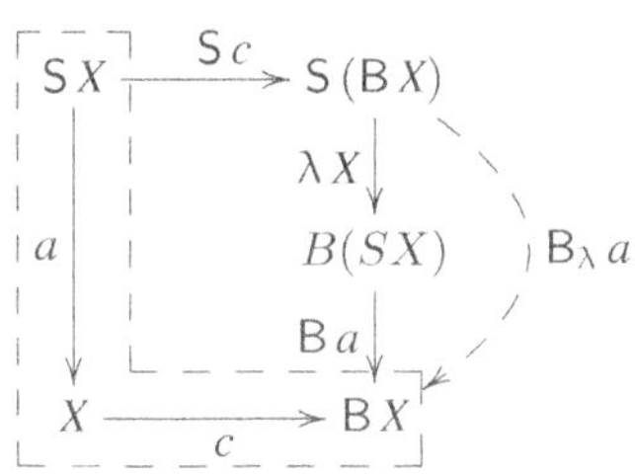

Here we can see that c is not only a B-coalgebra, but also an S-algebra homomorphism from $\langle X, a \rangle$ to $\langle \mathsf{B}\,X, \mathsf{B}\,a \cdot \lambda\,X \rangle$.

We can characterize this situation as lifting the endofunctor $\mathsf{B} : \mathscr{C} \to \mathscr{C}$ to a functor on S-algebras; we will give it the name $\mathsf{B}_\lambda : \mathsf{S}\text{-}\mathbf{Alg}(\mathscr{C}) \to \mathsf{S}\text{-}\mathbf{Alg}(\mathscr{C})$, and define it as,

$$\mathsf{B}_\lambda \langle X, a : \mathsf{S}\,X \to X \rangle = \langle \mathsf{B}\,X, \mathsf{B}\,a \cdot \lambda\,X : \mathsf{S}\,(\mathsf{B}\,X) \to \mathsf{B}\,X \rangle \ , \quad (6.1)$$

$$\mathsf{B}_\lambda\, h = \mathsf{B}\,h \ . \quad (6.2)$$

For notational simplicity, we shall employ lifted functors synecdochically: by $\mathsf{B}_\lambda\, a$ we mean $\mathsf{B}_\lambda \langle X, a \rangle$, a is used *pars pro toto*, and in certain contexts, $\mathsf{B}_\lambda\, a$ is used *totum pro parte* for the arrow of the resultant algebra, $\mathsf{B}\,a \cdot \lambda\,X$. That B_λ is a functor follows from a more general construction given in Appendix B. For reference, we record that it preserves S-algebra homomorphisms.

$$\mathsf{B}\,h : \mathsf{B}_\lambda\, a \to \mathsf{B}_\lambda\, b : \mathsf{S}\text{-}\mathbf{Alg} \iff h : a \to b : \mathsf{S}\text{-}\mathbf{Alg} \quad (6.3)$$

Therefore, we can give c, viewed as an algebra homomorphism, the more succinct type $c : a \to \mathsf{B}_\lambda\, a : \mathsf{S}\text{-}\mathbf{Alg}$.

Dually, a is both an S-algebra and a B-coalgebra homomorphism, with the type $a : \mathsf{S}^\lambda\, c \to c : \mathsf{B}\text{-}\mathbf{Coalg}$, where the lifted functor $\mathsf{S}^\lambda : \mathsf{B}\text{-}\mathbf{Coalg}(\mathscr{C}) \to \mathsf{B}\text{-}\mathbf{Coalg}(\mathscr{C})$ is defined as,

$$\mathsf{S}^\lambda \langle X, c : X \to \mathsf{B}\,X \rangle = \langle \mathsf{S}\,X, \lambda\,X \cdot \mathsf{S}\,c : \mathsf{S}\,X \to \mathsf{B}\,(\mathsf{S}\,X) \rangle \ , \quad (6.4)$$

$$\mathsf{S}^\lambda\, h = \mathsf{S}\,h \ . \quad (6.5)$$

By duality, S^λ is functorial, as well.

6.2 Initial and Final Objects

Our initial λ-bialgebra will be $\langle \mu\mathsf{S}, in, (\!|\mathsf{B}_\lambda\, in|\!) \rangle$, as depicted below.

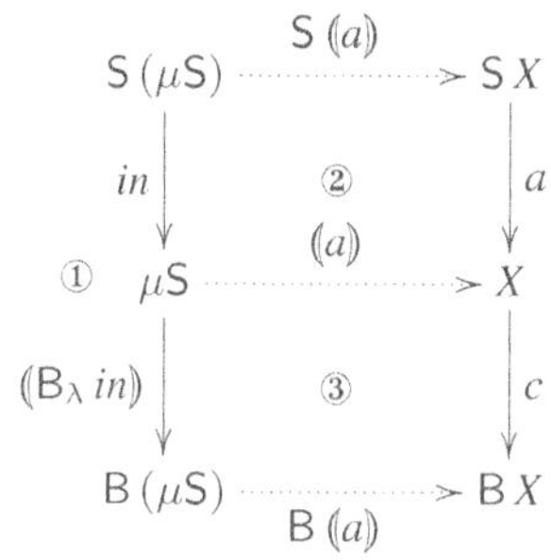

We have three proof obligations. First we must show that the triple $\langle \mu\mathsf{S}, in, (\!|\mathsf{B}_\lambda\, in|\!) \rangle$ is indeed a λ-bialgebra (①)—it has the right types, but it must also satisfy (5.1).

$$\begin{aligned}
& (\!|\mathsf{B}_\lambda\, in|\!) \cdot in \\
= \ & \{ \text{ fold computation (§A) } \} \\
& \mathsf{B}_\lambda\, in \cdot \mathsf{S}\,(\!|\mathsf{B}_\lambda\, in|\!) \\
= \ & \{ \text{ definition of } \mathsf{B}_\lambda \text{ (6.1) } \} \\
& \mathsf{B}\, in \cdot \lambda\,(\mu\mathsf{S}) \cdot \mathsf{S}\,(\!|\mathsf{B}_\lambda\, in|\!)
\end{aligned}$$

The second obligation, that $(\!|a|\!)$ is an S-algebra homomorphism is by construction—the top half of the diagram commutes (②). Moreover, the uniqueness of this arrow comes for free. Finally, we must show that $(\!|a|\!)$ is also a B-coalgebra homomorphism—that the bottom half of the diagram commutes (③).

$$\begin{aligned}
& c \cdot (\!|a|\!) = \mathsf{B}\,(\!|a|\!) \cdot (\!|\mathsf{B}_\lambda\, in|\!) \\
\Longleftrightarrow \ & \{ \text{ fold fusion (§A) with } c : a \to \mathsf{B}_\lambda\, a : \mathsf{S}\text{-}\mathbf{Alg} \ \} \\
& (\!|\mathsf{B}_\lambda\, a|\!) = \mathsf{B}\,(\!|a|\!) \cdot (\!|\mathsf{B}_\lambda\, in|\!) \\
\Longleftarrow \ & \{ \text{ fold fusion (§A) } \} \\
& \mathsf{B}\,(\!|a|\!) : \mathsf{B}_\lambda\, in \to \mathsf{B}_\lambda\, a : \mathsf{S}\text{-}\mathbf{Alg} \\
\Longleftarrow \ & \{ \ \mathsf{B}_\lambda \text{ functor (6.3) } \} \\
& (\!|a|\!) : in \to a : \mathsf{S}\text{-}\mathbf{Alg}
\end{aligned}$$

We can dualize the results above. We have just used Finn's coalgebra to construct the initial λ-bialgebra, so naturally we will use Iniga's algebra to construct the final λ-bialgebra. Indeed, $\langle \nu\mathsf{B}, [\!(\mathsf{S}^\lambda\, out)\!], out \rangle$ is the final λ-bialgebra; and $[\!(c)\!]$ is the unique homomorphism from any λ-bialgebra $\langle X, a, c \rangle$ to the final λ-bialgebra. The duality extends to the satisfaction of the proof obligations.

We have defined the initial and final λ-bialgebras, and we are now in a position to state the homomorphism between them—the semantic function from syntax to behaviour $\mu\mathsf{S} \to \nu\mathsf{B}$.

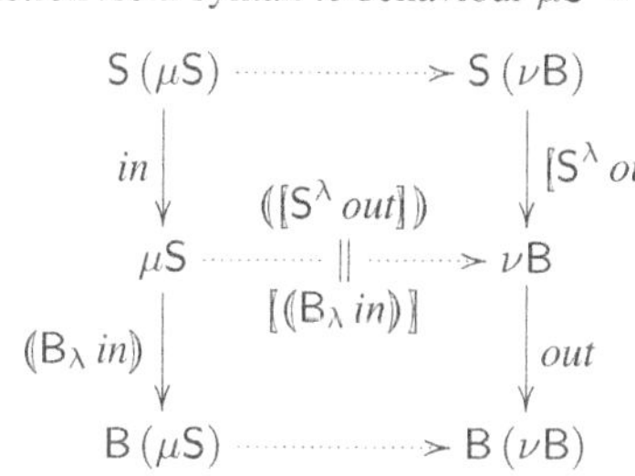

The semantic arrow is unique, and we can give two justifications for it being so: namely that it is the unique homomorphism both from the initial λ-bialgebra and to the final λ-bialgebra. For the same two reasons, we can give two definitions of this arrow, and by uniqueness they are equal. And just like that, we have the basic resolution of Iniga and Finn's seemingly opposing points of view.

In a manner of speaking, Iniga and Finn's personalities would appear to be entwined. Iniga thought in terms of initial algebras and folds, but ended up constructing the final λ-bialgebra, and vice versa for Finn. This is not a coincidence as the category of λ-bialgebras is isomorphic to a category of algebras over coalgebras.

$$
\begin{aligned}
& \langle X, a, c\rangle : \lambda\text{-}\mathbf{Bialg}(\mathscr{C}) \\
\iff\ & \{ \text{definition of } \lambda\text{-bialgebra} \} \\
& c \cdot a = \mathsf{B}\, a \cdot \lambda X \cdot \mathsf{S}\, c \\
\iff\ & \{ \text{definition of } \mathsf{S}^{\lambda}\ (6.4) \} \\
& c \cdot a = \mathsf{B}\, a \cdot \mathsf{S}^{\lambda}\, c \\
\iff\ & \{ \text{definition of B-coalgebra homomorphism} \} \\
& a : \mathsf{S}^{\lambda}\, \langle X, c\rangle \to \langle X, c\rangle : \mathsf{B}\text{-}\mathbf{Coalg}(\mathscr{C}) \\
\iff\ & \{ \text{definition of an } \mathsf{S}^{\lambda}\text{-algebra} \} \\
& \langle\langle X, c\rangle, a\rangle : \mathsf{S}^{\lambda}\text{-}\mathbf{Alg}(\mathsf{B}\text{-}\mathbf{Coalg}(\mathscr{C}))
\end{aligned}
$$

The proof shows that the objects are in one-to-one correspondence. A similar calculation establishes a bijection between arrows.

$$
\begin{aligned}
& h : \langle X_1, a_1, c_1\rangle \to \langle X_2, a_2, c_2\rangle \\
\iff\ & \{ \text{definition of } \lambda\text{-bialgebra homomorphism} \} \\
& h \cdot a_1 = a_2 \cdot \mathsf{S}\, h \ \wedge\ \mathsf{B}\, h \cdot c_1 = c_2 \cdot h \\
\iff\ & \{ \text{definition of B-coalgebra homomorphism} \} \\
& h \cdot a_1 = a_2 \cdot \mathsf{S}\, h \ \wedge\ h : \langle X_1, c_1\rangle \to \langle X_2, c_2\rangle : \mathsf{B}\text{-}\mathbf{Coalg}(\mathscr{C}) \\
\iff\ & \{ \text{definition of } \mathsf{S}^{\lambda}\text{-algebra homomorphism} \} \\
& h : \langle\langle X_1, c_1\rangle, a_1\rangle \to \langle\langle X_2, c_2\rangle, a_2\rangle : \mathsf{S}^{\lambda}\text{-}\mathbf{Alg}(\mathsf{B}\text{-}\mathbf{Coalg}(\mathscr{C}))
\end{aligned}
$$

As a summary of our construction above, for the categorically enlightened, the final λ-bialgebra is determined by the final S^{λ}-algebra. Recall that the *final* S-algebra is $\langle 1, !_{\mathsf{S}\,1}\rangle$. Consequently, the final S^{λ}-algebra is $\langle 1, !_{\mathsf{S}^{\lambda}\,1}\rangle = \langle\langle \nu\mathsf{B}, \mathit{out}\rangle, [\![\mathsf{S}^{\lambda}\ \mathit{out}]\!]\rangle$ as $\langle \nu\mathsf{B}, \mathit{out}\rangle$ is the final object in $\mathsf{B}\text{-}\mathbf{Coalg}(\mathscr{C})$.

Dually, we can view a bialgebra as a coalgebra over algebras.

$$
\lambda\text{-}\mathbf{Bialg}(\mathscr{C}) \cong \begin{cases} \mathsf{S}^{\lambda}\text{-}\mathbf{Alg}(\mathsf{B}\text{-}\mathbf{Coalg}(\mathscr{C})) \\ \mathsf{B}_{\lambda}\text{-}\mathbf{Coalg}(\mathsf{S}\text{-}\mathbf{Alg}(\mathscr{C})) \end{cases} \qquad (6.6)
$$

The double isomorphism says that there are actually two ways to determine initial and final objects in $\lambda\text{-}\mathbf{Bialg}(\mathscr{C})$. The reader is encouraged to work out the details.

7. A Step along the Categorical Brick Road...

Distributive laws of type $\mathsf{S}\circ\mathsf{B} \dot{\to} \mathsf{B}\circ\mathsf{S}$ are not sufficiently expressive to model the recursion equations for *bird* and *fib* as their right-hand sides consist of more than one layer of syntax. In general, we need terms, elements of the free monad for the syntax functor. However, rather than making a beeline for free monads, we will visit *pointed functors* as a stepping stone. This is an adventure with category theory after all, and the fun is in the journey.

Example 7.1. Suspend your disbelief and suppose that you need the identity operator on streams, defined by the equation,

$$
\mathit{id}\ (\mathit{Cons}\ m\ s) = m \prec s\ .
$$

A system containing this equation cannot be turned into a distributive law $\lambda : \mathsf{S}\circ\mathsf{B} \dot{\to} \mathsf{B}\circ\mathsf{S}$ as the stream s is not an element of the syntax functor S. To solve this, we can allow for variables or constructors of S.

$$
\begin{aligned}
&\mathbf{data}\ \mathsf{P}\ x = \mathit{Var}\ x \mid \mathit{Con}\ (\mathsf{S}\ x) \\
&\mathbf{data}\ \mathsf{S}\ x = \mathit{Id}\ x \mid \mathit{One} \mid \ldots
\end{aligned}
$$

A system of recursion equations is now captured by a natural transformation ρ of type $\mathsf{S}\circ\mathsf{B} \dot{\to} \mathsf{B}\circ\mathsf{P}$.

$$
\begin{aligned}
&\rho\ (\mathit{Id}\ (\mathit{Cons}\ (m, s))) = \mathit{Cons}\ (m, \mathit{Var}\ s) \\
&\rho\ (\mathit{One}) \qquad\qquad\quad\ = \mathit{Cons}\ (1, \mathit{Con}\ \mathit{One}) \quad \ldots
\end{aligned}
$$

Note that we have only replaced S on the right-hand side, where there is a need. We shall later restore symmetry and show how to turn ρ into a distributive law (Section 7.3). Furthermore, this is a very limited introduction of variables: one can either have a variable, or a constructor, but no variables as arguments. □

The Haskell type P is the so-called free pointed functor of S [13]. We will discuss pointed functors in general and then return to the free construction in Section 7.1.

Definition 7.2. We say that an endofunctor $\mathsf{T} : \mathscr{C} \to \mathscr{C}$ is *pointed* if it is equipped with a natural transformation $\eta : \mathsf{Id} \dot{\to} \mathsf{T}$.

We are going to build on the picture we laid out in the previous section by replacing the plain endofunctor with a pointed functor. The extra structure that we have introduced with η has two implications: first with regards to the distributive law λ and second with regards to constructing algebras of pointed functors.

Condition 7.3. A distributive law $\lambda : \mathsf{T}\circ\mathsf{B} \dot{\to} \mathsf{B}\circ\mathsf{T}$ for a pointed functor T has an additional coherence condition to satisfy:

$$
\lambda \cdot \eta\circ\mathsf{B} = \mathsf{B}\circ\eta\ . \qquad (7.1)
$$

Condition 7.4. If we construct an algebra $\langle X, a : \mathsf{T}\, X \to X\rangle$ of a pointed functor T, then it must respect η:

$$
a \cdot \eta X = \mathit{id}_X\ . \qquad (7.2)
$$

For full specificity we will say that $(\mathsf{T}, \eta)\text{-}\mathbf{Alg}(\mathscr{C})$ is the category of T-algebras that respect η. This is a full subcategory of $\mathsf{T}\text{-}\mathbf{Alg}(\mathscr{C})$. Henceforth, we will be working with λ-bialgebras based on (T, η)-algebras and B-coalgebras.

The double isomorphism (6.6) succinctly tells the story of initial and final objects in λ-**Bialg**. In a sense, Conditions 7.3 and 7.4 ensure that we can establish an analogous isomorphism for pointed functors. The following two properties prepare the ground.

Property 7.5. Let $c : X \to \mathsf{B}\, X$ be a B-coalgebra, then

$$
\eta X : c \to \mathsf{T}^{\lambda}\, c : \mathsf{B}\text{-}\mathbf{Coalg}(\mathscr{C})\ , \qquad (7.3)
$$

is the lifting of η to a B-coalgebra homomorphism.

Proof.

$$
\begin{aligned}
& \mathsf{T}^{\lambda}\, c \cdot \eta X \\
=\ & \{ \text{definition of } \mathsf{T}^{\lambda}\ (6.4) \} \\
& \lambda X \cdot \mathsf{T}\, c \cdot \eta X \\
=\ & \{ \eta : \mathsf{Id} \dot{\to} \mathsf{T} \text{ is natural} \} \\
& \lambda X \cdot \eta(\mathsf{B}\, X) \cdot c \\
=\ & \{ \text{coherence of } \lambda \text{ with } \eta\ (7.1) \} \\
& \mathsf{B}\, (\eta X) \cdot c \quad \square
\end{aligned}
$$

In other words, the lifted functor T^{λ} is pointed as well and we can form $(\mathsf{T}^{\lambda}, \eta)\text{-}\mathbf{Alg}(\mathsf{B}\text{-}\mathbf{Coalg}(\mathscr{C}))$.

Property 7.6. The functor B_{λ} preserves respect for η.

$$
\mathsf{B}_{\lambda}\, a \cdot \eta(\mathsf{B}\, X) = \mathit{id}_{\mathsf{B}\, X} \iff a \cdot \eta X = \mathit{id}_X \qquad (7.4)
$$

Proof.

$$\begin{aligned} & \mathsf{B}_\lambda\, a \cdot \eta(\mathsf{B}\, X) \\ = & \quad \{ \text{ definition of } \mathsf{B}_\lambda \text{ (6.1) } \} \\ & \mathsf{B}\, a \cdot \lambda X \cdot \eta(\mathsf{B}\, X) \\ = & \quad \{ \text{ coherence of } \lambda \text{ with } \eta \text{ (7.1) } \} \\ & \mathsf{B}\, a \cdot \mathsf{B}\, (\eta X) \\ = & \quad \{ \mathsf{B} \text{ functor and assumption } a \cdot \eta X = id_X \} \\ & id_{\mathsf{B}\, X} \quad \square \end{aligned}$$

In other words, B_λ is an endofunctor on $(\mathsf{T},\eta)\text{-}\mathbf{Alg}(\mathscr{C})$ and we can form $\mathsf{B}_\lambda\text{-}\mathbf{Coalg}((\mathsf{T},\eta)\text{-}\mathbf{Alg}(\mathscr{C}))$.

Summary

Properties 7.5 and 7.6 imply that the double isomorphism (6.6) carries over to the new setting.

$$\lambda\text{-}\mathbf{Bialg}(\mathscr{C}) \cong \begin{cases} (\mathsf{T}^\lambda,\eta)\text{-}\mathbf{Alg}(\mathsf{B}\text{-}\mathbf{Coalg}(\mathscr{C})) \\ \mathsf{B}_\lambda\text{-}\mathbf{Coalg}((\mathsf{T},\eta)\text{-}\mathbf{Alg}(\mathscr{C})) \end{cases} \tag{7.5}$$

7.1 Free Pointed Functor

Let $\mathsf{S} : \mathscr{C} \to \mathscr{C}$ be an endofunctor. There is a canonical pointed functor, with pleasant properties, that we can construct from S. This is the *free* pointed functor of S [13], the categorical version of the Haskell type P we saw in Example 7.1,

$$\mathsf{P}\, X = X + \mathsf{S}\, X \ . \tag{7.6}$$

The natural transformation $\eta : \mathsf{Id} \dot{\to} \mathsf{P}$ that equips the free pointed functor is simply $\eta = inl$. Our λ-bialgebras now have P-algebras, but what about all the S-algebras that we have used previously? All is not lost, in fact far from it.

Theorem 7.1. *The category of algebras for the free pointed functor is isomorphic to the category of* S*-algebras:*

$$(\mathsf{P},\eta)\text{-}\mathbf{Alg}(\mathscr{C}) \cong \mathsf{S}\text{-}\mathbf{Alg}(\mathscr{C}) \ .$$

The following definitions are the witnesses to this isomorphism.

$$\lceil \langle X, a : \mathsf{S}\, X \to X \rangle \rceil = \langle X, id_X \triangledown a : \mathsf{P}\, X \to X \rangle \qquad \lceil h \rceil = h \tag{7.7}$$

$$\lfloor \langle X, b : \mathsf{P}\, X \to X \rangle \rfloor = \langle X, b \cdot inr : \mathsf{S}\, X \to X \rangle \qquad \lfloor h \rfloor = h \tag{7.8}$$

In particular, $\lceil - \rceil$ *preserves and reflects homomorphisms.*

$$h : \lceil a \rceil \to \lceil b \rceil : (\mathsf{P},\eta)\text{-}\mathbf{Alg}(\mathscr{C}) \iff h : a \to b : \mathsf{S}\text{-}\mathbf{Alg}(\mathscr{C}) \tag{7.9}$$

Proof. (i) Given an S-algebra a, we can cast it up to a P-algebra $\lceil a \rceil$. Likewise, we can cast a P-algebra b down to an S-algebra $\lfloor b \rfloor$. The following proves both directions of the isomorphism.

$$\begin{aligned} & \lfloor \lceil a \rceil \rfloor && \lceil \lfloor b \rfloor \rceil \\ = & \quad \{ \text{ definition of } \lceil - \rceil \} & = & \quad \{ \text{ defs. of } \lfloor - \rfloor \text{ and } \lceil - \rceil \} \\ & \lfloor id_X \triangledown a \rfloor && id_X \triangledown b \cdot inr \\ = & \quad \{ \text{ definition of } \lfloor - \rfloor \} & = & \quad \{ b \text{ respects } \eta \text{ (7.2) } \} \\ & (id_X \triangledown a) \cdot inr && b \cdot inl \triangledown b \cdot inr \\ = & \quad \{ \text{ join comp. (§A) } \} & = & \quad \{ \text{ join fusion and refl. (§A) } \} \\ & a && b \end{aligned}$$

(ii) $\lfloor - \rfloor$ is functorial as $inr : \mathsf{S} \dot{\to} \mathsf{P}$ and $\lfloor - \rfloor = inr\text{-}\mathbf{Alg}$ (cf. §3).

(iii) $\lceil - \rceil$ maps S-homomorphisms to P-homomorphisms. For the proof we refer to the full paper [11].

(iv) Finally, $\lceil \langle X, a \rangle \rceil$ has to be an algebra for the pointed functor. That $\lceil a \rceil$ respects η (7.2), unfolds to $(id \triangledown a) \cdot inl = id$, and this is just an instance of the join computation law (§A). $\square$

7.2 Initial and Final Objects

The double isomorphism (7.5) immediately suggests how to define initial and final objects in the new setting. Nonetheless, we will slow down a bit and go through the construction step by step.

In Section 6 we explored λ-bialgebras over S and B, the functors representing syntax and behaviour, respectively. Despite the fact that we are now using the free pointed functor of S, the carrier of the initial λ-bialgebra will remain the same, as we are not changing our objects of syntax. Instead, we are generalizing the evaluation of our syntax. The initial λ-bialgebra will be $\langle \mu\mathsf{S}, a : \mathsf{P}\,(\mu\mathsf{S}) \to \mu\mathsf{S}, c : \mu\mathsf{S} \to \mathsf{B}\,(\mu\mathsf{S}) \rangle$, for some a and c that we will now determine.

Previously the algebra component of the initial λ-bialgebra was simply $in : \mathsf{S}\,(\mu\mathsf{S}) \to \mu\mathsf{S}$. This can no longer be the case; we need an algebra $a : \mathsf{P}\,(\mu\mathsf{S}) \to \mu\mathsf{S}$. However, now that we can freely cast between S and (P,η)-algebras, we can use $\lceil in \rceil : \mathsf{P}\,(\mu\mathsf{S}) \to \mu\mathsf{S}$.

The previous coalgebra component was $(\!|\mathsf{B}_\lambda\, in|\!)$, and this also no longer has the right type, as our λ has changed. Now B_λ lifts the functor B to a functor on (P,η)-algebras, not S-algebras; $(\!|-|\!)$ expects an S-algebra, and in is an S-algebra. We can satisfy these expectations with selective usage of casting: we can cast in up to a (P,η)-algebra so that we can apply B_λ, and furthermore, we can cast the image of $\mathsf{B}_\lambda \lceil in \rceil$ down so that it is an S-algebra that we can fold. The claim is that $\langle \mu\mathsf{S}, \lceil in \rceil, (\!|\lfloor \mathsf{B}_\lambda \lceil in \rceil \rfloor|\!) \rangle$ is the initial λ-bialgebra and $(\!|\lfloor a \rfloor|\!)$ is the unique homomorphism to any λ-bialgebra $\langle X, a, c \rangle$. There are the three usual proof obligations we must satisfy. For reasons that will become clear, we will start by showing that $(\!|\lfloor a \rfloor|\!)$ is (P,η)-algebra homomorphism.

$$(\!|\lfloor a \rfloor|\!) : \lceil in \rceil \to a : (\mathsf{P},\eta)\text{-}\mathbf{Alg} \tag{7.10}$$

This is a direct consequence of Theorem 7.1.

$$\begin{aligned} & (\!|\lfloor a \rfloor|\!) : \lceil in \rceil \to a : (\mathsf{P},\eta)\text{-}\mathbf{Alg} \\ \iff & \quad \{ \text{ isomorphism } (\mathsf{P},\eta)\text{-}\mathbf{Alg} \cong \mathsf{S}\text{-}\mathbf{Alg} \text{ (7.9) } \} \\ & (\!|\lfloor a \rfloor|\!) : in \to \lfloor a \rfloor : \mathsf{S}\text{-}\mathbf{Alg} \end{aligned}$$

Next we will show that $\langle \mu\mathsf{S}, \lceil in \rceil, (\!|\lfloor \mathsf{B}_\lambda \lceil in \rceil \rfloor|\!) \rangle$ is indeed a λ-bialgebra, in that it satisfies the pentagonal law (5.1).

$$\begin{aligned} & (\!|\lfloor \mathsf{B}_\lambda \lceil in \rceil \rfloor|\!) \cdot \lceil in \rceil \\ = & \quad \{ (\!|\lfloor \mathsf{B}_\lambda \lceil in \rceil \rfloor|\!) : \lceil in \rceil \to \mathsf{B}_\lambda \lceil in \rceil : (\mathsf{P},\eta)\text{-}\mathbf{Alg} \text{ (7.10) } \} \\ & \mathsf{B}_\lambda \lceil in \rceil \cdot \mathsf{P}\,(\!|\lfloor \mathsf{B}_\lambda \lceil in \rceil \rfloor|\!) \\ = & \quad \{ \text{ definition of } \mathsf{B}_\lambda \text{ (6.1) } \} \\ & \mathsf{B} \lceil in \rceil \cdot \lambda\,(\mu\mathsf{S}) \cdot \mathsf{P}\,(\!|\lfloor \mathsf{B}_\lambda \lceil in \rceil \rfloor|\!) \end{aligned}$$

Furthermore, (7.2) is satisfied since $\lceil - \rceil$ creates such an algebra.

Finally, we will show that $(\!|\lfloor a \rfloor|\!)$ is a B-coalgebra homomorphism. We know from the pentagonal law that c is a (P,η)-algebra homomorphism, $c : a \to \mathsf{B}_\lambda\, a : (\mathsf{P},\eta)\text{-}\mathbf{Alg}$. By (7.9) c is also an S-algebra homomorphism, $c : \lfloor a \rfloor \to \lfloor \mathsf{B}_\lambda\, a \rfloor : \mathsf{S}\text{-}\mathbf{Alg}$, and as a direct consequence of fold fusion (§A), $c \cdot (\!|\lfloor a \rfloor|\!) = (\!|\lfloor \mathsf{B}_\lambda\, a \rfloor|\!)$.

$$\begin{aligned} & c \cdot (\!|\lfloor a \rfloor|\!) = \mathsf{B}\,(\!|\lfloor a \rfloor|\!) \cdot (\!|\lfloor \mathsf{B}_\lambda \lceil in \rceil \rfloor|\!) \\ \iff & \quad \{ \text{ fold fusion (§A) with } c : \lfloor a \rfloor \to \lfloor \mathsf{B}_\lambda\, a \rfloor : \mathsf{S}\text{-}\mathbf{Alg} \} \\ & (\!|\lfloor \mathsf{B}_\lambda\, a \rfloor|\!) = \mathsf{B}\,(\!|\lfloor a \rfloor|\!) \cdot (\!|\lfloor \mathsf{B}_\lambda \lceil in \rceil \rfloor|\!) \\ \Longleftarrow & \quad \{ \text{ fold fusion (§A) } \} \\ & \mathsf{B}\,(\!|\lfloor a \rfloor|\!) : \lfloor \mathsf{B}_\lambda \lceil in \rceil \rfloor \to \lfloor \mathsf{B}_\lambda\, a \rfloor : \mathsf{S}\text{-}\mathbf{Alg} \\ \iff & \quad \{ \text{ isomorphism } (\mathsf{P},\eta)\text{-}\mathbf{Alg} \cong \mathsf{S}\text{-}\mathbf{Alg} \text{ (7.9) } \} \\ & \mathsf{B}\,(\!|\lfloor a \rfloor|\!) : \mathsf{B}_\lambda \lceil in \rceil \to \mathsf{B}_\lambda\, a : (\mathsf{P},\eta)\text{-}\mathbf{Alg} \\ \Longleftarrow & \quad \{ \mathsf{B}_\lambda \text{ functor (6.3) } \} \\ & (\!|\lfloor a \rfloor|\!) : \lceil in \rceil \to a : (\mathsf{P},\eta)\text{-}\mathbf{Alg} \end{aligned}$$

We have already shown that the last statement holds (7.10).

As before, the final λ-bialgebra is $\langle \nu\mathsf{B}, [\mathsf{P}^{\lambda}\, out], out\rangle$. The unique λ-bialgebra homomorphism to the final λ-bialgebra from any λ-bialgebra $\langle X, a, c\rangle$ is $[c]$. There is one final proof obligation: we have to show that $[\mathsf{P}^{\lambda}\, out]$ respects η (7.2).

$$
\begin{aligned}
& [\mathsf{P}^{\lambda}\, out] \cdot \eta(\nu\mathsf{B}) = id_{\nu\mathsf{B}} \\
\iff\; & \{ \text{ unfold reflection (§A) } \} \\
& [\mathsf{P}^{\lambda}\, out] \cdot \eta(\nu\mathsf{B}) = [out] \\
\Longleftarrow\; & \{ \text{ unfold fusion (§A) } \} \\
& \eta(\nu\mathsf{B}) : out \to \mathsf{P}^{\lambda}\, out
\end{aligned}
$$

The last statement holds as P^{λ} is pointed (7.3).

Putting things together, we can give a new statement of the semantic function $\mu\mathsf{S} \to \nu\mathsf{B}$.

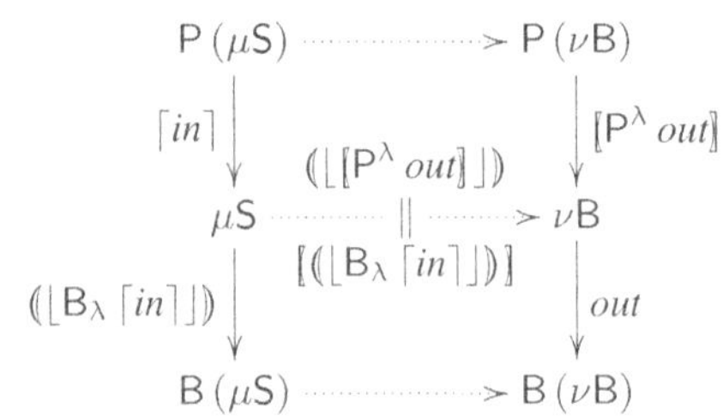

We are in a more expressive setting, yet thanks to Theorem 7.1, we can hold on to our resolution of Iniga and Finn's viewpoints.

7.3 Constructing a Distributive Law

In Section 6 we modelled a stream program by a distributive law of type $\mathsf{S}\circ\mathsf{B} \dot{\to} \mathsf{B}\circ\mathsf{S}$. With the introduction of the free pointed functor, stream equations have become slightly more expressive. A program, such as in Example 7.1, now gives rise to a natural transformation $\rho : \mathsf{S}\circ\mathsf{B} \dot{\to} \mathsf{B}\circ\mathsf{P}$. The pointed functor appears only on the right. On the left we keep S, as a stream equation defines a constructor of S, not a variable. From $\rho : \mathsf{S}\circ\mathsf{B} \dot{\to} \mathsf{B}\circ\mathsf{P}$ we seek to *construct* a distributive law $\lambda : \mathsf{P}\circ\mathsf{B} \dot{\to} \mathsf{B}\circ\mathsf{P}$ such that

$$
c \cdot \lceil a \rceil = \mathsf{B}\,\lceil a \rceil \cdot \lambda X \cdot \mathsf{P}\, c \iff c \cdot a = \mathsf{B}\,\lceil a \rceil \cdot \rho X \cdot \mathsf{S}\, c \;. \quad (7.11)
$$

Since P is a coproduct, λ has to be defined by a case analysis. Though obvious, we will calculate λ from the specification above as this will serve nicely as a blueprint for later sections.

$$
\begin{aligned}
& c \cdot a = \mathsf{B}\,\lceil a \rceil \cdot \rho X \cdot \mathsf{S}\, c \\
\iff\; & \{ \text{ equality of joins } \} \\
& c \mathbin{\triangledown} c \cdot a = c \mathbin{\triangledown} \mathsf{B}\,\lceil a \rceil \cdot \rho X \cdot \mathsf{S}\, c \\
\iff\; & \{ \lceil a \rceil \text{ respects } \eta \text{ (7.2) and B functor } \} \\
& c \mathbin{\triangledown} c \cdot a = \mathsf{B}\,\lceil a \rceil \cdot \mathsf{B}\,(\eta X) \cdot c \mathbin{\triangledown} \mathsf{B}\,\lceil a \rceil \cdot \rho X \cdot \mathsf{S}\, c \\
\iff\; & \{ \text{ join fusion and functor fusion (§A) } \} \\
& c \cdot (id \mathbin{\triangledown} a) = \mathsf{B}\,\lceil a \rceil \cdot (\mathsf{B}\,(\eta X) \mathbin{\triangledown} \rho X) \cdot (c + \mathsf{S}\, c) \\
\iff\; & \{ \text{ definitions of } \lceil - \rceil \text{ (7.7) and P (7.6) } \} \\
& c \cdot \lceil a \rceil = \mathsf{B}\,\lceil a \rceil \cdot (\mathsf{B}\,(\eta X) \mathbin{\triangledown} \rho X) \cdot \mathsf{P}\, c
\end{aligned}
$$

The specification (7.11) can be satisfied if we set $\lambda = \mathsf{B}\circ\eta \mathbin{\triangledown} \rho$, which is easily seen to satisfy the coherence condition (7.1).

8. ... to Monad City

With pointed functors we made a limited introduction of variables. The next step is to allow constructors to be nested. In this section we are going to build on our picture of λ-bialgebras again, augmenting pointed functors to monads.

Example 8.1. Let us look at an example comparable to those of Section 2. Here is a stream equation for the natural numbers.

$$
nat = 0 \prec nat + 1
$$

We need more than a single syntax constructor to represent $nat + 1$. To solve this, we build terms with variables and constructors of S.

```
data M x = Var x | Com (S (M x))
data S x = One | Plus (x, x) | Nat
```

A system of recursion equations is now captured by a natural transformation ρ of type $\mathsf{S}\circ\mathsf{B} \dot{\to} \mathsf{B}\circ\mathsf{M}$.

$$
\begin{aligned}
& \rho\ One \\
& \quad = Cons\ (1, Com\ One) \\
& \rho\ (Plus\ (Cons\ (m, s), Cons\ (n, t))) \\
& \quad = Cons\ (m + n, Com\ (Plus\ (Var\ s, Var\ t))) \\
& \rho\ Nat \\
& \quad = Cons\ (0, Com\ (Plus\ (Com\ Nat, Com\ One)))
\end{aligned}
$$

Note that we only have terms on the right-hand side. Arguments of *Cons* on the left can be embedded into variables on the right, and as shown in the case of *Nat*, we can use more than one level of syntax. Again, we shall restore symmetry later, showing how to derive a distributive law from ρ (Section 8.3). □

The Haskell type M is the so-called free monad of S. We will discuss monads in general and then return to the free construction in Section 8.1.

Definition 8.2. We say that $\mathsf{T} : \mathscr{C} \to \mathscr{C}$ is a *monad* if there are natural transformations $\eta : \mathsf{Id} \dot{\to} \mathsf{T}$ and $\mu : \mathsf{T}\circ\mathsf{T} \dot{\to} \mathsf{T}$ such that

$$
\mu \cdot \eta\circ\mathsf{T} = id_{\mathsf{T}} \;, \quad (8.1a)
$$

$$
\mu \cdot \mathsf{T}\circ\eta = id_{\mathsf{T}} \;, \quad (8.1b)
$$

$$
\mu \cdot \mu\circ\mathsf{T} = \mu \cdot \mathsf{T}\circ\mu \;. \quad (8.1c)
$$

A monad extends a pointed functor with a second natural transformation $\mu : \mathsf{T}\circ\mathsf{T} \dot{\to} \mathsf{T}$. In the previous section we saw that η must be respected when constructing algebras and also by the distributive law of the λ-bialgebra; these same conditions extend to μ.

Condition 8.3. The following are the necessary coherence conditions for a distributive law $\lambda : \mathsf{T}\circ\mathsf{B} \dot{\to} \mathsf{B}\circ\mathsf{T}$ over a monad T:

$$
\lambda \cdot \eta\circ\mathsf{B} = \mathsf{B}\circ\eta \;, \quad (8.2a)
$$

$$
\lambda \cdot \mu\circ\mathsf{B} = \mathsf{B}\circ\mu \cdot \lambda\circ\mathsf{T} \cdot \mathsf{T}\circ\lambda \;. \quad (8.2b)
$$

Condition 8.4. If we construct an algebra $\langle X, a : \mathsf{T}\,X \to X\rangle$ of a monad T, then it must respect both η and μ.

$$
a \cdot \eta X = id_X \;, \quad (8.3a)
$$

$$
a \cdot \mu X = a \cdot \mathsf{T}\, a \;. \quad (8.3b)
$$

In the same manner as for pointed functors, we will say that (T, η, μ)-$\mathbf{Alg}(\mathscr{C})$ is the category of T-algebras that respect η and μ, a full subcategory of T-$\mathbf{Alg}(\mathscr{C})$. Henceforth, we will be working with λ-bialgebras based on (T, η, μ)-algebras and B-coalgebras.

As in Section 7, the additional conditions ensure that the double isomorphism (6.6) is maintained. We have shown previously that η can be lifted to a B-coalgebra homomorphism (7.3). There is an analogous property for μ:

Property 8.5. Let $c : X \to \mathsf{B}\,X$ be a B-coalgebra, then

$$
\mu X : \mathsf{T}^{\lambda}\,(\mathsf{T}^{\lambda}\, c) \to \mathsf{S}^{\lambda}\, c : \mathsf{B}\text{-}\mathbf{Coalg}(\mathscr{C}) \;, \quad (8.4)
$$

is the lifting of μ to a B-coalgebra homomorphism.

Proof.

$$\begin{aligned}
&\mathsf{T}^{\lambda}\, c \cdot \mu X \\
=\;& \{\ \text{definition of } \mathsf{T}^{\lambda}\ (6.4)\ \} \\
&\lambda X \cdot \mathsf{T}\, c \cdot \mu X \\
=\;& \{\ \mu : \mathsf{T}{\circ}\mathsf{T} \dot{\to} \mathsf{T} \text{ is natural}\ \} \\
&\lambda X \cdot \mu(\mathsf{B}\, X) \cdot \mathsf{T}\,(\mathsf{T}\, c) \\
=\;& \{\ \text{coherence of } \lambda \text{ with } \mu\ (8.2b)\ \} \\
&\mathsf{B}\,(\mu X) \cdot \lambda\,(\mathsf{T}\, X) \cdot \mathsf{T}\,(\lambda X) \cdot \mathsf{T}\,(\mathsf{T}\, c) \\
=\;& \{\ \mathsf{T} \text{ functor and definition of } \mathsf{T}^{\lambda}\ (6.4)\ \} \\
&\mathsf{B}\,(\mu X) \cdot \mathsf{T}^{\lambda}\,(\mathsf{T}^{\lambda}\, c) \quad \square
\end{aligned}$$

In other words, the lifted functor T^{λ} is a monad as well and we can form $(\mathsf{T}^{\lambda}, \eta, \mu)\text{-}\mathbf{Alg}(\mathsf{B}\text{-}\mathbf{Coalg}(\mathscr{C}))$.

We also have shown that B_{λ} preserves respect for η (7.4). Again, there is an analogous property for μ:

Property 8.6. The lifted functor B_{λ} preserves respect for μ.

$$\mathsf{B}_{\lambda}\, a \cdot \mu(\mathsf{B}\, X) = \mathsf{B}_{\lambda}\, a \cdot \mathsf{T}\,(\mathsf{B}_{\lambda}\, a) \quad \Longleftarrow \quad a \cdot \mu X = a \cdot \mathsf{T}\, a \qquad (8.5)$$

Proof.

$$\begin{aligned}
&\mathsf{B}_{\lambda}\, a \cdot \mu(\mathsf{B}\, X) \\
=\;& \{\ \text{definition of } \mathsf{B}_{\lambda}\ (6.1)\ \} \\
&\mathsf{B}\, a \cdot \lambda X \cdot \mu(\mathsf{B}\, X) \\
=\;& \{\ \text{coherence of } \lambda \text{ with } \mu\ (8.2b)\ \} \\
&\mathsf{B}\, a \cdot \mathsf{B}\,(\mu X) \cdot \lambda\,(\mathsf{T}\, X) \cdot \mathsf{T}\,(\lambda X) \\
=\;& \{\ \mathsf{B} \text{ functor and assumption } a \cdot \mu X = a \cdot \mathsf{T}\, a\ \} \\
&\mathsf{B}\, a \cdot \mathsf{B}\,(\mathsf{T}\, a) \cdot \lambda\,(\mathsf{T}\, X) \cdot \mathsf{T}\,(\lambda X) \\
=\;& \{\ \lambda : \mathsf{T}{\circ}\mathsf{B} \dot{\to} \mathsf{B}{\circ}\mathsf{T} \text{ is natural}\ \} \\
&\mathsf{B}\, a \cdot \lambda X \cdot \mathsf{T}\,(\mathsf{B}\, a) \cdot \mathsf{T}\,(\lambda X) \\
=\;& \{\ \mathsf{T} \text{ functor and definition of } \mathsf{B}_{\lambda}\ (6.1)\ \} \\
&\mathsf{B}_{\lambda}\, a \cdot \mathsf{T}\,(\mathsf{B}_{\lambda}\, a) \quad \square
\end{aligned}$$

Thus, B_{λ} is an endofunctor on $(\mathsf{T}, \eta, \mu)\text{-}\mathbf{Alg}(\mathscr{C})$ and we can form $\mathsf{B}_{\lambda}\text{-}\mathbf{Coalg}((\mathsf{T}, \eta, \mu)\text{-}\mathbf{Alg}(\mathscr{C}))$.

Summary

As before the category of bialgebras can be seen as a category of algebras over coalgebras or as a category of coalgebras over algebras.

$$\lambda\text{-}\mathbf{Bialg}(\mathscr{C}) \cong \begin{cases} (\mathsf{T}^{\lambda}, \eta, \mu)\text{-}\mathbf{Alg}(\mathsf{B}\text{-}\mathbf{Coalg}(\mathscr{C})) \\ \mathsf{B}_{\lambda}\text{-}\mathbf{Coalg}((\mathsf{T}, \eta, \mu)\text{-}\mathbf{Alg}(\mathscr{C})) \end{cases} \qquad (8.6)$$

8.1 Free Monad

Let $\mathsf{S} : \mathscr{C} \to \mathscr{C}$ be an endofunctor representing our syntax. There is a canonical monad, with pleasant properties, that we can construct from S. To do so we will first define the *free* S-algebra.

The free S-algebra over X is an algebra $\langle \mathsf{M}\, X, com \rangle$ equipped with an arrow $var : X \to \mathsf{M}\, X$. We think of elements of $\mathsf{M}\, X$ as terms built from our syntax functor S and variables drawn from X. There are two ways to construct a term: *var* embeds a variable into a term; and $com : \mathsf{S}\,(\mathsf{M}\, X) \to \mathsf{M}\, X$ constructs a composite term from a level of syntax over subterms.

If we have an algebra $a : \mathsf{S}\, X \to X$, we can evaluate a term with $(\!|a|\!) : \mathsf{M}\, X \to X$ (pronounce "eval"). Given an arrow $g : Y \to X$ to evaluate variables and an S-algebra a to evaluate composites, evaluation of terms is characterized by the uniqueness property,

$$f = (\!|a|\!) \cdot \mathsf{M}\, g \iff f \cdot var = g \;\wedge\; f \cdot com = a \cdot \mathsf{S}\, f\ , \qquad (8.7)$$

for all $f : \mathsf{M}\, Y \to X$. The equivalence states that a compositional evaluation of a term, second conjunct, is uniquely defined by an evaluation of variables, first conjunct. (For the clued-in reader, all of this information comes from the adjunction of the free and forgetful functors between $\mathsf{S}\text{-}\mathbf{Alg}(\mathscr{C})$ and $\mathscr{C}$.)

The initial algebra emerges as a special case: $\mu\mathsf{S} \cong \mathsf{M}\, 0$. It represents the closed terms. Modulo this isomorphism, we have $in = com_0$ and $(\!|a|\!) = (\!|a|\!) \cdot \mathsf{M}\, i_A$. (Again, this relation is induced by the aforementioned adjunction.)

There are two simple consequences of the uniqueness property. If we set the evaluation of variables to the identity ($g = id$), we get the computation laws:

$$(\!|a|\!) \cdot var = id\ , \qquad (8.8a)$$

$$(\!|a|\!) \cdot com = a \cdot \mathsf{S}\,(\!|a|\!)\ . \qquad (8.8b)$$

As *var* and *com* are the constructors of terms, we can read these as defining equations of $(\!|-|\!)$. The uniqueness property also implies that *var* and *com* are natural in X and that $(\!|-|\!)$ preserves naturality.

The free monad of the functor S is $\langle \mathsf{M}, \eta, \mu \rangle$, where $\eta = var$ and $\mu = (\!|com|\!)$. The $\mu : \mathsf{M}{\circ}\mathsf{M} \dot{\to} \mathsf{M}$ of the monad flattens a term whose variables are terms. It does so by evaluating the term with the composite constructor—the action of the free algebra.

Theorem 8.1. *The category of algebras for the free monad of* S *is isomorphic to the category of* S*-algebras:*

$$(\mathsf{M}, \eta, \mu)\text{-}\mathbf{Alg}(\mathscr{C}) \cong \mathsf{S}\text{-}\mathbf{Alg}(\mathscr{C})\ .$$

The following definitions are the witnesses to this isomorphism.

$$\lceil \langle X, a : \mathsf{S}\, X \to X \rangle \rceil = \langle X, (\!|a|\!) : \mathsf{M}\, X \to X \rangle \qquad \lceil h \rceil = h\ , \qquad (8.9)$$

$$\lfloor \langle X, b : \mathsf{M}\, X \to X \rangle \rfloor = \langle X, b \cdot \theta X : \mathsf{S}\, X \to X \rangle \qquad \lfloor h \rfloor = h\ , \qquad (8.10)$$

where $\theta = com \cdot \mathsf{S}{\circ}\eta : \mathsf{S} \dot{\to} \mathsf{M}$, *which turns a level of syntax into a term. The map* $\lceil - \rceil$ *preserves and reflects homomorphisms.*

$$h : \lceil a \rceil \to \lceil b \rceil : (\mathsf{M}, \eta, \mu)\text{-}\mathbf{Alg}(\mathscr{C}) \iff h : a \to b : \mathsf{S}\text{-}\mathbf{Alg}(\mathscr{C}) \qquad (8.11)$$

Proof. (i) $\lfloor \lceil \langle X, a \rangle \rceil \rfloor = \langle X, a \rangle$:

$$\begin{aligned}
&\lfloor \lceil a \rceil \rfloor \\
=\;& \{\ \text{definitions of } \lceil - \rceil\ (8.9) \text{ and } \lfloor - \rfloor\ (8.10)\ \} \\
&(\!|a|\!) \cdot com \cdot \mathsf{S}\,(\eta X) \\
=\;& \{\ \text{eval computation (8.8b) and } \mathsf{S} \text{ functor}\ \} \\
&a \cdot \mathsf{S}\,((\!|a|\!) \cdot \eta X) \\
=\;& \{\ \text{eval computation (8.8a) and } \mathsf{S} \text{ functor}\ \} \\
&a
\end{aligned}$$

An instance of this property is $com = \lfloor \lceil com \rceil \rfloor = \mu X \cdot \theta(\mathsf{M}\, X)$. In the opposite direction, $\lceil \lfloor \langle X, b \rangle \rfloor \rceil = \langle X, b \rangle$:

$$\begin{aligned}
&\lceil \lfloor b \rfloor \rceil = b \\
\iff\;& \{\ \text{definitions of } \lceil - \rceil\ (8.9) \text{ and } \lfloor - \rfloor\ (8.10)\ \} \\
&(\!|b \cdot \theta X|\!) = b \\
\iff\;& \{\ \text{uniqueness of eval (8.7)}\ \} \\
&b \cdot \eta X = id \;\wedge\; b \cdot com = b \cdot \theta X \cdot \mathsf{S}\, b
\end{aligned}$$

The first conjunct follows from the fact that b respects η (8.3a). For the second conjunct we reason:

$$\begin{aligned}
&b \cdot \theta X \cdot \mathsf{S}\, b \\
=\;& \{\ \theta : \mathsf{S} \dot{\to} \mathsf{M} \text{ is natural}\ \} \\
&b \cdot \mathsf{M}\, b \cdot \theta(\mathsf{M}\, X) \\
=\;& \{\ b \text{ respects } \mu\ (8.3b)\ \}
\end{aligned}$$

$$\begin{aligned}
& b \cdot \mu X \cdot \theta(\mathsf{M}\,X) \\
= \;& \{\ \mu X \cdot \theta(\mathsf{M}\,X) = com, \text{ see above }\} \\
& b \cdot com\ .
\end{aligned}$$

(ii) $\lfloor - \rfloor$ is functorial as $\theta : \mathsf{S} \dot{\to} \mathsf{M}$ is natural and $\lfloor - \rfloor = \theta\text{-}\mathbf{Alg}$.

(iii) $\lceil - \rceil$ maps S-homomorphisms to M-homomorphisms.

$$\begin{aligned}
& h \cdot (\!|a|\!) = (\!|b|\!) \cdot \mathsf{M}\,h \\
\iff\; & \{\ \text{uniqueness of eval (8.7)}\ \} \\
& h \cdot (\!|a|\!) \cdot \eta X = h \ \wedge\ h \cdot (\!|a|\!) \cdot com = b \cdot \mathsf{S}\,(h \cdot (\!|a|\!))
\end{aligned}$$

The first conjunct is a direct consequence of computation (8.8a). For the second conjunct we reason:

$$\begin{aligned}
& h \cdot (\!|a|\!) \cdot com \\
= \;& \{\ \text{eval computation (8.8b)}\ \} \\
& h \cdot a \cdot \mathsf{S}\,(\!|a|\!) \\
= \;& \{\ \text{assumption } h : a \to b : \mathsf{S}\text{-}\mathbf{Alg} \text{ and } \mathsf{S} \text{ functor}\ \} \\
& b \cdot \mathsf{S}\,(h \cdot (\!|a|\!))
\end{aligned}$$

(iv) Finally, $\lceil \langle A, a \rangle \rceil$ is an algebra for the monad. That $\lceil a \rceil$ respects η (8.3a), unfolds to, $(\!|a|\!) \cdot \eta X = id$, which is the first computation law (8.8a). That $\lceil a \rceil$ respects μ (8.3b), unfolds to, $(\!|a|\!) \cdot \mu X = (\!|a|\!) \cdot \mathsf{M}\,(\!|a|\!)$, and this follows from part (iii)

$$\begin{aligned}
& (\!|a|\!) \cdot \mu X = (\!|a|\!) \cdot \mathsf{M}\,(\!|a|\!) \\
\Longleftarrow\; & \{\ \lceil - \rceil \text{ maps } \mathsf{S}\text{- to } \mathsf{M}\text{-homomorphisms and } \mu = (\!|com|\!)\ \} \\
& (\!|a|\!) \cdot com = a \cdot \mathsf{S}\,(\!|a|\!)
\end{aligned}$$

and the second computation law (8.8b). □

8.2 Initial and Final Objects

Now that we have completed another round of generalization, from free pointed functors to free monads, it is appropriate to examine what the new initial and final λ-bialgebras are. Again, they can be derived from the double isomorphism (8.6), and again, we will highlight the salient details.

Superficially, the initial λ-bialgebra has not changed: it remains $\langle \mu\mathsf{S}, \lceil in \rceil, (\!|\lfloor \mathsf{B}^{\lambda}\,\lceil in \rceil \rfloor|\!) \rangle$. What *has* changed are the definitions of $\lceil - \rceil$ and $\lfloor - \rfloor$. The usual three proof obligations are all discharged by the proofs provided in previous section. All of the proof steps have analogues in this section—in particular, Theorem 7.1 has been succeeded by Theorem 8.1.

The final λ-bialgebra is $\langle \nu\mathsf{B}, [\mathsf{M}^{\lambda}\,out], out \rangle$; the single change is replacing P^{λ} with M^{λ}. The unique λ-bialgebra homomorphism to the final λ-bialgebra from any λ-bialgebra $\langle X, a, C \rangle$ is still $[c]$. Just as in Section 7.2, there is one final proof obligation: we have to show that $[\mathsf{M}^{\lambda}\,out]$ is an algebra for M. Previously we showed that $[\mathsf{P}^{\lambda}\,out]$ respects η, and this proof suffices to show the same of $[\mathsf{M}^{\lambda}\,out]$ (8.3a). It remains to show that μ is respected (8.3b):

$$\begin{aligned}
& [\mathsf{M}^{\lambda}\,out] \cdot \mu(\nu\mathsf{B}) = [\mathsf{M}^{\lambda}\,out] \cdot \mathsf{M}\,[\mathsf{M}^{\lambda}\,out] \\
\iff\; & \{\ \text{unfold fusion (§A)} \\
& \quad \text{with } \mu(\nu\mathsf{B}) : \mathsf{M}^{\lambda}\,(\mathsf{M}^{\lambda}\,out) \to \mathsf{M}^{\lambda}\,out \text{ (8.4)}\ \} \\
& [\mathsf{M}^{\lambda}\,(\mathsf{M}^{\lambda}\,out)] = [\mathsf{M}^{\lambda}\,out] \cdot \mathsf{M}\,[\mathsf{M}^{\lambda}\,out] \\
\Longleftarrow\; & \{\ \text{unfold fusion (§A)}\ \} \\
& \mathsf{M}\,[\mathsf{M}^{\lambda}\,out] : \mathsf{M}^{\lambda}\,(\mathsf{M}^{\lambda}\,out) \to \mathsf{M}^{\lambda}\,out \\
\Longleftarrow\; & \{\ \mathsf{M}^{\lambda} \text{ functor}\ \} \\
& [\mathsf{M}^{\lambda}\,out] : \mathsf{M}^{\lambda}\,out \to out\ .
\end{aligned}$$

Finally, we can give another statement of the semantic function $\mu\mathsf{S} \to \nu\mathsf{B}$, in the setting of $\lambda : \mathsf{M} \circ \mathsf{B} \dot{\to} \mathsf{B} \circ \mathsf{M}$.

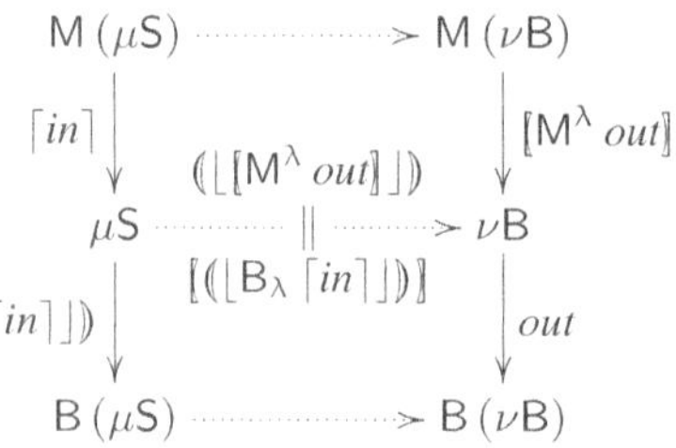

We have upgraded pointed functors to monads and Theorem 8.1 ensures that Iniga and Finn still see eye to eye. However, we will need to repeat the exercise of Section 7.3.

8.3 Constructing a Distributive Law

Given a program that is modelled by a natural transformation of type $\rho : \mathsf{S} \circ \mathsf{B} \dot{\to} \mathsf{B} \circ \mathsf{M}$, we seek to derive a distributive law $\lambda : \mathsf{M} \circ \mathsf{B} \dot{\to} \mathsf{B} \circ \mathsf{M}$ such that

$$c \cdot \lceil a \rceil = \mathsf{B}\,\lceil a \rceil \cdot \lambda X \cdot \mathsf{M}\,c \iff c \cdot a = \mathsf{B}\,\lceil a \rceil \cdot \rho X \cdot \mathsf{S}\,c\ . \quad (8.12)$$

Let us calculate.

$$\begin{aligned}
& c \cdot a = \mathsf{B}\,\lceil a \rceil \cdot \rho X \cdot \mathsf{S}\,c \\
\iff\; & \{\ \text{isomorphism } (\mathsf{M}, \eta, \mu)\text{-}\mathbf{Alg} \cong \mathsf{S}\text{-}\mathbf{Alg} \text{ (8.11)}\ \} \\
& c \cdot \lceil a \rceil = \lceil \mathsf{B}\,\lceil a \rceil \cdot \rho X \rceil \cdot \mathsf{M}\,c \\
\iff\; & \{\ \text{see below}\ \} \\
& c \cdot \lceil a \rceil = \mathsf{B}_{\lambda}\,\lceil a \rceil \cdot \mathsf{M}\,c \\
\iff\; & \{\ \text{definition of } \mathsf{B}_{\lambda} \text{ (6.1)}\ \} \\
& c \cdot \lceil a \rceil = \mathsf{B}\,\lceil a \rceil \cdot \lambda X \cdot \mathsf{M}\,c
\end{aligned}$$

The specification (8.12) holds if $\mathsf{B}_{\lambda}\,\lceil a \rceil = \lceil \mathsf{B}\,\lceil a \rceil \cdot \rho X \rceil$. To turn this property into a definition for λ, we have to delve a bit deeper into the theory. Applegate [3] discovered that distributive laws $\lambda : \mathsf{M} \circ \mathsf{B} \dot{\to} \mathsf{B} \circ \mathsf{M}$ are in one-to-one correspondence to lifted functors $\bar{\mathsf{B}} : (\mathsf{M}, \eta, \mu)\text{-}\mathbf{Alg} \to (\mathsf{M}, \eta, \mu)\text{-}\mathbf{Alg}$, where a functor $\bar{\mathsf{B}}$ is a lifting of B if its action on carriers and homomorphisms is given by B. It is useful to make explicit what it means for $\bar{\mathsf{B}}$ to preserve algebra homomorphisms (as before, $\bar{\mathsf{B}}\,a$ is synecdochic, see §6.1).

$$\mathsf{B}\,h \cdot \bar{\mathsf{B}}\,a = \bar{\mathsf{B}}\,b \cdot \mathsf{M}\,(\mathsf{B}\,h) \Longleftarrow h \cdot a = b \cdot \mathsf{M}\,h \quad (8.13)$$

This property immediately implies that $\bar{\mathsf{B}}$ takes natural algebras of type $\mathsf{M} \circ \mathsf{F} \dot{\to} \mathsf{F}$ to natural algebras of type $\mathsf{M} \circ \mathsf{B} \circ \mathsf{F} \dot{\to} \mathsf{B} \circ \mathsf{F}$.

Looking back, we note that we have already made extensive use of the correspondence in one direction, turning a distributive law into a lifting B_{λ}; now we need the opposite direction. Given a lifting $\bar{\mathsf{B}}$, we can construct a distributive law as follows. The uniqueness property (8.7) states that homomorphisms of type $\mathsf{M}\,X \to A$ are in one-to-one correspondence to arrows of type $X \to A$. We aim to construct $\lambda : \mathsf{M} \circ \mathsf{B} \dot{\to} \mathsf{B} \circ \mathsf{M}$, so we need a natural transformation of type $\mathsf{B} \dot{\to} \mathsf{B} \circ \mathsf{M}$. The composition $\mathsf{B} \circ \eta$ will do nicely. We obtain:

$$\lambda_{\bar{\mathsf{B}}} = \bar{\mathsf{B}}\,\mu \cdot \mathsf{M} \circ \mathsf{B} \circ \eta\ , \quad (8.14)$$

where $\bar{\mathsf{B}}\,\mu : \mathsf{M} \circ \mathsf{B} \circ \mathsf{M} \dot{\to} \mathsf{B} \circ \mathsf{M}$ is the M-algebra for the carrier $\mathsf{B} \circ \mathsf{M}$. We must show that $\lambda_{\bar{\mathsf{B}}}$ coheres with η and μ per equations (8.2a) and (8.2b). For the proof we refer to the full paper [11].

The mappings $\lambda \mapsto \mathsf{B}_{\lambda}$ and $\bar{\mathsf{B}} \mapsto \lambda_{\bar{\mathsf{B}}}$ then establish the one-to-one correspondence between distributive laws and lifted functors.

Returning to the task at hand, constructing a distributive law from ρ, we use the property $\mathsf{B}_{\lambda}\,\lceil a \rceil = \lceil \mathsf{B}\,\lceil a \rceil \cdot \rho X \rceil$ to define:

$$\begin{aligned}
\bar{\mathsf{B}}\,\langle X, b : \mathsf{M}\,X \to X \rangle &= \langle \mathsf{B}\,X, \lceil \mathsf{B}\,b \cdot \rho X \rceil : \mathsf{M}\,(\mathsf{B}\,X) \to \mathsf{B}\,X \rangle\ , \\
\bar{\mathsf{B}}\,h &= \mathsf{B}\,h\ .
\end{aligned}$$

This defines a lifting because $\lceil - \rceil = (\!|-|\!)$ is one that lifts $\mathsf{S}\,(\mathsf{B}\,X) \to \mathsf{B}\,X$ to $\mathsf{M}\,(\mathsf{B}\,X) \to \mathsf{B}\,X$. Putting things together, the distributive law $\lambda = \lambda_{\mathsf{B}}$ expressed as a composition of natural transformations is:

$$\lambda = (\!|\mathsf{B}\circ\mu \cdot \rho\circ\mathsf{M}|\!) \cdot \mathsf{M}\circ\mathsf{B}\circ\eta \ . \qquad (8.15)$$

8.4 Distributive Laws à la Carte

Distributive laws can be constructed modularly from a system of recursion equations. In this modular development we will have different syntax functors S and we need to construct the free monad for each, so we will replace the notation M by the more informative S^*. The mapping $(-)^*$ is actually a higher-order functor whose arrow part takes a natural transformation $\alpha : \mathsf{S} \dot\to \mathsf{T}$ to a natural transformation $\alpha^* : \mathsf{S}^* \dot\to \mathsf{T}^*$. Think of α^* as a term converter.

First let us consider an alternative definition of *fib* (cf. §2.2).

$$\mathit{fib} = 0 \prec (1 \prec \mathit{fib}) + \mathit{fib}$$

Note that there is a nested occurrence of $\prec$. We can support nested stream constructors if we embed the behaviour into the syntax. The new syntax-with-behaviour functor is $\mathsf{T}\,X = \mathsf{B}\,X + \mathsf{S}\,X$. Given a system of recursion equations $\rho : \mathsf{S}\circ\mathsf{B} \dot\to \mathsf{B}\circ\mathsf{T}^*$, we can construct a symmetric system σ as,

$$\sigma = \mathsf{B}\circ \mathit{inl}^* \cdot \mathsf{B}\circ\theta_{\mathsf{B}} \triangledown \rho = \mathsf{B}\circ(\theta_{\mathsf{T}} \cdot \mathit{inl}) \triangledown \rho : \mathsf{T}\circ\mathsf{B} \dot\to \mathsf{B}\circ\mathsf{T}^* \ ,$$

where $\mathit{inl} : \mathsf{B} \dot\to \mathsf{T}$ and $\theta_{\mathsf{F}} : \mathsf{F} \dot\to \mathsf{F}^*$. A distributive law $\lambda : \mathsf{T}^*\circ\mathsf{B} \dot\to \mathsf{B}\circ\mathsf{T}^*$ can then be constructed by Section 8.3.

Embedding behaviour into syntax is a special case of extending a system of recursion equations. Specifically, given a base system $\rho_1 : \mathsf{S}_1\circ\mathsf{B} \dot\to \mathsf{B}\circ\mathsf{S}_1^*$ and an extension $\rho_2 : \mathsf{S}_2\circ\mathsf{B} \dot\to \mathsf{B}\circ\mathsf{S}^*$, where $\mathsf{S}\,X = \mathsf{S}_1\,X + \mathsf{S}_2\,X$, we can form a combined system as follows:

$$\rho = \mathsf{B}\circ\mathit{inl}^* \cdot \rho_1 \triangledown \rho_2 : \mathsf{S}\circ\mathsf{B} \dot\to \mathsf{B}\circ\mathsf{S}^* \ .$$

The idea is that ρ_2 can use the operators of S_1 *and* S_2 to define the operators of S_2. Compare this with Example 8.1: we can model *One* and *Plus* with an S_1 and ρ_1, and *Nat* with an S_2 and ρ_2, where *Nat* is defined in terms of itself as well as *One* and *Plus*.

Returning to the embedding of behaviour into syntax, by setting $\mathsf{S}_1 = \mathsf{B}$ and $\rho_1 = \mathsf{B}\circ\theta_{\mathsf{B}}$, the embedding emerges as a special case. A minor variation is the merge of two independent systems of recursion equations,

$$\rho = \mathsf{B}\circ\mathit{inl}^* \cdot \rho_1 \triangledown \mathsf{B}\circ\mathit{inr}^* \cdot \rho_2 \ ,$$

where $\rho_1 : \mathsf{S}_1\circ\mathsf{B} \dot\to \mathsf{B}\circ\mathsf{S}_1^*$ and $\rho_2 : \mathsf{S}_2\circ\mathsf{B} \dot\to \mathsf{B}\circ\mathsf{S}_2^*$. We can further modularize our modelling of Example 8.1 as the recursion equations for *One* and *Plus* are independent. It is clear that we can develop distributive laws modularly: if we have a collection of recursion equations with acyclic dependencies, then we can combine them into a single system using the two techniques described above. In the same fashion as Swierstra's *Data types à la carte* [20], we can create distributive laws à la carte.

There is one final thing to be said on this topic. The embedding of behaviour makes the constructors of B available in the syntax. Often, one also wishes to embed an element of $\nu\mathsf{B}$: consider the equation $x = 0 \prec \mathit{evenfib'} + x$ from Section 2. The stream *evenfib'* is defined by a previous system, in fact, two systems; we wish to reuse it at this point. This can be accommodated by setting $\mathsf{S}_1\,X = \nu\mathsf{B}$ and $\rho_1 = \mathsf{B}\circ\mathit{com} \cdot \mathit{out}$. Here S_1 is a constant functor—elements of $\nu\mathsf{B}$ are embedded as constants. It is important to note that merging the systems for *fib'*, *even* and x is *not* an option as *even* uses a different definitional style and, as we have pointed out, we cannot mix styles. Of course, we have to show that *even* is uniquely defined and this is what we do in Section 9.

8.5 Proving the Unique Fixed-Point Principle Correct

Let us now return to our original problem of proving the unique fixed-point principle correct. Also, a brief summary is perhaps not amiss. A system of recursion equations is modelled by a natural transformation $\rho : \mathsf{S}\circ\mathsf{B} \dot\to \mathsf{B}\circ\mathsf{S}^*$, where S is the syntax functor and B the behaviour functor. The type of ρ captures the slogan *consume at most one, produce at least one*. Using the trick of embedding behaviour into syntax we can consume nothing (the argument is reassembled on the right) and we can produce more than one. Systems of this form are quite liberal; most, but not all of the examples in the literature satisfy the restrictions. We will get back to this point in Section 9.

A solution of a system modelled by ρ consists of an S-algebra and a B-coalgebra over a common carrier that satisfies:

$$c \cdot a = \mathsf{B}\,\lceil a \rceil \cdot \rho\,X \cdot \mathsf{S}\,c \ .$$

We can now replay the calculations of Section 4. If the coalgebra is final, then a is uniquely determined, which establishes the UFP:

$$\begin{aligned}
& \mathit{out} \cdot a = \mathsf{B}\,\lceil a \rceil \cdot \rho\,(\nu\mathsf{B}) \cdot \mathsf{S}\,\mathit{out} \\
\iff & \{\ \lambda \text{ given by (8.15) which satisfies (8.12)}\ \} \\
& \mathit{out} \cdot \lceil a \rceil = \mathsf{B}\,\lceil a \rceil \cdot \lambda\,(\nu\mathsf{B}) \cdot \mathsf{M}\,\mathit{out} \\
\iff & \{\ \text{definition of } \mathsf{M}^{\lambda} \text{ and uniqueness of unfold (3.2)}\ \} \\
& \lceil a \rceil = [\!(\mathsf{M}^{\lambda}\ \mathit{out})\!] \\
\iff & \{\ \text{isomorphism } (\mathsf{M}, \eta, \mu)\text{-}\mathbf{Alg} \cong \mathsf{S}\text{-}\mathbf{Alg}\ (8.1)\ \} \\
& a = \lfloor [\!(\mathsf{M}^{\lambda}\ \mathit{out})\!] \rfloor \ .
\end{aligned}$$

Conversely, if the algebra is initial, then c is fixed: $c = (\!|\lfloor \mathsf{B}_{\lambda}\ \lceil \mathit{in} \rceil \rfloor|\!)$. Since the data defines initial and final objects in λ-$\mathbf{Bialg}(\mathscr{C})$, we can furthermore conclude that the two ways of defining the semantic function of type $\mu\mathsf{S} \to \nu\mathsf{B}$ coincide: $(\!|a|\!) = [\!(c)\!]$.

9. Echoes from the Second Dimension

Thus far, we have been living in a single dimension: we have incrementally augmented the syntax functor S, first to P, the free pointed functor of S, and then to M, the free monad of S. A second dimension arises as the dual of the first; just as we replaced S with P, we can do so dually with B and C, the *cofree copointed functor* of B. Of course, the progression continues predictably on to N, the *cofree comonad* of B. The developments of C and N are the duals of Sections 7 and 8, respectively; the details are spelled out in [11].

Let us take a moment to characterize the natural transformations with which we are modelling recursion equations: they take the general form of $\rho : \mathsf{S}\circ\mathit{lhs} \dot\to \mathsf{B}\circ\mathit{rhs}$. In Section 6 we took the simplest case, where $\mathit{lhs} = \mathsf{B}$, $\mathit{rhs} = \mathsf{S}$, and thus ρ was exactly our distributive law λ. The duality of the dimensions can be seen in how they affect the expressive power of these natural transformations.

The first dimension, the one we have focused on hitherto, corresponds to the sophistication with which we can build syntax on the right-hand side of equations; the progression first replaced a constructor by a constructor or a variable, and then by terms, nested constructors with variables. This culminated in a ρ where $\mathit{lhs} = \mathsf{B}$, $\mathit{rhs} = \mathsf{M}$, and λ is defined in terms of ρ using the structure of M.

The second dimension corresponds to the left-hand side of equations, and rather than constructing syntax, this is about destructing or patterning matching on behaviour. The *cofree copointed functor* C, defined as $\mathsf{C}\,X = X \times \mathsf{B}\,X$, gives a categorical modelling of Haskell's *as-patterns*, where *var*@*pat* gives the name *var* to the value being matched by *pat*—B represents a level of behaviour and C gives a label to that level. Therefore, a ρ, where $\mathit{lhs} = \mathsf{C}$, models an equation that consumes at most one, rather than strictly one. This can also be achieved, albeit in an indirect way, by embedding behaviour in syntax, as described in Section 8.4. For example, consider the stream operator that interleaves two streams:

$$\mathit{interleave}\ (\mathit{Cons}\ m\ s)\ (\mathit{Cons}\ n\ t) = m \prec \mathit{interleave}\ (n \prec t)\ s \ .$$

The result of *interleave* $(0\,2\,4\,..)\,(1\,3\,5\,..)$ is $0\,1\,2\,3\,..$, the natural numbers. In this definition we are unnecessarily deconstructing the second parameter into its head and tail, we simply need the whole stream. A more natural definition is:

$$interleave\ (Cons\ m\ s)\ t = m \prec interleave\ t\ s\ .$$

Sometimes we want the head, tail, *and* the whole stream. Consider the stream operator that performs an ordered merge of two streams:

$$\begin{aligned}&merge\ s@(Cons\ m\ s')\ t@(Cons\ n\ t')\\ &\quad = \textbf{if}\ m \leqslant n\ \textbf{then}\ m \prec merge\ s'\ t\ \textbf{else}\ n \prec merge\ s\ t'\ .\end{aligned}$$

From this we are able to construct a natural transformation $\rho : \mathsf{S}\circ\mathsf{C} \dot{\to} \mathsf{B}\circ\mathsf{S}$ to model *interleave* and *merge* without the need to reconstruct behaviour on the right-hand side.

$$\begin{aligned}&\textbf{data}\ \mathsf{C}\ x = As\ x\ (\mathsf{B}\ x)\\ &\rho\ (Interleave\ (As\ \_\ (Cons\ (m,s)), As\ t\ \_))\\ &\quad = Cons\ (m, Interleave\ (t,s))\\ &\rho\ (Merge\ (As\ s\ (Cons\ (m,s')), As\ t\ (Cons\ (n,t'))))\\ &\quad = \textbf{if}\ m \leqslant n\ \textbf{then}\\ &\qquad\quad Cons\ (m, Merge\ (s',t))\\ &\qquad \textbf{else}\\ &\qquad\quad Cons\ (n,\ Merge\ (t,\ t'))\end{aligned}$$

Finally, the *cofree comonad* permits the inspection of behaviour to an arbitrary depth—unlimited consumption. This is exactly what we need to model the equations that consume more than they produce, such as the stream operator *even*, which we saw in Section 2.

$$even\ (Cons\ m\ (Cons\ n\ u)) = m \prec even\ u$$

We can render the *cofree comonad* in Haskell as,

$$\textbf{data}\ \mathsf{N}\ x = Root\ x\ (\mathsf{B}\ (\mathsf{N}\ x))\ ,$$

and *even* is captured by a natural transformation $\rho : \mathsf{S}\circ\mathsf{N} \dot{\to} \mathsf{B}\circ\mathsf{S}$,

$$\begin{aligned}&\rho\ (Even\ (Root\ s\ (Cons\ (m, Root\ t\ (Cons\ (n, Root\ u\ \_))))))\\ &\quad = Cons\ (m, Even\ u)\ .\end{aligned}$$

We can form a distributive law $\lambda : \mathsf{S}\circ\mathsf{N} \dot{\to} \mathsf{N}\circ\mathsf{S}$ from ρ, by following the dual of the derivation outlined in Section 8.3.

There are three points in each dimension, leading to a total of nine different instantiations of $\rho : \mathsf{S}\circ lhs \dot{\to} \mathsf{B}\circ rhs$, which correspond to nine combinations of expressive power. A natural transformation $\rho : \mathsf{S}\circ\mathsf{N} \dot{\to} \mathsf{B}\circ\mathsf{M}$ is the most general: it captures recursion equations that have an arbitrary depth of pattern matching on the left-hand side, with an arbitrary term on the right-hand side. And in some sense it is too general, as it unclear how to derive the corresponding distributive law $\lambda : \mathsf{M}\circ\mathsf{N} \dot{\to} \mathsf{N}\circ\mathsf{M}$, or if there should be such a derivation. We leave this determination as future work.

The sweet spot of expressivity is $\rho : \mathsf{S}\circ\mathsf{C} \dot{\to} \mathsf{B}\circ\mathsf{M}$, where M is the free monad of syntax with embedded behaviour, which captures the slogan mentioned in Section 8.5: *consume at most one, produce at least one*. The use of C makes the nature of the consumption more explicit. Let us showcase this sweet spot.

There is a sequence of numbers called the Hamming numbers, which can be characterized as the numbers that only have 2, 3 or 5 as prime factors. They are named after the Turing award winner Richard Hamming, who posed the problem of generating these numbers in ascending order. Dijkstra [6] presented a solution in SASL, attributed to J. L. A. van de Snepscheut, and proved its correctness. Here we will replicate the same solution, which is in fact a slightly simplified version for numbers that only have 2 and 3 as prime factors. The stream is,

$$ham = 1 \prec merge\ (times\ 2\ ham, times\ 3\ ham)\ ,$$

where the definition of *merge* is given above and *times* is,

$$times\ n\ (Cons\ m\ s) = n \times m \prec times\ n\ s\ .$$

Again, we can capture the recursion equations *merge*, *times* and *ham* by a natural transformation $\rho : \mathsf{S}\circ\mathsf{C} \dot{\to} \mathsf{B}\circ\mathsf{M}$:

$$\begin{aligned}&\rho\ (Merge\ (As\ s\ (Cons\ (m,s')), As\ t\ (Cons\ (n,t'))))\\ &\quad = \textbf{if}\ m \leqslant n\ \textbf{then}\\ &\qquad\quad Cons\ (m, Com\ (Merge\ (Var\ s', Var\ t)))\\ &\qquad \textbf{else}\\ &\qquad\quad Cons\ (n,\ Com\ (Merge\ (Var\ t,\ Var\ t')))\\ &\rho\ (Times\ n\ (As\ \_\ (Cons\ (m,s))))\\ &\quad = Cons\ (n \times m, Com\ (Times\ n\ (Var\ s)))\\ &\rho\ Ham\\ &\quad = Cons\ (1, Com\ (Merge\ (Com\ (Times\ 2\ (Com\ Ham)),\\ &\qquad\qquad\qquad\qquad\qquad Com\ (Times\ 3\ (Com\ Ham)))))\ .\end{aligned}$$

The details of the construction of the distributive law $\lambda : \mathsf{M}\circ\mathsf{C} \dot{\to} \mathsf{C}\circ\mathsf{M}$ can be found in Hinze and James [11]. By the naturality of ρ and thus the constructed λ, we have a proof (as an alternative to Dijkstra's) that *ham* uniquely defines a stream.

10. Related Work

The theoretical foundations of our work exist in the literature, originally in Turi and Plotkin [21] and refined in Lenisa et al. [13]. We see our work as an application of, and an exercise in, this theory.

The work that is closest in spirit to ours is Bartels [4]. It is centered around the coinduction proof principle, in contrast to the UFP. Bartels looks at two out of the nine points that we have identified, the simplest $\lambda : \mathsf{S}\circ\mathsf{B} \dot{\to} \mathsf{B}\circ\mathsf{S}$, and our sweet spot $\lambda : \mathsf{M}\circ\mathsf{C} \dot{\to} \mathsf{C}\circ\mathsf{M}$, but for space reasons does not explore any others. Bartels introduces a construction *homomorphism up-to*, which is a homomorphism from a coalgebra to a bialgebra, and uses it as a definitional principle. We simply use bialgebra homomorphisms, following the original theory of Turi and Plotkin [21], which nicely exhibits the duality of Iniga and Finn's viewpoints.

Rutten and Silva have presented two coinductive calculi, one for streams [17] and one for binary trees [19], also using coinduction as a proof principle. They have a uniqueness proof for each: Theorem 3.1 and Appendix A in Rutten [17]; and Theorem 2 in Silva and Rutten [19]. Our approach treats streams and infinite trees, and *behaviour* in general, in a datatype generic way—the same proofs apply, only varying in the chosen functors for syntax and behaviour. Moreover, we emphasize a compositional, functional style.

Our task of determining that a recursion equation has a unique solution is related to the task of determining that corecursive definitions are productive [18]. This is crucial in dependently typed programming and proof languages, where the logical consistency of the system requires it. In Coq this is enforced by the guardedness condition [8], which is particularly conservative: it has no means to propagate information through function calls, so corecursive calls are forbidden to appear anywhere other than as a direct argument of a constructor. Compositionality is the first casualty. The situation is similar in Agda [2].

Hughes et al. [12] were the first to talk about the notion of *sized-types*, and used it as part of a type-based analysis that guarantees termination and liveness of embedded functional programs. Following this, there have been a whole host of proposed type systems incorporating size annotations. MiniAgda [1, 15] is a tangible implementation of a dependently typed core language with sized types, able to track the productivity of corecursive definitions. Type signatures are mandatory and contain sizes explicitly, which is in contrast to our ρ functions, the naturality of which is easy to infer.

Specific to streams, Endrullis et al. [7] introduce what they call *data-oblivious* productivity: productivity that can be decided without inspecting the stream elements. They present three classes of stream specifications. Their analysis is provably optimal for the *flat* class, where stream functions cannot contain nested function applications. Our slogan "consume at most one, produce at least one" corresponds to their *friendly nesting* class. A competing approach appears in Zantema [22], who reduces the determination of uniqueness to the termination of a term rewriting system (TRS). A stream specification has a unique solution if its *observational variant* TRS is terminating, a TRS that is very like Rutten's stream definitions.

Acknowledgements

Ralf would like to thank Jan Rutten for pointing him to distributive laws and bialgebras. Daniel is funded by a DTA Studentship from the Engineering and Physical Sciences Research Council.

References

[1] A. Abel. MiniAgda: Integrating Sized and Dependent Types. *Electronic Proceedings in Theoretical Computer Science*, 43:14–28, 2010.

[2] A. Abel and T. Altenkirch. A predicative analysis of structural recursion. *JFP*, 12(1):1–41, 2002.

[3] H. Applegate. *Acyclic models and resolvent functors*. PhD thesis, Columbia University, 1965.

[4] F. Bartels. Generalised coinduction. *Mathematical Structures in Computer Science*, 13(2):321–348, 2003.

[5] R. S. Bird and O. De Moor. *Algebra of Programming*, volume 100 of *International Series in Computing Science*. Prentice Hall, 1997.

[6] E. W. Dijkstra. Hamming's exercise in SASL. Personal Note EWD792, 1981.

[7] J. Endrullis, C. Grabmayer, and D. Hendriks. Data-oblivious stream productivity. In *Logic for Programming, Artificial Intelligence, and Reasoning*, volume 5330 of *LNCS*, pages 79–96. Springer, 2008.

[8] E. Giménez. Codifying guarded definitions with recursive schemes. In *Types for Proofs and Programs*, volume 996 of *LNCS*, pages 39–59. Springer, 1995.

[9] R. Hinze. The Bird tree. *JFP*, 19(5):491–508, 2009.

[10] R. Hinze. Concrete stream calculus—an extended study. *JFP*, 20(5–6):463–535, 2010.

[11] R. Hinze and D. W. H. James. Proving the Unique-Fixed Point Principle Correct. Technical Report RR-11-03, Department of Computer Science, University of Oxford, 2011.

[12] J. Hughes, L. Pareto, and A. Sabry. Proving the correctness of reactive systems using sized types. In *POPL*, pages 410–423. ACM, 1996.

[13] M. Lenisa, J. Power, and H. Watanabe. Distributivity for endofunctors, pointed and co-pointed endofunctors, monads and comonads. *Electronic Notes in Theoretical Computer Science*, 33:230–260, 2000.

[14] C. McBride and R. Paterson. Applicative programming with effects. *JFP*, 18(1):1–13, 2008.

[15] K. Mehltretter. Termination checking for a dependently typed language. Master's thesis, LMU Munich, 2007.

[16] M. Niqui and J. J. M. M. Rutten. Sampling, splitting and merging in coinductive stream calculus. In *MPC*, volume 6120 of *LNCS*, pages 310–330. Springer, 2010.

[17] J. J. M. M. Rutten. Fundamental study: Behavioural differential equations: A coinductive calculus of streams, automata, and power series. *Theoretical Computer Science*, 308:1–53, 2003.

[18] B. A. Sijtsma. On the productivity of recursive list definitions. *ACM Trans. Program. Lang. Syst.*, 11(4):633–649, 1989.

[19] A. Silva and J. J. M. M. Rutten. A coinductive calculus of binary trees. *Information and Computation*, 208:578–593, 2010.

[20] W. Swierstra. Data types à la carte. *JFP*, 18(04):423–436, 2008.

[21] D. Turi and G. Plotkin. Towards a mathematical operational semantics. In *Logic in Computer Science*, pages 280–291. IEEE, 1997.

[22] H. Zantema. Well-definedness of streams by transformation and termination. *Logical Methods in Computer Science*, 6(3:21), 2010.

A. Miscellaneous Laws

$$id = inl \triangledown inr \qquad \text{join reflection}$$

$$(g_1 \triangledown g_2) \cdot inl = g_1 \qquad \text{join computation}$$

$$(g_1 \triangledown g_2) \cdot inr = g_2 \qquad \text{join computation}$$

$$k \cdot (g_1 \triangledown g_2) = k \cdot g_1 \triangledown k \cdot g_2 \qquad \text{join fusion}$$

$$(g_1 \triangledown g_2) \cdot (h_1 + h_2) = g_1 \cdot h_1 \triangledown g_2 \cdot h_2 \qquad \text{join functor fusion}$$

$$(\!|a|\!) \cdot in = a \cdot \mathsf{F}\,(\!|a|\!) \qquad \text{fold computation}$$

$$h \cdot (\!|a|\!) = (\!|b|\!) \iff h \cdot a = b \cdot \mathsf{F}\,h \qquad \text{fold fusion}$$

$$[\!(out)\!] = id \qquad \text{unfold reflection}$$

$$[\!(d)\!] = [\!(c)\!] \cdot h \iff \mathsf{F}\,h \cdot d = c \cdot h \qquad \text{unfold fusion}$$

B. Lifting

The underlying or forgetful functor $\mathsf{U} : \mathsf{F}\text{-}\mathbf{Alg}(\mathscr{C}) \to \mathscr{C}$ is defined

$$\mathsf{U}\,\langle A, a\rangle = A \ , \qquad \mathsf{U}\,h = h \ .$$

A functor $\bar{\mathsf{H}} : \mathsf{F}\text{-}\mathbf{Alg}(\mathscr{C}) \to \mathsf{G}\text{-}\mathbf{Alg}(\mathscr{D})$ is a *lifting of* $\mathsf{H} : \mathscr{C} \to \mathscr{D}$ if $\mathsf{U} \circ \bar{\mathsf{H}} = \mathsf{H} \circ \mathsf{U}$.

$$\begin{array}{ccc} \mathsf{F}\text{-}\mathbf{Alg}(\mathscr{C}) & \xrightarrow{\bar{\mathsf{H}}} & \mathsf{G}\text{-}\mathbf{Alg}(\mathscr{D}) \\ {\scriptstyle \mathsf{U}}\downarrow & & \downarrow{\scriptstyle \mathsf{U}} \\ \mathscr{C} & \xrightarrow[\mathsf{H}]{} & \mathscr{D} \end{array}$$

Given a natural transformation $\lambda : \mathsf{G} \circ \mathsf{H} \dot{\to} \mathsf{H} \circ \mathsf{F}$, we can define a lifting $\mathsf{H}_\lambda : \mathsf{F}\text{-}\mathbf{Alg}(\mathscr{C}) \to \mathsf{G}\text{-}\mathbf{Alg}(\mathscr{D})$ of H as follows:

$$\mathsf{H}_\lambda\,\langle X, a : \mathsf{F}\,X \to X\rangle = \langle \mathsf{H}\,X, \mathsf{H}\,a \cdot \lambda X : \mathsf{G}\,(\mathsf{H}\,X) \to \mathsf{H}\,X\rangle \ , \quad \text{(B.1)}$$

$$\mathsf{H}_\lambda\,h = \mathsf{H}\,h \ . \quad \text{(B.2)}$$

Since H_λ's action on carriers and homomorphisms is given by H, it preserves identity and composition. It remains to show that it takes F-homomorphisms to G-homomorphisms.

$$\mathsf{H}\,h : \mathsf{H}_\lambda\,a \to \mathsf{H}_\lambda\,b : \mathsf{G}\text{-}\mathbf{Alg}(\mathscr{D}) \iff h : a \to b : \mathsf{F}\text{-}\mathbf{Alg}(\mathscr{C}) \ ,$$

where $a : \mathsf{F}\,X \to X$ and $b : \mathsf{F}\,Y \to Y$. (As throughout this paper, and as explained in Section 6.1, we use lifted functors synecdochically.) We reason

$$\begin{aligned} & \mathsf{H}\,h \cdot \mathsf{H}_\lambda\,a \\ = \ & \{ \text{definition of } \mathsf{H}_\lambda \text{ (B.1)} \} \\ & \mathsf{H}\,h \cdot \mathsf{H}\,a \cdot \lambda X \\ = \ & \{ \mathsf{H} \text{ functor and assumption } h : a \to b : \mathsf{F}\text{-}\mathbf{Alg}(\mathscr{C}) \} \\ & \mathsf{H}\,b \cdot \mathsf{H}\,(\mathsf{F}\,h) \cdot \lambda X \\ = \ & \{ \lambda : \mathsf{G} \circ \mathsf{H} \dot{\to} \mathsf{H} \circ \mathsf{F} \text{ is natural} \} \\ & \mathsf{H}\,b \cdot \lambda Y \cdot \mathsf{G}\,(\mathsf{H}\,h) \\ = \ & \{ \text{definition of } \mathsf{H}_\lambda \text{ (B.1)} \} \\ & \mathsf{H}_\lambda\,b \cdot \mathsf{G}\,(\mathsf{H}\,h) \ . \end{aligned}$$

The functor α-$\mathbf{Alg}$ emerges as a special case with $\mathsf{H} = \mathsf{Id}$ and $\lambda = \alpha$. Also, S_λ is an instance of the scheme with $\mathsf{F} = \mathsf{G}$, which consequently restricts H to endofunctors.

The construction dualizes to categories of coalgebras.

Linearity and PCF: a Semantic Insight!

Marco Gaboardi

Dip. di Scienze dell'Informazione, Università di Bologna, INRIA Focus Team, Mura Anteo Zamboni 7, 40127 Bologna, Italy

gaboardi@cs.unibo.it

Luca Paolini

Dipartimento di Informatica, Università degli Studi di Torino - Corso Svizzera 185, 10149 Torino, Italy

paolini@di.unito.it

Mauro Piccolo

Dipartimento di Informatica, Università degli Studi di Torino - Corso Svizzera 185, 10149 Torino, Italy

piccolo@di.unito.it

Abstract

Linearity is a multi-faceted and ubiquitous notion in the analysis and the development of programming language concepts. We study linearity in a denotational perspective by picking out programs that correspond to linear functions between coherence spaces.

We introduce a language, named $\mathcal{S}\ell\text{PCF}_\star$, that increases the higher-order expressivity of a linear core of PCF by means of new operators related to exception handling and parallel evaluation. $\mathcal{S}\ell\text{PCF}_\star$ allows us to program all the finite elements of the model and, consequently, it entails a full abstraction result that makes the reasoning on the equivalence between programs simpler.

Denotational linearity provides also crucial information for the operational evaluation of programs. We formalize two evaluation machineries for the language. The first one is an abstract and concise operational semantics designed with the aim of explaining the new operators, and is based on an infinite-branching search of the evaluation space. The second one is more concrete and it prunes such a space, by exploiting the linear assumptions. This can also be regarded as a base for an implementation.

Categories and Subject Descriptors D.3.1 [*Programming Languages*]: Formal Definitions and Theory—Semantics, Syntax; D.3.3 [*Programming Languages*]: Language Constructs and Features—Control structures; F.3.2 [*Logics and meanings of programs*]: Semantics of programming languages—Denotational semantics, Operational semantics

General Terms Languages, Theory, Design

Keywords PCF, Linear Logic, Denotational Semantics, Operational Semantics

1. Introduction

Linearity is a key tool in order to support a conscious use of resources in programming languages. A non-exhaustive list of its uses includes garbage collection, memory management and aliasing control, description of digital circuits, process channels and messages management, languages for quantum computations, etc. A survey of several variants of linear type systems proposed in literature is [34]. This broad spectrum of applications highlights the fact that linearity is a multifaceted abstract concept which can be considered in different perspectives. For instance, notions of **syntactical linearity** can be considered when variables are used once (in suitable senses), e.g. [4, 21]. On the other hand, if redexes cannot be discarded or duplicated during reduction [21] then a kind of **operational linearity** is achieved. This is related to the notion of *simple term* [24] in λ-calculus which suggests a kind of linearity on reductions, unrelated from a specific strategy.

Although some ideas that can be tracked to linearity have been implicitly used in programming languages for many years, the introduction of linear logic [19] is a redoubtable milestone in this setting. Linear logic arises from a sharp semantic analysis of stable domains where stable functions have been decomposed into linear functions and exponential domain constructors. Such a decomposition is patently reflected in the syntax of linear logic. Moreover, it suggests a new approach to linearity: **denotational linearity**. In a programming perspective, denotational linearity says that programs (i.e., closed terms) should correspond via a suitable interpretation to linear function on some specific domains, e.g. the linear models introduced in [13, 14, 19, 22]. By tackling this correspondence minutely some important contributions to the theory of programming can be obtained. If the considered domain includes all the computable functions (usually, they do it), then the analysis provides Turing-complete languages with weak syntactic linear constraints on variables, and new linear operators that, in a higher-type computability perspective [25, 27] increase the expressivity of linear languages.

To advance in this research line, we aim to pick out all and only (recursive) linear functions in a **linear model** built as the full subcategory of coherence spaces and linear functions [19] identified by the type structure of numerals and arrows. The language $\mathcal{S}\ell\text{PCF}$ proposed in [30] is correct for this linear model, so it is denotationally linear. Moreover, it grasps a limited completeness, namely $\mathcal{S}\ell\text{PCF}$ is sufficient to assure the definability of all the tokens ("prime elements" in domain terms) of the linear model. From this follows a restricted full abstraction result for terms without free stable variables (i.e. variables used for recursion). A more general result was erroneously claimed in [30, Corollary 3]; see Section 3 for more details.

In this paper we propose $\mathcal{S}\ell\text{PCF}_\star$ a language extending $\mathcal{S}\ell\text{PCF}$ by the operator ℓ`et`-ℓ`or`. This operator provides a linear counterpart of the `gor` operator introduced in [29], and increases the non-deterministic expressiveness of the language. Indeed, this extension allows us to gain a **finite definability** result [15], i.e. the definability of all the finite cliques of the considered linear model. In fact, a crucial role in the proof of our finite definability result is played not only by the ℓ`et`-ℓ`or` operator but also by the $\mathcal{S}\ell\text{PCF}$ operator `which?`. In [30], the `which?` operator has been proposed as an example of interesting higher-order linear operator providing runtime information, in order to give a flavor of our research line. However, it was not necessary for the token-definability and the limited full abstraction results. Here, we show how to use `which?` (together with the new ℓ`et-`ℓ`or` operator) in order to reach the finite definability.

By using the finite definability, we prove that $\mathcal{S}\ell$PCF$_\star$ is **fully abstract** with respect to the considered linear model. That is, the *operational equivalence* coincides with the *denotational equivalence*. This result allows us to reason on programs in a compositional way. This is important because even if the operational equivalence is defined for closed ground contexts, since it relies on the operational formal machine evaluating programs, sometimes one wants just to replace a subterm with another one and preserve the equivalence. So, we need to consider also open sub-terms that form our programs. In our case, tackling the equivalence also when terms contain open variables is particularly challenging due to the presence of stable variables, used for recursion. Besides, we prove the coincidence of three different definitions of operational equivalence that make simpler the reasoning on the equivalence between programs by permitting to consider only contexts of a restricted shape. Moreover, the proof of this result uses non-trivial syntactical and denotational arguments that are to our knowledge new and of wider interest.

We remark that $\mathcal{S}\ell$PCF$_\star$ is neither syntactically linear nor operationally linear in a tight sense, albeit its finitary fragment (the set of programs which does not involve recursion) enjoys some syntactical and operational forms of linearity. For instance, it is syntactically linear for slices, and when only slices are considered it can be evaluated without duplicating redexes. Besides, we conclude the paper by giving an operational semantics inducing an efficient evaluation of $\mathcal{S}\ell$PCF$_\star$ terms. This operational semantics traces out and records linear information to drastically prune the infinite branching search tree of the evaluation of $\mathcal{S}\ell$PCF$_\star$.

Outline In Section 2 we introduce in an informal way the contributions that will be technically presented in the rest of the paper. In Section 3 we introduce the background needed to understand the technical results of this paper. In Section 4 we show that $\mathcal{S}\ell$PCF lacks the full abstraction. In Section 5 we introduce the language $\mathcal{S}\ell$PCF$_\star$ and we give some programming examples. In Section 6 we prove the finite definability and the full abstraction for $\mathcal{S}\ell$PCF$_\star$. In Section 7 we show the coincidence of the three operational equivalence introduced. In Section 8 we give an abstract machine for $\mathcal{S}\ell$PCF$_\star$ that traces the linear use of terms and it provides the base for an efficient implementation of our language.

2. Contributions: An Informal Account

In this paper, we propose an extension of the language $\mathcal{S}\ell$PCF introduced in [30]. $\mathcal{S}\ell$PCF is a PCF-like language enriched with the `which?` operator, that is correct for the considered linear model. In particular, linearity is obtained by means of some constraints on clever variable management. $\mathcal{S}\ell$PCF is based on three kinds of variables: ground $\mathtt{x}^\iota$ and stable variables $\mathit{f}^{\sigma\multimap\tau}$, that can be weakened and contracted, and linear ones $\mathtt{f}^{\sigma\multimap\tau}$ that cannot. Ground and linear variables can be λ-abstracted, stable variables cannot. Stable variables can be bound by a dedicated binder (the μ-abstraction) and they are used to define recursive functions. In $\mathcal{S}\ell$PCF, an argument `N` supplied to λ`x.M` is evaluated by using a call-by-value policy in case `x` is ground, a call-by-name policy otherwise. More details can be found in Section 3.2.

The denotational insights

The basic components of the model are *tokens*. A token is a tuple of natural numbers that complies with the structure of types. For instance

$$\begin{array}{c}((\iota \multimap \iota) \multimap \iota) \multimap (\iota \multimap \iota) \multimap \iota \\ (((0\ ,\ 1)\ ,\ 2)\ ,\ (3\ ,\ 4)\ ,\ 5)\end{array}$$

The second row of the formula above describes a token belonging to the coherence space corresponding to the type written in the first row (clearly, ι is the type of natural numbers while $\multimap$ is the linear arrow). $\mathcal{S}\ell$PCF is able to define all the tokens which belong to coherence spaces corresponding to the types [30]. For instance, the following term defines the token written above:

$$\lambda\mathtt{f}.\lambda\mathtt{g}.\ell\mathtt{if}\ \Big(\big(\mathtt{f}\big(\lambda\mathtt{x}.\ell\mathtt{if}\ (\mathtt{x} \doteq \underline{0})\ \underline{1}\ \Omega\big) \doteq \underline{2}\big)\ \mathtt{and}\ (\mathtt{g}\ \underline{3} \doteq \underline{4})\Big)\ \underline{5}\ \Omega\,.$$

To program a token means to verify that each input coincides with the one described by the token, in the example there are two input (i.e. $((0,1),2)$ and $(3,4)$).

The elements of the linear model as usual in coherence spaces are *cliques*, i.e. sets of *coherent* tokens. The coherence relation ensures that cliques describes only *traces* of functions (where the trace is an economic way to describe the graph of a function). In particular, coherence establishes when two tokens can coexists in the trace of a function. Consider a simple clique of a linear function:

$$\left\{\begin{array}{l}((0,0)\ ,\ ((5,7)\ ,\ 0)\ ,\ 0)\\ ((2,0)\ ,\ ((3,9)\ ,\ 1)\ ,\ 1)\\ ((2,1)\ ,\ ((3,9)\ ,\ 1)\ ,\ 2)\end{array}\right\}$$

Above three tokens have two input arguments, respectively of type $\iota \multimap \iota$ and $(\iota \multimap \iota) \multimap \iota$. Coherence ensures that, for each pair of tokens, there exists an input argument allowing to decide what is the unique token being (eventually) involved in the computation. For instance, by applying the first argument to $\underline{2}$ we can distinguish between the second and the third token, in fact the sub-tokens $(2,0)$ and $(2,1)$ are incoherent indeed they cannot coexist in the same function. Likewise, by applying the second argument to $\lambda\mathtt{x}^\iota.\ell\mathtt{if}\ (\mathtt{x} \doteq \underline{5})\ \underline{7}\ (\ell\mathtt{if}\ (\mathtt{x} \doteq \underline{3})\ \underline{9}\ \Omega)$, we can distinguish the first token from both the second and the third. Indeed $((3,9),1)$ and $((5,7),0)$ are incoherent and they cannot coexist in the same function.

These properties are important in order to program linear functions, however, linearity gives no information about how to locate such observations. In particular, when higher-order types are considered this becomes quite tricky, and parallelism is necessary.

Is $\mathcal{S}\ell$PCF able to program (at least) all the finite cliques?

Anticipating, we say immediately that the answer is negative: $\mathcal{S}\ell$PCF allows us to program some finite cliques but not all of them. The extension we propose in this paper however fills this gap. That is, $\mathcal{S}\ell$PCF$_\star$ permits one to program all the finite cliques.

Let us now go in more details. $\mathcal{S}\ell$PCF is Turing-complete. This means that it is able to program all the first order (computable) cliques. For instance denoting with $*$ the multiplication between numerals, the following term

$$\mu\mathit{f}.\lambda\mathtt{x}.\ell\mathtt{if}\ (\mathtt{x} \doteq 0)\ 1\ (\mathtt{x} * (\mathit{f}\ (\mathbf{p}\mathtt{x}^\iota)))$$

defines the clique $\{(n, \mathtt{factorial}(n)) \mid n \in \mathbf{N}\}$. So at the first order, $\mathcal{S}\ell$PCF is able to program not only all the finite cliques but all the computable infinite ones. When higher-order functions are considered, however, the situation becomes more difficult. For instance, if we want to define the following clique

$$\left\{\begin{array}{l}(((0,3)\ ,\ 0)\ ,\ 1)\\ (((1,4)\ ,\ 0)\ ,\ 2)\end{array}\right\}$$

we cannot discriminate the two given tokens just by looking at the result of the evaluation of the argument applied to the term $\mathtt{N}$ — $\lambda\mathtt{x}.\ell\mathtt{if}\ (\mathtt{x} \doteq \underline{0})\ \underline{3}\ (\ell\mathtt{if}\ (\mathtt{x} \doteq \underline{1})\ \underline{4}\ \Omega)$, because it corresponds to $\underline{0}$ for both tokens. In order to discriminate them, we need to grasp some intensional aspect of the above evaluation, more specifically, we need to identify the value passed to N (i.e. $\underline{0}$ in the first token and $\underline{1}$ in the second). Information like this can be retrieved by an appropriate use of the `which?` operator, introduced in [30]. The `which?` operator corresponds to a primitive form of exception handling: it allows to obtain besides the result of an evaluation also the information on what has been used during that evaluation. More examples are in Section 5.1.

The `which?` operator increases the expressivity of the language. However, there are still some finite cliques that cannot be programmed in $\mathcal{S}\ell$PCF. For instance,

$$\left\{ \begin{array}{l} ((0,0),\ (1,0),\ (0,1),\ 0) \\ ((0,1),\ (0,0),\ (1,0),\ 1) \\ ((1,0),\ (0,1),\ (0,0),\ 2) \end{array} \right\} \qquad (1)$$

The reason is that we cannot identify *a priori* which is the observation that should be done. In particular, we are not able to determine which argument we should observe first and what is the value we should supply to it. Suppose we want to realize the program defining the clique in Equation 1, writing a term of the following shape

$$\lambda \mathtt{f}_1.\lambda \mathtt{f}_2.\lambda \mathtt{f}_3.\Big(\lambda \mathtt{x}.\ell\mathtt{if}\ (\mathtt{x} \doteq \underline{0})\ \mathtt{P}_1\ \big(\ell\mathtt{if}\ (\mathtt{x} \doteq \underline{1})\ \mathtt{P}_2\ \mathtt{P}_3\big)\Big)(\mathtt{f}_1\underline{0})$$

This means that we start the observation from the first argument $\mathtt{f}_1$ and we apply $\underline{0}$ to it. This term diverges if we supply as first argument a term defining $(1,0)$ and any other term as second and third argument. However, this behavior can be admitted by the third token. Something similar happens if we start the observation from an other argument and/or if we choose to apply $\underline{1}$ instead of $\underline{0}$ to it. Such a behavior would be not desirable.

To solve this circularity, we need to make available a parallel operator. This kind of parallelism is well known in *stable domains*, where so called Gustave's functions exists [6, 8]. Following [29], we could add a *gustave-or* operator where linearity is carefully forced. That is, a gustave-or typed as follows:

$$\frac{\Gamma \vdash \mathtt{M}_1 : \iota \quad \Gamma \vdash \mathtt{M}_2 : \iota \quad \Gamma \vdash \mathtt{M}_3 : \iota}{\Gamma \vdash \mathtt{Gor}\ (\mathtt{M}_1, \mathtt{M}_2, \mathtt{M}_3) : \iota}$$

with the provision that the basis Γ does not contain linear variables. This operator can then be equipped by the following semantics:

$$\frac{\mathtt{M}_1 \Downarrow \underline{0} \quad \mathtt{M}_2 \Downarrow \underline{\mathtt{n}+1}}{\mathtt{Gor}\ (\mathtt{M}_1, \mathtt{M}_2, \mathtt{M}_3) \Downarrow \underline{\mathtt{n}}} \quad \frac{\mathtt{M}_2 \Downarrow \underline{0} \quad \mathtt{M}_3 \Downarrow \underline{\mathtt{n}+1}}{\mathtt{Gor}\ (\mathtt{M}_1, \mathtt{M}_2, \mathtt{M}_3) \Downarrow \underline{\mathtt{n}}} \quad \frac{\mathtt{M}_3 \Downarrow \underline{0} \quad \mathtt{M}_1 \Downarrow \underline{\mathtt{n}+1}}{\mathtt{Gor}\ (\mathtt{M}_1, \mathtt{M}_2, \mathtt{M}_3) \Downarrow \underline{\mathtt{n}}}$$

Adding it to $\mathcal{S}\ell$PCF however is not sufficient to program the clique defined in Equation 1 (actually, to extend $\mathcal{S}\ell$PCF by `Gor` does not add any linear function!). We need something enabling a limited form of contraction on linear variable to permit parallel observations of the same linear variable on different arguments. One way to do this is by introducing a further control operator, that can be described as a `let`-like operator:

$$\frac{\Gamma \vdash \mathtt{N} : \sigma \multimap \tau \qquad \digamma : \sigma \multimap \tau, \Delta \vdash \mathtt{M} : \iota}{\Gamma, \Delta \vdash \mathtt{let}\ \digamma^{\sigma \multimap \tau} = \mathtt{N}\ \mathtt{in}\ \mathtt{M} : \iota}$$

where the variable $\digamma$ can be weakened and contracted, i.e. it does not respect any occurrence constraint. The operational meaning of this `let`-like operator can be described by the following rule:

$$\frac{[\![\mathtt{P}]\!] = \{a\} \subseteq [\![\mathtt{N}]\!] \qquad \mathtt{M}[\mathtt{P}/\digamma] \Downarrow \underline{\mathtt{n}} \qquad \mathtt{M}[\Omega/\digamma] \Uparrow}{\mathtt{let}\ \digamma^{\sigma \multimap \tau} = \mathtt{N}\ \mathtt{in}\ \mathtt{M} \Downarrow \underline{\mathtt{n}}}$$

Such an operator appears to have the flavor of the co-dereliction of Differential Linear Logic [16]. The idea motivating the above rule is that:

> *Denotational linearity* allow several observations of a *clique*, as long as they are performed on the *same token*.

Following this intuition, the side condition $[\![\mathtt{P}]\!] = \{a\} \subseteq [\![\mathtt{N}]\!]$ says that P is interpreted as the unique token of N that can be so observed several time in evaluating $\mathtt{M}[\mathtt{P}/\digamma]$. The third condition $\mathtt{M}[\Omega/\digamma] \Uparrow$ instead is here just to ensure that the token is actually really used.

A clever combination of the two above operators allows to program the clique described in Equation 1 (such combination will be detailed in Section 5.1). We remark some drawbacks of `let`.

1. Its operational rule given above is not effective, due to the presence of the third condition $\mathtt{M}[\Omega/\digamma] \Uparrow$.
2. It limits the understanding of the program control flow. It can be checked only at run-time that the same token has been observed.

The first drawback can be solved by designing an ad-hoc operational semantics, the second one is more problematic since it could make the understanding of programs really problematic. For these two reasons, we extend $\mathcal{S}\ell$PCF by a single operator, combining together `Gor` and `let`. The ℓ`et`-ℓ`or` (considering only a linear variable `f`) is typed as follows:

$$\frac{\Gamma \vdash \mathtt{N} : \sigma \quad \mathtt{f} : \sigma, \Delta \vdash \mathtt{M}_1 : \iota \quad \mathtt{f} : \sigma, \Delta \vdash \mathtt{M}_2 : \iota \quad \mathtt{f} : \sigma, \Delta \vdash \mathtt{M}_3 : \iota}{\Gamma, \Delta \vdash \underline{\ell\mathtt{et}}\ \mathtt{f}^{\sigma} = \mathtt{N}\ \underline{\mathtt{in}\ell\mathtt{or}}\ \mathtt{M}_1\ \mathtt{M}_2\ \mathtt{M}_3 : \iota}$$

again with the provision that the basis Δ does not contain linear variables. Note that now the $\underline{\ell\mathtt{et}}$-bounded variable `f` is linear, albeit used in three program-branches. The ℓ`et`-ℓ`or` evaluation can now be described using rules as follows:

$$\frac{\mathtt{M}_1[\mathtt{P}/\mathtt{f}] \Downarrow \underline{0} \quad \mathtt{M}_2[\mathtt{P}/\mathtt{f}] \Downarrow \underline{\mathtt{n}+1} \quad [\![\mathtt{P}]\!] = \{a\} \subseteq [\![\mathtt{N}]\!]}{\underline{\ell\mathtt{et}}\ \mathtt{f}^{\sigma \multimap \tau} = \mathtt{N}\ \underline{\mathtt{in}\ell\mathtt{or}}\ \mathtt{M}_1\ \mathtt{M}_2\ \mathtt{M}_3 \Downarrow \underline{\mathtt{n}}}$$

(we give just one rule, the other two are analogous). Thanks to a generalized ℓ`et`-ℓ`or` operator, the resulting language $\mathcal{S}\ell$PCF$_\star$ permits to program all the finite cliques. So, the *full abstraction* follows.

The operational Insights

The full abstraction result mentioned above ensures as usual that a *compositional* theory of program equivalence can be defined. That is, program equivalence is a congruence. Concretely, the full abstraction is proved with respect to a non-standard notion of contextual equivalence $\sim$, named *fix-point equivalence* defined as:

$$\mathtt{M} \sim \mathtt{N} \quad \text{iff} \quad \mathtt{C}[\mathtt{M}[\vec{\mathtt{P}^{\sigma}}/\vec{\digamma^{\sigma}}]] \Downarrow \underline{\mathtt{n}} \iff \mathtt{C}[\mathtt{N}[\vec{\mathtt{P}^{\sigma}}/\vec{\digamma^{\sigma}}]] \Downarrow \underline{\mathtt{n}}$$

where all the $\mathtt{P}_i^{\sigma_i}$ are closed terms. This notion of equivalence makes explicit the fact that for reasoning in a compositional way about programs we need to permit to substitute general terms to stable variables, even if such variables are only used for dealing with recursion. It is exactly to program the $\mathtt{P}_i$ that the definability of all the finite cliques is needed in order to get full abstraction. Indeed, in [30] a full abstraction result for terms without open stable variables was proved. Anyway, the definition of fix-point equivalence seems ad-hoc with respect to the usual notion of contextual equivalence:

$$\mathtt{M} \approx \mathtt{N} \quad \text{iff} \quad \mathtt{C}[\mathtt{M}] \Downarrow \underline{\mathtt{n}} \iff \mathtt{C}[\mathtt{N}] \Downarrow \underline{\mathtt{n}}$$

So, it is natural to consider the following question:

> Do the relations $\sim$ and $\approx$ coincide?

Anticipating, the answer to this question is positive. Although, proving this result is quite technical. Intuitively, the reason is that stable variables can only be μ-abstracted. More precisely, suppose $\mathtt{M} \not\sim \mathtt{N}$ and suppose they have a free stable variable $\digamma$ of type $\sigma_1 \multimap \ldots \multimap \sigma_k \multimap \iota$. We have that there is a context C and a term P such that $\mathtt{C}[\mathtt{M}[\mathtt{P}/\digamma]] \Downarrow \underline{\mathtt{n}}$ and $\mathtt{C}[\mathtt{N}[\mathtt{P}/\digamma]] \not\Downarrow \underline{\mathtt{n}}$. Intuitively, to prove that also $\mathtt{M} \not\approx \mathtt{N}$ holds, one could think to build a (pseudo)-context

$$\mathtt{C}' = \mathtt{C}[(\lambda\digamma.[\,])\mathtt{P}]$$

such that $\mathtt{C'[M]} \Downarrow \underline{\mathtt{n}}$ and $\mathtt{C'[N]} \not\Downarrow \underline{\mathtt{n}}$. Unfortunately, this context cannot be built since the stable variable $\mathcal{F}$ cannot be λ-abstracted but can only μ-abstracted. So, the best that one can hope to get is a context

$$\mathtt{C''} = \mathtt{C}_1[\mu\mathcal{F}.\mathtt{C}_2[\,]]$$

acting similarly to $\mathtt{C'}$. We will show in Section 7 how to build a such context. Here, we propose an example. Suppose that M and N can be distinguished in the empty context [.], by using P (for simplicity, we assume $\mathcal{F}$, P typed $\iota \multimap \iota$, and $[\![\mathtt{P}]\!] = \{(n, m)\}$ with $n \neq 0$). So, we consider a term $\mathtt{P'} : \iota \multimap \iota$ defining the clique $\{(0,0),(n,m)\}$. We can define $\mathtt{C''}$ as

$$\mu\mathcal{F}.\lambda\mathtt{y}.\Big(\Big(\lambda\mathtt{x}^{\iota}.\ell\mathtt{if}\ (\mathtt{x} \doteq \underline{\mathtt{0}})\ [.]\big(\ell\mathtt{if}\ (\mathtt{x} \doteq \underline{\mathtt{m}})\ \underline{\mathtt{m}}\ \Omega\big)\Big)(\mathtt{P'}\ \mathtt{y})\Big)$$

Therefore, this context can be used to build the terms $\mathtt{C''[N]}\underline{\mathtt{0}}$ and $\mathtt{C''[M]}\underline{\mathtt{0}}$. After one recursion step, the terms $\mathtt{N}[\mathtt{C''[N]}/\mathcal{F}]$ and $\mathtt{M}[\mathtt{C''[M]}/\mathcal{F}]$ are obtained. However, in the next recursive step $\mathtt{C''[N]}$ and $\mathtt{C''[M]}$ will behave exactly as P and so the two terms can be distinguished. One can doubt that this construction cannot be always done. However, the properties of the linear model ensure that finite cliques are never *maximal* with respect to the set theoretical inclusion. This for instance does not happen in *stable models* in general. This means that given a finite clique x one can always find a *new coherent token* that can be added to it and that can be used to control the recursion. The proof just generalizes this example.

Besides the equivalence of programs, *linearity* provides also crucial information for the operational evaluation of programs. As instance, the side condition $[\![\mathtt{P}]\!] = \{a\} \subseteq [\![\mathtt{N}]\!]$ in the rule of ℓ**et**-ℓ**or** above assumes the existence of such a P, but it does not give any hints on its search. If we face a concrete implementation of SℓPCF$_\star$ then this could be a problem. An exhaustive search of such a token a is intrinsically inefficient. So, it is natural to consider the following question:

> Is there a reasonable way to drive the evaluation of SℓPCF$_\star$ programs?

The answer to this question as we will show in Section 8 is positive, and again *linearity* comes in our help. It ensures two important properties: first that such a token a exists, and second that it is unique. From these properties we can devise a finer implementation of the language. Consider again the rule

$$\frac{\mathtt{M}_1[\mathtt{P}/\mathtt{f}] \Downarrow \underline{\mathtt{0}} \quad \mathtt{M}_2[\mathtt{P}/\mathtt{f}] \Downarrow \underline{\mathtt{n+1}} \quad [\![\mathtt{P}]\!] = \{a\} \subseteq [\![\mathtt{N}]\!]}{\underline{\ell\mathtt{et}}\ \mathtt{f}^{\sigma\multimap\tau} = \mathtt{N}\ \underline{\mathtt{in}\ell\mathtt{or}}\ \mathtt{M}_1\ \mathtt{M}_2\ \mathtt{M}_3 \Downarrow \underline{\mathtt{n}}}$$

Instead of evaluating $\mathtt{M}_i[\mathtt{P}/\mathtt{f}]$ one can think to evaluate $\mathtt{M}_i$ in an environment e storing the information about variables. So, we associate f to the term N. When the term N is used, we record its observed token a (conveniently encoded by a term P). In particular, the above ℓ**et**-ℓ**or** rule becomes, roughly:

$$\frac{\langle \mathtt{M}_1 | e_0[\mathtt{f} := \mathtt{N}]\rangle \Downarrow_T \langle \underline{\mathtt{0}} | e_1[\mathtt{f} := \mathtt{P}]\rangle \quad \langle \mathtt{M}_2 | e_1[\mathtt{f} := \mathtt{P}]\rangle \Downarrow_T \langle \underline{\mathtt{m}} | e_2\rangle}{\langle \underline{\ell\mathtt{et}}\ \mathtt{f} = \mathtt{N}\ \underline{\mathtt{in}\ell\mathtt{or}}\ \mathtt{M}_1\ \mathtt{M}_2\ \mathtt{M}_3 | e_0\rangle \Downarrow_T \langle \underline{\mathtt{m}} | e_2\rangle}$$

Note that the above reasoning relies on an effective tracing of all evaluated terms. For instance an evaluation of the term $(\lambda\mathtt{x}^{\iota}.\mathtt{M})\mathtt{Q}$ is done using a rule as

$$\frac{\langle \mathtt{Q} | e_0\rangle \Downarrow_T \langle \underline{\mathtt{m}} | e_1\rangle \quad \langle \mathtt{M} | e_1[\mathtt{x} := \underline{\mathtt{m}}]\rangle \Downarrow_T \langle \underline{\mathtt{n}} | e_2\rangle}{\langle \mathtt{fQ} | e_0[\mathtt{f} := \lambda\mathtt{x}^{\iota}.\mathtt{M}^{\iota}]\rangle \Downarrow_T \langle \underline{\mathtt{n}} | e_2[\mathtt{f} := \langle \underline{\mathtt{m}}, \underline{\mathtt{n}}\rangle]\rangle}$$

that traces the information of the used token, i.e. it puts $\langle \underline{\mathtt{m}}, \underline{\mathtt{n}}\rangle$ into the environment. A tracing evaluation of SℓPCF$_\star$ programs will be devised in Section 8. Note that this kind of evaluation can be considered a kind of linear call-by-need evaluation where only one evaluation is done and where further observations are used to check the consistency of the information.

Synopsis

In summary, the key contributions of this paper are:

- The definition of a new linear operator ℓ**et**-ℓ**or** (Definition 13) that permits to establish a bridge between denotational and syntactical linearity through a full abstraction result (Corollary 2).
- A finite definability result (Theorem 6). It gives evidence that SℓPCF$_\star$ is able to program a broader class of linear programs than other linear programming languages.
- The coincidence of different operational equivalences (Corollary 5). This makes simpler the reasoning on the equivalence between linear programs.
- An efficient reduction semantics exploiting linear properties in order to provide a concrete running evaluation of SℓPCF$_\star$ that avoids exhaustive evaluation searches, by tracing and recording explicitly the linear use of subterms.

3. Background

3.1 Coherence Spaces

Coherence spaces are a simple framework for Berry's stable functions [7], developed by Girard [19]. More details are in [20].

A *coherence space* X is a pair $\langle |X|, \frown\!\!\!\!\smile_X\rangle$ where $|X|$ is a set of *tokens* called the *web* of X and $\frown\!\!\!\!\smile_X$ is a reflexive and symmetric relation between tokens of $|X|$ called the *coherence relation* on X. The *strict incoherence* $\smile_X$ is the complementary relation of $\frown\!\!\!\!\smile_X$; the *incoherence* $\asymp_X$ is the union of relations $\smile_X$ and $=$; the *strict coherence* $\frown_X$ is the complementary relation of $\asymp_X$. A *clique* x of X is a subset of $|X|$ containing pairwise coherent tokens. The set of cliques of X is denoted $\mathcal{C}l(X)$, while the set of finite cliques is denoted $\mathcal{C}l_{fin}(X)$.

The basis of our model is the infinite flat domain. Let $\mathbf{N}$ denotes the space of natural numbers, namely $(|\mathbf{N}|, \frown\!\!\!\!\smile_{\mathbf{N}})$ such that $|\mathbf{N}| = \mathbb{N}$ and $m \frown\!\!\!\!\smile_{\mathbf{N}} n$ if and only if $m = n$, for all $m, n \in |\mathbf{N}|$.

Definition 1. *Let X and Y be coherence spaces and $f : \mathcal{C}l(X) \longrightarrow \mathcal{C}l(Y)$ be a monotone function. Then, f is* linear *whenever $\forall x \in \mathcal{C}l(X), \forall b \in f(x)\ \exists! a \in x$ s.t. $b \in f(\{a\})$.*

Linear functions can be represented as cliques.

Definition 2. *Let X and Y be coherence spaces. $X \multimap Y$ is the coherence space having $|X \multimap Y| = |X| \times |Y|$ as web, while $(a, b) \frown_{X\multimap Y} (a', b')$ iff $a \frown\!\!\!\!\smile_X a'$ implies $b \frown_Y b'$.*

The *trace* of a linear function $f : \mathcal{C}l(X) \to \mathcal{C}l(Y)$ is $\mathcal{T}r(f) = \{(a, b) \mid a \in |X|, b \in f(\{a\})\}$. Given $t \in \mathcal{C}l(X \multimap Y)$ and $x \in \mathcal{C}l(X)$, let us define the map $\mathcal{F}(t) : \mathcal{C}l(X) \to \mathcal{C}l(Y)$ as

$$\mathcal{F}(t)(x) = \{b \in |Y| \mid \exists a \in x, (a, b) \in t\} \tag{2}$$

Lemma 1. *If $f : \mathcal{C}l(X) \to \mathcal{C}l(Y)$ is a linear function then $\mathcal{T}r(f) \in \mathcal{C}l(X \multimap Y)$. If $t \in \mathcal{C}l(X \multimap Y)$ then $\mathcal{F}(t) : \mathcal{C}l(X) \to \mathcal{C}l(Y)$ is a linear function.*

Definition 3 (Linear Model). *The* Linear Model $\mathcal{L}$ *is the type structure generated by the coherence space* $\mathbf{N}$ *and the arrow* $\multimap$.

3.2 The language SℓPCF

SℓPCF has been introduced in [17, 30] to be the syntactical counterpart of the above mentioned linear model.

Definition 4. *The set* $\mathbb{T}$ *of* linear types *is defined by the grammar:* $\sigma, \tau \ ::= \ \iota \mid \sigma \multimap \tau$ *, where ι is the only* ground *type.*

For the sake of clearness we introduce three kinds of variables, in order to remark their different explicit use.

Definition 5. *Let* Var^{σ} *be numerable sets of variables of type σ. Let* SVar^{σ} $(\sigma \neq \iota)$ *be numerable sets of variables disjoint from*

$$\frac{}{\vdash \mathbf{0} : \iota}\,(z) \quad \frac{}{\vdash \mathbf{s} : \iota \multimap \iota}\,(s) \quad \frac{}{\vdash \mathbf{p} : \iota \multimap \iota}\,(p) \quad \frac{}{\varkappa^{\sigma} \vdash \varkappa : \sigma}\,(v) \quad \frac{}{\vdash \texttt{which?} : ((\iota \multimap \iota) \multimap \iota) \multimap \iota}\,(w)$$

$$\frac{\Gamma \vdash \mathtt{M} : \tau}{\Gamma, \mathtt{x}^{\iota} \vdash \mathtt{M} : \tau}\,(gw) \quad \frac{\Gamma, \mathtt{x_1}^{\iota}, \mathtt{x_2}^{\iota} \vdash \mathtt{M} : \tau}{\Gamma, \mathtt{x}^{\iota} \vdash \mathtt{M}[\mathtt{x}/\mathtt{x_1}, \mathtt{x_2}] : \tau}\,(gc) \quad \frac{\Gamma, \mathtt{x}^{\sigma} \vdash \mathtt{M} : \tau}{\Gamma \vdash \lambda \mathtt{x}^{\sigma}.\mathtt{M} : \sigma \multimap \tau}\,(\lambda) \quad \frac{\Gamma \cap \Delta = \emptyset \quad \Gamma \vdash \mathtt{M} : \iota \quad \Delta \vdash \mathtt{L} : \iota \quad \Delta \vdash \mathtt{R} : \iota}{\Gamma, \Delta \vdash \ell\texttt{if}\ \mathtt{M}\ \mathtt{L}\ \mathtt{R} : \iota}\,(lif)$$

$$\frac{\Gamma \vdash \mathtt{M} : \tau}{\Gamma, \digamma^{\sigma} \vdash \mathtt{M} : \tau}\,(sw) \quad \frac{\Gamma, \digamma_1^{\sigma}, \digamma_2^{\sigma} \vdash \mathtt{M} : \tau}{\Gamma, \digamma^{\sigma} \vdash \mathtt{M}[\digamma/\digamma_1, \digamma_2] : \tau}\,(sc) \quad \frac{\Gamma, \digamma^{\sigma} \vdash \mathtt{M} : \sigma \quad \Gamma \restriction \ell = \emptyset}{\Gamma \vdash \mu \digamma.\mathtt{M} : \sigma}\,(\mu) \quad \frac{\Gamma \cap \Delta = \emptyset \quad \Gamma \vdash \mathtt{M} : \sigma \multimap \tau \quad \Delta \vdash \mathtt{N} : \sigma}{\Gamma, \Delta \vdash \mathtt{MN} : \tau}\,(ap)$$

$$\frac{}{\mathbf{0} \Downarrow \mathbf{0}}\,(0) \quad \frac{\mathtt{M} \Downarrow \underline{\mathtt{n}}}{\mathbf{s}\mathtt{M} \Downarrow \mathbf{s}\underline{\mathtt{n}}}\,(s) \quad \frac{\mathtt{M} \Downarrow \mathbf{s}\underline{\mathtt{n}}}{\mathbf{p}\mathtt{M} \Downarrow \underline{\mathtt{n}}}\,(p) \quad \frac{\mathtt{M} \Downarrow \mathbf{0} \quad \mathtt{L} \Downarrow \underline{\mathtt{m}}}{\ell\texttt{if}\ \mathtt{M}\ \mathtt{L}\ \mathtt{R} \Downarrow \underline{\mathtt{m}}}\,(ifl) \quad \frac{\mathtt{M} \Downarrow \mathbf{s}(\underline{\mathtt{n}}) \quad \mathtt{R} \Downarrow \underline{\mathtt{m}}}{\ell\texttt{if}\ \mathtt{M}\ \mathtt{L}\ \mathtt{R} \Downarrow \underline{\mathtt{m}}}\,(ifr) \quad \frac{\mathtt{M}[\mathtt{N}/\mathtt{f}]\mathtt{P}_1 \cdots \mathtt{P}_i \Downarrow \underline{\mathtt{v}}}{(\lambda \mathtt{f}^{\sigma \multimap \tau}.\mathtt{M})\mathtt{N}\mathtt{P}_1 \cdots \mathtt{P}_i \Downarrow \underline{\mathtt{v}}}\,(\lambda^{\multimap})$$

$$\frac{\mathtt{M}[\mu \digamma.\mathtt{M}/\digamma]\mathtt{P}_1 \cdots \mathtt{P}_i \Downarrow \underline{\mathtt{v}}}{(\mu \digamma.\mathtt{M})\mathtt{P}_1 \cdots \mathtt{P}_i \Downarrow \underline{\mathtt{v}}}\,(\mu) \quad \frac{\mathtt{N} \Downarrow \underline{\mathtt{m}} \quad \mathtt{M}[\underline{\mathtt{m}}/\mathtt{x}]\mathtt{P}_1 \cdots \mathtt{P}_i \Downarrow \underline{\mathtt{v}}}{(\lambda \mathtt{x}^{\iota}.\mathtt{M})\mathtt{N}\mathtt{P}_1 \cdots \mathtt{P}_i \Downarrow \underline{\mathtt{v}}}\,(\lambda^{\iota}) \quad \frac{\mathtt{M}(\lambda \mathtt{x}^{\iota}.\ell\texttt{if}(\overbrace{\mathbf{p} \ldots \mathbf{p}}^{\underline{\mathtt{k}}}\ \mathtt{x})\ \underline{\mathtt{k}}\ (\mathbf{p}\mathbf{0})) \Downarrow \underline{\mathtt{n}}}{\texttt{which?}\,\mathtt{M}^{(\iota \multimap \iota) \multimap \iota} \Downarrow \lceil \underline{\mathtt{n}}, \underline{\mathtt{k}} \rceil}\,(w)$$

$$[\![\mathbf{0}^{\iota}]\!]\rho = \{0\} \quad [\![\mathbf{s}^{\iota \multimap \iota}]\!]\rho = \{(n, n+1) \mid n \in \mathbb{N}\} \quad [\![\mathbf{p}^{\iota \multimap \iota}]\!]\rho = \{(0,0)\} \cup \{(n, n-1) \mid n \in \mathbb{N} \wedge n > 0\} \quad [\![\mathtt{x}^{\sigma}]\!]\rho = \{\rho(\mathtt{x}^{\sigma})\}$$

$$[\![\digamma^{\sigma}]\!]\rho = \rho(\digamma^{\sigma}) \quad [\![\mathtt{M}^{\sigma \multimap \tau}\mathtt{N}^{\sigma}]\!]\rho = \mathcal{F}([\![\mathtt{M}]\!]\rho)[\![\mathtt{N}]\!]\rho \quad [\![\lambda \mathtt{x}^{\sigma}.\mathtt{M}^{\tau}]\!]\rho = \{(a_0, b) \in |[\![\sigma \multimap \tau]\!]| \mid b \in [\![\mathtt{M}]\!]\rho[\mathtt{x}^{\sigma} := a_0]\}$$

$$[\![(\ell\texttt{if}\ \mathtt{M}^{\iota}\ \mathtt{N}^{\iota}\ \mathtt{L}^{\iota})^{\iota}]\!]\rho = \{n \in \mathbb{N} \mid [\![\mathtt{M}^{\iota}]\!]\rho = \{0\} \wedge [\![\mathtt{N}^{\iota}]\!]\rho = \{n\}\} \cup \{n \in \mathbb{N} \mid [\![\mathtt{M}^{\iota}]\!]\rho = \{m+1\} \wedge [\![\mathtt{L}^{\iota}]\!]\rho = \{n\}, m \in \mathbb{N}\}$$

$$[\![(\mu \digamma^{\sigma}.\mathtt{M}^{\sigma})^{\sigma}]\!]\rho = \texttt{fix}(\lambda x \in \mathcal{C}l([\![\sigma]\!]).\textstyle\bigcup_{x' \subseteq_{fin} x}[\![\mathtt{M}]\!]\rho[\digamma := x']) \quad [\![\texttt{which?}]\!]\rho = \{(((n,n),r), \lceil r, n \rceil) \mid n, r \in \mathbb{N}\}$$

Table 1. (a) Type system, (b) operational semantics and (c) linear interpretation for SℓPCF

Var^{σ}. *Variables in* Var^{ι} *are named* ground variables. *Variables in* $\ell\mathrm{Var} = \bigcup_{\sigma, \tau \in \mathbb{T}} \mathrm{Var}^{\sigma \multimap \tau}$ *are named* linear variables. *Variables in* $\mathbb{S}\mathrm{Var} = \bigcup_{\sigma \neq \iota} \mathbb{S}\mathrm{Var}^{\sigma}$ *are named* stable variables.

Note that there are no stable variables of type ι. Latin letters $\mathtt{x}^{\sigma}, \mathtt{y}^{\sigma}, \mathtt{f}^{\sigma}, \ldots$ denote variables in Var^{σ}. We use types to explicitly distinguish between ground, e.g. $\mathtt{x}^{\iota}$, and linear variables, e.g. $\mathtt{x}^{\sigma \multimap \tau}$. Moreover, $\digamma_0^{\sigma}, \digamma_1^{\sigma}, \digamma_2^{\sigma}, \ldots$ denote stable variables. Last, $\varkappa$ is a wild-card for all the variables.

We define terms (Definition 7) as the pre-terms (Definition 6) that can be typed using the type system in Table 1.a.

Definition 6. Pre-terms *are defined by the grammar:*

$$\mathtt{M} ::= \varkappa^{\tau} \mid \mathbf{0} \mid \mathbf{s} \mid \mathbf{p} \mid \ell\texttt{if}\ \mathtt{M}\ \mathtt{M}\ \mathtt{M} \mid (\mathtt{MM}) \mid (\lambda \mathtt{x}^{\sigma}.\mathtt{M}) \mid \mu \digamma.\mathtt{M} \mid \texttt{which?}$$

We write $\underline{\mathtt{n}}$ for $\mathbf{s}(\cdots(\mathbf{s}\mathbf{0})\cdots)$ where $\mathbf{s}$ is applied n-times to $\mathbf{0}$, and we denote $\mathcal{N} = \{\mathbf{0}, \ldots, \underline{\mathtt{n}}, \ldots\}$ the set of *numerals*.

We consider typing judgments of the shape $\Gamma \vdash \mathtt{M} : \sigma$ where $\mathtt{M}$ is a pre-term, σ is a linear type and Γ is a *basis*, that is a finite list of variables in Var, where each variable appears at most once. We denote $\Gamma \restriction \mathbb{S}$ (resp $\Gamma \restriction \iota$, $\Gamma \restriction \ell$) the restriction of the basis Γ containing only variables in $\mathbb{S}\mathrm{Var}$ (resp. in Var^{ι}, $\ell\mathrm{Var}$). We denote Γ, Δ and $\Gamma \cap \Delta$ the union and the intersection of two basis respectively. We can now define SℓPCF terms.

Definition 7. *The* terms *of* SℓPCF *are the pre-terms typable by using the type system in Table 1.a.*

Sometimes, we write $\mathtt{M}^{\sigma}$ when, for some Γ, we have $\Gamma \vdash \mathtt{M} : \sigma$. Free variables of any kind (FV), free linear variables (ℓFV), free stable variables ($\mathbb{S}$FV), closed and open terms are defined as expected. We denote $\mathcal{P} = \{\mathtt{M}^{\iota} \in \mathrm{S\ell PCF} \mid \mathrm{FV}(\mathtt{M}^{\iota}) = \emptyset\}$ the set of *programs*. As usual, $\mathtt{M}[\mathtt{N}/\varkappa]$ denotes the capture-free substitution of all free occurrences of $\varkappa$ in $\mathtt{M}$ by $\mathtt{N}$.

Lemma 2 (Substitution). *Let* $\mathtt{M}^{\tau}, \mathtt{N}^{\sigma} \in \mathrm{S\ell PCF}$.

- *If* $\ell\mathrm{FV}(\mathtt{M}^{\tau}) \cap \ell\mathrm{FV}(\mathtt{N}^{\sigma}) = \emptyset$ *and* $\mathtt{x}^{\sigma} \in \ell\mathrm{Var}$ *then* $\mathtt{M}^{\tau}[\mathtt{N}^{\sigma}/\mathtt{x}^{\sigma}] \in \mathrm{S\ell PCF}$.
- *If* $\ell\mathrm{FV}(\mathtt{N}^{\tau}) = \emptyset$ *then* $\mathtt{M}^{\tau}[\mathtt{N}^{\sigma}/\digamma^{\sigma}] \in \mathrm{S\ell PCF}$.
- *If* $\ell\mathrm{FV}(\mathtt{N}^{\tau}) = \emptyset$ *then* $\mathtt{M}[\mathtt{N}/\varkappa_1, \ldots, \mathtt{N}/\varkappa_n] \in \mathrm{S\ell PCF}$.

Pairing (i.e. mapping pair of numerals on one numeral) and *projections function* will be used everywhere in the paper. We will denote with $\lceil \underline{\mathtt{n}}, \underline{\mathtt{m}} \rceil$ the numeral $\underline{\mathtt{k}}$ encoding the ordered pair of $\underline{\mathtt{n}}$ and $\underline{\mathtt{m}}$ and we write $\pi_1(\underline{\mathtt{k}})$ for the numeral $\underline{\mathtt{n}}$ and $\pi_2(\underline{\mathtt{k}})$ for the numeral $\underline{\mathtt{m}}$. SℓPCF-terms defining them can be found in [30]. We avoided to explicitly use the product-types in syntax and semantics just for sake of simplicity, albeit a such extension can be pursued.

Definition 8. *The* evaluation relation $\Downarrow \subseteq \mathcal{P} \times \mathcal{N}$ *is the smallest relation inductively satisfying the rules of Table 1.b. If there exists a numeral* $\underline{\mathtt{n}}$ *such that* $\mathtt{M} \Downarrow \underline{\mathtt{n}}$ *then we say that* $\mathtt{M}$ converges, *and we write* $\mathtt{M} \Downarrow$, *otherwise we say that it* diverges, *and we write* $\mathtt{M} \Uparrow$.

Remark that $\mathbf{p}$ is a partial operator, namely $\mathbf{p}\,\mathbf{0}$ diverges. Moreover, note that as stressed in Section 2, the result of the evaluation of the operator $\texttt{which?}$ applied to a term $\mathtt{M}$ consists of a pair $\lceil \underline{\mathtt{n}}, \underline{\mathtt{k}} \rceil$ where $\underline{\mathtt{n}}$ is the result of the evaluation of $\mathtt{M}(\lambda \mathtt{x}^{\iota}.\mathtt{x})$ while $\underline{\mathtt{k}}$ is the unique (thanks to linearity) numeral that $\mathtt{M}$ gives as argument to $\lambda \mathtt{x}^{\iota}.\mathtt{x}$.

The set of σ-*context* Ctx_{σ} is defined as:

$$\begin{aligned}\mathtt{C}[\sigma] \quad ::= \; & [\sigma] \mid \varkappa^{\tau} \mid \mathbf{0} \mid \mathbf{s} \mid \mathbf{p} \mid \ell\texttt{if}\ \mathtt{C}[\sigma]\ \mathtt{C}[\sigma]\ \mathtt{C}[\sigma] \\ & \mid \texttt{which?} \mid (\mathtt{C}[\sigma]\mathtt{C}[\sigma]) \mid (\lambda \mathtt{x}^{\sigma}.\mathtt{C}[\sigma]) \mid \mu \digamma.\mathtt{C}[\sigma]\end{aligned}$$

$\mathtt{C}[\mathtt{N}^{\sigma}]$ denotes the result obtained by replacing all the occurrences of $[\sigma]$ in the context $\mathtt{C}[\sigma]$ by the term $\mathtt{N}^{\sigma}$ and by allowing the capture of its free variables.

Definition 9 (Standard Operational Equivalence). *Let* $\mathtt{M}^{\sigma}, \mathtt{N}^{\sigma} \in$ SℓPCF.

- $\mathtt{M} \lessapprox_{\sigma} \mathtt{N}$ *whenever, for all* $\mathtt{C}[\sigma]$ *s.t.* $\mathtt{C}[\mathtt{M}], \mathtt{C}[\mathtt{N}] \in \mathcal{P}$, *if* $\mathtt{C}[\mathtt{M}] \Downarrow \underline{\mathtt{n}}$ *then* $\mathtt{C}[\mathtt{N}] \Downarrow \underline{\mathtt{n}}$.
- $\mathtt{M} \approx_{\sigma} \mathtt{N}$ *if and only if* $\mathtt{M} \lessapprox_{\sigma} \mathtt{N}$ *and* $\mathtt{N} \lessapprox_{\sigma} \mathtt{M}$.

We are interested in a language for which the linear model $\mathcal{L}$ is fully abstract under a *standard interpretation* $[\![-]\!]$, i.e. ground types are interpreted on flat posets (see [33]). The standard interpretation is such that $[\![\iota]\!] = \mathbf{N}$ and $[\![\sigma \multimap \tau]\!] = [\![\sigma]\!] \multimap [\![\tau]\!]$.

An *environment* $\rho \in \mathrm{Env}$ is a partial function mapping a variable $\mathtt{x}^{\sigma}$ in a token $a \in |[\![\sigma]\!]|$ and a stable variable $\digamma^{\sigma}$ in a finite clique $x \in \mathcal{C}l_{fin}([\![\sigma]\!])$. The set of environments is denoted by Env. Let $\vec{a}$ be a sequence of tokens of a coherence space, let

$\vec{x}$ be a sequence of non-stable variables of the same length of $\vec{a}$; $\rho[\vec{x} := \vec{a}]$ is the environment such that $\rho[\vec{x} := \vec{a}](x') = a_i$ in case x' is the i-th element of $\vec{x}$, otherwise $\rho[\vec{x} := \vec{a}](x') = \rho(x')$. If $\vec{x}$ is a sequence of finite cliques and $\vec{\digamma}$ is a sequence of stable variables of the same length then $\rho[\vec{\digamma} := \vec{x}]$ is defined likewise.

Definition 10. *Let* $M^\sigma, N^\sigma \in \mathcal{S}\ell\mathrm{PCF}$ *and* $\rho \in \mathrm{Env}$. *The* linear interpretation $[\![M^\sigma]\!] : \mathrm{Env} \to \mathcal{C}l([\![\sigma]\!])$ *is defined in Table 1.c using* $\mathcal{F}$ *as defined in* Equation 2 *and* $\mathtt{fix}$ *which is the least fix point operator.*

3.3 Stable Closed Full Abstraction

We recall the main properties of $\mathcal{S}\ell\mathrm{PCF}$ [30, 32]. First, the linear interpretation is adequate and correct.

Theorem 1 ([30]). *Let* $M^\iota \in \mathcal{P}$ *and* $N^\sigma, L^\sigma \in \mathcal{S}\ell\mathrm{PCF}$.

Adequacy: $M^\iota \Downarrow \underline{n} \iff [\![M^\iota]\!] = [\![\underline{n}]\!]$.
Correctness: $[\![N^\sigma]\!] = [\![L^\sigma]\!] \Rightarrow N \approx^\sigma L$

In $\mathcal{S}\ell\mathrm{PCF}$ all the tokens of the linear model $\mathcal{L}$ can be defined. Moreover, as shown in [30], this can be done without using the `which?` operator.

Theorem 2 (Token Definability).
If $u \in |[\![\sigma]\!]|$ *then there exists a closed* $M^\sigma \in \mathcal{S}\ell\mathrm{PCF}$ *such that* $[\![M]\!] = \{u\}$.

Token definability permits to define the separating terms used in the next lemma. This in contrast to what happens in [29, 33] where a finite definability is needed.

Lemma 3 (Separability). *Let* $\sigma \in \mathbb{T}$. *For all distinct* $f, g \in \mathcal{C}l([\![\sigma]\!])$ *there exists a closed term* $P^{\sigma \multimap \iota}$ *such that* $\mathcal{F}([\![P]\!])(f) \neq \mathcal{F}([\![P]\!])(g)$.

From this follows that full abstraction holds for all the terms that do not contain free *stable* variables. We stress that such a result was erroneously claimed in [30] to be of more generality. Indeed, we show in the next section that the unrestricted full abstraction fails.

Theorem 3 (Stable Closed Completeness). *Let* $M^\sigma, N^\sigma \in \mathcal{S}\ell\mathrm{PCF}$ *and* $\mathcal{S}\mathrm{FV}(M^\sigma) = \mathcal{S}\mathrm{FV}(N^\sigma) = \emptyset$. *Then:*

$$M \approx_\sigma N \Rightarrow [\![M]\!] = [\![N]\!]$$

Proof. Let us prove the contrapositive. Let us assume $[\![M]\!]\rho \neq [\![N]\!]\rho$, for an environment ρ. By Separability Lemma 3, there exists a closed $P^{\sigma\multimap\iota}$ such that $\mathcal{F}([\![P]\!]\rho)([\![M]\!]\rho) = n_1 \neq \mathcal{F}([\![P]\!])([\![N]\!]\rho)$. Moreover, by Token Definability Theorem 2 we can build a context $C[^\iota]$ such that $[\![P\ M]\!]\rho = [\![C[P\ M]]\!]\emptyset$ and $[\![P\ N]\!]\rho = [\![C[P\ N]]\!]\emptyset$ where $\emptyset$ is the empty environment. So, by adequacy we have $(C[P\ M]) \Downarrow \underline{n_1}$ and $(C[P\ N]) \not\Downarrow \underline{n_1}$. So $M \not\approx_\sigma N$. □

Note that, in the above proof the Token Definability Theorem 2 allows us to build the context $C[^\iota]$ only because we have assumed that the two terms have no stable variables. In the next section, we prove that in order to relax this constraint the language must to be extended.

Corollary 1 (Stable Closed Full Abstraction). *Let* $M^\sigma, N^\sigma \in \mathcal{S}\ell\mathrm{PCF}$ *and* $\mathcal{S}\mathrm{FV}(M^\sigma) = \mathcal{S}\mathrm{FV}(N^\sigma) = \emptyset$. *Then:*

$$M \approx_\sigma N \iff [\![M]\!] = [\![N]\!]$$

4. Lack of Full abstraction

$\mathcal{S}\ell\mathrm{PCF}$ does not enjoy the unrestricted full abstraction. In this section, we show that the Corollary 1 cannot be extended to terms having free occurrences of stable variables, since they are interpreted in finite cliques. We prove that $\mathcal{S}\ell\mathrm{PCF}$ is not able to define all finite cliques of the model by presenting a linear function that is not definable in $\mathcal{S}\ell\mathrm{PCF}$, since it is not strongly stable [12]. We use this function to define two terms having free occurrences of stable variables which are operationally equivalent, albeit they are interpreted into two different linear functions.

4.1 Token enumeration

First, we introduce some abbreviations that are useful in order to simplify the rest of the paper. We use $(M\ \mathtt{and}\ N)$ to abbreviate $(\ell\mathtt{if}\ M\ (\ell\mathtt{if}\ N\ \underline{0}\ \underline{1})\ \underline{1})$. The equivalence among numerals, denoted $\doteq$ used in infix notation, is encoded as $\mu\digamma^{\iota\multimap\iota\multimap\iota}.\lambda x^\iota.\lambda y^\iota.\ell\mathtt{if}\ x\ (\ell\mathtt{if}\ y\ \underline{0}\ \underline{1})\ (\ell\mathtt{if}\ y\ \underline{1}\ (\digamma\,(\mathbf{p}x)(\mathbf{p}y)))$. Moreover, we define a family of diverging terms by induction on types, $\Omega^\iota = \mathbf{p}\underline{0}$ and, if $\sigma_0 = \mu_1 \multimap \ldots \multimap \mu_m \multimap \iota$ for some $m \in \mathbb{N}$ then $\Omega^{\sigma_0 \multimap \ldots \multimap \sigma_n \multimap \iota}$ is

$$\lambda x_0^{\sigma_0} \ldots x_n^{\sigma_n}.\ell\mathtt{if}(\Omega^\tau x_1^{\sigma_1} \ldots x_n^{\sigma_n})(x_0\Omega^{\mu_1} \ldots \Omega^{\mu_m})(x_0\Omega^{\mu_1} \ldots \Omega^{\mu_m})$$

Clearly, $\Omega^{\sigma_1 \multimap \ldots \sigma_n \multimap \iota} M_1^{\sigma_1} \ldots M_n^{\sigma_n} \Uparrow$ for each $M_1^{\sigma_1}, \ldots, M_n^{\sigma_n}$.

We can define an encoding $(\!|-|\!) : |[\![\sigma]\!]| \to \mathbb{N}$ from tokens of the coherence space $[\![\sigma]\!]$ to natural numbers as:

- $(\!|n|\!) = n$ if $\sigma = \iota$;
- $(\!|(a_1, a_2)|\!) = \lceil (\!|a_1|\!), (\!|a_2|\!) \rceil$ if $\sigma = \tau_1 \multimap \tau_2$.

It provides an enumeration of the tokens of our model. Remark that the Theorem 2 implies that there is a family of terms $\mathtt{Sgl}_n^\sigma : \sigma$ (short for *singleton*) being an enumeration of terms that can be interpreted on (single) tokens. Concretely, we define $\mathtt{Sgl}_n^\sigma : \sigma$ by mutual induction with terms $\mathtt{Chk}_n^{(\sigma)} : \sigma \multimap \iota$ that checks whether a token is included in the operational behavior of a term typed σ.

Definition 11. *The terms* $\mathtt{Sgl}_n^\sigma : \sigma$ *and* $\mathtt{Chk}_n^{(\sigma)} : \sigma \multimap \iota$ *are defined by mutual induction on* σ.
If $\sigma = \iota$, $\mathtt{Sgl}_n^\iota = \underline{n}$ *and* $\mathtt{Chk}_n^{(\iota)} = \lambda y^\iota.\ell\mathtt{if}\ (\underline{n} \doteq y)\ \underline{0}\ \Omega^\iota$.
If $\sigma = \sigma_1 \multimap \sigma_2$, *let* $\sigma_2 = \tau_1 \multimap \ldots \multimap \tau_k \multimap \iota$ *for some* k, *without loss of generality, then* $\mathtt{Sgl}_n^\sigma$ *is*

$$\lambda f^{\sigma_1}\lambda g_1^{\tau_1} \ldots \lambda g_k^{\tau_k}.\ell\mathtt{if}\ (\mathtt{Chk}_{\pi_1(n)}^{(\sigma_1)} f)(\mathtt{Sgl}_{\pi_2(n)}^{\sigma_2} g_1 \ldots g_k)(\Omega^{\sigma_2} g_1 \ldots g_k)$$

and $\mathtt{Chk}_n^{(\sigma)}$ *is* $\lambda f^\sigma.\ell\mathtt{if}\ (\mathtt{Chk}_{\pi_2(n)}^{(\sigma_2)}(f\ \mathtt{Sgl}_{\pi_1(n)}^{(\sigma_1)}))\ \underline{0}\ \Omega^\iota$.

In $\mathtt{Chk}_n^{(\sigma)}$ we use (σ) as a short for $\sigma \multimap \iota$. As an instance, if $\underline{n} = \lceil \underline{n_1}, \underline{n_2} \rceil$ then the term $\mathtt{Sgl}_n^{\iota\multimap\iota}$ is operationally equivalent to the term $\lambda x^\iota.\ell\mathtt{if}\ (x \doteq \underline{n_1})\ \underline{n_2}\ \Omega^\iota$, while the term $\mathtt{Chk}_n^{(\iota\multimap\iota)}$ is operationally equivalent to the term $\lambda f^{\iota\multimap\iota}\ell\mathtt{if}\ (f\ \underline{n_1} \doteq \underline{n_2})\ \underline{0}\ \Omega^\iota$.

Lemma 4. *Let us fix a type* σ. *If* $a \in |[\![\sigma]\!]|$ *and* $n = (\!|a|\!)$, *then:*

1. $[\![\mathtt{Sgl}_n^{(\sigma)}]\!]\rho = \{a\}$, *for all* ρ;
2. *if* $[\![\mathtt{Chk}_n^{(\sigma)}\ N]\!]\rho = [\![\underline{0}]\!]\rho$ *then* $a \in [\![N]\!]\rho$, *for all* ρ.

4.2 Fix-point operational equivalence

In order to simplify the reasoning about programs, we introduce a non-standard notion of operational equivalence.

Definition 12. *Let assume* M^σ, N^σ *be terms of* $\mathcal{S}\ell\mathrm{PCF}$, *such that* $\mathcal{S}\mathrm{FV}(M), \mathcal{S}\mathrm{FV}(N) \subseteq \{\digamma_1^{\sigma_1}, \ldots, \digamma_n^{\sigma_n}\}$.

- $M \lesssim_\sigma N$ *whenever, for all* $P_1^{\sigma_1}, \ldots P_n^{\sigma_n}$, *for all* $C[\sigma]$ *s.t.* $C[M[P_1/\digamma_1, \ldots, P_n/\digamma_n]], C[N[P_1/\digamma_1, \ldots, P_n/\digamma_n]] \in \mathcal{P}$ *if* $C[M[P_1/\digamma_1, \ldots, P_n/\digamma_n]] \Downarrow \underline{n} \Rightarrow C[N[P_1/\digamma_1, \ldots, P_n/\digamma_n]] \Downarrow \underline{n}$.
- $M \sim_\sigma N$ *if and only if* $M \lesssim_\sigma N$ *and* $N \lesssim_\sigma M$

It is easy to verify that $\lesssim_\sigma$ is a preorder and $\sim_\sigma$ is an equivalence. Note that the comparison between the fix-point operational equivalence and the standard one is not immediate. Indeed, proving that the two coincide corresponds to prove that $\sim_\sigma$ is also a *congruence*. For instance, let us assume that both M^ι, N^ι contain just one free variable $\digamma^\sigma$. If $M \not\sim_\sigma N$ then it is not easy to build contexts $C[\sigma]$ and $\mu\digamma.C'[\sigma]$ (depending from the common substitution to $\digamma$) such that $C[\mu\digamma.C'[M]] \Downarrow$ and $C[\mu\digamma.C'[N]] \not\Downarrow$, i.e. $M \not\approx_\sigma N$.

The standard interpretation is correct with respect to the fix-point operational equivalence too.

Proposition 1. *Let* $\mathtt{M}^\sigma, \mathtt{N}^\sigma \in \mathcal{S}\ell\mathrm{PCF}$. $[\![\mathtt{M}]\!] = [\![\mathtt{N}]\!] \Rightarrow \mathtt{M} \sim^\sigma \mathtt{N}$.

For clarity, we anticipate that the fix-point equivalence coincide with the standard contextual equivalence (see Section 7).

4.3 Full Abstraction Counterexample

We use the second-order *gustave-or* operator $\mathtt{G\overset{2}{o}r}$: $(\iota \multimap \iota) \multimap (\iota \multimap \iota) \multimap (\iota \multimap \iota) \multimap \iota$, introduced in [30], and equipped with the following evaluation.

$$\frac{\mathtt{P}_0\underline{0} \Downarrow \underline{0} \quad \mathtt{P}_1\underline{1} \Downarrow \underline{0} \quad \mathtt{P}_2\underline{0} \Downarrow \underline{1}}{\mathtt{G\overset{2}{o}r}^{\mathtt{L}}\ \mathtt{P}_0\mathtt{P}_1\mathtt{P}_2 \Downarrow \underline{0}}\ (\mathtt{G}_0) \qquad \frac{\mathtt{P}_0\underline{0} \Downarrow \underline{1} \quad \mathtt{P}_1\underline{0} \Downarrow \underline{0} \quad \mathtt{P}_2\underline{1} \Downarrow \underline{0}}{\mathtt{G\overset{2}{o}r}^{\mathtt{L}}\ \mathtt{P}_0\mathtt{P}_1\mathtt{P}_2 \Downarrow \underline{1}}\ (\mathtt{G}_1)$$

$$\frac{\mathtt{P}_0\underline{1} \Downarrow \underline{0} \quad \mathtt{P}_1\underline{0} \Downarrow \underline{1} \quad \mathtt{P}_2\underline{0} \Downarrow \underline{0}}{\mathtt{G\overset{2}{o}r}^{\mathtt{L}}\ \mathtt{P}_0\mathtt{P}_1\mathtt{P}_2 \Downarrow \underline{2}}\ (\mathtt{G}_2) \qquad \frac{\mathtt{P}_0\underline{1} \Downarrow \underline{1} \quad \mathtt{P}_1\underline{1} \Downarrow \underline{1} \quad \mathtt{P}_2\underline{1} \Downarrow \underline{1}}{\mathtt{G\overset{2}{o}r}^{\mathtt{L}}\ \mathtt{P}_0\mathtt{P}_1\mathtt{P}_2 \Downarrow \underline{3}}\ (\mathtt{G}_3)$$

The operator $\mathtt{G\overset{2}{o}r}$, non-deterministically provides inputs to its three branches and it looks for their outputs (ex-ante, it is not possible to choose inputs). As soon as the evaluation terminates by using a rule, the other rules cannot terminate anywise, i.e. ex-post the evaluation determines a unique rule which converges. The operator $\mathtt{G\overset{2}{o}r}$ is the operational counterpart of the following clique

$$g = \left\{ \begin{array}{l} ((0,0)\,,\,(1,0)\,,\,(0,1)\,,\,0) \\ ((0,1)\,,\,(0,0)\,,\,(1,0)\,,\,1) \\ ((1,0)\,,\,(0,1)\,,\,(0,0)\,,\,2) \\ ((1,1)\,,\,(1,1)\,,\,(1,1)\,,\,3) \end{array} \right\} \qquad (3)$$

The following result has been proved in [30].

Theorem 4. $\mathtt{G\overset{2}{o}r}$ *is not* $\mathcal{S}\ell$*PCF-definable*

Based on the statement above, we can build the desired counter-example. Here we make use of fix-point operational equivalence. Let $\mathtt{M} = \mathit{I}\ \Omega^{\iota\multimap\iota}\Omega^{\iota\multimap\iota}\Omega^{\iota\multimap\iota}$ and

$$\mathtt{N} = \ell\mathtt{if} \left(\begin{array}{l} \mathit{I}\ (\mathtt{Sgl}^{\iota\multimap\iota}_{\lceil \underline{0},\underline{0} \rceil})(\mathtt{Sgl}^{\iota\multimap\iota}_{\lceil \underline{1},\underline{0} \rceil})(\mathtt{Sgl}^{\iota\multimap\iota}_{\lceil \underline{0},\underline{1} \rceil}) \doteq \underline{0} \text{ and} \\ \mathit{I}\ (\mathtt{Sgl}^{\iota\multimap\iota}_{\lceil \underline{0},\underline{1} \rceil})(\mathtt{Sgl}^{\iota\multimap\iota}_{\lceil \underline{0},\underline{0} \rceil})(\mathtt{Sgl}^{\iota\multimap\iota}_{\lceil \underline{1},\underline{0} \rceil}) \doteq \underline{1} \text{ and} \\ \mathit{I}\ (\mathtt{Sgl}^{\iota\multimap\iota}_{\lceil \underline{1},\underline{0} \rceil})(\mathtt{Sgl}^{\iota\multimap\iota}_{\lceil \underline{0},\underline{1} \rceil})(\mathtt{Sgl}^{\iota\multimap\iota}_{\lceil \underline{0},\underline{0} \rceil}) \doteq \underline{2} \text{ and} \\ \mathit{I}\ (\mathtt{Sgl}^{\iota\multimap\iota}_{\lceil \underline{1},\underline{1} \rceil})(\mathtt{Sgl}^{\iota\multimap\iota}_{\lceil \underline{1},\underline{1} \rceil})(\mathtt{Sgl}^{\iota\multimap\iota}_{\lceil \underline{1},\underline{1} \rceil}) \doteq \underline{3} \end{array} \right) \underline{7}\ \Omega^\iota$$

be $\mathcal{S}\ell$PCF terms such that $\mathit{I}^{(\iota\multimap\iota)\multimap(\iota\multimap\iota)\multimap(\iota\multimap\iota)\multimap\iota} \vdash \mathtt{M}, \mathtt{N} : \iota$. It is easy to see that $[\![\mathtt{M}]\!]\rho \neq [\![\mathtt{N}]\!]\rho$, by taking $\rho(\mathit{I}) = g$ as defined in Equation 3. Instead, $\mathtt{M} \sim_\iota \mathtt{N}$ since to separate the two terms a term behaving like $\mathtt{G\overset{2}{o}r}$ is necessary. However, such a term is not definable in $\mathcal{S}\ell$PCF as shown by Theorem 4.

5. The extended language

To recover the problem presented in the previous section, $\mathcal{S}\ell\mathrm{PCF}_\star$ extends the $\mathcal{S}\ell$PCF language by means of a new $\ell\mathtt{et}$-$\ell\mathtt{or}$ operator.

Definition 13. *The* $\mathcal{S}\ell\mathrm{PCF}_\star$ pre-terms *are defined by extending the grammar of pre-terms as follows:*

$$\mathtt{M} ::= \cdots \mid \underline{\ell\mathtt{et}}\,\mathtt{f}_1^{\sigma_1\multimap\tau_1} = \mathtt{M}, \ldots, \mathtt{f}_k^{\sigma_k\multimap\tau_k} = \mathtt{M}\ \underline{\mathtt{in}\ell\mathtt{or}}\ \mathtt{M}\,\mathtt{M}\,\mathtt{M}$$

The terms *of* $\mathcal{S}\ell\mathrm{PCF}_\star$ *are the pre-terms typable by using the type system in Table 1.a extended by the rules in Table 2.a.*

The $\ell\mathtt{et}$-$\ell\mathtt{or}$ generalizes the behavior of the $\mathtt{G\overset{2}{o}r}$ operator presented in the previous section by forcing a linear evaluation. It is worth noticing that the contexts of the terms $\mathtt{M}_i$ in the ($\ell\mathtt{et}$-$\ell\mathtt{or}$) rule are managed in an additive way, contracting common (ground, linear and stable) variables. However, note that a $\ell\mathtt{et}$-$\ell\mathtt{or}$ binds all the linear variables in its three branches. So, a form of syntactic linearity (*by slice* [19]) for linear variables is preserved.

Definition 14. *A* slice *of a term* M *is a new term where:*

- *each subterm* $\ell\mathtt{if}\ \mathtt{P}\ \mathtt{M}_0\ \mathtt{M}_1$ *of* M *is replaced by, either* $(\lambda\mathtt{z}^\iota.\mathtt{M}_0)\mathtt{P}$ *or* $(\lambda\mathtt{z}^\iota.\mathtt{M}_1)\mathtt{P}$ *where* $\mathtt{z}$ *is a fresh variable;*
- *each subterm* $\underline{\ell\mathtt{et}}\,\mathtt{f}_1 = \mathtt{N}_1, \ldots, \mathtt{f}_k = \mathtt{N}_k\ \underline{\mathtt{in}\ell\mathtt{or}}\ \mathtt{M}_1\ \mathtt{M}_2\ \mathtt{M}_3$ *is replaced by,* $(\lambda\mathtt{f}_1 \ldots \mathtt{f}_k.\mathtt{M}_i)\mathtt{N}_1 \ldots \mathtt{N}_k$ *where* $1 \le i \le 3$.

Morally, a slice of a term chooses one branch of each $\ell\mathtt{if}$ and one branch of $\ell\mathtt{et}$-$\ell\mathtt{or}$. Indeed, a slice contains neither $\ell\mathtt{if}$ nor $\ell\mathtt{et}$-$\ell\mathtt{or}$. It is easy to verify that each linear variable $\mathtt{f}^{\sigma\multimap\tau}$ occurs in a slice of a term M at most once. This says that $\mathcal{S}\ell\mathrm{PCF}_\star$ is syntactically linear by slices. However, as expected, a term containing n $\ell\mathtt{if}$ and m $\ell\mathtt{et}$-$\ell\mathtt{or}$ has $2^n 3^m$ slices which can eventually coincide.

In order to deal with the $\ell\mathtt{et}$-$\ell\mathtt{or}$ operator without violating the semantic linearity we need a careful evaluation of terms, this is described using the terms $\mathtt{Sgl}^\sigma_n$ and $\mathtt{Chk}^{(\sigma)}_n$ introduced in the previous section.

Definition 15. *The* evaluation relation $\Downarrow \subseteq \mathcal{P} \times \mathcal{N}$ *for* $\mathcal{S}\ell\mathrm{PCF}_\star$ *programs is the smallest relation satisfying the rules in Table 1.b extended by the rules in Table 2.b.*

The evaluation rules for $\ell\mathtt{et}$-$\ell\mathtt{or}$ are patterns for infinite rules, likewise the rule for $\mathtt{which?}$ (see previous sections) and for $\exists$ in [33]. The evaluation of the $\ell\mathtt{et}$-$\ell\mathtt{or}$ operator is obtained by three distinct rules that explore pairwisely the $\ell\mathtt{et}$-$\ell\mathtt{or}$ branches. The evaluation of a $\ell\mathtt{et}$-$\ell\mathtt{or}$ can be performed only in the case two between $\mathtt{M}_1, \mathtt{M}_2$ and $\mathtt{M}_3$ evaluate to the values $\underline{0}$ and $\underline{\mathtt{m}+1}$ respectively by using a *single* tuple (i.e., a token) of the traces in the $\ell\mathtt{et}$-$\ell\mathtt{or}$-argument $\mathtt{N}_\mathtt{i}$, for $i \le k$. For instance, the $(\mathtt{1lgor})$ can be applied in the case $\mathtt{M}_1[\mathtt{N}_1/\mathtt{f}_1, \ldots, \mathtt{N}_k/\mathtt{f}_k] \Downarrow \underline{0}$ and $\mathtt{M}_2[\mathtt{N}_1/\mathtt{f}_1, \ldots, \mathtt{N}_k/\mathtt{f}_k] \Downarrow \underline{\mathtt{sm}}$ and the same *single* information of each $\mathtt{N}_j$ coded on numerals n_j is used in both evaluations. The *check* of this constraints is the motivation for introducing the terms $\mathtt{Sgl}^\sigma_n$ and $\mathtt{Chk}^{(\sigma)}_n$ above. Albeit ex-ante we don't know what is the right pair of $\ell\mathtt{et}$-$\ell\mathtt{or}$ branches to evaluate, they are established during the course of the evaluation, so ex-post only one of the three rules can converge. The interpretation of the $\ell\mathtt{et}$-$\ell\mathtt{or}$ operator follows these ideas.

Definition 16. *Let* $\mathtt{M}^\sigma, \mathtt{N}^\sigma \in \mathcal{S}\ell\mathrm{PCF}_\star$ *and* $\rho \in \mathrm{Env}$. *The* linear interpretation $[\![\mathtt{M}^\sigma]\!] : \mathrm{Env} \to \mathcal{C}l([\![\sigma]\!])$ *is defined by the equations in Table 1.c extended by the ones for the* $\ell\mathtt{et}$-$\ell\mathtt{or}$ *operator in Table 2.c.*

It is not difficult to see that the correctness w.r.t. the linear model (Theorem 1) still holds for $\mathcal{S}\ell\mathrm{PCF}_\star$.

5.1 $\mathcal{S}\ell\mathrm{PCF}_\star$ program examples

We show how to use the $\ell\mathtt{et}$-$\ell\mathtt{or}$ operator in order to program in $\mathcal{S}\ell\mathrm{PCF}_\star$ the operator $\mathtt{G\overset{2}{o}r}$ presented in Section 4. This should so suggest how to recover the counterexample to full abstraction.

In fact, we show something more. We describe how to program a family of terms $\mathtt{G\overset{2}{o}r}^{\mathtt{L}}$ that generalize the behavior of the operator $\mathtt{G\overset{2}{o}r}$. The terms $\mathtt{G\overset{2}{o}r}^{\mathtt{L}}$, are parametrized over an ordered list L of four numerals $\underline{\mathtt{k}_0}, \underline{\mathtt{k}_1}, \underline{\mathtt{k}_2}, \underline{\mathtt{k}_3}$ representing the output returned in the case the assumptions of one of the rule $(\mathtt{G}_0)$, $(\mathtt{G}_1)$, $(\mathtt{G}_2)$ or $(\mathtt{G}_3)$ respectively, are satisfied. So, in particular $\mathtt{G\overset{2}{o}r}^{\mathtt{L}} = \mathtt{G\overset{2}{o}r}$ when $\mathtt{L} = \{\underline{0}, \underline{1}, \underline{2}, \underline{3}\}$ is considered. In order to proceed in a modular way, we introduce also a notation in order to consider restrictions of $\mathtt{G\overset{2}{o}r}^{\mathtt{L}}$ which use only a subset of the four rules. Precisely, a $\bullet$ in the list L is used to denote the operator obtained omitting the corresponding rules. For instance, $\mathtt{G\overset{2}{o}r}^{\mathtt{L}_0}$ where $\mathtt{L}_0 = \underline{0}, \underline{2}, \bullet, \bullet$ is defined as

$$\begin{array}{l} \lambda\mathtt{f}_1^{\iota\multimap\iota}\mathtt{f}_2^{\iota\multimap\iota}\mathtt{f}_3^{\iota\multimap\iota}. \\ \left(\begin{array}{l} \lambda\mathtt{w}.\ell\mathtt{if}\ \mathtt{w} \doteq \underline{0}(\ell\mathtt{if}\ (\mathtt{f}_2\underline{1} \doteq \underline{0} \text{ and } \mathtt{f}_3\underline{0} \doteq \underline{1})\ \underline{0}\ \Omega^\iota) \\ \quad (\ell\mathtt{if}\ \mathtt{w} \doteq \underline{1}(\ell\mathtt{if}\ (\mathtt{f}_2\underline{0} \doteq \underline{0} \text{ and } \mathtt{f}_3\underline{1} \doteq \underline{0})\ \underline{2}\ \Omega^\iota)\ \Omega^\iota) \end{array} \right) (\mathtt{f}_1\underline{0}) \end{array}$$

All the $\mathtt{G\overset{2}{o}r}^{\mathtt{L}}$ defined by just two rules, i.e. for L containing two occurrences of $\bullet$, can be defined likewise. Thus, $\mathtt{G\overset{2}{o}r}^{\mathtt{L}_1}$ with parameter

$$\frac{\Gamma \cap \Delta = \emptyset \quad \Delta \restriction \ell = \mathtt{f}_1^{\sigma_1}, \ldots, \mathtt{f}_k^{\sigma_k} \quad \Gamma_1 \vdash \mathtt{N}_1 : \sigma_1 \ \ldots \ \Gamma_k \vdash \mathtt{N}_k : \sigma_k \quad \Delta \vdash \mathtt{M}_i : \iota \ (1 \le i \le 3)}{\Delta \restriction \mathcal{S}, \Delta \restriction \iota, \Gamma_1, \ldots, \Gamma_k \vdash \underline{\ell\mathtt{et}}\, \mathtt{f}_1 = \mathtt{N}_1, \ldots, \mathtt{f}_k = \mathtt{N}_k\, \underline{\mathtt{in}\ell\mathtt{or}}\ \mathtt{M}_1\, \mathtt{M}_2\, \mathtt{M}_3 : \iota} \ (\ell\mathtt{et}\text{-}\ell\mathtt{or})$$

$$\frac{\mathtt{M}_1[\mathtt{Sgl}_{\mathtt{n}_1}^{\sigma_1}/\mathtt{f}_1, \ldots, \mathtt{Sgl}_{\mathtt{n}_k}^{\sigma_k}/\mathtt{f}_k] \Downarrow \underline{0} \quad \mathtt{M}_2[\mathtt{Sgl}_{\mathtt{n}_1}^{\sigma_1}/\mathtt{f}_1, \ldots, \mathtt{Sgl}_{\mathtt{n}_k}^{\sigma_k}/\mathtt{f}_k] \Downarrow \mathtt{s}\underline{\mathtt{m}} \quad \mathtt{Chk}_{\mathtt{n}_j}^{(\sigma_k)}\mathtt{N}_j \Downarrow \underline{0} \quad (j \in \{1,\ldots,k\})}{\underline{\ell\mathtt{et}}\, \mathtt{f}_1^{\sigma_1} = \mathtt{N}_1, \ldots, \mathtt{f}_k^{\sigma_k} = \mathtt{N}_k\, \underline{\mathtt{in}\ell\mathtt{or}}\ \mathtt{M}_1\, \mathtt{M}_2\, \mathtt{M}_3 \Downarrow \underline{\mathtt{m}}} \ (\mathtt{1lgor})$$

$$\frac{\mathtt{M}_2[\mathtt{Sgl}_{\mathtt{n}_1}^{\sigma_1}/\mathtt{f}_1, \ldots, \mathtt{Sgl}_{\mathtt{n}_k}^{\sigma_k}/\mathtt{f}_k] \Downarrow \underline{0} \quad \mathtt{M}_3[\mathtt{Sgl}_{\mathtt{n}_1}^{\sigma_1}/\mathtt{f}_1, \ldots, \mathtt{Sgl}_{\mathtt{n}_k}^{\sigma_k}/\mathtt{f}_k] \Downarrow \mathtt{s}\underline{\mathtt{m}} \quad \mathtt{Chk}_{\mathtt{n}_j}^{(\sigma_k)}\mathtt{N}_j \Downarrow \underline{0} \quad (j \in \{1,\ldots,k\})}{\underline{\ell\mathtt{et}}\, \mathtt{f}_1^{\sigma_1} = \mathtt{N}_1, \ldots, \mathtt{f}_k^{\sigma_k} = \mathtt{N}_k\, \underline{\mathtt{in}\ell\mathtt{or}}\ \mathtt{M}_1\, \mathtt{M}_2\, \mathtt{M}_3 \Downarrow \underline{\mathtt{m}}} \ (\mathtt{2lgor})$$

$$\frac{\mathtt{M}_3[\mathtt{Sgl}_{\mathtt{n}_1}^{\sigma_1}/\mathtt{f}_1, \ldots, \mathtt{Sgl}_{\mathtt{n}_k}^{\sigma_k}/\mathtt{f}_k] \Downarrow \underline{0} \quad \mathtt{M}_1[\mathtt{Sgl}_{\mathtt{n}_1}^{\sigma_1}/\mathtt{f}_1, \ldots, \mathtt{Sgl}_{\mathtt{n}_k}^{\sigma_k}/\mathtt{f}_k] \Downarrow \mathtt{s}\underline{\mathtt{m}} \quad \mathtt{Chk}_{\mathtt{n}_j}^{(\sigma_k)}\mathtt{N}_j \Downarrow \underline{0} \quad (j \in \{1,\ldots,k\})}{\underline{\ell\mathtt{et}}\, \mathtt{f}_1^{\sigma_1} = \mathtt{N}_1, \ldots, \mathtt{f}_k^{\sigma_k} = \mathtt{N}_k\, \underline{\mathtt{in}\ell\mathtt{or}}\ \mathtt{M}_1\, \mathtt{M}_2\, \mathtt{M}_3 \Downarrow \underline{\mathtt{m}}} \ (\mathtt{3lgor})$$

$$\begin{aligned}
[\![\underline{\ell\mathtt{et}}\, \vec{\mathtt{f}} = \vec{\mathtt{N}}\, \underline{\mathtt{in}\ell\mathtt{or}}\ \mathtt{M}_1\, \mathtt{M}_2\, \mathtt{M}_3]\!]\rho \ = \ & \left\{ n \in \mathbb{N} \,\middle|\, \exists \vec{a} \in \overrightarrow{[\![\mathtt{N}]\!]\rho} \ \begin{matrix} [\![\mathtt{M}_3]\!]\rho[\vec{\mathtt{f}} := \vec{a}] = \{0\} \wedge \\ [\![\mathtt{M}_1]\!]\rho[\vec{\mathtt{f}} := \vec{a}] = \{n+1\} \end{matrix} \right\} \cup \left\{ n \in \mathbb{N} \,\middle|\, \exists \vec{a} \in \overrightarrow{[\![\mathtt{N}]\!]\rho} \ \begin{matrix} [\![\mathtt{M}_1]\!]\rho[\vec{\mathtt{f}} := \vec{a}] = \{0\} \wedge \\ [\![\mathtt{M}_2]\!]\rho[\vec{\mathtt{f}} := \vec{a}] = \{n+1\} \end{matrix} \right\} \\
\cup \ & \left\{ n \in \mathbb{N} \,\middle|\, \exists \vec{a} \in \overrightarrow{[\![\mathtt{N}]\!]\rho} \ \begin{matrix} [\![\mathtt{M}_2]\!]\rho[\vec{\mathtt{f}} := \vec{a}] = \{0\} \wedge \\ [\![\mathtt{M}_3]\!]\rho[\vec{\mathtt{f}} := \vec{a}] = \{n+1\} \end{matrix} \right\}
\end{aligned}$$

Table 2. (a) Type system, (b) operational semantics and (c) linear interpretation for the ℓet-ℓor operator.

$\mathtt{L}_1 = \underline{1}, \bullet, \underline{0}, \underline{0}$ can be defined using the ℓet-ℓor operator as

$$\begin{aligned}&\lambda \mathtt{f}_1\mathtt{f}_2\mathtt{f}_3.\underline{\ell\mathtt{et}}\ \mathtt{g}_1 = \mathtt{f}_1, \mathtt{g}_2 = \mathtt{f}_2, \mathtt{g}_3 = \mathtt{f}_3\ \underline{\mathtt{in}\ell\mathtt{or}} \\ &\quad (\mathtt{G\ell or}^{\underline{0},\bullet,\underline{1},\bullet}\ \mathtt{g}_1\mathtt{g}_2\mathtt{g}_3)(\mathtt{G\ell or}^{\underline{2},\bullet,\bullet,\underline{0}}\ \mathtt{g}_1\mathtt{g}_2\mathtt{g}_3)(\mathtt{G\ell or}^{\bullet,\bullet,\underline{0},\underline{1}}\ \mathtt{g}_1\mathtt{g}_2\mathtt{g}_3)\end{aligned}$$

and $\mathtt{G\ell or}^{\mathtt{L}_2}$ with parameter $\mathtt{L}_2 = \bullet, \underline{0}, \underline{3}, \underline{4}$ can be defined as

$$\begin{aligned}&\lambda \mathtt{f}_1\mathtt{f}_2\mathtt{f}_3.\underline{\ell\mathtt{et}}\ \mathtt{g}_1 = \mathtt{f}_1, \mathtt{g}_2 = \mathtt{f}_2, \mathtt{g}_3 = \mathtt{f}_3\ \underline{\mathtt{in}\ell\mathtt{or}} \\ &\quad (\mathtt{G\ell or}^{\bullet,\underline{0},\underline{4},\bullet}\ \mathtt{g}_1\mathtt{g}_2\mathtt{g}_3)(\mathtt{G\ell or}^{\bullet,\underline{1},\bullet,\underline{0}}\ \mathtt{g}_1\mathtt{g}_2\mathtt{g}_3)(\mathtt{G\ell or}^{\bullet,\bullet,\underline{0},\underline{5}}\ \mathtt{g}_1\mathtt{g}_2\mathtt{g}_3)\end{aligned}$$

Finally, $\mathtt{G\ell or}^{\mathtt{L}_3}$ with parameter $\mathtt{L}_3 = \underline{0}, \underline{1}, \underline{2}, \underline{3}$ can be defined as

$$\begin{aligned}&\lambda \mathtt{f}_1^{\iota \multimap \iota}\mathtt{f}_2^{\iota \multimap \iota}\mathtt{f}_3^{\iota \multimap \iota}\underline{\ell\mathtt{et}}\ \mathtt{g}_1 = \mathtt{f}_1, \mathtt{g}_2 = \mathtt{f}_2, \mathtt{g}_3 = \mathtt{f}_3 \\ &\quad \underline{\mathtt{in}\ell\mathtt{or}}(\mathtt{G\ell or}^{\mathtt{L}_0}\ \mathtt{g}_1\mathtt{g}_2\mathtt{g}_3)(\mathtt{G\ell or}^{\mathtt{L}_1}\ \mathtt{g}_1\mathtt{g}_2\mathtt{g}_3)(\mathtt{G\ell or}^{\mathtt{L}_2}\ \mathtt{g}_1\mathtt{g}_2\mathtt{g}_3)\end{aligned}$$

For every parameter L, all the $\mathtt{G\ell or}^{\mathtt{L}}$ can be built analogously. As expected, the ℓet-ℓor operator is fundamental for the above construction.

We give here also a flavor on how to use the which? operator to define programming constructs useful to collect run-time information. These programming constructs (called $@\mathtt{wh?}_\tau^\sigma$) are a generalization of the operators introduced in [30, Section 3.1] and will be used in the next Section to prove the Finite Definability Theorem 6. Let us introduce the operators $@\mathtt{wh?}_\tau^\sigma : (\sigma \multimap \tau) \multimap \sigma \multimap \tau$, with the following operational semantics:

$$\frac{(\mathtt{M}^{\sigma \multimap \tau}\mathtt{Sgl}_{\underline{\mathtt{m}}}^{(\sigma)})\mathtt{P}_1 \ldots \mathtt{P}_k \Downarrow \underline{\mathtt{n}} \qquad \mathtt{Chk}_{\underline{\mathtt{m}}}^{(\sigma)}\ \mathtt{N} \Downarrow \underline{0}}{(@\mathtt{wh?}_\tau^\sigma\, \mathtt{M}^{\sigma \multimap \tau}\ \mathtt{N}^\sigma)\mathtt{P}_1 \ldots \mathtt{P}_k \Downarrow \lceil \underline{\mathtt{n}}, \underline{\mathtt{m}} \rfloor}$$

Observe that $(@\mathtt{wh?}\ \mathtt{M}\,\mathtt{N})\mathtt{P}_1 \ldots \mathtt{P}_k \Downarrow$ if and only if $\mathtt{M}\mathtt{N}\mathtt{P}_1 \ldots \mathtt{P}_k \Downarrow$. This control operator gives back the result $\underline{\mathtt{n}}$ of the evaluation of $\mathtt{M}\mathtt{N}\ \mathtt{P}_1 \ldots \mathtt{P}_k$ together with the numeral $\underline{\mathtt{m}}$ encoding the part of the trace of N used for the evaluation. This information will be essential in the proof of the Finite Definability Theorem 6.

@wh? can be programmed in $\mathcal{S}\ell$PCF$_\star$ using which?.

Theorem 5. *$@\mathtt{wh?}_\tau^\sigma$ is $\mathcal{S}\ell$PCF$_\star$ programmable.*

Proof. The proof is by structural induction on σ. The base case is simple observing that the term
$\lambda \mathtt{f}^{\iota \multimap \tau}\lambda \mathtt{x}^\iota \lambda \mathtt{g}_1^{\tau_1}, \ldots, \mathtt{g}_k^{\tau_k}.\mathtt{which?}(\lambda \mathtt{h}^{\iota \multimap \iota}.\mathtt{f}(\mathtt{hx})\mathtt{g}_1 \ldots \mathtt{g}_k)$
behaves as $@\mathtt{wh?}_\tau^\iota$, with $\tau = \tau_1 \multimap \ldots \multimap \tau_k \multimap \iota$. The inductive case is a bit more complicated. The idea is to generalize the behavior of the term above where the variable h acts like an observer which retrieves the used trace. □

6. Finite Definability and Full Abstraction

In this section we prove that the linear model $\mathcal{L}$ is *fully abstract* with respect to $\mathcal{S}\ell$PCF$_\star$. This result relies on the *completeness* of the linear interpretation with respect to the operational semantics and on the *definability* of all the finite cliques by means of $\mathcal{S}\ell$PCF$_\star$ terms. In particular, we prove the completeness with respect to the Fix-Point equivalence. In the next section (Proposition 2 and Theorem 8) we then prove that the Fix-Point and the Standard operational equivalences coincide. From this, full abstraction holds also with respect to the latter.

Finite definability asserts that all finite cliques can be defined by means of $\mathcal{S}\ell$PCF$_\star$ terms. Our proof follows a standard scheme for proofs of this kind, e.g. [33],[29]. Non trivial uses of @wh? and ℓet-ℓor constructors are needed in the inductive high-order steps.

Definition 17. *Let u be a finite clique of a coherence space in $\mathcal{L}$. A term* M defines *u if and only if $[\![\mathtt{M}]\!] = u$. The class of closed terms having u as interpretation is denoted by $\lceil u \rfloor$* [1]*, hence $\lceil u \rfloor = \{\mathtt{M} \mid [\![\mathtt{M}]\!] = u\}$. By abuse of notation, in the following we denote $\lceil x \rfloor$ a term M such that $\mathtt{M} = \lceil x \rfloor$.*

To prove definability, we use the following auxiliary lemma.

Lemma 5. *Let $(a_0, \ldots, a_n, a), (b_0, \ldots, b_n, b) \in |[\![\tau_0 \multimap \cdots \multimap \tau_n \multimap \iota]\!]|$. Then:*

1. *$(a_0, \ldots, a_n, a) \frown (b_0, \ldots, b_n, b)$ iff $\exists k \le n$: $a_k \smile b_k$.*
2. *$(a_0, \ldots, a_n, a) \asymp (b_0, \ldots, b_n, b)$ iff $\forall k \le n$: $a_k \supset b_k$.*

Some measures are needed in the next theorem: the *cardinality* of a clique u is denoted $\|u\|$; the RK of a type is inductively defined as: $\mathrm{RK}(\iota) = 1$; $\mathrm{RK}(\sigma \multimap \tau) = \mathrm{RK}(\sigma) + \mathrm{RK}(\tau)$.

Theorem 6 (Finite Definability). *If $u \in \mathcal{C}l_{fin}([\![\sigma]\!])$ then there exists a closed $\mathtt{M} \in \mathcal{S}\ell$PCF$_\star$ such that $\mathtt{M} = \lceil \mathtt{u} \rfloor$.*

Proof. Let $\sigma = \tau_1 \multimap \cdots \multimap \tau_k \multimap \iota$ for some $k \ge 0$. The proof is by induction on the triple $\langle\ \mathrm{RK}(\sigma), k, \|u\|\ \rangle$ ordered in a lexicographic way.

- Consider $\mathrm{RK}(\sigma) = 1$, then $\sigma = \iota$ and $[\![\sigma]\!] = \mathbf{N}$. Thus, Ω^ι and numerals define all possible finite cliques, since $\mathcal{C}l_{fin}(\mathbf{N}) = \{\emptyset\} \cup \{\{n\} \,/\, n \in |\mathbb{N}|\}$.

[1] In general, we use $\lceil a^1, \ldots, a^k \rfloor$ as an abbreviation for $\lceil \{a^1, \ldots, a^k\} \rfloor$.

- Consider $\mathrm{RK}(\sigma) = 2$, then $\sigma = \iota \multimap \iota$.

  - If $\|u\| = 0$ then $u = \emptyset$ is defined by $\Omega^{\iota \multimap \iota}$.
  - If $\|u\| \geq 1$, then $u = u' \cup \{(a, b)\}$ for $a, b \in \mathbb{N}$. By induction hypothesis we have $\lceil u' \rfloor$, hence $\lceil u \rfloor = \lambda \mathtt{z}.\ell\mathtt{if}\ (\mathtt{z} \doteq \lceil a \rfloor)\ \lceil b \rfloor\ (\lceil u' \rfloor \mathtt{z})$.

- Consider $\mathrm{RK}(\sigma) \geq 3$ and $k = 1$, then $\sigma = \tau \multimap \iota$ with $\tau = \sigma_1 \multimap \cdots \sigma_r \multimap \iota$.

  - If $\|u\| = 0$ then $u = \emptyset$ is defined by $\Omega^{\tau \multimap \iota}$.
  - If $\|u\| = 1$, then $u = \{(a, b)\}$ for $a \in [\![\tau]\!]$ and $b \in \mathbb{N}$. Suppose $a = (a_1, \ldots, a_r, c)$ where $a_i \in [\![\sigma_i]\!]$ and $c \in \mathbb{N}$ $(1 \leq i \leq r)$. By induction hypothesis we have $\lceil a_1 \rfloor, \ldots, \lceil a_r \rfloor, \lceil c \rfloor$ and $\lceil b \rfloor$, hence: $\lceil u \rfloor = \lambda \mathtt{f}.\ell\mathtt{if}\ (\mathtt{f} \lceil a_1 \rfloor \cdots \lceil a_r \rfloor \doteq \lceil c \rfloor)\ \lceil b \rfloor\ \Omega^{\iota}$.
  - If $\|u\| > 1$, then $u = \{(a^0, b^0), \ldots, (a^m, b^m)\}$ for $a^i \in [\![\tau]\!]$ and $b^i \in \mathbb{N}$ $(0 \leq i \leq m)$. Suppose $a^i = (a^i_1, \ldots, a^i_r, c^i)$ where $a^i_j \in [\![\sigma_j]\!]$ and $c^i \in \mathbb{N}$ $(1 \leq j \leq r)$. By Lemma 5.1, we have $a^h \smile a^k$ $(0 \leq h \neq k \leq m)$, so by Lemma 5.2 $a^h_j \circ a^k_j$ $(1 \leq j \leq r)$. Hence, take $v_j = \{a^i_j \mid 1 \leq i \leq m\}$. Moreover, for sake of simplicity, we write just $\underline{\mathtt{a}^{\mathtt{i}}_{\mathtt{j}}}$ in place of $(\!|a^i_j|\!)$, i.e. the natural number encoding a^i_j.
  By induction hypothesis we have $\lceil v_j \rfloor$, $\lceil c^i \rfloor$ for every $0 \leq i \leq m$, $1 \leq j \leq r$ and $1 \leq k \leq s$. So, we can define:

$$\lceil u \rfloor = \lambda \mathtt{F}^{\tau}.\Big(\lambda \mathtt{z}^{\iota}.$$

$$\ell\mathtt{if}\ (\boldsymbol{\pi}^r_1(z) \doteq \underline{\mathtt{c}^0} \text{ and } \boldsymbol{\pi}^{r-1}_1(\boldsymbol{\pi}_2(z)) \doteq \underline{\mathtt{a}^0_1} \ \ldots\ \boldsymbol{\pi}_2(z) \doteq \underline{\mathtt{a}^0_r})\ \underline{\mathtt{b}^0}$$

$$\ell\mathtt{if}\ (\boldsymbol{\pi}^r_1(z) \doteq \underline{\mathtt{c}^1} \text{ and } \boldsymbol{\pi}^{r-1}_1(\boldsymbol{\pi}_2(z)) \doteq \underline{\mathtt{a}^1_1} \ \ldots\ \boldsymbol{\pi}_2(z) \doteq \underline{\mathtt{a}^1_r})\ \underline{\mathtt{b}^1}$$

$$\vdots$$

$$\ell\mathtt{if}\ (\boldsymbol{\pi}^r_1(z) \doteq \underline{\mathtt{c}^m} \text{ and } \boldsymbol{\pi}^{r-1}_1(\boldsymbol{\pi}_2(z)) \doteq \underline{\mathtt{a}^m_1} \ \ldots\ \boldsymbol{\pi}_2(z) \doteq \underline{\mathtt{a}^m_r})\ \underline{\mathtt{b}^m}$$

$$)\cdots\Big)\big(@\mathtt{wh}?^{\sigma_r}_{\iota}(\ldots(@\mathtt{wh}?^{\sigma_1}_{\sigma_2 \multimap \cdots \sigma_r \multimap \iota}(\mathtt{F})(\lceil \mathtt{v}_1 \rfloor))\ldots)(\lceil \mathtt{v}_r \rfloor)\big)$$

- Consider $\mathrm{RK}(\sigma) \geq 3$ and $k > 1$.

  - If $\|u\| = 0$, then $u = \emptyset$ is defined by $\Omega^{\tau_1 \multimap \cdots \multimap \tau_k \multimap \iota}$.
  - If $\|u\| = 1$, then $u = \{(a_1, \ldots a_k, b)\}$ where $a_i \in [\![\tau_i]\!]$ $(1 \leq i \leq k)$ and $b \in \mathbb{N}$. Thus,

$$\lceil u \rfloor = \lambda \mathtt{f}_1 \ldots \mathtt{f}_k.$$

$$\ell\mathtt{if}\ ((\mathtt{Chk}^{(\sigma_1)}_{\underline{\mathtt{a}_1}} \mathtt{f}_1) \text{ and} \cdots \text{and } (\mathtt{Chk}^{(\sigma_k)}_{\underline{\mathtt{a}_k}} \mathtt{f}_k))\ \lceil \mathtt{b} \rfloor\ \Omega^{\iota}$$

  - if $\|u\| = 2$ then $u = \{(a^1_1, \ldots, a^1_k, b^1), (a^2_1, \ldots, a^2_k, b^2)\}$. We know that there is $i \in [1, k]$ such that $a^1_i \smile a^2_i$. If $\tau_i = \iota$ then a^1_1 and a^2_i are two different numbers: thus the term defining u is the following

$$\lceil u \rfloor = \lambda \mathtt{f}_1 \ldots . \mathtt{f}_k.\ell\mathtt{if}\ (\mathtt{f}_\mathtt{i} \doteq \lceil a^1_i \rfloor)\Big(\ell\mathtt{if}\ (\mathtt{Chk}^{(\sigma_1)}_{\underline{\mathtt{a}^1_1}} \mathtt{f}_1) \text{ and} \cdots$$

$$\text{and } (\mathtt{Chk}^{(\sigma_k)}_{\underline{\mathtt{a}^1_k}} \mathtt{f}_k)\ \lceil b^1 \rfloor\ \Omega\Big)\Big(\ell\mathtt{if}((\mathtt{f}_\mathtt{i} \doteq \lceil a^2_i \rfloor) \text{ and}$$

$$(\mathtt{Chk}^{(\sigma_1)}_{\underline{\mathtt{a}^2_1}} \mathtt{f}_1) \text{ and} \cdots \text{and } ((\mathtt{Chk}^{(\sigma_1)}_{\underline{\mathtt{a}^2_k}} \mathtt{f}_k))\ \lceil b^2 \rfloor\ \Omega\Big)$$

  If $\tau = \nu_1 \multimap \ldots \nu_l \multimap \iota$ then we have that $a^1_i = (e^1_1, \ldots, e^1_l, c^1)$ and $a^2_i = (e^2_1, \ldots, e^2_l, c^2)$. Since $a^1_i \smile a^2_i$, we have that for all $j \in [1, l]$ the sets $\{e^1_j, e^2_j\}$ are cliques of lower rank. Thus by inductive hypothesis we have terms $\mathtt{N}_\mathtt{j}$ defining them. Thus the term defining u is the following

$$\lceil u \rfloor = \lambda \mathtt{f}_1 \ldots . \mathtt{f}_k.\Big(\lambda \mathtt{x}^{\iota}.\ell\mathtt{if}\ \Big(\boldsymbol{\pi}^1_1 \mathtt{x} \doteq \underline{\mathtt{c}^1} \text{ and } \boldsymbol{\pi}^{1-1}_1(\boldsymbol{\pi}_2 \mathtt{x}) \doteq \underline{\mathtt{e}^1_1}$$

$$\text{and} \ldots \boldsymbol{\pi}_2 \mathtt{x} \doteq \underline{e^1_l}\Big)\Big(\ell\mathtt{if}\big(\mathtt{Chk}^{(\tau_1)}_{\underline{\mathtt{a}^1_1}} \mathtt{f}_1 \text{ and } \ldots$$

$$\mathtt{Chk}^{(\tau_{i-1})}_{\underline{\mathtt{a}^1_{i-1}}} \mathtt{f}_{i-1} \text{ and } \mathtt{Chk}^{(\tau_{i+1})}_{\underline{\mathtt{a}^1_{i+1}}} \mathtt{f}_{i+1} \text{ and } \ldots \mathtt{Chk}^{(\tau_k)}_{\underline{\mathtt{a}^1_k}} \mathtt{f}_k\big)\ \lceil \mathtt{b}^1 \rfloor\ \Omega\Big)$$

$$\Big(\ell\mathtt{if}\big(\boldsymbol{\pi}^l_1 \mathtt{x} \doteq \underline{c^2} \text{ and } \boldsymbol{\pi}^{l-1}_1(\boldsymbol{\pi}_2 \mathtt{x}) \doteq \underline{e^2_1} \text{ and} \ldots \boldsymbol{\pi}_2 \mathtt{x} \doteq \underline{e^2_l} \text{ and}$$

$$\mathtt{Chk}^{(\tau_1)}_{\underline{\mathtt{a}^2_1}} \mathtt{f}_1 \text{ and } \ldots \mathtt{Chk}^{(\tau_{i-1})}_{\underline{\mathtt{a}^2_{i-1}}} \mathtt{f}_{i-1} \text{ and}$$

$$\mathtt{Chk}^{(\tau_{i+1})}_{\underline{\mathtt{a}^2_{i+1}}} \mathtt{f}_{i+1} \text{ and} \ldots \mathtt{Chk}^{(\tau_k)}_{\underline{\mathtt{a}^2_k}} \mathtt{f}_k\big)\ \lceil \mathtt{b}^2 \rfloor\ \Omega\Big)$$

$$\Big)\Big(@\mathtt{wh}?^{\nu_l}_{\iota}(\ldots(@\mathtt{wh}?^{\nu_1}_{\nu_2 \multimap \ldots \nu_l \multimap \iota}(\mathtt{f}_\mathtt{i})(\mathtt{N}_1))\ldots)\mathtt{N}_1\Big)$$

  - If $\|u\| > 2$, then $u = \{d^1, \ldots, d^m\}$ where $d^j = (a^j_1, \ldots, a^j_k, b^j)$, $a^j_i \in [\![\tau_i]\!]$ and $b^j \in \mathbb{N}$ $(1 \leq j \leq m,\ 1 \leq i \leq k)$. We denote by $d^j[b]$ the token $(a^j_1, \ldots, a^j_k, b)$. By Lemma 5.1 there exists $1 \leq h \leq k$ such that $a^1_h \frown a^2_h$, so we can build the following finite cliques:

$$w_1 = \{d^1[0], d^2[b^2 + 1]\ \}$$

$$w_2 = \{d^1[b^1 + 1]\} \cup \{d^r[0] \mid 2 < r \leq m\ \}$$

$$w_3 = \{d^2[0]\} \cup \{d^r[b^r + 1] \mid 2 < r \leq m\ \}$$

  Note that $\|w_s\| < \|u\|$ for $s = 1, 2, 3$. So, by induction hypothesis we have $\lceil w_1 \rfloor$, $\lceil w_2 \rfloor$ and $\lceil w_3 \rfloor$. Hence:

$$\lceil u \rfloor = \lambda \mathtt{f}_1 \ldots \mathtt{f}_k.\underline{\mathtt{let}}\ \mathtt{g}_1 = \mathtt{f}_1, \ldots, \mathtt{g}_k = \mathtt{f}_k$$

$$\underline{\mathtt{in}\ell or}\ (\lceil w_1 \rfloor \mathtt{g}_1 \cdots \mathtt{g}_k)(\lceil w_2 \rfloor \mathtt{g}_1 \cdots \mathtt{g}_k)(\lceil w_3 \rfloor \mathtt{g}_1 \cdots \mathtt{g}_k)$$

  and this concludes the proof. □

The definability of finite cliques is the key ingredient to extend the Stable Closed Completeness Theorem 3 to all the terms of $\mathcal{S}\ell\mathrm{PCF}_\star$ as follows.

Theorem 7 (Completeness). *Let* $\mathtt{M}^\sigma, \mathtt{N}^\sigma \in \mathcal{S}\ell\mathrm{PCF}_\star$.

$$\mathtt{M} \sim_\sigma \mathtt{N} \Rightarrow [\![\mathtt{M}]\!] = [\![\mathtt{N}]\!]$$

Proof. Let $\Gamma \vdash \mathtt{M}, \mathtt{N} : \sigma$ with $\Gamma \restriction \mathcal{S} = \{I^{\tau_1}_1, \ldots, I^{\tau_n}_n\}$ and $\Gamma \restriction \ell, \Gamma \restriction \iota = \{\mathtt{x_1}^{\sigma_1}, \ldots, \mathtt{x_m}^{\sigma_m}\}$. Assume $[\![\mathtt{M}]\!] \neq [\![\mathtt{N}]\!]$, then there exists ρ such that $[\![\mathtt{M}]\!]\rho \neq [\![\mathtt{N}]\!]\rho$. By the Separability Lemma 3, there exists a closed term $\mathtt{P}^{\sigma \multimap \iota}$ such that $\mathcal{F}([\![\mathtt{P}]\!])([\![\mathtt{M}]\!]\rho) \neq \mathcal{F}([\![\mathtt{P}]\!])([\![\mathtt{N}]\!]\rho)$. By the Finite Definability Theorem 6, for all I_i in $\Gamma \restriction \mathcal{S}$ there is a term $\mathtt{P_i} = \lceil \rho(I_i) \rfloor$ and for all $\mathtt{x_i}$ in $\Gamma \restriction \ell, \Gamma \restriction \iota$ there is a term $\mathtt{N_i} = \lceil \rho(\mathtt{x_i}) \rfloor$. So, we can build $\mathtt{C} = \mathtt{P}(\lambda \mathtt{x}^{\sigma_1}_1 \ldots \mathtt{x}^{\sigma_m}_m.[\cdot^\sigma]\mathtt{N}_1 \cdots \mathtt{N}_m)$. Without loss of generality, let us assume $\mathcal{F}([\![\mathtt{P}]\!])([\![\mathtt{M}]\!]\rho) = \{k\}$. By adequacy $\mathtt{C}[\mathtt{M}[\mathtt{P}_1/I_1, \ldots, \mathtt{P}_n/I_n]] \Downarrow \underline{\mathtt{k}}$ but $\mathtt{C}[\mathtt{N}[\mathtt{P}_1/I_1, \ldots, \mathtt{P}_n/I_n]] \not\Downarrow \underline{\mathtt{k}}$. This concludes the proof. □

By soundness and completeness the full abstraction follows.

Corollary 2 (Full Abstraction). *Let* $\mathtt{M}^\sigma, \mathtt{N}^\sigma \in \mathcal{S}\ell\mathrm{PCF}_\star$.

$$\mathtt{M} \sim_\sigma \mathtt{N} \iff [\![\mathtt{M}]\!] = [\![\mathtt{N}]\!]$$

7. Coincidence of operational equivalences

In this section we prove the coincidence between the standard operational equivalence (Definition 9) and the fix-point operational equivalence (Definition 12). Therefore, the full abstraction holds also for the standard operational equivalence and a *compositional* theory of program equivalence can be effectively defined.

The fix-point equivalence coincides with the denotational equivalence by Corollary 2. The proof follows of the next proposition directly by the correctness of the denotational semantics w.r.t the standard operational equivalence.

Proposition 2. *Let* $\mathtt{M}^\sigma, \mathtt{N}^\sigma \in \mathcal{S\ell}\mathrm{PCF}_\star$. $\mathtt{M} \sim_\sigma \mathtt{N} \Rightarrow \mathtt{M} \approx_\sigma \mathtt{N}$.

The opposite direction is more difficult and it requires a semantic reasoning. First, we prove an auxiliary result claiming that in a coherence space $X \in \mathcal{L}$ (i.e in our type structure) different from $\mathbf{N}$, finite cliques are never maximal w.r.t. set-theoretical inclusion (Corollary 3)[2]. Then, we use this fact, together with Adequacy (Theorem 1) and Finite Definability (Theorem 6) to prove the result in the ground case (Lemma 8), which implies the general result (Theorem 8).

The fact that finite cliques in a coherence space $X \in \mathcal{L}$ different from $\mathbf{N}$ are never maximal w.r.t. set-theoretical inclusion follows from the next lemmas.

Lemma 6.

1. *Let x be a non-empty finite set of tokens in $|[\![\sigma]\!]|$ s.t. $\exists a \in x \forall b \in x . a \asymp b$. Then $\exists a' \notin x \forall b \in x . a' \smile b$.*
2. *Let x be a non-empty finite set of tokens in $|[\![\sigma]\!]|$ $(\sigma \neq \iota)$ s.t. $\exists a \in x \forall b \in x . a \supset b$. Then $\exists a' \notin x . \forall b \in x . a \frown b$.*

Corollary 3. *Let $x \in Cl_{fin}([\![\sigma]\!])$, with $\sigma \neq \iota$. Then there is $a \in |[\![\sigma]\!]|$ such that $a \notin x$ and $x \cup \{a\} \in Cl([\![\sigma]\!])$.*

Given an environment ρ, a term M, a stable variable F^σ and an infinite clique $x \in Cl([\![\sigma]\!])$, with a slight abuse of notation in the sequel we write $[\![\mathtt{M}]\!]\rho[F := x]$ to denote $\bigcup_{y \subseteq_{fin} x} [\![\mathtt{M}]\!]\rho[F := y]$. The next auxiliary lemma will be useful in what follows.

Lemma 7. *Let* $\mathtt{M}^\sigma, \mathtt{N}^\tau \in \mathcal{S\ell}\mathrm{PCF}_\star$ *and* $\rho \in \mathrm{Env}$. *If* $\mathtt{M}^\sigma[\mathtt{N}/F^\tau] \in \mathcal{S\ell}\mathrm{PCF}_\star$, *then* $[\![\mathtt{M}^\sigma[\mathtt{N}/F^\tau]]\!]\rho = \bigcup_{x \subseteq_{fin} [\![\mathtt{N}]\!]\rho} [\![\mathtt{M}]\!]\rho[F^\tau := x]$

Now, we show that by using fixpoints it is possible to build contexts that allow us to discriminate as much as we can do by using substitutions.

Lemma 8. *If* $\Gamma \vdash \mathtt{M}, \mathtt{N} : \iota$ *with* $\Gamma\restriction_\ell = \emptyset$. $\mathtt{M} \approx_\iota \mathtt{N} \Rightarrow \mathtt{M} \sim_\iota \mathtt{N}$.

Proof. We prove the contrapositive. Let $F_1^{\sigma_1}, \ldots, F_n^{\sigma_n}$ be such that $\mathcal{SFV}(\mathtt{M}), \mathcal{SFV}(\mathtt{N}) \subseteq \{F_1, \ldots, F_n\}$. Let $\mathtt{C}[\cdot^\iota]$ be a context and $\vec{\mathtt{P}}$ be closed terms such that $\mathtt{C}[\mathtt{M}[\vec{\mathtt{P}}/\vec{F}]] \Downarrow \underline{\mathtt{n}}$ and $\mathtt{C}[\mathtt{N}[\vec{\mathtt{P}}/\vec{F}]] \not\Downarrow \underline{\mathtt{n}}$. We prove by induction on n that there is a $\mathtt{C}'$ such that $\mathtt{C}'[\mathtt{M}] \Downarrow \underline{\mathtt{n}}'$ and $\mathtt{C}'[\mathtt{M}] \not\Downarrow \underline{\mathtt{n}}'$.

Base case. Since $n = 0$ the two terms have no free occurrence of stable variables, thus we can take $\mathtt{C}' = \mathtt{C}$.

Inductive case. The fix-point (in)equivalence implies that there is a context $\mathtt{C}[.^\iota]$ and there are closed terms $\mathtt{P}_1, \ldots, \mathtt{P}_{n+1}$, such that $\mathtt{C}[\mathtt{M}[\mathtt{P}_1/F_1^{\sigma_1}, \ldots, \mathtt{P}_{n+1}/F_{n+1}^{\sigma_{n+1}}]] \Downarrow \underline{\mathtt{k}}$ but $\mathtt{C}[\mathtt{N}[\mathtt{P}_1/F_1^{\sigma_1}, \ldots, \mathtt{P}_{n+1}/F_{n+1}^{\sigma_{n+1}}]] \not\Downarrow \underline{\mathtt{k}}$. Thus, by Correctness, there exists a ρ such that

$$[\![\mathtt{M}]\!]\rho[F_1^{\sigma_1} := [\![\mathtt{P}_1]\!]\rho, \ldots, F_{n+1}^{\sigma_{n+1}} := [\![\mathtt{P}_{n+1}]\!]\rho] \neq [\![\mathtt{N}]\!]\rho[F_1^{\sigma_1} := [\![\mathtt{P}_1]\!]\rho, \ldots, F_{n+1}^{\sigma_{n+1}} := [\![\mathtt{P}_{n+1}]\!]\rho]$$

In the following, we define $\rho_1 = \rho[F_1^{\sigma_1} := [\![\mathtt{P}_1]\!]\rho, \ldots, F_n^{\sigma_n} := [\![\mathtt{P}_n]\!]\rho]$. Let us observe that both $[\![\mathtt{M}]\!]\rho_1[F_{n+1}^{\sigma_{n+1}} := [\![\mathtt{P}_{n+1}]\!]\rho]$ and $[\![\mathtt{N}]\!]\rho_1[F_{n+1}^{\sigma_{n+1}} := [\![\mathtt{P}_{n+1}]\!]\rho]$ are finite sets (in particular, they have at most one element and they cannot be both empty). Thus, without loss of generality, we assume that $[\![\mathtt{M}]\!]\rho_1[F_{n+1}^{\sigma_{n+1}} := [\![\mathtt{P}_{n+1}]\!]\rho] = \{k\}$. So by Lemma 7 there exists $x \subseteq_{fin} [\![\mathtt{P}_{n+1}]\!]\rho$ such that

$$[\![\mathtt{M}]\!]\rho_1[F_{n+1} := [\![\mathtt{P}_{n+1}]\!]\rho] = [\![\mathtt{M}]\!]\rho_1[F_{n+1} := x] \neq [\![\mathtt{N}]\!]\rho_1[F_{n+1} := x] \subseteq [\![\mathtt{N}]\!]\rho_1[F_{n+1} := [\![\mathtt{P}_{n+1}]\!]\rho]$$

Since stable variables are never of ground type, we can let $\sigma_{n+1} = \tau_1 \multimap \ldots \multimap \tau_m \multimap \iota$ and $m \geq 1$. Let $x = \{(a_1^1, \ldots, a_m^1, h^1), \ldots, (a_1^p, \ldots, a_m^p, h^p)\}$ with $p \geq 0$ and $a_1^i \in |[\![\tau_1]\!]|, \ldots, a_m^i \in |[\![\tau_m]\!]|, h^i \in \mathbb{N}$ for all $i \in [1, p]$. Furthermore, by Corollary 3 there is a token $(a_1^*, \ldots, a_m^*, h^*) \notin x$ such that $x^* = x \cup \{(a_1^*, \ldots, a_m^*, h^*)\}$ is still a clique. Observe that it is not restrictive to assume $h^* \notin \{h_1, \ldots, h_p\}$, since changing of outputs preserves the coherence of tokens. By Finite Definability, there is a term P defining the clique x^*. Now, let us consider the context

$$\begin{aligned}\mathtt{D} = \mu F_{n+1}.\lambda \mathtt{f}_1^{\tau_1} \ldots \mathtt{f}_m^{\tau_m}.\Big(\lambda \mathtt{x}^\iota. \; & \ell\mathtt{if}\ (\mathtt{x} \doteq \underline{\mathtt{h}^*}) \quad [\cdot^\iota] \\ & \ell\mathtt{if}\ (\mathtt{x} \doteq \underline{\mathtt{h}_1}) \quad \underline{\mathtt{h}_1} \\ & \vdots \\ & \ell\mathtt{if}\ (\mathtt{x} \doteq \underline{\mathtt{h}_\mathtt{p}}) \quad \underline{\mathtt{h}_\mathtt{p}}\ \Omega^\iota\Big)\Big(\mathtt{P}\,\mathtt{f}_1 \ldots \mathtt{f}_\mathtt{m}\Big)\end{aligned}$$

Observe that $\mathtt{D}[\mathtt{M}], \mathtt{D}[\mathtt{N}] \in \mathcal{S\ell}\mathrm{PCF}_\star$ because we hypothesized that M, N have no free occurrences of linear variables. If $q_1 = (\!|a_1^*|\!), \ldots, q_m = (\!|a_m^*|\!)$, it is not difficult to see that $[\![\mathtt{D}[\mathtt{M}]\ \mathtt{Sgl}_{\mathtt{q}_1}^{(\tau_1)} \ldots \mathtt{Sgl}_{\mathtt{q}_\mathtt{m}}^{(\tau_\mathtt{m})}]\!]\rho_1 = [\![\mathtt{M}]\!]\rho_1[F_{n+1} := [\![\mathtt{P}_{n+1}]\!]\rho] = \{\mathtt{k}\}$ and $[\![\mathtt{D}[\mathtt{N}]\ \mathtt{Sgl}_{\mathtt{q}_1}^{(\tau_1)} \ldots \mathtt{Sgl}_{\mathtt{q}_\mathtt{m}}^{(\tau_\mathtt{m})}]\!]\rho_1 \subseteq [\![\mathtt{N}]\!]\rho_1[F_{n+1} := [\![\mathtt{P}_{n+1}]\!]\rho]$ which is either empty or it is a singleton $\{k'\}$ different from k.

By Lemma 7, adequacy and definition of fix-point equivalence we have $\mathtt{D}[\mathtt{M}]\ \mathtt{Sgl}_{\mathtt{q}_1}^{(\tau_1)} \ldots \mathtt{Sgl}_{\mathtt{q}_\mathtt{m}}^{(\tau_\mathtt{m})} \not\sim_\iota \mathtt{D}[\mathtt{N}]\ \mathtt{Sgl}_{\mathtt{q}_1}^{(\tau_1)} \ldots \mathtt{Sgl}_{\mathtt{q}_\mathtt{m}}^{(\tau_\mathtt{m})}$. Thus, we can apply inductive hypothesis (since the number of free stable variables has decreased), to conclude the proof. □

The above lemma can be used to prove the general case.

Theorem 8. *Let* $\mathtt{M}^\sigma, \mathtt{N}^\sigma \in \mathcal{S\ell}\mathrm{PCF}_\star$. $\mathtt{M} \approx_\sigma \mathtt{N} \Rightarrow \mathtt{M} \sim_\sigma \mathtt{N}$.

Proof. We prove the contrapositive statement. Let $F_1^{\sigma_1}, \ldots, F_n^{\sigma_n}$ be such that $\mathcal{SFV}(\mathtt{M}), \mathcal{SFV}(\mathtt{N}) \subseteq \{F_1, \ldots, F_n\}$. Let C be a context and $\vec{\mathtt{P}}$ be closed terms such that $\mathtt{C}[\mathtt{M}[\vec{\mathtt{P}}/\vec{F}]] \Downarrow \underline{\mathtt{n}}$ and $\mathtt{C}[\mathtt{N}[\vec{\mathtt{P}}/\vec{F}]] \not\Downarrow \underline{\mathtt{n}}$ for some numeral $\underline{\mathtt{n}}$. In particular, observe that $\mathtt{C}[\mathtt{M}] \not\sim_\iota \mathtt{C}[\mathtt{N}]$, by definition of Fix-Point Operational Equivalence. Moreover, by construction $\mathtt{C}[\mathtt{M}]$ and $\mathtt{C}[\mathtt{N}]$ have no free occurrence of linear variables. Thus, by Lemma 8 there is a context D such that $\mathtt{D}[\mathtt{C}[\mathtt{M}]] \Downarrow \underline{\mathtt{m}}$ and $\mathtt{D}[\mathtt{C}[\mathtt{M}]] \not\Downarrow \underline{\mathtt{m}}$. So, the proof is done. □

Corollary 4. *The equivalence $\sim_\sigma$ is a congruence.*

7.1 Applicative Operational Equivalence

We conclude the section by defining an applicative operational equivalence obtained by considering only special kinds of contexts (*Applicative Contexts*) to test the equality of terms.

Definition 18 (Applicative Operational Equivalence). *Let* $\mathtt{M}^\sigma, \mathtt{N}^\sigma \in \mathcal{S\ell}\mathrm{PCF}_\star$ *such that* $\mathcal{SFV}(\mathtt{M}), \mathcal{SFV}(\mathtt{N}) \subseteq \{F_1^{\sigma_1}, \ldots, F_n^{\sigma_n}\}$.

- $\mathtt{M} \lesssim_\sigma^\mathtt{A} \mathtt{N}$ *whenever, for all context* C *of the form* $(\lambda \vec{\mathtt{f}}.[.^\sigma])\ \mathtt{P}_1 \ldots \mathtt{P}_\mathtt{m}$ *and for all closed terms* $\mathtt{L}_1^{\sigma_1}, \ldots, \mathtt{L}_n^{\sigma_1}$, *if* $\mathtt{C}[\mathtt{M}[\vec{\mathtt{L}}/\vec{F}]] \Downarrow \underline{\mathtt{n}}$ *then* $\mathtt{C}[\mathtt{N}[\vec{\mathtt{L}}/\vec{F}]] \Downarrow \underline{\mathtt{n}}$
- $\mathtt{M} \sim_\sigma^\mathtt{A} \mathtt{N}$ *iff* $\mathtt{M} \lesssim_\sigma^\mathtt{A} \mathtt{N}$ *and* $\mathtt{N} \lesssim_\sigma^\mathtt{A} \mathtt{M}$.

Theorem 9. *Let* $\mathtt{M}^\sigma, \mathtt{N}^\sigma \in \mathcal{S\ell}\mathrm{PCF}_\star$. $\mathtt{M} \sim_\sigma^\mathtt{A} \mathtt{N} \Rightarrow [\![\mathtt{M}]\!] = [\![\mathtt{N}]\!]$.

Proof. Just by observing that the context used in the proof of Theorem 7 is an applicative context. □

The applicative equivalence still coincides with the previous ones, so it provides a convenient tool for reasoning on programs.

[2] Observe that this fact is not true in the general case of stable functions: for example in the coherence space $!\mathbf{N} \multimap \mathbf{N}$, the finite clique $\{(\emptyset, 0)\}$ is maximal.

Corollary 5 (Equivalences Coincidence). *Let* $\mathtt{M}^\sigma, \mathtt{N}^\sigma \in \mathcal{S}\ell\mathrm{PCF}_\star$.

$$\mathtt{M} \sim_\sigma \mathtt{N} \iff \mathtt{M} \approx_\sigma \mathtt{N} \iff \mathtt{M} \sim_\sigma^{\mathtt{A}} \mathtt{N}$$

8. A Tracing Evaluation Semantics

The operational semantics of $\mathcal{S}\ell\mathrm{PCF}_\star$ presented in the previous sections is effective, but quite inefficient. Indeed, the rules for `which?` and `ℓet-ℓor` non-deterministically face a potentially infinite number of evaluation branches. Consequently, its bovine implementation should try an exhaustive search of the right branch among the infinite ones. In this section, we introduce a *tracing evaluation semantics* which is able to drastically prune such infinite-branching search tree.

Roughly, denotational linearity provides the certainty that each term is applied to a unique sequence of arguments. That is, only one token of the corresponding *trace* is used. So, an efficient evaluation can be obtained by storing an argument N in an environment e, and when the evaluation of N is done, by replacing the term in the environment by its trace. This way of evaluating programs is a kind of higher-order call-by-need evaluation where the trace of the term is stored instead of the value. In order to simplify the evaluation of the new operators, we record such sequence-information along the evaluation tree. The idea is "to recursively trace" the arguments supplied to functions. The so-obtained pruned search-tree is finite-branching and it induces a clever and more efficient evaluation.

A key role in order to trace all the information is played by the environment.

Definition 19. *An* **environment** e *is a function from a finite set of variables (ground or linear) to either a term (named* subject*) or a numeral (named* trace*).*
Let $\mathtt{x}^\sigma$ *be a variable in the domain of* e. *If* $\sigma = \iota$ *then* $e(\mathtt{x})$ *is always the trace. If* σ *is an arrow then either* $e(\mathtt{x})$ *is a term typed* σ *(the subject) or it is the trace typed* ι.
We note $e[\mathtt{z} := \mathtt{M}]$ *the new environment* e' *such that* $e'(\mathtt{z}) = \mathtt{M}$ *and* $e'(\mathtt{y}) = e(\mathtt{y})$, *for each* $\mathtt{y} \neq \mathtt{z}$. *Last, we note* $e\restriction_{\{\mathtt{x}\}}$ *the restricted environment obtained by deleting the variable* x.

Note that, the environments associate terms to type union, i.e. a variable could refer either to a term or to a numeral (encoding the trace). Moreover, in the case of a ground variable we just need to store a numeral because of the call-by-value policy that makes subjects and traces coincide.

The use of an environment to manage substitutions and the presence of a recursion operator raise the issue of clashes between variable-names. For sake of simplicity, we do not introduce closures. We overcame clashes by assuming a whole bunch of fresh variables and by doing the appropriate renaming at run-time in the reduction rules. Another reason for following that approach is that fresh variables are anyway necessary to trace the evaluation of `which?` arguments.

As expected, the rules of our machine will be driven by *states* (i.e. term in environment); they are denoted by $\langle \mathtt{M} | e \rangle$. Given a state, the environment contains as usual the subterms to be substituted to all the free variables and, sometimes, also some additional variables recording traces. Indeed, during the evaluation, sometimes an operational rule "fetches" an head redex and extends the environment with a fresh variable associated to a new subject. When arguments are supplied, the operational rules carefully substitute the subject by the convenient numeral encoding the trace. In this way, if a variable x contains a trace then, it has recorded the use done during the evaluation of the subject initially associated to the variable x itself. For sake of clarity, we explicitly remove not used variables from environments.

We note $\sharp$ the empty environment, so if M is a ground closed term then we can obtain its evaluation, by supplying the state $\langle \mathtt{M} | \sharp \rangle$ to the tracing machine.

Definition 20. *The* tracing evaluation $\Downarrow_{\mathrm{T}}$ *is the effective relation from states (ground terms in environments) to states (numerals in environments) defined by the rules of Table 3. If* $\langle \mathtt{M} | \sharp \rangle \Downarrow_{\mathrm{T}} \langle \underline{\mathtt{n}} | e_1 \rangle$ *then we say that* M converges, *and we write simply* $\mathtt{M} \Downarrow_{\mathrm{T}}$, *otherwise we say that it* diverges, *and we write* $\mathtt{M} \Uparrow_{\mathrm{T}}$.

We emphasize that all the states in rules of table 3 are driven by the head of a ground term. In order to facilitate the comprehension of the tracing machine we have devised its rules in two parts. The rules in the higher Part (a) take into account all possible shapes of the head of terms, except the case of a head variable that is tackled by the rules in the lower Part (b).

The rules in the higher part are quite easy to understand, so we comment only the rules involving non-standard operators. The rule (`w`) extends the incoming environment e_0 by a fresh variable h associated to the term M that we plan to trace, and evaluates h applied to the identity $\mathtt{I} = \lambda\mathtt{x}.\mathtt{x}$ (recall that if `which?`(M) converges, by rules in the Table 1.c, then MI also converges). The result of this evaluation gives back a state $\langle \underline{\mathtt{n}} | e_1 \rangle$ where e_1 reports the observed trace of M. From this, the result is built. Likewise, the three `ℓet-ℓor` rules start by evaluating a branch. If such a branch converges, the reported traces are used in order to start the evaluation of the other branch. In this case we supply as subjects of the involved variables terms having (exactly) the behavior of the reported trace (recall the Lemma 4). Therefore, a rule converges only in case the two branches do the same observations on the list of arguments supplied to a linear variable.

The lower part of Table 3 is a bit more complex. All the rules fetch head-variables, so the discriminating factor that drives their behavior is found in the shape of the subject associated in the environment to the head variable itself. Indeed, it is easy to see that there is one rule for all possible shape of the "head-subject". We remark that `ℓet-ℓor` is not taken into account, since a term having a `ℓet-ℓor` as head is certainly typed ground and ground terms are evaluated before to be stored in the environment (because of the call-by-value policy).

The rule (Hgvar) is easy. (Hvar) considers the case where the subject associated to the head variable is another variable-name, it forwards the evaluation by using the subject. (Happ) is a key rule. It applies in the case the subject associated to the head variable is an application MN. In this case, it shifts N in the term of the state driving the rules. Such approach allows us to collect sufficient information to report the needed traces. The rules (Hs), (Hp) and (Hμ) are quite simple. Likewise to the rule (`w`) presented above, the rule (H`w`) is interesting: it uses the information collected by the fresh variable h to produce the right outcome and the trace of the `which?` itself (since it is a subject of the incoming environment). Finally, the rules (Hλ^ι_ι), (H$\lambda^\iota_\multimap$), (H$\lambda^\multimap_\iota$) and (H$\lambda^\multimap_\multimap$) consider the cases arising from an head variable associated to an abstraction in the environment. There are four rules depending from two types, i.e. the type of the body of the abstraction and the type of the abstracted variable; mnemonically, the rule's names use as superscript the type of the variable and as subscript the type of the body. The rules (Hλ^ι_ι) and (H$\lambda^\iota_\multimap$) need first to evaluate the ground argument in order to comply the call-by-value policy. All the rules compose the sub-traces information in the rule-premises to obtain the traces that they must provide in the rule-conclusion.

We now prove that the trace evaluation machine is correct and complete with respect to the evaluation semantics presented in Table 1 and Table 2. It is easy to check by induction that the rules of Table 3 preserve the following property: if $\mathrm{FV}(\mathtt{M}) = \{\varkappa_1, \ldots, \varkappa_n\}$ for some $n \geq 0$ then such variables are in the domain of e.

$$\frac{}{\langle \underline{0}|e\rangle \Downarrow_T \langle \underline{0}|e\rangle}\ (0) \qquad \frac{\langle M|e_0\rangle \Downarrow_T \langle \underline{n}|e_1\rangle}{\langle \mathbf{s}\,M|e_0\rangle \Downarrow_T \langle \mathbf{s}\,\underline{n}|e_1\rangle}\ (s) \qquad \frac{\langle M|e_0\rangle \Downarrow_T \langle \mathbf{s}\,\underline{n}|e_1\rangle}{\langle \mathbf{p}\,M|e_0\rangle \Downarrow_T \langle \underline{n}|e_1\rangle}\ (p) \qquad \frac{f' \text{ fresh},\ \ \langle M[f'/f]P_1\ldots P_k|e_0[f':=N]\rangle \Downarrow_T \langle \underline{n}|e_1\rangle}{\langle (\lambda f^{\sigma\multimap\tau}.M)NP_1\ldots P_k|e_0\rangle \Downarrow_T \langle \underline{n}|e_1\restriction_{\{f'\}}\rangle}\ (\lambda^{\multimap})$$

$$\frac{\langle M|e_0\rangle \Downarrow_T \langle \underline{0}|e_1\rangle \quad \langle L|e_1\rangle \Downarrow_T \langle \underline{m}|e_2\rangle}{\langle \ell\mathtt{if}\ M\ L\ R\,|e_0\rangle \Downarrow_T \langle \underline{m}|e_2\rangle}\ (\text{ifl}) \qquad \frac{\langle M|e_0\rangle \Downarrow_T \langle \mathbf{s}\underline{n}|e_1\rangle \quad \langle R|e_1\rangle \Downarrow_T \langle \underline{m}|e_2\rangle}{\langle \ell\mathtt{if}\ M\ L\ R\,|e_0\rangle \Downarrow_T \langle \underline{m}|e_2\rangle}\ (\text{ifr}) \qquad \frac{\langle M[\mu F.M/F]P_1\ldots P_k|e_0\rangle \Downarrow_T \langle \underline{n}|e_1\rangle}{\langle (\mu F.M)P_1\ldots P_k|e_0\rangle \Downarrow_T \langle \underline{n}|e_1\rangle}\ (\mu)$$

$$\frac{x' \text{ fresh},\ \ \langle N|e_0\rangle \Downarrow_T \langle \underline{n}'|e_1\rangle \quad \langle M[x'/x]P_1\ldots P_k|e_1[x':=\underline{n}']\rangle \Downarrow_T \langle \underline{n}|e_2\rangle}{\langle (\lambda x^{\iota}.M)NP_1\ldots P_k|e_0\rangle \Downarrow_T \langle \underline{n}|e_2\restriction_{\{x'\}}\rangle}\ (\lambda^{\iota}) \qquad \frac{h^{(\iota\multimap\iota)\multimap\iota} \text{ fresh},\ \ \langle hI|e_0[h:=M]\rangle \Downarrow_T \langle \underline{n}|e_1\rangle \quad \underline{k}=\pi_1\pi_1 e_1(h)}{\langle \mathtt{which?}\,M^{(\iota\multimap\iota)\multimap\iota}|e_0\rangle \Downarrow_T \langle \lceil \underline{n},\underline{k}\rceil|e_1\restriction_{\{h\}}\rangle}\ (w)$$

$$\frac{f'_i \text{ fresh } (1\le i\le k),\ \ \begin{array}{l}\langle M_1[f'_1/f_1,\ldots,f'_k/f_k]|e_0[f'_1:=N_1,\ldots,f'_k:=N_k]\rangle \Downarrow_T \langle \underline{0}|e_1\rangle\\ \langle M_2[f'_1/f_1,\ldots,f'_k/f_k]|e_1[f'_1:=\mathtt{Sgl}^{\sigma_1}_{e_1(f'_1)},\ldots,f'_k:=\mathtt{Sgl}^{\sigma_k}_{e_1(f'_k)}]\rangle \Downarrow_T \langle \mathbf{s}\underline{m}|e_2\rangle\end{array}}{\langle \underline{\ell\mathtt{et}}\,f_1^{\sigma_1}=N_1,\ldots,f_k^{\sigma_k}=N_k\ \underline{\mathtt{in}\ell\mathtt{or}}\ M_1\ M_2\ M_3|e_0\rangle \Downarrow_T \langle \underline{m}|e_2\restriction_{\{f'_1,\ldots,f'_k\}}\rangle}\ (\text{1lgor})$$

$$\frac{f'_i \text{ fresh } (1\le i\le k),\ \ \begin{array}{l}\langle M_2[f'_1/f_1,\ldots,f'_k/f_k]|e_0[f'_1:=N_1,\ldots,f'_k:=N_k]\rangle \Downarrow_T \langle \underline{0}|e_1\rangle\\ \langle M_3[f'_1/f_1,\ldots,f'_k/f_k]|e_1[f'_1:=\mathtt{Sgl}^{\sigma_1}_{e_1(f'_1)},\ldots,f'_k:=\mathtt{Sgl}^{\sigma_k}_{e_1(f'_k)}]\rangle \Downarrow_T \langle \mathbf{s}\underline{m}|e_2\rangle\end{array}}{\langle \underline{\ell\mathtt{et}}\,f_1^{\sigma_1}=N_1,\ldots,f_k^{\sigma_k}=N_k\ \underline{\mathtt{in}\ell\mathtt{or}}\ M_1\ M_2\ M_3|e_0\rangle \Downarrow_T \langle \underline{m}|e_2\restriction_{\{f'_1,\ldots,f'_k\}}\rangle}\ (\text{2lgor})$$

$$\frac{f'_i \text{ fresh } (1\le i\le k),\ \ \begin{array}{l}\langle M_3[f'_1/f_1,\ldots,f'_k/f_k]|e_0[f'_1:=N_1,\ldots,f'_k:=N_k]\rangle \Downarrow_T \langle \underline{0}|e_1\rangle\\ \langle M_1[f'_1/f_1,\ldots,f'_k/f_k]|e_1[f'_1:=\mathtt{Sgl}^{\sigma_1}_{e_1(f'_1)},\ldots,f'_k:=\mathtt{Sgl}^{\sigma_k}_{e_1(f'_k)}]\rangle \Downarrow_T \langle \mathbf{s}\underline{m}|e_2\rangle\end{array}}{\langle \underline{\ell\mathtt{et}}\,f_1^{\sigma_1}=N_1,\ldots,f_k^{\sigma_k}=N_k\ \underline{\mathtt{in}\ell\mathtt{or}}\ M_1\ M_2\ M_3|e_0\rangle \Downarrow_T \langle \underline{m}|e_2\restriction_{\{f'_1,\ldots,f'_k\}}\rangle}\ (\text{3lgor})$$

$$\frac{e(x)=\underline{n}}{\langle x^{\iota}|e\rangle \Downarrow_T \langle \underline{n}|e\rangle}\ (\text{Hgvar}) \qquad \frac{\langle hP_1\ldots P_k|e_0\restriction_{\{f\}}\rangle \Downarrow_T \langle \underline{n}|e_1\rangle}{\langle fP_1\ldots P_k|e_0[f:=h]\rangle \Downarrow_T \langle \underline{n}|e_1[f:=e_1(h)]\rangle}\ (\text{Hvar}) \qquad \frac{h \text{ fresh},\ \ \langle hNP_1\ldots P_k|e_0[h:=M]\restriction_{\{f\}}\rangle \Downarrow_T \langle \underline{n}|e_1\rangle}{\langle fP_1\ldots P_k|e_0[f:=M^{\sigma\multimap\tau}N]\rangle \Downarrow_T \langle \underline{n}|e_1[f:=(\pi_2 e_1(h))]\restriction_{\{h\}}\rangle}\ (\text{Happ})$$

$$\frac{\langle M|e_0\restriction_{\{f\}}\rangle \Downarrow_T \langle \underline{n}|e_1\rangle}{\langle f^{\iota\multimap\iota}M|e_0[f:=\mathbf{s}]\rangle \Downarrow_T \langle \mathbf{s}\underline{n}|e_1[f:=\lceil \underline{n},\mathbf{s}\underline{n}\rceil]\rangle}\ (\text{Hs}) \qquad \frac{\langle M|e_0\restriction_{\{f\}}\rangle \Downarrow_T \langle \mathbf{s}\,\underline{n}|e_1\rangle}{\langle f^{\iota\multimap\iota}M|e_0[f:=\mathbf{p}]\rangle \Downarrow_T \langle \underline{n}|e_1[f:=\lceil \mathbf{s}\underline{n},\underline{n}\rceil]\rangle}\ (\text{Hp})$$

$$\frac{\langle fP_1\ldots P_k|e_0[f:=(M[\mu F.M/F])]\rangle \Downarrow_T \langle \underline{n}|e_1\rangle}{\langle fP_1\ldots P_k|e_0[f:=(\mu F.M)]\rangle \Downarrow_T \langle \underline{n}|e_1\rangle}\ (\text{H}\mu) \qquad \frac{h \text{ fresh},\ \ \langle hI|e_0[h:=M]\restriction_{\{f\}}\rangle \Downarrow_T \langle \underline{n}|e_1\rangle \quad \underline{k}=\pi_1\pi_1 e_1(h)}{\langle fM|e_0[f:=\mathtt{which?}]\rangle \Downarrow_T \langle \lceil \underline{n},\underline{k}\rceil|e_1[f:=\lceil\lceil\lceil \underline{k},\underline{k}\rceil,\underline{n}\rceil,\lceil \underline{n},\underline{k}\rceil\rceil]\restriction_{\{h\}}\rangle}\ (\text{Hw})$$

$$\frac{\begin{array}{l} z \text{ fresh},\\ \langle P|e_0\restriction_{\{f\}}\rangle \Downarrow_T \langle \underline{m}|e_1\rangle \quad \langle M[z/x]|e_1[z:=\underline{m}]\rangle \Downarrow_T \langle \underline{n}|e_2\rangle\end{array}}{\langle fP|e_0[f:=\lambda x^{\iota}.M^{\iota}]\rangle \Downarrow_T \langle \underline{n}|e_2[f:=\lceil \underline{m},\underline{n}\rceil]\restriction_{\{z\}}\rangle}\ (\text{H}\lambda^{\iota}_{\iota}) \qquad \frac{\begin{array}{l} h,z \text{ fresh},\\ \langle P_1|e_0\restriction_{\{f\}}\rangle \Downarrow_T \langle \underline{n}|e_1\rangle \quad \langle hP_2\ldots P_k|e_1[z:=\underline{n},h:=M[z/x]]\rangle \Downarrow_T \langle \underline{n}|e_2\rangle\end{array}}{\langle fP_1\ldots P_k|e_0[f:=\lambda x^{\iota}.M^{\sigma\multimap\tau}]\rangle \Downarrow_T \langle \underline{n}|e_2[f:=\lceil e_2(z),e_2(h)\rceil]\restriction_{\{z,h\}}\rangle}\ (\text{H}\lambda^{\iota}_{\multimap})$$

$$\frac{g' \text{ fresh},\ \ \langle M[g'/g]|e_0[g':=P]\restriction_{\{f\}}\rangle \Downarrow_T \langle \underline{n}|e_1\rangle}{\langle fP|e_0[f:=\lambda g^{\sigma\multimap\tau}.M^{\iota}]\rangle \Downarrow_T \langle \underline{n}|e_1[f:=\lceil e_1(g'),\underline{n}\rceil]\restriction_{\{g'\}}\rangle}\ (\text{H}\lambda^{\multimap}_{\iota}) \qquad \frac{h,g' \text{ fresh},\ \ \langle hP_2\ldots P_k|e_1[g':=P_1,h:=M[g'/g]]\restriction_{\{f\}}\rangle \Downarrow_T \langle \underline{n}|e_2\rangle}{\langle fP_1\ldots P_k|e_0[f:=\lambda g^{\sigma\multimap\sigma'}.M^{\tau\multimap\tau'}]\rangle \Downarrow_T \langle \underline{n}|e_2[f:=\lceil e_2(g'),e_2(h)\rceil]\restriction_{\{h,g'\}}\rangle}\ (\text{H}\lambda^{\multimap}_{\multimap})$$

Table 3. Tracing Semantics - Part (a) and Part (b).

Note that e associates to a variable $\varkappa$ a term N that can contain variables which are also in the domain of e. We show that we can avoid the use of cyclic environments. Let e_0 be an environment such that $dom(e_0) = \{\varkappa_1,\ldots,\varkappa_n\}$, let $\langle M|e\rangle$ be a state, let N be $M[e(\varkappa_1)/\varkappa_1,\ldots,e(\varkappa_n)/\varkappa_n]$. We define $\mathcal{T}$ to be the function from state to state, defined as follows: $\mathcal{T}(\langle M|e\rangle) = \langle N|e\restriction_{\{FV(N)\}}\rangle$. We plan to transform a state $\langle M|e\rangle$ in a closed ground term by iterating $\mathcal{T}$ until the environments becomes (eventually) empty. If such procedure is terminating then the state is said **acyclic**.

Lemma 9. *The evaluation of acyclic states only uses acyclic states.*

Proof. Since we add only fresh variables to the environments and the environments is always finite. □

From now on, we consider only acyclic states. Since $\langle M|\sharp\rangle$ is trivially acyclic, we can define $\mathcal{T}_\infty(\langle M|e\rangle)$ to be the closed ground term obtained by iterating $\mathcal{T}$ until the environment becomes empty.

Lemma 10. *Let* $\tau = \sigma_1 \multimap \ldots \multimap \sigma_k \multimap \gamma$.
If $\langle f^{\tau}P_1\ldots P_k|e_0\rangle \Downarrow_T \langle \underline{n}|e_1\rangle$ *then* $\mathtt{Chk}^{(\tau)}_{e_1(f)}(e_0(f)) \Downarrow \underline{0}$ *and* $\langle \mathtt{Sgl}_{e_1(f)}P_1\ldots P_k|e_0\rangle \Downarrow_T \langle \underline{n}|e_1\restriction_{\{f\}}\rangle$

Proof. Easy by induction on the tracing reduction rules. □

We can prove the trace evaluation machine to be correct and complete, by using the previous lemmas.

Theorem 10. *Let* $\mathcal{T}_\infty(\langle M|e_0\rangle) = P$.

Correctness. *If* $\langle M|e_0\rangle \Downarrow_T \langle \underline{n}|e_1\rangle$ *then* $P \Downarrow \underline{n}$.
Completeness. *If* $P \Downarrow \underline{n}$ *then* $\langle M|e_0\rangle \Downarrow_T \langle \underline{n}|e_1\rangle$.

Note that the tracing evaluation machine is a concrete improvement with respect to the evaluation machine presented in Table 1 and Table 2, in the sense that it prunes the infinite branching search trees of the evaluation rules for which? and ℓet-ℓor. So, it can be regarded as a guideline for a reasonable implementation.

Example Let us see the effectiveness of the tracing machine, by showing the evaluation of the term $\mathtt{which?}(\lambda f^{\iota\multimap\iota}.\mathbf{s}(f\underline{3}))$. In the following, we denote with e the environment $\sharp[f' = I]$.

$$\dfrac{\dfrac{\dfrac{\dfrac{\dfrac{\vdots}{\langle \underline{3}|e\rangle \Downarrow_T \langle \underline{3}|e\rangle} \quad \dfrac{}{\langle z|e[z=\underline{3}]\rangle \Downarrow_T \langle \underline{3}|e[z=\underline{3}]\rangle}\ (\text{Hgvar})}{\langle f'\underline{3}|e\rangle \Downarrow_T \langle \underline{3}|\sharp[f'=\lceil \underline{3},\underline{3}\rceil]\rangle}\ (\text{H}\lambda^{\iota}_{\iota})}{\langle \mathbf{s}(f'\underline{3})|e\rangle \Downarrow_T \langle \underline{4}|\sharp[f'=\lceil \underline{3},\underline{3}\rceil]\rangle}\ (s)}{\langle h\ I|\sharp[h=\lambda f.\mathbf{s}(f\underline{3})]\rangle \Downarrow_T \langle \underline{3},\sharp[h=\lceil\lceil \underline{3},\underline{3}\rceil,\underline{4}\rceil]\rangle}\ (\text{H}\lambda^{\multimap}_{\iota})}{\langle \mathtt{which?}(\lambda f^{\iota\multimap\iota}.\mathbf{s}(f\underline{3}))|\sharp\rangle \Downarrow_T \langle \lceil \underline{4},\underline{3}\rceil|\sharp\rangle}\ (w)$$

It can be noted here that the rules $(\text{H}\lambda^{\multimap}_{\iota})$ and $(\text{H}\lambda^{\iota}_{\iota})$ are crucial to trace out the use of terms being substituted to the fresh head variables h and f'. The rule $(\text{H}\lambda^{\multimap}_{\iota})$ traces the term $\lambda f.\mathbf{s}(f\underline{3})$ applied to I. The rule $(\text{H}\lambda^{\iota}_{\iota})$ traces the term I applied to $\underline{3}$.

9. Related works

The study of the relations between languages and models is a classic theme in denotational semantics [15, 28]. The full abstraction for PCF has led to the development of very sophisticated semantics techniques (as [2, 23]) and revealed relevant programming principles and operational constructions. In particular, several works have studied how to extend PCF by different operators in order to achieve full abstraction compared to some classical models. For example, this approach has been followed by Plotkin [33] for the continuous Scott model, by Berry and Curien [9] for the sequential algorithms model, by Abramsky and McCusker [1] for a particular game model, by Longley [26] for the strongly stable model and by Paolini [29] for the stable model. Remark that all higher-type operators introduced in the works above [9, 26, 29, 33] cannot be directly interpreted in the linear model. This motivates our search for new operators.

Many linear languages with different goals have been proposed so far in the literature. Recently, in the studies of syntactical linearity, Alves et al. have proposed several syntactical linear languages in order to characterize different classes of computable functions [3–5]. Such languages are syntactically linear but do not have extra operators that are key ingredients of $\mathcal{SL}$PCF$_\star$.

Two PCF-like languages embedding linearity notions have been proposed in [10, 11]. These languages are not denotationally linear, in the sense that not all their closed terms are in correspondence with linear functions of a suitable domain. In particular, they cannot be interpreted in the linear model considered here. Despite this fact, the authors of [10, 11] give some interesting results on the relations between several forms of operational reasoning, in the context of the linear decomposition. Our results on the coincidence of three operational equivalences can be viewed as further contributions in those topics.

10. Conclusions and Future Works

The results presented in this paper are part of a wider project (started with the works [17, 30]) aiming to extend the expressive power of linear programming languages. Our aim is to study particular denotational models embedding a notion of linearity, in order to extract programming languages that are fully abstract or fully complete (universal) with respect to the model, and that have new interesting operational features. Our study is also related to higher-type computability [25, 27], since the higher-type of new operators arising from these analysis.

A first interesting direction is to extend the results obtained in this paper in order to prove the universality of $\mathcal{SL}$PCF$_\star$ with respect to the linear model, i.e. to find the language able to define all the *recursive cliques* of the model. Another interesting direction is the study of $\mathcal{SL}$PCF$_\star$ semantics with respect to other model notions. In particular, we would pursue the study started in [31] about a model for $\mathcal{SL}$PCF$_\star$ based on linear processes. Moreover, we would pursue the study about categorical models for $\mathcal{SL}$PCF$_\star$ [18].

Last, we guess that an even more efficient evaluation of $\mathcal{SL}$PCF is possible. In particular, it would be interesting to study a new evaluation machine having an optimized memory management. That is, an evaluation machine that does not need neither fresh variables nor closures and where the heap will be used only for trace out sub-programs.

References

[1] S. Abramsky and G. McCusker. Linearity, sharing and state: a fully abstract game semantics for idealized algol with active expressions. *ENTCS*, 3, 1996.

[2] S. Abramsky, P. Malacaria, and R. Jagadeesan. Full abstraction for PCF. *I & C*, 163(2):409–470, 2000.

[3] S. Alves, M. Fernández, M. Florido, and I. Mackie. The power of linear functions. In *LNCS* 4207, pages 119–134. 2006.

[4] S. Alves, M. Fernández, M. Florido, and I. Mackie. Linear recursive functions. In *LNCS* 4600, pages 182–195. 2007.

[5] S. Alves, M. Fernndez, M. Florido, and I. Mackie. Gdel's system t revisited. *TCS*, 411(11-13):1484 – 1500, 2010.

[6] R. Amadio and P. L. Curien. *Domains and Lambda-Calculi* Cambridge University Press, 1998.

[7] G. Berry. Stable models of typed λ-calculi. In *LNCS* 62, pages 72–89. 1978.

[8] G. Berry. *Modèles completement adequats et stable du lambda-calcul typé*. PhD thesis, Université de Paris VII, France, 1979.

[9] G. Berry and P. L. Curien. Sequential algorithms on concrete data structures. *TCS*, 20:265–321, 1982.

[10] G. M. Bierman. Program equivalence in a linear functional language. *JFP*, 10(2):167–190, 2000.

[11] G. M. Bierman, A. M. Pitts, and C. V. Russo. Operational properties of lily, a polymorphic linear lambda calculus with recursion. *ENTCS*, 41(3), 2000.

[12] A. Bucciarelli and T. Ehrhard. Sequentiality and strong stability. In *Proc. LICS'91*, pages 138–145, 1991.

[13] A. Bucciarelli and T. Ehrhard. A theory of sequentiality. *TCS*, 113(2): 273–291, 7 June 1993.

[14] A. Bucciarelli, A. Carraro, T. Ehrhard, and A. Salibra. On linear information systems. In *EPTCS* 22, pages 38 – 48, 2010.

[15] P. L. Curien. Definability and full abstraction. *ENTCS*, 172:301–310, 2007.

[16] T. Ehrhard and L. Regnier. Differential interaction nets. *TCS*, 364(2): 166–195, 2006.

[17] M. Gaboardi and L. Paolini. Syntactical, operational and denotational linearity. In *Workshop LOGIC*. 2007.

[18] M. Gaboardi and M. Piccolo. Categorical models for a semantically linear λ-calculus. In *EPTCS* 22, pages 1 – 13, 2010.

[19] J. Y. Girard. Linear logic. *TCS*, 50:1–102, 1987.

[20] J. Y. Girard, Y. Lafont, and P. Taylor. *Proofs and Types*. Cambridge University Press, 1989.

[21] J. R. Hindley. BCK-combinators and linear λ-terms have types. *TCS*, 64:97–105, 1989.

[22] M. Huth. Linear domains and linear maps. In *LNCS* 802, pages 438–453. 1993.

[23] J. M. E. Hyland and L. C.-H. Ong. On full abstraction for PCF: I, II, and III. *I & C*, 163(2):285–408, 2000.

[24] J. W. Klop. New fix point combinators from old. In *Reflections on Type Theory*. Radboud University Nijmegen, 2007.

[25] J. R. Longley. Notions of computability at higher types I. In *Lecture Notes in Logic*, pages 32–142. 2000.

[26] J. R. Longley. The sequentially realizable functionals. *APAL*, 117: 1–93, 2002.

[27] D. Normann. Computing with functionals - computability theory or computer science? *Bulletin of Symbolic Logic*, 12(1):43–59, 2006.

[28] C.-H. Luke Ong. Correspondence between operational and denotational semantics: the full abstraction for PCF. In *Handbook of Logic in Computer Science* pages 269–356. Oxford University Press, 1995.

[29] L. Paolini. A stable programming language. *I & C*, 204(3):339–375, 2006.

[30] L. Paolini and M. Piccolo. Semantically linear programming languages. In *PPDP'08*, pages 97–107. ACM, 2008.

[31] L. Paolini and M. Piccolo. A process-model for linear programs. In *LNCS* 5497, pages 289–305. 2009.

[32] M. Piccolo. *Linearity and Beyond in Denotational Semantics*. PhD thesis, Universitá di Torino/Université de Paris VII, 2009.

[33] G. D. Plotkin. LCF considerd as a programming language. *TCS*, 5: 225–255, 1977.

[34] D. Walker. *Advanced Topics in Types and Programming Languages*, chapter Substructural Type Systems. The MIT Press, 2005.

Generalising and Dualising the Third List-Homomorphism Theorem

Functional Pearl

Shin-Cheng Mu
Academia Sinica, Taiwan
scm@iis.sinica.edu.tw

Akimasa Morihata
Tohoku University, Japan
morihata@riec.tohoku.ac.jp

Abstract

The third list-homomorphism theorem says that a function is a list homomorphism if it can be described as an instance of both a *foldr* and a *foldl*. We prove a dual theorem for unfolds and generalise both theorems to trees: if a function generating a list can be described both as an *unfoldr* and an *unfoldl*, the list can be generated from the middle, and a function that processes or builds a tree both upwards and downwards may independently process/build a subtree and its one-hole context. The point-free, relational formalism helps to reveal the beautiful symmetry hidden in the theorem.

Categories and Subject Descriptors D.1.1 [*Programming Techniques*]: Applicative (Functional) Programming; F.3.1 [*Logics and Meanings of Programs*]: Specifying and Verifying and Reasoning about Programs

General Terms Algorithms, Theory

Keywords program derivation, third list homomorphism theorem

1. Introduction

As multicore hardware has become standard in recent years, parallel programming rekindles as an important potential application of functional programming. The *skeletal parallel programming* [3] paradigm proposes the idea of developing parallel programs by combining parallel skeletons — functions that capture useful parallel programming patterns. Among the important parallel skeletons is list homomorphism [1], one that satisfies the equation

$$h\,(xs +\!\!+\, ys) = h\,xs \odot h\,ys,$$

which says that to compute h, one may arbitrarily split the input list into $xs +\!\!+\, ys$, compute h on them recursively in parallel, and combine the results using an associative operator $(\odot)$.

A well-known *third list-homomorphism theorem* [6] says that a function is a list homomorphism if it can be described as an instance of both *foldr* and *foldl*. For example, since $sum = foldr\ (+)\ 0 = foldl\ (+)\ 0$, there exists some $(\odot)$ such that $sum\,(xs +\!\!+\, ys) = sum\,xs \odot sum\,ys$, — for this simple example, $(\odot)$ happens to be $(+)$ as well. One naturally wonders whether $(\odot)$ can be mechanically constructed. Such methods have been proposed [5, 9, 11], and even generalised to trees [10].

Less noticed, however, is that the theorem and its proof dualise very well to unfolds on lists. Consider the function $fromTo\ (x, y) = [x, x+1 \ldots y]$. One may imagine three possible implementations: generating the list from the left, from the right, and from some arbitrary point in the middle. Is it true that any function that can be defined as both an *unfoldr* and an *unfoldl* can be written as one that generates the list from the middle?

We show in this pearl that the answer is positive. This is not only of theoretical interest but could also have a practical impact. First, there are several efficient algorithms that are based on divide-and-conquer sequence generation, such as Quicksort. Moreover, the performance bottleneck in distributed parallel computing often lies in data distribution. Being able to generate the list anywhere allows us to distribute seeds of sublists and simultaneously generate from them, and thereby reduce communication costs and increase parallelism.

List homomorphisms and the third list-homomorphism theorem are reviewed in Section 2, before we present a dualised theorem in Section 3 and apply it, in Section 4, to examples including sorting and parallel scan. In Section 5, the results are further generalised to trees, before we conclude in Section 6.

ICFP'11, September 19–21, 2011, Tokyo, Japan.

2. The Third List-Homomorphism Theorem

As is well known, in the world of sets and total functions, the equations

$$\begin{aligned} h\,[\,] &= e \\ h\,(x : xs) &= f_{\triangleleft}\,(x, h\,xs), \end{aligned} \qquad (1)$$

where $e :: b$ and $f_{\triangleleft} :: (a \times b) \to b$, have a unique solution for $h :: [a] \to b$, denoted by $foldr\ f_{\triangleleft}\ e$. We deviate from the standard and let $f_{\triangleleft}$ be uncurried since it is more convenient in point-free style, where programs are described by function composition rather than application. In fact, we will also introduce uncurried constructor $cons\ (x, xs) = x : xs$, and let $(f \times g)\,(x, y) = (f\,x, g\,y)$, which satisfies a law $(f \times g) \circ (h \times k) = (f \circ h \times g \circ k)$, which we will refer to as "product functor". Thus (1) can be written

$$h \circ cons = f_{\triangleleft} \circ (id \times h).$$

We define a variation of *foldr* that takes the base case as an extra argument,

$$\begin{aligned} &foldrr :: ((a \times b) \to b) \to ([a], b) \to b \\ &foldrr\ f_{\triangleleft}\ ([\,], e) = e \\ &foldrr\ f_{\triangleleft}\ (x : xs, e) = f_{\triangleleft}\,(x, foldrr\ f_{\triangleleft}\ (xs, e)), \end{aligned}$$

It can be seen as a "resumed" version of *foldr* (hence the suffix "r" in the name), that is, if $h = foldr\ f_\triangleleft\ e$, one can easily show by induction on xs that

$$h\ (xs + ys) = foldrr\ f_\triangleleft\ (xs, h\ ys). \qquad (2)$$

Let $cat\ (xs, ys) = xs + ys$, (2) can be written point-free as

$$h \circ cat = foldrr\ f_\triangleleft \circ (id \times h). \qquad (3)$$

Symmetrically, let $snoc\ (xs, x) = xs + [x]$. It is known that $foldl\ f_\triangleright\ e$ is the unique solution for $h :: [a] \to b$ in

$$\begin{aligned} h\,[\,] &= e \\ h \circ snoc &= f_\triangleright \circ (h \times id), \end{aligned}$$

where $f_\triangleright :: (b \times a) \to b$. Defining resumable *foldl* as

$$\begin{aligned} &foldlr :: ((b \times a) \to b) \to (b, [a]) \to b \\ &foldlr\ f_\triangleright\ (e, [\,]) = e \\ &foldlr\ f_\triangleright\ (e, xs + [x]) = f_\triangleright\ (foldlr\ f_\triangleright\ (e, xs), x), \end{aligned}$$

we have, if $h = foldl\ f_\triangleright\ e$, that

$$h \circ cat = foldlr\ f_\triangleright \circ (h \times id). \qquad (4)$$

A function $h :: [a] \to b$ is a *list homomorphism* if there exist $e :: b$, $k :: a \to b$, and $f :: (b \times b) \to b$ such that

$$\begin{aligned} h\,[\,] &= e \\ h\,[x] &= k\ x \\ h\ (xs + ys) &= f\ (h\ xs, h\ ys). \end{aligned}$$

In such a case we denote h by $hom\ f\ k\ e$. The equations imply that f is associative, on the range of h, with unit e. To compute a list homomorphism h, one may split the input list arbitrarily into two parts, recursively compute h on both parts, and combine the results using f, implying a potential for parallel computation. If f and k are constant-time operations, a list homomorphism can be evaluated in time $O(n/p + \log p)$, where n is the length of the input list and p the number of processors, and we get almost linear speedups with respect to p.

Some famous theorems relate *foldr*, *foldl* and list homomorphisms. Firstly, since the input list can be split arbitrarily, we may of course choose a biased split, reducing a list homomorphism to a *foldr* or a *foldl*.

Theorem 1 (the 2nd list-hom. theorem [1]). If $h = hom\ f\ k\ e$ then $h = foldr\ f_\triangleleft\ e = foldl\ f_\triangleright\ e$, where $f_\triangleleft\ (x, v) = f\ (k\ x, v)$ and $f_\triangleright\ (v, x) = f\ (v, k\ x)$. □

Somewhat surprisingly, if a function can be computed both by a *foldr* and a *foldl*, it is a list homomorphism.

Theorem 2 (the 3rd list-hom. theorem [6]). $h = foldr\ f_\triangleleft\ e = foldl\ f_\triangleright\ e$ implies $h = hom\ f\ k\ e$ for some f and k.

Proof. The only possible choice for k is $k\ x = h\ [x]$. The aim is to find f such that $h \circ cat = f \circ (h \times h)$. A function f^{-1} is called a *right inverse* of f if for all y in the range of f, we have $f\ (f^{-1}\ y) = y$. Equivalently, $f \circ f^{-1} \circ f = f$. In a set-theoretical model, a right inverse always exists but may not be unique.

While a semantical proof was given by Gibbons [6], we will provide a proof having a more equational flavour. We reason:

$$\begin{aligned} & h \circ cat \\ =\ & \{\ (3)\ \} \\ & foldrr\ f_\triangleleft \circ (id \times h) \\ =\ & \{\ h = h \circ h^{-1} \circ h, \text{ product functor }\ \} \\ & foldrr\ f_\triangleleft \circ (id \times h) \circ (id \times h^{-1}) \circ (id \times h) \\ =\ & \{\ (3) \text{ backwards, and } (4)\ \} \\ & foldlr\ f_\triangleright \circ (h \times id) \circ (id \times h^{-1}) \circ (id \times h) \\ =\ & \{\ h = h \circ h^{-1} \circ h, \text{ product functor }\ \} \\ & foldlr\ f_\triangleright \circ (h \times id) \circ (h^{-1} \times h^{-1}) \circ (h \times h) \\ =\ & \{\ (4) \text{ backwards }\ \} \\ & h \circ cat \circ (h^{-1} \times h^{-1}) \circ (h \times h). \end{aligned}$$

Thus the theorem holds if we pick $f = h \circ cat \circ (h^{-1} \times h^{-1})$. □

Theorem 2 in fact provides hints how to construct list homomorphisms. For example, since $sum = foldr\ (+)\ 0 = foldl\ (+)\ 0$, Theorem 2 states that sum can be written as $sum = hom\ f\ k\ 0$ where $k\ x = sum\ [x] = x$ and $f\ (v, w) = sum\ (g\ v + g\ w)$ for any right inverse g of sum. One may simply pick $g\ x = [x]$, and $f\ (v, w)$ simplifies to $v + w$.

Readers might have noticed something odd in the proof: the property much talked about, that h being both a *foldr* and a *foldl*, could be weakened — properties (3) and (4) were merely used to push h to the right. In fact, $h \circ cat$ is never expanded in the proof. One thus wonders whether there is something more general waiting to be discovered, which is indeed what we will see in the following sections. The syntactical approach makes such generalisations much easier to spot.

3. Dual of Third List-Homomorphism Theorem

The function *unfoldr*, a dual of *foldr* that generates a list from left to right, may be defined as follows. [1]

$$\begin{aligned} &unfoldr :: (b \to (a, b)) \to (b \to Bool) \to b \to [a] \\ &unfoldr\ g_\triangleright\ p\ v \mid p\ v = [\,] \\ &\qquad\qquad\qquad \mid (x, v') \leftarrow g_\triangleright\ v = x : unfoldr\ g_\triangleright\ p\ v'. \end{aligned}$$

Symmetrically, the function *unfoldl* is defined by

$$\begin{aligned} &unfoldl :: (b \to (b, a)) \to (b \to Bool) \to b \to [a] \\ &unfoldl\ g_\triangleleft\ p\ v \mid p\ v = [\,] \\ &\qquad\qquad\qquad \mid (v', x) \leftarrow g_\triangleleft\ v = unfoldl\ g_\triangleleft\ p\ v' + [x]. \end{aligned}$$

Typically, unfolds are defined for coinductive, possibly infinite lists. Since we want the unfolded lists to have both a left end and a right end, and for another important technical reason to be mentioned later, our "unfolds" in this pearl return inductive, finite lists and require separate proofs that all successive applications of $g_\triangleright$ and $g_\triangleleft$ eventually reaches some v for which $p\ v$ is true. Due to space constraints, however, the proof of termination is usually treated informally.

Finally, we denote a function $k :: b \to [a]$ by $unhom\ g\ f\ p\ q$ if it satisfies

$$\begin{aligned} k\ v &\mid p\ v = [\,] \\ &\mid q\ v = [f\ v] \\ &\mid (v_1, v_2) \leftarrow g\ v = k\ v_1 + k\ v_2. \end{aligned}$$

[1] The "pattern guard" $(x, v') \leftarrow g_\triangleright\ v$ matches the result of $g_\triangleright$ in the guard.

We also demand that successive applications of g eventually produce seeds for which either p or q is true, and thus k generates finite lists.

Regrettably, Theorem 1 does not dualise to unfolds.

Lemma 3. There exists h such that $h = \mathit{unhom}\ g\ f\ p\ q$ for which there exist neither $g_\triangleright$ satisfying $h = \mathit{unfoldr}\ g_\triangleright\ p$ nor $g_\triangleleft$ satisfying $h = \mathit{unfoldl}\ g_\triangleleft\ p$.

Proof. Let $\mathit{exp} :: \mathit{Int} \to [\mathit{Int}]$ generate a list of 1's of length 2^n for given n. It can be defined by $\mathit{unhom}\ g\ f\ p\ q$ where $f\ 0 = 1$, $q = (0 ==)$, $p = (0 >)$, and $g\ (1+n) = (n, n)$, but not by an $\mathit{unfoldr}$ or $\mathit{unfoldl}$. An intuitive reason is that there is not always an m such that $2^n - 1 = 2^m$. One may use the theories of Gibbons et al. [7] for a proof. □

Does Theorem 2 have an unfold counterpart? To establish that $k = \mathit{unhom}\ g\ f\ p'\ q$ given $k = \mathit{unfoldr}\ g_\triangleright\ p = \mathit{unfoldl}\ g_\triangleleft\ p$, we can pick $p' = p$, $q = p \circ \mathit{snd} \circ g_\triangleright$, and $f = \mathit{fst} \circ g_\triangleright$. The challenge is to construct g. To do so, we introduce some concepts dual to those for folds. While foldrr and foldlr resume a partially computed fold, their duals pause during generation of lists. During the generation of a list there are many places where we may pause. The following functions $\mathit{unfoldrp}$ and $\mathit{unfoldlp}$ ("p" for pause) return, in a list, all intermediate lists and seeds during list generation:

$$\begin{array}{l}
\mathit{unfoldrp} :: (b \to (a, b)) \to (b \to \mathit{Bool}) \to b \to [([a], b)] \\
\mathit{unfoldrp}\ g_\triangleright\ p\ v = \mathit{iter}_\triangleright\ ([\,], v) \quad \textbf{where} \\
\quad \mathit{iter}_\triangleright\ (xs, v) \mid p\ v = [(xs, v)] \\
\qquad\qquad\qquad\ \mid (x, v') \leftarrow g_\triangleright\ v = (xs, v) : \mathit{iter}_\triangleright\ (xs +\!\!+ [x], v'),
\end{array}$$

$$\begin{array}{l}
\mathit{unfoldlp} :: (b \to (b, a)) \to (b \to \mathit{Bool}) \to b \to [(b, [a])] \\
\mathit{unfoldlp}\ g_\triangleleft\ p\ v = \mathit{iter}_\triangleleft\ (v, [\,]) \quad \textbf{where} \\
\quad \mathit{iter}_\triangleleft\ (v, xs) \mid p\ v = [(v, xs)] \\
\qquad\qquad\qquad\ \mid (v', x) \leftarrow g_\triangleleft\ v = \mathit{iter}_\triangleleft\ (v', x : xs) +\!\!+ [(v, xs)].
\end{array}$$

We may think of them as returning the "traces" of unfolding. For example, $\mathit{unfoldrp}\ g_\triangleright\ p\ v_0$ yields the list $[([\,], v_0), ([x_1], v_1), ([x_1, x_2], v_2) \ldots]$, etc, if $(x_{i+1}, v_{i+1}) = g_\triangleright\ v_i$.

A crucial property relating $\mathit{unfoldr}$ and $\mathit{unfoldrp}$ is that if $k = \mathit{unfoldr}\ g_\triangleright\ p$ we have

$$\mathit{splits} \circ k = \mathit{map}\ (\mathit{id} \times k) \circ \mathit{unfoldrp}\ g_\triangleright\ p, \tag{5}$$

where $\mathit{splits} :: [a] \to ([a], [a])$ returns all the "splits" of the given list (e.g. $\mathit{splits}\ [1,2] = [([], [1,2]), ([1], [2]), ([1,2], [])]$). Similarly, we have that

$$\mathit{splits} \circ k = \mathit{map}\ (k \times \mathit{id}) \circ \mathit{unfoldlp}\ g_\triangleleft\ p, \tag{6}$$

if $k = \mathit{unfoldl}\ g_\triangleleft\ p$. Notice how they roughly resemble the "converses" of (3) and (4): functions next to the composition $(\circ)$ are swapped; instead of $f \circ \mathit{cat}$ we have $\mathit{splits} \circ k$ on the left hand sides of the equalities; $(\mathit{id} \times k)$ in (5) is on the lefthand side of $(\circ)$, and is lifted to lists by map due to the type, etc.

A relational perspective We could have proceeded from (5) and (6) to construct g and thereby prove the dual theorem. However, we would like to take a bold approach and ask the readers to see paused unfolding as a relation. Functional programmers appear to regard relations as an arcane creation, which is an unfortunate misunderstanding. Dijkstra argued that, for program derivation, non-determinism should be the norm and determinism a special case [4], and this pearl is indeed a case where one has to bring up relations to appreciate the nice duality between the theorems for folding and unfolding.

For this pearl we need only a one-paragraph introduction to relations. A function $f :: a \to b$ is a subset of $(b \times a)$ where $(y, x) \in f$ means that x is mapped to y by f, or y is a result to which f maps the argument x, with the constraint that $(y, x) \in f$ and $(y', x) \in f$ implies $y = y'$. The constraint is relaxed for relations, allowing x to be mapped to multiple ys. Composition of relations is defined by

$$(z, x) \in (R \circ S) \equiv (\exists y :: (z, y) \in R \wedge (y, x) \in S).$$

Given $R :: a \to b$, its *converse* $R^\circ :: b \to a$ is defined by $(x, y) \in R^\circ \equiv (y, x) \in R$. We have $(R^\circ)^\circ = R$, $\mathit{id}^\circ = \mathit{id}$, and that converse distributes covariantly over product, and contravariantly over composition:

$$\begin{array}{l}
(R \times S)^\circ = (R^\circ \times S^\circ), \\
(R \circ S)^\circ = S^\circ \circ R^\circ.
\end{array}$$

In this pearl we view unfolds as the relational converse of folds, which is another reason why we restrict ourselves to finite lists — our "unfolds" are actually converses of folds in disguise, and an unhom is the relational converse of a list homomorphism.

Let the relation $\mathit{mem} :: [a] \to a$ relate a list to any of its members, and let

$$\begin{array}{l}
\mathit{unfr}\ g_\triangleright\ p = \mathit{mem} \circ \mathit{unfoldrp}\ g_\triangleright\ p, \\
\mathit{unfl}\ g_\triangleleft\ p = \mathit{mem} \circ \mathit{unfoldlp}\ g_\triangleleft\ p.
\end{array}$$

While $\mathit{unfoldrp}$ and $\mathit{unfoldlp}$ generate the entire trace, unfr and unfl map the input seed to one arbitrary intermediate state. That is, $\mathit{unfr}\ g_\triangleright\ p$ maps v_0 to each of $([\,], v_0)$, $([x_1], v_1)$, $([x_1, x_2], v_2)$, etc., if $(x_{i+1}, v_{i+1}) = g_\triangleright\ v_i$. The equality (5) can be expressed relationally — if $k = \mathit{unfoldr}\ g_\triangleright\ p$ we have

$$\mathit{cat}^\circ \circ k = (\mathit{id} \times k) \circ \mathit{unfr}\ g_\triangleright\ p. \tag{7}$$

Both sides relate the input seed, say v, to a *pair* of lists. On the left hand side, the list returned by $k\ v$ is arbitrarily split into (xs, ys). The equation says that $xs +\!\!+ ys = k\ v$ if and only if xs can be generated by $\mathit{unfr}\ g_\triangleright\ p$ and ys can be generated by k starting from where $\mathit{unfr}\ g_\triangleright\ p$ left off. For $k = \mathit{unfoldl}\ g_\triangleleft\ p$, a symmetric property holds:

$$\mathit{cat}^\circ \circ k = (k \times \mathit{id}) \circ \mathit{unfl}\ g_\triangleleft\ p. \tag{8}$$

Recall that our aim is to construct g. It suffices to find a g such that

$$\mathit{cat}^\circ \circ k = (k \times k) \circ g.$$

That is, $k\ v = xs +\!\!+ ys$ if and only if xs and ys can be generated from seeds produced by $g\ v$.

Notice that by applying the converse operator $(\_)^\circ$ to both sides of (7) and (8), we get equations that are almost (3) and (4) apart from having converses of k and unfolds in the formulae:

$$\begin{array}{l}
k^\circ \circ \mathit{cat} = (\mathit{unfr}\ g_\triangleright\ p)^\circ \circ (\mathit{id} \times k^\circ), \\
k^\circ \circ \mathit{cat} = (\mathit{unfl}\ g_\triangleleft\ p)^\circ \circ (k^\circ \times \mathit{id}).
\end{array}$$

The proof of Theorem 2, however, proceeds the same way even if the components are not functions! In the realm of relations, part of the proof of Theorem 2 can be generalised to:

Theorem 4. If $R \circ \mathit{cat} = S_\triangleright \circ (\mathit{id} \times R) = S_\triangleleft \circ (R \times \mathit{id})$ and $R \circ R' \circ R = R$ for some R', then $R \circ \mathit{cat} = R \circ \mathit{cat} \circ (R^\circ \times R^\circ) \circ (R \times R)$.

Proof. The same as that of Theorem 2. We will prove a more general Theorem 7 later. □

The desired dual theorem thus follows:

Corollary 5. If $k = \mathit{unhom}\ g\ f\ p\ q$ for some g, f, and q, then $k = \mathit{unfoldr}\ g_\triangleright\ p = \mathit{unfoldl}\ g_\triangleleft\ p$.

Proof. We have talked about f and q, and now we aim to find g such that $\mathit{cat}^\circ \circ k = (k \times k) \circ g$. Using (7) and (8) as antecedents of Theorem 4, we get

$$\mathit{cat}^\circ \circ k = (k \times k) \circ (k^\circ \times k^\circ) \circ \mathit{cat}^\circ \circ k,$$

thus g can be any functional subset of $(k^\circ \times k^\circ) \circ \mathit{cat}^\circ \circ k$. □

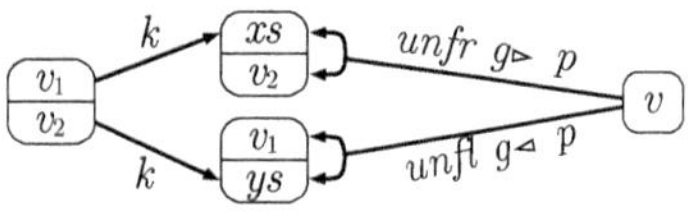

Figure 1. Depicting $((k^{\circ} \times id) \circ unfr\ g_{\triangleright}\ p) \cap ((id \times k^{\circ}) \circ unfl\ g_{\triangleleft}\ p)$.

Calculating g The expression $(k^{\circ} \times k^{\circ}) \circ cat^{\circ} \circ k$, however, is not easy to simplify. To calculate g we often use a lemma that, if $k = unfoldr\ g_{\triangleright}\ p = unfoldl\ g_{\triangleleft}\ p$, we can refine $(k^{\circ} \times k^{\circ}) \circ cat^{\circ} \circ k$ to

$$((k^{\circ} \times id) \circ unfr\ g_{\triangleright}\ p) \cap ((id \times k^{\circ}) \circ unfl\ g_{\triangleleft}\ p).$$

For readers who are not familiar with intersection and converses, Figure 1 offers some intuition. Given a seed v, $unfr\ g_{\triangleright}\ p$ and $unfl\ g_{\triangleleft}\ p$ non-deterministically pause somewhere and respectively generate (xs, v_2) and (v_1, ys). The intersection means that they stop when they "meet in the middle", that is, when $k\ v_1 = xs$ and $k\ v_2 = ys$. The new pair of seeds, a possible result of g, is (v_1, v_2).

The lemma has a functional formulation that may be more friendly to readers. Writing the list membership predicate $elem :: a \to [a] \to Bool$ in the Haskell Standard Prelude in infix position as $(\in)$, we have,

Lemma 6. Assume that $k = unfoldr\ g_{\triangleright}\ p = unfoldl\ g_{\triangleleft}\ p$. A function g is a subset of $(k^{\circ} \times k^{\circ}) \circ cat^{\circ} \circ k$ if, for all v, $g\ v = (v_1, v_2)$ where v_1 and v_2 satisfy $(k\ v_1, v_2) \in unfoldrp\ g_{\triangleright}\ p\ v$ and $(v_1, k\ v_2) \in unfoldlp\ g_{\triangleleft}\ p$.

From now on we will use Lemma 6 and restrict ourselves to functions when we calculate g.

4. Generating Sequences from Middle

In this section we look at two examples using the dual theorem for list generation.

4.1 Quicksort

While Gibbons [6] demonstrated how to derive merge sort from insertion sort using the third list homomorphism theorem, we use the dual theorem to derive quicksort from selection sort. [2]

We regard the input as a set and denote disjoint union by $\uplus$. One may come up with two definitions of selection sort: $sort = unfoldr\ g_{\triangleright}\ p = unfoldl\ g_{\triangleleft}\ p$, where $p = null$ and

$$g_{\triangleright}\ zs \mid zs \neq \varnothing, x \leftarrow min\ zs = (x, zs - \{x\}),$$
$$g_{\triangleleft}\ zs \mid zs \neq \varnothing, x \leftarrow max\ zs = (zs - \{x\}, x).$$

Let $xs \mathrel{\dot{\leq}} ys \equiv (\forall x \in xs, y \in ys :: x \leq y)$. One can see that

$$(sort\ xs, ys) \in unfoldrp\ g_{\triangleright}\ p\ zs,$$
$$(xs, sort\ ys) \in unfoldlp\ g_{\triangleleft}\ p\ zs,$$

if $xs \uplus ys = zs$ and $xs \mathrel{\dot{\leq}} ys$. We show only the proof of the first membership, for which we show that

$$(ws \mathbin{+\!\!+} sort\ xs, ys) \in iter_{\triangleright}\ (ws, zs) \Leftarrow xs \uplus ys = zs \wedge xs \mathrel{\dot{\leq}} ys. \quad (9)$$

Property (9) can be proved by induction on the size of zs. For $zs = \varnothing$ the property trivially holds. The nonempty case is shown in Figure 2.

By Lemma 6 we may thus choose $g\ zs = (xs, ys)$ for any $xs \uplus ys = zs \wedge xs \mathrel{\dot{\leq}} ys$. That is, we split the set zs into two, such that all elements in one set are no larger than any element in the other set, and sort them recursively. That gives rise to the equation,

$$sort\ (xs \uplus ys) \mid xs \mathrel{\dot{\leq}} ys \;=\; sort\ xs \mathbin{+\!\!+} sort\ ys.$$

Despite being valid, the equation does not form a definition — as a program $sort$ might not terminate since, for example, xs could be empty and the size of ys equals that of zs. For this example, one may come up with a terminating definition by enforcing that the neither xs nor ys is empty. We thus have $sort = unhom\ g\ f\ p\ q$ where $g\ zs = (xs, ys)$ for some non-empty xs and ys such that $xs \uplus ys = zs \wedge xs \mathrel{\dot{\leq}} ys$, $f\ \{x\} = x$, $p\ xs \equiv xs = \varnothing$, and $q\ xs$ holds if xs is singleton. By "unfolding" $sort$ by one step we come up with the definition

$$\begin{array}{ll} sort\ \varnothing & = [\,] \\ sort\ (xs \uplus \{x\} \uplus ys) & \mid\ xs \mathrel{\dot{\leq}} \{x\} \mathrel{\dot{\leq}} ys \\ & \quad = sort\ xs \mathbin{+\!\!+} [x] \mathbin{+\!\!+} sort\ ys. \end{array}$$

$$\begin{array}{ll}
 & (ws \mathbin{+\!\!+} sort\ xs, ys) \in iter_{\triangleright}\ (ws, zs) \\
\equiv & \quad \{\ zs \neq \varnothing, \text{let } z = min\ zs\ \} \\
 & (ws \mathbin{+\!\!+} sort\ xs, ys) = (ws, zs) \vee \\
 & (ws \mathbin{+\!\!+} sort\ xs, ys) \in iter_{\triangleright}\ (ws \mathbin{+\!\!+} [z], zs - \{z\}) \\
\Leftarrow & \quad \{\ \text{for non-empty } xs, \text{let } x = min\ xs\ \} \\
 & (xs = \varnothing \wedge ys = zs) \vee \\
 & (ws \mathbin{+\!\!+} [x] \mathbin{+\!\!+} sort\ (xs - \{x\}), ys) \in iter_{\triangleright}\ (ws \mathbin{+\!\!+} [z], zs - \{z\}) \\
\Leftarrow & \quad \{\ \text{induction}\ \} \\
 & (xs = \varnothing \wedge ys = zs) \vee \\
 & ((xs - \{x\} \uplus ys = zs - \{z\} \wedge xs \mathrel{\dot{\leq}} ys \wedge x = z) \\
\equiv & xs \uplus ys = zs \wedge xs \mathrel{\dot{\leq}} ys.
\end{array}$$

$$\begin{array}{ll}
 & (ws \mathbin{+\!\!+} s\ (e, xs), (e \oplus r\ xs, ys)) \in iter_{\triangleright}\ (ws, (e, z : zs)) \\
\equiv & (ws \mathbin{+\!\!+} s\ (e, xs), (e \oplus r\ xs, ys)) = (ws, (e, z : zs)) \vee \\
 & (ws \mathbin{+\!\!+} s\ (e, xs), (e \oplus r\ xs, ys)) \in iter_{\triangleright}\ (ws \mathbin{+\!\!+} [e], (e \oplus z, zs)) \\
\Leftarrow & \quad \{\ \text{let } xs = x : xs' \text{ for the non-empty case}\ \} \\
 & (xs = [\,] \wedge ys = z : zs) \vee \\
 & (ws \mathbin{+\!\!+} [e] \mathbin{+\!\!+} s\ (e \oplus x, xs'), (e \oplus x \oplus r\ xs', ys)) \in \\
 & \qquad iter_{\triangleright}\ (ws \mathbin{+\!\!+} [e], (e \oplus z, zs)) \\
\Leftarrow & \quad \{\ \text{induction}\ \} \\
 & (xs = [\,] \wedge ys = z : zs) \vee (xs' \mathbin{+\!\!+} ys = zs \wedge x = z) \\
\equiv & xs \mathbin{+\!\!+} ys = z : zs.
\end{array}$$

Figure 2. Proofs of properties (9) and (10). In the latter proof, $scan$ and $reduce$ are respectively abbreviated to s and r.

4.2 Parallel Scan

It is known that the Haskell prelude function $scanl\ (\oplus)\ e$, when $(\oplus)$ is associative and $e = \iota_{\oplus}$, the unit of $(\oplus)$, is both a $foldr$ and a $foldl$. Geser and Gorlatch [5] in fact showed how the following list homomorphism can be derived using the third list homomorphism theorem:

$$\begin{array}{l} scanl\ (\oplus)\ \iota_{\oplus}\ (xs \mathbin{+\!\!+} ys) \\ \quad \mid\ xs' \mathbin{+\!\!+} [x] \leftarrow scanl\ (\oplus)\ \iota_{\oplus}\ xs \\ \quad = xs' \mathbin{+\!\!+} [x] \mathbin{+\!\!+} map\ (x\oplus)\ (scanl\ (\oplus)\ \iota_{\oplus}\ ys). \end{array}$$

In an actual implementation, however, one would like to avoid having to perform $map\ (x\oplus)$. Here we demonstrate that an attention to unfolds leads to a faster program.

For a concise presentation we again consider a slightly different variation. The following $scan$ discards the right-most element of

[2] What we derive here, however, is the toy Quicksort well-known among functional programmers. It is arguable that the essence of real Quicksort is the algorithm for partition, which is not addressed here.

the input list:

$$scan\ (e, [\,]) = [\,]$$
$$scan\ (e, x : xs) = e : scan\ (e \oplus x, xs).$$

For example, $scan\ (e, [1, 2, 3]) = [e, e \oplus 1, e \oplus 1 \oplus 2]$. It is not hard to show that

$$scan\ (e, xs + [x]) = scan\ (e, xs) + [e \oplus reduce\ xs],$$

where $reduce = hom\ (\oplus)\ id\ \iota_\oplus$. We thus have $scan = unfoldr\ g_\triangleright\ p = unfoldl\ g_\triangleleft\ p$, where $p = null \circ snd$ and

$$g_\triangleright\ (e, x : xs) = (e, (e \oplus x, xs)),$$
$$g_\triangleleft\ (e, xs + [\_]) = ((e, xs), e \oplus reduce\ xs),$$

where the domains of $g_\triangleright$ and $g_\triangleleft$ are pairs whose second components are non-empty.

To construct g, we show that for $xs + ys = zs$ we have

$$(scan\ (e, xs), (e \oplus reduce\ xs, ys)) \in unfoldrp\ g_\triangleright\ p\ (e, zs),$$
$$((e, xs), scan\ (e \oplus reduce\ xs, ys)) \in unfoldlp\ g_\triangleleft\ p\ (e, zs).$$

Again we prove only the first property, for which we need to prove a slight generalisation,

$$(ws + scan\ (e, xs), (e \oplus reduce\ xs, ys)) \in iter_\triangleright\ (ws, (e, zs)), \quad (10)$$

if $xs + ys = zs$. The proof is an uninteresting induction on zs, and the inductive case is shown in Figure 2.

Thus we pick $g\ (e, zs) = ((e, xs), (e \oplus reduce\ xs, ys))$ for some $xs + ys = zs$. For termination we want xs and ys to be both non-empty, which gives rise to the definition

$$scan\ (e, [\,]) = [\,]$$
$$scan\ (e, [x]) = [e]$$
$$scan\ (e, xs + ys)\ \mid\ xs \neq [\,] \wedge ys \neq [\,]$$
$$= scan\ (e, xs) + scan\ (e \oplus reduce\ xs, ys).$$

This is not yet an efficient implementation. To avoid repeated calls to $reduce$, one typically performs a *tupling*. Let

$$sr\ (e, xs) = (scan\ (e, xs), reduce\ xs).$$

One may calculate a definition for sr:

$$sr\ (e, [\,]) = ([\,], \iota_\oplus)$$
$$sr\ (e, [x]) = ([e], x)$$
$$sr\ (e, xs + ys)\ \mid\ xs \neq [\,] \wedge ys \neq [\,]$$
$$= \mathbf{let}\ (s_1, r_1) = sr\ (e, xs)$$
$$(s_2, r_2) = sr\ (e \oplus r_1, ys)$$
$$\mathbf{in}\ (s_1 + s_2, r_1 \oplus r_2).$$

However, the second call to sr in the $xs + ys$ case demands the value of r_1, which is a result of the first call to sr. This prevents the two calls to sr from being executed in parallel.

Instead, we compute $scan$ in two phases: all the r's are first computed and cached, which are then used in the second phase to compute $scan$. For that we need a data structure storing the r's. Consider the following binary tree, with a function val extracting the value at the root,

$$\mathbf{data}\ Tree\ a = \mathsf{L}\ a \mid \mathsf{N}\ (Tree\ a)\ a\ (Tree\ a),$$
$$val\ (\mathsf{L}\ n) = n$$
$$val\ (\mathsf{N}\ \_\ n\ \_) = n.$$

The following function builds a tree out of a non-empty list, with the invariant that $val\ (build\ xs) = reduce\ xs$:

$$build\ [x] = \mathsf{L}\ x$$
$$build\ (xs + ys)\ \mid\ xs \neq [\,] \wedge ys \neq [\,]$$
$$= \mathbf{let}\ t = build\ xs;\ u = build\ ys$$
$$\mathbf{in}\ \mathsf{N}\ t\ (val\ t \oplus val\ u)\ u.$$

The key to construct an efficient implementation of $scan$ is to perform $build$ in a separate phase and use only the results stored in the tree. That is, we wish to construct some function f such that

$$scan\ (e, xs) = f\ (e, build\ xs).$$

The singleton case is easy: $f\ (e, \mathsf{L}\ x) = [e]$. For inputs of length at least two, we calculate (for non-empty xs and ys):

$$\begin{aligned}
& scan\ (e, xs + ys) \\
= \ & scan\ (e, xs) + scan\ (e \oplus reduce\ xs, ys) \\
= \ & \quad \{\ \text{since } val\ (build\ xs) = reduce\ xs\ \} \\
& scan\ (e, xs) + scan\ (e \oplus val\ (build\ xs), ys) \\
= \ & \quad \{\ \text{induction: } scan\ (e, xs) = f\ (e, build\ xs)\ \} \\
& f\ (e, build\ xs) + f\ (e \oplus val\ (build\ xs), build\ ys) \\
= \ & \quad \{\ \text{let } \mathsf{N}\ t\ v\ u = build\ (xs + ys)\ \} \\
& f\ (e, t) + f\ (e \oplus val\ t, u) \\
= \ & \quad \{\ \text{let } f\ (e, \mathsf{N}\ t\ _\ u) = f\ (e, t) + f\ (e \oplus val\ t,\ u)\ \} \\
& f\ (e, build\ (xs + ys)).
\end{aligned}$$

We rename f to acc since it accumulates the result:

$$scan\ (e, [\,]) = [\,]$$
$$scan\ (e, xs) = acc\ (e, build\ xs),$$
$$acc\ (e, \mathsf{L}\ x) = [e]$$
$$acc\ (e, \mathsf{N}\ t\ \_\ u) = acc\ (e, t) + acc\ (e \oplus val\ t,\ u).$$

By constructing a balanced binary tree, the evaluation can be performed in $O(\log n)$ time given a sufficient number of processors, or in $O(n/p + \log p)$ time if $p \ll n$ where p is the number of processors. We have in fact reconstructed a well-known efficient implementation of $scan$ recorded by, for example, Blelloch [2].

5. Generalising to Trees

As mentioned earlier, when looking at the proof of Theorem 2 in detail, one notices that further generalisation is possible. Indeed, the presence of $R \circ cat$ in Theorem 4 is superficial, and the theorem can still be generalised.

Theorem 7. $R = U \circ (id \times S) = V \circ (T \times id)$, $S \circ S^\circ \circ S = S$, and $T \circ T^\circ \circ T = T$ imply $R = R \circ (T^\circ \times S^\circ) \circ (T \times S)$.

Proof.

$$\begin{aligned}
R &= U \circ (id \times S) \\
&= U \circ (id \times S) \circ (id \times S^\circ) \circ (id \times S) \\
&= R \circ (id \times S^\circ) \circ (id \times S) \\
&= V \circ (T \times id) \circ (id \times S^\circ) \circ (id \times S) \\
&= V \circ (T \times id) \circ (T^\circ \times S^\circ) \circ (T \times S) \\
&= R \circ (T^\circ \times S^\circ) \circ (T \times S).
\end{aligned}$$

□

However, the conclusion of the theorem, that $R = R \circ (T^\circ \times S^\circ) \circ (T \times S)$, does not have much structure hinting at how this theorem can be useful. The use-cases we found are when S is a sub-expression of R (for example, to prove Corollary 5, we used $R = k^\circ \circ cat$ and $S = T = k^\circ$. We do not require $S = T$ in general), and we use Theorem 7 to establish recursive equations about S, hoping to construct a terminating definition of S.

5.1 Third Homomorphism Theorem on Trees Revisited

Consider the $Tree$ datatype defined in Section 4.2 and assume that we wish to efficiently compute a function on trees by distributing the work to multiple processors. One slight annoyance is that splitting a tree into two at an arbitrary point yields not two trees, but one tree and a context containing a single hole that can be filled by a tree. The concept of contexts of a datatype was proposed by Huet [8] as the *zipper*. In particular, the context for $Tree$ can be modelled by

$$\begin{aligned} &\mathbf{type}\ Cxt\ a = [Z\ a], \\ &\mathbf{data}\ Z\ a \ = \mathsf{Nl}\ a\ (Tree\ a) \mid \mathsf{Nr}\ (Tree\ a)\ a, \end{aligned}$$

with a function $fill :: (Cxt\ a, Tree\ a) \to Tree\ a$ that fills the hole of the context by a tree:

$$\begin{aligned} &fill\ ([\,], t) &&= t \\ &fill\ (\mathsf{Nl}\ x\ u : xs, t) &&= fill\ (xs, \mathsf{N}\ t\ x\ u) \\ &fill\ (\mathsf{Nr}\ t\ x : xs, u) &&= fill\ (xs, \mathsf{N}\ t\ x\ u). \end{aligned}$$

For example, consider the tree

$$t = \mathsf{N}\,(\mathsf{N}\,(\mathsf{L}\,1)\,2\,(\mathsf{L}\,3))\,4\,(\mathsf{N}\,(\mathsf{N}\,(\mathsf{L}\,5)\,6\,(\mathsf{L}\,7))\,8\,(\mathsf{L}\,9)).$$

What remains after taking out the subtree $u = \mathsf{N}\,(\mathsf{L}\,5)\,6\,(\mathsf{L}\,7)$ is

$$cx = [\mathsf{Nl}\,8\,(\mathsf{L}\,9), \mathsf{Nr}\,(\mathsf{N}\,(\mathsf{L}\,1)\,2\,(\mathsf{L}\,3))\,4],$$

with $fill\ (cx, u) = t$.

To parallelise a function $f :: Tree\ a \to b$, we must have a variation $f' :: Cxt\ a \to b$ defined on contexts. Instantiating R, S, and T in Theorem 7 respectively to $f \circ fill$, f, and f', we see that $f\ t$ can be computed in terms of $f'\ cx$ and $f\ u$,

$$f \circ fill = f \circ fill \circ (f'^{\circ} \times f^{\circ}) \circ (f' \times f),$$

if there exist U and V such that

$$f \circ fill = U \circ (id \times f) \wedge \qquad (11)$$

$$f \circ fill = V \circ (f' \times id). \qquad (12)$$

Equation (11) basically says that f is *outwards* — $f\ (fill\ (cx, u))$ can be computed from cx and $f\ u$, while (12) says that f is also *inwards* — $f\ (fill\ (cx, u))$ can be computed from $f'\ cx$ and u. This is another way to view the previous work of Morihata et al. [10].

5.2 Generating Trees from the Middle

One naturally wonders whether the result can also be dualised to generating trees rather than consuming them. Again the answer is yes: if a tree can be generated both upwards and downwards, it can be generated "from the middle." We will formalise what we mean below.

Let b be the type of seeds. Unfolding a tree downwards from the root using a function $g_\downarrow :: b \to (b, a, b)$ is relatively familiar:

$$\begin{aligned} &unf_\downarrow :: (b \to (b,a,b), b \to a, b \to Bool) \to b \to Tree\ a \\ &unf_\downarrow\ (fs@(g_\downarrow, f_\downarrow, p))\ v \\ &\quad \mid p\ v = \mathsf{L}\ (f_\downarrow\ v) \\ &\quad \mid (v_1, x, v_2) \leftarrow g_\downarrow\ v = \mathsf{N}\ (unf_\downarrow\ fs\ v_1)\ x\ (unf_\downarrow\ fs\ v_2). \end{aligned}$$

As in the case of lists, our unfolds are actually converses of folds in disguise and are well-defined only if they terminate and produce finite trees. We consider paused versions of unfolding, which yields $(Cxt\ a, b)$, a context and a seed. The function $unfp_\downarrow$ returns a list containing all such pairs of contexts and seeds:

$$\begin{aligned} &unfp_\downarrow :: (b \to (b,a,b), b \to a, b \to Bool) \to b \to [(Cxt\ a, b)] \\ &unfp_\downarrow\ (fs@(g_\downarrow, f_\downarrow, p))\ v = iter_\downarrow\ ([\,], v), \ \ \mathbf{where} \\ &iter_\downarrow\ (xs, v) \mid p\ v = [(xs, v)] \\ &\qquad \mid (v_1, x, v_2) \leftarrow g_\downarrow\ v = \\ &\qquad\quad (xs, v) : iter_\downarrow\ (\mathsf{Nl}\ x\ (unf_\downarrow\ fs\ v_2) : xs, v_1) + \\ &\qquad\qquad iter_\downarrow\ (\mathsf{Nr}\ (unf_\downarrow\ fs\ v_1)\ x : xs, v_2). \end{aligned}$$

With the definition we have, for $k = unf_\downarrow\ (g_\downarrow, f_\downarrow, p)$, that

$$fill^{\circ} \circ k = (id \times k) \circ mem \circ unfp_\downarrow\ (g_\downarrow, f_\downarrow, p). \qquad (13)$$

By generating a tree "from the middle" we mean to find $g :: b \to (b, b)$ and $k' :: b \to Cxt\ a$ such that

$$\begin{aligned} &k\ v \mid p\ v = \mathsf{L}\ (f_\downarrow\ v) \\ &\quad \mid (v_\uparrow, v_\downarrow) \leftarrow g\ v = fill\ (k'\ v_\uparrow)\ (k\ v_\downarrow). \end{aligned}$$

That is, the tree returned by k, if not a leaf, can be split into a context and a subtree that can be generated separately from the two seeds returned by g. It suffices for g and k' to satisfy

$$fill^{\circ} \circ k = (k' \times k) \circ g.$$

Generating a tree "upwards" intuitively means to start from a leaf and find the path back to the root. With application of Theorem 7 in mind, we want to come up with a function $unfp_\uparrow\ (g_\uparrow, f_\uparrow) :: b \to [(b, Tree\ a)]$ that satisfies, for some k',

$$fill^{\circ} \circ k = (k' \times id) \circ mem \circ unfp_\uparrow\ (g_\uparrow, f_\uparrow), \qquad (14)$$

thus each of (13) and (14) matches one antecedent of Theorem 7.

To grow a tree upwards from a leaf, we use a function $g_\uparrow$ having type $G_\uparrow\ a\ b = b \to [(b, (a,b) + (b,a))]$ (where $\mathbf{data}\ a + b = \mathsf{Lt}\ a \mid \mathsf{Rt}\ b$). If $g_\uparrow\ v$ is empty, we have reached the root. If it contains $(v', \mathsf{Lt}\ (x, v_r))$, we go up by using the current tree as the left child, v_r the seed for the right child, and v' the seed going up. Similarly with Rt. We could have grown a $Tree\ a$. To reuse the function later, however, we grow a context instead. Define $cxtp_\uparrow\ g_\uparrow :: b \to [(b, Cxt\ a)]$ that generates all (seed, context) pairs when one goes upwards:

$$\begin{aligned} &cxtp_\uparrow\ g_\uparrow\ v = iter_\uparrow\ (v, [\,]), \ \mathbf{where} \\ &\quad iter_\uparrow\ (v, cx) = (v, cx) : [y \mid (v', lr) \leftarrow g_\uparrow\ v, \\ &\qquad\qquad y \leftarrow iter_\uparrow\ (v', cx + [up\ lr])], \\ &\quad up\ (\mathsf{Lt}\ (x, v_r)) = \mathsf{Nl}\ x\ (k\ v_r) \\ &\quad up\ (\mathsf{Rt}\ (v_l, x)) = \mathsf{Nr}\ (k\ v_l)\ x. \end{aligned}$$

To generate all the splits, we need to be able to start from any leaf. Thus we let $f_\uparrow :: b \to [(b, a)]$ return the list of values on each leaf, paired with a seed to go up with. We may then define $unfp_\uparrow$ by

$$\begin{aligned} &unfp_\uparrow :: (G_\uparrow\ a\ b, b \to [(b,a)]) \to b \to [(b, Tree\ a)] \\ &unfp_\uparrow\ (g_\uparrow, f_\uparrow)\ v = [(v'', fill\ (cx, \mathsf{L}\ x)) \mid \\ &\qquad (v', x) \leftarrow f_\uparrow\ v,\ (v'', cx) \leftarrow cxtp_\uparrow\ g_\uparrow\ v']. \end{aligned}$$

While $cxtp_\uparrow$ and $unfp_\uparrow$ return the entire history of upwards tree generation, their non-pausing version, $cxt_\uparrow$ and $unf_\uparrow$, keep only completed contexts and trees (those which have reached the root):

$$\begin{aligned} &cxt_\uparrow\ g_\uparrow\ v = [cx \mid (v', cx) \leftarrow cxtp_\uparrow\ g_\uparrow\ v, null\ (p\ v')], \\ &unf_\uparrow\ (g_\uparrow, f_\uparrow)\ v = [t \mid (v', t) \leftarrow unfp_\uparrow\ (g_\uparrow, f_\uparrow)\ v, null\ (p\ v')]. \end{aligned}$$

Equation (14) is satisfiable if $k = mem \circ unf_\uparrow\ (g_\uparrow, f_\uparrow)$ is a function (that is, all routes from leaves to the root yields the same tree), and $k' = mem \circ cxt_\uparrow\ g_\uparrow\ v$.

With (13) and (14), we therefore obtain from Theorem 7 that

$$fill^{\circ} \circ k = (k' \times k) \circ (k'^{\circ} \times k^{\circ}) \circ fill^{\circ} \circ k,$$

if $k = unf_\downarrow\ (g_\downarrow, f_\downarrow, p) = mem \circ unf_\uparrow\ (g_\uparrow, f_\uparrow)$ and $k' = mem \circ cxt_\uparrow\ g_\uparrow\ v$. To compute k "from the middle", we may pick g to be a subset of $(k'^{\circ} \times k^{\circ}) \circ fill^{\circ} \circ k$.

6. Conclusions

By formulating the third list homomorphism theorem in point-free, relational style, we have dualised the theorem to unfolds, as well as generalised the theorem to both folds and unfolds for trees. While the original theorem establishes a connection between insertion sort and merge sort, the dual theorem shows a similar connection between selection sort and quicksort. We have also derived an efficient parallel algorithm for scan based on unfolds. To the best of the authors' knowledge, while there has been many studies on parallel programming based on structural recursion, none have considered the dual — list generation in the form of $unhom$.

The theorem generalises nicely to trees: if a function processes or generates a tree both downwards and upwards, it may process or generate the tree from the middle. Finally, we have also presented an example that shows how a relational view may shed new light on an old topic by revealing its hidden symmetry. The authors believe that relational methods deserve to be appreciated more among functional programmers.

As a remark, in practice, for both list and tree generation one might need different types of seeds for left/right or inwards/outwards unfolding. That is, we have $k = unfoldr\ g_{\triangleright}\ p \circ i_1 = unfoldl\ g_{\triangleleft}\ p \circ i_2$ or $k = unf_{\downarrow}\ fs_{\downarrow} \circ i_1 = unf_{\uparrow}\ fs_{\uparrow} \circ i_2$, for some i_1 and i_2 that initialise the seeds. This is also covered by Theorem 7. We leave it to the readers to work out the details.

Acknowledgements The authors would like to thank Jeremy Gibbons, José Nuno Oliveira, and Janis Voigtländer for comments on earlier drafts, and to the anonymous referees for their valuable comments. This pearl was inspired by a question proposed by Zhenjiang Hu, who also cooperated with the authors throughout the development of this paper and made plenty of important technical contributions.

References

[1] R. S. Bird. An introduction to the theory of lists. In M. Broy, editor, *Logic of Programming and Calculi of Discrete Design*, volume 36 of *NATO ASI Series F*, pages 3–42. Springer-Verlag, New York, NY, USA, 1987. *Technical Monograph PRG-56*.

[2] G. E. Blelloch. Prefix sums and their applications. In J. E. Reif, editor, *Synthesis of Parallel Algorithms*. Morgan Kaufmann Publishers Inc., San Francisco, CA, USA, 1993.

[3] M. I. Cole. *Algorithmic Skeletons: Structural Management of Parallel Computation*. MIT Press, 1989.

[4] E. W. Dijkstra. *A Discipline of Programming*. Prentice Hall PTR, 1976.

[5] A. Geser and S. Gorlatch. Parallelizing functional programs by generalization. *Journal of Functional Programming*, 9(6):649–673, 1999.

[6] J. Gibbons. The third homomorphism theorem. *Journal of Functional Programming*, 6(4):657–665, 1996.

[7] J. Gibbons, G. Hutton, and T. Altenkirch. When is a function a fold or an unfold? *Electr. Notes Theor. Comput. Sci.*, 44(1), 2001.

[8] G. P. Huet. The zipper. *Journal of Functional Programming*, 7(5): 549–554, 1997.

[9] A. Morihata, K. Matsuzaki, Z. Hu, and M. Takeichi. Program parallelization by candidate generation and conformity testing. *IPSJ Transaction on Programming*, 2(2):132–143, 2009. (In Japanese).

[10] A. Morihata, K. Matsuzaki, Z. Hu, and M. Takeichi. The third homomorphism theorem on trees: Downward & upward lead to divide-and-conquer. In *Proceedings of the 36th ACM SIGPLAN-SIGACT Symposium on Principles of Programming Languages, POPL 2009, Savannah, Georgia, USA, January 21-23, 2009*, pages 177–185. ACM, 2009.

[11] K. Morita, A. Morihata, K. Matsuzaki, Z. Hu, and M. Takeichi. Automatic inversion generates divide-and-conquer parallel programs. In J. Ferrante and K. S. McKinley, editors, *Proceedings of the ACM SIGPLAN 2007 Conference on Programming Language Design and Implementation, San Diego, California, USA, June 10-13, 2007*, pages 146–155. ACM, 2007.

Incremental Updates for Efficient Bidirectional Transformations

Meng Wang
Computer Science and Engineering
Chalmers University of Technology
412 96 Göteborg, Sweden
wmeng@chalmers.se

Jeremy Gibbons
Department of Computer Science
University of Oxford
Wolfson Building, Parks Road
Oxford OX1 3QD, UK
jeremy.gibbons@cs.ox.ac.uk

Nicolas Wu
Well-Typed LLP
Oxford, UK
nick@well-typed.com

Abstract

A bidirectional transformation is a pair of mappings between *source* and *view* data objects, one in each direction. When the view is modified, the source is updated accordingly. The key to handling large data objects that are subject to relatively small modifications is to process the updates incrementally. Incrementality has been explored in the semi-structured settings of relational databases and graph transformations; this flexibility in structure makes it relatively easy to divide the data into separate parts that can be transformed and updated independently. The same is not true if the data is to be encoded with more general-purpose algebraic datatypes, with transformations defined as functions: dividing data into well-typed separate parts is tricky, and recursions typically create interdependencies. In this paper, we study transformations that support incremental updates, and devise a constructive process to achieve this incrementality.

Categories and Subject Descriptors D.3.2 [*Programming Languages*]: Language Classifications—Applicative (functional) languages, Specialized application languages; D.3.3 [*Programming Languages*]: Language Constructs and Features—Data types and structures, Polymorphism

General Terms Languages, Design, Performance, Theory

Keywords Functional Programming, Bidirectional Programming, Incremental Computing, Program Transformation, View-update Problem

1. Introduction

From a programming perspective, bidirectional programming is an exercise in writing programs that execute both forwards and backwards. This goal is not always achievable: non-injective functions obscure the route back, while non-surjective functions leave the 'backward' execution partial. Nevertheless, the need to invert a computation does arise in many contexts in which pairs of programs naturally interact with one another; parser/printer, embedding/projection, marshalling/unmarshalling, and compression/decompression are typical examples. For decades, the needs of bidirectionality have been fulfilled by individually crafted pairs of programs. This is a significant duplication of work, because the two programs in a pair are closely related. Furthermore, maintaining the relationship between these progams becomes a source of errors, where changes to only one of the programs may lead to an inconsistency within the pair.

A more promising solution to the challenge of bidirectional programming is to design languages that execute bidirectionally. In such languages, any user-defined program, mapping a source into a view, is coupled with an automatically generated 'backward' version, whose correctness with regards to certain bidirectional properties is guaranteed. An obvious bidirectional property is invertibility. For a given program fwd, its inverse bwd satisfies $fwd \circ bwd = id$ and $bwd \circ fwd = id$. While this invertibility is elegant, it restricts the expressiveness of the approach, since fwd must be bijective. Modulo information encoded in fwd itself, the source and view necessarily contain exactly the same information, probably with different presentations. This is an unrealistically strong assumption, and has driven research into more widely applicable frameworks:

> "More generally, bijective transformations are the exception rather than the rule: the fact that one model contains information not represented in the other is part of the reason for having separate models." [27]

1.1 Semi-Invertibility

To circumvent the bijectivity restriction, other languages have been designed with particular applications in mind, where less demanding constraints such as one-sided invertibility are imposed: left-invertibility ($fwd \circ bwd = id$) in [24], and right-invertibility ($bwd \circ fwd = id$) in [31]. A more dramatic diversion from the invertibility framework is the *lens* approach [10, 4, 12, 11, 3, 18], which originated from the study of the *view-update problem* of databases [7, 2, 14]. In the setting of lenses, (all or part of) the original source is copied and is used in the 'backward' computation: a 'get' function has type $s \to v$ from source to view, while a 'put' function has type $(v, s) \to s$. We make the following notational convention: for a 'get' function f, the counterpart 'put' function is written as $f^{<}$. The task of a 'put' function is to discover the connection between a view update and an appropriate corresponding source update. This 'appropriateness' is defined by the *definitional properties* [6, 27]:

Consistency $f\ (f^{<}\ (v, s)) = v$

Acceptability $f^{<}\ (f\ s, s) = s$

Here *consistency* (also known as the PutGet law) roughly corresponds to right-invertibility, basically ensuring that all updates on a view are captured by the updated source, and *acceptability* (also known as the GetPut law) roughly corresponds to left-invertibility, prohibiting changes to the source if no update has been made on the view. Bidirectional transformations satisfying the above two laws

ICFP'11, September 19–21, 2011, Tokyo, Japan.

are sometimes called *well-behaved* [10]. In addition to these laws, an optional *undoability* property is sometimes introduced:

Undoability $f^{<} \, (f \, s, f^{<} \, (v', s)) = s$

This property states that the result of an update can be undone through the view. For the sake of this paper, we will present our proposal within the lenses framework, with the understanding that the same technique applies to invertible languages as well.

1.2 State-Based and Operation-Based Approaches

The word 'update' is commonly found in the bidirectional transformation literature, and used to describe changes both in views and in sources. In the sequel, we restrict the use of the term 'update' to the transformed effect on a source, as a result of an *edit* to the view. Despite being fundamental to bidirectional transformation, there is no universal agreement on what constitutes an edit. Roughly speaking, opinions are divided as to whether one should look into the mechanism of an edit or simply its result. Translated into language design, one can either take an operation-based approach, considering an editing function that changes a view, or a state-based approach, which only sees the unedited and edited views. It happens that the majority of existing bidirectional frameworks take the latter approach, due to its mathematical simplicity and good compatibility. The bidirectional laws discussed above are specified from a state-based perspective. Since only the edited view is required for the 'put' function, it is easier to design a bidirectional framework independently of any editing system. On the other hand, a state-based approach necessarily discards information about an edit, and must reverse-engineer it later by performing some kind of difference analysis on the two view values. Consequently, the run-time performance of a state-based 'put' function is bound by the difference analysis that is required: even a small change to the view implies a complete re-traversal.

Meertens [23] observed that to maintain constraints between two structures, it is useful to know how a view is edited. Consider the scenario where two lists are connected by a mapping relation (i.e. each is the result of *map*ping some function over the other); an edit to one list, say deletion at a particular position, can be translated to a deletion at the same position in the other list. In this setting, a lot more information about the edit is made available to the bidirectional framework, including where (the location) and what (a deletion) has changed. As a result, the updating process could be more straightforward compared to a state-based approach—in the latter, all that is known is that one list is changed into another list that is one element shorter, which is fairly ambiguous. In addition, having an operation for source update potentially achieves better-than-linear runtime performance.

If run-time performance is the only concern, the 'where' part of the knowledge of an edit is the key. For a given edit-affected view fragment, once the corresponding source fragment is picked out, a state-based approach could perform the changes as efficiently as an operation-based counterpart, without the undesired complications that the latter brings. This idea is not new. As a matter of fact, for bidirectional systems in the neighbouring fields of databases and software engineering, incrementality of source updates is the norm rather than the exception [5, 8, 15]. With the more recent upsurge in (mostly functional) programming language approaches to bidirectional transformation [19, 10, 21, 28, 25, 29], fresh challenges emerge: structured data cannot easily be divided into separate parts to be transformed and updated independently; and recursions typically create interdependencies. As a result, in contrast to the situation with databases and model transformations, none of the existing bidirectional languages supports any kind of incremental behaviour.

1.3 A Change-Based Approach

In this paper, we propose a novel *change-based* framework for bidirectional transformation. Instead of inventing from first principles to add to the already burgeoning population of bidirectional languages, we focus on the preservation and propagation of user-provided editing information. In a sense, our proposal can be seen as a generic optimiser of certain given state-based bidirectional frameworks: we exploit any locality in the editing of views, and try to translate it into incrementality in the updating of sources. Obviously, such preservation of locality does not hold for arbitrary transformations. Identifying the semantic properties, or *conditions*, required forms one of the major technical contributions of this paper. The ultimate goal of our framework is to reduce an update of a (large) structure into one of a (small) delta, and then outsource the hopefully much smaller problem of actually translating the update to an existing state-based frameworks. This step positively impacts the run-time behaviour of 'put', due to the newly gained incrementality.

Our proposal aims at modularity: there is a clearly defined interface that decouples any editing system from our framework; and different state-based bidirectional approaches can be plugged in as black boxes, whatever their manifestation as purpose-built bidirectional languages or syntactic/semantic transformations of unidirectional programs. As a result, a change-based bidirectional framework arises automatically from a given state-based one, while preserving the bidirectional properties of the latter.

We choose Haskell [26] as the language of discourse, but no specific language feature other than algebraic datatypes is required for our technique to apply.

1.4 A Small Example

As a motivating example, consider the structure of a binary tree:

data *Tree a* = *Empty*
  | *Fork a* (*Tree a*) (*Tree a*)

One possible 'get' function from this source is an inorder traversal, which produces a list, and can be defined as follows:

inorder :: *Tree a* → [*a*]
inorder Empty = [ ]
inorder (*Fork a t u*) = *inorder t* ++ [*a*] ++ *inorder u*

For instance, a traversal of the source

Fork 5 (*Fork* 6 (*Fork* 7 *Empty Empty*) *Empty*)
  (*Fork* 8 (*Fork* 4 *Empty Empty*) (*Fork* 9 *Empty Empty*))

yields the list [7,6,5,4,8,9]. Now, suppose the number 4 is deleted from this view. A state-based 'put' function will take the edited view and try to construct a tree without the deleted element; and hopefully the new source remains similar to the original one, so that unnecessary changes are kept to a minimum. (Note that we have deliberately kept all the functions abstract, because our proposal is not dependent on any particular implementation.)

The method described above takes effort proportional to the size of the data, not to the size of the change. Assuming a functional cons-list, the deletion of 4 involves traversing the view list to the location of the deletion, and changing only the sublist [4,8,9] rooted at that location; a more efficient approach is to update only the source subtree (*Fork* 8 (*Fork* 4 *Empty Empty*) (*Fork* 9 *Empty Empty*)) that is responsible for generating the view fragment [4,8,9]. That is to say, the bidirectional updating should be incremental. Better still, in the case of lists, where a deletion is local and does not induce subsequent changes to a substructure, a more refined analysis may discover that only the subtree (*Fork* 4 *Empty Empty*) is really affected by the edit, and updating this is sufficient.

We were able to conclude above that the view sublist $[4,8,9]$ corresponds to the source subtree (*Fork* 8 (*Fork* 4 *Empty Empty*) (*Fork* 9 *Empty Empty*)), because all elements in the former can be found in the latter, and the 'get' function (inorder traversal) happens to have certain properties that allow structure correspondences to be derived from element correspondences. In the sequel, we will discuss in detail how 'get' functions that support incremental updates can be identified; and present a constructive method for performing the said update in a change-based framework. Assuming a fairly balanced source tree, the complexity of our algorithm is $O(m \times \log n + f\ m)$ where n is the size of the source tree, m is the size of the affected source part, and f is the complexity function of a state-based 'put' function. The update itself takes time proportional to m; but it takes $m \times \log n$ time to locate the target source location.

The rest of the paper is structured as follows. Section 2 gives the overall setting of change-based bidirectional frameworks. Section 3 discusses the propagation of locality of view editing to the level of source updating, and Section 4 presents a constructive method for deriving change-based 'put' functions. We then refine the technique for list views (Section 5), and discuss related issues (Section 6), before surveying related work (Section 7) and concluding (Section 8).

2. The Overall Setting

We restrict our attention to polymorphically typed tree-structured data, and polymorphic 'get' functions. To be explicit about our assumptions, we express our requirements in terms of a type class *TypeFunctor*:

```
class TypeFunctor s where
  bimap :: (a → b) → (c → d) → s a c → s b d
  arity  :: s a b → Int
  select :: s a b → Int → b
  lab :: s (Label, a) Labels → Labels
  data Delta s :: * → * → *
  close :: Delta s a b → b → s a b
```

The remainder of Section 2 elaborates on these requirements.

2.1 Algebraic Datatypes

We restrict attention to regular datatypes—that is, defined in terms of sums, products, and least fixed points. We assume that the type functor is (as the name suggests) a bifunctor, satisfying the functor laws

```
bimap id id          = id
bimap (f ∘ g) (h ∘ k) = bimap f h ∘ bimap g k
```

The type functor determines the shape of the tree; polymorphic tree terms are then formed by taking the fixpoint (in the second argument) of this bifunctor.

```
data TypeFunctor s ⇒ Term s a = InT {outT :: s a (Term s a)}
```

For example, the binary tree type from Section 1.4 is represented by the following definitions:

```
data TreeF a b = EmptyF | ForkF a b b
type Tree a = Term TreeF a
```

with the obvious definition of *bimap*.

In the interests of brevity, we will usually write binary type constructors s in the type class *TypeFunctor* as single bold capitals $\mathbf{S}$; and in an abuse of notation, we will often omit the element type, writing just $\mu\mathbf{S}$ for *Term s a*.

As usual, the type functor induces a fold operator for consuming tree terms:

```
fold :: TypeFunctor s ⇒ (s a b → b) → Term s a → b
fold f t = f (bimap id (fold f) (outT t))
```

The idea is that 'get' functions should be written as polymorphic instances of *fold*. For example, with an appropriate type functor definition for lists:

```
data ListF a b = NilF | ConsF a b
type List a    = Term ListF a
```

we could implement the *inorder* transformation as follows:

```
inorder :: Tree a → List a
inorder t = fold step t (InT NilF) where
  step EmptyF         = id
  step (ForkF a f g) = f ∘ InT ∘ ConsF a ∘ g
```

2.2 Tree Navigation

We use functions

```
arity  :: TypeFunctor s ⇒ s a b → Int
select :: TypeFunctor s ⇒ s a b → Int → b
```

to capture the number of recursive components in an $\mathbf{S}$-structure, and to select one of those components. For example, for binary trees we have

```
arity EmptyF          = 0
arity (ForkF _ _ _) = 2
select (ForkF _ t _) 0 = t
select (ForkF _ _ u) 1 = u
```

Note that *select* is a partial function, and *select x i* is defined iff $0 \leqslant i < arity\ x$. As a shorthand, we write x_i for *select x i*, and $x_{i \mapsto t}$ to denote the substitution of t for x_i in x. We define a function *child* to select an immediate subterm of a term:

```
child :: TypeFunctor s ⇒ Term s a → Int → Term s a
child t i = (outT t)_i
```

and a function *zoom* to select an arbitrarily deep subterm, following a path represented as a list of positions:

```
type Path = [Int]
zoom :: TypeFunctor s ⇒ Term s a → Path → Term s a
zoom = foldl child
```

2.3 Labelling

We assume that all tree elements are associated with unique labels; for this purpose we assume an abstract type *Label*, and a corresponding type *Labels* of sets of labels. (For example, the unique label associated with an element at a particular node might be formed out of the path from the root of the tree to that node, together with a disambiguating index in case there are multiple elements at the same node.)

```
type Label  = ...
type Labels = Set Label
```

Generally speaking, the labels should be thought of as being behind the scenes, inaccessible to normal functions; that is why we insist that 'get' functions should be polymorphic. In particular, we assume that the 'get' function cannot invent labels: all the labels that turn up in a view subterm originated from the corresponding source term. But for the purposes of discussing labels and labelsets themselves, we require the type functor to provide a mechanism for combining the labelsets from subterms to make the labelset for a term itself:

```
lab :: TypeFunctor s ⇒ s (Label, a) Labels → Labels
```

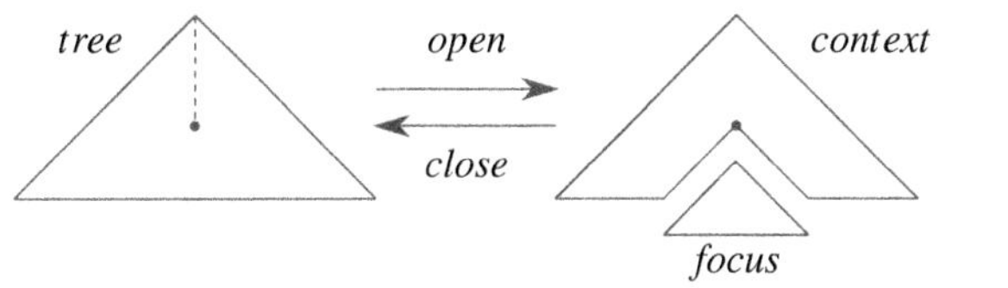

Figure 1. The context-focus representation.

For example, for binary trees we have

$$lab\ EmptyF = \emptyset$$
$$lab\ (ForkF\ (l,a)\ x\ y) = singleton\ l \cup x \cup y$$

This forms an **S**-algebra, which can be exploited by a partly polymorphic fold to compute the labelset of a labelled term:

type *LTerm s a* = *Term s* (*Label*, *a*)
labels :: *TypeFunctor s* ⇒ *LTerm s a* → *Labels*
labels = *fold lab*

We will often use the shorthand $\langle t \rangle$ to denote *labels t*; we extend this notation to **S**-structures of $\mu\mathbf{S}'$ trees $x :: \mathbf{S}\ \mu\mathbf{S}'$ by writing '$\langle x \rangle$' for '$labs_{\mathbf{S}}\ (\mathbf{S}\ labels_{\mu\mathbf{S}'}\ x)$', and, as a shorthand, write '$\langle x_{\neq i} \rangle$' for '$labs_{\mathbf{S}}\ (\mathbf{S}\ labels_{\mu\mathbf{S}'}\ x)_{i \mapsto \emptyset}$'.

Splitting an **S**-structure into one component and the remainder yields an exhaustive and (at least for **S**-structures arising directly from a $\mu\mathbf{S}$-structure) disjoint partition of the label sets: for $x :: \mathbf{S}\ \mu\mathbf{S}'$ and for any valid i,

$$\langle x_{\neq i} \rangle \cup \langle x_i \rangle = \langle x \rangle$$

and for $s :: \mu\mathbf{S}$ and any valid i,

$$\langle (outT\ s)_{\neq i} \rangle \# \langle (outT\ s)_i \rangle$$

where # denotes disjointness, that is, $x \# y = (x \cap y = \emptyset)$. Note that $(x \subseteq y) \wedge (y \# z) \Rightarrow (x \# z)$ by monotonicity of intersection, so we allow ourselves to write derivations of the form '$w \subseteq x \# y \supseteq z$', with a chain of inclusions, a disjointness, and a chain of containments, and conclude from it that $w \# z$.

2.4 Tree Contexts

As implemented by function *zoom*, a subtree of interest can be accessed by navigating from the root of a tree and following a given path. Such a path need not represent a traversal from the root all the way to a leaf: paths may point to internal nodes in a tree. The traversal of a tree following a path 'opens' that tree into two disjoint structures: one represents the subtree below the node reached by the path, known as the current *focus*; the other represents the rest of the tree and is known as the *context* of the focus (see Figure 1). On typing grounds, we only consider as valid those paths that lead to recursive components; for example, the focus of the binary tree datatype above can descend to the left or the right subtree, but not to the element stored in a node.

We represent a context as a tree with a hole in it, denoting the location of the subtree given by the focus. This can be captured in terms of a type function *Delta*, such that *Delta s a b* is the type of one-hole contexts for *s a b*. That is, a value of type *Delta s a b* is equivalent to one of type *s a b* that is missing one value of type *b*; so the type functor should be equipped with the corresponding operation to 'close' a *Delta s a b* around the missing *b* to make an *s a b*.

data *Delta s* :: ∗ → ∗ → ∗
close :: *TypeFunctor s* ⇒ *Delta s a b* → *b* → *s a b*

Then a one-hole context for a tree consists of a list of one-hole contexts for nodes; we have chosen to represent that list outermost context first, so that 'closing' is a *foldr*.

type *Context s a* = [*Delta s a* (*Term s a*)]
(⋖) :: *TypeFunctor s* ⇒ *Context s a* → *Term s a* → *Term s a*
cs ⋖ *t* = *foldr* (λ*d u* → *InT* (*close d u*)) *t cs*

For example, for binary trees, there are two ways of making a *TreeF a b* that is missing a single *b*, one for each side of a *Fork* node—but there is no way for an *Empty* node to have a hole:

data *Delta TreeF a b* = *LForkF a b* | *RForkF a b*
close (*LForkF a u*) *t* = *ForkF a t u*
close (*RForkF a t*) *u* = *ForkF a t u*

In fact, the context type *Delta s* follows directly from the structure *s* of the tree; contexts are a type-indexed data type [17], and can be defined generically [16, 22].

2.5 Subterms

We prohibit trees with 'junk' structures that are not labelled, because such structures break the one-to-one correspondence between subtrees of a given tree and their labelsets, a property required for tracing structure transformations using labels.

REQUIREMENT 1 (No Junk). *Given a tree t,* $\langle child\ t\ i \rangle \subset \langle t \rangle$*, for any valid index i.* □

The no-junk condition enforces that the labelset of any subtree tree must be a proper subset of that of its parent. For many datatypes, similar to the representation of binary trees above, this no-junk condition is enforced by the constructors. But for other datatypes such as leaf-labelled trees

data *LTree a* = *EmptyL*
  | *Leaf a*
  | *Bin* (*LTree a*) (*LTree a*)

one can construct invalid values such as *Bin EmptyL* (*Leaf* 1), where *Leaf* 1 is a strict subterm of *Bin EmptyL* (*Leaf* 1), but has the same labelset. In this paper, we rule out datatypes like this that do not enforce the no-junk requirement.

Tree navigation induces a subterm ordering on trees.

DEFINITION 2 (Subterm Ordering). *Given trees r and t, we say r is a subterm of t, written* $r \preccurlyeq t$*, if* $r = zoom\ t\ p$ *for some p. We say that a subterm r is trivial if* $\langle r \rangle = \emptyset$*.* □

Throughout this paper, we assume non-trivial subterms unless otherwise stated.

COROLLARY 3 (Distinct Subterms). *Because tree elements are uniquely labelled, when* $r \preccurlyeq t$ *(and r is non-trivial), then r is in fact at the end of a unique path; that is, there is a (partial) function* $locate :: \mu\mathbf{S} \to \mu\mathbf{S} \to Path$ *satisfying*

$$locate\ t\ r = p \quad \Leftrightarrow \quad r = zoom\ t\ p$$

We say that 'r is at depth n in t' when $n = length\ (locate\ t\ r)$*.* □

DEFINITION 4 (Orderedness). *We say r and t are ordered, written as* $r \sim t$*, if* $r \preccurlyeq t \vee t \preccurlyeq r$*.* □

A consequence of the no-junk requirement is a close correlation between the subterm relation and inclusion among labelsets.

COROLLARY 5 (Labels of Subterms). *The subterm relationship is a refinement of inclusion of labelsets:* $r \preccurlyeq t \Rightarrow \langle r \rangle \subseteq \langle t \rangle$*. And for ordered trees* $r \sim t$*, the converse holds too:* $r \preccurlyeq t \Leftarrow \langle r \rangle \subseteq \langle t \rangle$*.* □

Another consequence is that the labelsets of two ordered trees intersect.

COROLLARY 6. *We have* $r \sim t \Rightarrow (\langle r \rangle \cap \langle t \rangle \neq \emptyset)$ *for non-trivial trees r,t.* □

The operator $(\lessdot)$ that closes a context around a tree has a partial inverse $(/)$, in the sense that

$$c \lessdot r = t \quad \Leftrightarrow \quad t \,/\, r = c$$

when $r \preccurlyeq t$; in particular, $(t \,/\, r) \lessdot r = t$ and $(c \lessdot r) \,/\, r = c$. One might think of $t \,/\, r$ as the result of subtracting subtree r from tree t. The two operators $(\lessdot)$ and $(/)$ associate to the right, and $(/)$ has a higher precedence than $(\lessdot)$; we can therefore nest them:

PROPOSITION 7 (Nesting). *Given that* $r \preccurlyeq s \preccurlyeq t$, *then* $t \,/\, s \lessdot s \,/\, r \lessdot q = t \,/\, r \lessdot q$. □

Subtraction is related to substition:

PROPOSITION 8. *For trees r and t and position i,* $InT\ (outT\ r)_{i \mapsto t} = r \,/\, (outT\ r)_i \lessdot t$. □

Closing extends the input tree, as captured by the following monotonicity condition.

PROPOSITION 9 (Monotonicity). $t \preccurlyeq (c \lessdot t)$ □

Lastly, all holes are equal.

REQUIREMENT 10 (Hole Equality). $s \,/\, s = t \,/\, t$. □

COROLLARY 11 (Left Unit). $s \,/\, s \lessdot t = t$. □

2.6 Local Editing

An *editing function* is an endofunction $edit :: v \rightarrow v$; we will consider editing functions only on views. We require all editing functions to be total, so that they can always be applied to a subterm of a view. We treat editing functions as being in some sense location-independent: they can be applied to any superterm enclosing the subterm that is actually affected by the edit.

DEFINITION 12 (Locality). *We say an editing function e is local to a subterm* u_0 *of a view v if*

$$\forall u.\ u_0 \preccurlyeq u \preccurlyeq v \Rightarrow e\ v = v \,/\, u \lessdot e\ u$$

□

In the above definition, applying the local editing function e to any subterm u of v enclosing the affected subterm u_0 has the same effect as applying the function to v. For example, as we have seen in the binary tree example, deleting 4 from the sublist $[4,8,9]$ and combining the result with the context $[7,6,5]$ is the same as deleting 4 from the complete view $[7,6,5,4,8,9]$. From the equality of holes, we can conclude that the trivial locality always holds.

COROLLARY 13. *Given a view v, any editing function is local to subterm v of v.* □

Beyond the trivial one, there is certainly an ordering among different levels of locality, based on the subterm ordering, which falls out from the above definition. In this sense, a context-sensitive (path-based) editing function, always requiring traversing from the root, fixes u_0 to be v, which implies very poor locality characteristics. We will discuss an option for remedying this in Section 6.1.

In our proposal, the subterm u_0 to which an editing function is local is user-provided; our approach is based on the assumption that u_0 is significantly smaller than v. We pair the editing function with an additional function that returns the affected subterm.

$$\textbf{data}\ Edit\ a = E\ \{edit :: a \rightarrow a, affect :: a \rightarrow a\}$$

(The above declaration creates a polymorphic record type *Edit* with named fields *edit* and *affect*, each of which is a function. The field extractors are named after the fields; so given a value $e :: Edit\ a$, the two functions encapsulated in it can be retrieved as $edit\ e :: a \rightarrow a$ and $affect\ e :: a \rightarrow a$. We require that $edit\ e$ is local to $affect\ e$.)

2.7 Change-Based Bidirectional Frameworks

A change-based bidirectional framework consists of two functions: a 'get' function $f :: s \rightarrow v$ from source to view, and a change-based 'put' function $f^{\lessdot}_{ch} :: Edit\ v \rightarrow s \rightarrow s$. We only consider 'get' functions that are regular structural recursions, because they are more likely to benefit from our proposed improvement. We will discuss this choice in detail in Section 3.2. We also rule out 'get' functions involving duplication of labels, so that uniqueness of identifiers is preserved. The function $f^{\lessdot}_{ch}$ is higher-order, in contrast to $f^{\lessdot}_{st} :: (v,s) \rightarrow s$ in a state-based setting. Thus $f^{\lessdot}_{ch}$ no longer constructs an updated source from an edited view, but from the original source; any information in the edited view can be derived from the editing function and the original source. In contrast to an operation-based approach, $f^{\lessdot}_{ch}$ is not dependent on the actual editing functions.

Bidirectional laws semantically equivalent to those developed for state-based bidirectional frameworks can be specified in the new setting.

Consistency $f\ (f^{\lessdot}_{ch}\ e\ s) = edit\ e\ (f\ s)$

Acceptability $f^{\lessdot}_{ch}\ (E\ \{edit = id\}) = id$

Undoability $f^{\lessdot}_{ch}\ (e\ \{edit = (edit\ e)^{\circ}\}) \circ f^{\lessdot}_{ch}\ e = id$.

The relationships between different view values are expressed through explicit editing functions. For acceptability, we construct a record with the identity edit (and leave the *affect* field unspecified). For undoability, a record is updated with the left-inverse $((edit\ e)^{\circ})$ of its editing function to cancel its effect on the source.

Moving from a state-based framework to a change-based framework potentially improves run-time performance, as we exploit the locality of updating. We look into the details in the next section.

3. Locality Preservation

Incremental updates can be achieved if the locality of an editing function is propagated to the source level. Figure 2 shows how a 'get' function may relate subterms in the source to subterms in the view. The idea is that the subterm v of the view depends only on the subterm s of the source. Furthermore, the sequences of source contexts $sc_1, ..., sc_n$ and view contexts $vc_1, ..., vc_m$ maintain this relationship, so that $vc_1 \lessdot v$ depends only on $sc_1 \lessdot s$, and so on, until $vc_m \lessdot ... \lessdot vc_1 \lessdot v$ depends only on $sc_n \lessdot ... \lessdot sc_1 \lessdot s$. Note that we can always arrange the two columns in a way that both have the same length (i.e., $m = n$); when one subterm on one side matches with multiple ones on the other side, we only need to insert a few empty contexts (since $[\,] \lessdot t = t$) to realign the two sides. This kind of locality preservation is determined by the 'get' function, which defines the connection between a view and its source.

3.1 Alignment

DEFINITION 14 (Alignment). *We say 'get' function f aligns at subterm r of s iff for all t we have*

$$f\ (s \,/\, r \lessdot t) = f\ s \,/\, f\ r \lessdot f\ t$$

We call r an alignment position in s with respect to f. □

When a 'get' function f and a source s are unambiguous, the term r may be referred to as an alignment position, where f is said to align at r. The above definition not only characterizes the matching of source subterms r to corresponding view subterms $f\ r$, but also a kind of isolation between them. An alignment position can be seen as a 'resistive barrier' between the construction of a subterm and its

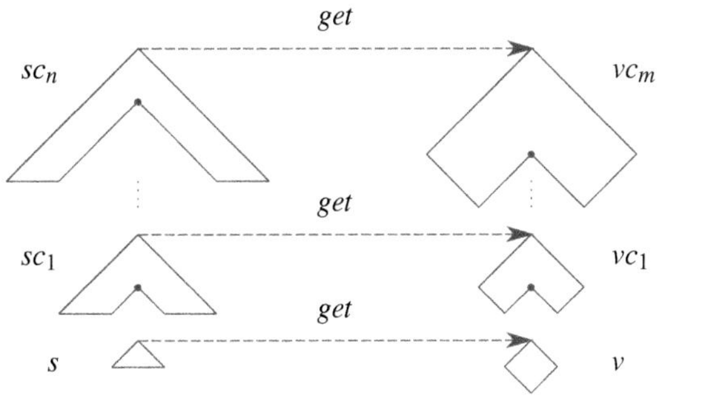

Figure 2. Source-view alignment.

context, through which information does not flow. At an alignment position, $f\ r$ is independent of s / r and $f\ s / f\ r$ is independent of r.

The significance of alignment positions is that they capture the mapping between the locality to $f\ r$ in the view and the locality to r in the source. As a result, if $f\ r$ can be locally edited, then r can be locally updated:

$$f^{\lessdot}_{st'}\ (f\ s / f\ r \lessdot v', s) = s / r \lessdot f^{\lessdot}_{st}\ (v', r)$$

The above defines an optimization of an existing 'put' function. Basically, to process an edited view $f\ s / f\ r \lessdot v'$, we only need to process v' (the edited $f\ r$), provided f aligns at r. To show that the above transformation is correct, we prove the consistency of $f^{\lessdot}_{st'}$.

$$\begin{array}{ll} & f\ (f^{\lessdot}_{st'}\ (f\ s / f\ r \lessdot v', s)) \\ = & \{\text{definition of } f^{\lessdot}_{st'}\} \\ & f\ (s / r \lessdot f^{\lessdot}_{st}\ (v', r)) \\ = & \{f \text{ aligns at } r\} \\ & f\ s / f\ r \lessdot f\ (f^{\lessdot}_{st}\ (v', r)) \\ = & \{\text{consistency of } f^{\lessdot}_{st}\} \\ & f\ s / f\ r \lessdot v' \end{array}$$

Other bidirectional properties hold as well; we postpone their proofs until Section 4, where the complete solution is presented.

Not all view subterms match exactly with a source subterm; sometimes we need to resort to a looser fit.

DEFINITION 15. *Given a 'get' function f, we say an alignment position s covers v if $v \preccurlyeq_f s$.*

We now show some example 'get' functions that preserve different degrees of alignment. Consider a function that returns the mirror image of a tree.

mirror :: *Tree a* → *Tree a*
mirror Empty = *Empty*
mirror (*Fork a l r*) = *Fork a* (*mirror r*) (*mirror l*)

Every subtree in the source is an alignment position, because the constructions of the view and of the source coincide.

Another such function is *inorder*, defined in Section 1.4. In this case, only the right subtrees are alignment positions, because the left subtrees do not correspond to subterms in the view.

Yet another example is the function *spine* that extracts the elements on the spine of a tree:

spine :: *Tree a* → [*a*]
spine Empty = [ ]
spine (*Fork a l r*) = *a* : *spine r*

In this case, all subterms of the source are alignment positions, though the left subtrees, which always correspond to the empty list in the view, are not very interesting.

3.2 Exploiting Regularity

Change-based 'put' functions are only interesting when there are plenty of alignment positions to choose from, so that view subterms can be covered 'tightly'. As alignment positions represent matches between source and view constructions, for a recursive 'get' function, this matching of constructions suggests a kind of structural recursion pattern. Though not a sufficient condition, regularity of the recursion pattern is likely to positively impact the availability of alignment positions. Thus, we focus on regular structural recursions—functions that can be implemented as folds. For a regular structural recursion, a source is deconstructed in a uniform way, which leaves the fold body to determine whether the construction of a view matches up.

To explain the intuition behind how 'get' functions determine alignment positions, let us revisit the function *spine*. A fold deconstructs a non-empty input tree into two source subterms l and r and a single element a; for the *spine* computation, the fold body discards l and adds the element a to *spine r*. The recursive calls always produce a view recursive component (such as *spine r*) from a source subterm (r); whether the view recursive component so produced is made into a view subterm by the fold body determines the possibility of alignment. For example, recursive component *spine r* is a subterm of a : *spine r*, which makes r an alignment position. In this case, any edit local to *spine r* can be addressed by updating r. In contrast, if we define *spine* as

spineRev (*Fork a l r*) = *spineRev r* ++ [*a*]

then the view construction is the 'opposite' of the source construction, with the parent a at the bottom (tail end) of the list. This misalignment manifests itself by causing *spineRev r* not to form a subterm in the view. Any edit to the view affects a sublist including a, which implies an update to the complete source tree.

In the case of *spine*, a view subterm not only has a recursive component as its origin, but also as its exclusive origin: *spine r* is copied to the view without modification. This exclusivity is necessary for producing alignment positions. Consider a variant of *spine* that breaks this rule:

spineRot (*Fork a l r*) = *a* : *reverse* (*spineRot r*)

The recursive component *spineRot r* is changed by *reverse*; and its manifestation in the view depends on its context, which decides how many times *reverse* is applied to it. Though at each individual recursive step *reverse* (*spineRot r*) is a subterm of *a* : *reverse* (*spineRot r*), a subsequent step does not preserve this property: *reverse* (*spineRot r*) ceases to be a subterm of *b* : (*reverse* (*a* : *reverse* (*spineRot r*))). In this case, only three alignment positions (the complete source and the root's two immediate children) exist, which is not very interesting.

3.2.1 The Well-Aligning Condition

We formalize the above observation into a condition on the bodies of 'get' functions defined as folds that guarantees the availability of alignment positions.

DEFINITION 16 (Well-aligning). *We say a fold body b is well-aligning if for all x such that arity $x \neq 0$, and for all non-trivial subterms u of $b\ x$, we have*

$$\exists i.\ u \sim x_i \wedge \forall w.\ b\ x_{i \mapsto w} = b\ x / x_i \lessdot w$$

Further, we say that f = fold b is well-aligning if its body b is. □

We do not worry about the case when there are no recursive components in x (i.e., *arity* $x = 0$), as they are terminals in construction, and will not affect alignment. There are two parts to the condition: the first part ($u \sim x_i$) enforces that each non-trivial view subterm u has a recursive component as its origin; the second part

$(\forall w.\, b\, x_{i \mapsto w} = b \,/\, x_i \lessdot w)$ guarantees the exclusivity of the origins (with no influence by external factors)—the recursive component in question is copied unchanged to the view. It is important for the expressiveness of 'get' functions that this copying requirement only applies to selected recursive components; some, that will appear as subterms of $b\,x$, are taken as opaque blocks, leaving the rest to be broken up for gluing the blocks together.

For example, consider the following functions:

$$
\begin{aligned}
vlr\,(v, ls, rs) &= [v] \mathbin{+\!\!+} ls \mathbin{+\!\!+} rs \\
lvr\,(v, ls, rs) &= ls \mathbin{+\!\!+} [v] \mathbin{+\!\!+} rs \\
lrv\,(v, ls, rs) &= ls \mathbin{+\!\!+} rs \mathbin{+\!\!+} [v]
\end{aligned}
$$

The functions *vlr*, *lvr*, and *lrv* (standing for 'visit, left, right', etc) correspond to individual cases of the fold bodies for traversing binary trees in pre-, in-, and post-order, respectively. There are two inputs to the functions that are recursive view components, namely *ls* and *rs*. Functions *vlr* and *lvr* are well-aligning, as *rs* is ordered with respect to all the view subterms that are visited, whereas *lrv* is not.

Generalizing the definition to the semantics of transformations, we say that a 'get' function is well-aligning if all cases of its body are well-aligning. By that definition, *preorder*, *inorder*, *unzip*, *mirror*, *spine*, *filter*, *map* are examples of well-aligning 'get' functions, while *postorder* is not. (However, we will discuss how this function can be made well-aligning in Section 5.)

3.2.2 Availability of Alignment Positions

The well-aligning property guarantees the availability of alignment positions; and we can state a declarative result about how they may be found.

THEOREM 17. *Given a well-aligning 'get' function f such that $f\,s = v$, we have that f aligns at subterm r of s if there exists a non-trivial subterm u of v such that $u \preccurlyeq f\,r$.* □

The well-aligning condition tells us clearly that some selected recursive components become subterms in the view; and the source subterms producing the selected subcomponents are alignment positions. The key to proving Theorem 17 is to establish the fact that recursive component $f\,r$ is among those selected due to the premise $u \preccurlyeq f\,r$; this can be achieved by connecting the unique labels in u with those in $f\,r$.

As preparation for formally proving Theorem 17, we state some properties regarding labels of trees under transformation. As mentioned at the beginning of Section 2, one important requirement of 'get' functions is that they do not invent labels.

REQUIREMENT 18 (Conservation of Labels). *Given a 'get' function $f = fold\ b$, we have that b does not invent labels:*

$$\forall x.\ \langle b\,x\rangle \subseteq lab\ x$$

and hence, neither does $f = fold\ b$ invent labels:

$$\forall s.\ \langle f\,s\rangle \subseteq \langle s\rangle$$

□

An important consequence of the fact that 'get' functions do not invent labels is that labels cannot reappear after they have been dropped during the construction of a view. Conversely, if a label set $\langle v\rangle$ has been generated after processing subterm r of t by the 'get' function f (that is, $r \preccurlyeq t$ and $\langle v\rangle \subseteq \langle f\,r\rangle$), and $\langle v\rangle$ is still present after processing t itself (that is, $\langle v\rangle \subseteq \langle f\,t\rangle$), then $\langle v\rangle$ is present at every intermediate stage too ($\langle v\rangle \subseteq \langle f\,s\rangle$ for every s such that $r \preccurlyeq s \preccurlyeq t$). This is a kind of 'convexity' property of label sets.

More importantly in what follows, a similar result holds for subterms, rather than their projections to label sets; but for this, we need the additional assumption that the 'get' function f is well-aligning. The primary result (Corollary 20) is a convexity property for terms: given sources r, t with $r \preccurlyeq t$ such that $v \preccurlyeq f\,r$ and $v \preccurlyeq f\,t$, then also $v \preccurlyeq f\,s$ for any s such that $r \preccurlyeq s \preccurlyeq t$. (In fact, $v \preccurlyeq f\,t$ is not strictly required; $\langle v\rangle \subseteq \langle f\,t\rangle$ suffices.) The essential step (Lemma 19) is the one from the outermost term t to one of its immediate children: if view subterm v shows up after processing a subterm r within the ith child $(outT\ t)_i$ of t, and v is still present after processing t, then v must have come from the ith child: $v \preccurlyeq f\,(outT\ t)_i$. Note that, for both of these results, we make use of our implicit assumption that v is non-trivial.

LEMMA 19 (Maintaining terms). *Suppose a well-aligning 'get' function $f = fold\ b$. For source terms r, t with $r \preccurlyeq (outT\ t)_i$, if $v \preccurlyeq f\,r$ and $v \preccurlyeq f\,t$, then also $v \preccurlyeq f\,(outT\ t)_i$.*

PROOF. Let $x = \mathbf{S}f\,(outT\ t)$, so that $f\,t = b\,x$ and $f\,(outT\ t)_i = x_i$. Since b is well-aligning, and v is a non-trivial subterm of $b\,x$, there exists a j such that $v \sim x_j = f\,(outT\ t)_j$. In fact, this j must be i:

$$
\begin{aligned}
& \langle v\rangle \\
\subseteq\ & \{\text{labels of subterms (Corollary 5); } v \preccurlyeq f\,r\text{, by assumption}\} \\
& \langle f\,r\rangle \\
\subseteq\ & \{f \text{ does not invent labels}\} \\
& \langle r\rangle \\
\subseteq\ & \{r \preccurlyeq (outT\ t)_i\text{; Corollary 5 again}\} \\
& \langle (outT\ t)_i\rangle \\
\#\ & \{\text{disjointness of labels}\} \\
& \langle (outT\ t)_{\neq i}\rangle \\
\supseteq\ & \{f \text{ does not invent labels; monotonicity of intersection}\} \\
& \langle (\mathbf{S}f\,(outT\ t))_{\neq i}\rangle \\
=\ & \{\text{definition of } x\} \\
& \langle x_{\neq i}\rangle
\end{aligned}
$$

and so $\langle v\rangle \# \langle x_{\neq i}\rangle$, and hence $\langle v\rangle \subseteq \langle x_i\rangle$ by disjointness of labels. Finally, $v \sim x_i$ and $\langle v\rangle \subseteq \langle x_i\rangle$ imply $v \preccurlyeq x_i$, by Corollary 5. □

COROLLARY 20 (Term convexity). *Suppose a well-aligning 'get' function $f = fold\ b$. For source terms r, t with $r \preccurlyeq t$, if $v \preccurlyeq f\,r$ and $v \preccurlyeq f\,t$, then also $v \preccurlyeq f\,s$ for every s such that $r \preccurlyeq s \preccurlyeq t$.*

PROOF. The proof is by induction over the length of *locate t r*. The base case is when the path is empty, so $r = t$; then the lemma is trivially true. For the inductive case, assume the statement is valid for paths of length n. Suppose that $r \preccurlyeq t$, and that r is at depth $n+1$ in t (so that $r \preccurlyeq (outT\ t)_i$ for some unique index i, and $locate\ (outT\ t)_i\ r$ has length n), and that $v \preccurlyeq f\,r$ and $v \preccurlyeq f\,t$. By Lemma 19, we get $v \preccurlyeq f\,(outT\ t)_i$; then by induction we get $v \preccurlyeq f\,s$ for every s with $r \preccurlyeq s \preccurlyeq (outT\ t)_i$ too; and the final case $s = t$ trivially holds. □

Theorem 17 follows directly from the following result: given a well-aligning 'get' function f, and sources r,s such that $r \preccurlyeq s$, if there exists any view subterm v such that $v \preccurlyeq f\,r$ and $v \preccurlyeq f\,s$, then f aligns at subterm r of s. (Again, we assume that v is non-trivial.)

LEMMA 21 (Get alignment). *Given a well-aligning 'get' function f, sources r, t with $r \preccurlyeq t$, and view v such that $v \preccurlyeq f\,r$ and $v \preccurlyeq f\,t$, then f aligns at subterm r of t.*

PROOF. Again, by induction over the length of *locate t r*. The base case is when the path is empty; then $t = r$ and the theorem is trivially true (since f necessarily aligns at the root t of source t). For the inductive case, we assume that the statement is valid for paths of length n; we are given terms r, t with $r \preccurlyeq t$ and r at depth $n+1$ in t, and a term v with $v \preccurlyeq f\,r$ and $v \preccurlyeq f\,t$, and we have to show that f aligns at subterm r of t.

Suppose that r is within the i'th child of t, that is, $r \preccurlyeq s$ where $s = (outT\ t)_i$. Then by Corollary 20, we have $v \preccurlyeq f\ s$, and by induction, f aligns at subterm r of s. Let $x = \mathbf{S} f\ (outT\ t)$, so that $f\ t = b\ x$ and $f\ (outT\ t)_i = x_i$. Because b is well-aligning and $v \preccurlyeq b\ x$, there exists a j such that $v \sim x_j$ and $b\ x_{j \mapsto w} = b\ x \,/\, x_j \lessdot w$ for any w. In fact, that j must be i, by the same argument as in the proof of Lemma 19. In particular, $f\ s = x_i \preccurlyeq b\ x$, a fact that we shall use below. Finally, we show that f aligns at subterm r of t. For an arbitrary source term p, we have:

$$
\begin{array}{ll}
 & f\ (t \,/\, r \lessdot p) \\
= & \quad \{\text{since } r \preccurlyeq s \preccurlyeq t\} \\
 & f\ (t \,/\, s \lessdot (s \,/\, r \lessdot p)) \\
= & \quad \{\text{Proposition 8---} s = (outT\ t)_i\} \\
 & f\ (InT\ (outT\ t)_{i \mapsto (s/r \lessdot p)}) \\
= & \quad \{\text{evaluation rule for } f = \mathit{fold}\ b\} \\
 & b\ (\mathbf{S} f\ (outT\ t)_{i \mapsto (s/r \lessdot p)}) \\
= & \quad \{\text{naturality of } \mathit{select}\} \\
 & b\ (\mathbf{S} f\ (outT\ t))_{i \mapsto (f\ (s/r \lessdot p))} \\
= & \quad \{b \text{ is well-aligning; discussion above}\} \\
 & b\ (\mathbf{S} f\ (outT\ t)) \,/\, f\ (outT\ t)_i \lessdot f\ (s \,/\, r \lessdot p) \\
= & \quad \{\text{evaluation rule for } f \text{ again; } s = (outT\ t)_i\} \\
 & f\ t \,/\, f\ s \lessdot f\ (s \,/\, r \lessdot p) \\
= & \quad \{\text{induction}\} \\
 & f\ t \,/\, f\ s \lessdot (f\ s \,/\, f\ r \lessdot f\ p) \\
= & \quad \{\text{nesting}\} \\
 & f\ t \,/\, f\ r \lessdot f\ p
\end{array}
$$

□

So far, we have established well-alignment as a sufficient condition for the availability of alignment positions (Definition 16), and proved a declarative result about how alignment positions can be found (Theorem 17). Next, we move on to devise a constructive method of finding alignment positions, and deriving a change-based 'put' function based on this method.

4. Change-Based 'Put' Functions

The derivation of a 'put' function is divided into three steps: (i) finding an alignment position covering the edited view subterm; (ii) using a state-based 'put' function to map the view subterm to a source subterm; and (iii) merging the original source context with the updated source subterm. The key part of this process is step (i); the other two follow on quite naturally. Taking the previous result, we know that a source subterm is an alignment position if there is a corresponding subterm in the view. A standard way of establishing the source/view correspondence semantically is to trace the uniquely identifying labels.

4.1 Labelling and Reflecting

Unique identifiers are created using paths in the source, from the root to the node constructors of the elements. As a result, a node is at the root position of the subterm identified by the path. As far as 'get' functions are concerned, an element and its label form an atomic unit; an element in the view originates from an element in the source associated with the same label. (It is worth noting that the labels only represent paths in the source, not those in the view.) Given an edit-affected view subterm v, a sensible alignment position should include all the labels in $\langle v \rangle$; the path leading to such a source subterm is the maximum common prefix $mcp\ \langle v \rangle$ of all the paths to nodes with these labels.

Consider a simple example with *mirror* as the 'get' function (see Figure 3). Note that the labels in the source—the list component of each pair in the diagram—are copied over to the view. Suppose we insert a new node at the location labelled $[1]$ in the view, affecting the element 68 at location $[1]$ and the locations below it $[[1,1],[1,2]]$. (Note that we don't require a concrete label for the newly inserted node since it will not contribute to the identification of the affected source.) The maximum common prefix of the affected labels $[[1],[1,1],[1,2]]$ is $[1]$. Now tracing the pedigree of the path $[1]$ back to the source, we conclude that it is the subtree with root element 68 that needs to be changed.

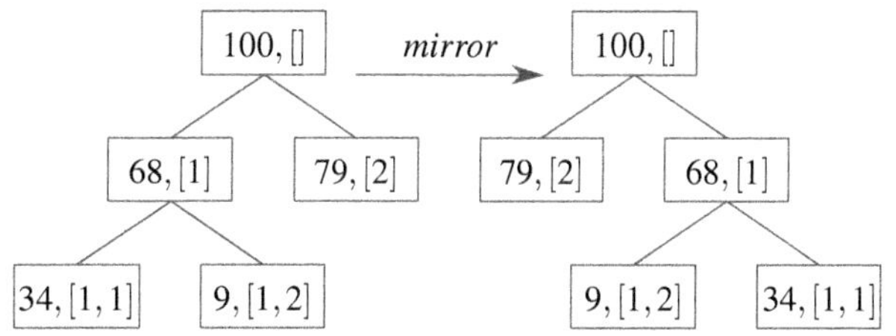

Figure 3. Using *mirror* as a 'get' function.

The key to demonstrating the correctness of the above process is to show that the subset relation between label sets corresponds to the subterm relation between trees.

LEMMA 22. *Given a well-aligning 'get' function $f = fold\ b$, and source terms s, t with $s \preccurlyeq t$, and view term v, if $v \preccurlyeq f\ t$ and $\langle v \rangle \subseteq \langle s \rangle$ then $v \preccurlyeq f\ s$.*

PROOF. Again, by induction over the length of *locate t s*. The base case is when the path is empty; then $s = t$, and the result trivially holds. For the inductive case, assume that the result holds for paths of length n, and that s is at depth $n+1$ in t. Let i be such that $s \preccurlyeq (outT\ t)_i$, so that $locate\ (outT\ t)_i\ s$ has length n. We will show that $v \preccurlyeq f\ (outT\ t)_i$; then we can conclude $v \preccurlyeq f\ s$ by appeal to the inductive hypothesis.

Let $x = \mathbf{S} f\ (outT\ t)$, so $f\ t = b\ x$ and $f\ (outT\ t)_i = x_i$. Since v is a non-trivial subterm of $b\ x$, and b is well-aligning, there exists a j such that $v \sim x_j$. By the usual argument, that j must be i:

$$
\begin{array}{ll}
 & \langle v \rangle \\
\subseteq & \quad \{\text{assumption}\} \\
 & \langle s \rangle \\
\subseteq & \quad \{\text{hypothesis, and Corollary 5}\} \\
 & \langle (outT\ t)_i \rangle \\
\# & \quad \{\text{disjointness of labels}\} \\
 & \langle (outT\ t)_{\neq i} \rangle \\
\supseteq & \quad \{f \text{ does not invent labels}\} \\
 & \langle (\mathbf{S} f\ (outT\ t))_{\neq i} \rangle \\
= & \quad \{\text{definition}\} \\
 & \langle x_{\neq i} \rangle
\end{array}
$$

So $v \sim x_i$. Moreover, $\langle v \rangle \subseteq \langle x_i \rangle$, by disjointness of labels, since by assumption we have $v \preccurlyeq f\ t$ and hence $\langle v \rangle \subseteq \langle f\ t \rangle = \langle b\ x \rangle \subseteq \langle x \rangle$, and we have just shown that $\langle v \rangle \# \langle x_{\neq i} \rangle$. Therefore, by Corollary 5 we conclude $v \preccurlyeq x_i = f\ (outT\ t)_i$. □

As a side remark, so far we have been oblivious to the fact that the source and view nodes are now labelled, and have assumed that the 'get' and 'put' functions work uniformly on them. This is certainly correct given parametrically polymorphic datatypes and functions; free theorems [30] provide the guarantee we need. It is straightforward to relax this fully-parametric type restriction to constrained polymorphic types. For example, we can use equality in the transformation by introducing the following:

$$
\begin{array}{l}
f \;\; :: Eq\ a \Rightarrow s\ a \rightarrow v\ a \\
f^{\preccurlyeq}_{st} :: Eq\ a \Rightarrow (v\ a, s\ a) \rightarrow s\ a
\end{array}
$$

and a generic instance to bypass the labels:

instance $Eq\ a \Rightarrow Eq\ (Label, a)$ **where**
$(\equiv)\ (\_, a)\ (\_, b) = a \equiv b$

This kind of generic definition is all that is required to introduce constrained polymorphism. For example, consider a function that filters the labels of a tree and returns them as a list.

$filterT :: Eq\ a \Rightarrow (a, Tree\ a) \to [a]$
$filterT\ (x, Empty) \quad = [\,]$
$filterT\ (x, Fork\ a\ l\ r) = \textbf{if}\ a \equiv x\ \textbf{then}\ lr\ \textbf{else}\ a : lr$
$\quad \textbf{where}\ lr = filterT\ l +\!\!+ filterT\ r$

Function *filterT* is well-aligning, and our technique is applicable without modification.

It is worth mentioning that labelling tree elements uniquely and exploiting parametricity to establish connections between source and view is not limited to finding subterm correspondence. In [28], 'get' functions are applied to source values with elements replaced by labels, which allows one to conduct a kind of forensic examination of the transformation, determining its effect without examining its implementation; with such information a 'put' function can be constructed. We will discuss in more detail in Section 7 the connection between our technique and the approach in [28].

4.2 The Change-Based 'Put' Function

We are now ready to present the change-based 'put' function. For any $f_{st}^{<}$, a generic $f_{ch}^{<}$ function can be defined as follows:

$f_{ch}^{<} :: Edit\ v \to s \to s$
$f_{ch}^{<}\ e\ s = s \,/\, r \lessdot (f_{st}^{<} \circ ((edit\ e \circ f) \vartriangle id))\ r$
$\quad \textbf{where}\ r = zoom\ i\ s$
$\qquad\qquad i = mcp\ \langle affect\ e\ (f\ s) \rangle$

The function $f_{ch}^{<}$ maps an edit operation on views, e, into an update operation on sources. The evaluation of $f_{ch}^{<}$ is illustrated in Figure 4, which shows how an updated source is obtained by an indirect route. A source is firstly mapped into a view via f, with the affected view subterm of the edit extracted via *affect e*. After that, the labels in the affected view subterm are collected and are used to identify an alignment position, r, covering the affected view subterm. A view of the alignment position is then constructed by applying f, and is edited before the state-based 'put' function $f_{st}^{<}$ maps it into an updated source subterm. Finally, the standard split operator, $\vartriangle$, with type $(a \to b) \to (a \to c) \to (a \to (b, c))$, is used to produce a pair containing the result of applying two functions to a value. Here it combines the newly created source subterm with the original context that remains unchanged. (The straightforward re-labelling of the newly generated source subterm with i as the root label is omitted.)

As shown in Figure 4, there are several passes across the source/view boundary, and apart from the initial 'get' function application, all of them concern only the edit-affected subterms. Assuming the editing and 'get' functions have no worse runtime performance than the 'put' function, the complexity of $f_{ch}^{<}$ is $O\ (m \times \log n + c\ m)$ where n and m are the sizes of the source s and the change r, and c is the complexity function for $f_{st}^{<}$. Note that $affect\ e\ (f\ s)$ will have been executed prior to the 'put' function execution, and is not included in the performance analysis. The cost of computing $s \,/\, r$ is not considered because the context $s \,/\, r$ can be computed together with the focus r when the zooming is performed. The $m \times \log n$ part of the above complexity function comes from the computation of *mcp*, where m labels of size $\log n$ need to be processed.

The function $f_{ch}^{<}$ is expected to preserve the bidirectional properties of $f_{st}^{<}$. This is established when $f_{ch}^{<}$ operates at alignment positions.

THEOREM 23. *Given a well-aligning 'get' function f such that $f\ s = v$, then for all source subterms r of s and view subterms u of v, $zoom\ (mcp\ \langle u \rangle)\ s$ is the smallest alignment position covering u.*

PROOF. By definition, we have $\langle u \rangle \subseteq \langle zoom\ (mcp\ \langle u \rangle)\ s \rangle$.

$\langle u \rangle \subseteq \langle zoom\ (mcp\ \langle u \rangle)\ s \rangle \wedge u \preccurlyeq f\ s\ \wedge$
$\langle zoom\ (mcp\ \langle u \rangle)\ s \rangle \preccurlyeq s$
$\Rightarrow \quad \{\text{lemma } 22\}$
$u \preccurlyeq f\ (zoom\ (mcp\ \langle u \rangle)\ s) \wedge u \preccurlyeq f\ s\ \wedge$
$\langle zoom\ (mcp\ \langle u \rangle)\ s \rangle \preccurlyeq s$
$\Rightarrow \quad \{\text{theorem } 17\}$
f aligns at subterm $zoom\ (mcp\ \langle u \rangle)\ s$ of s

Also from the definition of *mcp*, there exists no r such that $r \prec zoom\ (mcp\ \langle u \rangle)\ s$ and $\langle u \rangle \subseteq \langle r \rangle$. Thus, $zoom\ (mcp\ \langle u \rangle)\ s$ is the smallest alignment position covering u. □

We can state the bidirectional properties of $f_{ch}^{<}$.

THEOREM 24 (Consistency). $f\ (f_{ch}^{<}\ e\ s) = edit\ e\ (f\ s)$

PROOF.

$f\ (f_{ch}^{<}\ e\ s)$
$= \quad \{\text{definition of } f_{ch}^{<}\}$
$f\ (s \,/\, r \lessdot (f_{st}^{<} \circ ((edit\ e \circ f) \vartriangle id))\ r))$
$= \quad \{r \text{ is an alignment position}\}$
$f\ s \,/\, f\ r \lessdot (f \circ f_{st}^{<} \circ ((edit\ e \circ f) \vartriangle id))\ r)$
$= \quad \{\text{consistency of } f_{st}^{<}\}$
$f\ s \,/\, f\ r \lessdot (edit\ e \circ f)\ r$
$= \quad \{r \text{ covers } affect\ e\ (f\ s), \text{ and locality of } edit\}$
$edit\ e\ (f\ s \,/\, f\ r \lessdot f\ r)$
$= \quad \{r \text{ is an alignment position}\}$
$edit\ e\ (f\ (s \,/\, r \lessdot r))$
$= \quad \{\text{cancellation}\}$
$edit\ e\ (f\ s)$

□

For acceptability, we need an 'identity' edit that does not change the view.

THEOREM 25 (Acceptability). $f_{ch}^{<}\ (E\ \{edit = id\}) = id$.

PROOF.

$f_{ch}^{<}\ (E\ \{edit = id\})\ s$
$= \quad \{\text{definition of } f_{ch}^{<}\}$
$s \,/\, r \lessdot (f_{st}^{<} \circ ((id \circ f) \vartriangle id))\ r$
$= \quad \{\text{acceptability of } f_{st}^{<}\}$
$s \,/\, r \lessdot r$
$= \quad \{\text{cancellation}\}$
s

□

Undoability involves inverting an edit as a function.

THEOREM 26 (Undoability). $f_{ch}^{<}\ (e\ \{edit = (edit\ e)^{\circ}\}) \circ f_{ch}^{<}\ e = id$.

PROOF.

$(f_{ch}^{<}\ (e\ \{edit = (edit\ e)^{\circ}\}) \circ f_{ch}^{<}\ e)\ s$
$= \quad \{\text{definition of } f_{ch}^{<}, \text{ and constant } affect \text{ in } e\}$
$s \,/\, r \lessdot (f_{st}^{<} \circ ((edit\ e)^{\circ} \circ f \vartriangle id))\ ((f_{st}^{<} \circ (edit\ e \circ f \vartriangle id))\ r)$
$= \quad \{\text{definition of } \vartriangle\}$
$s \,/\, r \lessdot f_{st}^{<}\ (((edit\ e)^{\circ} \circ f \circ f_{st}^{<})\ ((edit\ e \circ f)\ r, r),$
$\qquad f_{st}^{<}\ ((edit\ e \circ f)\ r, r))$

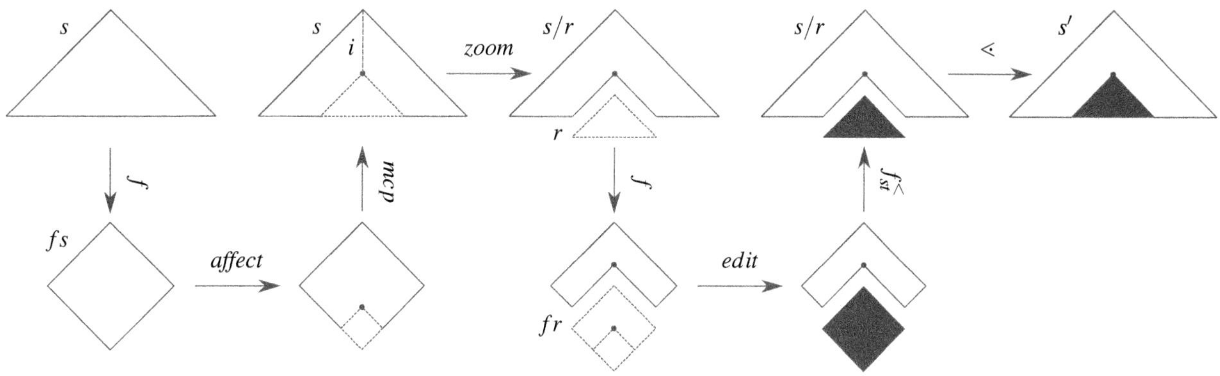

Figure 4. Change-based 'put' execution, showing relationship between source (top) and associated view (bottom) during transformation.

$$\begin{array}{ll}
= & \{\text{consistency of } f_{st}^{<}\} \\
 & s\,/\,r \lessdot f_{st}^{<}\ (((edit\ e)^{\circ} \circ edit\ e \circ f)\ r, f_{st}^{<}\ ((edit\ e \circ f)\ r, r)) \\
= & \{(edit\ e)^{\circ} \circ edit\ e = id\} \\
 & s\,/\,r \lessdot f_{st}^{<}\ (f\ r, f_{st}^{<}\ ((edit\ e \circ f)\ r, r)) \\
= & \{\text{undoability of } f_{st}^{<}\} \\
 & s\,/\,r \lessdot r \\
= & \{\text{cancellation}\} \\
 & s
\end{array}$$

□

5. More Refined Locality

As we have seen, the performance of our proposal depends on the height of the source tree and the size of the affected region (i.e., the degree of locality of the edit). The former is clearly beyond the control of any bidirectional framework, and the latter is largely decided by the structure of the view. For fairly balanced trees, the majority of nodes are deep in the structure, so it is reasonable to suppose that the majority of edits will be too; given structure alignment, this implies a good degree of locality. A problem arises when the view tree is skewed, such as in a list, since the likelihood that a node appears at any depth is the same. If a node high in the structure is affected by an edit, such as a deletion, the affected subtree could be rather large.

This problem has already manifested itself in our binary-tree traversal example (see Section 1.4, where it is excessive to mark the whole sublist [4,8,9] as affected). A better alternative is to recognize the sublist [8,9] as unaffected context too.

Another example is post-order tree traversal, where any non-empty sublist of the view contains the head of the source, which results in very poor locality preservation. As a matter of fact, post-order traversal is excluded through the well-aligning condition.

Nevertheless, being a special kind of tree, lists enjoy a number of unique properties. We notice that unlike general trees, where a separate datatype is needed for contexts, the context type for lists is isomorphic to the list type itself, and so we can simply use lists as both contexts and foci, and use the append function $(+\!\!+)$ as the close function $(\lessdot)$. Given the symmetry of $(+\!\!+)$, either the context or the focus can be edited, and all the definitions and results dualize. For example, consider the *reverse* function. Editing the front of the list view can be localized to a prefix of the view and mapped back to a suffix of the source.

As a result, it makes sense to try to capture a lower (right) bound of an edit-affected sublist, in addition to the upper (left) bound. Instead of splitting a list view into a prefix (context) and a suffix (focus), we can now see it as $l_1 +\!\!+ l_2 +\!\!+ l_3$. To reflect this specialization, we overload the infix operator $\lessdot$ and define its list version as $(l_1, l_3) \lessdot l_2 = l_1 +\!\!+ l_2 +\!\!+ l_3$. (In a sense, this is treating lists as semi-structured data, similar to traditional treatments of relational databases and graphs, and not as an algebraic datatype.) All the other definitions developed for general trees remain valid.

Now instead of always picking out a complete suffix or prefix, we can mark an interior list segment as affected by editing, and the same definition of $f_{ch}^{<}$ directly applies. For example, deleting 4 from [7,6,5,4,8,9] only affects the interior segment [4], leaving both contexts [7,6,5] and [8,9] unaffected. Correspondingly, the alignment positions now match subterms in the source with segments (rather than with tails) in the view.

6. Discussion

6.1 Context-Sensitive Editing

The editing system we have looked at so far is context-independent; this is particularly convenient for local editing, since the same edit can be applied both to a structure and to its subterms. For tree-structured views, it is sometimes useful to provide a full (or partial) path to the intended editing location, to narrow down the search. In this case, the editing becomes context sensitive, because the starting point of the path matters. Consider a path-based editing system.

$$\mathbf{type}\ EditP\ t = \{edit :: Path \to t \to t, affect :: Path \to t \to Path\}$$

An edit operation now finds its target in a structure following a path, and produces the edited structure together with the path leading to the affected subterm. Note that these paths in the view should not be confused with labels of nodes that represent paths in the source.

The definition of $f_{ch}^{<}$ can be adapted for the new editing system. We separate all interesting steps into **where** clauses to facilitate explanation.

$$\begin{array}{ll}
f_{ch}^{<} :: Edit\ v \to Path \to s \to s & \\
f_{ch}^{<}\ e\ p\ s = (s\,/\,r) \lessdot f_{st}^{<}\ (edit\ e\ p_3\ u', r)\ \mathbf{where} & \\
\quad v = f\ s & \\
\quad p_1 = affect\ e\ p\ v & \\
\quad u = zoom\ p_1\ v & \text{-- affected subterm} \\
\quad i = mcp\ \langle u \rangle & \\
\quad r = zoom\ i\ s & \\
\quad u' = f\ r & \\
\quad p_2 = travelUntil\ (p_1, v)\ u' & \text{-- path to } u' \\
\quad Just\ p_3 = stripPrefix\ p_2\ p_1 & \text{-- relative editing path}
\end{array}$$

Note that we keep the path information of the edit explicit, so that it can be modified along with the shifting of focus. Compared with the context-independent version, there are a few additional steps. As the editing function returns a path locating the affected subterm, we need to open the view to get to it (u in the third clause above). A bigger challenge posed by this context-sensitivity is to find a relative editing path when the starting point is moved to the root of subterm u'. We denote the path from the root of a structure x to its subterm y as $x \rightsquigarrow y$. Since we know the subterm relations $u \preccurlyeq u' \preccurlyeq v$ among the affected subterm, the view of the alignment position and the complete view, the path $p_3 = u' \rightsquigarrow u$ is the difference between $p_1 = v \rightsquigarrow u$ and $p_2 = v \rightsquigarrow u'$. We already know p_1; traversing p_1 until the root of u' gives us p_2, before we can perform path arithmetic to recover the correspondence between the path and structure inputs of *edit e*. Function *travelUntil* follows a path down a tree until it reaches a given subtree; the part of the path travelled is returned as the output. Function *stripPrefix* is a standard Haskell function of type $Eq\ a \Rightarrow [a] \rightarrow [a] \rightarrow Maybe\ [a]$ that strips the first input from the second one; since we know that p_2 is a prefix of p_1, the execution of *stripPrefix* $p_2\ p_1$ is always going to succeed. A concern here is that the additional computation does impose a performance overhead: travelling the path takes time linear in the height of the view tree. Clearly, the multiple traversals in the above code can be combined; we have presented them in separate steps for clarity.

6.2 Totality of 'Put' Functions

The proofs of bidirectional properties in Section 4.2 are done in a total setting, where the state-based transformations are assumed to execute successfully when given well-defined terms. Since the 'get' functions are regular structural recursions, it is reasonable to expect that if the execution over a complete source is successful, then the evaluation over subterms will also succeed. Establishing a similar safety property for 'put' functions is much harder; 'put' functions are often partial due to the conflicts between the edited view and the original source (though advanced type systems may help to specify their domains [10]), and usually do not expose their semantics other than through the bidirectional laws.

Since our approach employs state-based bidirectional frameworks as black-boxes, it is impossible to conclude that the approach is universally safe. Nevertheless, there are patterns to follow: most bidirectional frameworks create 'put' functions that try to trace the original 'get' execution backwards, and recursively deconstruct their view and source inputs in parallel, until a discrepancy is encountered, which is the point where the 'put' function has to either resolve the conflict or fail. Our change-based approach reduces the scope of a 'put' function by removing a context that is known to be unaffected by the edit. Consequently, we expect that failures, if there are any, happen within the processing of the alignment position, and so moving from a state-based approach to the change-based approach preserves the safety property.

7. Related Work

Incremental updates have been studied in the context of model transformation, for improving speed [13], and for achieving more refined semantics [8]. Similar to our design, both of these approaches also require additional specification of the effect of an edit. In contrast to tree-like datatypes, models are loosely-connected untyped graphs, which are more easily divided into independent fragments to be updated separately; whereas our well-aligning property of typed and overlapping subtrees is much harder to establish. In their work on graph transformations via structural recursion, Hidaka et al. [15] use a simplified assumption that different parts of the graph are always independent. As a result, the structural recursion is effectively reduced to a *concatMap* operation. However, this assumption is not valid in general; and as a result, the acceptability property does not hold in their framework.

The concept of an alignment position is also known as an *exclusive data source* in the database literature [9], and is used to prevent 'side effects' on the view that is edited (similar to our consistency requirement). Exclusive data sources are commonly computed by establishing *lineages* between a database and its view through tracing identifiers of data [5]. Databases are typically large, so it is never practical to process them completely for an update; as a result, identifying exclusive data sources is not considered as an optimization, but the core part of the update. Despite the obvious similarity of these ideas, techniques developed for databases are not applicable in our setting, due to the very different representations of data and transformations.

Despite being in a unidirectional setting, the concept of *adaptive programming* [1] is closely related to incremental updates. The basic idea of adaptive programming is to build up a complete input-output dependency graph for a given input, from some syntactic annotations to the program. Based on the dependency, a corresponding output change can be derived from an input change, which hopefully has a much better run-time performance compared to re-executing the program with the new input. However, it is not obvious how the technique can be applied in a bidirectional setting, where we need to derive an input change from an output change. Nevertheless, this would be an interesting future direction to explore.

Explicit caching of intermediate computations is another way of achieving incremental execution. If an input change can be described as a loop increment, an incremental version of the program under the change can be constructed and benefit from previously computed results [20]. In a sense, the contexts in our approach can be seen as cached values, and the focuses can be seen as increments. Since in our case the closing operation ($\lessdot$) that combines the cached result and the newly computed increment is not dependent on the transformations, we do not need to 'improve' the transformations to achieve incrementality.

Indexed elements in source structures and parametricity arising from polymorphic 'get' functions are the key components of *semantic bidirectionalization* [28] – deriving a 'put' function without inspecting the syntactic definition of the 'get' function. Similar to our approach, the indices in [28] are unique and cannot be created by 'get' transformations, so that individual elements in the view can be mapped back to their source origins, as can any edits. Nevertheless, there has not been any attempt to derive structure correspondences from the element correspondences, as we do in this paper. Consequently, editing view structures is not permitted in semantic bidirectionalization, while our approach only optimizes a given 'put' function instead of creating one.

Maintaining proper alignment between ordered source and view is itself an important semantic issue of bidirectional programming, as view editing may cause mismatchings between view/source data. *Matching lenses* [3] aims at addressing this issue without hard-wiring alignment strategies into bidirectional systems. Though our use of alignment in this paper is intended for optimization purposes, we note that a change-based 'put' function should preserve the alignment semantics of the state-based 'put' function it uses, because the unaffected context that is not processed will have no impact on alignment.

The connection between alignment and incrementality is speculated in [18]. However, as far as we are aware, there has not been any concrete proposal before.

8. Conclusions

We have developed a change-based bidirectional transformation framework that focuses on changes rather than data. The technique we have presented is very general, and most existing state-based frameworks may draw benefits from its adoption, so long as the 'get' function is well-aligning. This condition is semantic; there is no restriction on the language that is used for implementation.

In the future, we plan to look at ways of dealing with monomorphic functions, which are widely used in XML transformations. In contrast to the polymorphic case presented in this paper, the labelling of tree nodes does require some adjustment of a state-based bidirectional framework. It will be interesting to see whether such adjustments can be made in a systematic way.

Acknowledgements

We are grateful to Ralf Hinze for his valuable comments on an early draft of the paper; and the ICFP reviewers for their detailed and insightful reviews. The work was partly conducted when the first author was at the University of Oxford supported by the UK EPSRC grant *Generic and Indexed Programming* (EP/E02128X).

References

[1] U. A. Acar, G. E. Blelloch, and R. Harper. Adaptive functional programming. *ACM Transactions on Programming Languages and Systems*, 28:990–1034, November 2006.

[2] F. Bancilhon and N. Spyratos. Update semantics of relational views. *ACM Transactions on Database Systems*, 6(4):557–575, 1981.

[3] D. M. Barbosa, J. Cretin, N. Foster, M. Greenberg, and B. C. Pierce. Matching lenses: alignment and view update. In *International Conference on Functional Programming (ICFP)*, pages 193–204, New York, NY, USA, 2010. ACM.

[4] A. Bohannon, J. N. Foster, B. C. Pierce, A. Pilkiewicz, and A. Schmitt. Boomerang: Resourceful lenses for string data. In *Principles of Programming Languages*, pages 407–419, New York, NY, USA, Jan. 2008. ACM.

[5] Y. Cui, J. Widom, and J. L. Wiener. Tracing the lineage of view data in a warehousing environment. *ACM Transactions on Database Systems*, 25:179–227, June 2000.

[6] K. Czarnecki, J. N. Foster, Z. Hu, R. Lämmel, A. Schürr, and J. F. Terwilliger. Bidirectional transformations: A cross-discipline perspective. In *Theory and Practice of Model Transformations*, pages 260–283, Berlin, Heidelberg, 2009. Springer-Verlag.

[7] U. Dayal and P. A. Bernstein. On the correct translation of update operations on relational views. *ACM Transactions on Database Systems*, 7(3):381–416, 1982.

[8] Z. Diskin, Y. Xiong, and K. Czarnecki. From state- to delta-based bidirectional model transformations. In *Theory and Practice of Model Transformations*, ICMT'10, pages 61–76, Berlin, Heidelberg, 2010. Springer-Verlag.

[9] L. Fegaras. Propagating updates through XML views using lineage tracing. In *International Conference on Data Engineering*, pages 309–320, Los Alamitos, CA, USA, 2010. IEEE Computer Society.

[10] J. N. Foster, M. B. Greenwald, J. T. Moore, B. C. Pierce, and A. Schmitt. Combinators for bidirectional tree transformations: A linguistic approach to the view update problem. *ACM Transactions on Programming Languages and Systems*, 29(3), May 2007. Preliminary version in POPL '05.

[11] J. N. Foster, B. C. Pierce, and S. Zdancewic. Updatable security views. In *Computer Security Foundations*, pages 60–74, Washington, DC, USA, 2009. IEEE Computer Society.

[12] J. N. Foster, A. Pilkiewicz, and B. C. Pierce. Quotient lenses. In *International Conference on Functional Programming (ICFP)*, pages 383–396, New York, NY, USA, 2008. ACM.

[13] H. Giese and R. Wagner. From model transformation to incremental bidirectional model synchronization. *Software and Systems Modeling*, 8:21–43, 2009. 10.1007/s10270-008-0089-9.

[14] G. Gottlob, P. Paolini, and R. Zicari. Properties and update semantics of consistent views. *ACM Transactions on Database Systems*, 13(4):486–524, 1988.

[15] S. Hidaka, Z. Hu, K. Inaba, H. Kato, K. Matsuda, and K. Nakano. Bidirectionalizing graph transformations. In *International Conference on Functional Programming (ICFP)*, ICFP '10, pages 205–216, New York, NY, USA, 2010. ACM.

[16] R. Hinze and J. Jeuring. Functional Pearl: Weaving a web. *Journal of Functional Programming*, 11(6):681–689, nov 2001.

[17] R. Hinze, J. Jeuring, and A. Löh. Type-indexed data types. *Science of Computer Programming*, 51(1-2):117–151, 2004.

[18] M. Hofmann, B. Pierce, and D. Wagner. Symmetric lenses. In *Principles of Programming Languages (POPL)*, POPL '11, pages 371–384, New York, NY, USA, 2011. ACM.

[19] Z. Hu, S.-C. Mu, and M. Takeichi. A programmable editor for developing structured documents based on bidirectional transformations. In *Workshop on Partial Evaluation and Program Manipulation (PEPM)*, pages 178–189, New York, NY, USA, 2004. ACM.

[20] Y. A. Liu, S. D. Stoller, and T. Teitelbaum. Static caching for incremental computation. *ACM Transactions on Programming Languages and Systems*, 20:546–585, May 1998.

[21] K. Matsuda, Z. Hu, K. Nakano, M. Hamana, and M. Takeichi. Bidirectionalization transformation based on automatic derivation of view complement functions. In *International Conference on Functional Programming (ICFP)*, pages 47–58, New York, NY, USA, 2007. ACM.

[22] C. McBride. The derivative of a regular type is its type of one-hole contexts (extended abstract). `http://strictlypositive.org/diff.pdf`, University of Durham, 2001.

[23] L. Meertens. Designing constraint maintainers for user interaction. `ftp://ftp.kestrel.edu/pub/papers/meertens/dcm.ps`, CWI, Amsterdam, 1998.

[24] S.-C. Mu, Z. Hu, and M. Takeichi. An injective language for reversible computation. In *Mathematics of Program Construction*, volume 3125 of *Lecture Notes in Computer Science*, pages 289–313. Springer, 2004.

[25] H. Pacheco and A. Cunha. Generic point-free lenses. In C. Bolduc, J. Desharnais, and B. Ktari, editors, *Mathematics of Program Construction*, volume 6120 of *Lecture Notes in Computer Science*, pages 331–352. Springer Berlin / Heidelberg, 2010.

[26] S. Peyton Jones, editor. *Haskell 98 Language and Libraries: The Revised Report*. Cambridge University Press, 2003.

[27] P. Stevens. Bidirectional model transformations in QVT: semantic issues and open questions. *Software and Systems Modeling*, 9:7–20, 2010.

[28] J. Voigtländer. Bidirectionalization for free! (Pearl). In *Principles of Programming Languages (POPL)*, pages 165–176, New York, NY, USA, 2009. ACM.

[29] J. Voigtländer, Z. Hu, K. Matsuda, and M. Wang. Combining syntactic and semantic bidirectionalization. In *International Conference on Functional Programming (ICFP)*, pages 181–192, New York, NY, USA, 2010. ACM.

[30] P. Wadler. Theorems for free! In *Functional Programming Languages and Computer Architecture*, pages 347–359, New York, NY, USA, 1989. ACM.

[31] M. Wang, J. Gibbons, K. Matsuda, and Z. Hu. Gradual refinement: Blending pattern matching with data abstraction. In C. Bolduc, J. Desharnais, and B. Ktari, editors, *Mathematics of Program Construction*, volume 6120 of *Lecture Notes in Computer Science*, pages 397–426. Springer Berlin / Heidelberg, 2010.

Modular Verification of Preemptive OS Kernels

Alexey Gotsman
IMDEA Software Institute
Alexey.Gotsman@imdea.org

Hongseok Yang
University of Oxford
Hongseok.Yang@cs.ox.ac.uk

Abstract

Most major OS kernels today run on multiprocessor systems and are preemptive: it is possible for a process running in the kernel mode to get descheduled. Existing modular techniques for verifying concurrent code are not directly applicable in this setting: they rely on scheduling being implemented correctly, and in a preemptive kernel, the correctness of the scheduler is interdependent with the correctness of the code it schedules. This interdependency is even stronger in mainstream kernels, such as Linux, FreeBSD or XNU, where the scheduler and processes interact in complex ways.

We propose the first logic that is able to decompose the verification of preemptive multiprocessor kernel code into verifying the scheduler and the rest of the kernel separately, even in the presence of complex interdependencies between the two components. The logic hides the manipulation of control by the scheduler when reasoning about preemptable code and soundly inherits proof rules from concurrent separation logic to verify it thread-modularly. This is achieved by establishing a novel form of refinement between an operational semantics of the real machine and an axiomatic semantics of OS processes, where the latter assumes an abstract machine with each process executing on a separate virtual CPU. The refinement is local in the sense that the logic focuses only on the relevant state of the kernel while verifying the scheduler. We illustrate the power of our logic by verifying an example scheduler, modelled on the one from Linux 2.6.11.

Categories and Subject Descriptors D.2.4 [*Software Engineering*]: Software/Program Verification; F.3.1 [*Logics and Meanings of Programs*]: Specifying and Verifying and Reasoning about Programs; D.4.1 [*Operating Systems*]: Process Management

General Terms Languages, Theory, Verification

Keywords Verification, Concurrency, Scheduling, Modularity

1. Introduction

Developments in formal verification now allow us to consider the full verification of an operating system (OS) kernel, one of the most crucial components in any system today. Several recent projects have demonstrated that formal verification can tackle realistic OS kernels, such as a variant of the L4 microkernel [17] and Microsoft's Hyper-V hypervisor [3]. Having dealt with relatively small microkernels, these projects nevertheless give us hope that in the future we will be able to verify the likes of kernels from today's mainstream operating systems, such as Windows and Linux.

In this paper, we tackle one of the main challenges in realising this hope—handling kernel preemption in a multiprocessor system. Most major OS kernels are designed to run with multiple CPUs and are preemptive: it is possible for a process running in the kernel mode to get descheduled. Reasoning about such kernels is difficult for the following reasons.

First of all, in a multiprocessor system several invocations of a system call may be running concurrently in a shared address space, so reasoning about the call needs to consider all possible interactions among them. This is a notoriously difficult problem; however, we now have a number of logics [3–5, 13, 20, 23] that can reason about concurrent code. The way the logics make verification tractable is by using thread-modular reasoning principles that consider every thread of computation in isolation under some assumptions about its environment and thus avoid direct reasoning about all possible interactions.

The problem is that all these logics can verify code only under so-called interleaving semantics, expressed by the well-known operation semantics rule:

$$\frac{C_k \longrightarrow C_k'}{C_1 \parallel \ldots \parallel C_k \parallel \ldots \parallel C_n \longrightarrow C_1 \parallel \ldots \parallel C_k' \parallel \ldots \parallel C_n}$$

This rule effectively assumes an abstract machine where every process C_k has its own CPU, whereas in reality, the processes are multiplexed onto available CPUs by a scheduler. Furthermore, in a preemptive kernel, the scheduler is part of the kernel being verified and its correctness is *interdependent* with the correctness of the rest of the kernel (which, in the following, we refer to as just the kernel). Thus, what you see in a C implementation of OS system calls and what most logics reason about is not what you execute in such a kernel. When reasoning about a system call implementation in reality, we have to consider the possibility of context-switch code getting executed at almost every program point. Upon a context switch, the state of the system call will be stored in kernel data structures and subsequently loaded for execution again, possibly on a different CPU. A bug in the scheduling code can load an incorrect state of the system call implementation upon a context switch, and a bug in the system call can corrupt the scheduler's data structures. It is, of course, possible to reason about the kernel together with the scheduler as a whole, using one of the available logics. However, in a mainstream kernel, where kernel preemption is enabled most of the time, such reasoning would quickly become intractable.

In this paper we propose a logic that is able to decompose the verification of safety properties of preemptive OS code into verifying the scheduler and preemptable code separately. This is the first logic that can handle interdependencies between the scheduler and the kernel present in mainstream OS kernels, such as Linux, FreeBSD and XNU. Our logic consists of two proof systems, which we call high-level and low-level. The high-level system verifies preemptable code assuming that the scheduler is implemented cor-

ICFP'11, September 19–21, 2011, Tokyo, Japan.

rectly (Section 4.3). It hides the complex manipulation of control by the scheduler, which stores program counters of processes (describing their continuations) and jumps to one of them during a context switch. In this way, the high-level proof system provides the illusion that every process has its own virtual CPU—the control moves from one program point in the process code to the next without changing its state. This illusion is justified by verifying the scheduler code separately from the kernel in the low-level proof system (Section 4.4).

A common way to simplify reasoning about program components sharing an address space, such as the scheduler and the kernel, is to introduce the notion of *ownership* of memory areas: only the component owning an area of memory has the right to access it. The main difficulty of decomposing the verification of the mainstream OS kernels mentioned above lies in the fact that in such kernels there is no static address space separation between data structures owned by the scheduler and the rest of the kernel: the boundary between these changes according to a protocol for transferring the ownership of memory cells and permissions to access them in a certain way. For example, when an implementation of the `fork` system call asks the scheduler to make a new process runnable, the scheduler usually gains the ownership of the process descriptor provided by the system call implementation. This leads to several technical challenges our logic has to deal with.

First, this setting introduces an obligation to prove that the scheduler and the kernel do not corrupt each other's data structures. To this end, we base our proof systems on concurrent separation logic [20], which allows us to track the dynamic memory partitioning between the scheduler and the rest of the kernel and prohibit memory accesses that cross the partitioning boundary. For example, assertions in the high-level proof system talk only about the memory belonging to the kernel and completely hide the memory belonging to the scheduler. A *frame property*, validated by concurrent separation logic, implies that in this case any memory not mentioned in the assertions, e.g., the memory belonging to the scheduler, is guaranteed not to be changed by the kernel. A realistic interface between the scheduler and the kernel is supported by proof rules for ownership transfer of logical assertions between the two components describing permissions to access memory cells.

Second, in reasoning about mainstream operating systems, the ownership transfer between the scheduler and the kernel can involve not only fixed memory cells, but arbitrary logical facts describing them (Section 4.3). Such ownership transfers make even formalising the notion of scheduler correctness non-trivial, as they are difficult to accommodate in an operational semantics of the abstract machine with one CPU per process the scheduler is supposed to implement. In this paper we resolve this problem by introducing a concept of *logical refinement* between an operational semantics of the real machine and an axiomatic (as opposed to operational) semantics of the abstract machine, defined in our logic by the high-level proof system. Namely, desired properties of OS code are proved with respect to the abstract machine using the high-level proof system; the low-level system then relates the concrete and the abstract machines. However, proofs in neither of the two systems are interpreted with respect to any semantics alone, as would be the case in the usual semantic refinement. Instead, our soundness statement (Section 6) interprets a proof of the kernel in the high-level system and a proof of the scheduler in the low-level one together with respect to the semantics of the concrete machine.

Finally, while we would like to hide the scheduler state completely when reasoning about the kernel, the converse is not true: the scheduler has to be able to access at least some of the local state of every process, such as its register values. For this reason, the low-level proof system (Section 4.4) includes special assertions to describe the state of the OS processes the scheduler manages. These assertions are also interpreted as exclusive permissions to schedule the corresponding processes, which allows us to reason about scheduling on multiprocessors. A novel feature of the low-level proof system that allows verifying schedulers separately from the rest of the kernel is its *locality*: proofs about the scheduler focus only on a small relevant part of the state of processes.

Even though all of the OS verification projects carried out so far had to deal with a scheduler (see Section 7 for a discussion), to our knowledge they have not produced methods for handling practical multiprocessor schedulers with a complicated scheduler/kernel interface. We illustrate the power of our logic by verifying an example scheduler, modelled on the one from Linux 2.6.11 (Sections 2.2 and 5), which exhibits the issues mentioned above.

2. Informal development

We first explain our results informally, sketching the machine we use for formalising them (Section 2.1), illustrating the challenges of reasoning about schedulers by an example (Section 2.2) and describing the approach we take in our program logic (Section 2.3).

2.1 Example machine

To keep the presentation tractable, we formalise our results for a simple machine, defined in Section 3. Here we present it informally to the extent needed for understanding the rest of this section.

We consider a machine with multiple CPUs, identified by integers from 1 to `NCPUS`, communicating via the shared memory. We assume that the program the machine executes is stored separately from the heap and may not be modified; its commands are identified by labels. For simplicity we also assume that programs can synchronise using a set of built-in locks (in reality they would be implemented as spin-locks). Every CPU has a single interrupt, with its handler located at a distinguished label `schedule`, which a scheduler can use to trigger a context switch. There are four special-purpose registers, `ip`, `if`, `ss` and `sp`, and m general-purpose ones, $\texttt{gr}_1, \ldots, \texttt{gr}_m$. The `ip` register is the instruction pointer. The `if` register controls interrupts: they are disabled on the corresponding CPU when it is zero and enabled otherwise. As `if` affects only one CPU, we might have several instances of the scheduler code executing in parallel on different CPUs. Upon an interrupt, the CPU sets `if` to 0, which prevents nested interrupts. The `ss` register keeps the starting address of the stack, and `sp` points to the top of the stack, i.e., its first free slot. The stack grows upwards, so we always have $\texttt{ss} < \texttt{sp}$.

Since we are primarily interested in interactions of components within an OS kernel, our machine does not make a distinction between the user mode and the kernel mode—all processes can potentially access all available memory and execute all commands.

The machine executes programs in a minimalistic assembly-like programming language. It is described in full in Section 3; for now it suffices to say that the language includes standard commands for accessing registers and memory, and the following special ones:

- $\texttt{lock}(\ell)$ and $\texttt{unlock}(\ell)$ acquire and release the lock ℓ.
- $\texttt{savecpuid}(e)$ stores the identifier of the CPU executing it at the address e.
- $\texttt{call}(l)$ is a call to the function that starts at the label l. It pushes the label of the next instruction in the program and the values of the general-purpose registers onto the stack, and jumps to the label l. $\texttt{icall}(l)$ behaves the same as $\texttt{call}(l)$, except that it also disables interrupts by modifying the `if` register.
- `ret` is the return command. It pops the return label and the saved general-purpose registers off the stack, updates the registers with the new values, and jumps to the return label. `iret` is a variant of `ret` that additionally enables interrupts.

2.2 Motivating example

Figure 1 presents an implementation of the scheduler we use as a running example. We would like to be able to verify safety properties of OS processes managed by this scheduler using off-the-shelf concurrency logics, i.e., as though every process has its own virtual CPU. The scheduler uses data structures and an interface with the rest of the kernel similar to the ones in Linux 2.6.11 [2][1]. To concentrate on key issues of scheduler verification, we make some simplifying assumptions: we do not consider virtual memory and assume that processes are never removed and never go to sleep. We have also omitted the code for data structure initialisation.

The scheduler's interface consists of two functions: `schedule` and `create`. The former is called as the interrupt handler or directly by a process and is responsible for switching the process running on the CPU and migrating processes between CPUs. The latter can be called by the kernel implementation of the `fork` system call and is responsible for inserting a newly created process into the scheduler's data structures, thereby making it runnable. Both functions are called by processes using the `icall` command that disables interrupts, thus, the scheduler routines always execute with interrupts disabled.

Programming language. Even though we formalise our results for a machine executing a minimalistic programming language, we present the example in C. We now explain how a C program, such as the one in Figure 1, is mapped to our machine.

We assume that global variables are allocated at fixed addresses in memory. Local variable declarations allocate local variables on the stack in the activation records of the corresponding procedures; these variables are then addressed via the `sp` register. When the variables go out of scope, they are removed from the stack by decrementing the `sp` register. The general-purpose registers are used to store intermediate values while computing complex expressions. We allow the `ss` and `sp` registers to be accessed directly as `_ss` and `_sp`. Function calls and returns are implemented using the `call` and `ret` commands of the machine. By default, parameters and return values are passed via the stack; in particular, a zero-filled slot for a return value is allocated on the stack before calling a function. Parameters of functions annotated with `_regparam` (such as `create`) are passed via registers. We assume macros `lock`, `unlock`, `savecpuid` and `iret` for the corresponding machine commands. We also use some library functions: e.g., `remove_node` deletes a node from the doubly-linked list it belongs to, and `insert_node_after` inserts the node given as its second argument after the list node given as its first argument.

Data structures. Every process is associated with a process descriptor of type `Process`. Its `prev` and `next` fields are used by the scheduler to connect descriptors into doubly-linked lists of processes it manages (runqueues). The scheduler uses per-CPU runqueues with dummy head nodes pointed to by the entries in the `runqueue` array. These are protected by the locks in the `runqueue_lock` array, meaning that a runqueue can only be accessed with the corresponding lock held. The entries in the `current` array point to the descriptors of the processes running on the corresponding CPUs; these descriptors are not members of any runqueue. Thus, every process descriptor is either in the `current` array or in some runqueue. Note that every CPU always has at least one process to run—the one in the corresponding slot of the `current` array. Every process has its own kernel stack of a fixed size `StackSize`, represented by the `kernel_stack` field of its de-

[1] We modelled our scheduler on an older version of the Linux kernel (from 2005) because it uses simpler data structures. Newer versions use more efficient data structures [18] that would only complicate our running example without adding anything interesting.

```
#define FORK_FRAME   sizeof(Process*)
#define SCHED_FRAME  sizeof(Process*)+sizeof(int)

struct Process  {
  Process *prev, *next;
  word kernel_stack[StackSize];
  word *saved_sp;
  int timeslice; };
Lock *runqueue_lock[NCPUS];
Process *runqueue[NCPUS];
Process *current[NCPUS];

void schedule() {
  int cpu;
  Process *old_process;
  savecpuid(&cpu);
  load_balance(cpu);
  old_process = current[cpu];
  if (--old_process->timeslice) iret();
  old_process->timeslice = SCHED_QUANTUM;
  lock(runqueue_lock[cpu]);
  insert_node_after(runqueue[cpu]->prev, old_process);
  current[cpu] = runqueue[cpu]->next;
  remove_node(current[cpu]);
  old_process->saved_sp = _sp;
  _sp = current[cpu]->saved_sp;
  savecpuid(&cpu);
  _ss = &(current[cpu]->kernel_stack[0]);
  unlock(runqueue_lock[cpu]);
  iret();
}

void load_balance(int cpu) {
  int cpu2;
  Process *proc;
  if (random(0, 1)) return;
  do { cpu2 = random(0, NCPUS-1); } while (cpu == cpu2);
  if (cpu < cpu2) {
    lock(runqueue_lock[cpu]); lock(runqueue_lock[cpu2]);
  } else {
    lock(runqueue_lock[cpu2]); lock(runqueue_lock[cpu]);
  }
  if (runqueue[cpu2]->next != runqueue[cpu2]) {
    proc = runqueue[cpu2]->next;
    remove_node(proc);
    insert_node_after(runqueue[cpu], proc);
  }
  unlock(runqueue_lock[cpu]);
  unlock(runqueue_lock[cpu2]);
}

_regparam void create(Process *new_process) {
  int cpu;
  savecpuid(&cpu);
  new_process->timeslice = SCHED_QUANTUM;
  lock(runqueue_lock[cpu]);
  insert_node_after(runqueue[cpu], new_process);
  unlock(runqueue_lock[cpu]);
  iret();
}

int fork() {
  Process *new_process;
  new_process = malloc(sizeof(Process));
  memcpy(new_process->kernel_stack, _ss, StackSize);
  new_process->saved_sp = new_process->kernel_stack+
    _sp-_ss-FORK_FRAME+SCHED_FRAME;
  _icall create(new_process);
  return 1;
}
```

Figure 1. The example scheduler

activation records	ip	$\mathtt{gr}_1$	...	$\mathtt{gr}_m$	cpu	old_process	...

↑ saved_sp

Figure 2. The invariant of the stack of a preempted process

scriptor. When a process is preempted, the `saved_sp` field is used to save the value of the stack pointer register `sp`. Finally, while a process is running, the `timeslice` field gives the remaining time from its scheduling time quantum and is periodically updated by the scheduler.

Apart from the data structures described above, a realistic kernel would contain many others not related to scheduling, including additional fields in process descriptors. The kernel data structures reside in the same address space as the ones belonging to the scheduler, thus, while verifying the OS, we have to prove that the two components do not corrupt each other's data structures.

The* `schedule` *function. According to the semantics of our machine, when `schedule` starts executing, interrupts are disabled and the previous values of `ip` and the general-purpose registers are saved on the top of the stack. The scheduler uses the empty slots on the stack of the process it has preempted to store activation records of its procedures and thus expects the kernel to leave enough of these. Intuitively, while a process is running, only this process has the right to access its stack, i.e., *owns* it. When the scheduler preempts the process, the right to access the empty slots on the stack (their *ownership*) is transferred to the scheduler. When the scheduler returns the control to this process, it transfers the ownership of the stack slots back. This is one example of ownership transfer we have to reason about.

The `schedule` function first calls `load_balance`, which migrates processes between CPUs to balance the load; we describe it below. The function then decrements the timeslice of the currently running process, and if it becomes zero, schedules another one. The processes are scheduled in a round-robin fashion, thus, the function inserts the current process at the end of the local runqueue and dequeues the process at the front of the runqueue, making it current. The function also refills the scheduling quantum of the process being descheduled. The runqueue manipulations are done with the corresponding lock held. Note that in a realistic OS choosing a process to run would be more complicated, but still based on scheduler-private data structures protected by runqueue locks.

To save the state of the process being preempted, `schedule` copies `sp` into the `saved_sp` field of the process descriptor. This field, together with the `kernel_stack` of the process forms its saved state. The stack of a preempted process contains the activation records of functions called before the process was preempted, the label of the instruction to resume the process from, the values of general-purpose registers saved upon the interrupt, and the activation record of `schedule`, as shown in Figure 2. This invariant holds for descriptors of all preempted processes.

The actual context switch is performed by the assignment to `sp`, which switches the current stack to another one satisfying the invariant in Figure 2. Since this changes the activation record of `schedule`, the function has to update the `cpu` variable, which lets it then retrieve and load the new value of `ss`. The `iret` command at the end of `schedule` loads the values of the registers stored on the stack and enables interrupts, thus completing the context switch.

The* `load_balance` *function checks if the CPU given as its parameter is underloaded and, if it is the case, tries to migrate a process from another CPU to this one. The particular way the function performs the check and chooses the process is irrelevant for our purposes, and is thus abstracted by a random choice. To migrate a process, the function chooses a runqueue to steal a process from and locks it together with the current runqueue in the order determined by the corresponding CPU identifiers, to avoid deadlocks. The function then removes one process from the victim runqueue, if it is non-empty, and inserts it into the current one. Note that two concurrent scheduler invocations executing `load_balance` on different CPUs may access the same runqueue. While verifying the OS, we have to ensure they synchronise their accesses correctly.

The* `create` *function inserts the descriptor of a newly created process with the address given as its parameter into the runqueue of the current CPU. We pass the parameter via a register, as this simplifies the following treatment of the example. The descriptor must be initialised like that of a preempted process, hence, its stack must satisfy the invariant in Figure 2. To prevent deadlocks, `create` must be called using `icall`, which disables interrupts. Upon a call to `create`, the ownership of the descriptor is transferred from the kernel to the scheduler.

The* `fork` *function is not part of the scheduler. It illustrates how the rest of the kernel can use `create` to implement a common system call that creates a clone of the current process. This function allocates a new descriptor, copies the stack of the current process to it and initialises the stack as expected by `create` (Figure 2). This amounts to discarding the topmost activation record of `fork` and pushing a fake activation record of `schedule` (note that the values of registers the new process should start from have been saved on the stack upon the call to `fork`). Since stack slots for return values are initialised with zeros, this is what `fork` in the child process will return; we return 1 in the parent process.

The need for modularity. We could try to verify the scheduler and the rest of the kernel as a whole, modelling every CPU as a process in one of the existing program logics for concurrency [3–5, 13, 20, 23]. However, in this case our proofs would have to consider the possibility of the control-flow going from any statement in a process to the `schedule` function, and from there to any other process. Thus, in reasoning about a system call implementation we would end up having to reason explicitly about invariants and actions of both `schedule` and all other processes, making the reasoning unintuitive and, most likely, intractable. In the rest of the paper we propose a logic that avoids this pitfall.

2.3 Approach

Before presenting our logic in detail, we give an informal overview of the reasoning principles behind it.

Modular reasoning via memory partitioning. The first issue we have to deal with while designing the logic is how to verify the scheduler and the kernel separately, despite the fact that they share the same address space. To this end, our logic partitions the memory into two disjoint parts. The memory cells in each of the parts are *owned* by the corresponding component, meaning that only this component can access them. It is important to note that this partitioning does not exist in the semantics, but is enforced by proofs in the logic to enable modular reasoning about the system. Modular reasoning becomes possible because, while reasoning about one component, one does not have to consider the memory partition owned by the other, since it cannot influence the behaviour of the component. An important feature of our logic, required for handling schedulers from mainstream kernels, is that the memory partitioning is not required to be static: the logic permits ownership transfer of memory cells between the areas owned by the scheduler and the kernel according to an axiomatically defined interface. For example, in reasoning about the scheduler of Section 2.2, the logic permits the transfer of the descriptor for a new process from the kernel to the scheduler at a call to `create`.

As we have noted before, our logic consists of two proof systems: the high-level system (Section 4.3) for verifying the kernel and the low-level one for the scheduler (Section 4.4). These proof systems implement a form of assume-guarantee reasoning between the two components, where one component assumes that the other does not touch its memory partition and provides well-formed pieces of memory at ownership transfer points.

Concurrent separation logic. We use concurrent separation logic [20] as a basis for modular reasoning within a given component, i.e., either among concurrent OS processes or concurrent scheduler invocations on different CPUs. This choice was guided by the convenience of presentation; see Section 8 for a discussion of how more advanced logics can be integrated. However, the use of a version of separation logic is crucial, because we inherently rely on the *frame property* validated by the logic: the memory that is not mentioned in the assertions in a proof of a command is guaranteed not to be changed by it. While reasoning about a component, we consider only the memory partition belonging to it. Hence, we automatically know that the component cannot modify the others.

Concurrent separation logic achieves modular reasoning by further partitioning the memory owned by the component under consideration into disjoint process-local parts (one for each process or scheduler invocation on a given CPU) and protected parts (one for each free lock). A process-local part can only be accessed by the corresponding process or scheduler invocation, and a lock-protected part only when the process holds the lock. The resulting partitioning of the system state is illustrated in Figure 3. The frame property guarantees that a process cannot access the partition of the heap belonging to another one. To reason modularly about parts of the state protected by locks, the logic associates with every lock an assertion—its *lock invariant*—that describes the part of the state it protects. Resource invariants restrict how processes can change the protected state, and hence, allow reasoning about them in isolation.

Scheduler-agnostic verification of kernel code. The high-level proof system (Section 4.3) reasons about preemptable code assuming an abstract machine where every process has its own virtual CPU. It relies on the partitioned view of memory described above to hide the state of the scheduler, with all the remaining state split among processes and locks accessible to them, as illustrated in Figure 4. We have primed process identifiers in the figure to emphasise that the virtual state of the process can be represented differently in the abstract and physical machines: for example, if a process is not running, the values of its local registers can be stored in scheduler-private data structures, rather than in CPU registers.

Apart from hiding the state of the scheduler, the high-level system also hides the complex manipulation of the control-flow performed by it: the proof system assumes that the control moves from one point in the process code to the next without changing its state, ignoring the possibility of the scheduler getting executed upon an interrupt. Explicit calls to the scheduler are treated as if they were executed atomically.

Technically, the proof system is a straightforward adaptation of concurrent separation logic, which is augmented with proof rules axiomatising the effect of scheduler routines explicitly called by processes. The novelty here is that we can use such a scheduler-agnostic logic in this context at all.

Proving schedulers correct via logical refinement. The use of the high-level proof system is justified by verifying the scheduler implementation using a low-level proof system (Section 4.4). What does it mean for a scheduler to be functionally correct? Intuitively, a scheduler must provide an illusion of a system where every process has its own virtual CPU with a dedicated set of registers. To formalise this, we could define a semantics of such an abstract system and prove that any behaviour of the concrete system is reproducible in the abstract one, thus establishing a refinement between the two systems. The main technical challenge we have to

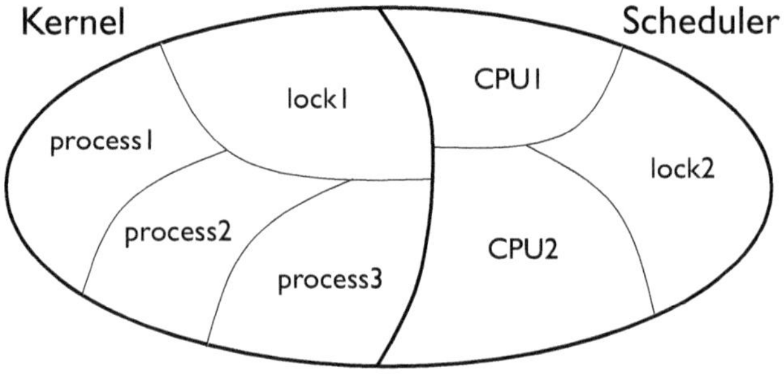

Figure 3. The partitioning of the system state enforced by the logic. The memory is partitioned into two parts, owned by the scheduler and the kernel, respectively. The memory of each component is further partitioned into parts local to processes or scheduler invocations on a given CPU, and parts protected by locks.

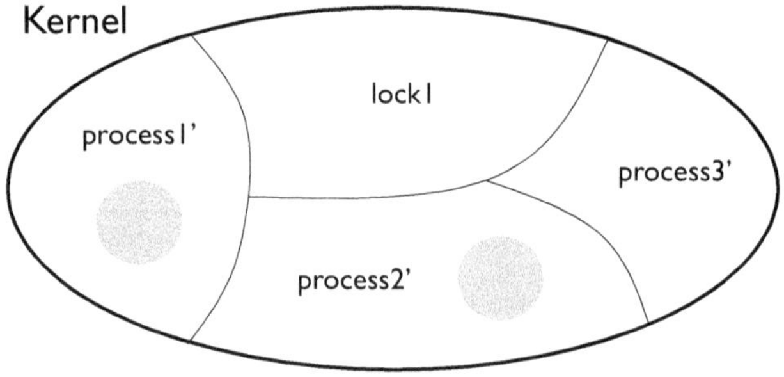

Figure 4. The state of the abstract system with one virtual CPU per process. Process identifiers are primed to emphasise that the virtual state of the process can be represented differently in the abstract and physical machines (cf. Figure 3). Dark regions illustrate the parts of process state that are tracked by a scheduler invocation running on a particular physical CPU.

deal with in this paper is that for realistic OS schedulers, defining a semantics for the abstract system a scheduler implements is difficult. This is because, in reasoning about mainstream operating systems, the ownership transfer between the scheduler and the kernel can involve not only fixed memory cells, but arbitrary *logical* facts describing them, which is difficult to describe operationally (see the treatment of the desc predicate in Section 4.3).

In this paper we resolve this problem in a novel way. Instead of defining the semantics of the abstract machine operationally, we define it only axiomatically as the high-level proof system described above. As expected, the low-level proof system is used to reason about the correspondence between the concrete and the abstract system, with its assertions relating their states. However, proofs in neither of the two systems are interpreted with respect to any semantics alone: our soundness statement (Section 6) interprets a proof of the kernel in the high-level system and a proof of the scheduler in the low-level one together with respect to the semantics of the concrete machine. Thus, instead of relating sets of executions of the two systems, the soundness statement relates logical statements about the abstract system (given by high-level proofs) to logical statements about the concrete one (given by a constraint on concrete states). We call this form of establishing a correspondence between the two systems a *logical refinement*. Note that in this case the soundness statement for the logic does not yield a semantic statement of correctness for the scheduler being considered. Rather, its correctness is established indirectly by the fact that reasoning in the high-level proof system, which assumes

$$\begin{array}{ll}
\mathsf{Reg} = \{\mathtt{ip}, \mathtt{if}, \mathtt{ss}, \mathtt{sp}, \mathtt{gr}_1, \ldots, \mathtt{gr}_m\} & \mathsf{Loc} \subseteq \mathsf{Val} \\
\mathsf{Context} = \mathsf{Reg} \to \mathsf{Val} & \mathsf{CPUid} = \{1, \ldots, \mathtt{NCPUS}\} \\
\mathsf{GContext} = \mathsf{CPUid} \rightharpoonup \mathsf{Context} & \mathsf{Heap} = \mathsf{Loc} \rightharpoonup \mathsf{Val} \\
\mathsf{Lock} = \{\ell_1, \ell_2, \ldots, \ell_n\} & \mathsf{Lockset} = \mathcal{P}(\mathsf{Lock})
\end{array}$$

$$\mathsf{Config} = \mathsf{GContext} \times \mathsf{Heap} \times \mathsf{Lockset}$$

Figure 5. The set of machine configurations Config. We assume sets Loc of valid memory addresses and Val of values, respectively.

the abstract one-CPU-per-process machine, is sound with respect to the concrete machine.

To verify the scheduler separately from the processes it manages, low-level assertions focus only on a small relevant part of the state of the kernel, which we call *scheduler-visible*. Namely, the assertions relate the state local to a scheduler invocation on a particular CPU in the concrete system (e.g., the region marked CPU1 in Figure 3) to parts of abstract states of some of the OS processes (e.g., the dark regions in Figure 4). The latter parts can include, e.g., the values of registers of the virtual CPU of the process, but not the process-local memory. They are used in the low-level proof system to verify that the operations performed by the scheduler in the concrete machine correctly implement the required actions in the abstract machine. These parts also function as permissions to schedule the corresponding processes, i.e., a given part can be owned by at most one scheduler invocation at a time. For example, a scheduler invocation owning the parts of process states marked in Figure 4 has a permission to schedule processes 1 and 2, but not 3. Such a permission reading is crucial for handling scheduling on multiprocessors, as it ensures that a process may not be scheduled at two CPUs at the same time.

Summary. In the following we formalise the above approach for a particular class of schedulers. Despite the formalisaton being performed for this class, the technical methods we develop here can be reused in other settings (see Section 8 for a discussion). In particular, we propose the following novel ideas:

- exploiting a logic validating the frame property to hide the state of the scheduler while verifying the kernel and vice versa;
- using a logical refinement in a context where defining an abstract semantics refined by the concrete one is difficult; and
- focusing on relevant parts of the two systems related in the refinement and giving a permission interpretation to them.

3. Preliminaries

In this section, we give a formal semantics to the example machine informally presented in Section 2.1.

3.1 Storage model

Figure 5 gives a model for the set of configurations Config that can arise during an execution of the machine. A machine configuration is a triple with the components describing the values of registers of the CPUs in the machine, the state of the heap and the set of locks taken by some CPU. The configurations in which the heap or the global context is a partial function are not encountered in the semantics we define in this section. They come in handy in Sections 4 and 6 to give a semantics to the assertion language and express the soundness of our logic.

In this paper, we use the following notation for partial functions: $f[x : y]$ is the function that has the same value as f everywhere, except for x, where it has the value y; $[\,]$ is a nowhere-defined function; $f \uplus g$ is the union of the disjoint partial functions f and g.

3.2 Commands

Programs for our machine consist of primitive commands c:

$$\mathtt{r} \in \mathsf{Reg} - \{\mathtt{ip}\} \qquad \ell \in \mathsf{Lock} \qquad l \in \mathsf{Label} = \mathbb{N}$$

$$\begin{array}{rcl}
e & ::= & \mathtt{r} \mid 0 \mid 1 \mid 2 \mid \ldots \mid e + e \mid e - e \\
b & ::= & e = e \mid e \leq e \mid b \wedge b \mid b \vee b \mid \neg b \\
c & ::= & \mathtt{skip} \mid \mathtt{r} := e \mid \mathtt{r} := [e] \mid [e] := e \mid \mathtt{assume}(b) \\
& \mid & \mathtt{lock}(\ell) \mid \mathtt{unlock}(\ell) \mid \mathtt{savecpuid}(e) \\
& \mid & \mathtt{call}(l) \mid \mathtt{icall}(l) \mid \mathtt{ret} \mid \mathtt{iret}
\end{array}$$

In addition to the primitive commands listed in Section 2, we have the following ones: `skip` and $\mathtt{r} := e$ have the standard meaning; $\mathtt{r} := [e]$ reads the contents of a heap cell e and assigns the value read to `r`; $[e] := e'$ updates the contents of cell e by e'; $\mathtt{assume}(b)$ acts as a filter on the state space of programs, choosing those satisfying b. We write PComm for the set of primitive commands. Note that the commands cannot access the `ip` register directly.

Commands C are partial maps from Label to PComm $\times$ $\mathcal{P}$(Label). Intuitively, if $C(l) = (c, X)$, then c is labelled with l in C and is followed by commands with labels in X. In this case we let $\mathsf{comm}(C, l) = c$ and $\mathsf{next}(C, l) = X$. We denote the domain of C with $\mathsf{labels}(C)$ and the set of all commands with Comm.

The language constructs used in the example scheduler of Section 2, such as loops and conditionals, can be expressed as commands in a standard way, with conditions translated using `assume`.

3.3 Semantics

We now give a standard operational semantics to our programming language. We interpret primitive commands c using a transition relation $\rightsquigarrow_c$ of the following type:

$$\mathsf{State} = \mathsf{Context} \times \mathsf{Heap} \times \mathsf{Lockset}$$

$$\rightsquigarrow_c \;\subseteq\; (\mathsf{CPUid} \times \mathsf{State} \times \mathsf{Label}^2) \times (\mathsf{State} \times \mathsf{Label} \cup \{\top\})$$

The input to $\rightsquigarrow_c$ consists of four components. The first is the identifier of the CPU executing the command, and the next the configuration of the system projected to this CPU, which we call a state. The latter includes the context of the CPU and the information about the shared resources—the heap and locks. The last two components of the input are the labels of the command c and a primitive command following it in the program. Given this input, the transition relation $\rightsquigarrow_c$ for c nondeterministically computes the next state of the CPU after running c, together with the label of the primitive command to run next. The former may be a special $\top$ state signalling a machine crash. The latter may be different from the label given as the last component of the input, when c is a call or a return.

The relation $\rightsquigarrow_c$ appears in Figure 6. In the figure and in the rest of the paper, we write _ for an expression whose value is irrelevant and implicitly existentially quantified. The relation follows the informal meaning of primitive commands given in Sections 2.1 and 3.2. Note that $\rightsquigarrow_c$ may yield no post-state for a given pre-state. Unlike a transition to the $\top$ state, this represents the divergence of the command. For example, according to Figure 6, acquiring the same lock twice leads to a deadlock, and releasing a lock that is not held crashes the system. Note that we do not prevent a held lock from being released by a CPU that did not acquire it, so locks behave like binary semaphores.

The program our machine executes is given by a command C that includes a primitive command labelled `schedule`, serving as the entry point of the interrupt handler. For such a command C, we give its meaning using a small-step operational semantics, formalised by the transition relation $\to_C \;\subseteq\; \mathsf{Config} \times (\mathsf{Config} \cup \{\top\})$ in Figure 7. The first rule in the figure describes a normal execution, where the `ip` register of CPU k is used to choose the primitive command c to run. After choosing c, the machine picks the label l' of a following command, runs c according to the semantics $\rightsquigarrow_c$,

$$
\begin{array}{lll}
(k,(r,h[\llbracket e\rrbracket r:u],L),l,l') & \rightsquigarrow_{\mathtt{r:=[e]}} & ((r[\mathtt{r}:u],h[\llbracket e\rrbracket r:u],L),l') \\
(k,(r,h,L),l,l') & \rightsquigarrow_{\mathtt{assume}(b)} & ((r,h,L),l'),\ \text{if } \llbracket b\rrbracket r=\mathsf{true} \\
(k,(r,h,L),l,l') & \not\rightsquigarrow_{\mathtt{assume}(b)} & \text{if } \llbracket b\rrbracket r=\mathsf{false} \\
(k,(r,h,L),l,l') & \rightsquigarrow_{\mathtt{lock}(\ell)} & ((r,h,L\cup\{\ell\}),l'),\ \text{if } \ell\notin L \\
(k,(r,h,L),l,l') & \not\rightsquigarrow_{\mathtt{lock}(\ell)} & \text{if } \ell\in L \\
(k,(r,h,L),l,l') & \rightsquigarrow_{\mathtt{unlock}(\ell)} & ((r,h,L-\{\ell\}),l'),\ \text{if } \ell\in L \\
(k,(r,h[\llbracket e\rrbracket r:\_],L),l,l') & \rightsquigarrow_{\mathtt{savecpuid}(e)} & ((r,h[\llbracket e\rrbracket r:k],L),l')
\end{array}
$$

$$
\begin{array}{l}
(k,(r,h[r(\mathtt{sp}):\_,\ldots,r(\mathtt{sp})+m:\_],L),l,l') \\
\quad \rightsquigarrow_{\mathtt{call}(l'')} ((r[\mathtt{sp}:r(\mathtt{sp})+m+1], \\
\quad h[r(\mathtt{sp}):l',r(\mathtt{sp})+1:r(\mathtt{gr}_1),\ldots,r(\mathtt{sp})+m:r(\mathtt{gr}_m)],L),l'') \\
(k,(r,h[r(\mathtt{sp})-m-1:l'',r(\mathtt{sp})-m:g_1,\ldots,r(\mathtt{sp})-1:g_m],L),l,l') \\
\quad \rightsquigarrow_{\mathtt{ret}} ((r[\mathtt{sp}:r(\mathtt{sp})-m-1,\mathtt{gr}_1:g_1,\ldots,\mathtt{gr}_m:g_m], \\
\quad h[r(\mathtt{sp})-m-1:l'',r(\mathtt{sp})-m:g_1,\ldots,r(\mathtt{sp})-1:g_m],L),l'') \\
(k,(r,h,L),l,l') \rightsquigarrow_c \top,\ \text{otherwise}
\end{array}
$$

Figure 6. Semantics of primitive commands. We have omitted standard definitions for `skip` and most of assignments (see [21]). We have also omitted them for `icall` and `iret`: the definitions are the same as for `call` and `ret`, but additionally modify `if`. In the figure $\rightsquigarrow_c \top$ indicates that the command c crashes, and $\not\rightsquigarrow_c$ means that it does not crash, but diverges. The function $\llbracket\cdot\rrbracket r$ evaluates expressions with respect to the context r.

$$\frac{r(\mathtt{ip})=l\in\mathsf{labels}(C) \qquad l'\in\mathsf{next}(C,l) \qquad (k,(r,h,L),l,l')\rightsquigarrow_{\mathsf{comm}(C,l)}((r',h',L'),l'')}{(R[k:r],h,L)\to_C(R[k:r'[\mathtt{ip}:l'']],h',L')}$$

$$\frac{r(\mathtt{ip})=l\in\mathsf{labels}(C) \qquad r(\mathtt{if})=1 \qquad (k,(r,h,L),l,l)\rightsquigarrow_{\mathtt{icall(schedule)}}((r',h',L'),l'')}{(R[k:r],\ h,\ L)\to_C(R[k:r'[\mathtt{ip}:l'']],\ h',\ L')}$$

$$\frac{r(\mathtt{ip})=l\in\mathsf{labels}(C) \qquad l'\in\mathsf{next}(C,l) \qquad (k,(r,h,L),l,l')\rightsquigarrow_{\mathsf{comm}(C,l)}\top}{(R[k:r],h,L)\to_C\top}$$

$$\frac{r(\mathtt{ip})\notin\mathsf{labels}(C)}{(R[k:r],h,L)\to_C\top}$$

$$\frac{r(\mathtt{if})=1 \quad \{r(\mathtt{sp}),\ldots,r(\mathtt{sp})+m\}\not\subseteq\mathsf{dom}(h)}{(R[k:r],\ h,\ L)\to_C\top}$$

Figure 7. Operational semantics of the machine

and uses the result of this run to update the registers of CPU k and the heap and the lockset of the machine. The next rule concerns interrupts. Upon an interrupt, the interrupt handler label `schedule` is loaded into `ip`, and the label of the command to execute after the handler returns is pushed onto the stack together with the values of the general-purpose registers. The remaining rules deal with crashes arising from erroneous execution of primitive commands, undefined command labels and a stack overflow upon an interrupt.

4. The logic

In this paper we consider schedulers whose interface consists of two routines: `create` and `schedule`. Like in our example scheduler (Section 2.2), `create` makes a new process runnable, and `schedule` performs a context-switch. (Our results can be extended when new scheduler routines are introduced; see Section 8 for a discussion.) Our logic thus reasons about programs of the form:

$$\mathsf{C}\uplus[l_c:(\mathtt{iret},\{l_c{+}1\})]\uplus\mathsf{S}\uplus[l_s:(\mathtt{iret},\{l_s{+}1\})]\uplus\mathsf{K} \quad \text{(OS)}$$

where C and S are pieces of code implementing the `create` and `schedule` routines of the scheduler and K is the rest of the kernel code. Our high-level proof system is designed for proving K, and the low-level system for proving C and S.

We place several restrictions on programs. First, we require that C and S define primitive commands labelled `create` and `schedule`, which are meant to be the entry points for the corresponding scheduler routines. The `create` routine expects the address of the descriptor of the new process to be stored in the register $\mathtt{gr}_1$. By our convention `schedule` also marks the entry point of the interrupt handler. Thus, `schedule` may be called both directly by a process or by an interrupt. For simplicity, we assume that the scheduler data structures are properly initialised when the program starts executing.

To ensure that the scheduler routines execute with interrupts disabled, we require that C and S may not contain `icall`, `iret` and assignments accessing the `if` register. We also need to ensure that the kernel may not affect the status of interrupts, become aware of the particular CPU it is executing on, or change the stack address. Thus, K may not contain `savecpuid`, `icall` and `iret` (except calls to the scheduler routines `schedule` and `create`), assignments accessing `if` or writing to `ss`. In reality, a kernel might need to disable interrupts. We discuss how our results can be extended to handle this in Section 8. Finally, we require that the kernel K and the scheduler C and S access disjoint sets of locks. This condition simplifies the soundness statement in Section 6 and can be lifted.

The core part of our logic is the low-level proof system for verifying scheduler code, which we present in Section 4.4. It extends the high-level proof system used for verifying kernel code, which, in turn, adapts concurrent separation logic to our setting. For this reason, we present the high-level system first.

4.1 Assertion language

We now present the assertion language of the high-level proof system. Assertions describe properties of a single process, as if it were running on a separate virtual CPU. The state of the process thus consists of the values of the CPU registers (its context), the heap local to the process and the locks the process has a permission to release (its lockset). Mathematically, states of a process are just elements of State defined in Section 3.3: State $=$ Context $\times$ Heap $\times$ Lockset. However, unlike in the semantics of Section 3.3, a heap here can be a partial function, with its domain defining the part of the heap owned by the process. A lockset is now meant to contain only the set of locks that the process has a permission to release (in our logic such permissions can be transferred between processes).

To denote sets of process states in our logic, we use a minor extension of the assertion language of separation logic [21]. Let NVar and CVar be disjoint sets containing logical variables for values and contexts, respectively. Assertions are defined as follows:

$$x,y\in\mathsf{NVar} \qquad \gamma\in\mathsf{CVar}$$

$$\mathtt{r}\in\mathsf{Reg}-\{\mathtt{ip}\} \qquad \mathbf{r}\in\{\mathbf{ip},\mathbf{if},\mathbf{ss},\mathbf{sp},\mathbf{gr}_1,\ldots,\mathbf{gr}_m\}$$

$$
\begin{array}{l}
E ::= x \mid \mathtt{r} \mid 0 \mid 1 \mid \ldots \mid E{+}E \mid E{-}E \mid G(\mathbf{r}) \\
G ::= \gamma \mid [\mathbf{ip}:E,\mathbf{if}:E,\mathbf{ss}:E,\mathbf{sp}:E,\vec{\mathbf{gr}}:\vec{E}] \\
\Sigma ::= \varepsilon \mid E \mid \Sigma\,\Sigma \\
B ::= E{=}E \mid \Sigma{=}\Sigma \mid G{=}G \mid E{\le}E \mid B\wedge B \mid B\vee B \mid \neg B \\
P ::= B \mid \mathsf{true} \mid P\wedge P \mid \neg P \mid \exists x.\,P \mid \exists\gamma.\,P \mid \mathsf{emp} \\
\quad\ \mid E\mapsto E \mid E..E\mapsto\Sigma \mid P*P \mid \mathsf{dll}_\Lambda(E,E,E,E) \mid \mathsf{locked}(\ell)
\end{array}
$$

Expressions E and Booleans B are similar to those in programs, except that they allow logical variables to appear and include the lookup $G(\mathbf{r})$ of the value of the register $\mathbf{r}$ in the context G. A context G is either a logical variable or a finite map from register

$(r, h, L) \models_\eta B$ iff $[\![B]\!]_\eta r = \mathit{true}$
$(r, h, L) \models_\eta P_1 \wedge P_2$ iff $(r, h, L) \models_\eta P_1$ and $(r, h, L) \models_\eta P_2$
$(r, h, L) \models_\eta \mathsf{emp}$ iff $h = [\,]$ and $L = \emptyset$
$(r, h, L) \models_\eta E_0 \mapsto E_1$ iff $h = [[\![E_0]\!]_\eta r : [\![E_1]\!]_\eta r]$ and $L = \emptyset$
$(r, h, L) \models_\eta E_0..E_1 \mapsto \Sigma$ iff $\exists j \geq 0. \exists v_1, \ldots, v_j \in \mathsf{Val}.$
$L = \emptyset,\ j = [\![E_1]\!]_\eta r - [\![E_0]\!]_\eta r + 1,\ v_1 v_2 \ldots v_j = [\![\Sigma]\!]_\eta r$
and $h = [[\![E_0]\!]_\eta r : v_1, \ldots, [\![E_1]\!]_\eta r : v_j]$
$(r, h, L) \models_\eta \mathsf{locked}(\ell)$ iff $h = [\,]$ and $L = \{\ell\}$
$(r, h, L) \models_\eta P_1 * P_2$ iff $\exists h_1, h_2, L_1, L_2.\ h = h_1 \uplus h_2,$
$L = L_1 \uplus L_2,\ (r, h_1, L_1) \models_\eta P_1$ and $(r, h_2, L_2) \models_\eta P_2$

Predicate dll_Λ is the least one satisfying the equivalence below:

$$\mathsf{dll}_\Lambda(E_h, E_p, E_n, E_t) \Leftrightarrow \exists x. (E_h = E_n \wedge E_p = E_t \wedge \mathsf{emp}) \vee E_h.\mathtt{prev} \mapsto E_p * E_h.\mathtt{next} \mapsto x * \Lambda(E_h) * \mathsf{dll}_\Lambda(x, E_h, E_n, E_t)$$

Figure 8. Semantics of high-level assertions. We have omitted the standard clauses for most of the first-order connectives. The function $[\![\cdot]\!]_\eta r$ evaluates expressions with respect to the context r and the logical variable environment η.

labels **r** to expressions. We denote the set of assertions defined here with $\mathsf{Assert}_\mathsf{K}$. Let a logical variable environment η be a mapping from $\mathsf{NVar} \cup \mathsf{CVar}$ to $\mathsf{Val} \cup \mathsf{Context}$ that respects the types of variables. Assertions denote sets of states from State as defined by the satisfaction relation $\models_\eta$ in Figure 8. For an environment η and an assertion P, we denote with $[\![P]\!]_\eta$ the set of states satisfying P.

The assertions in the first line of the definition of P except emp are connectives from the first-order logic with the standard semantics. We can define the missing connectives from the given ones. The following assertions from emp up to the dll_Λ predicate are standard assertions of separation logic [21]. Informally, emp describes the empty heap, and $E \mapsto E'$ the heap with only one cell at the address E containing E'. The assertion $E..E' \mapsto \Sigma$ is the generalisation of the latter to several consecutive cells at the addresses from E to E' inclusive containing the sequence of values Σ. For a value u of a C type $\mathtt{t}$ taking several cells, we shorten $E..(E+\mathtt{sizeof(t)}-1) \mapsto u$ to just $E \mapsto u$. For a field $\mathtt{f}$ of a C structure, we use $E.\mathtt{f} \mapsto E'$ as a shortcut for $E + \mathit{off} \mapsto E'$, where off is the offset of $\mathtt{f}$ in the structure. The separating conjunction $P_1 * P_2$ talks about the splitting of the local state, which consists of the heap and the lockset of the process. It says that a pair (h, L) can be split into two disjoint parts, such that one part (h_1, L_1) satisfies P_1 and the other (h_2, L_2) satisfies P_2.

The assertion $\mathsf{dll}_\Lambda(E_h, E_p, E_n, E_t)$ is an inductive predicate describing a segment of a doubly-linked list. It assumes a C structure definition with fields `prev` and `next`. Here E_h is the address of the head of the list, E_t the address of its tail, E_p the pointer in the `prev` field of the head node, and E_n the pointer in the `next` field of the tail node. The Λ parameter is a formula with one free logical variable describing the shape of each node in the list, excluding the `prev` and `next` fields; the logical variable defines the address of the node. For instance, a simple doubly-linked list can be expressed using $\Lambda(x) = \mathsf{emp}$. We included dll_Λ to describe the runqueues of the scheduler in our example. Predicates for other data structures can be added straightforwardly [21].

Finally, the assertion $\mathsf{locked}(\ell)$ is specific to reasoning about concurrent programs and denotes states with an empty local heap and the lockset consisting of ℓ, i.e., it denotes a permission to release the lock ℓ. Note that $\mathsf{locked}(\ell) * \mathsf{locked}(\ell)$ is inconsistent: acquiring the same lock twice leads to a deadlock.

To summarise, our assertion language extends that of concurrent separation logic with expressions to denote contexts and locked assertions to keep track of permissions to release locks.

4.2 Interface parameters

As we noted in Section 2.3, our logic can be viewed as implementing a form of assume-guarantee reasoning between the scheduler and the kernel. In particular, interactions between them involve ownership transfer of memory cells at points where the control crosses the boundary between the two components. Hence, the high- and low-level proof systems have to agree on the description of the memory areas being transferred and the properties they have to satisfy. These descriptions form the specification of the interface between the scheduler and the kernel, and, correspondingly, between the two proof systems. Here we describe parameters used to formulate it. We note that the interface parameters we present here are tied to a particular class of schedulers for which we present our logic. As we argue in Section 8, our results can be carried over to schedulers with more elaborate interfaces.

Ownership transfer happens at calls to and returns from the scheduler routines `create` and `schedule`. When the kernel calls the `create` routine of the scheduler, the latter should get the ownership of the process descriptor supplied as the parameter. In the two proof systems, we specify this descriptor using an assertion $\mathsf{desc}(d, \gamma) \in \mathsf{Assert}_\mathsf{K}$ with two free logical variables and no register occurrences. Our intention is that it describes the descriptor of a process with the context γ, allocated at the address d. However, the user of our logic is free to choose any assertion, depending on a particular scheduler implementation being verified. As the scheduler and the kernel access disjoint sets of locks, we require that all states in $[\![\mathsf{desc}(d, \gamma)]\!]_\eta$ have an empty lockset.

We fix the piece of state transferred from the kernel to the `schedule` routine upon an interrupt to be the free part of the stack of the process being preempted. The parameters determining its size are the size of the stack $\mathtt{StackSize} \in \mathbb{N}$ and the upper bound $\mathtt{StackBound} \in \mathbb{N}$ on the stack usage by the kernel (excluding the scheduler). To ensure that the stack does not overflow while calling an interrupt hander, we require that $\mathtt{StackSize} - \mathtt{StackBound} \geq m+1$, where m is the number of general-purpose registers.

4.3 High-level proof system

The high-level proof system reasons about the kernel code K. It is obtained by adapting concurrent separation logic to our setting and adding proof rules axiomatising the effect of scheduler routines.

The judgements of the high-level proof system are of the form $I, \Delta \vdash C$, where $I : \mathsf{Lock} \rightharpoonup \mathsf{Assert}_\mathsf{K}$ is a partial mapping from locks accessible in the kernel code to their invariants (see Section 2.3) and $\Delta : \mathsf{Label} \to \mathsf{Assert}_\mathsf{K}$ is a total mapping from code labels to preconditions. The parameter Δ in our judgement specifies local states of the process at various program points, which induce pre- and post-conditions for all primitive commands in C. When considering a complete system in Section 4.5, we restrict Δ so that it is false everywhere except at labels in the kernel code. An example of a lock invariant is

$$\exists x, y.\ 10.\mathtt{prev} \mapsto y * 10.\mathtt{next} \mapsto x * \mathsf{dll}_\Lambda(x, 10, 10, y),$$

where $\Lambda(x) = \mathsf{emp}$. It states that the lock protects a non-empty cyclic doubly-linked list with the head node at address 10. We forbid lock invariants to contain registers or free occurrences of logical variables. We consider a version of concurrent separation logic where resource invariants are allowed to be imprecise [20] at the expense of excluding the conjunction rule from the proof system [12].

The rule PROG-H for deriving the judgements is given in Figure 9. The first premise of the rule says that all assertions in Δ have to satisfy some restrictions regarding stack usage, formulated using parameters `StackSize` and `StackBound` introduced in Section 4.2. These ensure that the interrupt handler can safely execute on the stack of the process it preempts:

$$\frac{\begin{array}{c}\forall l \in \mathsf{Label}(C).\, \exists P \in \mathsf{Assert}_{\mathsf{K}}.\, \Delta(l) \Leftrightarrow (0 \leq \mathtt{sp}{-}\mathtt{ss} \leq \mathtt{StackBound} \land P * \mathtt{sp}..(\mathtt{ss}{+}\mathtt{StackSize}{-}1) \mapsto \_) \\ \forall l \in \mathsf{labels}(C).\, \forall l' \in \mathsf{next}(C,l).\, (I,\Delta \rhd_{l'} \{\Delta(l)\}\ \mathsf{comm}(C,l)\ \{\Delta(l')\})\end{array}}{I,\Delta \vdash C}\ \textsc{Prog-h}$$

$$\frac{P \Rightarrow P' \quad I,\Delta \rhd_l \{P'\}\, c\, \{Q'\} \quad Q' \Rightarrow Q}{I,\Delta \rhd_l \{P\}\, c\, \{Q\}}\ \textsc{Conseq} \qquad \frac{I,\Delta \rhd_l \{P\}\, c\, \{Q\} \quad \mathsf{notCallRet}(c)}{I,\Delta \rhd_l \{\exists x.\, P\}\, c\, \{\exists x.\, Q\}}\ \textsc{Exists}$$

$$\frac{I,\Delta \rhd_l \{P_1\}\, c\, \{Q_1\} \quad I,\Delta \rhd_l \{P_2\}\, c\, \{Q_2\}}{I,\Delta \rhd_l \{P_1 \lor P_2\}\, c\, \{Q_1 \lor Q_2\}}\ \textsc{Disj} \qquad \frac{I,\Delta \rhd_l \{P\}\, c\, \{Q\} \quad \mathsf{mod}(c) \cap \mathsf{free}(F) = \emptyset \quad \mathsf{notCallRet}(c)}{I,\Delta \rhd_l \{P * F\}\, c\, \{Q * F\}}\ \textsc{Frame}$$

$$\frac{}{I,\Delta \rhd_l \{P\}\ \mathtt{assume}(b)\ \{P \land b\}}\ \textsc{Assume} \qquad \frac{}{I,\Delta \rhd_l \{e \mapsto \_\}\ [e]{:=}e'\ \{e \mapsto e'\}}\ \textsc{Store}$$

$$\frac{}{I,\Delta \rhd_l \{\mathsf{emp}\}\ \mathtt{lock}(\ell)\ \{I(\ell) * \mathsf{locked}(\ell)\}}\ \textsc{Lock} \qquad \frac{}{I,\Delta \rhd_l \{I(\ell) * \mathsf{locked}(\ell)\}\ \mathtt{unlock}(\ell)\ \{\mathsf{emp}\}}\ \textsc{Unlock}$$

$$\frac{(P * (\mathtt{sp}..(\mathtt{sp}{+}m) \mapsto l\, \mathbf{gr}_1 \ldots \mathbf{gr}_m)) \ \Rightarrow\ (\Delta(l')[\mathtt{sp}{+}m{+}1/\mathtt{sp}])}{I,\Delta \rhd_l \{P * (\mathtt{sp}..(\mathtt{sp}{+}m) \mapsto \_)\}\ \mathtt{call}(l')\ \{Q\}}\ \textsc{Call} \qquad \frac{}{I,\Delta \rhd_l \{P\}\ \mathtt{icall\ (schedule)}\ \{P\}}\ \textsc{Sched}$$

$$\frac{\forall l' \in \mathsf{Label}.\ (P * ((\mathtt{sp}{-}m{-}1)..(\mathtt{sp}{-}1) \mapsto E'\vec{E}) \land E' = l') \ \Rightarrow\ (\Delta(l')[\mathtt{sp}{-}m{-}1/\mathtt{sp}][\vec{E}/\vec{\mathtt{gr}}])}{I,\Delta \rhd_l \{P * ((\mathtt{sp}{-}m{-}1)..(\mathtt{sp}{-}1) \mapsto E'\vec{E})\}\ \mathtt{ret}\ \{Q\}}\ \textsc{Ret}$$

$$\frac{\mathsf{free}(P) \cap \mathsf{Reg} = \emptyset \qquad \forall l' \in \mathsf{Label}.\ (\exists \gamma.\, \mathsf{id} = \gamma \land \gamma(\mathbf{ip}) = l' \land \mathtt{sp}..(\mathtt{ss}{+}\mathtt{StackSize}{-}1) \mapsto \_ * P) \ \Rightarrow\ \Delta(l')}{I,\Delta \rhd_l \{\exists \gamma.\, \gamma(\mathbf{if}) = 1 \land \mathsf{desc}(\mathbf{gr}_1,\gamma) * P * Q\}\ \mathtt{icall(create)}\ \{\exists \gamma.\, Q\}}\ \textsc{Create}$$

Figure 9. High-level proof system. Here $\mathsf{mod}(c)$ is the set of registers modified by c, $\mathsf{free}(F)$ is the set of registers appearing in F, and $\mathsf{notCallRet}(c)$ means that c is not one of `call`, `icall`, `ret` and `iret`. Finally, $\mathsf{id} = [\mathbf{ip} : \_, \mathbf{if} : \mathtt{if}, \mathbf{ss} : \mathtt{ss}, \mathbf{sp} : \mathtt{sp}, \vec{\mathbf{gr}} : \vec{\mathtt{gr}}]$.

- the free part of the stack of the process must always be in its local state so that it can be transferred to the handler at any time;
- this part must always be large enough for the handler to run without a stack overflow; and
- the assertions should be independent of any changes to the empty slots of the stack, which may be modified by the handler.

The other condition in the PROG-H rule is that for every primitive command c in C and the label l' of a command following c, we have to prove $I,\Delta \rhd_{l'} \{\Delta(l)\}\ c\ \{\Delta(l')\}$. This informally means that, if c is run from an initial state satisfying $\Delta(l)$, then *it accesses only the memory specified by* $\Delta(l)$ and either terminates normally and ends up in a state satisfying $\Delta(l')$, or jumps to a label l'' whose assertion $\Delta(l'')$ holds in the current state. Note that the italicised clause enforces the frame property (Section 2.3). The proof rules for such judgements are also given in Figure 9. The rules CONSEQ, DISJ and EXISTS are standard rules of Hoare logic. The FRAME rule is inherited from separation logic; it states that executing a command in a bigger local state does not change its behaviour. The rule is useful to restrict the reasoning about primitive commands to the memory they actually access. To keep the logic sound we have to forbid EXISTS and FRAME to be applied to calls or returns. The logic also provides standard separation logic axioms for primitive commands. In Figure 9 we show two of them, ASSUME and STORE, and omit the others to save space; see [21].

The LOCK and UNLOCK axioms are inherited from concurrent separation logic and provide tools for modular reasoning about concurrent processes. The LOCK axiom says that, upon acquiring a lock, the process gets the ownership of its invariant and a permission to release it. According to UNLOCK, before releasing the lock, the process must have the corresponding permission and must re-establish the lock invariant. When the lock is released, the process gives up the ownership of the permission and the invariant.

The CALL and RET axioms mirror the operational semantics of `call` and `ret` (see Section 2.1 and Figure 6). CALL requires us to provide enough space on the stack to store the values of registers before a call. The precondition together with the modified stack then has to establish the assertion given by Δ at the target label. RET similarly requires the precondition to establish the assertion at the target label after the values of general-purpose registers and `ip` (denoted with $\vec{E}$ and E') have been loaded from the stack.

The axioms CALL and RET provide only a very rudimentary treatment of procedures. In particular, our logic does not have analogues of the usual modular Hoare proof rules for procedures and does not allow applying the FRAME rule over a procedure call. This is because soundly formulating such proof rules in the setting where the stack is visible to procedure code and can potentially be modified by it is non-trivial. This issue is orthogonal to the problem of scheduler verification we are concerned with, thus, in this paper we chose the simplest high-level logic possible. See Section 8 for pointers to more expressive logics for procedures.

What we have presented so far is just an adaptation of concurrent separation logic to our setting. We now provide axioms for calling the scheduler routines `schedule` and `create`, which are specific to our logic. As the high-level proof system hides the implementation of scheduler routines, the corresponding axioms are significantly different from CALL. In particular, the axioms are formulated as if after these `icall` commands the control just proceeded to the next statement in the program instead of jumping to the implementation of the routines. This is despite the fact that after a call to `schedule`, the process may be preempted and the control-flow given to any other process in the system. In this way, the axioms abstract from the scheduler implementation.

The SCHED axiom states that invoking `schedule` has no effect from the point of view of the process—if it is preempted, the scheduler resumes it in the same context, and no other process can touch its local heap. The axiom does not place any requirements on the process, as the preconditions necessary for the execution of `schedule`, which anyway can be invoked at any time as the interrupt handler, are established by the first condition in PROG-H.

The CREATE axiom is more complicated. First, it requires the caller of `create` to provide a new descriptor $\mathsf{desc}(\mathbf{gr}_1,\gamma)$ for the process being created with the context γ. We pass the parameter via the register $\mathbf{gr}_1$ and not via the stack, as this simplifies the following technical presentation. The context is required to have **if** set, since after the context switch is finished, the process starts executing with interrupts enabled. Note that the descriptor is not present in the postcondition: it gets transferred to the scheduler and reappears in the precondition of the implementation of `create` (Section 4.5). The axiom also allows us to transfer the ownership of the part of the heap given by P to the newly created process, thus providing it with an initial local state. This is a typical idiom for high-level reasoning about processes in separation logics [13]. The premise of the rule correspondingly requires that, after the registers and the stack are properly initialised, the state P we are transferring should establish the assertion at the label the process starts executing from. The effect of loading registers from γ is formulated using the context id.

For the example scheduler in Section 2.2, $\mathsf{desc}(d,\gamma)$ should describe a process descriptor with the stack initialised according to the invariant of a preempted process pictured in Figure 2: $\mathsf{desc}(d,\gamma) = d.\mathtt{prev} \mapsto \_ * d.\mathtt{next} \mapsto \_ * \mathsf{desc}_0(d,\gamma)$, where

$$\begin{aligned}&\mathsf{desc}_0(d,\gamma) \Leftrightarrow \gamma(\mathbf{if}){=}1 \wedge \gamma(\mathbf{ss}){=}d.\mathtt{kernel\_stack} \wedge\\ &\quad 0 \le \gamma(\mathbf{sp}){-}\gamma(\mathbf{ss}) \le \mathtt{StackBound} \wedge d.\mathtt{timeslice} \mapsto \_ *\\ &\quad d.\mathtt{saved\_sp} \mapsto (\gamma(\mathbf{sp}){+}m{+}1{+}\mathtt{SCHED\_FRAME}) *\\ &\quad \gamma(\mathbf{sp})..(\gamma(\mathbf{sp}){+}m) \mapsto \gamma(\mathbf{ip})\gamma(\vec{\mathbf{gr}}) *\\ &\quad (\gamma(\mathbf{sp}){+}m{+}1)..(\gamma(\mathbf{ss}){+}\mathtt{StackSize}{-}1) \mapsto \_\end{aligned}$$

and SCHED_FRAME is the size of the activation record of `schedule` (Figure 1). The descriptor does not include filled stack slots; they can be passed to the process directly in the precondition P.

As we have noted before, $\mathsf{desc}(d,\gamma)$ can be an arbitrary logical predicate. In some cases, e.g., when it is imprecise [20], its transfer from the kernel to the scheduler is hard to express operationally when defining a semantics of the kernel separately from the implementation of the scheduler; see [12] for a discussion. The situation would be worse had we based our logic on one of advanced modular concurrency logics, such as deny-guarantee [4], which are needed to handle real OS code. This is because proofs of soudness for such logics do not give an operational semantics to separate components of a program. The above difficulties with an operational definition of ownership transfer are a prime reason for using logical refinement in this paper.

The high-level proof system provides modern tools for modular reasoning about concurrent processes using proof rules of concurrent separation logic. The PROG-H rule of the system subsumes the usual sequential composition rule of Hoare logic, which assumes that the control-flow follows the structure of the process code and ignores the possibility of scheduler code getting executed at an interrupt. The axioms SCHED and CREATE abstract the implementation of scheduler routines by treating them like atomic commands. Thus, the state and the control-flow of the scheduler is completely hidden by the proof system. The soundness of such an illusion is established by verifying the scheduler code using a low-level proof system, which we describe next.

4.4 Low-level proof system

We now present the core of our logic—the low-level proof system, which is used to prove that the commands C and S of the OS program implement scheduling correctly. As we explained in Section 2.3, assertions of the proof system relate the states of the concrete machine and an abstract one, where every process has its own virtual CPU. The state of the concrete machine can be described using separation logic assertions introduced in Section 4.1. To describe states of the abstract machine, we extend the assertion language of Section 4.3 with an additional predicate: $P ::= \ldots \mid \mathsf{Process}(G)$, where G ranges over context expressions. We denote the set of such assertions with $\mathsf{Assert}_\mathsf{S}$. The $\mathsf{Process}(G)$ predicate

$$\begin{aligned}&(r,h,L),M \models_\eta \mathsf{Process}(G) \text{ iff } h=[\,],\ L=\emptyset,\ M=\{[\![G]\!]_\eta r\}\\ &(r,h,L),M \models_\eta P*Q \text{ iff } \exists h_1,h_2,L_1,L_2,M_1,M_2.\\ &\qquad h=h_1\uplus h_2,\ L=L_1\uplus L_2,\ M=M_1\uplus M_2,\\ &\qquad (r,h_1,L_1),M_1\models_\eta P \text{ and } (r,h_2,L_2),M_2\models_\eta Q\\ &(r,h,L),M \models_\eta \mathsf{emp} \quad \text{iff } h=[\,],\ L=\emptyset \text{ and } M=\emptyset\\ &(r,h,L),M \models_\eta P\wedge Q \text{ iff}\\ &\qquad (r,h,L),M\models_\eta P \text{ and } (r,h,L),M\models_\eta Q\end{aligned}$$

Figure 10. Semantics of low-level assertions. The $\uplus$ operation on multisets adds up the number of occurrences of each element in its operands.

describes a process with the values of registers of its virtual CPU given by the context G.

The addition of the Process predicate changes objects described by assertions: they now denote relations defined by subsets of $\mathsf{RelState} = \mathsf{State} \times \mathcal{M}(\mathsf{Context})$, where $\mathcal{M}(A)$ is the set of all finite multisets with elements from A. Relations in RelState connect the states of the concrete machine and the abstract machine with one CPU per process. As we have noted before, these relations do not describe the full state of the machines. The first component in a relation describes the local state of a scheduler invocation running on a CPU, including its context and the heap and the lockset local to it (e.g., the region marked CPU1 in Figure 3). The multiset in the second part records the scheduler-visible states of processes described by Process predicates in the assertion, i.e., parts of their local states that may be referred to by proofs about the scheduler (cf. the dark regions in Figure 4). These include the context of a process, but exclude its local heap and lockset: the latter are irrelevant for the schedulers we consider here and are therefore invisible to them. The low-level logic we present in this section is based on separation logic, hence, the invisibility of parts of process state to the scheduler automatically guarantees that it cannot access them.

Apart from keeping track of the state of a process, a Process predicate serves in the logic as an exclusive permission for the scheduler invocation owning it to schedule the corresponding process. To enforce this, the semantics of assertions defined below forbids the duplication of Process predicates: $\mathsf{Process}(G) \not\Rightarrow \mathsf{Process}(G) * \mathsf{Process}(G)$. Furthermore, the proof obligations for the scheduler we define in Section 4.5 state that it needs a Process predicate to schedule a process. Such a permission interpretation of Process is a key feature of our logic that allows us to reason about schedulers for multiprocessors: it ensures that, at a given time, only one scheduler invocation can own a Process predicate for a process, and hence, it can be scheduled only on one CPU at a time.

We give the formal semantics of assertions using the satisfaction relation $\models_\eta$ in Figure 10, parameterised by environments η. The first two cases in the figure are the most interesting ones. $\mathsf{Process}(G)$ relates a scheduler invocation having the empty heap and the empty lockset to a single process with the register values G. To be related by the separating conjunction $P * Q$, all parts of the state-multiset pair except the context should be split such that the first part is related by P and the second by Q. The semantic definitions of the remaining assertions are obtained from the corresponding cases in our high-level proof system (Figure 8) either by requiring the multiset component M to be empty, like in the case of emp, or by propagating M to their sub-assertions, like in the case of $P \wedge Q$. We denote with $[\![P]\!]_\eta$ the set of states satisfying P.

The judgements of the low-level proof system have the form $I, \Delta \vdash_k C$, where $k \in \mathsf{CPUid}$, $I : \mathsf{Lock} \rightharpoonup \mathsf{Assert}_\mathsf{S}$ is a vector of resource invariants for locks accessible to the scheduler, and $\Delta : \mathsf{Label} \to \mathsf{Assert}_\mathsf{S}$ is a mapping from program positions to low-level assertions. When considering a complete system in Section 4.5, we restrict Δ so that it is false everywhere except at labels in the scheduler code. The intuitive meaning of the judgements is the same as in the high-level system (Section 4.3), with the component describing scheduler-visible process states unchanged during the execution of scheduler commands. The judgements thus express how the scheduler code changes the relationship between the state of the scheduler on the CPU k and those of processes running on the machine. The proof rule for deriving our judgements is:

$$\frac{\forall l \in \mathsf{labels}(C).\, \forall l' \in \mathsf{next}(C,l).\quad I, \Delta \rhd^k_{l'} \{\Delta(l)\}\ \mathsf{comm}(C,l)\ \{\Delta(l')\}}{I, \Delta \vdash_k C}\ \textsc{Prog-L}$$

Note that the syntactic structure of the OS program (see the beginning of Section 4) ensures that the scheduler always executes with interrupts disabled. Thus, in the rule we are able to follow the control flow of C. The low-level system inherits the proof rules for deriving judgements for primitive commands $I, \Delta \rhd_l \{P\}\ c\ \{Q\}$ in Figure 9, adding the superscript k to $\rhd_l$ and ignoring the rules for `icall(schedule)` and `icall(create)`. It also has a rule for `savecpuid`, which makes use of the index k:

$$\frac{}{I, \Delta \rhd^k_l \{e \mapsto \_\}\ \mathtt{savecpuid}(e)\ \{e \mapsto k\}}\ \textsc{CPUid}$$

4.5 Putting the two proof systems together

The proof systems presented in Sections 4.3 and 4.4 allow us to reason about the kernel and the scheduler code. We now describe a rule for combining judgements from the two systems, which defines proof obligations for the OS components. This allows us to prove the OS program defined at the beginning of Section 4.

As can be seen from the example of Section 2.2, a scheduler might need to maintain some data structures related to every CPU, which can be accessed by a scheduler invocation on it. A data structure of this kind in our example scheduler is the element of the `current` array corresponding to the current CPU. Let J_k be an invariant of such data structures for CPU k, which is meant to be maintained when the scheduler is not running on it. Similarly to lock invariants, we forbid J_k to contain free logical variables or registers, except ss. In this case we can allow ss because we have previously required that the kernel cannot modify it. We denote with J the vector of invariants J_k.

Consider assertions $I_\mathsf{K}, \Delta_\mathsf{K}$ and $I_\mathsf{S}, \Delta^k_\mathsf{S}$ for all $k \in \mathsf{CPUid}$, such that:

- $\mathsf{dom}(I_\mathsf{K}) \cap \mathsf{dom}(I_\mathsf{S}) = \emptyset$;
- $\forall l.\, l \notin \mathsf{dom}(\mathsf{K}) \Rightarrow \Delta_\mathsf{K}(l) = \mathsf{false}$;
- $\forall l.\, l \notin \mathsf{dom}(S) \uplus \mathsf{dom}(C) \uplus \{l_s, l_c\} \Rightarrow \Delta^k_\mathsf{S}(l) = \mathsf{false}$.

The proof rule for the program OS is as follows:

$$\frac{\begin{array}{l} I_\mathsf{K}, \Delta_\mathsf{K} \vdash \mathsf{K} \\ \forall k \in \mathsf{CPUid}.\ I_\mathsf{S}, \Delta^k_\mathsf{S} \vdash_k \mathsf{S},\ \ I_\mathsf{S}, \Delta^k_\mathsf{S} \vdash_k \mathsf{C} \\ \forall k \in \mathsf{CPUid}.\ \Delta^k_\mathsf{S}(\mathtt{schedule}) = \Delta^k_\mathsf{S}(l_s) = \Delta^k_\mathsf{S}(l_c) = \mathsf{SchedState}_k \\ \forall k \in \mathsf{CPUid}.\ \Delta^k_\mathsf{S}(\mathtt{create}) = (\exists \gamma.\, \gamma(\mathbf{if}){=}1\ \wedge \\ \qquad\qquad \mathsf{SchedState}_k * \mathsf{desc}(\mathsf{gr}_1, \gamma) * \mathsf{Process}(\gamma)) \end{array}}{I_\mathsf{K}, \Delta_\mathsf{K} \mid I_\mathsf{S}, \{\Delta^k_\mathsf{S}\}_{k \in \mathsf{CPUid}} \mid J \vdash (\mathsf{S}, \mathsf{C}, \mathsf{K})}$$

where

$$\begin{array}{l} \mathsf{SchedState}_k = \exists l, \vec{g}.\, \mathtt{if}{=}0 \wedge 0 \le \mathtt{sp}{-}\mathtt{ss}{-}m{-}1 \le \mathtt{StackBound} \\ \wedge\ (\mathtt{sp}{-}m{-}1)..(\mathtt{sp}{-}1) \mapsto l\vec{g} * \mathtt{sp}..(\mathtt{ss}{+}\mathtt{StackSize}{-}1) \mapsto \_ * \\ \quad J_k * \mathsf{Process}([\mathbf{ip} : l, \mathbf{if} : 1, \mathbf{ss} : \mathtt{ss}, \mathbf{sp} : \mathtt{sp}{-}m{-}1, \vec{\mathbf{gr}} : \vec{g}]) \end{array}$$

The first three premises require us to prove the kernel and the scheduler code in their respective proof systems. The rest define pre- and postconditions for `schedule` and `create` by fixing the assertions at the corresponding labels. This is done using the predicate $\mathsf{SchedState}_k$, which describes the state of a scheduler invocation at CPU k right after it is called using `icall` or before it returns by executing `iret`.

When `schedule` is called, the stack satisfies the bound on stack usage and interrupts are disabled. The scheduler gets the ownership of the per-CPU data structure J_k, a part of the stack of the process being preempted (which contains the values of registers saved upon the call together with the empty slots), and a Process predicate consistent with the registers saved on the stack. The predicate certifies that, when the scheduler starts executing, the state of the preempted process in the machine corresponds to its state in the abstract machine. The `schedule` routine has to re-establish the same assertion before returning. In the case when it schedules a different process, this will be done using a different Process predicate. However, since the scheduler can only get a Process predicate in the precondition of `schedule` (and when a new process is created; see below), its postcondition guarantees that the process being scheduled has the same register values it had last time it was preempted. Note that the precondition of `schedule` mirrors the first premise of the Prog-H rule. Thus, the assumptions it makes about the kernel are justified by the proof of the latter in the high-level system.

The precondition of `create` is similar to that of `schedule`, but additionally assumes a process descriptor for a new process with the address in gr_1, and a corresponding Process assertion initialised according to the information in the descriptor. This descriptor is guaranteed to be provided by the kernel by the precondition of the Create rule. Adding the new Process assertion can be understood intuitively as creating a fresh virtual CPU for the new process in the abstract machine.

5. Verifying the example scheduler

We have used the logic to manually construct a proof of the example scheduler of Section 2.2, establishing the judgements about `schedule` and `create` required by the proof rule in Section 4.5. By the soundness theorem for our logic (presented in Section 6), this implies that any property of a piece of high-level code proved in concurrent separation logic, including memory safety and functional correctness, holds of the code when it is managed by the example scheduler. The detailed proof is given in [14, Appendix A]. Here we present only lock and per-CPU scheduler invariants together with some informal explanations.

The invariants of runqueue locks are as follows:

$$\begin{array}{l} I(\mathtt{runqueue\_lock}[k]) = \exists x, y, z.\, \mathtt{runqueue}[k] \mapsto z\ * \\ \quad \mathsf{desc}_0(z, \_) * z.\mathtt{prev} \mapsto y * z.\mathtt{next} \mapsto x * \mathsf{dll}_\Lambda(x, z, z, y) \end{array}$$

where $\Lambda(d) = \exists \gamma.\, \mathsf{desc}_0(d, \gamma) * \mathsf{Process}(\gamma)$ and desc_0 is defined in Section 4.3. The per-CPU scheduler invariants are:

$$\begin{array}{l} J_k = \exists d.\, (d.\mathtt{kernel\_stack}{=}\mathtt{ss}) \wedge \mathtt{current}[k] \mapsto d\ * \\ d.\mathtt{prev} \mapsto \_ * d.\mathtt{next} \mapsto \_ * d.\mathtt{timeslice} \mapsto \_ * d.\mathtt{saved\_sp} \mapsto \_ \end{array}$$

According to these definitions, a runqueue for a CPU k contains a list of descriptors of preempted processes together with Process predicates matching the state stored in them. When an invocation of `schedule` acquires the runqueue lock and removes a node from the list, it gets the ownership of the corresponding Process predicate, which lets it schedule the process by establishing the postcondition $\mathsf{SchedState}_k$ of `schedule` (see Section 4.5). The descriptor of the process just scheduled, pointed to by an entry in the `current` array, forms the scheduler's per-CPU state and is described by J_k. When the process is preempted again, `schedule` receives the Process predicate in its precondition $\mathsf{SchedState}_k$. This predicate and the state in J_k let the scheduler insert the descriptor back into the runqueue while maintaining its invariant.

6. Soundness

In this section, we explain the guarantees about the entire kernel that follow from proofs in our logic. Consider a program OS of the form introduced in Section 4. We formulate a theorem, proved in [14, Appendix B], which describes how proofs of a scheduler and the kernel in our logic can be combined to construct an inductive invariant of the entire system. To aid understanding, we first state the theorem and explain the components used to formulate it informally. Only after this do we provide formal definitions.

THEOREM 1. *If* $I_{\mathsf{K}}, \Delta_{\mathsf{K}} \mid I_{\mathsf{S}}, \{\Delta_{\mathsf{S}}^k\}_{k \in \mathsf{CPUid}} \mid J \vdash (\mathsf{S}, \mathsf{C}, \mathsf{K})$, *then for all environments* η, *the following set of configurations* $\mathcal{R}_k$ *is preserved by* $\rightarrow_{\mathsf{OS}}$:

$$\begin{aligned}\mathsf{compose}(&\textstyle\bigcup_{L \uplus L' = \mathsf{dom}(I_{\mathsf{S}})} \mathsf{held}_{\mathsf{S}}(L) \cap (\mathsf{lowinv}_\eta \star_{\mathsf{S}} \mathsf{lowlock}_{L'}),\\ &\textstyle\bigcup_{L \uplus L' = \mathsf{dom}(I_{\mathsf{K}})} \mathsf{held}_{\mathsf{K}}(L) \cap (\mathsf{highinv}_\eta \star_{\mathsf{K}} \mathsf{highlock}_{L'}))\end{aligned}$$

Informal explanation. The invariant $\mathcal{R}$ is constructed in several steps by conjoining the descriptions of pieces of program state owned by different OS components. First, from assertions Δ_{S}^k and J in the proof of the scheduler, we construct a predicate

$$\mathsf{lowinv}_\eta \subseteq \mathsf{RelConfig} \stackrel{\text{def}}{=} \mathsf{Config} \times \mathcal{M}(\mathsf{Context})$$

Consider $((R, h, L), M) \in \mathsf{lowinv}_\eta$. For register values of the CPUs in the machine given by R, the components h and L describe the part of the machine state belonging to the scheduler, and M the contexts of the processes it has a permission to schedule. Similarly, from assertions Δ_{K} in the proof of the kernel, we construct a predicate

$$\mathsf{highinv}_\eta \subseteq \mathsf{HighConfig} \stackrel{\text{def}}{=} \mathcal{M}(\mathsf{Context}) \times \mathsf{Heap} \times \mathsf{Lockset}$$

Consider $(M, h, L) \in \mathsf{highinv}_\eta$. For any set of processes with the contexts given by M, the components h and L describe the part of the machine state belonging to these processes.

To construct the complete machine state, we also have to take into account the parts of the heap protected by free locks. Thus, for any set of free locks L' accessible to the scheduler, from resource invariants I_{S} we construct a predicate $\mathsf{lowlock}_{L'} \subseteq \mathsf{RelConfig}$ describing the state protected by the locks. A similar predicate $\mathsf{highlock}_{L'} \subseteq \mathsf{HighConfig}$, constructed from I_{K}, describes the state protected by a set of free locks L' accessible to the kernel. The predicates $\mathsf{lowlock}_{L'}$ and $\mathsf{highlock}_{L'}$ are then combined with lowinv_η and $\mathsf{highinv}_\eta$ using operations

$$\begin{aligned}\star_{\mathsf{S}} &: \mathcal{P}(\mathsf{RelConfig}) \times \mathcal{P}(\mathsf{RelConfig}) \rightarrow \mathcal{P}(\mathsf{RelConfig})\\ \star_{\mathsf{K}} &: \mathcal{P}(\mathsf{HighConfig}) \times \mathcal{P}(\mathsf{HighConfig}) \rightarrow \mathcal{P}(\mathsf{HighConfig})\end{aligned}$$

To ensure that L' is indeed the set of all free locks, we require that the rest of the locks L are held by intersecting the result with $\mathsf{held}_{\mathsf{S}}(L) \subseteq \mathcal{P}(\mathsf{RelConfig})$ or $\mathsf{held}_{\mathsf{K}}(L) \subseteq \mathcal{P}(\mathsf{HighConfig})$.

Finally, we connect the resulting predicates describing the states of the scheduler and the kernel using a form of relational composition, implemented by

$$\mathsf{compose} : \mathcal{P}(\mathsf{RelConfig}) \times \mathcal{P}(\mathsf{HighConfig}) \rightarrow \mathcal{P}(\mathsf{Config})$$

The operation conjoins the heaps and locksets described by the predicates and makes sure that the scheduler-visible states of processes they describe match. The result is an invariant of the entire machine maintained by each step of the kernel or the scheduler.

We now formally define the above operations and predicates.

Composition operations. Each of the operations $\star_{\mathsf{S}}$, $\star_{\mathsf{K}}$ and compose is obtained by lifting a partial function in $A \times B \rightharpoonup C$ to a function in $\mathcal{P}(A) \times \mathcal{P}(B) \rightarrow \mathcal{P}(C)$ pointwise. To define $\star_{\mathsf{K}}$ we lift the operation $\bullet_{\mathsf{K}}$ on HighConfig that combines the information about processes, heaps and locksets:

$$(M_1, h_1, L_1) \bullet_{\mathsf{K}} (M_2, h_2, L_2) = (M_1 \uplus M_2, h_1 \uplus h_2, L_1 \uplus L_2)$$

(Recall that the $\uplus$ operation on multisets adds up the number of occurrences of each element in its operands.)

To define $\star_{\mathsf{S}}$ we similarly lift $\bullet_{\mathsf{S}}$ on RelConfig that combines the information about contexts, heaps, locksets and processes:

$$\begin{aligned}&((R_1, h_1, L_1), M_1) \bullet_{\mathsf{S}} ((R_2, h_2, L_2), M_2)\\ &\quad = ((R_1 \uplus R_2, h_1 \uplus h_2, L_1 \uplus L_2), M_1 \uplus M_2)\end{aligned}$$

Finally, we lift $\bullet_{\mathsf{compose}} : \mathsf{RelConfig} \times \mathsf{HighConfig} \rightharpoonup \mathsf{Config}$ that combines heaps and locksets provided the scheduler-visible states of processes in both arguments match:

$$((R, h_1, L_1), M_1) \bullet_{\mathsf{compose}} (M_2, h_2, L_2) = (R, h_1 \uplus h_2, L_1 \uplus L_2)$$

if both unions are defined and $M_1 = M_2$; undefined otherwise. It is this operation that carries over statements proved in the high-level proof system about the abstract machine with one virtual CPU per process to the concrete machine: the second operand (M_2, h_2, L_2) represents the state owned by the processes running on the abstract machine, and the first $((R, h_1, L_1), M_1)$ relates the scheduler state in the concrete machine to the processes it has permissions to schedule. The components M_1 and M_2 are used to ensure that the two operands describe the same set of processes.

Predicate definitions. Consider $p \subseteq \mathsf{RelState}$ and $q \subseteq \mathsf{State}$. Given $k \in \mathsf{CPUid}$ and $r \in \mathsf{Context}$, we define the following embedding operations converting states to configurations:

$$\begin{aligned}\lfloor p \rfloor_k &= \{(([k : r], h, L), M) \in \mathsf{RelConfig} \mid ((r, h, L), M) \in p\}\\ \lfloor q \rfloor_r &= \{(\{r\}, h, L) \in \mathsf{HighConfig} \mid\\ &\qquad (r, h \uplus [r(\mathtt{sp})..(r(\mathtt{ss}){+}\mathtt{StackSize}{-}1) : \_], L) \in q\}\\ \lfloor p \rfloor &= \{(([\,], h, L), M) \in \mathsf{RelConfig} \mid ((r, h, L), M) \in p\}\\ \lfloor q \rfloor &= \{(\emptyset, h, L) \in \mathsf{HighConfig} \mid (r, h, L) \in q\}\end{aligned}$$

The first one tags states with CPU identifiers and is used to construct lowinv_η. The second selects the states with a given context r and is used for $\mathsf{highinv}_\eta$. For technical reasons it removes the empty slots of the process stack, which are accounted for in the scheduler state (see the definition of $\mathsf{SchedSleep}_k$ below). The remaining two operations are used for $\mathsf{lowlock}_{L'}$ and $\mathsf{highlock}_{L'}$. As resource invariants do not restrict registers, they ignore contexts. We also need predicates defining states where the CPU is at a particular label l, or configurations with a particular lockset L:

$$\begin{aligned}\mathsf{at}_{\mathsf{S}}(l) &= \{((r, h, L), M) \in \mathsf{RelState} \mid r(\mathtt{ip}) = l\}\\ \mathsf{held}_{\mathsf{S}}(L) &= \{((R, h, L), M) \in \mathsf{RelConfig}\}\\ \mathsf{held}_{\mathsf{K}}(L) &= \{(M, h, L) \in \mathsf{HighConfig}\}\end{aligned}$$

The following predicate describes the state of the scheduler on CPU k, when a process is running on this CPU and is at label l:

$$\begin{aligned}\mathsf{SchedSleep}_k(l) = J_k * \mathtt{sp}..(\mathtt{ss}{+}\mathtt{StackSize}{-}1) \mapsto \_ *&\\ \mathsf{Process}([\mathbf{ip} : l, \mathbf{if} : 1, \mathbf{ss} : \mathtt{ss}, \mathbf{sp} : \mathtt{sp}, \vec{\mathbf{gr}} : \vec{\mathtt{gr}}])&\end{aligned}$$

Finally, let $\circledast_{\mathsf{S}}$ and $\circledast_{\mathsf{K}}$ be the iterated versions of $\star_{\mathsf{S}}$ and $\star_{\mathsf{K}}$.

Using the above notation, we can define the predicates from the theorem. For $L_{\mathsf{S}} \subseteq \mathsf{dom}(I_{\mathsf{S}})$ and $L_{\mathsf{K}} \subseteq \mathsf{dom}(I_{\mathsf{K}})$, we have:

$$\begin{aligned}\mathsf{lowinv}_\eta = \mathop{\circledast_{\mathsf{S}}}_{k \in \mathsf{CPUid}} &(\textstyle\bigcup_{l \in \mathsf{labels}(\mathsf{K})} \lfloor [\![\mathsf{SchedSleep}_k(l)]\!]_\eta \cap \mathsf{at}_{\mathsf{S}}(l) \rfloor_k \cup\\ &\textstyle\bigcup_{l \in (\mathsf{labels}(\mathsf{S} \uplus \mathsf{C}) \uplus \{l_s, l_c\})} \lfloor [\![\Delta_{\mathsf{S}}^k(l)]\!]_\eta \cap \mathsf{at}_{\mathsf{S}}(l) \rfloor_k)\end{aligned}$$

$$\mathsf{highinv}_\eta = \bigcup_{M \in \mathcal{M}(\mathsf{Context})} \mathop{\circledast_{\mathsf{K}}}_{r \in M} \lfloor [\![\Delta_{\mathsf{K}}(r(\mathtt{ip}))]\!]_\eta \rfloor_r$$

$$\mathsf{lowlock}_{L_{\mathsf{S}}} = \mathop{\circledast_{\mathsf{S}}}_{\ell \in L_{\mathsf{S}}} \lfloor [\![I_{\mathsf{S}}(\ell)]\!] \rfloor$$

$$\mathsf{highlock}_{L_{\mathsf{K}}} = \mathop{\circledast_{\mathsf{K}}}_{\ell \in L_{\mathsf{K}}} \lfloor [\![I_{\mathsf{K}}(\ell)]\!] \rfloor$$

The definitions follow the informal explanation given at the beginning of this section. To determine the state of the scheduler on a given CPU when defining lowinv_η, we branch over all possible program positions l of that CPU. Depending on whether l is in the scheduler or the kernel code, we use either the assertion in the scheduler proof or the invariant $\mathsf{SchedSleep}_k$, describing the state of the scheduler when it is not running. Since assertions do not restrict the value of the `ip` register, we have to do this explicitly using at_S. Note that, although assertions in the high-level proof system mention the empty slots of the process stack, the slots in fact belong to the scheduler when the process is preempted. For simplicity we choose always to count them in the scheduler state (the assertion in Δ_S^k or the scheduler invariant $\mathsf{SchedSleep}_k$).

To define $\mathsf{highinv}_\eta$ we branch over all possible finite multisets of contexts M, representing processes that may run on the machine. For every context r in M, the local state of the corresponding process is then determined by the assertion in the proof of the kernel at the program point $r(\mathtt{ip})$, restricted to the states with the context r. Note that the comprehension $r \in M$ over a multiset M considers every duplicate of an element in the multiset separately.

Finally, $\mathsf{lowlock}_{L_\mathsf{S}}$ and $\mathsf{highlock}_{L_\mathsf{K}}$ are straightforward combinations of resource invariants for the given sets of locks.

Ownership transfer. It is instructive to analyse how ownership transfer between the scheduler and the kernel is handled by our soundness statement. For example, consider a transfer of a new process descriptor $\mathsf{desc}(d, \gamma)$ from the kernel to the scheduler at a call to `create`. Since the CREATE axiom requires the descriptor in its precondition, before the kernel calls `create`, the state partitioning defined by $\mathcal{R}$ counts the descriptor as part of $\mathsf{highinv}_\eta$. Since the implementation of `create` receives the descriptor in its precondition, in the configuration immediately after the call to `create`, $\mathcal{R}$ defines it to be part of lowinv_η. Thus, ownership transfer repartitions program state among the parts defined in Theorem 1.

Consequences. Theorem 1 allows us to check invariance properties of preemptable code. For example, assume that the initial configuration satisfies $\mathcal{R}$. Then the soundness statement ensures that the machine cannot reach an error label l_e on any CPU, provided the assertion at this program point in all high-level proofs is false. Indeed, in this case the invariant $\mathcal{R}$ does not contain any states where one of the CPUs is at l_e. Note that the functional correctness of an OS kernel is usually formulated as a simulation between the kernel and its specification. As an OS kernel does not usually make any assumptions about user processes, proving the simulation can be reduced to proving an invariance property relating the two (e.g., [10, 17]). Thus, Theorem 1 can be also used to justify such proofs.

7. Related work

There have been a number of OS verification projects; see [16] for a survey. To our knowledge, none of these has included the verification of a scheduler in a preemptive kernel with the realistic features we consider. A representative example is the L4.verified project [17], which verified the L4 microkernel as a whole, together with the scheduler. There, proofs about kernel components other than the scheduler had to ensure the preservation of its invariants, e.g., the preservation of its runqueue. The proof was still tractable because the kernel was running on a uniprocessor and preemption was disabled most of the time. However, such architecture is not used by mainstream operating systems.

The closest work to ours is the one by Feng et al. [6–8], who verified an idealised scheduler without dynamic process creation. Their logic considers a uniprocessor and does not handle ownership transfer between the scheduler and processes. Like us, they have separate proof systems for the scheduler and preemptable code. However, their high-level system is non-modular in that it does not have a notion of a process-local state. Their approach to low-level reasoning and proving the soundness of the logic is also different from ours. Because Feng et al. consider a restricted scheduler and high-level proof system, they are able to avoid designing a special relational low-level logic. Instead, they view calls to and returns from the scheduler as jumps and compile proofs of the scheduler and the rest of the system into OCAP [6], a logic supporting first-class code pointers. According to our understanding, extending this approach to handle multiprocessing, ownership transfer and a modular high-level proof system would be non-trivial.

Maeda and Yonezawa have proved a simple context-switch routine using an extension of alias types [19]. Their proof expresses the disjointness of data structures belonging to the scheduler and the rest of the kernel using the tensor operator of alias types, which corresponds to our separating conjunction. However, their type system does not hide the internal data structures of the scheduler while proving the rest of the kernel, and is thus non-modular.

Yang and Hawblitzel [24] have recently proposed a kernel where most of the codebase is typechecked and therefore cannot directly access data structures belonging to the core part of the kernel, including the scheduler. However, the guarantees established by the type system do not take into account the contents of data structures, so the kernel can still subvert the scheduler by leaving them in an inconsistent state. The OS resorts to runtime checks in such cases, introducing a performance penalty. The relationship to this work is that of a trade-off: type safety guarantees are easier to get, but are not as strong as those provided by a program logic.

Refinement is a well-known approach in verification of both operating systems and general concurrent programs [1, 10, 15, 17, 22]. We advance it further by proposing its novel form where the target of the refinement is defined axiomatically and refinement relations focus only on the relevant state of the systems related. This allows us to handle systems with complex ownership transfers.

8. Discussion

In this paper we have neither verified a complete operating system nor built an automatic tool. Instead, we have proposed a proof rule that allows decomposing the verification of a preemptive OS kernel into two simpler tasks—verifying the scheduler and preemptable code separately. Such a result is relevant no matter what type of formal analysis of OS code one is performing: manual or automatic verification, or even bug-finding. Moreover, as we argued in Section 2.2, the straightforward approach of verifying the scheduler together with the rest of the kernel makes reasoning intractable; thus, a result such as ours is in fact indispensable for verifying realistic OS kernels.

The only way we could communicate the proposed reasoning principles understandably is by presenting our results in a simplified setting. Besides, we could not cover all the interesting features of mainstream OS kernels, even in regards to scheduling, in one paper. Below we list some of the limitations of our results and possible ways to lift them, which also provide avenues for future work:

- We based our logic for preemptable code on concurrent separation logic, which would not be able to handle complicated concurrency mechanisms employed in modern OS kernels. The proof of soundness of our logic follows an approach that has been applied extensively to various concurrent derivatives of separation logic [11, 12]. This leads us to believe that we can integrate more advanced logics from this class [4, 5, 23] without problems.
- Our treatment of procedure calls is naive in that it does not allow us to reason about procedures modularly. We consider this problem orthogonal to our goal and believe that our logic can be combined with more powerful logics for procedures in low-level code, such as [9].

- We have considered schedulers with only two procedures in their interface, and fixed the piece of state transferred between the scheduler and the kernel at `schedule` to be the empty slots of the process stack. It is straightforward to add new procedures and define their pre- and postconditions abstractly, like desc in the precondition of `create`. The real issue is how to restrict the ways the scheduler is allowed to change the state it receives before giving the state back to the kernel. For example, in some operating systems (e.g., XNU), `schedule` can receive the ownership of the whole stack of the process being preempted and may reallocate the stack when it schedules the process again, while preserving its contents. Such an interference is routinely described in combinations of separation logic and rely-guarantee [4, 5, 23] and can be integrated into our logic.
- Modern OS kernels have a number of features that break through the abstraction of a virtual CPU implemented by the scheduler. For example, they allow preemptable code to disable interrupts, e.g., to access data structures local to a particular CPU. The effects of such features can be axiomatised in the high-level logic in much the same way as we axiomatise the effect of the `create` routine of the scheduler. We plan to report on extensions of our logic to such features in future papers.
- Our logic is designed for proving safety properties only. Proof methods for liveness properties or the absence of deadlocks usually rely on modular methods for safety properties. Thus, our logic is a prerequisite for attacking liveness in the future.

Despite the above limitations, our logic is the first to handle patterns of interaction between the scheduler and the kernel that are present in mainstream operating systems. Even though the logic has been formalised in a particular setting, its key technical ideas—the use of proof systems validating the frame property, logical refinement and a local way of establishing it—are transferable and can be reused in OS verification projects.

Acknowledgements

We would like to thank Anindya Banerjee, Xinyu Feng, Boris Koepf, Mark Marron, Peter O'Hearn, Matthew Parkinson, Noam Rinetzky, Zhong Shao, Viktor Vafeiadis and Jules Villard for comments and discussions that helped improve the paper. Yang was supported by EPSRC.

References

[1] R.-J. Back. On correct refinement of programs. *Journal of Computer and System Sciences*, 23:49–68, 1981.

[2] D. Bovet and M. Cesati. *Understanding the Linux Kernel, 3rd ed.* O'Reilly, 2005.

[3] E. Cohen, W. Schulte, and S. Tobies. Local verification of global invariants in concurrent programs. In *CAV'10: Conference on Computer-Aided Verification*, volume 6174 of *LNCS*, pages 480–494. Springer, 2010.

[4] T. Dinsdale-Young, M. Dodds, P. Gardner, M. Parkinson, and V. Vafeiadis. Concurrent abstract predicates. In *ECOOP'10: European Conference on Object-Oriented Programming*, pages 504–528. Springer, 2010.

[5] X. Feng, R. Ferreira, and Z. Shao. On the relationship between concurrent separation logic and assume-guarantee reasoning. In *ESOP'07: European Conference on Programming*, volume 4421 of *LNCS*, pages 173–188. Springer, 2007.

[6] X. Feng, Z. Ni, Z. Shao, and Y. Guo. An open framework for foundational proof-carrying code. In *TLDI'07: Workshop on Types in Language Design and Implementation*, pages 67–78. ACM, 2007.

[7] X. Feng, Z. Shao, Y. Dong, and Y. Guo. Certifying low-level programs with hardware interrupts and preemptive threads. In *PLDI'08: Conference on Programming Language Design and Implementation*, pages 170–182. ACM, 2008.

[8] X. Feng, Z. Shao, Y. Guo, and Y. Dong. Combining domain-specific and foundational logics to verify complete software systems. In *VSTTE'08: Conference on Verified Software: Theories, Tools, Experiments*, volume 5295 of *LNCS*, pages 54–69. Springer, 2008.

[9] X. Feng, Z. Shao, A. Vaynberg, S. Xiang, and Z. Ni. Modular verification of assembly code with stack-based control abstractions. In *PLDI'06: Conference on Programming Language Design and Implementation*, pages 401–414. ACM, 2006.

[10] M. Gargano, M. Hillebrand, D. Leinenbach, and W. Paul. On the correctness of operating system kernels. In *TPHOLs: Conference on Theorem Proving in Higher Order Logics*, volume 3603 of *LNCS*, pages 1–16. Springer, 2005.

[11] A. Gotsman. Logics and analyses for concurrent heap-manipulating programs. PhD Thesis, University of Cambridge, 2009.

[12] A. Gotsman, J. Berdine, and B. Cook. Precision and the conjunction rule in concurrent separation logic. In *MFPS'11: Conference on Mathematical Foundations of Programming Semantics*, 2011. To appear.

[13] A. Gotsman, J. Berdine, B. Cook, N. Rinetzky, and M. Sagiv. Local reasoning for storable locks and threads. In *APLAS'07: Asian Symposium on Programming Languages and Systems*, volume 4807 of *LNCS*, pages 19–37. Springer, 2007.

[14] A. Gotsman and H. Yang. Modular verification of preemptive OS kernels (extended version). Available from `www.software.imdea.org/~gotsman`.

[15] C. Jones. Splitting atoms safely. *Theoretical Computer Science*, 375:109–119, 2007.

[16] G. Klein. Operating system verification–an overview. *Sādhanā*, 34:26–69, 2009.

[17] G. Klein, K. Elphinstone, G. Heiser, J. Andronick, D. Cock, P. Derrin, D. Elkaduwe, K. Engelhardt, R. Kolanski, M. Norrish, T. Sewell, H. Tuch, and S. Winwood. seL4: Formal verification of an OS kernel. In *SOSP'09: Symposium on Operating Systems Principles*, pages 207–220. ACM, 2009.

[18] R. Love. *Linux Kernel Development, 3rd ed.* Addison Wesley, 2010.

[19] T. Maeda and A. Yonezawa. Writing an OS kernel in a strictly and statically typed language. In *Formal to Practical Security*, volume 5458 of *LNCS*, pages 181–197. Springer, 2009.

[20] P. W. O'Hearn. Resources, concurrency and local reasoning. *Theoretical Computer Science*, 375:271–307, 2007.

[21] J. Reynolds. Separation logic: A logic for shared mutable data structures. In *LICS'02: Symposium on Logic in Computer Science*, pages 55–74. IEEE, 2002.

[22] A. Turon and M. Wand. A separation logic for refining concurrent objects. In *POPL'11: Symposium on Principles of Programming Languages*, pages 247–258. ACM, 2011.

[23] V. Vafeiadis and M. J. Parkinson. A marriage of rely/guarantee and separation logic. In *CONCUR'07: Conference on Concurrency Theory*, volume 4703 of *LNCS*, pages 256–271. Springer, 2007.

[24] J. Yang and C. Hawblitzel. Safe to the last instruction: automated verification of a type-safe operating system. In *PLDI'10: Conference on Programming Language Design and Implementation*, pages 99–110. ACM, 2010.

Characteristic Formulae for the Verification of Imperative Programs

Arthur Charguéraud
Max Planck Institute for Software Systems (MPI-SWS)
charguer@mpi-sws.org

Abstract

In previous work, we introduced an approach to program verification based on characteristic formulae. The approach consists of generating a higher-order logic formula from the source code of a program. This characteristic formula is constructed in such a way that it gives a sound and complete description of the semantics of that program. The formula can thus be exploited in an interactive proof assistant to formally verify that the program satisfies a particular specification.

This previous work was, however, only concerned with purely-functional programs. In the present paper, we describe the generalization of characteristic formulae to an imperative programming language. In this setting, characteristic formulae involve specifications expressed in the style of Separation Logic. They also integrate the frame rule, which enables local reasoning. We have implemented a tool based on characteristic formulae. This tool, called CFML, supports the verification of imperative Caml programs using the Coq proof assistant. Using CFML, we have formally verified nontrivial imperative algorithms, as well as CPS functions, higher-order iterators, and programs involving higher-order stores.

Categories and Subject Descriptors D.2.4 [*Software/Program Verification*]: Formal methods

General Terms Verification

1. Introduction

This paper addresses the problem of building formal proofs of correctness for higher-order imperative programs. It describes an effective technique for verifying that a program satisfies a specification, and for proving termination of that program. This technique supports the verification of arbitrarily-complex properties, thanks to the use of an interactive proof assistant based on higher-order logic. The work described in this paper is based on the notion of *characteristic formula* of a program. A characteristic formula is a higher-order logic formula that fully characterizes the semantics of a program, and may thus be used to prove properties about the behavior of that program.

In previous work, we have shown how to build and exploit characteristic formulae for purely-functional programs [9]. In this paper, we extend those results to an imperative programming language. Let $[\![t]\!]$ denote the characteristic formula of a imperative term t. The application of the predicate $[\![t]\!]$ to a pre-condition H and to a post-condition Q yields the proposition $[\![t]\!]\ H\ Q$. By construction of characteristic formulae, this proposition is true if and only if the term t admits H as pre-condition and Q as post-condition. The proposition $[\![t]\!]\ H\ Q$ may be established through interactive proofs, using a combination of general-purpose tactics and tactics specialized for the manipulation of characteristic formulae.

Characteristic formulae are designed to be easily readable and easily manipulable from inside an interactive proof assistant. A characteristic formula has a size linear in that of the program it describes. Moreover, a characteristic formula can be displayed in a way that closely resembles the source code that it describes, thanks to the use of an appropriate system of notation. With this notation system, the proof obligation $[\![t]\!]\ H\ Q$ stating that "the term t admits H as pre-condition and Q as post-condition" is displayed in a way that reads as "$t\ H\ Q$". This display feature makes it easy to relate proof obligations to the piece of code they arose from.

The notion of characteristic formulae originates in process calculi. In this context, two processes are behaviorally equivalent if and only if their characteristic formulae are logically equivalent [16]. An algorithm for building the characteristic formula of any process was proposed in the 80's [14]. More recently, Honda, Berger and Yoshida adapted this idea from process logics to program logics [18]. They gave an algorithm for building the pair of the weakest pre-condition and of the strongest post-condition of any PCF program. Note that their algorithm differs from weakest pre-condition calculus in that the PCF program considered is not assumed to be annotated with any invariant. Honda *et al* suggested that characteristic formulae could be used in program verification. However, they did not find a way to encode the ad-hoc logic that they were using for stating specifications into a standard logic. Since the construction of a theorem prover dedicated to this logic would have required a tremendous effort, Honda *et al*'s work remained theoretical and did not result in an effective program verification tool.

In prior work [9], we showed how to construct characteristic formulae that are expressed in a standard higher-order logic. Moreover, we showed that characteristic formulae can be made of linear size and that they can be pretty-printed like the source code they describe. Those formulae are therefore suitable for manipulation inside an existing proof assistant such as Coq [11]. We have implemented a tool, called CFML (short for *Characteristic Formulae for ML*) that parses a Caml program [24] and produces its characteristic formula in the form of a Coq statement. Using CFML, we were able to verify more than half of the content of Okasaki's reference book *Purely Functional Data Structures* [37]. Since then, we have generalized characteristic formulae to support reasoning about mutable state, and have updated CFML accordingly. In the

ICFP'11, September 19–21, 2011, Tokyo, Japan.

present paper, we report on this generalization, making the following contributions.

- We show that characteristic formulae for imperative programs can still be pretty printed in a way that closely resambles the source code they describe, in spite of the fact that their semantics now involves a memory store that is implicitly threaded throughout the execution of the program.
- In order to support local reasoning, we adapt characteristic formulae to handle specifications stated in the style of Separation Logic [39], and we introduce a predicate transformer for integrating the frame rule into characteristic formulae.
- We accompany the definition of characteristic formulae not only with a proof of soundness, but also with a proof of completeness. Completeness ensures that any correct specification can be established using characteristic formulae.
- We report on the verification of a nontrivial imperative algorithm, Dijkstra's shortest path algorithm. We also demonstrate the ability of CFML to reason about interactions between first-class functions and mutable state.

The content of this paper is organized in three main parts. Section 2 describes the key ideas involved in the construction, the pretty-printing and the manipulation of characteristic formulae for imperative programs. Section 3 gives details on the formalization of memory states, on the algorithm for generating characteristic formulae and on the soundness and completeness theorems. Section 4 contains a presentation of several examples that were specified and formalized using CFML. Due to space limitations, several aspects of CFML could only be summarized. All the details can be found in the author's PhD dissertation [8], and all the Coq proofs mentioned in this paper can be found online.[1]

2. Overview

2.1 Verification through characteristic formulae

The characteristic formula of a term t, written $[\![t]\!]$, relates a description of the input heap in which the term t is executed with a description of the output value and a description of the output heap produced by the execution of t. Characteristic formulae are hence closely related to Hoare triples [17], and, more precisely, to *total correctness* Hoare triples, which also account for termination. A total correctness Hoare triple $\{H\}\ t\ \{Q\}$ asserts that, when executed in a heap satisfying the predicate H, the term t terminates and returns a value v in a heap satisfying $Q\ v$. Note that the post-condition Q is used to specify both the output heap *and* the output value. When t has type τ, the pre-condition H has type $\mathsf{Heap} \rightarrow \mathsf{Prop}$ and the post-condition Q has type $\langle\tau\rangle \rightarrow \mathsf{Heap} \rightarrow \mathsf{Prop}$, where Heap is the type of a heap and where $\langle\tau\rangle$ is the Coq type that corresponds to the ML type τ.

The characteristic formula $[\![t]\!]$ is a predicate such that $[\![t]\!]\ H\ Q$ captures exactly the same proposition as the triple $\{H\}\ t\ \{Q\}$. There is however a fundamental difference between Hoare triples and characteristic formulae. A Hoare triple $\{H\}\ t\ \{Q\}$ is a three-place relation, whose second argument is a representation of the syntax of the term t. On the contrary, $[\![t]\!]\ H\ Q$ is a logical proposition, expressed in terms of standard higher-order logic connectives, such as $\wedge$, $\exists$, $\forall$ and $\Rightarrow$. Importantly, this proposition does not refer to the syntax of the term t. Whereas Hoare-triples need to be established by application of derivation rules specific to Hoare logic, characteristic formulae can be proved using only basic higher-order logic reasoning, without involving external derivation rules.

[1] `http://arthur.chargueraud.org/research/2011/cfml/`

We have used characteristic formulae for building CFML, a tool that supports the verification of imperative Caml programs using the Coq proof assistant. CFML takes as input source code written in a large subset of Caml, and it produces as output a set of Coq axioms that correspond to the characteristic formulae of each top-level definition. It is worth noting that CFML generates characteristic formulae without knowledge of the specification nor of the invariants of the source code. The specification of each top-level definition is instead provided by the user, in the form of the statement of a Coq theorem. The user may prove such a theorem by exploiting the axiom generated by CFML for that definition, and he is to provide information such as loop invariants during the interactive proof.

When reasoning about a program through its characteristic formula, a proof obligation typically takes the form $[\![t]\!]\ H\ Q$, asserting that the piece of code t admits H as pre-condition and Q as post-condition. The user can make progress in the proof by invoking the custom tactics provided by CFML. Proof obligations thereby get decomposed into simpler subgoals, following the structure of the code. When reaching a leaf of the source code, some facts need to be established in order to justify the correctness of the program. Those facts, which no longer contain any reference to characteristic formulae, can be proved using general-purpose Coq tactics, including calls to decision procedures and to proof-search algorithms.

The rest of this section presents the key ideas involved in the construction of characteristic formulae, covering the treatment of let bindings, the frame rule and functions.

2.2 Characteristic formula of a let-binding

To evaluate a term of the form "$\mathsf{let}\,x = t_1\,\mathsf{in}\,t_2$", one first evaluates the subterm t_1 and then computes the result of the evaluation of t_2, in which x denotes the result produced by t_1. To prove that the expression "$\mathsf{let}\,x = t_1\,\mathsf{in}\,t_2$" admits H as pre-condition and Q as post-condition, one thus needs to find a valid post-condition Q' for t_1. This post-condition, when applied to the result x produced by t_1, describes the state of memory after the execution of t_1 and before the execution of t_2. So, $Q'\,x$ denotes the pre-condition for t_2. The corresponding Hoare-logic rule for reasoning on let-bindings is:

$$\frac{\{H\}\ t_1\ \{Q'\} \qquad \forall x.\ \{Q'\,x\}\ t_2\ \{Q\}}{\{H\}\ (\mathsf{let}\,x = t_1\,\mathsf{in}\,t_2)\ \{Q\}}\ \text{LET}$$

The characteristic formula for a let-binding is built as follows:

$$[\![\mathsf{let}\,x = t_1\,\mathsf{in}\,t_2]\!] \ \equiv\ \lambda H.\lambda Q.\ \exists Q'.\ [\![t_1]\!]\,H\,Q' \ \wedge\ \forall x.\ [\![t_2]\!]\,(Q'\,x)\,Q$$

This formula closely resembles the corresponding Hoare-logic rule. The only real difference is that, in the characteristic formula, the intermediate post-condition Q' is explicitly introduced with an existential quantifier, whereas this quantification is implicit in the Hoare-logic derivation rule. The existential quantification of unknown specifications, which is made possible by the strength of higher-order logic, plays a central role here. This existential quantification of specifications contrasts with traditional program verification approaches where intermediate specifications, including loop invariants, have to be included in the source code.

Next, we introduce a notation system for pretty-printing characteristic formulae. The aim is to make proof obligations easily readable and closely related to the source code. For let-bindings, the piece of notation defined is:

$$(\mathbf{let}\ x = \mathcal{F}_1\ \mathbf{in}\ \mathcal{F}_2) \ \equiv\ \lambda H.\lambda Q.\ \exists Q'.\ \mathcal{F}_1\,H\,Q' \ \wedge\ \forall x.\ \mathcal{F}_2\,(Q'\,x)\,Q$$

Hereafter, bold keywords correspond to notation for logical formulae, whereas plain keywords correspond to constructors from the programming language syntax. The definition of the characteristic formula of a let-binding can now be reformulated as:

$$[\![\mathsf{let}\, x = t_1 \,\mathsf{in}\, t_2]\!] \quad \equiv \quad (\mathbf{let}\ x = [\![t_1]\!]\ \mathbf{in}\ [\![t_2]\!])$$

The generation of characteristic formulae, which is a translation from program syntax to higher-order logic, therefore boils down to a re-interpretation of the programming language keywords.

Notation for characteristic formulae can be defined in a similar fashion for all the other constructions of the programming language. It follows that characteristic formulae may be pretty-printed exactly like the source code they describe. Hence, during the verification of a program, a proof-obligation appears to the user as a piece of source code followed with its pre-condition and its post-condition. Note that this convenient display applies not only to a top-level program definition t but also to all of the subterms of t involved during the verification of t.

CFML provides a set of tactics for making progress in the analysis of a characteristic formula. For example, the tactic `xlet` applies to a goal of the form "$(\mathbf{let}\ x = \mathcal{F}_1\ \mathbf{in}\ \mathcal{F}_2)\ H\ Q$". It introduces a unification variable, call it Q', and produces two subgoals. The first one is $\mathcal{F}_1\ H\ Q'$. The second one is $\mathcal{F}_2\,(Q'\,x)\,Q$, under a context extended with a fresh variable named x. The intermediate specification Q' introduced here typically gets instantiated through unification when solving the first subgoal. The pre-condition for $\mathcal{F}_2$ is thus known when starting to reason about the second subgoal. The instantiation of Q' may also be provided by the user explicitly, as argument of the tactic `xlet`. More generally, CFML provides one such "x-tactic" for each language construction. As a result, one can verify a program using characteristic formulae even without any knowledge about the construction of characteristic formulae.

2.3 Integration of the frame rule

Local reasoning [36] refers to the ability to verify a piece of code by reasoning only about the memory cells that are involved in the execution of that code. With local reasoning, all the memory cells that are not explicitly mentioned are implicitly assumed to remain unchanged. The concept of local reasoning is very elegantly captured by the "frame rule", which originates in Separation Logic [39]. The frame rule states that if a program expression transforms a heap described by a predicate H_1 into heap described by a predicate H_1', then, for any heap predicate H_2, the same program expression also transforms a heap of the form $H_1 * H_2$ into a state of the form $H_1' * H_2$. The star symbol, called separating conjunction, captures a disjoint union of two pieces of heap. The frame rule can be formulated in terms of Hoare triples as shown next.

$$\frac{\{H_1\}\ t\ \{Q_1\}}{\{H_1 * H_2\}\ t\ \{Q_1 \star H_2\}}\ \text{FRAME}$$

Above, the symbol $(\star)$ is like $(*)$ except that it extends a post-condition with a piece of heap. Technically, $Q_1 \star H_2$ is defined as "$\lambda x.\,(Q_1\,x) * H_2$", where the variable x denotes the output value and $Q_1\,x$ describes the output heap.

To integrate the frame rule in characteristic formulae, we rely on a predicate called local. This predicate is defined in such a way that, to prove the proposition "$\mathsf{local}\,[\![t]\!]\ H\ Q$", it suffices to find a decomposition of H of the form $H_1 * H_2$, a decomposition of Q of the form $Q_1 \star H_2$, and to prove $[\![t]\!]\ H_1\ Q_1$. Intuitively, the predicate local can be defined as follows.

$$\begin{array}{lll}\mathsf{local}\,\mathcal{F} & \equiv & \lambda H.\,\lambda Q.\ \exists H_1.\exists H_2.\exists Q_1. \\ & & \quad H = H_1 * H_2 \ \wedge\ \mathcal{F}\,H_1\,Q_1 \ \wedge\ Q = Q_1 \star H_2\end{array}$$

The frame rule is not syntax-directed, meaning that one cannot guess from the shape of the term t when the frame rule needs to be applied. Yet, our goal is to generate characteristic formulae in a systematic manner from the syntax of the source code. Since we do not know where to insert applications of the predicate local, we may simply insert applications of this predicate at every node of characteristic formulae. For example, the previous definition for let-bindings gets updated as follows.

$$\begin{array}{l}(\mathbf{let}\ x = \mathcal{F}_1\ \mathbf{in}\ \mathcal{F}_2) \ \equiv \\ \quad \mathsf{local}\,(\lambda H.\,\lambda Q.\ \exists Q'.\ \mathcal{F}_1\,H\,Q' \ \wedge\ \forall x.\ \mathcal{F}_2\,(Q'\,x)\,Q)\end{array}$$

This aggressive strategy allows us to apply the frame rule at any time during program verification. If there is no need to apply the frame rule, then the local predicate may be simply ignored. Indeed, given a formula $\mathcal{F}$, the proposition "$\mathcal{F}\ H\ Q$" is always a sufficient condition for proving "$\mathsf{local}\,\mathcal{F}\ H\ Q$". (It suffices to instantiate H_2 as the specification of the empty heap.) We will later generalize the approach described here for handling the frame rule so as to also handle applications of the rule of consequence, which is used to strengthen pre-conditions and weaken post-conditions, and to enable the discarding of memory cells, for simulating garbage collection.

2.4 Translation of types

Higher-order logic can naturally be used to state properties about basic values such as purely-functional lists. Indeed, the list data structure defined in Coq perfectly matches the list data structure from Caml. However, particular care is required when specifying and reasoning about program functions. Indeed, programming language functions cannot be directly represented as logical functions, because of a mismatch between the two: program functions may be partial, whereas logical functions must always be total. To address this issue, we introduce a new data type, called Func, used to represent functions. To the user of characteristic formulae, the type Func is presented as an abstract data type. In the proof of soundness, however, a value of type Func is interpreted as the syntax of the source code of a function.

Another particularity of the reflection of program values into Coq values is the treatment of pointers. When reasoning through characteristic formulae, the type and the contents of memory cells are described explicitly through heap predicates, so there is no need for pointers to carry the type of the memory cell they point to. All pointers are therefore described in the logic through an abstract data type called Loc. In the proof of soundness, a value of type Loc is interpreted as a store location.

The translation of Caml types into Coq types is formalized through an operator, written $\langle\cdot\rangle$, that maps all arrow types to the type Func and maps all reference types to the type Loc. A Caml value of type τ is thus represented as a Coq value of type $\langle\tau\rangle$. For simplicity, program integers are idealized and are simply mapped to Coq values of type $\mathbb{Z}$. However, it would also be possible to map the type int to the Coq type int64 for reasoning about overflows. The definition of the operator $\langle\cdot\rangle$ can be summarized as follows.

$$\begin{array}{lll}\langle \mathsf{int}\rangle & \equiv & \mathbb{Z} \\ \langle \tau_1 \times \tau_2\rangle & \equiv & \langle\tau_1\rangle \times \langle\tau_2\rangle \\ \langle \tau_1 + \tau_2\rangle & \equiv & \langle\tau_1\rangle + \langle\tau_2\rangle \\ \langle \tau_1 \rightarrow \tau_2\rangle & \equiv & \mathsf{Func} \\ \langle \mathsf{ref}\,\tau\rangle & \equiv & \mathsf{Loc}\end{array}$$

The translation from Caml types to Coq types is in fact conducted in two steps. A well-typed ML program gets first translated into a well-typed *weak-ML* program, and this weak-ML program is then fed to the characteristic formula generator. Weak-ML corresponds to a relaxed version of ML that does not keep track of the type of pointers nor of the type of functions. Moreover, weak-ML does not impose any constraint on the typing of applications nor on the typing of dereferencing.

Since weak-ML imposes strictly fewer constraints than ML, any program well-typed in ML is also well-typed in weak-ML. Weak-ML nevertheless enforces strong enough invariants to justify the soundness of characteristic formulae. So, although memory safety is not obtained by weak-ML, it is guaranteed by the proofs of correctness established using a characteristic formula generated from a well-typed weak-ML program.

Although it is possible to generate characteristic formulae directly from ML programs, the use of weak-ML as an intermediate type system serves three important purposes. First, weak-ML helps simplifying the definition of the characteristic formula generation algorithm. Second, it enables the verification of programs that are well-typed in weak-ML but not in ML, such as programs exploiting System F functions, null pointers, or strong updates (i.e., type-varying updates of a reference cell). Third, weak-ML plays a crucial role in proving the soundness and completeness of characteristic formulae. This latter aspect of weak-ML is not discussed in this paper, however it is described in author's PhD dissertation [8].

2.5 Reasoning about functions

To specify the behavior of functions, we rely on a predicate, called App, which also appears to the user as an abstract predicate. Intuitively, the proposition "$\mathsf{App}\, f\, v\, H\, Q$" asserts that the application of the function f to v in a heap satisfying H terminates and returns a value v' in a heap satisfying $Q\, v'$. The predicates H and Q correspond to the pre- and post-conditions of the application of the function f to the argument v. It follows that the characteristic formula for an application of a function f to a value v is simply built as the partial application of App to f and v.

$$[\![f\, v]\!] \quad \equiv \quad \mathsf{App}\, f\, v$$

The function f is viewed in the logic as a value of type Func. If f takes as argument a value v described in Coq at type A and returns a value described in Coq at type B, then the pre-condition H has type Hprop, a shorthand for Heap $\rightarrow$ Prop, and the post-condition Q has type $B \rightarrow$ Hprop. So, the predicate App has type:

$$\forall A\, B.\ \mathsf{Func} \rightarrow A \rightarrow \mathsf{Hprop} \rightarrow (B \rightarrow \mathsf{Hprop}) \rightarrow \mathsf{Prop}$$

For example, the specification of the function incr, which increments the content of a memory cell containing an integer, takes the form of a theorem stated in terms of the predicate App:

$$\forall r.\ \forall n.\ \mathsf{App}\, \mathsf{incr}\, r\, (r \hookrightarrow n)\, (\lambda\_.\ r \hookrightarrow n+1)$$

Above, the heap predicate $(r \hookrightarrow n)$ describes the memory state expected by the function: it consists of a single memory cell located at address r and whose content is the value n. Similarly, the heap predicate $(r \hookrightarrow n+1)$ describes the memory state posterior to the function execution. The abstraction "$\lambda\_.$" is used to discard the unit value returned by the function incr.

By construction, a statement of the form "$\mathsf{App}\, f\, v\, H\, Q$" describes the behavior of an application. As we have just seen, App can be used to write specifications. It remains to explain where assumptions of the form "$\mathsf{App}\, f\, v\, H\, Q$" can be obtained from. Such assumptions are provided by characteristic formulae associated with function definitions. If a function f is defined as the abstraction "$\lambda x.\, t$", then, given a particular argument v, one can derive an instance of "$\mathsf{App}\, f\, v\, H\, Q$" simply by proving that the body t, in which x is instantiated with v, admits the pre-condition H and the post-condition Q.

In what follows, we explain how to build characteristic formula for local functions and then for top-level function. For a local function definition, the characteristic formula is as follows:

$$[\![\mathsf{let\ rec}\, f = \lambda x.\, t \,\mathsf{in}\, t']\!] \;\equiv\; \lambda H.\, \lambda Q.\ \forall f.\ \mathcal{H} \Rightarrow [\![t']\!]\, H\, Q$$
$$\text{where } \mathcal{H} \;\equiv\; (\forall x\, H'\, Q'.\ [\![t]\!]\, H'\, Q' \Rightarrow \mathsf{App}\, f\, x\, H'\, Q')$$

For a top-level function definition of the form "$\mathsf{let\ rec}\, f = \lambda x.\, t$", CFML generates two Coq axioms. The first one has name f and type Func. This Coq variable f corresponds to the Caml function f. The second axiom describes the semantics of f, through the following statement: "$\forall x\, H\, Q.\ [\![t]\!]\, H\, Q \Rightarrow \mathsf{App}\, f\, x\, H\, Q$". Note that the soundness theorem proved for characteristic formulae ensures that adding this axiom does not introduce any logical inconsistency.

For example, consider the top-level function definition "$\mathsf{let}\, f = \lambda r.\, (\mathsf{incr}\, r\, ;\, \mathsf{incr}\, r)$", which expects a reference and increments its content twice. This function may be specified through a theorem whose statement is "$\forall rn.\ \mathsf{App}\, f\, r\, (r \hookrightarrow n)\, (\lambda\_.\ r \hookrightarrow n+2)$". To establish this theorem, the first step consists in applying the second axiom generated for the function f. The resulting proof obligation is "$(\mathbf{app}\ \mathsf{incr}\, r\, \mathbf{;}\ \mathbf{app}\ \mathsf{incr}\, r)\, (r \hookrightarrow n)\, (\lambda\_.\ r \hookrightarrow n+2)$", where "**app**" and "**;**" correspond to the pieces of notation defined for the characteristic formulae of applications and of sequences, respectively. This proof obligation can be discharged with help of the tactic `xseq`, for reasoning about the sequence, and of the tactic `xapp`, for reasoning about the two applications. In fact, for such a simple function, one may establish correctness through a simple invocation of a tactic called `xgo`, which repeatedly applies the appropriate x-tactic until some information is required from the user.

Two observations are worth making about the treatment of functions. First, characteristic formulae do not involve any specific treatment of recursivity. Indeed, to prove that a recursive function satisfies a given specification, it suffices to conduct a proof that the function satisfies that specification by induction. The induction may be conducted on a measure or on a well-founded relation, using the induction facility from the interactive theorem prover being used. So, characteristic formulae for recursive functions do not need to include any induction hypothesis. A similar observation was also made by Honda *et al* in their work on program logics [18].

The second observation concerns first-class functions. As explained through this section, a function f is specified with a statement of the form "$\mathsf{App}\, f\, v\, H\, Q$". Because this statement is a proposition like any other (it has type Prop), it may appear inside the pre-condition or the post-condition of any another function (thanks to the impredicativity of Prop). This statement may also appear in the specification of the content of a memory cell. The predicate App therefore supports reasoning about higher-order functions (functions taking functions as arguments) and higher-order stores (memory stores containing functions).

3. Characteristic formula generation

This section of the paper explains in more details how characteristic formulae are constructed. It presents weak-ML types, the source language, the translation of Caml values into Coq values, and the predicates used to describe heaps. It then describes the algorithm used to generated characteristic formulae. Note that it is safe to read Section 4, which is concerned with examples, before this one.

3.1 From ML types to Weak-ML types and Coq types

In what follows, we describe the grammar of ML types and weak-ML types, and then formalize the translation from ML types to weak-ML types, and the translation from weak-ML types to Coq types. Hereafter, A denotes a type variable, C denotes the type constructor for an algebraic data type, τ denotes an ML type, and σ denotes a ML type scheme. Furthermore, the overbar notation denotes a list of items. The grammar of ML types is:

$$\tau \;:=\; A \;\mid\; \mathsf{int} \;\mid\; C\,\overline{\tau} \;\mid\; \tau \rightarrow \tau \;\mid\; \mathsf{ref}\,\tau \;\mid\; \mu A.\tau$$
$$\sigma \;:=\; \forall \overline{A}.\tau$$

Note that sum types, product types, the boolean type and the unit type can be defined as algebraic data types.

$$
\begin{array}{lcl}
\langle A\rangle & \equiv & A \\
\langle \mathsf{int}\rangle & \equiv & \mathsf{int} \\
\langle C\,\overline{\tau}\rangle & \equiv & C\,\langle\overline{\tau}\rangle \\
\langle \tau_1 \to \tau_2\rangle & \equiv & \mathsf{func} \\
\langle \mathsf{ref}\,\tau\rangle & \equiv & \mathsf{loc} \\
\langle \forall\overline{A}.\,\tau\rangle & \equiv & \forall\overline{B}.\,\langle\tau\rangle \quad \text{where } \overline{B} = \overline{A}\cap \mathsf{fv}(\langle\tau\rangle) \\
\langle \mu A.\tau\rangle & \equiv & \left|\begin{array}{ll} \langle\tau\rangle & \text{if } A \notin \langle\tau\rangle \\ \text{program rejected} & \text{otherwise}\end{array}\right.
\end{array}
$$

Figure 1. Translation from ML types to weak-ML types

Weak-ML types are obtained from ML types by mapping all arrow types to a constant type called func and mapping all reference types to the constant type called loc. Let T denote a weak-ML type and S denote a weak-ML type scheme. The grammar of weak-ML types is as follows:

$$
\begin{array}{lcl}
T & := & A \mid \mathsf{int} \mid C\,\overline{T} \mid \mathsf{func} \mid \mathsf{loc} \\
S & := & \forall\overline{A}.T
\end{array}
$$

The translation of an ML type τ into the corresponding weak-ML type, written $\langle\tau\rangle$, appears in Figure 1. The treatment of polymorphism and of recursive types is explained next. When translating a type scheme, the list of quantified variables might shrink. For example, the ML type scheme "$\forall AB.\ A + (B \to B)$" is mapped to "$\forall A.\ A + \mathsf{func}$", which no longer involves the type variable B. Weak-ML includes algebraic data types, but does not support general equi-recursive types. Nevertheless, some recursive ML types can be translated into weak-ML, because the recursion involved might vanish when erasing arrow types. For example, the recursive ML type "$\mu A.(A \times \mathsf{int})$" does not have any counterpart in weak-ML, however the recursive ML type "$\mu A.(A \to B)$" gets mapped to the weak-ML type func. The verification approach described in the present paper therefore supports reasoning about functions with an equi-recursive type.

When building the characteristic formula of a weak-ML program, weak-ML types get translated into Coq types. This translation is almost the identity, because every type constructor from weak-ML is directly mapped to the corresponding Coq type constructor. Algebraic type definitions are translated into corresponding Coq inductive definitions. Note that the positivity requirement associated with Coq inductive types is not a problem here: since there is no arrow type in weak-ML, the translation from weak-ML types to Coq types never produces a negative occurrence of an inductive type in its own definition. In summary, the Coq translation of a weak-ML type T, written $[\![T]\!]$, is defined as follows.

$$
\begin{array}{lcl|lcl}
[\![\mathsf{int}]\!] & \equiv & \mathbb{Z} & [\![A]\!] & \equiv & A \\
[\![\mathsf{loc}]\!] & \equiv & \mathsf{Loc} & [\![C\,\overline{T}]\!] & \equiv & C\,[\![\overline{T}]\!] \\
[\![\mathsf{func}]\!] & \equiv & \mathsf{Func} & [\![\forall\overline{A}.T]\!] & \equiv & \forall\overline{A}.\,[\![T]\!]
\end{array}
$$

3.2 Typed source language

Before generating characteristic formulae, programs first need to be put in an *administrative normal form*. Through this process, programs are arranged so that all intermediate results and all functions become bound by a let-definition. One notable exception is the application of simple total functions such as addition and subtraction. For example, the application "$f\,(v_1 + v_2)$" is considered to be in normal form although "$f\,(g\,v_1\,v_2)$" is not in normal form in general. The normalization process, which is similar to A-normalization [13], preserves the semantics and greatly simplifies formally reasoning about programs. Moreover, it is straightforward to implement. Similar transformations have appeared in previous work on program verification (e.g., [18, 38]). In this paper, we omit a formal description of the normalization process and only show the grammar of terms in normal form.

The characteristic formula generator expects a program in administrative normal form. It moreover expects this program to be typed, in the sense that all its subterms should be annotated with their weak-ML type. To formally define characteristic formulae, we therefore need to introduce the syntax of typed programs in normal forms. This syntax is formalized as follows, where $\hat{t}$ ranges over typed term and $\hat{v}$ ranges over typed values.

$$
\begin{array}{lcl}
\hat{v} & := & n \mid x\,\overline{T} \mid D\,\overline{T}(\hat{v},\ldots,\hat{v}) \mid \\
& & \mathsf{ref} \mid \mathsf{get} \mid \mathsf{set} \mid \mathsf{cmp} \mid \mathsf{null} \\
\hat{t} & := & \hat{v} \mid (\hat{v}\,\hat{v}) \mid \mathsf{crash} \mid \mathsf{if}\,\hat{v}\,\mathsf{then}\,\hat{t}\,\mathsf{else}\,\hat{t} \mid \\
& & \mathsf{let}\,x = \hat{t}\,\mathsf{in}\,\hat{t} \mid \mathsf{let}\,x = \Lambda\overline{A}.\,\hat{v}\,\mathsf{in}\,\hat{t} \mid \hat{t}\,;\,\hat{t} \mid \\
& & \mathsf{let\,rec}\,f = \Lambda\overline{A}.\lambda x.\hat{t}\,\mathsf{in}\,\hat{t}
\end{array}
$$

Note that locations and function closures do not exist in source programs, so they are not included in the above grammar. The letter n denotes an integer a memory location. The functions ref, get and set are used to allocate, read and write reference cells, respectively, and the function cmp enables comparison of two memory locations. The null pointer, written null, is a particular location that never gets allocated. Typed programs carry explicit information about generalized type variables, so a polymorphic function definition takes the form "$\mathsf{let\,rec}\,f = \Lambda\overline{A}.\lambda x.\hat{t}_1\ \mathsf{in}\ \hat{t}_2$" and a polymorphic let-binding takes the form "$\mathsf{let}\,x = \Lambda\overline{A}.\,\hat{v}\,\mathsf{in}\,\hat{t}$". Due to the value restriction, the general form "$\mathsf{let}\,x = \Lambda\overline{A}.\,\hat{t}_1\ \mathsf{in}\,\hat{t}_2$" is not allowed. The syntax of typed programs also keeps track of type applications, which take place either on a polymorphic variable x, written $x\,\overline{T}$, or on a polymorphic data constructor D, written $D\,\overline{T}$. For-loops and while-loops are discussed later on (§3.7).

3.3 Reflection of values in the logic

Constructing characteristic formulae requires a translation of all the Caml values that appear in the program source code into the corresponding Coq values. This translation, called *decoding*, and written $\lceil\hat{v}\rceil$, transforms a weak-ML value $\hat{v}$ of type T into the corresponding Coq value, which has type $[\![T]\!]$. The definition of $\lceil\hat{v}\rceil$ is shown below. Values on the left-hand side are well-typed weak-ML values whereas values on the right-hand side are (well-typed) Coq values.

$$
\begin{array}{lcl}
\lceil n\rceil & \equiv & n \\
\lceil x\,\overline{T}\rceil & \equiv & x\,[\![\overline{T}]\!] \\
\lceil D\,\overline{T}(\hat{v}_1,\ldots,\hat{v}_2)\rceil & \equiv & D\,[\![\overline{T}]\!]\,(\lceil\hat{v}_1\rceil,\ldots,\lceil\hat{v}_2\rceil) \\
\lceil\Lambda\overline{A}.\,\hat{v}\rceil & \equiv & \lambda\overline{A}.\,\lceil\hat{v}\rceil
\end{array}
$$

Above, a program integer n is mapped to the corresponding Coq integer. If x is a non-polymorphic variable, then it is simply mapped to itself. However, if x is a polymorphic variable applied to some types $\overline{T}$, then this occurrence is translated as the application of x to the translations of each of the types from the list $\overline{T}$. A program data constructor D is mapped to the corresponding Coq inductive constructor, and if the constructor is polymorphic then its type arguments get translated into Coq types. The primitive functions for manipulating references (e.g., get) are mapped to corresponding abstract Coq values of type Func.

The decoding of a polymorphic value $\Lambda\overline{A}.\,\hat{v}$ is a Coq function that expects some types $\overline{A}$ and returns the decoding of the value $\hat{v}$. For example, the polymorphic pair (nil, nil) has type "$\forall A.\forall B.\ \mathsf{list}\,A \times \mathsf{list}B$". The Coq translation of this value is "`fun A B : Type => (@nil A, @nil B)`", where the prefix `@` indicates that type arguments are given explicitly. The Coq expert might feel sceptical about the fact that the type variables A and B get assigned the kind Type. Since a weak-ML type variable is to be instantiated with a weak-ML type T, a Coq type variable occuring in a characteristic formula should presumably be instantiated only with a Coq type of the form $[\![T]\!]$. Nevertheless, we have proved that it is not needed to consider the kind defined as the image of the operator $[\![\cdot]\!]$, because it remains sound to assign the kind Type to the type variables quantified in characteristic formulae. The proof can be found in [8], Section 6.4.

3.4 Heap predicates

This section explains how heaps are represented, how operations on heaps are defined, and how heap predicates are built in the style of Separation Logic. Note that all the operations and predicates on heaps are completely formalized in Coq.

The semantics of a source program involves a memory store, which is a finite map from locations to program values. The Coq object that corresponds to a memory store is called a *heap*. The type Heap is defined in Coq as the type of finite maps from locations to dependent pairs, where a dependent pair is a pair of a Coq type $\mathcal{T}$ and of a Coq value V of type $\mathcal{T}$. With this definition, the set of Coq values of type Heap is isomorphic to the set of well-typed memory stores.

Operations on heaps are defined in terms of operations on maps. The empty heap, written $\varnothing$, is a heap built on the empty map. Similarly, a singleton heap, written $l \rightarrow_{\mathcal{T}} V$, is a heap built on a singleton map binding a location l to a dependent pair made of a type $\mathcal{T}$ and a value V of type $\mathcal{T}$. Two heaps are said to be disjoint, written $h_1 \perp h_2$, when their underlying maps have disjoint domains. The union of two heaps, written $h_1 + h_2$, returns the union of the two underlying finite maps. We are only concerned with disjoint unions here, so it does not matter how the map union operator is defined for maps with overlapping domains.

Using those basic operations on heaps, one can define predicates for specifying heaps in the style of Separation Logic, as is done for example in Ynot [10]. Heap predicates are simply predicates over values of type Heap, so they have the type Heap $\rightarrow$ Prop, abbreviated as Hprop. A singleton heap that binds a non-null location l to a value V of type $\mathcal{T}$ is characterized by the predicate $l \hookrightarrow_{\mathcal{T}} V$, which is defined as $\lambda h.\ l \neq \mathsf{null} \wedge h = (l \rightarrow_{\mathcal{T}} V)$. The heap predicate $H_1 * H_2$ holds of a disjoint union of a heap satisfying H_1 and of a heap satisfying H_2. It is defined as $\lambda h.\ \exists h_1\, h_2.\ h_1 \perp h_2 \ \wedge\ h = h_1 + h_2 \ \wedge\ H_1\, h_1 \ \wedge\ H_2\, h_2$.

In order to describe local invariants of data structures, propositions are lifted as heap predicates. More precisely, the predicate $[\mathcal{P}]$ holds of an empty heap if the proposition $\mathcal{P}$ is true. So, $[\mathcal{P}]$ is defined as $\lambda h.\ \mathcal{P} \wedge h = \varnothing$. In particular, the empty heap is characterized by the predicate $[\,]$, which is short for [True]. Similarly, existential quantifiers are lifted: $\exists x.\, H$ holds of a heap h if there exists a value x such that H holds of that heap[2].

The present work ignores the disjunction construct ($H_1 \vee H_2$). To reason on the content of the heap by case analysis, we instead rely on heap predicates of the form "if P then H_1 else H_2", which are defined using the builtin conditional construct from classical logic. The present work also does not make use of non-separating conjunction ($H_1 \wedge H_2$). It therefore does not include the rule of conjunction, which can be found in a number of formalizations of Separation Logic. From a pratical perspective, we never felt the need for the conjunction rule. From a theoretical perspective, the conjunction rule is not needed for characteristic formulae to achieve completeness. (It is not yet known whether characteristic formulae would be able to accomodate the conjunction rule or not.)

Reasoning about heaps is generally conducted in terms of an entailment relation, written $H_1 \rhd H_2$, which asserts that any heap satisfying H_1 also satisfies H_2. It is defined as $\forall h.\ H_1\, h \Rightarrow H_2\, h$. Similarly, an entailment relation is provided for post-conditions. It is written $Q_1 \blacktriangleright Q_2$ and defined as $\forall x.\ Q_1\, x \rhd Q_2\, x$. A number of lemmas (not shown) allow reasoning about heap entailment without having to unfold the definition of this relation. Moreover, several tactics are provided to automate the application of these lemmas. As a result, apart from the setting up of the core definition and lemmas in the CFML library, the proofs never refer to objects of type Heap directly: program verification is carried out solely in terms of heap predicates of type Hprop (like done, e.g., in Ynot [10]).

Observe that the Separation Logic used here is not intuitionistic. In general, the entailment $H_1 * H_2 \rhd H_1$ is false. (It only holds when H_2 describes an empty heap.) With an intuitionistic Separation Logic, one may discard pieces of heap at any time during the reasoning on heap entailment. Here, garbage collection is instead modelled by having an explicit garbage heap mentioned in the definition of the predicate local, as described next.

3.5 Local predicates

In the introduction, we suggested how to define the predicate transformer "local" to account for applications of the frame rule. We now present the general definition of this predicate, a definition that also accounts for the rule of consequence and for the rule of garbage collection. Moreover, it supports the extraction of propositions and existentially-quantified variables from pre-conditions. We also introduce a predicate, called "islocal", that is useful for manipulating formulae of the form "local $\mathcal{F}$".

The predicate local applies to a formula $\mathcal{F}$ with a type of the form Hprop $\rightarrow$ ($A \rightarrow$ Hprop) $\rightarrow$ Prop, for some type A. Its definition is:

$$\begin{aligned}\mathsf{local}\,\mathcal{F} \ \equiv\ \lambda H\, Q.\ \forall h.\ H\, h \Rightarrow \exists H_1\, H_2\, H_3\, Q_1.\\ (H_1 * H_2)\, h \ \wedge\ \mathcal{F}\, H_1\, Q_1 \ \wedge\ Q_1 \star H_2 \blacktriangleright Q \star H_3\end{aligned}$$

where H describes the initial heap, H_1 corresponds to the part of the heap with which the formula $\mathcal{F}$ is concerned, H_2 corresponds to the part of the heap that is being framed out, H_3 corresponds to the part of the heap that gets discarded, Q describes the final result and final heap, and Q_1 is such that Q is equivalent to $Q_1 \star H_2$. (Recall that the latter is defined as $\lambda x.\ Q_1\, x * H_2$.) Note that the definition of the predicate local shows some similarities with the definition of the "STsep" monad from Hoare Type Theory [32], in the sense that both aim at baking the Separation Logic frame condition into a system originally defined in terms of heaps describing the whole memory.

One can prove that the predicate local may be safely discarded during reasoning, in the sense that "$\mathcal{F}\, H\, Q$" is a sufficient condition for proving "local $\mathcal{F}\, H\, Q$". Another useful property of the predicate local is its idempotence: for any predicate $\mathcal{F}$, the predicate "local $\mathcal{F}$" is equivalent to the predicate "local (local $\mathcal{F}$)". Other properties of local can be expressed in terms of a predicate called islocal, defined as:

$$\mathsf{islocal}\,\mathcal{F} \quad \equiv \quad (\mathcal{F} = \mathsf{local}\,\mathcal{F})$$

This definition asserts that the predicate $\mathcal{F}$ is extensionally equivalent to "local $\mathcal{F}$". In such a case, the formula $\mathcal{F}$ is called a *local* formula. Note that "islocal (local $\mathcal{F}$)" is true for any $\mathcal{F}$.

Now, assuming that $\mathcal{F}$ is a local formula, all the reasoning rules shown in Figure 2 can be exploited. The interest of introducing the predicates islocal is that it conveniently allows us to apply any of the reasoning rules from Figure 2, an arbitrary number of times,

[2] The formal definition for existentials properly handles binders. It actually takes the form hexists J, where J is a predicate. Formally:
hexists (A : Type) ($J : A \rightarrow$ Hprop) $\equiv \lambda(h : \mathsf{Heap}).\ \exists(x : A).\ J\, x\, h$.

FRAME :	$\mathcal{F}\,H\,Q \;\Rightarrow\; \mathcal{F}\,(H * H')\,(Q \star H')$
GC-PRE :	$\mathcal{F}\,H\,Q \;\Rightarrow\; \mathcal{F}\,(H * H')\,Q$
GC-POST :	$\mathcal{F}\,H\,(Q \star H') \;\Rightarrow\; \mathcal{F}\,H\,Q$
CONSEQUENCE-PRE :	$\mathcal{F}\,H\,Q \;\wedge\; H' \rhd H \;\Rightarrow\; \mathcal{F}\,H'\,Q$
CONSEQUENCE-POST :	$\mathcal{F}\,H\,Q \;\wedge\; Q \blacktriangleright Q' \;\Rightarrow\; \mathcal{F}\,H\,Q'$
EXTRACT-PROP :	$(\mathcal{P} \Rightarrow \mathcal{F}\,H\,Q) \;\Rightarrow\; \mathcal{F}\,([\mathcal{P}] * H)\,Q$
EXTRACT-EXISTS :	$(\forall x.\ \mathcal{F}\,H\,Q) \;\Rightarrow\; \mathcal{F}\,(\exists x.\,H)\,Q$

Figure 2. Reasoning rules applicable to a *local* formula $\mathcal{F}$

$$
\begin{array}{l}
[\![\hat{v}]\!] \;\equiv \\
\quad \mathsf{local}\,(\lambda HQ.\ H \rhd Q\,\lceil \hat{v} \rceil) \\
[\![\hat{v}_1\,\hat{v}_2]\!] \;\equiv \\
\quad \mathsf{local}\,(\lambda HQ.\ \mathsf{App}\,\lceil \hat{v}_1 \rceil\,\lceil \hat{v}_2 \rceil\,H\,Q) \\
[\![\mathsf{let}\,x = \hat{t}_1\,\mathsf{in}\,\hat{t}_2]\!] \;\equiv \\
\quad \mathsf{local}\,(\lambda HQ.\ \exists Q'.\ [\![\hat{t}_1]\!]\,H\,Q' \wedge\ \forall x.\ [\![\hat{t}_2]\!]\,(Q'\,x)\,Q) \\
[\![\hat{t}_1\,;\,\hat{t}_2]\!] \;\equiv \\
\quad \mathsf{local}\,(\lambda HQ.\ \exists Q'.\ [\![\hat{t}_1]\!]\,H\,Q' \wedge\ [\![\hat{t}_2]\!]\,(Q'\,tt)\,Q) \\
[\![\mathsf{let\,rec}\,f = \Lambda\overline{A}.\lambda x.\hat{t}_1\,\mathsf{in}\,\hat{t}_2]\!] \;\equiv \\
\quad \mathsf{local}\,(\lambda HQ.\ \forall f.\ \mathcal{H} \Rightarrow [\![\hat{t}_2]\!]\,H\,Q) \\
\qquad \mathsf{with}\ \mathcal{H} \equiv \forall \overline{A} x H' Q'.\ [\![\hat{t}_1]\!]\,H'\,Q' \Rightarrow \mathsf{App}\,f\,x\,H'\,Q' \\
[\![\mathsf{if}\,\hat{v}\,\mathsf{then}\,\hat{t}_1\,\mathsf{else}\,\hat{t}_2]\!] \;\equiv \\
\quad \mathsf{local}\,(\lambda HQ.\quad (\lceil \hat{v} \rceil = \mathsf{true} \Rightarrow [\![\hat{t}_1]\!]\,H\,Q) \\
\qquad\qquad\qquad \wedge\ (\lceil \hat{v} \rceil = \mathsf{false} \Rightarrow [\![\hat{t}_2]\!]\,H\,Q)) \\
[\![\mathsf{crash}]\!] \;\equiv \\
\quad \mathsf{local}\,(\lambda HQ.\ \mathsf{False}) \\
[\![\mathsf{let}\,x = \Lambda\overline{A}.\,\hat{v}\,\mathsf{in}\,\hat{t}]\!] \;\equiv \\
\quad \mathsf{local}\,(\lambda HQ.\ \forall x.\ x = \lambda\overline{A}.\lceil \hat{v} \rceil \Rightarrow [\![\hat{t}]\!]\,H\,Q)
\end{array}
$$

Figure 3. Generation of characteristic formulae

and in any order. Moreover, the predicate islocal plays a key role in the characteristic formulae of for-loops and while-loops (see §3.7).

3.6 Characteristic formula construction

We are now ready to describe the algorithm for constructing characteristic formulae. The characteristic formula of a typed term $\hat{t}$ is written $[\![\hat{t}]\!]$. If $\hat{t}$ admits the weak-ML type T, then the formula $[\![\hat{t}]\!]$ has type $\mathsf{Hprop} \to ([\![T]\!] \to \mathsf{Hprop}) \to \mathsf{Prop}$. Recall that Hprop is an abbreviation for $\mathsf{Heap} \to \mathsf{Prop}$. The rules for constructing characteristic formulae appear in Figure 3. Before describing each rule individually, two observations are worth making about the figure. First, every definition starts with an application of the predicate local. The presence of this predicate at every node of a characteristic formula enables us to apply any of the reasoning rules from Figure 2 at any point during the verification of a program. Second, all the program values get translated into Coq values. This is done through applications of the decoding operator, written $\lceil \hat{v} \rceil$.

The first rule from Figure 3 states that a value v admits a pre-condition H and a post-condition Q if the current heap, which is described by H, also satisfies the predicate $Q\,\lceil \hat{v} \rceil$. The characteristic formula of an application is obtained directly by applying the special predicate App. The treatment of let-bindings has already been explained in the introduction. The case of a sequence is a specialized version of that of let-bindings, where the result of the first term is always the unit value (written tt).

The treatment of functions has also already been explained, except for the treatment of polymorphism. A polymorphic function is written "let rec $f = \Lambda\overline{A}.\lambda x.\hat{t}_1$", where $\overline{A}$ denotes the list of type variables involved in the type-checking of the body of the function. The type variables from the list $\overline{A}$ are quantified in the hypothesis $\mathcal{H}$ provided by the characteristic formula for reasoning about the body of the function. Here again, the type variables are given the kind Type in Coq. Note that, in weak-ML, a polymorphic function admits the type func, just like any other function. So, the variable f admits in Coq the type Func.

To show that a conditional of the form "if v then t_1 else t_2" admits a given specification, one needs to prove that t_1 admits that specification when v is true and that t_2 admits that same specification when v is false. The definition of the characteristic formula of the instruction crash, which corresponds to a dead branch in the code, requires the programmer to prove that this point in the code can never be reached. This is equivalent to showing that the set of assumptions accumulated before reaching this point contains a logical inconsistency, i.e., that False is derivable.

The last definition from Figure 3 is slightly more technical. A polymorphic let-binding takes the form "let $x = \Lambda\overline{A}.\,\hat{v}$ in $\hat{t}$", where $\hat{v}$ is a polymorphic value with free type variables $\overline{A}$. If $\hat{v}$ has type T, then the program variable x has type $\forall\overline{A}.T$. The characteristic formula associated with this let-binding quantifies over a Coq variable x of type $\forall\overline{A}.[\![T]\!]$, and it provides the assumption that x is the Coq value that corresponds to the program value $\hat{v}$. This assumption is stated through an extensional equality, written $x = \lambda\overline{A}.\lceil \hat{v} \rceil$. This equality implies that, for any list of weak-ML types $\overline{U}$, the application "$x\,[\![\overline{U}]\!]$" yields the Coq value that corresponds to the program value $\lceil \overline{A} \to \overline{U} \rceil\,\hat{v}$.

This completes the description of Figure 3. The characteristic formulae of loops are explained in the next section. The treatment of n-ary functions, mutually-recursive functions, assertions and pattern matching could not be described in this paper due to space limitations. This material can be found in the author's dissertation [8].

For each construction of the programming language, a custom Coq notation is defined for pretty-printing it in a way that resembles the source code. We have already seen how to pretty-print formulae for let-bindings. Additional examples concerning values, applications and function definitions are shown below.

$$
\begin{array}{l}
(\mathbf{ret}\ V) \;\equiv\; \mathsf{local}\,(\lambda HQ.\ H \rhd Q\,V) \\
(\mathbf{app}\ V_1\ V_2) \;\equiv\; \mathsf{local}\,(\lambda HQ.\ \mathsf{App} V_1 V_2 H Q) \\
(\mathbf{let\ rec} f = (\mathbf{fun}\ \overline{A}\,x := \mathcal{F}_1)\ \mathbf{in}\ \mathcal{F}_2) \;\equiv\; \mathsf{local}\,(\lambda HQ. \\
\qquad \forall f.\ (\forall \overline{A} x H' Q'.\ \mathcal{F}_1\,H'\,Q' \Rightarrow \mathsf{App}\,f\,x\,H'\,Q') \Rightarrow \mathcal{F}_2\,H\,Q)
\end{array}
$$

Finally, consider the specification of the functions for manipulating references:

$$
\begin{array}{ll}
\forall A\,v. & \mathsf{App}\,\mathsf{ref}\,v\,[\,]\,(\lambda r.\ r \hookrightarrow_A v) \\
\forall A\,r\,v. & \mathsf{App}\,\mathsf{get}\,r\,(r \hookrightarrow_A v)\,(\lambda x.\ [x = v] * r \hookrightarrow_A v) \\
\forall A\,A'\,r\,v\,v'. & \mathsf{App}\,\mathsf{set}\,(r, v)\,(r \hookrightarrow_{A'} v')\,(\lambda\_.\ r \hookrightarrow_A v) \\
\forall r\,r'. & \mathsf{App}\,\mathsf{cmp}\,(r, r')\,[\,]\,(\lambda x.\ [x = \mathsf{true} \Leftrightarrow r = r'])
\end{array}
$$

Above, the functions being specified have type Func, v has type A, v' has type A', and r and r' have type Loc. Observe that the specification of set allows for strong updates, that is, for changes in the type of the content of a reference cell.

3.7 Characteristic formulae for loops

Since the source language already contains recursive functions, there is, from a theoretical perspective, no need do discuss the treatment of loops. That said, loops admit direct characteristic formulae whose use greatly shortens verification proof scripts in practice. To understand the characteristic formula of a while loop, it is useful to first study an example.

Consider the term "while (get $r > 0$) do (decr r ; incr s)", and call this term t. Let us prove that, for any non-negative integer n and any integer m, the term t admits the pre-condition "$(r \hookrightarrow n) * (s \hookrightarrow m)$" and the post-condition "$(r \hookrightarrow 0) * (s \hookrightarrow m + n)$". We can prove this statement by induction on n. According to the semantics of a while loop, the term t admits the same semantics as the term "if (get $r > 0$) then (decr r ; incr s ; t) else tt". If the content of r is zero, then n is equal to zero, and it is straightforward to check that the pre-condition matches the post-condition. Otherwise, the decrement and increment functions are called, and the state after their execution is described as "$(r \hookrightarrow n - 1) * (s \hookrightarrow m + 1)$". At this point, we need to reason about the nested occurrence of t, that is, about the subsequent iterations of the loop. To that end, we invoke the induction hypothesis and derive the post-condition "$(r \hookrightarrow 0) * (s \hookrightarrow (m + 1) + (n - 1))$", which matches the required post-condition.

This example illustrates how the reasoning about a while loop is equivalent to the reasoning about a conditional whose first branch ends with a call to the same while loop. The characteristic formula of "while t_1 do t_2" builds upon this idea. It involves a quantification over an abstract variable R, which denotes the semantics of the while loop, in the sense that $R\,H'\,Q'$ holds if and only if the loop admits H' as pre-condition and Q' as post-condition. The main assumption provided about R states that, to establish the proposition $R\,H'\,Q'$ for a particular H' and Q', it suffices to prove that the term "if t_1 then (t_2 ; while t_1 do t_2) else tt" admits H' as pre-condition and Q' as post-condition. This latter statement is expressed with the help of the notation introduced for pretty-printing characteristic formulae. The characteristic formula for while loops is therefore as follows. (The role of the hypothesis "islocal R" is explained afterwards.)

$$\begin{array}{l} [\![\mathsf{while}\ \hat{t}_1\ \mathsf{do}\ \hat{t}_2]\!] \ \equiv \\ \quad \mathsf{local}\,(\lambda HQ.\ \ \forall R.\ \mathsf{islocal}\ R \wedge \mathcal{H} \Rightarrow R\,H\,Q) \\ \mathsf{with}\ \mathcal{H} \equiv \forall H'Q'. \\ \quad (\mathbf{if}\ [\![\hat{t}_1]\!]\ \mathbf{then}\ ([\![\hat{t}_2]\!]\,;R)\ \mathbf{else\ ret}\ tt)\ H'\,Q' \ \Rightarrow\ R\,H'\,Q' \end{array}$$

With the characteristic formula shown above, the verification of a while-loop can be conducted by induction on any well-founded relation. CFML also provides tactics to address the typical case where the proof is conducted using a loop invariant and a termination measure.

To reflect the fact that the predicate R supports application of the frame rule as if it were a characteristic formula, the definition shown above provides the assumption that R is a local formula. For example, this assumption would be useful for reasoning about the traversal of an imperative list using a while-loop. At every iteration of this loop, one cell is traversed. This cell may be framed out from the reasoning about the subsequent iterations, thanks to the assumption "islocal R". Such an application of the frame rule makes it possible to verify the list trasversal using only the simple list representation predicate, avoiding the need to involve the list-segment representation predicate. A similar observation about the usefulness of applying the frame rule during the execution of a loop was also recently made by Tuerk [41].

The characteristic formula of a for-loop is somewhat similar to that of a while-loop. The main difference is that the predicate R is replaced with a predicate S which takes as extra argument the current value of the loop counter, here named i. The definition is:

$$\begin{array}{l} [\![\mathsf{for}\ i = \hat{v}_1\ \mathsf{to}\ \hat{v}_2\ \mathsf{do}\ \hat{t}]\!] \ \equiv \\ \quad \mathsf{local}\,(\lambda HQ.\forall S.\ (\forall i.\,\mathsf{islocal}\,(S\,i)) \wedge \mathcal{H} \Rightarrow S\,\lceil \hat{v}_1 \rceil\,H\,Q) \\ \mathsf{with}\ \mathcal{H} \equiv \forall i H'Q'. \\ (\mathbf{if}\ i \le \lceil \hat{v}_2 \rceil\ \mathbf{then}\ ([\![\hat{t}]\!]\,;S\,(i+1))\ \mathbf{else\ ret}\ tt)\ H'\,Q' \Rightarrow S\,i\,H'\,Q' \end{array}$$

3.8 Soundness and completeness

Characteristic formulae are both sound and complete. The soundness theorem states that if the characteristic formula of a program holds of some specification, then this program indeed satisfies that specification. More precisely, if the characteristic formula of a term t holds of a pre-condition H and a post-condition Q, then the execution of t, starting from a state h satisfying the pre-condition H, terminates and produces a value v in a final state h' such that the post-condition Q holds of v and h'. The semantics judgment involved here is written $\hat{t}_{/h} \Downarrow \hat{v}_{/h'}$. The formal statement shown below also takes into account the fact the final heap may contain some garbage values, which are gathered in a sub-heap called h''.

Theorem 3.1 (Soundness) *Let $\hat{t}$ be a well-typed, closed weak-ML term. Let H and Q be a pre- and a post-condition, and h be a heap.*

$$[\![\hat{t}]\!]\ H\ Q\ \wedge\ H\,h\ \Rightarrow\ \exists \hat{v}\,h'\,h''.\ \hat{t}_{/h} \Downarrow \hat{v}_{/(h'+h'')}\ \wedge\ Q\,\lceil \hat{v} \rceil\,h'$$

Above, H has type "Heap $\to$ Prop" and Q has type "$[\![T]\!] \to$ Heap $\to$ Prop", where T is the type of $\hat{t}$.

The completeness theorem asserts that, reciprocally, if a program admits a given specification, then it is possible to prove that the characteristic formula of this program holds of that specification. This completeness statement is, of course, relative to the expressiveness power of the logic of Coq. More precisely, the statement of completeness states the following: if one is able to establish, with respect to a deep embedding of the source language in Coq, that a given program terminates and produces a value satisfying a given post-condition, then it is possible to establish in Coq that the characteristic formula of this program holds of the given post-condition.

Due to space limitations, the present paper does not include the general statement of the completeness theorem, which involves the notion of most-general specification and that of typed reduction, but only a specialized version for the case of an ML program producing an integer result. This simplified statement reads as follows: if t is a closed ML program whose execution produces an integer n, then the characteristic formula of t holds of a pre-condition that characterizes the empty heap and of a post-condition asserting that the output value is exactly equal to n.

Theorem 3.2 (Completeness —particular case) *Let t be a closed ML term, and let $\hat{t}$ denote the corresponding weak-ML term. Let n be an integer and let h be a memory state. Then,*

$$t_{/\emptyset} \Downarrow n_{/h}\quad \Rightarrow\quad [\![\hat{t}]\!]\ [\,]\ (\lambda x.\,[x = n])$$

The completeness theorem is relative to the expressive power of Coq because the hypothesis $t_{/\emptyset} \Downarrow n_{/h}$ is interpreted as the statement of a fact provable in Coq. More precisely, this hypothesis asserts the existence of a Coq proof term witnessing the fact that the configuration $t_{/\emptyset}$ is related to the configuration $n_{/h}$ by the inductively-defined evaluation judgment ($\Downarrow$).

The proofs of the soundness and completeness theorems are quite involved. They amounts to about 30 pages of the author's PhD dissertation [8]. In addition to those paper-and-pencil proofs, we considered a simple imperative programming language (including while loops but no functions) and mechanized the theory of characteristic formulae for this language. More precisely, we formalized the syntax and semantics of this language, defined a characteristic formula generator for it, and then proved in Coq that the formulae produced by this generator are both sound and complete.

4. Examples

This section describes four examples. The first one is Dijsktra's shortest path algorithm. It illustrates how CFML supports the reasoning about modular code involving complex invariants. The other examples focus on the treatment of imperative first-class functions, covering a counter function with an abstract local state, Reynold's CPS-append function, and an iterator on imperative lists.

Conducting proofs using CFML involves two additional ingredients that have not yet been described. The first one is the predicate App_n, which generalizes the predicate App to n-ary applications. For example, "$\mathsf{App}_2\ f\ x\ y\ H\ Q$" asserts that the application of f to x and y admits H and Q as pre- and post-conditions. The predicate App_1 is the same as App, and the predicates App_n can be defined in terms of App_1.

The second key ingredient is the notion of a representation predicate. A heap predicate of the form $v \rightsquigarrow T\,V$ is used to relate the mutable data structure found at location v with the mathematical value V that it represents. Here, T is a representation predicate: it characterizes the relationship between v, V and the piece of memory state spanned by the data structure under consideration. In fact, $v \rightsquigarrow T\,V$ is simply defined as $T\,V\,v$, where T can be any predicate of type $A \to B \to \mathsf{Hprop}$. This section contains examples showing how to use and how to define representation predicates.

4.1 Dijkstra's shortest path

In this first example, describe the specification and verification of a particular implementation of Dijkstra's algorithm. This implementation uses a priority queue that does not support the decrease-key operation. Using such a queue makes the proofs slightly more involved, because the invariants need to account for the fact that the queue may contain superseded values. The algorithm involves three mutable data structures: v, an array of boolean used to mark the nodes for which the best distance is already known; b, an array of distances used to store the best know distance for every node (distances may be infinite); and q, a priority queue for efficiently identifying the next nodes to be visited.

The Caml source code is 20 lines long, and it is organized around a main while-loop. Inside the loop, the higher-order function List.iter is used for traversing an adjacency list. The implementation of the priority queue is left abstract: the source code is implemented as a Caml functor, whose argument corresponds to a priority queue module. Similarly, the verification script is implemented as a Coq functor. This functor expects two arguments: a module representing the implementation of the priority queue, and a module representing the proofs of correctness of that queue implementation. This strategy allows us to achieve modular verification of modular code.

The specification of the function dijkstra is as follows:

$$\begin{array}{l}\forall gxyG.\ \mathsf{nonnegative\_edges}\,G \wedge x \in \mathsf{nodes}\,G \wedge y \in \mathsf{nodes}\,G \\ \Rightarrow \mathsf{App}_3\ \mathsf{dijkstra}\ g\ x\ y\ (g \rightsquigarrow \mathsf{GraphAdjList}\,G) \\ \qquad\qquad (\lambda d.\ [d = \mathsf{dist}\,G\,x\,y] * (g \rightsquigarrow \mathsf{GraphAdjList}\,G))\end{array}$$

It states that if g is the location of a data structure that represents a mathematical graph G through adjacency lists, if the edges in G all have nonnegative weights, and if x and y are indices of two nodes from that graph, then the application of the function dijkstra to g, x and y returns a value d that is equal to the length of the shortest path between x and y in the graph G. Moreover, the above specification asserts that the structure of the graph is not modified by the execution of the function.

The representation predicate GraphAdjList is used to relate a mathematical graph with its representation as an array of lists of pairs. It is defined as:

$$\begin{array}{l}\mathsf{GraphAdjList}\,G\,g\ \equiv\ \exists N.\ (g \rightsquigarrow \mathsf{Array}\,N) * \\ \quad [\forall x.\ x \in \mathsf{nodes}\,G \Leftrightarrow x \in \mathsf{dom}\,N] * \\ \quad [\forall x \in \mathsf{nodes}.\ \forall yw.\ (x,y,w) \in \mathsf{edges}\,G \Leftrightarrow \mathsf{mem}(y,w)\,N[x]]\end{array}$$

Above, g denotes a value of type Loc, G denotes a mathematical graph whose nodes are indexed by integers and whose edges have integer weight, and N is a finite map from integers to lists of pairs of integers. The definition asserts that x is an index in N if and only if it is the index of a node in G, and that a pair (y, w) belongs to the list $N[x]$ if and only if the graph G has an edge of weight w between the nodes x and y.

The invariant of the main loop of Dijkstra's algorithm, written "$\mathsf{hinv}\ V\ B\ Q$" describes the state of the data structures in terms of three data structures: V is a finite map describing the array v, B is a finite map describing the array b, and Q is a multiset of pairs describing the priority queue q. Several logical invariants enforce constraints ocharacteristic formulae.n the content of V, B and Q. Those invariants are captured by a record of propositions, written "$\mathsf{inv}\ V\ B\ Q$". The definition of this record is not shown here but, for example, the first field of this record ensures that if $V[z]$ contains the value true then $B[z]$ contains exactly the length of the shortest path between the source x and the node z in the graph G. The heap description specifying the memory state at each iteration of the main loop therefore takes the following form.

$$\begin{array}{l}\mathsf{hinv}\ V\ B\ Q\ \equiv \\ \qquad (g \rightsquigarrow \mathsf{GraphAdjList}\,G) * (v \rightsquigarrow \mathsf{Array}\,V) \\ \qquad * (b \rightsquigarrow \mathsf{Array}\,B) * (q \rightsquigarrow \mathsf{Pqueue}\,Q) * [\mathsf{inv}\ V\ B\ Q]\end{array}$$

The proof that the function dijkstra satisfies its specification consists of two parts. The first part is concerned with a number of mathematical theorems that justify the method used by Dijkstra's algorithm for computing shortest paths. This part, which amounts to 180 lines of Coq scripts, is totally independent of characteristic formulae and would presumably be needed in any approach to program verification. The second part consists of one theorem, whose statement is the specification given earlier on, and whose purpose is to establish that the source code correctly implements Dijkstra's algorithm. The proof of this theorem follows the structure of the characteristic formula generated, and therefore also follows the structure of the source code.

Figure 4 show the beginning of the proof script for this verification theorem. The script contains three kind of tactics. First, x-tactics are used to make progress through the characteristic formula. For example, the tactic `xwhile_inv` is used to provide the loop invariant and the termination relation. Here, termination is justified by a lexicographical order whose first component is the size of the number of node treated (this number increases from zero up to the total number of nodes) and whose second component is the size of the priority queue. Second, general-purpose Coq tactics (all those whose name does not start with the letter "x") are typically used to name variables, unfold invariants, and discharge simple side-conditions. Third, the proof script contains invocations of the mathematical theorems mentioned earlier on. For example, the script contains a reference to the lemma `inv_start`, which justifies that the loop invariant holds at the first iteration of the loop. Overall, this verification proof contains a total of 48 lines, including 8 lines of statement of the invariants, and Coq is able to verify the proof in 8 seconds on a 3 GHz machine.

Figure 5 gives an example of a proof obligation that arises during the verification of the function dijkstra. The set of hypotheses appears above the dashed line. Observe that all the hypotheses are short and well-named. Those names are provided explicitly in the proof script. Providing names is not mandatory, however it generally helps to increase readability and robustness. The proof obligation appears below the dashed line. It consists of a characteristic formula being applied to a pre-condition and to a post-condition. Note that, in Coq, characteristic formula are pretty-printed using capitalized keywords instead of bold keywords and the sequence operator is written "`;;`".

```
xcf. introv Pos Ns De. unfold GraphAdjList at 1.
hdata_simpl. xextract as N Neg Adj. xapp. intros Ln.
rewrite <- Ln in Neg. xapps. xapps. xapps.
xapps. set (data := fun B V Q => g ~> Array N \*
  v ~> Array V \* b ~> Array B \* q ~> Heap Q).
set (hinv := fun VQ => let '(V,Q) := VQ in Hexists B,
  data B V Q \* [inv G n s V B Q (crossing G s V)]).
xseq (fun _ => Hexists V, hinv (V,\)).
set (W := lexico2 (binary_map (count (= true)) (upto n))
                  (binary_map card (downto 0))).
xwhile_inv W hinv.
(* -- initial state satisfies the invariant -- *)
refine (ex_intro' (_,_)). unfold hinv,data. hsimpl.
 applys_eq inv_start 2. permut_simpl.
(* -- verification of the loop -- *)
intros [V Q]. unfold hinv. xextract as B Inv. xwhilebody.
```

Figure 4. Beginning of the proof script for Dijkstra's algorithm

```
Pos : nonnegative_edges G
Ns : s \in nodes G
Ne : e \in nodes G
Neg : nodes_index G n
Adj : forall x y w : int, x \in nodes G ->
      Mem (y, w) (N\(x)) = has_edge G x y w
Nx : x \in nodes G
Vx : ~ V\(x)
Dx : Finite dx = dist G s x
Inv : inv G n s V' B Q (new_crossing G s x L' V)
EQ : N\(x) = rev L' ++ (y, w) :: L
Ew : has_edge G x y w
Ny : y \in nodes G
-------------------------------------------------(1/6)
(Let dy := Ret (dx + w) in
  Let fy := App ml_array_get b y ; in
   If Match
       (Case fy = Finite d [d] Then Ret (dy < d) Else
       (Case fy = Infinite Then Ret true Else Done))
   Then (App ml_array_set b y (Finite dy) ;) ;;
          App push (y, dy) h ; Else (Ret tt))
(q ~> Pqueue Q \* b ~> Array B \*
  v ~> Array V' \* g ~> Array N)
(fun _:unit => hinv' L)
```

Figure 5. Example of a proof obligation

4.2 Counter function

This example illustrates the treatment of functions with an abstract local state. A counter function is a function that, every time it is called, returns the successor of the integer that it returned on the previous call. The function create constructs a new counter function. It allocates a fresh reference r with initial contents 0, and builds a function whose body increments r and returns its contents.

$$\text{create} \;\equiv\; \lambda\_.\ \text{let}\, r = \text{ref}\,0\,\text{in}\,(\lambda\_.\ (\text{incr}\,r\,;\ \text{get}\,r))$$

To specify the function create in an abstract manner, we use a representation predicate, called Cntr. The heap predicate "$f \leadsto \text{Cntr}\,n$" asserts that f is a counter function whose last call returned the value n. The definition of Cntr involves an existential quantification over a predicate I of type "int $\rightarrow$ Hprop", as shown below:

$$\text{Cntr}\,n\,f \;\equiv\; \exists I.\,(I\,n) * [\forall m.\ \text{App}_1\,f\,tt\,(I\,m)\,(\lambda x.\,[x = m+1] * I\,(m+1))]$$

The existential quantification of I allows us to state that a call to the counter function f takes the counter from a state "$I\,m$" to a state "$I\,(m+1)$" and returns the value $m+1$, without revealing any details of the implementation of this counter function.

The function create is then specified as producing a function f that is a counter with internal state 0.

$$\text{App}\,\text{create}\,tt\,[\,]\,(\lambda f.\,f \leadsto \text{Cntr}\,0)$$

This specification is sufficient for reasoning about all the calls to a counter function produced by the function create. That said, we can go even further in terms of abstraction. Instead of forcing the client of the function create to manipulate the definition of Cntr, we can make the definition of the predicate Cntr completely abstract and instead provide a direct lemma for reasoning about calls to counter functions. This lemma takes the following form:

$$\forall f n.\ \text{App}\,f\,tt\,(f \leadsto \text{Cntr}\,n)\,(\lambda x.\,[x = n{+}1] * f \leadsto \text{Cntr}\,(n{+}1))$$

This example illustrates how the abstract local state of a function can be entirely packed into a representation predicate.

4.3 Continuations

The CPS-append function has been proposed as a verification challenge by Reynolds [39], for testing the ability to specify and reason about continuations that are used in a nontrivial way. The CPS-append function takes as an argument two lists x and y, as well as an initial continuation k. In the end, the function calls the continuation k on the concatenation of this lists x and y. What makes this function nontrivial is that it does not build the list $x{+\!\!+}y$ explicitly. Instead, the function calls itself recursively using a different continuation at every iteration. The nested execution of those continuations starts from the list y and eventually produces the list $x{+\!\!+}y$. This list is then passed as an argument to the original continuation k. The code of the CPS-append function is:

```
let rec cpsapp (x y:'a list) (k:'a list->'b) : 'b =
  match x with
  | [] -> k y
  | v::x' -> cpsapp x' y (fun z -> k (v::z))
```

Its specification is as follows, where k has type Func, x and y have type "list$A$", and $+\!\!+$ denotes the concatenation of two Coq lists:

$$\forall AxykHQ.\ \text{App}_1\,k\,(x{+\!\!+}y)\,H\,Q \;\Rightarrow\; \text{App}_3\,\text{cpsapp}\,x\,y\,k\,H\,Q$$

Slightly more challenging is the verification of the imperative counterpart of the CPS-append function. It is based on the same principle as the purely-functional version, except that x and y are now pointers to mutable lists and that the continuations mutate pointers in the list x in order to build the concatenation of the two lists in place. The specification of this imperative version is:

$$\forall AxykLMHQ.\ (\forall z.\ \text{App}_1\,k\,z\,(H * (z \leadsto \text{Mlist}\,(L{+\!\!+}M)))\,Q) \Rightarrow \text{App}_3\,\text{cpsapp'}\,x\,y\,k\,(H * (x \leadsto \text{Mlist}\,L) * (y \leadsto \text{Mlist}\,M))\,Q$$

Above, the pre-condition asserts that the locations x and y (of type Loc) correspond to lists called L and M, respectively. The pre-condition also mentions an abstract heap predicate H, which is needed because the frame rule usually does not apply when reasoning about CPS functions. Indeed, the entire heap needs to be passed on to the continuation[3]. The continuation k is ultimately called on a location z that corresponds to the list $L{+\!\!+}M$. The proof that the imperative CPS-append function satisfies its specification is conducted by induction on L. It is only 8 lines long.

4.4 Imperative list iterator

This last example requires a generalized version of the representation predicate for lists. So far, we have used heap predicates of the form $m \leadsto \text{Mlist}\,L$. This works well when the values in the list are of some base type, however in general the values stored in the list

[3] Thielecke [40] suggested that answer-type polymorphism could be used to design reasoning rules that would save the need for quantifying over the heap H passed on to the continuation. However, his technique has limitations, in particular it does not support recursion through the store.

need to be described using their own representation predicate, call it T. To that end, we use a more general parametric representation predicate, written $\mathsf{Mlistof}\, T$. (The predicate Mlist used so far can be obtained as the application of $\mathsf{Mlistof}$ to the identity representation predicate, which is defined as "$\lambda X.\, \lambda x.\, [x = X]$".) For example, we will later use the heap predicate "$m \rightsquigarrow \mathsf{Mlistof}\,\mathsf{Cntr}\, L$" to describe a mutable list that starts at location m and contains a list of counter functions whose internal states are described by the integer values from the Coq list L.

We are now ready to describe the specification of an higher-order iterator on mutable lists. This iterator, called iter, is implemented using a while loop. The execution of "$\mathsf{iter}\, f\, m$" results in the function f being applied to all the values stored in the list whose head is located as address m. This execution may result in two effects. First, it may modify the values stored in the list. Second, it may affect the state of other mutable data structures. Thus, if the initial state is described as $H * (m \rightsquigarrow \mathsf{Mlistof}\, T\, L)$, then the final state generally takes the form $H' * (m \rightsquigarrow \mathsf{Mlistof}\, T\, L')$, where H and H' are two heap descriptions and L and L' are two Coq lists. To introduce some abstraction, we use a predicate called I. The intention is that the proposition $I\, L\, L'\, H\, H'$ captures the fact that, for any m, the term "$\mathsf{iter}\, f\, m$" admits the pre-condition $H * (m \rightsquigarrow \mathsf{Mlistof}\, T\, L)$ and the post-condition $\lambda\_.\ H' * (m \rightsquigarrow \mathsf{Mlistof}\, T\, L')$.

Two assumptions are provided for reasoning about the predicate I. The first one concerns the case where the list is empty. In this case, both L and L' are empty, and H' must match H. The second one concerns the case where the list is not empty. In this case, a call to f is first performed and then a recursive call to the function iter is made. The initial state of the list is then of the form $X :: L$ and the final state is of the form $X' :: L'$. The values X and X' are related by the specification of the function f. This specification also relates the input state H with an intermediate state H'', which corresponds to the state after the call to f and before the recursive call to iter. The formal statement of the assumptions about I are:

$$\begin{array}{lll} \mathcal{H}_1 & \equiv & \forall H.\ I\, \mathsf{nil}\, \mathsf{nil}\, H\, H \\ \mathcal{H}_2 & \equiv & \forall X X' L L' H H' H''. \\ & & (\forall x.\ \mathsf{App}_1\, f\, x\, (H * x \rightsquigarrow T\, X)\, (H'' * x \rightsquigarrow T\, X')) \\ & & \wedge\ I\, L\, L'\, H''\, H' \quad \Rightarrow\ I\, (X :: L)\, (X' :: L')\, H\, H' \end{array}$$

Above, L and L' have type $\mathsf{list}A$, f has type Func, X has type A, x has type B, and T has type $A \to B \to \mathsf{Hprop}$.

To establish that the term "$\mathsf{iter}\, f\, m$" admits the pre-condition $H * (m \rightsquigarrow \mathsf{Mlistof}\, T\, L)$ and the post-condition $\lambda\_.\ H' * (m \rightsquigarrow \mathsf{Mlistof}\, T\, L')$, it suffices to prove the proposition $I\, L\, L'\, H\, H'$, where I is an abstract predicate for which only the assumptions $\mathcal{H}_1$ and $\mathcal{H}_2$ are provided. This result is captured by the specification of iter shown next:

$$\begin{array}{l} \forall A B T f m L L' H H'.\ (\forall I.\ \mathcal{H}_1 \wedge \mathcal{H}_2 \Rightarrow I\, L\, L'\, H\, H') \\ \quad \Rightarrow\ \mathsf{App}_2\, \mathsf{iter}\, f\, m\, (H * (m \rightsquigarrow \mathsf{Mlistof}\, T\, L)) \\ \qquad\qquad\qquad (\lambda\_.\ H' * (m \rightsquigarrow \mathsf{Mlistof}\, T\, L')) \end{array}$$

To check the usability of this specification, we describe an example, which involves a list m of distinct counter functions (as defined in §4.2). The idea is to make a call to each of those counters. The results of those calls are simply ignored. What matters here is that every counter sees its current state incremented by one. The function steps implements this scenario.

$$\mathsf{steps} \quad \equiv \quad \lambda m.\ \mathsf{iter}\, (\lambda f.\, \mathsf{ignore}\, (f\, tt))\, m$$

The heap predicate "$m \rightsquigarrow \mathsf{Mlistof}\,\mathsf{Cntr}\, L$" asserts that the mutable list starting at location m contains a list of counter functions whose internal states are described by the integer values from the Coq list L. A call to the function steps on the list m increments the internal state of every counter, so the the final state is described by the heap predicate "$m \rightsquigarrow \mathsf{Mlistof}\,\mathsf{Cntr}\, L'$", where L' is obtained by adding one to all the elements in L. Thus, steps is specified as:

$$\begin{array}{l} \forall m L.\ \mathsf{App}_1\, \mathsf{steps}\, m\, (m \rightsquigarrow \mathsf{Mlistof}\,\mathsf{Cntr}\, L) \\ \qquad\qquad (\lambda\_.\ m \rightsquigarrow \mathsf{Mlistof}\,\mathsf{Cntr}\, (\mathsf{map}\, (+1)\, L)) \end{array}$$

This example demonstrates the ability of CFML to formally verify the application of a polymorphic higher-order iterator to an imperative list of first-class functions with abstract local state.

5. Related work

Program logics A program logic consists of a specification language and of a set of reasoning rules that can be used to establish that a program satisfies a specification. Program logics do not directly provide an effective program verification tool, but they may serve as a basis for justifying the correctness of such a tool. Hoare logic [17] is probably the most well-known program logic. Separation Logic [39] is an extension of Hoare logic that supports local reasoning. A number of verification tools have been built upon ideas from Separation Logic, for example Smallfoot [5]. Separation Logic frequently been exploited inside standard interactive proof assistants (e.g., [1, 10, 26, 27, 30]), including the present paper. Dynamic Logic [15] is another program logic. In this modal logic, the formula "$H_1 \to \langle t \rangle\, H_2$" asserts that, in any heap satisfying H_1, the sequence of commands t terminates and produces a heap satisfying H_2. Dynamic Logic serves as the foundation of the KeY system [4], which targets the verification of Java programs. One problem with Dynamic Logics is that they depart from standard mathematical logic, precluding the use of a standard proof assistant.

The aforementioned logics usually do not support reasoning about higher-order functions. A program logic supporting them has been developed by Honda, Berger and Yoshida [6]. The specification language of Honda *et al*'s logic is a nonstandard first-order logic, which features an ad-hoc construction, called *evaluation formula* and written $\{H\}\, v \bullet v' \searrow x\, \{H'\}$. This proposition asserts that under a heap satisfying H, the application of the value v to the value v' produces a result named x in a heap satisfying H'. This evaluation formula plays a similar role as that of the predicate App. Another specificity of the specification language is that its values are the values of the programming language, including non-terminating functions. This use of such a nonstandard specification language prevented Honda *et al* from building a practical verification tool on top of an existing theorem prover. In contrast, the characteristic formulae that we generate are expressed in terms of a standard higher-order logic predicates.

Verification condition generators A Verification Condition Generator (VCG) is a tool that, given a program annotated with its specification and its invariants, extracts a set of proof obligations that entails the correctness of the program. A large number of VCGs targeting various programming languages have been implemented in the last decades. For example, the Spec-# tool [2] parses annotated C# programs, and then produces proof obligations that can then be sent to an SMT solver. Because most SMT solvers can only cope with first-order logic, the specification language is usually restricted to this fragment, and therefore does not benefit from the expressiveness, modularity, and elegance of higher-order logic.

A few tools support higher-order logic. One notable example is the tool Why [12]. When the proof obligations produced by Why cannot be verified automatically by at an SMT solver, they can be discharged using an interactive proof assistant such as Coq. Recent work has focused on trying to extend Why with support for higher-order functions [20], building upon ideas developed for the tool Pangolin [38]. Another tool that supports higher-order logic is Jahob [42], which targets the verification of programs written in a subset of Java. For discharging proof obligations, Jahob relies on a translation from (a subset of) higher-order logic into first order logic, as well as on automated theorem provers extended with specialized decision procedures for reasoning on lists, trees, sets and maps. A key feature of Jahob is its *integrated proof language*, which allows the user to include proof hints directly inside the source code. Those hints are intended to guide automated theorem provers, in particular by indicating how to instantiate existential variables. When trying to verify complex programs, the central difficulty is to come up with the correct invariants, a process that usually requires a great number of iterations. With a VCG tool such as Why or Jahob, if the user changes, say, a local loop invariant, then he needs to run the VCG tool, wait for the SMT solvers to try and discharge the proof obligations, and then read the remaining obligations. On the contrary, with characteristic formulae, the user works in an interactive setting that provides nearly-instantaneous feedback on changes to the invariants.

Shallow embeddings The shallow embedding approach to program verification aims at relating a source program to a corresponding logical definition. The relationship can take three forms.

First, one can write a logical definition and use an extraction mechanism (e.g., [25]) to translate the code into a conventional programming language. For example, Leroy's certified C compiler [23] is developed in this way. Also based on extraction is the tool Ynot [10], which implements Hoare Type Theory (HTT) [33], by axiomatically extending the Coq language with a monad for encapsulating side effects and partial functions. HTT was also later re-implemented by Nanevski *et al* [34] without using any axioms, yet at the expense of loosing the ability to reason on higher-order stores. In HTT, the monad involved has a type of the form "$\mathsf{STsep}\,P\,Q$", and it correponds to a partial-correctness specification with pre-condition P and post-condition Q. Verification proofs take the form of Coq typing derivations for the source code. So, program verification is done at the same time as type-checking the source code. This is a significant difference with characteristic formulae, which allow verifying programs after they have been written, without requiring the source code to be modified in any way. Moreover, characteristic formulae are able to target an existing programming language, whereas the Ynot programming language has to fit into the logic it is implemented in. For example, supporting handy features such as alias-patterns and when-clauses would be a real challenge for Ynot. (Pattern matching is so deeply hard-wired in Coq that it would be very hard to modify it.)

Another technical difficulty faced by HTT is the treatment of auxiliary variables. A specification of the form "$\mathsf{STsep}\,P\,Q$" does not naturally allow for auxiliary variables to be used for sharing information between the pre- and the post-condition. Indeed, if P and Q both refer to a auxiliary variable x quantified outside of the type "$\mathsf{STsep}\,P\,Q$", then x is considered as a computationally-relevant value and thus it will appear in the extracted code. Ynot [10] relies on a hack for simulating the Implicit Calculus of Constructions [3], in which computationally-irrelevant value are tagged explicitly. A danger of this approach is that forgetting to tag a variable as auxiliary does not produce any warning yet results in the extracted code being inefficient. Other implementation of HTT have taken a different approach by relying on post-conditions that may also refer not only to the output heap but also to the input heap [33, 34]. The use of such *binary post-conditions* makes it possible to eliminate auxiliary variables by duplicating the pre-condition inside the post-condition. Typically, in informal notation, "$\forall x.\ \mathsf{STsep}\,P\,Q$" gets encoded as "$\mathsf{STsep}\,(\exists x.P)\,(\forall x.\,P\ \Rightarrow\ Q)$". HTT [34] then provides tactics to try and avoid the duplication of proof obligations. However, duplication typically remains visible in specifications, which is problematic. Indeed, specifications are part of the trusted base, so their statement should be as simple as possible.

The second way of relating a source program to a logical definition consists in decompiling a piece of conventional source code into a set of logical definitions. This approach is used in the LOOP compiler [19] and also in Myreen and Gordon's work [31]. The LOOP compiler takes Java programs and compiles them into PVS definitions. The proof tactics rely on a weakest-precondition calculus to achieve a high degree of automation. However, interactive proofs require a lot of expertise: LOOP requires the user to understand the compilation scheme involved [19]. By contrast, the tactics manipulating characteristic formulae allow conducting interactive proofs of correctness without detailed knowledge on the construction of those formulae. Myreen and Gordon showed how to decompile machine code into HOL4 functions [31]. The lemmas proved interactively about the generated HOL4 functions can then be automatically transformed into lemmas about the behavior of the corresponding pieces of machine code. Importantly, the translation into HOL4 is possible only because the functional translation of a while loop is a tail-recursive function, and because tail-recursive functions can be accepted as logical definitions in HOL4 without compromising the soundness of the logic even when the function is non-terminating. Without exploiting this peculiarity of tail-recursive functions, the automated translation of source code into HOL4 would not be possible. For this reason, it seems hard to apply this decompilation-based approach to the verification of code featuring general recursion and higher-order functions.

A third approach to using a shallow embedding consists in writing the program to be verified twice, once as a program definition and once as a logical definition, and then proving that the two are related. This approach has been employed in the verification of a microkernel as part of the Sel4 project [22]. Compared with Myreen and Gordon's work [29, 31], the main difference is that the low-level code is not decompiled automatically but instead decompiled by hand, and that this decompilation phase is then proved correct using semi-automated tactics. The Sel4 approach thus allows for more flexibility in the choice of the logical definitions, yet at the expense of a bigger investment from the user. Moreover, like in Myreen and Gordon's work, general recursion is problematic: all the code of the Sel4 microkernel written in the shallow embedding had to avoid any form of nontrivial recursion [21].

In summary, all approaches based on shallow embedding share one central difficulty: the need to overcome the discrepancies between the programming language and the logical language, in particular with respect to the treatment of imperative functions, partial functions, and recursive functions. In contrast, characteristic formulae rely on the first-order data type Func for representing functions. As established by the completeness theorem, this approach supports reasoning about all forms of first-class functions.

Deep embeddings A deep embedding consists of describing the syntax and the semantics of a programming language in the logic of a proof assistant, using inductive definitions. In theory, a deep embedding can be used to verify programs written in any programming language, without any restrictions in terms of expressiveness (apart from those of the proof assistant). Mehta and Nipkow [28] have set up the first proof-of-concept by formalizing a basic procedural language in Isabelle/HOL and proving Hoare-style reasoning rules correct with respect to the semantics of that language. More recently, Shao *et al* have developed the frameworks such as XCAP [35] for reasoning in Coq about short but complex assembly routines. In previous work [7], the author has worked on a deep embedding of the pure fragment of Caml inside the Coq proof assistant. This work then lead to the development of characteristic formulae, which can be viewed as an abstract layer built on top of a deep embedding: characteristic formulae hide the technical details associated with the explicit representation of syntax while retaining the high expressiveness of that approach. In particular, characteristic formulae avoid the explicit representation of syntax, which is associated with many technical difficulties (including the representation of binders). Moreover, when moving to characteristic formulae, specifications can be greatly simplified because program values such as tuples and functional lists become directly represented with their logical counterpart.

6. Conclusion

In this paper, we have explained how to build characteristic formulae for imperative programs, and we have shown how to use those formulae in practice to formally verify programs involving nontrivial interactions between first-class functions and mutable state.

References

[1] Andrew W. Appel. Tactics for separation logic. *Unpublished draft, http://www.cs.princeton.edu/appel/papers/septacs.pdf*, 2006.

[2] Mike Barnett, Rob DeLine, Manuel Fähndrich, K. Rustan M. Leino, and Wolfram Schulte. Verification of object-oriented programs with invariants. *Journal of Object Technology*, 3(6), 2004.

[3] Bruno Barras and Bruno Bernardo. The implicit calculus of constructions as a programming language with dependent types. In *FoSSaCS*, volume 4962 of *LNCS*, pages 365–379. Springer, 2008.

[4] Bernhard Beckert, Reiner Hähnle, and Peter H. Schmitt. *Verification of Object-Oriented Software: The KeY Approach*, volume 4334 of *LNCS*. Springer-Verlag, Berlin, 2007.

[5] Josh Berdine, Cristiano Calcagno, and Peter W. O'Hearn. Smallfoot: Modular automatic assertion checking with separation logic. In *International Symposium on Formal Methods for Components and Objects*, volume 4111 of *LNCS*, pages 115–137. Springer, 2005.

[6] Martin Berger, Kohei Honda, and Nobuko Yoshida. A logical analysis of aliasing in imperative higher-order functions. In *ICFP*, pages 280–293, 2005.

[7] Arthur Charguéraud. Verification of call-by-value functional programs through a deep embedding. 2009. Unpublished. http://arthur.chargueraud.org/research/2009/deep/.

[8] Arthur Charguéraud. *Characteristic Formulae for Mechanized Program Verification*. PhD thesis, Université Paris-Diderot, 2010.

[9] Arthur Charguéraud. Program verification through characteristic formulae. In *ICFP*, pages 321–332. ACM, 2010.

[10] Adam Chlipala, Gregory Malecha, Greg Morrisett, Avraham Shinnar, and Ryan Wisnesky. Effective interactive proofs for higher-order imperative programs. In *ICFP*, 2009.

[11] The Coq Development Team. *The Coq Proof Assistant Reference Manual, Version 8.2*, 2009.

[12] Jean-Christophe Filliâtre. Verification of non-functional programs using interpretations in type theory. *Journal of Functional Programming*, 13(4):709–745, 2003.

[13] Cormac Flanagan, Amr Sabry, Bruce F. Duba, and Matthias Felleisen. The essence of compiling with continuations. In *PLDI*, pages 237–247, 1993.

[14] Susanne Graf and Joseph Sifakis. A modal characterization of observational congruence on finite terms of CCS. *Information and Control*, 68(1-3):125–145, 1986.

[15] David Harel, Dexter Kozen, and Jerzy Tiuryn. *Dynamic Logic*. The MIT Press, Cambridge, Massachusetts, 2000.

[16] Matthew Hennessy and Robin Milner. On observing nondeterminism and concurrency. In *ICALP*, volume 85 of *LNCS*, pages 299–309. Springer-Verlag, 1980.

[17] C. A. R. Hoare. An axiomatic basis for computer programming. *Communications of the ACM*, 12(10):576–580, 583, 1969.

[18] Kohei Honda, Martin Berger, and Nobuko Yoshida. Descriptive and relative completeness of logics for higher-order functions. In *ICALP*, volume 4052 of *LNCS*. Springer, 2006.

[19] Bart Jacobs and Erik Poll. Java program verification at nijmegen: Developments and perspective. In *ISSS*, volume 3233 of *LNCS*, pages 134–153. Springer, 2003.

[20] Johannes Kanig and Jean-Christophe Filliâtre. Who: a verifier for effectful higher-order programs. In *ML'09: Proceedings of the 2009 ACM SIGPLAN workshop on ML*, pages 39–48. ACM, 2009.

[21] Gerwin Klein, Philip Derrin, and Kevin Elphinstone. Experience report: seL4: formally verifying a high-performance microkernel. In *ICFP*, pages 91–96. ACM, 2009.

[22] Gerwin Klein, Kevin Elphinstone, Gernot Heiser, June Andronick, David Cock, Philip Derrin, Dhammika Elkaduwe, Kai Engelhardt, Rafal Kolanski, Michael Norrish, Thomas Sewell, Harvey Tuch, and Simon Winwood. seL4: Formal verification of an OS kernel. In *Proceedings of the 22nd Symposium on Operating Systems Principles (SOSP), Operating Systems Review (OSR)*, pages 207–220, Big Sky, MT, 2009. ACM SIGOPS.

[23] Xavier Leroy. Formal certification of a compiler back-end or: programming a compiler with a proof assistant. In *POPL*, pages 42–54, 2006.

[24] Xavier Leroy, Damien Doligez, Jacques Garrigue, Didier Rémy, and Jérôme Vouillon. *The Objective Caml system*, 2005.

[25] Pierre Letouzey. *Programmation fonctionnelle certifiée – l'extraction de programmes dans l'assistant Coq*. PhD thesis, Université Paris 11, 2004.

[26] Nicolas Marti, Reynald Affeldt, and Akinori Yonezawa. Towards formal verification of memory properties using separation logic, 2005.

[27] Andrew McCreight. Practical tactics for separation logic. In *TPHOLs*, volume 5674 of *LNCS*, pages 343–358. Springer, 2009.

[28] Farhad Mehta and Tobias Nipkow. Proving pointer programs in higher-order logic. *Information and Computation*, 199(1–2), 2005.

[29] Magnus O. Myreen. *Formal Verification of Machine-Code Programs*. PhD thesis, University of Cambridge, 2008.

[30] Magnus O. Myreen. Separation logic adapted for proofs by rewriting. In *Interactive Theorem Proving (ITP)*, volume 6172 of *LNCS*, pages 485–489. Springer, 2010.

[31] Magnus O. Myreen and Michael J. C. Gordon. Verified LISP implementations on ARM, x86 and powerPC. In *TPHOLs*, volume 5674 of *LNCS*, pages 359–374. Springer, 2009.

[32] Aleksandar Nanevski and Greg Morrisett. Dependent type theory of stateful higher-order functions. Technical Report TR-24-05, Harvard University, 2005.

[33] Aleksandar Nanevski, J. Gregory Morrisett, and Lars Birkedal. Hoare type theory, polymorphism and separation. *Journal of Functional Programming*, 18(5-6):865–911, 2008.

[34] Aleksandar Nanevski, Viktor Vafeiadis, and Josh Berdine. Structuring the verification of heap-manipulating programs. In *POPL*, pages 261–274. ACM, 2010.

[35] Zhaozhong Ni and Zhong Shao. Certified assembly programming with embedded code pointers. In *POPL*, 2006.

[36] Peter O'Hearn, John Reynolds, and Hongseok Yang. Local reasoning about programs that alter data structures. In *CSL*, volume 2142 of *LNCS*, pages 1–19, Berlin, 2001. Springer-Verlag.

[37] Chris Okasaki. *Purely Functional Data Structures*. Cambridge University Press, 1999.

[38] Yann Régis-Gianas and François Pottier. A Hoare logic for call-by-value functional programs. In *MPC*, 2008.

[39] John C. Reynolds. Separation logic: A logic for shared mutable data structures. In *LICS*, pages 55–74, 2002.

[40] Hayo Thielecke. Frame rules from answer types for code pointers. In *POPL*, pages 309–319, 2006.

[41] Thomas Tuerk. Local reasoning about while-loops. In *VSTTE LNCS*, 2010.

[42] Karen Zee, Viktor Kuncak, and Martin C. Rinard. An integrated proof language for imperative programs. In *PLDI*, pages 338–351. ACM, 2009.

An Equivalence-Preserving CPS Translation via Multi-Language Semantics *

Amal Ahmed
Indiana University
amal@cs.indiana.edu

Matthias Blume
Google
blume@google.com

Abstract

Language-based security relies on the assumption that all potential attacks follow the rules of the language in question. When programs are compiled into a different language, this is true only if the translation process preserves observational equivalence.

To prove that a translation preserves equivalence, one must show that if two program fragments cannot be distinguished by any source context, then their translations cannot be distinguished by any target context. Informally, target contexts must be no more powerful than source contexts, i.e., for every target context there exists a source context that "behaves the same." This seems to amount to being able to "back-translate" arbitrary target terms. However, that is simply not viable for practical compilers where the target language is lower-level and, thus, contains expressions that have no source equivalent.

In this paper, we give a CPS translation from a less expressive source language (STLC) to a more expressive target language (System F) and prove that the translation preserves observational equivalence. The key to our equivalence-preserving compilation is the choice of the right type translation: a source type σ mandates a set of behaviors and we must ensure that its translation σ^+ mandates semantically equivalent behaviors at the target level. Based on this type translation, we demonstrate how to prove that for every target term of type σ^+, there exists an equivalent source term of type σ — even when sub-terms of the target term are not necessarily "back-translatable" themselves. A key novelty of our proof, resulting in a pleasant proof structure, is that it leverages a multi-language semantics where source and target terms may interoperate.

Categories and Subject Descriptors D.3.1 [*Programming Languages*]: Formal Definitions and Theory—Semantics

General Terms Languages, Reliability, Security, Theory

Keywords full abstraction, equivalence-preserving compilation, continuation-passing style, multi-language semantics, logical relations, back-translation

* In electronic versions of this paper, we use blue to typeset our source language and red to typeset the target. The paper will be much easier to read if viewed/printed in color.

ICFP'11, September 19–21, 2011, Tokyo, Japan.

1. Introduction

Abstraction is a key tool for ensuring the reliability and security of large, complex systems. We modularize such systems into components, define *interfaces* between these components, and let each component's *implementation* depend only on the interfaces of other components, not their implementation. With the advent of languages like Java and C#, developers increasingly rely on programming language techniques for enforcing abstraction.

Language-based security relies on an *abstraction theorem* [40] which effectively states that no user of a component can observe the difference between two different implementations of that component (i.e., the two implementations are *contextually equivalent*) if all manifestations of that difference in the interface are masked by an *abstract type*. If we think of the context as the adversary, the potential attacker, it becomes clear that language-based security requires that the attacker obey the typing rules of the same language.

Most programs written in some language S (*source*) are compiled to another language T (*target*) from where they are then executed. Thus, components e_S and e'_S might be compiled to e_T and e'_T, which would then interact with a target context C_T. But what if there exists some C_T that can observe a difference between e_T and e'_T, even if e_S and e'_S are contextually equivalent? This is a question that programmers *should* care about! It is critical for a programmer writing code in language S be able to reason about the properties of her code by *thinking* in S—that is, by only considering the behavior of other S components that may interact with her code in a type-safe manner. (In particular, to reason about the properties of an S component, she *should not* have to consider all possible interactions with components written in a different language, such as the target language T.) This can only be achieved if compilation both *preserves* and *reflects* contextual equivalence and is, therefore, *fully abstract*.

If the set of possible contexts in T is restricted to exactly those that can be obtained by translating S contexts, then it would be easy to show that no C_T can distinguish between code fragments not distinguishable by S contexts. However, this is usually not the case. For instance, Microsoft's Common Language Runtime (CLR) was specifically designed to be the target of compilers for multiple source languages, and most traditional compilers generate machine code that can then be linked with other machine code, possibly obtained by compiling code written in other source languages. In these situations, it is possible that the target language contains features that have no source-level equivalent, leading to T contexts that are *too powerful* in the sense that they can make observations that S contexts cannot. In fact, Kennedy [26] describes a number of ways in which abstractions were broken in the process of compiling C# to the CLR intermediate language. Similar problems with Java have been previously examined by Abadi [1].

There are three approaches to repairing failures of full abstraction. First, we could add features to the source language so that every target-level observation has a source-level counterpart. But this is hardly a desirable solution as it amounts to weakening the abstraction facilities of the source language. Second, we could remove features from the target language until it becomes, in some sense, merely an alternative notation for source programs, thereby guaranteeing that the only expressible target contexts trivially correspond to source contexts. This might work in some specialized situations, but it does not apply to foreign-function interfaces, plugin architectures, or multi-language frameworks such as .NET. (As we discuss in Section 9, much of the existing work on proving full abstraction resorts to one of these two approaches.)

The third approach is to change the translation. Specifically, we advocate engineering the translation so that it uses target-level abstraction facilities in a clever enough fashion so that well-typed target contexts have no choice but to respect the original abstractions. Put another way, instead of removing features from the target language, engineer the type translation to use types at the target level to restrict the set of contexts that a compiled source component can interact (or be linked) with. Of course, this assumes the presence of a rich enough type system at the target language. Fortunately, JVM bytecode, the CLR, and Typed Assembly Language (TAL) [36] may already provide most of the necessary features.

Assuming that the translation can be engineered in this way, it is still not clear how to *prove* that the result really is fully abstract. Full abstraction for a full-fledged C#-to-CLR is currently too hard a problem to tackle. A nontrivial first step would be to attempt full abstraction for a more idealized compiler such as that from System F to TAL [36] (which was mentioned in that paper as future work).

In prior work [4], we proved that typed closure conversion as defined by Morrisett *et al.* [36] is fully abstract. For typed closure conversion the key target language feature required was existential types, while the particular way the translation assigns existential types to closure records is what makes full abstraction work.

An interesting aspect of our earlier proof—which, unfortunately, significantly limits the situations where that proof strategy may be used—is that it takes advantage of a setup where source language S and target language T are the *same* language. Of course, source and target languages are rarely the same in practice, but we argued there that as long as the "real" target language is *less* expressive than the source language (i.e., if the compiler "compiles away" certain high-level source features), there is no loss of generality. Simply speaking, if contexts in the more expressive target language T (where $T = S$) cannot distinguish between two target language expressions, then contexts in the less expressive "real" target language cannot make the distinction either. Thus, our earlier proof methodology suffices when the source language is at least as expressive as the target, but *not* when the latter is more expressive.

However, there are usually some features in typical target languages that have no source equivalent. A common example for this is *control*: low-level languages tend to have explicit representations of the program counter and the program's control stack. In this setting the assumption of having equally powerful source and target languages does not work. To prove full abstraction when it holds, a different proof technique is required.

In this paper we investigate the full abstraction problem for CPS translation from a *less expressive source language* to a *more expressive target language*. Since CPS conversion makes continuations explicit, it represents the above-mentioned situation of a target language with explicit control. Next, we show that the "standard" typed CPS translation is not fully abstract, after which we discuss the specific contributions of this paper.

"Standard" CPS Conversion is Not Fully Abstract As we have discussed, full abstraction is at least as much a property of the translation as it is one of the target language. Therefore, a particular translation scheme can fail to be fully abstract even if the source- and target languages are identical. Consider the simply-typed λ-calculus. In this setting, it is easy to see that the following two terms A and B are contextually equivalent:

$$A = \lambda(f : \mathrm{int} \to \mathrm{int}, g : \mathrm{int} \to \mathrm{int}).(f\,0;\ g\,0;\ 0)$$
$$B = \lambda(f : \mathrm{int} \to \mathrm{int}, g : \mathrm{int} \to \mathrm{int}).(g\,0;\ f\,0;\ 0).$$

When applied to concrete arguments, the results of calling f and g are ignored in either case, and the overall answer is always 0.

Now consider A' and B', which are the results of translating A and B using the standard typed CPS-conversion approach (see, e.g., [20]) which makes use of a global abstract answer type ans. (We omit the type annotation int $\times$ (int $\to$ ans) $\to$ ans on f, g):

$$A' = \lambda(f, g, k : \mathrm{int} \to \mathrm{ans}).f(0, \lambda\_.\ g(0, \lambda\_.\ k\,0))$$
$$B' = \lambda(f, g, k : \mathrm{int} \to \mathrm{ans}).g(0, \lambda\_.\ f(0, \lambda\_.\ k\,0))$$

The following context C distinguishes between A' and B':

$$C = \lambda k.\ [\cdot]\,(\lambda(\_, \_).\ k\,1,\ \lambda(\_, \_).\ k\,2,\ k)$$

Substituting A' for the hole applies k to 1, while plugging in B' applies k to 2. The problem is that the values given for f and g take advantage of the explicit representation of continuations. They do something that our non-CPS functions cannot do: they ignore their own continuation and directly invoke a different one, thereby exposing the previously invisible difference in evaluation order within the bodies of A and B. Thus, this particular CPS-translation is not fully abstract.

The difference could be observed by source contexts if we added more powerful control operators to our source language, such as `call/cc` or even just exceptions. But we want a fully abstract translation without enriching the source language and weakening its abstractions to make more observations possible. The key idea is to take advantage of the target language type system in such a way that it rules out any target contexts that could make observations that are not possible at the source. One option, that has been studied extensively (e.g., Berdine *et al.* [10, 11]), is to ascribe linear types to continuations thus ensuring that they are used exactly once. As we will explain, in this paper, we eschew adding linear (or affine) types to the target and instead use polymorphism.

Contributions Our source language λ^{S} is the simply typed λ-calculus, while our target calculus λ^{T} is System F. (Section 3). We prove full abstraction for a CPS translation where each computation term is *locally* polymorphic in its answer type (Section 4). This translation has been studied before [48], but we are unaware of any work on proving it fully abstract. Although our target type system itself is not substructural, the locally polymorphic answer type is sufficient to enforce that continuations be used *at least once*—that is, continuations must be *relevant* in the terminology of substructural logics. Intuitively, enforcing relevance of continuations suffices in our setting because in a purely functional, terminating language such as λ^{T} it is impossible to distinguish between a single use and multiple uses of a continuation.

Our proof of full abstraction uses elementary operational techniques; there is no use of sophisticated machinery such as domain theory or game semantics. While the proof technique we used in prior work [4] relied on the source and target language being identical, our current proof technique works even if the two languages are different. To illustrate this point, we have picked a target (System F) that is more expressive than the source (STLC)—e.g., we can encode arithmetic operations in System F but not in STLC. In addition, like Morrisett *et al.*'s CPS target language [36], our λ^{T} requires terms to be in CPS form (in the spirit of compilers like SML/NJ [7, 45], Rabbit [47], Orbit [28], and more recently, Kennedy's SML.NET compiler [27], though our syntax is not as restrictive, e.g., we do not distinguish functions from continuations.)

Thus, neither language is a sub-language of the other. An interesting aspect of our proof technique is that it draws upon work on *language interoperability*. We define a *combined* language λ^{ST} that incorporates both λ^{S}, λ^{T}, and has two new *boundary* forms that let us interface terms of one language with the other (Section 5). This setup allows us to neatly decompose our proof into three parts (Section 6).

We discuss the addition of recursion to both the source and target in Section 8 but the details are beyond the scope of this paper. We have elided most proofs here. Detailed proofs may be found in the online technical appendix [5].

2. Main Ideas

Multi-language scenario and interoperability. Consider two source terms e_S and e'_S and their corresponding translation terms e_T and e'_T. To show full abstraction we need to establish equivalence *reflection* and equivalence *preservation*. Reflection is closely related to "compiler correctness" in the sense that we deem the translation fundamentally broken if non-equivalent source terms translate to equivalent target terms. The hard part of the proof, however, is to establish preservation: terms that are equivalent at source level should translate to equivalent target terms.

A natural way of proving equivalence preservation is to take an indirect approach: assume that e_T and e'_T are *not* equivalent and derive a contradiction. If e_T and e'_T are not contextually equivalent, there has to be a target context C_T that exposes the difference: $C_T[e_T]$ evaluates to true_T while $C_T[e'_T]$ evaluates to false_T. The idea is to show the existence of a *source* context C_S such that $C_S[e_S]$ evaluates to true_S while $C_S[e'_S]$ evaluates to false_S. In our previous work [4] we were able to construct C_S directly from C_T with the help of "wrapper" terms. This technique does not apply directly to the current setting of mutually incompatible source- and target languages.

However, it is possible to apply the technique—at least in an intuitive sense—if we take a page out of the work on interoperability [31] and define a combined language in which S- and T-terms can interoperate in a controlled way. The discriminating target context C_T gives rise to a discriminating context C_{ST} for e_S and e'_S. What remains to be done now is to show that C_{ST} can be converted to a context C_S that is equally discriminating.

Relevant continuations via parametricity. Our version of typed CPS-conversion differs from the "standard" account that uses a single, globally abstract answer type. Our answer type is individually abstract at each point where a continuation argument appears. In essence, each computation term of type $(\tau \to \mathrm{ans}) \to \mathrm{ans}$ becomes $\forall\alpha\,.\,(\tau \to \alpha) \to \alpha$. The polymorphic type variable α replaces the single answer type ans. As a result, the computation has less freedom in how it can use its continuation. In particular, to produce its own answer of type α, it has no choice but to invoke *its own* continuation (which ensures that the continuation is used at least once). It turns out that this typing of CPS code prevents any "bad" target terms (for example those whose source equivalent is a variant of `call/cc`) from being well typed. The technical underpinnings of this intuition is a *free theorem* [50] that applies to computation terms that are polymorphic in their answer type.

Back-translation. The remaining hurdle is to show that CPS-typed target contexts can be "back-translated" to corresponding source contexts. The difficulty lies in the fact that the type only governs the interface of a term without preventing the presence of arbitrary subterms, so for a term to have translation type does not immediately imply that it can be back-translated. However, as we will show, we are always able to eliminate occurrences of inconvenient subterms by partially reducing them. For instance, whenever

Types	σ	$::=$	$\mathsf{bool} \mid \sigma_1 \to \sigma_2$
Values	v	$::=$	$\mathsf{x} \mid \mathsf{true} \mid \mathsf{false} \mid \lambda\mathsf{x}:\sigma.\,\mathsf{e}$
Terms	e	$::=$	$\mathsf{v} \mid \mathsf{if\ e\ then\ e_1\ else\ e_2} \mid \mathsf{e_1\ e_2}$
Eval. Contexts	E	$::=$	$[\cdot]_{\mathsf{S}} \mid \mathsf{if\ E\ then\ e_1\ else\ e_2} \mid \mathsf{E\ e} \mid \mathsf{v\ E}$

$\boxed{\mathsf{e} \longmapsto \mathsf{e}'}$

$$\mathsf{if\ true\ then\ e_1\ else\ e_2} \longmapsto \mathsf{e_1}$$
$$\mathsf{if\ false\ then\ e_1\ else\ e_2} \longmapsto \mathsf{e_2}$$
$$(\lambda\mathsf{x}:\sigma.\,\mathsf{e})\ \mathsf{v} \longmapsto \mathsf{e}[\mathsf{v}/\mathsf{x}]$$
$$\frac{\mathsf{e} \longmapsto \mathsf{e}'}{\mathsf{E}[\mathsf{e}] \longmapsto \mathsf{E}[\mathsf{e}']}$$

Figure 1. λ^{S}: Syntax and Dynamic Semantics

we have a term of the form $\mathbf{v}\ [\tau]\ \mathbf{v}_1$—application of a polymorphic function $\mathbf{v}$ to type τ and then to an argument $\mathbf{v}_1$—of translation type σ^+, either $\mathbf{v}$ will have a translation type $(\sigma_1 \to \sigma_2)^+$ (and therefore can be related to a source term of type $\sigma_1 \to \sigma_2$), or it will be a lambda term that can be applied to τ and $\mathbf{v}_1$, yielding a term $\mathbf{e}$ of type σ^+. The latter term can now be back-translated. This is well-founded because the result term is "smaller" in that it will reduce to a value in fewer steps. The metric for well-foundedness of our "back-translation" relation is a combination of length of reduction sequence, structure of the type of the term being back-translated, and the structure of the expression. We explain the details in Section 6.2.

3. The Source and Target Languages

We typeset the terms, types, and contexts of our source language λ^{S} using a blue sans-serif font, and those of our target language λ^{T} using a **bold red font with serifs**.

3.1 The Source Language (λ^{S})

Our source language λ^{S} is the call-by-value simply-typed λ-calculus with booleans. The syntax and dynamic semantics of λ^{S} are shown in Figure 1. We define a small-step operational semantics for λ^{S}, using evaluation contexts E to lift the primitive reductions to a standard left-to-right call-by-value semantics for the language.

λ^{S} typing judgments have the form $\Gamma \vdash \mathsf{e} : \sigma$, where the value environment Γ tracks the set of free term variables in scope, along with their types. The typing rules are entirely standard so we omit them here. (They appear later as part of Figure 3 when we define the CPS translation by induction on the structure of $\Gamma \vdash \mathsf{e} : \sigma$.)

λ^{S} Contextual Equivalence A λ^{S} context C is an expression with a single hole $[\cdot]_{\mathsf{S}}$ in it. Typing judgments for contexts have the form $\vdash \mathsf{C} : (\Gamma \vdash \sigma) \Rightarrow (\Gamma' \vdash \sigma')$, where $(\Gamma \vdash \sigma)$ indicates the type of the hole. Essentially, this judgment says that if e is an expression such that $\Gamma \vdash \mathsf{e} : \sigma$, then $\Gamma' \vdash \mathsf{C}[\mathsf{e}] : \sigma'$. The typing rule for a hole is as follows:

$$\frac{\Gamma \subseteq \Gamma'}{\vdash [\cdot]_{\mathsf{S}} : (\Gamma \vdash \sigma) \Rightarrow (\Gamma' \vdash \sigma)}$$

The other rules are straightforward (see our online appendix [5]).

We define contextual approximation ($\Gamma \vdash \mathsf{e_1} \precsim^{ctx}_{\mathsf{S}} \mathsf{e_2} : \sigma$) to mean that, for any well-typed program context C with a hole of the type of $\mathsf{e_1}$ and $\mathsf{e_2}$, and result type bool, if $\mathsf{C}[\mathsf{e_1}]$ evaluates to the boolean value v then so does $\mathsf{C}[\mathsf{e_2}]$. Contextual equivalence ($\Gamma \vdash \mathsf{e_1} \approx^{ctx}_{\mathsf{S}} \mathsf{e_2} : \sigma$) is then defined as contextual approximation in both directions.

Definition 3.1 (λ^S **Contextual Approximation & Equivalence)**
Let $\Gamma \vdash e_1 : \sigma$ *and* $\Gamma \vdash e_2 : \sigma$.

$$\begin{array}{l}\Gamma \vdash e_1 \precsim_S^{ctx} e_2 : \sigma \stackrel{\text{def}}{=} \\ \quad \forall C, v_1.\ \vdash C : (\Gamma \vdash \sigma) \Rightarrow (\cdot \vdash \text{bool}) \ \wedge\ C[e_1] \Downarrow v_1 \implies \\ \qquad \exists v_2.\ C[e_2] \Downarrow v_2 \ \wedge\ v_1 = v_2\end{array}$$

$$\Gamma \vdash e_1 \approx_S^{ctx} e_2 : \sigma \stackrel{\text{def}}{=} \Gamma \vdash e_1 \precsim_S^{ctx} e_2 : \sigma \ \wedge\ \Gamma \vdash e_2 \precsim_S^{ctx} e_1 : \sigma$$

λ^S ***CIU equivalence*** Note that evaluation contexts E (Figure 1) are a subset of general contexts C. Since only closed terms can be placed in an evaluation context, the type of the hole always has the form $\cdot \vdash \sigma$.

We define the notion of *ciu-equivalence* (uses of closed instantiations, first introduced by Mason and Talcott [30]) and show that it is a consequence of contextual equivalence. Two closed terms of type σ are ciu-equivalent if, in any evaluation context E with hole type σ and result type bool, they evaluate to the same value. This notion is often easier to work with than contextual equivalence since it cuts down on the number of contexts under consideration. The notion is extended to open terms by closing the terms with a value substitution γ that maps variables x to values v; we write $\vdash \gamma : \Gamma$ when $\text{dom}(\gamma) = \text{dom}(\Gamma)$ and for all $x \in \text{dom}(\Gamma)$, $\vdash \gamma(x) : \Gamma(x)$.

Definition 3.2 (λ^S **CIU Approximation & Equivalence)**
Let $\Gamma \vdash e_1 : \sigma$ *and* $\Gamma \vdash e_2 : \sigma$.

$$\begin{array}{l}\Gamma \vdash e_1 \precsim_S^{ciu} e_2 : \sigma \stackrel{\text{def}}{=} \\ \quad \forall E, \gamma, v_1.\ \vdash E : (\cdot \vdash \sigma) \Rightarrow (\cdot \vdash \text{bool}) \ \wedge\ \vdash \gamma : \Gamma \ \wedge\ E[\gamma(e_1)] \Downarrow v_1 \implies \\ \qquad \exists v_2.\ E[\gamma(e_2)] \Downarrow v_2 \ \wedge\ v_1 = v_2\end{array}$$

$$\Gamma \vdash e_1 \approx_S^{ciu} e_2 : \sigma \stackrel{\text{def}}{=} \Gamma \vdash e_1 \precsim_S^{ciu} e_2 : \sigma \ \wedge\ \Gamma \vdash e_2 \precsim_S^{ciu} e_1 : \sigma$$

Lemma 3.3 (λ^S**: Contextual Approx Implies CIU Approx)**
If $\Gamma \vdash e_1 \precsim_S^{ctx} e_2 : \sigma$ *then* $\Gamma \vdash e_1 \precsim_S^{ciu} e_2 : \sigma$.

3.2 The Target Language (λ^T)

Our CPS target language λ^T is call-by-value System F with booleans and pairs. The λ^T syntax and dynamic semantics are given in Figure 2 (top). Following Morrisett *et al.* [36], our CPS target language syntactically enforces continuation-passing style. λ^T code is nearly linear—consisting of a series of let bindings followed by a function call—with the exception of the if construct which forms a tree containing two subexpressions. Also following Morrisett *et al.*, we combine the types $\forall$ and $\rightarrow$ into $\forall[\alpha].\tau_1 \rightarrow \tau_2$ and have only one abstraction mechanism (λ) which binds both type and term variables. Finally, we have pairs in λ^T so we can express CPS conversion without the need to introduce more curried functions.

We define a small-step, call-by-value operational semantics. Notice that evaluation contexts in λ^T are redundant since the syntactic restriction to CPS results in a unique order of evaluation; we introduce them primarily to permit a more uniform treatment of λ^S and λ^T when they are incorporated into the multi-language semantics in Section 5.

λ^T typing judgments have the form $\Delta; \Gamma \vdash e : \tau$, where the environments Δ and Γ are defined in Figure 2. The type environment Δ tracks the type variables in scope. The value environment Γ tracks the term variables in scope along with their types τ which must be well formed in environment Δ (written $\Delta \vdash \tau$ and defined as $\text{ftv}(\tau) \subseteq \Delta$, where $\text{ftv}(\tau)$ denotes the set of type variables that appear free in type τ). The typing rules are standard, so we only show a few rules in Figure 2 (middle).

Syntactic Sugar We abbreviate $\forall[\alpha].\tau_1 \rightarrow \tau_2$ as $\tau_1 \rightarrow \tau_2$ when $\alpha \notin (\text{ftv}(\tau_1) \cup \text{ftv}(\tau_2))$; we similarly abbreviate $\lambda[\alpha](x:\tau_1).e$ to $\lambda(x:\tau_1).e$, when α does not appear free in τ_1 or e; and we abbreviate $v\,[\tau]\,v_1$ to $v\ v_1$ when v has type $\tau_1 \rightarrow \tau_2$. We also use the following shorthand (and in the first three cases below, we have analogous shorthand for λ^S):

$$\begin{array}{rcll}\lambda x.e & = & \lambda(x:\tau).e & ;\ \tau \text{ inferred from context} \\ \text{let } x = v \text{ in } e & = & (\lambda x.e)\ v & \\ \text{id} & = & \lambda x.x & \\ \text{let } (x_1, x_2) = z \text{ in } e & = & \text{let } x_1 = \pi_1 z \text{ in } (\text{let } x_2 = \pi_2 z \text{ in } e) & \\ \lambda[\alpha]((x_1, x_2) : \tau_1 \times \tau_2).e & = & & \\ & & \lambda[\alpha](z : \tau_1 \times \tau_2).\text{let } (x_1, x_2) = z \text{ in } e & \end{array}$$

$$\begin{array}{llcl}\textit{Types} & \tau & ::= & \text{bool} \mid \tau_1 \times \tau_2 \mid \alpha \mid \forall[\alpha].\tau_1 \rightarrow \tau_2 \\ \textit{Values} & v & ::= & x \mid \text{true} \mid \text{false} \mid (v_1, v_2) \mid \lambda[\alpha](x:\tau).e \\ \textit{Terms} & e & ::= & v \mid \text{if } v \text{ then } e_1 \text{ else } e_2 \mid \text{let } x = \pi_i v \text{ in } e \mid v_1\,[\tau]\,v_2 \\ \textit{Eval. Ctxts} & E & ::= & [\cdot]_T\end{array}$$

$$\boxed{e \longmapsto e'} \quad \begin{array}{rcl}\text{if true then } e_1 \text{ else } e_2 & \longmapsto & e_1 \\ \text{if false then } e_1 \text{ else } e_2 & \longmapsto & e_2 \\ \text{let } x = \pi_i(v_1, v_2) \text{ in } e & \longmapsto & e[v_i/x] \\ (\lambda[\alpha](x:\tau_1).e)\,[\tau]\,v & \longmapsto & e[\tau/\alpha][v/x]\end{array}$$

$$\frac{e \longmapsto e'}{E[e] \longmapsto E[e']}$$

$$\begin{array}{llcl}\textit{Type Environments} & \Delta & ::= & \cdot \mid \Delta, \alpha \\ \textit{Value Environments} & \Gamma & ::= & \cdot \mid \Gamma, x : \tau\end{array}$$

$$\boxed{\Delta; \Gamma \vdash e : \tau} \quad \frac{x : \tau \in \Gamma}{\Delta; \Gamma \vdash x : \tau} \quad \cdots \quad \frac{\Delta; \Gamma \vdash v_1 : \tau_1 \qquad \Delta; \Gamma \vdash v_2 : \tau_2}{\Delta; \Gamma \vdash (v_1, v_2) : \tau_1 \times \tau_2}$$

$$\frac{\Delta; \Gamma \vdash v : \tau_1 \times \tau_2 \qquad \Delta; \Gamma, x : \tau_i \vdash e : \tau}{\Delta; \Gamma \vdash \text{let } x = \pi_i v \text{ in } e : \tau}$$

$$\frac{\Delta, \alpha; \Gamma, x : \tau_1 \vdash e : \tau_2}{\Delta; \Gamma \vdash \lambda[\alpha](x:\tau_1).e : \forall[\alpha].\tau_1 \rightarrow \tau_2}$$

$$\frac{\Delta; \Gamma \vdash v_1 : \forall[\alpha].\tau_2 \rightarrow \tau \qquad \Delta \vdash \tau' \qquad \Delta; \Gamma \vdash v_2 : \tau_2[\tau'/\alpha]}{\Delta; \Gamma \vdash v_1\,[\tau']\,v_2 : \tau[\tau'/\alpha]}$$

$$\begin{array}{llcl}\textit{Value Contexts} & C^V & ::= & [\cdot]_T^V \mid (C^V, v_2) \mid (v_1, C^V) \mid \lambda[\alpha](x:\tau).C \\ \textit{Contexts} & C & ::= & [\cdot]_T \mid C^V \mid \text{if } C^V \text{ then } e_1 \text{ else } e_2 \mid \\ & & & \text{if } e \text{ then } C \text{ else } e_2 \mid \text{if } e \text{ then } e_1 \text{ else } C \mid \\ & & & \text{let } x = \pi_i C^V \text{ in } e \mid \text{let } x = \pi_i v \text{ in } C \mid \\ & & & C^V\,[\tau]\,v_2 \mid v_1\,[\tau]\,C^V\end{array}$$

Figure 2. λ^T: Syntax, Dynamic + Static Semantics, Contexts

λ^T ***Contextual Equivalence and CIU Equivalence*** The syntax of λ^T contexts is given at the bottom of Figure 2. A λ^T context C is an expression with a single hole in it, but the hole may be either of the form $[\cdot]_T^V$, a hole that expects a value, or of the form $[\cdot]_T$, a hole that expects any term. We write C^V (respectively, C) for a context that *once filled*, regardless of the kind of hole in it, yields a value (respectively, a term). Typing rules for λ^T contexts are analogous to those for λ^S contexts, except that typing judgments have the form $\vdash C : (\Delta; \Gamma \vdash \tau) \Rightarrow (\Delta'; \Gamma' \vdash \tau')$. Hence, if e is a term such that $\Delta; \Gamma \vdash e : \tau$, then $\Delta'; \Gamma' \vdash C[e] : \tau'$. The typing rules for holes $[\cdot]_T^V$ and $[\cdot]_T$ are identical so we show just one:

$$\frac{\Delta \subseteq \Delta' \qquad \Gamma \subseteq \Gamma'}{\vdash [\cdot]_T^V : (\Delta; \Gamma \vdash \tau) \Rightarrow (\Delta'; \Gamma' \vdash \tau)}$$

The remaining rules are straightforward (see online appendix [5]). The definition of contextual approximation and equivalence for λ^T are analogous to those for λ^S, except that we now also have to account for the environment Δ. Also, we must make sure that the terms $C[e_1]$ and $C[e_2]$ are syntactically well formed λ^T terms. The extra checks are needed because the hole in a context C may be of the form $[\cdot]_{\mathrm{T}}$ or $[\cdot]_{\mathrm{T}}^{\mathrm{v}}$. If it's of the form $[\cdot]_{\mathrm{T}}$, then any well-typed term e may be placed in C. However, if it's of the form $[\cdot]_{\mathrm{T}}^{\mathrm{v}}$, then $\mathrm{C}[\mathrm{e}]$ will not be a well-formed term unless e is a value.

Definition 3.4 **(λ^{T} Contextual Approximation & Equivalence)**
Let $\Delta;\Gamma \vdash \mathrm{e}_1 : \tau$ *and* $\Delta;\Gamma \vdash \mathrm{e}_2 : \tau$.

$$\begin{array}{l}\Delta;\Gamma \vdash \mathrm{e}_1 \precsim^{ctx}_{\mathrm{T}} \mathrm{e}_2 : \tau \stackrel{\mathrm{def}}{=} \\ \quad \forall \mathrm{C}, \mathrm{v}_1.\ \vdash \mathrm{C} : (\Delta;\Gamma \vdash \tau) \Rightarrow (\cdot;\cdot \vdash \mathrm{bool})\ \wedge\ \cdot;\cdot \vdash \mathrm{C}[\mathrm{e}_1] : \mathrm{bool}\ \wedge \\ \qquad\qquad \cdot;\cdot \vdash \mathrm{C}[\mathrm{e}_2] : \mathrm{bool}\ \wedge\ \mathrm{C}[\mathrm{e}_1] \Downarrow \mathrm{v}_1 \implies \\ \qquad\qquad \exists \mathrm{v}_2.\ \mathrm{C}[\mathrm{e}_2] \Downarrow \mathrm{v}_2\ \wedge\ \mathrm{v}_1 = \mathrm{v}_2\end{array}$$

$$\Delta;\Gamma \vdash \mathrm{e}_1 \approx^{ctx}_{\mathrm{T}} \mathrm{e}_2 : \tau \stackrel{\mathrm{def}}{=} \Delta;\Gamma \vdash \mathrm{e}_1 \precsim^{ctx}_{\mathrm{T}} \mathrm{e}_2 : \tau \wedge \Delta;\Gamma \vdash \mathrm{e}_2 \precsim^{ctx}_{\mathrm{T}} \mathrm{e}_1 : \tau$$

λ^{T} evaluation contexts are essentially degenerate. Nonetheless we define ciu-equivalence for λ^{T} since the notion will later be more convenient to work with than contextual equivalence. As before, closed terms of closed type τ are ciu-equivalent if, in any evaluation context E with hole type τ and result type bool, they evaluate to the same value. The notion is extended to open terms by closing the type τ and the terms with substitutions δ and γ. The type substitution δ is a finite map from type variables α to closed types τ; we write $\delta \models \Delta$ whenever $\mathrm{dom}(\delta) = \Delta$. The value substitution γ now maps variables x to values v and $\vdash \gamma : \Gamma$ means that γ maps variables to values that are well-typed according to Γ.

Definition 3.5 **(λ^{T} CIU Approximation & Equivalence)**
Let $\Delta;\Gamma \vdash \mathrm{e}_1 : \tau$ *and* $\Delta;\Gamma \vdash \mathrm{e}_2 : \tau$.

$$\begin{array}{l}\Delta;\Gamma \vdash \mathrm{e}_1 \precsim^{ciu}_{\mathrm{T}} \mathrm{e}_2 : \tau \stackrel{\mathrm{def}}{=} \\ \quad \forall \mathrm{E}, \delta, \gamma, \mathrm{v}_1.\ \vdash \mathrm{E} : (\cdot;\cdot \vdash \delta(\tau)) \Rightarrow (\cdot;\cdot \vdash \mathrm{bool})\ \wedge \\ \qquad\qquad \delta \models \Delta\ \wedge\ \vdash \gamma : \delta(\Gamma)\ \wedge\ \mathrm{E}[\delta(\gamma(\mathrm{e}_1))] \Downarrow \mathrm{v}_1 \implies \\ \qquad\qquad \exists \mathrm{v}_2.\ \mathrm{E}[\delta(\gamma(\mathrm{e}_2))] \Downarrow \mathrm{v}_2\ \wedge\ \mathrm{v}_1 = \mathrm{v}_2\end{array}$$

$$\Delta;\Gamma \vdash \mathrm{e}_1 \approx^{ciu}_{\mathrm{T}} \mathrm{e}_2 : \tau \stackrel{\mathrm{def}}{=} \Delta;\Gamma \vdash \mathrm{e}_1 \precsim^{ciu}_{\mathrm{T}} \mathrm{e}_2 : \tau \wedge \Delta;\Gamma \vdash \mathrm{e}_2 \precsim^{ciu}_{\mathrm{T}} \mathrm{e}_1 : \tau$$

Lemma 3.6 **(λ^{T}: Contextual Approx Implies CIU Approx)**
If $\Delta;\Gamma \vdash \mathrm{e}_1 \precsim^{ctx}_{\mathrm{T}} \mathrm{e}_2 : \tau$ *then* $\Delta;\Gamma \vdash \mathrm{e}_1 \precsim^{ciu}_{\mathrm{T}} \mathrm{e}_2 : \tau$.

4. Typed CPS Translation

CPS translation maps source values of type σ to target values of type σ^+. The type translation is given in Figure 3 (top).

As mentioned earlier, our version of typed CPS-conversion differs from the "standard" account. Instead of using a single, globally abstract answer type, we make the answer type individually abstract at each point where a continuation argument appears. As shown in Figure 3 (top left), each function of type $\sigma_1 \to \sigma_2$ acquires a type parameter α and an additional term parameter of type $\sigma_2{}^+ \to \alpha$ representing the continuation. The polymorphic type variable α acts as the *answer* type. The consequence of this is that a function of CPS type has less freedom in how it can use continuations. In particular, to produce its own answer of type α, it has no choice but to invoke *its own* continuation. Of course, the function can invoke its continuation multiple times, but in a purely functional setting it is impossible to tell the difference between one use of the continuation and multiple uses. As discussed earlier, this typing of CPS code prevents any "bad" target terms from being well typed. The polymorphic type of each continuation lets us take advantage of a *free theorem* [50] that captures the above intuitions and plays a key role in our proof; see discussion of Lemma 6.10 in Section 6.3.

Figure 3 (bottom) shows the rules for CPS translation in combination with declarative typing rules for the source language λ^{S}. To this end, the typing judgment $\Gamma \vdash \mathrm{e} : \sigma$ is extended to a translation judgment $\Gamma \vdash \mathrm{e} : \sigma \rightsquigarrow \mathrm{v}$, where v describes a CPS *computation* of type $\forall[\alpha].(\sigma^+ \to \alpha) \to \alpha$ (which we abbreviate as $\sigma^{\div}$). A computation is a suspended term awaiting its continuation. It is polymorphic in the answer type of the continuation and, like functions, it will be forced to invoke its own continuation to produce its answer of type α.

Note that for v to have the type $\sigma^{\div}$, it has to be considered under the translated environment Γ^+ (defined in Figure 3, top right). Therefore, notice that variables x in the source term are replaced by variables x in the target term. For instance, in the variable translation rule, the source variable x changes to x in the target. Also, in the function rule, note that v in the premise may contain a free occurrence of $\mathrm{x} : \sigma_1{}^+$. This x is captured in the conclusion by a binding occurrence of x. We could parametrize our translation with a mapping from source variables to target variables and use that to perform renaming. To avoid this unnecessary complication, we work with a fixed a-priori mapping and adopt the convention that for each x, y, z, etc., there exists a unique x, y, z, respectively, that we can use in the translated term.

The rules are designed with clarity, not optimality, in mind. A translation term v will usually contain many "administrative" redexes that can easily be eliminated with subsequent optimization.

$$\begin{array}{llcl} \textit{Types} & \varphi & ::= & \sigma \mid \tau \\ \textit{Terms} & \mathrm{e} & ::= & \ldots \mid {}^{\sigma}\mathcal{ST}\,\mathrm{e} \\ & \mathrm{e} & ::= & \ldots \mid \mathrm{let}\ \mathrm{x} = (\mathcal{TS}^{\,\sigma}\,\mathrm{e})\ \mathrm{in}\ \mathrm{e} \\ & e & ::= & \mathrm{e} \mid \mathrm{e} \\ \textit{Values} & v & ::= & \mathrm{v} \mid \mathrm{v} \\ \textit{Eval. Contexts} & \mathrm{E} & ::= & \ldots \mid {}^{\sigma}\mathcal{ST}\,\mathrm{E} \\ & \mathrm{E} & ::= & \ldots \mid \mathrm{let}\ \mathrm{x} = (\mathcal{TS}^{\,\sigma}\,\mathrm{E})\ \mathrm{in}\ \mathrm{e} \\ & E & ::= & \mathrm{E} \mid \mathrm{E} \end{array}$$

$$\boxed{e \longmapsto e'}$$

$$\begin{array}{rcl} {}^{\mathsf{bool}}\mathcal{ST}\,\mathrm{true} & \longmapsto & \mathsf{true} \\ {}^{\mathsf{bool}}\mathcal{ST}\,\mathrm{false} & \longmapsto & \mathsf{false} \\ {}^{\sigma_1 \to \sigma_2}\mathcal{ST}\,\mathrm{v} & \longmapsto & \lambda \mathsf{x} : \sigma_1.\ {}^{\sigma_2}\mathcal{ST}\,(\mathrm{let}\ \mathrm{z} = (\mathcal{TS}^{\,\sigma_1}\,\mathsf{x})\ \mathrm{in}\ (\mathrm{v}\ [\sigma_2{}^+]\ (\mathrm{z}, \mathrm{id}))) \end{array}$$

$$\begin{array}{rcl} \mathrm{let}\ \mathrm{y} = (\mathcal{TS}^{\,\mathsf{bool}}\,\mathsf{true})\ \mathrm{in}\ \mathrm{e} & \longmapsto & \mathrm{e}[\mathrm{true}/\mathrm{y}] \\ \mathrm{let}\ \mathrm{y} = (\mathcal{TS}^{\,\mathsf{bool}}\,\mathsf{false})\ \mathrm{in}\ \mathrm{e} & \longmapsto & \mathrm{e}[\mathrm{false}/\mathrm{y}] \\ \mathrm{let}\ \mathrm{y} = (\mathcal{TS}^{\,\sigma_1 \to \sigma_2}\,\mathsf{v})\ \mathrm{in}\ \mathrm{e} & \longmapsto & \mathrm{e}[\mathrm{v}/\mathrm{y}] \end{array}$$

$$\text{where } \mathrm{v} = \lambda[\alpha]\,((\mathrm{x}, \mathrm{k}) : \sigma_1{}^+ \times (\sigma_2{}^+ \to \alpha)).\ \mathrm{let}\ \mathrm{z} = (\mathcal{TS}^{\,\sigma_2}\,(\mathsf{v}\,({}^{\sigma_1}\mathcal{ST}\,\mathrm{x})))\ \mathrm{in}\ \mathrm{k}\ \mathrm{z}$$

$$\frac{e \longmapsto e'}{E[e] \longmapsto E[e']}$$

$$\begin{array}{llcl} \textit{Type Environments} & \Delta & ::= & \cdot \mid \Delta, \alpha \\ \textit{Value Environments} & \Gamma & ::= & \cdot \mid \Gamma, \mathsf{x} : \sigma \mid \Gamma, \mathrm{x} : \tau \end{array}$$

$$\boxed{\Delta;\Gamma \vdash e : \varphi}$$

$$\ldots \quad \frac{\Delta;\Gamma \vdash \mathrm{e} : \sigma^+}{\Delta;\Gamma \vdash {}^{\sigma}\mathcal{ST}\,\mathrm{e} : \sigma} \qquad \frac{\Delta;\Gamma \vdash \mathsf{e} : \sigma \qquad \Delta;\Gamma, \mathrm{x} : \sigma^+ \vdash \mathrm{e} : \tau}{\Delta;\Gamma \vdash \mathrm{let}\ \mathrm{x} = (\mathcal{TS}^{\,\sigma}\,\mathsf{e})\ \mathrm{in}\ \mathrm{e} : \tau}$$

$$\begin{array}{lrcl} \textit{Contexts} & \mathsf{C} & ::= & \ldots \mid {}^{\sigma}\mathcal{ST}\,\mathrm{C} \\ & \mathrm{C} & ::= & \ldots \mid \mathrm{let}\ \mathrm{x} = (\mathcal{TS}^{\,\sigma}\,\mathsf{C})\ \mathrm{in}\ \mathrm{e} \mid \mathrm{let}\ \mathrm{x} = (\mathcal{TS}^{\,\sigma}\,\mathsf{e})\ \mathrm{in}\ \mathrm{C} \\ & C & ::= & \mathsf{C} \mid \mathrm{C} \end{array}$$

Figure 4. λ^{ST}: Syntax, Dynamic + Static Semantics, Contexts

5. Multi-Language Semantics

In this section, we present the language λ^{ST} designed for interoperability of terms from the source and target languages λ^{S} and λ^{T} and give a definition of contextual equivalence (written $\approx^{ctx}_{\mathrm{ST}}$) for the language.

The λ^{ST} multi-language system, presented in Figure 4, embeds the source and target languages λ^{S} and λ^{T} so that both languages have natural access to foreign values (i.e., values from the other

$$\boxed{\sigma^{+}} \qquad (\mathsf{bool})^{+} = \mathsf{bool} \qquad (\sigma_1 \to \sigma_2)^{+} = \forall[\alpha].(\sigma_1^{+} \times (\sigma_2^{+} \to \alpha)) \to \alpha$$

$$\boxed{\Gamma^{+}} \qquad (\cdot)^{+} = \cdot \qquad (\Gamma, \mathsf{x} : \sigma)^{+} = \Gamma^{+}, \mathsf{x} : \sigma^{+}$$

$$\boxed{\Gamma \vdash \mathsf{e} : \sigma \rightsquigarrow \mathsf{v}} \quad \text{where } \cdot; \Gamma^{+} \vdash \mathsf{v} : \sigma^{\div} \text{ and we define } \sigma^{\div} = \forall[\alpha].(\sigma^{+} \to \alpha) \to \alpha$$

$$\frac{}{\Gamma \vdash \mathsf{true} : \mathsf{bool} \rightsquigarrow \lambda[\alpha]\,(\mathsf{k} : \mathsf{bool}^{+} \to \alpha).\,\mathsf{k}\ \mathsf{true}} \qquad \frac{}{\Gamma \vdash \mathsf{false} : \mathsf{bool} \rightsquigarrow \lambda[\alpha]\,(\mathsf{k} : \mathsf{bool}^{+} \to \alpha).\,\mathsf{k}\ \mathsf{false}}$$

$$\frac{\Gamma \vdash \mathsf{e} : \mathsf{bool} \rightsquigarrow \mathsf{v} \qquad \Gamma \vdash \mathsf{e}_1 : \sigma \rightsquigarrow \mathsf{v}_1 \qquad \Gamma \vdash \mathsf{e}_2 : \sigma \rightsquigarrow \mathsf{v}_2}{\Gamma \vdash \mathsf{if\ e\ then\ e_1\ else\ e_2} : \sigma \rightsquigarrow \lambda[\alpha]\,(\mathsf{k} : \sigma^{+} \to \alpha).\ \mathsf{v}\,[\alpha]\,(\lambda(\mathsf{x} : \mathsf{bool}).\,\mathsf{if\ x\ then}\ (\mathsf{v}_1\,[\alpha]\,\mathsf{k})\ \mathsf{else}\ (\mathsf{v}_2\,[\alpha]\,\mathsf{k}))}$$

$$\frac{\mathsf{x} : \sigma \in \Gamma}{\Gamma \vdash \mathsf{x} : \sigma \rightsquigarrow \lambda[\alpha]\,(\mathsf{k} : \sigma^{+} \to \alpha).\,\mathsf{k}\ \mathsf{x}} \qquad \frac{\Gamma, \mathsf{x} : \sigma_1 \vdash \mathsf{e} : \sigma_2 \rightsquigarrow \mathsf{v}}{\Gamma \vdash \lambda \mathsf{x} : \sigma_1.\,\mathsf{e} : \sigma_1 \to \sigma_2 \rightsquigarrow \lambda[\alpha]\,(\mathsf{k} : (\sigma_1 \to \sigma_2)^{+} \to \alpha).\ \mathsf{k}\,(\lambda[\beta]\,((\mathsf{x}, \mathsf{k}') : \sigma_1^{+} \times (\sigma_2^{+} \to \beta)).\,(\mathsf{v}\,[\beta]\,\mathsf{k}'))}$$

$$\frac{\Gamma \vdash \mathsf{e}_1 : \sigma_2 \to \sigma \rightsquigarrow \mathsf{v}_1 \qquad \Gamma \vdash \mathsf{e}_2 : \sigma_2 \rightsquigarrow \mathsf{v}_2}{\Gamma \vdash \mathsf{e}_1\,\mathsf{e}_2 : \sigma \rightsquigarrow \lambda[\alpha]\,(\mathsf{k} : \sigma^{+} \to \alpha).\ \mathsf{v}_1\,[\alpha]\,(\lambda(\mathsf{x}_1 : (\sigma_2 \to \sigma)^{+}).\,\mathsf{v}_2\,[\alpha]\,(\lambda(\mathsf{x}_2 : \sigma_2^{+}).\,\mathsf{x}_1\,[\alpha]\,(\mathsf{x}_2, \mathsf{k})))}$$

Figure 3. CPS: Type and Environment Translation (top); Term Translation (bottom)

language). They receive foreign boolean values as native values, and can call foreign functions as native functions. The design is inspired by Matthews and Findler's multi-language system for (pared down) ML and Scheme [31], but crafted with the CPS translation in mind.

To the original core languages, we add new syntax, evaluation contexts, and reduction rules that define syntactic boundaries, written ${}^{\sigma}\mathcal{ST}$ and $\mathcal{TS}^{\sigma}$ to allow cross-language communication. The term ${}^{\sigma}\mathcal{ST}\,\mathsf{e}$ (target inside, source outside) allows a term e of target type σ^{+} to be used as a term of source type σ, while $\mathcal{TS}^{\sigma}\,\mathsf{e}$ (source inside, target outside) allows a term of source type σ to be used as a term of target type σ^{+}. Since code in our CPS target language is (nearly) linear, we let-bind $\mathcal{TS}^{\sigma}\,\mathsf{e}$ instead of simply adding $\mathcal{TS}^{\sigma}\,\mathsf{e}$ to the grammar for terms. (Here, we do not require e to be a value since, informally, e lives on the source side of the boundary and the source language does not mandate the linear code structure of the target.) In the interest of brevity, we will often abbreviate $\mathsf{let}\ \mathsf{z} = (\mathcal{TS}^{\sigma}\,\mathsf{e})\ \mathsf{in}\ C[\mathsf{z}]$ to just $C[\mathcal{TS}^{\sigma}\,\mathsf{e}]$ even if C requires a value.

We define reduction rules for boundaries annotated bool that convert boolean values from one language to the other. To convert functions across languages, we use native proxy functions. We represent a target function v in the source at type $\sigma_1 \to \sigma_2$ by a new function that takes an argument of type σ_1, converts it to its equivalent in the target, passes that and the identity continuation as an argument to the original target function v (instantiated with the result type $\sigma_2{}^{+}$), and converts the result back to source at type σ_2. Converting source functions to target functions is a little more involved. We represent a source function v in the target at type $(\sigma_1 \to \sigma_2)^{+}$ by a new function that takes type parameter α, an argument $\mathsf{x} : \sigma_1{}^{+}$ and a continuation $\mathsf{k} : \sigma_2{}^{+} \to \alpha$, converts the argument x to its equivalent in the source, passes that to the original source function v, converts the result back to target at type $\sigma_2{}^{+}$, and finally passes that to the continuation k. In both cases, notice that the direction of the conversion (and the boundary used) reverses for function arguments.

Typing judgments for λ^{ST} have the form $\Delta; \Gamma \vdash e : \varphi$, where the environments Δ and Γ are defined in Figure 4. Note that the environment Γ now tracks both source variables of type σ and target variables of type τ. The typing rules include all the λ^{S} typing rules, but augmented with the additional environment Δ; all the λ^{T} typing rules, unchanged; and rules for the two boundary constructs, shown in Figure 4.

λ^{ST} Contextual Equivalence and CIU Equivalence The grammar for contexts from λ^{S} and λ^{T} is augmented to define λ^{ST} contexts as shown in Figure 4 (bottom). The typing rules for contexts are straightforward (see online appendix [5]), largely following the ideas discussed before for λ^{T}. The definition of contextual equivalence for λ^{ST} is similar to that for λ^{T} and is given below. In the definition below, we could equivalently have chosen the context C's result type to be bool instead of bool. As is usually the case for contextual equivalence in a terminating language, any base type of the language would suffice.

Definition 5.1 (Contextual Approximation & Equivalence)
Let $\Delta; \Gamma \vdash e_1 : \varphi$ *and* $\Delta; \Gamma \vdash e_2 : \varphi$.

$$\begin{aligned} &\Delta; \Gamma \vdash e_1 \lesssim^{ctx}_{\mathrm{ST}} e_2 : \varphi \stackrel{\mathrm{def}}{=} \\ &\quad \forall C, v_1.\ \vdash C : (\Delta; \Gamma \vdash \varphi) \Rightarrow (\cdot; \cdot \vdash \mathsf{bool})\ \wedge\ \cdot; \cdot \vdash C[e_1] : \mathsf{bool}\ \wedge \\ &\qquad \cdot; \cdot \vdash C[e_2] : \mathsf{bool}\ \wedge\ C[e_1] \Downarrow v_1 \implies \\ &\qquad \exists v_2.\ C[e_2] \Downarrow v_2\ \wedge\ v_1 = v_2 \end{aligned}$$

$$\Delta; \Gamma \vdash e_1 \approx^{ctx}_{\mathrm{ST}} e_2 : \varphi \stackrel{\mathrm{def}}{=} \Delta; \Gamma \vdash e_1 \lesssim^{ctx}_{\mathrm{ST}} e_2 : \varphi \wedge \Delta; \Gamma \vdash e_2 \lesssim^{ctx}_{\mathrm{ST}} e_1 : \varphi$$

We define ciu-equivalence for λ^{ST} below. It is analogous to the definition of ciu-equivalence for λ^{T}. As before, the substitution δ maps type variables α to closed types τ. The substitution γ now maps both source variables (to values v) and target variables (to values v) in Γ.

Definition 5.2 (λ^{ST} CIU Approximation & Equivalence)
Let $\Delta; \Gamma \vdash e_1 : \varphi$ *and* $\Delta; \Gamma \vdash e_2 : \varphi$.

$$\begin{aligned} &\Delta; \Gamma \vdash e_1 \lesssim^{ciu}_{\mathrm{ST}} e_2 : \varphi \stackrel{\mathrm{def}}{=} \\ &\quad \forall E, \delta, \gamma, v_1.\ \vdash E : (\cdot; \cdot \vdash \delta(\varphi)) \Rightarrow (\cdot; \cdot \vdash \mathsf{bool})\ \wedge \\ &\qquad \delta \models \Delta\ \wedge\ \vdash \gamma : \delta(\Gamma)\ \wedge\ E[\delta(\gamma(e_1))] \Downarrow v_1 \implies \\ &\qquad \exists v_2.\ E[\delta(\gamma(e_2))] \Downarrow v_2\ \wedge\ v_1 = v_2 \end{aligned}$$

$$\Delta; \Gamma \vdash e_1 \approx^{ciu}_{\mathrm{ST}} e_2 : \varphi \stackrel{\mathrm{def}}{=} \Delta; \Gamma \vdash e_1 \lesssim^{ciu}_{\mathrm{ST}} e_2 : \varphi \wedge \Delta; \Gamma \vdash e_2 \lesssim^{ciu}_{\mathrm{ST}} e_1 : \varphi$$

Lemma 5.3 (λ^{ST}: Contextual Approx Implies CIU Approx)
If $\Delta; \Gamma \vdash e_1 \lesssim^{ctx}_{\mathrm{ST}} e_2 : \varphi$ *then* $\Delta; \Gamma \vdash e_1 \lesssim^{ciu}_{\mathrm{ST}} e_2 : \varphi$.

6. Equivalence Preservation

Having defined λ^{ST} for source-language interoperability, the proof of equivalence preservation can be decomposed into three parts:

1. if $\Gamma \vdash \mathsf{e}_1 \approx^{ctx}_{\mathrm{S}} \mathsf{e}_2 : \sigma$ then $\Gamma \vdash \mathsf{e}_1 \approx^{ctx}_{\mathrm{ST}} \mathsf{e}_2 : \sigma$ (Section 6.2);
2. if $\Gamma \vdash \mathsf{e}_1 \approx^{ctx}_{\mathrm{ST}} \mathsf{e}_2 : \sigma$ then $\cdot; \Gamma^{+} \vdash \mathsf{v}_1 \approx^{ctx}_{\mathrm{ST}} \mathsf{v}_2 : \sigma^{\div}$, where $\Gamma \vdash \mathsf{e}_1 : \sigma \rightsquigarrow \mathsf{v}_1$ and $\Gamma \vdash \mathsf{e}_2 : \sigma \rightsquigarrow \mathsf{v}_2$ (Section 6.3); and

$$\mathrm{Atom}[\varphi_1, \varphi_2] = \{ (e_1, e_2) \mid \cdot;\cdot \vdash e_1 : \varphi_1 \wedge \cdot;\cdot \vdash e_2 : \varphi_2 \}$$

$$\mathrm{Rel}[\tau_1, \tau_2] = \{ R \in \mathscr{P}(\mathrm{Atom}^{\mathrm{val}}[\tau_1, \tau_2]) \mid \forall(v_1, v_2) \in R.\ \forall v_2'.\ v_2 \precsim^{ciu}_{\mathrm{ST}} v_2' : \tau_2 \implies (v_1, v_2') \in R \}$$

Shorthand: $\mathrm{Atom}[\varphi]\rho = \mathrm{Atom}[\rho_1(\varphi), \rho_2(\varphi)]$

$$\mathcal{V}\,[\![\mathsf{bool}]\!]\,\rho = \{ (\mathsf{v}, \mathsf{v}) \in \mathrm{Atom}[\mathsf{bool}]\rho \mid \mathsf{v} = \mathsf{true} \vee \mathsf{v} = \mathsf{false} \}$$

$$\mathcal{V}\,[\![\sigma \to \sigma']\!]\,\rho = \{ (\lambda \mathsf{x} : \sigma.\, \mathsf{e}_1, \lambda \mathsf{x} : \sigma.\, \mathsf{e}_2) \in \mathrm{Atom}[\sigma \to \sigma']\rho \mid \forall(\mathsf{v}_1, \mathsf{v}_2) \in \mathcal{V}\,[\![\sigma]\!]\,\rho.\ (\mathsf{e}_1[\mathsf{v}_1/\mathsf{x}], \mathsf{e}_2[\mathsf{v}_2/\mathsf{x}]) \in \mathcal{E}\,[\![\sigma']\!]\,\rho \}$$

$$\mathcal{V}\,[\![\alpha]\!]\,\rho = R \qquad \text{where } \rho(\alpha) = (\tau_1, \tau_2, R)$$

$$\mathcal{V}\,[\![\mathtt{bool}]\!]\,\rho = \{ (\mathtt{v}, \mathtt{v}) \in \mathrm{Atom}[\mathtt{bool}]\rho \mid \mathtt{v} = \mathtt{true} \vee \mathtt{v} = \mathtt{false} \}$$

$$\mathcal{V}\,[\![\tau \times \tau']\!]\,\rho = \{ ((\mathtt{v}_1, \mathtt{v}_1'), (\mathtt{v}_2, \mathtt{v}_2')) \in \mathrm{Atom}[\tau \times \tau']\rho \mid (\mathtt{v}_1, \mathtt{v}_2) \in \mathcal{V}\,[\![\tau]\!]\,\rho \wedge (\mathtt{v}_1', \mathtt{v}_2') \in \mathcal{V}\,[\![\tau']\!]\,\rho \}$$

$$\begin{aligned}\mathcal{V}\,[\![\forall[\alpha].\tau \to \tau']\!]\,\rho = {} & \{ (\Lambda[\alpha]\,(\mathtt{x} : \rho_1(\tau)).\, \mathtt{e}_1, \Lambda[\alpha]\,(\mathtt{x} : \rho_2(\tau)).\, \mathtt{e}_2) \in \mathrm{Atom}[\forall[\alpha].\tau \to \tau']\rho \mid \\ & \forall \tau_1, \tau_2, R \in \mathrm{Rel}[\tau_1, \tau_2]. \\ & \forall (\mathtt{v}_1, \mathtt{v}_2) \in \mathcal{V}\,[\![\tau]\!]\,\rho[\alpha \mapsto (\tau_1, \tau_2, R)]. \\ & (\mathtt{e}_1[\tau_1/\alpha][\mathtt{v}_1/\mathtt{x}], \mathtt{e}_2[\tau_2/\alpha][\mathtt{v}_2/\mathtt{x}]) \in \mathcal{E}\,[\![\tau']\!]\,\rho[\alpha \mapsto (\tau_1, \tau_2, R)] \}\end{aligned}$$

$$\mathcal{E}\,[\![\varphi]\!]\,\rho = \{ (e_1, e_2) \in \mathrm{Atom}[\varphi]\rho \mid \forall v_1.\ e_1 \longmapsto^* v_1 \implies \exists v_2.\ e_2 \longmapsto^* v_2 \wedge (v_1, v_2) \in \mathcal{V}\,[\![\varphi]\!]\,\rho \}$$

$$\mathcal{D}\,[\![\cdot]\!] = \{ \emptyset \}$$

$$\mathcal{D}\,[\![\Delta, \alpha]\!] = \{ \rho[\alpha \mapsto (\tau_1, \tau_2, R)] \mid \rho \in \mathcal{D}\,[\![\Delta]\!] \wedge R \in \mathrm{Rel}[\tau_1, \tau_2] \}$$

$$\mathcal{G}\,[\![\cdot]\!]\,\rho = \{ (\emptyset, \emptyset) \}$$

$$\mathcal{G}\,[\![\Gamma, x : \varphi]\!]\,\rho = \{ (\gamma_1[x \mapsto v_1], \gamma_2[x \mapsto v_2]) \mid (\gamma_1, \gamma_2) \in \mathcal{G}\,[\![\Gamma]\!]\,\rho \wedge (v_1, v_2) \in \mathcal{V}\,[\![\varphi]\!]\,\rho \}$$

$$\begin{aligned}\Delta; \Gamma \vdash e_1 \precsim^{log}_{\mathrm{ST}} e_2 : \varphi \stackrel{\mathrm{def}}{=} {} & \Delta; \Gamma \vdash e_1 : \varphi \wedge \Delta; \Gamma \vdash e_2 : \varphi \wedge \\ & \forall \rho, \gamma_1, \gamma_2.\ \rho \in \mathcal{D}\,[\![\Delta]\!] \wedge (\gamma_1, \gamma_2) \in \mathcal{G}\,[\![\Gamma]\!]\,\rho \implies \\ & (\rho_1(\gamma_1(e_1)), \rho_2(\gamma_2(e_2))) \in \mathcal{E}\,[\![\varphi]\!]\,\rho\end{aligned}$$

$$\Delta; \Gamma \vdash e_1 \approx^{log}_{\mathrm{ST}} e_2 : \varphi \stackrel{\mathrm{def}}{=} \Delta; \Gamma \vdash e_1 \precsim^{log}_{\mathrm{ST}} e_2 : \varphi \wedge \Delta; \Gamma \vdash e_2 \precsim^{log}_{\mathrm{ST}} e_1 : \varphi$$

Figure 5. Combined Language (λ^{ST}): Logical Relation

3. if $\cdot; \Gamma^+ \vdash \mathtt{v}_1 \approx^{ctx}_{\mathrm{ST}} \mathtt{v}_2 : \sigma^{\div}$ then $\cdot; \Gamma^+ \vdash \mathtt{v}_1 \approx^{ctx}_{\mathrm{T}} \mathtt{v}_2 : \sigma^{\div}$ (Section 6.4).

We shall see that parts (1) and (2) are the nontrivial parts of the proof. Informally, part (1) says that embedding λ^{S} into λ^{ST} preserves λ^{S} equivalences, while part (2) says that the translation preserves equivalences within λ^{ST}. Once we have proved (1), (2), and (3), our main result is immediate:

Theorem 6.1 (CPS Translation is Equivalence Preserving)
If $\Gamma \vdash \mathsf{e}_1 : \sigma \rightsquigarrow \mathtt{v}_1$, $\Gamma \vdash \mathsf{e}_2 : \sigma \rightsquigarrow \mathtt{v}_2$, *and* $\Gamma \vdash \mathsf{e}_1 \approx^{ctx}_{\mathrm{S}} \mathsf{e}_2 : \sigma$, *then* $\cdot; \Gamma^+ \vdash \mathtt{v}_1 \approx^{ctx}_{\mathrm{T}} \mathtt{v}_2 : \sigma^{\div}$.

We start in Section 6.1 by setting up some machinery for our proof. We define a logical relation for λ^{ST} and prove that it coincides with contextual equivalence. Proving contextual equivalence directly can be hard or even intractable due to the quantification over all contexts C in the definition of $\approx^{ctx}_{\mathrm{ST}}$. The logical relation provides us with a convenient method for carrying out proofs of contextual equivalence. Next, in Sections 6.2-6.4, we present the three parts of the proof.

6.1 Logical Relation for λ^{ST} and Two Key Lemmas

The basic idea of logical relations is to define an equivalence (or approximation) relation on program terms by induction on the structure of their types. For instance, we would say that two functions are logically related at the type $\sigma_1 \to \sigma_2$ iff, when applied to arguments that are logically related at σ_1, they yield results that are logically related at σ_2. To take the example of product types, we would say that two pairs are logically related at the type $\tau_1 \times \tau_2$ iff their first and second components are pairwise related at the types τ_1 and τ_2, respectively.

Figure 5 presents the definition of the logical relation for λ^{ST}. The big picture is that we define a relation $\mathcal{V}\,[\![\varphi]\!]$ that relates closed values at type φ and a relation $\mathcal{E}\,[\![\varphi]\!]$ that relates closed terms at type φ, and then generalize the definition of relatedness to open terms (written $\Delta; \Gamma \vdash e_1 \precsim^{log}_{\mathrm{ST}} e_2 : \varphi$). So far these relations define logical approximation and are intended to capture the notion of contextual approximation; we define logical equivalence (written $\Delta; \Gamma \vdash e_1 \approx^{log}_{\mathrm{ST}} e_2 : \varphi$) as logical approximation in both directions.

In more detail, the value relation $\mathcal{V}\,[\![\varphi]\!]$ is parametrized by a parameter ρ that provides relational interpretations R for the free type variables in φ. We must make sure that these relations R satisfy certain requirements (enforced by requiring that R belong to $\mathrm{Rel}[\tau_1, \tau_2]$, which we explain momentarily). The first requirement is that R should relate only well-typed closed values. To this end, we first define $\mathrm{Atom}[\varphi_1, \varphi_2]$ to be the set of all pairs of well-typed closed terms e_1 and e_2 of types φ_1 and φ_2, respectively. We write $\mathrm{Atom}^{\mathrm{val}}$ to restrict the above set to pairs of values. The second requirement is that R must be *equivalence-respecting*. The latter means that R must be closed under equivalence (or more precisely under approximation): if $(v_1, v_2) \in R$ (where $v_2 : \tau_2$) and $v_2 \precsim^{ciu}_{\mathrm{ST}} v_2' : \tau_2$, then $(v_1, v_2') \in R$. Both of these requirements are enforced by $\mathrm{Rel}[\tau_1, \tau_2]$, which we define as the set of all relations R that contain values of types τ_1 and τ_1 with the additional requirement that these relations must be equivalence-respecting. (Note that the equivalence-respecting requirement is needed to prove that our logical relation is *complete* with respect to contextual equivalence.)

The parameter ρ is a finite map from type variables α to triples (τ_1, τ_2, R), where τ_1 and τ_2 are closed types and $R \in \mathrm{Rel}[\tau_1, \tau_2]$. We define abbreviations for projecting the type components of the triple as follows. If $\rho(\alpha) = (\tau_1, \tau_2, R)$, then $\rho_1(\alpha) = \tau_1$ and $\rho_2(\alpha) = \tau_2$.

The rest of the definition of the logical relation is essentially standard. All value relations $\mathcal{V}\,[\![\varphi]\!]\,\rho$ consist of pairs (v_1, v_2) where $\cdot;\cdot \vdash v_1 : \rho_1(\varphi)$ and $\cdot;\cdot \vdash v_2 : \rho_2(\varphi)$ (and similarly for term relations $\mathcal{E}\,[\![\varphi]\!]\,\rho$). Two values are related at the type α if they are in the relation R in $\rho(\alpha)$. Two values are related at the type bool (similarly, $\mathtt{bool}$) if they are equal. Two functions are related at $\sigma \to \sigma'$ if, when applied to arguments related at σ, they beta reduce to terms related at σ'—i.e., the latter must be terms that belong to the term relation $\mathcal{E}\,[\![\sigma']\!]$. The term relation $\mathcal{E}\,[\![\varphi]\!]\,\rho$ relates terms e_1 and e_2 if, when e_1 evaluates to v_1, then e_2 evaluates to some v_2 such that v_1 and v_2 are related in $\mathcal{V}\,[\![\varphi]\!]\,\rho$. Finally, the relation $\mathcal{V}\,[\![\forall[\alpha].\tau \to \tau']\!]\,\rho$, relates polymorphic functions. As expected, it considers arbitrary types τ_1, τ_2, together with an arbitrary relation $R \in \mathrm{Rel}[\tau_1, \tau_2]$, and two arguments $\mathtt{v}_1$ and $\mathtt{v}_2$ related at τ (with ρ extended to map α to (τ_1, τ_2, R), since α may appear free in τ). Then, the two polymorphic functions are considered related at type $\forall[\alpha].\tau \to \tau'$ if, when applied, respectively, to the type arguments τ_1 and τ_2, and the value arguments $\mathtt{v}_1$ and $\mathtt{v}_2$, they beta reduce to terms that are related at type τ' (again, with $\rho[\alpha \mapsto (\tau_1, \tau_2, R)]$).

The definitions of logical approximation and equivalence for open terms (at the bottom of Figure 5) rely on the relational semantics ascribed to the contexts Δ and Γ. We say that ρ belongs to the relational interpretation of Δ if $\mathrm{dom}(\rho) = \Delta$, and whenever

$\rho(\alpha) = (\tau_1, \tau_2, R)$, R is a well-formed relational interpretation (i.e., $R \in \text{Rel}[\tau_1, \tau_2]$). We say the value substitutions γ_1 and γ_2 are related at Γ if they map variables in $\text{dom}(\Gamma)$ to related values.

The definition of the logical relation for open terms, $\Delta; \Gamma \vdash e_1 \precsim^{log}_{\text{ST}} e_2 : \varphi$ (pronounced "e_1 logically approximates e_2"), is also standard. It says that given a relational interpretation ρ for Δ and value substitutions γ_1, γ_2 related at Γ, the closed terms $\rho_1(\gamma_1(e_1))$ and $\rho_2(\gamma_2(e_2))$ are related at the type φ. Finally, we say that e_1 and e_2 are logically equivalent, $\Delta; \Gamma \vdash e_1 \approx^{log}_{\text{ST}} e_2 : \varphi$, if they logically approximate each other.

Properties of the Logical Relation We prove the fundamental property of logical relations, which says that if a term is well typed, then it is related to itself. This follows from the proofs of a series of compatibility lemmas (e.g., see [38]). The proofs of most of these lemmas are standard, exactly as for any logical relation for System F. The two that are interesting are the compatibility lemmas for boundaries, which we state below. These require the following "bridge" lemma. (Further details and proofs are given in the online technical appendix [5].)

Lemma 6.2 (Bridge Lemma)

1. If $(\mathrm{e}_1, \mathrm{e}_2) \in \mathcal{E}\llbracket\sigma^+\rrbracket\,\emptyset$ *then* $({}^{\sigma}\mathcal{ST}\,\mathrm{e}_1, {}^{\sigma}\mathcal{ST}\,\mathrm{e}_2) \in \mathcal{E}\llbracket\sigma\rrbracket\,\emptyset$.

2. If $(\mathrm{e}_1, \mathrm{e}_2) \in \mathcal{E}\llbracket\sigma\rrbracket\,\emptyset$
and $(\lambda(\mathrm{x}:\sigma^+).\,\mathrm{e}_1{}', \lambda(\mathrm{x}:\sigma^+).\,\mathrm{e}_2{}') \in \mathcal{V}\llbracket\sigma^+ \to \tau\rrbracket\,\rho$, *then*
$(\text{let } \mathrm{x} = (\mathcal{TS}^{\,\sigma}\,\mathrm{e}_1) \text{ in } \mathrm{e}_1{}', \text{let } \mathrm{x} = (\mathcal{TS}^{\,\sigma}\,\mathrm{e}_2) \text{ in } \mathrm{e}_2{}') \in \mathcal{E}\llbracket\tau\rrbracket\,\rho$.

Lemma 6.3 (Compatibility $\mathcal{ST}$)
If $\Delta; \Gamma \vdash \mathrm{e}_1 \precsim^{log}_{\text{ST}} \mathrm{e}_2 : \sigma^+$ *then* $\Delta; \Gamma \vdash {}^{\sigma}\mathcal{ST}\,\mathrm{e}_1 \precsim^{log}_{\text{ST}} {}^{\sigma}\mathcal{ST}\,\mathrm{e}_2 : \sigma$.

Lemma 6.4 (Compatibility $\mathcal{TS}$)
If $\Delta; \Gamma \vdash e_1 \precsim^{log}_{\text{ST}} e_2 : \sigma$ *and* $\Delta; \Gamma, \mathrm{x} : \sigma^+ \vdash \mathrm{e}_1 \precsim^{log}_{\text{ST}} \mathrm{e}_2 : \tau$ *then* $\Delta; \Gamma \vdash \text{let } \mathrm{x} = (\mathcal{TS}^{\,\sigma}\,e_1) \text{ in } \mathrm{e}_1 \precsim^{log}_{\text{ST}} \text{let } \mathrm{x} = (\mathcal{TS}^{\,\sigma}\,e_2) \text{ in } \mathrm{e}_2 : \tau$.

Theorem 6.5 (λ^{ST} Fundamental Property)
If $\Delta; \Gamma \vdash e : \varphi$ *then* $\Delta; \Gamma \vdash e \precsim^{log}_{\text{ST}} e : \varphi$.

Proof By induction on the derivation $\Delta; \Gamma \vdash e : \varphi$. Each case follows from the corresponding compatibility lemma. □

Next, we prove that the λ^{ST} logical relation is *sound* and *complete* with respect to contextual equivalence. The key thing here is that the following lemmas (along with the property that $\precsim^{ctx}_{\text{ST}}$ implies $\precsim^{ciu}_{\text{ST}}$, Lemma 5.3), together establish that logical approximation $\precsim^{log}_{\text{ST}}$, ciu-approximation $\precsim^{ciu}_{\text{ST}}$, and contextual approximation $\precsim^{ctx}_{\text{ST}}$ all coincide. Therefore, in subsequent sections, when proving contextual equivalence properties, we are free to switch to whichever definition is most convenient to work with for proving the property at hand.

Theorem 6.6 (λ^{ST}: Soundness w.r.t. Contextual Approx)
If $\Delta; \Gamma \vdash e_1 \precsim^{log}_{\text{ST}} e_2 : \varphi$ *then* $\Delta; \Gamma \vdash e_1 \precsim^{ctx}_{\text{ST}} e_2 : \varphi$.

Lemma 6.7 (λ^{ST}: CIU Approx Implies Logical Approx)
If $\Delta; \Gamma \vdash e_1 \precsim^{ciu}_{\text{ST}} e_2 : \varphi$ *then* $\Delta; \Gamma \vdash e_1 \precsim^{log}_{\text{ST}} e_2 : \varphi$.

Theorem 6.8 (λ^{ST}: Completeness w.r.t. Contextual Approx)
If $\Delta; \Gamma \vdash e_1 \precsim^{ctx}_{\text{ST}} e_2 : \varphi$ *then* $\Delta; \Gamma \vdash e_1 \precsim^{log}_{\text{ST}} e_2 : \varphi$.

Proof Immediate from Lemmas 5.3 and 6.7. □

Two Key Lemmas We use our logical relation to establish two key properties that we will need repeatedly when proving parts (1) and (2).

The first is *boundary cancellation*, which essentially says that if you embed e into the source using $\mathcal{ST}$, and then embed that into the target using $\mathcal{TS}$, the resulting term is contextually equivalent to the original. Analogously, embedding e into the target via $\mathcal{TS}$ and then embedding the latter into the source via $\mathcal{ST}$, also results in a term that is contextually equivalent to the original.

Lemma 6.9 (Boundary Cancellation)

- *Let* $\Delta; \Gamma \vdash \mathrm{e} : \sigma$. *Then* $\Delta; \Gamma \vdash \mathrm{e} \approx^{log}_{\text{ST}} {}^{\sigma}\mathcal{ST}\,(\mathcal{TS}^{\,\sigma}\,\mathrm{e}) : \sigma$.
- *Let* $\Delta; \Gamma \vdash \mathrm{e} : \sigma^+$. *Then* $\Delta; \Gamma \vdash \mathrm{e} \approx^{log}_{\text{ST}} \mathcal{TS}^{\,\sigma}\,({}^{\sigma}\mathcal{ST}\,\mathrm{e}) : \sigma^+$.

Proof By induction on the structure of σ. □

The second key property is a *free theorem* [50] regarding terms of (computation) type $\forall\,[\alpha].(\sigma^+ \to \alpha) \to \alpha$. (We prove an analogous free theorem for terms of type $\forall\,[\alpha].(\sigma_1{}^+ \times (\sigma_2{}^+ \to \alpha)) \to \alpha$, but we will not show that here.) This free theorem captures the essence of what we gain from switching from a CPS type translation that makes use of a global answer type, to one that makes each continuation's answer type individually abstract: namely, that a computation (or function) of the above type *must* invoke its continuation at least once, and that it does not matter (in our purely functional setting) if it invokes it more than once. The free theorem can be proved using our logical relation; a similar theorem is given in Wadler [50]. We take a notational liberty in the statement of this theorem, which we discuss next.

Lemma 6.10 (Free Theorem: Continuation Shuffling)
Let $\Delta; \Gamma \vdash \mathrm{v}_f : \forall\,[\alpha].(\tau \to \alpha) \to \alpha$, *and* $\Delta; \Gamma \vdash \mathrm{v}_k : \tau \to \tau_k$.
Then $\Delta; \Gamma \vdash \mathrm{v}_f\,[\tau_k]\,\mathrm{v}_k \approx^{log}_{\text{ST}} \mathrm{v}_k\,(\mathrm{v}_f\,[\tau]\,\mathrm{id}) : \tau_k$.

Notice that $\mathrm{v}_k\,(\mathrm{v}_f\,[\tau]\,\mathrm{id})$ is not a syntactically well-formed term in λ^{ST}! We use this essentially as shorthand to avoid a much longer (and less intuitive) statement of the theorem. Strictly speaking, the conclusion of the above lemma should be written as follows:

$$\begin{array}{l} \text{Then: } \forall\rho \in \mathcal{D}\llbracket\Delta\rrbracket\,.\,\forall(\gamma_1, \gamma_2) \in \mathcal{G}\llbracket\Gamma\rrbracket\,\rho. \\ \quad \text{if } \rho_2(\gamma_2(\mathrm{v}_f\,[\tau]\,\mathrm{id})) \longmapsto^* \mathrm{v} \text{ then} \\ \quad\quad (\rho_1(\gamma_1(\mathrm{v}_f\,[\tau_k]\,\mathrm{v}_k)), (\rho_2(\gamma_2(\mathrm{v}_k)))\,\mathrm{v}) \in \mathcal{E}\llbracket\tau_k\rrbracket\,\rho \\ \quad \text{and} \\ \quad \text{if } \rho_1(\gamma_1(\mathrm{v}_f\,[\tau]\,\mathrm{id})) \longmapsto^* \mathrm{v} \text{ then} \\ \quad\quad ((\rho_1(\gamma_1(\mathrm{v}_k)))\,\mathrm{v}, \rho_2(\gamma_2(\mathrm{v}_f\,[\tau_k]\,\mathrm{v}_k))) \in \mathcal{E}\llbracket\tau_k\rrbracket\,\rho \end{array}$$

The intuition here is that we close off the expression $\mathrm{v}_f\,[\tau]\,\mathrm{id}$ with appropriate type and term substitutions and evaluate it to get a value v that we then pass to the (appropriately closed) continuation v_k. The two clauses are required because our underlying relation $\mathcal{E}\llbracket\cdot\rrbracket$ is an approximation while what we want here is equivalence.

6.2 Proving Part (1)

We start with the top layer of the proof of equivalence preservation. Our goal here is to prove that if $\Gamma \vdash \mathrm{e}_1 \approx^{ctx}_{\text{S}} \mathrm{e}_2 : \sigma$ then $\cdot; \Gamma \vdash \mathrm{e}_1 \approx^{ctx}_{\text{ST}} \mathrm{e}_2 : \sigma$. As discussed in Section 2, given an arbitrary λ^{ST} context C with a hole of type $(\cdot; \Gamma \vdash \sigma)$, we need to "back-translate" C to an equivalent λ^{S} context C. The fact that this can be done at all may seem surprising, since λ^{ST} is a more expressive language than λ^{S}. Specifically, λ^{ST} includes System F in which we can encode, e.g., Church numerals, and operations like addition and multiplication; but natural numbers, addition and multiplication cannot be encoded in our source language λ^{S}. As another example, λ^{ST} contains pairs (from λ^{T}), but pairs cannot be encoded in our source language λ^{S}. Thus, we consider this "back-translation" method and its accompanying insights to be a significant contribution of this work.

"Back-translating" λ^{ST} to λ^{S} As discussed above, we wish to "back-translate" an arbitrary λ^{ST} context C with a hole of type $(\cdot; \Gamma \vdash \sigma)$. Such a context can simply be treated as an expression $\lambda\mathrm{x} : \sigma.\, C[\mathrm{x}]$ which has type $\sigma \to \mathrm{bool}$. This type is significant. Informally, the type represents the interface for this component and, in this case, it tells us that the component behaves like a term of source type (if we have our translation right, that is) and expects to interact with terms that behave similarly (which, technically, will mean terms of some source type σ or translation type σ^+). Thus, we have to be able to "back-translate" λ^{ST} terms of source type.

$\boxed{\cdot;\Gamma \vdash e : \sigma \twoheadrightarrow \mathsf{e}}$ $\boxed{\cdot;\Gamma \vdash^{+} e : \sigma^{+} \twoheadrightarrow \mathsf{e}}$

where $\Gamma ::= \cdot \mid \Gamma, \mathsf{x} : \sigma \mid y : \sigma^{+}$
and $\mathsf{e} \in \lambda^{S}$ and $\Gamma^{\twoheadrightarrow} \vdash \mathsf{e} : \sigma$

and where $\Gamma^{\twoheadrightarrow}$ is defined as

$$(\cdot)^{\twoheadrightarrow} = \cdot \qquad (\Gamma, \mathsf{x}:\sigma)^{\twoheadrightarrow} = \Gamma^{\twoheadrightarrow}, \mathsf{x}:\sigma \qquad (\Gamma, y:\sigma^{+})^{\twoheadrightarrow} = \Gamma^{\twoheadrightarrow}, \mathsf{y}:\sigma$$

$$\frac{}{\cdot;\Gamma \vdash \mathsf{true} : \mathsf{bool} \twoheadrightarrow \mathsf{true}} \qquad \frac{}{\cdot;\Gamma \vdash \mathsf{false} : \mathsf{bool} \twoheadrightarrow \mathsf{false}} \qquad \frac{\cdot;\Gamma \vdash \mathsf{e} : \mathsf{bool} \twoheadrightarrow \mathsf{e}' \quad \cdot;\Gamma \vdash \mathsf{e}_1 : \sigma \twoheadrightarrow \mathsf{e}_1' \quad \cdot;\Gamma \vdash \mathsf{e}_2 : \sigma \twoheadrightarrow \mathsf{e}_2'}{\cdot;\Gamma \vdash \mathsf{if\ e\ then\ e_1\ else\ e_2} : \sigma \twoheadrightarrow \mathsf{if\ e'\ then\ e_1'\ else\ e_2'}}$$

$$\frac{\mathsf{x}:\sigma \in \Gamma}{\cdot;\Gamma \vdash \mathsf{x} : \sigma \twoheadrightarrow \mathsf{x}} \qquad \frac{\cdot;\Gamma, \mathsf{x}:\sigma_1 \vdash \mathsf{e} : \sigma_2 \twoheadrightarrow \mathsf{e}'}{\cdot;\Gamma \vdash \lambda \mathsf{x}:\sigma_1.\,\mathsf{e} : \sigma_1 \rightarrow \sigma_2 \twoheadrightarrow \lambda \mathsf{x}:\sigma_1.\,\mathsf{e}'} \qquad \frac{\cdot;\Gamma \vdash \mathsf{e}_1 : \sigma_2 \rightarrow \sigma \twoheadrightarrow \mathsf{e}_1' \quad \cdot;\Gamma \vdash \mathsf{e}_2 : \sigma_2 \twoheadrightarrow \mathsf{e}_2'}{\cdot;\Gamma \vdash \mathsf{e}_1\ \mathsf{e}_2 : \sigma \twoheadrightarrow \mathsf{e}_1'\ \mathsf{e}_2'} \qquad \frac{\cdot;\Gamma \vdash^{+} e : \sigma^{+} \twoheadrightarrow \mathsf{e}}{\cdot;\Gamma \vdash {}^{\sigma}\mathcal{ST}\, e : \sigma \twoheadrightarrow \mathsf{e}}$$

$$\frac{}{\cdot;\Gamma \vdash^{+} true : \mathsf{bool}^{+} \twoheadrightarrow \mathsf{true}} \qquad \frac{}{\cdot;\Gamma \vdash^{+} false : \mathsf{bool}^{+} \twoheadrightarrow \mathsf{false}} \qquad \frac{\cdot;\Gamma \vdash^{+} v : \mathsf{bool}^{+} \twoheadrightarrow \mathsf{e} \quad \cdot;\Gamma \vdash^{+} e_1 : \sigma^{+} \twoheadrightarrow \mathsf{e}_1 \quad \cdot;\Gamma \vdash^{+} e_2 : \sigma^{+} \twoheadrightarrow \mathsf{e}_2}{\cdot;\Gamma \vdash^{+} \mathtt{if}\ v\ \mathtt{then}\ e_1\ \mathtt{else}\ e_2 : \sigma^{+} \twoheadrightarrow \mathsf{if\ e\ then\ e_1\ else\ e_2}}$$

$$\frac{y : \sigma^{+} \in \Gamma}{\cdot;\Gamma \vdash^{+} y : \sigma^{+} \twoheadrightarrow \mathsf{y}} \qquad \frac{\cdot;\Gamma, y : {\sigma_1}^{+} \vdash^{+} e[{\sigma_2}^{+}/\alpha][id/k] : {\sigma_2}^{+} \twoheadrightarrow \mathsf{e}}{\cdot;\Gamma \vdash^{+} \lambda[\alpha]\,((y,k) : ({\sigma_1}^{+} \times ({\sigma_2}^{+} \rightarrow \alpha))).\,e : \forall[\alpha].({\sigma_1}^{+} \times ({\sigma_2}^{+} \rightarrow \alpha)) \rightarrow \alpha \twoheadrightarrow \lambda \mathsf{y}:\sigma_1.\,\mathsf{e}}$$

$$\frac{\cdot;\Gamma \vdash \mathsf{e}_1 : \sigma_1 \twoheadrightarrow \mathsf{e}_1' \quad \cdot;\Gamma, x : {\sigma_1}^{+} \vdash^{+} e : \sigma^{+} \twoheadrightarrow \mathsf{e}}{\cdot;\Gamma \vdash^{+} \mathtt{let}\ x = (\mathcal{TS}^{\sigma_1}\, \mathsf{e}_1)\ \mathtt{in}\ e : \sigma^{+} \twoheadrightarrow \mathsf{let\ x = e_1'\ in\ e}} \qquad \frac{\cdot;\Gamma \vdash v : \tau_1 \times \tau_2 \quad v = (v_1, v_2) \quad \cdot;\Gamma \vdash^{+} e[v_i/x] : \sigma^{+} \twoheadrightarrow \mathsf{e}}{\cdot;\Gamma \vdash^{+} \mathtt{let}\ x = \pi_i v\ \mathtt{in}\ e : \sigma^{+} \twoheadrightarrow \mathsf{e}}$$

$$\frac{\begin{array}{c}\cdot;\Gamma \vdash v_1 : \forall[\alpha].\tau_2 \rightarrow \tau \quad \cdot \vdash \tau' \quad \cdot;\Gamma \vdash v_2 : \tau_2[\tau'/\alpha] \\ \sigma^{+} = \tau[\tau'/\alpha] \quad v_1 = \lambda[\alpha]\,(z:\tau_2).\,e \quad \cdot;\Gamma \vdash^{+} e[\tau'/\alpha][v_2/z] : \sigma^{+} \twoheadrightarrow \mathsf{e}\end{array}}{\cdot;\Gamma \vdash^{+} v_1\,[\tau']\,v_2 : \sigma^{+} \twoheadrightarrow \mathsf{e}} \ (\nexists \sigma_1.\ {\sigma_1}^{+} = \forall[\alpha].\tau_2 \rightarrow \tau)$$

$$\frac{\tau' = \sigma^{+} \quad v_2 = (v_a, \lambda(z:{\sigma_2}^{+}).\,e_k) \quad \cdot;\Gamma \vdash^{+} v_1 : (\sigma_1 \rightarrow \sigma_2)^{+} \twoheadrightarrow \mathsf{e}_1 \quad \cdot;\Gamma \vdash^{+} v_a : {\sigma_1}^{+} \twoheadrightarrow \mathsf{e}_a \quad \cdot;\Gamma, z : {\sigma_2}^{+} \vdash^{+} e_k : \sigma^{+} \twoheadrightarrow \mathsf{e}_k}{\cdot;\Gamma \vdash^{+} v_1\,[\tau']\,v_2 : \sigma^{+} \twoheadrightarrow \mathsf{let\ z = e_1\ e_a\ in\ e_k}}$$

Figure 6. "Back-translation": Relating λ^{ST} terms to λ^{S} terms

Translating all the λ^{S} terms embedded in λ^{ST} is straightforward—they remain unchanged—until we get to a boundary term ${}^{\sigma}\mathcal{ST}\, e$. At this point, we have to be able to translate e which has type σ^{+}. As discussed before, e may contain subterms that are not "back-translatable". However, the whole term e has type σ^{+} so it should be back-translatable. Intuitively, the idea here is to partially evaluate e till you have a term whose subterms are all back-translatable (of type σ or σ^{+}). Of course, the result of partial evaluation will be equivalent to the original e. The remaining issue is: can we always partially evaluate till we get to such a point? We will show that this is always the case.

With that in mind, we set up two judgments that "back-translate" e to some $\mathsf{e} \in \lambda^{S}$ (see Figure 6). They have the form $\cdot;\Gamma \vdash e : \sigma \twoheadrightarrow \mathsf{e}$ (for translating σ terms) and $\cdot;\Gamma \vdash^{+} e : \sigma^{+} \twoheadrightarrow \mathsf{e}$ (for translating σ^{+} terms). Here Γ may only contain mappings of the form $\mathsf{x} : \sigma$ or $y : \sigma^{+}$—that is, Γ may *only* contain variables of source type or translation type. (This is an important restriction as we shall see.) $\Gamma^{\twoheadrightarrow}$ denotes the environment Γ with all mappings of the form $y : \sigma^{+}$ replaced by $\mathsf{y} : \sigma$. $\Gamma^{\twoheadrightarrow}$ is the environment used to type-check e.

The "back-translation" rules are given in Figure 6. The rules for translating λ^{ST} terms $\mathsf{e} : \sigma$ are straightforward, defined by induction on the structure of the term. The only interesting case is the boundary ${}^{\sigma}\mathcal{ST}\, e$. This is where we switch to the other judgment ($\vdash^{+}$) which translates terms e that have type σ^{+}. We translate target boolean values by converting them to equivalent source booleans and target $\mathtt{if}$ expressions are easy to translate because all of the subterms are of translation type.

When translating λ terms of type $\sigma_1 \rightarrow {\sigma_2}^{+}$, which have a type parameter α and two value parameters $y : {\sigma_1}^{+}$ and $k : {\sigma_2}^{+} \rightarrow \alpha$, we can only add $y : {\sigma_1}^{+}$ to the environment Γ; since k is not of source type or translation type it cannot be added to Γ, and we can never add type variables to the type environment Δ (it always remains empty). Hence, we substitute ${\sigma_2}^{+}$ for α in the body of the function and the identity continuation id for k. As a result, our premise has a term of translation type ${\sigma_2}^{+}$ that we can continue to back-translate. The reason this rule is well founded is because the type of the term (${\sigma_2}^{+}$) in the premise is smaller than the type of the term in the conclusion.

Translating the (let form for) boundary $\mathcal{TS}^{\sigma}\, \mathsf{e}_1$ is straightforward, since the subterms have either source type or translation type.

The term $\mathtt{let}\ x = \pi_i v\ \mathtt{in}\ e$ is more interesting. Here v must have type $\tau_1 \times \tau_2$. But since the latter is not a source type σ or a translation type σ^{+}, v cannot be a variable! (This is why the restriction on the codomain of Γ is critical.) Therefore, v must be a pair, which means partial evaluation is possible. We project the i-th component and substitute it for x in the let body e. The resulting term has type σ^{+} so we continue to back-translate. Note that this rule is well founded because $e[v_i/x]$ will reduce in fewer steps than $\mathtt{let}\ x = \pi_i v\ \mathtt{in}\ e$.

The two rules for $v_1\,[\tau']\,v_2$ are more involved but follow similar reasoning. In the first of these rules the function v_1 is not of translation type. That means that it cannot be a variable. This permits partial evaluation (by applying v_1 to τ' and v_2, which yields a term that can be back-translated (since it has type σ^{+}) and will reduce in fewer steps. In the second rule (last rule in Figure 6), v_1 is of type $(\sigma_1 \rightarrow \sigma_2)^{+}$ (so it may be a variable), but that means that v_2 must be a pair so it cannot be a variable. Therefore, we take apart the argument v_a and the continuation in that pair. The continuation also is not of translation type, so it cannot be variable. We then separately back-translate these and reassemble to get the final back-translation for $v_1\,[\tau']\,v_2$. This rule is well founded since it only requires back-translation of subterms of the original term.

Our rules are exhaustive, in the sense that all possible terms of type σ and σ^{+} have been covered.

Next we show that for every term of type σ and σ^{+}, it is possible to construct a finite back-translation derivation, and that the back-translation e is equivalent to the original e. Note that for the equivalence statement, on the right-hand side we have to replace all target y variables with $\mathcal{TS}^{\sigma}$ y since $\Gamma^{\twoheadrightarrow}$ contains y : σ in place of y : σ^+.

Lemma 6.11 (From λ^{ST} term : σ / σ^+ to equivalent λ^{S} term)
Let $\Gamma ::= \cdot \mid \Gamma, x:\sigma \mid y:\sigma^+$

1. *If* $\cdot;\Gamma \vdash e : \sigma$ *then there exists* $e \in \lambda^{\mathrm{S}}$ *s.t.* $\cdot;\Gamma \vdash e : \sigma \twoheadrightarrow e$ *and* $\cdot;\Gamma^{\twoheadrightarrow} \vdash e[(\mathcal{TS}^{\Gamma^{\twoheadrightarrow}(y)}\, y)/y] \approx^{log}_{\mathrm{ST}} e : \sigma$.
2. *If* $\cdot;\Gamma \vdash e : \sigma^+$ *then there exists* $e \in \lambda^{\mathrm{S}}$ *s.t.* $\cdot;\Gamma \vdash^{+} e : \sigma^+ \twoheadrightarrow e$ *and* $\cdot;\Gamma^{\twoheadrightarrow} \vdash {}^{\sigma}\mathcal{ST}\,(e[(\mathcal{TS}^{\Gamma^{\twoheadrightarrow}(y)}\, y)/y]) \approx^{log}_{\mathrm{ST}} e : \sigma$.

Proof (1) and (2) are proved by simultaneous induction since the σ and σ^+ translation rules are mutually dependent. We then proceed by induction on the length of the reduction sequence for e, nested induction on the type σ, and innermost induction on the structure of the term e. □

Wrapping Up Proof of Part (1) Our desired lemma, that $\Gamma \vdash e_1 \approx^{ctx}_{\mathrm{S}} e_2 : \sigma$ implies $\cdot;\Gamma \vdash e_1 \approx^{ctx}_{\mathrm{ST}} e_2 : \sigma$, follows as a corollary from the lemma below.

Lemma 6.12 (Ciu-equiv in λ^{S} implies ciu-equiv in λ^{ST})
Let Γ *be a* λ^{S} *environment, and let* e_1 *and* e_2 *be* λ^{S} *terms.*
If $\Gamma \vdash e_1 \lesssim^{ciu}_{\mathrm{S}} e_2 : \sigma$ *then* $\cdot;\Gamma \vdash e_1 \lesssim^{ciu}_{\mathrm{ST}} e_2 : \sigma$.

Proof Suppose $E : (\cdot;\cdot \vdash \sigma \Rightarrow (\cdot;\cdot \vdash \mathsf{bool})$, and $\gamma_{st} : \Gamma$ and $E[\gamma_{st}(e_1)] \Downarrow v$ where $v : \mathsf{bool}$. Show: $E[\gamma_{st}(e_2)] \Downarrow v$.
We back-translate E (or, to be precise, $\lambda x{:}\sigma.\, E[x]$) and γ_{st} to e_E and γ_s. By Lemma 6.11 these are equivalent to the original E and γ_{st}. Hence, $E[\gamma_{st}(e_1)] \approx^{ctx}_{\mathrm{ST}} e_E(\gamma_s(e_1)) : \mathsf{bool}$. Hence, the latter evaluates to v. Now, we instantate the premise with e_E (after morphing it into a valid evaluation context), and γ_s. Hence, $e_E(\gamma_s(e_2))$ evaluates to v. Since $e_E(\gamma_s(e_2)) \approx^{ctx}_{\mathrm{ST}} E[\gamma_{st}(e_2)] : \mathsf{bool}$, the latter evaluates to v. □

6.3 Proving Part (2)

We now tackle the middle layer of the proof of equivalence preservation. Our goal in this section is to prove that if e_1 and e_2 translate to v_1 and v_2, then $e_1 \approx^{ctx}_{\mathrm{ST}} e_2$ at type σ implies that $v_1 \approx^{ctx}_{\mathrm{ST}} v_2$ at type $\sigma^{\div}$.

Below, we prove that our CPS translation is both semantics preserving (typically referred to as compiler correctness) and semantics reflecting. We use the logical relation for our multi-language system to do these proofs. Our statements of semantics preservation and reflection are novel in that they rely on our multi-language semantics. As we discuss in Section 8, as compared to work on semantics-preserving compilation that uses cross-language logical relations [8, 9, 17] (which relate source terms to target terms), it seems simpler to understand how to set up the definitions and machinery for such proofs using a multi-language system and logical relation.

Finally, we wrap up by showing that the main result of this section (Lemma 6.17), namely the proof that translation preserves equivalence (within λ^{ST}), which follows easily from the fact that CPS translation preserves and reflects semantics.

Translation Preserves and Reflects Semantics With the boundary cancellation and continuation-shuffling lemmas in hand, we can prove that our CPS translation preserves and reflects semantics. In the statement of these lemmas, we will have a λ^{S} term e on one side and its translation, a λ^{T} term v, on the other side. Wherever e contains a variable $x : \sigma$, v will have the variable $x : \sigma^+$. Therefore, we will need related (source and target) substitutions γ_{S} and γ_{T} to obtain closed terms.

Definition 6.13 (Related Source-Target Substitutions)
Let Γ *be a finite map from variables* x *to types* σ. *Let* γ_{S} *be a finite map from variables* x *to (closed) values* v. *Let* γ_{T} *be a finite map from variables* x *to (closed) values* v.
We define $\Gamma \vdash \gamma_{\mathrm{S}} \lesssim \gamma_{\mathrm{T}}$ *as follows:*

$$\begin{array}{rcl} \cdot \vdash \emptyset \lesssim \emptyset & \text{iff} & (\textit{unconditionally}) \\ \Gamma, x:\sigma \vdash \gamma_{\mathrm{S}}, x \mapsto v \lesssim \gamma_{\mathrm{T}}, x \mapsto v & \text{iff} & \Gamma \vdash \gamma_{\mathrm{S}} \lesssim \gamma_{\mathrm{T}} \\ & & \wedge \vdash v \lesssim^{log}_{\mathrm{ST}} {}^{\sigma}\mathcal{ST}\, v : \sigma \end{array}$$

We define $\Gamma \vdash \gamma_{\mathrm{S}} \gtrsim \gamma_{\mathrm{T}}$ *as follows:*

$$\begin{array}{rcl} \cdot \vdash \emptyset \gtrsim \emptyset & \text{iff} & (\textit{unconditionally}) \\ \Gamma, x:\sigma \vdash \gamma_{\mathrm{S}}, x \mapsto v \gtrsim \gamma_{\mathrm{T}}, x \mapsto v & \text{iff} & \Gamma \vdash \gamma_{\mathrm{S}} \gtrsim \gamma_{\mathrm{T}} \\ & & \wedge \vdash {}^{\sigma}\mathcal{ST}\, v \lesssim^{log}_{\mathrm{ST}} v : \sigma \end{array}$$

We define $\Gamma \vdash \gamma_{\mathrm{S}} \simeq \gamma_{\mathrm{T}}$ *as follows:*

$$\Gamma \vdash \gamma_{\mathrm{S}} \simeq \gamma_{\mathrm{T}} \quad \text{iff} \quad \Gamma \vdash \gamma_{\mathrm{S}} \lesssim \gamma_{\mathrm{T}} \wedge \Gamma \vdash \gamma_{\mathrm{S}} \gtrsim \gamma_{\mathrm{T}}$$

Notice that in the definition of $\Gamma \vdash \gamma_{\mathrm{S}} \gtrsim \gamma_{\mathrm{T}}$, we require $\vdash {}^{\sigma}\mathcal{ST}\, v \lesssim^{log}_{\mathrm{ST}} v : \sigma$. Using boundary cancellation and the compatibility lemmas for boundaries, we can conclude that this is equivalent to $\vdash v \lesssim^{log}_{\mathrm{ST}} \mathcal{TS}^{\sigma}\, v : \sigma^+$. (This observation might make it slightly easier to understand the statement of Lemma 6.15.)

Informally, the following lemma says that if e evaluates to some value v_1, then its CPS translation, when applied to the identity continuation will evaluate to some $v_2 : \sigma^+$ that can be converted to a source value v_2 such that v_1 and v_2 are related at σ.

Lemma 6.14 (CPS is semantics preserving)
If $\Gamma \vdash e : \sigma \rightsquigarrow v$ *and* $\Gamma \vdash \gamma_{\mathrm{S}} \lesssim \gamma_{\mathrm{T}}$
then $\vdash \gamma_{\mathrm{S}}(e) \lesssim^{log}_{\mathrm{ST}} {}^{\sigma}\mathcal{ST}\,(\gamma_{\mathrm{T}}(v)\ [\sigma^+]\ \mathrm{id}) : \sigma$.

Proof By induction on the structure of e. □

The statement that CPS translation is semantics reflecting is a bit more involved. Informally, the following lemma says that suppose that the computation v (which is the CPS translation of e), when applied to a type τ_a and some continuation $v_k : \sigma^+ \rightarrow \tau_a$, evaluates to the value $v_1 : \tau_a$. Then if we convert e to a target value $v' : \sigma^+$, and then invoke the continuation v_k (or to be precise, a continuation that's related to v_k) with v', this will result in a value v_2 such that v_1 and v_2 are related at the type τ_a.

Lemma 6.15 (CPS is semantics reflecting)
If $\Gamma \vdash e : \sigma \rightsquigarrow v$ *and* $\Gamma \vdash \gamma_{\mathrm{S}} \gtrsim \gamma_{\mathrm{T}}$ *then*
$\vdash \gamma_{\mathrm{T}}(v) \lesssim^{log}_{\mathrm{ST}} \Lambda[\alpha]\,(k:\sigma^+ \rightarrow \alpha).\ \mathrm{let}\ z = (\mathcal{TS}^{\sigma}\, \gamma_{\mathrm{S}}(e))\ \mathrm{in}\ k\ z : \sigma^{\div}$.

Proof By induction on the structure of e. □

The following is a corollary of semantics preservation and reflection. Notice that by boundary cancellation, the conclusion is equivalent to $\vdash \mathcal{TS}^{\sigma}\,(\gamma_{\mathrm{S}}(e)) \approx^{log}_{\mathrm{ST}} (\gamma_{\mathrm{T}}(v)\ [\sigma^+]\ \mathrm{id}) : \sigma^+$. (This explains why we call it "translation is equivalent to embedding.")

Corollary 6.16 (Translation is Equivalent to Embedding)
Let $\Gamma \vdash e : \sigma \rightsquigarrow v$ *and* $\Gamma \vdash \gamma_{\mathrm{S}} \simeq \gamma_{\mathrm{T}}$.
Then $\vdash \gamma_{\mathrm{S}}(e) \approx^{log}_{\mathrm{ST}} {}^{\sigma}\mathcal{ST}\,(\gamma_{\mathrm{T}}(v)\ [\sigma^+]\ \mathrm{id}) : \sigma$.

Lemma 6.17 (Translation Preserves Equivalence in λ^{ST})
Let e_1 *and* e_2 *be* λ^{S} *terms. If* $\Gamma \vdash e_1 : \sigma \rightsquigarrow v_1$, $\Gamma \vdash e_2 : \sigma \rightsquigarrow v_2$, *and* $\cdot;\Gamma \vdash e_1 \lesssim^{log}_{\mathrm{ST}} e_2 : \sigma$, *then* $\cdot;\Gamma \vdash v_1 \lesssim^{log}_{\mathrm{ST}} v_2 : \sigma^{\div}$.

Proof Follows from Lemmas 6.14 and 6.15 and the transitivity of $\lesssim^{log}_{\mathrm{ST}}$. □

6.4 Proving Part (3)

For the final (bottom) layer of our proof of equivalence preservation, we must show that if $\cdot;\Gamma^+ \vdash v_1 \approx^{ctx}_{\mathrm{ST}} v_2 : \sigma^{\div}$ then $\cdot;\Gamma^+ \vdash v_1 \approx^{ctx}_{\mathrm{T}} v_2 : \sigma^{\div}$. The latter is immediate from the following more general lemma.

Lemma 6.18 (Equivalence in λ^{ST} implies equivalence in λ^{T})
Let e_1 *and* e_2 *be* λ^{T} *terms.*
If $\Delta;\Gamma \vdash e_1 \lesssim^{ctx}_{\mathrm{ST}} e_2 : \tau$ *then* $\Delta;\Gamma \vdash e_1 \lesssim^{ctx}_{\mathrm{T}} e_2 : \tau$.

The proof is straightforward, intuitively, because λ^{T} contexts are a subset of λ^{ST} contexts. Given an arbitrary λ^{T} context C of the appropriate type, we must show that if C[e₁] evaluates to v (which will be of type bool) then so does C[e₁]. We can instantiate the premise with the context ${}^{\text{bool}}\mathcal{ST}$ [C[·]]. The rest easily follows from the fact that there is a one-to-one correspondence between the evaluation of a λ^{T} expression in λ^{ST} and in λ^{T}, and from noting that the reduction rule for ${}^{\text{bool}}\mathcal{ST}\,\cdot$ simply converts true to true and false to false.

7. Equivalence Reflection

Equivalence reflection is a direct consequence of semantics preservation. Semantics preservation states that source programs (closed λ^{S} terms of base type, i.e., bool) and their translations in λ^{T} behave analogously:

Lemma 7.1 (Semantics preservation)
Let $\cdot \vdash$ e : bool $\rightsquigarrow$ v. *If* e $\longmapsto^{*}$ true *then* v [bool] id $\longmapsto^{*}$ true *and if* e $\longmapsto^{*}$ false *then* v [bool] id $\longmapsto^{*}$ false.

Proof Immediate from Lemma 6.16. □

The next observation we need concerns the structural behavior of the CPS translation:

Lemma 7.2 (Context translation)
Let $\Gamma \vdash$ C[e₁] : σ *and* $\Gamma \vdash$ C[e₂] : σ. *Then there exist* C, v_1, v_2 *such that* $\Gamma \vdash$ C[e₁] : $\sigma \rightsquigarrow$ C[v_1] *and* $\Gamma \vdash$ C[e₂] : $\sigma \rightsquigarrow$ C[v_2].

Proof By induction on the structure of C, using the definition of the CPS translation relation. □

Equivalence reflection now follows almost immediately from Lemmas 7.1 and 7.2:

Theorem 7.3 (Equivalence reflection)
Let $\Gamma \vdash e_1 : \sigma \rightsquigarrow v_1$ *and* $\Gamma \vdash e_2 : \sigma \rightsquigarrow v_2$. *If* $\cdot;\Gamma^{+} \vdash v_1 \approx^{ctx}_{T} v_2 : \sigma^{\div}$ *then* $\Gamma \vdash e_1 \approx^{ctx}_{S} e_2 : \sigma$.

Proof Indirect: Suppose the conclusion does not hold, which means there exists some C such that $\cdot \vdash$ C[e₁] : bool and $\cdot \vdash$ C[e₂] : bool where (w.l.o.g.) C[e₁] $\longmapsto^{*}$ true while C[e₂] $\longmapsto^{*}$ false. By Lemma 7.2 there must exist a C such that $\cdot \vdash$ C[e₁] : bool $\rightsquigarrow$ C[v_1] and $\cdot \vdash$ C[e₂] : bool $\rightsquigarrow$ C[v_2]. At this point Lemma 7.1 tells us that (C[v_1]) [bool] id $\longmapsto^{*}$ true while (C[v_2]) [bool] id $\longmapsto^{*}$ false. Thus, (C[·]) [bool] id is a context that discriminates between v_1 and v_2, which is a contradiction. □

8. Discussion and Future Work

Supporting Additional Language Features For this paper, we chose simply-typed λ-calculus and System F as our source and target languages so that we could highlight the main ideas underlying our proof technique, in particular, the use of multi-language semantics and how back-translation can leverage partial evaluation given the right type translation. We now sketch how to extend our theorem and its proof to source and target langauges with more advanced features.

If the source and target language have *non-terminating* terms, then we are faced with two difficulties: ensuring well-foundedness of the back-translation (which affects Lemma 6.11) and proving the continuation-shuffling lemma (Lemma 6.10).

To address the first problem, ensuring well-foundedness of the back-translation relation, we add a new case wherever back-translation performs computation steps: if the term to be partially evaluated is non-terminating (i.e., contextually equivalent to a term that diverges), simply make its translation a non-terminating source term of appropriate type. Notice that this definition does not yield an algorithm for back-translation but merely a relation. However, since back-translation is merely a proof device, it does not need to be an algorithm. We explain this is greater detail in the technical appendix [5] (see §1.1): we add divergent terms to both λ^{S} and λ^{T} and present the changes required to the back-translation rules.

The second problem, proving the continuation-shuffling lemma, is more difficult to deal with: in the presence of non-termination, Lemma 6.10 cannot be proved by parametricity alone; parametricity only gives us an approximation relation and not an equivalence relation. However, there is an alternative, syntactic proof for the continuation-shuffling lemma in this case. The details are beyond the scope of the current work; we will present that result in a future paper.

Recursive types give rise to non-termination, so everything said above applies here as well. In particular, though, recursive types make it somewhat trickier to define the semantics of our multi-language boundary terms. However, the technique for defining "wrapper" terms in our full abstraction proof for closure conversion [4] can be adapted to deal with this issue. Also, in the presence of recursive types we will need to switch to a step-indexed logical relation [3] for λ^{ST} to ensure well-foundedness of the logical relation. Thus, all parts of the proof that make use of the λ^{ST} logical relation will become more involved. Again, we plan to report on this result in a future paper.

Adding *polymorphism* to the source language is not difficult to deal with. The main idea is for boundary terms to not "peek under" abstraction barriers but to simply leave abstract things abstract. We have successfully applied this idea before in our work on fully abstract closure conversion [4] and do not foresee any difficulties when adapting it to the case of CPS translation.

Our longer-term goal is to show that a compiler from *System F* (with recursion, and later, with state) *to typed assembly language* is equivalence preserving. Thus far we have considered two phases of compilation, namely CPS (this paper) and typed closure conversion [4], where the type translations were precisely the key to ensuring that the target terms that compiled code interacts with are sufficiently well behaved. Thus, the type translations were the key to proving that the translations were equivalence preserving. To formulate an equivalence-preserving translation from CPS-and-closure-converted code down to assembly, we will need a target-level type system rich enough to be able to express invariants about local state, separation of state, and so on. We believe that an assembly language based on Hoare Type Theory [37] can provide the features needed for imposing the necessary well-behavedness constraints on target contexts.

Finally, the reader may have wondered if we can prove that our CPS translation is fully abstract when the target language is System F *without the syntactic restriction that enforces continuation-passing style*. In the online technical appendix (see §1.3) we show that this is, in fact, the case. The main change to the proof is that the back-translation from this unrestricted System F to STLC becomes more complicated, intuitively, since a target language without the CPS restriction contains many more terms than λ^{T}.

Compiler Correctness Proofs Let us compare the statement of "CPS is Semantics Preserving" (Lemma 6.14) to roughly what one would expect in a semantics-preservation (compiler correctness) proof that uses a cross-language logical relation (e.g., [8, 9, 17]) relating source terms of type σ to target terms of type σ^{+} (though, relating to $\sigma^{\div}$ is a valid choice as well). In the absence of a combined language, the statement there cannot mention $\mathcal{ST}$. Instead it says that v_1 must be related to v_1 in the cross-language relation at the type σ (which would mean that v_1 would have type σ^{+}).

That means that to understand the definition of "relatedness" at each type, one would have to have a precise understanding of the cross-language relation. In the presence of features like recursive types (and eventually state), these logical relations get rather complicated, for instance using step-indexing and/or biorthogonality (e.g., [8, 9]), or advanced denotational models. Thus, it can be difficult for someone who simply wants to understand the statement of the semantics-preservation theorem, and not the mathematical machinery underlying the logical relation, to decipher exactly what that statement says. On the other hand, with the multi-language approach, to understand the statement of the theorem, one simply has to examine the reduction rules for boundaries. The details of the λ^{ST} logical relation are not important at this level; all one needs to know is that it is sound with respect to contextual equivalence.

Finally, defining the multi-language logical relation seems more straightforward than the cross-language logical relation. The multi-language logical relation is simply a combination of the logical relations for source and target; the desired relationship between source and target semantics is specified separately by defining the dynamic semantics for boundaries. The cross-language logical relation, meanwhile, must simultaneously provide a proof method and specify the desired relationship between source and target terms.

9. Related Work

Fully Abstract Denotational Models The earliest work on full abstraction was done in the context of denotational models of languages (e.g., [2, 16, 25, 33]). The denotation function can be thought of as a translation from a syntactic/operational calculus into a mathematical domain. The goal there is to ensure that the denotational semantics does not expose differences that are not operationally observable [35]. As typified by parallel OR in PCF [39], in a lot of this work, full abstraction is achieved by adding certain behaviors that are possible in the denotational semantics (target) to the operational semantics of the language being modeled (source). Our work differs somewhat from that on denotational models in that we are interested in proving full abstraction of *translations* (mostly compilers); here the target language also comes with an operational semantics. In particular, we focus on type-directed and type-preserving compilation and critically require a sufficiently "clever" type translation such that the types of compiled terms can impose well-behavedness constraints on any target-level term that might interact with the result of the translation, thus ensuring that target contexts cannot violate source-level abstractions.

Translation to Continuation-Passing Style CPS has been studied extensively in the literature. Here we only discuss work that seems most closely related to ours.

A number of papers have investigated full abstraction for CPS translation, but there is no prior full abstraction result for a CPS translation that uses a locally polymorphic answer type. Meyer and Riecke [32] pointed out that standard (untyped) CPS translation does not preserve observational equivalence and conjectured as to how this could be repaired.

Several papers have looked at the use of linear types to ensure that a function calls its continuation exactly once. Zdancewic and Myers [51] present a security-typed CPS target language with higher-order, imperative features where linear continuations are needed to ensure noninterference. They also give a translation from a security-typed, direct-style language into the afore-mentioned target language using linear typing of CPS and prove that the translation preserves well-typedness. Berdine *et al.* [10, 11] show that continuations are used linearly in a variety of situations, including procedure call/return, exception raising/handling, labelled jumps (`goto` statements) and process switching (coroutines). Neither Zdancewic and Myers [51] nor Berdine *et al.* [10, 11] present any full abstraction results for their CPS translation.

Berdine, O'Hearn, and Thielecke [12] use affine typing of CPS to extract the range of CPS for a call-by-value λ-calculus. Specifically, they restrict the grammar of types in the target to only those forms exercised by the CPS translation. They then define the grammar for target terms so that there is one syntactic category for terms of each type. This allows them to give a precise characterization of the range of CPS by showing that all terms in the target come from some term in the source—that is, they prove a "no junk" lemma (also known as full completeness) that states that for each term M in the target, there exists a term N in the source such that M is $\beta\eta$-equivalent to the CPS translation of N. The proof of this "no junk" lemma requires back-translating M to get N. The critical difference between Berdine *et al.*'s work [12] and ours that their target language is *exactly as expressive* as the source (i.e., every target term can be back-translated), while our target language is *more expressive* than the source (i.e., there exist well-typed target terms that cannot be back-translated, specifically, terms of type τ where τ is not a translation type.) Consequently, our proof framework allows for one target language to serve as the target for different source languages and compilers, and allows components written in these different source languages to interoperate at the target level (assuming the compilation strategies rely on similar representation invariants at the target level). As a concrete example, we could define a CPS translation from a second source language, System F, to our target langauge λ^{T}. Now source code written in λ^{S} can interoperate with source code written in System F *after* CPS translation to λ^{T}, as long as we have a well-typed program after "linking" the two compiled components in λ^{T}. This would not be possible if we had resorted to a strategy like Berdine *et al.*'s where back-translation requires that the target language be no more expressive than the source.

Sabry and Felleisen [43] study equational completeness of CPS based on $\beta\eta$-equality rather than observational equivalence. They present a CPS transformation and an inverse mapping (or "back-translation"). From the CPS transformation, they extract the precise language of CPS terms closed under $\beta\eta$-equality, arriving at almost exactly the same syntax (modulo "administrative" redexes) as Berdine *et al.* [12]. Sabry and Felleisen analyze the syntax of the output of CPS while Berdine *et al.* analyze the types of the output of CPS to arrive as almost exactly the same target language syntax. Hence, Berdine *et al.*'s back-translation is essentially Sabry and Felleisen's inverse mapping (from CPS to direct style).

Hasegawa [21] has proved a full completeness result for the linear CPS transformation in the setting of a simply typed λ-calculus using syntactic methods based on long $\beta\eta$-normal forms. Like Sabry and Felleisen [43], he considers only $\beta\eta$-equivalence, not observational equivalence.

Using categorical game semantics, Laird [29] showed that for call-by-value PCF one can recover full abstraction of CPS translation by imposing an *affine* typing discipline on continuations, essentially employing the idea of "linearly-used continuations" presented by Berdine *et al.* [11]. We feel that with proofs based on game semantics, it is hard for non-experts to understand even the *statements* of the main lemmas required for the proof. Therefore, a primary objective of our work has been to come up with an operational proof technique that's simpler to understand and could (plausibly) be used throughout all the stages of a compiler. The proof techniques described in this paper, combined with recent advances in step-indexed logical relations [3, 6] seem like they would scale when applied to richer languages and successive compilation phases.

Thielecke [48] seems to have been the first to study CPS transformation with a locally polymorphic answer type, though his work focuses on the role of answer type polymorphism in a language with control effects. He uses parametricity reasoning to observe the connection between linear typing of CPS and answer type polymorphism in a pure call-by-value setting, showing that functions without control effects do not impose any constraints on the answer type and so can have a locally polymorphic answer type. He essentially proves the equivalent of our continuation-shuffling lemma, a property that he calls naturality. He has also studied answer type polymorphism for the call-by-name CPS transform and used it to show that the latter satisfies the eta-law [49]. He does not, however, discuss full abstraction of CPS translations.

Danvy [18] presents a translation from CPS programs into direct-style (DS) programs in an untyped setting. His technique relies on syntactically characterizing CPS terms that can be translated back to DS. Specifically, to be back-translatable, a CPS term must satisfy certain *occurrence conditions* (see Danvy [18], Fig. 2) that ensure that the CPS term encodes a call-by-value left-to-right evaluation order, checked essentially by parsing the CPS term using a stack that holds the formal parameters of continuations. We, on the other hand, use types to *semantically* characterize terms that can be translated back to our direct-style λ^{S}, without requiring that all of their subterms also have back-translatable types. As a result, we can back-translate more terms. Finally, our CPS grammar does not distinguish between ordinary λ's and continuation λ's as Danvy's does, while he does not make use of partial evaluation as we do, i.e., to deal with subterms that are not, on their own, back-translatable.

Several researchers have investigated back-and-forth translations between direct-style and CPS semantics following Meyer and Wand's [34] work on *retractions*. An embedding-retraction pair (i, j) is a pair of functions such that $j \circ i$ is the identity function. Meyer and Wand work with the typed λ-calculus and use the "standard" type translation for CPS that we showed is not fully abstract in Section 1. They write σ' to denote their type translation of σ; let $\sigma^* = (\sigma' \rightarrow \text{ans}) \rightarrow \text{ans}$. They show that there exist embedding-retraction pairs (i_σ, j_σ) and (I_σ, J_σ)—definable in call-by-name λ-calculus (CBN)—where $i_\sigma : \sigma \rightarrow \sigma'$, $j_\sigma : \sigma' \rightarrow \sigma$, $I_\sigma : \sigma' \rightarrow \sigma^*$, and $J_\sigma : \sigma^* \rightarrow \sigma'$. Their main result is the Retraction Theorem which says that $(j_\sigma \circ J_\sigma)$ is the inverse of the CPS transform, i.e., $M =_{CBN} j_\sigma(J_\sigma(\overline{M}))$, where $\overline{M}$ is the CPS transform of M. The boundary terms $\mathcal{TS}^{\sigma}$ and ${}^{\sigma}\mathcal{ST}$ in our multi-language semantics are similar in spirit to i_σ and j_σ, respectively; the property that $(j_\sigma \circ i_\sigma) = \text{id}$ is analogous to (part 1) of our boundary cancellation property (Lemma 6.9); and their Retraction Theorem, which says that the retraction of a translation is equivalent to the original term, is analogous to our "translation is equivalent to embedding" lemma (Corollary 6.16). [1] But there are also important technical differences since our target language (System F) is more expressive than theirs (STLC), and due to the fact that we make use of a multi-language semantics. In particular, our boundary terms are "built-in" with an appropriate operational semantics; thus our embedding-retraction pairs do not have to be *definable* in the target language as is the case with retractions, and this makes our multi-language technique more general. With retractions, the source language is generally assumed to be a strict subset of the target and the Retraction Theorem proves equivalence with respect to the (larger) target language. Note that our λ^{S} is not a strict subset of λ^{T} since the latter syntactically enforces continuation-passing style. Meyer and Wand's Retraction Theorem is essentially analogous to our proof of Part (2). There is no analog to our Part (1) and no proof of full abstraction. In particular, Meyer and Riecke [32] subsequently showed that if we replace CBN $\beta\eta$-equational reasoning with call-by-value observational equivalence, then the embedding-retraction pairs defined in Meyer-Wand no longer suffice. In fact, Meyer and Riecke failed to prove a Retraction Theorem in this setting.

[1] In technical terms, our previous work on typed closure conversion seems closer to the work on retractions since there we do not use a multi-language semantics; instead the source and target are the same language and in this language we define wrapper functions $\mathcal{W}^{+}$ and $\mathcal{W}^{-}$ that are analogous to i and j, respectively, and we prove a theorem similar to Meyer and Wand's (except that it's for closure conversion, not CPS conversion).

Later Riecke [41] and Riecke and Viswanathan [41] investigated a semantic variation of the retraction approach with the goal of isolating side-effects in sequential programs. Also, Filinski [19] generalized Meyer and Wand's Retraction Theorem to a CPS transform for the monadic metalanguage. Like Meyer-Wand, Filinski's technique does not generalize to a language with divergence.

Berger, Honda, and Yoshida have studied fully abstract translations from various languages (with recursion [13], polymorphism [14, 15], control [23], state [22], and concurrency [22]) to linear or affinely typed—and in some cases polymorphic [14, 15]—π-calculus. They prove their translations fully abstract in the case of recursion (with source language PCF) [13], polymorphism (with source language System F) [14, 15], and control [23], but only speculate about full abstraction in the case of state and concurrency [22]. Since the usual translation of the λ-calculus into the π-calculus can be seen as a form of CPS translation, it may be useful to further investigate the connections between translations into the π-calculus and translations to continuation-passing style. Like us, Berger *et al.* rely on typing in the π-calculus to ensure that the translations are fully abstract. Unlike us, they rely on game semantics to prove their translations fully abstract. In this paper, we have shown that terms of translation type are *back-translatable*. Analogously, Berger *et al.* show that terms of translation type are *definable*. Definability says that for every π-calculus term P of translation type $\sigma^{\bullet}$, there exists a well-typed source term $M : \sigma$ (where they write $\sigma^{\bullet}$ to denote the translation of a source type σ). Like us, they note that one reason definability is difficult to establish is because subterms of P may not be of translation type, which means that the proof cannot be carried out simply by induction on typing derivations. Our strategy for dealing with subterms that are not of translation type was to show that it is always possible to perform some partial evaluation that gets rid of the problematic subterm, leaving only subterms that *are* of translation type. Their strategy is to show that every finite target term P of translation type can be represented by a *finite innocent function* that can be turned into a *finite canonical form*, which in turn is easily transformed into some source term M such that P is equivalent to the translation of M. Thus, they use the notion of *innocence* [24] from game semantics to establish, in essence, that translation types at the target level are inhabited by only well-behaved computations. They are, thus, able to perform induction on the size of the corresponding innocent functions. This approach is similar to that of Laird's [29] whose proof of full abstraction also relies on game semantics. Our proof method is more elementary as it relies on operational/syntactic techniques (coupled with typing) for back-translatability; expertise in game semantics is not required to follow the details.

Full Abstraction of Other Translations Most work on proving that translations preserve equivalence has typically resorted to adding precisely those target behaviors that are problematic to the source language. For instance, Riecke [42] investigates fully abstract translations between CBN, CBV, and lazy PCF, using denotational models of the languages that include the parallel conditional. This is needed to make the models fully abstract. Also, Sanjabi and Ong [44] investigate a translation from a core calculus of additive aspects to a target language with higher-order store in the style of ML references. After showing that their original translation is not fully abstract, they weaken the source language by endowing it with the power to construct "bad labels"—the analogue of the bad references at the target that were responsible for the failure of full abstraction.

Shikuma and Igarashi [46] prove full abstraction of a translation from STLC with seal and unseal operators to STLC with base types for each sealing authority. They use a syntactic proof method, but their back-translation is only applicable to terms *all* of whose *sub-*

terms are of translation type. Our back-translation is more general precisely because it does not impose this restriction.

Acknowledgments

The first author would like to thank Greg Morrisett for suggesting the problem of fully abstract compilation to her in Spring 2005. We thank Kyle Ross who helped us with this work in Spring 2010. We are also grateful to Amr Sabry and several anonymous reviewers for their many helpful suggestions on earlier versions of this paper.

References

[1] M. Abadi. Protection in programming-language translations. In *ICALP*, 1998.

[2] S. Abramsky, R. Jagadeesan, and P. Malacaria. Full abstraction for PCF. *Inf. Comput.*, 163(2):409–470, 2000.

[3] A. Ahmed. Step-indexed syntactic logical relations for recursive and quantified types. In *ESOP*, 2006.

[4] A. Ahmed and M. Blume. Typed closure conversion preserves observational equivalence. In *ICFP*, 2008.

[5] A. Ahmed and M. Blume. An equivalence-preserving CPS translation via multi-language semantics (technical appendix). Available at `http://www.cs.indiana.edu/~amal/papers/epc/`, July 2011.

[6] A. Ahmed, D. Dreyer, and A. Rossberg. State-dependent representation independence. In *POPL*, 2009.

[7] A. W. Appel. *Compiling with Continuations*. Cambridge University Press, 1992.

[8] N. Benton and C.-K. Hur. Biorthogonality, step-indexing and compiler correctness. In *ICFP*, 2009.

[9] N. Benton and C.-K. Hur. Realizability and compositional compiler correctness for a polymorphic language. Technical Report MSR-TR-2010-62, Microsoft Research, Apr. 2010.

[10] J. Berdine. Linear and affine typing of continuation-passing style. Technical Report RR-04-04, Queen Mary, Univ. of London, Jan. 2004.

[11] J. Berdine, P. O'Hearn, U. Reddy, and H. Thielecke. Linear continuation-passing. *Higher Order Symbol. Comput.*, 15(2-3):181–208, 2002.

[12] J. Berdine, P. O'Hearn, and H. Thielecke. Extracting the range of cps from affine typing: Extended abstract. In *Workshop on Linear Logic*, 2002.

[13] M. Berger, K. Honda, and N. Yoshida. Sequentiality and the π-calculus. In *TLCA*, 2001.

[14] M. Berger, K. Honda, and N. Yoshida. Genericity and the π-calculus. In *FOSSACS*, 2003.

[15] M. Berger, K. Honda, and N. Yoshida. Genericity and the π-calculus. *Acta Informatica*, 42:83–141, November 2005.

[16] R. Cartwright and M. Felleisen. Observable sequentiality and full abstraction. In *POPL*, 1992.

[17] A. Chlipala. A certified type-preserving compiler from lambda calculus to assembly language. In *PLDI*, 2007.

[18] O. Danvy. Back to direct style. *Science of Computer Programming*, 22(3):183–195, 1994.

[19] A. Filinski. Representing monads. In *POPL*, 1994.

[20] R. Harper and M. Lillibridge. Explicit polymorphism and CPS conversion. In *POPL*, 1993.

[21] M. Hasegawa. Linearly used effects: Monadic and CPS transformations into the linear lambda calculus. In *FLOPS*, 2002.

[22] K. Honda and N. Yoshida. A uniform type structure for secure information flow. In *POPL*, 2002.

[23] K. Honda, N. Yoshida, and M. Berger. Control in the π-calculus. In *Fourth ACM-SIGPLAN Continuations Workshop (CW '04)*, Jan. 2004.

[24] J. M. E. Hyland and C. H. L. Ong. On full abstraction for PCF: I, II, and III. *Information and Computation*, 163(2):285–408, 2000.

[25] A. Jeffrey. A fully abstract semantics for a concurrent functional language with monadic types. In *LICS*, 1995.

[26] A. Kennedy. Securing the .NET programming model. *Theoretical Computer Science*, 364(3):311–317, 2006.

[27] A. Kennedy. Compiling with continuations, continued. In *ICFP*, 2007.

[28] D. A. Kranz, R. A. Kelsey, J. A. Rees, P. Hudak, and J. Philbin. ORBIT: an optimizing compiler for Scheme. In *Proceedings of the ACM Symposium on Compiler Construction*, June 1986.

[29] J. Laird. Game semantics and linear CPS interpretation. *Theor. Comput. Sci.*, 333(1-2):199–224, 2005.

[30] I. A. Mason and C. L. Talcott. Equivalence in functional languages with effects. *J. Functional Programming*, 1(3):287–327, 1991.

[31] J. Matthews and R. B. Findler. Operational semantics for multi-language programs. In *POPL*, Nice, France, pages 3–10, Jan. 2007.

[32] A. Meyer and J. G. Riecke. Continuations may be unreasonable. In *Conf. on LISP and functional programming, LFP*, 1988.

[33] A. R. Meyer and K. Sieber. Towards fully abstract semantics for local variables. In *POPL*, 1988.

[34] A. R. Meyer and M. Wand. Continuation semantics in typed lambda-calculi. In R. Parikh, editor, *Logics of Programs (Brooklyn, June, 1985)*, volume 193 of *LNCS*, pages 219–224. Springer-Verlag, 1985.

[35] R. Milner. Fully abstract models of typed lambda calculi. *Theoretical Computer Science*, 4(1), 1977.

[36] G. Morrisett, D. Walker, K. Crary, and N. Glew. From System F to typed assembly language. *Transactions on Programming Languages and Systems*, 21(3):527–568, May 1999.

[37] A. Nanevski, A. Ahmed, G. Morrisett, and L. Birkedal. Abstract predicates and mutable adts in hoare type theory. In *ESOP*, 2007.

[38] A. M. Pitts. Typed operational reasoning. In B. C. Pierce, editor, *Advanced Topics in Types and Programming Languages*. MIT Press, 2005.

[39] G. D. Plotkin. LCF considered as a programming language. *Theoretical Computer Science*, 5:223–255, 1977.

[40] J. C. Reynolds. Types, abstraction, and parametric polymorphism. *Information Processing*, pages 513–523, 1983.

[41] J. Riecke and R. Viswanathan. Isolating side effects in sequential languages. In *POPL*, 1995.

[42] J. G. Riecke. Fully abstract translations between functional languages. In *POPL*, 1991.

[43] A. Sabry and M. Felleisen. Reasoning about programs in continuation-passing style. In *Conf. on LISP and functional programming, LFP*, 1992.

[44] S. B. Sanjabi and C.-H. L. Ong. Fully abstract semantics of additive aspects by translation. In *Proceedings of the 6th international conference on Aspect-oriented software development (AOSD)*, 2007.

[45] Z. Shao and A. W. Appel. A type-based compiler for Standard ML. In *PLDI*, 1995.

[46] N. Shikuma and A. Igarashi. Proving noninterference by a fully complete translation to the simply typed lambda-calculus. *Logical Methods in Computer Science*, 4(3:10):1–31, 2008.

[47] G. L. Steele. RABBIT: A compiler for SCHEME. Technical Report AI-TR-474, MIT, May 1978.

[48] H. Thielecke. From control effects to typed continuation passing. In *POPL*, 2003.

[49] H. Thielecke. Answer type polymorphism in call-by-name continuation passing. In *ESOP*, 2004.

[50] P. Wadler. Theorems for free! In *ACM Symposium on Functional Programming Languages and Computer Architecture (FPCA)*, 1989.

[51] S. Zdancewic and A. C. Myers. Secure information flow and CPS. In *ESOP*, 2001.

A Kripke Logical Relation for Effect-Based Program Transformations

Jacob Thamsborg
IT University of Copenhagen, Denmark
thamsborg@itu.dk

Lars Birkedal
IT University of Copenhagen, Denmark
birkedal@itu.dk

Abstract

We present a Kripke logical relation for showing the correctness of program transformations based on a type-and-effect system for an ML-like programming language with higher-order store and dynamic allocation.

We show how to use our model to verify a number of interesting program transformations that rely on effect annotations.

Our model is constructed as a step-indexed model over the standard operational semantics of the programming language. It extends earlier work [7, 8] that has considered, respectively, dynamically allocated first-order references and higher-order store for global variables (but no dynamic allocation). It builds on ideas from region-based memory management [21], and on Kripke logical relations for higher-order store, e.g. [12, 14].

Our type-and-effect system is region-based and includes a region-masking rule which allows to hide local effects. One of the key challenges in the model construction for dynamically allocated higher-order store is that the meaning of a type may change since references, conceptually speaking, may become dangling due to region-masking. We explain how our Kripke model can be used to show correctness of program transformations for programs involving references that, conceptually, are dangling.

Categories and Subject Descriptors D.3.1 [*PROGRAMMING LANGUAGES*]: Formal Definitions and Theory; F.3.1 [*LOGICS AND MEANINGS OF PROGRAMS*]: Specifying and Verifying and Reasoning about Programs

General Terms Languages, Theory, Verification

Keywords Kripke logical relation, ultrametric spaces, step-indexed model, type and effect system, program transformations, effect masking, dangling pointers

1. Introduction

A type system for a programming language classifies programs according to properties that the programs satisfy. An effect system is a type system that, in particular, classifies programs according to which side effects the programs may have. A variety of effect systems have been proposed for higher-order programming languages, e.g., [15, 18, 21], see [17] for a recent overview. Effect systems can often be understood as specifying the results of a static analysis, in the sense that it is possible to automatically infer types and effects. Effect systems can be used for different purposes: they were originally proposed by Lucassen and Gifford [18] for parallelization purposes but they have also, e.g., been used as the basis for implementing ML using a stack of regions for memory management [9, 21]. In a recent series of papers, Benton et. al. have argued that another important point of effect systems is that they can be used as the basis for effect-based program transformations, e.g., compiler optimizations, [5–8]. The idea is that certain program transformations are only sound under additional assumptions about which effects program phrases may, or rather may not, have. For example, in a higher-order language with references it is only sound to hoist an expression out a lambda abstraction if it is known that the expression neither allocates new references, nor reads or writes references.

While it is intuitively clear that effect information is important for validating program transformations, it is surprisingly challenging to develop semantic models that can be used to rigorously justify effect-based transformations. In earlier work, Benton et. al. developed semantic relational models of effect systems for a higher-order language with dynamically allocated first-order references (ground store) [7] and for a higher-order language with global variables for higher-order store (but no dynamic allocation) [8].

In this paper we present a Kripke logical relations model of a region-based effect system for a higher-order language with higher-order store *and* dynamic allocation, i.e., with general ML-like references. As pointed out in [8], this is a particularly challenging extension and one that is important for soundness of effect-based transformations for realistic ML-like languages. We now explain what the main challenges are; in Section 3 we give an intuitive overview of how we address these challenges.

The main challenge arises from effect masking: Our region-based effect system includes an effect masking rule that allows one to hide local uses of effects. This makes it possible to view a computation as pure even if it uses effects locally and makes the effect system stronger (it can justify more program transformations). To model effect masking we need to model references that, conceptually speaking, become dangling because they point into a region that is masked away. We say "conceptually speaking" because in the real operational semantics there is no deallocation of references (the operational semantics is completely standard); but in our model we have to reason *as if* regions could actually be allocated and deallocated.

Here is a simple concrete example: Consider the following expression e, typed as indicated:

$$\texttt{let x} = \texttt{ref}_\rho\,7\;\texttt{in let y} = \texttt{ref}_\sigma\,\texttt{x in}$$
$$\lambda z.\texttt{y} := \texttt{x} : 1 \overset{\{wr_\sigma\}}{\to} 1, \{al_\sigma\}$$

ICFP'11, September 19–21, 2011, Tokyo, Japan.

The program allocates two references, binds them to x and y, and then returns a trivial function from unit to unit that assigns x to y. The types indicate that x will be bound to a location in region ρ, say location 0, and that y will be bound to a location in region σ, say location 1. At location 0 the value 7 is stored and at location 1 the location 0 is stored. The so-called latent effect $\{wr_\sigma\}$ of the function type of the whole expression describes which effects the function may have when called. Finally the entire expression has the effect $\{al_\sigma\}$ as it allocates a location in region σ. It performs allocation in region ρ as well, but this effect has been masked out: since no ρ appears in the return type, the expression cannot leak location 0, and we can, conceptually, deallocate all locations in region ρ once the computation has run; this is what the masking rule captures. This particular example, however, was chosen to stress test the masking rule, as location 0 is in fact leaked: it is in the function closure that the expression returns. The function neither reads not writes location 0, but it does write it to the heap; our model must be able to cope with such conceptually dangling pointers. On the level of types, the meaning of the type $\texttt{ref}_\rho\ \texttt{int}$ of x changes: after the allocation of values for x and y, it contains location 0, but what should it contain after region ρ has been masked out? If, e.g., $\texttt{ref}_\rho\ \texttt{int}$ is taken to be empty, then the function is most likely no longer well-typed. We explain our answer to this question in Section 3.

Note that the effect annotations in the types are just annotations; the operational semantics is completely standard and regions only exist in our semantic model, not in the operational semantics. Further note that the issues in the above example do not arise for a language with only ground store.

Another challenge arises from the fact that since our language includes dynamically allocated general references, the existence of the logical relation is non-trivial; in particular, the set of worlds must be recursively defined. Here we build on our earlier work [12] and define the worlds as a solution to a recursive metric-space equation.

One may worry whether our resulting model now becomes much more complicated than the earlier, already non-trivial, models of Benton et. al. [7, 8]. As we shall explain in Section 8, that is not the case. Indeed, our model is arguably a bit simpler even though it applies to a richer language. Moreover, it also becomes simpler to verify equivalences using the model.

Our relational model is built directly over the operational semantics, using our metric approach to step-indexing. We could also have defined the model using a denotational model of the programming language; see the discussion in Section 8 — here we preferred the operational approach because it is perhaps more widely accessible.

We use our model to validate a number of interesting effect-based program transformations that, to the best of our knowledge, have not been proved correct before, see Section 7.

To focus the presentation on the core challenges, we here consider a monomorphically typed higher-order programming language with general references, but leave out universal and existential types as well as recursive types. However, we want to stress that since our semantic techniques (step-indexed Kripke logical relations over recursively defined worlds) do indeed scale well to universal, existential, and recursive types, e.g. [12, 14], it is straightforward to extend our model to a language with such types.[1] We conjecture that it is also possible to extend our model to richer effect systems involving region and effect polymorphism, but we have not done so yet.

[1] With type abstractions as values, we would have a latent effect on a polymorphic type, which would thus be of the form $\forall^\varepsilon \alpha.\tau$.

Throughout the paper we aim to explain the underlying intuitions of the technical definitions and how the different concepts interact. In particular, we have included a couple of selected proof cases, which serve to illuminate central points. A version of the paper with appendices containing more proof cases can be found online at `www.itu.dk/people/thamsborg/longcarnival.pdf`.

2. Language and Effect System

The expressions and values of our model language are defined in the grammar below. We use e to range over the set of expressions $\mathcal{E}$, v to range over the set of values $\mathcal{V}$, l to range over a countably infinite set of locations $\mathcal{L}$, and n to range over integers.

$$e ::= x \mid l \mid \underline{n} \mid () \mid (e_1, e_2) \mid \pi_1\, e \mid \pi_2\, e \mid \texttt{fix}\, f(x).e \mid e_1 e_2 \mid \texttt{ref}\; e \mid e_1 := e_2 \mid\ !e$$

$$v ::= l \mid \underline{n} \mid () \mid (v_1, v_2) \mid \texttt{fix}\, f(x).e$$

Note that expressions are not explicitly typed (we could also have worked with an explicitly typed language). The operational semantics is given by a small-step operational semantics in the standard way. We omit the full definition; suffice it to say that heaps $\mathcal{H}$ are finite maps from locations to closed values, and, for $e \in \mathcal{E}$, $h \in \mathcal{H}$ and $j \geq 0$, we write $\langle e, h\rangle \xrightarrow{j} \langle e', h'\rangle$ if $\langle e, h\rangle$ reduces to $\langle e', h'\rangle$ in j steps, counting all reduction steps. We write $\mathrm{irr}\langle e, h\rangle$ to state that no further reductions of $\langle e, h\rangle$ are possible, either because e is in fact a value or because we are stuck. To make some of the later proofs a little bit simpler, we assume that the allocation of a new location by evaluation of $\texttt{ref}\ e$ is deterministic. Runtime errors (such as trying to look up a non-existing location or trying to apply a number as a function) are modelled by the evaluation getting stuck.

Our effect system ensures that programs are well-typed in the standard sense of not getting stuck and, moreover, tracks dependencies and side-effects of computations on the heap.

The typing rules for our effect system are given in Figure 1. Types are defined by the following grammar:

$$\tau ::= \texttt{int} \mid \mathbf{1} \mid \tau_1 \times \tau_2 \mid \tau_1 \xrightarrow{\varepsilon} \tau_2 \mid \texttt{ref}_\rho\, \tau,$$

where ρ ranges over a countably infinite set of region variables $\mathcal{RV}$ and ε is ranges over the set of effects. An effect is a finite set of primitive effects, and a primitive effect is of one of the forms rd_ρ, wr_ρ, or al_ρ. The primitive effect rd_ρ specifies a read effect on region ρ. Likewise wr_ρ specifies a write effect and al_ρ specifies an allocation effect (that locations may be allocated in region ρ).

Note that, as usual, the function type $\tau_1 \xrightarrow{\varepsilon} \tau_2$ includes a *latent* effect ε; this is the effect that the function may have when called.

The effect type judgement defined in Figure 1 takes the form

$$\Pi \mid \Gamma \vdash e : \tau, \varepsilon,$$

with Γ a finite map from program variables to types, e an expression, τ a type, ε an effect, and Π a finite set of region variables, including all the region variables in Γ, τ, and ε.

The effect system is fairly standard. Note the inclusion of the effect masking rule T-MASKING; here $\varepsilon - \rho$ is defined as $\varepsilon - \{rd_\rho, wr_\rho, al_\rho\}$ and Π, ρ denotes the union of Π and $\{\rho\}$. We write $\mathrm{FRV}(\Gamma, \tau)$ for the region variables in the types of Γ and in τ. The masking rule expresses that to mask out primitive effects on ρ from ε, the region variable ρ must not be free in Γ, nor in τ. The idea is that in this case the remaining part of the computation cannot access ρ and thus we may hide the effects on ρ.

Also note that there is a standard notion of effect subtyping, given by finite set inclusion, which also yields a notion of subtyping (defined by the last three rules in the figure).

$$
\frac{}{\Pi \mid \Gamma, x{:}\tau \vdash x : \tau, \emptyset}
\qquad
\frac{}{\Pi \mid \Gamma \vdash () : \mathtt{1}, \emptyset}
\qquad
\frac{}{\Pi \mid \Gamma \vdash \underline{n} : \mathtt{int}, \emptyset}
\qquad
\frac{\Pi \mid \Gamma \vdash e : \mathtt{ref}_\rho \tau, \varepsilon}{\Pi \mid \Gamma \vdash\, !e : \tau, \varepsilon \cup \{rd_\rho\}}
$$

$$
\frac{\Pi \mid \Gamma \vdash e_1 : \mathtt{ref}_\rho \tau, \varepsilon_1 \qquad \Pi \mid \Gamma \vdash e_2 : \tau, \varepsilon_2}{\Pi \mid \Gamma \vdash e_1 {:=} e_2 : \mathtt{1}, \varepsilon_1 \cup \varepsilon_2 \cup \{wr_\rho\}}
\qquad
\frac{\Pi \mid \Gamma \vdash e : \tau, \varepsilon \qquad \rho \in \Pi}{\Pi \mid \Gamma \vdash \mathtt{ref}\ e : \mathtt{ref}_\rho \tau, \varepsilon \cup \{al_\rho\}}
$$

$$
\frac{\Pi \mid \Gamma \vdash e_1 : \tau_1, \varepsilon_1 \qquad \Pi \mid \Gamma \vdash e_2 : \tau_2, \varepsilon_2}{\Pi \mid \Gamma \vdash (e_1, e_2) : \tau_1 \times \tau_2, \varepsilon_1 \cup \varepsilon_2}
\qquad
\frac{\Pi \mid \Gamma \vdash e : \tau_1 \times \tau_2, \varepsilon}{\Pi \mid \Gamma \vdash \pi_1\, e : \tau_1, \varepsilon}
\qquad
\frac{\Pi \mid \Gamma \vdash e : \tau_1 \times \tau_2, \varepsilon}{\Pi \mid \Gamma \vdash \pi_2\, e : \tau_2, \varepsilon}
$$

$$
\frac{\Pi \mid \Gamma, f{:}\tau_1 \xrightarrow{\varepsilon} \tau_2, x{:}\tau_1 \vdash e : \tau_2, \varepsilon}{\Pi \mid \Gamma \vdash \mathtt{fix}\ f(x).e : \tau_1 \xrightarrow{\varepsilon} \tau_2, \emptyset}
\qquad
\frac{\Pi \mid \Gamma \vdash e_1 : \tau_1 \xrightarrow{\varepsilon} \tau_2, \varepsilon_1 \qquad \Pi \mid \Gamma \vdash e_2 : \tau_1, \varepsilon_2}{\Pi \mid \Gamma \vdash e_1 e_2 : \tau_2, \varepsilon \cup \varepsilon_1 \cup \varepsilon_2}
$$

$$
\frac{\Pi, \rho \mid \Gamma \vdash e : \tau, \varepsilon \qquad \rho \notin \mathrm{FRV}(\Gamma, \tau)}{\Pi \mid \Gamma \vdash e : \tau, \varepsilon - \rho}\ \text{T-MASKING}
$$

$$
\frac{\Pi \mid \Gamma \vdash e : \tau_1, \varepsilon_1 \qquad \Pi \mid \tau_1 \leq \tau_2 \qquad \varepsilon_1 \subseteq \varepsilon_2}{\Pi \mid \Gamma \vdash e : \tau_2, \varepsilon_2}\ \text{T-SUB}
$$

$$
\frac{}{\Pi \mid \tau \leq \tau}
\qquad
\frac{\Pi \mid \tau_1 \leq \tau_1' \qquad \Pi \mid \tau_2 \leq \tau_2'}{\Pi \mid \tau_1 \times \tau_2 \leq \tau_1' \times \tau_2'}
\qquad
\frac{\Pi \mid \tau_1' \leq \tau_1 \qquad \Pi \mid \tau_2 \leq \tau_2' \qquad \varepsilon_1 \subseteq \varepsilon_2}{\Pi \mid \tau_1 \xrightarrow{\varepsilon_1} \tau_2 \leq \tau_1' \xrightarrow{\varepsilon_2} \tau_2'}
$$

Figure 1. Effect System

Consider the example expression e from the introduction. Note that it is well-typed (`let`-expressions are definable as usual) since the judgement $\{\sigma\} \mid \emptyset \vdash e : \mathtt{1} \xrightarrow{\{wr_\sigma\}} \mathtt{1}, \{al_\sigma\}$ is derivable in the effect system. The last rule applied is the T-MASKING rule, which allows us to hide the local effect on ρ. Specifically, we apply the masking rule like this:

$$
\frac{\{\sigma, \rho\} \mid \emptyset \vdash e : \mathtt{1} \xrightarrow{\{wr_\sigma\}} \mathtt{1}, \{al_\rho, al_\sigma\}}{\{\sigma\} \mid \emptyset \vdash e : \mathtt{1} \xrightarrow{\{wr_\sigma\}} \mathtt{1}, \{al_\sigma\}}
$$

Thus we hide the allocation and use of the local reference bound to x.

Effect masking makes it possible to do more optimizations: Consider the familiar example of an efficient implementation *fib* of the fibonacci function using two local references. We can use the masking rule to give it type and effect $\mathtt{int} \xrightarrow{\emptyset} \mathtt{int}, \emptyset$. This allows us to view the imperative implementation as pure, and thus, e.g, by Theorem 7.1 we find that it is sound to optimize two identical calls to *fib* into one call. This sounds like a simple optimization, but the point is that a compiler can perform it automatically, just based on the effect types — and our model justifies that it is sound to do so. See [7, 8] for more examples.

Note though, that these earlier works either have ground store (only integers in memory) or no dynamic allocation, so many non-trivial uses of memory cannot be expressed. By contrast, we can write, say, a function that sorts a (functional) list of integers by doing an internal (imperative) heap sort, i.e., by building a heap in fresh memory, and returning a sorted list. Using the masking rule, we could type such a function as a pure function with no effects, and would know, e.g., that sorting the same list twice serves no purpose.

3. Overview of the Technical Development

Our point of departure is the Kripke logical relation reading of types for an ML-like programming langauge that has been explored extensively by the authors and others [2, 11, 12, 14]. The common approach is to augment the semantics — be it operational or denotational — with *worlds* that keep track of the layout of the heap: it knows the types of values stored at the allocated locations of the heap.[2] We then index type interpretations by worlds; this makes it possible to interpret `ref` τ as the set of allocated locations that hold values of type τ. A computation has the "precondition" that all locations hold well-typed values according to the world, and this property must be re-established after running the computation, i.e., it also serves as a "postcondition". As more locations are allocated, the world grows and the interpretation of types is set up to grow as well: it is a crucial property that interpreting types in future worlds yields more (or at least no fewer) values, this we refer to as *type monotonicity*.

Barring the masking rule, it is a mostly straightforward, if lengthy, exercise to extend this approach to the present region-based type-and-effect system. The worlds have to be partitioned into regions and interpreting $\mathtt{ref}_\rho\, \tau$ only considers region ρ of the world for locations that hold values of type τ. Also, computations now have effects and hence their behavior is more restricted: as "precondition" they only assume well-typedness of values at locations in the regions with read effects; as "postcondition" they are required to have performed only well-typed writes and allocations and, importantly, only in such regions as permitted, respectively, by the write and allocation effects.

The masking rule, however, introduces a new dimension to the development of worlds: in addition to adding new locations with types to existing regions as sketched above, we may now introduce new regions as well as *mask out* existing ones. One can loosely think of masking out region ρ as deallocating the locations of that region. A slightly revised intuition is that we just stop caring about region ρ: we expect never to touch it again and so we may safely relinquish control. On the level of worlds, we discard the region, i.e., lose the locations and the associated types. Whether the locations are actually deallocated or just float around in the surroundings does not matter: from our point of view they are gone.

As argued by example above, this leaves us the issue of dangling pointers. Phrased more concretely: how should the interpretation of

[2] In general, worlds may contain complex invariants of the heap; they may even vary over time and may thus be represented by state transition systems [14]. Here, we need only the invariant that values stored at locations belong to certain types.

types cope with region masking? What is, say, the interpretation of $\texttt{ref}_\rho\,\tau$ in a world where region ρ has been masked out? A natural choice is the empty set — after all, we know nothing about region ρ so what locations could we possibly choose. We, however, take a different approach: We generally interpret a type as all values with the properties you expect from that type. The more properties, the fever values and vice versa. A value v in $\texttt{ref}_\rho\,\tau$ is a reference to a location that we used to — but no longer — control. The value at the location may have changed or it may even have been deallocated: v is conceptually *dangling*. What can we reasonably do with a dangling pointer? We can neither read nor write it, indeed, we can do only things that go for all values, e.g., put it into a pair, project it out, etc. In other words, we expect no properties of dangling pointers and correspondingly interpret $\texttt{ref}_\rho\,\tau$ as the set of all values. We take a similar stand on functions: interpreting a function type that has effects on masked out regions gives the set of all values; such functions are somehow dangling too. Running such a function relies on preconditions outside our control, so we make no promises about the behavior.

This approach goes well with type monotonicity: the interpretation of types should not shrink under masking and, indeed, masking out region ρ enlarges $\texttt{ref}_\rho\,\tau$ to hold all values. There is a catch, though, since future worlds may introduce new regions as well, and reintroducing region ρ would not do. This is obvious from type monotonicity; a more conceptual explanation, however, is this: Assume that some function reads region ρ and that region ρ holds location l that stores values of some type. To run the function, we need to establish the precondition that a value of the proper type is stored at location l, because the function could very well read l. We then mask out region ρ, losing all information about l in the process, and afterwards reintroduce it. To run the function now, we verify that all locations in region ρ hold values of appropriate type — this is, after all, the precondition of the function — but as l is no longer in ρ, we cannot expect proper behavior of the function.

We solve this issue by tracking, in the worlds, the regions that have been masked out and prohibit their reintroduction. One viewpoint is that, as the world develops over time, a region goes through a life-cycle: Initially, it is unknown to the world, but at some point it gets initialized, joining the set of *live* regions. With further development of the world, locations with associated types are added to the region. This proceeds until the region is masked out; it loses all content and is moved to the set of *dead* regions. And this is a one-way street: once you are gone, you can't come back.

Local Reasoning Conceptually, a world does not describe the entire heap, just the part of it that the program sees or controls. On the level of definitions, this comes down to a frame property of our computations: a computation in a world runs in a world-adhering heap extended with a frame, and the latter remains unchanged. In addition, a computation may allocate locations that are not tracked by the ensuing world; these locations are conceptually transferred to the surroundings, they become part of the frame of the following computation. This is the fate of locations in regions that are masked out. In summa, we achieve a form of local reasoning by quantifying over frames, similarly to models of separation logic for higher-order languages [10].

4. Metric Spaces and Type-World Circularity

As argued above, we intend to augment our semantics with worlds that track the layout of the heap; hence we are faced with the construction of such worlds. Defining them directly will not do since, loosely, a world holds semantic types whilst semantic types are parameterized over worlds; this is the *type-world circularity* observed already by Ahmed in her thesis [1].

In recent work, Reus, Schwinghammer, Støvring, Yang and the authors [12] have proposed a general solution to such circularities, applying metric-space theory. The notion of worlds we require here is sufficiently simple that this solution is applicable off-the-shelf, so to speak. So we omit the machinery of the construction here and just present the worlds that is the result; after all, this is presently our object of interest. Details are given in the appendix of the long version of the paper. In addition, we will largely ignore the fact that we actually deal in metric spaces and not just plain sets. We emphasize that this is just for presentation purposes, worlds and types *are* metric spaces with certain properties; this is necessary to solve the circularity and must be taken into account, e.g., when interpreting types, see the appendix of the long version of the paper.

We face an additional challenge here: As described above, we intend to track dead regions to avoid recycling them. But if an expression is well-typed by the masking rule, then in terms of the development of worlds, it initializes and eventually masks out the very same region on each evaluation, and maybe we would like to run it more than once. Our solution to this is to introduce a layer of indirection, following ideas of earlier work [9, 21]: On the level of syntactic types, we have the region variables $\mathcal{RV}$ introduced above. In the worlds, however, we work with a countably infinite set of *region names* $\mathcal{RN}$. To interpret types we have *region environments*, i.e., injective maps $\mathcal{RV} \rightharpoonup_{fin} \mathcal{RN}$ with adequate domains; on each evaluation of an expression that performs masking, we then map the same region variable to a fresh region name. In the textual explanations below, however, we purposely blur the distinction between region variables, region names and the regions themselves.

The definition of worlds and types is given in Figure 2; the ordering on worlds relies on the world transitions given in Figure 3. Both warrant a few comments. $\mathrm{ParBij}(X, Y, \mathbf{Z})$ are finite partial bijections between X and Y decorated with elements from $\mathbf{Z}$; we write $\mathrm{dom}_1(P)$ for the set of first coordinates and $\mathrm{dom}_2(P)$ for the set of second coordinates. Worlds $\mathbf{W}$ have two components: the first is the *live* regions, these are partial bijections; the second the *dead* regions. No region can be both live and dead, nor can any location belong to more than one region.

Worlds may develop over time according to the transitions in Figure 3. The first transition adds a location pair with associated type to a live region; this corresponds to an actual allocation in the operational semantics and is a standard notion of world extension. The second and third transitions are orthogonal to the first. They give the region dynamics and have no counterpart in the operational semantics; they are, however, intimately connected to the masking rule. The first initializes a new empty region, the second masks out a live one, losing the partial bijection in the process. After being masked out, a region is considered dead and cannot be initialized once more.

The reflexive, transitive closure of the transitions is a preorder on worlds. We require of our types $\mathbf{T}$ that they are monotone with respect to that preorder and the standard set-theoretic inclusion on $\mathit{URel}(\mathcal{V})$; this is the type monotonicity. For any set X, $\mathit{URel}(X)$ is the set of indexed, downwards closed relations on X, i.e.,

$$\mathit{URel}(X) = \{R \subseteq \mathbb{N} \times X \times X \mid \forall (k, x_1, x_2) \in R.\, \forall j < k.\, (j, x_1, x_2) \in R\}.$$

The downwards closure is essential, it prevents values from fleeing types as the operational semantics progresses.[3] One minor issue remains: the types that decorate the partial bijections that are the regions belong to $\widehat{\mathbf{T}}$ and must be coerced into $\mathbf{T}$ by the isomor-

[3] The set $\mathit{URel}(X)$ has a natural metric [12] and the functions in $\mathbf{T}$ are not only monotone but also non-expansive; see the appendix of the long version of the paper for details.

$$\begin{aligned}
\mathrm{ParBij}(X,Y,\mathbf{Z}) &= \{P \subseteq_{fin} X \times Y \times \mathbf{Z} \mid \forall (x_1,y_1,z_1),(x_2,y_2,z_2) \in P.\\
&\qquad (x_1 = x_2 \Rightarrow y_1 = y_2 \wedge z_1 = z_2) \wedge (y_1 = y_2 \Rightarrow x_1 = x_2 \wedge z_1 = z_2)\}\\
\mathbf{W} &= \{(\varphi,\psi) \in (\mathcal{RN} \rightharpoonup_{fin} \mathrm{ParBij}(\mathcal{L},\mathcal{L},\widehat{\mathbf{T}})) \times \mathcal{P}_{fin}(\mathcal{RN}) \mid \mathrm{dom}(\varphi) \cap \psi = \emptyset \wedge\\
&\qquad \forall r,s \in \mathrm{dom}(\varphi).\, r \neq s \Rightarrow \mathrm{dom}_1(\varphi(r)) \cap \mathrm{dom}_1(\varphi(s)) = \emptyset = \mathrm{dom}_2(\varphi(r)) \cap \mathrm{dom}_2(\varphi(s))\}\\
w \sqsubseteq w' &\iff \exists n \in \mathbb{N}.\, \exists w_0, w_1, \ldots, w_n \in \mathbf{W}.\, w = w_0 \wedge w' = w_n \wedge\\
&\qquad \forall 0 \le i < n.\, (\exists r \in \mathcal{RN}.\, \exists l_1, l_2 \in \mathcal{L}.\, \exists \mu \in \widehat{\mathbf{T}}.\, w_i \to_{al(r,l_1,l_2,\mu)} w_{i+1}) \vee\\
&\qquad (\exists r \in \mathcal{RN}.\, w_i \to_{reg(r)} w_{i+1}) \vee (\exists r \in \mathcal{RN}.\, w_i \to_{mask(r)} w_{i+1})\\
\mathbf{T} &= \mathbf{W} \to_{mon} URel(\mathcal{V}), \quad \iota : \widehat{\mathbf{T}} \cong \frac{1}{2}\mathbf{T}
\end{aligned}$$

Figure 2. Our semantic footing: worlds and types. The former comes equipped with the preorder that is the reflexive, transitive closure of the transitions in Figure 3

$$\begin{aligned}
(\varphi,\psi) \to_{al(r,l_1,l_2,\mu)} (\varphi',\psi) &\iff r \in \mathrm{dom}(\varphi) \wedge l_1 \notin \mathrm{dom}_1(\varphi(r)) \wedge l_2 \notin \mathrm{dom}_2(\varphi(r)) \wedge\\
&\qquad \mathrm{dom}(\varphi') = \mathrm{dom}(\varphi) \wedge \varphi'(r) = \varphi(r) \cup \{(l_1,l_2,\mu)\} \wedge\\
&\qquad \forall s \in \mathrm{dom}(\varphi) \setminus \{r\}.\, \varphi'(s) = \varphi(s).\\
(\varphi,\psi) \to_{reg(r)} (\varphi',\psi) &\iff r \in \mathcal{RN} \setminus (\mathrm{dom}(\varphi) \cup \psi) \wedge \mathrm{dom}(\varphi') = \mathrm{dom}(\varphi) \cup \{r\} \wedge\\
&\qquad \varphi'(r) = \emptyset \wedge \forall s \in \mathrm{dom}(\varphi).\, \varphi'(s) = \varphi(s).\\
(\varphi,\psi) \to_{mask(r)} (\varphi',\psi') &\iff r \in \mathrm{dom}(\varphi) \wedge \mathrm{dom}(\varphi') = \mathrm{dom}(\varphi) \setminus \{r\} \wedge\\
&\qquad \psi' = \psi \cup \{r\} \wedge \forall s \in \mathrm{dom}(\varphi) \setminus \{r\}.\, \varphi'(s) = \varphi(s).
\end{aligned}$$

Figure 3. The three worlds transitions. We have $r \in \mathcal{RN}$ in all of them and additionally $l_1, l_2 \in \mathcal{L}$ and $\mu \in \widehat{\mathbf{T}}$ in the first. Transitions are, once parameters are given, partial maps from $\mathbf{W}$ to $\mathbf{W}$.

phism ι before they can be applied to a world. This isomorphism is what we get from the solution to the type-world circularity.

A bit of world-related notation will come in handy: For a world $w = (\varphi, \psi)$ we set $\mathrm{dom}(w) = \mathrm{dom}(\varphi)$ and $|w| = \mathrm{dom}(\varphi) \cup \psi$, i.e., $\mathrm{dom}(w)$ is the set of live regions and $|w|$ is the combined set of live and dead regions. We write $\mathrm{dom}_1(w)$ for the union of all first coordinates of all live regions; $\mathrm{dom}_2(w)$ is defined similarly. For $r \in \mathrm{dom}(w)$ we abuse notation and write $w(r)$ for $\varphi(r)$.

5. Types and the Logical Relation

The relational, world-indexed interpretation of types is given in Figure 4; the interpretation of function types relies on the interpretation of computations given in Figure 5. It is worthwhile to comment a bit on this. Note that both the interpretation of types and computations take a number of parameters, the requirements on those are given in the captions of the figures.

Overall, we follow the intuition laid out in Section 3. Integer, unit and product types are standard. Looking at the reference type there are three cases: If we interpret $\mathtt{ref}_\rho\ \tau$ in a world where $R(\rho)$ is unknown, we get the empty set. This we never do; it is just a dummy clause that is neutral with respect to type monotonicity, but we need it since we, for technical convenience, want interpreted types to be applicable to all worlds. The middle case is the proper one, here $R(\rho)$ is a live region and we go through it in search for location pairs that hold values of a type semantically identical to τ. The quantification over future worlds ensure type monotonicity and the k-equality is necessary for the step-indexed setup; both are quite standard. The latter means that the sets we compare are equal if we restrict to elements with index strictly less than k. In the last case we look for references to a masked region; these are conceptually dangling pointers that we make no assumption about, hence we return all (pairs of) values.

The function type proceeds along the same lines. The middle case is the proper one and it too is quite standard, except that we quantify only over future worlds in which $R(\mathrm{FRV}(\varepsilon))$ remain live. In worlds where this fails, we make no promise about the behavior.

The interpretations of computations is crucial. Note first that $\mathrm{rds}\,\varepsilon$ are all region variables with read effects in ε, $\mathrm{wrs}\,\varepsilon$ and $\mathrm{als}\,\varepsilon$ are defined similarly. $\mathbf{P}^R_\varepsilon\ w$ gives the precondition on heaps that computations running in world w with effects ε have: that all location pairs in all regions with read effects do, in fact, hold values of the appropriate type. If, now, the precondition holds and the left hand side terminates, then so does the right hand side, and there is a future world w' such that the results are in the desired type at w' and the resulting heaps satisfy the postcondition $\mathbf{Q}^R_\varepsilon\ w, w'$. The latter states, that any writes to existing locations are of the correct type and are permitted by a write effect; also any newly allocated locations tracked by w' hold well-typed values and are in regions with an allocation effect. That the postcondition speaks of the initial heaps as well as the final ones is seen in, e.g., Hoare Type Theory [19] as well. Also, since we do local reasoning, there may be parts of the heap outside our control; these are the frames f_1 and f_2, they must remain unmodified. And the computations may allocate locations that the future world does not track, these are the additional frames f_1' and f_2'.

Finally, it is worthwhile to remark that the region-dynamics of computations is quite restricted: the future world w' must have the same live regions as w. In other words, computations cannot mask out existing regions and if they initialize any new regions, they are obliged to mask them out before they terminate. Here we take inspiration from work on region-based memory management [9,

$$[\![\mathtt{1}]\!]^R w = \{(k,(),()) \mid k \in \mathbb{N}\} \qquad [\![\mathtt{int}]\!]^R w = \{(k,n,n) \mid k \in \mathbb{N} \wedge n \in \mathbb{Z}\}$$

$$[\![\tau_1 \times \tau_2]\!]^R w = \{(k,(v_{1,1},v_{2,1}),(v_{1,2},v_{2,2})) \mid (k,v_{1,1},v_{1,2}) \in [\![\tau_1]\!]^R w \wedge (k,v_{2,1},v_{2,2}) \in [\![\tau_2]\!]^R w\}$$

$$[\![\mathtt{ref}_\rho\,\tau]\!]^R w = \begin{cases} \emptyset & R(\rho) \notin |w| \\ \left\{(k,l_1,l_2) \mid \exists \mu \in \widehat{\mathbf{T}}.\,(l_1,l_2,\mu) \in w(R(\rho)) \wedge \forall w' \sqsupseteq w.\,[\![\tau]\!]^R w' \stackrel{k}{=} (\iota\,\mu)(w')\right\} & R(\rho) \in \mathrm{dom}(w) \\ \{(k,v_1,v_2) \mid k \in \mathbb{N} \wedge v_1,v_2 \in \mathcal{V}\} & R(\rho) \in |w| \setminus \mathrm{dom}(w). \end{cases}$$

$$[\![\tau_1 \xrightarrow{\varepsilon} \tau_2]\!]^R w = \begin{cases} \emptyset & R(\mathrm{FRV}(\varepsilon)) \not\subseteq |w| \\ \left\{ \begin{array}{c|c} (k,\mathtt{fix}\,f(x).e_1, & \forall w' \sqsupseteq w.\,R(\mathrm{FRV}(\varepsilon)) \subseteq \mathrm{dom}(w') \Rightarrow \\ \mathtt{fix}\,f(x).e_2) & \forall j \le k.\,\forall (v_1,v_2) \in \mathcal{V}\times\mathcal{V}.\,(j,v_1,v_2) \in [\![\tau_1]\!]^R w' \Rightarrow \\ & (j,(\mathtt{fix}\,f(x).e_1)\,v_1,(\mathtt{fix}\,f(x).e_2)\,v_2) \in [\![\mathrm{T}_\varepsilon\,\tau_2]\!]^R w' \end{array} \right\} & R(\mathrm{FRV}(\varepsilon)) \subseteq \mathrm{dom}(w) \\ \{(k,v_1,v_2) \mid k \in \mathbb{N} \wedge v_1,v_2 \in \mathcal{V}\} & \mathrm{dom}(w) \not\supseteq R(\mathrm{FRV}(\varepsilon)) \subseteq |w|. \end{cases}$$

Figure 4. Interpretation of types. We require $R : \mathcal{RV} \rightharpoonup_{fin} \mathcal{RN}$ injective with $\mathrm{FRV}(\tau) \subseteq \mathrm{dom}(R)$ and get $[\![\tau]\!]^R : \mathbf{W} \to_{mon} URel(\mathcal{V})$.

21] where regions are allocated and deallocated following a stack discipline.

Proposition 5.1. We have $[\![\tau]\!]^R \in \mathbf{T}$, i.e., it is a non-expansive and monotone map from $\mathbf{W}$ to $URel(\mathcal{H})$.

The proof of this proposition is deferred to the appendix of the long version of the paper.

When interpreting a type, we use region environments with possibly excessive domains. Clearly, the value of the region environments outside the region variables of the type does not matter; this is captured in the following lemma that we need below:

Lemma 5.2 (Environment Extension)**.** Let $R_1, R_2 : \mathcal{RV} \rightharpoonup_{fin} \mathcal{RN}$ be injective with $\mathrm{dom}(R_1) \supseteq \mathrm{FRV}(\tau) \subseteq \mathrm{dom}(R_2)$. If we have $R_1(\rho) = R_2(\rho)$ for all $\rho \in \mathrm{FRV}(\tau)$, then $[\![\tau]\!]^{R_1} = [\![\tau]\!]^{R_2}$.

The logical relation on expressions is defined in Figure 6. Π is a syntactic over-approximation of all region variables; together with the condition $R : \Pi \hookrightarrow |w|$ it ensures that we deal in live and dead regions only, not unknown ones. As for functions and computations, we require that the regions of the effects are live.

The logical relation is asymmetrical: the left hand side *approximates* the right hand side. We write $\Pi \mid \Gamma \models e_1 \sim e_2 : \tau, \varepsilon$ if the approximation goes both ways and consider the computations *equivalent* in that case. Our logical relation and subtyping are sound in the following, standard, sense:

Theorem 5.3 (Compatibility)**.** The logical relation in Figure 6 is compatible with the typing rules of Figure 1. That is, the formation of expressions according to the typing rules respects the logical relation.

Proposition 5.4. Interpreting subtypes gives subsets, i.e., we have that $\Pi \mid \tau_1 \le \tau_2$ implies $[\![\tau_1]\!]^R w \subseteq [\![\tau_2]\!]^R w$ for any region environment $R : \Pi \hookrightarrow \mathcal{RN}$ and any world $w \in \mathbf{W}$.

The proof of the theorem relies naturally on the proposition. The proofs are deferred to the next section and the appendix of the long version of the paper.

We have the Fundamental Lemma as corollary:

Lemma 5.5. (Fundamental)

$$\Pi \mid \Gamma \vdash e : \tau, \varepsilon \implies \Pi \mid \Gamma \models e \preceq e : \tau, \varepsilon.$$

Another standard corollary is *contextual equivalence*: Two equivalent computations that are placed inside the same closing, integer context, will co-terminate with the same value, when run in any two heaps. Observe, though, that the context must be typed according to the typing rules here, i.e., with effect annotations.

6. Soundness

In this section, we present some of the cases of the proof of the Compatibility Theorem stated just above. First off, two lemmas to handle some of the details, then we give detailed proofs of lookup, masking, and fixed points. See the appendix of the long version of the paper for more cases.

Lemma 6.1 (Precondition Strengthening)**.**

$$\varepsilon \subseteq \varepsilon' \implies \mathbf{P}^R_\varepsilon\, w \supseteq \mathbf{P}^R_{\varepsilon'}\, w.$$

Lemma 6.2 (Postcondition Weakening)**.**

$$\varepsilon \subseteq \varepsilon' \implies \mathbf{Q}^R_\varepsilon\, w, w' \subseteq \mathbf{Q}^R_{\varepsilon'}\, w, w'.$$

Lemma 6.3 (Lookup)**.** $\Pi \mid \Gamma \models e_1 \preceq e_2 : \mathtt{ref}_\rho\,\tau, \varepsilon$ implies $\Pi \mid \Gamma \models !\,e_1 \preceq !\,e_2 : \tau, \varepsilon \cup \{rd_\rho\}$.

Proof. We unroll the definition of the logical relation: Let $k \in \mathbb{N}$, $w \in \mathbf{W}$, $R : \Pi \hookrightarrow |w|$ and $\gamma_1, \gamma_2 \in \mathcal{V}^{|\Gamma|}$ be arbitrary. Assume $R(\mathrm{FRV}(\varepsilon \cup \{rd_\rho\})) \subseteq \mathrm{dom}(w)$ and that $(k, \gamma_1, \gamma_2) \in [\![\Gamma]\!]^R w$. We now must show that

$$(k, !\,e_1[\gamma_1/\Gamma], !\,e_2[\gamma_2/\Gamma]) \in [\![\mathrm{T}_{\varepsilon \cup \{\mathrm{rd}_\rho\}}\,\tau]\!]^R w.$$

We proceed to unroll the definition of computations: Let $j \le k$, $e''_1 \in \mathcal{E}$ and $h_1, h_2, f_1, f_2, g''_1 \in \mathcal{H}$ be arbitrary. Assume $(k, h_1, h_2) \in \mathbf{P}^R_{\varepsilon \cup \{rd_\rho\}}\, w$, that

$$\langle !\,e_1[\gamma_1/\Gamma], h_1 \cdot f_1\rangle \xrightarrow{j} \langle e''_1, g''_1\rangle$$

and $\mathrm{irr}\langle e''_1, g''_1\rangle$.

By the operational semantics, there must be $0 \le i \le j$, $e'_1 \in \mathcal{E}$ and $g'_1 \in \mathcal{H}$, such that

$$\langle e_1[\gamma_1/\Gamma], h_1 \cdot f_1\rangle \xrightarrow{i} \langle e'_1, g'_1\rangle, \quad \langle !\,e'_1, g'_1\rangle \xrightarrow{j-i} \langle e''_1, g''_1\rangle$$

and $\mathrm{irr}\langle e'_1, g'_1\rangle$ holds. The assumption of the lemma and Preconditioning Strengthening gives us $w' \sqsupseteq w$ with $\mathrm{dom}(w') = \mathrm{dom}(w)$ as well as $e'_2 \in \mathcal{E}$ and $g'_2, h'_1, h'_2, f'_1, f'_2$ such that

$$\langle e_2[\gamma_2/\Gamma], h_2 \cdot f_2\rangle \xrightarrow{*} \langle e'_2, g'_2\rangle,$$

with $g'_1 = h'_1 \cdot f'_1 \cdot f_1$, $g'_2 = h'_2 \cdot f'_2 \cdot f_2$ and $(k-i, e'_1, e'_2) \in [\![\mathtt{ref}_\rho\,\tau]\!]^R w'$ as well as $(k-i, h_1, h_2, h'_1, h'_2) \in \mathbf{Q}^R_\varepsilon\, w, w'$.

Let us ponder the fact $(k-i, e'_1, e'_2) \in [\![\mathtt{ref}_\rho\,\tau]\!]^R w'$. By assumption, $R(\rho) \in \mathrm{dom}(w) = \mathrm{dom}(w')$ and so we must have

$$
\begin{aligned}
&[\![\mathtt{T}_\varepsilon\,\tau]\!]^R w = \Big\{(k, e_1, e_2) \mid \\
&\quad \forall j \le k.\, \forall e_1' \in \mathcal{E}.\, \forall h_1, h_2, f_1, f_2, g_1' \in \mathcal{H}. \\
&\quad \Big[(k, h_1, h_2) \in \mathbf{P}^R_\varepsilon\, w \wedge \\
&\quad \langle e_1, h_1 \cdot f_1\rangle \xrightarrow{j} \langle e_1', g_1'\rangle \wedge \mathrm{irr}\langle e_1', g_1'\rangle\Big] \implies \\
&\quad \Big[\exists w' \sqsupseteq w.\, \exists e_2' \in \mathcal{E}.\, \exists g_2', h_1', h_2', f_1', f_2' \in \mathcal{H}. \\
&\quad \mathrm{dom}(w) = \mathrm{dom}(w') \wedge \\
&\quad \langle e_2, h_2 \cdot f_2\rangle \xrightarrow{*} \langle e_2', g_2'\rangle \wedge \\
&\quad g_1' = h_1' \cdot f_1' \cdot f_1 \wedge g_2' = h_2' \cdot f_2' \cdot f_2 \wedge \\
&\quad (k - j, h_1, h_2, h_1', h_2') \in \mathbf{Q}^R_\varepsilon\, w, w' \wedge \\
&\quad (k - j, e_1', e_2') \in [\![\tau]\!]^R w'\Big]\Big\}
\end{aligned}
$$

$$
\begin{aligned}
&(k, h_1, h_2) \in \mathbf{P}^R_\varepsilon\, w \iff \\
&\quad \mathrm{dom}(h_1) = \mathrm{dom}_1(w) \wedge \mathrm{dom}(h_2) = \mathrm{dom}_2(w) \wedge \\
&\quad \big(\forall \rho \in \mathrm{rds}\,\varepsilon.\, \forall (l_1, l_2, \mu) \in w(R(\rho)). \\
&\quad\quad k > 0 \Rightarrow (k - 1, h_1(l_1), h_2(l_2)) \in (\iota\,\mu)(w)\big)
\end{aligned}
$$

$$
\begin{aligned}
&(k, h_1, h_2, h_1', h_2') \in \mathbf{Q}^R_\varepsilon\, w, w' \iff \\
&\quad \mathrm{dom}(h_1) = \mathrm{dom}_1(w) \wedge \mathrm{dom}(h_2) = \mathrm{dom}_2(w) \wedge \\
&\quad \mathrm{dom}(h_1') = \mathrm{dom}_1(w') \wedge \mathrm{dom}(h_2') = \mathrm{dom}_2(w') \wedge \\
&\quad \big(\forall l_1 \in \mathrm{dom}(h_1).\, h_1(l_1) \ne h_1'(l_1) \Rightarrow \\
&\quad\quad \exists \rho \in \mathrm{wrs}\,\varepsilon.\, \exists (m_1, l_2, \mu) \in w(R(\rho)).\, l_1 = m_1 \wedge \\
&\quad\quad\quad k > 0 \Rightarrow (k - 1, h_1'(l_1), h_2'(l_2)) \in (\iota\,\mu)(w')\big) \wedge \\
&\quad \big(\forall l_2 \in \mathrm{dom}(h_2).\, h_2(l_2) \ne h_2'(l_2) \Rightarrow \\
&\quad\quad \exists \rho \in \mathrm{wrs}\,\varepsilon.\, \exists (l_1, m_2, \mu) \in w(R(\rho)) \wedge l_2 = m_2 \wedge \\
&\quad\quad\quad k > 0 \Rightarrow (k - 1, h_1'(l_1), h_2'(l_2)) \in (\iota\,\mu)(w')\big) \wedge \\
&\quad \big(\forall r \in \mathrm{dom}(w).\, \forall (l_1, l_2, \mu) \in w'(r) \setminus w(r).\, r \in R(\mathrm{als}\,\varepsilon) \wedge \\
&\quad\quad k > 0 \Rightarrow (k - 1, h_1'(l_1), h_2'(l_2)) \in (\iota\,\mu)(w')\big)
\end{aligned}
$$

Figure 5. Interpretation of computations with pre- and postconditions. There are implicit disjointness requirements on heaps: the heap compositions must all be well-defined. In all three cases we have $R : \mathcal{RV} \rightharpoonup_{fin} \mathcal{RN}$ injective and $w \in \mathbf{W}$. For $[\![\mathtt{T}_\varepsilon\,\tau]\!]^R w$ we require $\mathrm{FRV}(\varepsilon, \tau) \subseteq \mathrm{dom}(R)$ and $R(\mathrm{FRV}(\varepsilon)) \subseteq \mathrm{dom}(w)$. $\mathbf{P}^R_\varepsilon\, w$ is defined for $\mathrm{FRV}(\varepsilon) \subseteq \mathrm{dom}(R)$ and $R(\mathrm{FRV}(\varepsilon)) \subseteq \mathrm{dom}(w)$, $\mathbf{Q}^R_\varepsilon\, w, w'$ additionally requires $w' \in \mathbf{W}$ and $w \sqsubseteq w'$ with $\mathrm{dom}(w) = \mathrm{dom}(w')$.

$$
\begin{aligned}
&\Pi \mid \Gamma \models e_1 \preceq e_2 : \tau, \varepsilon \\
&\quad \iff \\
&\forall k \in \mathbb{N}.\, \forall w \in \mathbf{W}.\, \forall R : \Pi \hookrightarrow |w|.\, \forall \gamma_1, \gamma_2 \in \mathcal{V}^{|\Gamma|}. \\
&[R(\mathrm{FRV}(\varepsilon)) \subseteq \mathrm{dom}(w) \wedge (k, \gamma_1, \gamma_2) \in [\![\Gamma]\!]^R w] \Rightarrow \\
&(k, e_1[\gamma_1/\Gamma], e_2[\gamma_2/\Gamma]) \in [\![\mathtt{T}_\varepsilon\,\tau]\!]^R w.
\end{aligned}
$$

Figure 6. The logical relation. We require $\mathrm{FRV}(\Gamma, \tau, \varepsilon) \subseteq \Pi$ and, as always, $\mathrm{FV}(e_1, e_2) \in \Gamma$.

$l_1, l_2 \in \mathcal{L}$ and $\mu \in \widehat{\mathbf{T}}$ such that $e_1' = l_1$, $e_2' = l_2$, $(l_1, l_2, \mu) \in w'(R(\rho))$ and $[\![\tau]\!]^R w' \overset{k-i}{=} (\iota\,\mu)(w')$. Since $l_1 \in \mathrm{dom}_1(w') = \mathrm{dom}(h_1') \subseteq \mathrm{dom}(g_1')$ we must have $i < j$ since the alternative disproves $\mathrm{irr}\langle e_1'', g_1''\rangle$. Indeed, we must have $i = j - 1$ and the entire left hand side reduction must look like

$$\langle !\, e_1[\gamma_1/\Gamma], h_1 \cdot f_1\rangle \xrightarrow{j-1} \langle !\, l_1, g_1'\rangle \to \langle h_1'(l_1), g_1'\rangle,$$

in particular $e_1'' = h_1'(l_1)$ and $g_1'' = g_1'$. Moreover, since

$$\langle e_2[\gamma_2/\Gamma], h_2 \cdot f_2\rangle \xrightarrow{*} \langle l_2, g_2'\rangle,$$

and $l_2 \in \mathrm{dom}_2(w') = \mathrm{dom}(h_2') \subseteq \mathrm{dom}(g_2')$ we get a similar reduction on the right hand side

$$\langle !\, e_2[\gamma_2/\Gamma], h_2 \cdot f_2\rangle \xrightarrow{*} \langle !\, l_2, g_2'\rangle \to \langle h_2'(l_2), g_2'\rangle.$$

By Postcondition Weakening we are left to verify only that $(k - j, h_1'(l_1), h_2'(l_2)) \in [\![\tau]\!]^R w'$. Since $[\![\tau]\!]^R w' \overset{k-j+1}{=} (\iota\,\mu)(w')$, it suffices to prove $(k - j, h_1'(l_1), h_2'(l_2)) \in (\iota\,\mu)(w')$. We now branch on whether $(l_1, l_2, \mu) \in w(R(\rho))$ holds, i.e., whether locations we look up existed prior to the entire computation or were allocated along the way. If $(l_1, l_2, \mu) \in w'((R(\rho)) \setminus w(R(\rho))$, we get $(k - j, h_1'(l_1), h_2'(l_2)) \in (\iota\,\mu)(w')$ directly from $(k - i, h_1, h_2, h_1', h_2') \in \mathbf{Q}^R_\varepsilon\, w, w'$. If, on the other hand, it is the case that $(l_1, l_2, \mu) \in w(R(\rho))$ holds, then we get $(k - 1, h_1(l_1), h_2(l_2)) \in (\iota\,\mu)(w)$ from $\mathbf{P}^R_{\varepsilon \cup \{rd_\rho\}}$ because of the read effect rd_ρ. If the locations are not written during the computation, i.e., if $h_1(l_1) = h_1'(l_1)$ and $h_2(l_2) = h_2'(l_2)$, we get $(k - j, h_1'(l_1), h_2'(l_2)) \in (\iota\,\mu)(w')$ immediately. If, on the other hand, they are written, then we still get this, but this time from $(k - i, h_1, h_2, h_1', h_2') \in \mathbf{Q}^R_\varepsilon\, w, w'$. □

Lemma 6.4 (Masking). $\Pi, \rho \mid \Gamma \models e_1 \preceq e_2 : \tau, \varepsilon$ implies $\Pi \mid \Gamma \models e_1 \preceq e_2 : \tau, \varepsilon - \rho$ provided that $\rho \notin \mathrm{FRV}(\Gamma, \tau)$.

Proof. We unroll the definition of the logical relation: Let $k \in \mathbb{N}$, $w \in \mathbf{W}$, $R : \Pi \hookrightarrow |w|$ and $\gamma_1, \gamma_2 \in \mathcal{V}^{|\Gamma|}$ be arbitrary. Assume $R(\mathrm{FRV}(\varepsilon - \rho)) \subseteq \mathrm{dom}(w)$ and that $(k, \gamma_1, \gamma_2) \in [\![\Gamma]\!]^R w$. We now must show that

$$(k, e_1[\gamma_1/\Gamma], e_2[\gamma_2/\Gamma]) \in [\![\mathtt{T}_{\varepsilon - \rho}\,\tau]\!]^R w.$$

We proceed to unroll the definition of computations: Let $j \le k$, $e_1' \in \mathcal{E}$ and $h_1, h_2, f_1, f_2, g_1' \in \mathcal{H}$ be arbitrary. Assume that $(k, h_1, h_2) \in \mathbf{P}^R_{\varepsilon - \rho}\, w$, that $\langle e_1, h_1 \cdot f_1\rangle \xrightarrow{j} \langle e_1', g_1'\rangle$ and that $\mathrm{irr}\langle e_1', g_1'\rangle$. We now have to prove a range of things; to do so we make use of the assumptions of the lemma.

Pick $r \in \mathcal{RN} \setminus |w|$ and define $w' \in \mathbf{W}$ by the transition $w \to_{reg(r)} w'$. Let $R' = R[\rho \to r]$ be the corresponding extension of R. We have $R' : \Pi, \rho \to |w'|$, $R'(\mathrm{FRV}(\varepsilon)) \subseteq \mathrm{dom}(w')$ and $(k, \gamma_1, \gamma_2) \in [\![\Gamma]\!]^{R'} w'$, the latter by Environment Extension and monotonicity of semantic types. But then the assumption of the lemma buys us that

$$(k, e_1[\gamma_1/\Gamma], e_2[\gamma_2/\Gamma]) \in [\![\mathtt{T}_\varepsilon\,\tau]\!]^{R'} w'.$$

Observe, now, that $(k, h_1, h_2) \in \mathbf{P}^{R'}_\varepsilon\, w'$ because of type monotonicity and since $w'(R(\rho)) = \emptyset$. This means, that we have $w'' \sqsupseteq w'$ with $\mathrm{dom}(w'') = \mathrm{dom}(w')$ as well as $e_2' \in \mathcal{E}$, $g_2', h_1', h_2', f_1', f_2' \in \mathcal{H}$ such that $\langle e_2, h_2 \cdot f_2\rangle \xrightarrow{*} \langle e_2', g_2'\rangle$, $g_1' = h_1' \cdot f_1' \cdot f_1$, $g_2' = h_2' \cdot f_2' \cdot f_2$, $(k - j, e_1', e_2') \in [\![\tau]\!]^{R'} w''$ and $(k - j, h_1, h_2, h_1', h_2') \in \mathbf{Q}^{R'}_\varepsilon\, w', w''$.

Define $w''' \in \mathbf{W}$ by the transition $w'' \to_{mask(r)} w'''$, i.e., we mask out region r. We have $w''' \sqsupseteq w$ by transitivity. Also

$$\mathrm{dom}(w''') = \mathrm{dom}(w'') \setminus \{r\} = \mathrm{dom}(w') \setminus \{r\} = \mathrm{dom}(w).$$

By Environment Extension and monotonicity we get

$$(k-j, e_1', e_2') \in [\![\tau]\!]^{R'} w'' \subseteq [\![\tau]\!]^{R} w'''.$$

Write $h_1' = h_1^\dagger \cdot f_1^\dagger$ with $h_1^\dagger, f_1^\dagger \in \mathcal{H}$ and $\mathrm{dom}(f_1^\dagger) = \mathrm{dom}_1(w''')$. And similarly, write $h_2' = h_2^\dagger \cdot f_2^\dagger$ with $h_2^\dagger, f_2^\dagger \in \mathcal{H}$ and $\mathrm{dom}(f_2^\dagger) = \mathrm{dom}_2(w''')$. It remains to prove that $(k-j, h_1, h_2, h_1^\dagger, h_2^\dagger) \in \mathbf{Q}^R_{\varepsilon-\rho}\, w, w'''$; note that we have transferred to the frame whatever locations that were allocated in region r.

Take $l_1 \in \mathrm{dom}(h_1)$ and assume $h_1(l_1) \neq h_1^\dagger(l_1)$. We get $\sigma \in \mathrm{wrs}\,\varepsilon$ and $(m_1, l_2, \mu) \in w'(R(\sigma))$ with $l_1 = m_1$ and

$$k-j > 0 \Rightarrow (k-j-1, h_1'(l_1), h_2'(l_2)) \in (\iota\, \mu)(w'').$$

Since $w'(R(\rho)) = w'(r) = \emptyset$, we conclude $\sigma \neq \rho$ and so $\sigma \in \mathrm{wrs}\,\varepsilon - \rho$ and $(l_1, l_2, \mu) \in w(R(\sigma))$; all that remains is an application of type monotonicity. Writes to the right hand side heap is treated similarly. Assume, finally, that there is $s \in \mathrm{dom}(w)$ and $(l_1, l_2, \mu) \in w'''(s) \setminus w(s)$. Since $s \neq r$ we have $(l_1, l_2, \mu) \in w''(s) \setminus w'(s)$ and so there is $s \in R(\mathrm{als}\,\varepsilon)$ and

$$k-j > 0 \Rightarrow (k-j-1, h_1'(l_1), h_2'(l_2)) \in (\iota\, \mu)(w'').$$

Since we had $s \neq r = R(\rho)$, we must have $s \in R(\mathrm{als}\,\varepsilon - \rho)$ as well; type monotonicity takes us the last way if $k-j>0$ happens to hold. □

Lemma 6.5 (Fix). $\Pi \mid \Gamma, f : \tau_1 \xrightarrow{\varepsilon} \tau_2, x : \tau_1 \models e_1 \preceq e_2 : \tau_2, \varepsilon$ implies $\Pi \mid \Gamma \models \texttt{fix}\, f(x).e_1 \preceq \texttt{fix}\, f(x).e_2 : \tau_1 \xrightarrow{\varepsilon} \tau_2, \emptyset$.

Proof. We unroll the definition of the logical relation: Let $k \in \mathbb{N}$, $w \in \mathbf{W}$, $R : \Pi \hookrightarrow |w|$ and $\gamma_1, \gamma_2 \in \mathcal{V}^{|\Gamma|}$ be arbitrary. The assumption $R(\mathrm{FRV}(\emptyset)) \subseteq \mathrm{dom}(w)$ gives us nothing, but we do get that $(k, \gamma_1, \gamma_2) \in [\![\Gamma]\!]^R w$. Write $e_1' = \texttt{fix}\, f(x).e_1[\gamma_1/\Gamma]$ and $e_2' = \texttt{fix}\, f(x).e_2[\gamma_2/\Gamma]$, we must show that

$$(k, e_1', e_2') \in [\![\mathrm{T}_\emptyset\, \tau_1 \xrightarrow{\varepsilon} \tau_2]\!]^R w.$$

As both expressions are, in fact, values it will suffice to show

$$(k, e_1', e_2') \in [\![\tau_1 \xrightarrow{\varepsilon} \tau_2]\!]^R w.$$

Notice first that $R(\mathrm{FRV}(\varepsilon)) \subseteq |w|$. If $R(\mathrm{FRV}(\varepsilon)) \subseteq \mathrm{dom}(w)$ fails, then there is nothing left to show. Assume, hence, that the inclusion holds, we aim to prove by induction that for all $0 \leq j \leq k$ we have

$$(j, e_1', e_2') \in [\![\tau_1 \xrightarrow{\varepsilon} \tau_2]\!]^R w.$$

The base case is easy, since there is no termination in 0 steps here. So assume the above for $0 \leq j < k$, we must prove that

$$(j+1, e_1', e_2') \in [\![\tau_1 \xrightarrow{\varepsilon} \tau_2]\!]^R w.$$

is good too. Pick $w' \sqsupseteq w$ with $R(\mathrm{FRV}(\varepsilon)) \subseteq \mathrm{dom}(w')$. Let $i \leq j+1$ and $(v_1, v_2) \in \mathcal{V} \times \mathcal{V}$ with $(i, v_1, v_2) \in [\![\tau_1]\!]^R w'$ be arbitrary. We must show

$$(i, e_1' v_1, e_2' v_2) \in [\![\mathrm{T}_\varepsilon\, \tau_2]\!]^R w'.$$

So, let $i' \leq i$, $e_1'' \in \mathcal{E}$ and $h_1, h_2, f_1, f_2, g_1'' \in \mathcal{H}$ be arbitrary and assume $(i, h_1, h_2) \in \mathbf{P}^R_\varepsilon\, w'$ and

$$\langle e_1' v_1, h_1 \cdot f_1 \rangle \xrightarrow{i'} \langle e_1'', g_1'' \rangle$$

with $\mathrm{irr}\langle e_1'', g_1'' \rangle$.

Clearly, $i' > 0$, so the reduction must go like

$$\langle e_1' v_1, h_1 \cdot f_1 \rangle \to \langle e_1[\gamma_1/\Gamma, e_1'/f, v_1/x], h_1 \cdot f_1 \rangle \xrightarrow{i'-1} \langle e_1'', g_1'' \rangle$$

It is now time to make use of the assumption. Since $i'-1 \leq i-1 \leq j$, we can apply the induction hypothesis to get

$$(i'-1, e_1[\gamma_1/\Gamma, e_1'/f, v_1/x], e_2[\gamma_2/\Gamma, e_2'/f, v_2/x]) \in [\![\mathrm{T}_\varepsilon\, \tau_2]\!]^R w'.$$

All that is left is gathering the consequences. □

7. Applications

We now show applications of our logical relations model: we verify four effect-based program transformations. These transformations are also considered in [7], but only for a language with ground store.

Theorem 7.1 (Idempotent Computation). A computation with disjoint read and write effects and no allocation effects is idempotent. More precisely, assume that we have

$$\Pi \mid \Gamma \vdash e : \tau, \varepsilon$$

with $\mathrm{rds}\,\varepsilon \cap \mathrm{wrs}\,\varepsilon = \emptyset = \mathrm{als}\,\varepsilon$. Then it holds that

$$\Pi \mid \Gamma \models \texttt{let x} = e \texttt{ in let y} = e \texttt{ in (x,y)} \sim \texttt{let x} = e \texttt{ in (x,x)} : \tau \times \tau, \varepsilon.$$

Proof. We just prove that the left hand side approximates the right hand side, the other way round proceeds similarly. Let $k \in \mathbb{N}$, $w \in \mathbf{W}$, $R : \Pi \hookrightarrow |w|$ and $\gamma_1, \gamma_2 \in \mathcal{V}^{|\Gamma|}$ be arbitrary. Assume that $R(\mathrm{FRV}(\varepsilon)) \subseteq \mathrm{dom}(w)$ and that $(k, \gamma_1, \gamma_2) \in [\![\Gamma]\!]^R w$. We set

$$e_1 = \texttt{let x} = e[\gamma_1/\Gamma] \texttt{ in let y} = e[\gamma_1/\Gamma] \texttt{ in (x,y)}$$

and

$$e_2 = \texttt{let x} = e[\gamma_2/\Gamma] \texttt{ in (x,x)}$$

and have to prove $(k, e_1, e_2) \in [\![\mathrm{T}_\varepsilon\, \tau \times \tau]\!]^R w$.

We proceed to unroll the definition of computations: Let $j \leq k$, $e_1''' \in \mathcal{E}$ and $h_1, h_2, f_1, f_2, g_1''' \in \mathcal{H}$ be arbitrary. Assume that $(k, h_1, h_2) \in \mathbf{P}^R_\varepsilon\, w$, that

$$\langle e_1, h_1 \cdot f_1 \rangle \xrightarrow{j} \langle e_1''', g_1''' \rangle$$

and that $\mathrm{irr}\langle e_1''', g_1''' \rangle$.

By the definition of the operational semantics there must be $0 \leq i \leq j$, $e_1' \in \mathcal{E}$ and $g_1' \in \mathcal{H}$ such that the above reduction can be split into

$$\langle e_1, h_1 \cdot f_1 \rangle \xrightarrow{i} \langle \texttt{let x} = e_1' \texttt{ in let y} = e[\gamma_1/\Gamma] \texttt{ in (x,y)}, g_1' \rangle \xrightarrow{j-i} \langle e_1''', g_1''' \rangle$$

with

$$\langle e[\gamma_1/\Gamma], h_1 \cdot f_1 \rangle \xrightarrow{i} \langle e_1', g_1' \rangle$$

and $\mathrm{irr}\langle e_1', g_1' \rangle$.

From the Fundamental Lemma we get $(k, e[\gamma_1/\Gamma], e[\gamma_2/\Gamma]) \in [\![\mathrm{T}_\varepsilon\, \tau]\!]^R w$. But then we get $w' \sqsupseteq w$ with $\mathrm{dom}(w) = \mathrm{dom}(w')$ as well as $e_2' \in \mathcal{E}$ and $g_2', h_1', h_2', f_1', f_2' \in \mathcal{H}$ such that

$$\langle e[\gamma_2/\Gamma], h_2 \cdot f_2 \rangle \xrightarrow{*} \langle e_2', g_2' \rangle,$$

$g_1' = h_1' \cdot f_1' \cdot f_1$, $g_2' = h_2' \cdot f_2' \cdot f_2$, $(k-i, h_1, h_2, h_1', h_2') \in \mathbf{Q}^R_\varepsilon\, w, w'$ and $(k-i, e_1', e_2') \in [\![\tau]\!]^R w'$. The latter implies $e_1' \in \mathcal{V}$ and so we must have $i < j$ as the alternative would invalidate $\mathrm{irr}\langle e_1''', g_1''' \rangle$. Indeed, there must be $0 \leq i' \leq j-i-1$, $e_1'' \in \mathcal{E}$ and $g_1'' \in \mathcal{H}$ such that we can split the last $j-i$ steps further

$$\begin{aligned}&\langle \texttt{let x} = e_1' \texttt{ in let y} = e[\gamma_1/\Gamma] \texttt{ in (x,y)}, g_1' \rangle \\ &\to \langle \texttt{let y} = e[\gamma_1/\Gamma] \texttt{ in } (e_1', \texttt{y}), g_1' \rangle \\ &\xrightarrow{i'} \langle \texttt{let y} = e_1'' \texttt{ in } (e_1', \texttt{y}), g_1'' \rangle \\ &\xrightarrow{j-i-1-i'} \langle e_1''', g_1''' \rangle\end{aligned}$$

with

$$\langle e[\gamma_1/\Gamma], g_1' \rangle \xrightarrow{i'} \langle e_1'', g_1'' \rangle$$

and $\mathrm{irr}\langle e_1'', g_1'' \rangle$.

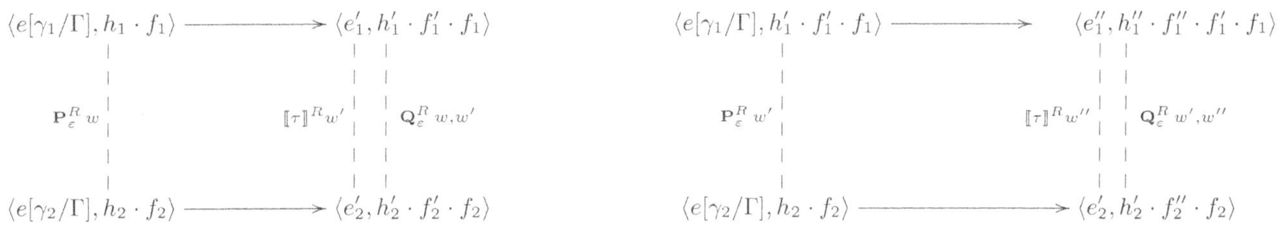

Figure 7. Illustrated proof of the Idempotent Computation Theorem.

Now for something odd: we reset the right hand side to the initial state. More precisely, we argue that $(k-i-1, h_1', h_2) \in \mathbf{P}^R_\varepsilon\, w'$, this is the crux of the entire proof: Notice initially, that not only is it the case that $\mathrm{dom}(w) = \mathrm{dom}(w')$, we also have $\forall r \in \mathrm{dom}(w).\, w(r) = w'(r)$ since $\mathrm{als}\,\varepsilon = \emptyset$; in particular we get $\mathrm{dom}_2(w) = \mathrm{dom}_2(w')$. Combining now the facts

$$\begin{aligned}&\forall \rho \in \mathrm{rds}\,\varepsilon.\, \forall (l_1, l_2, \mu) \in w(R(\rho)).\\ &\quad k > 0 \Rightarrow (k-1, h_1(l_1), h_2(l_2)) \in (\iota\,\mu)(w)\end{aligned}$$

and

$$\begin{aligned}&\forall l_1 \in \mathrm{dom}(h_1).\, h_1(l_1) \neq h_1'(l_1) \Rightarrow\\ &\quad \exists \rho \in \mathrm{wrs}\,\varepsilon.\, \exists (m_1, l_2, \mu) \in w(R(\rho)).\, l_1 = m_1 \wedge\\ &\qquad k > 0 \Rightarrow (k-1, h_1'(l_1), h_2'(l_2)) \in (\iota\,\mu)(w'),\end{aligned}$$

with $\mathrm{rds}\,\varepsilon \cap \mathrm{wrs}\,\varepsilon = \emptyset$ buys us

$$\begin{aligned}&\forall \rho \in \mathrm{rds}\,\varepsilon.\, \forall (l_1, l_2, \mu) \in w'(R(\rho)).\\ &\quad k-i-1 > 0 \Rightarrow (k-i-2, h_1'(l_1), h_2(l_2)) \in (\iota\,\mu)(w').\end{aligned}$$

Loosely speaking, the locations we are permitted to read held values of the correct type from the beginning and were not changed by the computation seen so far.

We proceed to use the fact that $(k-i-1, e[\gamma_1/\Gamma], e[\gamma_2/\Gamma]) \in [\![\mathrm{T}_\varepsilon\, \tau]\!]^R w'$ by a second application of the Fundamental Lemma. This yields $w'' \sqsupseteq w'$ with $\mathrm{dom}(w') = \mathrm{dom}(w'')$ as well as $e_2'' \in \mathcal{E}$ and $g_2'', h_1'', h_2'', f_1'', f_2'' \in \mathcal{H}$ such that

$$\langle e[\gamma_2/\Gamma], h_2 \cdot f_2\rangle \xrightarrow{*} \langle e_2'', g_2''\rangle,$$

$g_1'' = h_1'' \cdot f_1'' \cdot f_1' \cdot f_1$, $g_2'' = h_2'' \cdot f_2'' \cdot f_2$, $(k-i-1-i', h_1', h_2, h_1'', h_2'') \in \mathbf{Q}^R_\varepsilon\, w', w''$ and $(k-i-1-i', e_1'', e_2'') \in [\![\tau]\!]^R w''$. The latter implies $e_1'' \in \mathcal{V}$ and so we must have $i' < j-i-1$ since an equality would conflict with $\mathrm{irr}\langle e_1''', g_1'''\rangle$. Even more precisely, we must have $j-i-1-i' = 1$ and the final step in the entire reduction $\langle e_1, h_1 \cdot f_1\rangle \xrightarrow{j} \langle e_1''', g_1'''\rangle$ must be

$$\langle \mathtt{let}\ \mathtt{y}\ = e_1''\ \mathtt{in}\ (e_1', \mathtt{y}), g_1''\rangle \to \langle (e_1', e_1''), g_1''\rangle,$$

in particular $e_1''' = (e_1', e_1'')$ and $g_1''' = g_1''$.

We immediately get

$$\langle e_2, h_2 \cdot f_2\rangle \xrightarrow{*} \langle (e_2'', e_2''), g_2''\rangle.$$

In the proof, it now remains to prove $(k-j, h_1, h_2, h_1'', h_2'') \in \mathbf{Q}^R_\varepsilon\, w, w''$ and that $(k-j, (e_1', e_1''), (e_2'', e_2'')) \in [\![\tau]\!]^R_\varepsilon$ w". Notice initially, that by the determinism of the operational semantics and the fact that $e_2', e_2'' \in \mathcal{V}$ we have $e_2' = e_2''$ and $g_2' = g_2''$. Since $\mathrm{dom}_2(w') = \mathrm{dom}_2(w'')$ by $\mathrm{als}\,\varepsilon = \emptyset$ we furthermore get $h_2' = h_2''$ and $f_2' = f_2''$. Also recall $k-j = k-i-i'-2$.

On the first obligation, we take $l_1 \in \mathrm{dom}(h_1)$ and assume that $h_1(l_1) \neq h_1''(l_1)$. If also $h_1'(l_1) \neq h_1''(l_1)$ then the desired follows from $(k-i-1-i', h_1', h_2, h_1'', h_2'') \in \mathbf{Q}^R_\varepsilon\, w', w''$. Otherwise, we must have $h_1(l_1) \neq h_1'(l_1) = h_1''(l_1)$, but then $(k-i, h_1, h_2, h_1', h_2') \in \mathbf{Q}^R_\varepsilon\, w, w'$ paves the way. And the second obligation is met by recalling $(k-i, e_1', e_2') \in [\![\tau]\!]^R w'$ and $(k-i-1-i', e_1'', e_2'') \in [\![\tau]\!]^R w''$. □

Theorem 7.2 (Commuting Computations). Two computations commute if neither reads a region that the other writes, and there is no region they both write. More precisely, assume that we have

$$\Pi \mid \Gamma \vdash e : \tau, \varepsilon, \quad \Pi \mid \Gamma \vdash e' : \tau', \varepsilon'$$

with $\mathrm{rds}\,\varepsilon \cap \mathrm{wrs}\,\varepsilon' = \mathrm{rds}\,\varepsilon' \cap \mathrm{wrs}\,\varepsilon = \mathrm{wrs}\,\varepsilon \cap \mathrm{wrs}\,\varepsilon' = \emptyset$. Then we have the following equivalence:

$$\begin{aligned}\Pi \mid \Gamma \models\ &\mathtt{let}\ \mathtt{x}\ = e\ \mathtt{in}\ \mathtt{let}\ \mathtt{y}\ = e'\ \mathtt{in}\ (\mathtt{x}, \mathtt{y}) \sim\\ &\mathtt{let}\ \mathtt{y}\ = e'\ \mathtt{in}\ \mathtt{let}\ \mathtt{x}\ = e\ \mathtt{in}\ (\mathtt{x}, \mathtt{y}) : \tau \times \tau', \varepsilon \cup \varepsilon'.\end{aligned}$$

Proof. Again we give the details only one way: that the left hand side approximates the right hand side. Let $k \in \mathbb{N}$, $w \in \mathbf{W}$, $R : \Pi \hookrightarrow |w|$ and $\gamma_1, \gamma_2 \in \mathcal{V}^{|\Gamma|}$ be arbitrary. Assume that $R(\mathrm{FRV}(\varepsilon \cup \varepsilon')) \subseteq \mathrm{dom}(w)$ and that $(k, \gamma_1, \gamma_2) \in [\![\Gamma]\!]^R w$. Set

$$e_1 = \mathtt{let}\ \mathtt{x}\ = e[\gamma_1/\Gamma]\ \mathtt{in}\ \mathtt{let}\ \mathtt{y}\ = e'[\gamma_1/\Gamma]\ \mathtt{in}\ (\mathtt{x}, \mathtt{y})$$

and

$$e_2 = \mathtt{let}\ \mathtt{y}\ = e'[\gamma_2/\Gamma]\ \mathtt{in}\ \mathtt{let}\ \mathtt{x}\ = e[\gamma_2/\Gamma]\ \mathtt{in}\ (\mathtt{x}, \mathtt{y});$$

we have to prove $(k, e_1, e_2) \in [\![\mathrm{T}_{\varepsilon \cup \varepsilon}\, \tau \times \tau']\!]^R w$.

We proceed to unroll the definition of computations: Let $j \leq k$, $e_1''' \in \mathcal{E}$ and $h_1, h_2, f_1, f_2, g_1''' \in \mathcal{H}$ be arbitrary. Assume that $(k, h_1, h_2) \in \mathbf{P}^R_{\varepsilon \cup \varepsilon'}\, w$, that

$$\langle e_1, h_1 \cdot f_1\rangle \xrightarrow{j} \langle e_1''', g_1'''\rangle$$

and that $\mathrm{irr}\langle e_1''', g_1'''\rangle$.

By the definition of the operational semantics there must be $0 \leq i \leq j$, $e_1' \in \mathcal{E}$ and $g_1' \in \mathcal{H}$ such that the above reduction can be split into

$$\begin{aligned}\langle e_1, h_1 \cdot f_1\rangle &\xrightarrow{i} \langle\, \mathtt{let}\ \mathtt{x}\ = e_1'\ \mathtt{in}\ \mathtt{let}\ \mathtt{y}\ = e'[\gamma_1/\Gamma]\ \mathtt{in}\ (\mathtt{x}, \mathtt{y}), g_1'\rangle\\ &\xrightarrow{j-i} \langle e_1''', g_1'''\rangle\end{aligned}$$

with

$$\langle e[\gamma_1/\Gamma], h_1 \cdot f_1\rangle \xrightarrow{i} \langle e_1', g_1'\rangle$$

and $\mathrm{irr}\langle e_1', g_1'\rangle$.

From the Fundamental Lemma we get $(k, e[\gamma_1/\Gamma], e[\gamma_2/\Gamma]) \in [\![\mathrm{T}_\varepsilon\, \tau]\!]^R w$. By Precondition Strengthening we get a whole range of stuff, but we need only the following two facts: that $e_1' \in \mathcal{V}$ and that for $l_1 \in \mathrm{dom}(h_1)$ such that there is $r \in R(\mathrm{rds}\,\varepsilon')$ and $(m_1, l_2, \mu) \in w(r)$ with $m_1 = l_1$ we have $g_1'(l_1) = h_1(l_1)$. The latter is a consequence of $\mathrm{wrs}\,\varepsilon \cap \mathrm{rds}\,\varepsilon' = \emptyset$.

We must have $i < j$ as the alternative would invalidate $\mathrm{irr}\langle e_1''', g_1'''\rangle$. Indeed, there must be $0 \leq i' \leq j-i-1$, $e_1'' \in \mathcal{E}$

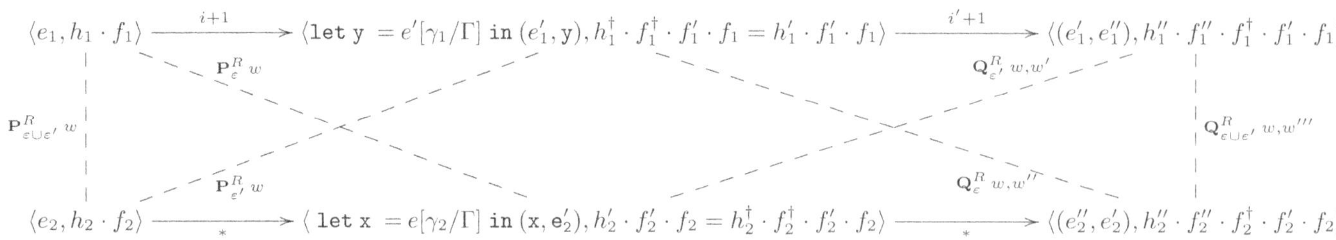

Figure 8. Illustrated proof of the Commuting Computations Theorem. Most of the dashed lines are slightly off, i.e., they do not point at the exact right subheaps.

and $g''_1 \in \mathcal{H}$ such that we can split the last $j - i$ steps further into

$$\begin{aligned}&\langle \texttt{let x} = e'_1\ \texttt{in let y} = e'[\gamma_1/\Gamma]\ \texttt{in}\ (\texttt{x}, \texttt{y}), g'_1\rangle\\ &\to \langle \texttt{let y} = e'[\gamma_1/\Gamma]\ \texttt{in}\ (e'_1, \texttt{y}), g'_1\rangle\\ &\overset{i'}{\to} \langle \texttt{let y} = e''_1\ \texttt{in}\ (e'_1, \texttt{y}), g''_1\rangle\\ &\overset{j-i-1-i'}{\to} \langle e'''_1, g'''_1\rangle\end{aligned}$$

with

$$\langle e'[\gamma_1/\Gamma], g'_1\rangle \overset{i'}{\to} \langle e''_1, g''_1\rangle$$

and $\mathrm{irr}\langle e''_1, g''_1\rangle$.

Much as in the previous proof, we now ditch our right hand side progress, but unlike that, we also lose our new future world. Notice first that the Fundamental Lemma gives us $(k - i - 1, e'[\gamma_1/\Gamma], e'[\gamma_2/\Gamma]) \in [\![\mathrm{T}_{\varepsilon'}\ \tau']\!]^R w$, we would like to apply that. Write $g'_1 = h_1^\dagger \cdot h_1^\circ$ for $h_1^\dagger, h_1^\circ \in \mathcal{H}$ with $\mathrm{dom}(h_1^\dagger) = \mathrm{dom}_1(w)$; the crucial observation now is that we have $(k-i-1, h_1^\dagger, h_2) \in \mathbf{P}^R_{\varepsilon'}\ w$. Hence we get $w' \sqsupseteq w$ with $\mathrm{dom}(w) = \mathrm{dom}(w')$ as well as $e'_2 \in \mathcal{E}$ and $g'_2, h''_1, h'_2, f''_1, f'_2 \in \mathcal{H}$ such that

$$\langle e'[\gamma_2/\Gamma], h_2 \cdot f_2\rangle \overset{*}{\to} \langle e'_2, g'_2\rangle,$$

$g''_1 = h''_1 \cdot f''_1 \cdot f_1^\circ, g'_2 = h'_2 \cdot f'_2 \cdot f_2, (k-i-1-i', h_1^\dagger, h_2, h''_1, h'_2) \in \mathbf{Q}^R_{\varepsilon'}\ w, w'$ and $(k - i - 1 - i', e''_1, e'_2) \in [\![\tau']\!]^R w'$.

Much as we have argued before, we now know that $e''_1 \in \mathcal{V}$, hence $j - i - 1 - i' = 1$ and the entire left hand side reduction must look like

$$\langle e_1, h_1 \cdot f_1\rangle \overset{j}{\to} \langle (e'_1, e''_1), g''_1\rangle,$$

in particular, $e'''_1 = (e'_1, e''_1)$ and $g'''_1 = g''_1$.

We have now, in some sense, considered the situation from the point of view of e', it is time to turn the tables. There are $h_2^\dagger, f_2^\dagger$ with $\mathrm{dom}(h_2^\dagger) = \mathrm{dom}_2(w)$ such that $h'_2 = h_2^\dagger \cdot f_2^\dagger$. So we have $(k, h_1, h_2^\dagger) \in \mathbf{P}^R_\varepsilon\ w$ by arguments as above, in particular we apply $\mathrm{wrs}\,\varepsilon' \cap \mathrm{rds}\,\varepsilon = \emptyset$. Now, we still have $(k, e[\gamma_1/\Gamma], e[\gamma_2/\Gamma]) \in [\![\mathrm{T}_\varepsilon\ \tau]\!]^R w$ and so there is $w'' \sqsupseteq w$ with $\mathrm{dom}(w) = \mathrm{dom}(w'')$ as well as $e''_2 \in \mathcal{E}$ and $g''_2, h'_1, h''_2, f'_1, f''_2 \in \mathcal{H}$ such that

$$\langle e[\gamma_2/\Gamma], h_2^\dagger \cdot f_2^\dagger \cdot f'_2 \cdot f_2\rangle \overset{*}{\to} \langle e''_2, g''_2\rangle,$$

$g'_1 = h'_1 \cdot f'_1 \cdot f_1, g''_2 = h''_2 \cdot f''_2 \cdot f_2^\dagger \cdot f'_2 \cdot f_2, (k-i, h_1, h_2^\dagger, h'_1, h''_2) \in \mathbf{Q}^R_\varepsilon\ w, w''$ and $(k - i, e'_1, e''_2) \in [\![\tau]\!]^R w^\dagger$. Write $h'_1 = h_1^\dagger \cdot f_1^\dagger$ for $f_1^\dagger \in \mathcal{H}$, in particular $g'_1 = h_1^\dagger \cdot f_1^\dagger \cdot f'_1 \cdot f_1$ and $g''_1 = h''_1 \cdot f''_1 \cdot f_1^\dagger \cdot f'_1 \cdot f_1$; this is notation we need soon. Observe first, though, that we have the right hand side reduction

$$\langle e_2, h_2 \cdot f_2\rangle \overset{*}{\to} \langle (e'_2, e''_2), g''_2\rangle.$$

We now build a world w''' with $\mathrm{dom}(w''') = \mathrm{dom}(w)$ and with both $w''' \sqsupseteq w'$ and $w''' \sqsupseteq w''$, i.e., a common future world. The natural choice is for the dead regions of w''' to be the dead regions of both w' and w''. For $r \in \mathrm{dom}(w)$ we set $w'''(r) = w'(r) \cup w''(r)$, but we must take care not to wreck the partial bijections nor their mutual disjointness: Let $r, s \in \mathrm{dom}(w)$ and take $(l'_1, l'_2, \mu') \in w'(r) \setminus w(r)$ and $(l''_1, l''_2, \mu'') \in w''(s) \setminus w(s)$; it will suffice to show $l'_1 \neq l''_1$ and $l'_2 \neq l''_2$. Now, we know that $l'_1 \in \mathrm{dom}_1(w') = \mathrm{dom}(h''_1)$, in particular we have $l'_1 \notin \mathrm{dom}(f_1^\dagger)$. Also $l'_1 \notin \mathrm{dom}_1(w) = \mathrm{dom}(h_1^\dagger)$. But $l''_1 \in \mathrm{dom}_1(w'') = \mathrm{dom}(h'_1)$ and since $h'_1 = h_1^\dagger \cdot f_1^\dagger$ we must have $l'_1 \neq l''_1$. Proving $l'_2 \neq l''_2$ proceeds similarly.

It shall now suffice to show

$$(k - j, h_1, h_2, h''_1 \cdot f_1^\dagger, h''_2 \cdot f_2^\dagger) \in \mathbf{Q}^R_{\varepsilon\cup\varepsilon'}\ w, w'''$$

as the remaining obligations are discharged already. We have

$$\begin{aligned}\mathrm{dom}_1(w''') &= \mathrm{dom}_1(w') \cup \mathrm{dom}_1(w'')\\ &= \mathrm{dom}(h''_1) \cup \mathrm{dom}(h_1^\dagger \cdot f_1^\dagger)\\ &= \mathrm{dom}(h''_1 \cdot f_1^\dagger)\end{aligned}$$

and get $\mathrm{dom}_2(w''') = \mathrm{dom}(h''_2 \cdot f_2^\dagger)$ similarly. So take $l_1 \in \mathrm{dom}(h_1)$ and assume that $h_1(l_1) \neq h''_1(l_1)$. If $h_1^\dagger(l_1) \neq h''_1(l_1)$ we get $\rho \in \mathrm{wrs}\,\varepsilon'$ and $(m_1, l_2, \mu) \in w(R(\rho))$ with $l_1 = m_1$ and $(k - j, h''_1(l_1), h''_2(l_2)) \in (\iota\,\mu)(w')$. And since $\mathrm{wrs}\,\varepsilon \cap \mathrm{wrs}\,\varepsilon = \emptyset$ we know that $h''_2(l_2) = h'_2(l_1)$. If, on the other hand, $h_1^\dagger(l_1) = h''_1(l_1)$ then we must have $h_1(l_1) \neq h_1^\dagger(l_1)$ and we get $\rho \in \mathrm{wrs}\,\varepsilon$ and $(m_1, l_2, \mu) \in w(R(\rho))$ with $l_1 = m_1$ and $(k - i - 1, h_1^\dagger(l_1), h''_2(l_2)) \in (\iota\,\mu)(w'')$.

It remains to consider allocation. So take $r \in \mathrm{dom}(w)$ and $(l_1, l_2, \mu) \in w'''(r) \setminus w(r)$. By the construction of w''' we get $(l_1, l_2, \mu) \in w'(r) \setminus w(r)$ or $(l_1, l_2, \mu) \in w'(r) \setminus w(r)$; in both cases we proceed similarly, so assume the former holds. Then we know $r \in R(\mathrm{als}\,\varepsilon')$ and that $(k - j, h''_1(l_1), h'_2(l_2)) \in (\iota\,\mu)(w')$. But as $l_2 \notin \mathrm{dom}_2(w)$ we must have $l_2 \in \mathrm{dom}(f_2^\dagger)$ and so $(h''_2 \cdot f_2^\dagger)(l_2) = f_2^\dagger(l_2) = h'_2(l_2)$ and we are done. □

In the remaining two applications we can prove only approximation, not equivalence, because of the possibility of non-termination. We defer the proofs to the appendix of the long version of the paper.

Theorem 7.3 (Neutral Computation)**.** A computation that performs no writes and has return type unit approximates the trivial computation. More precisely, having

$$\Pi \mid \Gamma \vdash e : \mathbf{1}, \varepsilon$$

with $\mathrm{wrs}\,\varepsilon = \emptyset$ implies

$$\Pi \mid \Gamma \models e \preceq () : \mathbf{1}, \varepsilon.$$

Theorem 7.4 (Pure Lambda Hoist)**.** A pure computation evaluated as part of a function can, up to approximation, be evaluated once and the result cached. More precisely, having

$$\Pi \mid \Gamma \vdash e : \tau_1, \emptyset, \quad \Pi \mid \Gamma, y : \tau_2, x : \tau_1 \vdash e' : \tau_3, \varepsilon.$$

gives us

$$\Pi \mid \Gamma \models \texttt{let x} = e \texttt{ in } \lambda y.\, e' \preceq \lambda y.\ \texttt{let x} = e \texttt{ in } e' : \tau_2 \xrightarrow{\varepsilon} \tau_3, \emptyset$$

8. Discussion

8.1 Work by Benton et. al

An important point of reference for our work is the relational model by Benton et. al. [7] of an effect system for a higher-order langauge with dynamic allocation and ground store, i.e., only integers in the heap. Indeed, apart from our extension to higher-order store, the type systems and examples considered are roughly the same.

Having said so, we remark that our take on the issue of masking is novel; in particular it is different from that of Benton et. al. Their approach does not scale easily, if at all, to the higher-order store setting: The pivot is the *Masking Lemma* [7, Lemma 3], stating that the interpretation of both types and computations in a world are preserved up to equality under masking, *provided* that the region masked out is not, syntactically, in the type respectively in the computation. Combined with ground store, this makes short work of soundness of the masking rule.

The Masking Lemma, however, does not scale easily to a higher-order store setting. Consider the computation from the introduction: The returned function has latent effect $\{wr_\sigma\}$ and correspondingly writes to location 1 in region σ. But the values stored at location 1 must be of type $\texttt{ref}_\rho\ \texttt{int}$, and that depends on the type `int` associated with location 0 in region ρ. In other words, the interpretation of a type may depend on regions that do not occur syntactically in the type; this is the antithesis to the Masking Lemma.

As described above, we take the different approach that interpretations of types should grow (or at least not shrink) under any application of masking, and only when we actually perform reads, writes and allocations do we require that the regions in question are still live. This also means that we can get by without a *silent region* [7, Sections 5 and 6]. This is a designated region of the world that tracks inaccessible parts of the heap in an untyped way; in *loc.cit.* it is necessary for the Masking Lemma to hold for computations.

That we have no silent region is not just a technical convenience: it means that our model permits *any* action on locations that have been masked out, including garbage collection or ownership transfer. The locations have left the world and we make no further assumptions on them, whatsoever. By contrast, locations in a silent region are still in the world and computations may assume that they remain allocated, even if the stored value cannot be changed. Indeed, computations may actually access such locations in extensionally invisible ways: we could, say, read a location in the silent region as long as we make no use of the read value.

Benton et. al.: Higher Order Store In more recent work, Benton et. al. [8] have given a relational model for a language with higher order store. The language has no dynamic allocation though, nor is there any masking rule.

Unlike our approach, however, they work with a denotational semantics of the language; in particular they prove existence of the logical relation by solving a non-trivial mixed-variance domain equation, extending the standard technique by Pitts [20] to do so. One advantage is transitivity of their logical relation; that is something we do not get. This is a general issue with step-indexed models observed first by Ahmed [3]; there are fixes, but a more proper take is to reason in a logic suited for step-indexing as done, e.g., by Dreyer et. al. [13]. We are convinced, however, that using the techniques developed by Støvring and the authors [11], we could also define a model based on a denotational semantics of the programming language, hence achieving transitivity.

Preservation of All Store Relations Throughout their work, Benton et. al. interpret computations by requiring preservation of *all* relations on heaps that respect the effects of the computations, i.e., that ensure well-typed reads at locations with read effects and is closed under well-typed writes to locations with write effects. Our approach is more simple-minded; we do, in some sense, just preserve one relation. But it is unclear what the additional relations buys, we know of no equivalences that fail due to our approach; indeed the two alternatives may very well be equivalent. What is clear, however, is that losing the many relations, as well as the absence of a silent region, simplify proofs considerably: writing out all details, as we do, obviously generates some mileage but in essence one may argue in simple diagrams as illustrated.

8.2 On Expressiveness

Consider the following variant of the so-called awkward example, discussed in detail in [14]. Let $\tau = (\texttt{1} \xrightarrow{\varepsilon_0} \texttt{1}) \xrightarrow{\varepsilon_1} \texttt{int}$ with $\varepsilon_0 = \{rd_\rho, wr_\rho\}$ and $\varepsilon_1 = \{rd_\rho, wr_\rho, rd_\sigma, wr_\sigma\}$ and define expressions e_1 and e_2, which both have type τ and effect $\{al_\sigma\}$, by

$$\begin{aligned} e_1 &= \texttt{let x} = \texttt{ref}_\sigma\, \texttt{0 in} \\ &\quad \lambda f.(x := 0; f(); x := 1; f(); !x) \\ e_2 &= \texttt{let x} = \texttt{ref}_\sigma\, \texttt{0 in} \\ &\quad \lambda f.(f(); f(); x := 1; !x). \end{aligned}$$

We have used the subscript σ to indicate that x will have the type $\texttt{ref}_\sigma\ \texttt{int}$. Since ρ and σ are distinct, f cannot read / write the reference bound to x; this ensures that both the left and the right hand side functions always return 1. Indeed we can show that e_1 and e_2 are contextually equivalent. We remark that if, on the other hand, we had typed e_1 and e_2 with the same region variable instead of two distinct region variables, then our semantic model would not be expressive enough to show that e_1 and e_2 are contextually equivalent. For that, we could extend our model using ideas from the model for non-effect-annotated types in [14]. In summa, effect information can be used to restrict the applicable contexts and can thus make it easier to show two expressions equivalent (for those restricted contexts). Note that a standard unification-based algorithm for inferring effects, would infer the type τ for e_1 with ρ and σ distinct.

9. Conclusion and Future Work

We have presented a solution to the open problem of constructing a relational model for an effect system for a higher-order language with dynamically allocated higher-order store. We have demonstrated that the model can be used to rigorously justify effect-based program transformations.

Future work includes extending the model to region and effect polymorphism, as found, e.g., in [21]. Moreover, we think our model could be adapted to a situation where the conceptual regions do not necessarily follow a stack-discipline [4, 16] by a slight modification of the interpretation of computations. In this paper we have focused on a relational model for verifying effect-based program transformations. We believe that the ideas of our model construction can also be used to construct models for other applications of effect systems for languages with higher-order store.

Acknowledgments

We thank Nick Benton, Lennart Beringer, Martin Hofmann and Andrew Kennedy for useful discussions. Kasper Svendsen and Filip Sieczkowski gave useful comments on a late draft of the paper. This research was funded in part by the ToMeSo project from the Danish Agency for Science, Technology and Innovation (grant number 274–08–0412).

References

[1] A. Ahmed. *Semantics of Types for Mutable State*. PhD thesis, Princeton University, 2004.

[2] A. Ahmed, D. Dreyer, and A. Rossberg. State-dependent representation independence. In *Proceedings of POPL*, 2009.

[3] A. J. Ahmed. Step-indexed syntactic logical relations for recursive and quantified types. In P. Sestoft, editor, *ESOP*, volume 3924 of *Lecture Notes in Computer Science*, pages 69–83. Springer, 2006. ISBN 3-540-33095-X.

[4] A. Aiken, M. Fähndrich, and R. Levien. Better static memory management: Improving region-based analysis of higher-order languages. In *Prcoeedings of PLDI*, 1995.

[5] N. Benton and P. Buchlovsky. Semantics of an effect analysis for exceptions. In *Proceedings of TLDI*, 2007.

[6] N. Benton, A. Kenney, M. Hofmann, and L. Beringer. Reading, writing and relations: Towards extensional semantics for effect analyses. In *Proceedings of APLAS*, 2006.

[7] N. Benton, L. Beringer, M. Hofmann, and A. Kennedy. Relational semantics for effect-based program transformations with dynamic allocation. In *Proceedings of PPDP*. ACM, 2007.

[8] N. Benton, L. Beringer, M. Hofmann, and A. Kennedy. Relational semantics for effect-based program transformations: Higher-order store. In *Proceedings of PPDP*. ACM, 2009.

[9] L. Birkedal, M. Tofte, and M. Vejlstrup. From region inference to von Neumann machines via region representation inference. In *Proceedings of POPL*, 1996.

[10] L. Birkedal, N. Torp-Smith, and H. Yang. Semantics of separation-logic typing and higher-order frame rules for algol-like langauges. *Logical Methods in Computer Science*, 2(5:1):1–33, 2006.

[11] L. Birkedal, K. Støvring, and J. Thamsborg. Realizability semantics of parametric polymorphism, general references, and recursive types. In *Proceedings of FOSSACS*, 2009.

[12] L. Birkedal, B. Reus, J. Schwinghammer, K. Støvring, J. Thamsborg, and H. Yang. Step-indexed Kripke models over recursive worlds. In *Proceedings of POPL*, pages 119–132, 2011.

[13] D. Dreyer, A. Ahmed, and L. Birkedal. Logical step-indexed logical relations. In *LICS*, pages 71–80. IEEE Computer Society, 2009. ISBN 978-0-7695-3746-7.

[14] D. Dreyer, G. Neis, and L. Birkedal. The impact of higher-order state and control effects on local relational reasoning. In *Proceedings of ICFP*, 2010.

[15] D. Gifford and J. Lucassen. Integrating functional and imperative programming. In *ACM Conference of LISP and Functional Programming*, 1986.

[16] F. Henglein, M. Makholm, and H. Niss. A direct approach to control-flow sensitive region-based memory management. In *Prcoeedings of PPDP*, 2001.

[17] F. Henglein, H. Makholm, and H. Niss. Effect types and region-based memory management. In B. Pierce, editor, *Advanced Topics in Types and Programming Languages*. MIT Press, 2005.

[18] J. Lucassen and D. Gifford. Polymorphic effect systems. In *Proceedings of POPL*, 1988.

[19] A. Nanevski, G. Morrisett, and L. Birkedal. Polymorphism and separation in hoare type theory. In J. H. Reppy and J. L. Lawall, editors, *ICFP*, pages 62–73. ACM, 2006. ISBN 1-59593-309-3.

[20] A. M. Pitts. Relational properties of domains. *Inf. Comput.*, 127(2): 66–90, 1996.

[21] M. Tofte and J.-P. Talpin. Implementation of the typed call-by-value λ-calculus using a stack of regions. In *Proceedings of POPL*, 1994.

Author Index

NOTES

NOTES

www.ingramcontent.com/pod-product-compliance
Ingram Content Group UK Ltd.
Pitfield, Milton Keynes, MK11 3LW, UK
UKHW051413290926
15471UKWH00009B/1582

9 781450 308656